Stan Lee PRESENTS

ESSENTIAL

the AMAZING SPIDER-MAN

VOL. 4

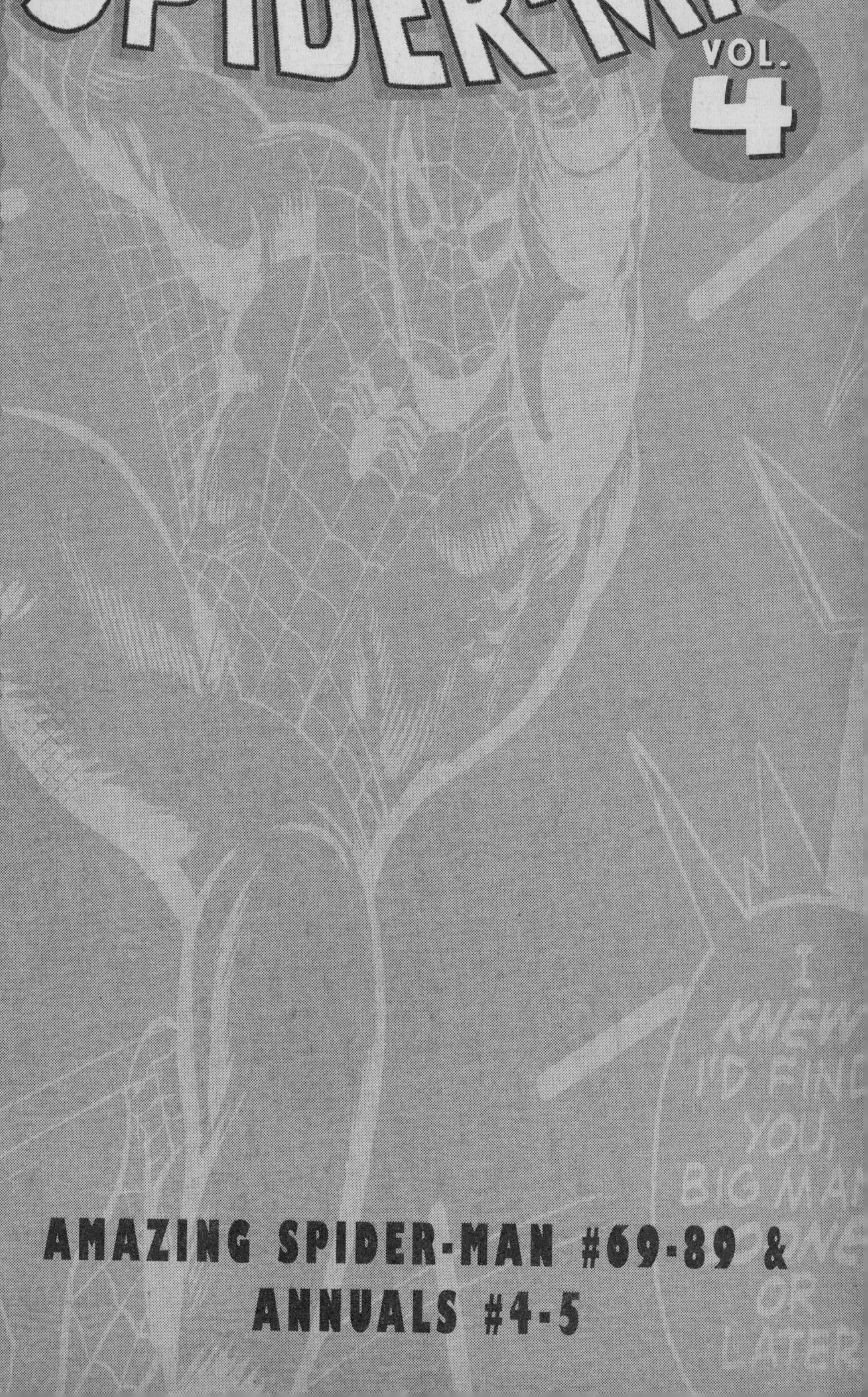
I
KNEW
I'D FIN
YOU
BIG MA
OR
LATER

AMAZING SPIDER-MAN #69-89 & ANNUALS #4-5

ESSENTIAL THE AMAZING SPIDER-MAN VOL. 4

THE AMAZING SPIDER-MAN #69

WRITER: STAN LEE
STORYTELLER: JOHN ROMITA
ILLUSTRATOR: JIM MOONEY
LETTERER: SAM ROSEN

THE AMAZING SPIDER-MAN #70

WRITER: STAN LEE
STORYTELLER: JOHN ROMITA
ILLUSTRATOR: JIM MOONEY
LETTERER: SAM ROSEN

THE AMAZING SPIDER-MAN #71

WRITER: STAN LEE
STORYTELLER: JOHN ROMITA
ILLUSTRATOR: JIM MOONEY
LETTERER: SAM ROSEN

THE AMAZING SPIDER-MAN #72

WRITER: STAN LEE
STORYTELLER: JOHN BUSCEMA
ILLUSTRATORS: JOHN ROMITA & JIM MOONEY
LETTERER: SAM ROSEN

The Amazing Spider-Man #73

WRITER: STAN LEE
STORYTELLER: JOHN ROMITA
ILLUSTRATORS: JOHN BUSCEMA & JIM MOONEY
LETTERER: SAM ROSEN

The Amazing Spider-Man #74

WRITER: STAN LEE
STORYTELLER: JOHN ROMITA
ILLUSTRATOR: JIM MOONEY
LETTERER: SAM ROSEN

The Amazing Spider-Man #75

WRITER: STAN LEE
STORYTELLER: JOHN ROMITA
ILLUSTRATOR: JIM MOONEY
LETTERER: ART SIMEK

The Amazing Spider-Man #76

WRITER: STAN LEE
STORYTELLER: JOHN BUSCEMA
ILLUSTRATOR: JIM MOONEY
LETTERER: SAM ROSEN

The Amazing Spider-Man #77

WRITER: STAN LEE
PLOT: JOHN ROMITA
STORYTELLER: JOHN BUSCEMA
ILLUSTRATOR: JIM MOONEY
LETTERER: SAM ROSEN

The Amazing Spider-Man #78

WRITER: STAN LEE
PLOT ASSISTS: JOHN ROMITA
STORYTELLER: JOHN BUSCEMA
ILLUSTRATOR: JIM MOONEY
LETTERER: SAM ROSEN

The Amazing Spider-Man Annual #4

WRITER: STAN LEE
STORYTELLER: LARRY LIEBER
INKER: MIKE ESPOSITO
LETTERER: JERRY FELDMANN

SPECIAL THANKS TO: Tom Brevoort
Ralph Macchio
Darby McShain
Ruben Molles
Jared Osborn
Shawnee Pugliese

ESSENTIAL SPIDER-MAN® VOL. 4 Contains material originally published in magazine form as AMAZING SPIDER-MAN #69 - 89 and AMAZING SPIDER-MAN ANNUALS #4 and #5. Second printing, February 2002. ISBN # 0-7851-0760-6. Published by MARVEL COMICS, a division of MARVEL ENTERTAINMENT GROUP, INC. OFFICE OF PUBLICATION: 10 EAST 40th STREET, NEW YORK, NY 10016. Copyright © 1969, 1970, 1971 and 2002 Marvel Characters, Inc. All rights reserved. Price $14.95 in the U.S. and $23.95 in Canada (GST #R127032852). No similarity between any of the names, characters, persons, and/or institutions in this publication with those of any living or dead person or institutions is intended, and any such similarity which may exist is purely coincidental. This publication may not be sold except by authorized dealers and is sold subject to the conditions that it shall not be sold or distributed with any part of its cover or markings removed, nor in a mutilated condition. SPIDER-MAN (including prominent characters featured in this publication and the distinctive likenesses thereof) is a trademark of MARVEL CHARACTERS, INC. Printed in Canada. PETER CUNEO, Chief Executive Officer; AVI ARAD, Chief Creative Officer; GUI KARYO, Chief Information Officer; STAN LEE, Chairman Emeritus.

10 9 8 7 6 5 4 3 2

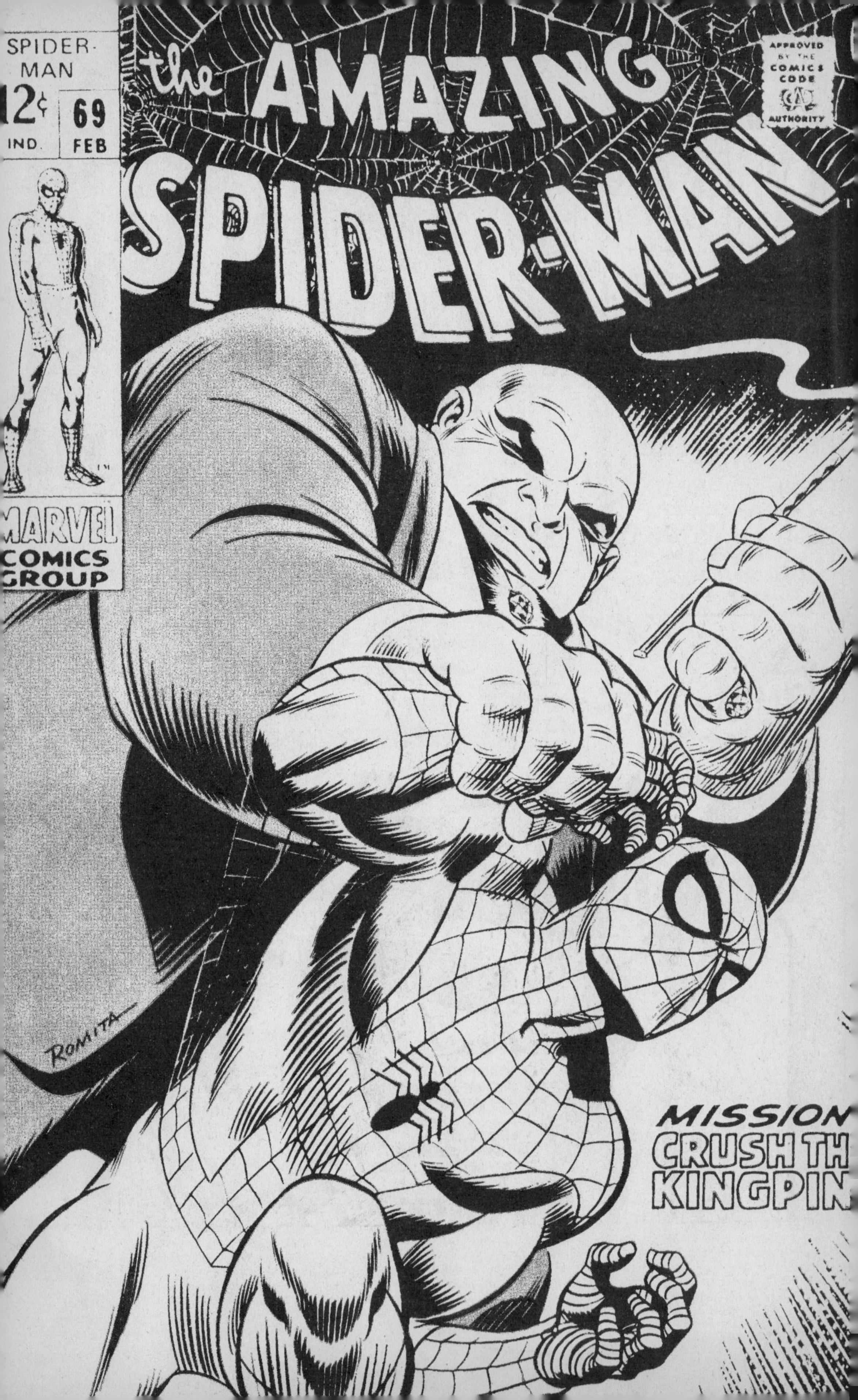
SPIDER-MAN
12¢
69
IND.
FEB
the AMAZING
SPIDER-MAN
APPROVED BY THE COMICS CODE AUTHORITY
MARVEL COMICS GROUP
ROMITA
MISSION
CRUSH TH
KINGPIN

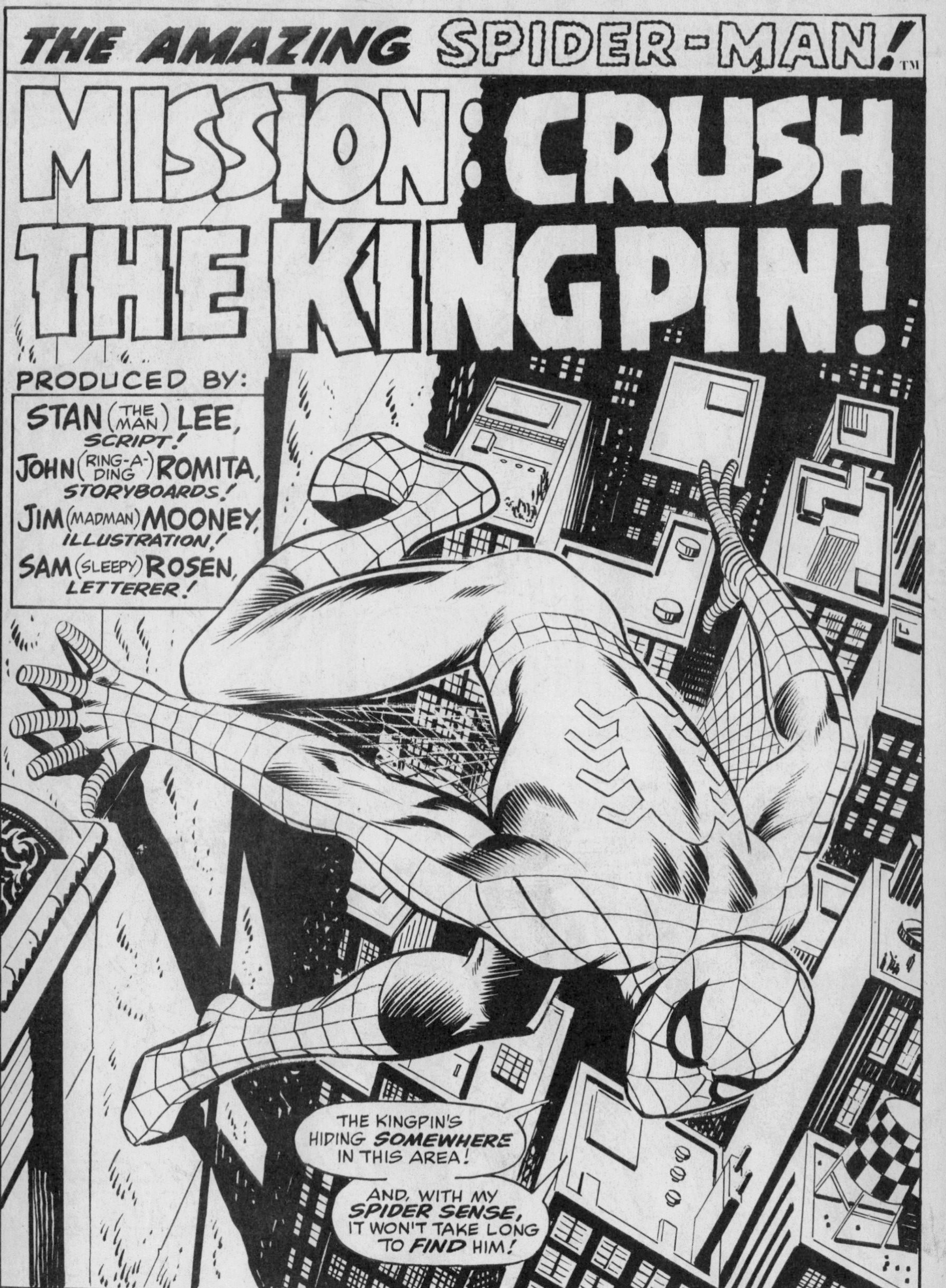
THE AMAZING SPIDER-MAN!™
MISSION: CRUSH THE KINGPIN!
PRODUCED BY:
STAN (THE MAN) LEE, SCRIPT!
JOHN (RING-A-DING) ROMITA, STORYBOARDS!
JIM (MADMAN) MOONEY, ILLUSTRATION!
SAM (SLEEPY) ROSEN, LETTERER!
THE KINGPIN'S HIDING SOMEWHERE IN THIS AREA!
AND, WITH MY SPIDER SENSE, IT WON'T TAKE LONG TO FIND HIM!

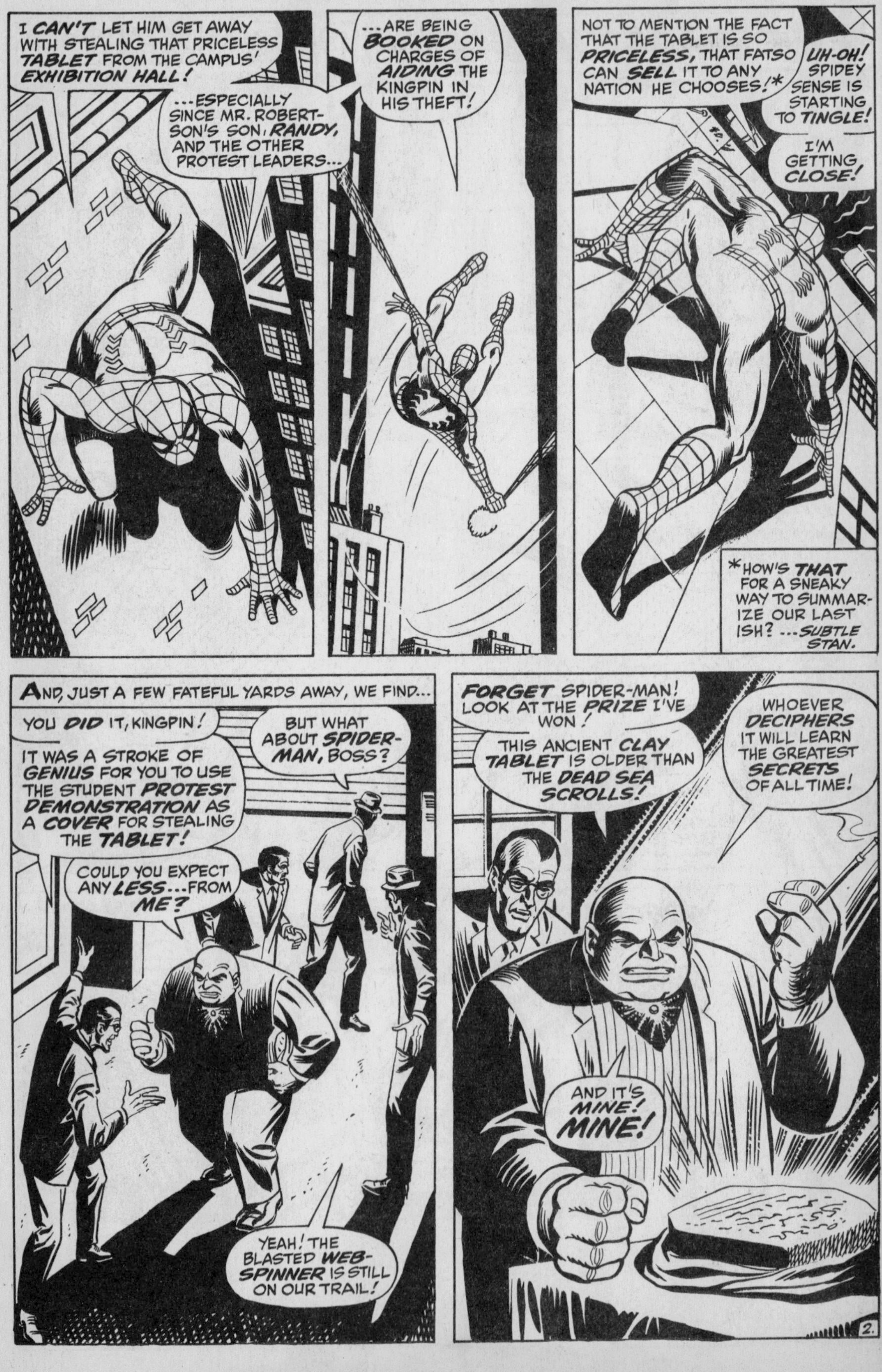
I CAN'T LET HIM GET AWAY WITH STEALING THAT PRICELESS TABLET FROM THE CAMPUS' EXHIBITION HALL!
...ESPECIALLY SINCE MR. ROBERTSON'S SON, RANDY, AND THE OTHER PROTEST LEADERS...
...ARE BEING BOOKED ON CHARGES OF AIDING THE KINGPIN IN HIS THEFT!
NOT TO MENTION THE FACT THAT THE TABLET IS SO PRICELESS, THAT FATSO CAN SELL IT TO ANY NATION HE CHOOSES!*
UH-OH! SPIDEY SENSE IS STARTING TO TINGLE!
I'M GETTING CLOSE!
*HOW'S THAT FOR A SNEAKY WAY TO SUMMARIZE OUR LAST ISH? ...SUBTLE STAN.
AND, JUST A FEW FATEFUL YARDS AWAY, WE FIND...
YOU DID IT, KINGPIN!
IT WAS A STROKE OF GENIUS FOR YOU TO USE THE STUDENT PROTEST DEMONSTRATION AS A COVER FOR STEALING THE TABLET!
BUT WHAT ABOUT SPIDER-MAN, BOSS?
COULD YOU EXPECT ANY LESS...FROM ME?
YEAH! THE BLASTED WEB-SPINNER IS STILL ON OUR TRAIL!
FORGET SPIDER-MAN! LOOK AT THE PRIZE I'VE WON!
THIS ANCIENT CLAY TABLET IS OLDER THAN THE DEAD SEA SCROLLS!
WHOEVER DECIPHERS IT WILL LEARN THE GREATEST SECRETS OF ALL TIME!
AND IT'S MINE! MINE!
2.

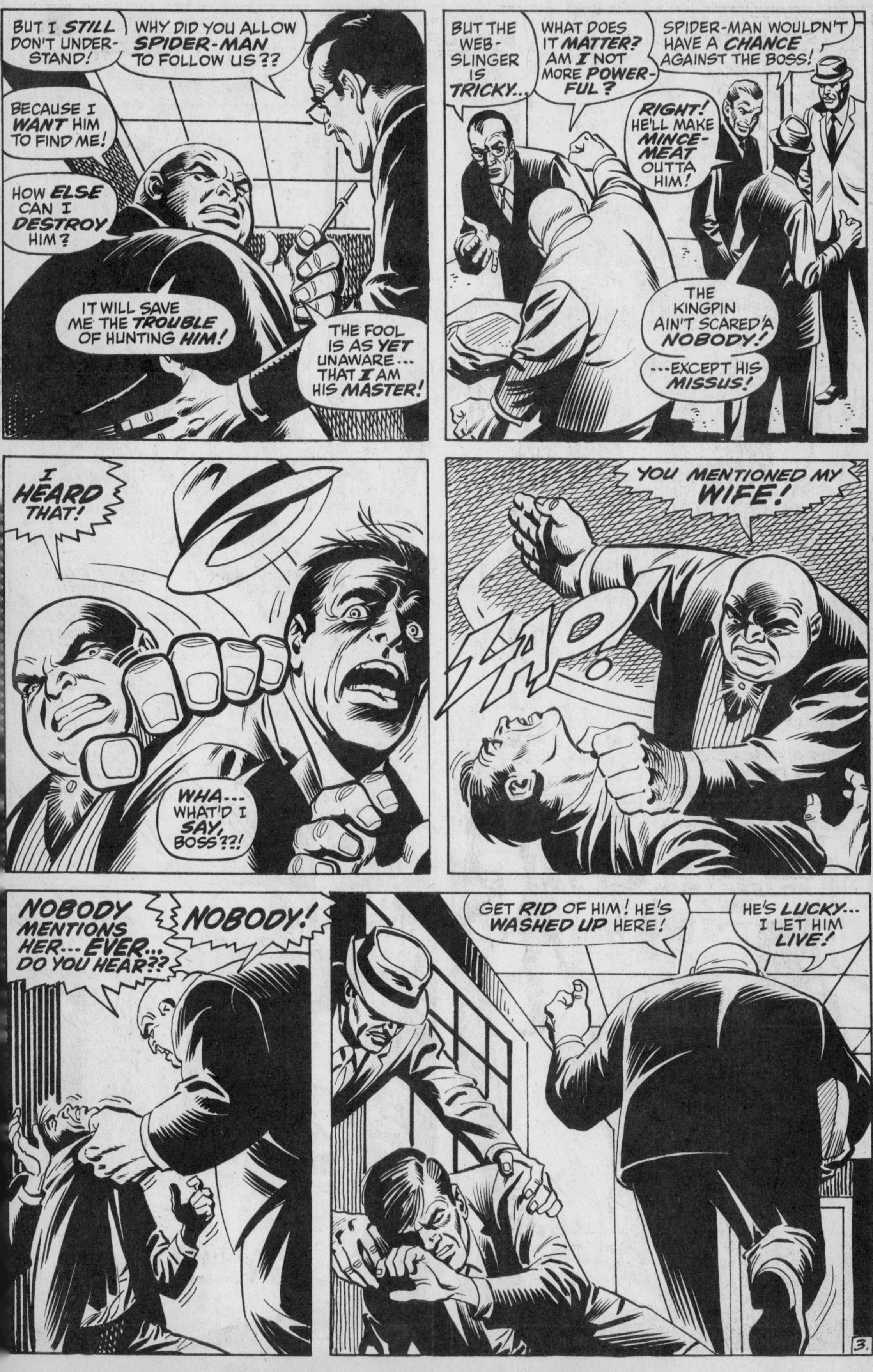
BUT I STILL DON'T UNDER-STAND!
WHY DID YOU ALLOW SPIDER-MAN TO FOLLOW US??
BECAUSE I WANT HIM TO FIND ME!
HOW ELSE CAN I DESTROY HIM?
IT WILL SAVE ME THE TROUBLE OF HUNTING HIM!
THE FOOL IS AS YET UNAWARE--- THAT I AM HIS MASTER!
BUT THE WEB-SLINGER IS TRICKY...
WHAT DOES IT MATTER? AM I NOT MORE POWER-FUL?
SPIDER-MAN WOULDN'T HAVE A CHANCE AGAINST THE BOSS!
RIGHT! HE'LL MAKE MINCE-MEAT OUTTA HIM!
THE KINGPIN AIN'T SCARED'A NOBODY!
---EXCEPT HIS MISSUS!
I HEARD THAT!
WHA... WHAT'D I SAY, BOSS??!
YOU MENTIONED MY WIFE!
SLAP!
NOBODY MENTIONS HER... EVER... DO YOU HEAR??
NOBODY!
GET RID OF HIM! HE'S WASHED UP HERE!
HE'S LUCKY... I LET HIM LIVE!

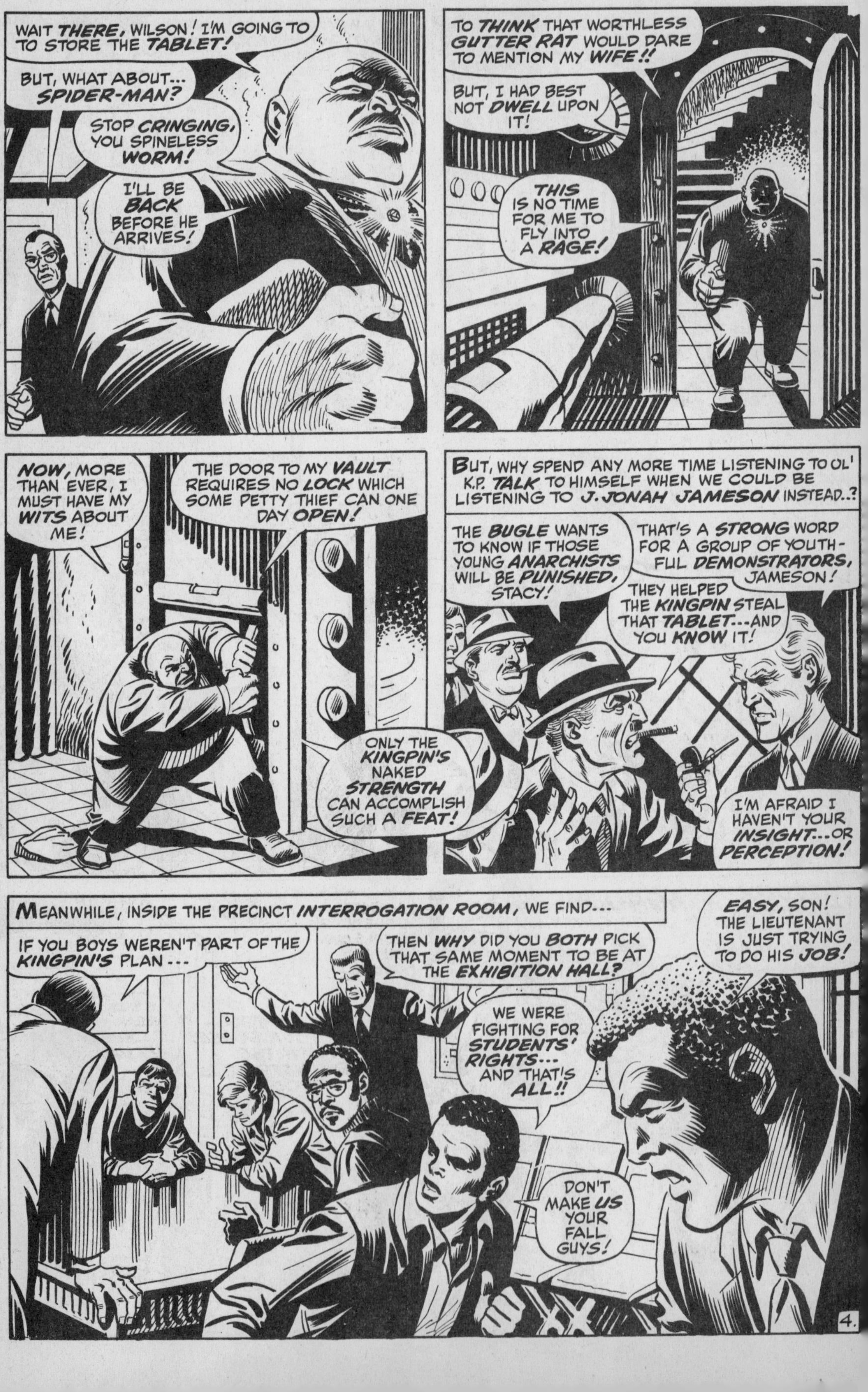
WAIT THERE, WILSON! I'M GOING TO TO STORE THE TABLET!
BUT, WHAT ABOUT... SPIDER-MAN?
STOP CRINGING, YOU SPINELESS WORM!
I'LL BE BACK BEFORE HE ARRIVES!
TO THINK THAT WORTHLESS GUTTER RAT WOULD DARE TO MENTION MY WIFE!!
BUT, I HAD BEST NOT DWELL UPON IT!
THIS IS NO TIME FOR ME TO FLY INTO A RAGE!
NOW, MORE THAN EVER, I MUST HAVE MY WITS ABOUT ME!
THE DOOR TO MY VAULT REQUIRES NO LOCK WHICH SOME PETTY THIEF CAN ONE DAY OPEN!
ONLY THE KINGPIN'S NAKED STRENGTH CAN ACCOMPLISH SUCH A FEAT!
BUT, WHY SPEND ANY MORE TIME LISTENING TO OL' K.P. TALK TO HIMSELF WHEN WE COULD BE LISTENING TO J. JONAH JAMESON INSTEAD..?
THE BUGLE WANTS TO KNOW IF THOSE YOUNG ANARCHISTS WILL BE PUNISHED, STACY!
THAT'S A STRONG WORD FOR A GROUP OF YOUTH-FUL DEMONSTRATORS, JAMESON!
THEY HELPED THE KINGPIN STEAL THAT TABLET---AND YOU KNOW IT!
I'M AFRAID I HAVEN'T YOUR INSIGHT...OR PERCEPTION!
MEANWHILE, INSIDE THE PRECINCT INTERROGATION ROOM, WE FIND---
IF YOU BOYS WEREN'T PART OF THE KINGPIN'S PLAN ---
THEN WHY DID YOU BOTH PICK THAT SAME MOMENT TO BE AT THE EXHIBITION HALL?
EASY, SON! THE LIEUTENANT IS JUST TRYING TO DO HIS JOB!
WE WERE FIGHTING FOR STUDENTS' RIGHTS... AND THAT'S ALL!!
DON'T MAKE US YOUR FALL GUYS!

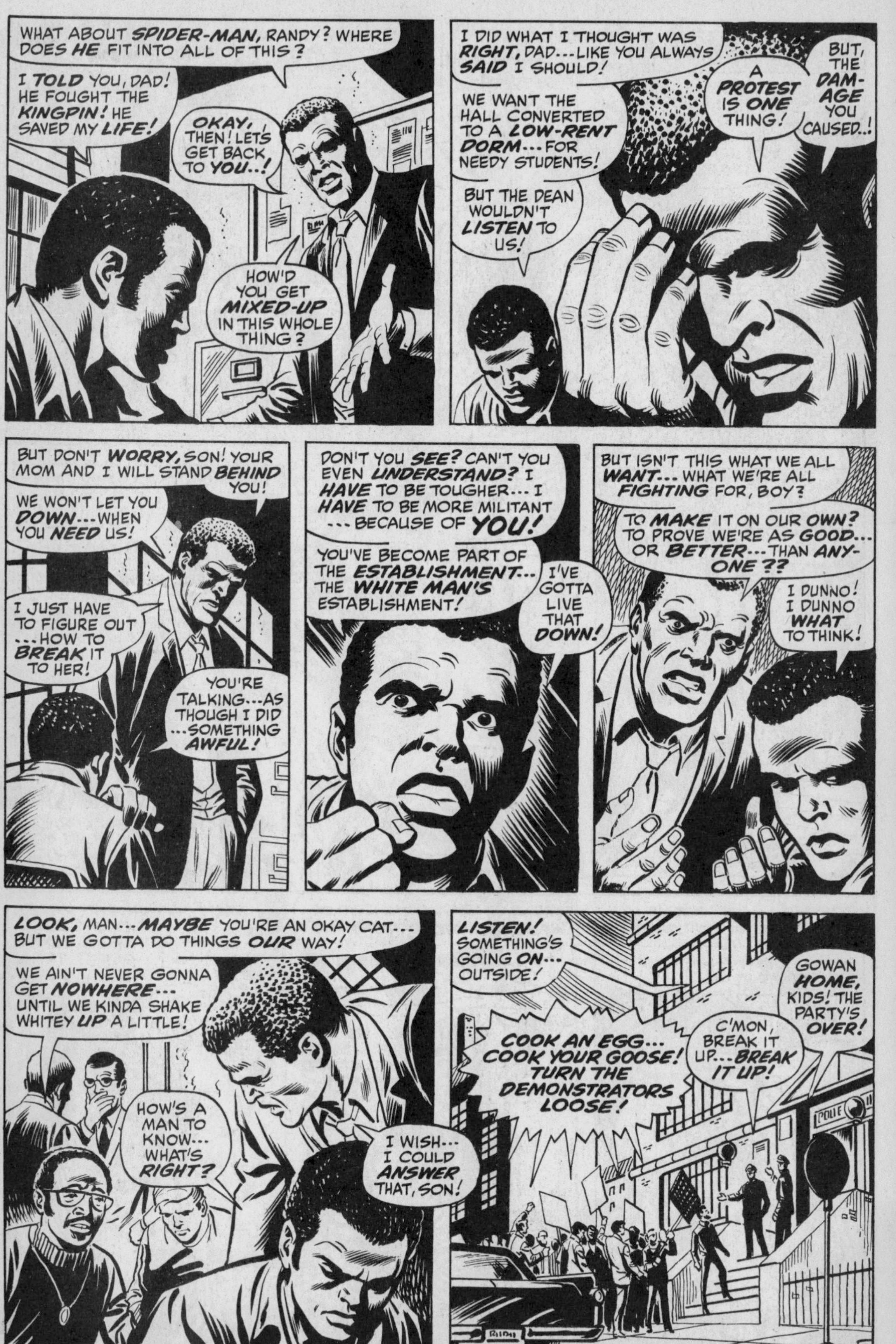
WHAT ABOUT SPIDER-MAN, RANDY? WHERE DOES HE FIT INTO ALL OF THIS?
I TOLD YOU, DAD! HE FOUGHT THE KINGPIN! HE SAVED MY LIFE!
OKAY, THEN! LET'S GET BACK TO YOU..!
HOW'D YOU GET MIXED-UP IN THIS WHOLE THING?
I DID WHAT I THOUGHT WAS RIGHT, DAD--LIKE YOU ALWAYS SAID I SHOULD!
WE WANT THE HALL CONVERTED TO A LOW-RENT DORM--FOR NEEDY STUDENTS!
BUT THE DEAN WOULDN'T LISTEN TO US!
A PROTEST IS ONE THING!
BUT, THE DAMAGE YOU CAUSED..!
BUT DON'T WORRY, SON! YOUR MOM AND I WILL STAND BEHIND YOU!
WE WON'T LET YOU DOWN--WHEN YOU NEED US!
I JUST HAVE TO FIGURE OUT ...HOW TO BREAK IT TO HER!
YOU'RE TALKING--AS THOUGH I DID ...SOMETHING AWFUL!
DON'T YOU SEE? CAN'T YOU EVEN UNDERSTAND? I HAVE TO BE TOUGHER... I HAVE TO BE MORE MILITANT ...BECAUSE OF YOU!
YOU'VE BECOME PART OF THE ESTABLISHMENT... THE WHITE MAN'S ESTABLISHMENT!
I'VE GOTTA LIVE THAT DOWN!
BUT ISN'T THIS WHAT WE ALL WANT... WHAT WE'RE ALL FIGHTING FOR, BOY?
TO MAKE IT ON OUR OWN? TO PROVE WE'RE AS GOOD... OR BETTER--THAN ANYONE??
I DUNNO! I DUNNO WHAT TO THINK!
LOOK, MAN...MAYBE YOU'RE AN OKAY CAT... BUT WE GOTTA DO THINGS OUR WAY!
WE AIN'T NEVER GONNA GET NOWHERE... UNTIL WE KINDA SHAKE WHITEY UP A LITTLE!
HOW'S A MAN TO KNOW... WHAT'S RIGHT?
I WISH... I COULD ANSWER THAT, SON!
LISTEN! SOMETHING'S GOING ON... OUTSIDE!
COOK AN EGG... COOK YOUR GOOSE! TURN THE DEMONSTRATORS LOOSE!
C'MON, BREAK IT UP... BREAK IT UP!
GOWAN HOME, KIDS! THE PARTY'S OVER!
POLICE
5

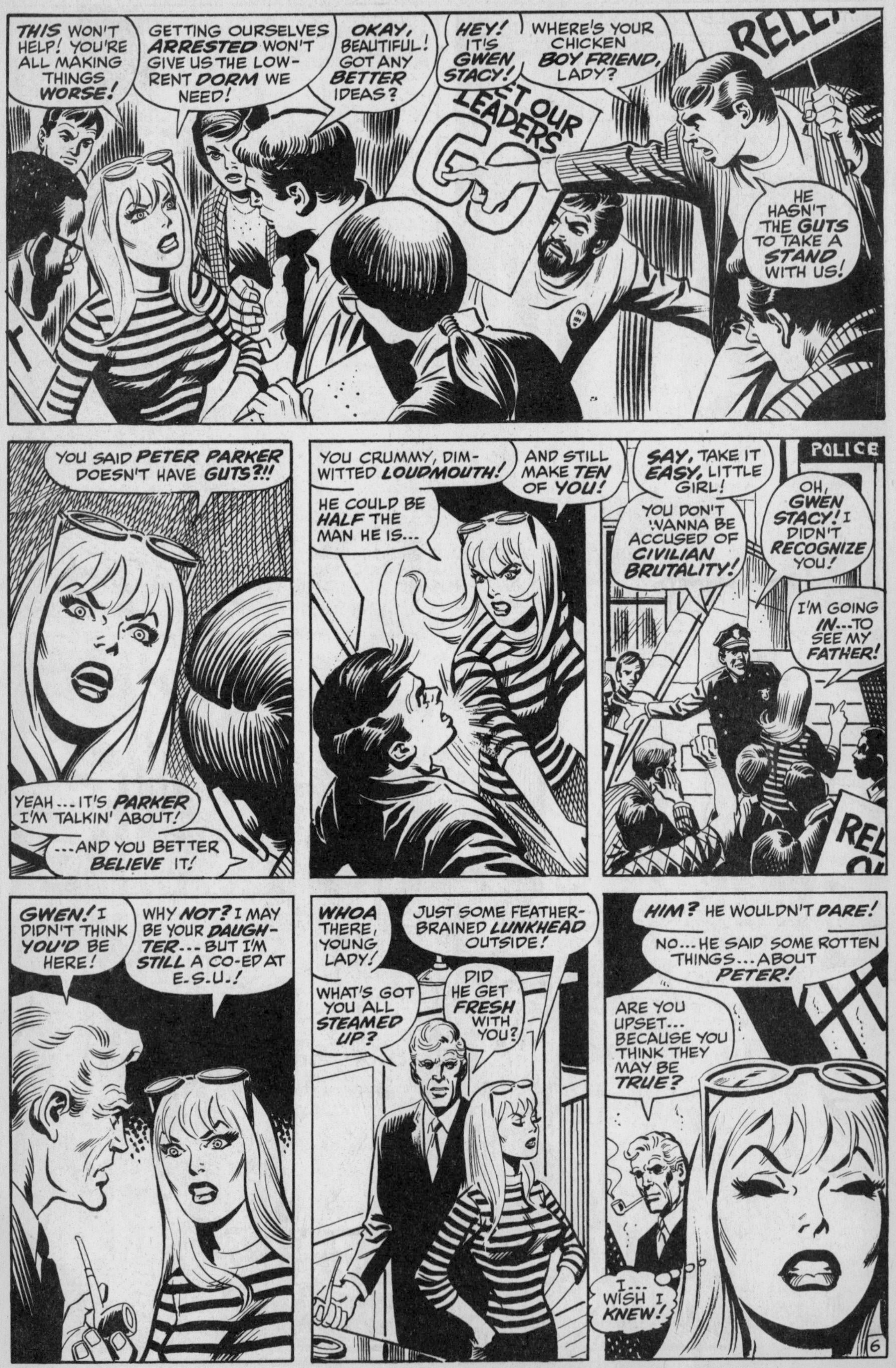
THIS WON'T HELP! YOU'RE ALL MAKING THINGS WORSE!
GETTING OURSELVES ARRESTED WON'T GIVE US THE LOW-RENT DORM WE NEED!
OKAY, BEAUTIFUL! GOT ANY BETTER IDEAS?
HEY! IT'S GWEN STACY!
WHERE'S YOUR CHICKEN BOY FRIEND, LADY?
HE HASN'T THE GUTS TO TAKE A STAND WITH US!
YOU SAID PETER PARKER DOESN'T HAVE GUTS?!!
YEAH... IT'S PARKER I'M TALKIN' ABOUT!
...AND YOU BETTER BELIEVE IT!
YOU CRUMMY, DIM-WITTED LOUDMOUTH!
HE COULD BE HALF THE MAN HE IS...
AND STILL MAKE TEN OF YOU!
SAY, TAKE IT EASY, LITTLE GIRL!
YOU DON'T WANNA BE ACCUSED OF CIVILIAN BRUTALITY!
POLICE
OH, GWEN STACY! I DIDN'T RECOGNIZE YOU!
I'M GOING IN--TO SEE MY FATHER!
GWEN! I DIDN'T THINK YOU'D BE HERE!
WHY NOT? I MAY BE YOUR DAUGHTER--- BUT I'M STILL A CO-ED AT E.S.U.!
WHOA THERE, YOUNG LADY!
WHAT'S GOT YOU ALL STEAMED UP?
JUST SOME FEATHER-BRAINED LUNKHEAD OUTSIDE!
DID HE GET FRESH WITH YOU?
HIM? HE WOULDN'T DARE!
NO... HE SAID SOME ROTTEN THINGS... ABOUT PETER!
ARE YOU UPSET... BECAUSE YOU THINK THEY MAY BE TRUE?
I... WISH I KNEW!

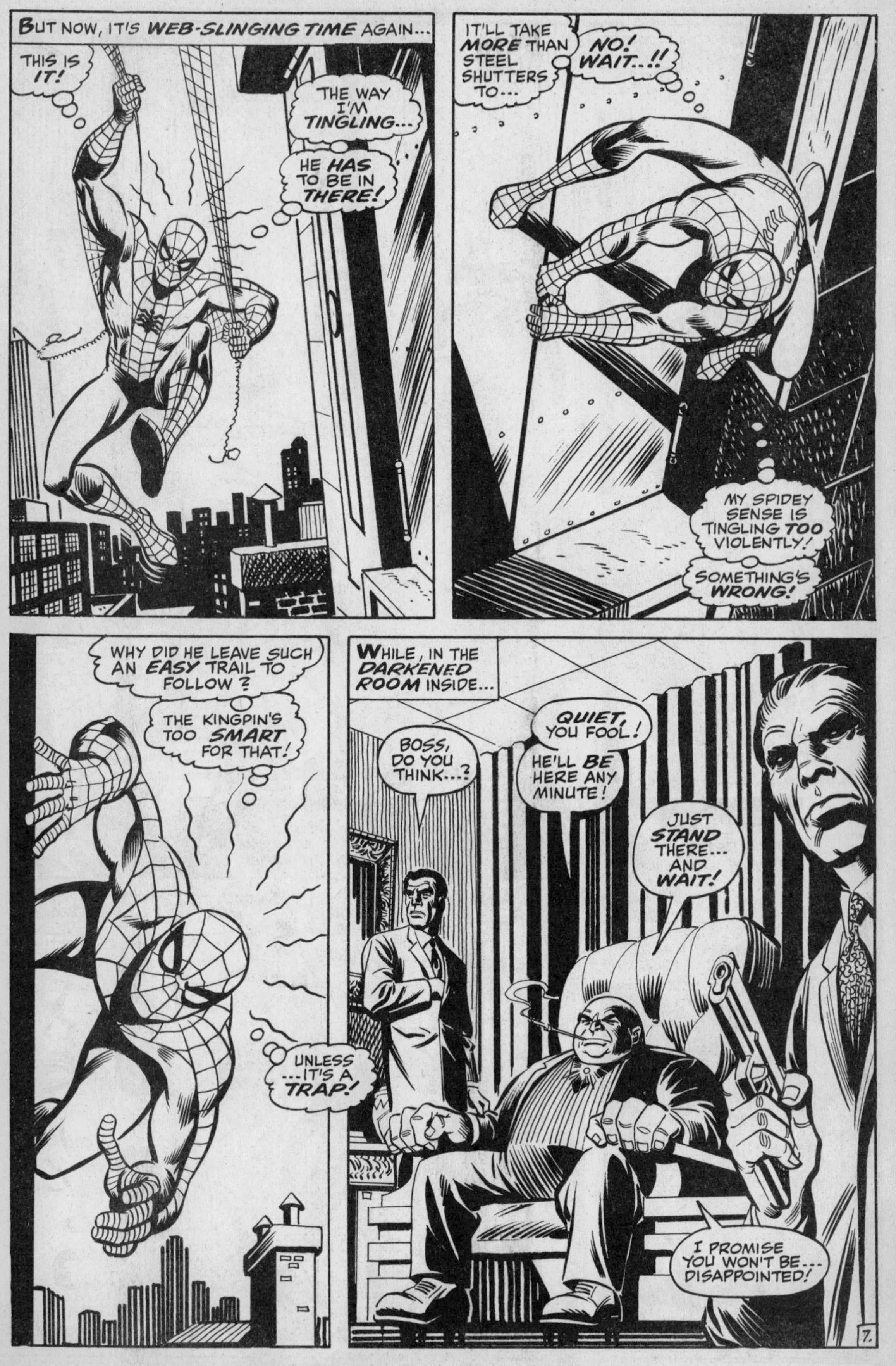

BUT NOW, IT'S WEB-SLINGING TIME AGAIN...
THIS IS IT!
THE WAY I'M TINGLING...
HE HAS TO BE IN THERE!
IT'LL TAKE MORE THAN STEEL SHUTTERS TO...
NO! WAIT...!!
MY SPIDEY SENSE IS TINGLING TOO VIOLENTLY!
SOMETHING'S WRONG!
WHY DID HE LEAVE SUCH AN EASY TRAIL TO FOLLOW?
THE KINGPIN'S TOO SMART FOR THAT!
UNLESS ...IT'S A TRAP!
WHILE, IN THE DARKENED ROOM INSIDE...
BOSS, DO YOU THINK...?
QUIET, YOU FOOL!
HE'LL BE HERE ANY MINUTE!
JUST STAND THERE... AND WAIT!
I PROMISE YOU WON'T BE... DISAPPOINTED!

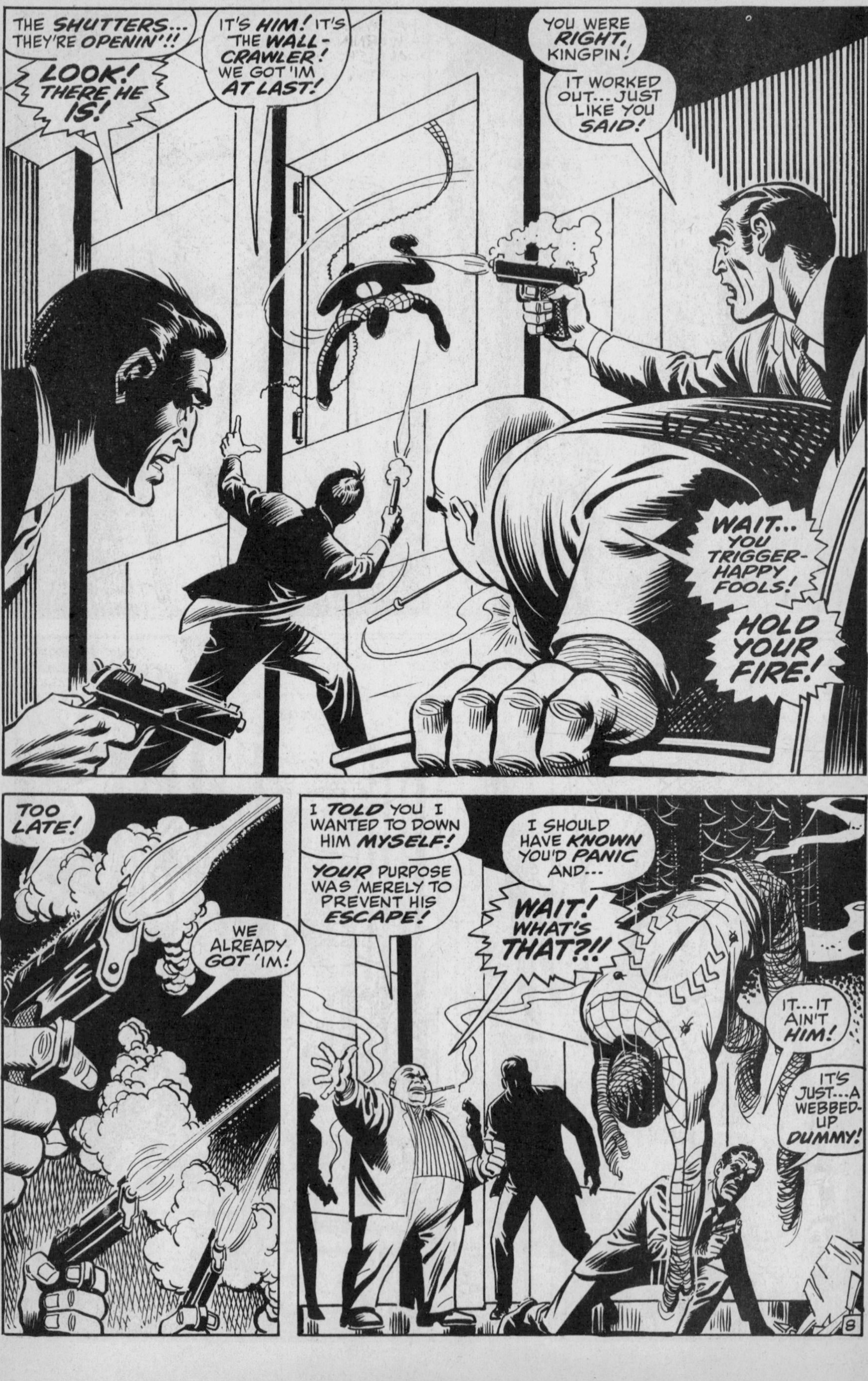
THE SHUTTERS... THEY'RE OPENIN'!!
LOOK! THERE HE IS!
IT'S HIM! IT'S THE WALL-CRAWLER! WE GOT 'IM AT LAST!
YOU WERE RIGHT, KINGPIN!
IT WORKED OUT... JUST LIKE YOU SAID!
WAIT... YOU TRIGGER-HAPPY FOOLS!
HOLD YOUR FIRE!
TOO LATE!
WE ALREADY GOT 'IM!
I TOLD YOU I WANTED TO DOWN HIM MYSELF!
YOUR PURPOSE WAS MERELY TO PREVENT HIS ESCAPE!
I SHOULD HAVE KNOWN YOU'D PANIC AND...
WAIT! WHAT'S THAT?!!
IT... IT AIN'T HIM!
IT'S JUST... A WEBBED-UP DUMMY!

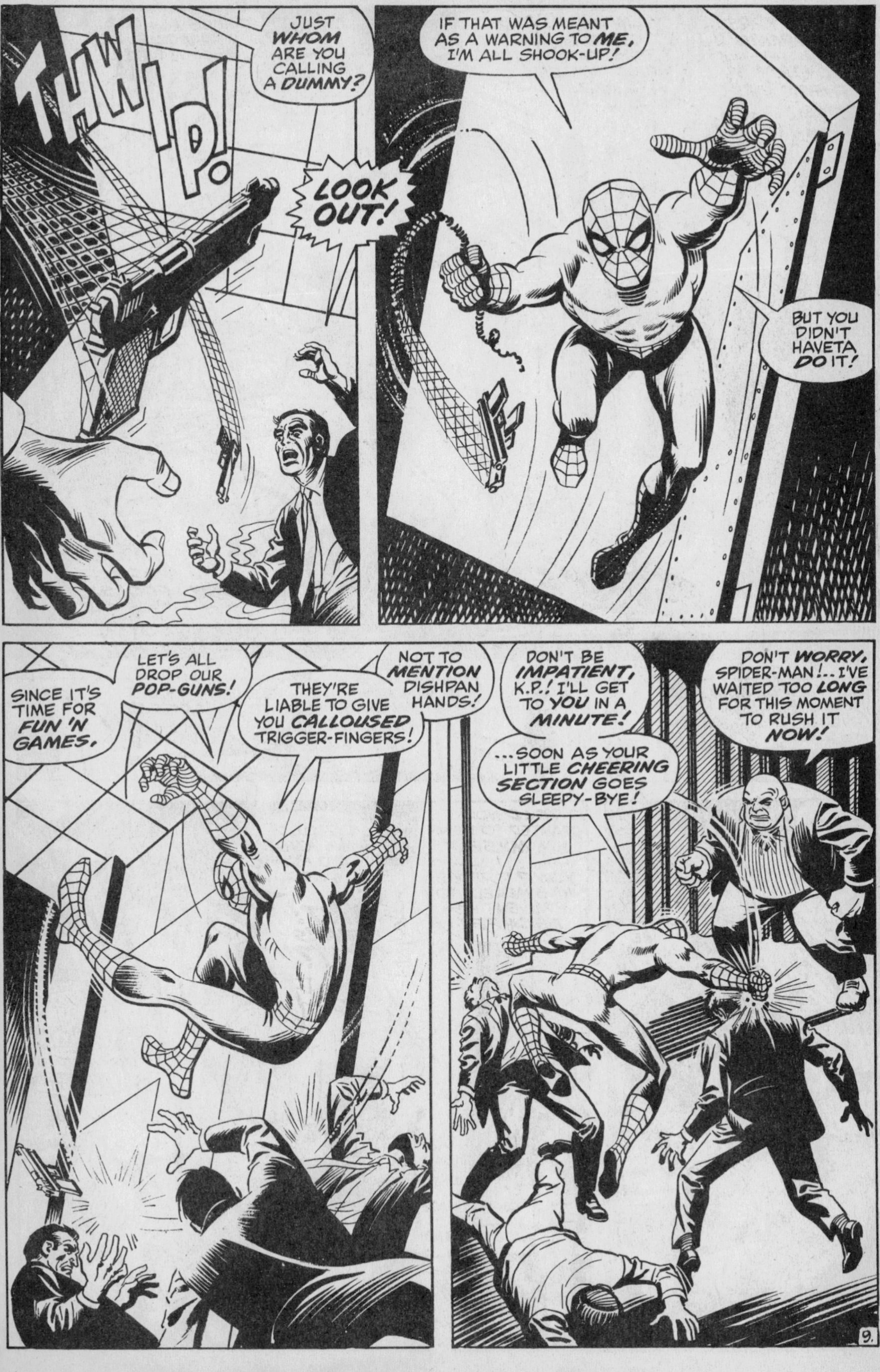
THWIP!
JUST WHOM ARE YOU CALLING A DUMMY?
LOOK OUT!
IF THAT WAS MEANT AS A WARNING TO ME, I'M ALL SHOOK-UP!
BUT YOU DIDN'T HAVETA DO IT!
SINCE IT'S TIME FOR FUN 'N GAMES,
LET'S ALL DROP OUR POP-GUNS!
THEY'RE LIABLE TO GIVE YOU CALLOUSED TRIGGER-FINGERS!
NOT TO MENTION DISHPAN HANDS!
DON'T BE IMPATIENT, K.P.! I'LL GET TO YOU IN A MINUTE!
...SOON AS YOUR LITTLE CHEERING SECTION GOES SLEEPY-BYE!
DON'T WORRY, SPIDER-MAN!... I'VE WAITED TOO LONG FOR THIS MOMENT TO RUSH IT NOW!
9.

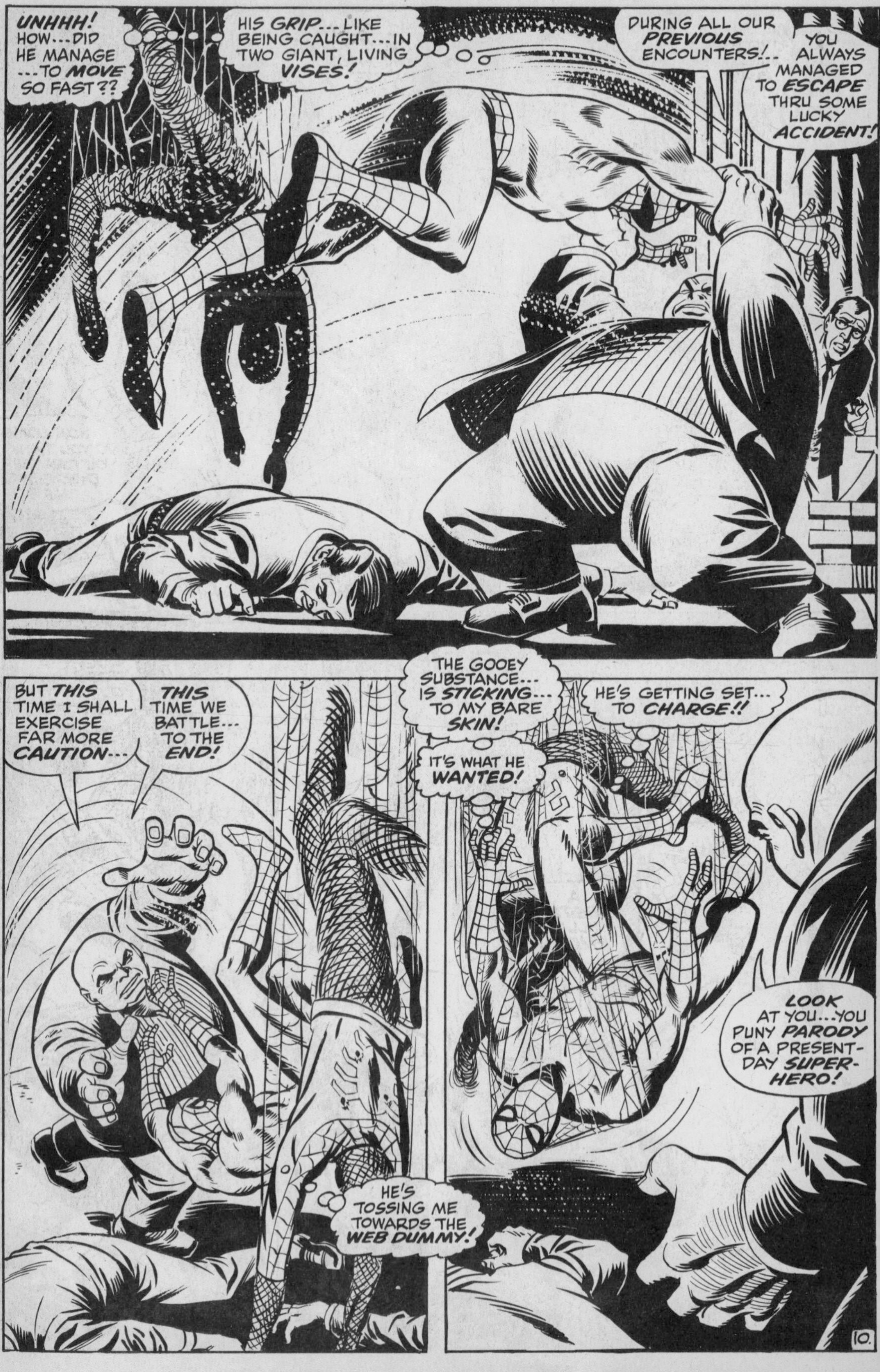
UNHHH! HOW...DID HE MANAGE ...TO MOVE SO FAST??
HIS GRIP...LIKE BEING CAUGHT...IN TWO GIANT, LIVING VISES!
DURING ALL OUR PREVIOUS ENCOUNTERS!..
YOU ALWAYS MANAGED TO ESCAPE THRU SOME LUCKY ACCIDENT!
BUT THIS TIME I SHALL EXERCISE FAR MORE CAUTION...
THIS TIME WE BATTLE...TO THE END!
HE'S TOSSING ME TOWARDS THE WEB DUMMY!
THE GOOEY SUBSTANCE...IS STICKING...TO MY BARE SKIN!
IT'S WHAT HE WANTED!
HE'S GETTING SET...TO CHARGE!!
LOOK AT YOU...YOU PUNY PARODY OF A PRESENT-DAY SUPER-HERO!
10.

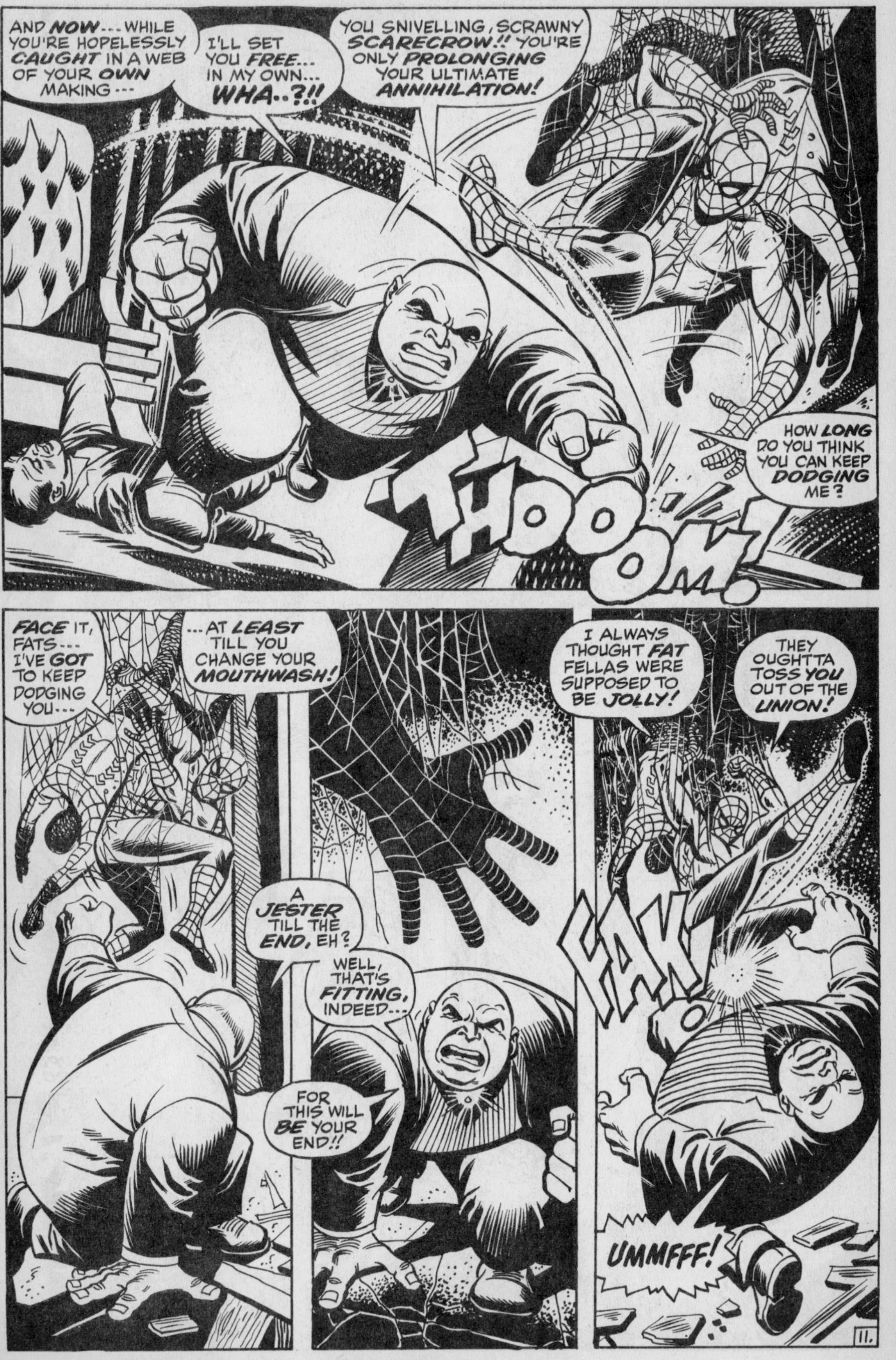

AND NOW... WHILE YOU'RE HOPELESSLY CAUGHT IN A WEB OF YOUR OWN MAKING---
I'LL SET YOU FREE... IN MY OWN... WHA..?!!
YOU SNIVELLING, SCRAWNY SCARECROW!! YOU'RE ONLY PROLONGING YOUR ULTIMATE ANNIHILATION!
HOW LONG DO YOU THINK YOU CAN KEEP DODGING ME?
THOOOOM!
FACE IT, FATS... I'VE GOT TO KEEP DODGING YOU...
...AT LEAST TILL YOU CHANGE YOUR MOUTHWASH!
A JESTER TILL THE END, EH?
WELL, THAT'S FITTING, INDEED...
FOR THIS WILL BE YOUR END!!
I ALWAYS THOUGHT FAT FELLAS WERE SUPPOSED TO BE JOLLY!
THEY OUGHTTA TOSS YOU OUT OF THE UNION!
CRAK
UMMFFF!

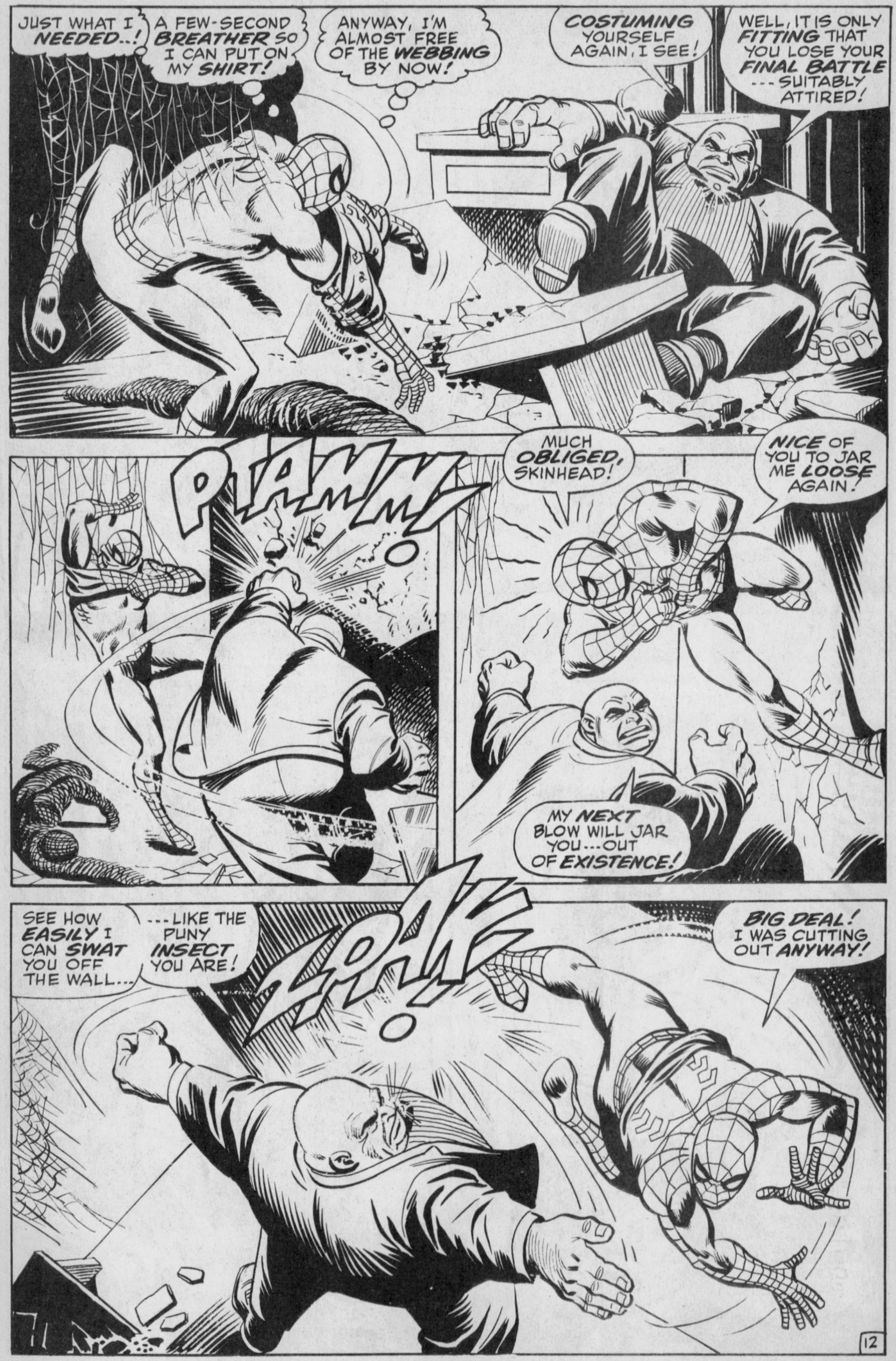
JUST WHAT I NEEDED..!
A FEW-SECOND BREATHER SO I CAN PUT ON MY SHIRT!
ANYWAY, I'M ALMOST FREE OF THE WEBBING BY NOW!
COSTUMING YOURSELF AGAIN, I SEE!
WELL, IT IS ONLY FITTING THAT YOU LOSE YOUR FINAL BATTLE --- SUITABLY ATTIRED!
PTAMMM!
MUCH OBLIGED, SKINHEAD!
NICE OF YOU TO JAR ME LOOSE AGAIN!
MY NEXT BLOW WILL JAR YOU---OUT OF EXISTENCE!
SEE HOW EASILY I CAN SWAT YOU OFF THE WALL...
---LIKE THE PUNY INSECT YOU ARE!
ZOAK!
BIG DEAL! I WAS CUTTING OUT ANYWAY!
12

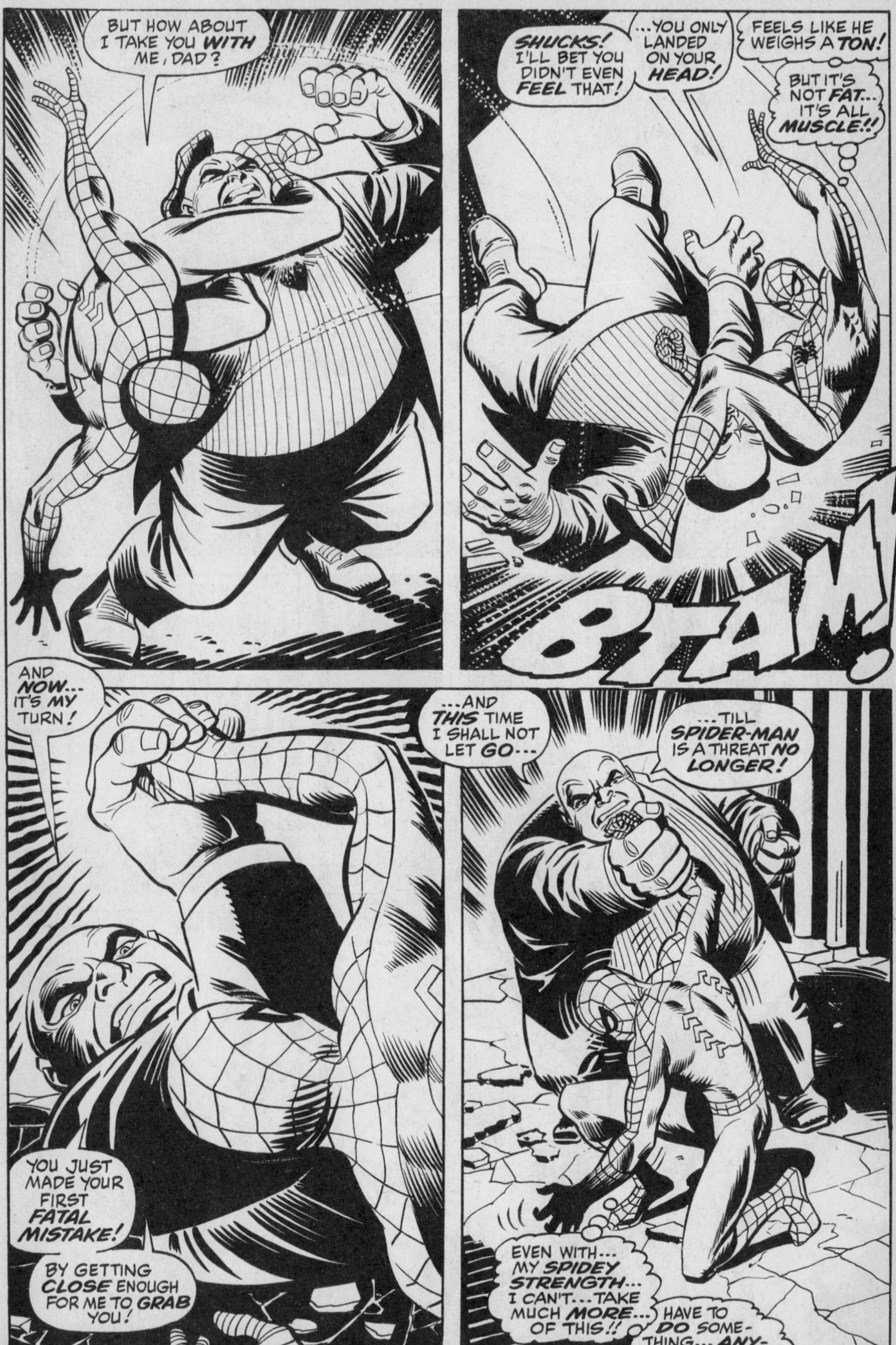

BUT HOW ABOUT I TAKE YOU WITH ME, DAD?
SHUCKS! I'LL BET YOU DIDN'T EVEN FEEL THAT!
...YOU ONLY LANDED ON YOUR HEAD!
FEELS LIKE HE WEIGHS A TON!
BUT IT'S NOT FAT... IT'S ALL MUSCLE!!
BTAM!
AND NOW... IT'S MY TURN!
YOU JUST MADE YOUR FIRST FATAL MISTAKE!
BY GETTING CLOSE ENOUGH FOR ME TO GRAB YOU!
...AND THIS TIME I SHALL NOT LET GO---
...TILL SPIDER-MAN IS A THREAT NO LONGER!
EVEN WITH... MY SPIDEY STRENGTH... I CAN'T... TAKE MUCH MORE... OF THIS!!
HAVE TO DO SOME-THING... ANY-THING... FAST!!

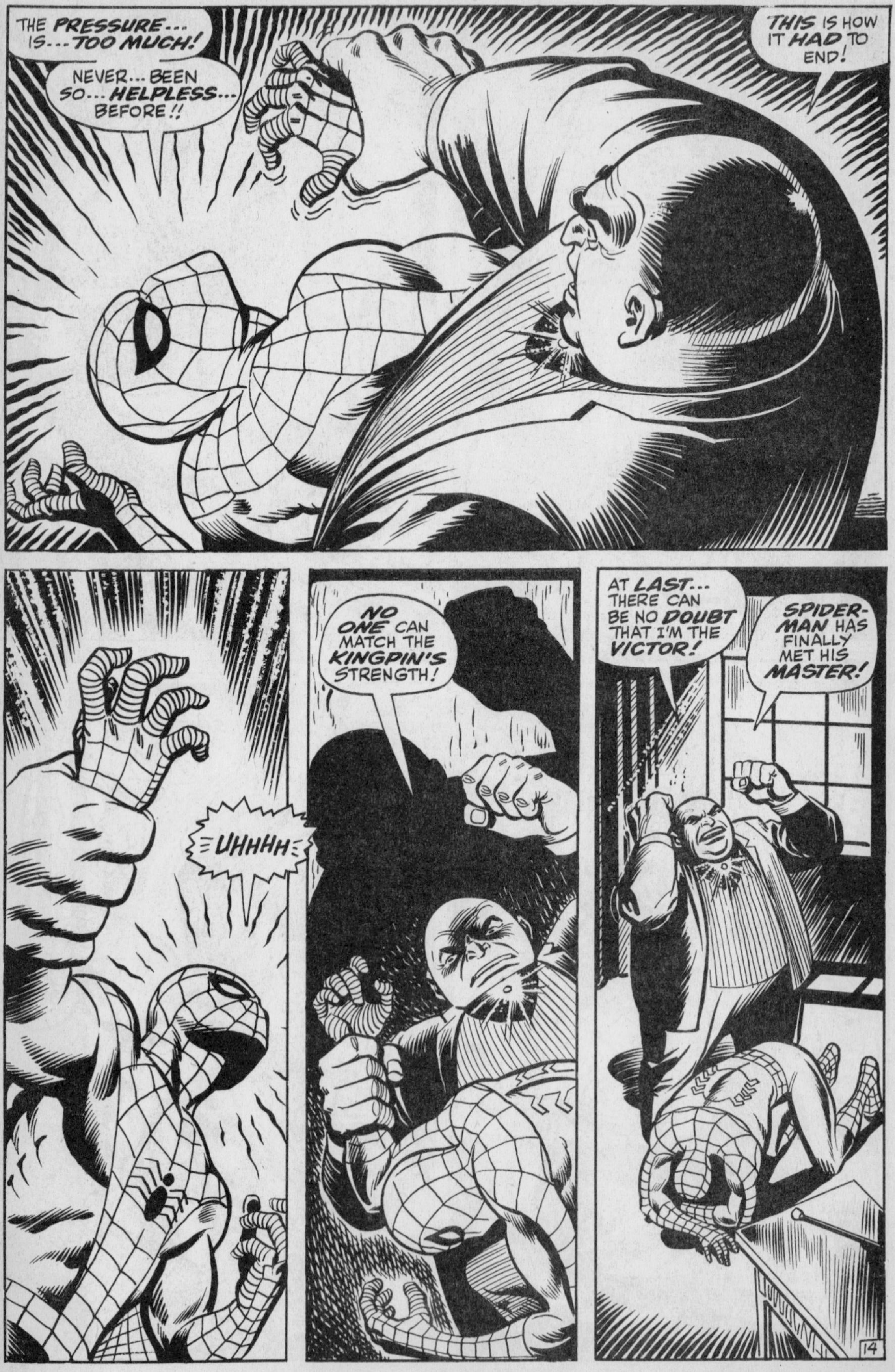
THE PRESSURE... IS...TOO MUCH!
NEVER... BEEN SO... HELPLESS... BEFORE!!
THIS IS HOW IT HAD TO END!
UHHHH
NO ONE CAN MATCH THE KINGPIN'S STRENGTH!
AT LAST... THERE CAN BE NO DOUBT THAT I'M THE VICTOR!
SPIDER-MAN HAS FINALLY MET HIS MASTER!
14

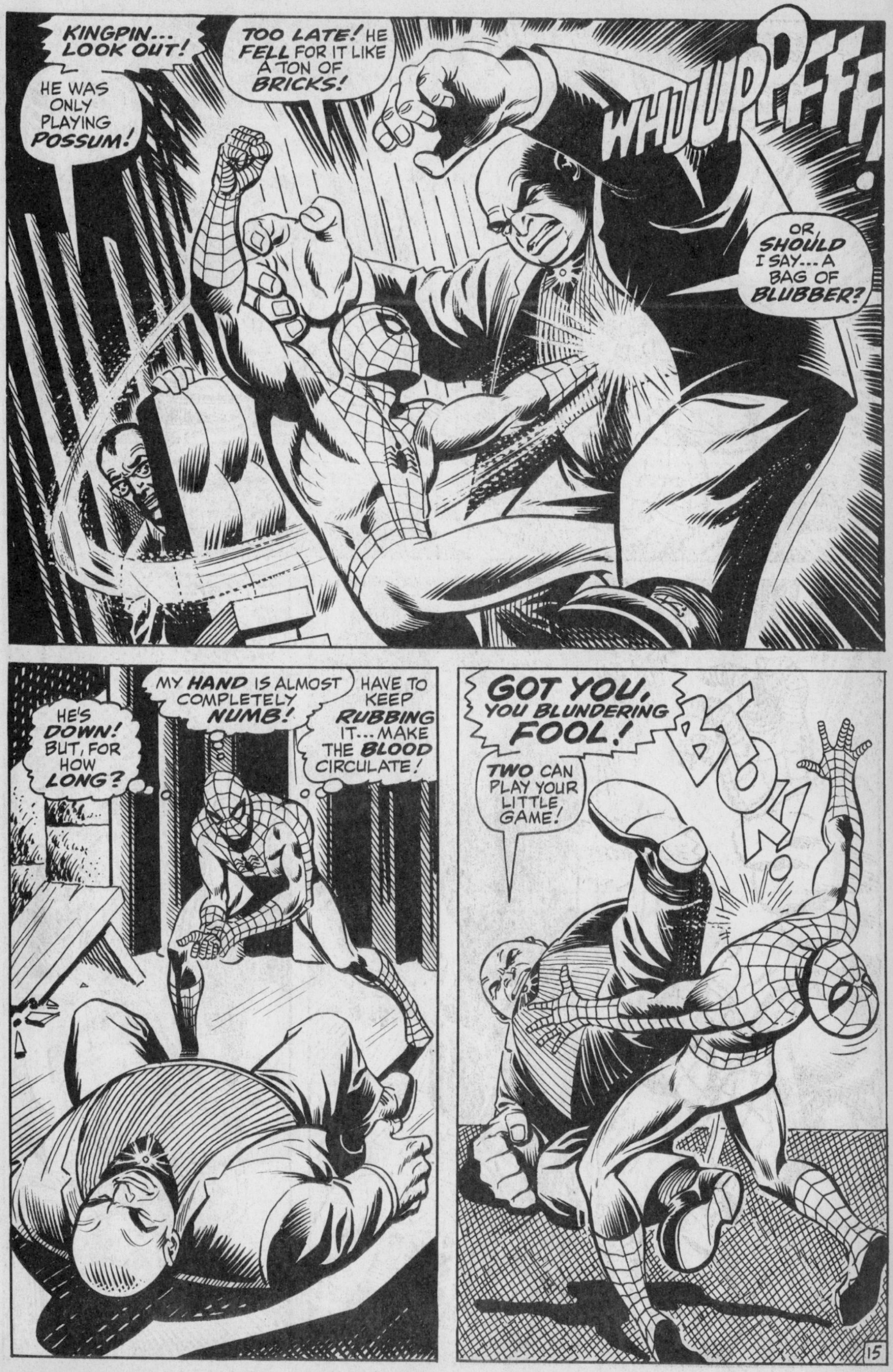
KINGPIN... LOOK OUT!
HE WAS ONLY PLAYING POSSUM!
TOO LATE! HE FELL FOR IT LIKE A TON OF BRICKS!
WHUUPPFFF!
OR, SHOULD I SAY... A BAG OF BLUBBER?
HE'S DOWN! BUT, FOR HOW LONG?
MY HAND IS ALMOST COMPLETELY NUMB!
HAVE TO KEEP RUBBING IT... MAKE THE BLOOD CIRCULATE!
GOT YOU, YOU BLUNDERING FOOL!
BTOK!
TWO CAN PLAY YOUR LITTLE GAME!
15

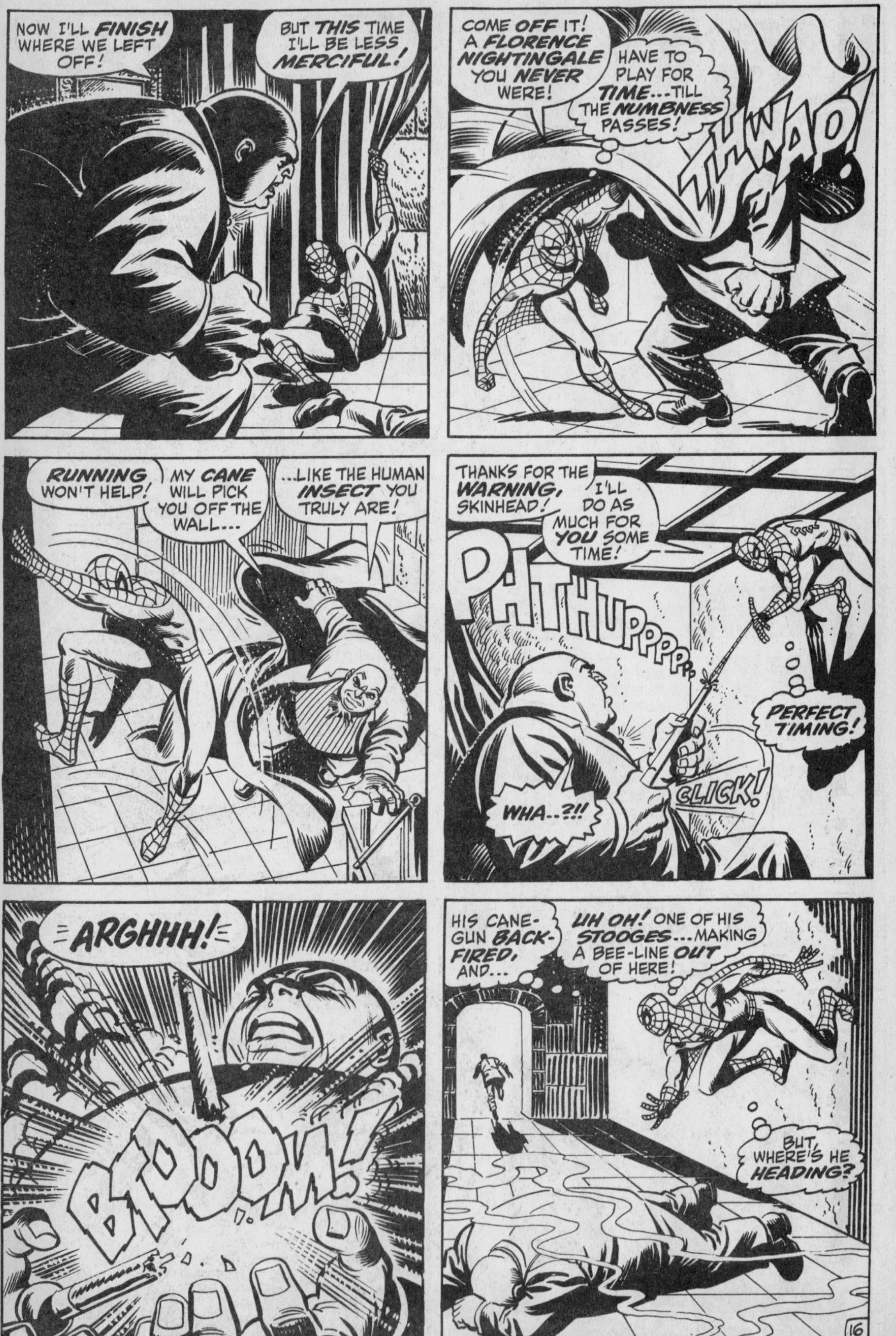
NOW I'LL FINISH WHERE WE LEFT OFF!
BUT THIS TIME I'LL BE LESS MERCIFUL!
COME OFF IT! A FLORENCE NIGHTINGALE YOU NEVER WERE!
HAVE TO PLAY FOR TIME...TILL THE NUMBNESS PASSES!
THWAP!
RUNNING WON'T HELP!
MY CANE WILL PICK YOU OFF THE WALL...
...LIKE THE HUMAN INSECT YOU TRULY ARE!
THANKS FOR THE WARNING, SKINHEAD!
I'LL DO AS MUCH FOR YOU SOME TIME!
PATHUPPPPP
PERFECT TIMING!
CLICK!
WHA..?!!
ARGHHH!
BTOOOM!
HIS CANE-GUN BACK-FIRED, AND...
UH OH! ONE OF HIS STOOGES...MAKING A BEE-LINE OUT OF HERE!
BUT, WHERE'S HE HEADING?
16

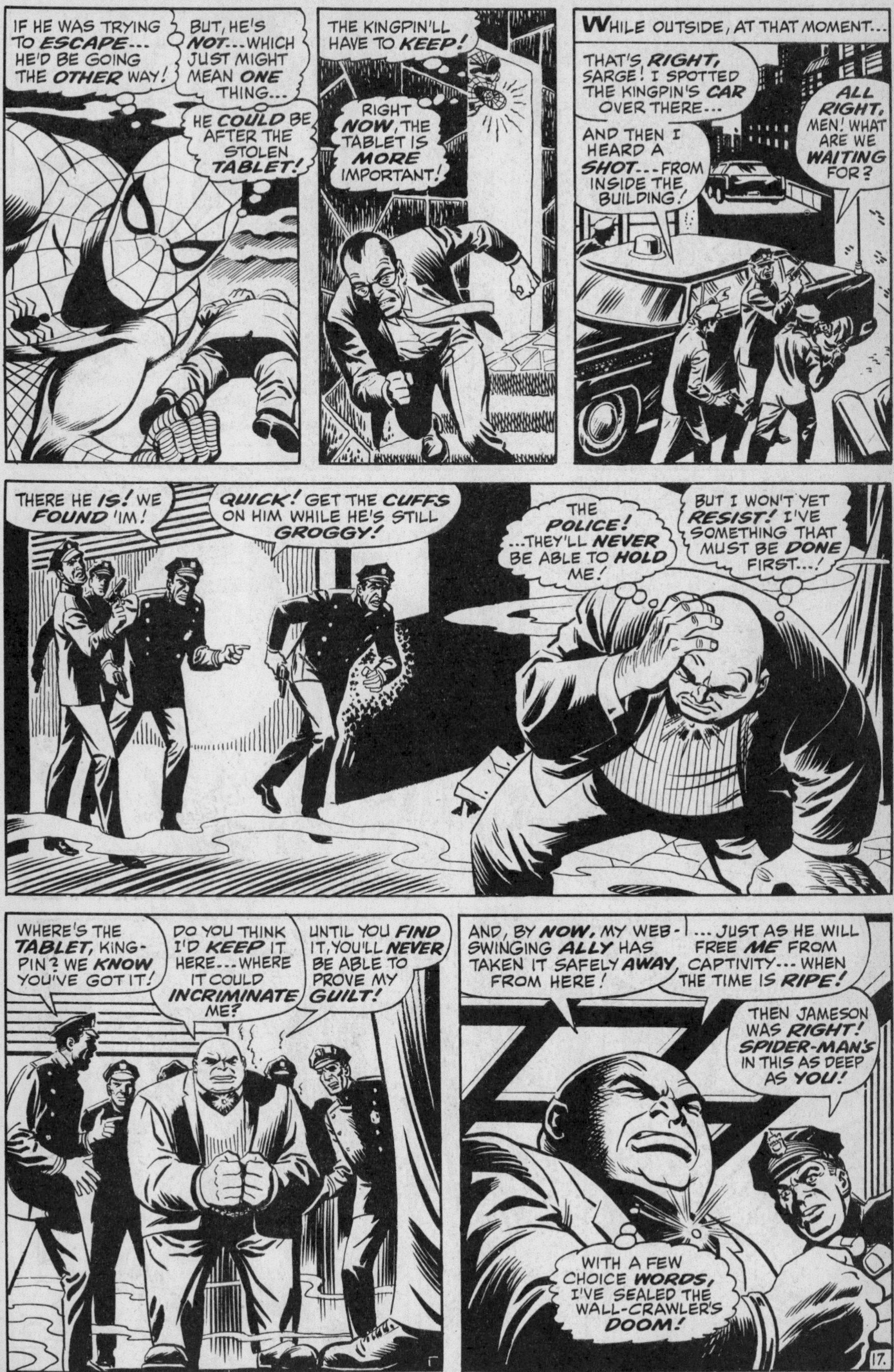

IF HE WAS TRYING TO ESCAPE... HE'D BE GOING THE OTHER WAY!
BUT, HE'S NOT... WHICH JUST MIGHT MEAN ONE THING...
HE COULD BE AFTER THE STOLEN TABLET!
THE KINGPIN'LL HAVE TO KEEP!
RIGHT NOW, THE TABLET IS MORE IMPORTANT!
WHILE OUTSIDE, AT THAT MOMENT...
THAT'S RIGHT, SARGE! I SPOTTED THE KINGPIN'S CAR OVER THERE...
AND THEN I HEARD A SHOT--- FROM INSIDE THE BUILDING!
ALL RIGHT, MEN! WHAT ARE WE WAITING FOR?
THERE HE IS! WE FOUND 'IM!
QUICK! GET THE CUFFS ON HIM WHILE HE'S STILL GROGGY!
THE POLICE! ...THEY'LL NEVER BE ABLE TO HOLD ME!
BUT I WON'T YET RESIST! I'VE SOMETHING THAT MUST BE DONE FIRST...!
WHERE'S THE TABLET, KING-PIN? WE KNOW YOU'VE GOT IT!
DO YOU THINK I'D KEEP IT HERE... WHERE IT COULD INCRIMINATE ME?
UNTIL YOU FIND IT, YOU'LL NEVER BE ABLE TO PROVE MY GUILT!
AND, BY NOW, MY WEB-SWINGING ALLY HAS TAKEN IT SAFELY AWAY FROM HERE!
... JUST AS HE WILL FREE ME FROM CAPTIVITY--- WHEN THE TIME IS RIPE!
THEN JAMESON WAS RIGHT! SPIDER-MAN'S IN THIS AS DEEP AS YOU!
WITH A FEW CHOICE WORDS, I'VE SEALED THE WALL-CRAWLER'S DOOM!
17.

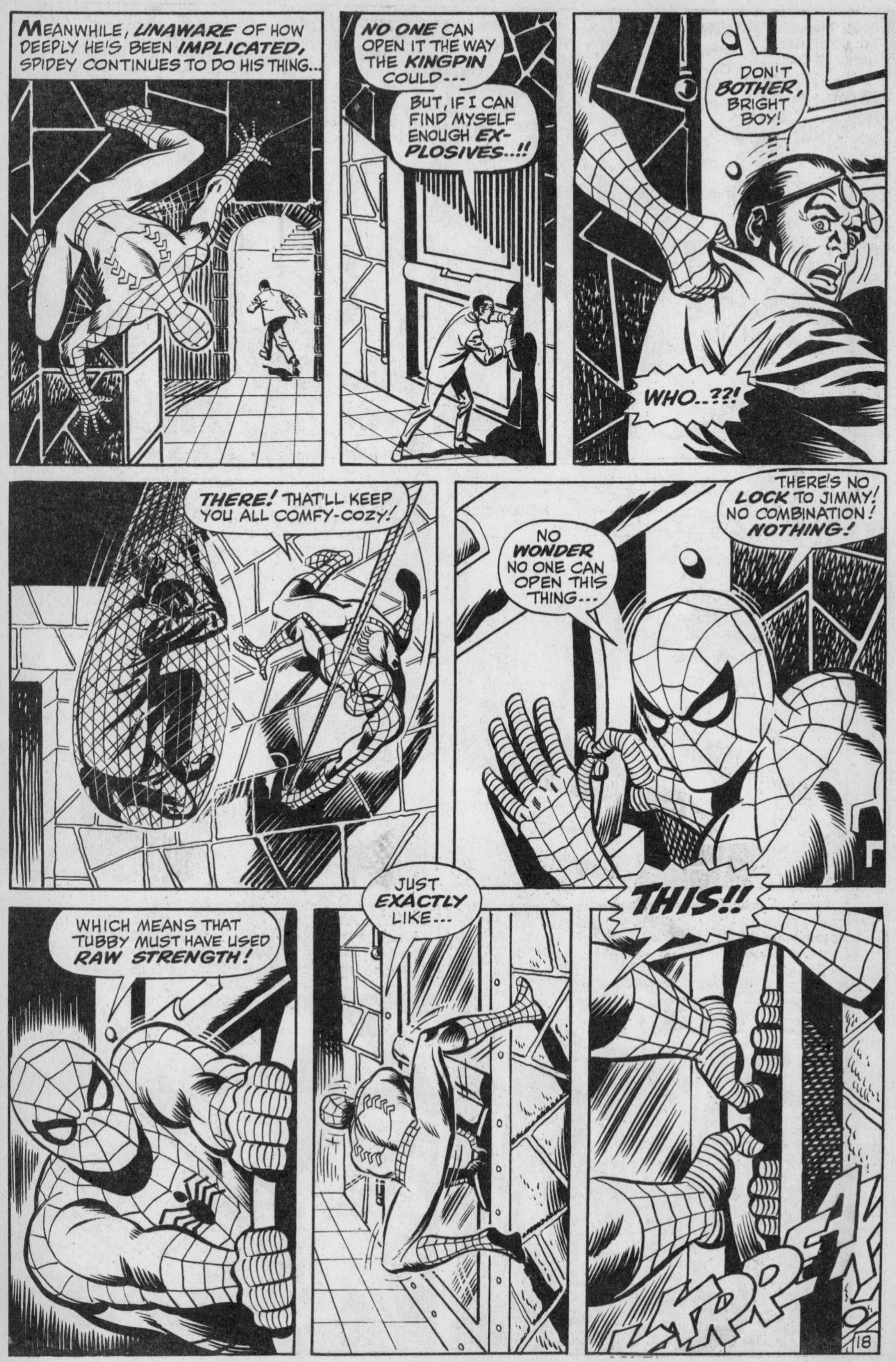
MEANWHILE, UNAWARE OF HOW DEEPLY HE'S BEEN IMPLICATED, SPIDEY CONTINUES TO DO HIS THING...
NO ONE CAN OPEN IT THE WAY THE KINGPIN COULD---
BUT, IF I CAN FIND MYSELF ENOUGH EX-PLOSIVES..!!
DON'T BOTHER, BRIGHT BOY!
WHO..??!
THERE! THAT'LL KEEP YOU ALL COMFY-COZY!
NO WONDER NO ONE CAN OPEN THIS THING...
THERE'S NO LOCK TO JIMMY! NO COMBINATION! NOTHING!
WHICH MEANS THAT TUBBY MUST HAVE USED RAW STRENGTH!
JUST EXACTLY LIKE...
THIS!!
KRRREAK
18

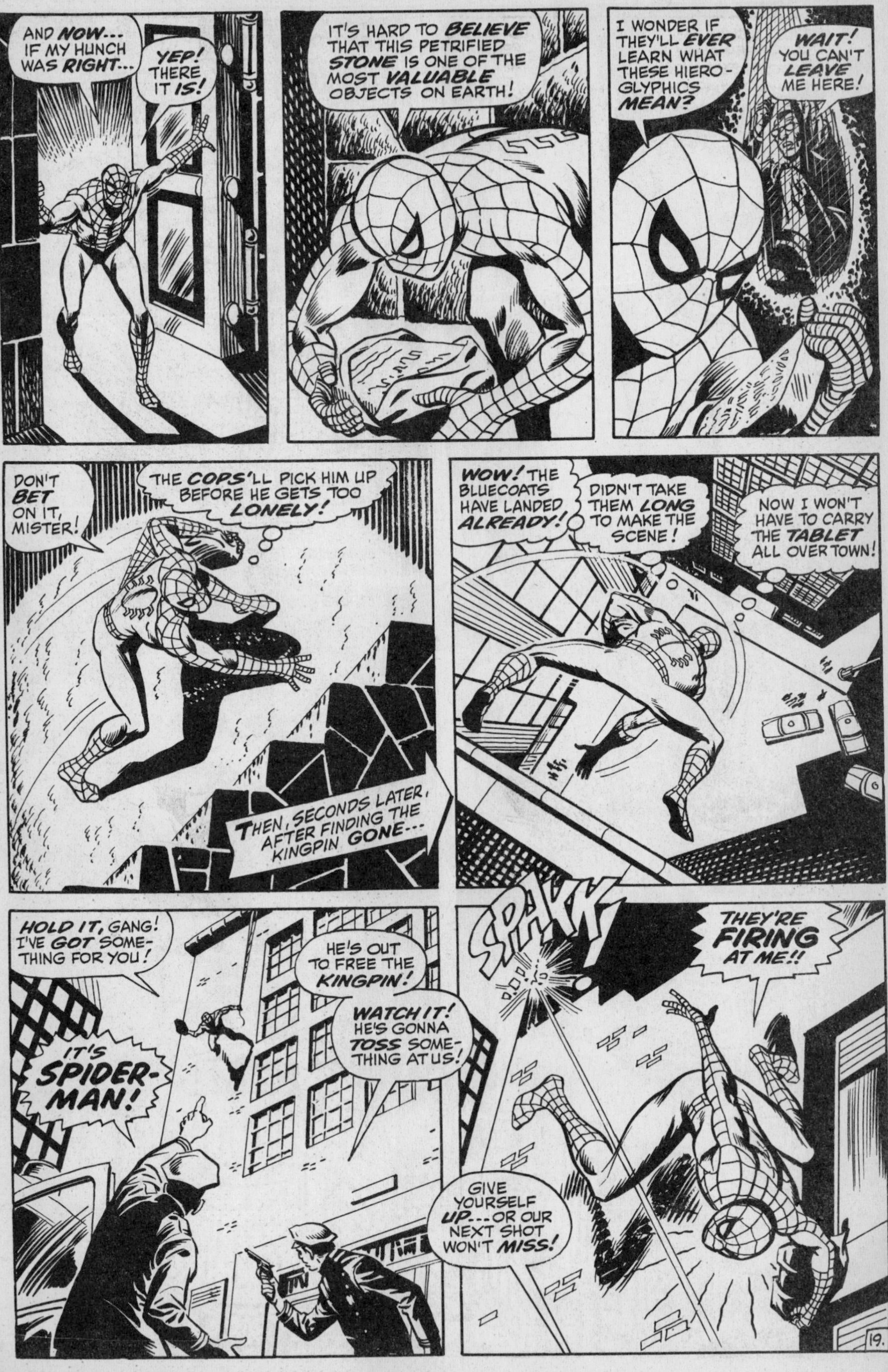
AND NOW... IF MY HUNCH WAS RIGHT...
YEP! THERE IT IS!
IT'S HARD TO BELIEVE THAT THIS PETRIFIED STONE IS ONE OF THE MOST VALUABLE OBJECTS ON EARTH!
I WONDER IF THEY'LL EVER LEARN WHAT THESE HIERO-GLYPHICS MEAN?
WAIT! YOU CAN'T LEAVE ME HERE!
DON'T BET ON IT, MISTER!
THE COPS'LL PICK HIM UP BEFORE HE GETS TOO LONELY!
THEN, SECONDS LATER, AFTER FINDING THE KINGPIN GONE---
WOW! THE BLUECOATS HAVE LANDED ALREADY!
DIDN'T TAKE THEM LONG TO MAKE THE SCENE!
NOW I WON'T HAVE TO CARRY THE TABLET ALL OVER TOWN!
HOLD IT, GANG! I'VE GOT SOME-THING FOR YOU!
HE'S OUT TO FREE THE KINGPIN!
WATCH IT! HE'S GONNA TOSS SOME-THING AT US!
IT'S SPIDER-MAN!
SPAKK!
THEY'RE FIRING AT ME!!
GIVE YOURSELF UP---OR OUR NEXT SHOT WON'T MISS!
19.

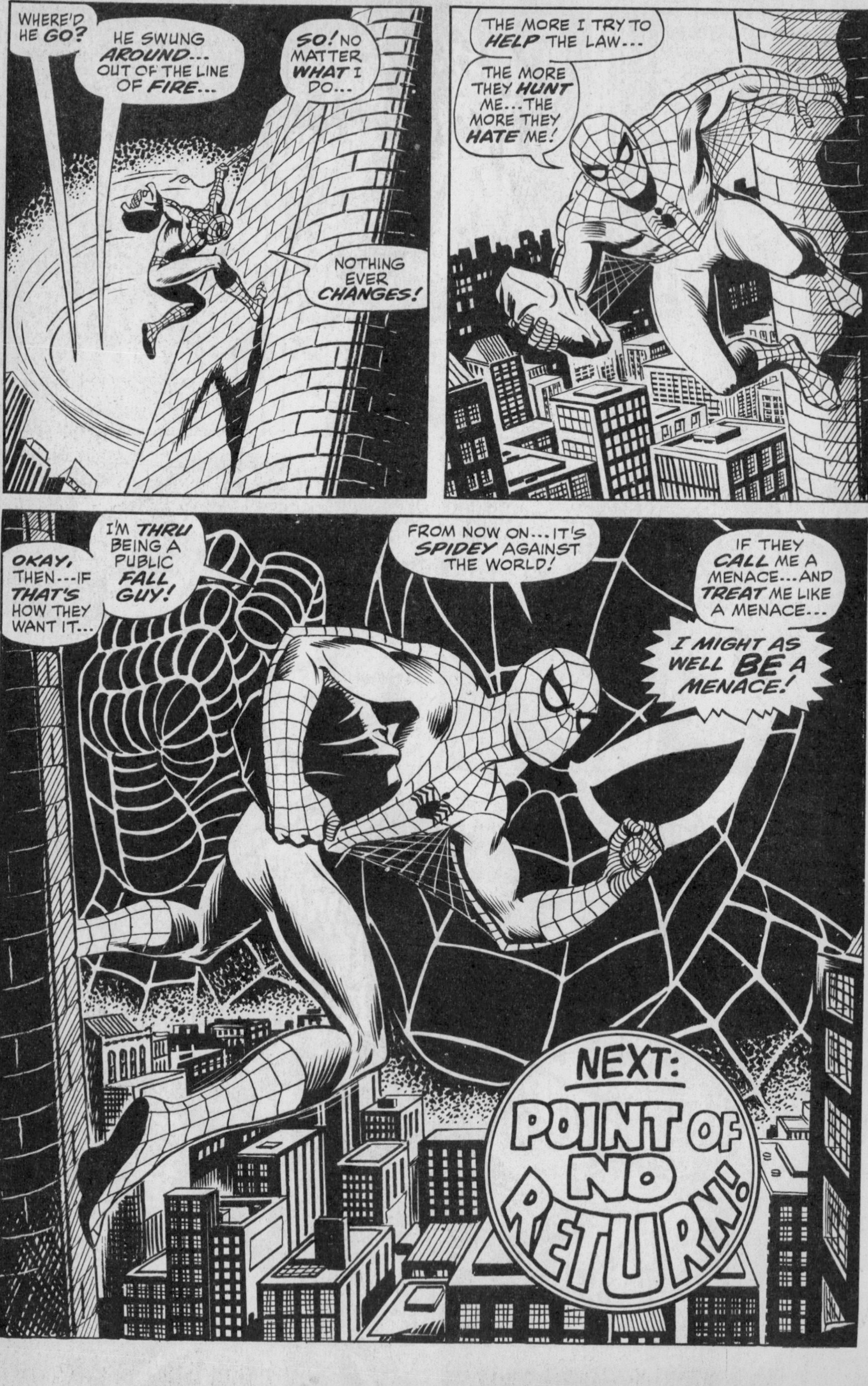
WHERE'D HE GO?
HE SWUNG AROUND... OUT OF THE LINE OF FIRE...
SO! NO MATTER WHAT I DO...
NOTHING EVER CHANGES!
THE MORE I TRY TO HELP THE LAW...
THE MORE THEY HUNT ME... THE MORE THEY HATE ME!
OKAY, THEN---IF THAT'S HOW THEY WANT IT...
I'M THRU BEING A PUBLIC FALL GUY!
FROM NOW ON... IT'S SPIDEY AGAINST THE WORLD!
IF THEY CALL ME A MENACE... AND TREAT ME LIKE A MENACE...
I MIGHT AS WELL BE A MENACE!
NEXT:
POINT OF NO RETURN!

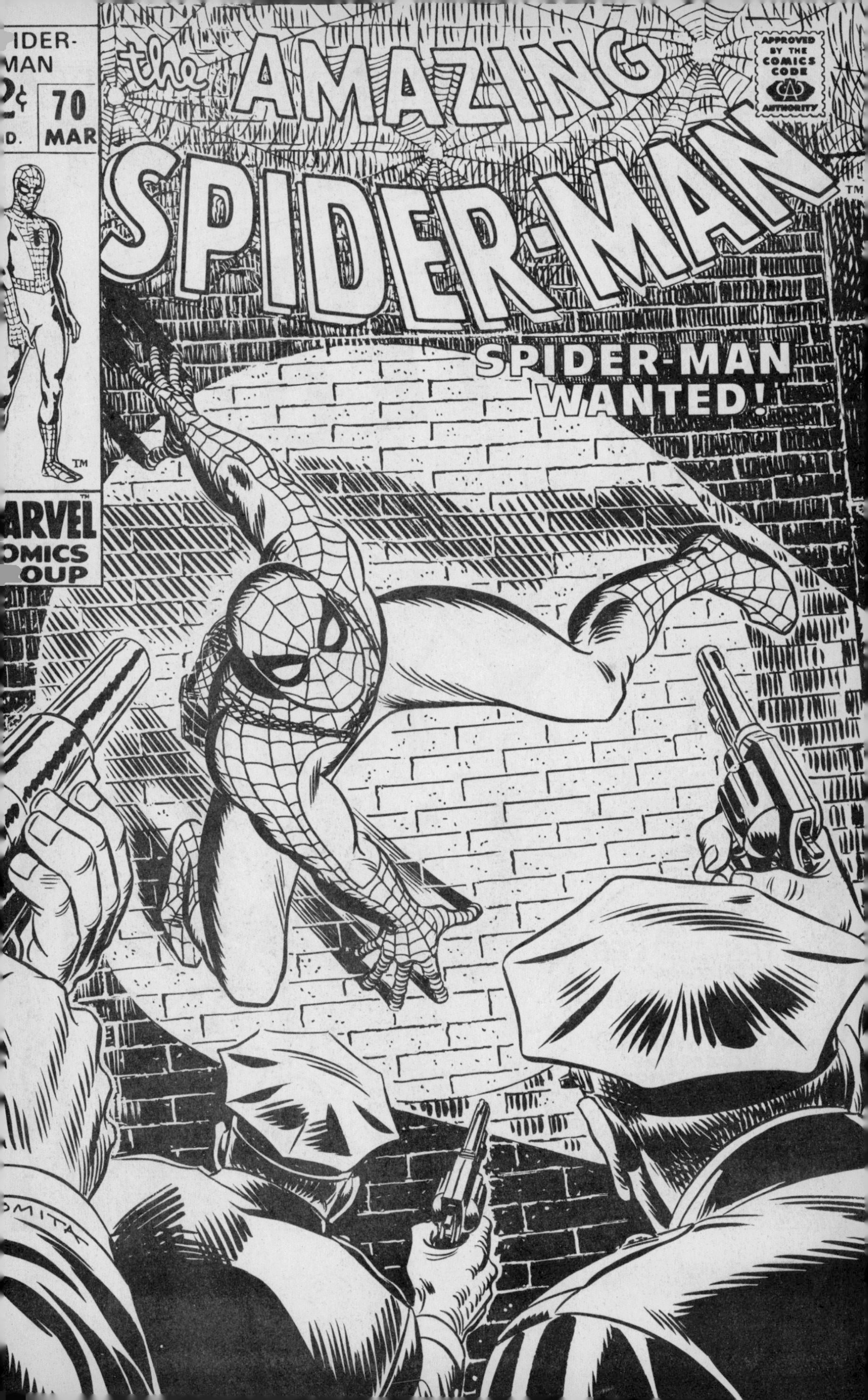
the AMAZING
SPIDER-MAN
70
MAR
APPROVED BY THE COMICS CODE AUTHORITY
SPIDER-MAN WANTED!
ROMITA

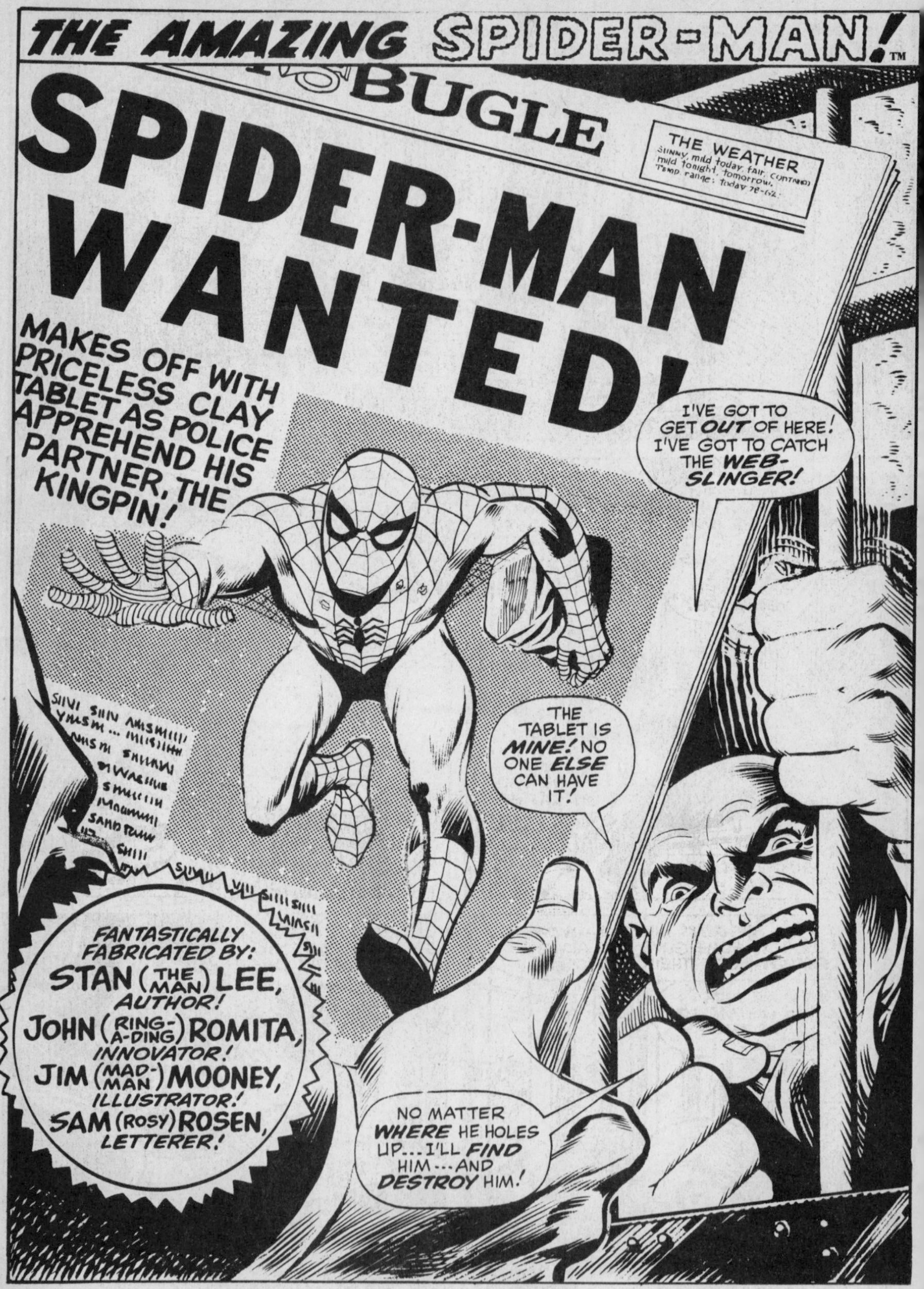

THE AMAZING SPIDER-MAN!™
BUGLE
SPIDER-MAN WANTED!
THE WEATHER
Sunny, mild today, fair, CONTINUED
mild tonight, tomorrow.
Temp range: today 78-62.
MAKES OFF WITH PRICELESS CLAY TABLET AS POLICE APPREHEND HIS PARTNER, THE KINGPIN!
I'VE GOT TO GET *OUT* OF HERE! I'VE GOT TO CATCH THE *WEB-SLINGER!*
THE TABLET IS *MINE!* NO ONE *ELSE* CAN HAVE IT!
NO MATTER *WHERE* HE HOLES UP... I'LL *FIND* HIM --- AND *DESTROY* HIM!
FANTASTICALLY FABRICATED BY:
STAN (THE MAN) LEE, *AUTHOR!*
JOHN (RING-A-DING) ROMITA, *INNOVATOR!*
JIM (MAD-MAN) MOONEY, *ILLUSTRATOR!*
SAM (ROSY) ROSEN, *LETTERER!*

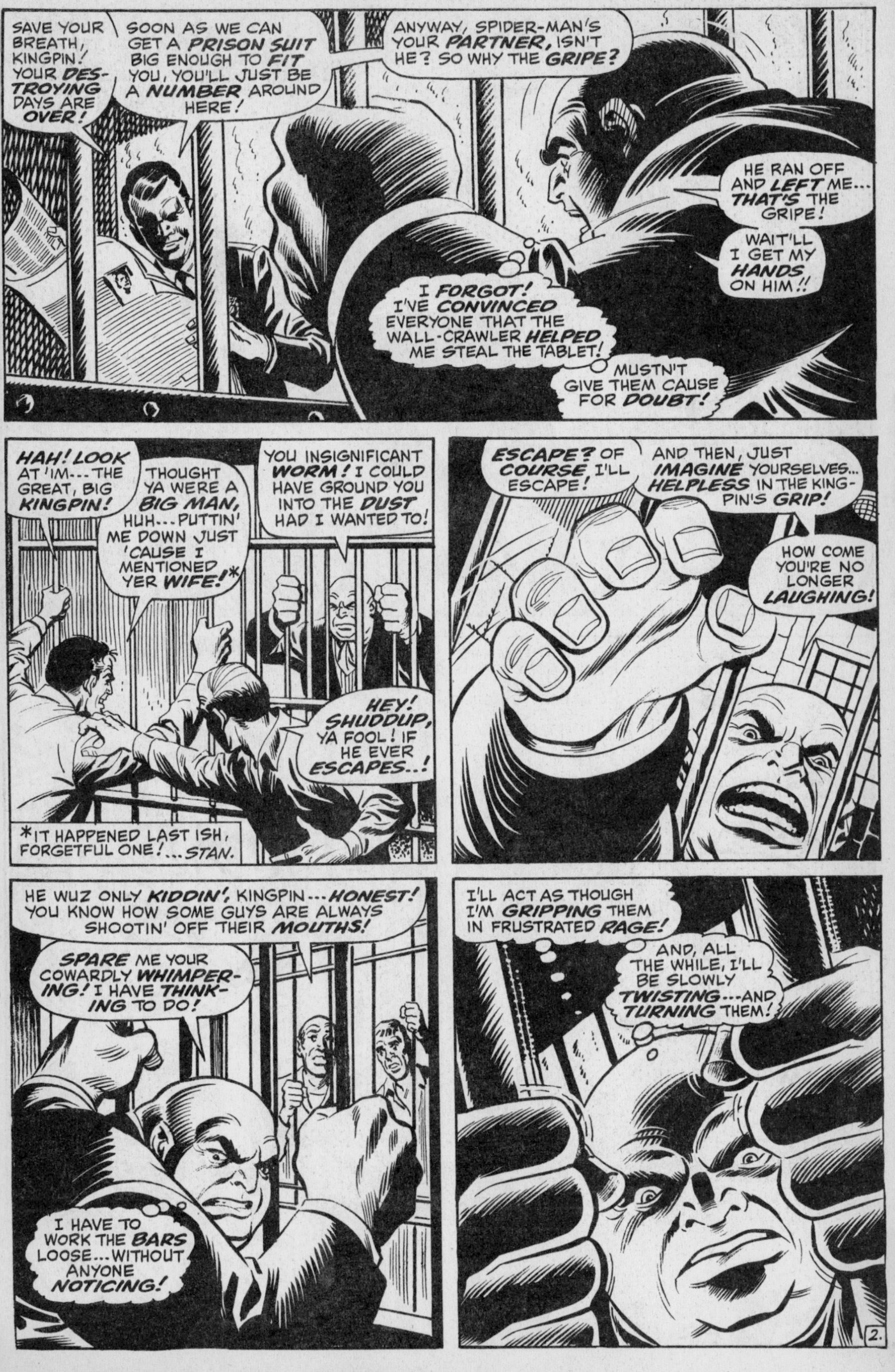
SAVE YOUR BREATH, KINGPIN! YOUR DESTROYING DAYS ARE OVER!
SOON AS WE CAN GET A PRISON SUIT BIG ENOUGH TO FIT YOU, YOU'LL JUST BE A NUMBER AROUND HERE!
ANYWAY, SPIDER-MAN'S YOUR PARTNER, ISN'T HE? SO WHY THE GRIPE?
HE RAN OFF AND LEFT ME... THAT'S THE GRIPE!
WAIT'LL I GET MY HANDS ON HIM!!
I FORGOT! I'VE CONVINCED EVERYONE THAT THE WALL-CRAWLER HELPED ME STEAL THE TABLET!
MUSTN'T GIVE THEM CAUSE FOR DOUBT!
HAH! LOOK AT 'IM--- THE GREAT, BIG KINGPIN!
THOUGHT YA WERE A BIG MAN, HUH--- PUTTIN' ME DOWN JUST 'CAUSE I MENTIONED YER WIFE!*
YOU INSIGNIFICANT WORM! I COULD HAVE GROUND YOU INTO THE DUST HAD I WANTED TO!
HEY! SHUDDUP, YA FOOL! IF HE EVER ESCAPES..!
*IT HAPPENED LAST ISH, FORGETFUL ONE! ... STAN.
ESCAPE? OF COURSE I'LL ESCAPE!
AND THEN, JUST IMAGINE YOURSELVES... HELPLESS IN THE KINGPIN'S GRIP!
HOW COME YOU'RE NO LONGER LAUGHING!
HE WUZ ONLY KIDDIN', KINGPIN --- HONEST! YOU KNOW HOW SOME GUYS ARE ALWAYS SHOOTIN' OFF THEIR MOUTHS!
SPARE ME YOUR COWARDLY WHIMPERING! I HAVE THINKING TO DO!
I HAVE TO WORK THE BARS LOOSE... WITHOUT ANYONE NOTICING!
I'LL ACT AS THOUGH I'M GRIPPING THEM IN FRUSTRATED RAGE!
AND, ALL THE WHILE, I'LL BE SLOWLY TWISTING---AND TURNING THEM!
2.

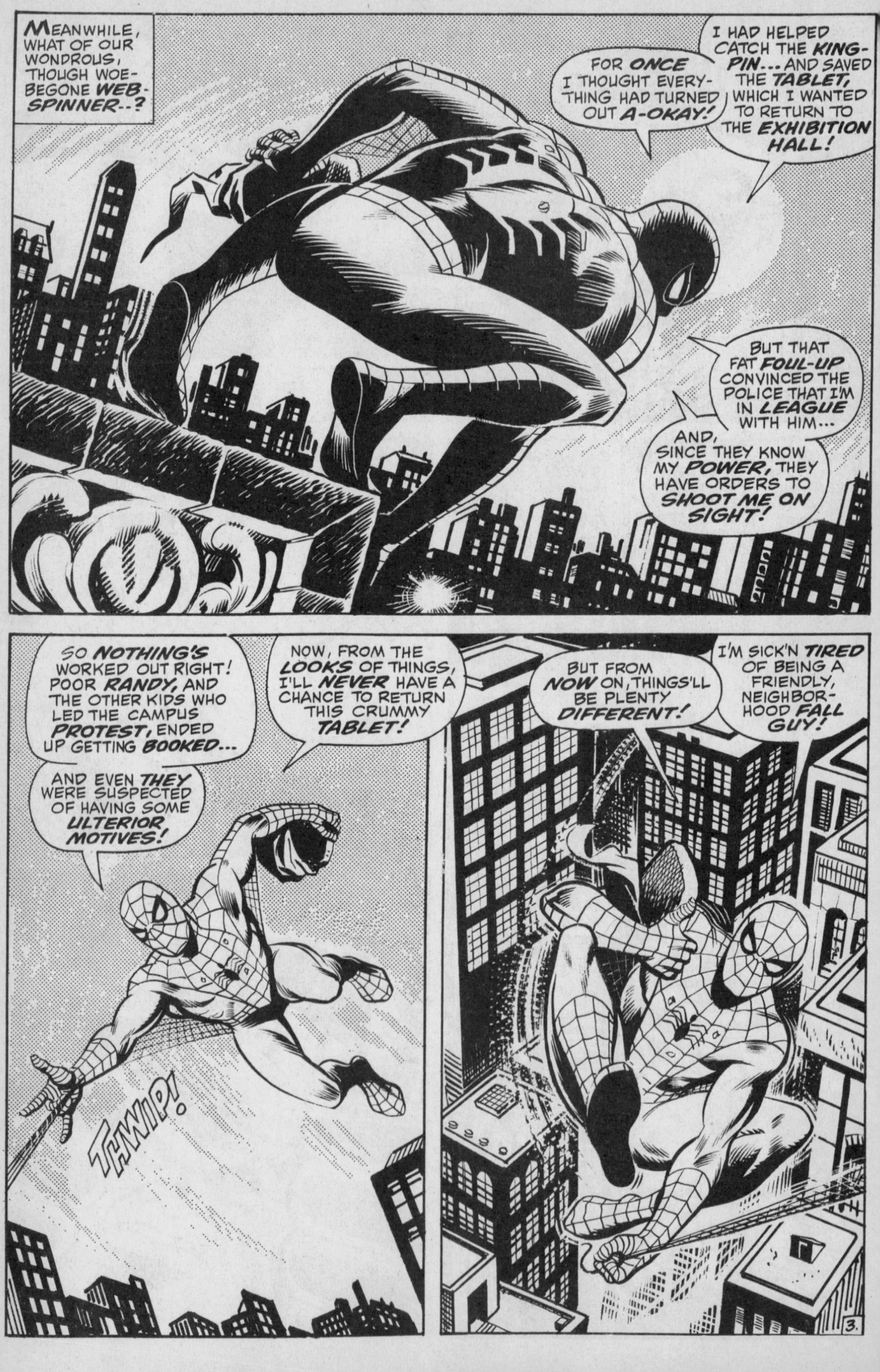
MEANWHILE, WHAT OF OUR WONDROUS, THOUGH WOE-BEGONE WEB-SPINNER--?
FOR ONCE I THOUGHT EVERY-THING HAD TURNED OUT A-OKAY!
I HAD HELPED CATCH THE KING-PIN... AND SAVED THE TABLET, WHICH I WANTED TO RETURN TO THE EXHIBITION HALL!
BUT THAT FAT FOUL-UP CONVINCED THE POLICE THAT I'M IN LEAGUE WITH HIM...
AND, SINCE THEY KNOW MY POWER, THEY HAVE ORDERS TO SHOOT ME ON SIGHT!
SO NOTHING'S WORKED OUT RIGHT! POOR RANDY, AND THE OTHER KIDS WHO LED THE CAMPUS PROTEST, ENDED UP GETTING BOOKED...
AND EVEN THEY WERE SUSPECTED OF HAVING SOME ULTERIOR MOTIVES!
NOW, FROM THE LOOKS OF THINGS, I'LL NEVER HAVE A CHANCE TO RETURN THIS CRUMMY TABLET!
THWIP!
BUT FROM NOW ON, THINGS'LL BE PLENTY DIFFERENT!
I'M SICK'N TIRED OF BEING A FRIENDLY, NEIGHBOR-HOOD FALL GUY!
3.

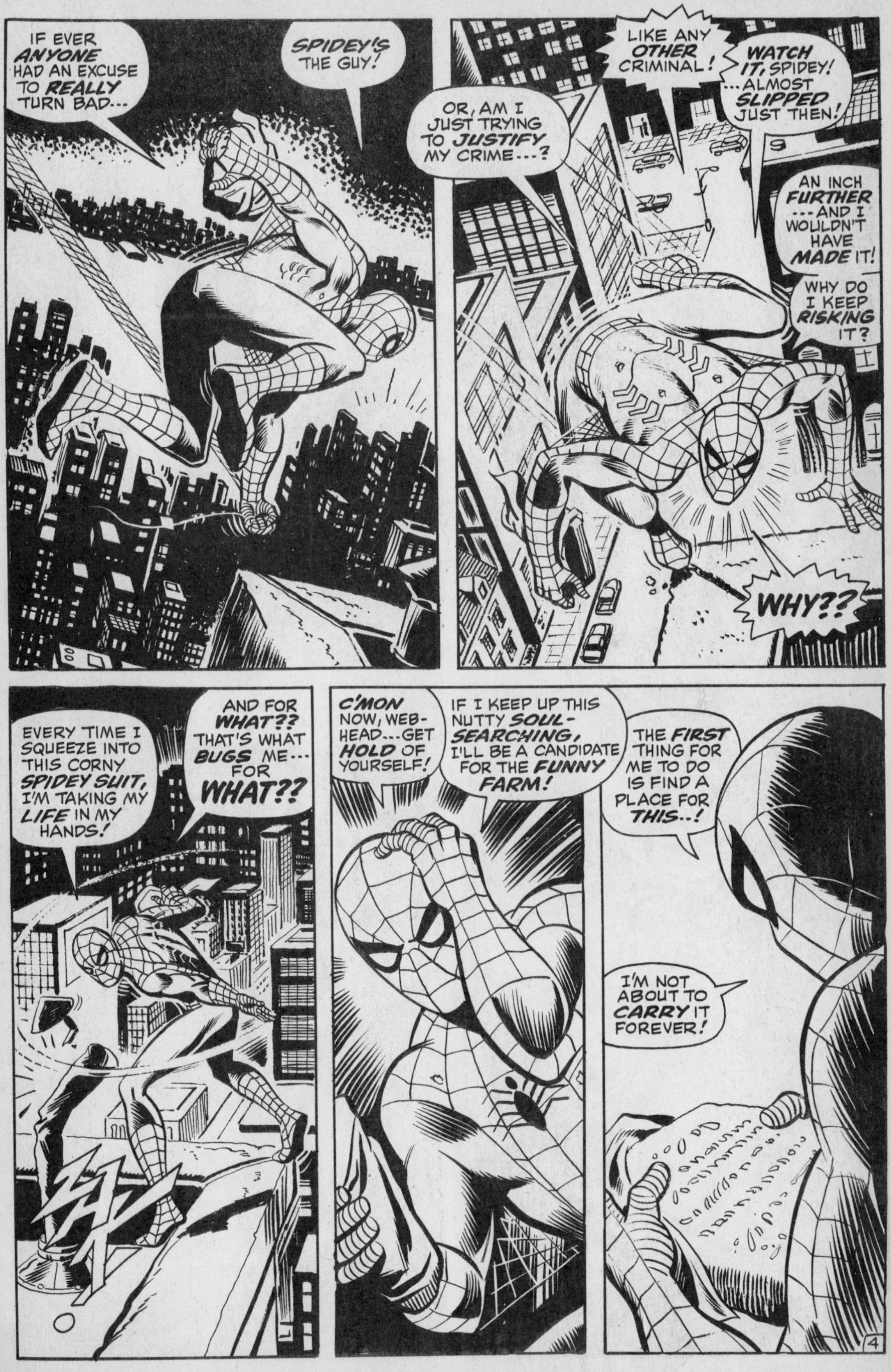
IF EVER ANYONE HAD AN EXCUSE TO REALLY TURN BAD...
SPIDEY'S THE GUY!
LIKE ANY OTHER CRIMINAL!
OR, AM I JUST TRYING TO JUSTIFY MY CRIME...?
WATCH IT, SPIDEY! ...ALMOST SLIPPED JUST THEN!
AN INCH FURTHER ---AND I WOULDN'T HAVE MADE IT!
WHY DO I KEEP RISKING IT?
WHY??
EVERY TIME I SQUEEZE INTO THIS CORNY SPIDEY SUIT, I'M TAKING MY LIFE IN MY HANDS!
AND FOR WHAT?? THAT'S WHAT BUGS ME--- FOR WHAT??
C'MON NOW, WEB-HEAD...GET HOLD OF YOURSELF!
IF I KEEP UP THIS NUTTY SOUL-SEARCHING, I'LL BE A CANDIDATE FOR THE FUNNY FARM!
THE FIRST THING FOR ME TO DO IS FIND A PLACE FOR THIS..!
I'M NOT ABOUT TO CARRY IT FOREVER!
4

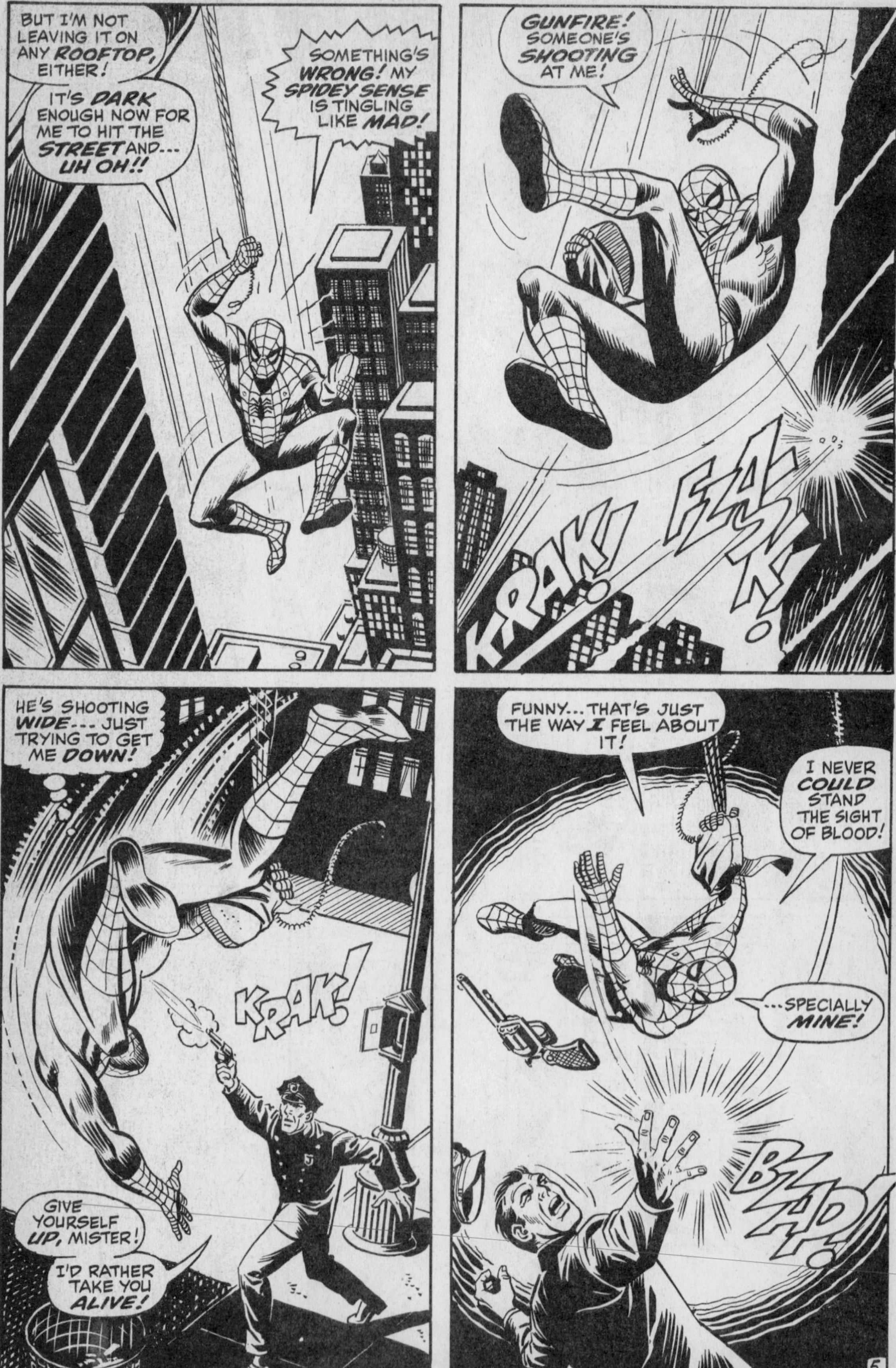
BUT I'M NOT LEAVING IT ON ANY ROOFTOP, EITHER!
IT'S DARK ENOUGH NOW FOR ME TO HIT THE STREET AND... UH OH!!
SOMETHING'S WRONG! MY SPIDEY SENSE IS TINGLING LIKE MAD!
GUNFIRE! SOMEONE'S SHOOTING AT ME!
KRAK! FLAK!
HE'S SHOOTING WIDE... JUST TRYING TO GET ME DOWN!
KRAK!
GIVE YOURSELF UP, MISTER!
I'D RATHER TAKE YOU ALIVE!
FUNNY... THAT'S JUST THE WAY I FEEL ABOUT IT!
I NEVER COULD STAND THE SIGHT OF BLOOD!
...SPECIALLY MINE!
BLAP!

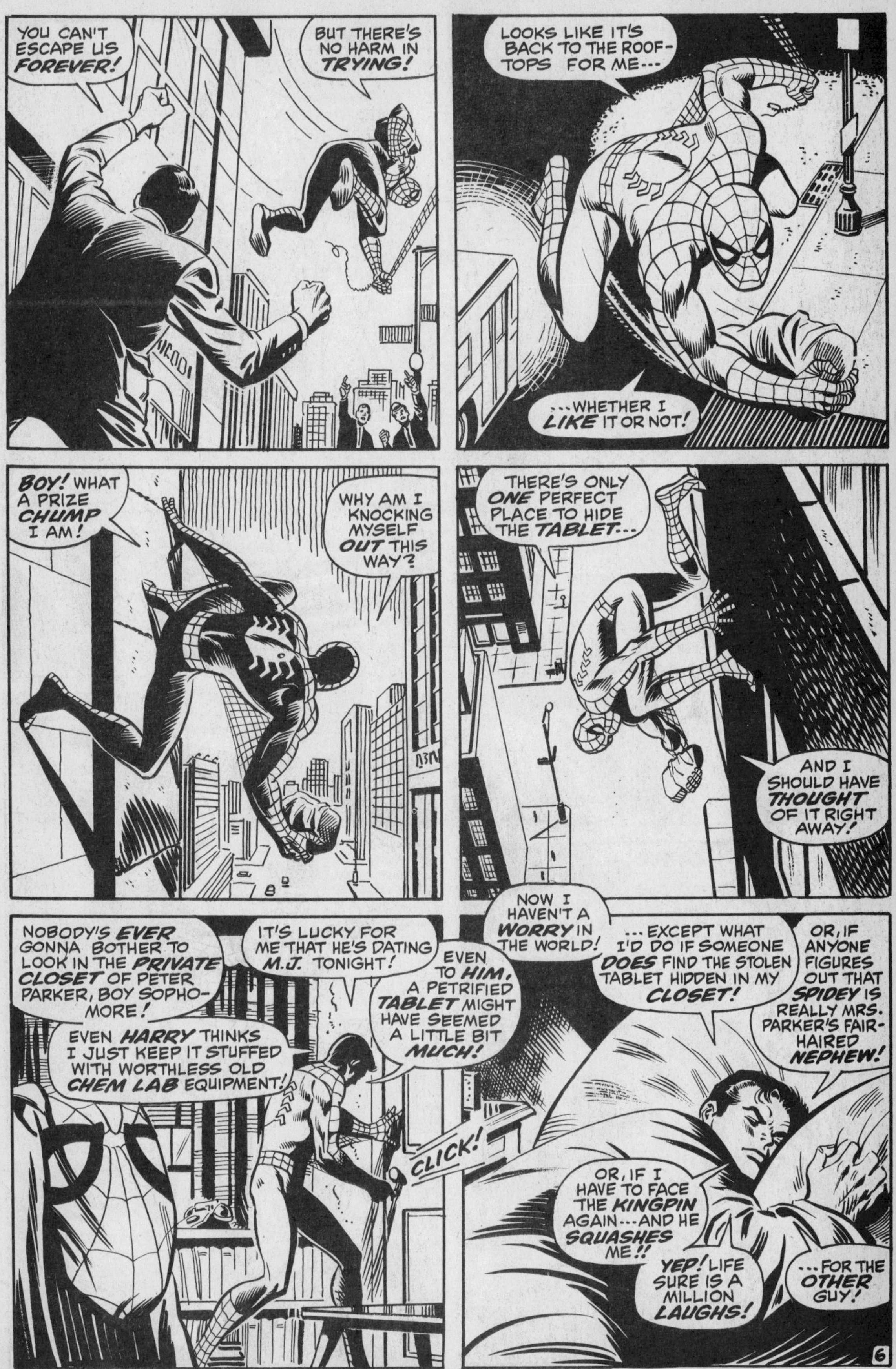
YOU CAN'T ESCAPE US FOREVER!
BUT THERE'S NO HARM IN TRYING!
LOOKS LIKE IT'S BACK TO THE ROOF-TOPS FOR ME---
---WHETHER I LIKE IT OR NOT!
BOY! WHAT A PRIZE CHUMP I AM!
WHY AM I KNOCKING MYSELF OUT THIS WAY?
THERE'S ONLY ONE PERFECT PLACE TO HIDE THE TABLET...
AND I SHOULD HAVE THOUGHT OF IT RIGHT AWAY!
NOBODY'S EVER GONNA BOTHER TO LOOK IN THE PRIVATE CLOSET OF PETER PARKER, BOY SOPHOMORE!
IT'S LUCKY FOR ME THAT HE'S DATING M.J. TONIGHT!
EVEN HARRY THINKS I JUST KEEP IT STUFFED WITH WORTHLESS OLD CHEM LAB EQUIPMENT!
EVEN TO HIM, A PETRIFIED TABLET MIGHT HAVE SEEMED A LITTLE BIT MUCH!
CLICK!
NOW I HAVEN'T A WORRY IN THE WORLD!
--- EXCEPT WHAT I'D DO IF SOMEONE DOES FIND THE STOLEN TABLET HIDDEN IN MY CLOSET!
OR, IF ANYONE FIGURES OUT THAT SPIDEY IS REALLY MRS. PARKER'S FAIR-HAIRED NEPHEW!
OR, IF I HAVE TO FACE THE KINGPIN AGAIN---AND HE SQUASHES ME!!
YEP! LIFE SURE IS A MILLION LAUGHS!
...FOR THE OTHER GUY!
6

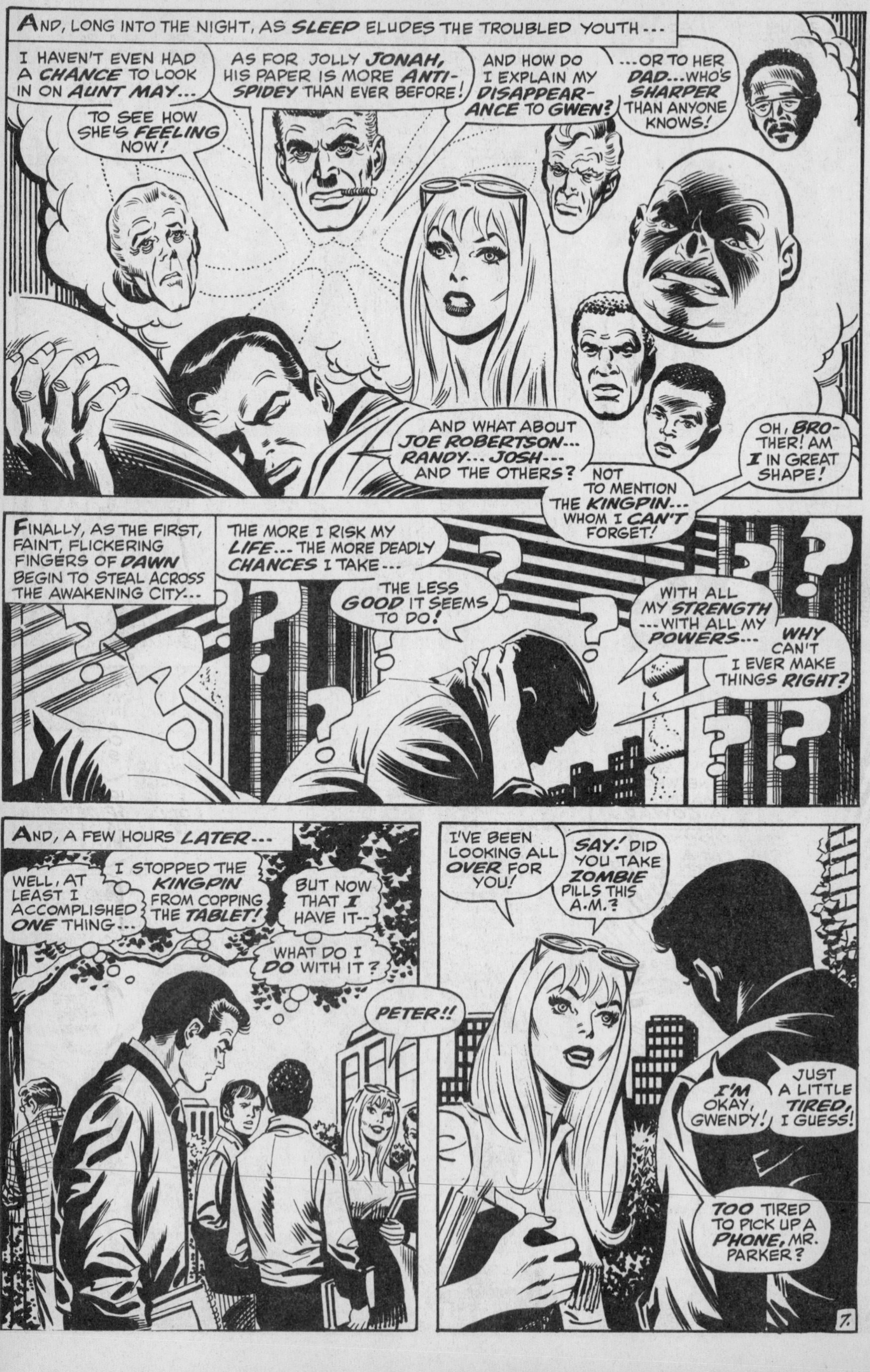

AND, LONG INTO THE NIGHT, AS SLEEP ELUDES THE TROUBLED YOUTH---
I HAVEN'T EVEN HAD A CHANCE TO LOOK IN ON AUNT MAY...
TO SEE HOW SHE'S FEELING NOW!
AS FOR JOLLY JONAH, HIS PAPER IS MORE ANTI-SPIDEY THAN EVER BEFORE!
AND HOW DO I EXPLAIN MY DISAPPEARANCE TO GWEN?
...OR TO HER DAD...WHO'S SHARPER THAN ANYONE KNOWS!
AND WHAT ABOUT JOE ROBERTSON... RANDY... JOSH--- AND THE OTHERS?
NOT TO MENTION THE KINGPIN... WHOM I CAN'T FORGET!
OH, BROTHER! AM I IN GREAT SHAPE!
FINALLY, AS THE FIRST, FAINT, FLICKERING FINGERS OF DAWN BEGIN TO STEAL ACROSS THE AWAKENING CITY...
THE MORE I RISK MY LIFE... THE MORE DEADLY CHANCES I TAKE---
THE LESS GOOD IT SEEMS TO DO!
WITH ALL MY STRENGTH ---WITH ALL MY POWERS...
WHY CAN'T I EVER MAKE THINGS RIGHT?
AND, A FEW HOURS LATER---
WELL, AT LEAST I ACCOMPLISHED ONE THING...
I STOPPED THE KINGPIN FROM COPPING THE TABLET!
BUT NOW THAT I HAVE IT--
WHAT DO I DO WITH IT?
PETER!!
I'VE BEEN LOOKING ALL OVER FOR YOU!
SAY! DID YOU TAKE ZOMBIE PILLS THIS A.M.?
I'M OKAY, GWENDY!
JUST A LITTLE TIRED, I GUESS!
TOO TIRED TO PICK UP A PHONE, MR. PARKER?
7.

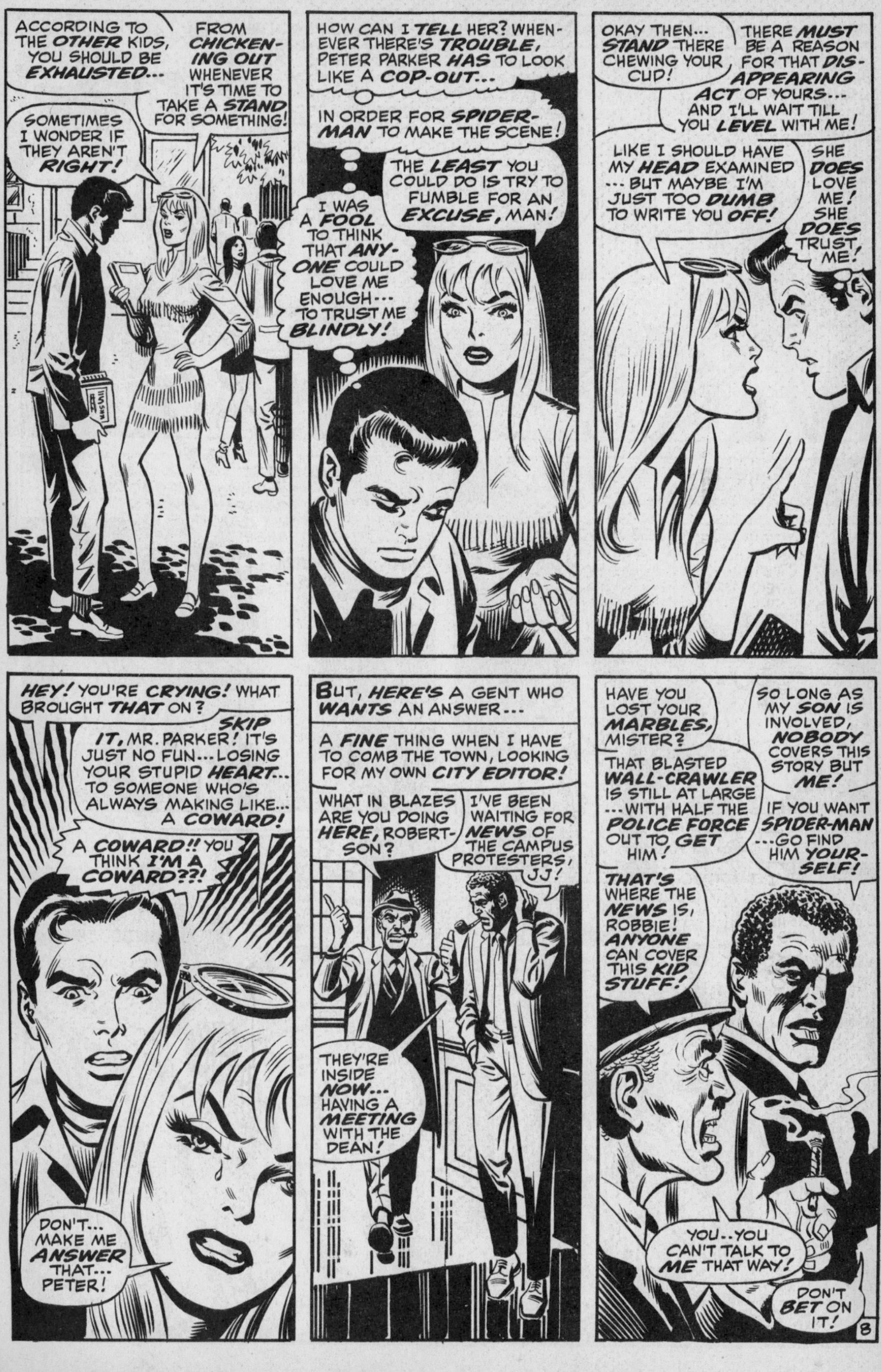
ACCORDING TO THE OTHER KIDS, YOU SHOULD BE EXHAUSTED...
FROM CHICKENING OUT WHENEVER IT'S TIME TO TAKE A STAND FOR SOMETHING!
SOMETIMES I WONDER IF THEY AREN'T RIGHT!
HOW CAN I TELL HER? WHENEVER THERE'S TROUBLE, PETER PARKER HAS TO LOOK LIKE A COP-OUT...
IN ORDER FOR SPIDER-MAN TO MAKE THE SCENE!
THE LEAST YOU COULD DO IS TRY TO FUMBLE FOR AN EXCUSE, MAN!
I WAS A FOOL TO THINK THAT ANYONE COULD LOVE ME ENOUGH--- TO TRUST ME BLINDLY!
OKAY THEN... STAND THERE CHEWING YOUR CUD!
THERE MUST BE A REASON FOR THAT DISAPPEARING ACT OF YOURS... AND I'LL WAIT TILL YOU LEVEL WITH ME!
LIKE I SHOULD HAVE MY HEAD EXAMINED --- BUT MAYBE I'M JUST TOO DUMB TO WRITE YOU OFF!
SHE DOES LOVE ME! SHE DOES TRUST ME!
HEY! YOU'RE CRYING! WHAT BROUGHT THAT ON?
SKIP IT, MR. PARKER! IT'S JUST NO FUN... LOSING YOUR STUPID HEART... TO SOMEONE WHO'S ALWAYS MAKING LIKE... A COWARD!
A COWARD!! YOU THINK I'M A COWARD??!
DON'T... MAKE ME ANSWER THAT... PETER!
BUT, HERE'S A GENT WHO WANTS AN ANSWER---
A FINE THING WHEN I HAVE TO COMB THE TOWN, LOOKING FOR MY OWN CITY EDITOR!
WHAT IN BLAZES ARE YOU DOING HERE, ROBERTSON?
I'VE BEEN WAITING FOR NEWS OF THE CAMPUS PROTESTERS, JJ!
THEY'RE INSIDE NOW... HAVING A MEETING WITH THE DEAN!
HAVE YOU LOST YOUR MARBLES, MISTER?
THAT BLASTED WALL-CRAWLER IS STILL AT LARGE ---WITH HALF THE POLICE FORCE OUT TO GET HIM!
THAT'S WHERE THE NEWS IS, ROBBIE! ANYONE CAN COVER THIS KID STUFF!
SO LONG AS MY SON IS INVOLVED, NOBODY COVERS THIS STORY BUT ME!
IF YOU WANT SPIDER-MAN ---GO FIND HIM YOURSELF!
YOU...YOU CAN'T TALK TO ME THAT WAY!
DON'T BET ON IT!
8

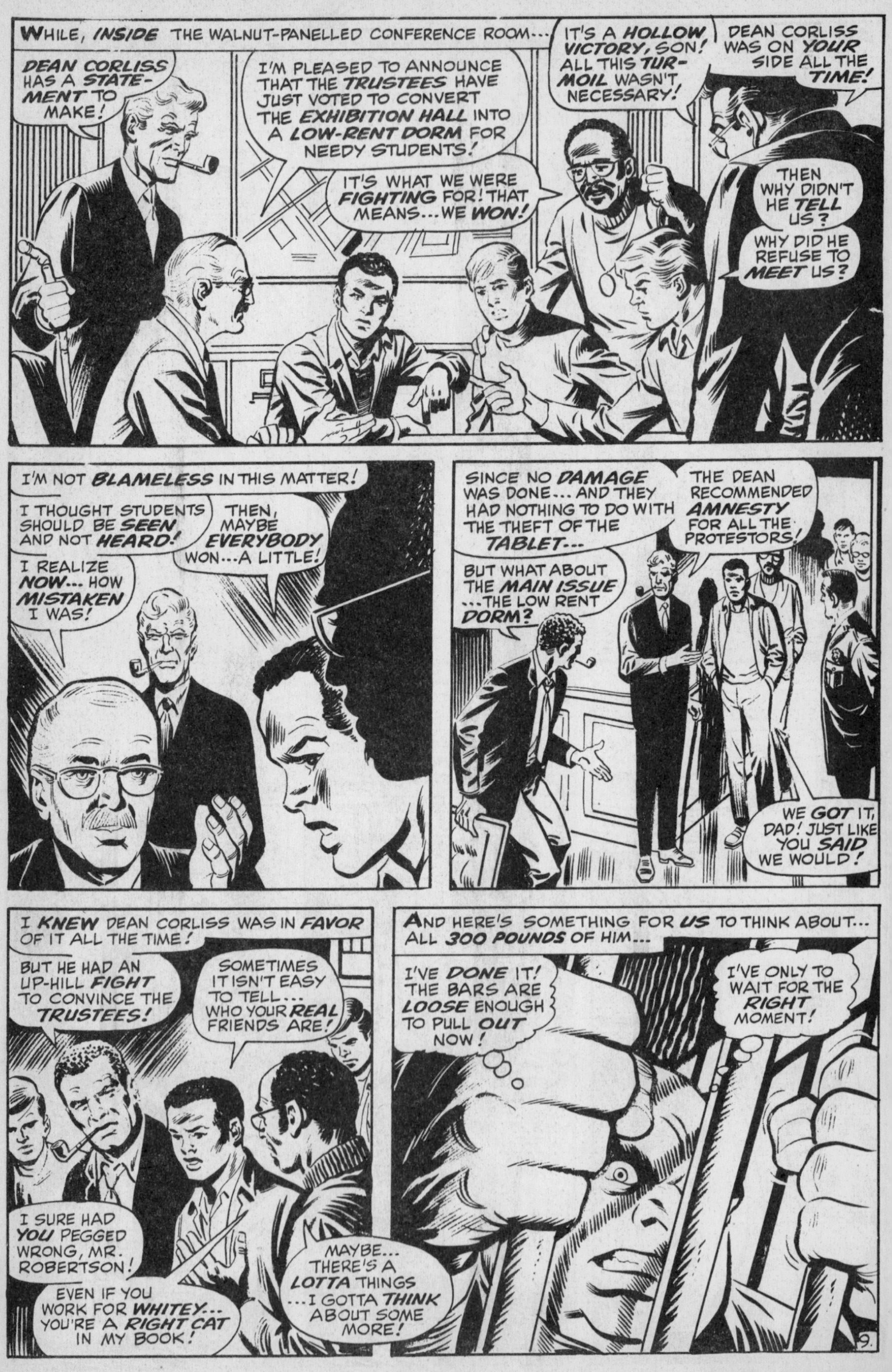
WHILE, INSIDE THE WALNUT-PANELLED CONFERENCE ROOM...
DEAN CORLISS HAS A STATEMENT TO MAKE!
I'M PLEASED TO ANNOUNCE THAT THE TRUSTEES HAVE JUST VOTED TO CONVERT THE EXHIBITION HALL INTO A LOW-RENT DORM FOR NEEDY STUDENTS!
IT'S WHAT WE WERE FIGHTING FOR! THAT MEANS... WE WON!
IT'S A HOLLOW VICTORY, SON! ALL THIS TURMOIL WASN'T NECESSARY!
DEAN CORLISS WAS ON YOUR SIDE ALL THE TIME!
THEN WHY DIDN'T HE TELL US?
WHY DID HE REFUSE TO MEET US?
I'M NOT BLAMELESS IN THIS MATTER!
I THOUGHT STUDENTS SHOULD BE SEEN AND NOT HEARD!
I REALIZE NOW... HOW MISTAKEN I WAS!
THEN, MAYBE EVERYBODY WON... A LITTLE!
SINCE NO DAMAGE WAS DONE... AND THEY HAD NOTHING TO DO WITH THE THEFT OF THE TABLET...
THE DEAN RECOMMENDED AMNESTY FOR ALL THE PROTESTORS!
BUT WHAT ABOUT THE MAIN ISSUE ...THE LOW RENT DORM?
WE GOT IT, DAD! JUST LIKE YOU SAID WE WOULD!
I KNEW DEAN CORLISS WAS IN FAVOR OF IT ALL THE TIME!
BUT HE HAD AN UP-HILL FIGHT TO CONVINCE THE TRUSTEES!
SOMETIMES IT ISN'T EASY TO TELL... WHO YOUR REAL FRIENDS ARE!
I SURE HAD YOU PEGGED WRONG, MR. ROBERTSON!
EVEN IF YOU WORK FOR WHITEY... YOU'RE A RIGHT CAT IN MY BOOK!
MAYBE... THERE'S A LOTTA THINGS ...I GOTTA THINK ABOUT SOME MORE!
AND HERE'S SOMETHING FOR US TO THINK ABOUT... ALL 300 POUNDS OF HIM...
I'VE DONE IT! THE BARS ARE LOOSE ENOUGH TO PULL OUT NOW!
I'VE ONLY TO WAIT FOR THE RIGHT MOMENT!
9.

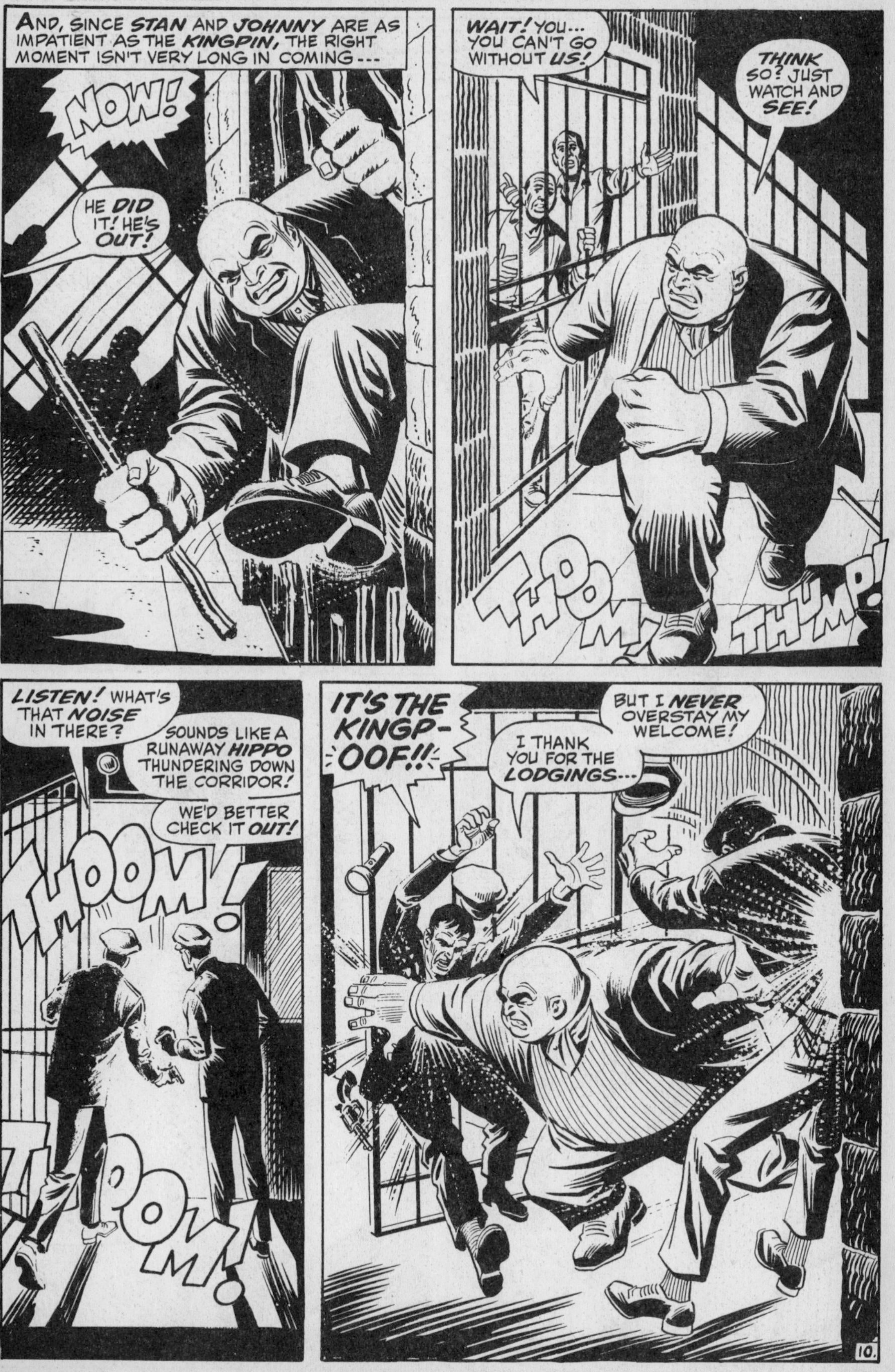
AND, SINCE STAN AND JOHNNY ARE AS IMPATIENT AS THE KINGPIN, THE RIGHT MOMENT ISN'T VERY LONG IN COMING---
NOW!
HE DID IT! HE'S OUT!
WAIT! YOU... YOU CAN'T GO WITHOUT US!
THINK SO? JUST WATCH AND SEE!
THOOM!
THUMP!
LISTEN! WHAT'S THAT NOISE IN THERE?
SOUNDS LIKE A RUNAWAY HIPPO THUNDERING DOWN THE CORRIDOR!
WE'D BETTER CHECK IT OUT!
THOOM!
THOOOM!
IT'S THE KINGP-OOF!!
I THANK YOU FOR THE LODGINGS...
BUT I NEVER OVERSTAY MY WELCOME!
10.

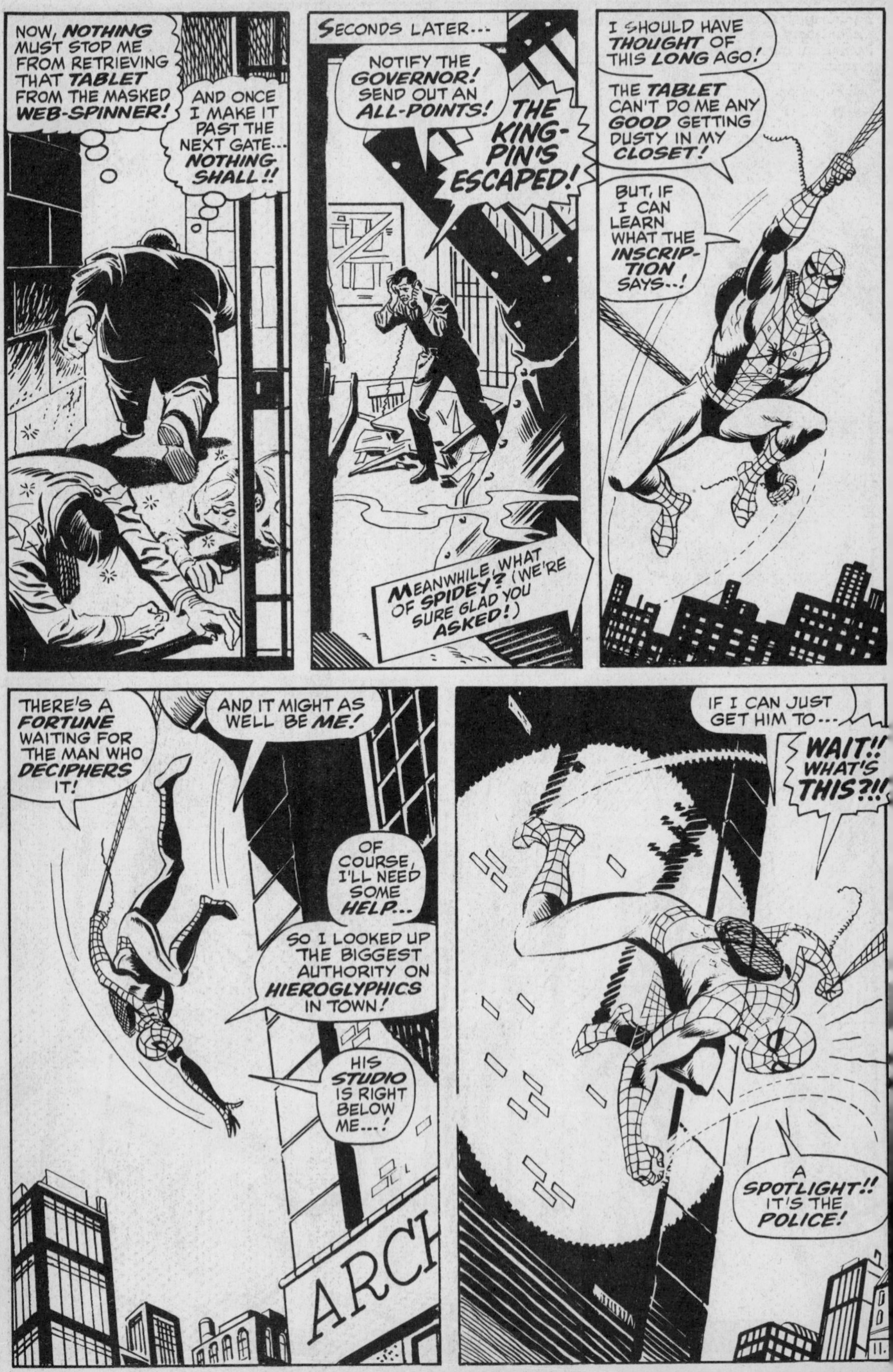

NOW, NOTHING MUST STOP ME FROM RETRIEVING THAT TABLET FROM THE MASKED WEB-SPINNER!
AND ONCE I MAKE IT PAST THE NEXT GATE... NOTHING SHALL!!
SECONDS LATER...
NOTIFY THE GOVERNOR! SEND OUT AN ALL-POINTS!
THE KING-PIN'S ESCAPED!
MEANWHILE, WHAT OF SPIDEY? (WE'RE SURE GLAD YOU ASKED!)
I SHOULD HAVE THOUGHT OF THIS LONG AGO!
THE TABLET CAN'T DO ME ANY GOOD GETTING DUSTY IN MY CLOSET!
BUT, IF I CAN LEARN WHAT THE INSCRIPTION SAYS...!
THERE'S A FORTUNE WAITING FOR THE MAN WHO DECIPHERS IT!
AND IT MIGHT AS WELL BE ME!
OF COURSE, I'LL NEED SOME HELP...
SO I LOOKED UP THE BIGGEST AUTHORITY ON HIEROGLYPHICS IN TOWN!
HIS STUDIO IS RIGHT BELOW ME...!
ARCH
IF I CAN JUST GET HIM TO...
WAIT!! WHAT'S THIS?!!
A SPOTLIGHT!! IT'S THE POLICE!
11.

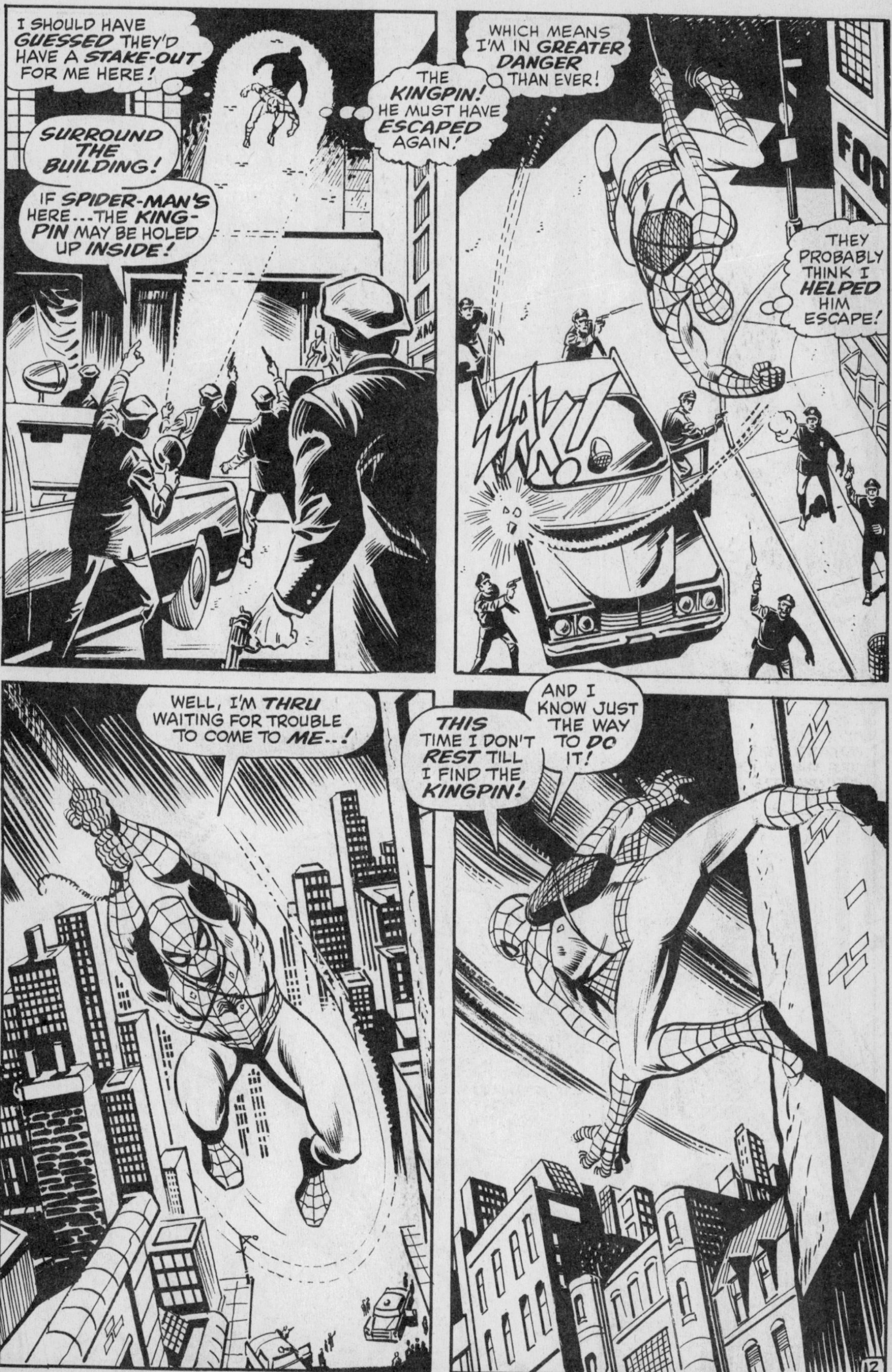
I SHOULD HAVE GUESSED THEY'D HAVE A STAKE-OUT FOR ME HERE!
SURROUND THE BUILDING!
IF SPIDER-MAN'S HERE...THE KING-PIN MAY BE HOLED UP INSIDE!
THE KINGPIN! HE MUST HAVE ESCAPED AGAIN!
WHICH MEANS I'M IN GREATER DANGER THAN EVER!
THEY PROBABLY THINK I HELPED HIM ESCAPE!
ZAK!
WELL, I'M THRU WAITING FOR TROUBLE TO COME TO ME..!
THIS TIME I DON'T REST TILL I FIND THE KINGPIN!
AND I KNOW JUST THE WAY TO DO IT!
12

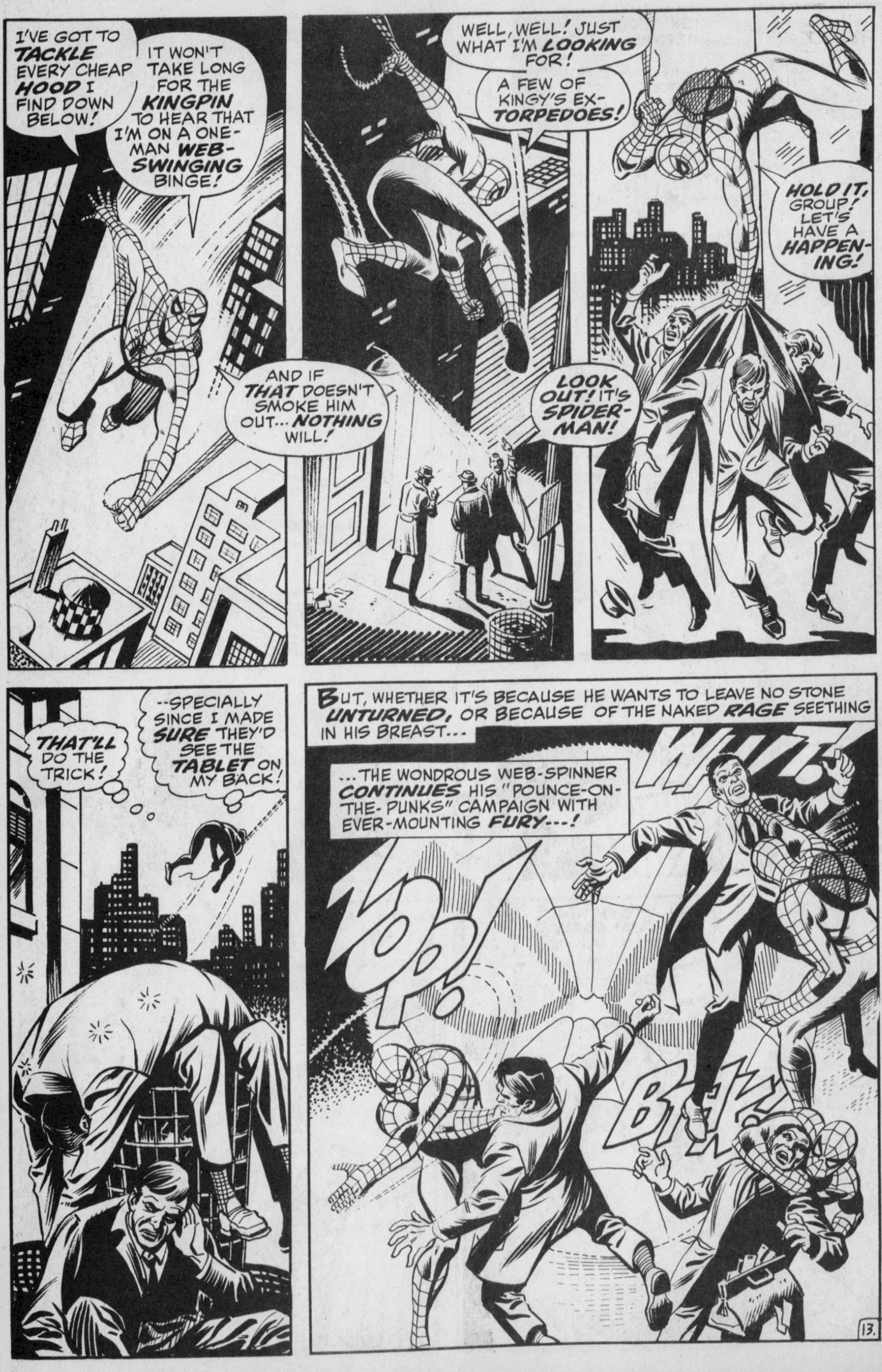

I'VE GOT TO TACKLE EVERY CHEAP HOOD I FIND DOWN BELOW!
IT WON'T TAKE LONG FOR THE KINGPIN TO HEAR THAT I'M ON A ONE-MAN WEB-SWINGING BINGE!
AND IF THAT DOESN'T SMOKE HIM OUT... NOTHING WILL!
WELL, WELL! JUST WHAT I'M LOOKING FOR!
A FEW OF KINGY'S EX-TORPEDOES!
HOLD IT, GROUP! LET'S HAVE A HAPPENING!
LOOK OUT! IT'S SPIDER-MAN!
THAT'LL DO THE TRICK!
--SPECIALLY SINCE I MADE SURE THEY'D SEE THE TABLET ON MY BACK!
BUT, WHETHER IT'S BECAUSE HE WANTS TO LEAVE NO STONE UNTURNED, OR BECAUSE OF THE NAKED RAGE SEETHING IN HIS BREAST...
...THE WONDROUS WEB-SPINNER CONTINUES HIS "POUNCE-ON-THE-PUNKS" CAMPAIGN WITH EVER-MOUNTING FURY---!
WHT!
WOOP!
BTK!

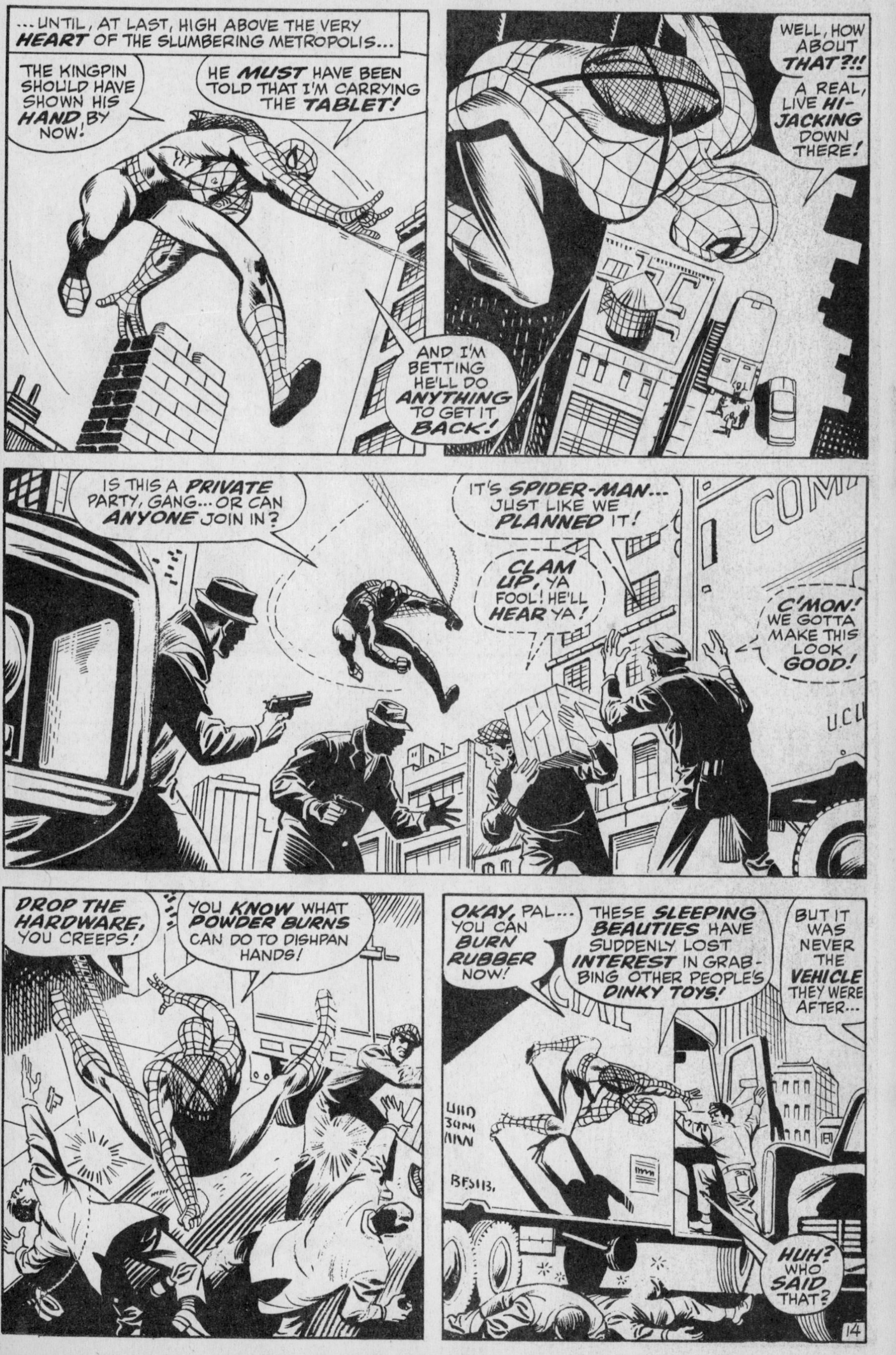
...UNTIL, AT LAST, HIGH ABOVE THE VERY HEART OF THE SLUMBERING METROPOLIS...
THE KINGPIN SHOULD HAVE SHOWN HIS HAND BY NOW!
HE MUST HAVE BEEN TOLD THAT I'M CARRYING THE TABLET!
AND I'M BETTING HE'LL DO ANYTHING TO GET IT BACK!
WELL, HOW ABOUT THAT?!!
A REAL, LIVE HI-JACKING DOWN THERE!
IS THIS A PRIVATE PARTY, GANG... OR CAN ANYONE JOIN IN?
IT'S SPIDER-MAN... JUST LIKE WE PLANNED IT!
CLAM UP, YA FOOL! HE'LL HEAR YA!
C'MON! WE GOTTA MAKE THIS LOOK GOOD!
DROP THE HARDWARE, YOU CREEPS!
YOU KNOW WHAT POWDER BURNS CAN DO TO DISHPAN HANDS!
OKAY, PAL... YOU CAN BURN RUBBER NOW!
THESE SLEEPING BEAUTIES HAVE SUDDENLY LOST INTEREST IN GRAB-BING OTHER PEOPLE'S DINKY TOYS!
BUT IT WAS NEVER THE VEHICLE THEY WERE AFTER...
HUH? WHO SAID THAT?

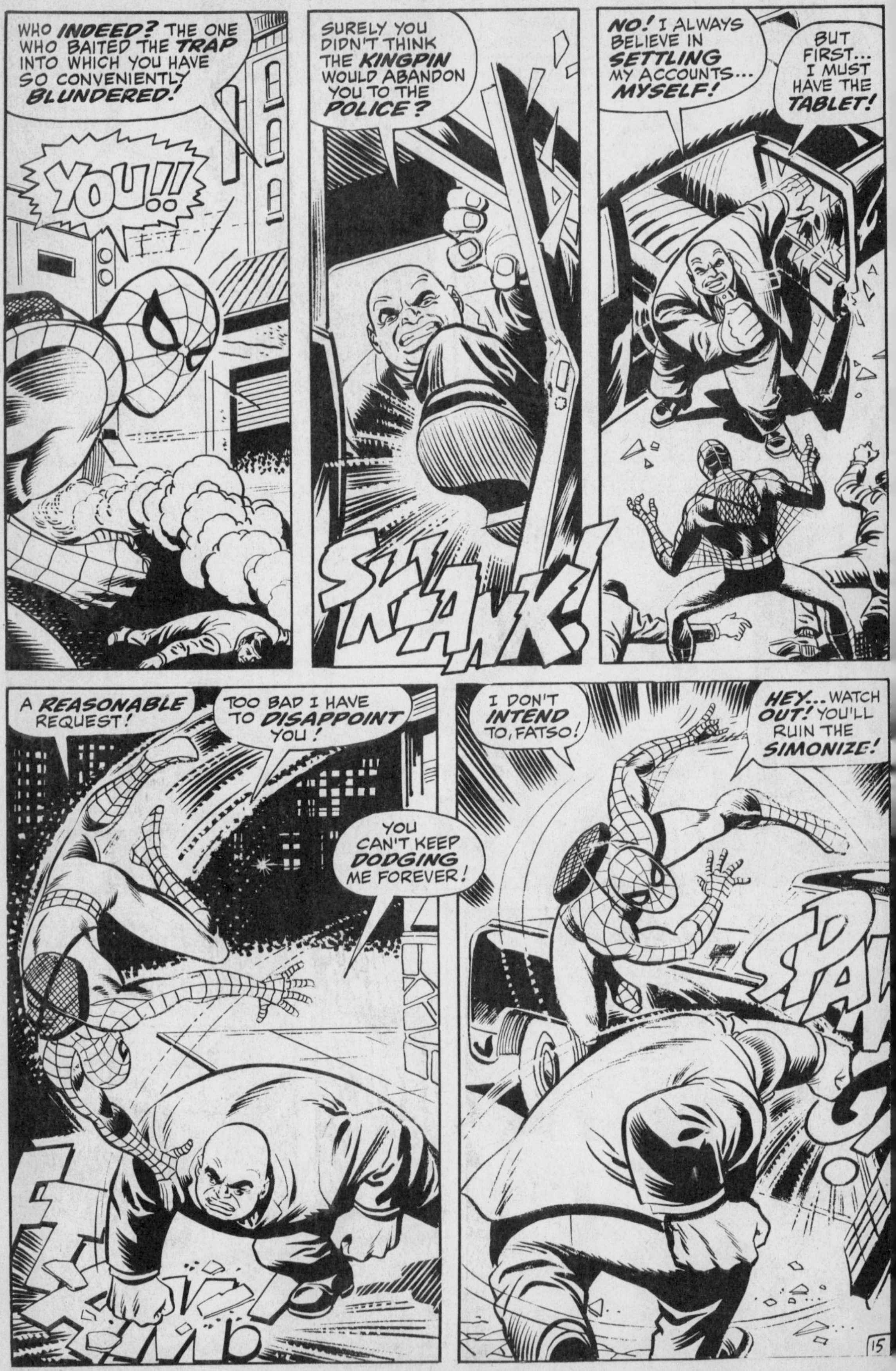
WHO INDEED? THE ONE WHO BAITED THE TRAP INTO WHICH YOU HAVE SO CONVENIENTLY BLUNDERED!
YOU!!
SURELY YOU DIDN'T THINK THE KINGPIN WOULD ABANDON YOU TO THE POLICE?
SKRANK!
NO! I ALWAYS BELIEVE IN SETTLING MY ACCOUNTS... MYSELF!
BUT FIRST... I MUST HAVE THE TABLET!
A REASONABLE REQUEST!
TOO BAD I HAVE TO DISAPPOINT YOU!
YOU CAN'T KEEP DODGING ME FOREVER!
I DON'T INTEND TO, FATSO!
HEY... WATCH OUT! YOU'LL RUIN THE SIMONIZE!

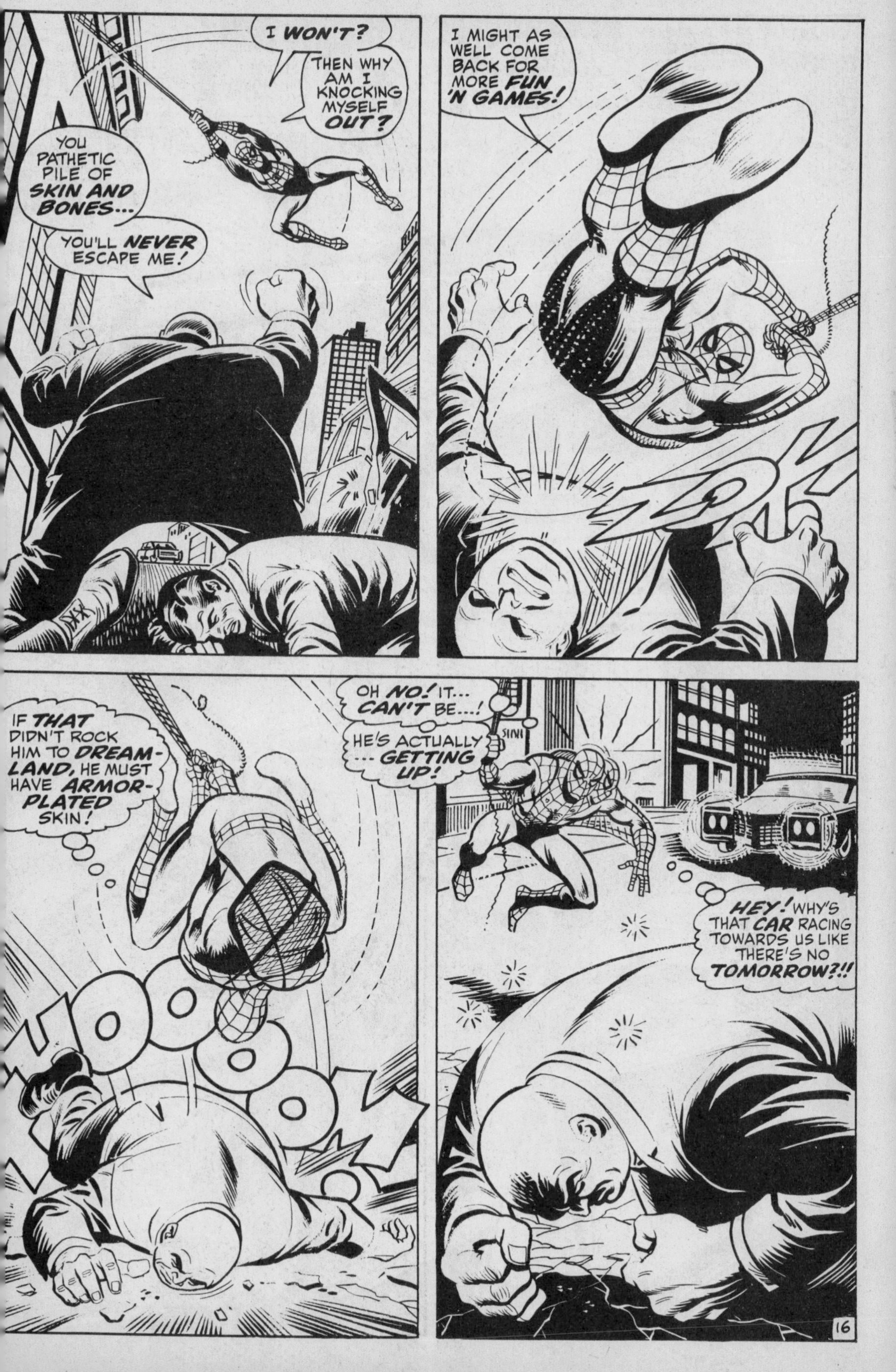
I WON'T?
THEN WHY AM I KNOCKING MYSELF OUT?
YOU PATHETIC PILE OF SKIN AND BONES...
YOU'LL NEVER ESCAPE ME!
I MIGHT AS WELL COME BACK FOR MORE FUN 'N GAMES!
ZOK
IF THAT DIDN'T ROCK HIM TO DREAM-LAND, HE MUST HAVE ARMOR-PLATED SKIN!
WOOOOK
OH NO! IT... CAN'T BE...!
HE'S ACTUALLY ...GETTING UP!
HEY! WHY'S THAT CAR RACING TOWARDS US LIKE THERE'S NO TOMORROW?!!
16

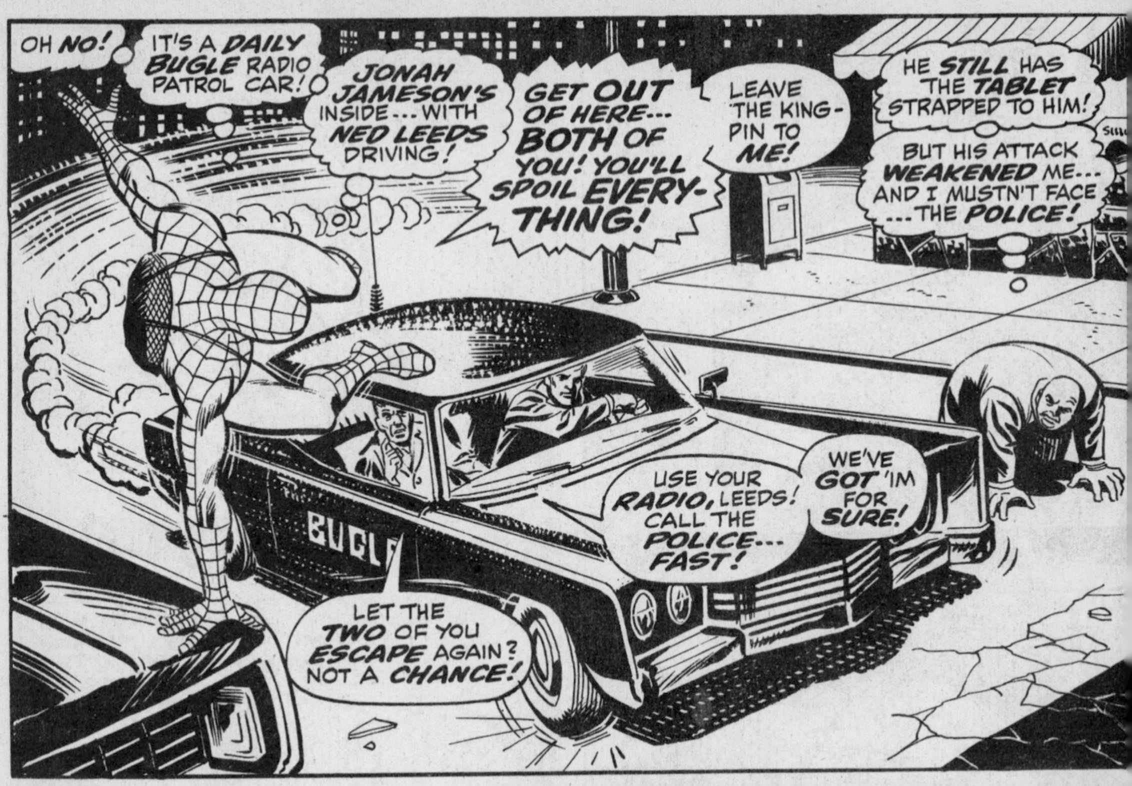
OH NO!
IT'S A DAILY BUGLE RADIO PATROL CAR!
JONAH JAMESON'S INSIDE--- WITH NED LEEDS DRIVING!
GET OUT OF HERE--- BOTH OF YOU! YOU'LL SPOIL EVERY-THING!
LEAVE THE KING-PIN TO ME!
HE STILL HAS THE TABLET STRAPPED TO HIM!
BUT HIS ATTACK WEAKENED ME--- AND I MUSTN'T FACE --- THE POLICE!
BUGLE
USE YOUR RADIO, LEEDS! CALL THE POLICE--- FAST!
WE'VE GOT 'IM FOR SURE!
LET THE TWO OF YOU ESCAPE AGAIN? NOT A CHANCE!

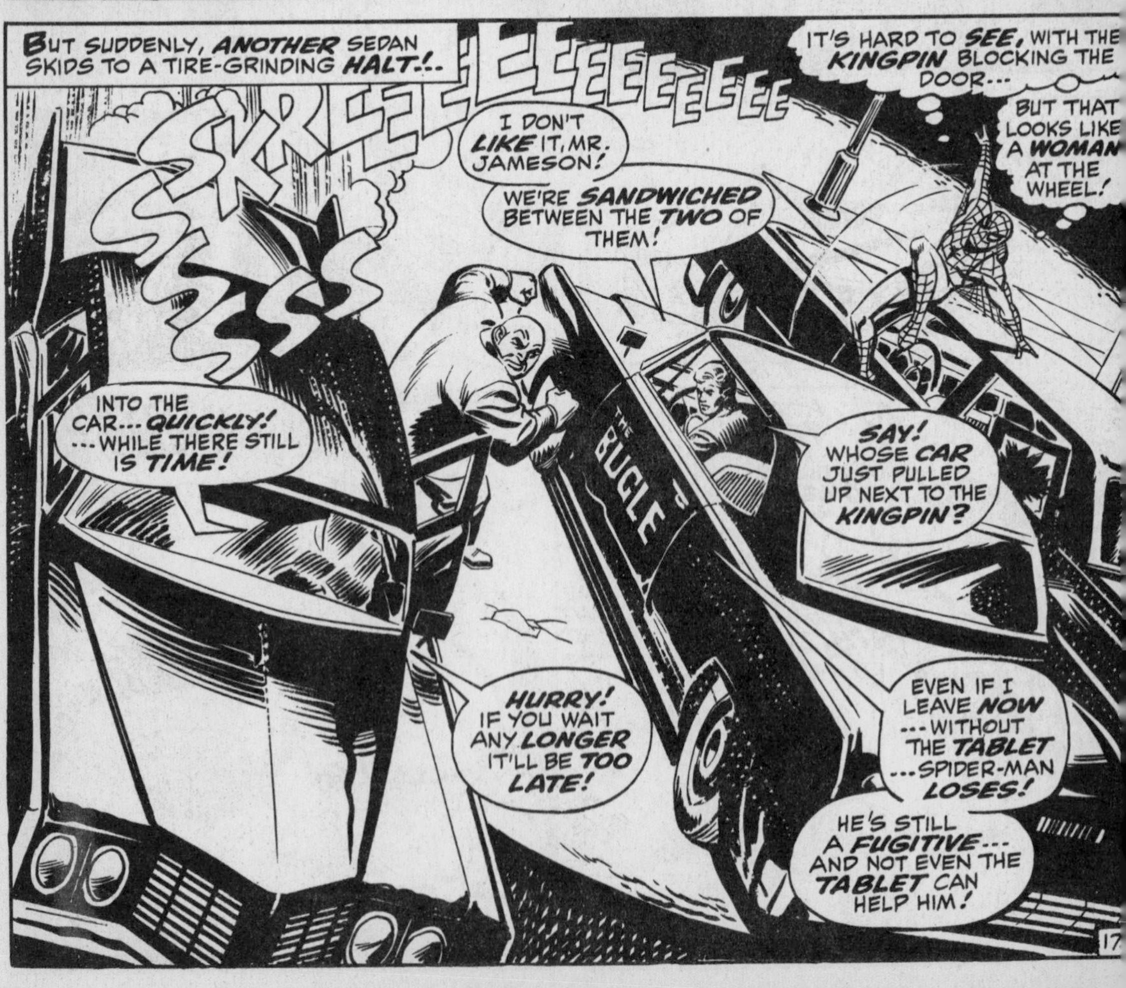
BUT SUDDENLY, ANOTHER SEDAN SKIDS TO A TIRE-GRINDING HALT!..
SKREEEEEEEEEEEEE
SSSSS
IT'S HARD TO SEE, WITH THE KINGPIN BLOCKING THE DOOR---
BUT THAT LOOKS LIKE A WOMAN AT THE WHEEL!
I DON'T LIKE IT, MR. JAMESON!
WE'RE SANDWICHED BETWEEN THE TWO OF THEM!
INTO THE CAR--- QUICKLY! --- WHILE THERE STILL IS TIME!
THE BUGLE
SAY! WHOSE CAR JUST PULLED UP NEXT TO THE KINGPIN?
HURRY! IF YOU WAIT ANY LONGER IT'LL BE TOO LATE!
EVEN IF I LEAVE NOW --- WITHOUT THE TABLET --- SPIDER-MAN LOSES!
HE'S STILL A FUGITIVE--- AND NOT EVEN THE TABLET CAN HELP HIM!

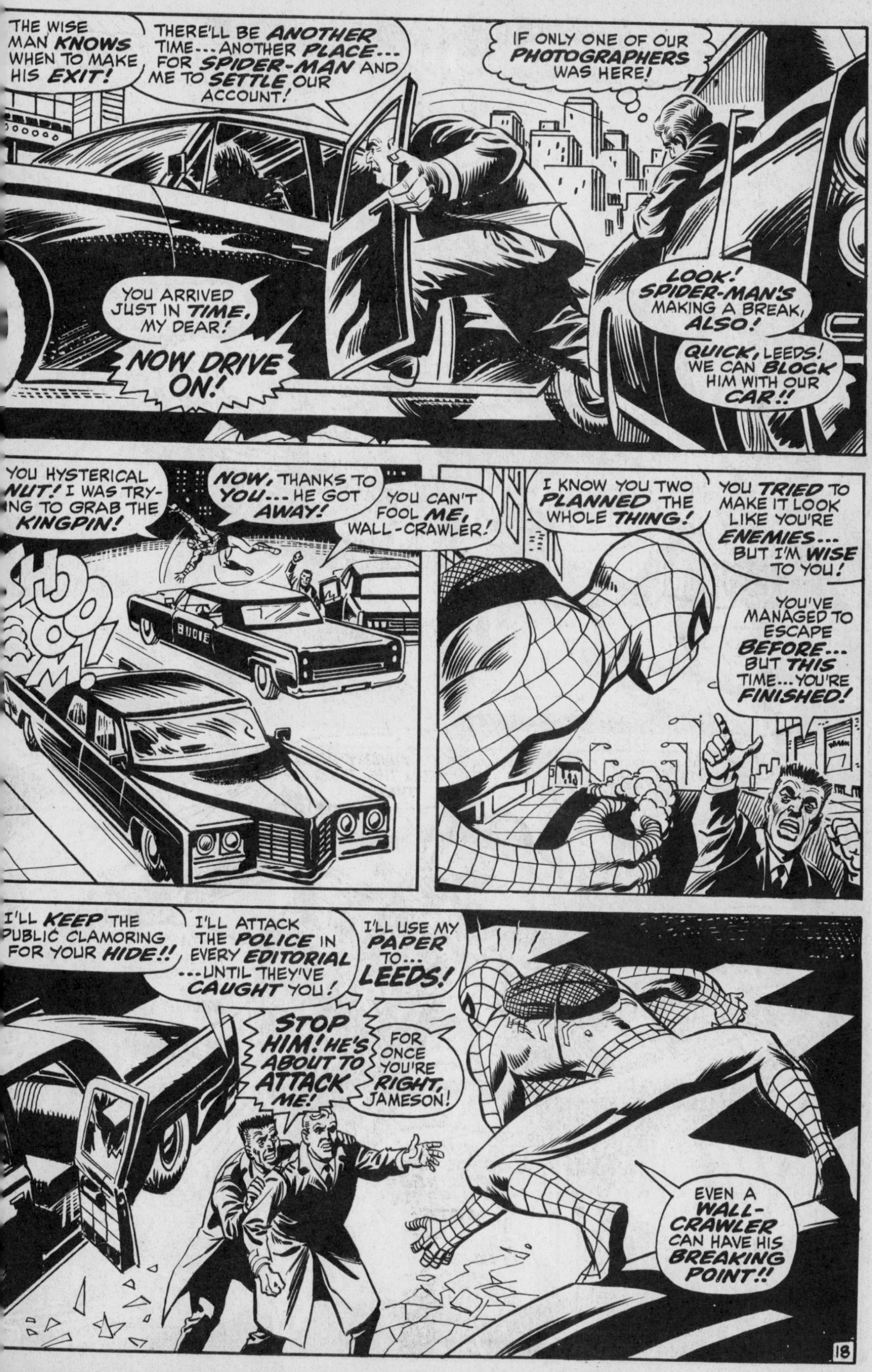
THE WISE MAN KNOWS WHEN TO MAKE HIS EXIT!
THERE'LL BE ANOTHER TIME... ANOTHER PLACE... FOR SPIDER-MAN AND ME TO SETTLE OUR ACCOUNT!
IF ONLY ONE OF OUR PHOTOGRAPHERS WAS HERE!
YOU ARRIVED JUST IN TIME, MY DEAR!
NOW DRIVE ON!
LOOK! SPIDER-MAN'S MAKING A BREAK, ALSO!
QUICK, LEEDS! WE CAN BLOCK HIM WITH OUR CAR!!
YOU HYSTERICAL NUT! I WAS TRYING TO GRAB THE KINGPIN!
NOW, THANKS TO YOU... HE GOT AWAY!
YOU CAN'T FOOL ME, WALL-CRAWLER!
SHOOOM!
I KNOW YOU TWO PLANNED THE WHOLE THING!
YOU TRIED TO MAKE IT LOOK LIKE YOU'RE ENEMIES... BUT I'M WISE TO YOU!
YOU'VE MANAGED TO ESCAPE BEFORE... BUT THIS TIME... YOU'RE FINISHED!
I'LL KEEP THE PUBLIC CLAMORING FOR YOUR HIDE!!
I'LL ATTACK THE POLICE IN EVERY EDITORIAL ...UNTIL THEY'VE CAUGHT YOU!
I'LL USE MY PAPER TO... LEEDS!
STOP HIM! HE'S ABOUT TO ATTACK ME!
FOR ONCE YOU'RE RIGHT, JAMESON!
EVEN A WALL-CRAWLER CAN HAVE HIS BREAKING POINT!!

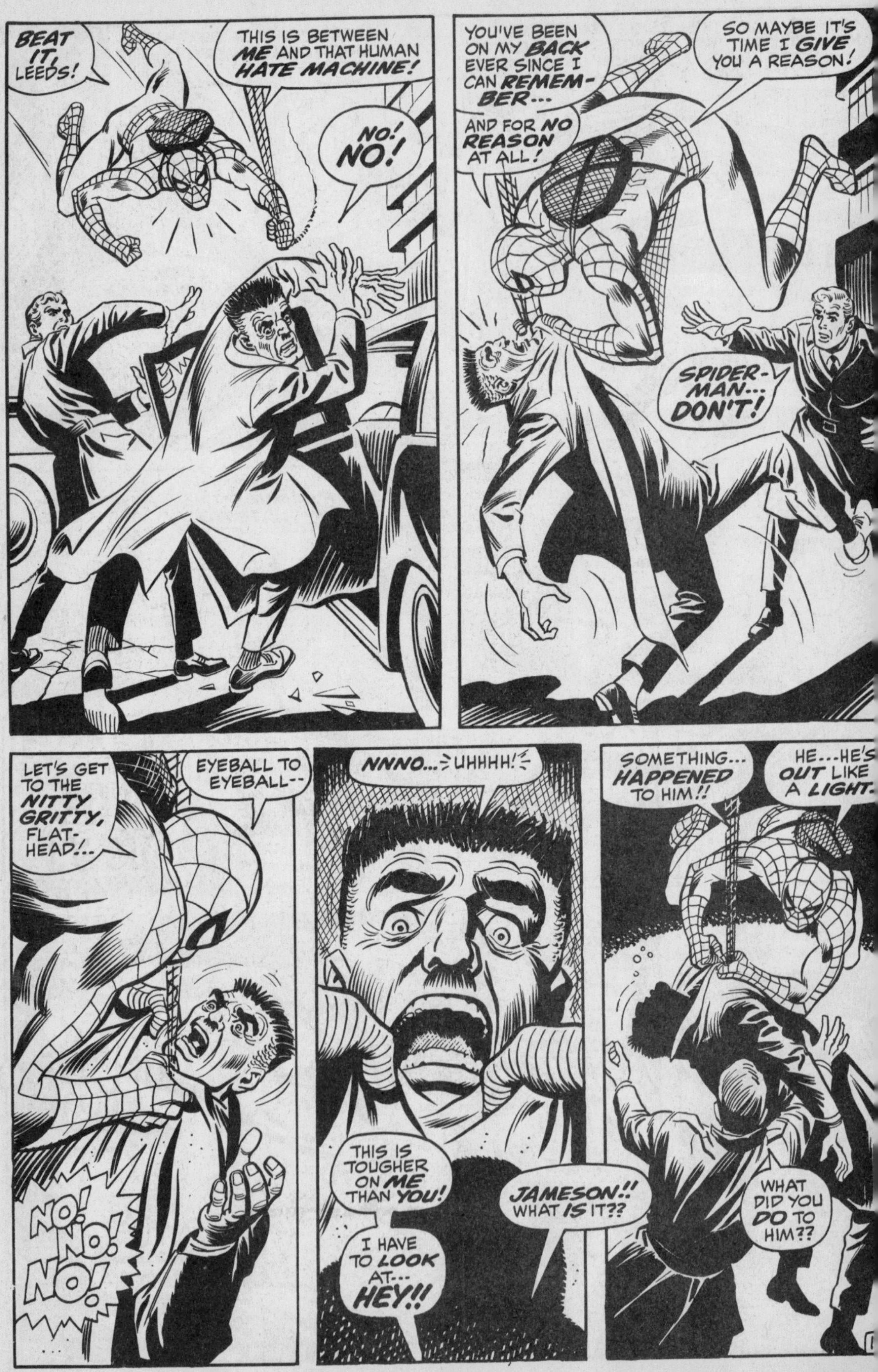
BEAT IT, LEEDS!
THIS IS BETWEEN ME AND THAT HUMAN HATE MACHINE!
NO! NO!
YOU'VE BEEN ON MY BACK EVER SINCE I CAN REMEMBER...
AND FOR NO REASON AT ALL!
SO MAYBE IT'S TIME I GIVE YOU A REASON!
SPIDER-MAN... DON'T!
LET'S GET TO THE NITTY GRITTY, FLAT-HEAD!..
EYEBALL TO EYEBALL--
NO! NO! NO!
NNNO...UHHHH!
THIS IS TOUGHER ON ME THAN YOU!
I HAVE TO LOOK AT... HEY!!
JAMESON!! WHAT IS IT??
SOMETHING... HAPPENED TO HIM!!
HE...HE'S OUT LIKE A LIGHT.
WHAT DID YOU DO TO HIM??

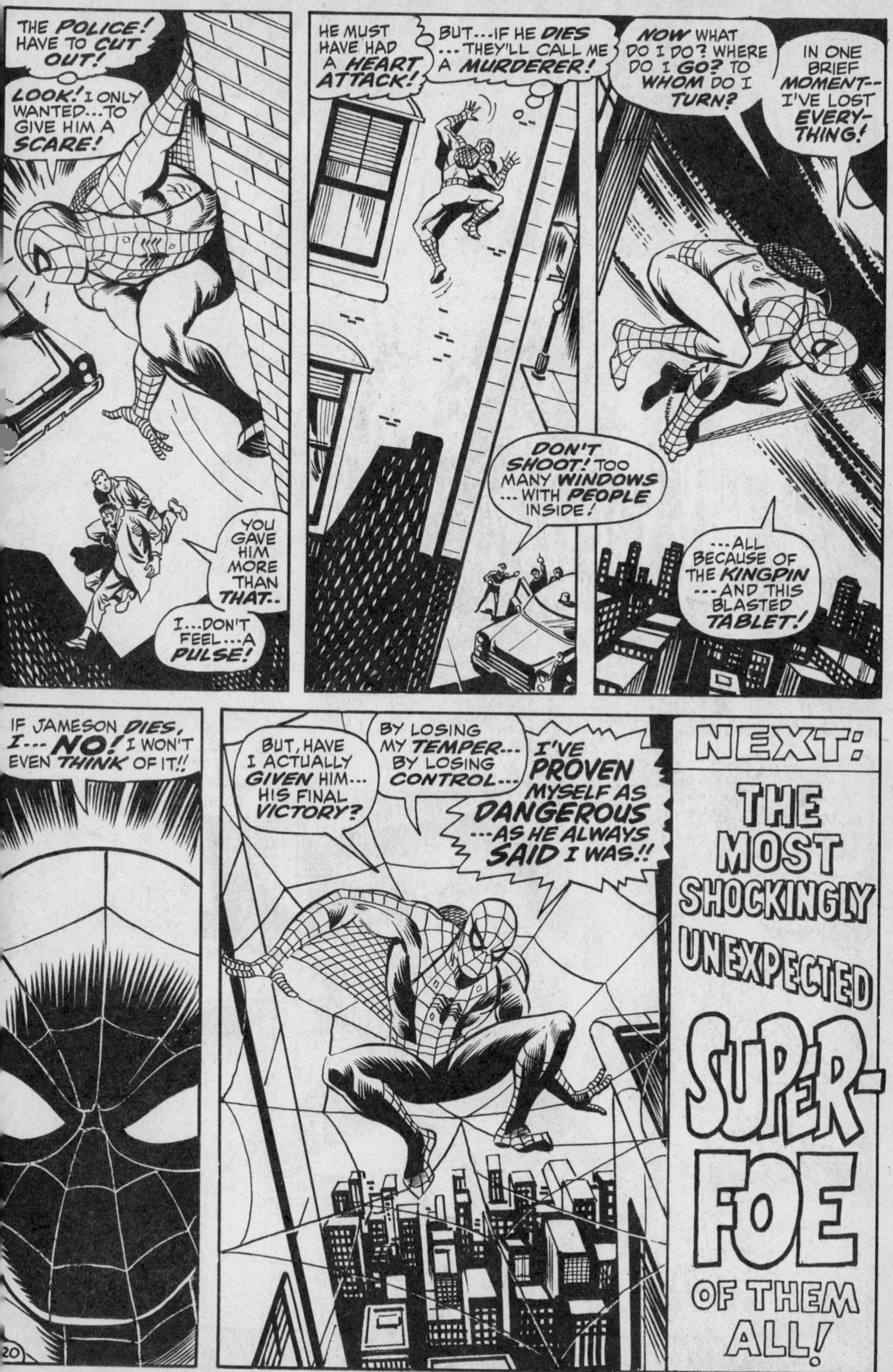
THE POLICE! HAVE TO CUT OUT!
LOOK! I ONLY WANTED...TO GIVE HIM A SCARE!
YOU GAVE HIM MORE THAN THAT..
I...DON'T FEEL...A PULSE!
HE MUST HAVE HAD A HEART ATTACK!
BUT...IF HE DIES ...THEY'LL CALL ME A MURDERER!
DON'T SHOOT! TOO MANY WINDOWS ...WITH PEOPLE INSIDE!
NOW WHAT DO I DO? WHERE DO I GO? TO WHOM DO I TURN?
IN ONE BRIEF MOMENT-- I'VE LOST EVERYTHING!
...ALL BECAUSE OF THE KINGPIN ---AND THIS BLASTED TABLET!
IF JAMESON DIES, I... NO! I WON'T EVEN THINK OF IT!!
BUT, HAVE I ACTUALLY GIVEN HIM... HIS FINAL VICTORY?
BY LOSING MY TEMPER... BY LOSING CONTROL...
I'VE PROVEN MYSELF AS DANGEROUS ---AS HE ALWAYS SAID I WAS!!
NEXT:
THE MOST SHOCKINGLY UNEXPECTED SUPER-FOE OF THEM ALL!
20

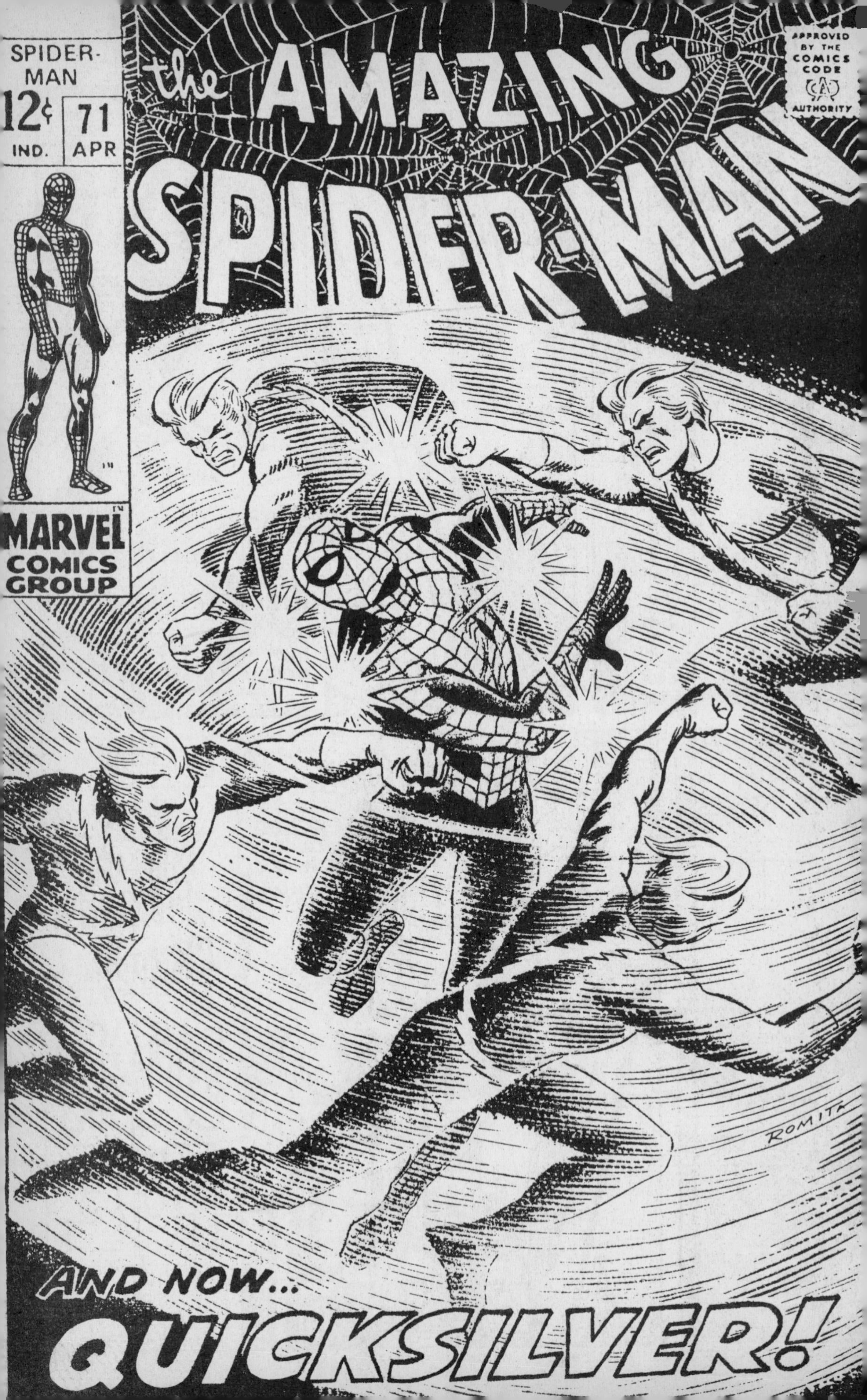
SPIDER-MAN
12¢
71
IND.
APR
the AMAZING
SPIDER-MAN
APPROVED BY THE COMICS CODE AUTHORITY
MARVEL COMICS GROUP
ROMITA
AND NOW...
QUICKSILVER!

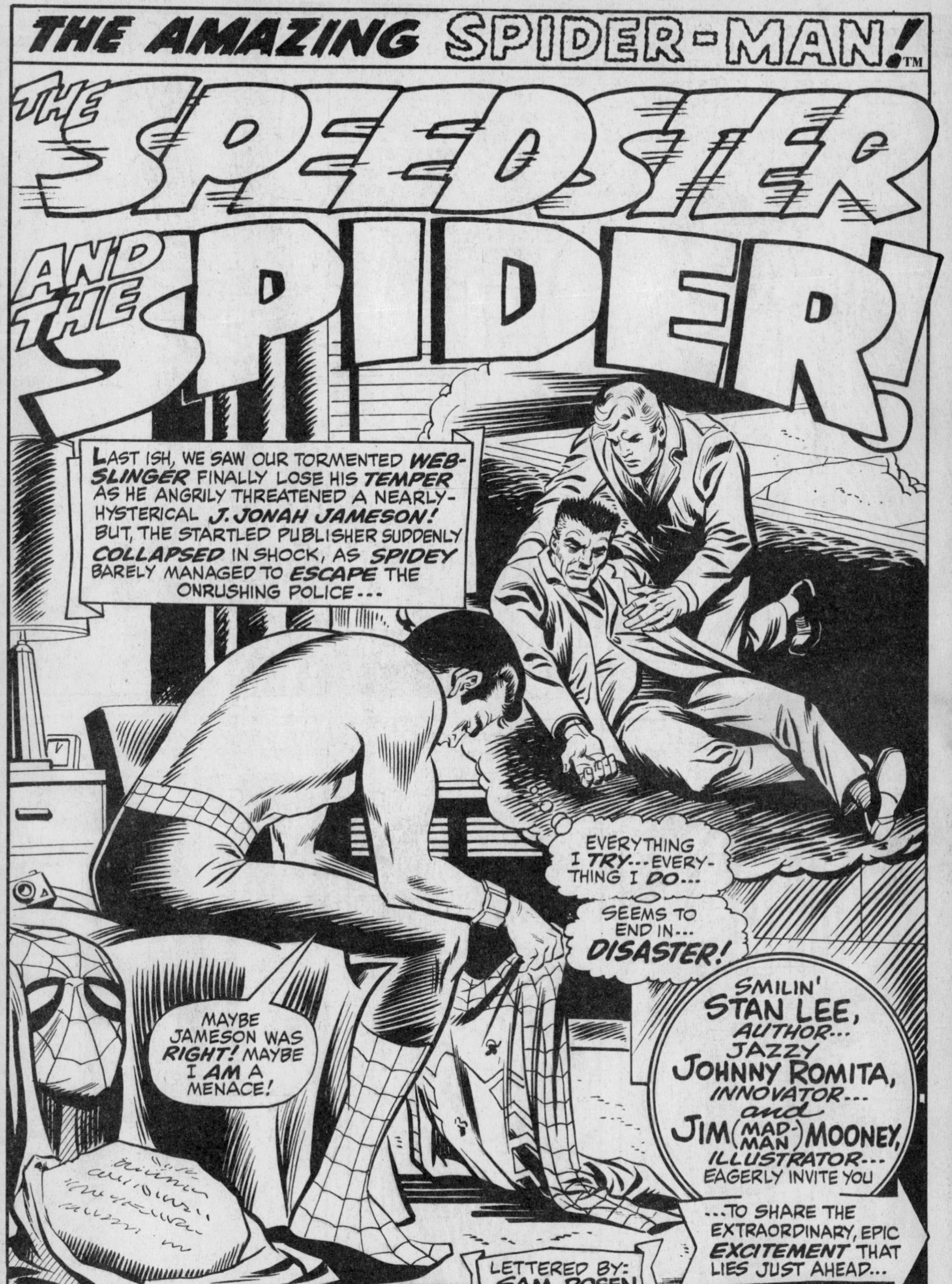
THE AMAZING SPIDER-MAN!™
THE SPEEDSTER AND THE SPIDER!
LAST ISH, WE SAW OUR TORMENTED WEB-SLINGER FINALLY LOSE HIS TEMPER AS HE ANGRILY THREATENED A NEARLY-HYSTERICAL J. JONAH JAMESON! BUT, THE STARTLED PUBLISHER SUDDENLY COLLAPSED IN SHOCK, AS SPIDEY BARELY MANAGED TO ESCAPE THE ONRUSHING POLICE---
EVERYTHING I TRY--- EVERYTHING I DO...
SEEMS TO END IN... DISASTER!
MAYBE JAMESON WAS RIGHT! MAYBE I AM A MENACE!
SMILIN' STAN LEE, AUTHOR... JAZZY JOHNNY ROMITA, INNOVATOR... and JIM (MAD-MAN) MOONEY, ILLUSTRATOR... EAGERLY INVITE YOU
...TO SHARE THE EXTRAORDINARY, EPIC EXCITEMENT THAT LIES JUST AHEAD...
LETTERED BY: SAM ROSEN

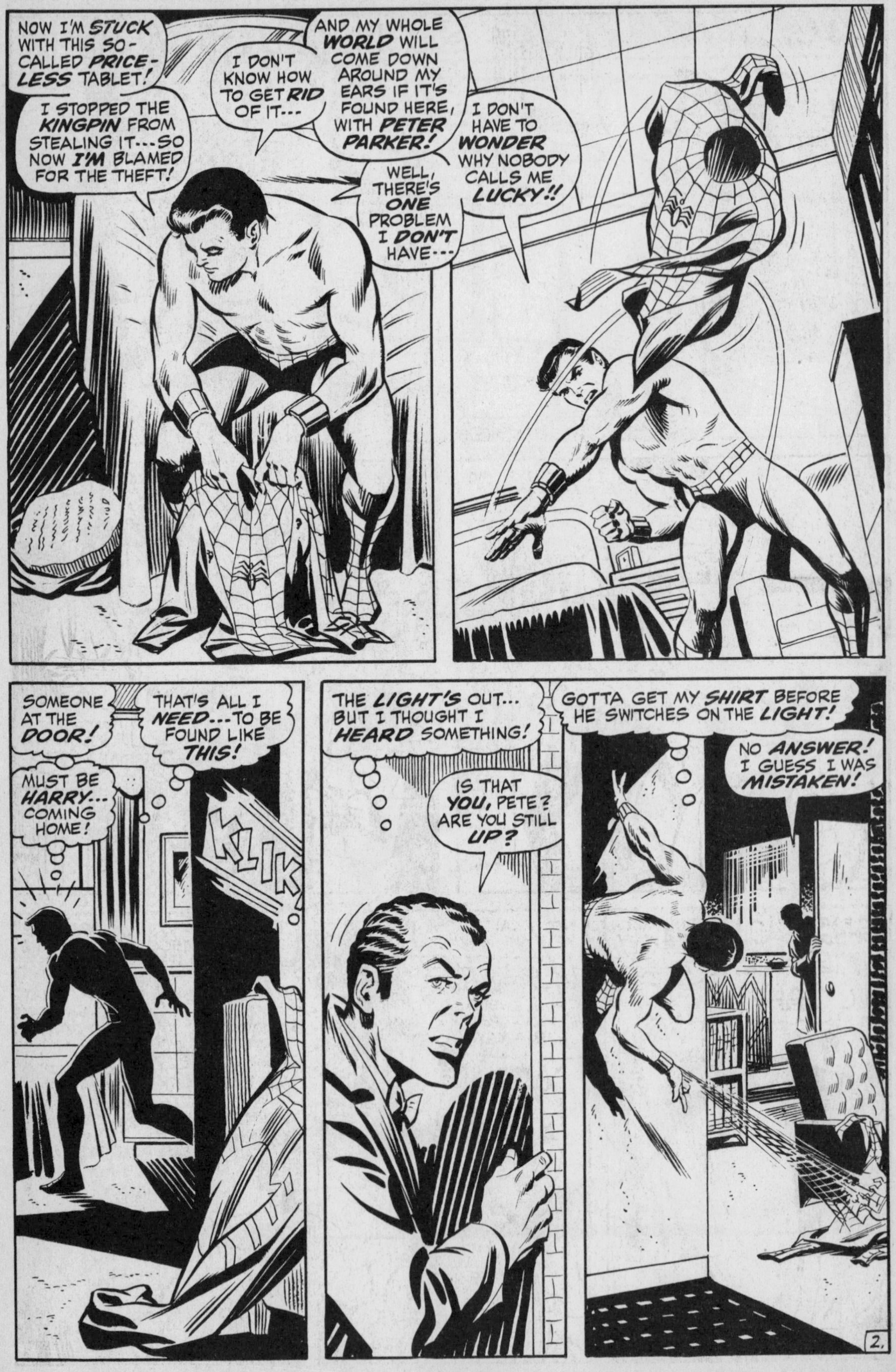

NOW I'M STUCK WITH THIS SO-CALLED PRICE-LESS TABLET!
I STOPPED THE KINGPIN FROM STEALING IT--- SO NOW I'M BLAMED FOR THE THEFT!
I DON'T KNOW HOW TO GET RID OF IT---
AND MY WHOLE WORLD WILL COME DOWN AROUND MY EARS IF IT'S FOUND HERE, WITH PETER PARKER!
WELL, THERE'S ONE PROBLEM I DON'T HAVE---
I DON'T HAVE TO WONDER WHY NOBODY CALLS ME LUCKY!!
SOMEONE AT THE DOOR!
MUST BE HARRY... COMING HOME!
THAT'S ALL I NEED--- TO BE FOUND LIKE THIS!
KLIK
THE LIGHT'S OUT... BUT I THOUGHT I HEARD SOMETHING!
IS THAT YOU, PETE? ARE YOU STILL UP?
GOTTA GET MY SHIRT BEFORE HE SWITCHES ON THE LIGHT!
NO ANSWER! I GUESS I WAS MISTAKEN!

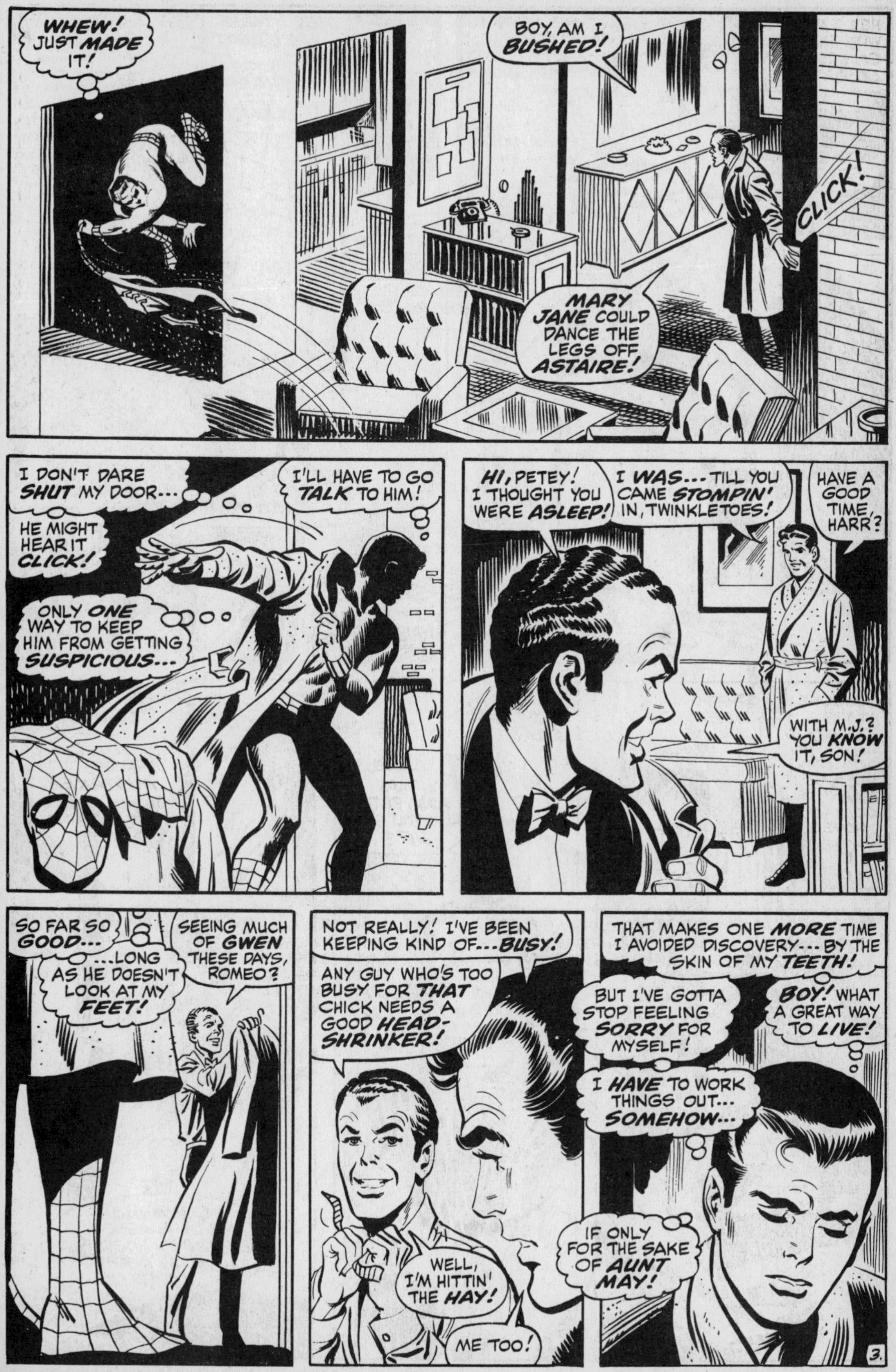

WHEW! JUST MADE IT!
BOY, AM I BUSHED!
CLICK!
MARY JANE COULD DANCE THE LEGS OFF ASTAIRE!
I DON'T DARE SHUT MY DOOR...
HE MIGHT HEAR IT CLICK!
I'LL HAVE TO GO TALK TO HIM!
ONLY ONE WAY TO KEEP HIM FROM GETTING SUSPICIOUS...
HI, PETEY! I THOUGHT YOU WERE ASLEEP!
I WAS... TILL YOU CAME STOMPIN' IN, TWINKLETOES!
HAVE A GOOD TIME, HARR?
WITH M.J.? YOU KNOW IT, SON!
SO FAR SO GOOD...
...LONG AS HE DOESN'T LOOK AT MY FEET!
SEEING MUCH OF GWEN THESE DAYS, ROMEO?
NOT REALLY! I'VE BEEN KEEPING KIND OF... BUSY!
ANY GUY WHO'S TOO BUSY FOR THAT CHICK NEEDS A GOOD HEAD-SHRINKER!
WELL, I'M HITTIN' THE HAY!
ME TOO!
THAT MAKES ONE MORE TIME I AVOIDED DISCOVERY... BY THE SKIN OF MY TEETH!
BUT I'VE GOTTA STOP FEELING SORRY FOR MYSELF!
BOY! WHAT A GREAT WAY TO LIVE!
I HAVE TO WORK THINGS OUT... SOMEHOW...
IF ONLY FOR THE SAKE OF AUNT MAY!
3.

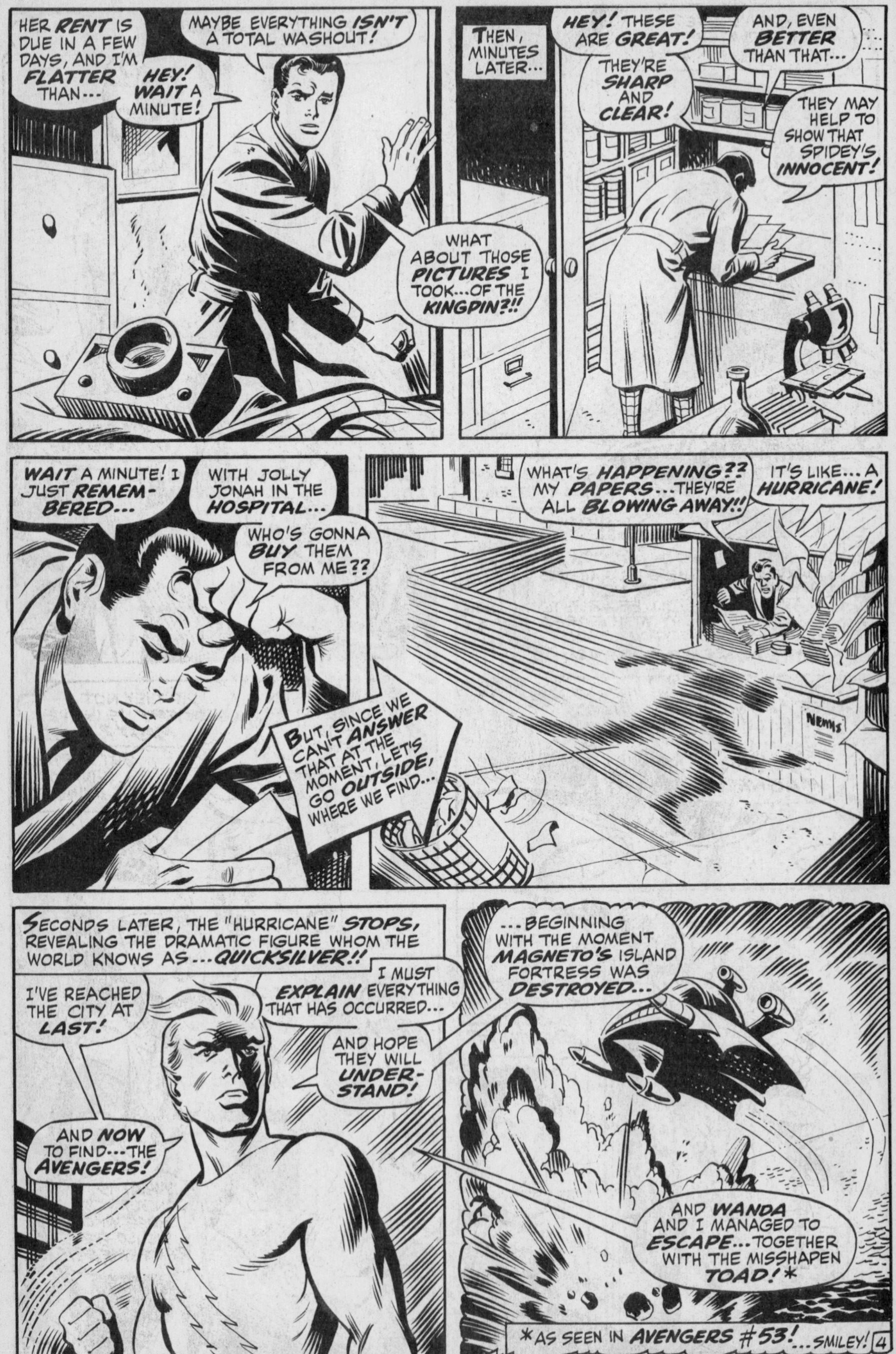
HER RENT IS DUE IN A FEW DAYS, AND I'M FLATTER THAN...
MAYBE EVERYTHING ISN'T A TOTAL WASHOUT!
HEY! WAIT A MINUTE!
WHAT ABOUT THOSE PICTURES I TOOK...OF THE KINGPIN?!!
THEN, MINUTES LATER...
HEY! THESE ARE GREAT!
THEY'RE SHARP AND CLEAR!
AND, EVEN BETTER THAN THAT...
THEY MAY HELP TO SHOW THAT SPIDEY'S INNOCENT!
WAIT A MINUTE! I JUST REMEMBERED...
WITH JOLLY JONAH IN THE HOSPITAL...
WHO'S GONNA BUY THEM FROM ME??
BUT, SINCE WE CAN'T ANSWER THAT AT THE MOMENT, LET'S GO OUTSIDE, WHERE WE FIND...
WHAT'S HAPPENING?? MY PAPERS...THEY'RE ALL BLOWING AWAY!!
IT'S LIKE...A HURRICANE!
NEWS
SECONDS LATER, THE "HURRICANE" STOPS, REVEALING THE DRAMATIC FIGURE WHOM THE WORLD KNOWS AS...QUICKSILVER!!
I'VE REACHED THE CITY AT LAST!
I MUST EXPLAIN EVERYTHING THAT HAS OCCURRED...
AND HOPE THEY WILL UNDERSTAND!
AND NOW TO FIND---THE AVENGERS!
...BEGINNING WITH THE MOMENT MAGNETO'S ISLAND FORTRESS WAS DESTROYED...
AND WANDA AND I MANAGED TO ESCAPE...TOGETHER WITH THE MISSHAPEN TOAD! *
*AS SEEN IN AVENGERS #53! ...SMILEY!
4

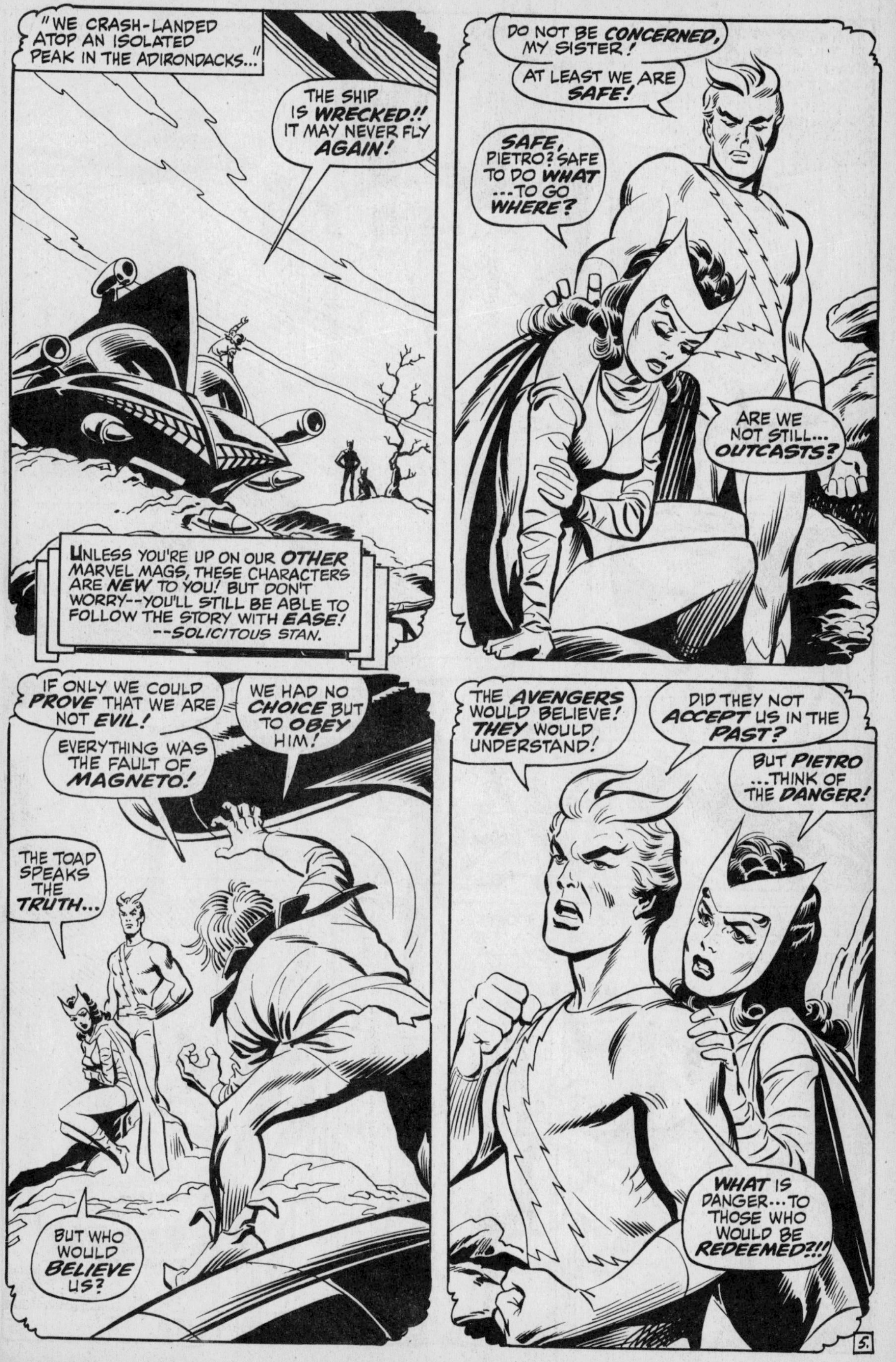
"WE CRASH-LANDED ATOP AN ISOLATED PEAK IN THE ADIRONDACKS..."
THE SHIP IS WRECKED!! IT MAY NEVER FLY AGAIN!
UNLESS YOU'RE UP ON OUR OTHER MARVEL MAGS, THESE CHARACTERS ARE NEW TO YOU! BUT DON'T WORRY--YOU'LL STILL BE ABLE TO FOLLOW THE STORY WITH EASE! --SOLICITOUS STAN.
DO NOT BE CONCERNED, MY SISTER!
AT LEAST WE ARE SAFE!
SAFE, PIETRO? SAFE TO DO WHAT ...TO GO WHERE?
ARE WE NOT STILL... OUTCASTS?
IF ONLY WE COULD PROVE THAT WE ARE NOT EVIL!
EVERYTHING WAS THE FAULT OF MAGNETO!
WE HAD NO CHOICE BUT TO OBEY HIM!
THE TOAD SPEAKS THE TRUTH...
BUT WHO WOULD BELIEVE US?
THE AVENGERS WOULD BELIEVE! THEY WOULD UNDERSTAND!
DID THEY NOT ACCEPT US IN THE PAST?
BUT PIETRO ...THINK OF THE DANGER!
WHAT IS DANGER...TO THOSE WHO WOULD BE REDEEMED?!!
5.

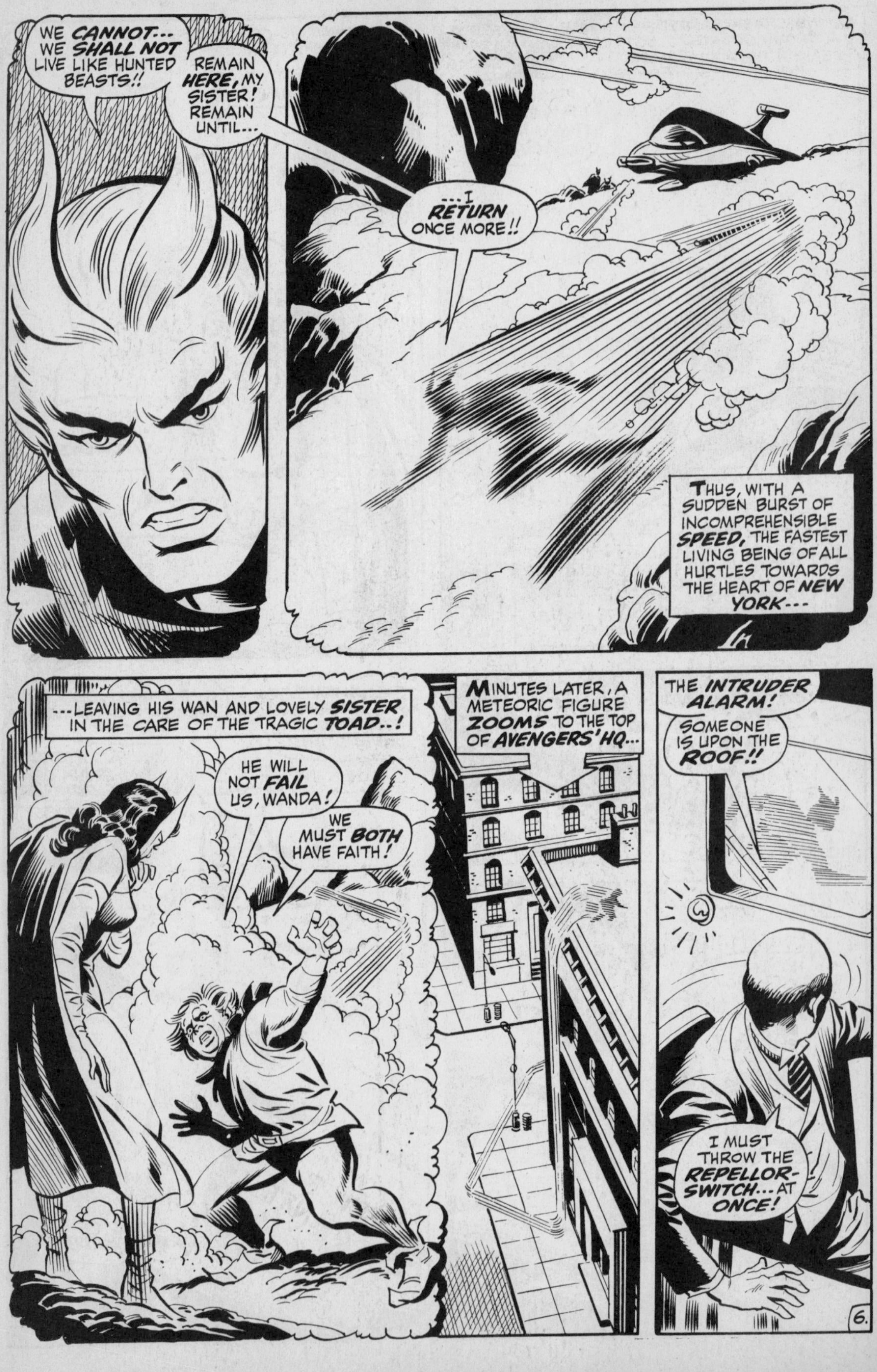
WE CANNOT... WE SHALL NOT LIVE LIKE HUNTED BEASTS!!
REMAIN HERE, MY SISTER! REMAIN UNTIL...
...I RETURN ONCE MORE!!
THUS, WITH A SUDDEN BURST OF INCOMPREHENSIBLE SPEED, THE FASTEST LIVING BEING OF ALL HURTLES TOWARDS THE HEART OF NEW YORK---
---LEAVING HIS WAN AND LOVELY SISTER IN THE CARE OF THE TRAGIC TOAD..!
HE WILL NOT FAIL US, WANDA!
WE MUST BOTH HAVE FAITH!
MINUTES LATER, A METEORIC FIGURE ZOOMS TO THE TOP OF AVENGERS' HQ...
THE INTRUDER ALARM!
SOMEONE IS UPON THE ROOF!!
I MUST THROW THE REPELLOR-SWITCH... AT ONCE!
6.

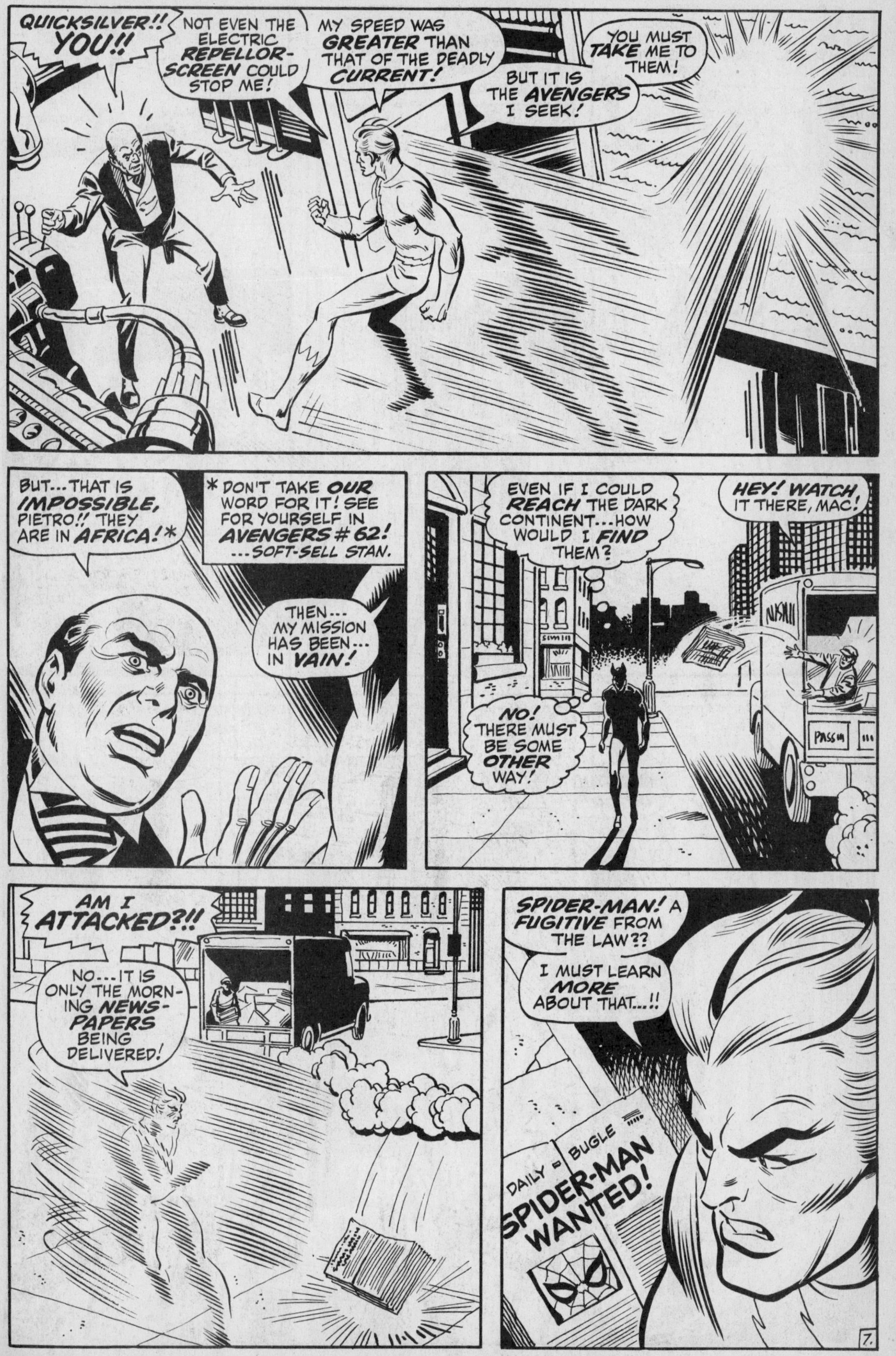
QUICKSILVER!! YOU!!
NOT EVEN THE ELECTRIC REPELLOR-SCREEN COULD STOP ME!
MY SPEED WAS GREATER THAN THAT OF THE DEADLY CURRENT!
BUT IT IS THE AVENGERS I SEEK!
YOU MUST TAKE ME TO THEM!
BUT... THAT IS IMPOSSIBLE, PIETRO!! THEY ARE IN AFRICA!*
* DON'T TAKE OUR WORD FOR IT! SEE FOR YOURSELF IN AVENGERS # 62! ---SOFT-SELL STAN.
THEN--- MY MISSION HAS BEEN... IN VAIN!
EVEN IF I COULD REACH THE DARK CONTINENT...HOW WOULD I FIND THEM?
HEY! WATCH IT THERE, MAC!
NO! THERE MUST BE SOME OTHER WAY!
AM I ATTACKED?!!
NO---IT IS ONLY THE MORNING NEWSPAPERS BEING DELIVERED!
SPIDER-MAN! A FUGITIVE FROM THE LAW??
I MUST LEARN MORE ABOUT THAT...!!
DAILY = BUGLE
SPIDER-MAN WANTED!
7.

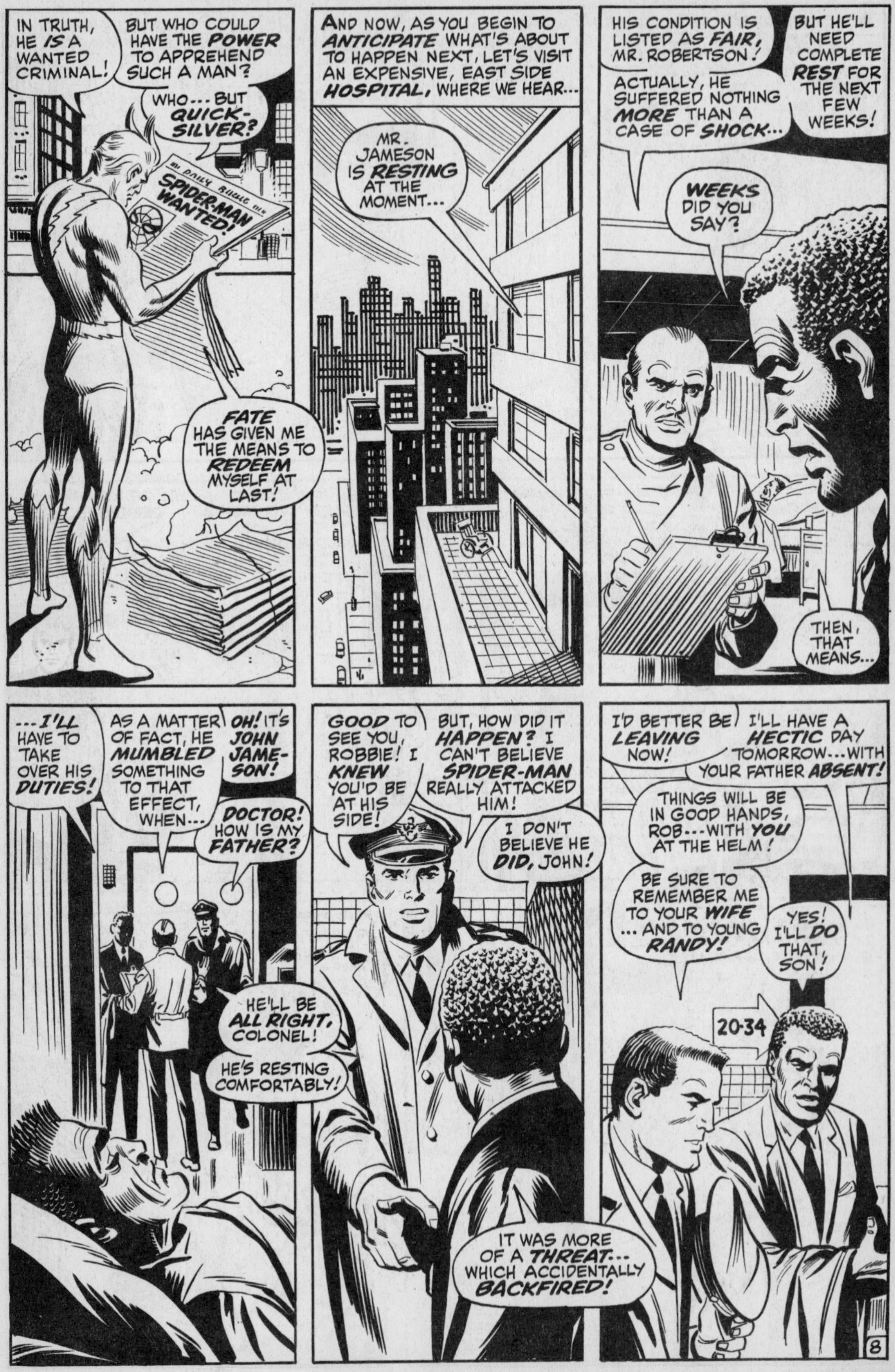
IN TRUTH, HE IS A WANTED CRIMINAL!
BUT WHO COULD HAVE THE POWER TO APPREHEND SUCH A MAN?
WHO... BUT QUICK-SILVER?
SPIDER-MAN WANTED!
FATE HAS GIVEN ME THE MEANS TO REDEEM MYSELF AT LAST!
AND NOW, AS YOU BEGIN TO ANTICIPATE WHAT'S ABOUT TO HAPPEN NEXT, LET'S VISIT AN EXPENSIVE, EAST SIDE HOSPITAL, WHERE WE HEAR...
MR. JAMESON IS RESTING AT THE MOMENT...
HIS CONDITION IS LISTED AS FAIR, MR. ROBERTSON!
ACTUALLY, HE SUFFERED NOTHING MORE THAN A CASE OF SHOCK...
BUT HE'LL NEED COMPLETE REST FOR THE NEXT FEW WEEKS!
WEEKS DID YOU SAY?
THEN, THAT MEANS...
...I'LL HAVE TO TAKE OVER HIS DUTIES!
AS A MATTER OF FACT, HE MUMBLED SOMETHING TO THAT EFFECT, WHEN...
OH! IT'S JOHN JAME-SON!
DOCTOR! HOW IS MY FATHER?
HE'LL BE ALL RIGHT, COLONEL!
HE'S RESTING COMFORTABLY!
GOOD TO SEE YOU, ROBBIE! I KNEW YOU'D BE AT HIS SIDE!
BUT, HOW DID IT HAPPEN? I CAN'T BELIEVE SPIDER-MAN REALLY ATTACKED HIM!
I DON'T BELIEVE HE DID, JOHN!
IT WAS MORE OF A THREAT... WHICH ACCIDENTALLY BACKFIRED!
I'D BETTER BE LEAVING NOW!
I'LL HAVE A HECTIC DAY TOMORROW... WITH YOUR FATHER ABSENT!
THINGS WILL BE IN GOOD HANDS, ROB... WITH YOU AT THE HELM!
BE SURE TO REMEMBER ME TO YOUR WIFE ... AND TO YOUNG RANDY!
YES! I'LL DO THAT, SON!
20-34
8

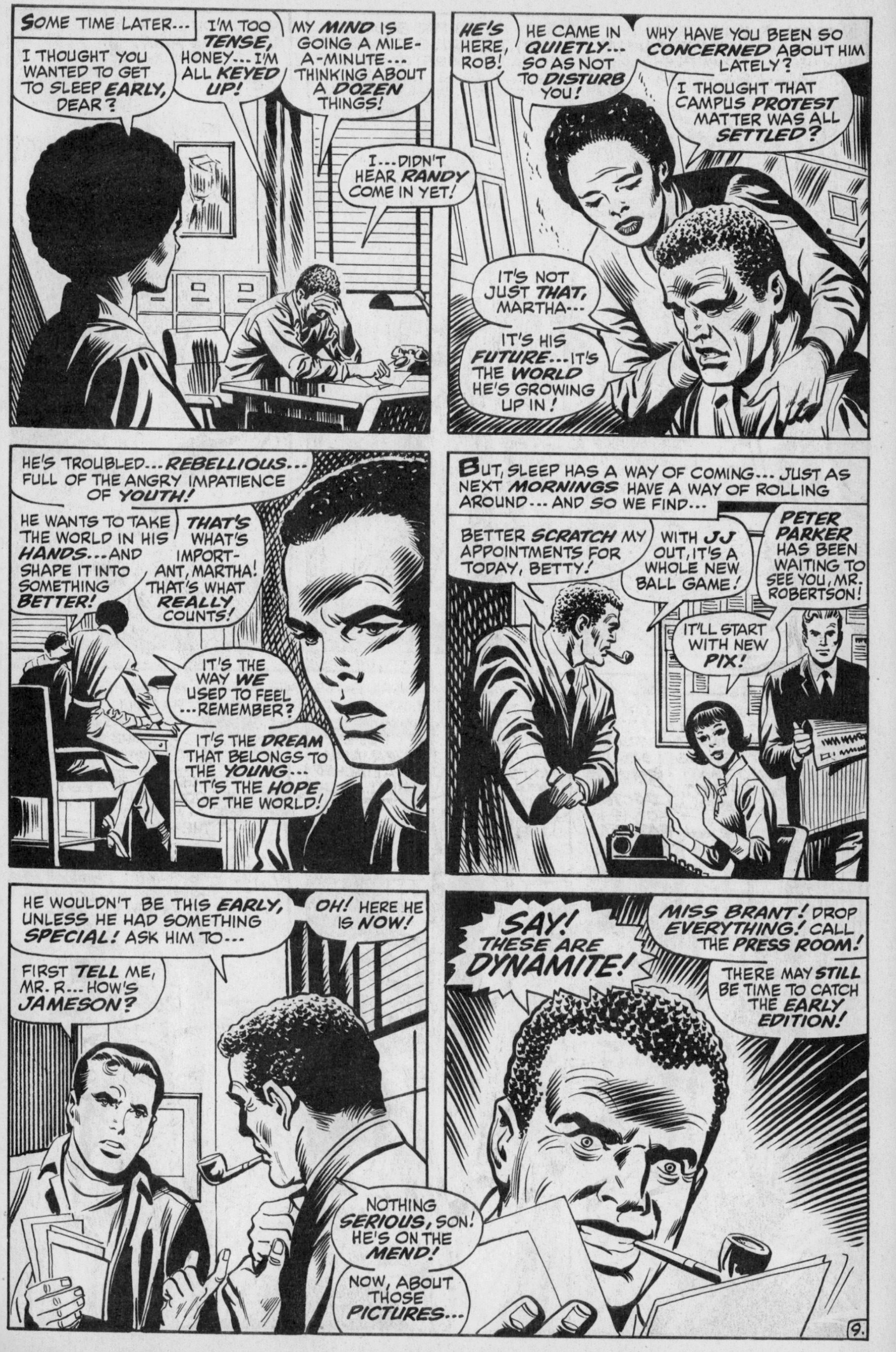
SOME TIME LATER...
I THOUGHT YOU WANTED TO GET TO SLEEP EARLY, DEAR?
I'M TOO TENSE, HONEY... I'M ALL KEYED UP!
MY MIND IS GOING A MILE-A-MINUTE... THINKING ABOUT A DOZEN THINGS!
I...DIDN'T HEAR RANDY COME IN YET!
HE'S HERE, ROB!
HE CAME IN QUIETLY... SO AS NOT TO DISTURB YOU!
WHY HAVE YOU BEEN SO CONCERNED ABOUT HIM LATELY?
I THOUGHT THAT CAMPUS PROTEST MATTER WAS ALL SETTLED?
IT'S NOT JUST THAT, MARTHA---
IT'S HIS FUTURE...IT'S THE WORLD HE'S GROWING UP IN!
HE'S TROUBLED...REBELLIOUS... FULL OF THE ANGRY IMPATIENCE OF YOUTH!
HE WANTS TO TAKE THE WORLD IN HIS HANDS...AND SHAPE IT INTO SOMETHING BETTER!
THAT'S WHAT'S IMPORTANT, MARTHA! THAT'S WHAT REALLY COUNTS!
IT'S THE WAY WE USED TO FEEL ...REMEMBER?
IT'S THE DREAM THAT BELONGS TO THE YOUNG... IT'S THE HOPE OF THE WORLD!
BUT, SLEEP HAS A WAY OF COMING... JUST AS NEXT MORNINGS HAVE A WAY OF ROLLING AROUND... AND SO WE FIND...
BETTER SCRATCH MY APPOINTMENTS FOR TODAY, BETTY!
WITH JJ OUT, IT'S A WHOLE NEW BALL GAME!
IT'LL START WITH NEW PIX!
PETER PARKER HAS BEEN WAITING TO SEE YOU, MR. ROBERTSON!
HE WOULDN'T BE THIS EARLY, UNLESS HE HAD SOMETHING SPECIAL! ASK HIM TO...
OH! HERE HE IS NOW!
FIRST TELL ME, MR. R... HOW'S JAMESON?
NOTHING SERIOUS, SON! HE'S ON THE MEND!
NOW, ABOUT THOSE PICTURES...
SAY! THESE ARE DYNAMITE!
MISS BRANT! DROP EVERYTHING! CALL THE PRESS ROOM!
THERE MAY STILL BE TIME TO CATCH THE EARLY EDITION!
9.

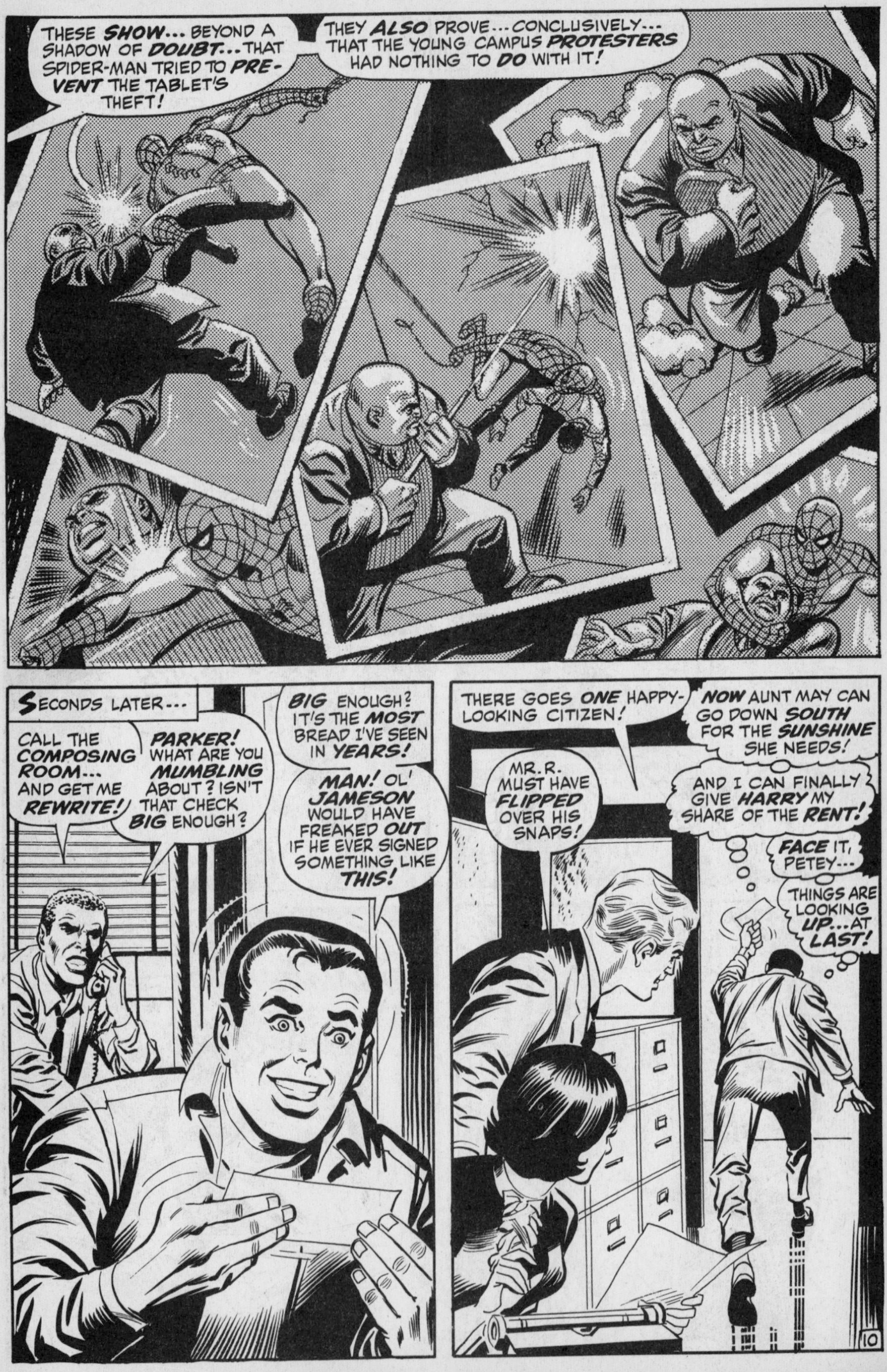
THESE SHOW... BEYOND A SHADOW OF DOUBT... THAT SPIDER-MAN TRIED TO PRE-VENT THE TABLET'S THEFT!
THEY ALSO PROVE... CONCLUSIVELY... THAT THE YOUNG CAMPUS PROTESTERS HAD NOTHING TO DO WITH IT!
SECONDS LATER...
CALL THE COMPOSING ROOM... AND GET ME REWRITE!
PARKER! WHAT ARE YOU MUMBLING ABOUT? ISN'T THAT CHECK BIG ENOUGH?
BIG ENOUGH? IT'S THE MOST BREAD I'VE SEEN IN YEARS!
MAN! OL' JAMESON WOULD HAVE FREAKED OUT IF HE EVER SIGNED SOMETHING LIKE THIS!
THERE GOES ONE HAPPY-LOOKING CITIZEN!
MR. R. MUST HAVE FLIPPED OVER HIS SNAPS!
NOW AUNT MAY CAN GO DOWN SOUTH FOR THE SUNSHINE SHE NEEDS!
AND I CAN FINALLY GIVE HARRY MY SHARE OF THE RENT!
FACE IT, PETEY...
THINGS ARE LOOKING UP... AT LAST!
10

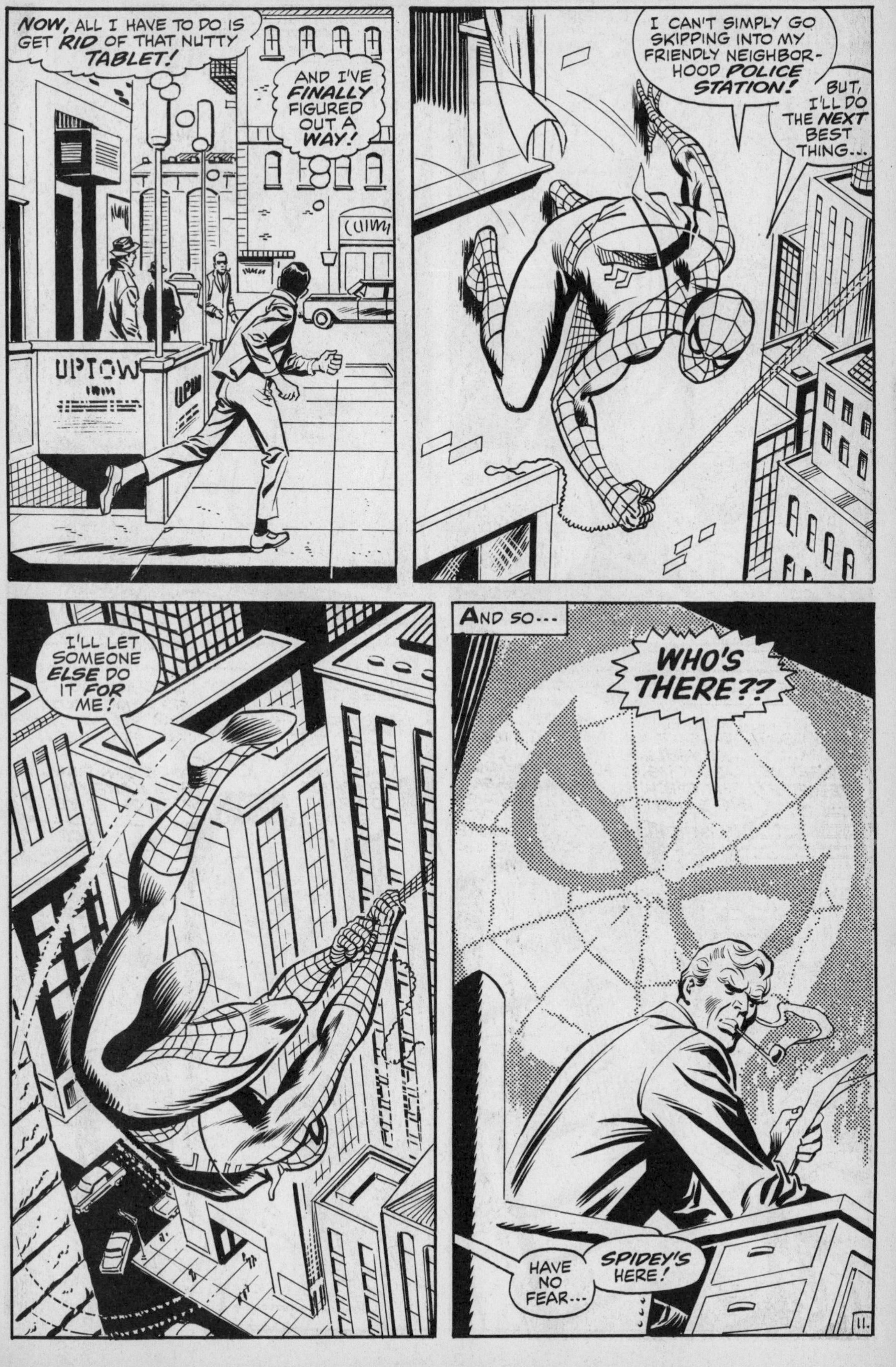
NOW, ALL I HAVE TO DO IS GET RID OF THAT NUTTY TABLET!
AND I'VE FINALLY FIGURED OUT A WAY!
UPTOW
I CAN'T SIMPLY GO SKIPPING INTO MY FRIENDLY NEIGHBOR-HOOD POLICE STATION!
BUT, I'LL DO THE NEXT BEST THING...
I'LL LET SOMEONE ELSE DO IT FOR ME!
AND SO...
WHO'S THERE??
HAVE NO FEAR...
SPIDEY'S HERE!
11.

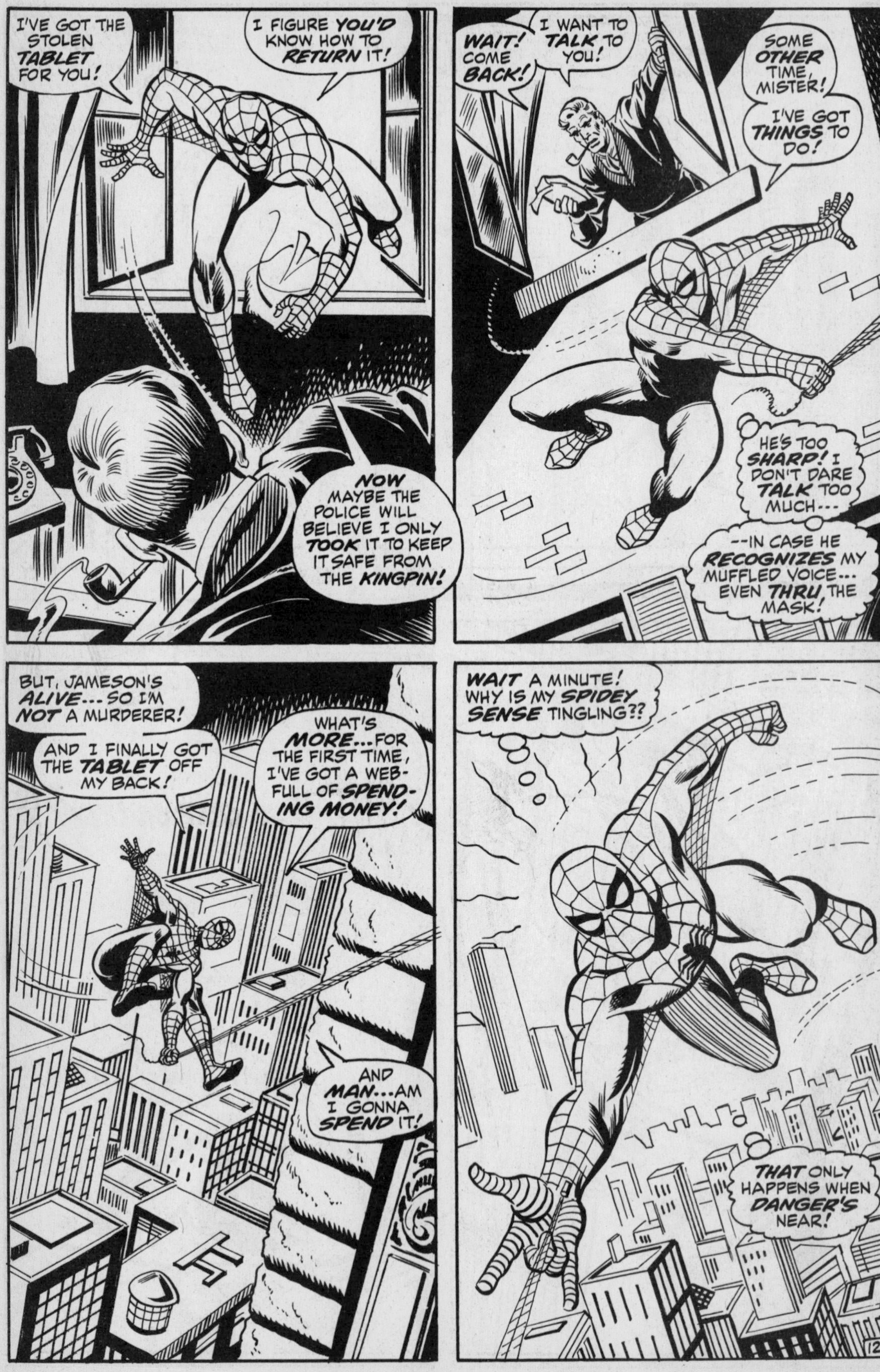

I'VE GOT THE STOLEN TABLET FOR YOU!
I FIGURE YOU'D KNOW HOW TO RETURN IT!
NOW MAYBE THE POLICE WILL BELIEVE I ONLY TOOK IT TO KEEP IT SAFE FROM THE KINGPIN!
WAIT! COME BACK!
I WANT TO TALK TO YOU!
SOME OTHER TIME, MISTER!
I'VE GOT THINGS TO DO!
HE'S TOO SHARP! I DON'T DARE TALK TOO MUCH---
--IN CASE HE RECOGNIZES MY MUFFLED VOICE... EVEN THRU THE MASK!
BUT, JAMESON'S ALIVE... SO I'M NOT A MURDERER!
AND I FINALLY GOT THE TABLET OFF MY BACK!
WHAT'S MORE... FOR THE FIRST TIME, I'VE GOT A WEB-FULL OF SPENDING MONEY!
AND MAN... AM I GONNA SPEND IT!
WAIT A MINUTE! WHY IS MY SPIDEY SENSE TINGLING??
THAT ONLY HAPPENS WHEN DANGER'S NEAR!
12

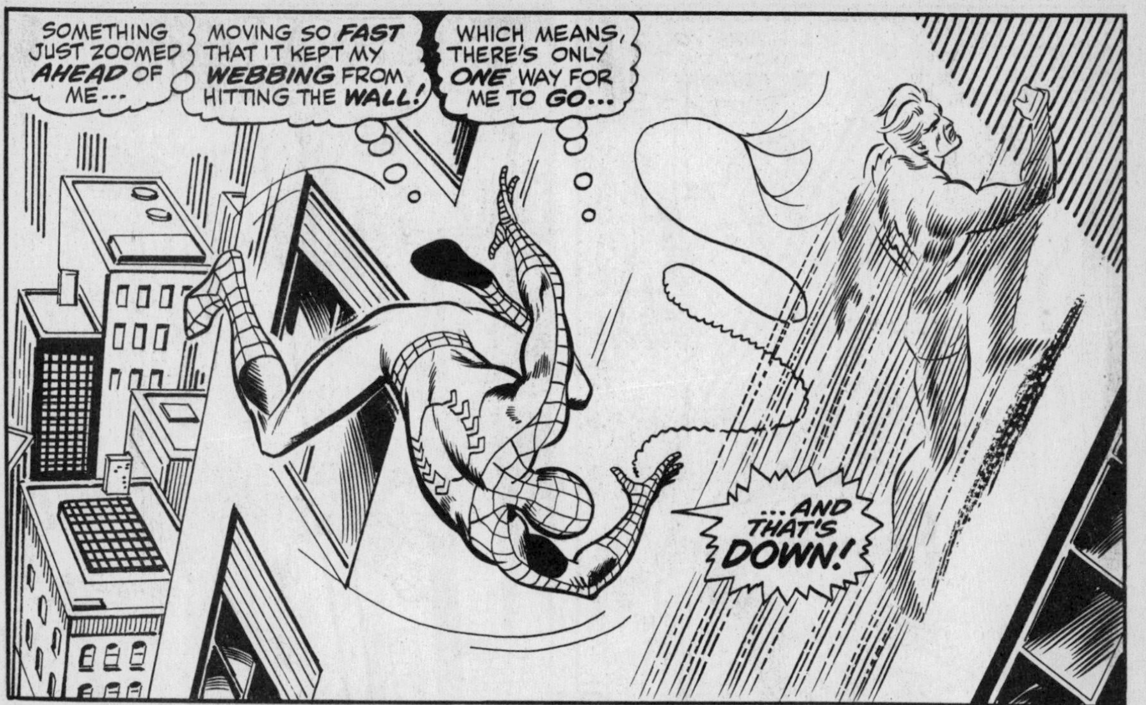
SOMETHING JUST ZOOMED AHEAD OF ME...
MOVING SO FAST THAT IT KEPT MY WEBBING FROM HITTING THE WALL!
WHICH MEANS, THERE'S ONLY ONE WAY FOR ME TO GO...
...AND THAT'S DOWN!

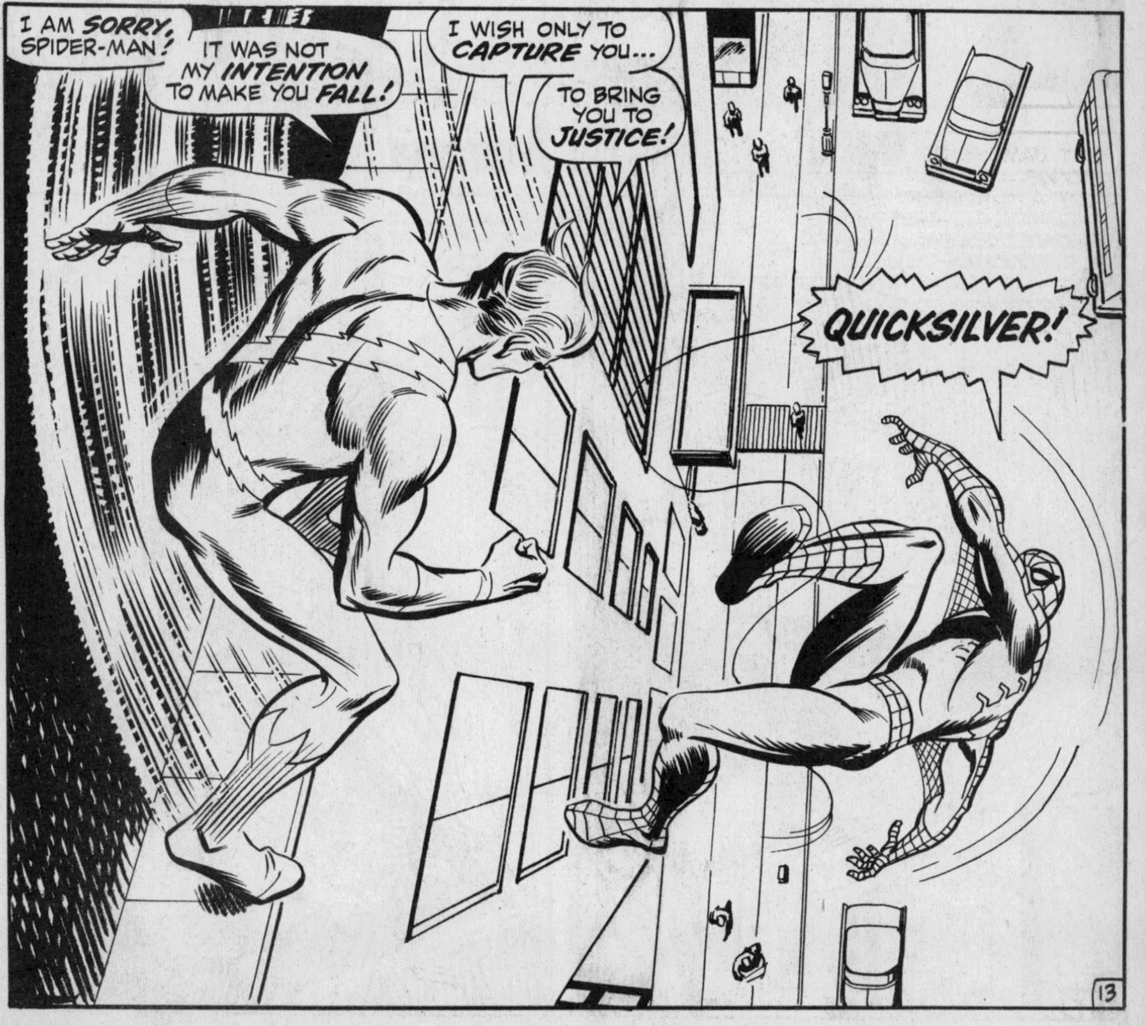
I AM SORRY, SPIDER-MAN!
IT WAS NOT MY INTENTION TO MAKE YOU FALL!
I WISH ONLY TO CAPTURE YOU...
TO BRING YOU TO JUSTICE!
QUICKSILVER!
13

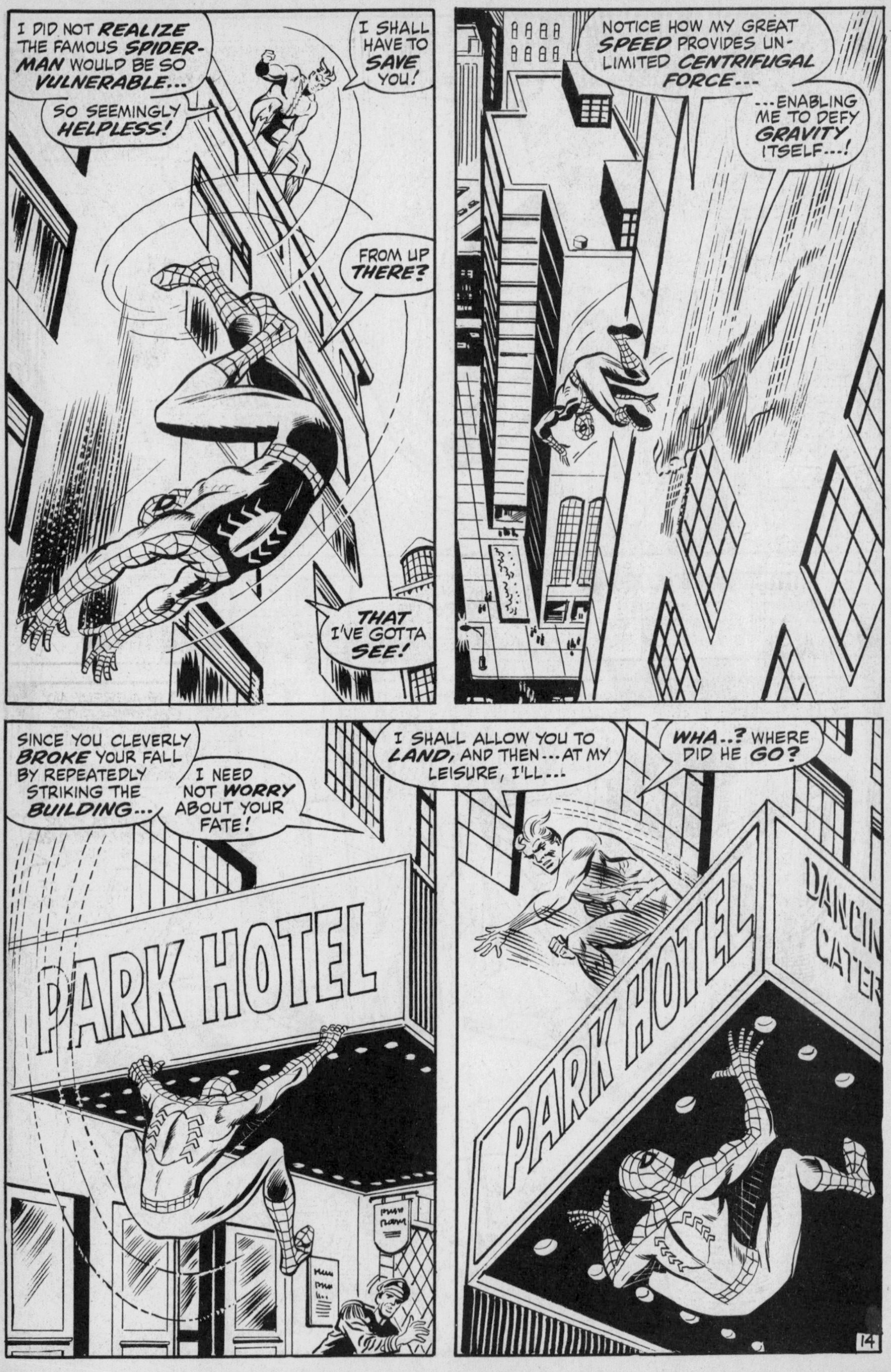
I DID NOT REALIZE THE FAMOUS SPIDER-MAN WOULD BE SO VULNERABLE...
SO SEEMINGLY HELPLESS!
I SHALL HAVE TO SAVE YOU!
FROM UP THERE?
THAT I'VE GOTTA SEE!
NOTICE HOW MY GREAT SPEED PROVIDES UN-LIMITED CENTRIFUGAL FORCE---
---ENABLING ME TO DEFY GRAVITY ITSELF---!
SINCE YOU CLEVERLY BROKE YOUR FALL BY REPEATEDLY STRIKING THE BUILDING...
I NEED NOT WORRY ABOUT YOUR FATE!
PARK HOTEL
I SHALL ALLOW YOU TO LAND, AND THEN---AT MY LEISURE, I'LL...
WHA..? WHERE DID HE GO?
PARK HOTEL
DANCIN
CATER
14

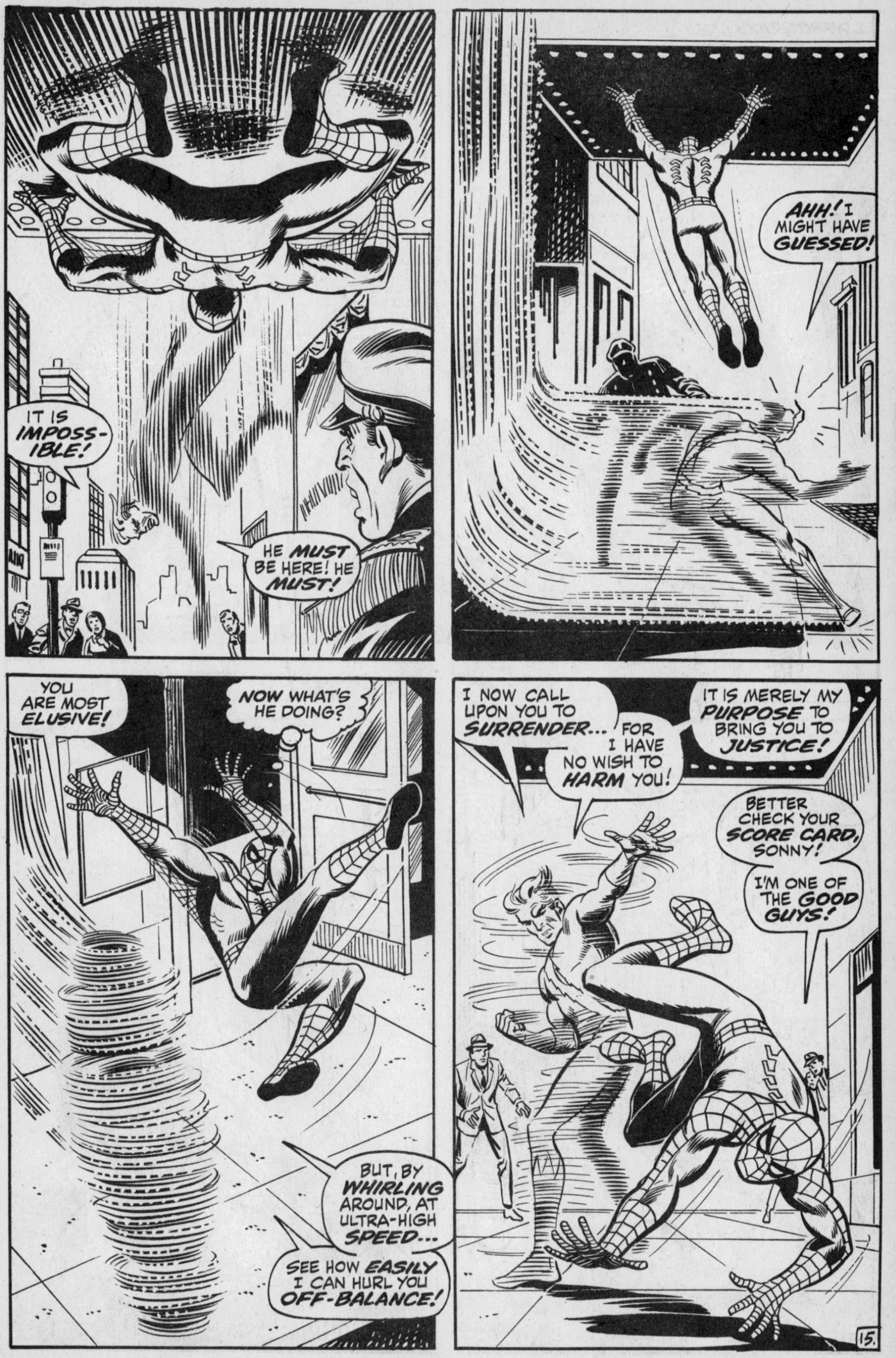

IT IS IMPOSS-IBLE!
HE MUST BE HERE! HE MUST!
AHH! I MIGHT HAVE GUESSED!
YOU ARE MOST ELUSIVE!
NOW WHAT'S HE DOING?
BUT, BY WHIRLING AROUND, AT ULTRA-HIGH SPEED...
SEE HOW EASILY I CAN HURL YOU OFF-BALANCE!
I NOW CALL UPON YOU TO SURRENDER... FOR I HAVE NO WISH TO HARM YOU!
IT IS MERELY MY PURPOSE TO BRING YOU TO JUSTICE!
BETTER CHECK YOUR SCORE CARD, SONNY!
I'M ONE OF THE GOOD GUYS!
15.

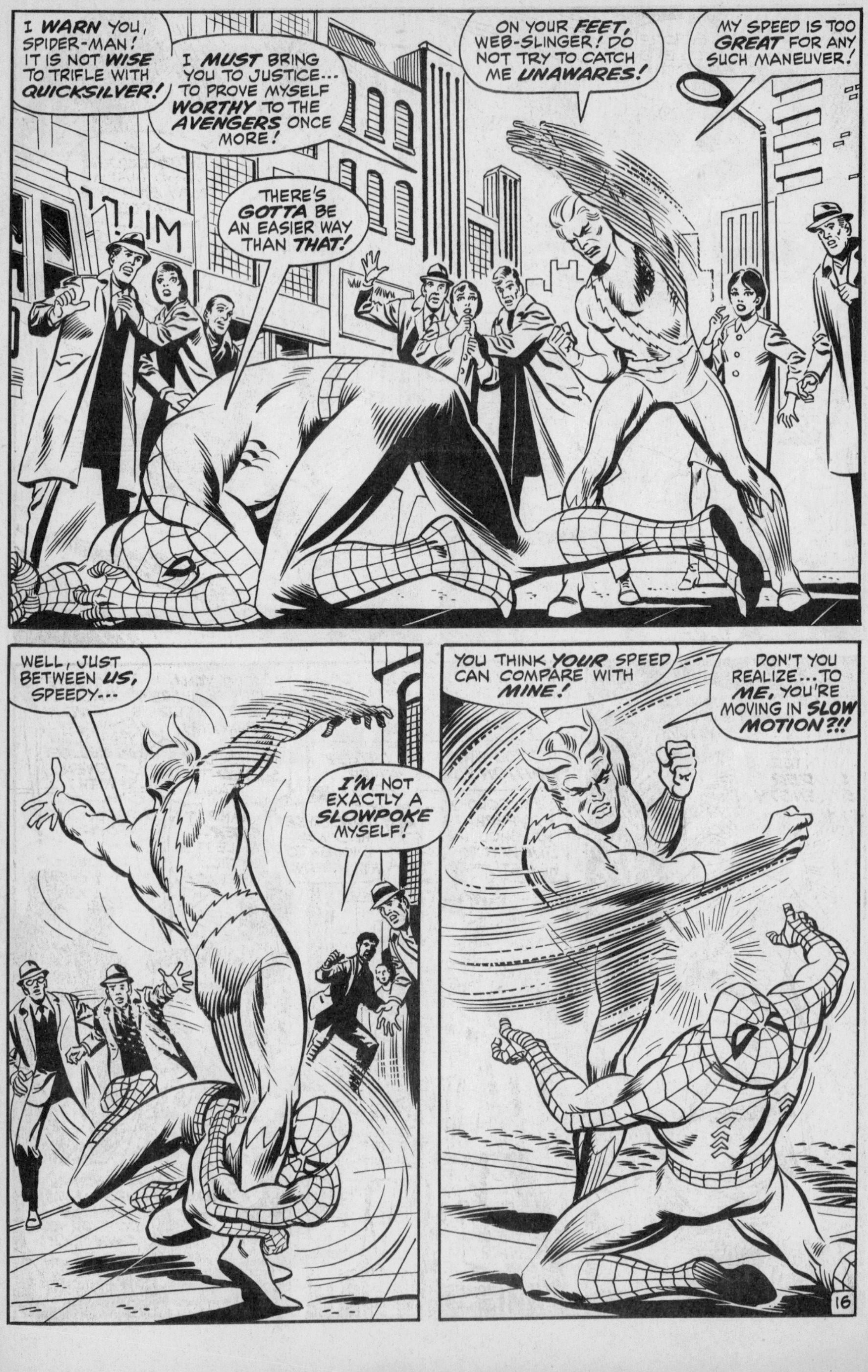

I WARN YOU, SPIDER-MAN! IT IS NOT WISE TO TRIFLE WITH QUICKSILVER!
I MUST BRING YOU TO JUSTICE... TO PROVE MYSELF WORTHY TO THE AVENGERS ONCE MORE!
THERE'S GOTTA BE AN EASIER WAY THAN THAT!
ON YOUR FEET, WEB-SLINGER! DO NOT TRY TO CATCH ME UNAWARES!
MY SPEED IS TOO GREAT FOR ANY SUCH MANEUVER!
WELL, JUST BETWEEN US, SPEEDY...
I'M NOT EXACTLY A SLOWPOKE MYSELF!
YOU THINK YOUR SPEED CAN COMPARE WITH MINE!
DON'T YOU REALIZE... TO ME, YOU'RE MOVING IN SLOW MOTION?!!
16

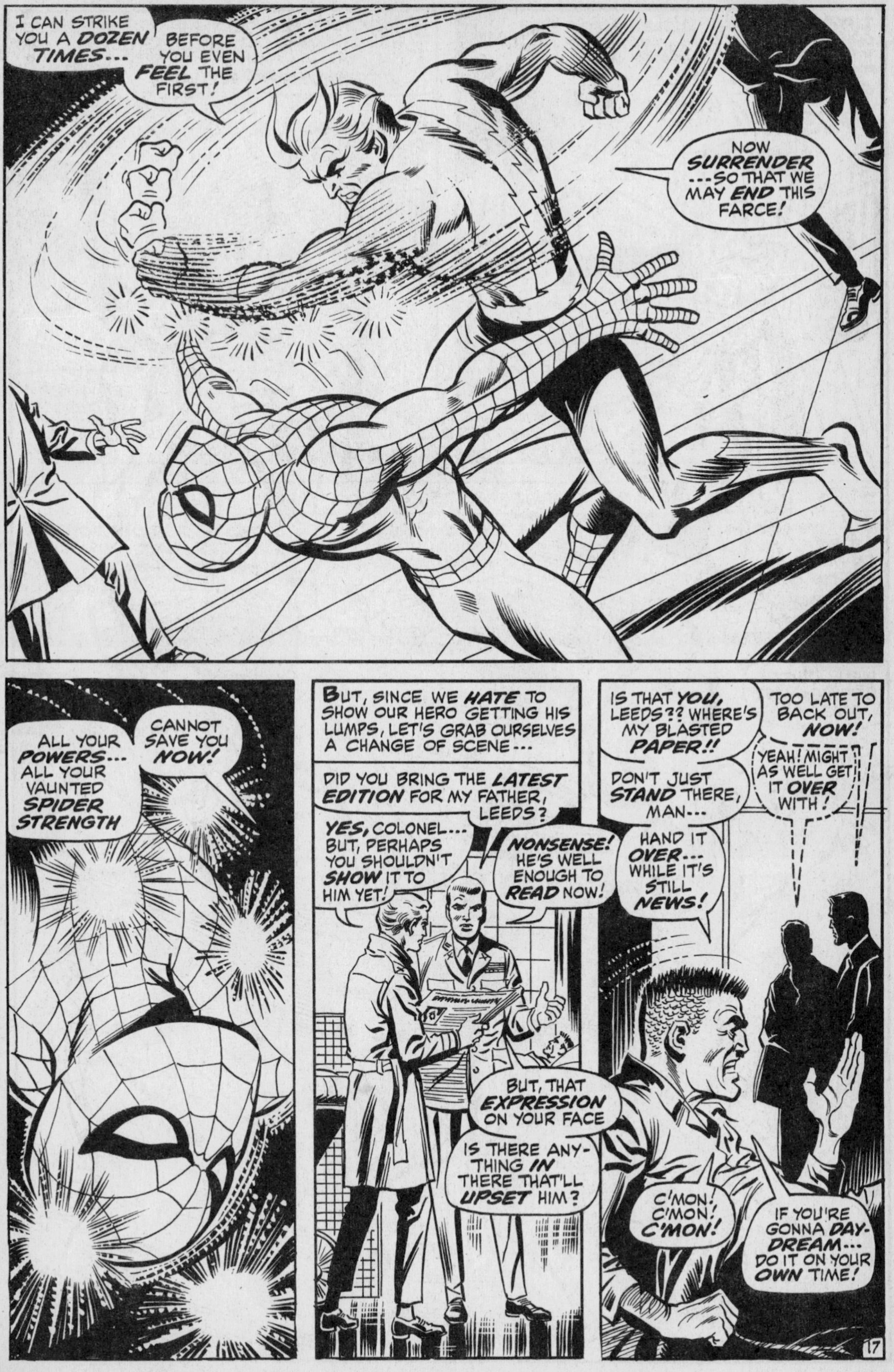
I CAN STRIKE YOU A DOZEN TIMES...
BEFORE YOU EVEN FEEL THE FIRST!
NOW SURRENDER ...SO THAT WE MAY END THIS FARCE!
ALL YOUR POWERS... ALL YOUR VAUNTED SPIDER STRENGTH
CANNOT SAVE YOU NOW!
BUT, SINCE WE HATE TO SHOW OUR HERO GETTING HIS LUMPS, LET'S GRAB OURSELVES A CHANGE OF SCENE---
DID YOU BRING THE LATEST EDITION FOR MY FATHER, LEEDS?
YES, COLONEL... BUT, PERHAPS YOU SHOULDN'T SHOW IT TO HIM YET!
NONSENSE! HE'S WELL ENOUGH TO READ NOW!
BUT, THAT EXPRESSION ON YOUR FACE
IS THERE ANYTHING IN THERE THAT'LL UPSET HIM?
IS THAT YOU, LEEDS?? WHERE'S MY BLASTED PAPER!!
DON'T JUST STAND THERE, MAN---
HAND IT OVER... WHILE IT'S STILL NEWS!
TOO LATE TO BACK OUT, NOW!
YEAH! MIGHT AS WELL GET IT OVER WITH!
C'MON! C'MON! C'MON!
IF YOU'RE GONNA DAY-DREAM... DO IT ON YOUR OWN TIME!
17

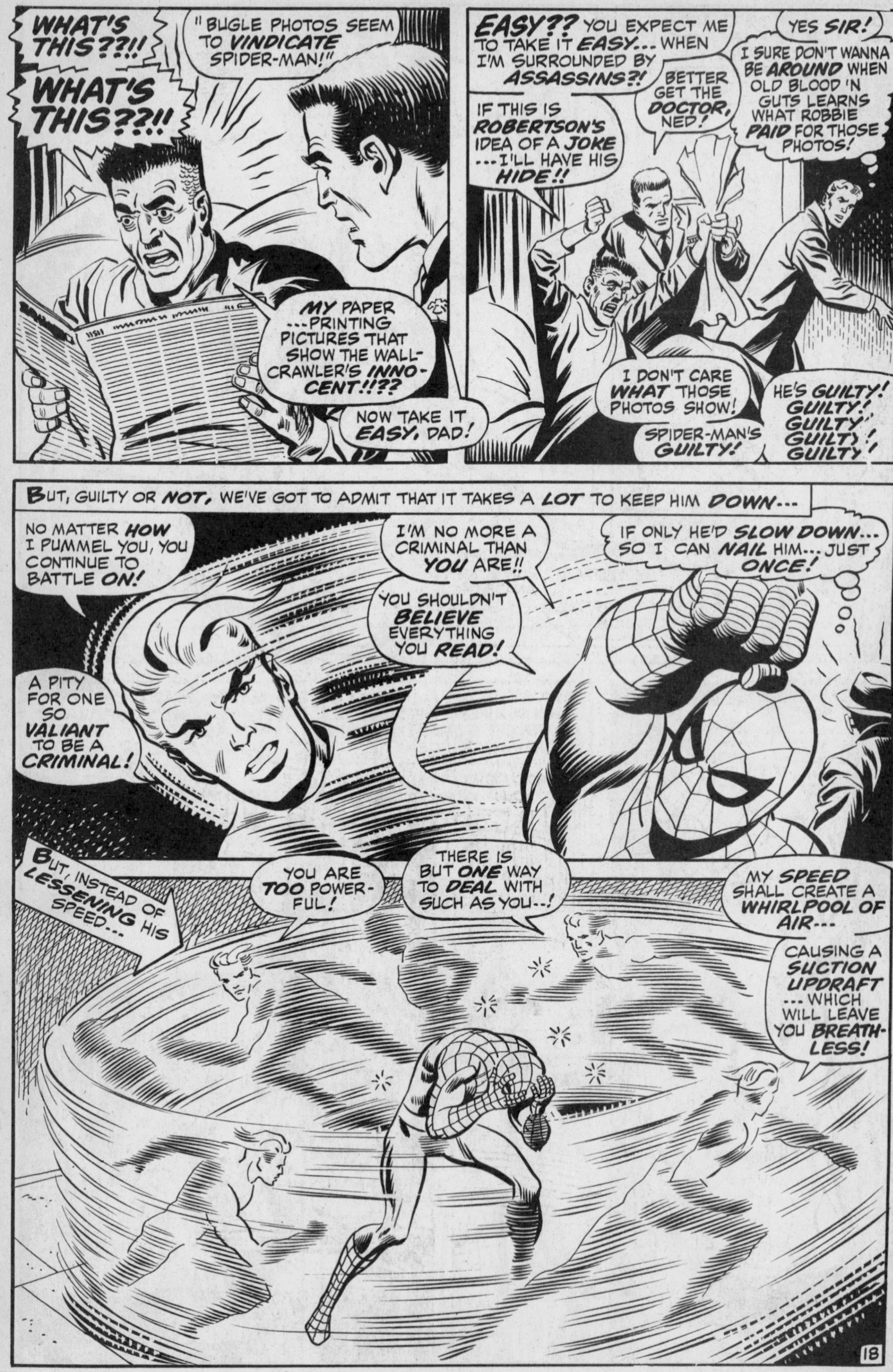
WHAT'S THIS??!!
WHAT'S THIS??!!
"BUGLE PHOTOS SEEM TO VINDICATE SPIDER-MAN!"
MY PAPER ---PRINTING PICTURES THAT SHOW THE WALL-CRAWLER'S INNO-CENT!!??
NOW TAKE IT EASY, DAD!
EASY?? YOU EXPECT ME TO TAKE IT EASY... WHEN I'M SURROUNDED BY ASSASSINS?!
IF THIS IS ROBERTSON'S IDEA OF A JOKE ---I'LL HAVE HIS HIDE!!
BETTER GET THE DOCTOR, NED!
YES SIR!
I SURE DON'T WANNA BE AROUND WHEN OLD BLOOD 'N GUTS LEARNS WHAT ROBBIE PAID FOR THOSE PHOTOS!
I DON'T CARE WHAT THOSE PHOTOS SHOW!
SPIDER-MAN'S GUILTY!
HE'S GUILTY! GUILTY! GUILTY! GUILTY! GUILTY!
BUT, GUILTY OR NOT, WE'VE GOT TO ADMIT THAT IT TAKES A LOT TO KEEP HIM DOWN---
NO MATTER HOW I PUMMEL YOU, YOU CONTINUE TO BATTLE ON!
A PITY FOR ONE SO VALIANT TO BE A CRIMINAL!
I'M NO MORE A CRIMINAL THAN YOU ARE!!
YOU SHOULDN'T BELIEVE EVERYTHING YOU READ!
IF ONLY HE'D SLOW DOWN... SO I CAN NAIL HIM... JUST ONCE!
BUT, INSTEAD OF LESSENING HIS SPEED...
YOU ARE TOO POWER-FUL!
THERE IS BUT ONE WAY TO DEAL WITH SUCH AS YOU--!
MY SPEED SHALL CREATE A WHIRLPOOL OF AIR---
CAUSING A SUCTION UPDRAFT --- WHICH WILL LEAVE YOU BREATH-LESS!

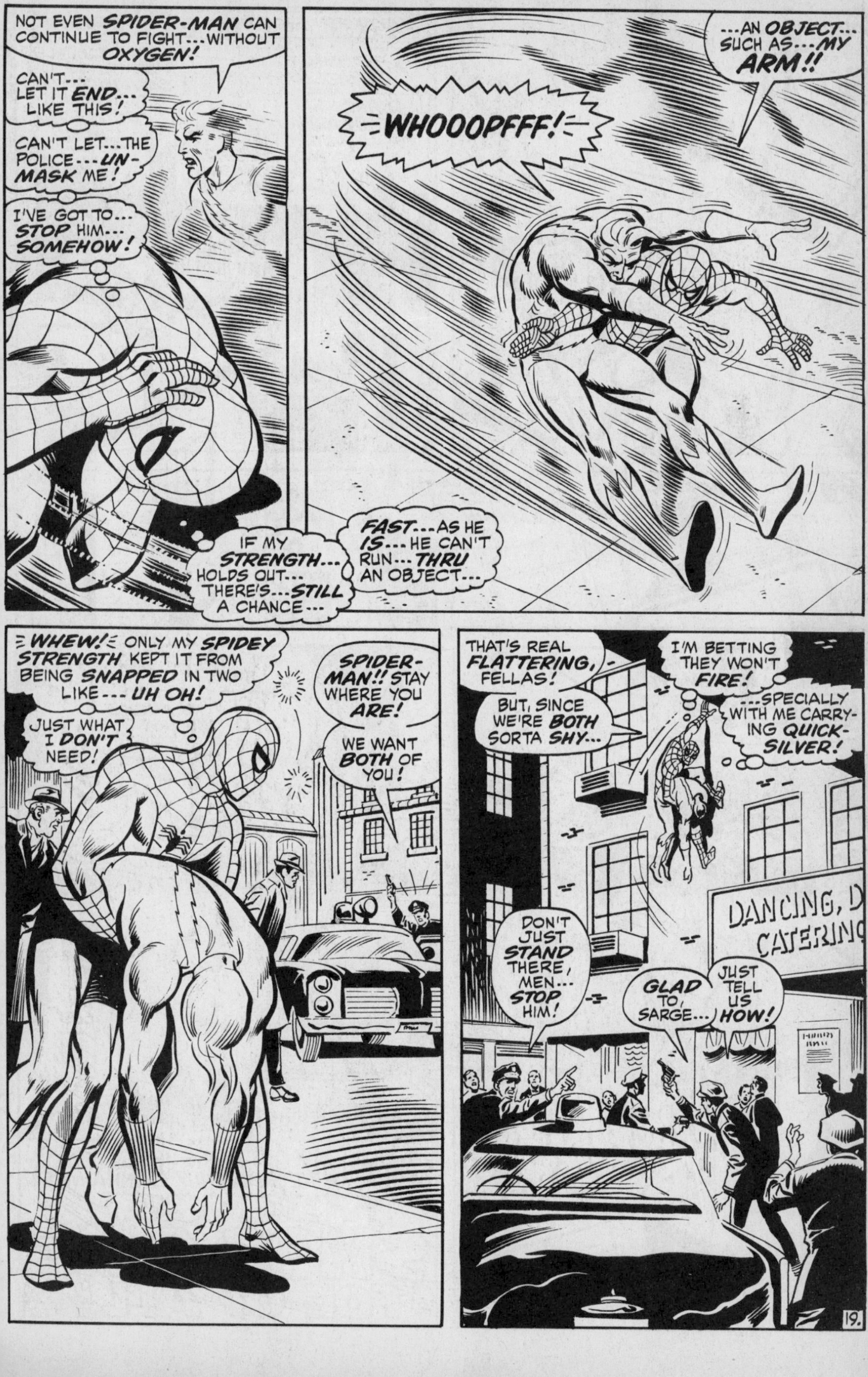
NOT EVEN SPIDER-MAN CAN CONTINUE TO FIGHT... WITHOUT OXYGEN!
CAN'T... LET IT END... LIKE THIS!
CAN'T LET... THE POLICE... UN-MASK ME!
I'VE GOT TO... STOP HIM... SOMEHOW!
IF MY STRENGTH... HOLDS OUT... THERE'S... STILL A CHANCE...
FAST... AS HE IS... HE CAN'T RUN... THRU AN OBJECT...
WHOOOPFFF!
...AN OBJECT... SUCH AS... MY ARM!!
WHEW! ONLY MY SPIDEY STRENGTH KEPT IT FROM BEING SNAPPED IN TWO LIKE... UH OH!
JUST WHAT I DON'T NEED!
SPIDER-MAN!! STAY WHERE YOU ARE!
WE WANT BOTH OF YOU!
THAT'S REAL FLATTERING, FELLAS!
BUT, SINCE WE'RE BOTH SORTA SHY...
I'M BETTING THEY WON'T FIRE!
...SPECIALLY WITH ME CARRYING QUICKSILVER!
DANCING, D
CATERING
DON'T JUST STAND THERE, MEN... STOP HIM!
GLAD TO, SARGE...
JUST TELL US HOW!
19.

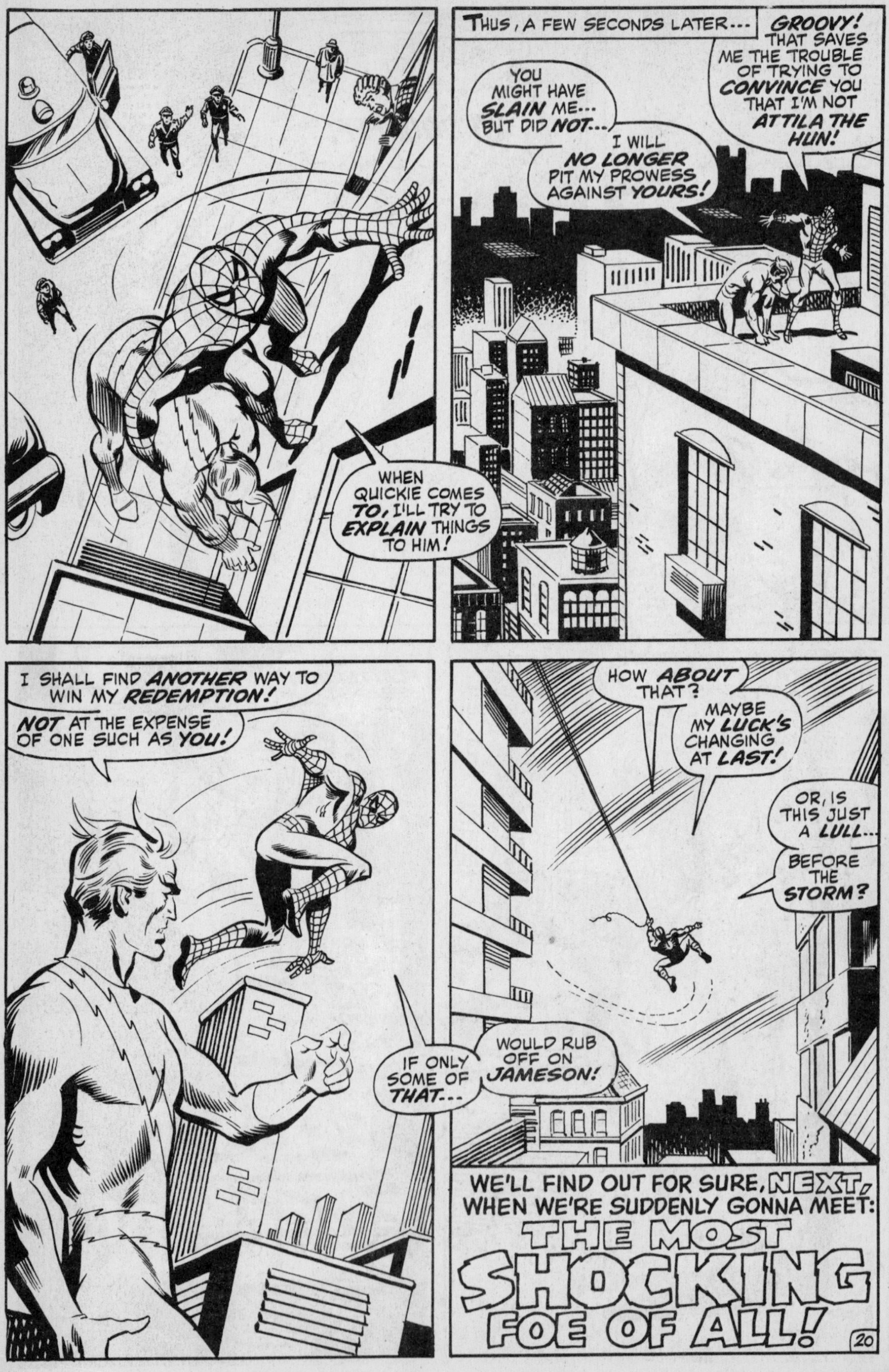
WHEN QUICKIE COMES TO, I'LL TRY TO EXPLAIN THINGS TO HIM!
THUS, A FEW SECONDS LATER...
YOU MIGHT HAVE SLAIN ME... BUT DID NOT...
I WILL NO LONGER PIT MY PROWESS AGAINST YOURS!
GROOVY! THAT SAVES ME THE TROUBLE OF TRYING TO CONVINCE YOU THAT I'M NOT ATTILA THE HUN!
I SHALL FIND ANOTHER WAY TO WIN MY REDEMPTION!
NOT AT THE EXPENSE OF ONE SUCH AS YOU!
IF ONLY SOME OF THAT...
WOULD RUB OFF ON JAMESON!
HOW ABOUT THAT?
MAYBE MY LUCK'S CHANGING AT LAST!
OR, IS THIS JUST A LULL...
BEFORE THE STORM?
WE'LL FIND OUT FOR SURE, NEXT, WHEN WE'RE SUDDENLY GONNA MEET:
THE MOST SHOCKING FOE OF ALL!
20

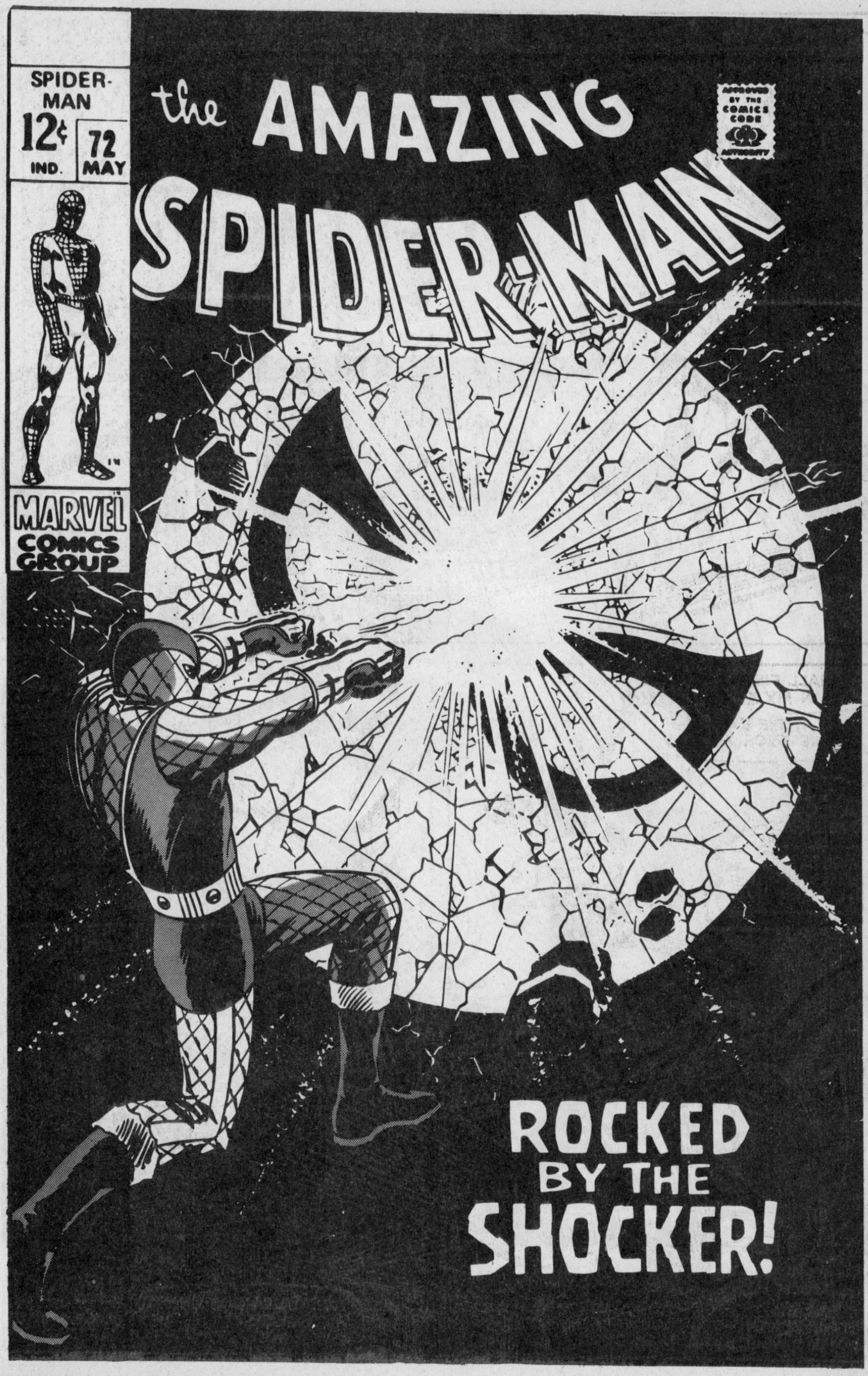
SPIDER-MAN
12¢
IND.
72
MAY
the AMAZING
SPIDER-MAN
APPROVED BY THE COMICS CODE AUTHORITY
MARVEL COMICS GROUP
ROCKED BY THE SHOCKER!

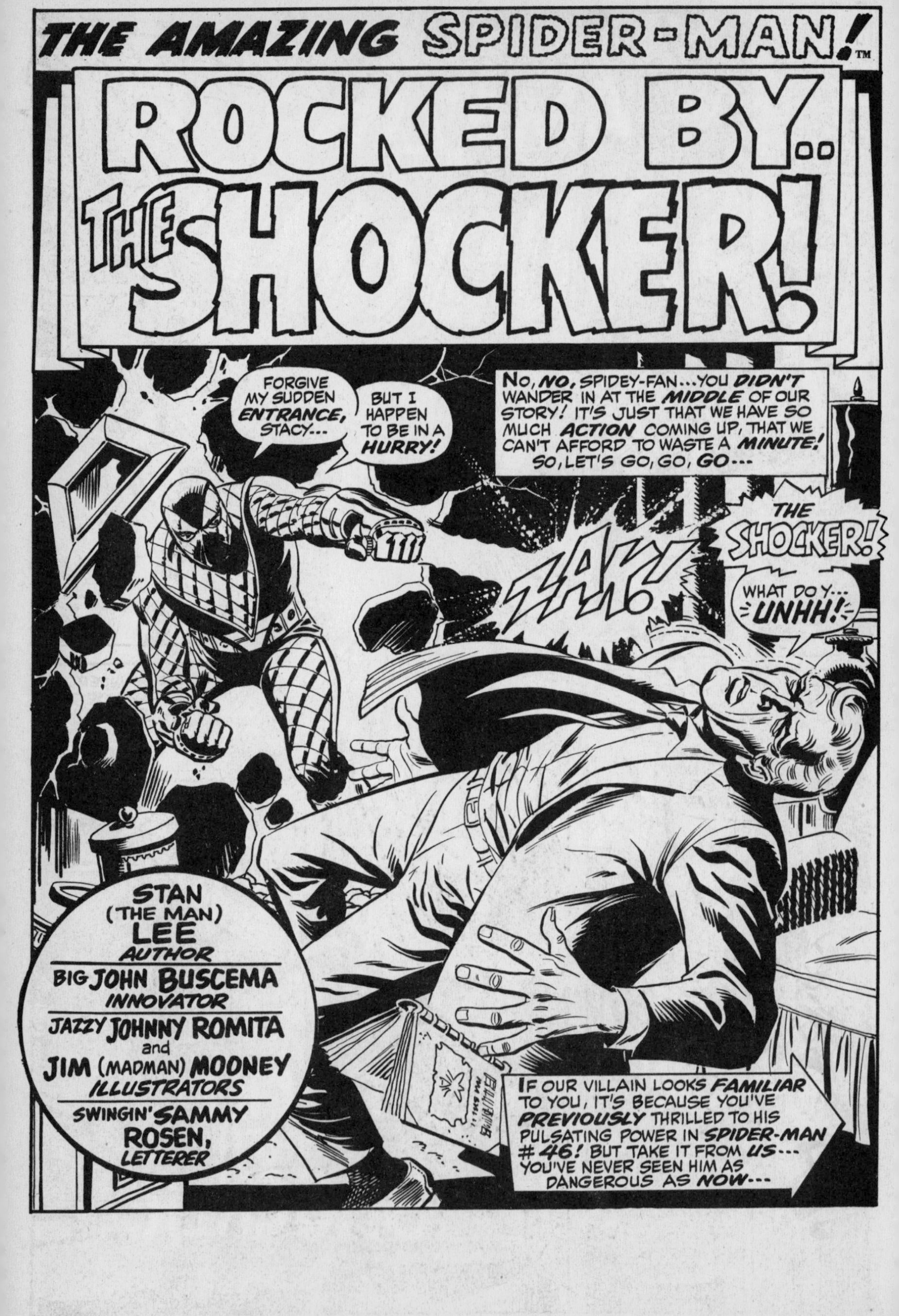
THE AMAZING SPIDER-MAN!™
ROCKED BY.. THE SHOCKER!
FORGIVE MY SUDDEN ENTRANCE, STACY...
BUT I HAPPEN TO BE IN A HURRY!
NO, NO, SPIDEY-FAN...YOU DIDN'T WANDER IN AT THE MIDDLE OF OUR STORY! IT'S JUST THAT WE HAVE SO MUCH ACTION COMING UP, THAT WE CAN'T AFFORD TO WASTE A MINUTE! SO, LET'S GO, GO, GO---
ZAK!
THE SHOCKER!
WHAT DO Y... UNHH!
STAN (THE MAN) LEE AUTHOR
BIG JOHN BUSCEMA INNOVATOR
JAZZY JOHNNY ROMITA and JIM (MADMAN) MOONEY ILLUSTRATORS
SWINGIN' SAMMY ROSEN, LETTERER
IF OUR VILLAIN LOOKS FAMILIAR TO YOU, IT'S BECAUSE YOU'VE PREVIOUSLY THRILLED TO HIS PULSATING POWER IN SPIDER-MAN #46! BUT TAKE IT FROM US--- YOU'VE NEVER SEEN HIM AS DANGEROUS AS NOW---

LUCKY FOR *HIM* I USED MY *VIBRO-POWER* AT ITS *WEAKEST* INTENSITY!

HE'LL BE *CONSCIOUS* AGAIN WITHIN A MATTER OF *MINUTES!*

ZZZAK KT

BUT, I'LL HAVE *FOUND* WHAT I SEEK BY THEN!

NO *SAFE* CAN RESIST MY VIBRATING *BLAST!*

ACCORDING TO THE *NEWSPAPERS,* THE PRICELESS CLAY *TABLET* SHOULD BE IN HERE...

SINCE *SPIDER-MAN* WAS DUMB ENOUGH NOT TO *KEEP* IT, AND SELL IT FOR *HIMSELF!*

BUT THE *SHOCKER* HAS NO SUCH *SCRUPLES!*

THE TABLET MUST BE *MINE!*

I'M IN *LUCK!*

STACY HASN'T YET *RETURNED* IT TO THE *COLLEGE!*

THIS ANCIENT PIECE OF PETRIFIED *STONE* IS WORTH A *KING'S RANSOM!*

DAD! DAD! WHAT WAS THAT *NOISE??*

IT SOUNDED LIKE PART OF THE *BUILDING* CAVING IN!!

DAD! WHERE *ARE* YOU? WHY DON'T YOU *ANSWER?*

WHAT'S *THAT?* ...FOOTSTEPS... RUNNING TOWARDS ME!

2

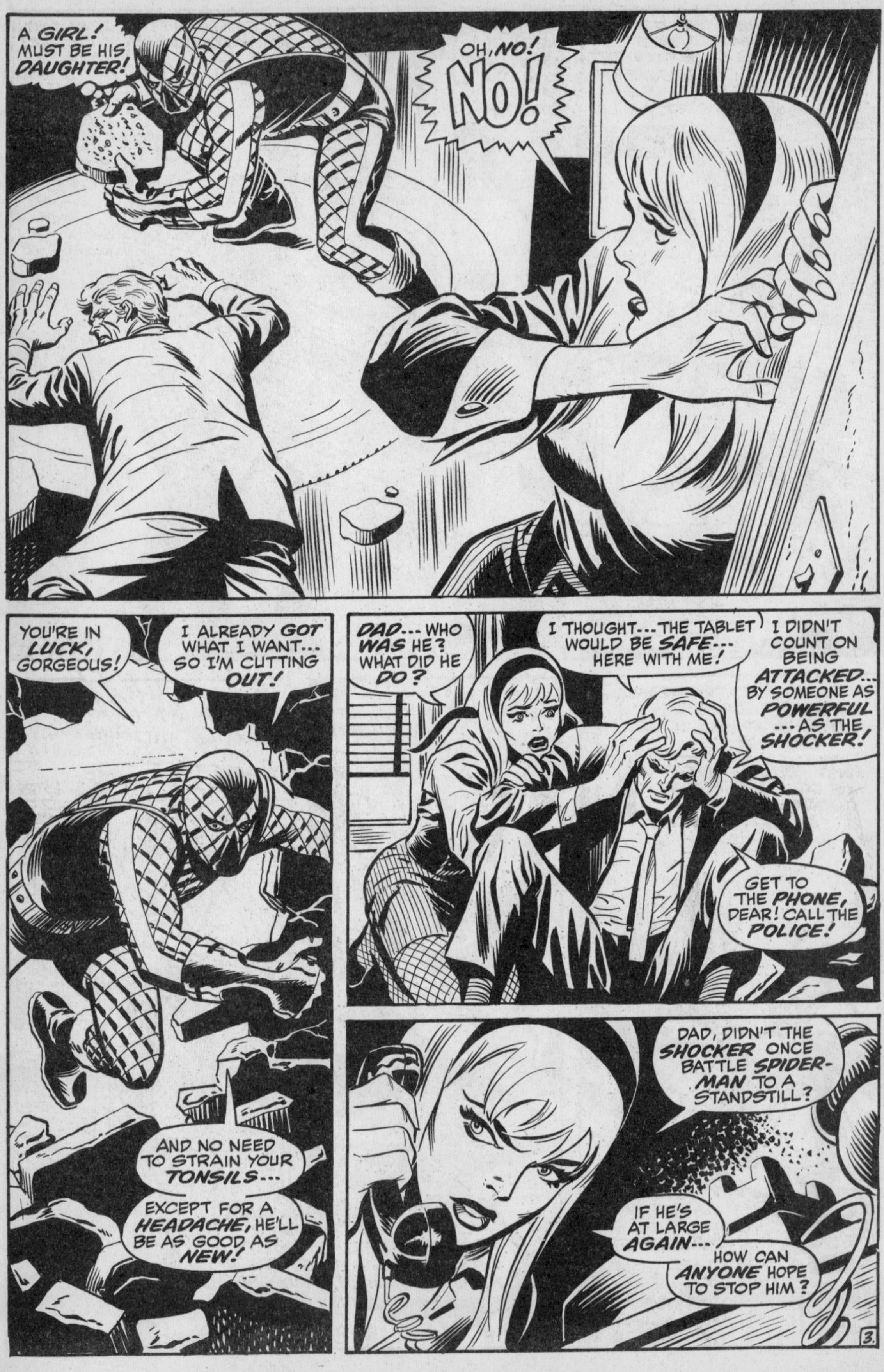
A GIRL! MUST BE HIS DAUGHTER!
OH, NO! NO!
YOU'RE IN LUCK, GORGEOUS!
I ALREADY GOT WHAT I WANT--- SO I'M CUTTING OUT!
AND NO NEED TO STRAIN YOUR TONSILS---
EXCEPT FOR A HEADACHE, HE'LL BE AS GOOD AS NEW!
DAD--- WHO WAS HE? WHAT DID HE DO?
I THOUGHT--- THE TABLET WOULD BE SAFE--- HERE WITH ME!
I DIDN'T COUNT ON BEING ATTACKED... BY SOMEONE AS POWERFUL --- AS THE SHOCKER!
GET TO THE PHONE, DEAR! CALL THE POLICE!
DAD, DIDN'T THE SHOCKER ONCE BATTLE SPIDER-MAN TO A STANDSTILL?
IF HE'S AT LARGE AGAIN---
HOW CAN ANYONE HOPE TO STOP HIM?
3.

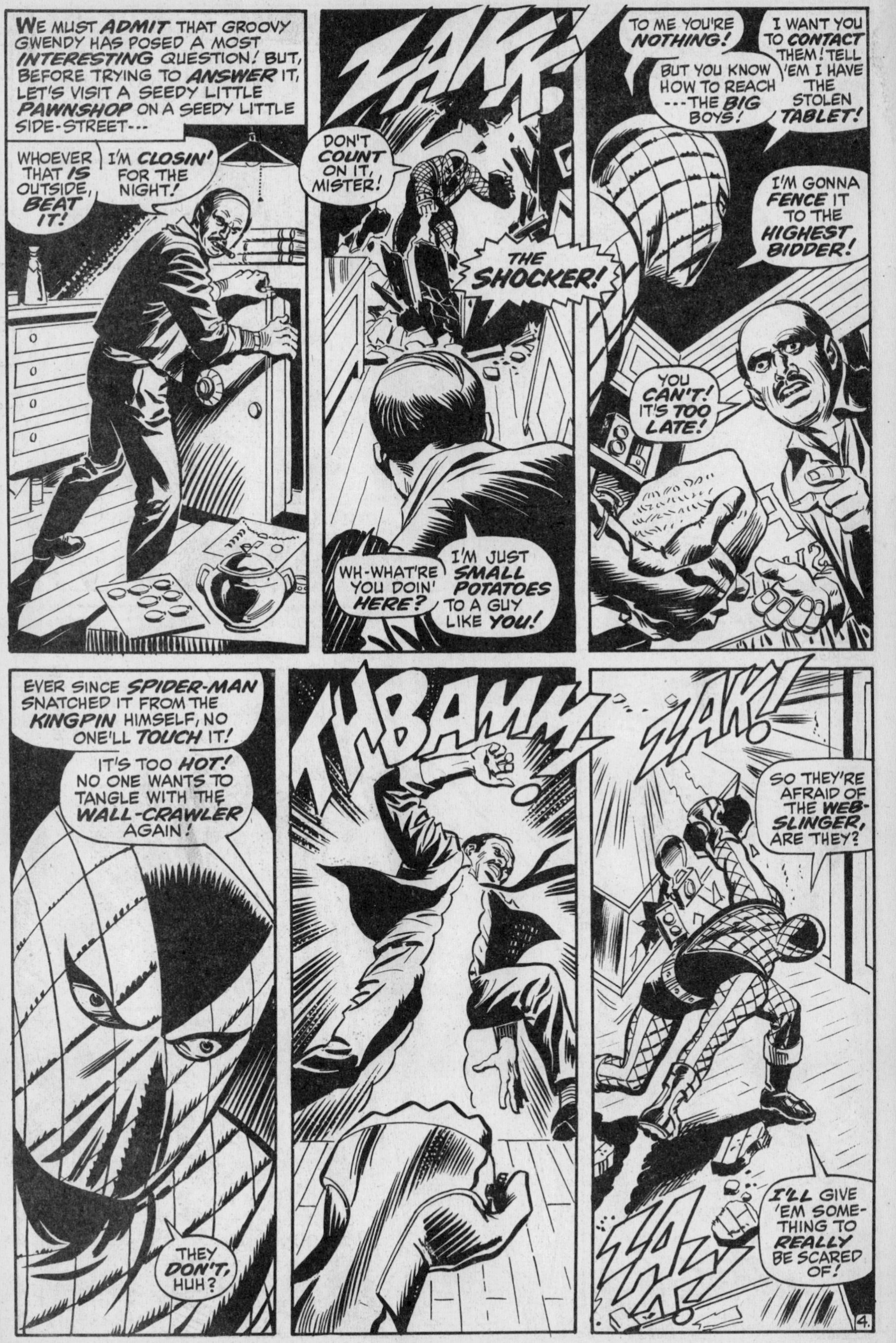
WE MUST ADMIT THAT GROOVY GWENDY HAS POSED A MOST INTERESTING QUESTION! BUT, BEFORE TRYING TO ANSWER IT, LET'S VISIT A SEEDY LITTLE PAWNSHOP ON A SEEDY LITTLE SIDE-STREET---
WHOEVER THAT IS OUTSIDE, BEAT IT!
I'M CLOSIN' FOR THE NIGHT!
ZAKK!
DON'T COUNT ON IT, MISTER!
THE SHOCKER!
WH-WHAT'RE YOU DOIN' HERE?
I'M JUST SMALL POTATOES TO A GUY LIKE YOU!
TO ME YOU'RE NOTHING!
BUT YOU KNOW HOW TO REACH ---THE BIG BOYS!
I WANT YOU TO CONTACT THEM! TELL 'EM I HAVE THE STOLEN TABLET!
I'M GONNA FENCE IT TO THE HIGHEST BIDDER!
YOU CAN'T! IT'S TOO LATE!
EVER SINCE SPIDER-MAN SNATCHED IT FROM THE KINGPIN HIMSELF, NO ONE'LL TOUCH IT!
IT'S TOO HOT! NO ONE WANTS TO TANGLE WITH THE WALL-CRAWLER AGAIN!
THEY DON'T, HUH?
THBAMM
ZAK!
SO THEY'RE AFRAID OF THE WEB-SLINGER, ARE THEY?
I'LL GIVE 'EM SOMETHING TO REALLY BE SCARED OF!
4.

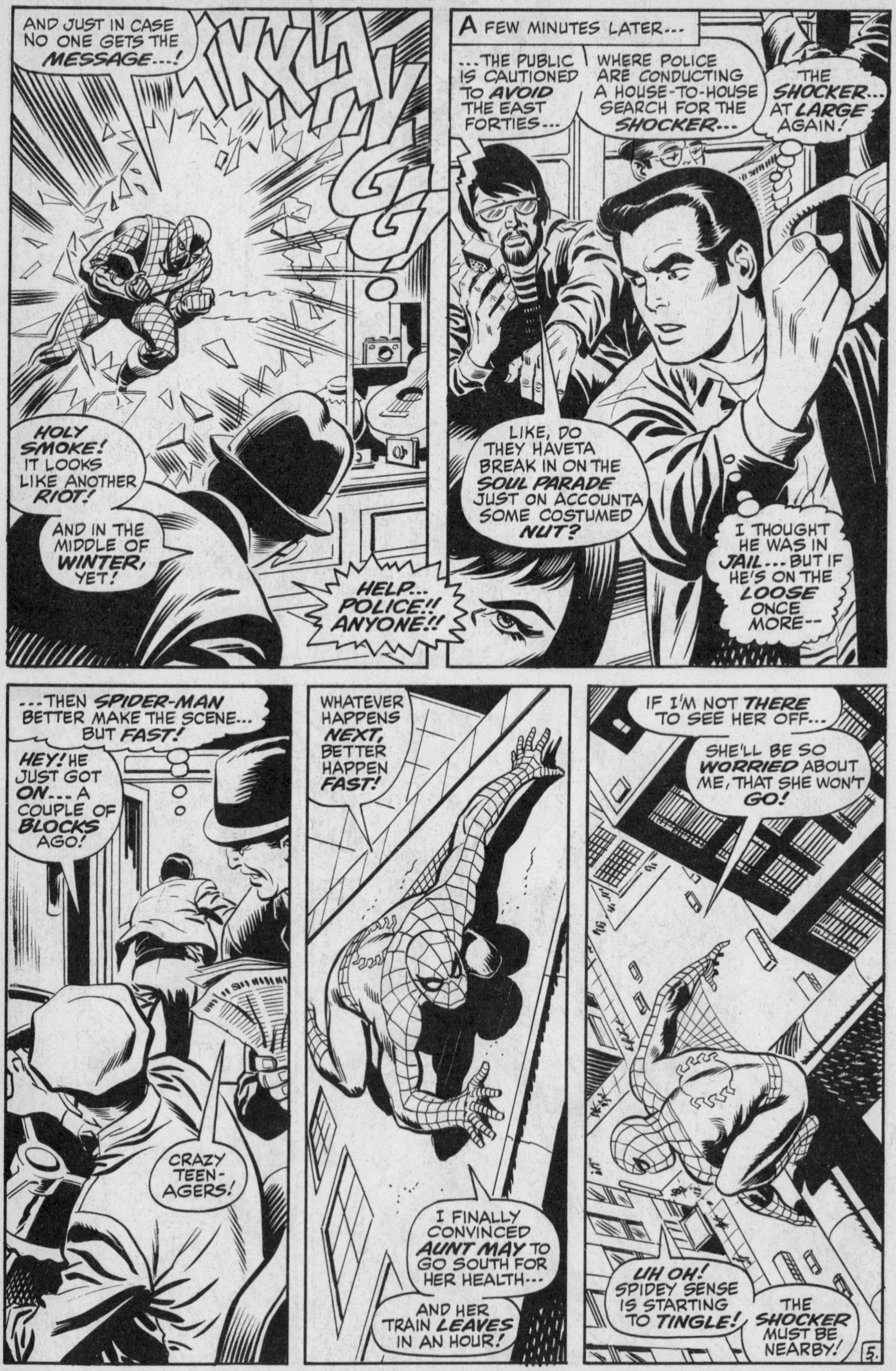
AND JUST IN CASE NO ONE GETS THE MESSAGE...!
HOLY SMOKE! IT LOOKS LIKE ANOTHER RIOT!
AND IN THE MIDDLE OF WINTER, YET!
HELP... POLICE!! ANYONE!!
A FEW MINUTES LATER...
...THE PUBLIC IS CAUTIONED TO AVOID THE EAST FORTIES...
WHERE POLICE ARE CONDUCTING A HOUSE-TO-HOUSE SEARCH FOR THE SHOCKER...
THE SHOCKER... AT LARGE AGAIN!
LIKE, DO THEY HAVETA BREAK IN ON THE SOUL PARADE JUST ON ACCOUNTA SOME COSTUMED NUT?
I THOUGHT HE WAS IN JAIL... BUT IF HE'S ON THE LOOSE ONCE MORE--
...THEN SPIDER-MAN BETTER MAKE THE SCENE... BUT FAST!
HEY! HE JUST GOT ON... A COUPLE OF BLOCKS AGO!
CRAZY TEEN-AGERS!
WHATEVER HAPPENS NEXT, BETTER HAPPEN FAST!
I FINALLY CONVINCED AUNT MAY TO GO SOUTH FOR HER HEALTH---
AND HER TRAIN LEAVES IN AN HOUR!
IF I'M NOT THERE TO SEE HER OFF...
SHE'LL BE SO WORRIED ABOUT ME, THAT SHE WON'T GO!
UH OH! SPIDEY SENSE IS STARTING TO TINGLE!
THE SHOCKER MUST BE NEARBY!
5.

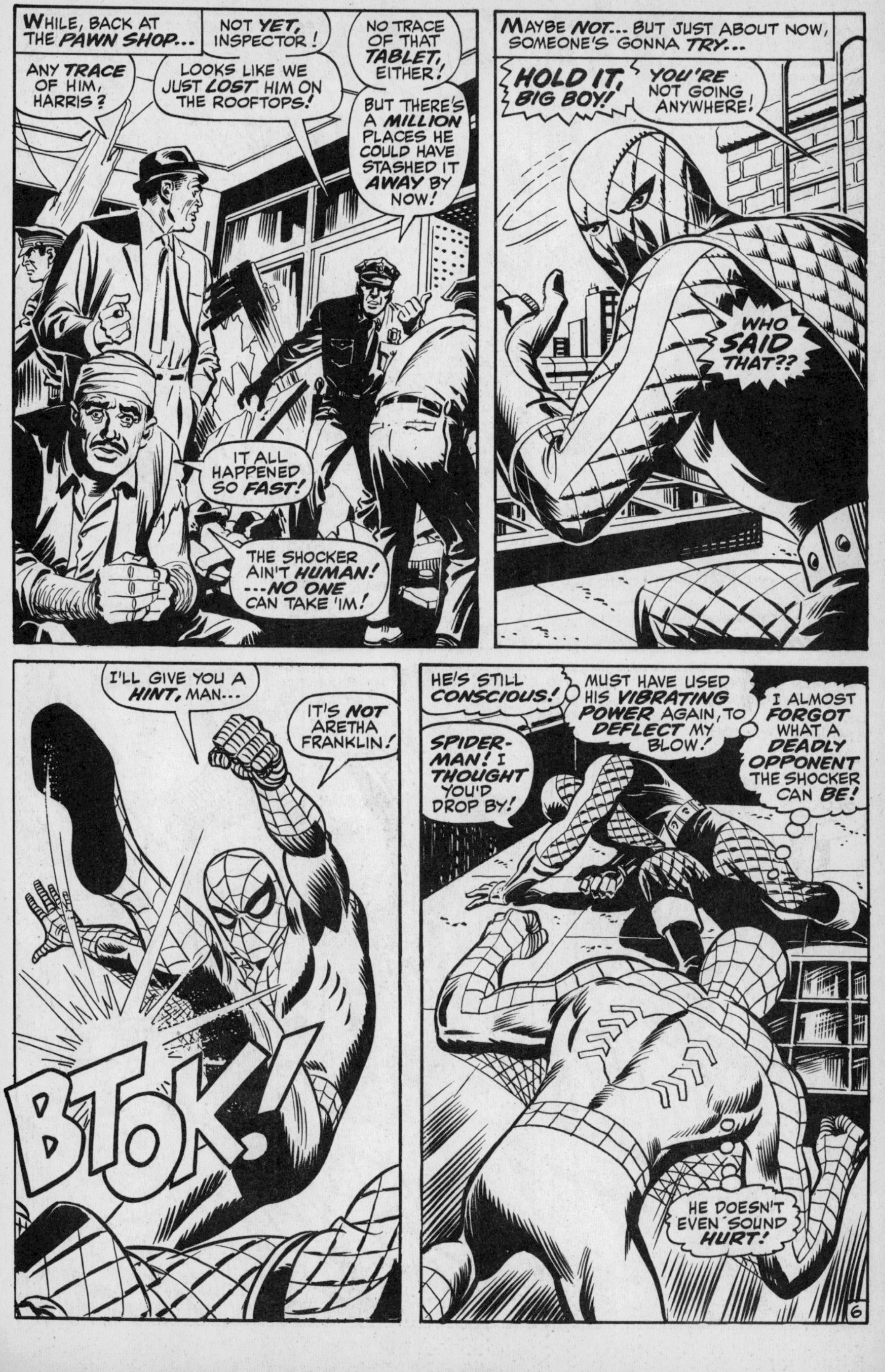
WHILE, BACK AT THE PAWN SHOP...
ANY TRACE OF HIM, HARRIS?
NOT YET, INSPECTOR!
LOOKS LIKE WE JUST LOST HIM ON THE ROOFTOPS!
NO TRACE OF THAT TABLET, EITHER!
BUT THERE'S A MILLION PLACES HE COULD HAVE STASHED IT AWAY BY NOW!
IT ALL HAPPENED SO FAST!
THE SHOCKER AIN'T HUMAN! ...NO ONE CAN TAKE 'IM!
MAYBE NOT... BUT JUST ABOUT NOW, SOMEONE'S GONNA TRY...
HOLD IT, BIG BOY!
YOU'RE NOT GOING ANYWHERE!
WHO SAID THAT??
I'LL GIVE YOU A HINT, MAN...
IT'S NOT ARETHA FRANKLIN!
BTOK!
HE'S STILL CONSCIOUS!
MUST HAVE USED HIS VIBRATING POWER AGAIN, TO DEFLECT MY BLOW!
I ALMOST FORGOT WHAT A DEADLY OPPONENT THE SHOCKER CAN BE!
SPIDER-MAN! I THOUGHT YOU'D DROP BY!
HE DOESN'T EVEN SOUND HURT!
6

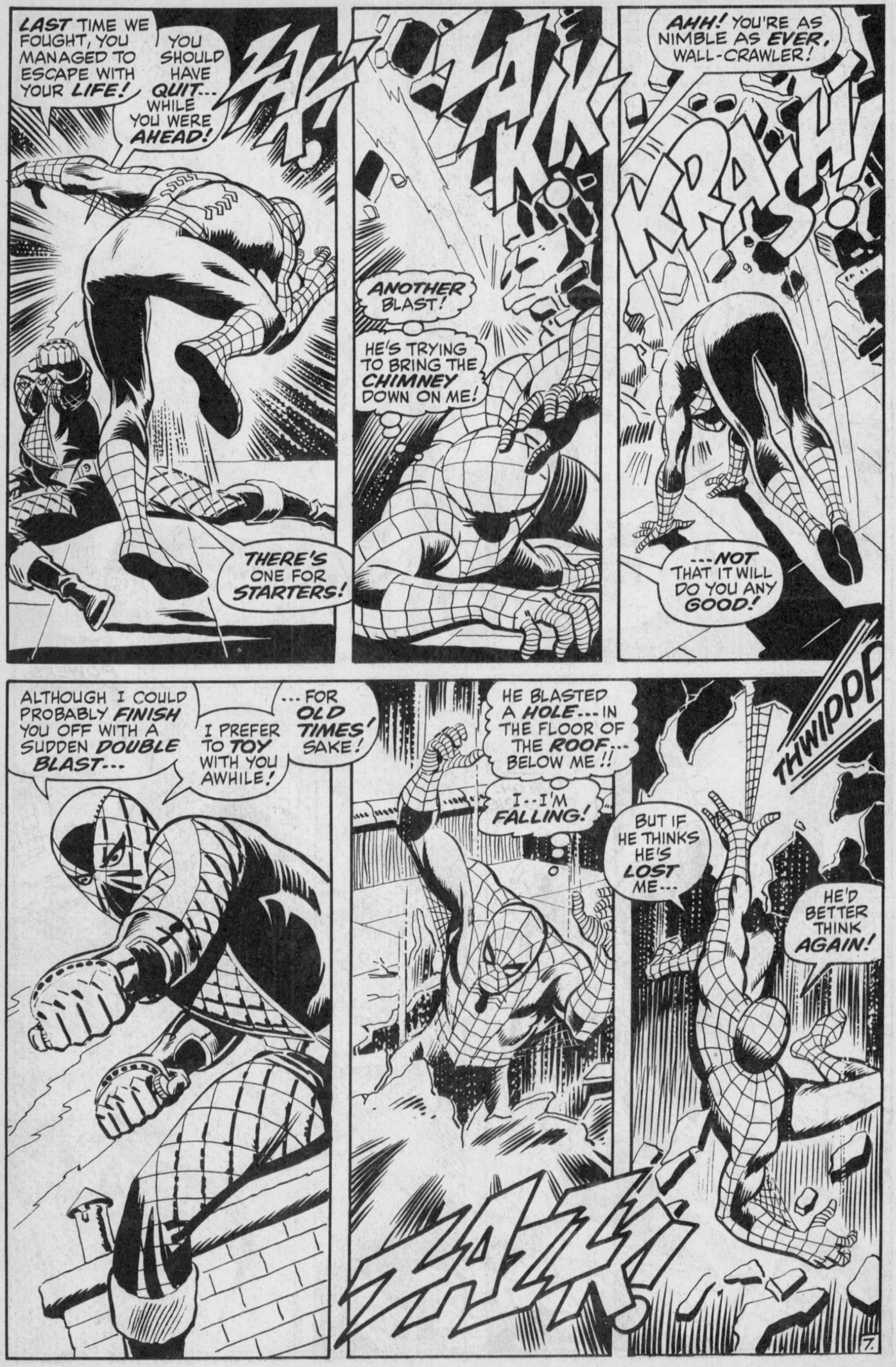
LAST TIME WE FOUGHT, YOU MANAGED TO ESCAPE WITH YOUR LIFE!
YOU SHOULD HAVE QUIT... WHILE YOU WERE AHEAD!
ZAKK!
THERE'S ONE FOR STARTERS!
ZAKK!
ANOTHER BLAST!
HE'S TRYING TO BRING THE CHIMNEY DOWN ON ME!
AHH! YOU'RE AS NIMBLE AS EVER, WALL-CRAWLER!
KRASH!
...NOT THAT IT WILL DO YOU ANY GOOD!
ALTHOUGH I COULD PROBABLY FINISH YOU OFF WITH A SUDDEN DOUBLE BLAST...
I PREFER TO TOY WITH YOU AWHILE!
...FOR OLD TIMES' SAKE!
HE BLASTED A HOLE... IN THE FLOOR OF THE ROOF... BELOW ME!!
I--I'M FALLING!
ZAKK!
THWIPPP
BUT IF HE THINKS HE'S LOST ME...
HE'D BETTER THINK AGAIN!
7.

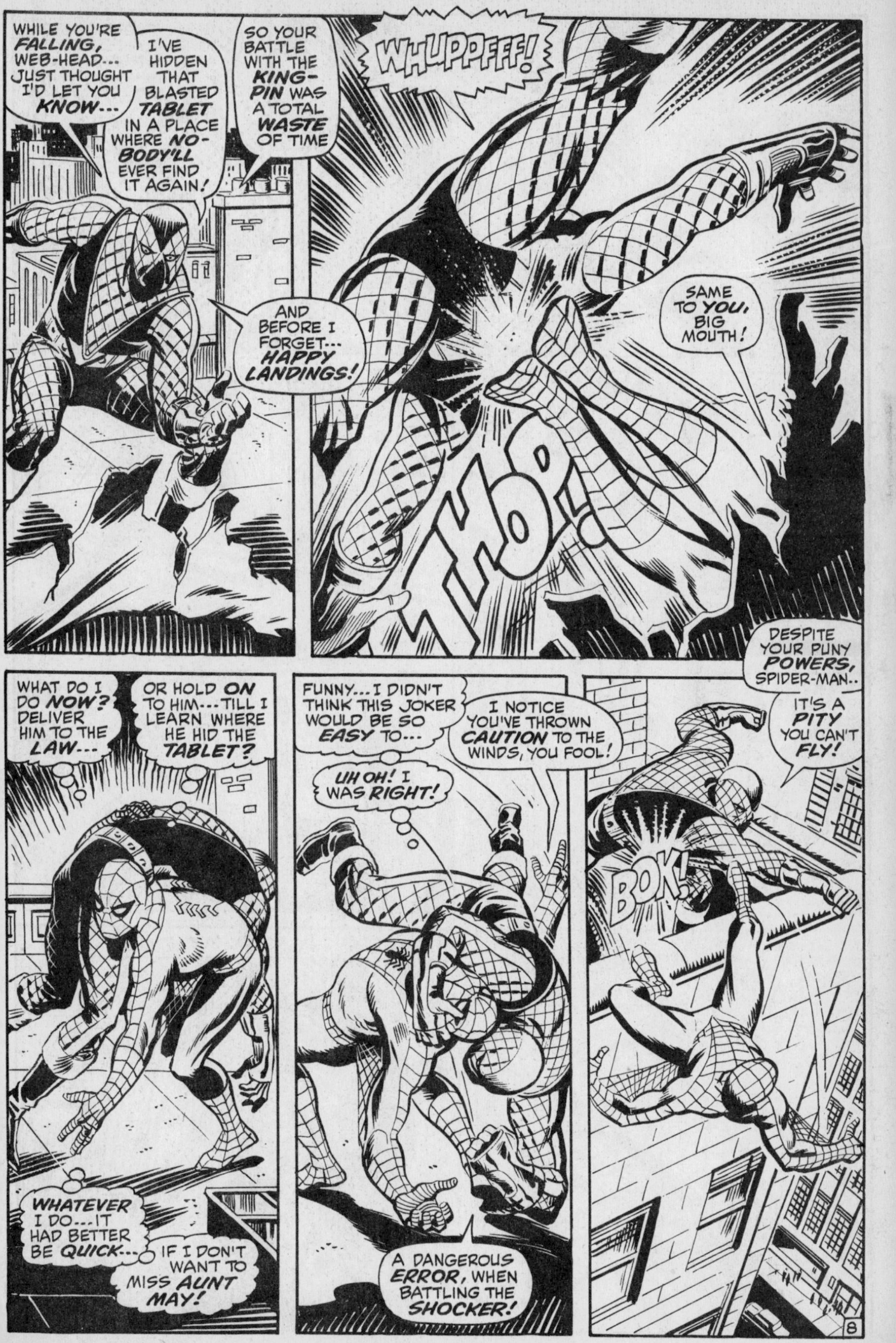
WHILE YOU'RE FALLING, WEB-HEAD... JUST THOUGHT I'D LET YOU KNOW---
I'VE HIDDEN THAT BLASTED TABLET IN A PLACE WHERE NO-BODY'LL EVER FIND IT AGAIN!
SO YOUR BATTLE WITH THE KING-PIN WAS A TOTAL WASTE OF TIME
AND BEFORE I FORGET--- HAPPY LANDINGS!
WHUPPFFF!
SAME TO YOU, BIG MOUTH!
THOP!
WHAT DO I DO NOW? DELIVER HIM TO THE LAW---
OR HOLD ON TO HIM---TILL I LEARN WHERE HE HID THE TABLET?
WHATEVER I DO---IT HAD BETTER BE QUICK---
IF I DON'T WANT TO MISS AUNT MAY!
FUNNY... I DIDN'T THINK THIS JOKER WOULD BE SO EASY TO...
I NOTICE YOU'VE THROWN CAUTION TO THE WINDS, YOU FOOL!
UH OH! I WAS RIGHT!
A DANGEROUS ERROR, WHEN BATTLING THE SHOCKER!
DESPITE YOUR PUNY POWERS, SPIDER-MAN..
IT'S A PITY YOU CAN'T FLY!
BOK!
8

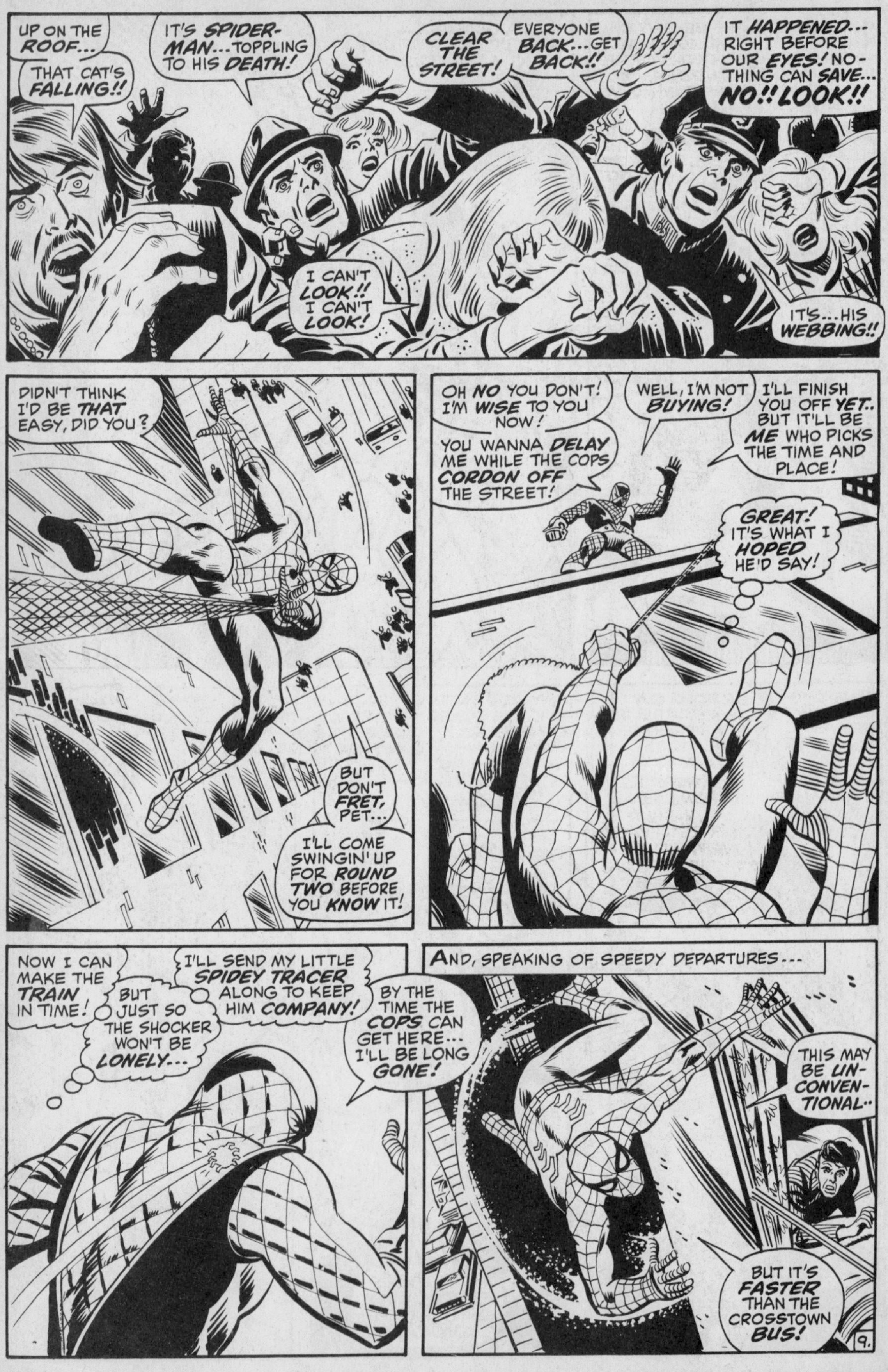
UP ON THE ROOF...
THAT CAT'S FALLING!!
IT'S SPIDER-MAN...TOPPLING TO HIS DEATH!
CLEAR THE STREET!
EVERYONE BACK...GET BACK!!
IT HAPPENED... RIGHT BEFORE OUR EYES! NOTHING CAN SAVE... NO!! LOOK!!
I CAN'T LOOK!! I CAN'T LOOK!
IT'S...HIS WEBBING!!
DIDN'T THINK I'D BE THAT EASY, DID YOU?
BUT DON'T FRET, PET...
I'LL COME SWINGIN' UP FOR ROUND TWO BEFORE YOU KNOW IT!
OH NO YOU DON'T! I'M WISE TO YOU NOW!
YOU WANNA DELAY ME WHILE THE COPS CORDON OFF THE STREET!
WELL, I'M NOT BUYING!
I'LL FINISH YOU OFF YET.. BUT IT'LL BE ME WHO PICKS THE TIME AND PLACE!
GREAT! IT'S WHAT I HOPED HE'D SAY!
NOW I CAN MAKE THE TRAIN IN TIME!
BUT JUST SO THE SHOCKER WON'T BE LONELY...
I'LL SEND MY LITTLE SPIDEY TRACER ALONG TO KEEP HIM COMPANY!
BY THE TIME THE COPS CAN GET HERE... I'LL BE LONG GONE!
AND, SPEAKING OF SPEEDY DEPARTURES...
THIS MAY BE UNCONVENTIONAL..
BUT IT'S FASTER THAN THE CROSSTOWN BUS!
9.

AND NOW, FOR THE BENEFIT OF AUNT MAY'S COUNTLESS FANS, WE HAPPILY PRESENT ONE OF THE FEW SCENES WHICH *DOESN'T* SHOW HER AT DEATH'S DOOR---

PETER, DEAR... ARE YOU *SURE* YOU CAN *AFFORD* THIS TICKET TO *FLORIDA* WHICH YOU BOUGHT ME?

YOU *KNOW* IT, AUNT MAY! WITH THE MONEY I GOT FOR THOSE *NEWS PIX* I SOLD TO THE *BUGLE,* I COULD SEND YOU TO THE MOON...

...BUT YOU WOULDN'T LIKE THE *ALTITUDE!*

HAVE A *GREAT* TIME...AND SOAK UP GOBS OF *SUN...* LIKE THE DOC *TOLD* YOU TO, HEAR?

AND *REMEMBER...*NO *DISCOTHEQUING* PAST FOUR A.M....AND DON'T OVERDO THE *JOGGING* AND *KARATE!*

SHE CAN'T *HEAR* ME THRU THE GLASS...BUT SHE GETS THE *MES-SAGE!*

BLESS HER HEART...THIS TRIP'S JUST WHAT SHE *NEEDED!*

SHE'S LOOKING HEALTHIER *ALREADY!*

AS FOR *ME,* I DON'T KNOW WHAT TO DO *FIRST!*

I *STILL* HAVE TO SQUARE MYSELF WITH *GWEN* ...AND THEN ...*HEY!!*

HOW ABOUT *THIS!* SPIDEY FINALLY GOT A DECENT *WRITE-UP!*

THINGS ARE REALLY LOOKING *UP* SINCE *JOLLY JONAH'S* IN THE HOSPITAL AND *JOE ROBERTSON* IS RUNNING THE PAPER!

SPIDER-MAN TACKLY STICK

SPIDER-MAN RISKS LIFE IN VALIANT EFFORT TO CAPTURE

SPIDER-MAN TACKLES SHOCKER

DAILY BUGLE

THEN, AS THE AMAZING YOUTH IDLY SCANS THE *REST* OF THE NEWSPAPER, HE SUDDENLY SEES A FATEFUL *ITEM...*

A WRITE-UP ABOUT *DR. CURT CONNORS!*

HE'S WORKING ON SOME NEW, VITAL, HIGHLY-SECRET *EXPERI-MENT* AT HIS LAB IN THE FLORIDA *EVERGLADES!*

IT'S BEEN *MONTHS* SINCE OUR PATHS LAST CROSSED!

HE'S ONE OF THE *GREATEST* MEN I'VE KNOWN!

"BUT, EXCEPT FOR HIS *WIFE,*...I'M THE ONLY *OTHER* PERSON WHO KNOWS THAT DOC CONNORS IS ALSO---THE DEADLY, SUPER-POWERFUL *LIZARD!!*"

10.

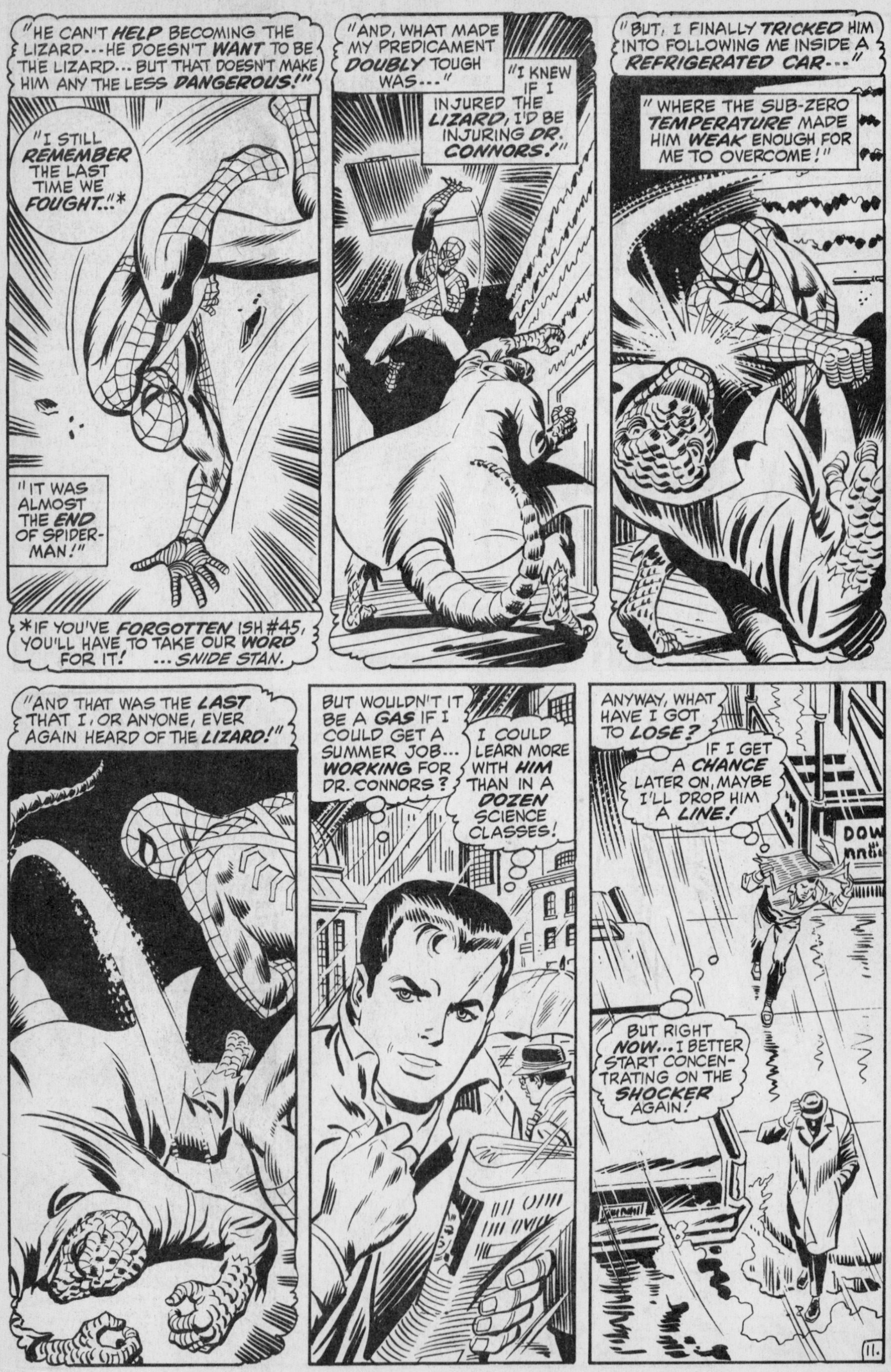
"HE CAN'T HELP BECOMING THE LIZARD---HE DOESN'T WANT TO BE THE LIZARD... BUT THAT DOESN'T MAKE HIM ANY THE LESS DANGEROUS!"
"I STILL REMEMBER THE LAST TIME WE FOUGHT...!"*
"IT WAS ALMOST THE END OF SPIDER-MAN!"
*IF YOU'VE FORGOTTEN ISH #45, YOU'LL HAVE TO TAKE OUR WORD FOR IT! ...SNIDE STAN.
"AND, WHAT MADE MY PREDICAMENT DOUBLY TOUGH WAS..."
"I KNEW IF I INJURED THE LIZARD, I'D BE INJURING DR. CONNORS!"
"BUT, I FINALLY TRICKED HIM INTO FOLLOWING ME INSIDE A REFRIGERATED CAR---"
"WHERE THE SUB-ZERO TEMPERATURE MADE HIM WEAK ENOUGH FOR ME TO OVERCOME!"
"AND THAT WAS THE LAST THAT I, OR ANYONE, EVER AGAIN HEARD OF THE LIZARD!"
BUT WOULDN'T IT BE A GAS IF I COULD GET A SUMMER JOB... WORKING FOR DR. CONNORS?
I COULD LEARN MORE WITH HIM THAN IN A DOZEN SCIENCE CLASSES!
ANYWAY, WHAT HAVE I GOT TO LOSE?
IF I GET A CHANCE LATER ON, MAYBE I'LL DROP HIM A LINE!
DOW
BUT RIGHT NOW... I BETTER START CONCEN-TRATING ON THE SHOCKER AGAIN!
11.

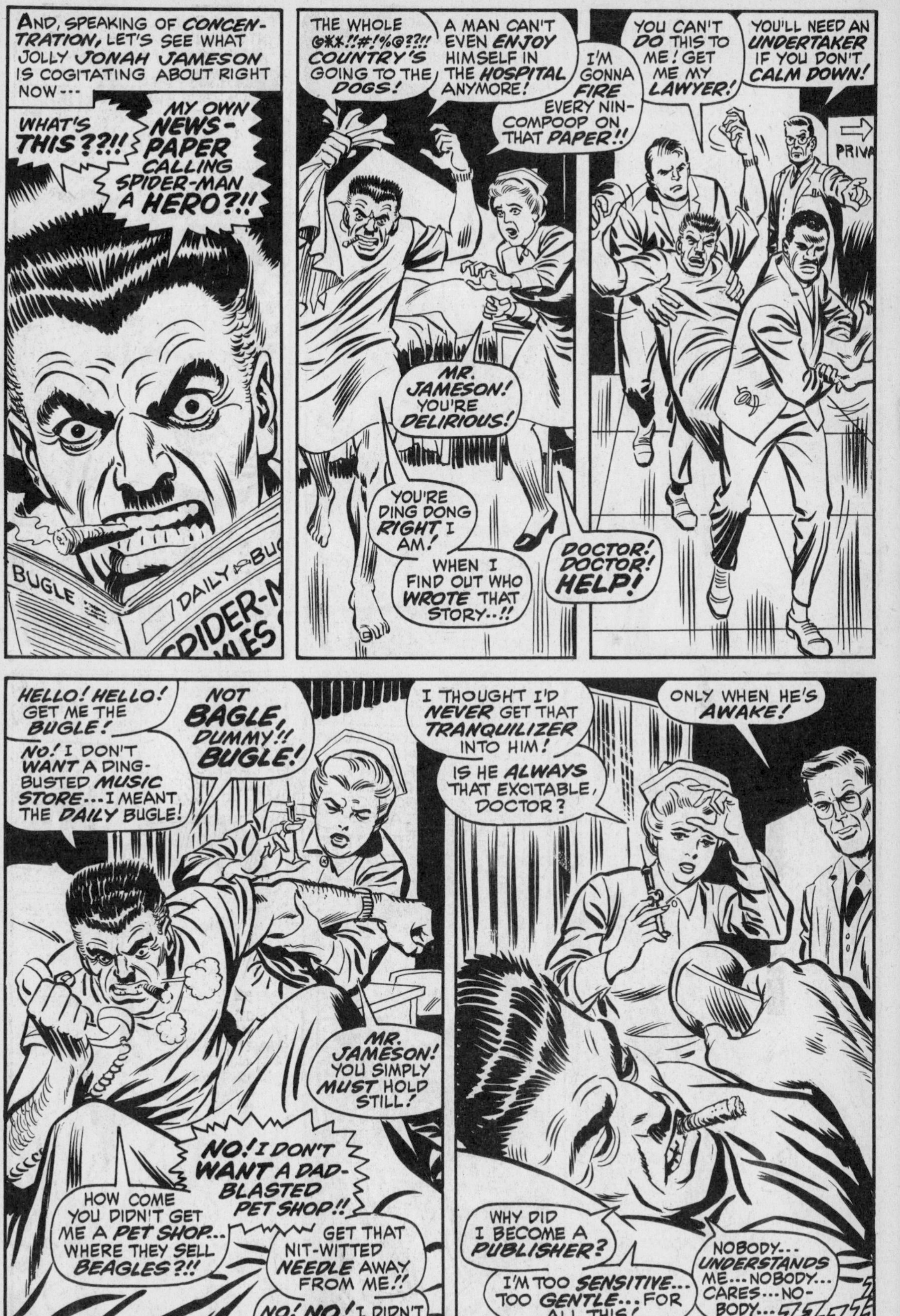

AND, SPEAKING OF CONCENTRATION, LET'S SEE WHAT JOLLY JONAH JAMESON IS COGITATING ABOUT RIGHT NOW---
WHAT'S THIS??!!
MY OWN NEWSPAPER CALLING SPIDER-MAN A HERO?!!
DAILY BUGLE
SPIDER-M
THE WHOLE @**!!#!%@??!! COUNTRY'S GOING TO THE DOGS!
A MAN CAN'T EVEN ENJOY HIMSELF IN THE HOSPITAL ANYMORE!
I'M GONNA FIRE EVERY NIN-COMPOOP ON THAT PAPER!!
MR. JAMESON! YOU'RE DELIRIOUS!
YOU'RE DING DONG RIGHT I AM!
WHEN I FIND OUT WHO WROTE THAT STORY--!!
DOCTOR! DOCTOR! HELP!
YOU CAN'T DO THIS TO ME! GET ME MY LAWYER!
YOU'LL NEED AN UNDERTAKER IF YOU DON'T CALM DOWN!
PRIVA
HELLO! HELLO! GET ME THE BUGLE!
NO! I DON'T WANT A DING-BUSTED MUSIC STORE...I MEANT THE DAILY BUGLE!
NOT BAGLE, DUMMY!! BUGLE!
MR. JAMESON! YOU SIMPLY MUST HOLD STILL!
NO! I DON'T WANT A DAD-BLASTED PET SHOP!!
HOW COME YOU DIDN'T GET ME A PET SHOP... WHERE THEY SELL BEAGLES?!!
GET THAT NIT-WITTED NEEDLE AWAY FROM ME!!
NO! NO! I DIDN'T MEAN YOU!
I THOUGHT I'D NEVER GET THAT TRANQUILIZER INTO HIM!
IS HE ALWAYS THAT EXCITABLE, DOCTOR?
ONLY WHEN HE'S AWAKE!
WHY DID I BECOME A PUBLISHER?
I'M TOO SENSITIVE... TOO GENTLE... FOR ALL THIS!
NOBODY... UNDERSTANDS ME... NOBODY... CARES... NO-BODY... ZZZZZ
12

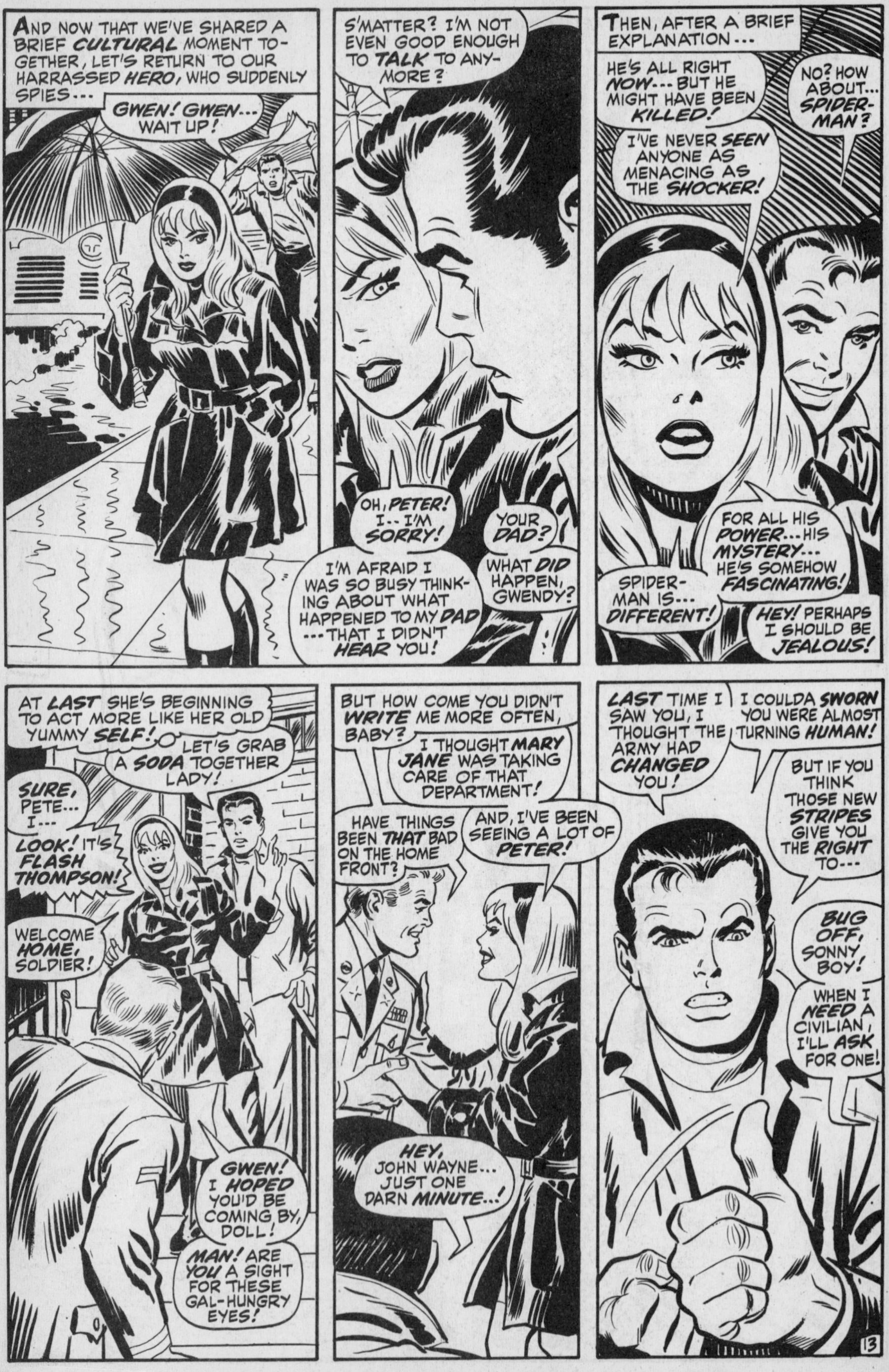
AND NOW THAT WE'VE SHARED A BRIEF CULTURAL MOMENT TOGETHER, LET'S RETURN TO OUR HARRASSED HERO, WHO SUDDENLY SPIES ---
GWEN! GWEN... WAIT UP!
S'MATTER? I'M NOT EVEN GOOD ENOUGH TO TALK TO ANYMORE?
OH, PETER! I-- I'M SORRY!
I'M AFRAID I WAS SO BUSY THINKING ABOUT WHAT HAPPENED TO MY DAD --- THAT I DIDN'T HEAR YOU!
YOUR DAD?
WHAT DID HAPPEN, GWENDY?
THEN, AFTER A BRIEF EXPLANATION ---
HE'S ALL RIGHT NOW--- BUT HE MIGHT HAVE BEEN KILLED!
I'VE NEVER SEEN ANYONE AS MENACING AS THE SHOCKER!
NO? HOW ABOUT... SPIDER-MAN?
SPIDER-MAN IS--- DIFFERENT!
FOR ALL HIS POWER--- HIS MYSTERY--- HE'S SOMEHOW FASCINATING!
HEY! PERHAPS I SHOULD BE JEALOUS!
AT LAST SHE'S BEGINNING TO ACT MORE LIKE HER OLD YUMMY SELF!
LET'S GRAB A SODA TOGETHER LADY!
SURE, PETE... I---
LOOK! IT'S FLASH THOMPSON!
WELCOME HOME, SOLDIER!
GWEN! I HOPED YOU'D BE COMING BY, DOLL!
MAN! ARE YOU A SIGHT FOR THESE GAL-HUNGRY EYES!
BUT HOW COME YOU DIDN'T WRITE ME MORE OFTEN, BABY?
I THOUGHT MARY JANE WAS TAKING CARE OF THAT DEPARTMENT!
HAVE THINGS BEEN THAT BAD ON THE HOME FRONT?
AND, I'VE BEEN SEEING A LOT OF PETER!
HEY, JOHN WAYNE... JUST ONE DARN MINUTE..!
LAST TIME I SAW YOU, I THOUGHT THE ARMY HAD CHANGED YOU!
I COULDA SWORN YOU WERE ALMOST TURNING HUMAN!
BUT IF YOU THINK THOSE NEW STRIPES GIVE YOU THE RIGHT TO---
BUG OFF, SONNY BOY!
WHEN I NEED A CIVILIAN, I'LL ASK FOR ONE!
13

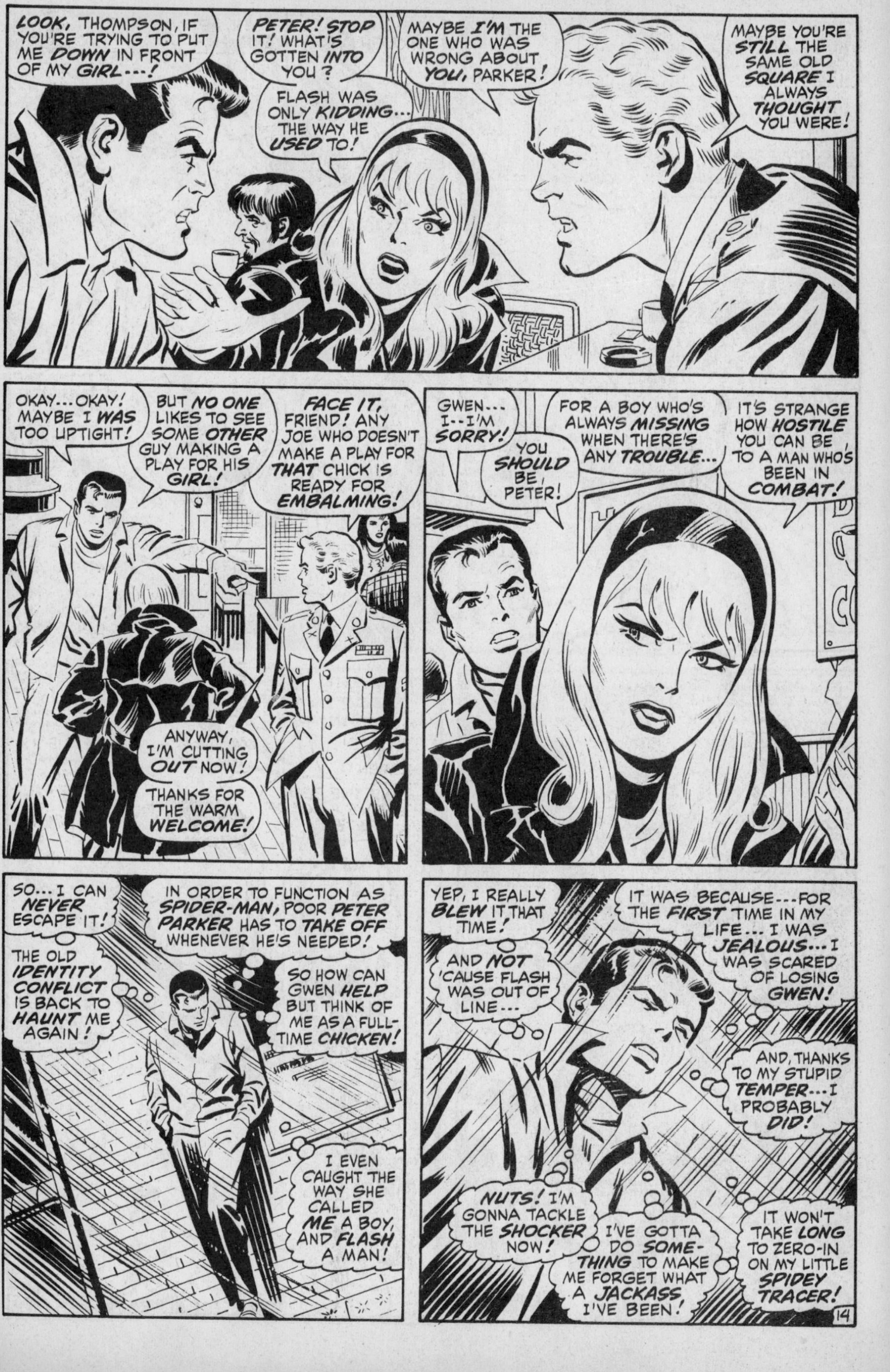

LOOK, THOMPSON, IF YOU'RE TRYING TO PUT ME DOWN IN FRONT OF MY GIRL---!
PETER! STOP IT! WHAT'S GOTTEN INTO YOU?
FLASH WAS ONLY KIDDING... THE WAY HE USED TO!
MAYBE I'M THE ONE WHO WAS WRONG ABOUT YOU, PARKER!
MAYBE YOU'RE STILL THE SAME OLD SQUARE I ALWAYS THOUGHT YOU WERE!
OKAY... OKAY! MAYBE I WAS TOO UPTIGHT!
BUT NO ONE LIKES TO SEE SOME OTHER GUY MAKING A PLAY FOR HIS GIRL!
FACE IT, FRIEND! ANY JOE WHO DOESN'T MAKE A PLAY FOR THAT CHICK IS READY FOR EMBALMING!
ANYWAY, I'M CUTTING OUT NOW!
THANKS FOR THE WARM WELCOME!
GWEN... I--I'M SORRY!
YOU SHOULD BE, PETER!
FOR A BOY WHO'S ALWAYS MISSING WHEN THERE'S ANY TROUBLE...
IT'S STRANGE HOW HOSTILE YOU CAN BE TO A MAN WHO'S BEEN IN COMBAT!
SO... I CAN NEVER ESCAPE IT!
IN ORDER TO FUNCTION AS SPIDER-MAN, POOR PETER PARKER HAS TO TAKE OFF WHENEVER HE'S NEEDED!
THE OLD IDENTITY CONFLICT IS BACK TO HAUNT ME AGAIN!
SO HOW CAN GWEN HELP BUT THINK OF ME AS A FULL-TIME CHICKEN!
I EVEN CAUGHT THE WAY SHE CALLED ME A BOY, AND FLASH A MAN!
YEP, I REALLY BLEW IT THAT TIME!
AND NOT 'CAUSE FLASH WAS OUT OF LINE---
IT WAS BECAUSE---FOR THE FIRST TIME IN MY LIFE... I WAS JEALOUS... I WAS SCARED OF LOSING GWEN!
AND, THANKS TO MY STUPID TEMPER---I PROBABLY DID!
NUTS! I'M GONNA TACKLE THE SHOCKER NOW!
I'VE GOTTA DO SOMETHING TO MAKE ME FORGET WHAT A JACKASS I'VE BEEN!
IT WON'T TAKE LONG TO ZERO-IN ON MY LITTLE SPIDEY TRACER!
14

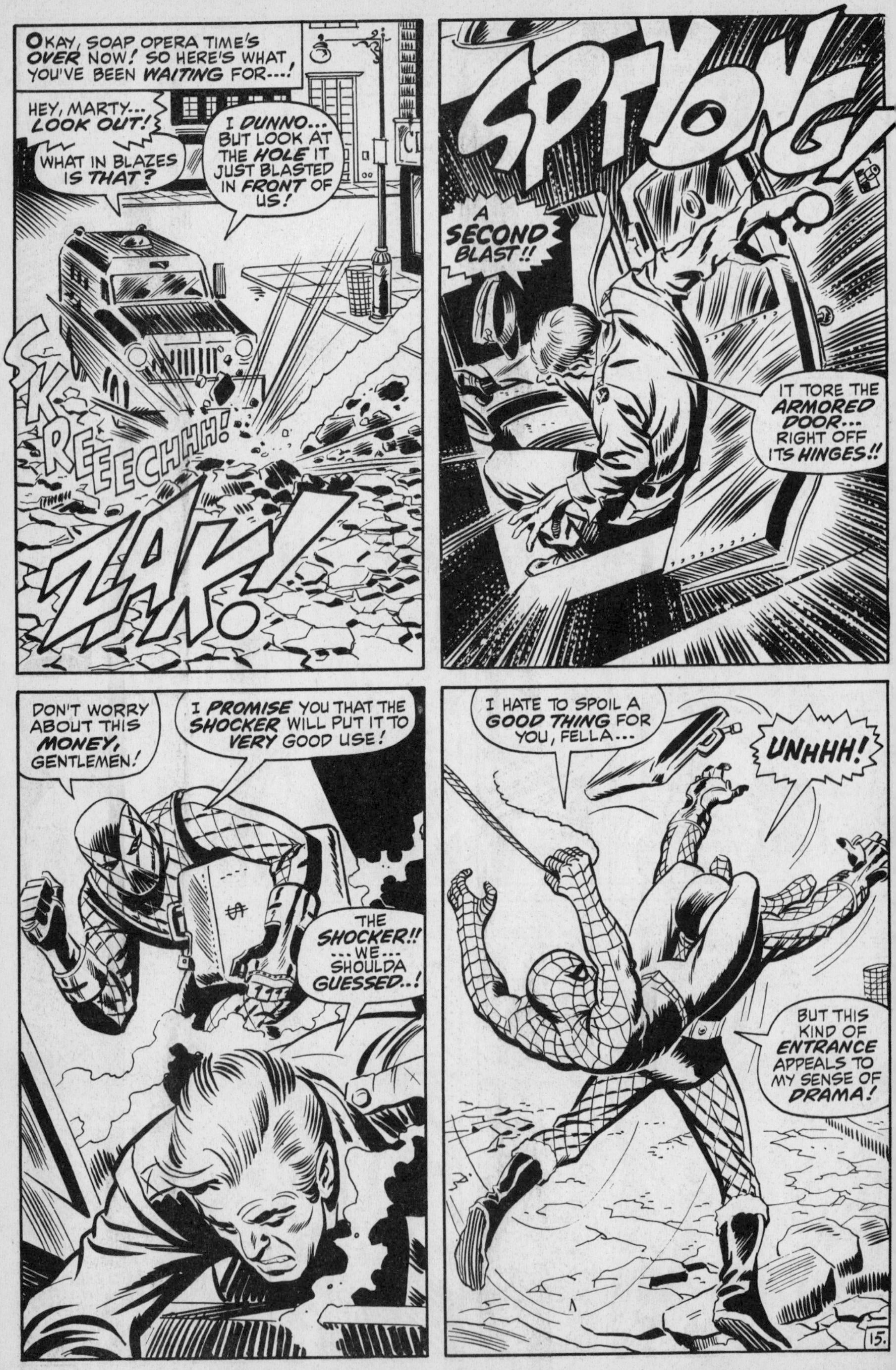
OKAY, SOAP OPERA TIME'S OVER NOW! SO HERE'S WHAT YOU'VE BEEN WAITING FOR---!
HEY, MARTY... LOOK OUT!
WHAT IN BLAZES IS THAT?
I DUNNO... BUT LOOK AT THE HOLE IT JUST BLASTED IN FRONT OF US!
SKREEECHHH!
ZAK!
SPTOOG!
A SECOND BLAST!!
IT TORE THE ARMORED DOOR... RIGHT OFF ITS HINGES!!
DON'T WORRY ABOUT THIS MONEY, GENTLEMEN!
I PROMISE YOU THAT THE SHOCKER WILL PUT IT TO VERY GOOD USE!
THE SHOCKER!! ...WE... SHOULDA GUESSED..!
I HATE TO SPOIL A GOOD THING FOR YOU, FELLA...
UNHHH!
BUT THIS KIND OF ENTRANCE APPEALS TO MY SENSE OF DRAMA!
15.

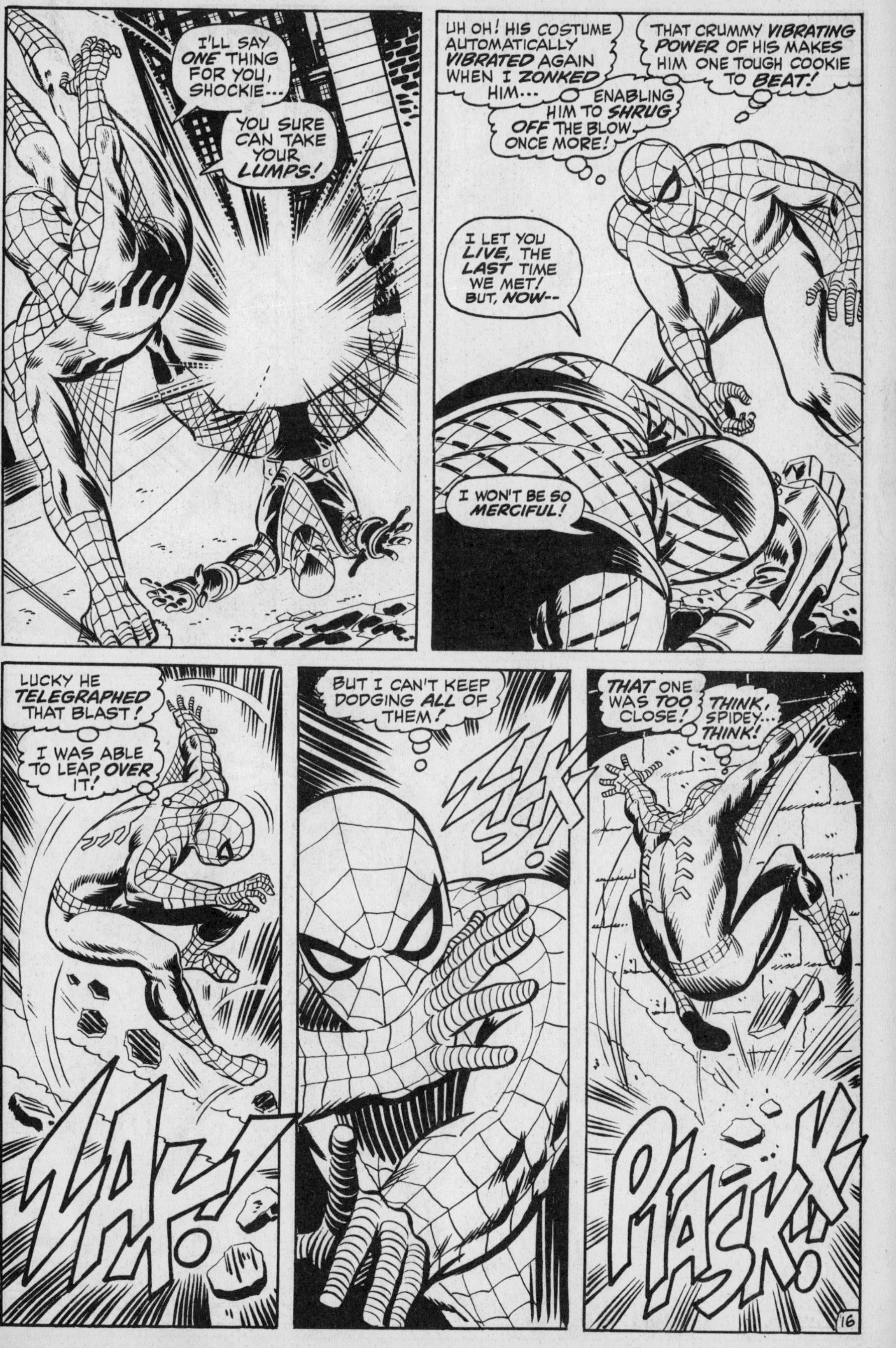

I'LL SAY ONE THING FOR YOU, SHOCKIE...
YOU SURE CAN TAKE YOUR LUMPS!
UH OH! HIS COSTUME AUTOMATICALLY VIBRATED AGAIN WHEN I ZONKED HIM...
ENABLING HIM TO SHRUG OFF THE BLOW ONCE MORE!
THAT CRUMMY VIBRATING POWER OF HIS MAKES HIM ONE TOUGH COOKIE TO BEAT!
I LET YOU LIVE, THE LAST TIME WE MET! BUT, NOW--
I WON'T BE SO MERCIFUL!
LUCKY HE TELEGRAPHED THAT BLAST!
I WAS ABLE TO LEAP OVER IT!
ZAK!
BUT I CAN'T KEEP DODGING ALL OF THEM!
ZZAK!
THAT ONE WAS TOO CLOSE!
THINK, SPIDEY... THINK!
PTAK!
16

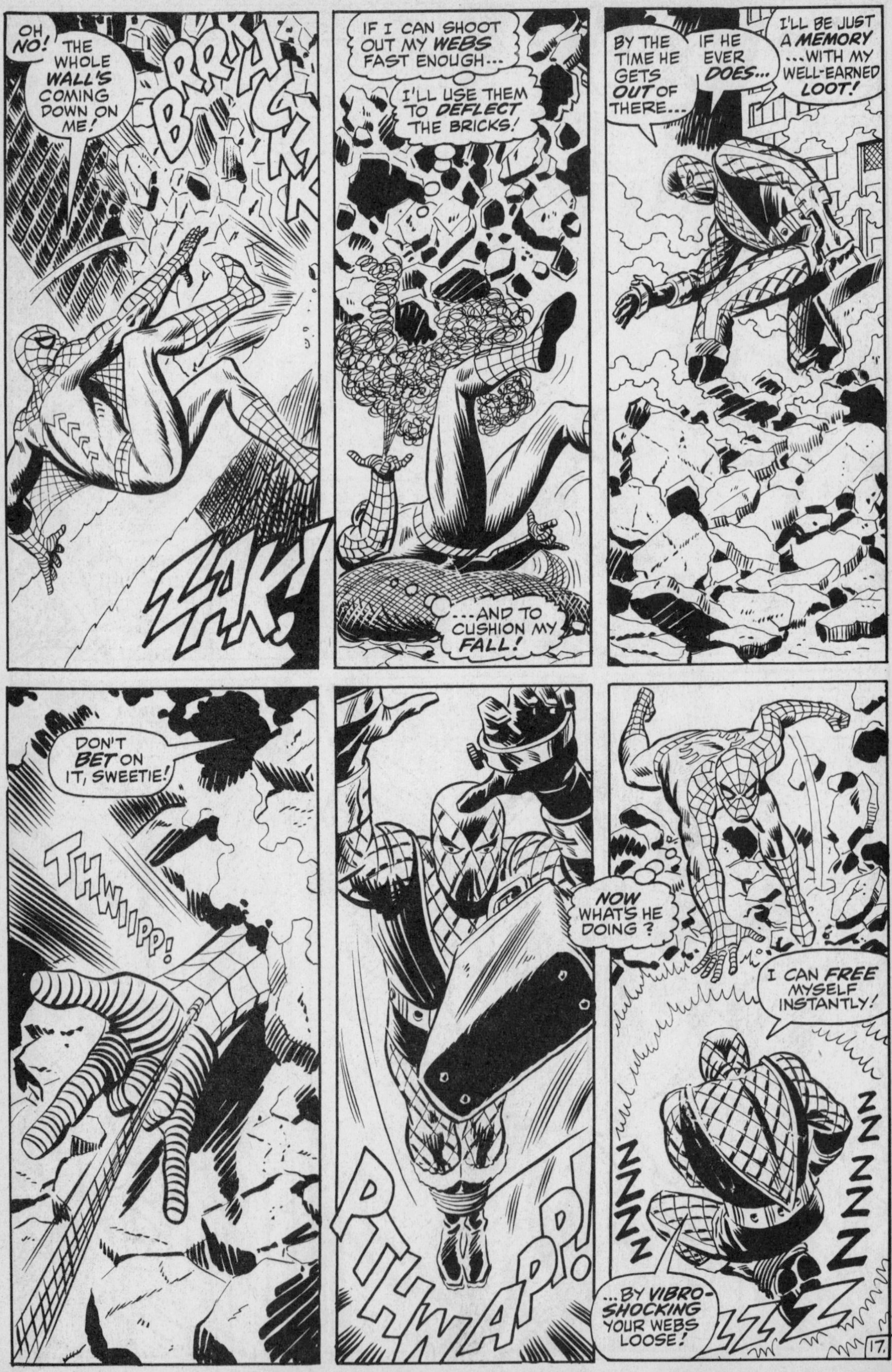
OH NO! THE WHOLE WALL'S COMING DOWN ON ME!
BRRAKK
ZAK!
IF I CAN SHOOT OUT MY WEBS FAST ENOUGH...
I'LL USE THEM TO DEFLECT THE BRICKS!
...AND TO CUSHION MY FALL!
BY THE TIME HE GETS OUT OF THERE...
IF HE EVER DOES...
I'LL BE JUST A MEMORY ...WITH MY WELL-EARNED LOOT!
DON'T BET ON IT, SWEETIE!
THWIIPP!
PTHWAP!
NOW WHAT'S HE DOING ?
I CAN FREE MYSELF INSTANTLY!
...BY VIBRO-SHOCKING YOUR WEBS LOOSE!
17.

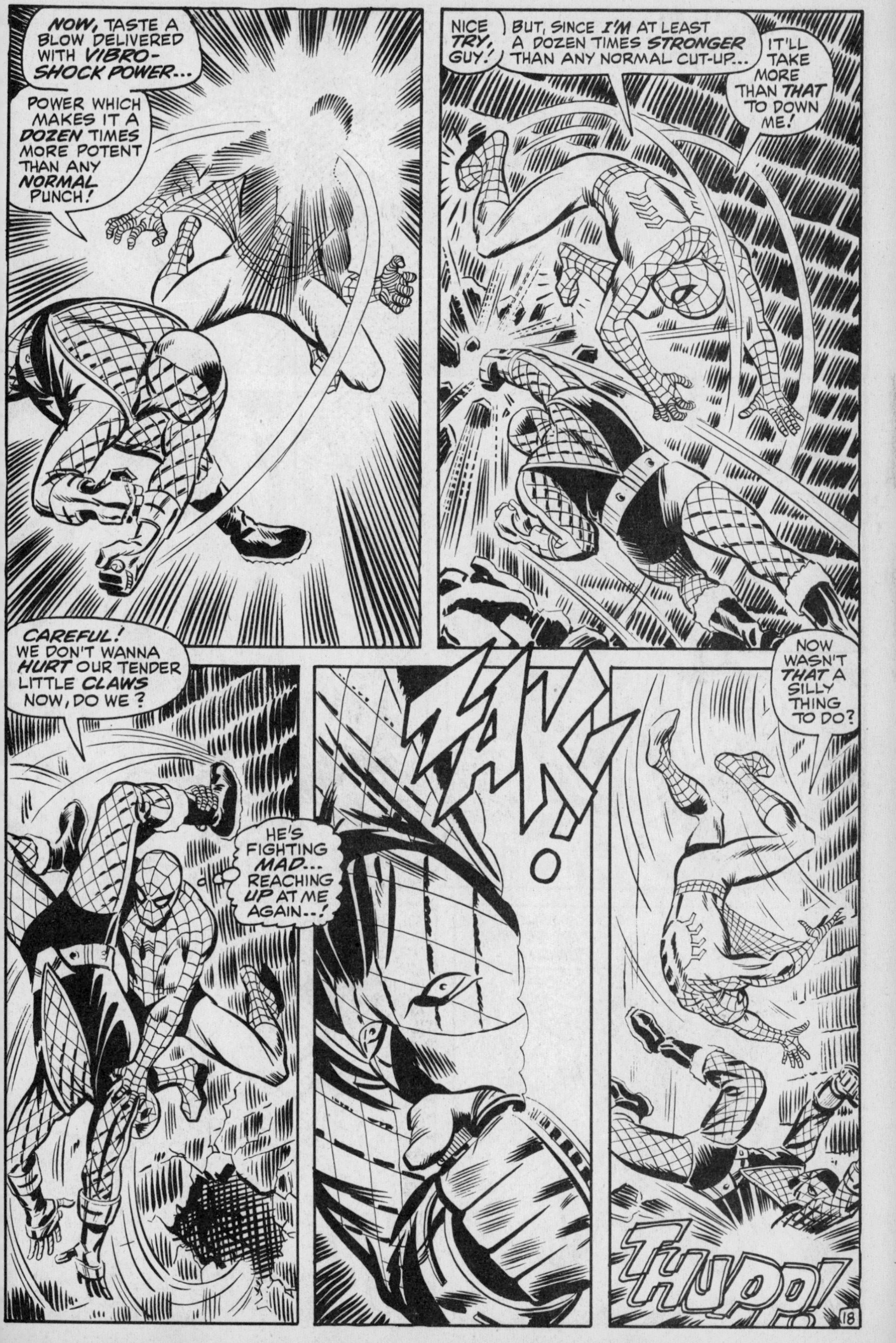
NOW, TASTE A BLOW DELIVERED WITH VIBRO-SHOCK POWER...
POWER WHICH MAKES IT A DOZEN TIMES MORE POTENT THAN ANY NORMAL PUNCH!
NICE TRY, GUY!
BUT, SINCE I'M AT LEAST A DOZEN TIMES STRONGER THAN ANY NORMAL CUT-UP...
IT'LL TAKE MORE THAN THAT TO DOWN ME!
CAREFUL! WE DON'T WANNA HURT OUR TENDER LITTLE CLAWS NOW, DO WE?
HE'S FIGHTING MAD... REACHING UP AT ME AGAIN...!
ZAK!
NOW WASN'T THAT A SILLY THING TO DO?
THUPP!
18

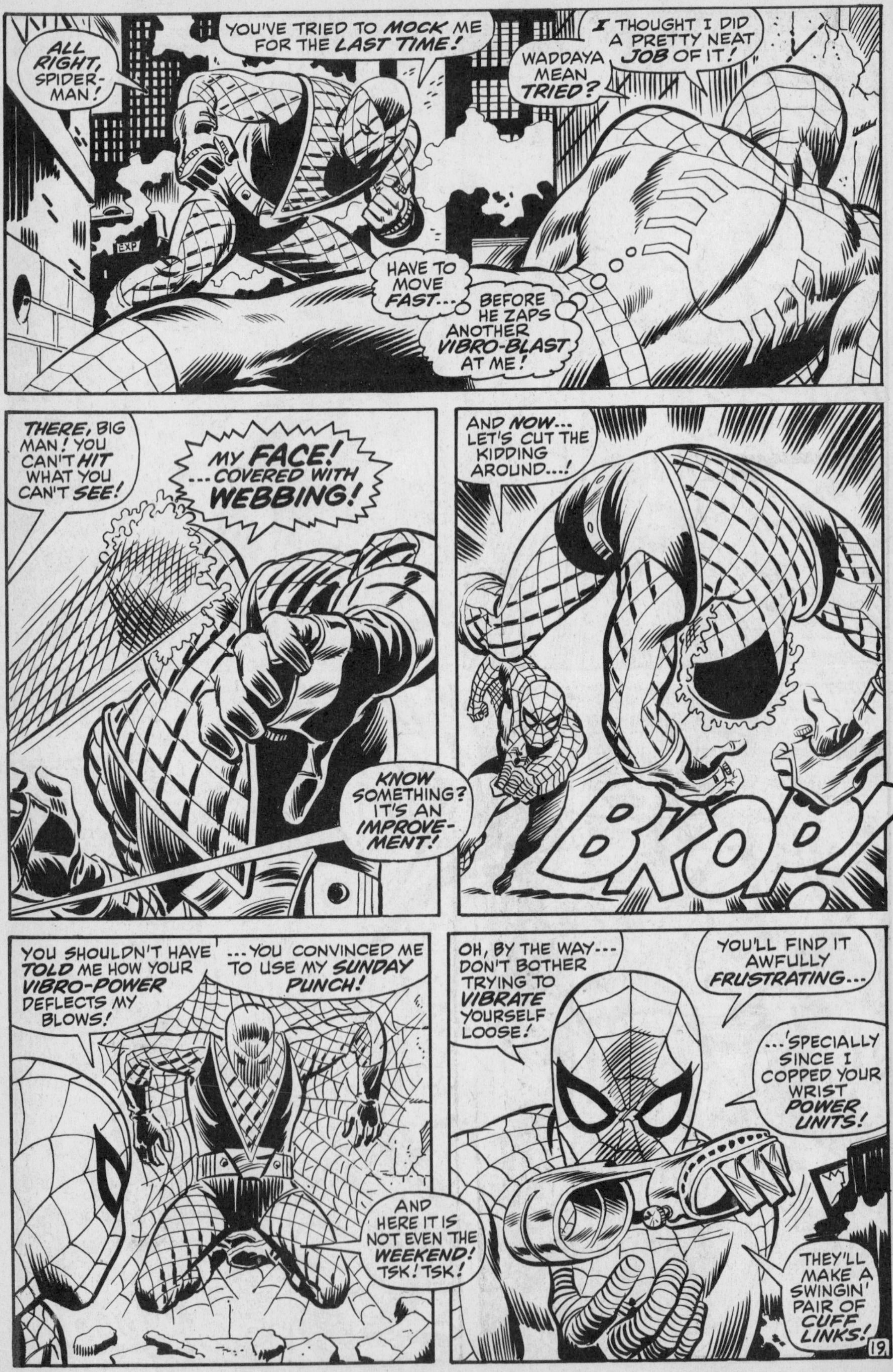
ALL RIGHT, SPIDER-MAN!
YOU'VE TRIED TO MOCK ME FOR THE LAST TIME!
WADDAYA MEAN TRIED?
I THOUGHT I DID A PRETTY NEAT JOB OF IT!
HAVE TO MOVE FAST...
BEFORE HE ZAPS ANOTHER VIBRO-BLAST AT ME!
EXP
THERE, BIG MAN! YOU CAN'T HIT WHAT YOU CAN'T SEE!
MY FACE! ...COVERED WITH WEBBING!
KNOW SOMETHING? IT'S AN IMPROVE-MENT!
AND NOW... LET'S CUT THE KIDDING AROUND...!
BROP!
YOU SHOULDN'T HAVE TOLD ME HOW YOUR VIBRO-POWER DEFLECTS MY BLOWS!
...YOU CONVINCED ME TO USE MY SUNDAY PUNCH!
AND HERE IT IS NOT EVEN THE WEEKEND! TSK! TSK!
OH, BY THE WAY--- DON'T BOTHER TRYING TO VIBRATE YOURSELF LOOSE!
YOU'LL FIND IT AWFULLY FRUSTRATING...
...'SPECIALLY SINCE I COPPED YOUR WRIST POWER UNITS!
THEY'LL MAKE A SWINGIN' PAIR OF CUFF LINKS!
19

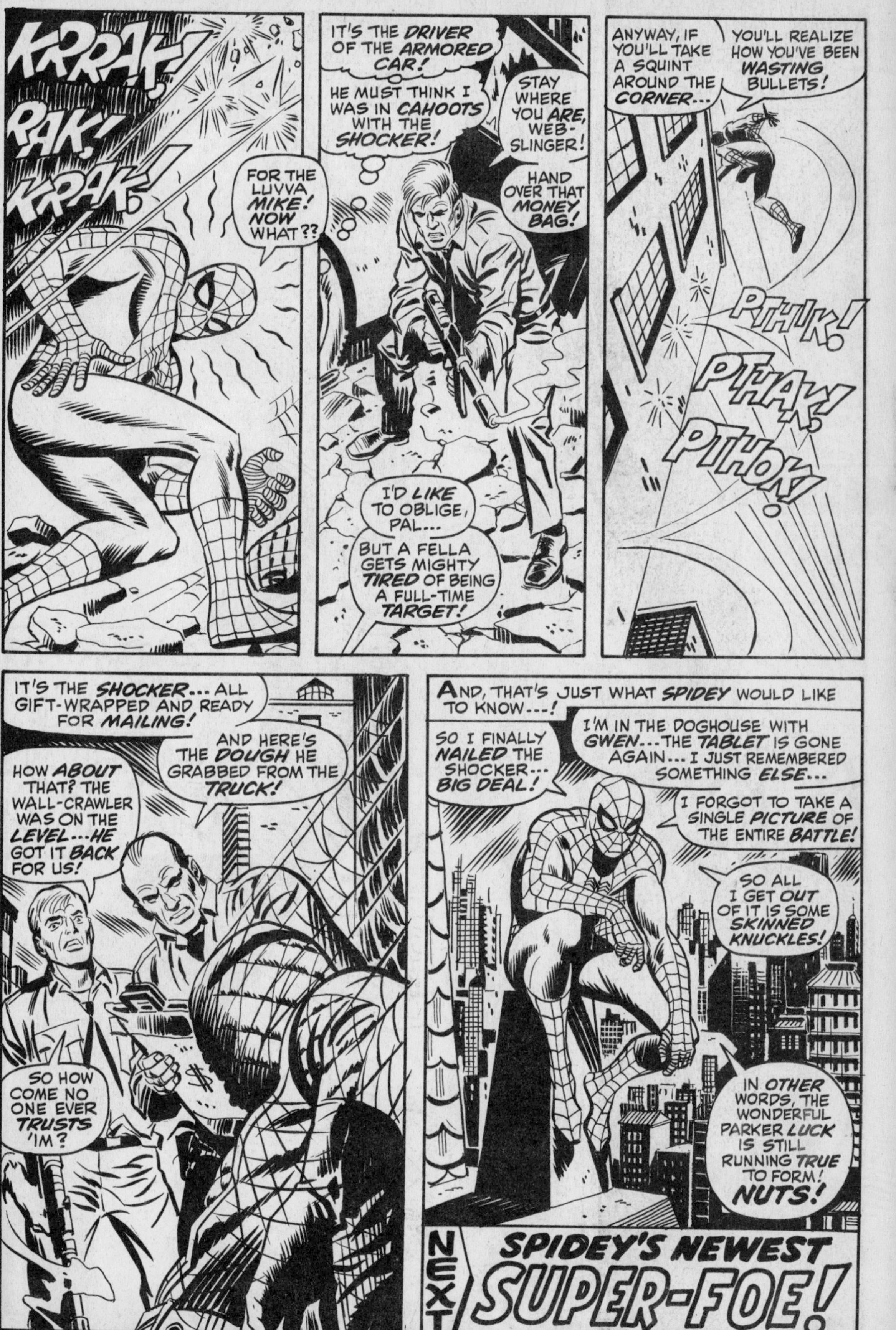
KRRAK!
RAK!
KRAK!
FOR THE LUVVA MIKE! NOW WHAT??
IT'S THE DRIVER OF THE ARMORED CAR!
HE MUST THINK I WAS IN CAHOOTS WITH THE SHOCKER!
STAY WHERE YOU ARE, WEB-SLINGER!
HAND OVER THAT MONEY BAG!
I'D LIKE TO OBLIGE, PAL...
BUT A FELLA GETS MIGHTY TIRED OF BEING A FULL-TIME TARGET!
ANYWAY, IF YOU'LL TAKE A SQUINT AROUND THE CORNER...
YOU'LL REALIZE HOW YOU'VE BEEN WASTING BULLETS!
PTHUK!
PTHAK!
PTHOK!
IT'S THE SHOCKER... ALL GIFT-WRAPPED AND READY FOR MAILING!
AND HERE'S THE DOUGH HE GRABBED FROM THE TRUCK!
HOW ABOUT THAT? THE WALL-CRAWLER WAS ON THE LEVEL... HE GOT IT BACK FOR US!
SO HOW COME NO ONE EVER TRUSTS 'IM?
AND, THAT'S JUST WHAT SPIDEY WOULD LIKE TO KNOW---!
SO I FINALLY NAILED THE SHOCKER... BIG DEAL!
I'M IN THE DOGHOUSE WITH GWEN... THE TABLET IS GONE AGAIN... I JUST REMEMBERED SOMETHING ELSE...
I FORGOT TO TAKE A SINGLE PICTURE OF THE ENTIRE BATTLE!
SO ALL I GET OUT OF IT IS SOME SKINNED KNUCKLES!
IN OTHER WORDS, THE WONDERFUL PARKER LUCK IS STILL RUNNING TRUE TO FORM! NUTS!
NEXT
SPIDEY'S NEWEST SUPER-FOE!

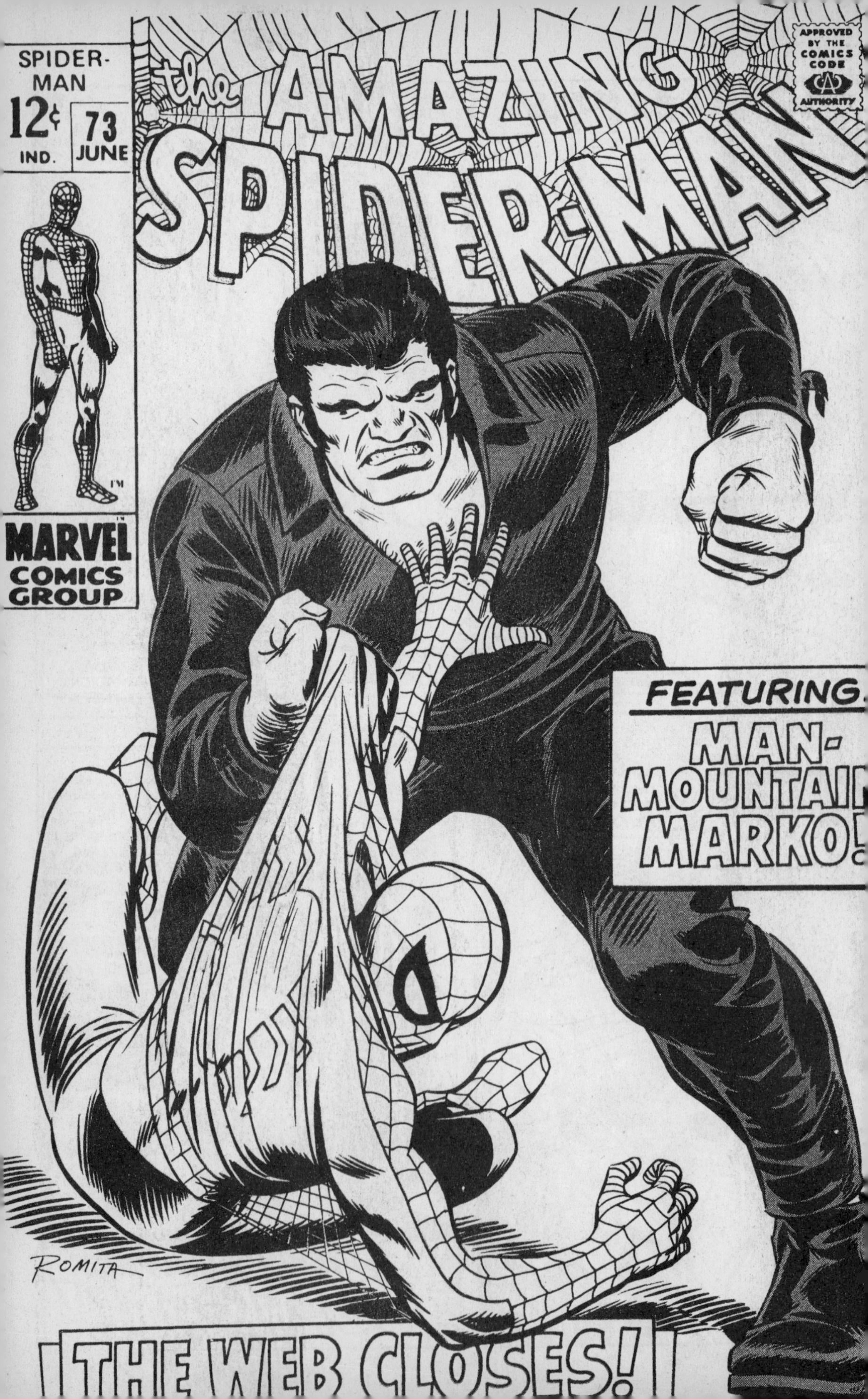

SPIDER-MAN
12¢ IND.
73 JUNE
the AMAZING SPIDER-MAN
APPROVED BY THE COMICS CODE AUTHORITY
MARVEL COMICS GROUP
FEATURING...
MAN-MOUNTAIN MARKO!
ROMITA
THE WEB CLOSES!

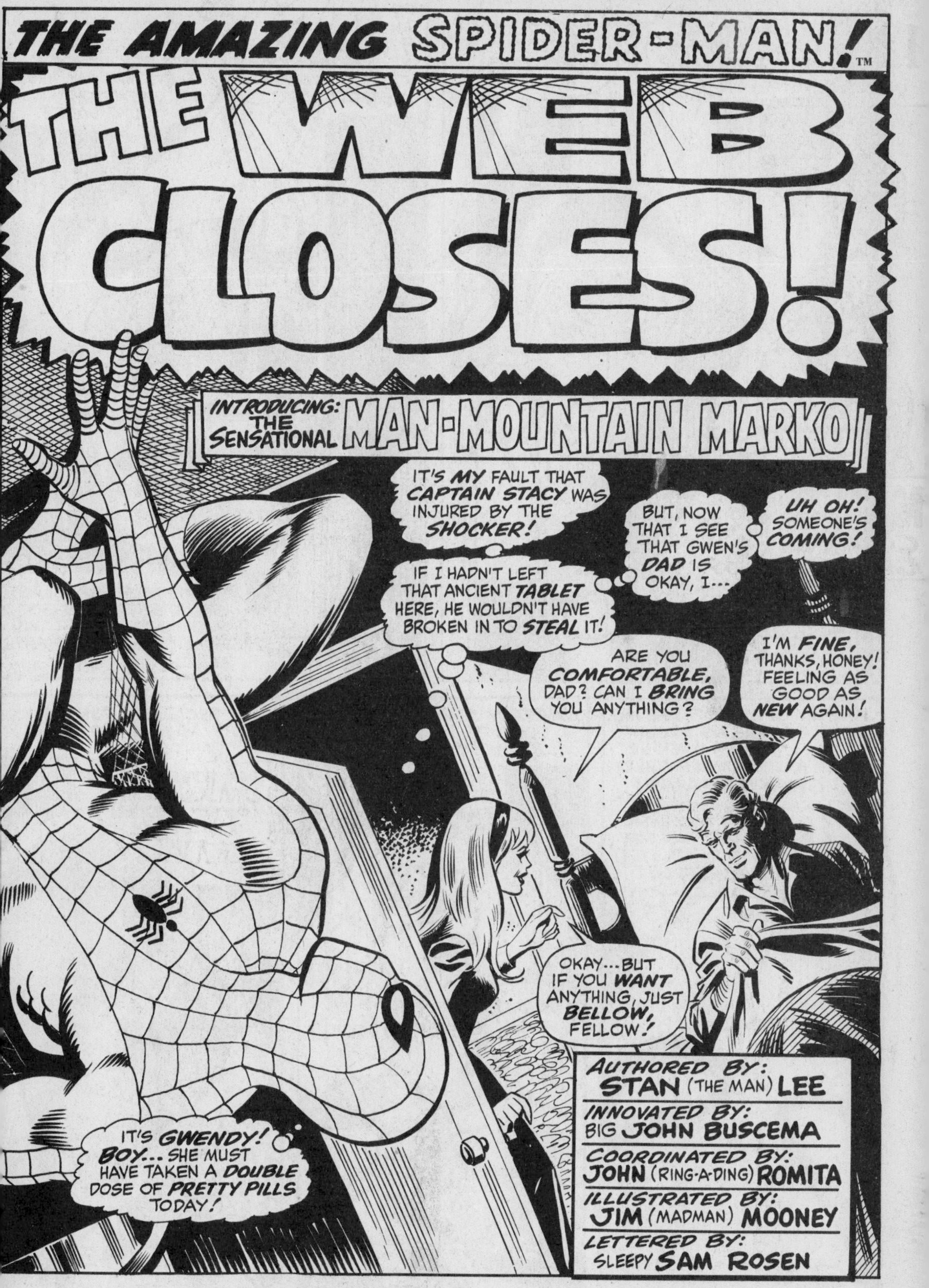
THE AMAZING SPIDER-MAN!™
THE WEB CLOSES!
INTRODUCING: THE SENSATIONAL MAN-MOUNTAIN MARKO
IT'S MY FAULT THAT CAPTAIN STACY WAS INJURED BY THE SHOCKER!
IF I HADN'T LEFT THAT ANCIENT TABLET HERE, HE WOULDN'T HAVE BROKEN IN TO STEAL IT!
BUT, NOW THAT I SEE THAT GWEN'S DAD IS OKAY, I...
UH OH! SOMEONE'S COMING!
ARE YOU COMFORTABLE, DAD? CAN I BRING YOU ANYTHING?
I'M FINE, THANKS, HONEY! FEELING AS GOOD AS NEW AGAIN!
OKAY...BUT IF YOU WANT ANYTHING, JUST BELLOW, FELLOW!
IT'S GWENDY! BOY... SHE MUST HAVE TAKEN A DOUBLE DOSE OF PRETTY PILLS TODAY!
AUTHORED BY: STAN (THE MAN) LEE
INNOVATED BY: BIG JOHN BUSCEMA
COORDINATED BY: JOHN (RING-A-DING) ROMITA
ILLUSTRATED BY: JIM (MADMAN) MOONEY
LETTERED BY: SLEEPY SAM ROSEN

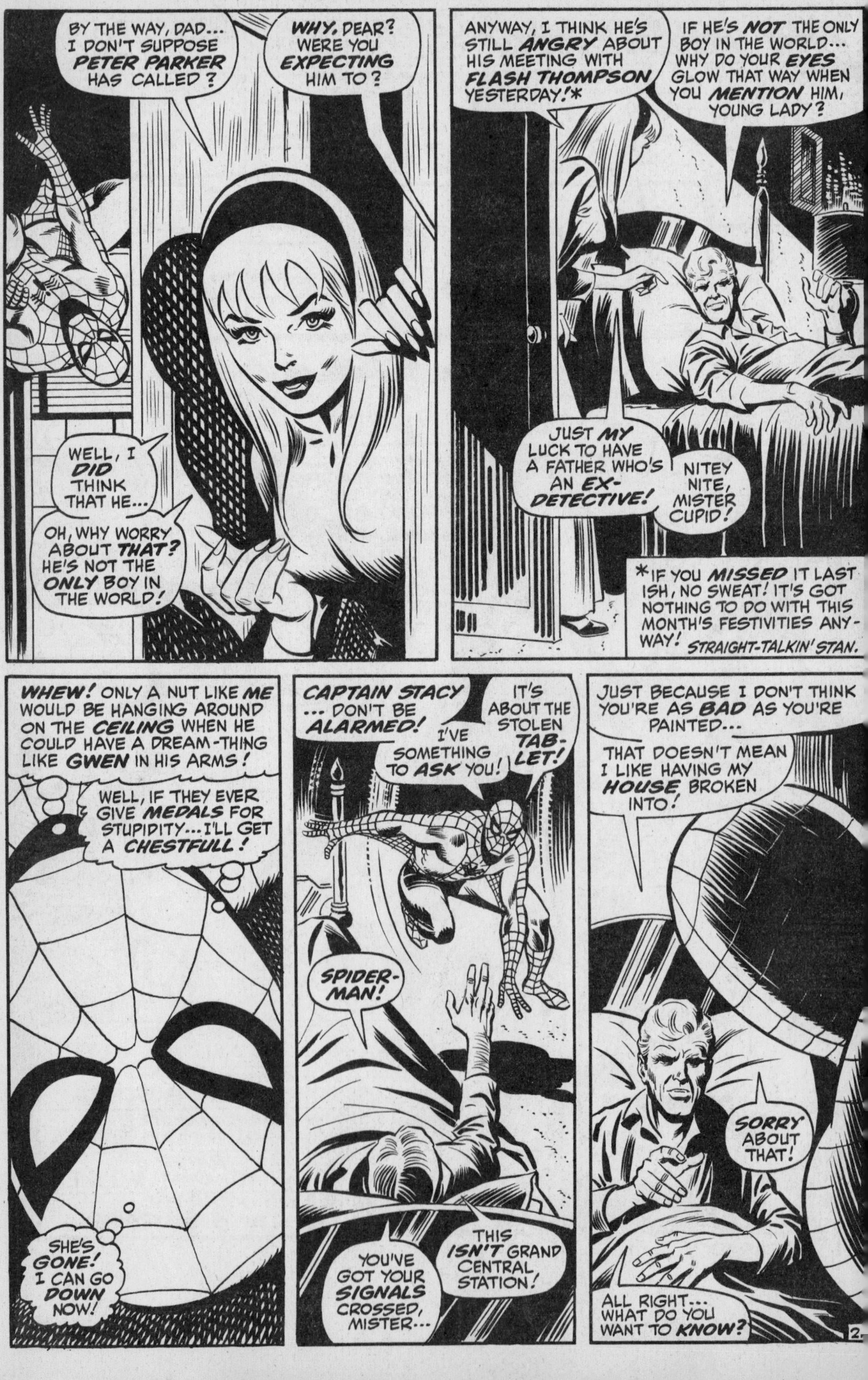
BY THE WAY, DAD... I DON'T SUPPOSE PETER PARKER HAS CALLED?
WHY, DEAR? WERE YOU EXPECTING HIM TO?
WELL, I DID THINK THAT HE...
OH, WHY WORRY ABOUT THAT? HE'S NOT THE ONLY BOY IN THE WORLD!
ANYWAY, I THINK HE'S STILL ANGRY ABOUT HIS MEETING WITH FLASH THOMPSON YESTERDAY!*
IF HE'S NOT THE ONLY BOY IN THE WORLD... WHY DO YOUR EYES GLOW THAT WAY WHEN YOU MENTION HIM, YOUNG LADY?
JUST MY LUCK TO HAVE A FATHER WHO'S AN EX-DETECTIVE!
NITEY NITE, MISTER CUPID!
*IF YOU MISSED IT LAST ISH, NO SWEAT! IT'S GOT NOTHING TO DO WITH THIS MONTH'S FESTIVITIES ANYWAY! STRAIGHT-TALKIN' STAN.
WHEW! ONLY A NUT LIKE ME WOULD BE HANGING AROUND ON THE CEILING WHEN HE COULD HAVE A DREAM-THING LIKE GWEN IN HIS ARMS!
WELL, IF THEY EVER GIVE MEDALS FOR STUPIDITY... I'LL GET A CHESTFULL!
SHE'S GONE! I CAN GO DOWN NOW!
CAPTAIN STACY ... DON'T BE ALARMED!
I'VE SOMETHING TO ASK YOU!
IT'S ABOUT THE STOLEN TABLET!
SPIDER-MAN!
YOU'VE GOT YOUR SIGNALS CROSSED, MISTER...
THIS ISN'T GRAND CENTRAL STATION!
JUST BECAUSE I DON'T THINK YOU'RE AS BAD AS YOU'RE PAINTED...
THAT DOESN'T MEAN I LIKE HAVING MY HOUSE BROKEN INTO!
SORRY ABOUT THAT!
ALL RIGHT... WHAT DO YOU WANT TO KNOW?
2

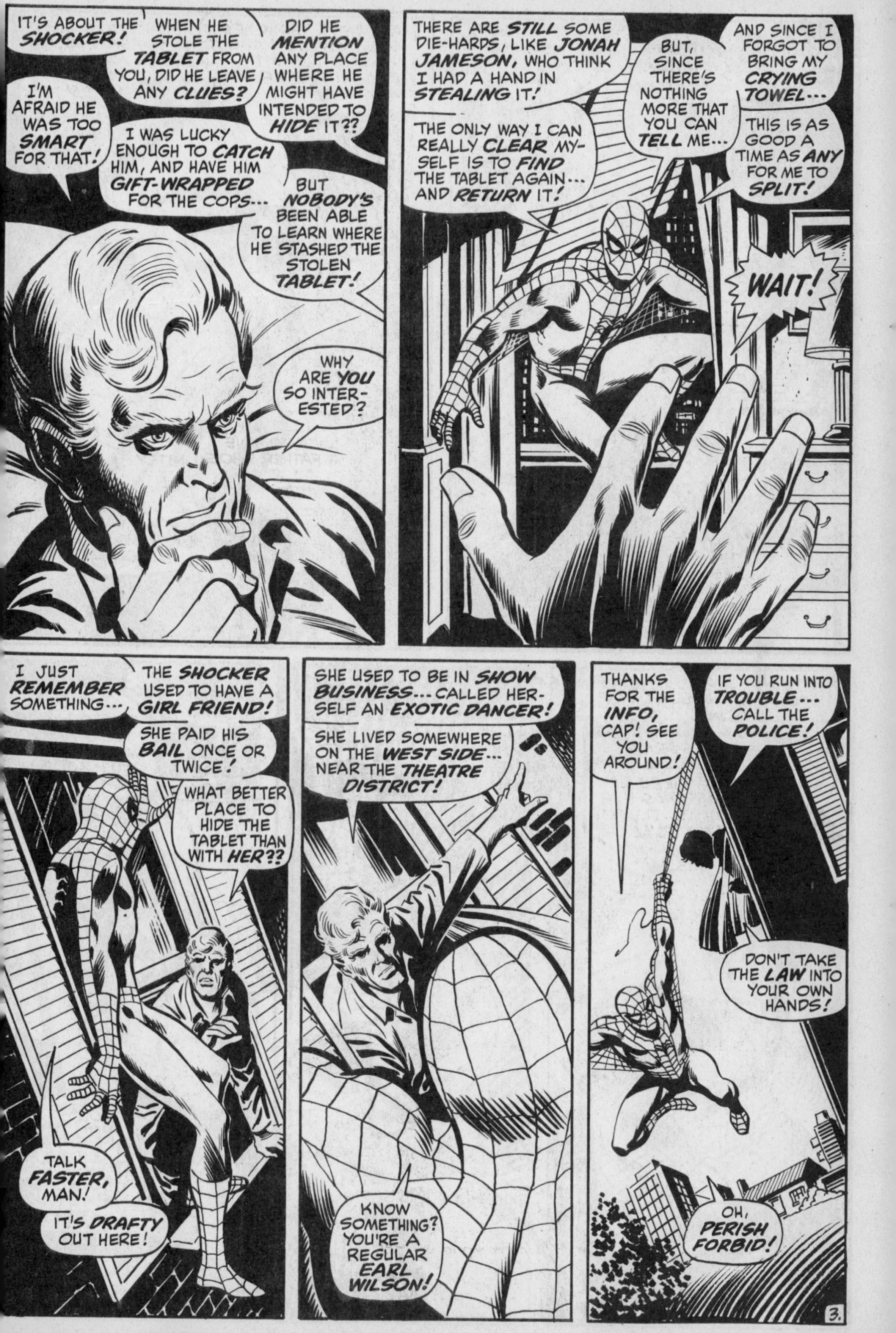
IT'S ABOUT THE SHOCKER!
WHEN HE STOLE THE TABLET FROM YOU, DID HE LEAVE ANY CLUES?
DID HE MENTION ANY PLACE WHERE HE MIGHT HAVE INTENDED TO HIDE IT??
I'M AFRAID HE WAS TOO SMART FOR THAT!
I WAS LUCKY ENOUGH TO CATCH HIM, AND HAVE HIM GIFT-WRAPPED FOR THE COPS...
BUT NOBODY'S BEEN ABLE TO LEARN WHERE HE STASHED THE STOLEN TABLET!
WHY ARE YOU SO INTER-ESTED?
THERE ARE STILL SOME DIE-HARDS, LIKE JONAH JAMESON, WHO THINK I HAD A HAND IN STEALING IT!
THE ONLY WAY I CAN REALLY CLEAR MY-SELF IS TO FIND THE TABLET AGAIN... AND RETURN IT!
BUT, SINCE THERE'S NOTHING MORE THAT YOU CAN TELL ME...
AND SINCE I FORGOT TO BRING MY CRYING TOWEL...
THIS IS AS GOOD A TIME AS ANY FOR ME TO SPLIT!
WAIT!
I JUST REMEMBER SOMETHING...
THE SHOCKER USED TO HAVE A GIRL FRIEND!
SHE PAID HIS BAIL ONCE OR TWICE!
WHAT BETTER PLACE TO HIDE THE TABLET THAN WITH HER??
TALK FASTER, MAN!
IT'S DRAFTY OUT HERE!
SHE USED TO BE IN SHOW BUSINESS... CALLED HER-SELF AN EXOTIC DANCER!
SHE LIVED SOMEWHERE ON THE WEST SIDE... NEAR THE THEATRE DISTRICT!
KNOW SOMETHING? YOU'RE A REGULAR EARL WILSON!
THANKS FOR THE INFO, CAP! SEE YOU AROUND!
IF YOU RUN INTO TROUBLE... CALL THE POLICE!
DON'T TAKE THE LAW INTO YOUR OWN HANDS!
OH, PERISH FORBID!
3.

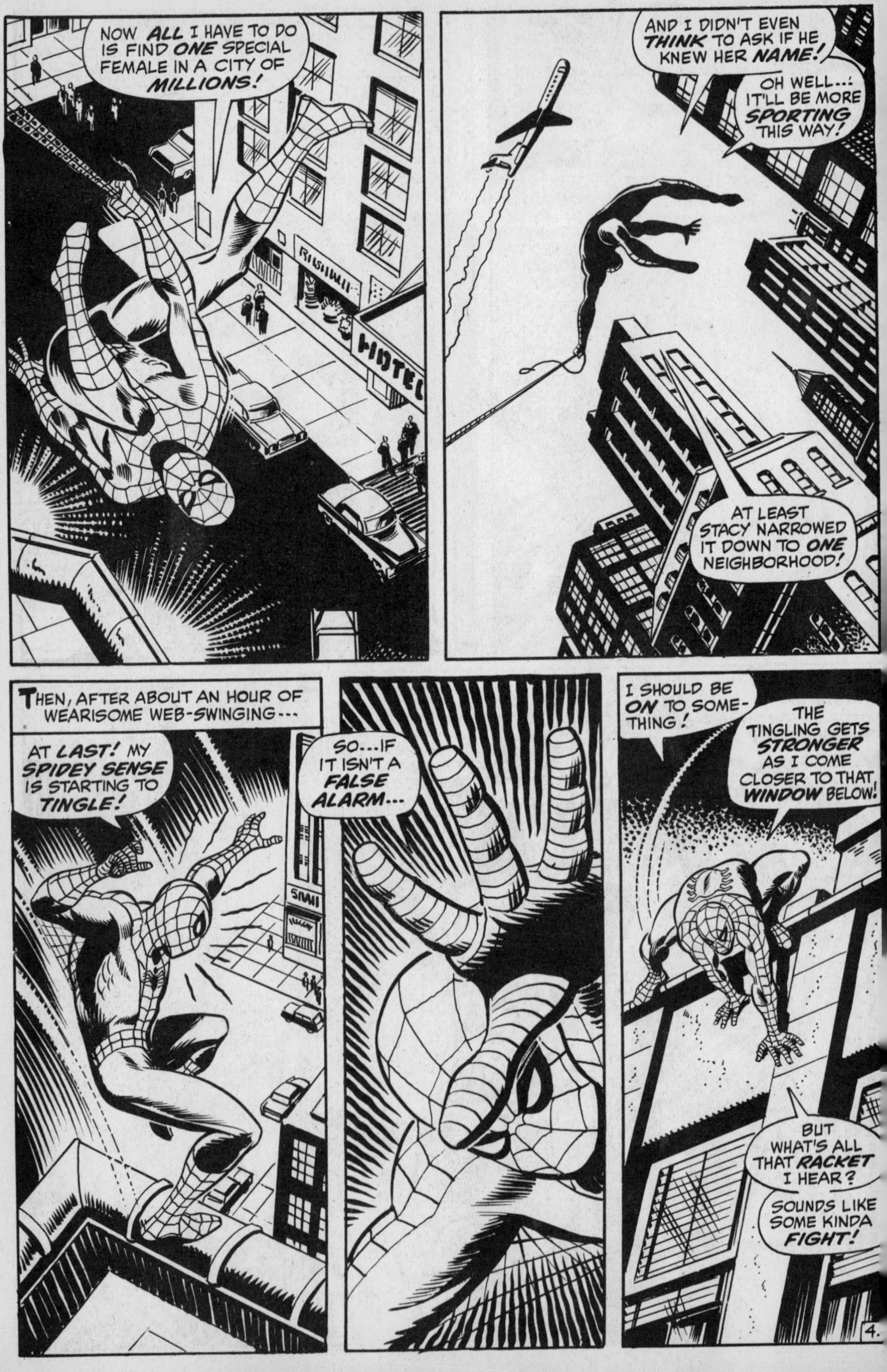

NOW ALL I HAVE TO DO IS FIND ONE SPECIAL FEMALE IN A CITY OF MILLIONS!
HOTEL
AND I DIDN'T EVEN THINK TO ASK IF HE KNEW HER NAME!
OH WELL..: IT'LL BE MORE SPORTING THIS WAY!
AT LEAST STACY NARROWED IT DOWN TO ONE NEIGHBORHOOD!
THEN, AFTER ABOUT AN HOUR OF WEARISOME WEB-SWINGING---
AT LAST! MY SPIDEY SENSE IS STARTING TO TINGLE!
SO...IF IT ISN'T A FALSE ALARM...
I SHOULD BE ON TO SOME-THING!
THE TINGLING GETS STRONGER AS I COME CLOSER TO THAT WINDOW BELOW!
BUT WHAT'S ALL THAT RACKET I HEAR?
SOUNDS LIKE SOME KINDA FIGHT!
4

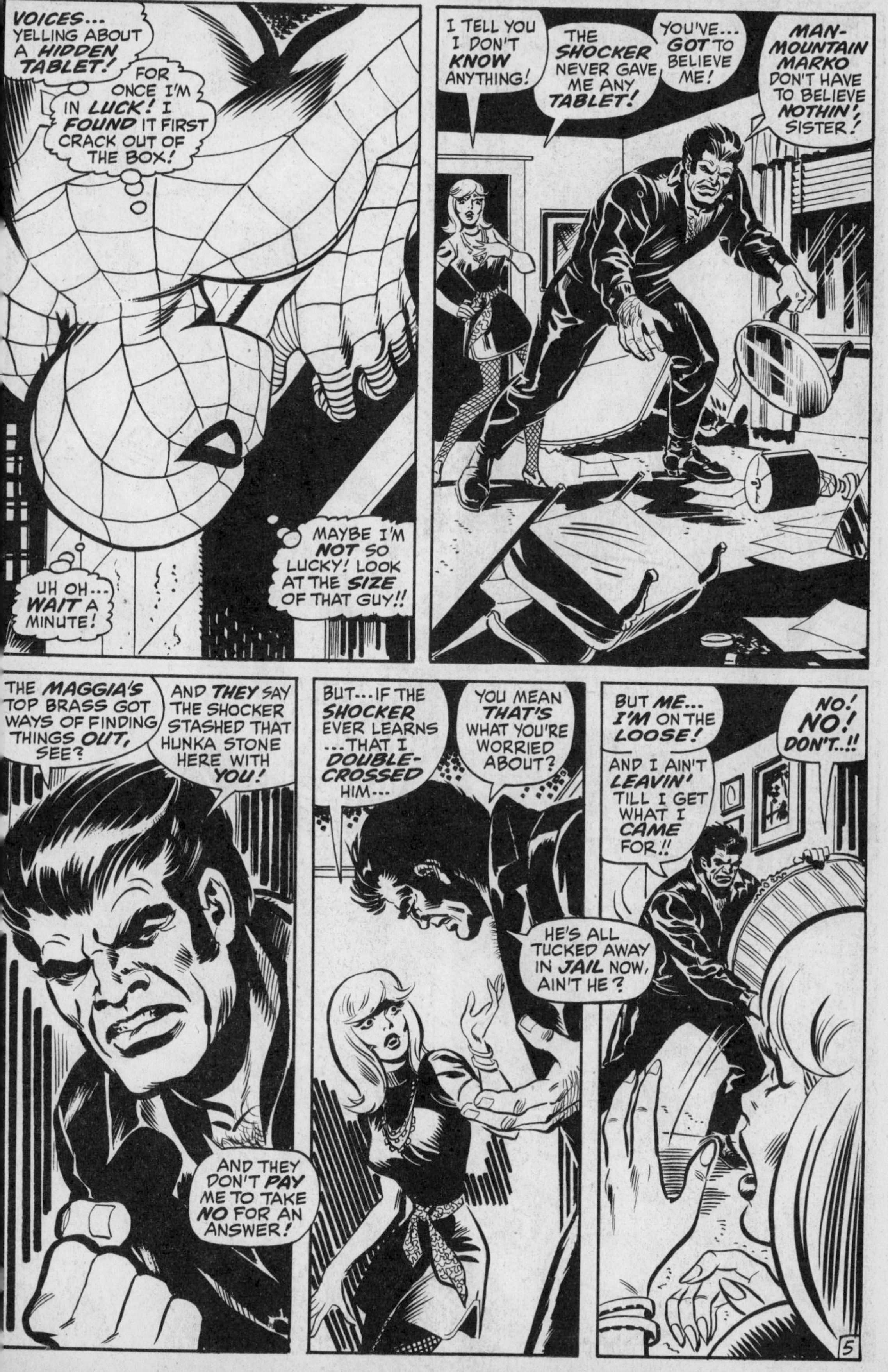
VOICES... YELLING ABOUT A HIDDEN TABLET!
FOR ONCE I'M IN LUCK! I FOUND IT FIRST CRACK OUT OF THE BOX!
UH OH... WAIT A MINUTE!
MAYBE I'M NOT SO LUCKY! LOOK AT THE SIZE OF THAT GUY!!
I TELL YOU I DON'T KNOW ANYTHING!
THE SHOCKER NEVER GAVE ME ANY TABLET!
YOU'VE... GOT TO BELIEVE ME!
MAN-MOUNTAIN MARKO DON'T HAVE TO BELIEVE NOTHIN', SISTER!
THE MAGGIA'S TOP BRASS GOT WAYS OF FINDING THINGS OUT, SEE?
AND THEY SAY THE SHOCKER STASHED THAT HUNKA STONE HERE WITH YOU!
AND THEY DON'T PAY ME TO TAKE NO FOR AN ANSWER!
BUT... IF THE SHOCKER EVER LEARNS ...THAT I DOUBLE-CROSSED HIM...
YOU MEAN THAT'S WHAT YOU'RE WORRIED ABOUT?
HE'S ALL TUCKED AWAY IN JAIL NOW, AIN'T HE?
BUT ME... I'M ON THE LOOSE!
AND I AIN'T LEAVIN' TILL I GET WHAT I CAME FOR!!
NO! NO! DON'T..!!
5

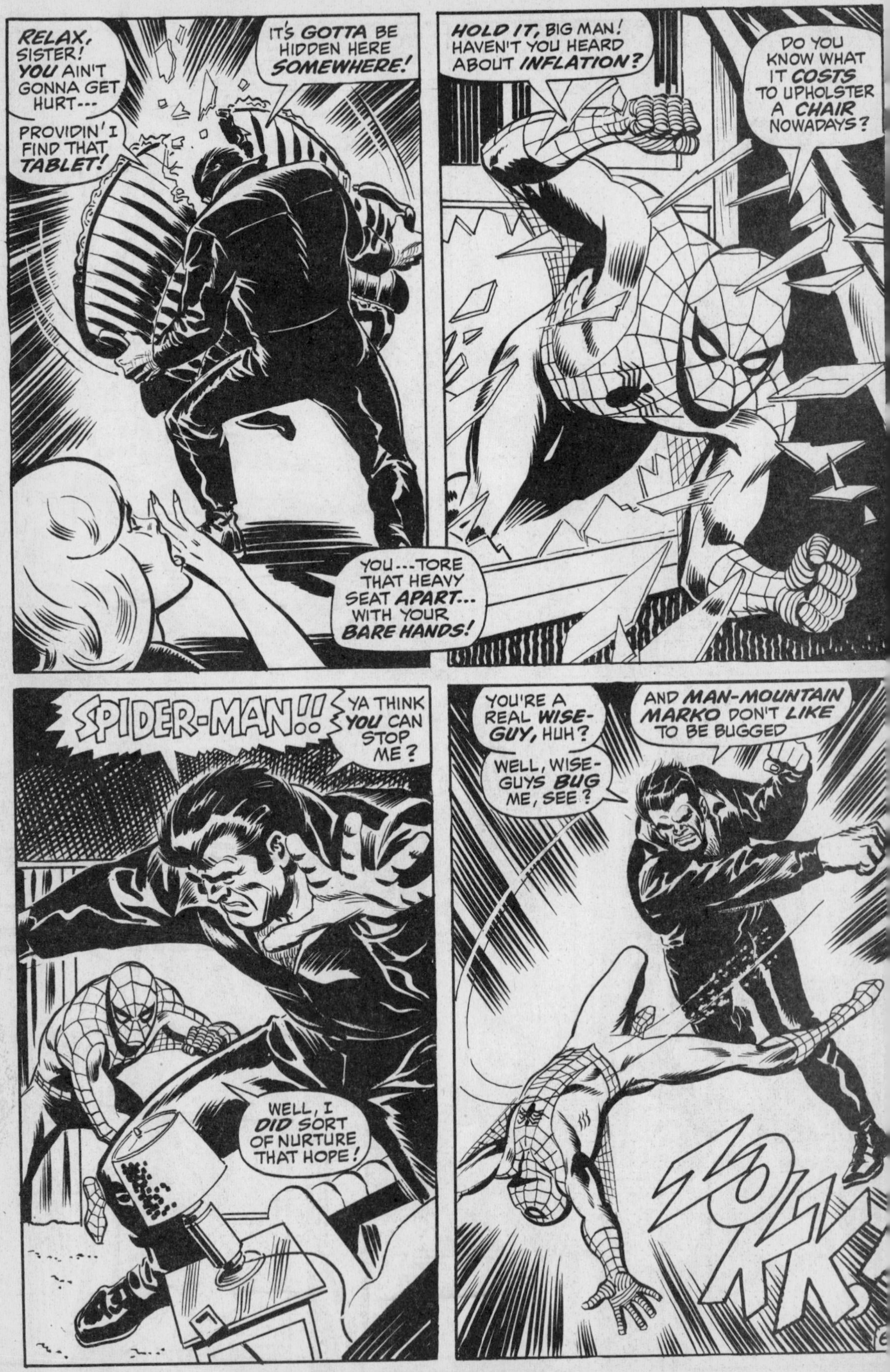

RELAX, SISTER! YOU AIN'T GONNA GET HURT---
PROVIDIN' I FIND THAT TABLET!
IT'S GOTTA BE HIDDEN HERE SOMEWHERE!
YOU---TORE THAT HEAVY SEAT APART... WITH YOUR BARE HANDS!
HOLD IT, BIG MAN! HAVEN'T YOU HEARD ABOUT INFLATION?
DO YOU KNOW WHAT IT COSTS TO UPHOLSTER A CHAIR NOWADAYS?
SPIDER-MAN!!
YA THINK YOU CAN STOP ME?
WELL, I DID SORT OF NURTURE THAT HOPE!
YOU'RE A REAL WISE-GUY, HUH?
WELL, WISE-GUYS BUG ME, SEE?
AND MAN-MOUNTAIN MARKO DON'T LIKE TO BE BUGGED

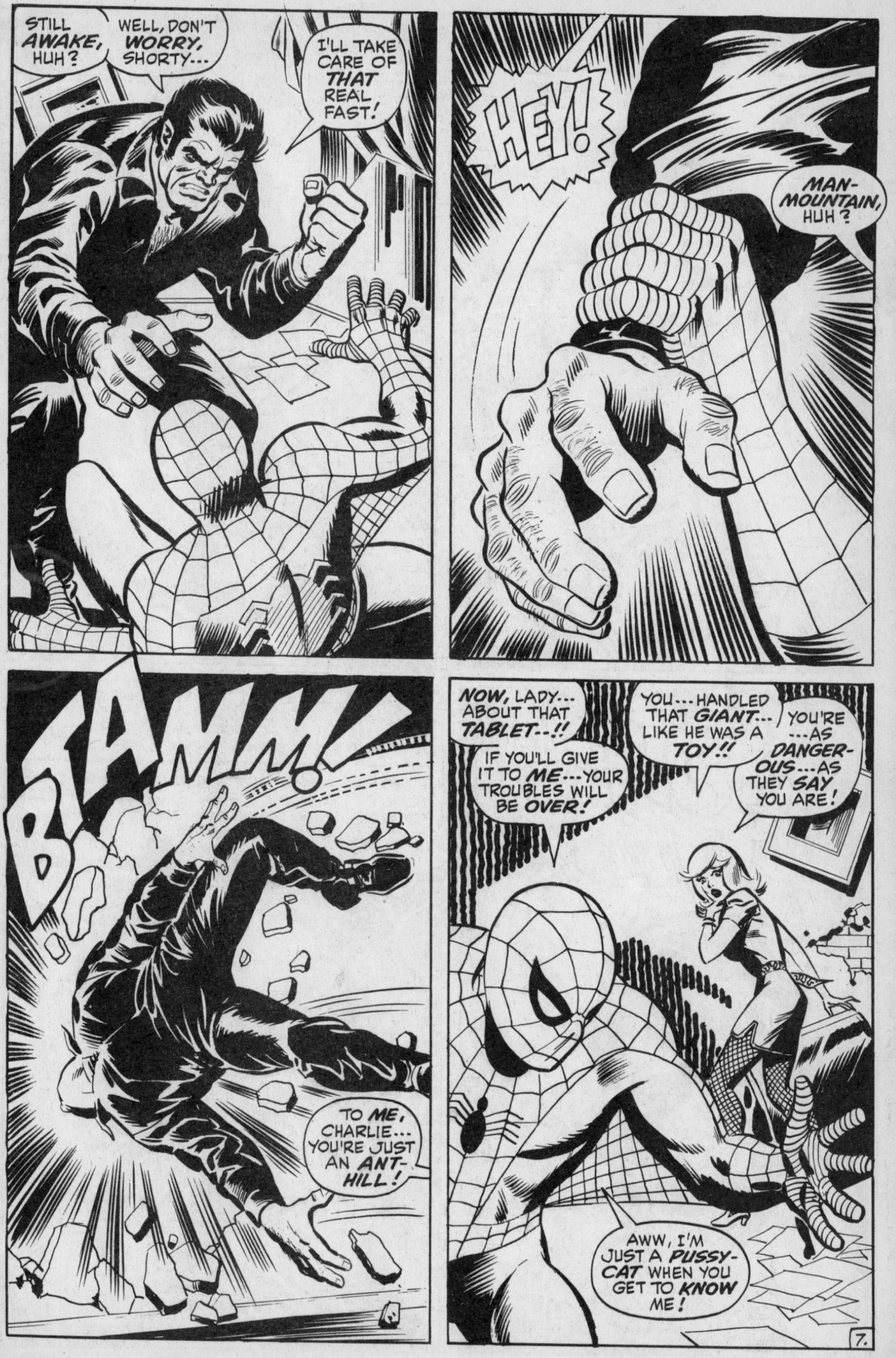
STILL AWAKE, HUH?
WELL, DON'T WORRY, SHORTY...
I'LL TAKE CARE OF THAT REAL FAST!
HEY!
MAN-MOUNTAIN, HUH?
BLAMM!
TO ME, CHARLIE... YOU'RE JUST AN ANT-HILL!
NOW, LADY... ABOUT THAT TABLET--!!
IF YOU'LL GIVE IT TO ME---YOUR TROUBLES WILL BE OVER!
YOU---HANDLED THAT GIANT... LIKE HE WAS A TOY!!
YOU'RE ---AS DANGER-OUS...AS THEY SAY YOU ARE!
AWW, I'M JUST A PUSSY-CAT WHEN YOU GET TO KNOW ME!
7.

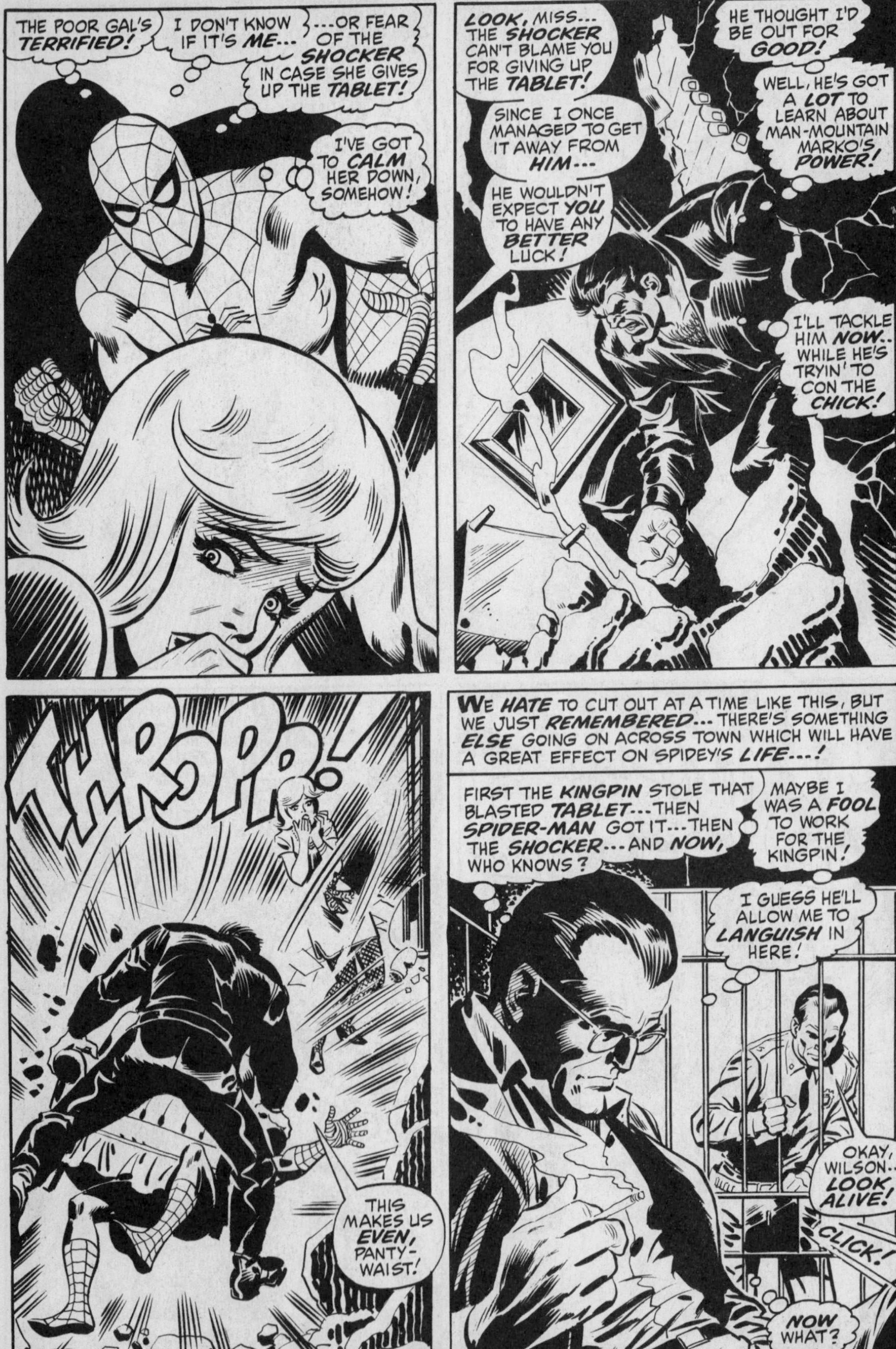
THE POOR GAL'S TERRIFIED!
I DON'T KNOW IF IT'S ME...
...OR FEAR OF THE SHOCKER IN CASE SHE GIVES UP THE TABLET!
I'VE GOT TO CALM HER DOWN, SOMEHOW!
LOOK, MISS... THE SHOCKER CAN'T BLAME YOU FOR GIVING UP THE TABLET!
SINCE I ONCE MANAGED TO GET IT AWAY FROM HIM---
HE WOULDN'T EXPECT YOU TO HAVE ANY BETTER LUCK!
HE THOUGHT I'D BE OUT FOR GOOD!
WELL, HE'S GOT A LOT TO LEARN ABOUT MAN-MOUNTAIN MARKO'S POWER!
I'LL TACKLE HIM NOW.. WHILE HE'S TRYIN' TO CON THE CHICK!
THROPP!
THIS MAKES US EVEN, PANTY-WAIST!
WE HATE TO CUT OUT AT A TIME LIKE THIS, BUT WE JUST REMEMBERED... THERE'S SOMETHING ELSE GOING ON ACROSS TOWN WHICH WILL HAVE A GREAT EFFECT ON SPIDEY'S LIFE---!
FIRST THE KINGPIN STOLE THAT BLASTED TABLET---THEN SPIDER-MAN GOT IT---THEN THE SHOCKER---AND NOW, WHO KNOWS?
MAYBE I WAS A FOOL TO WORK FOR THE KINGPIN!
I GUESS HE'LL ALLOW ME TO LANGUISH IN HERE!
OKAY, WILSON-- LOOK ALIVE!
CLICK!
NOW WHAT?
8

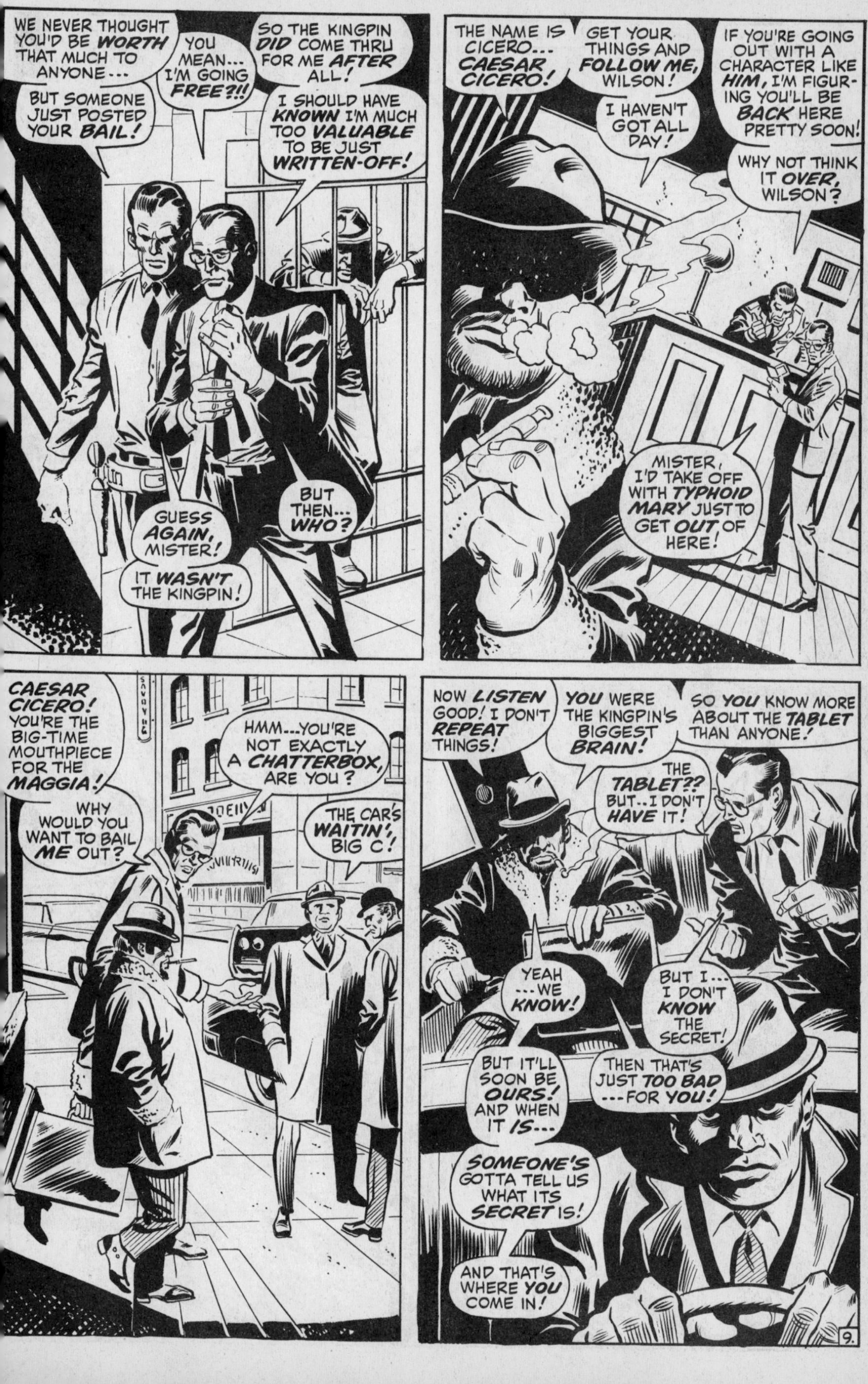
WE NEVER THOUGHT YOU'D BE WORTH THAT MUCH TO ANYONE---
BUT SOMEONE JUST POSTED YOUR BAIL!
YOU MEAN... I'M GOING FREE?!!
SO THE KINGPIN DID COME THRU FOR ME AFTER ALL!
I SHOULD HAVE KNOWN I'M MUCH TOO VALUABLE TO BE JUST WRITTEN-OFF!
GUESS AGAIN, MISTER!
IT WASN'T THE KINGPIN!
BUT THEN... WHO?
THE NAME IS CICERO... CAESAR CICERO!
GET YOUR THINGS AND FOLLOW ME, WILSON!
I HAVEN'T GOT ALL DAY!
IF YOU'RE GOING OUT WITH A CHARACTER LIKE HIM, I'M FIGURING YOU'LL BE BACK HERE PRETTY SOON!
WHY NOT THINK IT OVER, WILSON?
MISTER, I'D TAKE OFF WITH TYPHOID MARY JUST TO GET OUT OF HERE!
CAESAR CICERO! YOU'RE THE BIG-TIME MOUTHPIECE FOR THE MAGGIA!
WHY WOULD YOU WANT TO BAIL ME OUT?
HMM...YOU'RE NOT EXACTLY A CHATTERBOX, ARE YOU?
THE CAR'S WAITIN', BIG C!
NOW LISTEN GOOD! I DON'T REPEAT THINGS!
YOU WERE THE KINGPIN'S BIGGEST BRAIN!
SO YOU KNOW MORE ABOUT THE TABLET THAN ANYONE!
THE TABLET?? BUT..I DON'T HAVE IT!
YEAH ---WE KNOW!
BUT I... I DON'T KNOW THE SECRET!
BUT IT'LL SOON BE OURS! AND WHEN IT IS---
THEN THAT'S JUST TOO BAD ---FOR YOU!
SOMEONE'S GOTTA TELL US WHAT ITS SECRET IS!
AND THAT'S WHERE YOU COME IN!

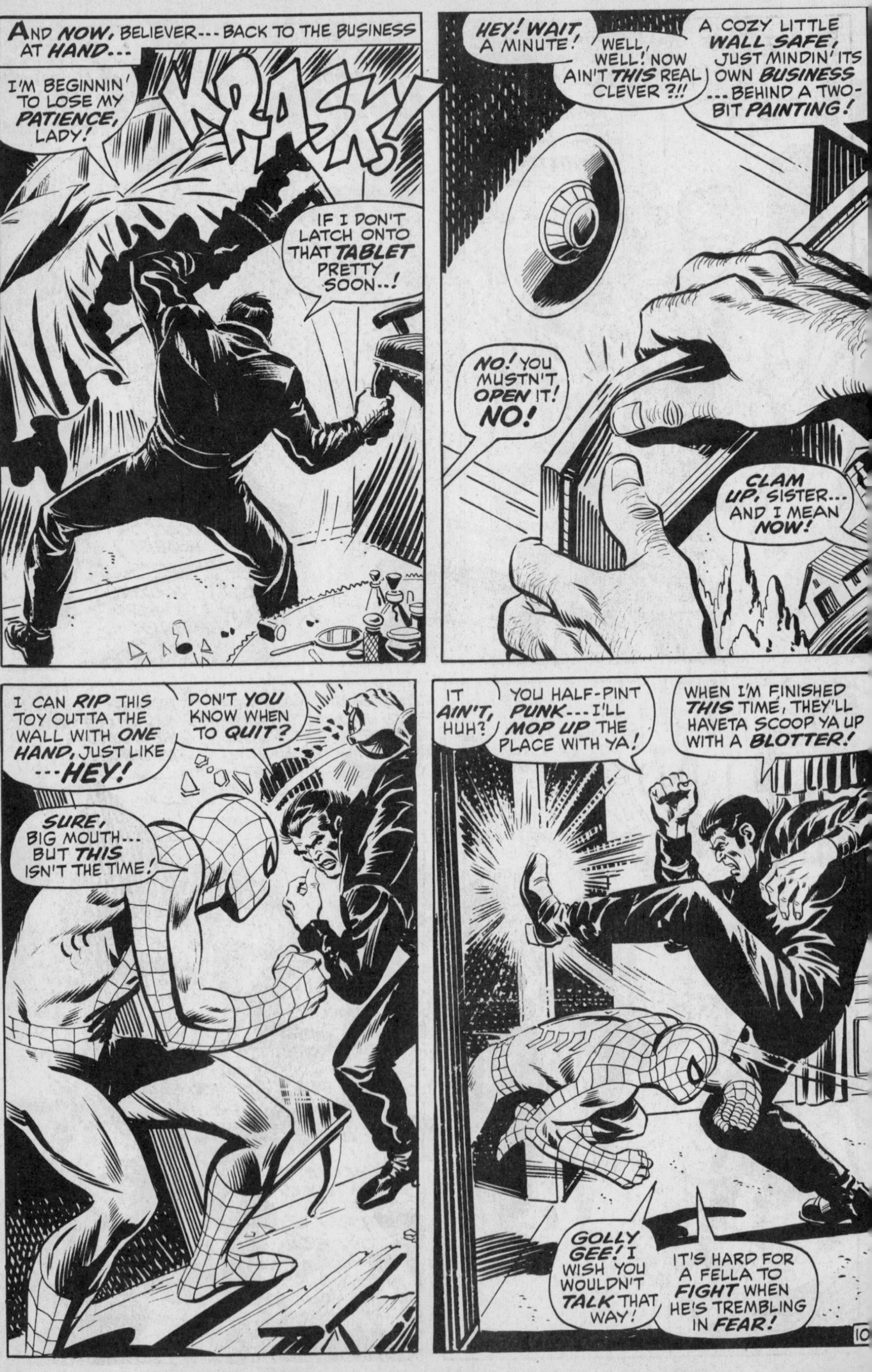
AND NOW, BELIEVER--- BACK TO THE BUSINESS AT HAND...
I'M BEGINNIN' TO LOSE MY PATIENCE, LADY!
KRASK!
IF I DON'T LATCH ONTO THAT TABLET PRETTY SOON..!
HEY! WAIT, A MINUTE!
WELL, WELL! NOW AIN'T THIS REAL CLEVER ?!!
A COZY LITTLE WALL SAFE, JUST MINDIN' ITS OWN BUSINESS ...BEHIND A TWO-BIT PAINTING!
NO! YOU MUSTN'T OPEN IT! NO!
CLAM UP, SISTER... AND I MEAN NOW!
I CAN RIP THIS TOY OUTTA THE WALL WITH ONE HAND, JUST LIKE ---HEY!
DON'T YOU KNOW WHEN TO QUIT?
SURE, BIG MOUTH... BUT THIS ISN'T THE TIME!
IT AIN'T, HUH?
YOU HALF-PINT PUNK---I'LL MOP UP THE PLACE WITH YA!
WHEN I'M FINISHED THIS TIME, THEY'LL HAVETA SCOOP YA UP WITH A BLOTTER!
GOLLY GEE! I WISH YOU WOULDN'T TALK THAT WAY!
IT'S HARD FOR A FELLA TO FIGHT WHEN HE'S TREMBLING IN FEAR!
10

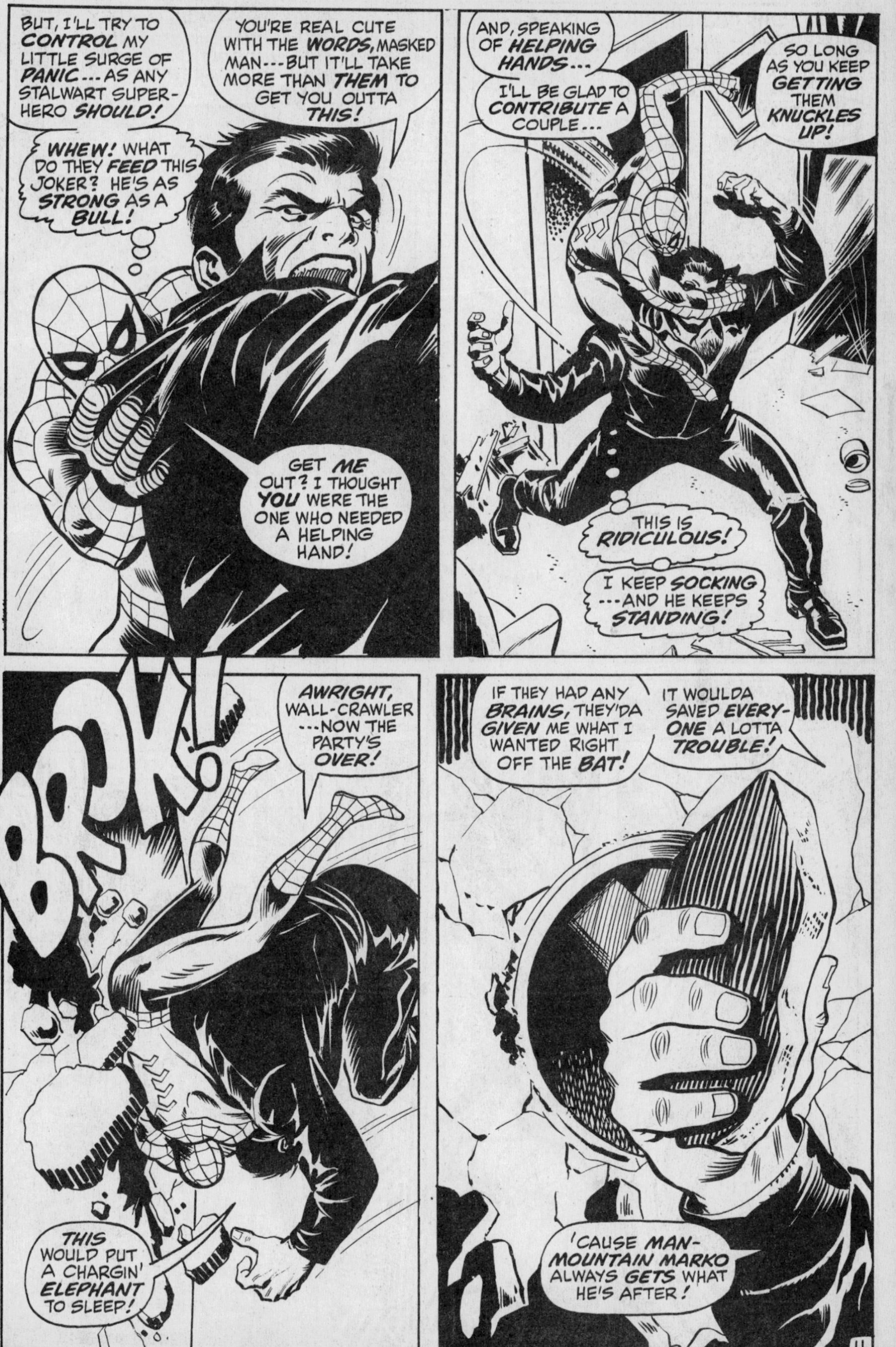
BUT, I'LL TRY TO CONTROL MY LITTLE SURGE OF PANIC... AS ANY STALWART SUPER-HERO SHOULD!
YOU'RE REAL CUTE WITH THE WORDS, MASKED MAN---BUT IT'LL TAKE MORE THAN THEM TO GET YOU OUTTA THIS!
WHEW! WHAT DO THEY FEED THIS JOKER? HE'S AS STRONG AS A BULL!
GET ME OUT? I THOUGHT YOU WERE THE ONE WHO NEEDED A HELPING HAND!
AND, SPEAKING OF HELPING HANDS...
I'LL BE GLAD TO CONTRIBUTE A COUPLE...
SO LONG AS YOU KEEP GETTING THEM KNUCKLES UP!
THIS IS RIDICULOUS!
I KEEP SOCKING ---AND HE KEEPS STANDING!
BROK!
AWRIGHT, WALL-CRAWLER ---NOW THE PARTY'S OVER!
THIS WOULD PUT A CHARGIN' ELEPHANT TO SLEEP!
IF THEY HAD ANY BRAINS, THEY'DA GIVEN ME WHAT I WANTED RIGHT OFF THE BAT!
IT WOULDA SAVED EVERY-ONE A LOTTA TROUBLE!
'CAUSE MAN-MOUNTAIN MARKO ALWAYS GETS WHAT HE'S AFTER!

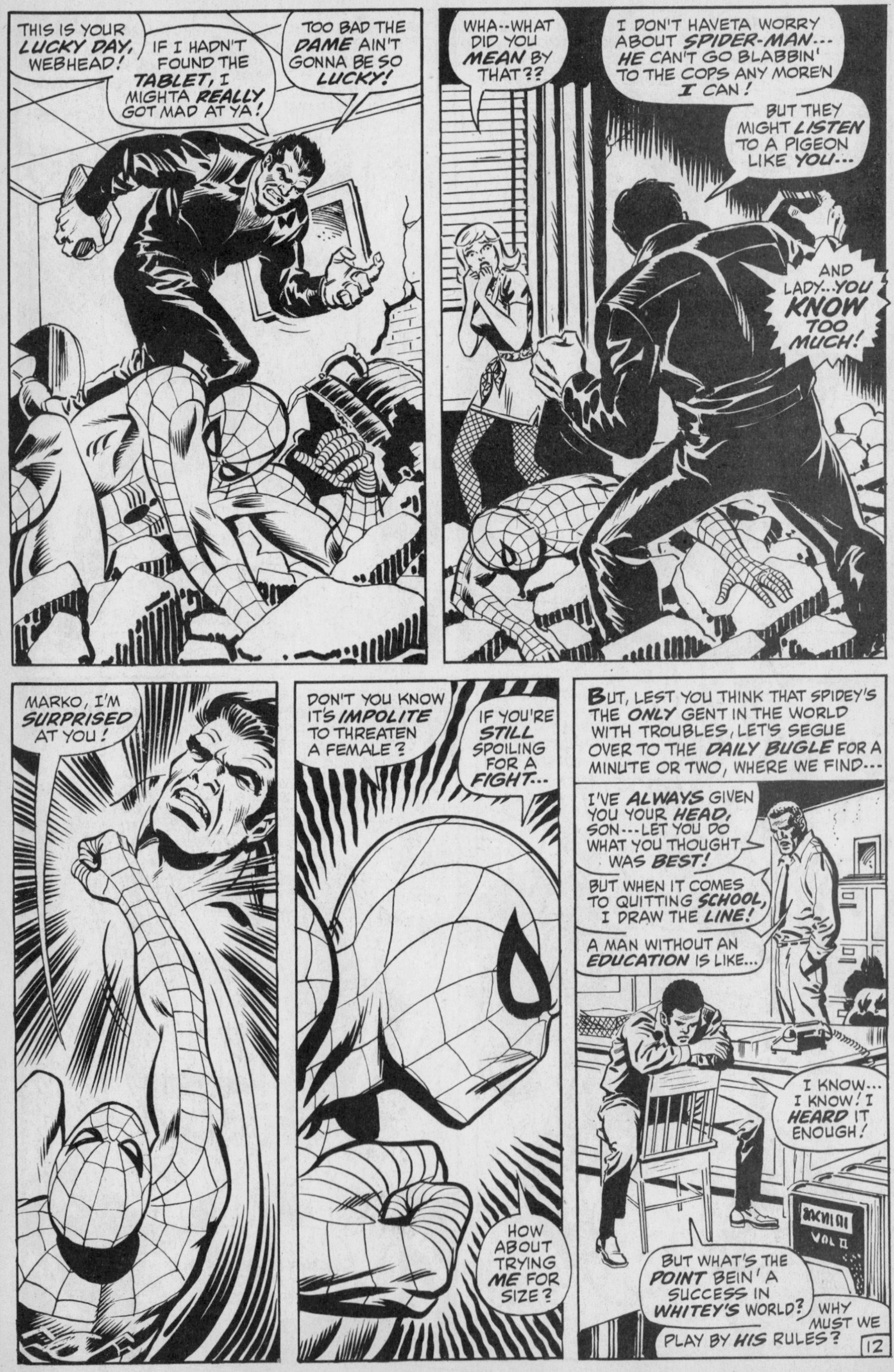
THIS IS YOUR LUCKY DAY, WEBHEAD!
IF I HADN'T FOUND THE TABLET, I MIGHTA REALLY GOT MAD AT YA!
TOO BAD THE DAME AIN'T GONNA BE SO LUCKY!
WHA--WHAT DID YOU MEAN BY THAT??
I DON'T HAVETA WORRY ABOUT SPIDER-MAN... HE CAN'T GO BLABBIN' TO THE COPS ANY MORE'N I CAN!
BUT THEY MIGHT LISTEN TO A PIGEON LIKE YOU...
AND LADY...YOU KNOW TOO MUCH!
MARKO, I'M SURPRISED AT YOU!
DON'T YOU KNOW IT'S IMPOLITE TO THREATEN A FEMALE?
IF YOU'RE STILL SPOILING FOR A FIGHT...
HOW ABOUT TRYING ME FOR SIZE?
BUT, LEST YOU THINK THAT SPIDEY'S THE ONLY GENT IN THE WORLD WITH TROUBLES, LET'S SEGUE OVER TO THE DAILY BUGLE FOR A MINUTE OR TWO, WHERE WE FIND---
I'VE ALWAYS GIVEN YOU YOUR HEAD, SON---LET YOU DO WHAT YOU THOUGHT WAS BEST!
BUT WHEN IT COMES TO QUITTING SCHOOL, I DRAW THE LINE!
A MAN WITHOUT AN EDUCATION IS LIKE...
I KNOW... I KNOW! I HEARD IT ENOUGH!
BUT WHAT'S THE POINT BEIN' A SUCCESS IN WHITEY'S WORLD?
WHY MUST WE PLAY BY HIS RULES?

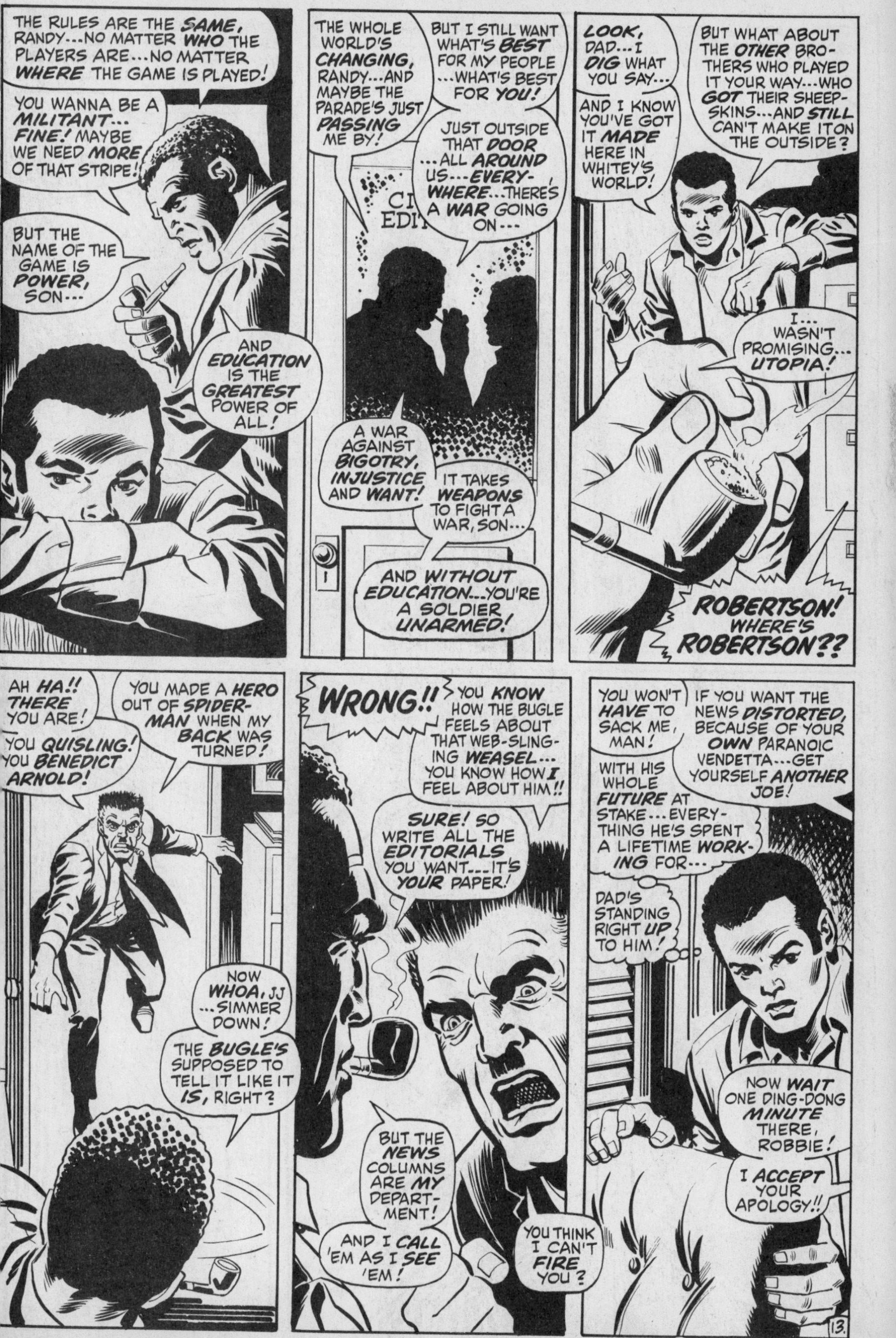

THE RULES ARE THE SAME, RANDY...NO MATTER WHO THE PLAYERS ARE...NO MATTER WHERE THE GAME IS PLAYED!
YOU WANNA BE A MILITANT... FINE! MAYBE WE NEED MORE OF THAT STRIPE!
BUT THE NAME OF THE GAME IS POWER, SON...
AND EDUCATION IS THE GREATEST POWER OF ALL!
THE WHOLE WORLD'S CHANGING, RANDY...AND MAYBE THE PARADE'S JUST PASSING ME BY!
BUT I STILL WANT WHAT'S BEST FOR MY PEOPLE ...WHAT'S BEST FOR YOU!
JUST OUTSIDE THAT DOOR ...ALL AROUND US...EVERY-WHERE...THERE'S A WAR GOING ON...
A WAR AGAINST BIGOTRY, INJUSTICE AND WANT!
IT TAKES WEAPONS TO FIGHT A WAR, SON...
AND WITHOUT EDUCATION...YOU'RE A SOLDIER UNARMED!
LOOK, DAD...I DIG WHAT YOU SAY...
AND I KNOW YOU'VE GOT IT MADE HERE IN WHITEY'S WORLD!
BUT WHAT ABOUT THE OTHER BRO-THERS WHO PLAYED IT YOUR WAY...WHO GOT THEIR SHEEP-SKINS...AND STILL CAN'T MAKE IT ON THE OUTSIDE?
I... WASN'T PROMISING... UTOPIA!
ROBERTSON! WHERE'S ROBERTSON??
AH HA!! THERE YOU ARE!
YOU QUISLING! YOU BENEDICT ARNOLD!
YOU MADE A HERO OUT OF SPIDER-MAN WHEN MY BACK WAS TURNED!
NOW WHOA, JJ ...SIMMER DOWN!
THE BUGLE'S SUPPOSED TO TELL IT LIKE IT IS, RIGHT?
WRONG!!
YOU KNOW HOW THE BUGLE FEELS ABOUT THAT WEB-SLING-ING WEASEL... YOU KNOW HOW I FEEL ABOUT HIM!!
SURE! SO WRITE ALL THE EDITORIALS YOU WANT...IT'S YOUR PAPER!
BUT THE NEWS COLUMNS ARE MY DEPART-MENT!
AND I CALL 'EM AS I SEE 'EM!
YOU THINK I CAN'T FIRE YOU?
YOU WON'T HAVE TO SACK ME, MAN!
IF YOU WANT THE NEWS DISTORTED, BECAUSE OF YOUR OWN PARANOIC VENDETTA...GET YOURSELF ANOTHER JOE!
WITH HIS WHOLE FUTURE AT STAKE...EVERY-THING HE'S SPENT A LIFETIME WORK-ING FOR...
DAD'S STANDING RIGHT UP TO HIM!
NOW WAIT ONE DING-DONG MINUTE THERE, ROBBIE!
I ACCEPT YOUR APOLOGY!!
13.

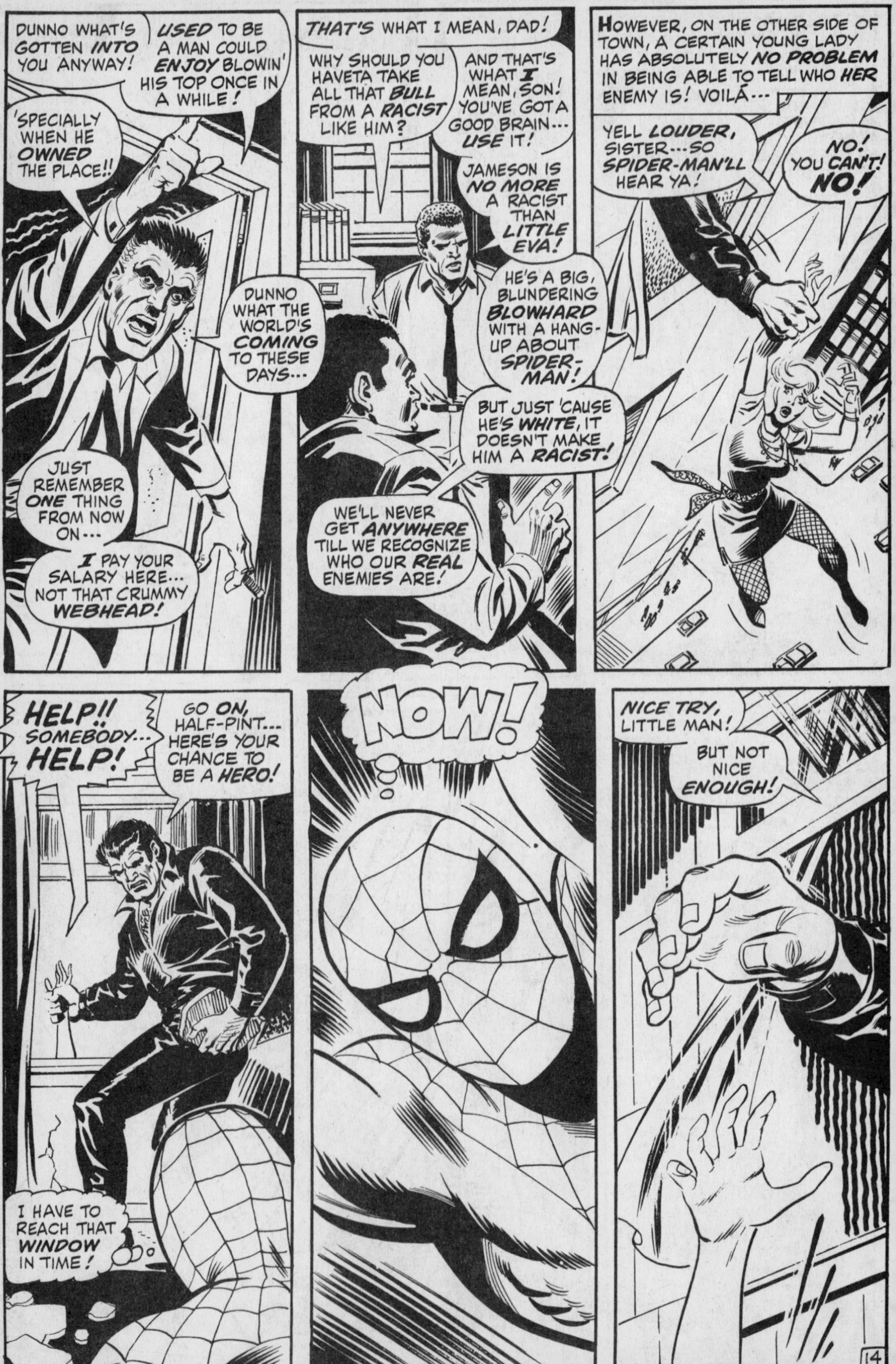
DUNNO WHAT'S GOTTEN INTO YOU ANYWAY!
USED TO BE A MAN COULD ENJOY BLOWIN' HIS TOP ONCE IN A WHILE!
'SPECIALLY WHEN HE OWNED THE PLACE!!
DUNNO WHAT THE WORLD'S COMING TO THESE DAYS...
JUST REMEMBER ONE THING FROM NOW ON...
I PAY YOUR SALARY HERE... NOT THAT CRUMMY WEBHEAD!
THAT'S WHAT I MEAN, DAD!
WHY SHOULD YOU HAVETA TAKE ALL THAT BULL FROM A RACIST LIKE HIM?
AND THAT'S WHAT I MEAN, SON! YOU'VE GOT A GOOD BRAIN... USE IT!
JAMESON IS NO MORE A RACIST THAN LITTLE EVA!
HE'S A BIG, BLUNDERING BLOWHARD WITH A HANG-UP ABOUT SPIDER-MAN!
BUT JUST 'CAUSE HE'S WHITE, IT DOESN'T MAKE HIM A RACIST!
WE'LL NEVER GET ANYWHERE TILL WE RECOGNIZE WHO OUR REAL ENEMIES ARE!
HOWEVER, ON THE OTHER SIDE OF TOWN, A CERTAIN YOUNG LADY HAS ABSOLUTELY NO PROBLEM IN BEING ABLE TO TELL WHO HER ENEMY IS! VOILÁ...
YELL LOUDER, SISTER... SO SPIDER-MAN'LL HEAR YA!
NO! YOU CAN'T! NO!
HELP!! SOMEBODY... HELP!
GO ON, HALF-PINT... HERE'S YOUR CHANCE TO BE A HERO!
I HAVE TO REACH THAT WINDOW IN TIME!
NOW!
NICE TRY, LITTLE MAN!
BUT NOT NICE ENOUGH!
14

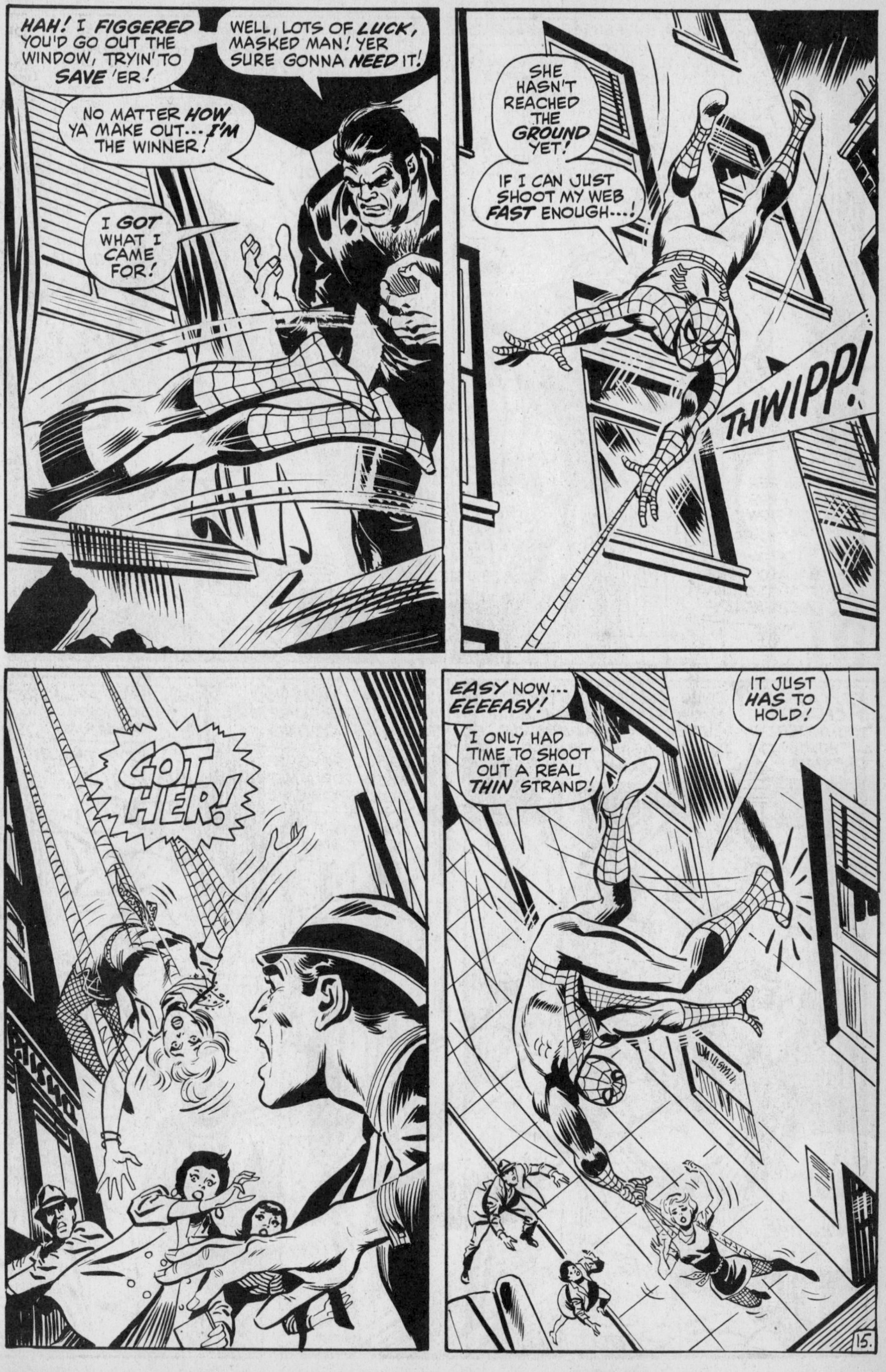
HAH! I FIGGERED YOU'D GO OUT THE WINDOW, TRYIN' TO SAVE 'ER!
WELL, LOTS OF LUCK, MASKED MAN! YER SURE GONNA NEED IT!
NO MATTER HOW YA MAKE OUT... I'M THE WINNER!
I GOT WHAT I CAME FOR!
SHE HASN'T REACHED THE GROUND YET!
IF I CAN JUST SHOOT MY WEB FAST ENOUGH...!
THWIPP!
GOT HER!
EASY NOW... EEEEASY!
I ONLY HAD TIME TO SHOOT OUT A REAL THIN STRAND!
IT JUST HAS TO HOLD!
15.

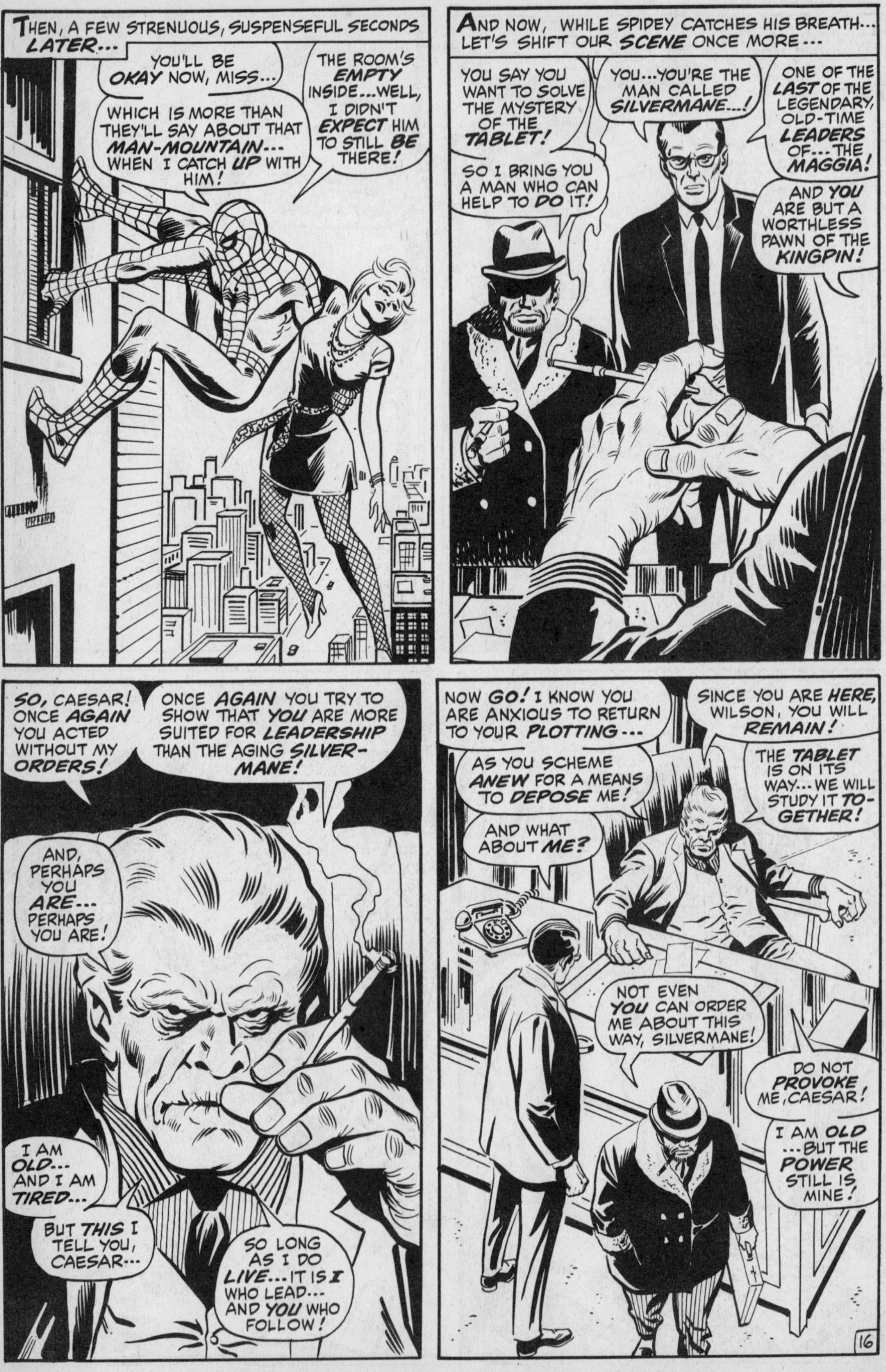
THEN, A FEW STRENUOUS, SUSPENSEFUL SECONDS LATER...
YOU'LL BE OKAY NOW, MISS...
WHICH IS MORE THAN THEY'LL SAY ABOUT THAT MAN-MOUNTAIN... WHEN I CATCH UP WITH HIM!
THE ROOM'S EMPTY INSIDE... WELL, I DIDN'T EXPECT HIM TO STILL BE THERE!
AND NOW, WHILE SPIDEY CATCHES HIS BREATH... LET'S SHIFT OUR SCENE ONCE MORE...
YOU SAY YOU WANT TO SOLVE THE MYSTERY OF THE TABLET!
SO I BRING YOU A MAN WHO CAN HELP TO DO IT!
YOU...YOU'RE THE MAN CALLED SILVERMANE...!
ONE OF THE LAST OF THE LEGENDARY, OLD-TIME LEADERS OF... THE MAGGIA!
AND YOU ARE BUT A WORTHLESS PAWN OF THE KINGPIN!
SO, CAESAR! ONCE AGAIN YOU ACTED WITHOUT MY ORDERS!
ONCE AGAIN YOU TRY TO SHOW THAT YOU ARE MORE SUITED FOR LEADERSHIP THAN THE AGING SILVER-MANE!
AND, PERHAPS YOU ARE... PERHAPS YOU ARE!
I AM OLD... AND I AM TIRED...
BUT THIS I TELL YOU, CAESAR...
SO LONG AS I DO LIVE... IT IS I WHO LEAD... AND YOU WHO FOLLOW!
NOW GO! I KNOW YOU ARE ANXIOUS TO RETURN TO YOUR PLOTTING...
AS YOU SCHEME ANEW FOR A MEANS TO DEPOSE ME!
SINCE YOU ARE HERE, WILSON, YOU WILL REMAIN!
THE TABLET IS ON ITS WAY... WE WILL STUDY IT TO-GETHER!
AND WHAT ABOUT ME?
NOT EVEN YOU CAN ORDER ME ABOUT THIS WAY, SILVERMANE!
DO NOT PROVOKE ME, CAESAR!
I AM OLD ...BUT THE POWER STILL IS MINE!
16

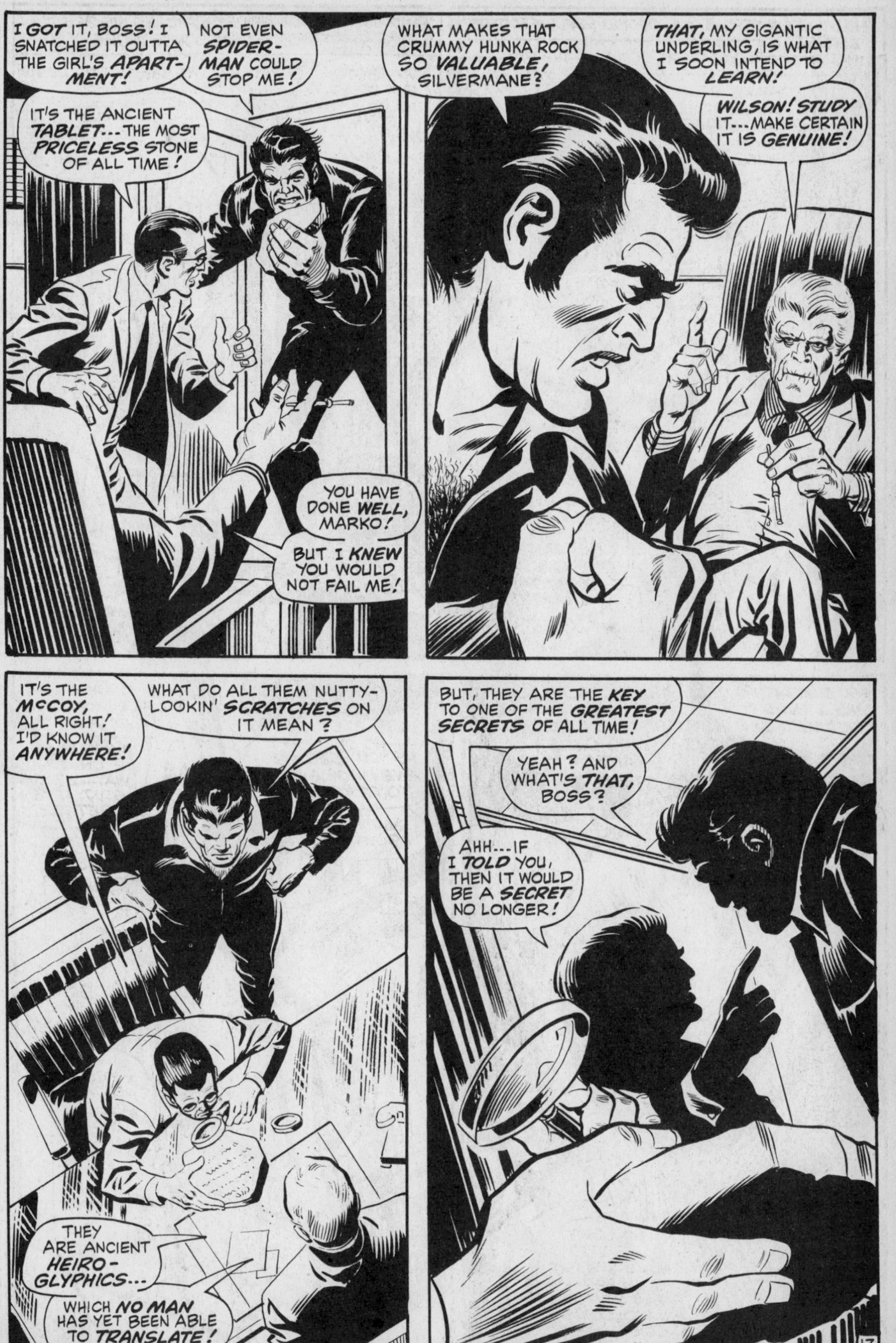
I GOT IT, BOSS! I SNATCHED IT OUTTA THE GIRL'S APARTMENT!
NOT EVEN SPIDER-MAN COULD STOP ME!
IT'S THE ANCIENT TABLET... THE MOST PRICELESS STONE OF ALL TIME!
YOU HAVE DONE WELL, MARKO!
BUT I KNEW YOU WOULD NOT FAIL ME!
WHAT MAKES THAT CRUMMY HUNKA ROCK SO VALUABLE, SILVERMANE?
THAT, MY GIGANTIC UNDERLING, IS WHAT I SOON INTEND TO LEARN!
WILSON! STUDY IT... MAKE CERTAIN IT IS GENUINE!
IT'S THE McCOY, ALL RIGHT! I'D KNOW IT ANYWHERE!
WHAT DO ALL THEM NUTTY-LOOKIN' SCRATCHES ON IT MEAN?
THEY ARE ANCIENT HEIRO-GLYPHICS...
WHICH NO MAN HAS YET BEEN ABLE TO TRANSLATE!
BUT, THEY ARE THE KEY TO ONE OF THE GREATEST SECRETS OF ALL TIME!
YEAH? AND WHAT'S THAT, BOSS?
AHH... IF I TOLD YOU, THEN IT WOULD BE A SECRET NO LONGER!
17.

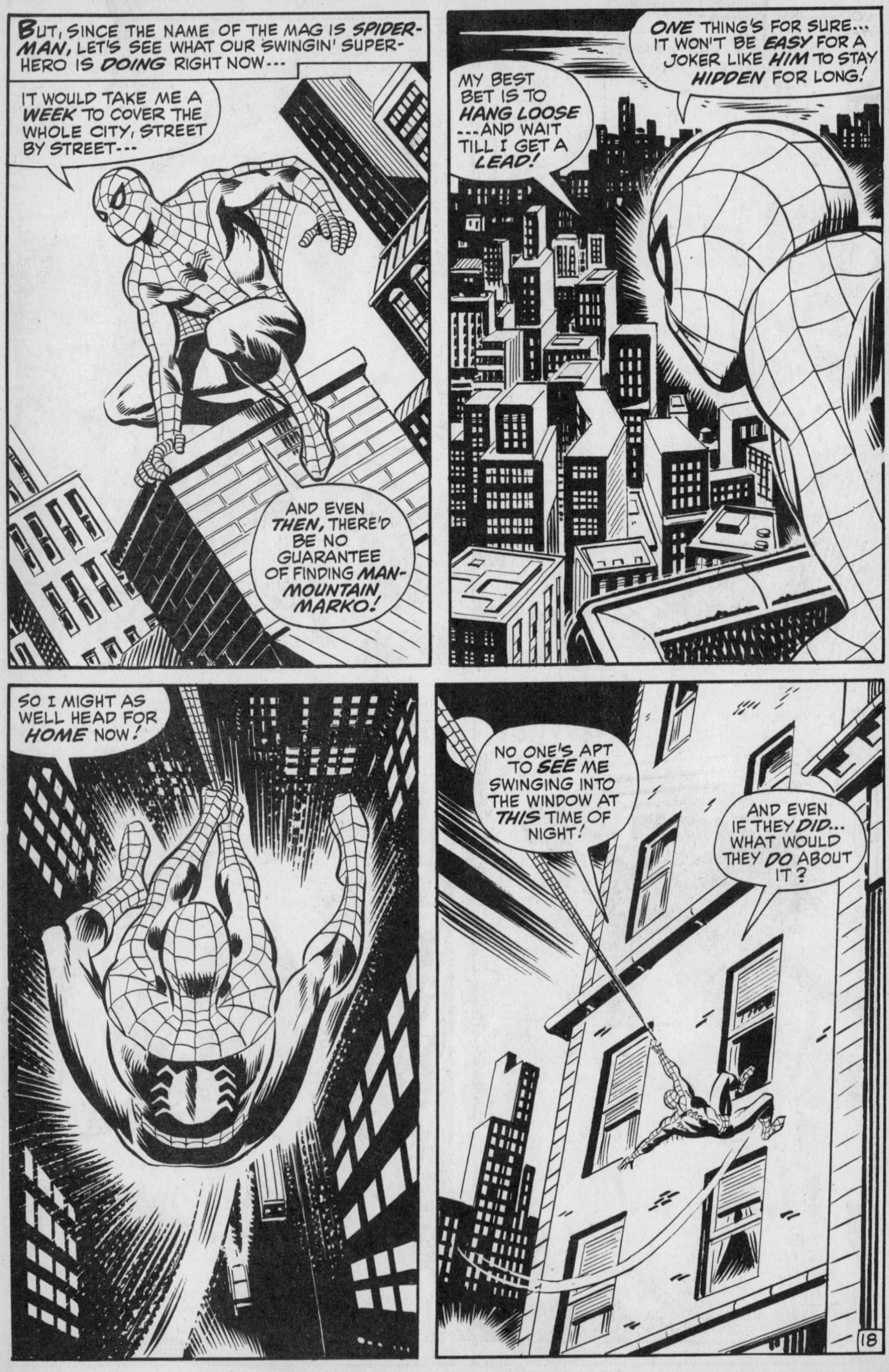
BUT, SINCE THE NAME OF THE MAG IS SPIDER-MAN, LET'S SEE WHAT OUR SWINGIN' SUPER-HERO IS DOING RIGHT NOW---
IT WOULD TAKE ME A WEEK TO COVER THE WHOLE CITY, STREET BY STREET---
AND EVEN THEN, THERE'D BE NO GUARANTEE OF FINDING MAN-MOUNTAIN MARKO!
MY BEST BET IS TO HANG LOOSE ---AND WAIT TILL I GET A LEAD!
ONE THING'S FOR SURE... IT WON'T BE EASY FOR A JOKER LIKE HIM TO STAY HIDDEN FOR LONG!
SO I MIGHT AS WELL HEAD FOR HOME NOW!
NO ONE'S APT TO SEE ME SWINGING INTO THE WINDOW AT THIS TIME OF NIGHT!
AND EVEN IF THEY DID... WHAT WOULD THEY DO ABOUT IT?
18

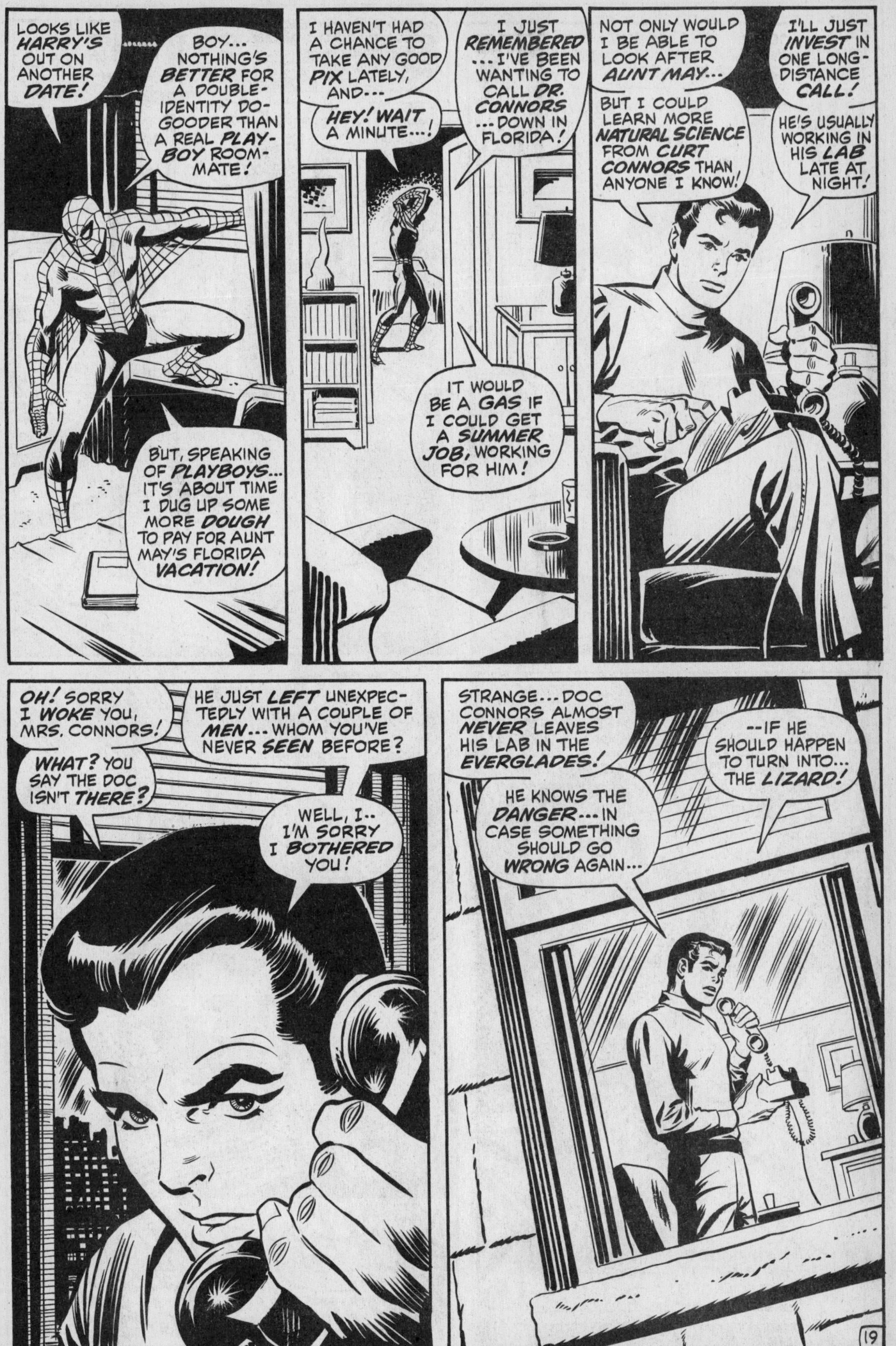

LOOKS LIKE HARRY'S OUT ON ANOTHER DATE!
BOY... NOTHING'S BETTER FOR A DOUBLE-IDENTITY DO-GOODER THAN A REAL PLAY-BOY ROOM-MATE!
BUT, SPEAKING OF PLAYBOYS... IT'S ABOUT TIME I DUG UP SOME MORE DOUGH TO PAY FOR AUNT MAY'S FLORIDA VACATION!
I HAVEN'T HAD A CHANCE TO TAKE ANY GOOD PIX LATELY, AND---
HEY! WAIT A MINUTE---!
I JUST REMEMBERED ---I'VE BEEN WANTING TO CALL DR. CONNORS ---DOWN IN FLORIDA!
IT WOULD BE A GAS IF I COULD GET A SUMMER JOB, WORKING FOR HIM!
NOT ONLY WOULD I BE ABLE TO LOOK AFTER AUNT MAY...
BUT I COULD LEARN MORE NATURAL SCIENCE FROM CURT CONNORS THAN ANYONE I KNOW!
I'LL JUST INVEST IN ONE LONG-DISTANCE CALL!
HE'S USUALLY WORKING IN HIS LAB LATE AT NIGHT!
OH! SORRY I WOKE YOU, MRS. CONNORS!
WHAT? YOU SAY THE DOC ISN'T THERE?
HE JUST LEFT UNEXPEC-TEDLY WITH A COUPLE OF MEN--- WHOM YOU'VE NEVER SEEN BEFORE?
WELL, I.. I'M SORRY I BOTHERED YOU!
STRANGE--- DOC CONNORS ALMOST NEVER LEAVES HIS LAB IN THE EVERGLADES!
HE KNOWS THE DANGER--- IN CASE SOMETHING SHOULD GO WRONG AGAIN...
--IF HE SHOULD HAPPEN TO TURN INTO... THE LIZARD!
19

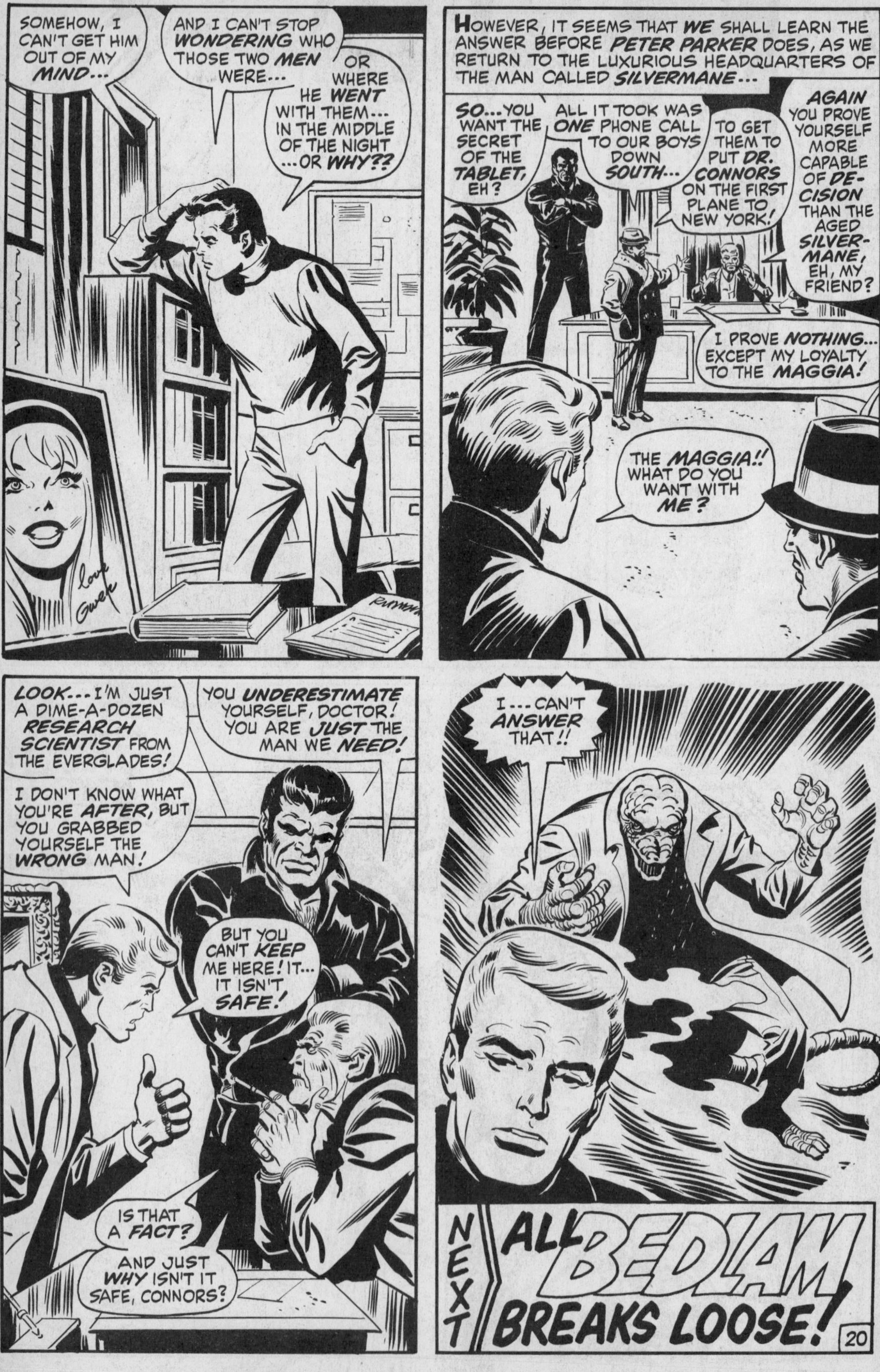

SOMEHOW, I CAN'T GET HIM OUT OF MY MIND...
AND I CAN'T STOP WONDERING WHO THOSE TWO MEN WERE...
OR WHERE HE WENT WITH THEM... IN THE MIDDLE OF THE NIGHT ...OR WHY??
Love Gwen
HOWEVER, IT SEEMS THAT WE SHALL LEARN THE ANSWER BEFORE PETER PARKER DOES, AS WE RETURN TO THE LUXURIOUS HEADQUARTERS OF THE MAN CALLED SILVERMANE...
SO...YOU WANT THE SECRET OF THE TABLET, EH?
ALL IT TOOK WAS ONE PHONE CALL TO OUR BOYS DOWN SOUTH...
TO GET THEM TO PUT DR. CONNORS ON THE FIRST PLANE TO NEW YORK!
AGAIN YOU PROVE YOURSELF MORE CAPABLE OF DECISION THAN THE AGED SILVERMANE, EH, MY FRIEND?
I PROVE NOTHING... EXCEPT MY LOYALTY TO THE MAGGIA!
THE MAGGIA!! WHAT DO YOU WANT WITH ME?
LOOK... I'M JUST A DIME-A-DOZEN RESEARCH SCIENTIST FROM THE EVERGLADES!
I DON'T KNOW WHAT YOU'RE AFTER, BUT YOU GRABBED YOURSELF THE WRONG MAN!
YOU UNDERESTIMATE YOURSELF, DOCTOR! YOU ARE JUST THE MAN WE NEED!
BUT YOU CAN'T KEEP ME HERE! IT... IT ISN'T SAFE!
IS THAT A FACT?
AND JUST WHY ISN'T IT SAFE, CONNORS?
I... CAN'T ANSWER THAT!!
NEXT
ALL BEDLAM BREAKS LOOSE!

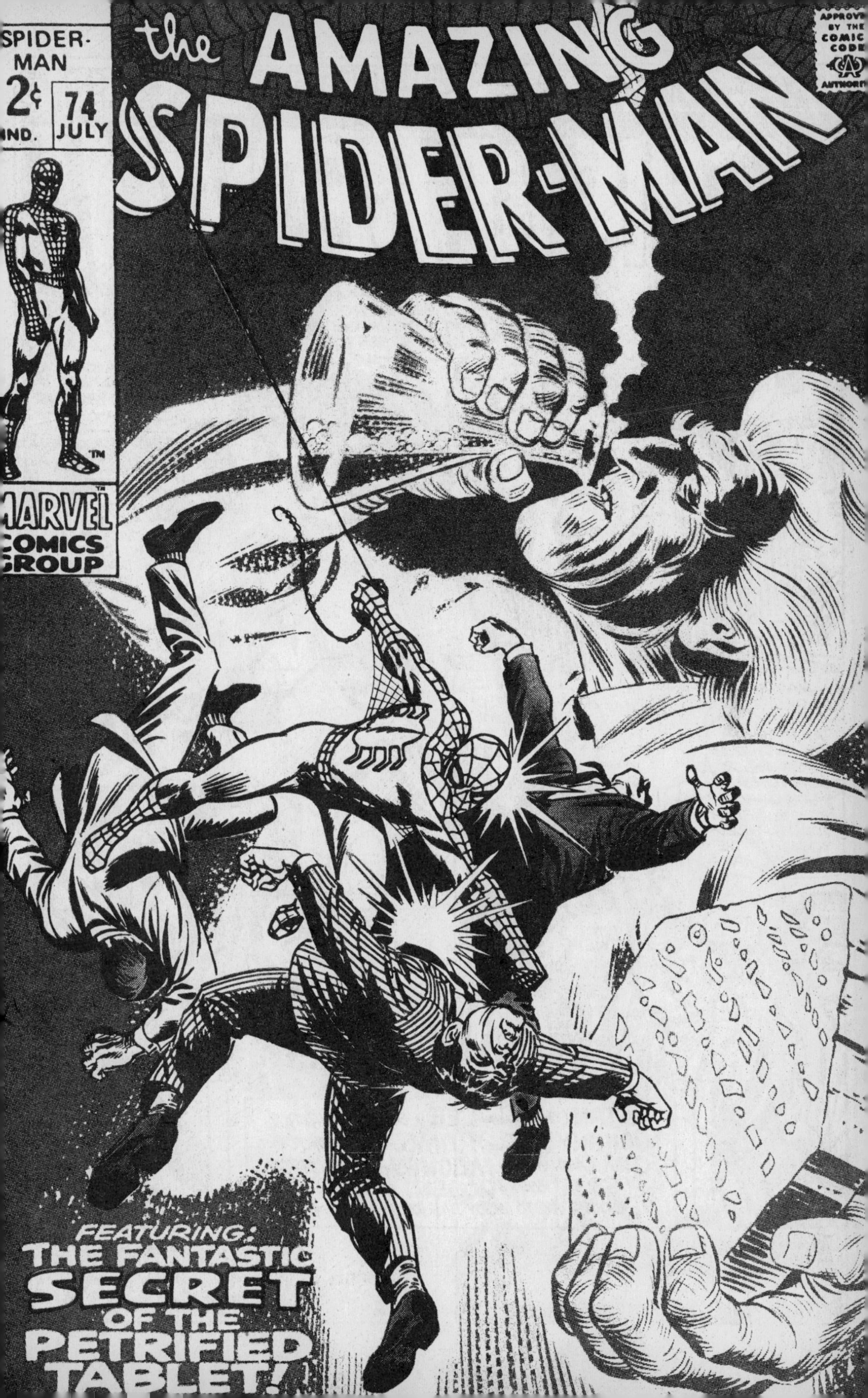

SPIDER-MAN
2¢
IND.
74
JULY
the AMAZING SPIDER-MAN
APPROVED BY THE COMICS CODE AUTHORITY
MARVEL COMICS GROUP
FEATURING:
THE FANTASTIC SECRET OF THE PETRIFIED TABLET!

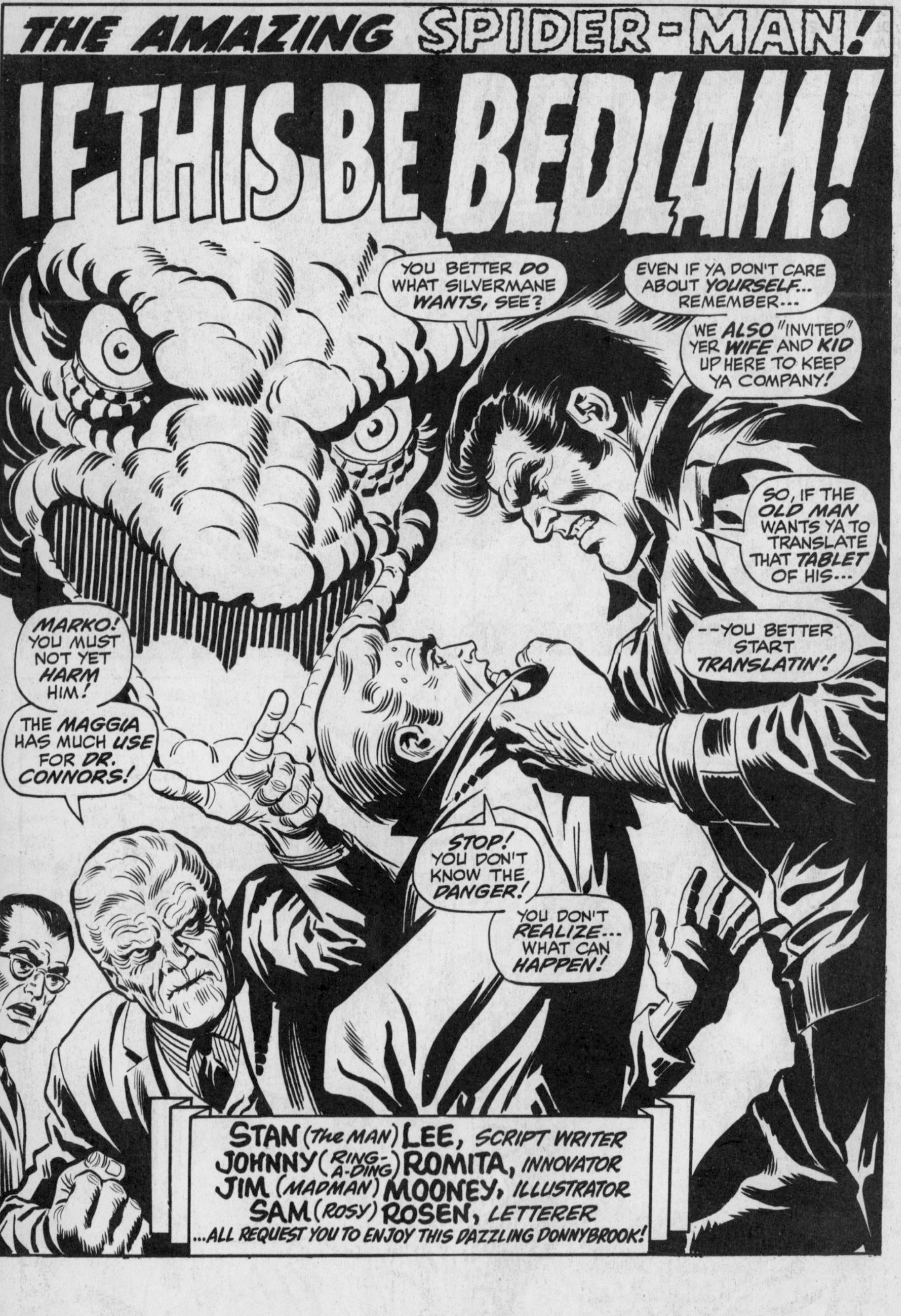
THE AMAZING SPIDER-MAN!
IF THIS BE BEDLAM!
YOU BETTER DO WHAT SILVERMANE WANTS, SEE?
EVEN IF YA DON'T CARE ABOUT YOURSELF... REMEMBER...
WE ALSO "INVITED" YER WIFE AND KID UP HERE TO KEEP YA COMPANY!
SO, IF THE OLD MAN WANTS YA TO TRANSLATE THAT TABLET OF HIS...
--YOU BETTER START TRANSLATIN'!
MARKO! YOU MUST NOT YET HARM HIM!
THE MAGGIA HAS MUCH USE FOR DR. CONNORS!
STOP! YOU DON'T KNOW THE DANGER!
YOU DON'T REALIZE... WHAT CAN HAPPEN!
STAN (The MAN) LEE, SCRIPT WRITER
JOHNNY (RING-A-DING) ROMITA, INNOVATOR
JIM (MADMAN) MOONEY, ILLUSTRATOR
SAM (ROSY) ROSEN, LETTERER
...ALL REQUEST YOU TO ENJOY THIS DAZZLING DONNYBROOK!

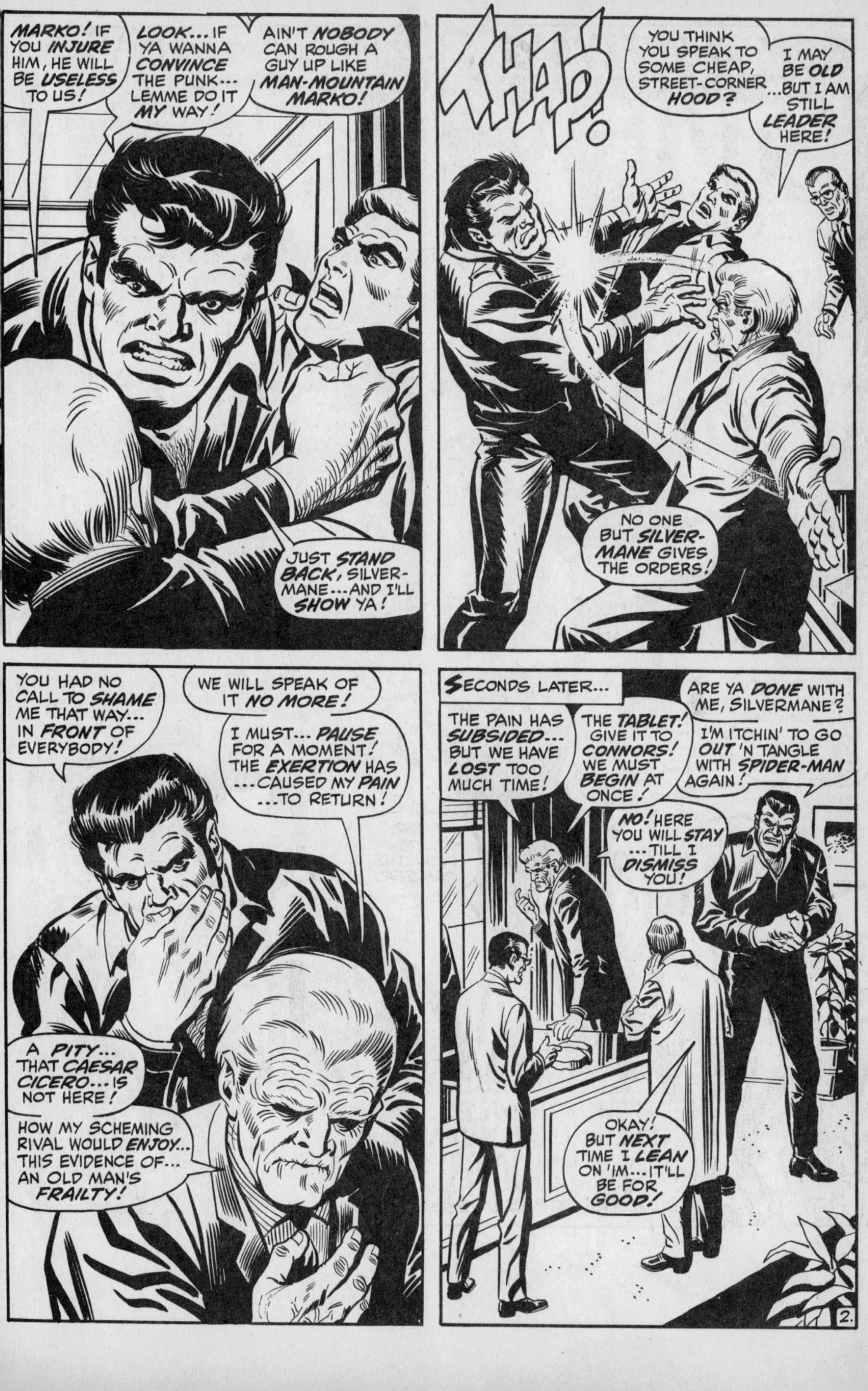
MARKO! IF YOU INJURE HIM, HE WILL BE USELESS TO US!
LOOK... IF YA WANNA CONVINCE THE PUNK... LEMME DO IT MY WAY!
AIN'T NOBODY CAN ROUGH A GUY UP LIKE MAN-MOUNTAIN MARKO!
JUST STAND BACK, SILVER-MANE... AND I'LL SHOW YA!
THAP!
YOU THINK YOU SPEAK TO SOME CHEAP, STREET-CORNER HOOD?
I MAY BE OLD ...BUT I AM STILL LEADER HERE!
NO ONE BUT SILVER-MANE GIVES THE ORDERS!
YOU HAD NO CALL TO SHAME ME THAT WAY... IN FRONT OF EVERYBODY!
WE WILL SPEAK OF IT NO MORE!
I MUST... PAUSE FOR A MOMENT! THE EXERTION HAS ...CAUSED MY PAIN ...TO RETURN!
A PITY... THAT CAESAR CICERO... IS NOT HERE!
HOW MY SCHEMING RIVAL WOULD ENJOY... THIS EVIDENCE OF... AN OLD MAN'S FRAILTY!
SECONDS LATER...
THE PAIN HAS SUBSIDED... BUT WE HAVE LOST TOO MUCH TIME!
THE TABLET! GIVE IT TO CONNORS! WE MUST BEGIN AT ONCE!
ARE YA DONE WITH ME, SILVERMANE?
I'M ITCHIN' TO GO OUT 'N TANGLE WITH SPIDER-MAN AGAIN!
NO! HERE YOU WILL STAY ...TILL I DISMISS YOU!
OKAY! BUT NEXT TIME I LEAN ON 'IM... IT'LL BE FOR GOOD!
2.

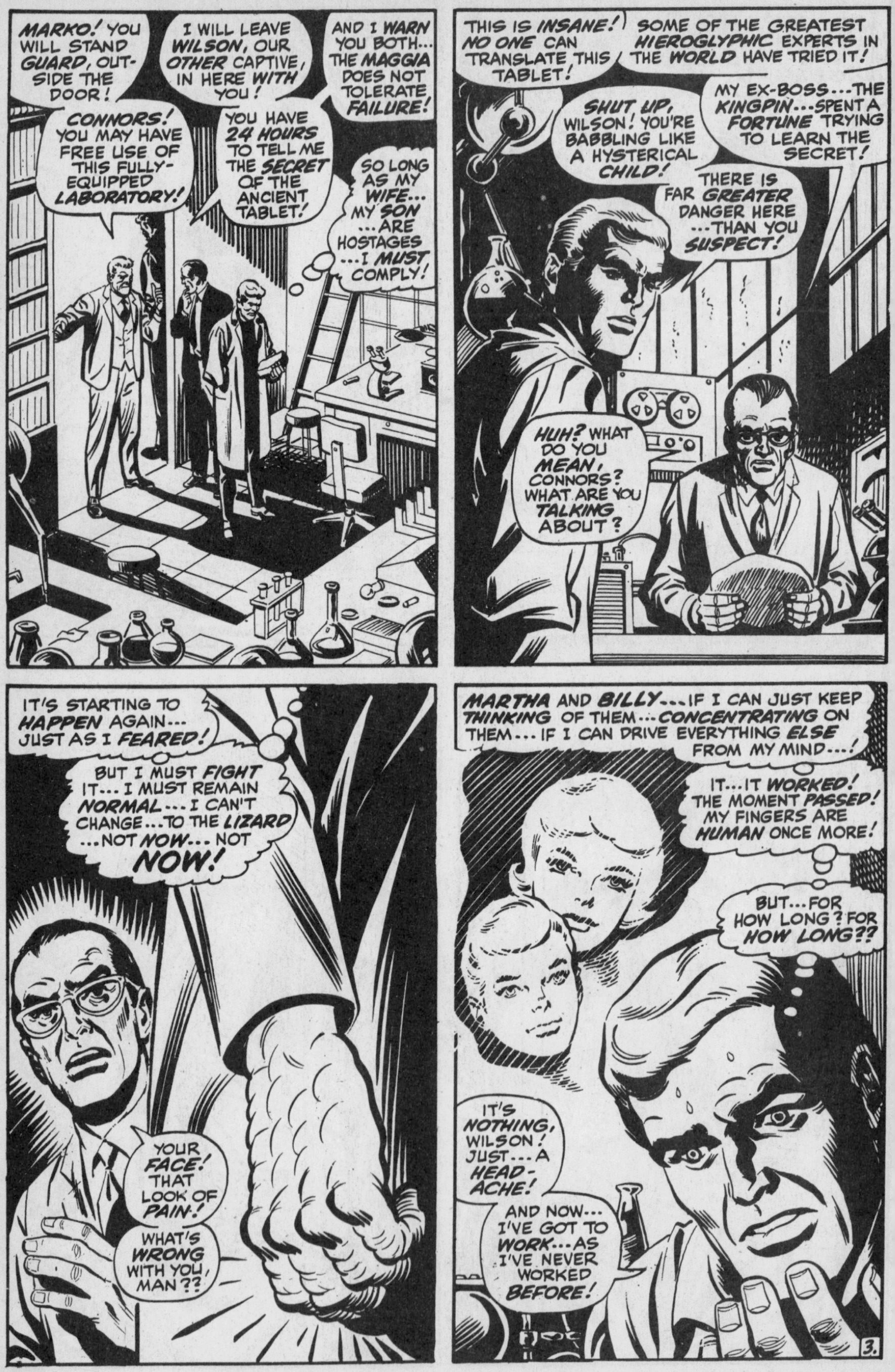
MARKO! YOU WILL STAND GUARD, OUTSIDE THE DOOR!
I WILL LEAVE WILSON, OUR OTHER CAPTIVE, IN HERE WITH YOU!
AND I WARN YOU BOTH... THE MAGGIA DOES NOT TOLERATE FAILURE!
CONNORS! YOU MAY HAVE FREE USE OF THIS FULLY-EQUIPPED LABORATORY!
YOU HAVE 24 HOURS TO TELL ME THE SECRET OF THE ANCIENT TABLET!
SO LONG AS MY WIFE... MY SON ...ARE HOSTAGES ...I MUST COMPLY!
THIS IS INSANE! NO ONE CAN TRANSLATE THIS TABLET!
SOME OF THE GREATEST HIEROGLYPHIC EXPERTS IN THE WORLD HAVE TRIED IT!
SHUT UP, WILSON! YOU'RE BABBLING LIKE A HYSTERICAL CHILD!
MY EX-BOSS...THE KINGPIN...SPENT A FORTUNE TRYING TO LEARN THE SECRET!
THERE IS FAR GREATER DANGER HERE ...THAN YOU SUSPECT!
HUH? WHAT DO YOU MEAN, CONNORS? WHAT ARE YOU TALKING ABOUT?
IT'S STARTING TO HAPPEN AGAIN... JUST AS I FEARED!
BUT I MUST FIGHT IT... I MUST REMAIN NORMAL... I CAN'T CHANGE...TO THE LIZARD ...NOT NOW... NOT NOW!
YOUR FACE! THAT LOOK OF PAIN!
WHAT'S WRONG WITH YOU, MAN??
MARTHA AND BILLY... IF I CAN JUST KEEP THINKING OF THEM... CONCENTRATING ON THEM... IF I CAN DRIVE EVERYTHING ELSE FROM MY MIND...!
IT...IT WORKED! THE MOMENT PASSED! MY FINGERS ARE HUMAN ONCE MORE!
BUT...FOR HOW LONG? FOR HOW LONG??
IT'S NOTHING, WILSON! JUST... A HEAD-ACHE!
AND NOW... I'VE GOT TO WORK...AS I'VE NEVER WORKED BEFORE!
3.

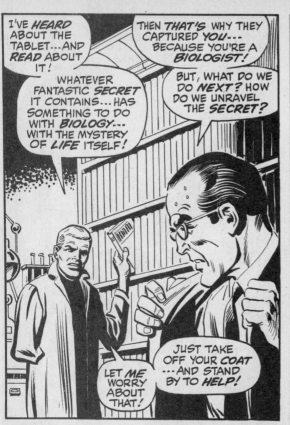

I'VE *HEARD* ABOUT THE *TABLET*...AND *READ* ABOUT IT!

WHATEVER FANTASTIC *SECRET* IT CONTAINS...HAS SOMETHING TO DO WITH *BIOLOGY*... WITH THE MYSTERY OF *LIFE* ITSELF!

THEN *THAT'S* WHY THEY CAPTURED *YOU*--- BECAUSE YOU'RE A *BIOLOGIST!*

BUT, WHAT DO WE DO *NEXT?* HOW DO WE UNRAVEL THE *SECRET?*

JUST TAKE OFF YOUR *COAT* ---AND STAND BY TO *HELP!*

LET *ME* WORRY ABOUT THAT!

SOME TIME *LATER*, IN ANOTHER PART OF THE CITY...

HUH?? ONE OF MY *PAPERS*... FLOATING *UP*... INTO THE *AIR!*

AND A *DIME*...COMING *DOWN*...OUT OF *NOWHERE!!*

NEWSPAPERS

NO...NOT EXACTLY OUT OF *NOWHERE*...AS WE SHALL SEE..

MAYBE THERE'S SOMETHING IN THE *BUGLE* THAT'LL GIVE ME A LEAD ON *MAN-MOUNTAIN MARKO!*

SAY! WHAT'S *THIS*...?

SOMEONE SPRUNG THE *KINGPIN'S* RIGHT-HAND MAN!

BUT...IT DOESN'T MAKE *SENSE*..!

IT WASN'T *FAT STUFF* WHO PUT UP THE *BAIL*...

IT WAS *CAESAR CICERO* ...THE *BIG-TIME MAGGIA* MOUTHPIECE! BUT... *WHY?*

KINGPIN'S CRIME LIEUTENANT BAILED OUT BY MAGGIA LAWYER

POLICE PONDER CONNECTION

CAESAR CICERO

LOUIS WILSON

4

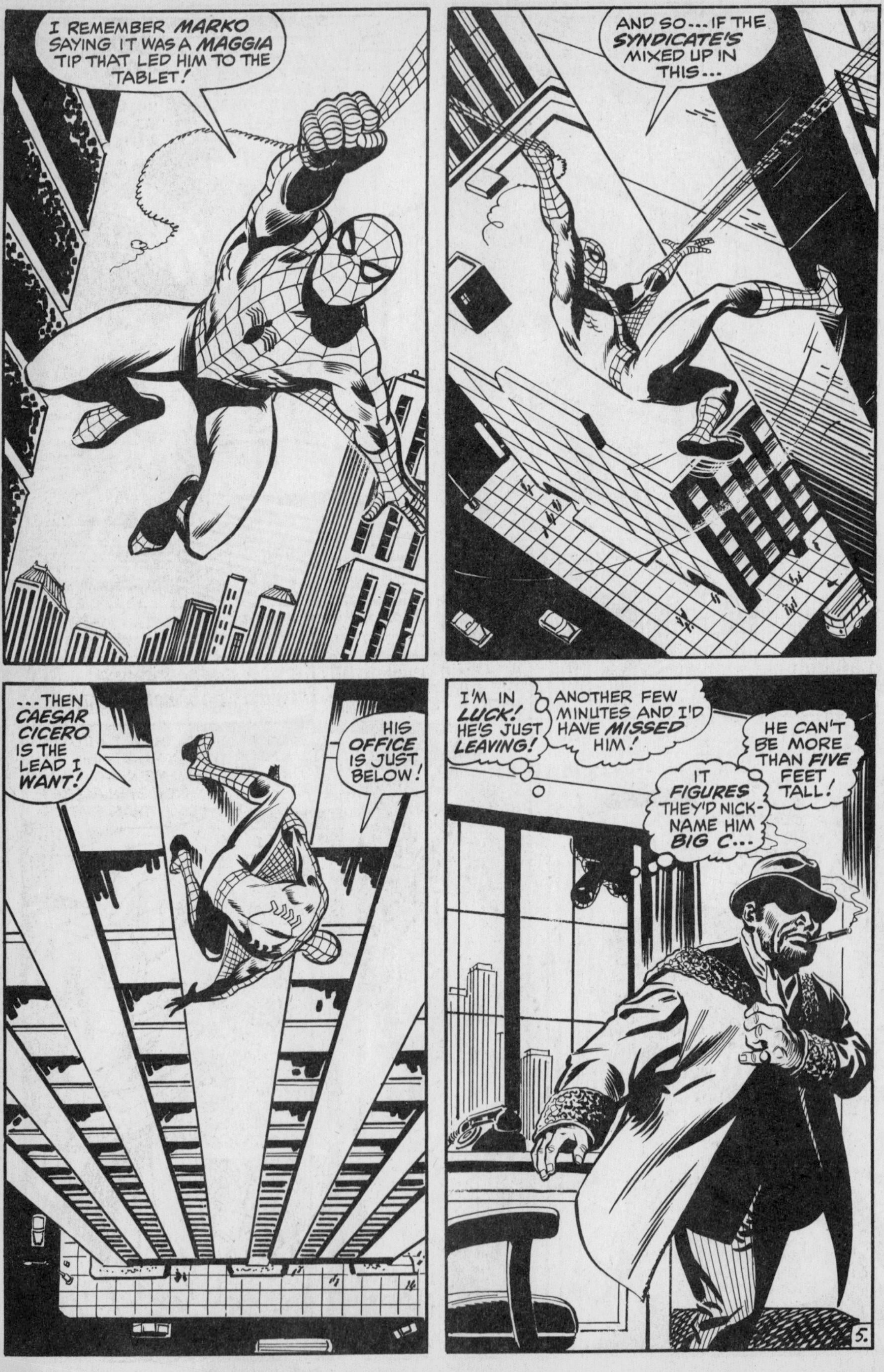
I REMEMBER MARKO SAYING IT WAS A MAGGIA TIP THAT LED HIM TO THE TABLET!
AND SO... IF THE SYNDICATE'S MIXED UP IN THIS...
...THEN CAESAR CICERO IS THE LEAD I WANT!
HIS OFFICE IS JUST BELOW!
I'M IN LUCK! HE'S JUST LEAVING!
ANOTHER FEW MINUTES AND I'D HAVE MISSED HIM!
HE CAN'T BE MORE THAN FIVE FEET TALL!
IT FIGURES THEY'D NICK-NAME HIM BIG C...
5.

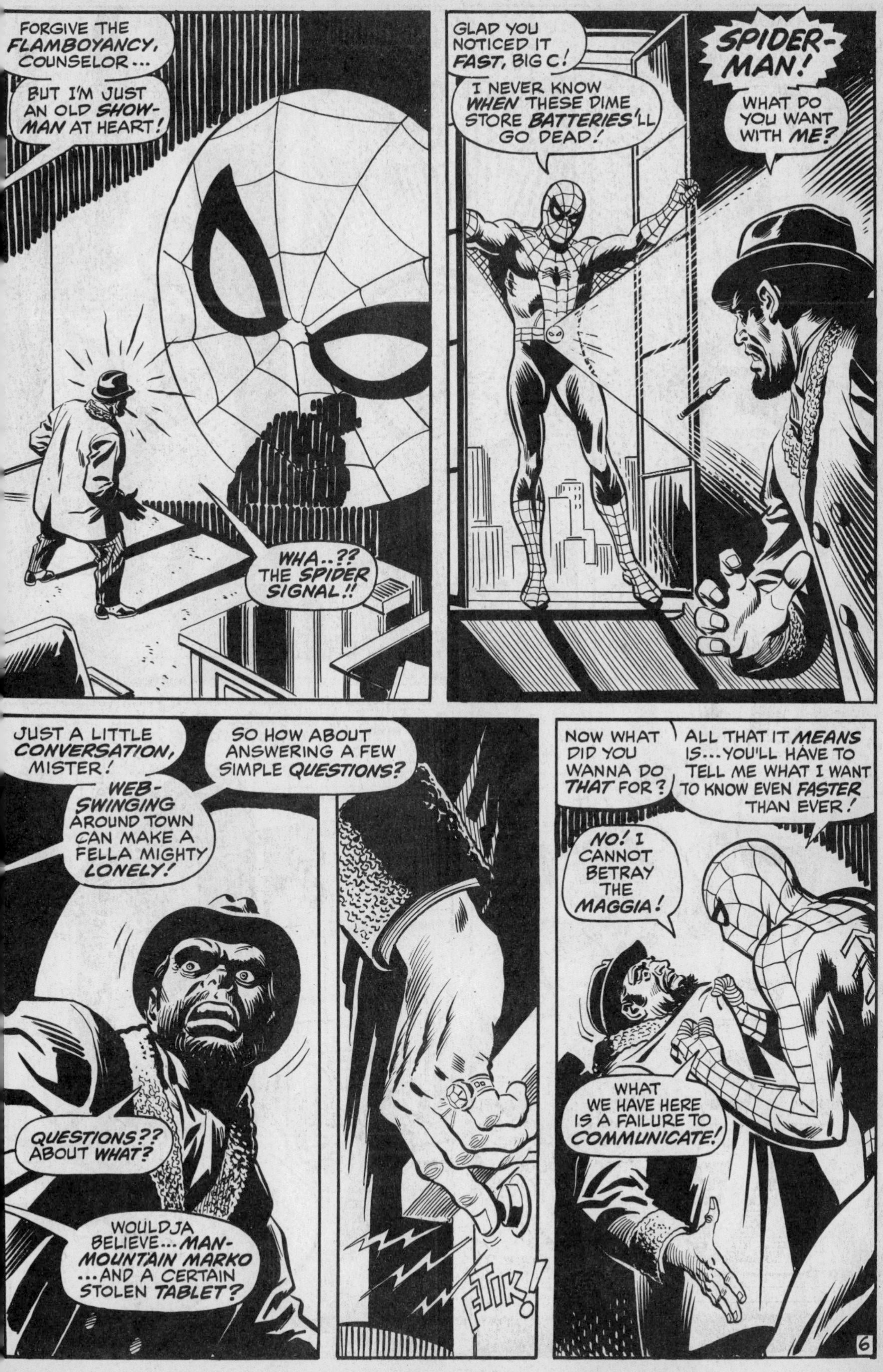
FORGIVE THE FLAMBOYANCY, COUNSELOR...
BUT I'M JUST AN OLD SHOW-MAN AT HEART!
WHA..?? THE SPIDER SIGNAL!!
GLAD YOU NOTICED IT FAST, BIG C!
I NEVER KNOW WHEN THESE DIME STORE BATTERIES'LL GO DEAD!
SPIDER-MAN!
WHAT DO YOU WANT WITH ME?
JUST A LITTLE CONVERSATION, MISTER!
WEB-SWINGING AROUND TOWN CAN MAKE A FELLA MIGHTY LONELY!
QUESTIONS?? ABOUT WHAT?
WOULDJA BELIEVE... MAN-MOUNTAIN MARKO ...AND A CERTAIN STOLEN TABLET?
SO HOW ABOUT ANSWERING A FEW SIMPLE QUESTIONS?
FTIK!
NOW WHAT DID YOU WANNA DO THAT FOR?
ALL THAT IT MEANS IS...YOU'LL HAVE TO TELL ME WHAT I WANT TO KNOW EVEN FASTER THAN EVER!
NO! I CANNOT BETRAY THE MAGGIA!
WHAT WE HAVE HERE IS A FAILURE TO COMMUNICATE!
6

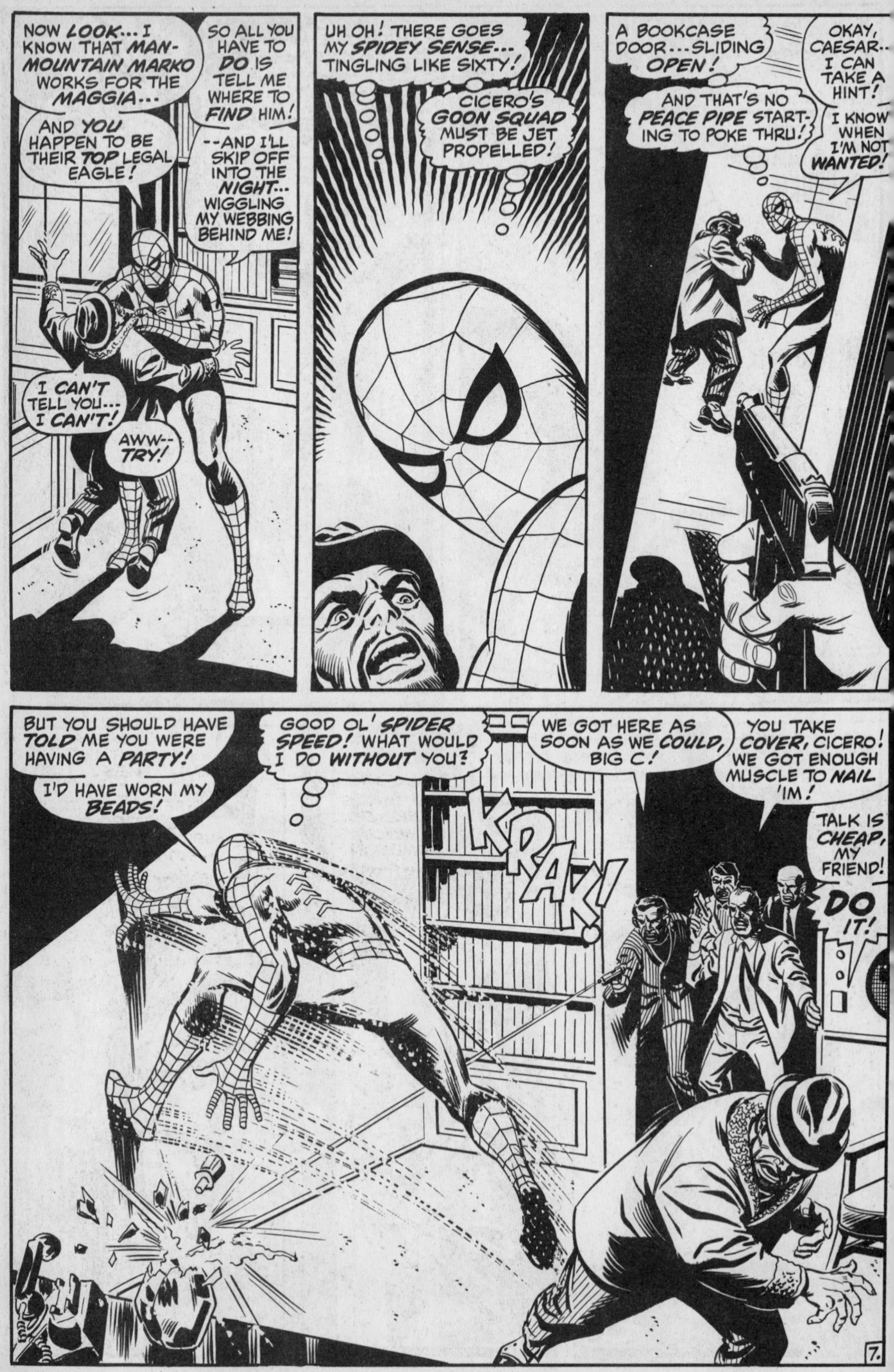

NOW LOOK... I KNOW THAT MAN-MOUNTAIN MARKO WORKS FOR THE MAGGIA...
AND YOU HAPPEN TO BE THEIR TOP LEGAL EAGLE!
SO ALL YOU HAVE TO DO IS TELL ME WHERE TO FIND HIM!
--AND I'LL SKIP OFF INTO THE NIGHT... WIGGLING MY WEBBING BEHIND ME!
I CAN'T TELL YOU... I CAN'T!
AWW--TRY!
UH OH! THERE GOES MY SPIDEY SENSE... TINGLING LIKE SIXTY!
CICERO'S GOON SQUAD MUST BE JET PROPELLED!
A BOOKCASE DOOR---SLIDING OPEN!
AND THAT'S NO PEACE PIPE STARTING TO POKE THRU!
OKAY, CAESAR.. I CAN TAKE A HINT!
I KNOW WHEN I'M NOT WANTED!
BUT YOU SHOULD HAVE TOLD ME YOU WERE HAVING A PARTY!
I'D HAVE WORN MY BEADS!
GOOD OL' SPIDER SPEED! WHAT WOULD I DO WITHOUT YOU?
KRAK!
WE GOT HERE AS SOON AS WE COULD, BIG C!
YOU TAKE COVER, CICERO! WE GOT ENOUGH MUSCLE TO NAIL 'IM!
TALK IS CHEAP, MY FRIEND!
DO IT!

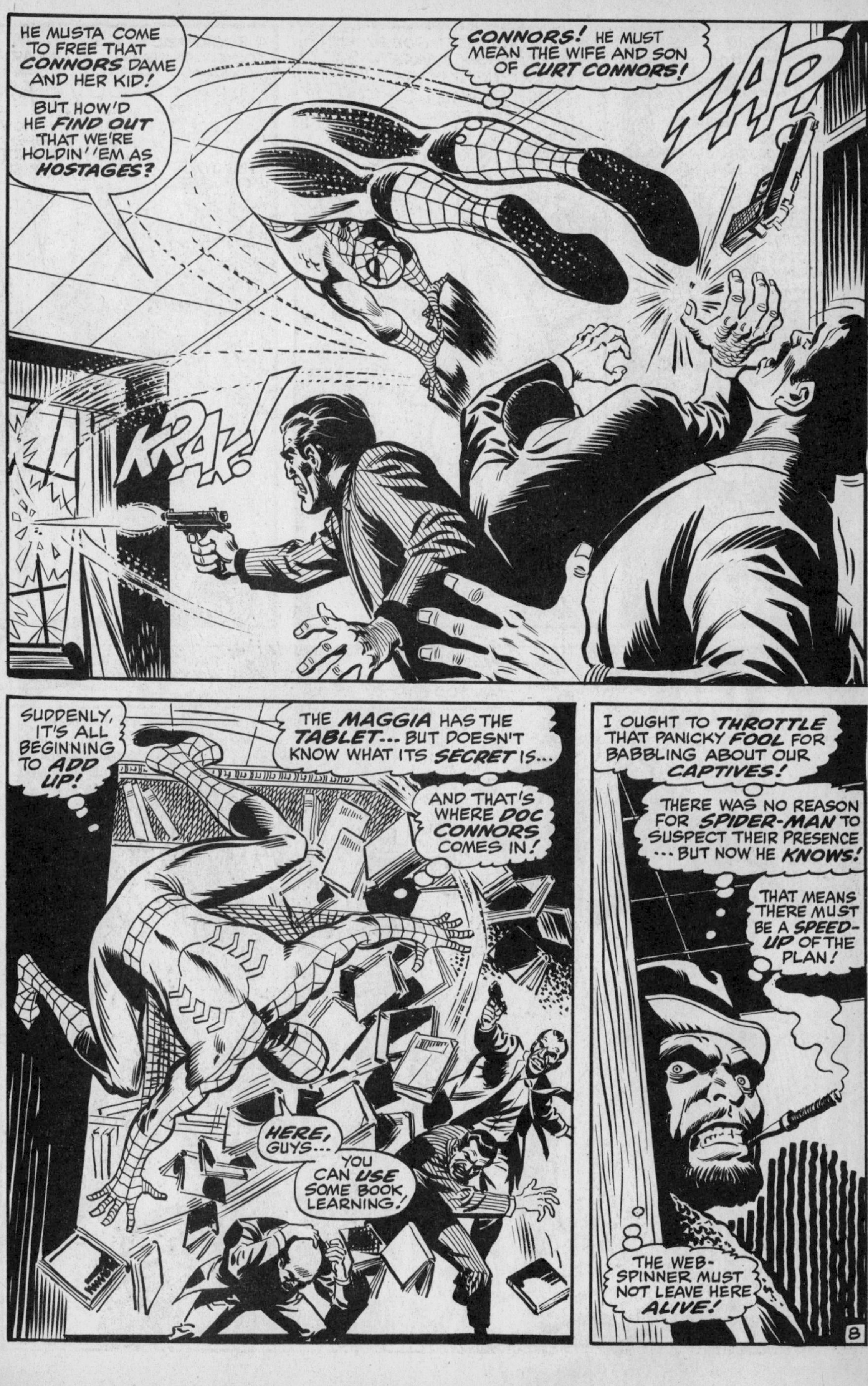

HE MUSTA COME TO FREE THAT CONNORS DAME AND HER KID!
BUT HOW'D HE FIND OUT THAT WE'RE HOLDIN' 'EM AS HOSTAGES?
CONNORS! HE MUST MEAN THE WIFE AND SON OF CURT CONNORS!
ZAP
KRAK!
SUDDENLY, IT'S ALL BEGINNING TO ADD UP!
THE MAGGIA HAS THE TABLET... BUT DOESN'T KNOW WHAT ITS SECRET IS...
AND THAT'S WHERE DOC CONNORS COMES IN!
HERE, GUYS... YOU CAN USE SOME BOOK LEARNING!
I OUGHT TO THROTTLE THAT PANICKY FOOL FOR BABBLING ABOUT OUR CAPTIVES!
THERE WAS NO REASON FOR SPIDER-MAN TO SUSPECT THEIR PRESENCE ... BUT NOW HE KNOWS!
THAT MEANS THERE MUST BE A SPEED-UP OF THE PLAN!
THE WEB-SPINNER MUST NOT LEAVE HERE ALIVE!

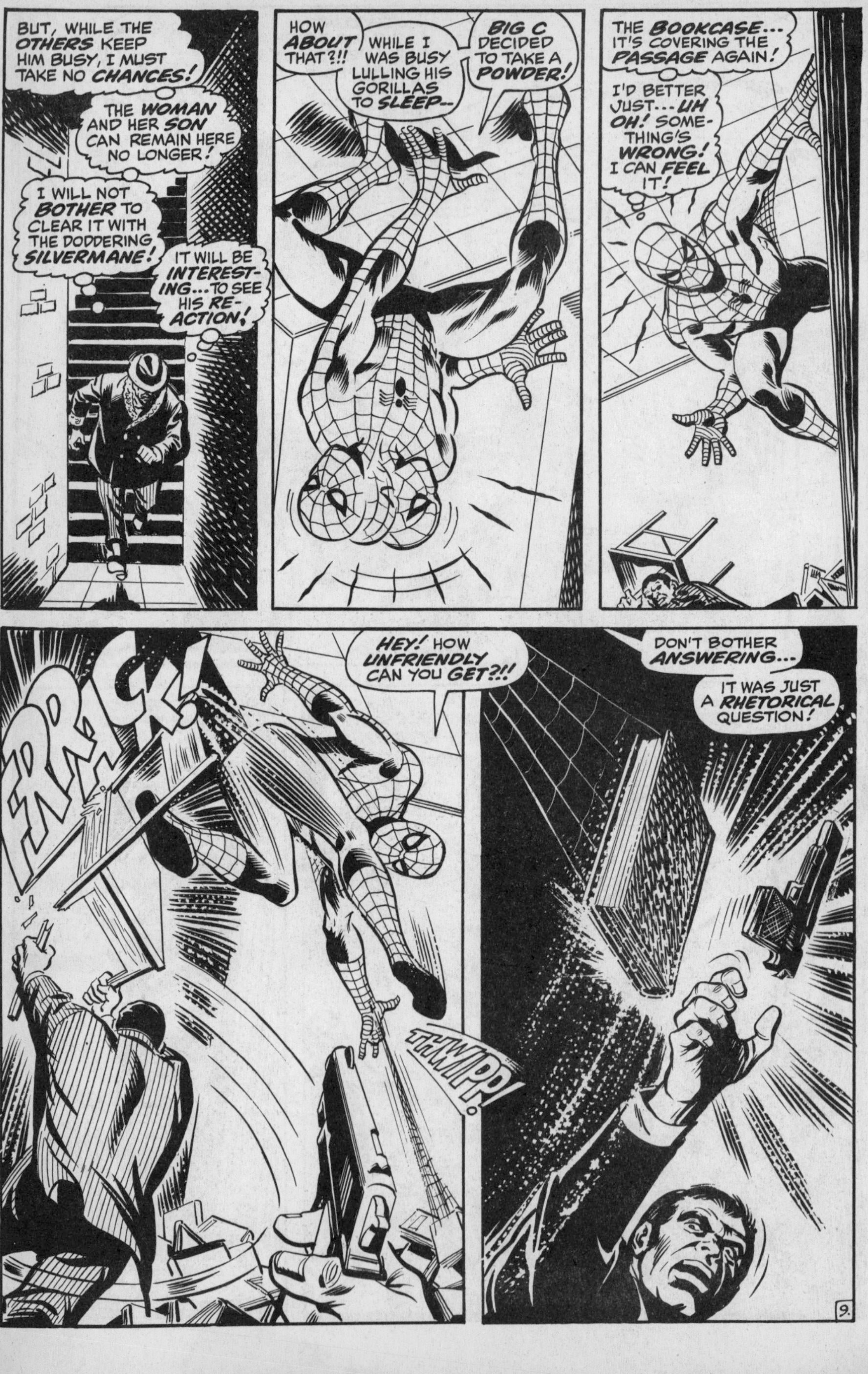
BUT, WHILE THE OTHERS KEEP HIM BUSY, I MUST TAKE NO CHANCES!
THE WOMAN AND HER SON CAN REMAIN HERE NO LONGER!
I WILL NOT BOTHER TO CLEAR IT WITH THE DODDERING SILVERMANE!
IT WILL BE INTERESTING... TO SEE HIS REACTION!
HOW ABOUT THAT?!!
WHILE I WAS BUSY LULLING HIS GORILLAS TO SLEEP--
BIG C DECIDED TO TAKE A POWDER!
THE BOOKCASE... IT'S COVERING THE PASSAGE AGAIN!
I'D BETTER JUST... UH OH! SOMETHING'S WRONG! I CAN FEEL IT!
KRRACK!
HEY! HOW UNFRIENDLY CAN YOU GET?!!
THWIPP!
DON'T BOTHER ANSWERING...
IT WAS JUST A RHETORICAL QUESTION!

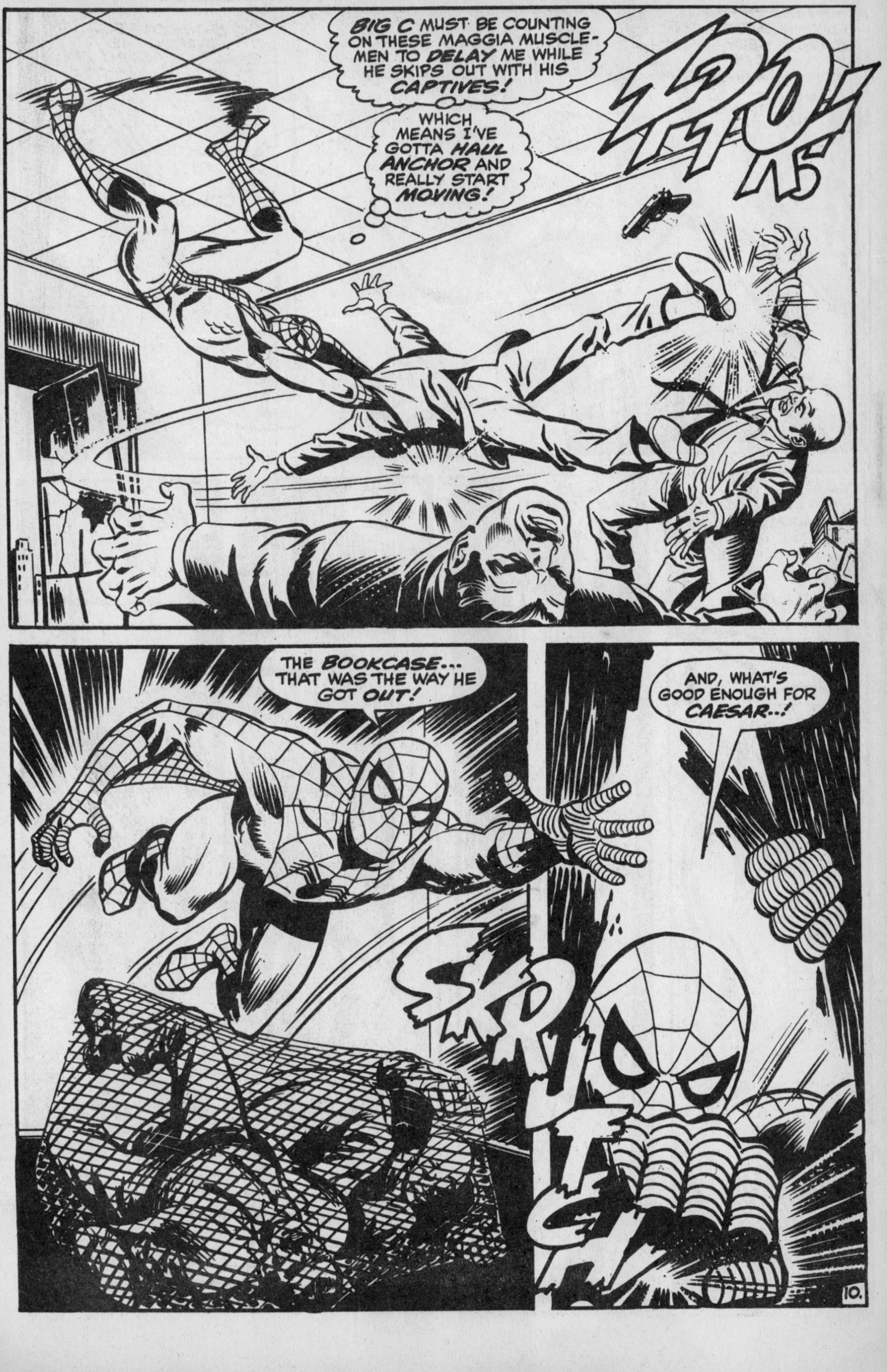
BIG C MUST BE COUNTING ON THESE MAGGIA MUSCLE-MEN TO DELAY ME WHILE HE SKIPS OUT WITH HIS CAPTIVES!
WHICH MEANS I'VE GOTTA HAUL ANCHOR AND REALLY START MOVING!
THE BOOKCASE... THAT WAS THE WAY HE GOT OUT!
AND, WHAT'S GOOD ENOUGH FOR CAESAR..!

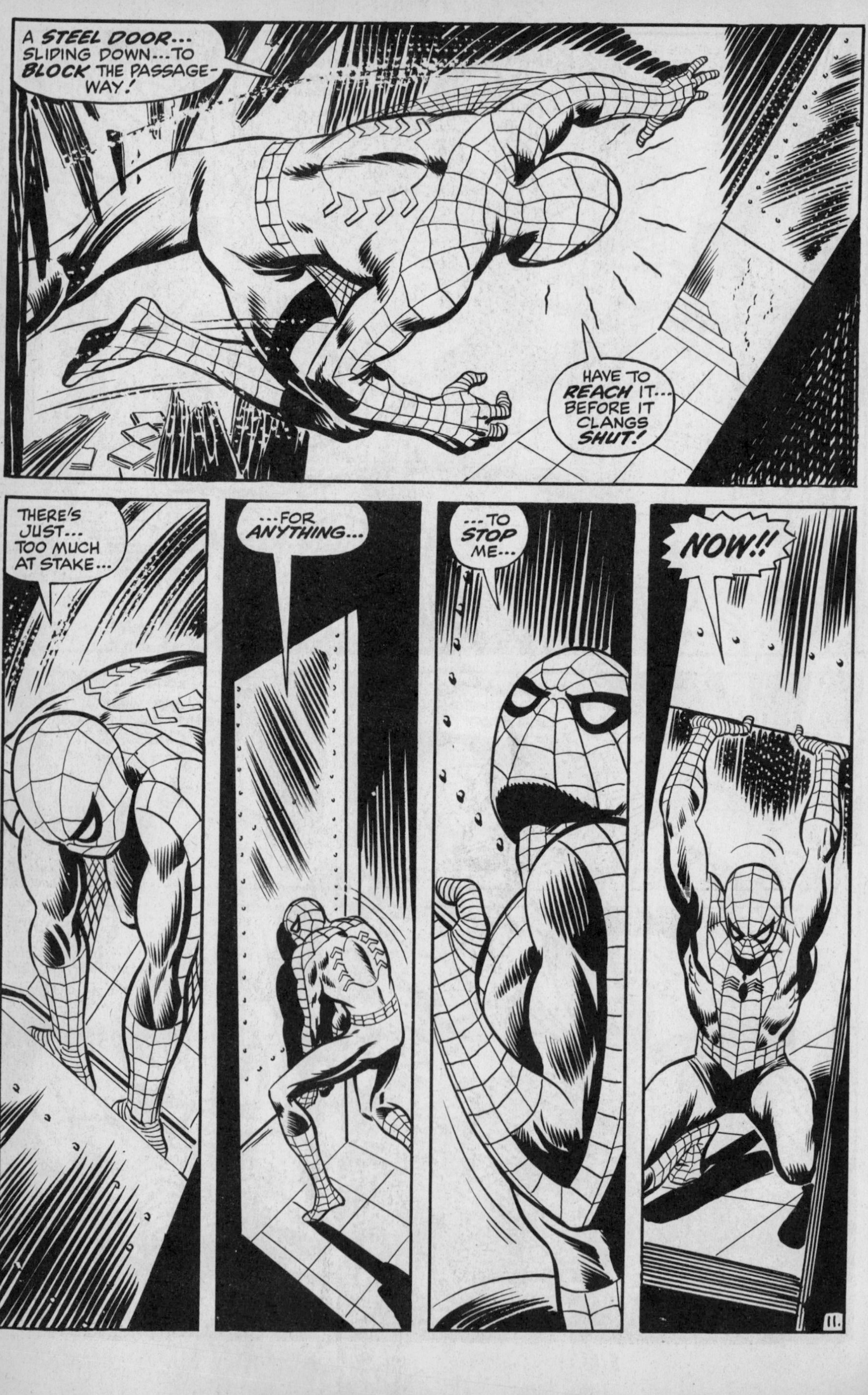
A STEEL DOOR... SLIDING DOWN...TO BLOCK THE PASSAGE-WAY!
HAVE TO REACH IT... BEFORE IT CLANGS SHUT!
THERE'S JUST... TOO MUCH AT STAKE...
...FOR ANYTHING...
...TO STOP ME...
NOW!!

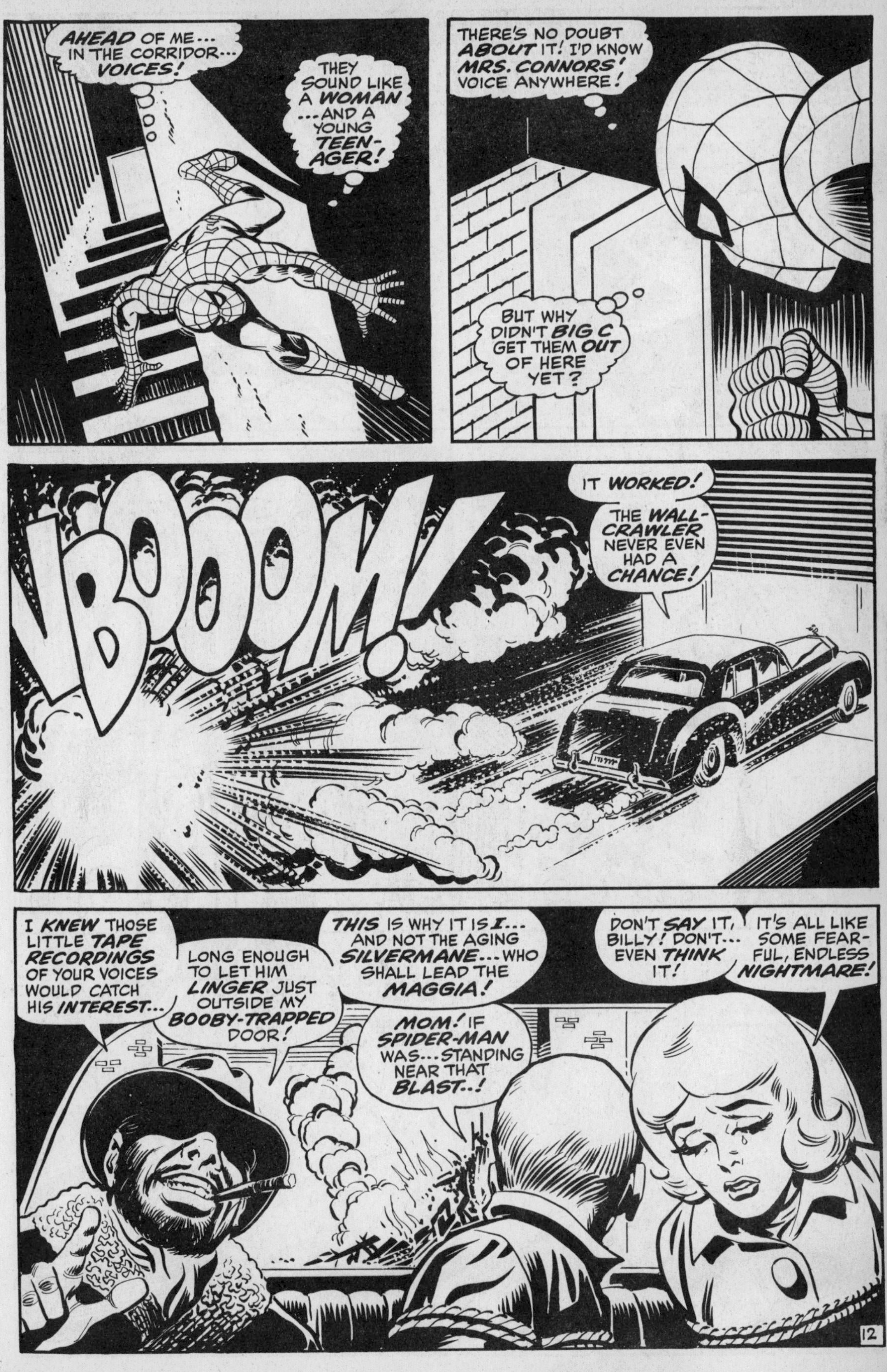
AHEAD OF ME... IN THE CORRIDOR... VOICES!
THEY SOUND LIKE A WOMAN ...AND A YOUNG TEEN-AGER!
THERE'S NO DOUBT ABOUT IT! I'D KNOW MRS. CONNORS' VOICE ANYWHERE!
BUT WHY DIDN'T BIG C GET THEM OUT OF HERE YET?
VBOOOM!
IT WORKED!
THE WALL-CRAWLER NEVER EVEN HAD A CHANCE!
I KNEW THOSE LITTLE TAPE RECORDINGS OF YOUR VOICES WOULD CATCH HIS INTEREST...
LONG ENOUGH TO LET HIM LINGER JUST OUTSIDE MY BOOBY-TRAPPED DOOR!
THIS IS WHY IT IS I... AND NOT THE AGING SILVERMANE... WHO SHALL LEAD THE MAGGIA!
MOM! IF SPIDER-MAN WAS... STANDING NEAR THAT BLAST..!
DON'T SAY IT, BILLY! DON'T... EVEN THINK IT!
IT'S ALL LIKE SOME FEAR-FUL, ENDLESS NIGHTMARE!
12

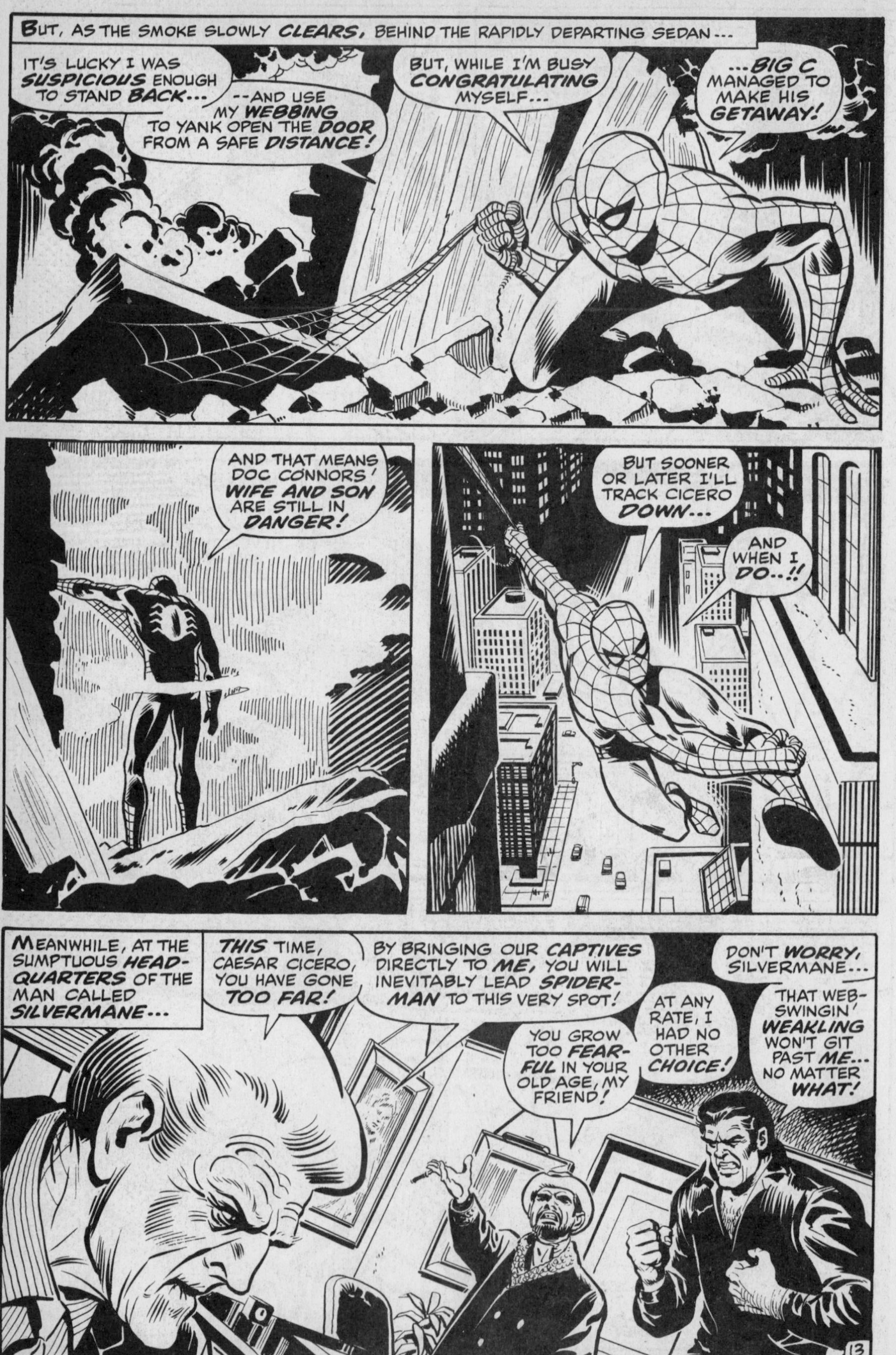
BUT, AS THE SMOKE SLOWLY CLEARS, BEHIND THE RAPIDLY DEPARTING SEDAN...
IT'S LUCKY I WAS SUSPICIOUS ENOUGH TO STAND BACK...
--AND USE MY WEBBING TO YANK OPEN THE DOOR FROM A SAFE DISTANCE!
BUT, WHILE I'M BUSY CONGRATULATING MYSELF...
...BIG C MANAGED TO MAKE HIS GETAWAY!
AND THAT MEANS DOC CONNORS' WIFE AND SON ARE STILL IN DANGER!
BUT SOONER OR LATER I'LL TRACK CICERO DOWN...
AND WHEN I DO..!!
MEANWHILE, AT THE SUMPTUOUS HEAD-QUARTERS OF THE MAN CALLED SILVERMANE...
THIS TIME, CAESAR CICERO, YOU HAVE GONE TOO FAR!
BY BRINGING OUR CAPTIVES DIRECTLY TO ME, YOU WILL INEVITABLY LEAD SPIDER-MAN TO THIS VERY SPOT!
YOU GROW TOO FEAR-FUL IN YOUR OLD AGE, MY FRIEND!
AT ANY RATE, I HAD NO OTHER CHOICE!
DON'T WORRY, SILVERMANE...
THAT WEB-SWINGIN' WEAKLING WON'T GIT PAST ME... NO MATTER WHAT!
13

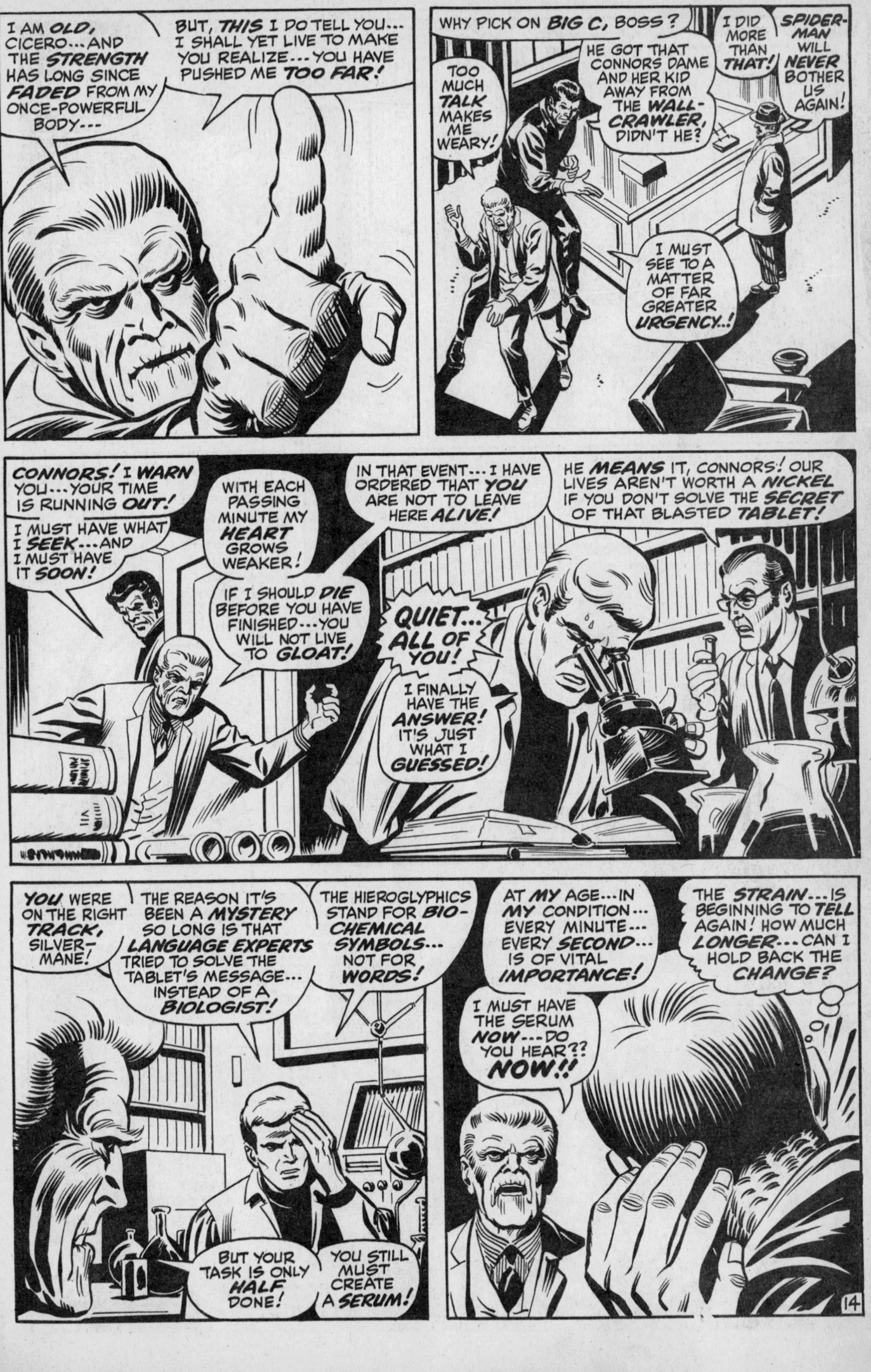

I AM OLD, CICERO... AND THE STRENGTH HAS LONG SINCE FADED FROM MY ONCE-POWERFUL BODY---
BUT, THIS I DO TELL YOU... I SHALL YET LIVE TO MAKE YOU REALIZE... YOU HAVE PUSHED ME TOO FAR!
WHY PICK ON BIG C, BOSS?
HE GOT THAT CONNORS DAME AND HER KID AWAY FROM THE WALL-CRAWLER, DIDN'T HE?
I DID MORE THAN THAT!
SPIDER-MAN WILL NEVER BOTHER US AGAIN!
TOO MUCH TALK MAKES ME WEARY!
I MUST SEE TO A MATTER OF FAR GREATER URGENCY..!
CONNORS! I WARN YOU... YOUR TIME IS RUNNING OUT!
I MUST HAVE WHAT I SEEK... AND I MUST HAVE IT SOON!
WITH EACH PASSING MINUTE MY HEART GROWS WEAKER!
IF I SHOULD DIE BEFORE YOU HAVE FINISHED... YOU WILL NOT LIVE TO GLOAT!
IN THAT EVENT... I HAVE ORDERED THAT YOU ARE NOT TO LEAVE HERE ALIVE!
HE MEANS IT, CONNORS! OUR LIVES AREN'T WORTH A NICKEL IF YOU DON'T SOLVE THE SECRET OF THAT BLASTED TABLET!
QUIET... ALL OF YOU!
I FINALLY HAVE THE ANSWER! IT'S JUST WHAT I GUESSED!
YOU WERE ON THE RIGHT TRACK, SILVER-MANE!
THE REASON IT'S BEEN A MYSTERY SO LONG IS THAT LANGUAGE EXPERTS TRIED TO SOLVE THE TABLET'S MESSAGE... INSTEAD OF A BIOLOGIST!
THE HIEROGLYPHICS STAND FOR BIO-CHEMICAL SYMBOLS... NOT FOR WORDS!
BUT YOUR TASK IS ONLY HALF DONE!
YOU STILL MUST CREATE A SERUM!
AT MY AGE... IN MY CONDITION... EVERY MINUTE... EVERY SECOND... IS OF VITAL IMPORTANCE!
I MUST HAVE THE SERUM NOW--- DO YOU HEAR?? NOW!!
THE STRAIN... IS BEGINNING TO TELL AGAIN! HOW MUCH LONGER... CAN I HOLD BACK THE CHANGE?
14

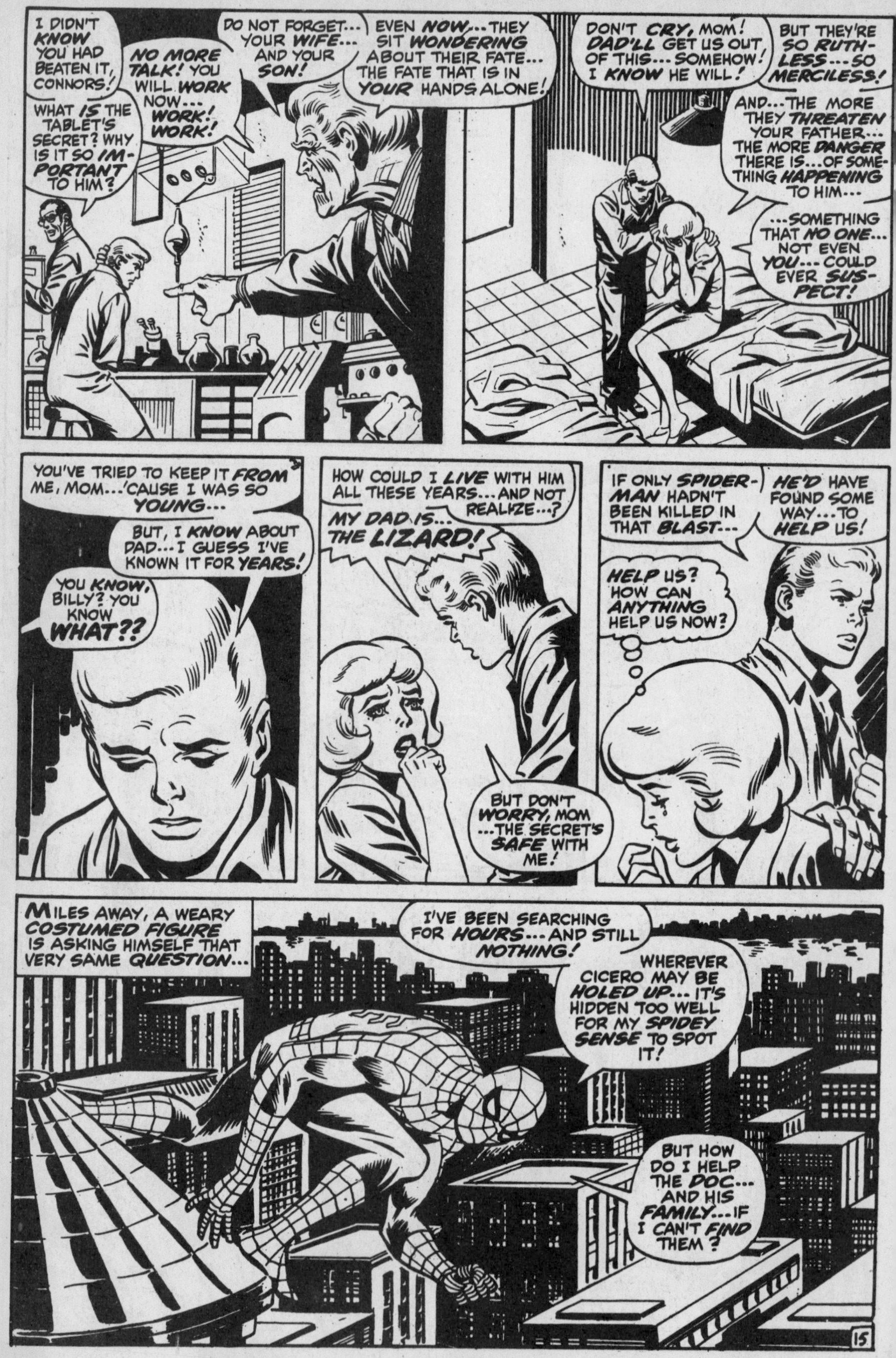

I DIDN'T KNOW YOU HAD BEATEN IT, CONNORS!
WHAT IS THE TABLET'S SECRET? WHY IS IT SO IMPORTANT TO HIM?
NO MORE TALK! YOU WILL WORK NOW... WORK! WORK!
DO NOT FORGET... YOUR WIFE... AND YOUR SON!
EVEN NOW... THEY SIT WONDERING ABOUT THEIR FATE... THE FATE THAT IS IN YOUR HANDS ALONE!
DON'T CRY, MOM! DAD'LL GET US OUT OF THIS... SOMEHOW! I KNOW HE WILL!
BUT THEY'RE SO RUTHLESS... SO MERCILESS!
AND... THE MORE THEY THREATEN YOUR FATHER... THE MORE DANGER THERE IS... OF SOMETHING HAPPENING TO HIM...
...SOMETHING THAT NO ONE... NOT EVEN YOU... COULD EVER SUSPECT!
YOU'VE TRIED TO KEEP IT FROM ME, MOM...'CAUSE I WAS SO YOUNG...
BUT, I KNOW ABOUT DAD... I GUESS I'VE KNOWN IT FOR YEARS!
YOU KNOW, BILLY? YOU KNOW WHAT??
HOW COULD I LIVE WITH HIM ALL THESE YEARS... AND NOT REALIZE...?
MY DAD IS... THE LIZARD!
BUT DON'T WORRY, MOM ...THE SECRET'S SAFE WITH ME!
IF ONLY SPIDER-MAN HADN'T BEEN KILLED IN THAT BLAST...
HE'D HAVE FOUND SOME WAY... TO HELP US!
HELP US? HOW CAN ANYTHING HELP US NOW?
MILES AWAY, A WEARY COSTUMED FIGURE IS ASKING HIMSELF THAT VERY SAME QUESTION...
I'VE BEEN SEARCHING FOR HOURS... AND STILL NOTHING!
WHEREVER CICERO MAY BE HOLED UP... IT'S HIDDEN TOO WELL FOR MY SPIDEY SENSE TO SPOT IT!
BUT HOW DO I HELP THE DOC... AND HIS FAMILY... IF I CAN'T FIND THEM?

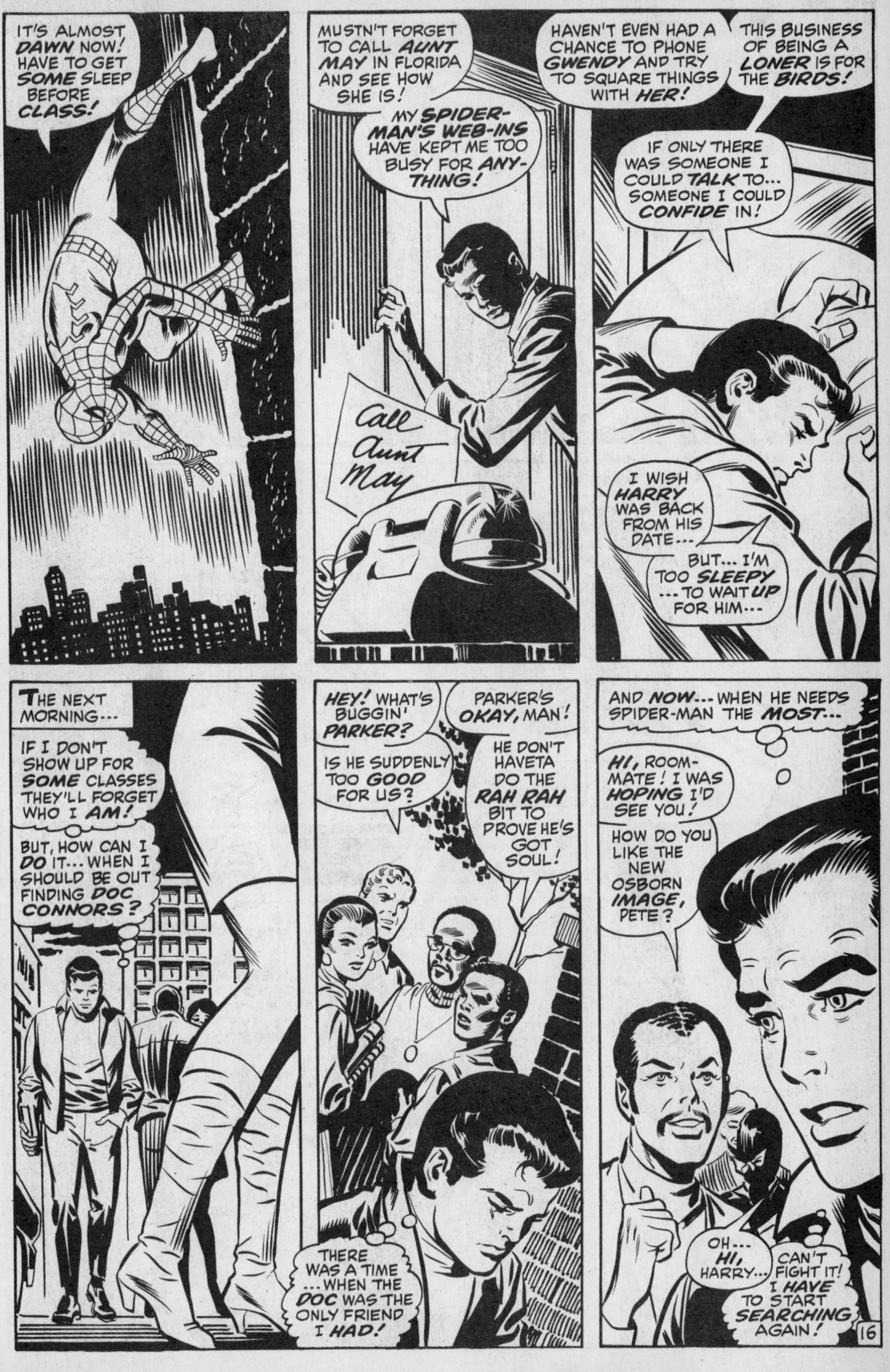

IT'S ALMOST DAWN NOW! HAVE TO GET SOME SLEEP BEFORE CLASS!
MUSTN'T FORGET TO CALL AUNT MAY IN FLORIDA AND SEE HOW SHE IS!
MY SPIDER-MAN'S WEB-INS HAVE KEPT ME TOO BUSY FOR ANY-THING!
Call Aunt May
HAVEN'T EVEN HAD A CHANCE TO PHONE GWENDY AND TRY TO SQUARE THINGS WITH HER!
THIS BUSINESS OF BEING A LONER IS FOR THE BIRDS!
IF ONLY THERE WAS SOMEONE I COULD TALK TO... SOMEONE I COULD CONFIDE IN!
I WISH HARRY WAS BACK FROM HIS DATE---
BUT... I'M TOO SLEEPY ---TO WAIT UP FOR HIM---
THE NEXT MORNING---
IF I DON'T SHOW UP FOR SOME CLASSES THEY'LL FORGET WHO I AM!
BUT, HOW CAN I DO IT... WHEN I SHOULD BE OUT FINDING DOC CONNORS?
HEY! WHAT'S BUGGIN' PARKER?
PARKER'S OKAY, MAN!
IS HE SUDDENLY TOO GOOD FOR US?
HE DON'T HAVETA DO THE RAH RAH BIT TO PROVE HE'S GOT SOUL!
THERE WAS A TIME ...WHEN THE DOC WAS THE ONLY FRIEND I HAD!
AND NOW... WHEN HE NEEDS SPIDER-MAN THE MOST...
HI, ROOM-MATE! I WAS HOPING I'D SEE YOU!
HOW DO YOU LIKE THE NEW OSBORN IMAGE, PETE?
OH... HI, HARRY...
CAN'T FIGHT IT! I HAVE TO START SEARCHING AGAIN!
16

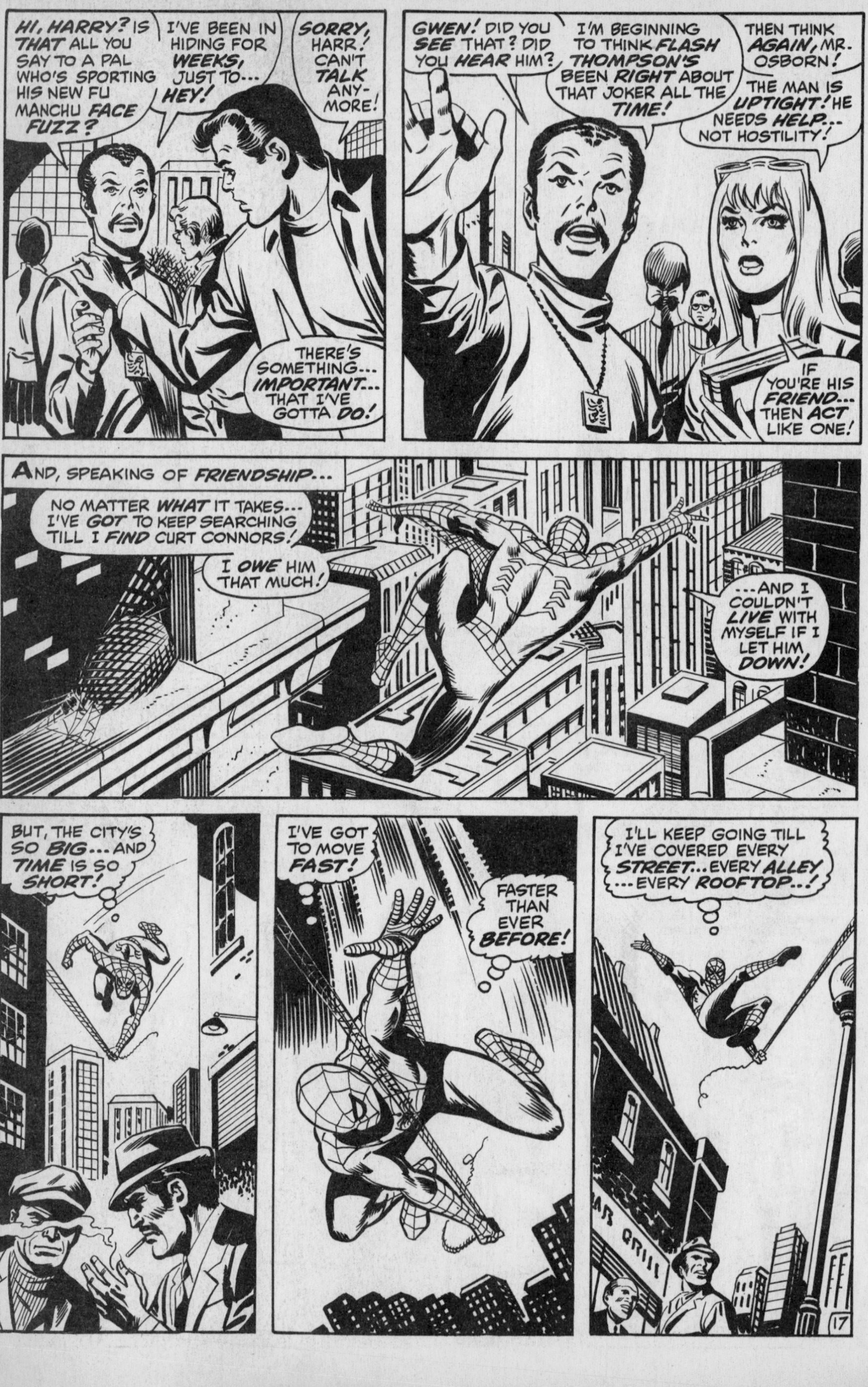
HI, HARRY? IS THAT ALL YOU SAY TO A PAL WHO'S SPORTING HIS NEW FU MANCHU FACE FUZZ?
I'VE BEEN IN HIDING FOR WEEKS, JUST TO... HEY!
SORRY, HARR! CAN'T TALK ANYMORE!
THERE'S SOMETHING... IMPORTANT... THAT I'VE GOTTA DO!
GWEN! DID YOU SEE THAT? DID YOU HEAR HIM?
I'M BEGINNING TO THINK FLASH THOMPSON'S BEEN RIGHT ABOUT THAT JOKER ALL THE TIME!
THEN THINK AGAIN, MR. OSBORN!
THE MAN IS UPTIGHT! HE NEEDS HELP... NOT HOSTILITY!
IF YOU'RE HIS FRIEND... THEN ACT LIKE ONE!
AND, SPEAKING OF FRIENDSHIP...
NO MATTER WHAT IT TAKES... I'VE GOT TO KEEP SEARCHING TILL I FIND CURT CONNORS!
I OWE HIM THAT MUCH!
...AND I COULDN'T LIVE WITH MYSELF IF I LET HIM DOWN!
BUT, THE CITY'S SO BIG... AND TIME IS SO SHORT!
I'VE GOT TO MOVE FAST!
FASTER THAN EVER BEFORE!
I'LL KEEP GOING TILL I'VE COVERED EVERY STREET... EVERY ALLEY ...EVERY ROOFTOP...!
BAR GRILL
17

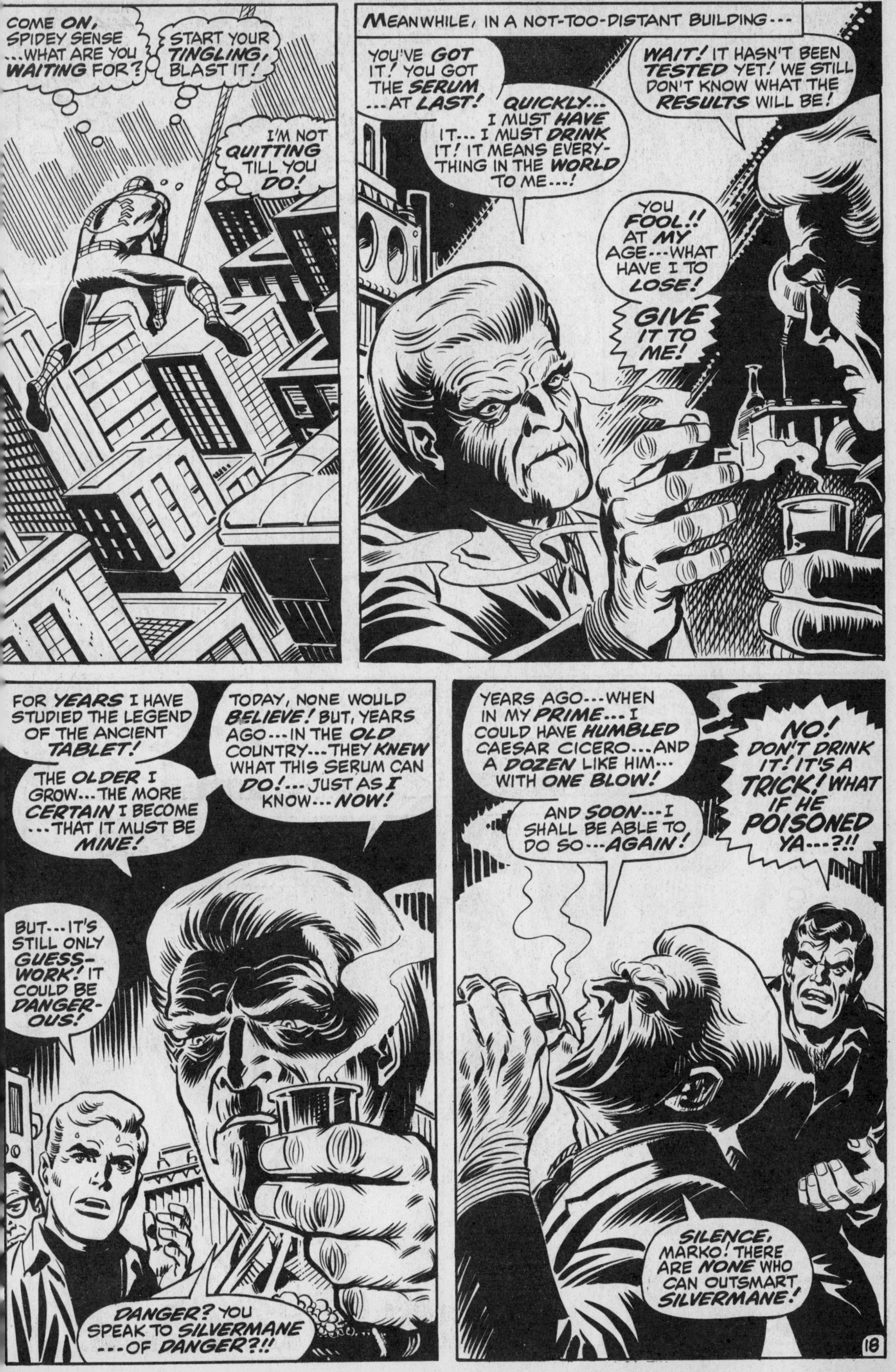
COME ON, SPIDEY SENSE ...WHAT ARE YOU WAITING FOR?
START YOUR TINGLING, BLAST IT!
I'M NOT QUITTING TILL YOU DO!
MEANWHILE, IN A NOT-TOO-DISTANT BUILDING---
YOU'VE GOT IT! YOU GOT THE SERUM ...AT LAST!
QUICKLY... I MUST HAVE IT... I MUST DRINK IT! IT MEANS EVERYTHING IN THE WORLD TO ME...!
WAIT! IT HASN'T BEEN TESTED YET! WE STILL DON'T KNOW WHAT THE RESULTS WILL BE!
YOU FOOL!! AT MY AGE---WHAT HAVE I TO LOSE!
GIVE IT TO ME!
FOR YEARS I HAVE STUDIED THE LEGEND OF THE ANCIENT TABLET!
THE OLDER I GROW... THE MORE CERTAIN I BECOME ---THAT IT MUST BE MINE!
TODAY, NONE WOULD BELIEVE! BUT, YEARS AGO---IN THE OLD COUNTRY---THEY KNEW WHAT THIS SERUM CAN DO!... JUST AS I KNOW... NOW!
BUT---IT'S STILL ONLY GUESS-WORK! IT COULD BE DANGER-OUS!
DANGER? YOU SPEAK TO SILVERMANE ---OF DANGER?!!
YEARS AGO---WHEN IN MY PRIME... I COULD HAVE HUMBLED CAESAR CICERO...AND A DOZEN LIKE HIM... WITH ONE BLOW!
AND SOON---I SHALL BE ABLE TO DO SO---AGAIN!
NO! DON'T DRINK IT! IT'S A TRICK! WHAT IF HE POISONED YA---?!!
SILENCE, MARKO! THERE ARE NONE WHO CAN OUTSMART SILVERMANE!
18

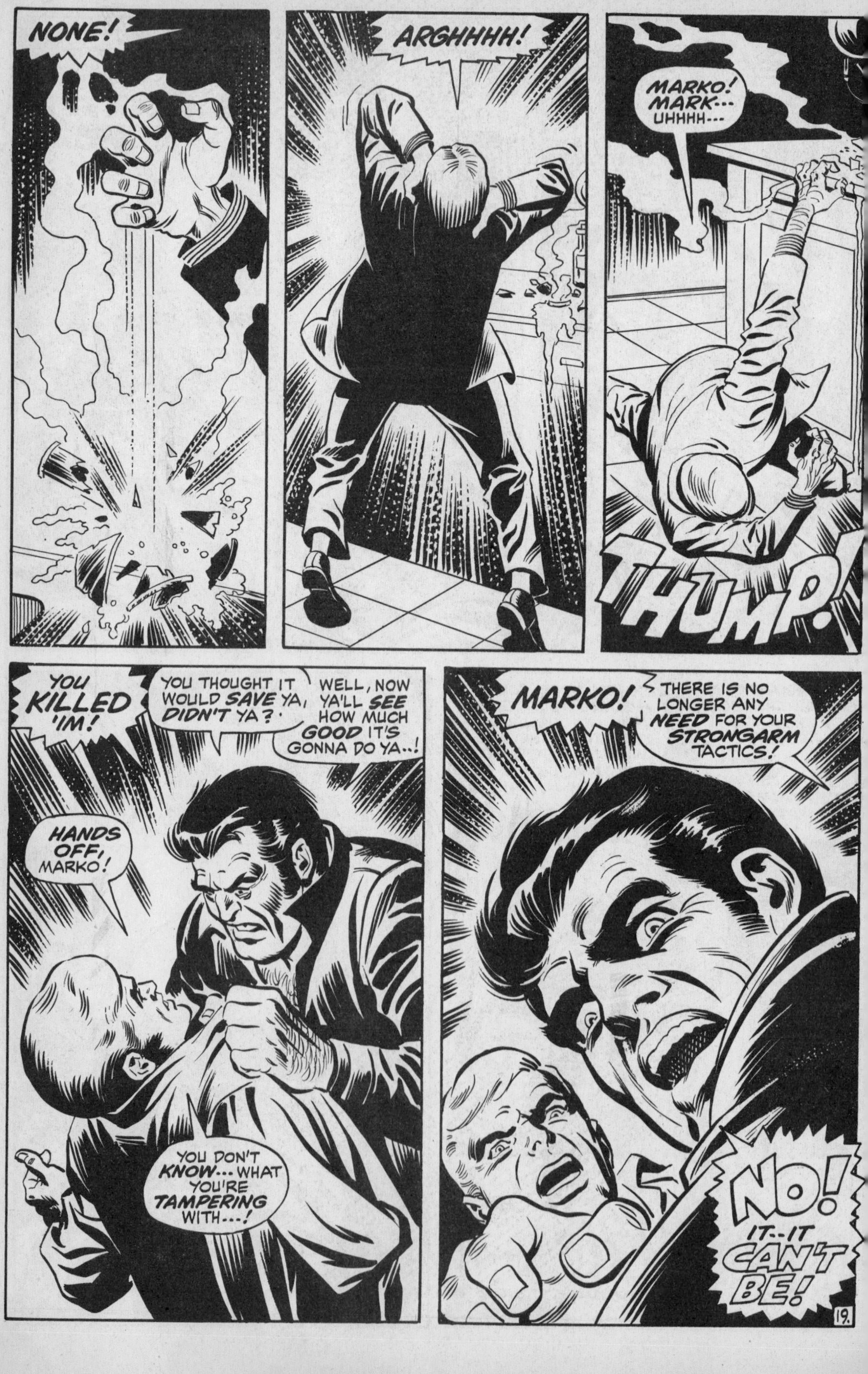
NONE!
ARGHHHH!
MARKO! MARK--- UHHHH---
THUMP!
YOU KILLED 'IM!
YOU THOUGHT IT WOULD SAVE YA, DIDN'T YA?
WELL, NOW YA'LL SEE HOW MUCH GOOD IT'S GONNA DO YA..!
HANDS OFF, MARKO!
YOU DON'T KNOW... WHAT YOU'RE TAMPERING WITH...!
MARKO!
THERE IS NO LONGER ANY NEED FOR YOUR STRONGARM TACTICS!
NO! IT--IT CAN'T BE!
19.

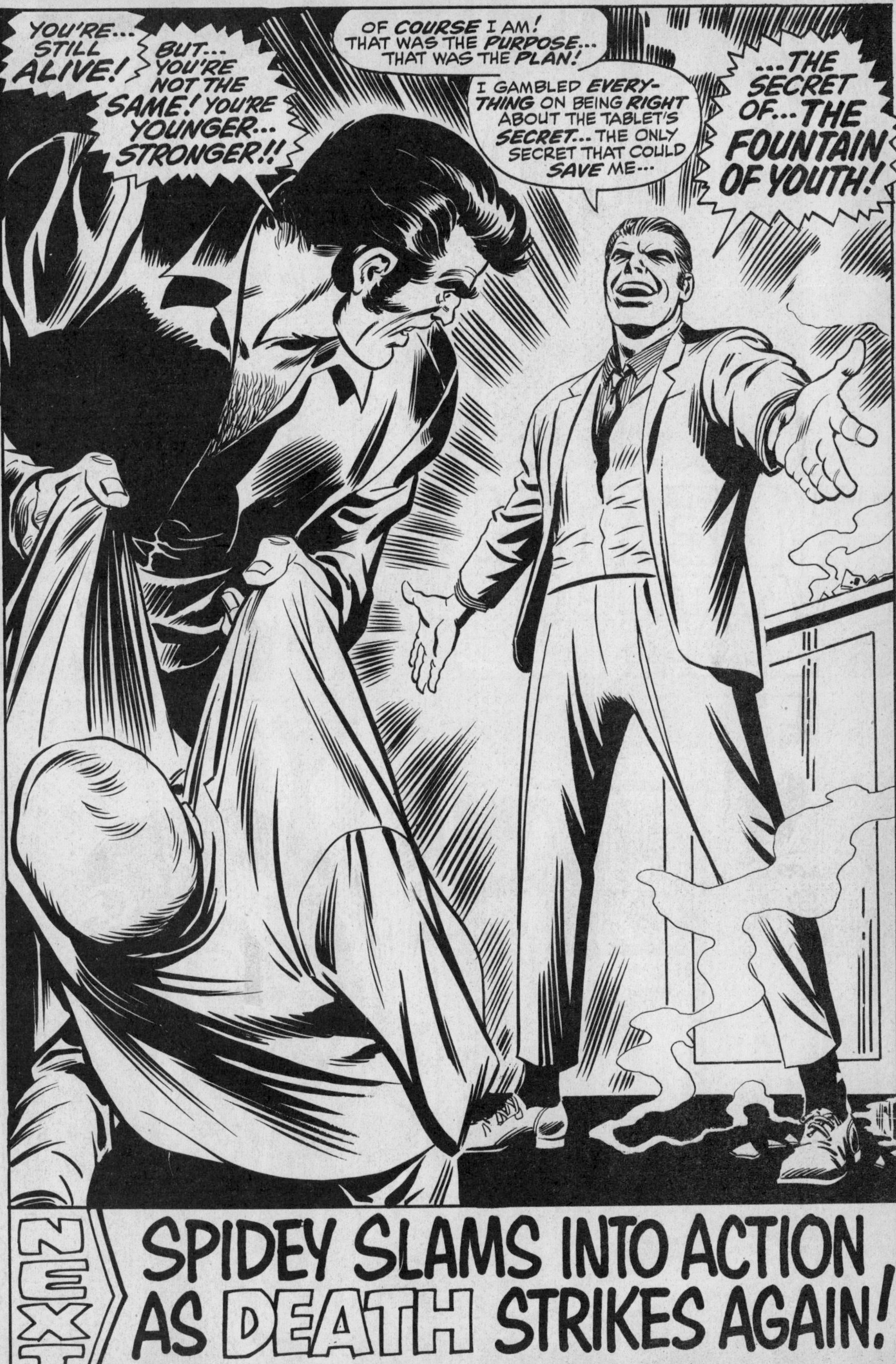
YOU'RE... STILL ALIVE!
BUT... YOU'RE NOT THE SAME! YOU'RE YOUNGER... STRONGER!!
OF COURSE I AM! THAT WAS THE PURPOSE... THAT WAS THE PLAN!
I GAMBLED EVERYTHING ON BEING RIGHT ABOUT THE TABLET'S SECRET... THE ONLY SECRET THAT COULD SAVE ME...
...THE SECRET OF... THE FOUNTAIN OF YOUTH!
NEXT
SPIDEY SLAMS INTO ACTION AS DEATH STRIKES AGAIN!

SPIDER-MAN
15¢
IND.
75
AUG
the AMAZING SPIDER-MAN
MARVEL COMICS GROUP
DEATH WITHOUT WARNING!

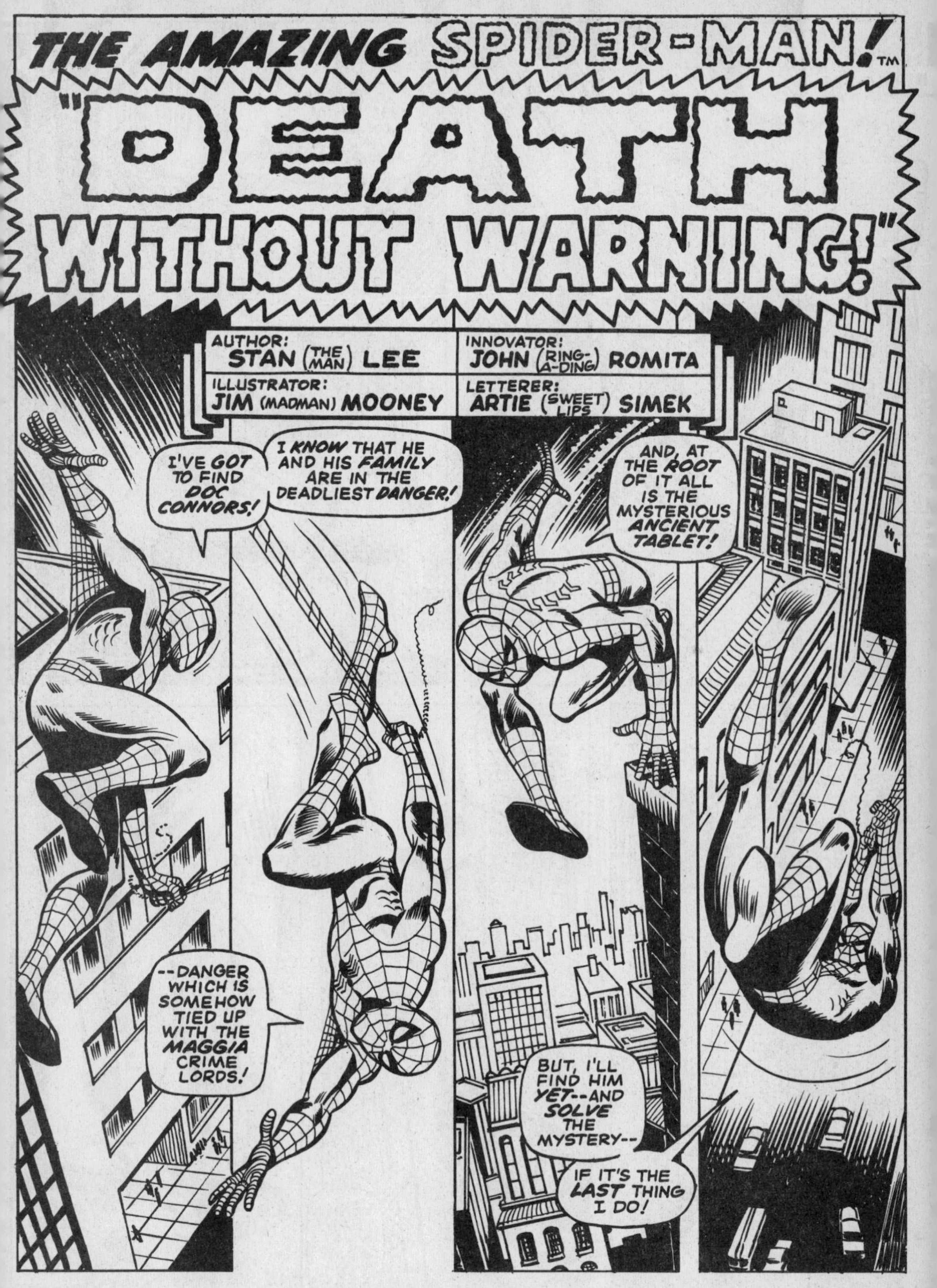

THE AMAZING SPIDER-MAN! TM
"DEATH WITHOUT WARNING!"
AUTHOR: STAN (THE MAN) LEE
INNOVATOR: JOHN (RING-A-DING) ROMITA
ILLUSTRATOR: JIM (MADMAN) MOONEY
LETTERER: ARTIE (SWEET LIPS) SIMEK
I'VE GOT TO FIND DOC CONNORS!
I KNOW THAT HE AND HIS FAMILY ARE IN THE DEADLIEST DANGER!
--DANGER WHICH IS SOMEHOW TIED UP WITH THE MAGGIA CRIME LORDS!
AND, AT THE ROOT OF IT ALL IS THE MYSTERIOUS ANCIENT TABLET!
BUT, I'LL FIND HIM YET--AND SOLVE THE MYSTERY--
IF IT'S THE LAST THING I DO!

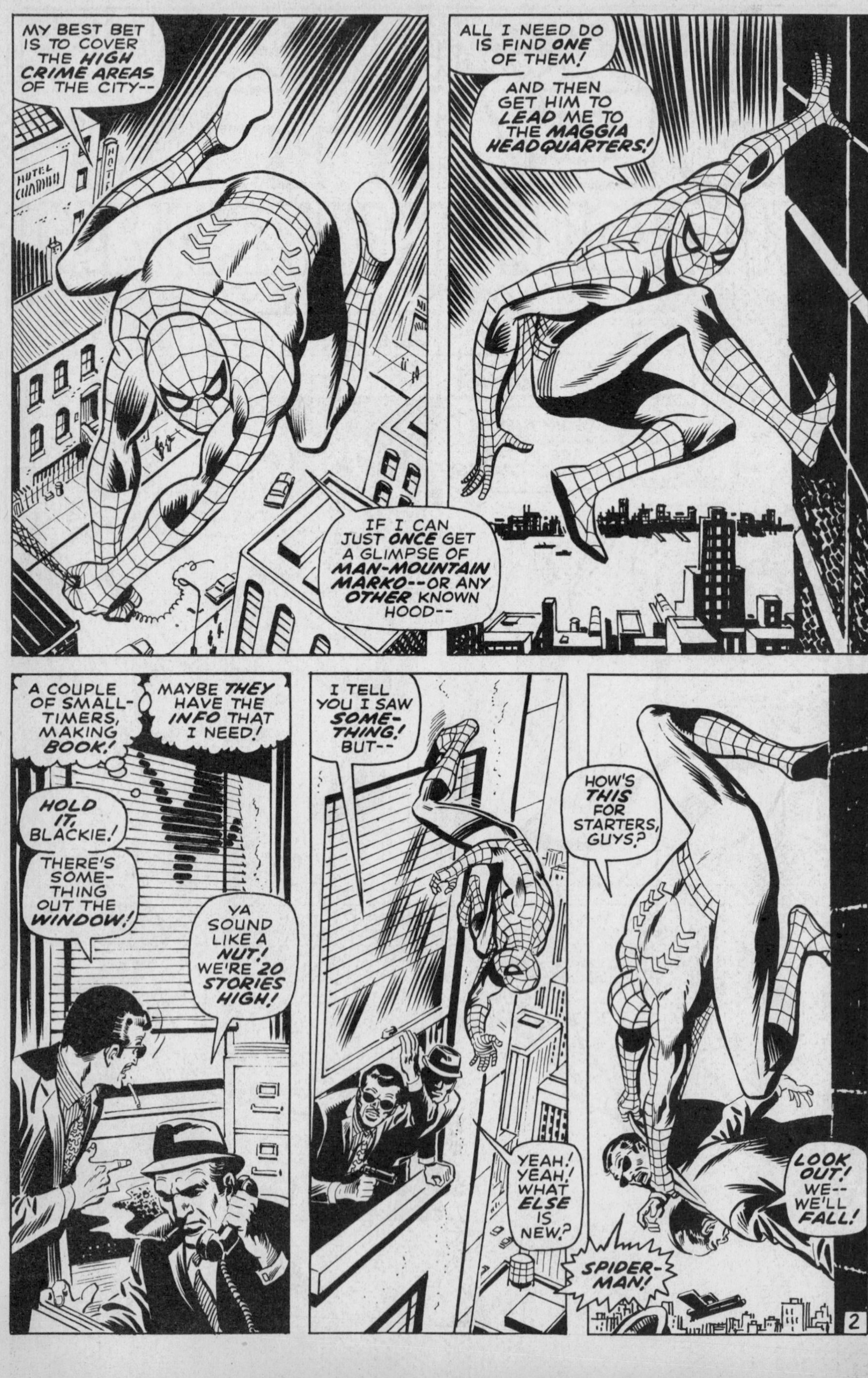
MY BEST BET IS TO COVER THE HIGH CRIME AREAS OF THE CITY--
HOTEL CHAMPION
ALL I NEED DO IS FIND ONE OF THEM!
AND THEN GET HIM TO LEAD ME TO THE MAGGIA HEADQUARTERS!
IF I CAN JUST ONCE GET A GLIMPSE OF MAN-MOUNTAIN MARKO--OR ANY OTHER KNOWN HOOD--
A COUPLE OF SMALL-TIMERS, MAKING BOOK!
MAYBE THEY HAVE THE INFO THAT I NEED!
HOLD IT, BLACKIE!
THERE'S SOME-THING OUT THE WINDOW!
YA SOUND LIKE A NUT! WE'RE 20 STORIES HIGH!
I TELL YOU I SAW SOME-THING! BUT--
YEAH! YEAH! WHAT ELSE IS NEW?
HOW'S THIS FOR STARTERS, GUYS?
LOOK OUT! WE-- WE'LL FALL!
SPIDER-MAN!

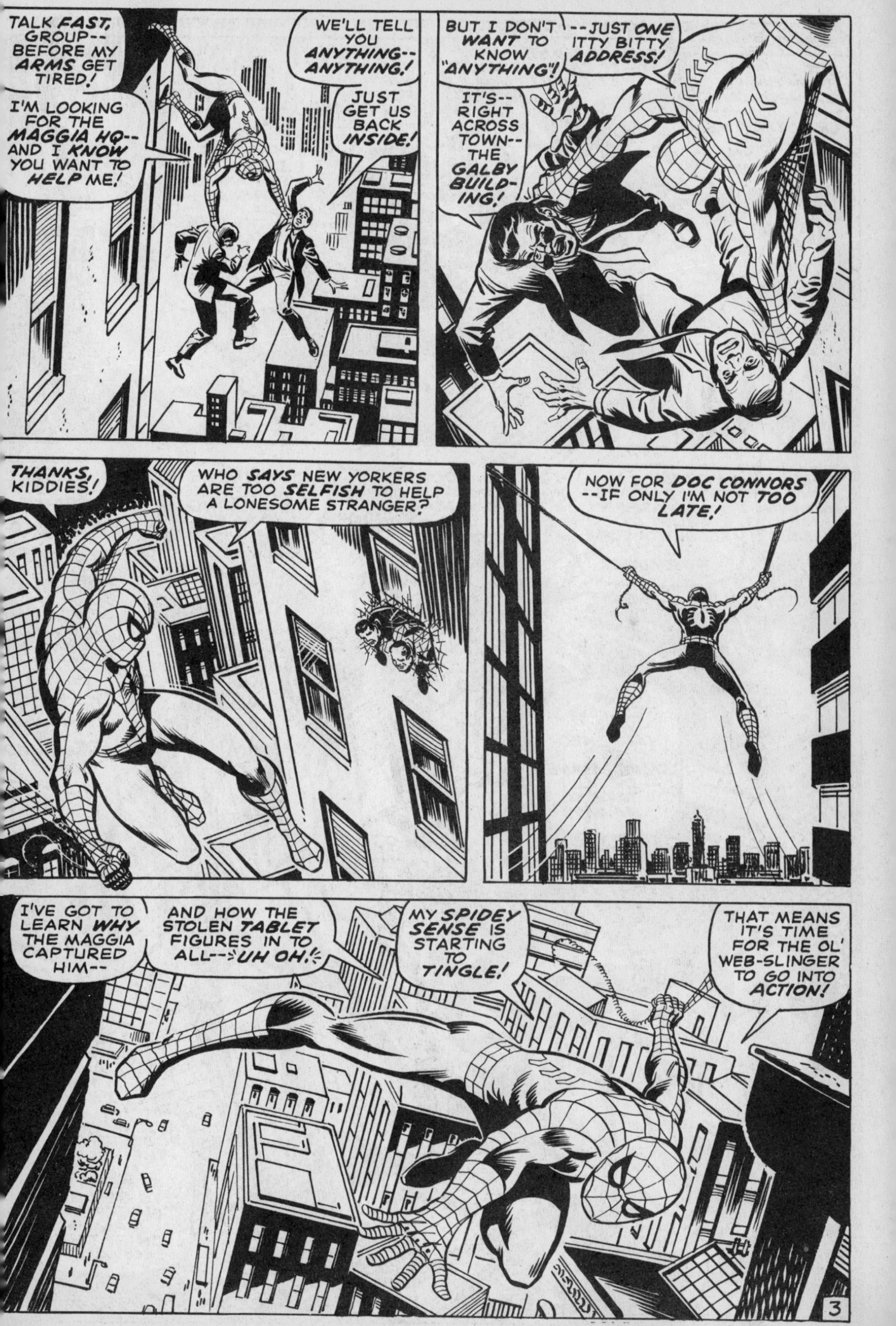
TALK FAST, GROUP-- BEFORE MY ARMS GET TIRED!
I'M LOOKING FOR THE MAGGIA HQ-- AND I KNOW YOU WANT TO HELP ME!
WE'LL TELL YOU ANYTHING-- ANYTHING!
JUST GET US BACK INSIDE!
BUT I DON'T WANT TO KNOW "ANYTHING"!
--JUST ONE ITTY BITTY ADDRESS!
IT'S-- RIGHT ACROSS TOWN-- THE GALBY BUILD-ING!
THANKS, KIDDIES!
WHO SAYS NEW YORKERS ARE TOO SELFISH TO HELP A LONESOME STRANGER?
NOW FOR DOC CONNORS --IF ONLY I'M NOT TOO LATE!
I'VE GOT TO LEARN WHY THE MAGGIA CAPTURED HIM--
AND HOW THE STOLEN TABLET FIGURES IN TO ALL-- UH OH!
MY SPIDEY SENSE IS STARTING TO TINGLE!
THAT MEANS IT'S TIME FOR THE OL' WEB-SLINGER TO GO INTO ACTION!
3

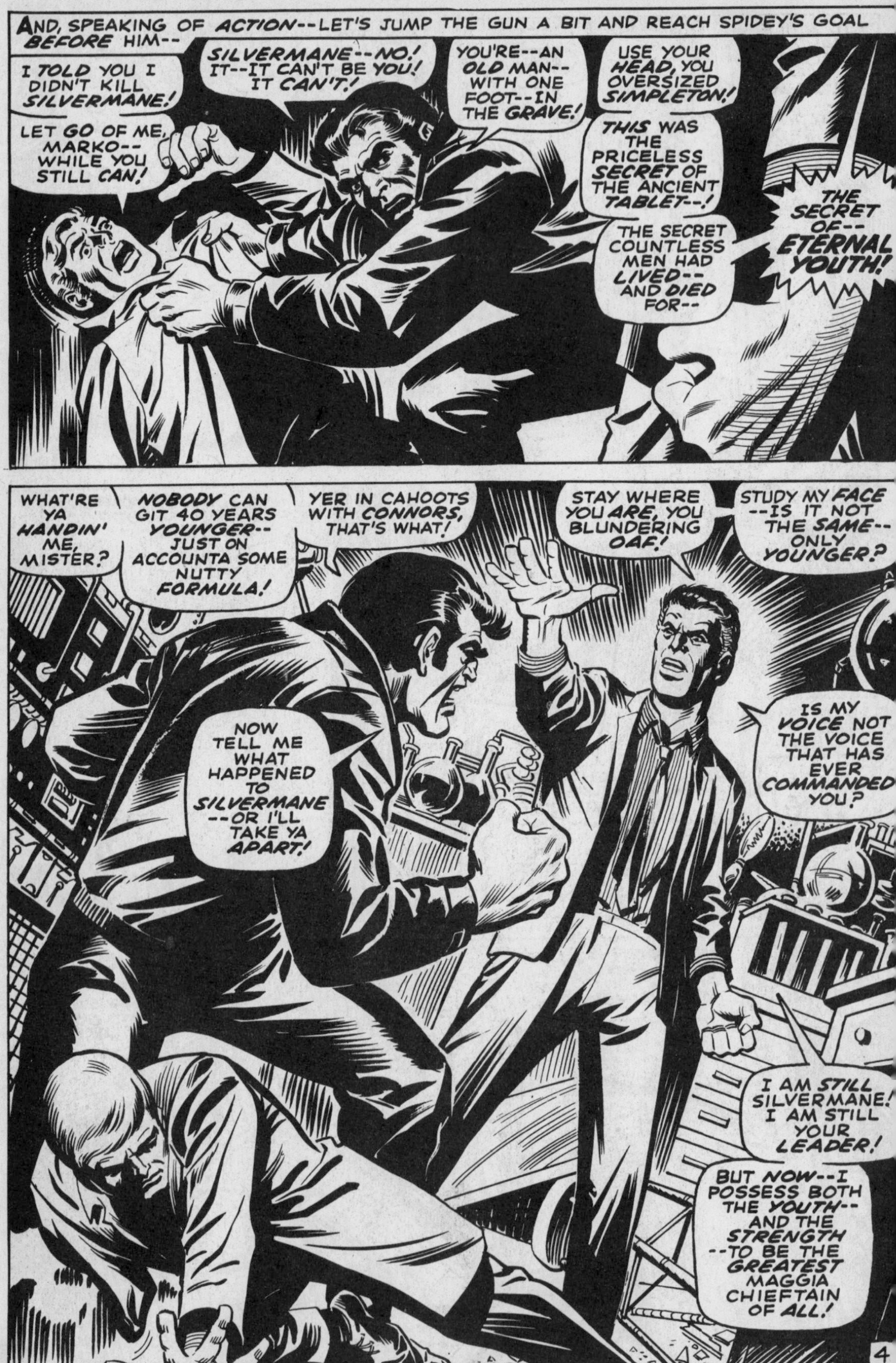

AND, SPEAKING OF ACTION--LET'S JUMP THE GUN A BIT AND REACH SPIDEY'S GOAL BEFORE HIM--
I TOLD YOU I DIDN'T KILL SILVERMANE!
LET GO OF ME, MARKO-- WHILE YOU STILL CAN!
SILVERMANE--NO! IT--IT CAN'T BE YOU! IT CAN'T!
YOU'RE--AN OLD MAN-- WITH ONE FOOT--IN THE GRAVE!
USE YOUR HEAD, YOU OVERSIZED SIMPLETON!
THIS WAS THE PRICELESS SECRET OF THE ANCIENT TABLET--!
THE SECRET COUNTLESS MEN HAD LIVED-- AND DIED FOR--
THE SECRET OF-- ETERNAL YOUTH!
WHAT'RE YA HANDIN' ME, MISTER?
NOBODY CAN GIT 40 YEARS YOUNGER-- JUST ON ACCOUNTA SOME NUTTY FORMULA!
YER IN CAHOOTS WITH CONNORS, THAT'S WHAT!
NOW TELL ME WHAT HAPPENED TO SILVERMANE --OR I'LL TAKE YA APART!
STAY WHERE YOU ARE, YOU BLUNDERING OAF!
STUDY MY FACE --IS IT NOT THE SAME-- ONLY YOUNGER?
IS MY VOICE NOT THE VOICE THAT HAS EVER COMMANDED YOU?
I AM STILL SILVERMANE! I AM STILL YOUR LEADER!
BUT NOW--I POSSESS BOTH THE YOUTH-- AND THE STRENGTH --TO BE THE GREATEST MAGGIA CHIEFTAIN OF ALL!

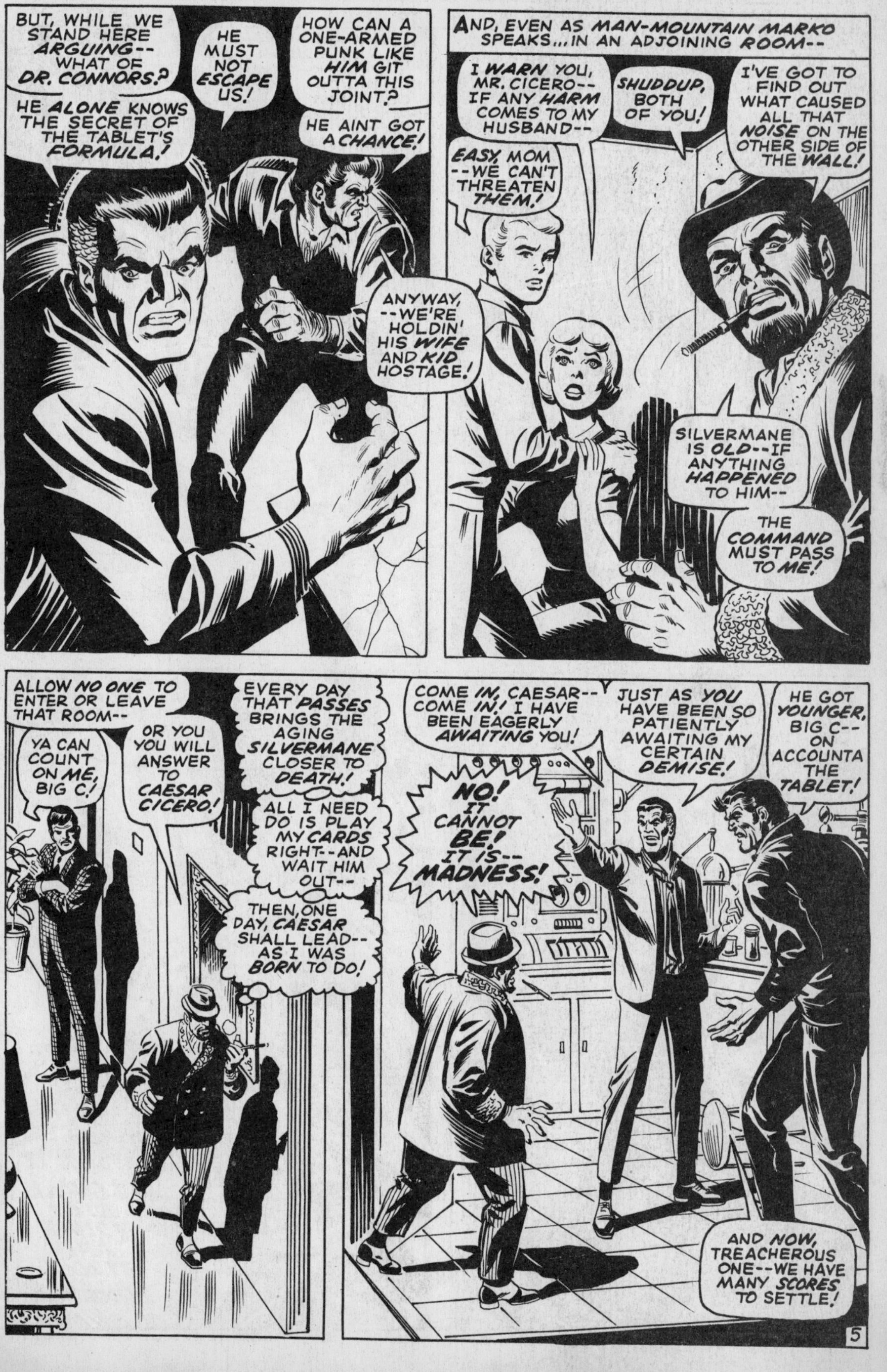
BUT, WHILE WE STAND HERE ARGUING-- WHAT OF DR. CONNORS?
HE ALONE KNOWS THE SECRET OF THE TABLET'S FORMULA!
HE MUST NOT ESCAPE US!
HOW CAN A ONE-ARMED PUNK LIKE HIM GIT OUTTA THIS JOINT?
HE AINT GOT A CHANCE!
ANYWAY, --WE'RE HOLDIN' HIS WIFE AND KID HOSTAGE!
AND, EVEN AS MAN-MOUNTAIN MARKO SPEAKS... IN AN ADJOINING ROOM--
I WARN YOU, MR. CICERO-- IF ANY HARM COMES TO MY HUSBAND--
EASY, MOM --WE CAN'T THREATEN THEM!
SHUDDUP, BOTH OF YOU!
I'VE GOT TO FIND OUT WHAT CAUSED ALL THAT NOISE ON THE OTHER SIDE OF THE WALL!
SILVERMANE IS OLD--IF ANYTHING HAPPENED TO HIM--
THE COMMAND MUST PASS TO ME!
ALLOW NO ONE TO ENTER OR LEAVE THAT ROOM--
OR YOU YOU WILL ANSWER TO CAESAR CICERO!
YA CAN COUNT ON ME, BIG C!
EVERY DAY THAT PASSES BRINGS THE AGING SILVERMANE CLOSER TO DEATH!
ALL I NEED DO IS PLAY MY CARDS RIGHT--AND WAIT HIM OUT--
THEN, ONE DAY, CAESAR SHALL LEAD-- AS I WAS BORN TO DO!
COME IN, CAESAR-- COME IN! I HAVE BEEN EAGERLY AWAITING YOU!
NO! IT CANNOT BE! IT IS-- MADNESS!
JUST AS YOU HAVE BEEN SO PATIENTLY AWAITING MY CERTAIN DEMISE!
HE GOT YOUNGER, BIG C-- ON ACCOUNTA THE TABLET!
AND NOW, TREACHEROUS ONE--WE HAVE MANY SCORES TO SETTLE!
5

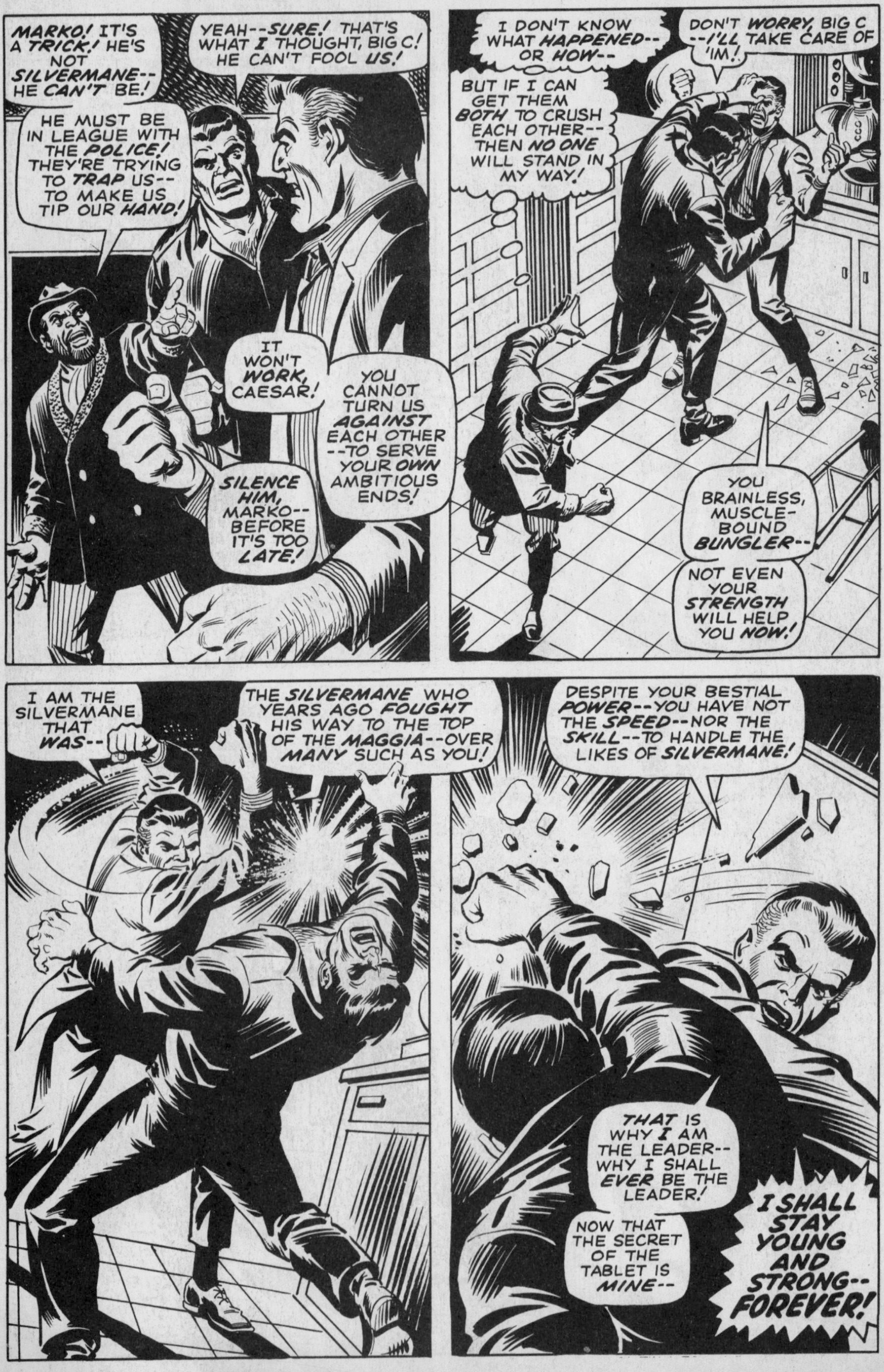

MARKO! IT'S A TRICK! HE'S NOT SILVERMANE-- HE CAN'T BE!
YEAH--SURE! THAT'S WHAT I THOUGHT, BIG C! HE CAN'T FOOL US!
HE MUST BE IN LEAGUE WITH THE POLICE! THEY'RE TRYING TO TRAP US-- TO MAKE US TIP OUR HAND!
IT WON'T WORK, CAESAR!
YOU CANNOT TURN US AGAINST EACH OTHER --TO SERVE YOUR OWN AMBITIOUS ENDS!
SILENCE HIM, MARKO-- BEFORE IT'S TOO LATE!
I DON'T KNOW WHAT HAPPENED-- OR HOW--
BUT IF I CAN GET THEM BOTH TO CRUSH EACH OTHER-- THEN NO ONE WILL STAND IN MY WAY!
DON'T WORRY, BIG C --I'LL TAKE CARE OF 'IM!
YOU BRAINLESS, MUSCLE-BOUND BUNGLER--
NOT EVEN YOUR STRENGTH WILL HELP YOU NOW!
I AM THE SILVERMANE THAT WAS--
THE SILVERMANE WHO YEARS AGO FOUGHT HIS WAY TO THE TOP OF THE MAGGIA--OVER MANY SUCH AS YOU!
DESPITE YOUR BESTIAL POWER--YOU HAVE NOT THE SPEED--NOR THE SKILL--TO HANDLE THE LIKES OF SILVERMANE!
THAT IS WHY I AM THE LEADER-- WHY I SHALL EVER BE THE LEADER!
NOW THAT THE SECRET OF THE TABLET IS MINE--
I SHALL STAY YOUNG AND STRONG-- FOREVER!

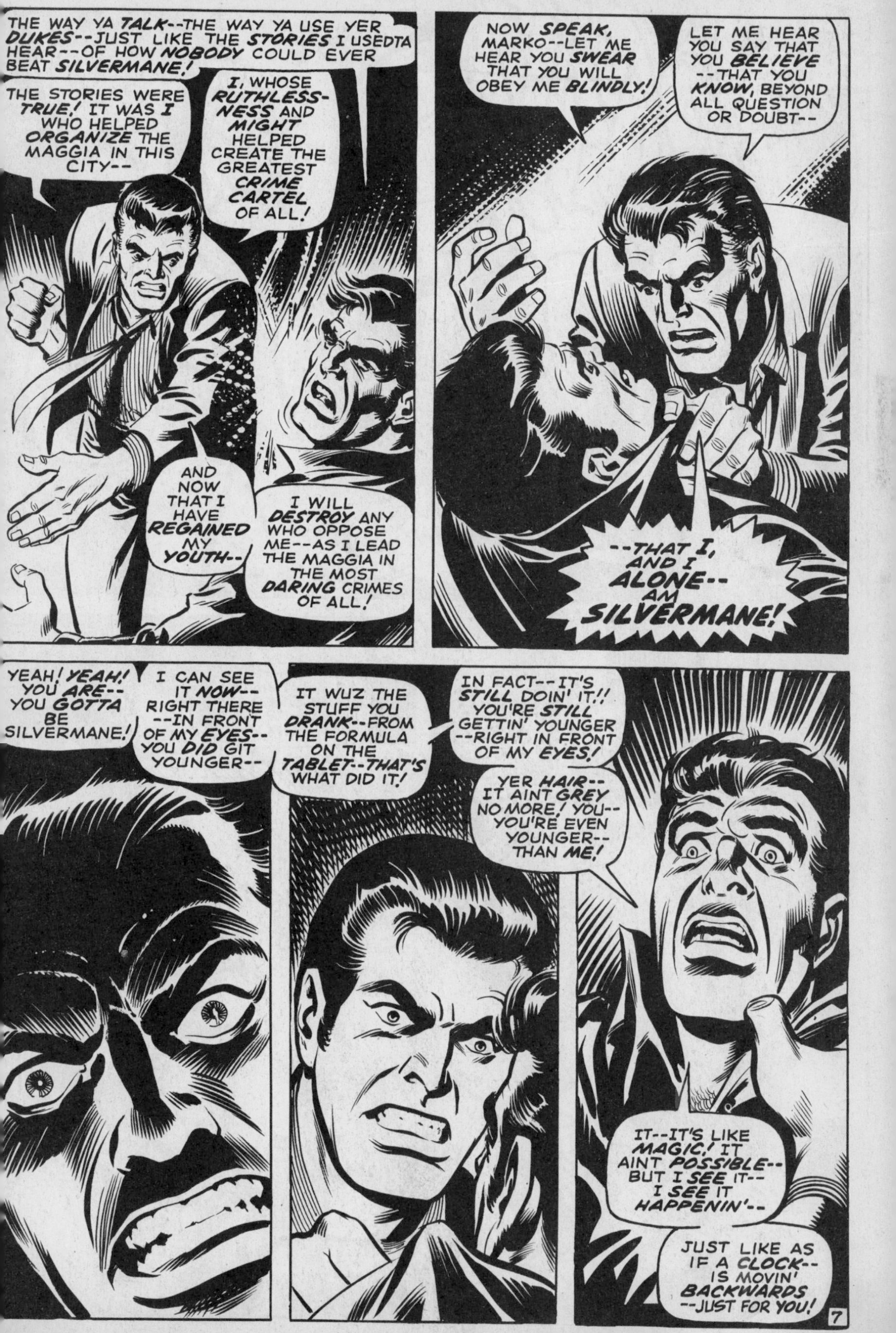
THE WAY YA TALK--THE WAY YA USE YER DUKES--JUST LIKE THE STORIES I USEDTA HEAR--OF HOW NOBODY COULD EVER BEAT SILVERMANE!
THE STORIES WERE TRUE! IT WAS I WHO HELPED ORGANIZE THE MAGGIA IN THIS CITY--
I, WHOSE RUTHLESS-NESS AND MIGHT HELPED CREATE THE GREATEST CRIME CARTEL OF ALL!
AND NOW THAT I HAVE REGAINED MY YOUTH--
I WILL DESTROY ANY WHO OPPOSE ME--AS I LEAD THE MAGGIA IN THE MOST DARING CRIMES OF ALL!
NOW SPEAK, MARKO--LET ME HEAR YOU SWEAR THAT YOU WILL OBEY ME BLINDLY!
LET ME HEAR YOU SAY THAT YOU BELIEVE --THAT YOU KNOW, BEYOND ALL QUESTION OR DOUBT--
--THAT I, AND I ALONE--AM SILVERMANE!
YEAH! YEAH! YOU ARE--YOU GOTTA BE SILVERMANE!
I CAN SEE IT NOW--RIGHT THERE --IN FRONT OF MY EYES--YOU DID GIT YOUNGER--
IT WUZ THE STUFF YOU DRANK--FROM THE FORMULA ON THE TABLET--THAT'S WHAT DID IT!
IN FACT--IT'S STILL DOIN' IT!! YOU'RE STILL GETTIN' YOUNGER --RIGHT IN FRONT OF MY EYES!
YER HAIR--IT AINT GREY NO MORE! YOU--YOU'RE EVEN YOUNGER--THAN ME!
IT--IT'S LIKE MAGIC! IT AINT POSSIBLE--BUT I SEE IT--I SEE IT HAPPENIN'--
JUST LIKE AS IF A CLOCK--IS MOVIN' BACKWARDS --JUST FOR YOU!
7

MARKO--LOOK OUT BEHIND YOU--!

KURASH!

SPIDER-MAN!

I KNEW I'D FIND YOU, BIG MAN-- SOONER OR LATER!

STOP 'IM! IF HE MANAGES TO-- -UNHHH!-

HE'S ALL ALONE! HE CAN'T-- -ARHHH!-

RELAX, GENT'S! I'LL HANDLE THINGS FROM HERE ON IN!

NOW, THE *FIRST* THING I WANT IS *DR. CONNORS!*

IF ANYTHING'S HAPPENED TO HIM--OR HIS *FAMILY*--

SHUT HIM UP, MARKO--AND DO IT *NOW!*

I WAS HOPIN' YA'D ASK ME, SILVER-MANE!

SILVER-MANE? THAT CAN'T BE HIM! HE SHOULD BE EIGHTY YEARS OLD!

8

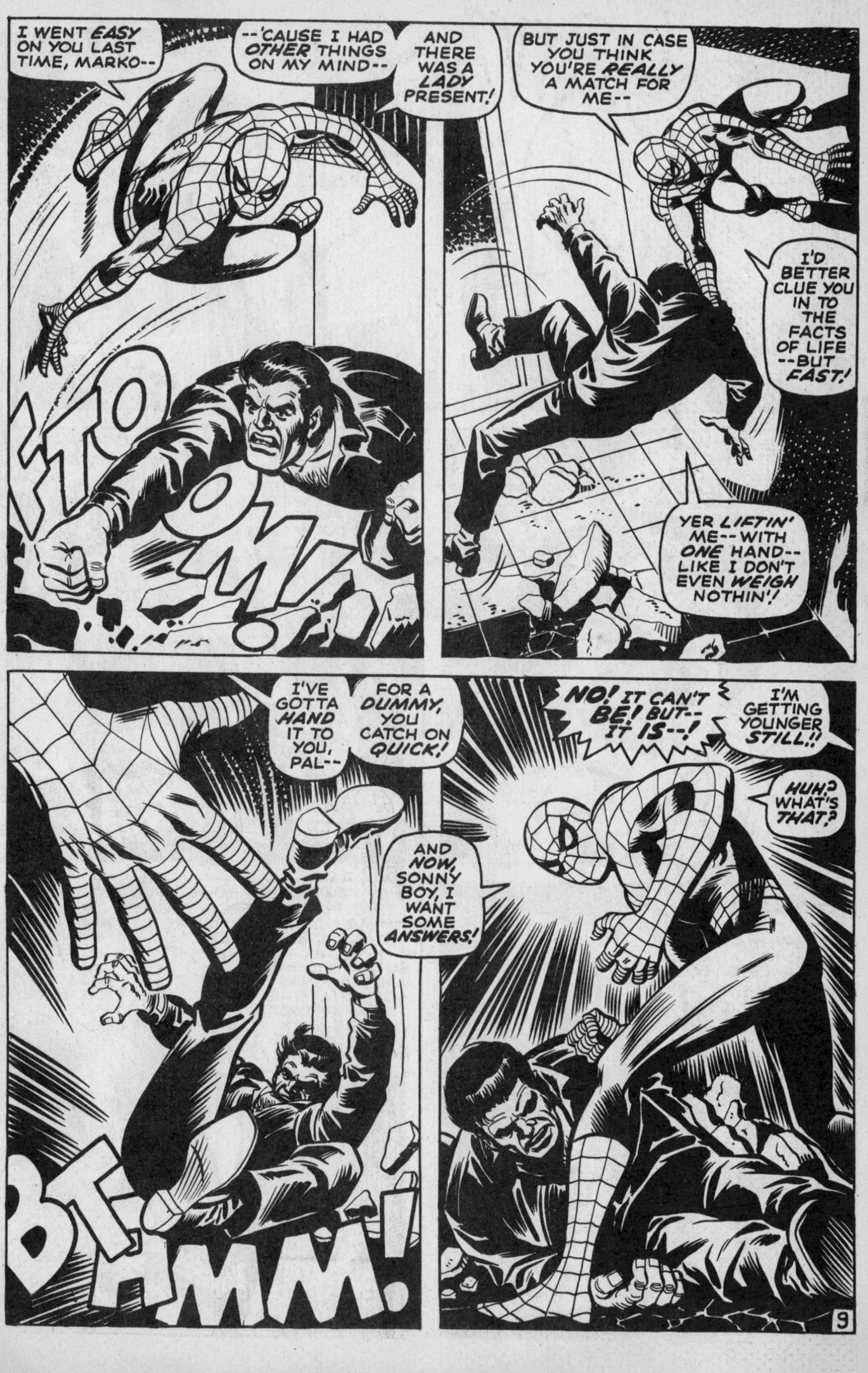
I WENT EASY ON YOU LAST TIME, MARKO--
--'CAUSE I HAD OTHER THINGS ON MY MIND--
AND THERE WAS A LADY PRESENT!
TOOM!
BUT JUST IN CASE YOU THINK YOU'RE REALLY A MATCH FOR ME--
I'D BETTER CLUE YOU IN TO THE FACTS OF LIFE --BUT FAST!
YER LIFTIN' ME--WITH ONE HAND--LIKE I DON'T EVEN WEIGH NOTHIN'!
I'VE GOTTA HAND IT TO YOU, PAL--
FOR A DUMMY, YOU CATCH ON QUICK!
AND NOW, SONNY BOY, I WANT SOME ANSWERS!
BTHMM!
NO! IT CAN'T BE! BUT-- IT IS--!
I'M GETTING YOUNGER STILL!!
HUH? WHAT'S THAT?

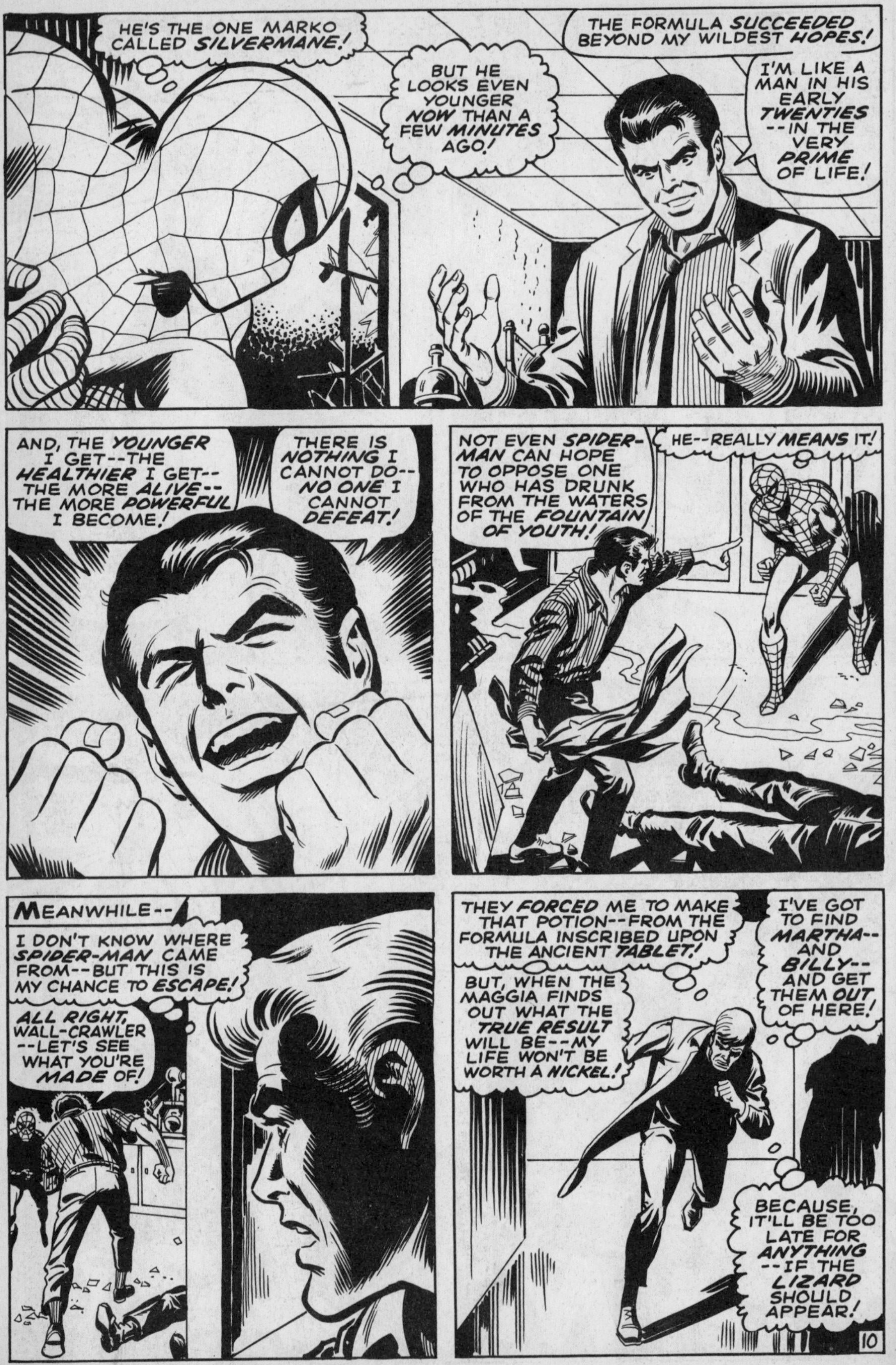
HE'S THE ONE MARKO CALLED SILVERMANE!
BUT HE LOOKS EVEN YOUNGER NOW THAN A FEW MINUTES AGO!
THE FORMULA SUCCEEDED BEYOND MY WILDEST HOPES!
I'M LIKE A MAN IN HIS EARLY TWENTIES --IN THE VERY PRIME OF LIFE!
AND, THE YOUNGER I GET--THE HEALTHIER I GET--THE MORE ALIVE--THE MORE POWERFUL I BECOME!
THERE IS NOTHING I CANNOT DO--NO ONE I CANNOT DEFEAT!
NOT EVEN SPIDER-MAN CAN HOPE TO OPPOSE ONE WHO HAS DRUNK FROM THE WATERS OF THE FOUNTAIN OF YOUTH!
HE--REALLY MEANS IT!
MEANWHILE--
I DON'T KNOW WHERE SPIDER-MAN CAME FROM--BUT THIS IS MY CHANCE TO ESCAPE!
ALL RIGHT, WALL-CRAWLER --LET'S SEE WHAT YOU'RE MADE OF!
THEY FORCED ME TO MAKE THAT POTION--FROM THE FORMULA INSCRIBED UPON THE ANCIENT TABLET!
BUT, WHEN THE MAGGIA FINDS OUT WHAT THE TRUE RESULT WILL BE--MY LIFE WON'T BE WORTH A NICKEL!
I'VE GOT TO FIND MARTHA--AND BILLY--AND GET THEM OUT OF HERE!
BECAUSE, IT'LL BE TOO LATE FOR ANYTHING --IF THE LIZARD SHOULD APPEAR!
10

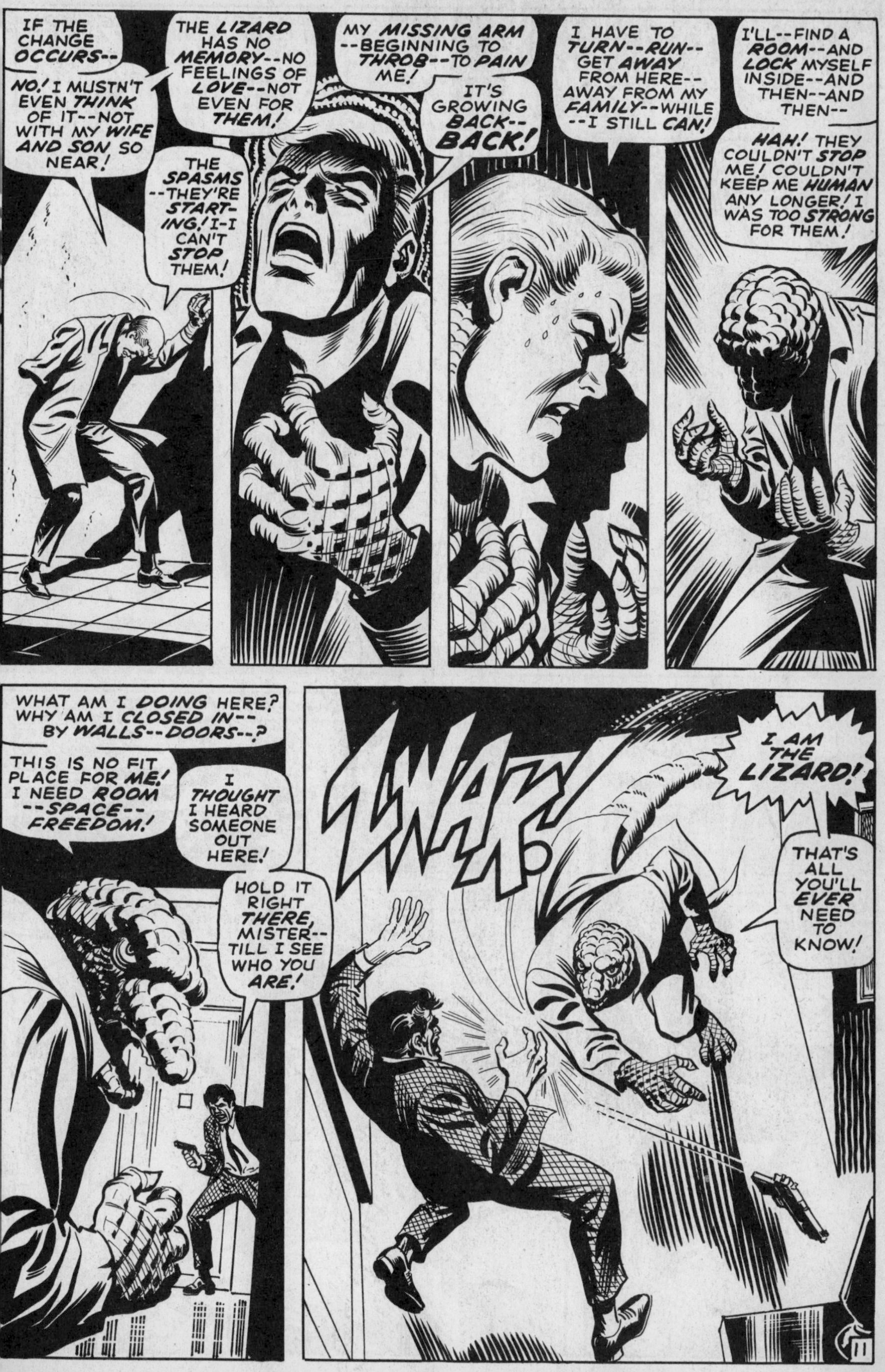

IF THE CHANGE OCCURS--
NO! I MUSTN'T EVEN THINK OF IT--NOT WITH MY WIFE AND SON SO NEAR!
THE LIZARD HAS NO MEMORY--NO FEELINGS OF LOVE--NOT EVEN FOR THEM!
THE SPASMS--THEY'RE STARTING! I-I CAN'T STOP THEM!
MY MISSING ARM--BEGINNING TO THROB--TO PAIN ME!
IT'S GROWING BACK--BACK!
I HAVE TO TURN--RUN--GET AWAY FROM HERE--AWAY FROM MY FAMILY--WHILE--I STILL CAN!
I'LL--FIND A ROOM--AND LOCK MYSELF INSIDE--AND THEN--AND THEN--
HAH! THEY COULDN'T STOP ME! COULDN'T KEEP ME HUMAN ANY LONGER! I WAS TOO STRONG FOR THEM!
WHAT AM I DOING HERE? WHY AM I CLOSED IN--BY WALLS--DOORS--?
THIS IS NO FIT PLACE FOR ME! I NEED ROOM--SPACE--FREEDOM!
I THOUGHT I HEARD SOMEONE OUT HERE!
HOLD IT RIGHT THERE, MISTER--TILL I SEE WHO YOU ARE!
ZWAP!
I AM THE LIZARD!
THAT'S ALL YOU'LL EVER NEED TO KNOW!
11

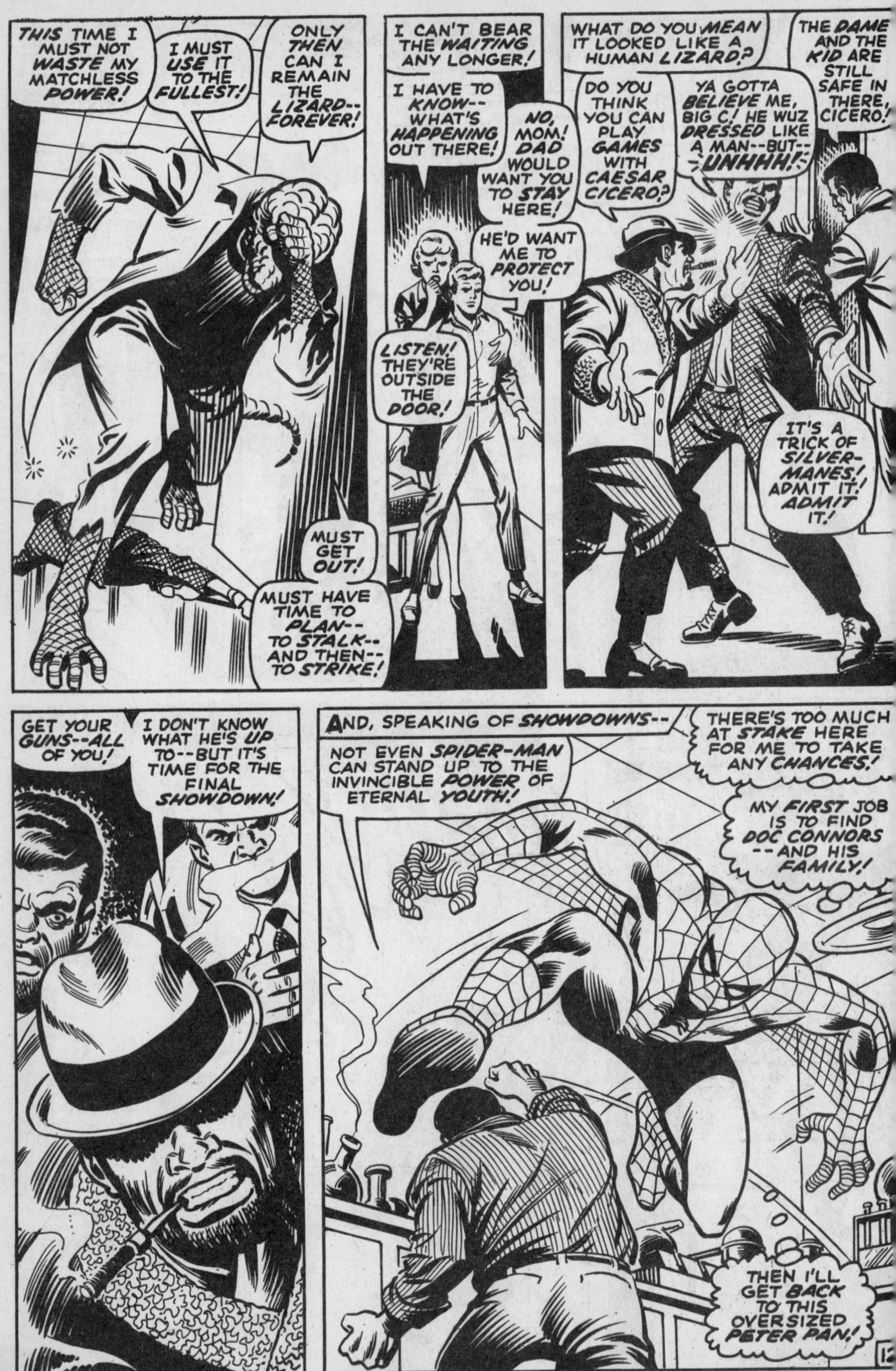
THIS TIME I MUST NOT WASTE MY MATCHLESS POWER!
I MUST USE IT TO THE FULLEST!
ONLY THEN CAN I REMAIN THE LIZARD-- FOREVER!
MUST GET OUT!
MUST HAVE TIME TO PLAN-- TO STALK-- AND THEN-- TO STRIKE!
I CAN'T BEAR THE WAITING ANY LONGER!
I HAVE TO KNOW-- WHAT'S HAPPENING OUT THERE!
NO, MOM! DAD WOULD WANT YOU TO STAY HERE!
HE'D WANT ME TO PROTECT YOU!
LISTEN! THEY'RE OUTSIDE THE DOOR!
WHAT DO YOU MEAN IT LOOKED LIKE A HUMAN LIZARD?
THE DAME AND THE KID ARE STILL SAFE IN THERE, CICERO!
DO YOU THINK YOU CAN PLAY GAMES WITH CAESAR CICERO?
YA GOTTA BELIEVE ME, BIG C.! HE WUZ DRESSED LIKE A MAN--BUT-- UNHHH!
IT'S A TRICK OF SILVERMANES! ADMIT IT! ADMIT IT!
GET YOUR GUNS--ALL OF YOU!
I DON'T KNOW WHAT HE'S UP TO--BUT IT'S TIME FOR THE FINAL SHOWDOWN!
AND, SPEAKING OF SHOWDOWNS--
NOT EVEN SPIDER-MAN CAN STAND UP TO THE INVINCIBLE POWER OF ETERNAL YOUTH!
THERE'S TOO MUCH AT STAKE HERE FOR ME TO TAKE ANY CHANCES!
MY FIRST JOB IS TO FIND DOC CONNORS --AND HIS FAMILY!
THEN I'LL GET BACK TO THIS OVERSIZED PETER PAN!

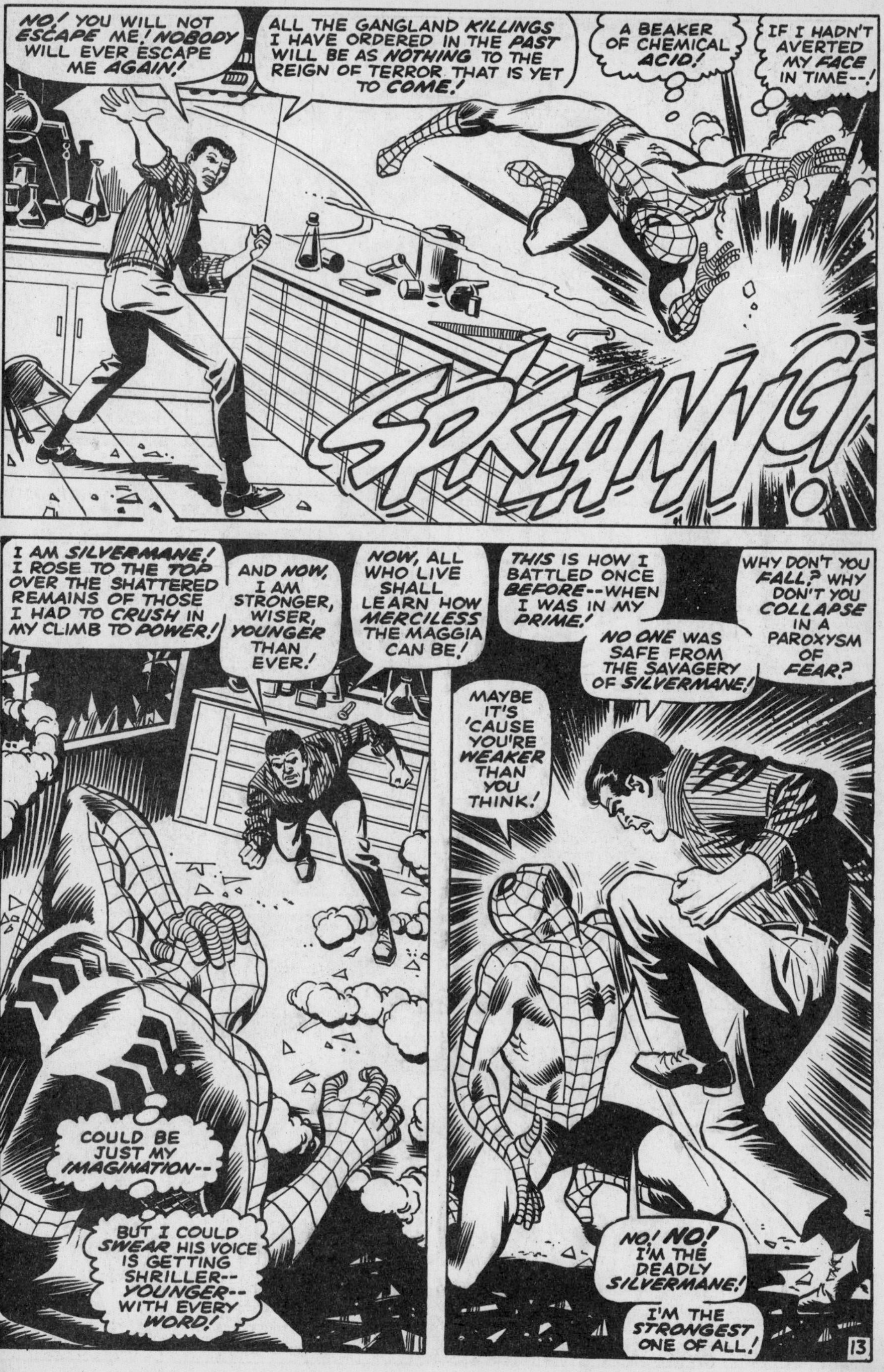
NO! YOU WILL NOT ESCAPE ME! NOBODY WILL EVER ESCAPE ME AGAIN!
ALL THE GANGLAND KILLINGS I HAVE ORDERED IN THE PAST WILL BE AS NOTHING TO THE REIGN OF TERROR THAT IS YET TO COME!
A BEAKER OF CHEMICAL ACID!
IF I HADN'T AVERTED MY FACE IN TIME--!
SPKLANNG!
I AM SILVERMANE! I ROSE TO THE TOP OVER THE SHATTERED REMAINS OF THOSE I HAD TO CRUSH IN MY CLIMB TO POWER!
AND NOW, I AM STRONGER, WISER, YOUNGER THAN EVER!
NOW, ALL WHO LIVE SHALL LEARN HOW MERCILESS THE MAGGIA CAN BE!
COULD BE JUST MY IMAGINATION--
BUT I COULD SWEAR HIS VOICE IS GETTING SHRILLER-- YOUNGER-- WITH EVERY WORD!
THIS IS HOW I BATTLED ONCE BEFORE--WHEN I WAS IN MY PRIME!
NO ONE WAS SAFE FROM THE SAVAGERY OF SILVERMANE!
WHY DON'T YOU FALL? WHY DON'T YOU COLLAPSE IN A PAROXYSM OF FEAR?
MAYBE IT'S 'CAUSE YOU'RE WEAKER THAN YOU THINK!
NO! NO! I'M THE DEADLY SILVERMANE!
I'M THE STRONGEST ONE OF ALL!
13

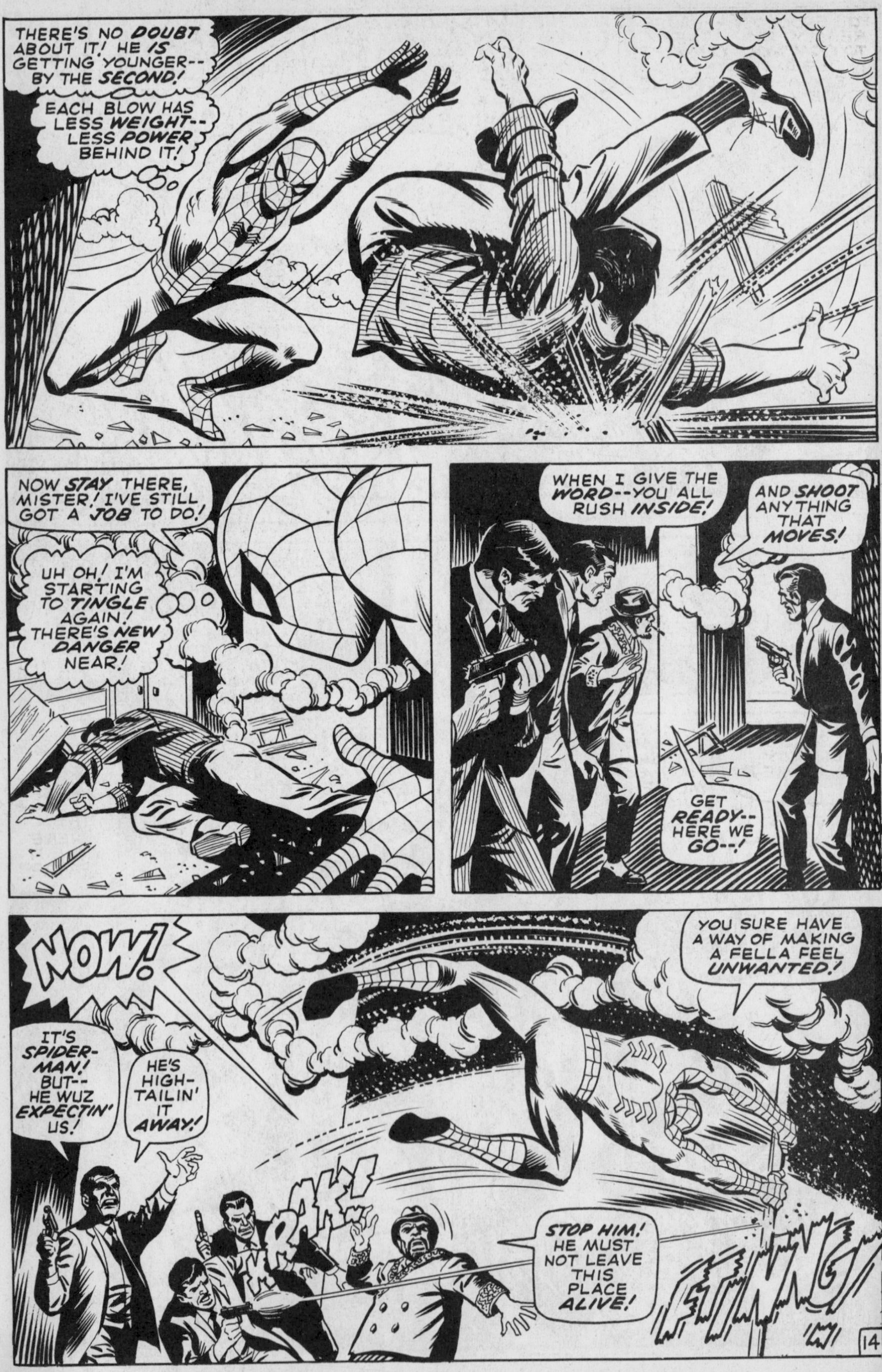
THERE'S NO DOUBT ABOUT IT! HE IS GETTING YOUNGER-- BY THE SECOND!
EACH BLOW HAS LESS WEIGHT-- LESS POWER BEHIND IT!
NOW STAY THERE, MISTER! I'VE STILL GOT A JOB TO DO!
UH OH! I'M STARTING TO TINGLE AGAIN! THERE'S NEW DANGER NEAR!
WHEN I GIVE THE WORD--YOU ALL RUSH INSIDE!
AND SHOOT ANYTHING THAT MOVES!
GET READY-- HERE WE GO--!
NOW!
YOU SURE HAVE A WAY OF MAKING A FELLA FEEL UNWANTED!
IT'S SPIDER-MAN! BUT-- HE WUZ EXPECTIN' US!
HE'S HIGH-TAILIN' IT AWAY!
KRAK!
STOP HIM! HE MUST NOT LEAVE THIS PLACE ALIVE!
FTING!

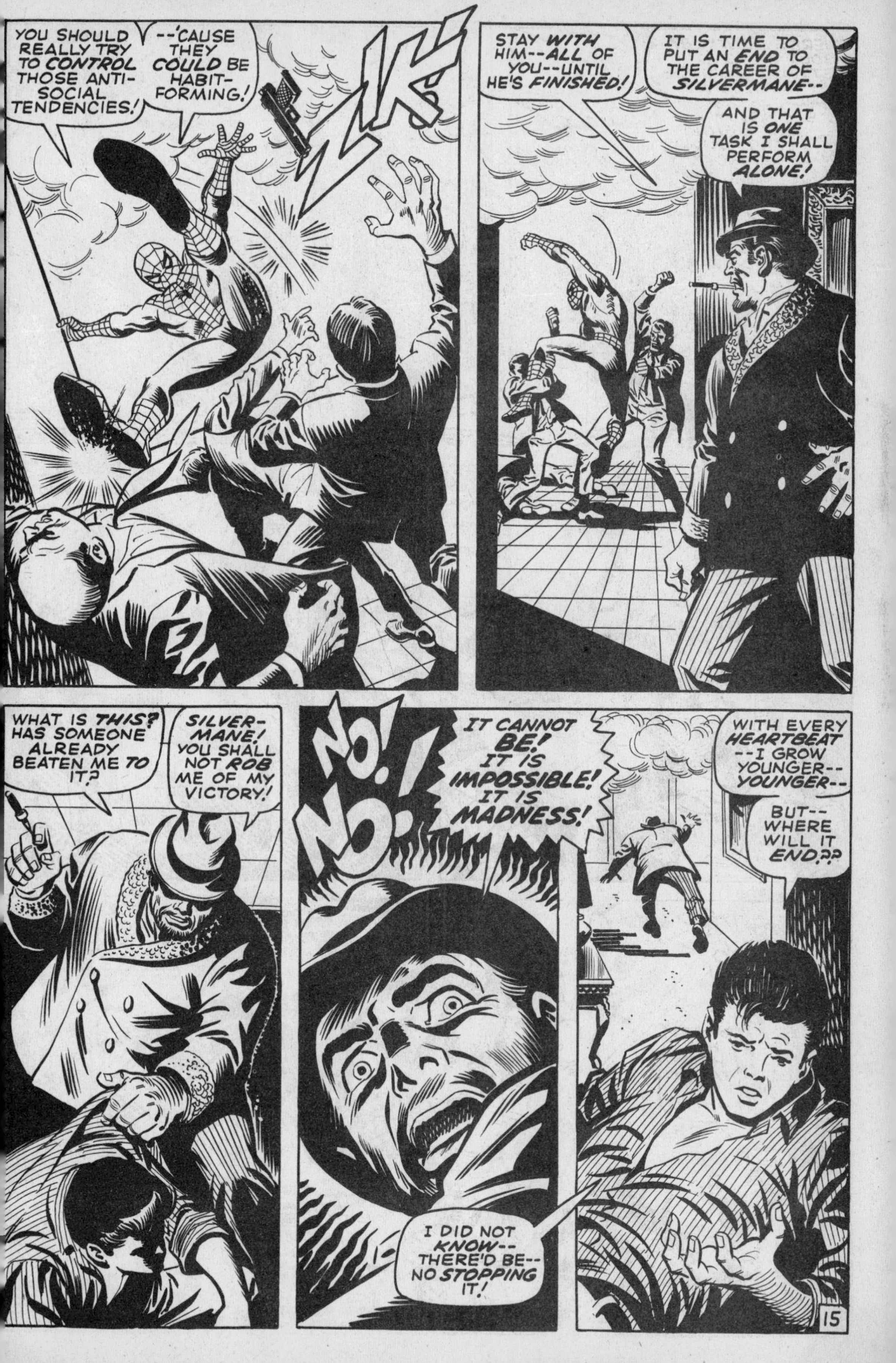
YOU SHOULD REALLY TRY TO CONTROL THOSE ANTI-SOCIAL TENDENCIES!
--'CAUSE THEY COULD BE HABIT-FORMING!
ZAK!
STAY WITH HIM--ALL OF YOU--UNTIL HE'S FINISHED!
IT IS TIME TO PUT AN END TO THE CAREER OF SILVERMANE--
AND THAT IS ONE TASK I SHALL PERFORM ALONE!
WHAT IS THIS? HAS SOMEONE ALREADY BEATEN ME TO IT?
SILVERMANE! YOU SHALL NOT ROB ME OF MY VICTORY!
NO! NO!
IT CANNOT BE! IT IS IMPOSSIBLE! IT IS MADNESS!
I DID NOT KNOW--THERE'D BE--NO STOPPING IT!
WITH EVERY HEARTBEAT--I GROW YOUNGER--YOUNGER--
BUT--WHERE WILL IT END???
15

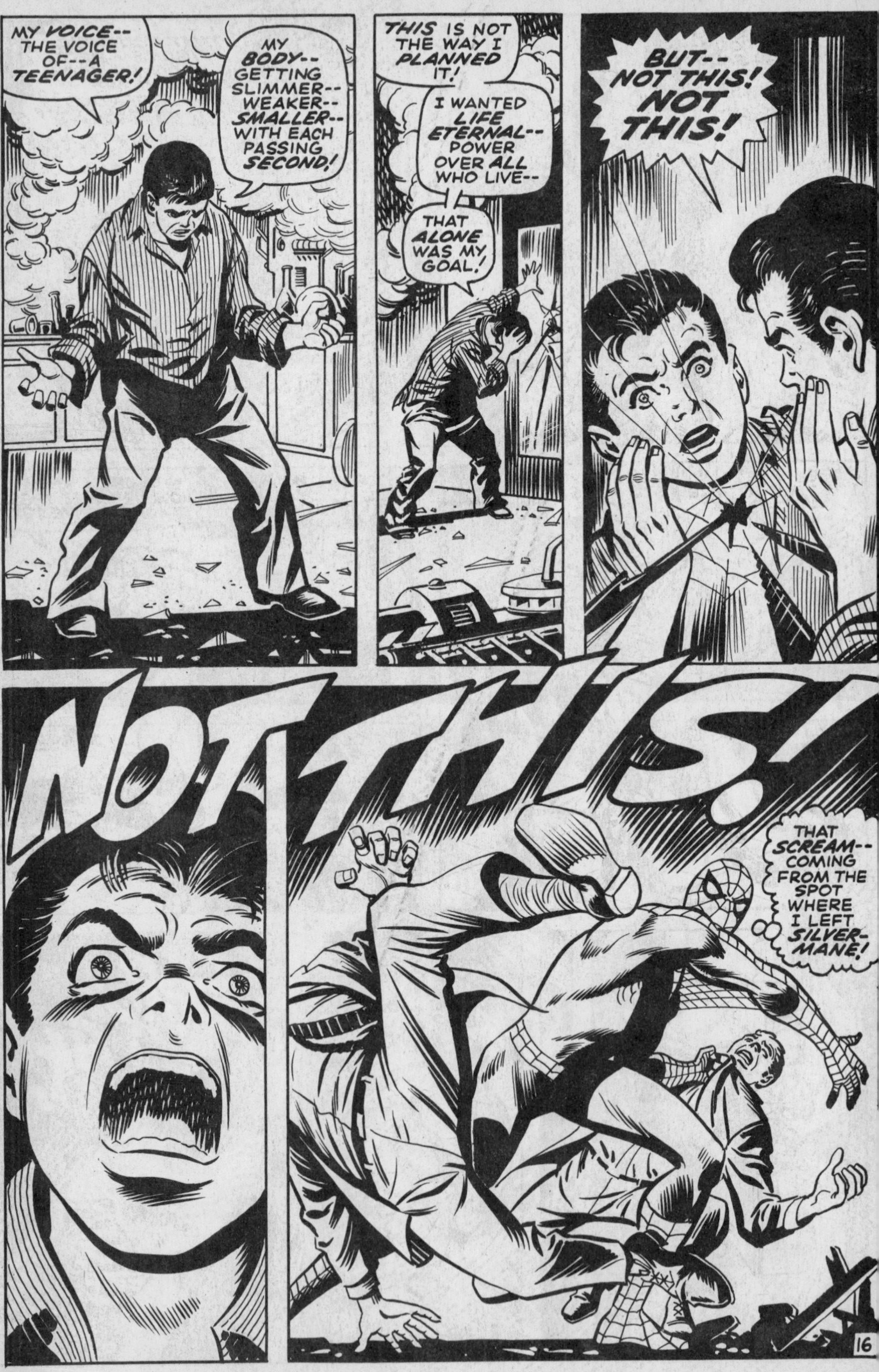
MY VOICE-- THE VOICE OF--A TEENAGER!
MY BODY-- GETTING SLIMMER-- WEAKER-- SMALLER-- WITH EACH PASSING SECOND!
THIS IS NOT THE WAY I PLANNED IT!
I WANTED LIFE ETERNAL-- POWER OVER ALL WHO LIVE--
THAT ALONE WAS MY GOAL!
BUT-- NOT THIS! NOT THIS!
NOT THIS!
THAT SCREAM-- COMING FROM THE SPOT WHERE I LEFT SILVER-MANE!
16

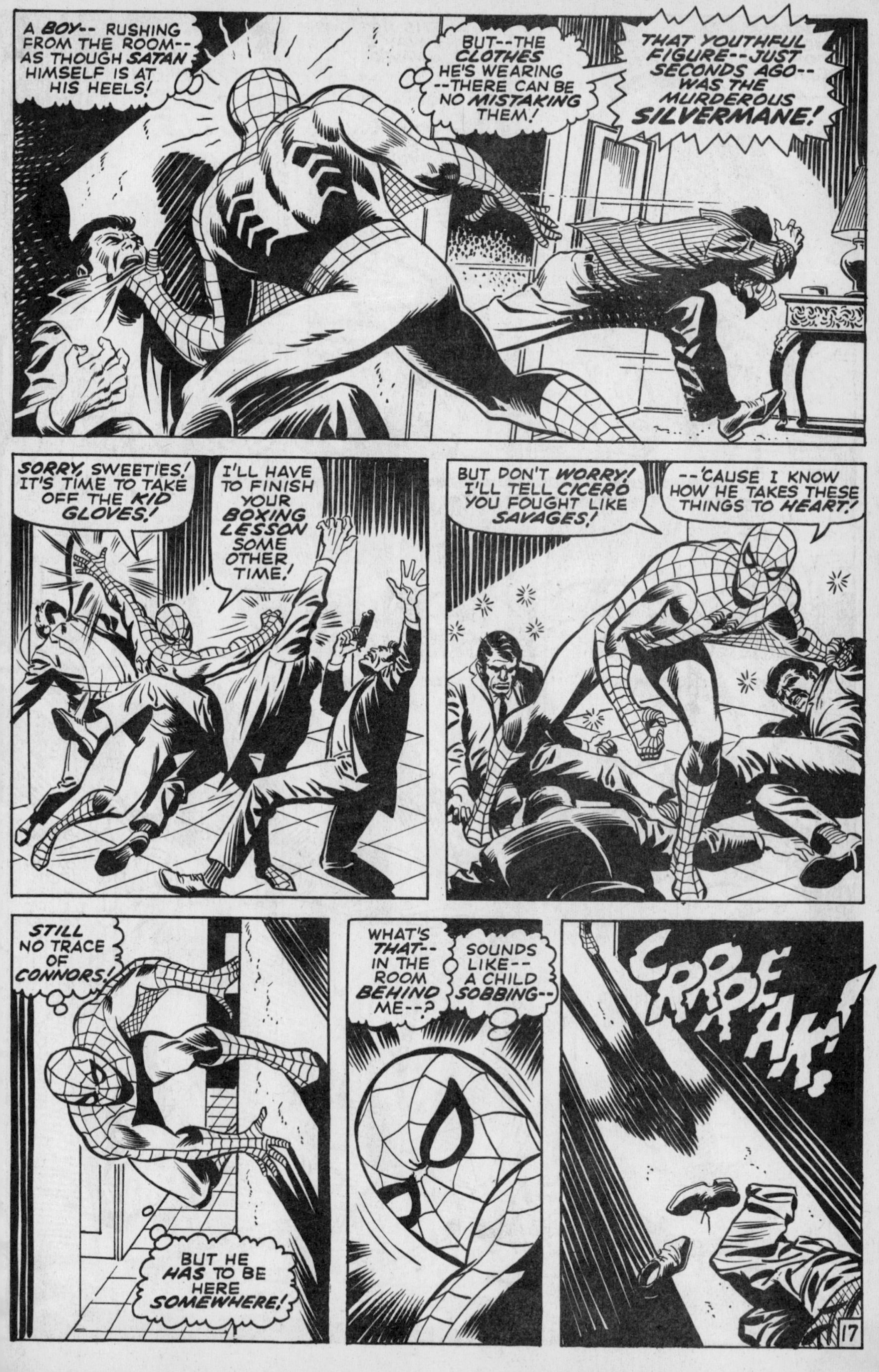
A BOY-- RUSHING FROM THE ROOM-- AS THOUGH SATAN HIMSELF IS AT HIS HEELS!
BUT--THE CLOTHES HE'S WEARING --THERE CAN BE NO MISTAKING THEM!
THAT YOUTHFUL FIGURE--JUST SECONDS AGO-- WAS THE MURDEROUS SILVERMANE!
SORRY, SWEETIES! IT'S TIME TO TAKE OFF THE KID GLOVES!
I'LL HAVE TO FINISH YOUR BOXING LESSON SOME OTHER TIME!
BUT DON'T WORRY! I'LL TELL CICERO YOU FOUGHT LIKE SAVAGES!
--'CAUSE I KNOW HOW HE TAKES THESE THINGS TO HEART!
STILL NO TRACE OF CONNORS!
BUT HE HAS TO BE HERE SOMEWHERE!
WHAT'S THAT-- IN THE ROOM BEHIND ME--?
SOUNDS LIKE-- A CHILD SOBBING--
CRRREAK!
17

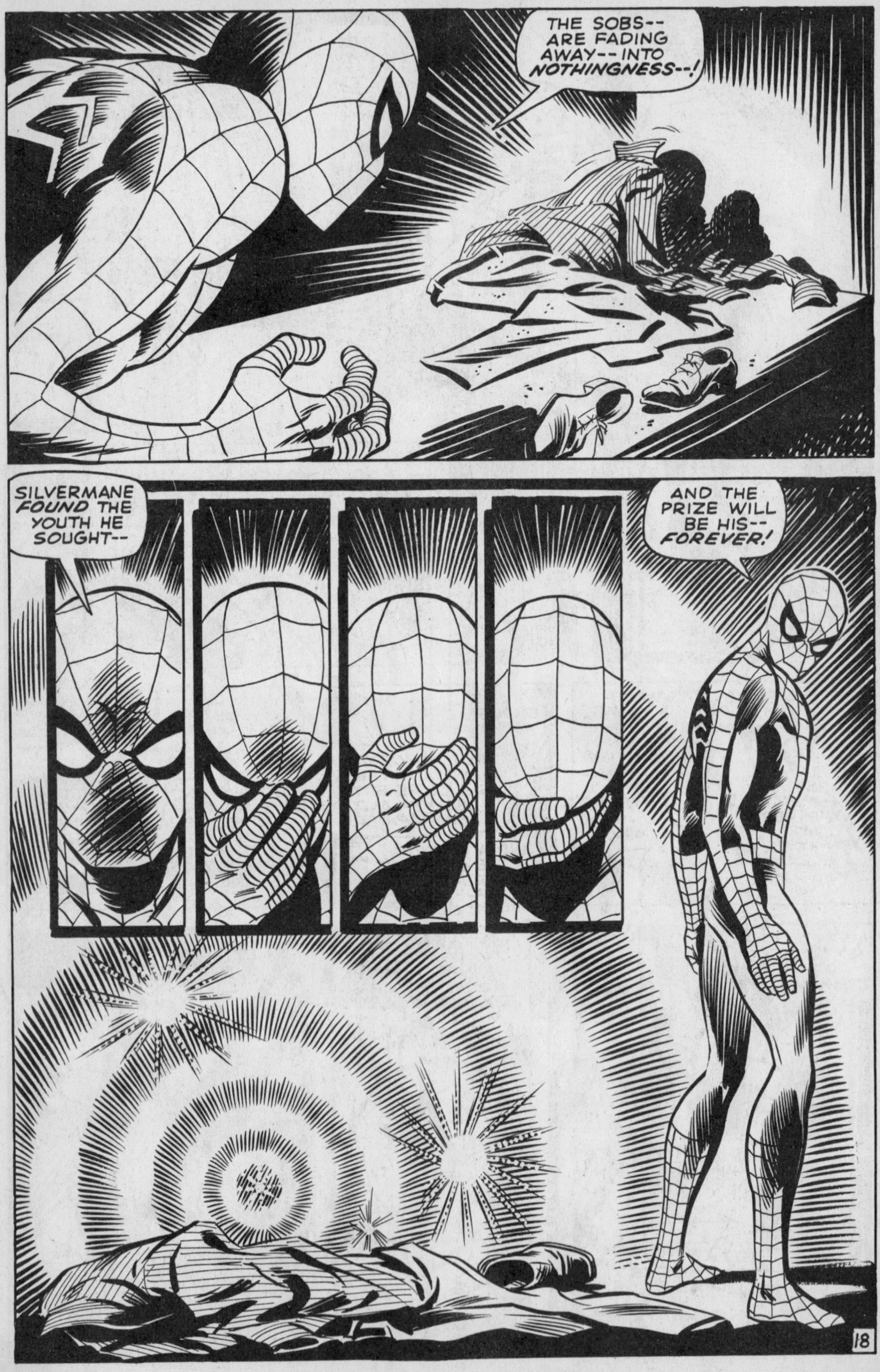
THE SOBS--
ARE FADING
AWAY--INTO
NOTHINGNESS--!
SILVERMANE
FOUND THE
YOUTH HE
SOUGHT--
AND THE
PRIZE WILL
BE HIS--
FOREVER!

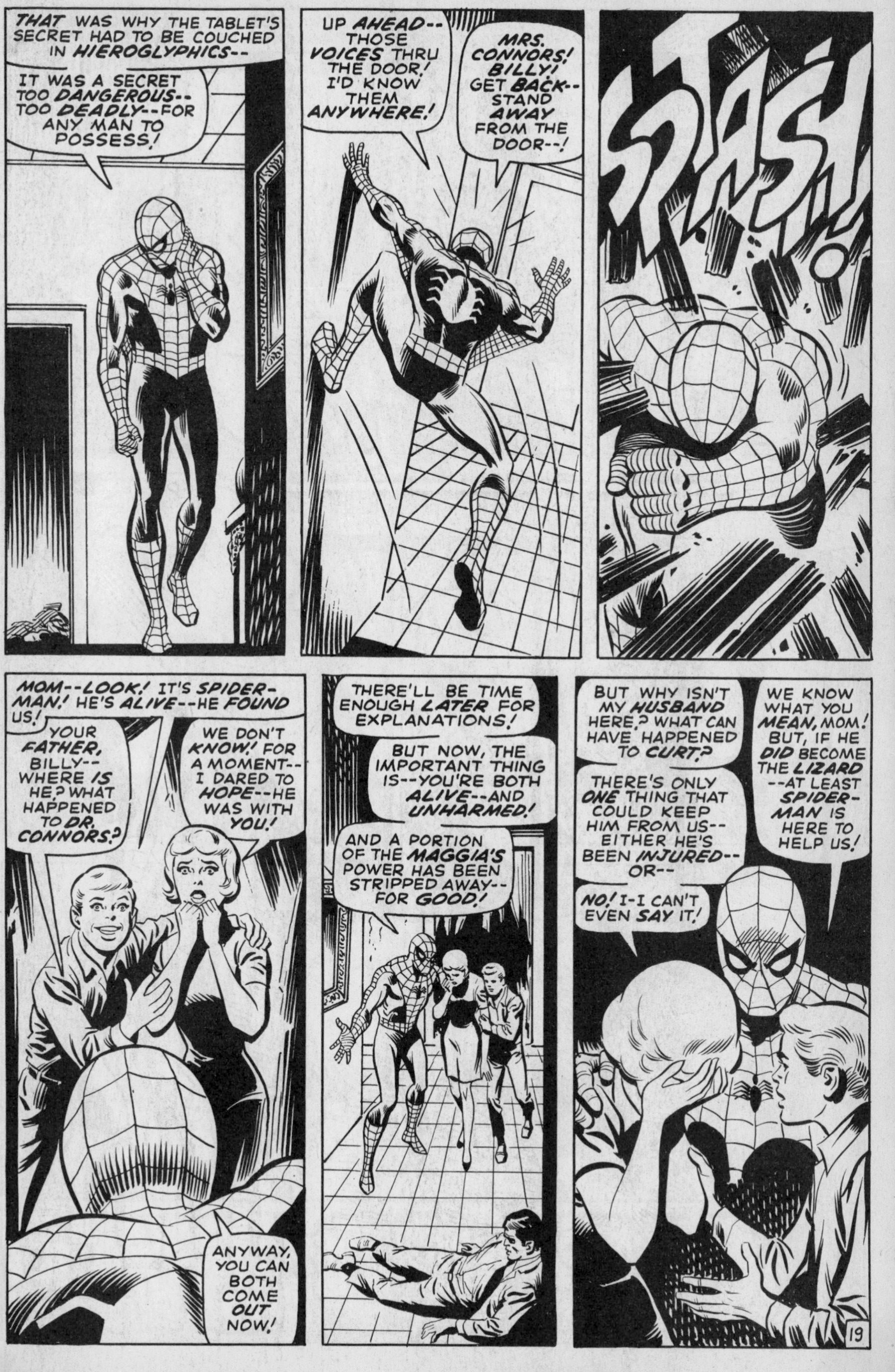
THAT WAS WHY THE TABLET'S SECRET HAD TO BE COUCHED IN HIEROGLYPHICS--
IT WAS A SECRET TOO DANGEROUS-- TOO DEADLY--FOR ANY MAN TO POSSESS!
UP AHEAD-- THOSE VOICES THRU THE DOOR! I'D KNOW THEM ANYWHERE!
MRS. CONNORS! BILLY! GET BACK-- STAND AWAY FROM THE DOOR--!
SPASH!
MOM--LOOK! IT'S SPIDER-MAN! HE'S ALIVE--HE FOUND US!
YOUR FATHER, BILLY-- WHERE IS HE? WHAT HAPPENED TO DR. CONNORS?
WE DON'T KNOW! FOR A MOMENT-- I DARED TO HOPE--HE WAS WITH YOU!
ANYWAY, YOU CAN BOTH COME OUT NOW!
THERE'LL BE TIME ENOUGH LATER FOR EXPLANATIONS!
BUT NOW, THE IMPORTANT THING IS--YOU'RE BOTH ALIVE--AND UNHARMED!
AND A PORTION OF THE MAGGIA'S POWER HAS BEEN STRIPPED AWAY-- FOR GOOD!
BUT WHY ISN'T MY HUSBAND HERE? WHAT CAN HAVE HAPPENED TO CURT?
THERE'S ONLY ONE THING THAT COULD KEEP HIM FROM US-- EITHER HE'S BEEN INJURED-- OR--
NO! I-I CAN'T EVEN SAY IT!
WE KNOW WHAT YOU MEAN, MOM! BUT, IF HE DID BECOME THE LIZARD --AT LEAST SPIDER-MAN IS HERE TO HELP US!
19

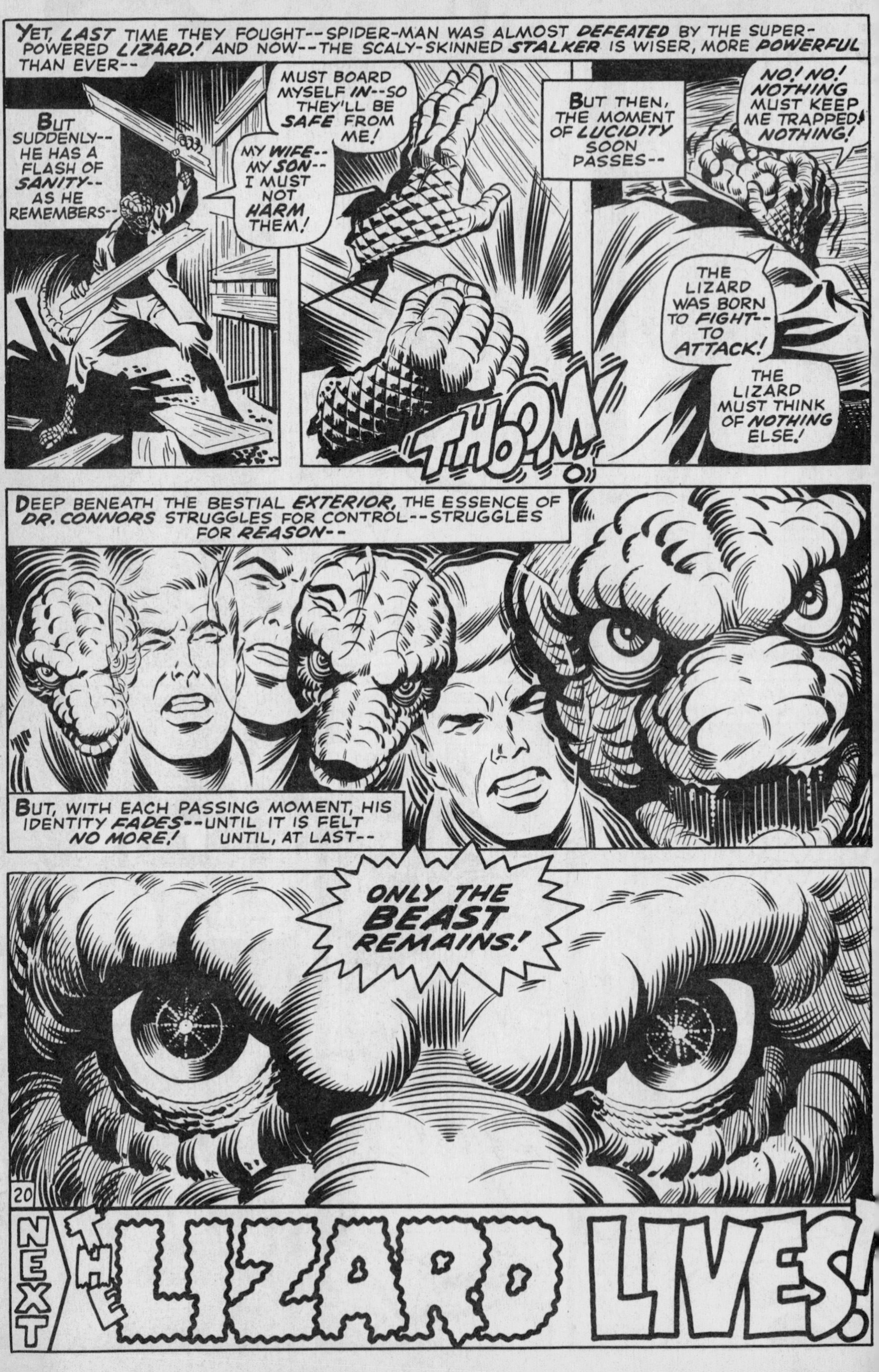
YET, LAST TIME THEY FOUGHT--SPIDER-MAN WAS ALMOST DEFEATED BY THE SUPER-POWERED LIZARD! AND NOW--THE SCALY-SKINNED STALKER IS WISER, MORE POWERFUL THAN EVER--
BUT SUDDENLY--HE HAS A FLASH OF SANITY--AS HE REMEMBERS--
MUST BOARD MYSELF IN--SO THEY'LL BE SAFE FROM ME!
MY WIFE--MY SON--I MUST NOT HARM THEM!
THOOM
BUT THEN, THE MOMENT OF LUCIDITY SOON PASSES--
NO! NO! NOTHING MUST KEEP ME TRAPPED! NOTHING!
THE LIZARD WAS BORN TO FIGHT--TO ATTACK!
THE LIZARD MUST THINK OF NOTHING ELSE!
DEEP BENEATH THE BESTIAL EXTERIOR, THE ESSENCE OF DR. CONNORS STRUGGLES FOR CONTROL--STRUGGLES FOR REASON--
BUT, WITH EACH PASSING MOMENT, HIS IDENTITY FADES--UNTIL IT IS FELT NO MORE! UNTIL, AT LAST--
ONLY THE BEAST REMAINS!
20
NEXT
THE LIZARD LIVES!

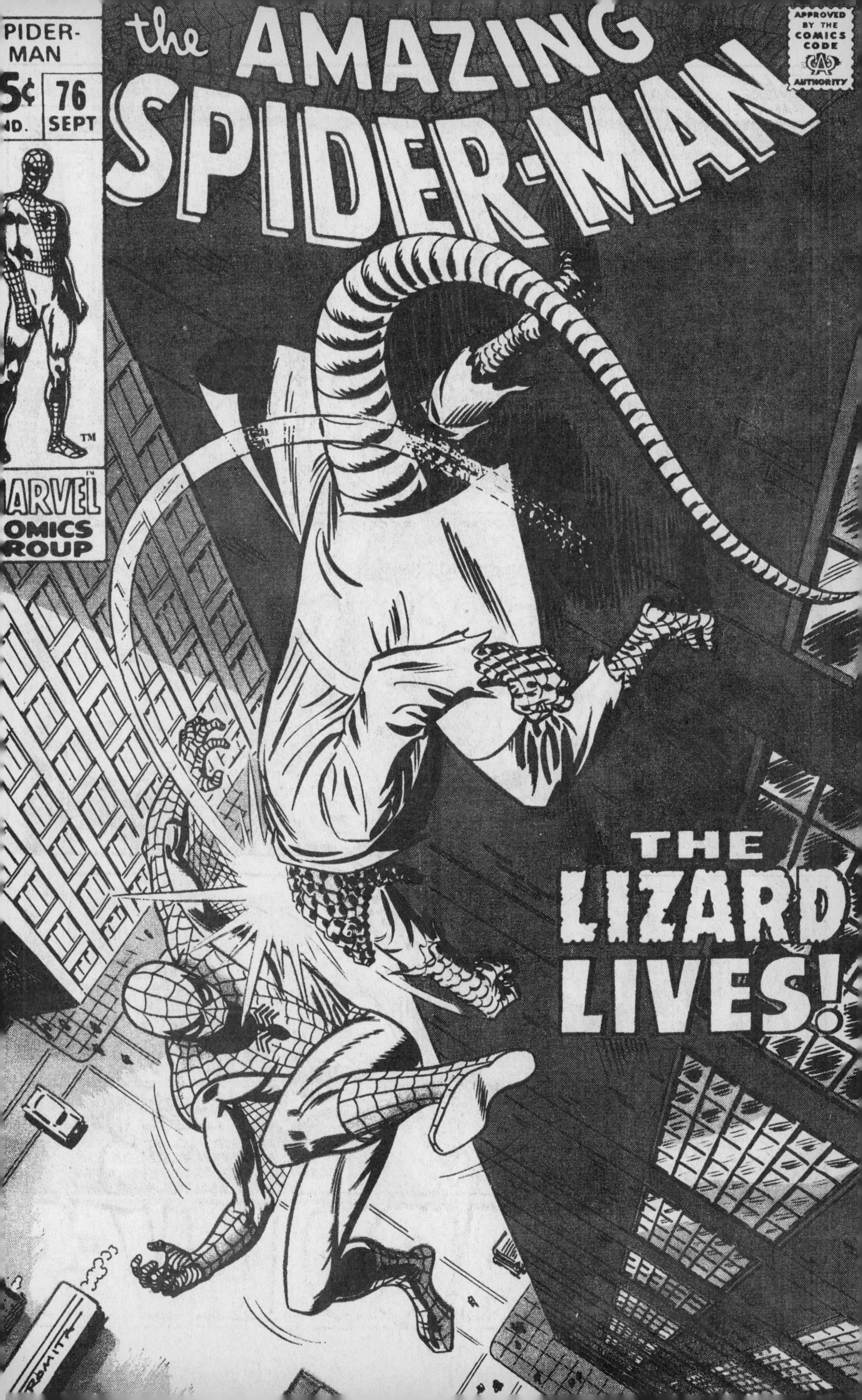
SPIDER-MAN
15¢
76
SEPT
IND.
APPROVED BY THE COMICS CODE AUTHORITY
the AMAZING SPIDER-MAN
MARVEL COMICS GROUP
THE LIZARD LIVES!
ROMITA

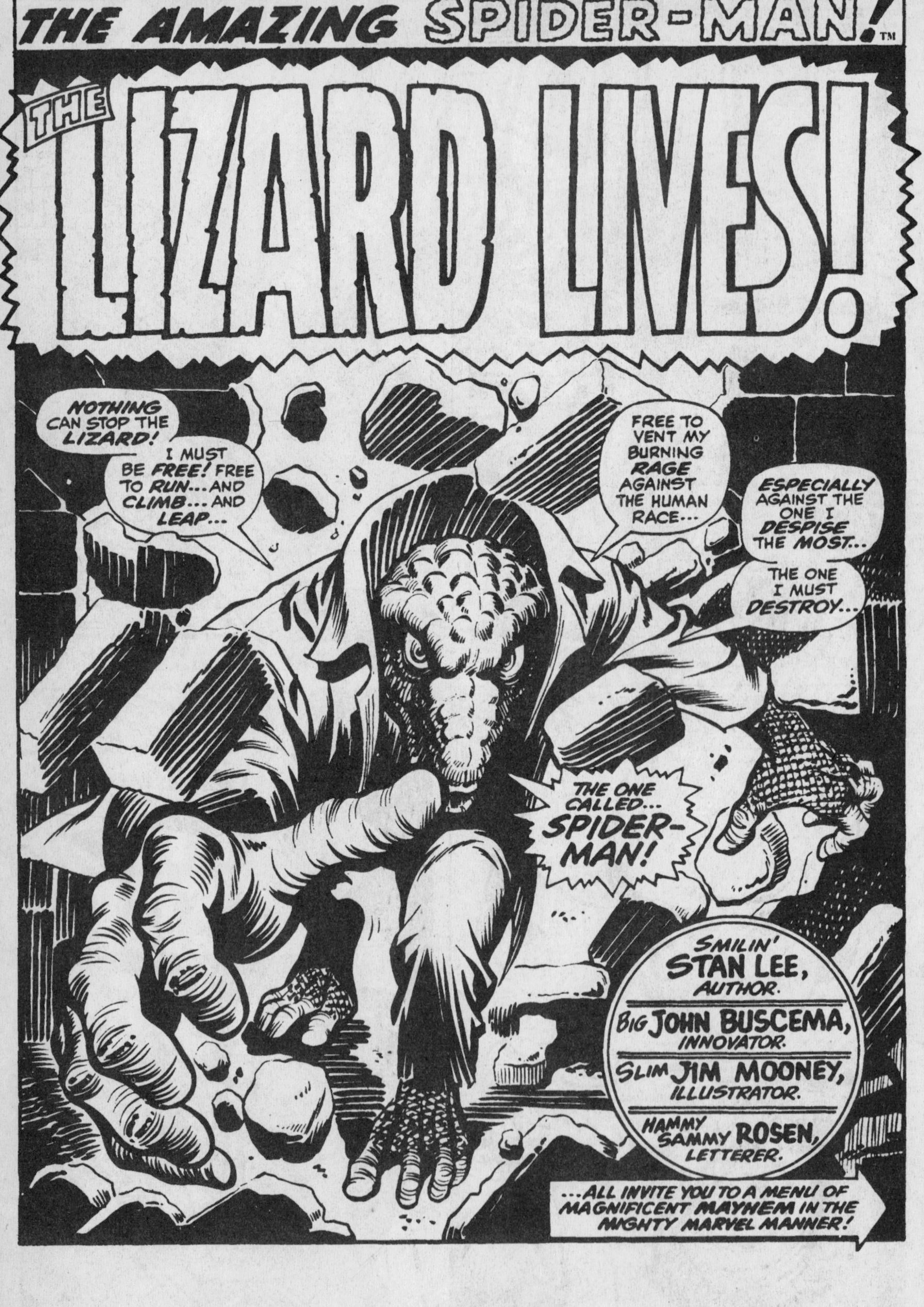
THE AMAZING SPIDER-MAN!™
THE LIZARD LIVES!
NOTHING CAN STOP THE LIZARD!
I MUST BE FREE! FREE TO RUN... AND CLIMB... AND LEAP...
FREE TO VENT MY BURNING RAGE AGAINST THE HUMAN RACE...
ESPECIALLY AGAINST THE ONE I DESPISE THE MOST...
THE ONE I MUST DESTROY...
THE ONE CALLED... SPIDER-MAN!
SMILIN' STAN LEE, AUTHOR.
BIG JOHN BUSCEMA, INNOVATOR.
SLIM JIM MOONEY, ILLUSTRATOR.
HAMMY SAMMY ROSEN, LETTERER.
...ALL INVITE YOU TO A MENU OF MAGNIFICENT MAYHEM IN THE MIGHTY MARVEL MANNER!

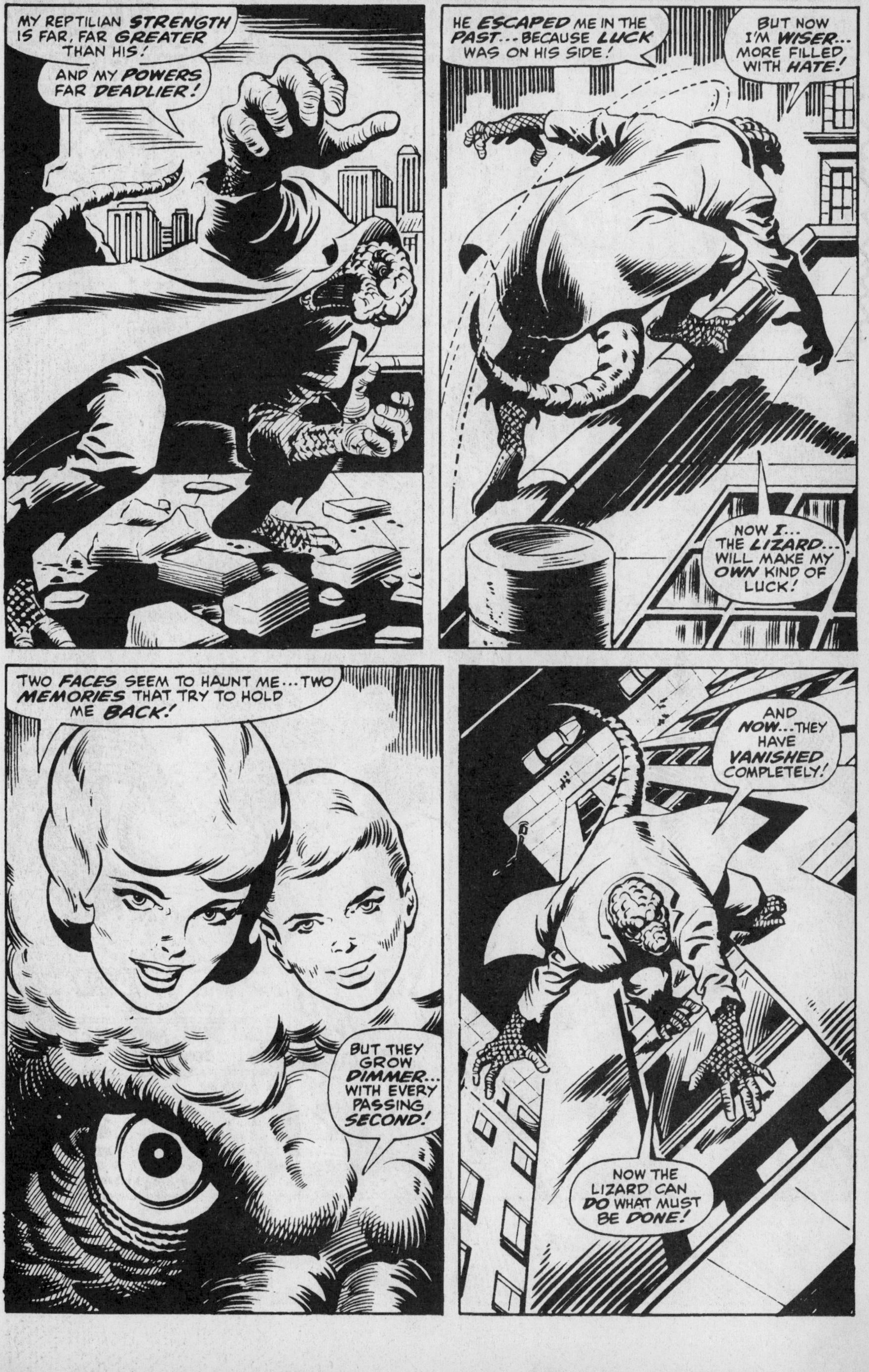
MY REPTILIAN STRENGTH IS FAR, FAR GREATER THAN HIS!
AND MY POWERS FAR DEADLIER!
HE ESCAPED ME IN THE PAST... BECAUSE LUCK WAS ON HIS SIDE!
BUT NOW I'M WISER... MORE FILLED WITH HATE!
NOW I... THE LIZARD... WILL MAKE MY OWN KIND OF LUCK!
TWO FACES SEEM TO HAUNT ME... TWO MEMORIES THAT TRY TO HOLD ME BACK!
BUT THEY GROW DIMMER... WITH EVERY PASSING SECOND!
AND NOW... THEY HAVE VANISHED COMPLETELY!
NOW THE LIZARD CAN DO WHAT MUST BE DONE!

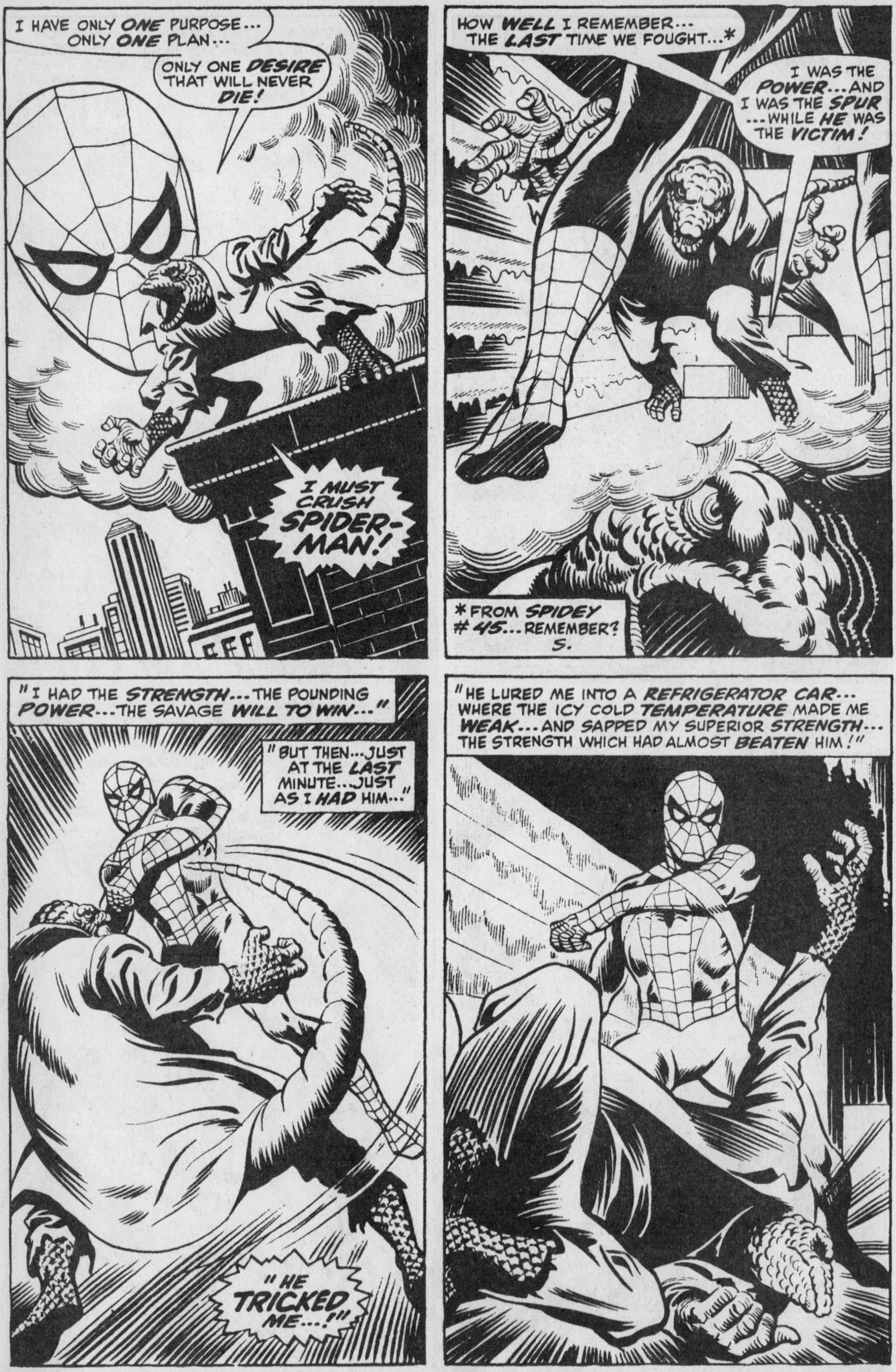

I HAVE ONLY ONE PURPOSE... ONLY ONE PLAN...
ONLY ONE DESIRE THAT WILL NEVER DIE!
I MUST CRUSH SPIDER-MAN!
HOW WELL I REMEMBER... THE LAST TIME WE FOUGHT...*
I WAS THE POWER...AND I WAS THE SPUR ...WHILE HE WAS THE VICTIM!
*FROM SPIDEY #45... REMEMBER? S.
"I HAD THE STRENGTH... THE POUNDING POWER... THE SAVAGE WILL TO WIN..."
"BUT THEN... JUST AT THE LAST MINUTE... JUST AS I HAD HIM..."
"HE TRICKED ME...!"
"HE LURED ME INTO A REFRIGERATOR CAR... WHERE THE ICY COLD TEMPERATURE MADE ME WEAK... AND SAPPED MY SUPERIOR STRENGTH... THE STRENGTH WHICH HAD ALMOST BEATEN HIM!"

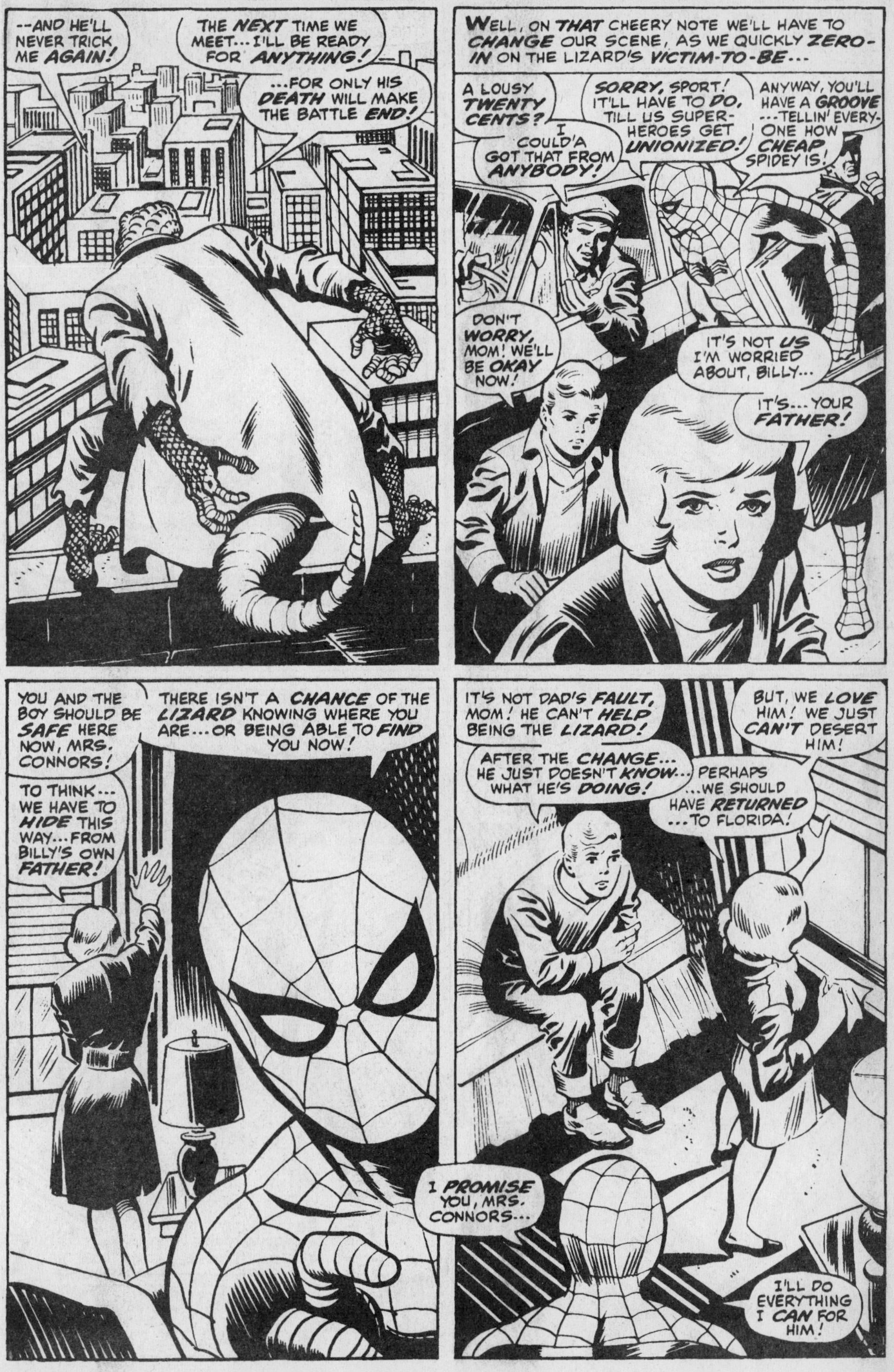
--AND HE'LL NEVER TRICK ME AGAIN!
THE NEXT TIME WE MEET... I'LL BE READY FOR ANYTHING!
...FOR ONLY HIS DEATH WILL MAKE THE BATTLE END!
WELL, ON THAT CHEERY NOTE WE'LL HAVE TO CHANGE OUR SCENE, AS WE QUICKLY ZERO-IN ON THE LIZARD'S VICTIM-TO-BE...
A LOUSY TWENTY CENTS?
I COULD'A GOT THAT FROM ANYBODY!
SORRY, SPORT! IT'LL HAVE TO DO, TILL US SUPER-HEROES GET UNIONIZED!
ANYWAY, YOU'LL HAVE A GROOVE ---TELLIN' EVERY-ONE HOW CHEAP SPIDEY IS!
DON'T WORRY, MOM! WE'LL BE OKAY NOW!
IT'S NOT US I'M WORRIED ABOUT, BILLY...
IT'S... YOUR FATHER!
YOU AND THE BOY SHOULD BE SAFE HERE NOW, MRS. CONNORS!
THERE ISN'T A CHANCE OF THE LIZARD KNOWING WHERE YOU ARE... OR BEING ABLE TO FIND YOU NOW!
TO THINK... WE HAVE TO HIDE THIS WAY... FROM BILLY'S OWN FATHER!
IT'S NOT DAD'S FAULT, MOM! HE CAN'T HELP BEING THE LIZARD!
BUT, WE LOVE HIM! WE JUST CAN'T DESERT HIM!
AFTER THE CHANGE... HE JUST DOESN'T KNOW... WHAT HE'S DOING!
PERHAPS ...WE SHOULD HAVE RETURNED ...TO FLORIDA!
I PROMISE YOU, MRS. CONNORS...
I'LL DO EVERYTHING I CAN FOR HIM!

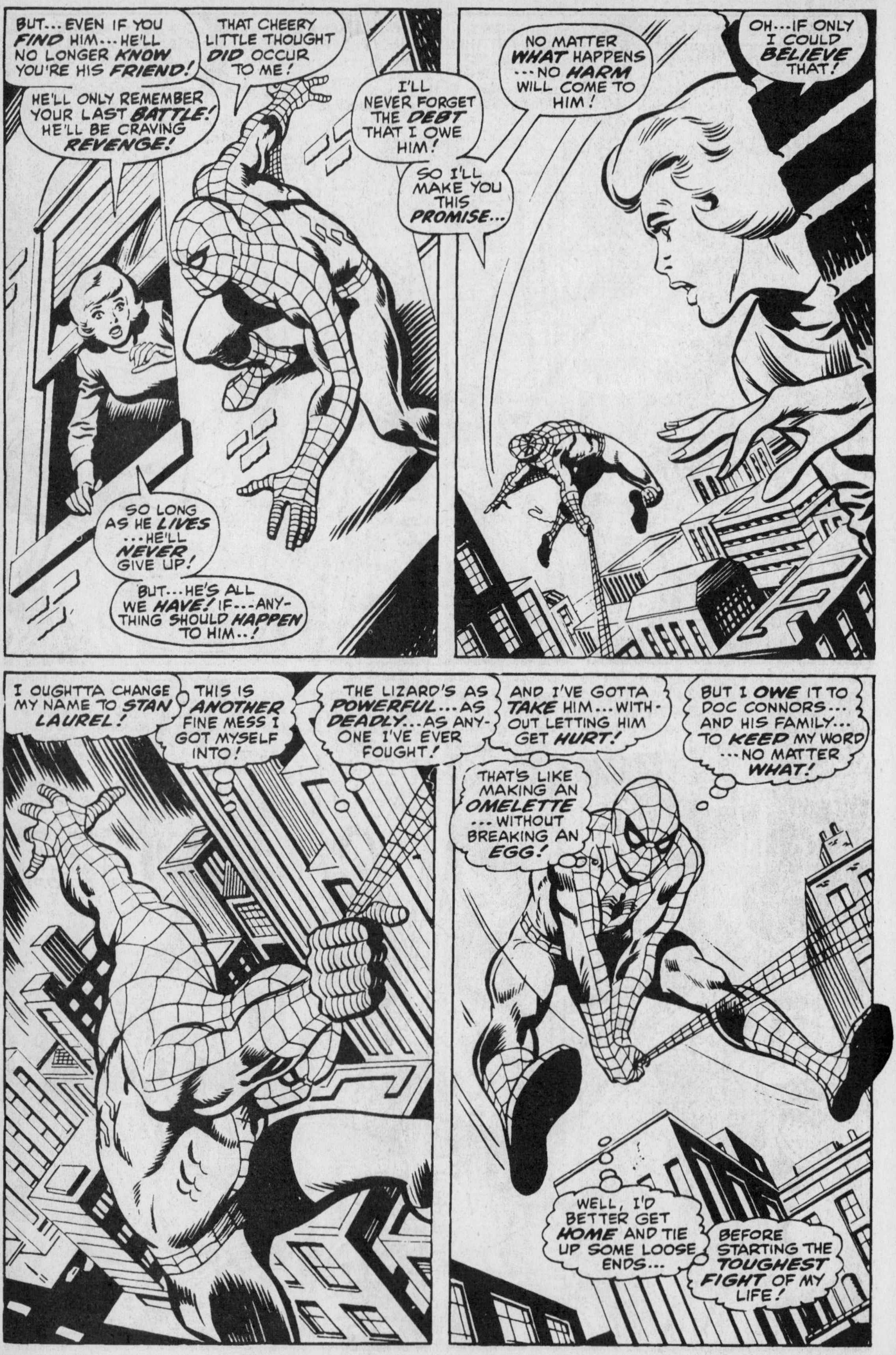

BUT... EVEN IF YOU FIND HIM... HE'LL NO LONGER KNOW YOU'RE HIS FRIEND!
THAT CHEERY LITTLE THOUGHT DID OCCUR TO ME!
HE'LL ONLY REMEMBER YOUR LAST BATTLE! HE'LL BE CRAVING REVENGE!
I'LL NEVER FORGET THE DEBT THAT I OWE HIM!
SO I'LL MAKE YOU THIS PROMISE...
SO LONG AS HE LIVES ...HE'LL NEVER GIVE UP!
BUT...HE'S ALL WE HAVE! IF...ANY-THING SHOULD HAPPEN TO HIM...!
NO MATTER WHAT HAPPENS ...NO HARM WILL COME TO HIM!
OH...IF ONLY I COULD BELIEVE THAT!
I OUGHTTA CHANGE MY NAME TO STAN LAUREL!
THIS IS ANOTHER FINE MESS I GOT MYSELF INTO!
THE LIZARD'S AS POWERFUL...AS DEADLY...AS ANY-ONE I'VE EVER FOUGHT!
AND I'VE GOTTA TAKE HIM...WITH-OUT LETTING HIM GET HURT!
THAT'S LIKE MAKING AN OMELETTE ...WITHOUT BREAKING AN EGG!
BUT I OWE IT TO DOC CONNORS... AND HIS FAMILY... TO KEEP MY WORD ...NO MATTER WHAT!
WELL, I'D BETTER GET HOME AND TIE UP SOME LOOSE ENDS...
BEFORE STARTING THE TOUGHEST FIGHT OF MY LIFE!

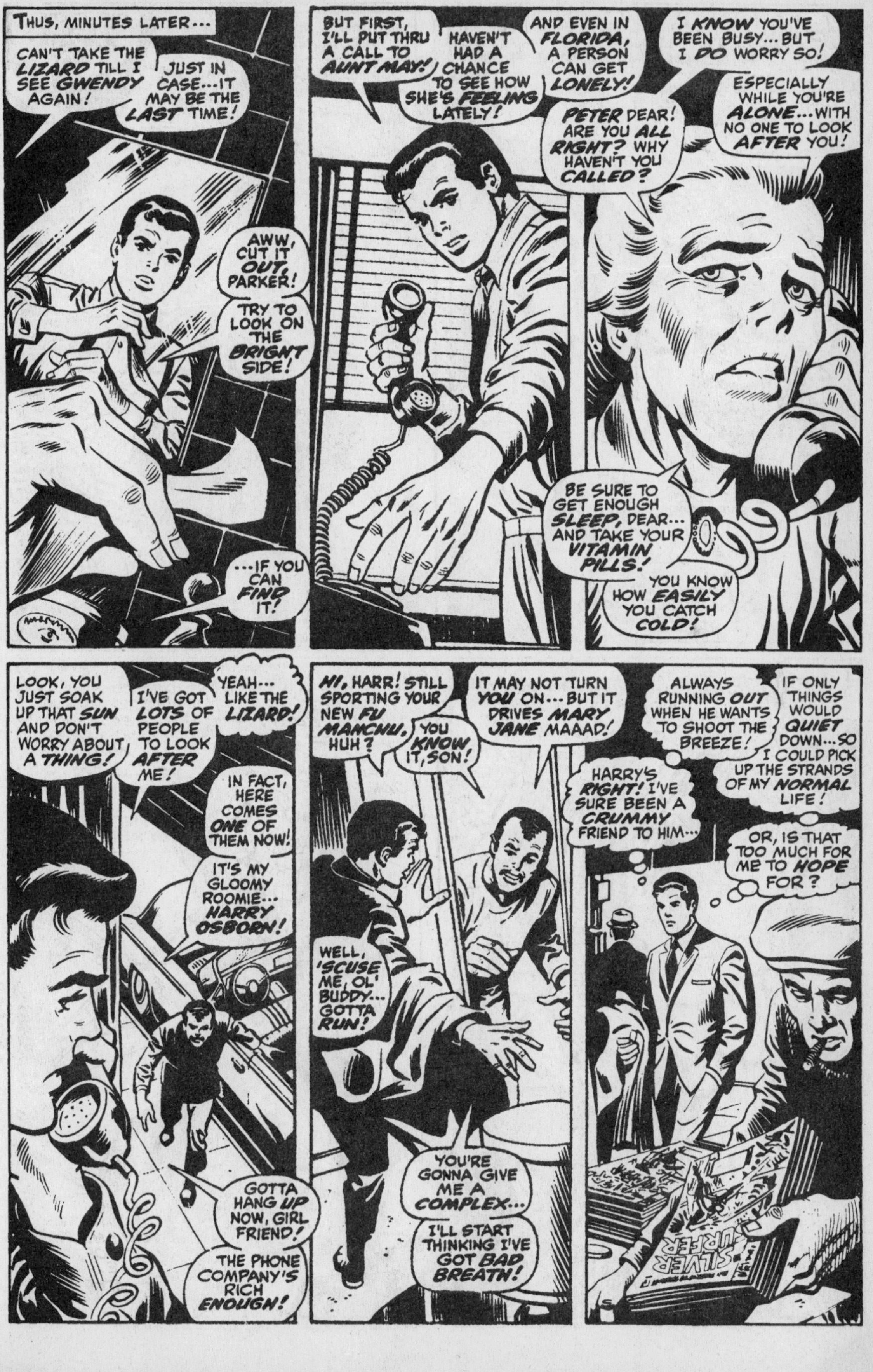
THUS, MINUTES LATER...
CAN'T TAKE THE LIZARD TILL I SEE GWENDY AGAIN!
JUST IN CASE...IT MAY BE THE LAST TIME!
AWW, CUT IT OUT, PARKER!
TRY TO LOOK ON THE BRIGHT SIDE!
...IF YOU CAN FIND IT!
BUT FIRST, I'LL PUT THRU A CALL TO AUNT MAY!
HAVEN'T HAD A CHANCE TO SEE HOW SHE'S FEELING LATELY!
AND EVEN IN FLORIDA, A PERSON CAN GET LONELY!
PETER DEAR! ARE YOU ALL RIGHT? WHY HAVEN'T YOU CALLED?
I KNOW YOU'VE BEEN BUSY...BUT I DO WORRY SO!
ESPECIALLY WHILE YOU'RE ALONE...WITH NO ONE TO LOOK AFTER YOU!
BE SURE TO GET ENOUGH SLEEP, DEAR... AND TAKE YOUR VITAMIN PILLS!
YOU KNOW HOW EASILY YOU CATCH COLD!
LOOK, YOU JUST SOAK UP THAT SUN AND DON'T WORRY ABOUT A THING!
I'VE GOT LOTS OF PEOPLE TO LOOK AFTER ME!
YEAH... LIKE THE LIZARD!
IN FACT, HERE COMES ONE OF THEM NOW!
IT'S MY GLOOMY ROOMIE... HARRY OSBORN!
GOTTA HANG UP NOW, GIRL FRIEND!
THE PHONE COMPANY'S RICH ENOUGH!
HI, HARR! STILL SPORTING YOUR NEW FU MANCHU, HUH?
YOU KNOW IT, SON!
IT MAY NOT TURN YOU ON...BUT IT DRIVES MARY JANE MAAAD!
WELL, 'SCUSE ME, OL' BUDDY... GOTTA RUN!
YOU'RE GONNA GIVE ME A COMPLEX...
I'LL START THINKING I'VE GOT BAD BREATH!
HARRY'S RIGHT! I'VE SURE BEEN A CRUMMY FRIEND TO HIM...
ALWAYS RUNNING OUT WHEN HE WANTS TO SHOOT THE BREEZE!
IF ONLY THINGS WOULD QUIET DOWN...SO I COULD PICK UP THE STRANDS OF MY NORMAL LIFE!
OR, IS THAT TOO MUCH FOR ME TO HOPE FOR?
SILVER SURFER

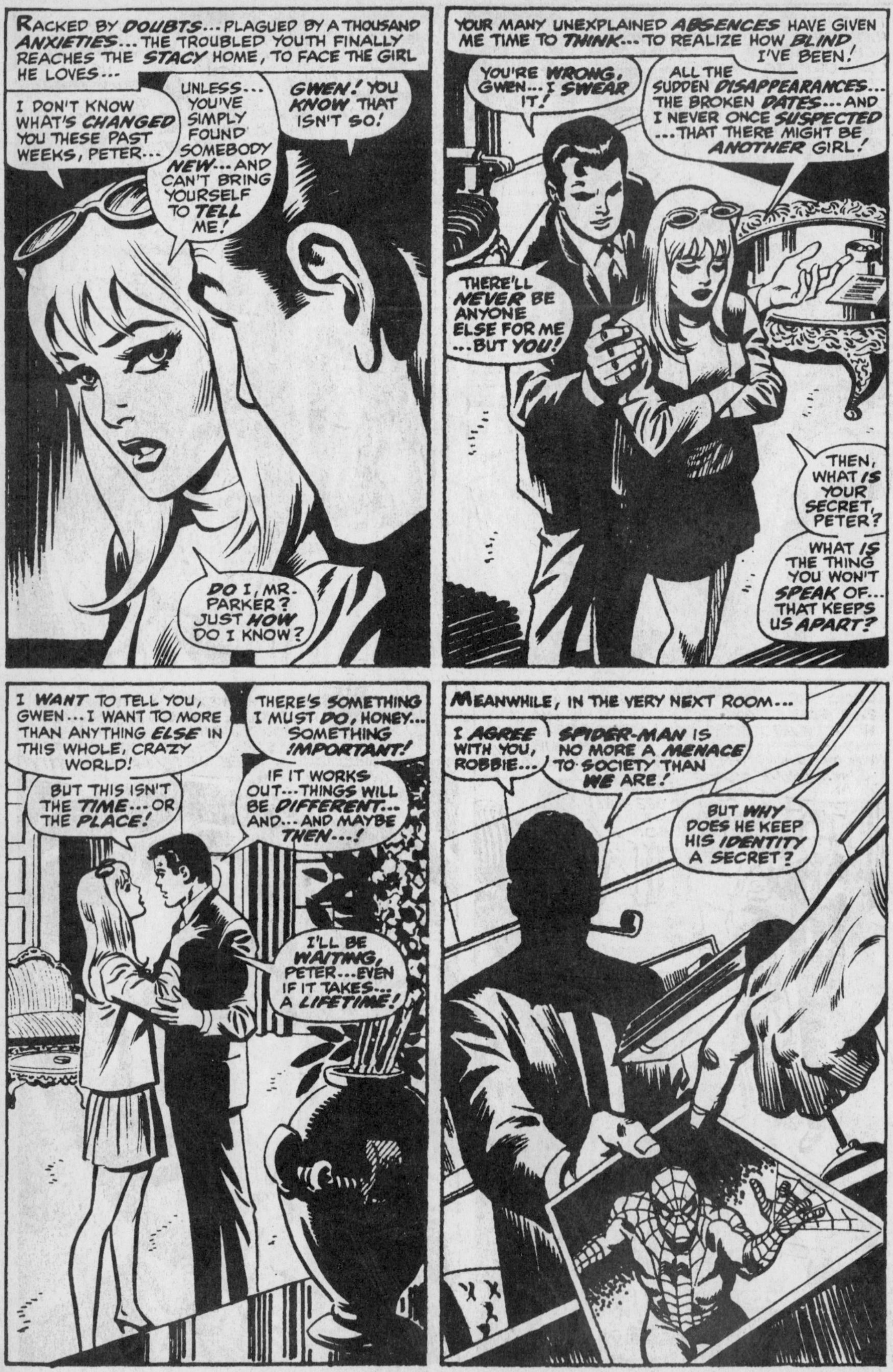
RACKED BY DOUBTS... PLAGUED BY A THOUSAND ANXIETIES... THE TROUBLED YOUTH FINALLY REACHES THE STACY HOME, TO FACE THE GIRL HE LOVES...
I DON'T KNOW WHAT'S CHANGED YOU THESE PAST WEEKS, PETER...
UNLESS... YOU'VE SIMPLY FOUND SOMEBODY NEW... AND CAN'T BRING YOURSELF TO TELL ME!
GWEN! YOU KNOW THAT ISN'T SO!
DO I, MR. PARKER? JUST HOW DO I KNOW?
YOUR MANY UNEXPLAINED ABSENCES HAVE GIVEN ME TIME TO THINK... TO REALIZE HOW BLIND I'VE BEEN!
YOU'RE WRONG, GWEN... I SWEAR IT!
ALL THE SUDDEN DISAPPEARANCES... THE BROKEN DATES... AND I NEVER ONCE SUSPECTED ...THAT THERE MIGHT BE ANOTHER GIRL!
THERE'LL NEVER BE ANYONE ELSE FOR ME ...BUT YOU!
THEN, WHAT IS YOUR SECRET, PETER?
WHAT IS THE THING YOU WON'T SPEAK OF... THAT KEEPS US APART?
I WANT TO TELL YOU, GWEN... I WANT TO MORE THAN ANYTHING ELSE IN THIS WHOLE, CRAZY WORLD!
BUT THIS ISN'T THE TIME... OR THE PLACE!
THERE'S SOMETHING I MUST DO, HONEY... SOMETHING IMPORTANT!
IF IT WORKS OUT... THINGS WILL BE DIFFERENT... AND... AND MAYBE THEN...!
I'LL BE WAITING, PETER... EVEN IF IT TAKES... A LIFETIME!
MEANWHILE, IN THE VERY NEXT ROOM...
I AGREE WITH YOU, ROBBIE...
SPIDER-MAN IS NO MORE A MENACE TO SOCIETY THAN WE ARE!
BUT WHY DOES HE KEEP HIS IDENTITY A SECRET?

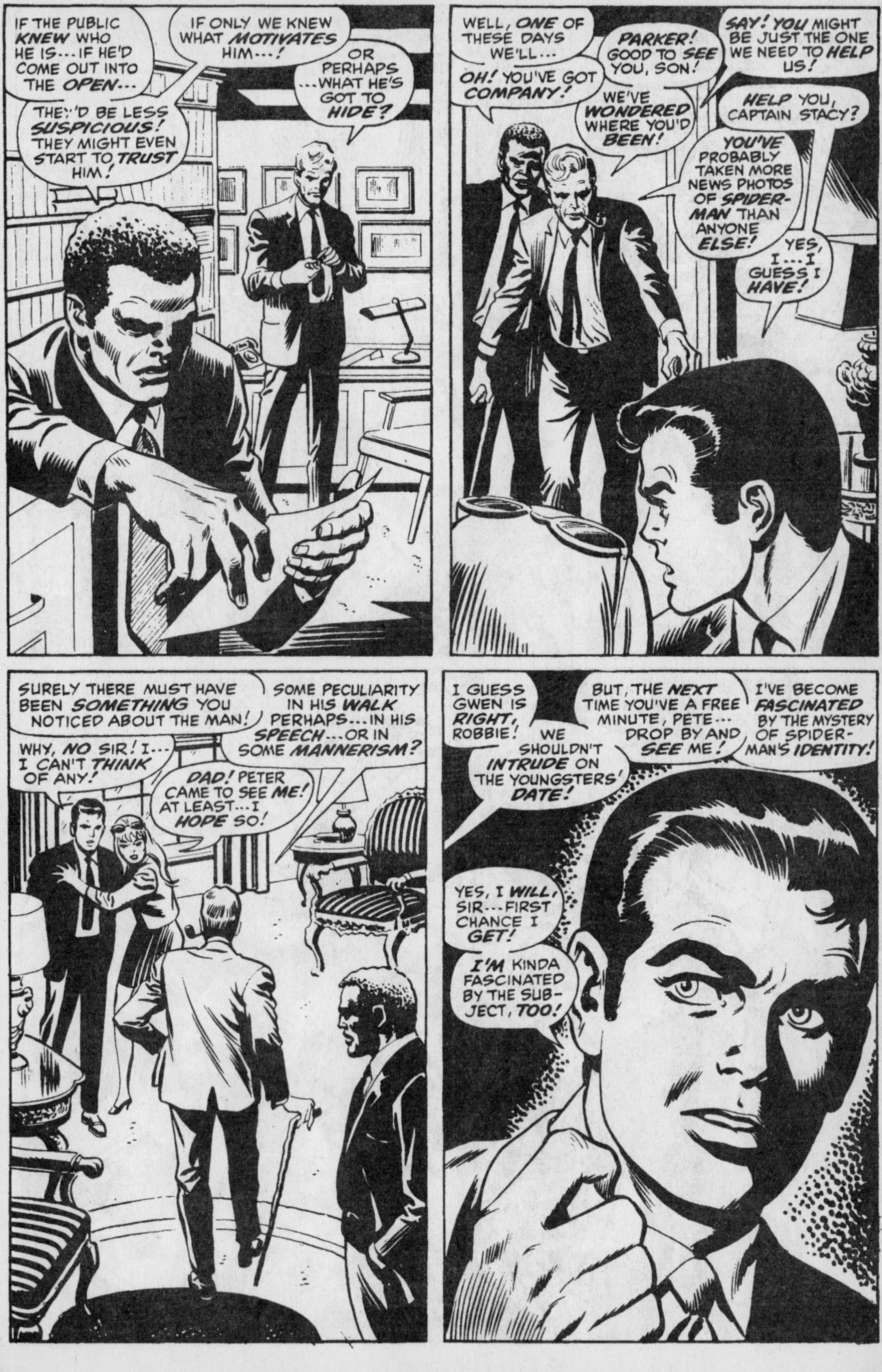
IF THE PUBLIC KNEW WHO HE IS... IF HE'D COME OUT INTO THE OPEN...
THEY'D BE LESS SUSPICIOUS! THEY MIGHT EVEN START TO TRUST HIM!
IF ONLY WE KNEW WHAT MOTIVATES HIM...!
OR PERHAPS ...WHAT HE'S GOT TO HIDE?
WELL, ONE OF THESE DAYS WE'LL...
OH! YOU'VE GOT COMPANY!
PARKER! GOOD TO SEE YOU, SON!
WE'VE WONDERED WHERE YOU'D BEEN!
SAY! YOU MIGHT BE JUST THE ONE WE NEED TO HELP US!
HELP YOU, CAPTAIN STACY?
YOU'VE PROBABLY TAKEN MORE NEWS PHOTOS OF SPIDER-MAN THAN ANYONE ELSE!
YES, I...I GUESS I HAVE!
SURELY THERE MUST HAVE BEEN SOMETHING YOU NOTICED ABOUT THE MAN!
SOME PECULIARITY IN HIS WALK PERHAPS... IN HIS SPEECH...OR IN SOME MANNERISM?
WHY, NO SIR! I... I CAN'T THINK OF ANY!
DAD! PETER CAME TO SEE ME! AT LEAST...I HOPE SO!
I GUESS GWEN IS RIGHT, ROBBIE!
WE SHOULDN'T INTRUDE ON THE YOUNGSTERS' DATE!
BUT, THE NEXT TIME YOU'VE A FREE MINUTE, PETE... DROP BY AND SEE ME!
I'VE BECOME FASCINATED BY THE MYSTERY OF SPIDER-MAN'S IDENTITY!
YES, I WILL, SIR---FIRST CHANCE I GET!
I'M KINDA FASCINATED BY THE SUB-JECT, TOO!

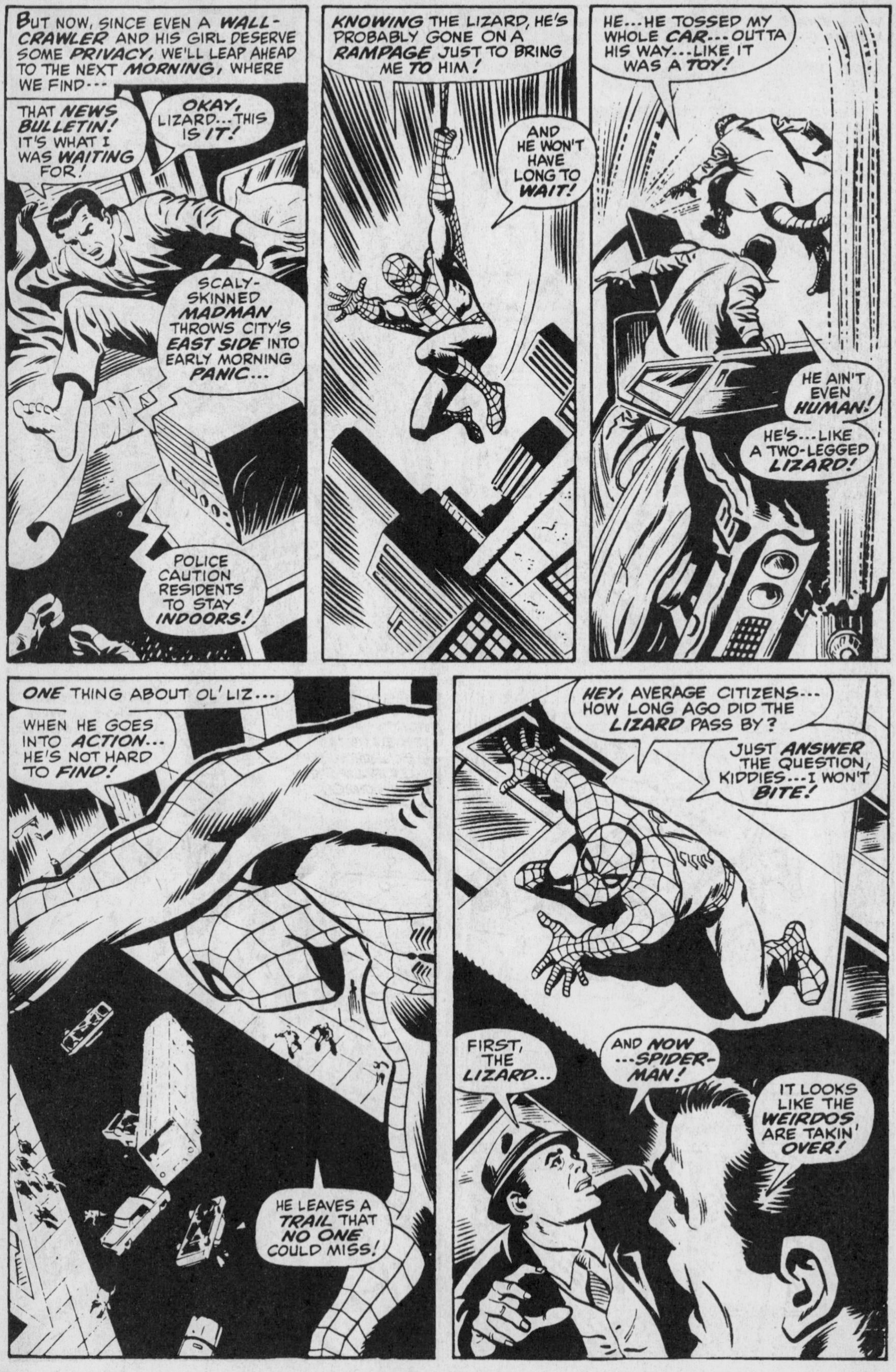

BUT NOW, SINCE EVEN A WALL-CRAWLER AND HIS GIRL DESERVE SOME PRIVACY, WE'LL LEAP AHEAD TO THE NEXT MORNING, WHERE WE FIND---
THAT NEWS BULLETIN! IT'S WHAT I WAS WAITING FOR!
OKAY, LIZARD...THIS IS IT!
SCALY-SKINNED MADMAN THROWS CITY'S EAST SIDE INTO EARLY MORNING PANIC...
POLICE CAUTION RESIDENTS TO STAY INDOORS!
KNOWING THE LIZARD, HE'S PROBABLY GONE ON A RAMPAGE JUST TO BRING ME TO HIM!
AND HE WON'T HAVE LONG TO WAIT!
HE...HE TOSSED MY WHOLE CAR...OUTTA HIS WAY...LIKE IT WAS A TOY!
HE AIN'T EVEN HUMAN!
HE'S...LIKE A TWO-LEGGED LIZARD!
ONE THING ABOUT OL' LIZ...
WHEN HE GOES INTO ACTION... HE'S NOT HARD TO FIND!
HE LEAVES A TRAIL THAT NO ONE COULD MISS!
HEY, AVERAGE CITIZENS... HOW LONG AGO DID THE LIZARD PASS BY?
JUST ANSWER THE QUESTION, KIDDIES...I WON'T BITE!
FIRST, THE LIZARD...
AND NOW ---SPIDER-MAN!
IT LOOKS LIKE THE WEIRDOS ARE TAKIN' OVER!

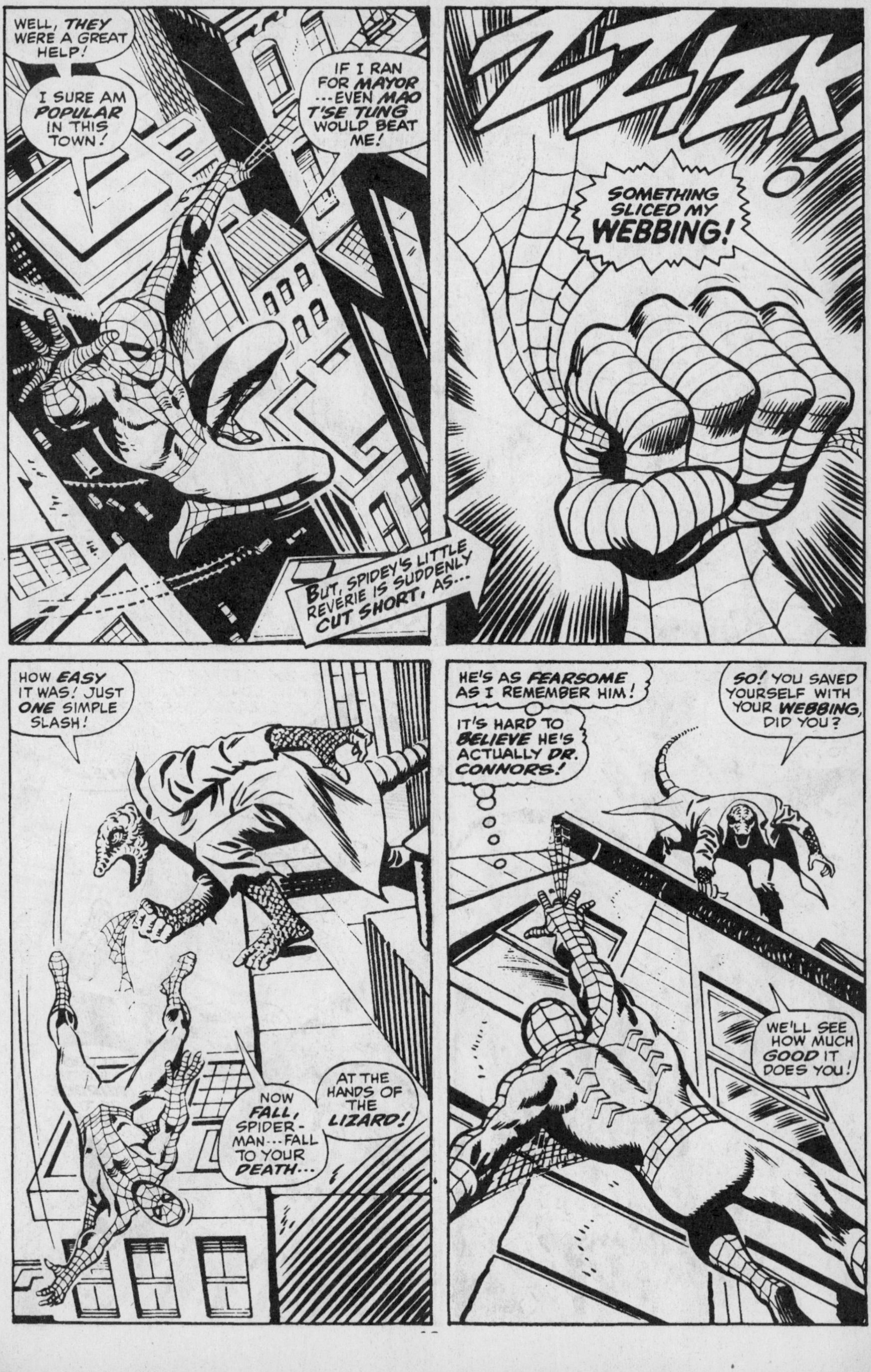
WELL, THEY WERE A GREAT HELP!
I SURE AM POPULAR IN THIS TOWN!
IF I RAN FOR MAYOR ...EVEN MAO T'SE TUNG WOULD BEAT ME!
BUT, SPIDEY'S LITTLE REVERIE IS SUDDENLY CUT SHORT, AS...
ZZZK
SOMETHING SLICED MY WEBBING!
HOW EASY IT WAS! JUST ONE SIMPLE SLASH!
NOW FALL, SPIDER-MAN... FALL TO YOUR DEATH...
AT THE HANDS OF THE LIZARD!
HE'S AS FEARSOME AS I REMEMBER HIM!
IT'S HARD TO BELIEVE HE'S ACTUALLY DR. CONNORS!
SO! YOU SAVED YOURSELF WITH YOUR WEBBING, DID YOU?
WE'LL SEE HOW MUCH GOOD IT DOES YOU!

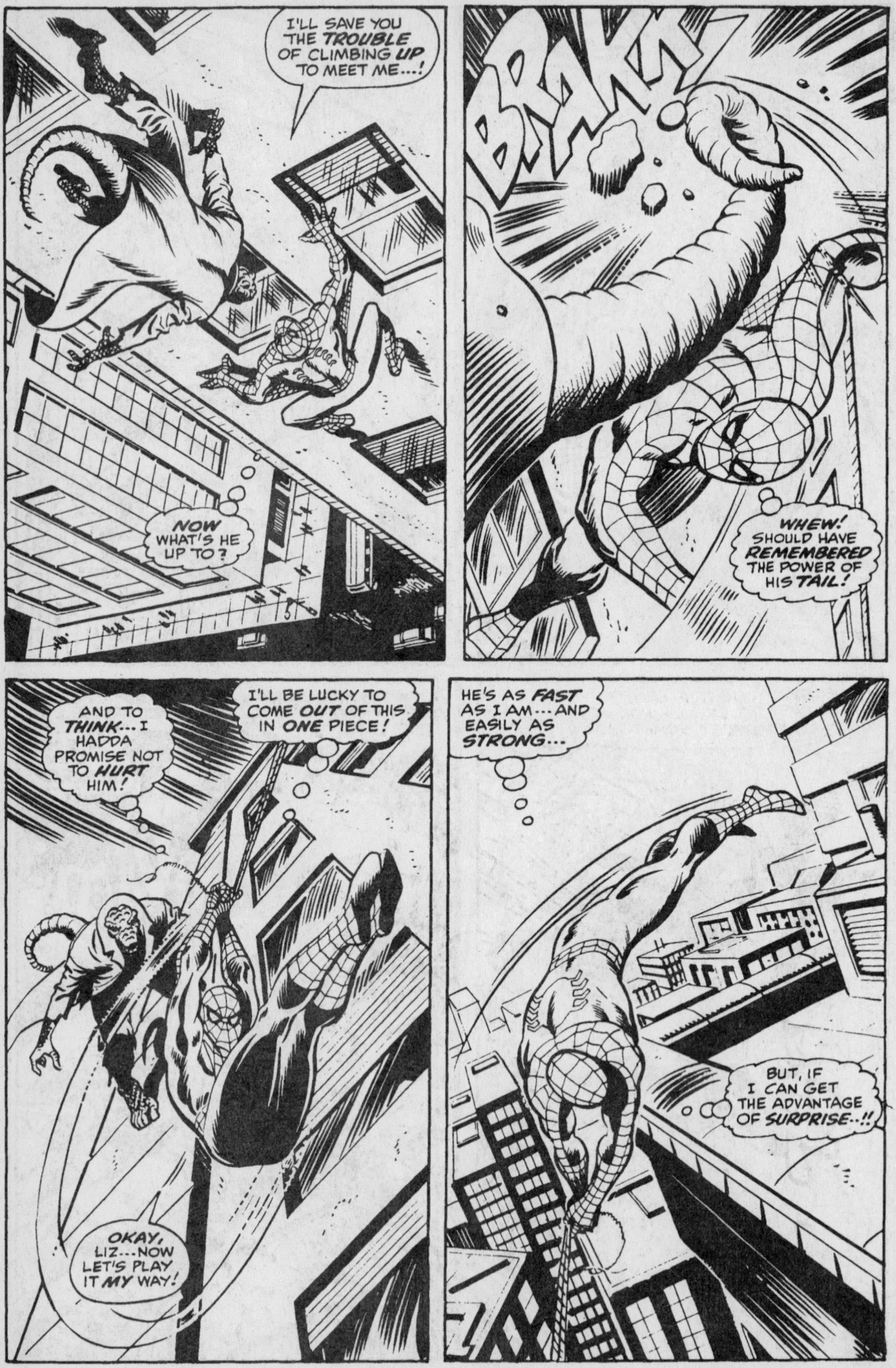
I'LL SAVE YOU THE TROUBLE OF CLIMBING UP TO MEET ME...!
NOW WHAT'S HE UP TO?
BRAKK
WHEW! SHOULD HAVE REMEMBERED THE POWER OF HIS TAIL!
AND TO THINK... I HADDA PROMISE NOT TO HURT HIM!
I'LL BE LUCKY TO COME OUT OF THIS IN ONE PIECE!
OKAY, LIZ... NOW LET'S PLAY IT MY WAY!
HE'S AS FAST AS I AM... AND EASILY AS STRONG...
BUT, IF I CAN GET THE ADVANTAGE OF SURPRISE..!!

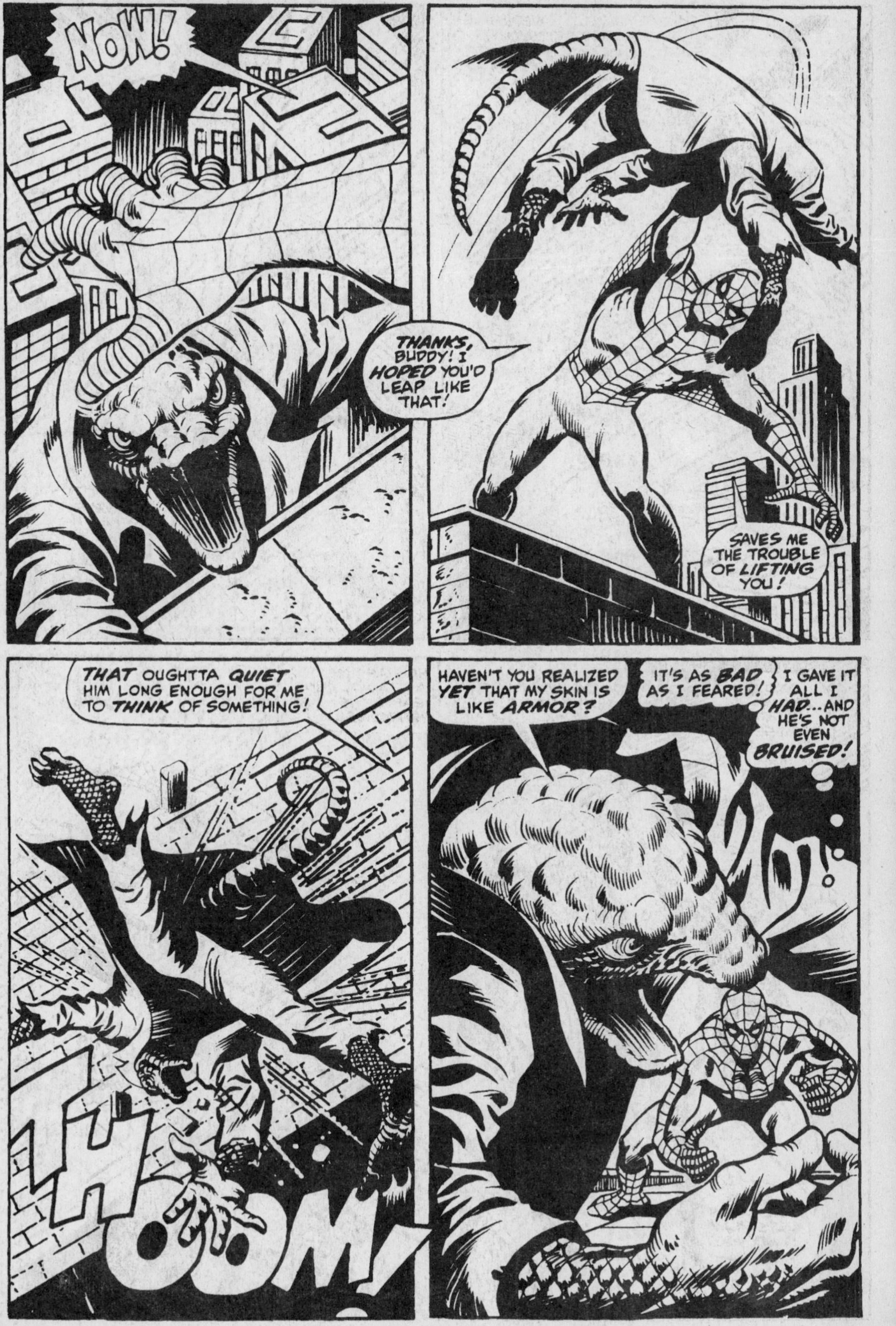
NOW!
THANKS, BUDDY! I HOPED YOU'D LEAP LIKE THAT!
SAVES ME THE TROUBLE OF LIFTING YOU!
THAT OUGHTTA QUIET HIM LONG ENOUGH FOR ME TO THINK OF SOMETHING!
THOOM!
HAVEN'T YOU REALIZED YET THAT MY SKIN IS LIKE ARMOR?
IT'S AS BAD AS I FEARED!
I GAVE IT ALL I HAD... AND HE'S NOT EVEN BRUISED!

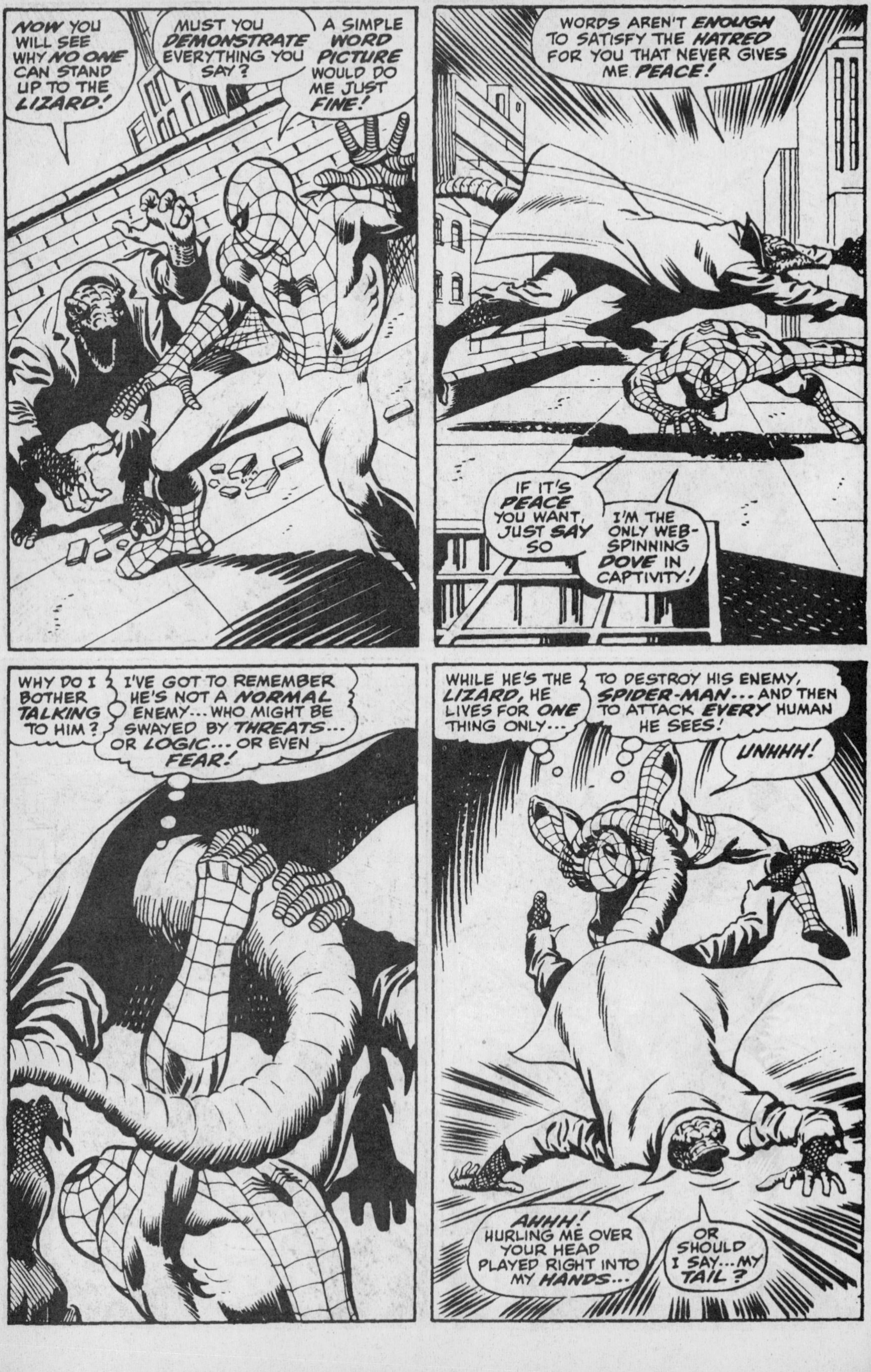
NOW YOU WILL SEE WHY NO ONE CAN STAND UP TO THE LIZARD!
MUST YOU DEMONSTRATE EVERYTHING YOU SAY?
A SIMPLE WORD PICTURE WOULD DO ME JUST FINE!
WORDS AREN'T ENOUGH TO SATISFY THE HATRED FOR YOU THAT NEVER GIVES ME PEACE!
IF IT'S PEACE YOU WANT, JUST SAY SO
I'M THE ONLY WEB-SPINNING DOVE IN CAPTIVITY!
WHY DO I BOTHER TALKING TO HIM?
I'VE GOT TO REMEMBER HE'S NOT A NORMAL ENEMY... WHO MIGHT BE SWAYED BY THREATS... OR LOGIC... OR EVEN FEAR!
WHILE HE'S THE LIZARD, HE LIVES FOR ONE THING ONLY...
TO DESTROY HIS ENEMY, SPIDER-MAN... AND THEN TO ATTACK EVERY HUMAN HE SEES!
UNHHH!
AHHH! HURLING ME OVER YOUR HEAD PLAYED RIGHT INTO MY HANDS...
OR SHOULD I SAY... MY TAIL?

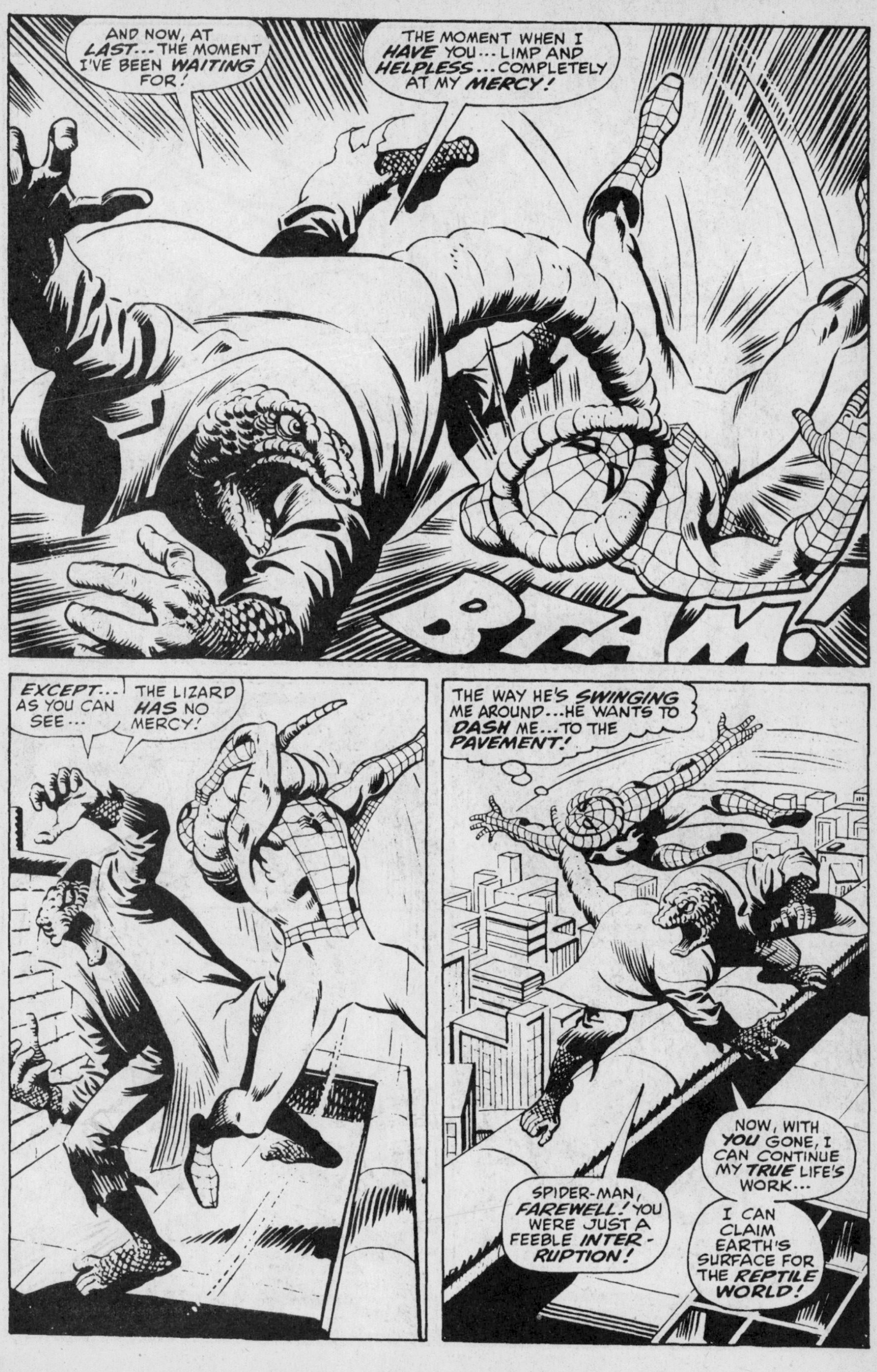
AND NOW, AT LAST... THE MOMENT I'VE BEEN WAITING FOR!
THE MOMENT WHEN I HAVE YOU... LIMP AND HELPLESS... COMPLETELY AT MY MERCY!
BLAM!
EXCEPT... AS YOU CAN SEE...
THE LIZARD HAS NO MERCY!
THE WAY HE'S SWINGING ME AROUND... HE WANTS TO DASH ME... TO THE PAVEMENT!
SPIDER-MAN, FAREWELL! YOU WERE JUST A FEEBLE INTER-RUPTION!
NOW, WITH YOU GONE, I CAN CONTINUE MY TRUE LIFE'S WORK...
I CAN CLAIM EARTH'S SURFACE FOR THE REPTILE WORLD!

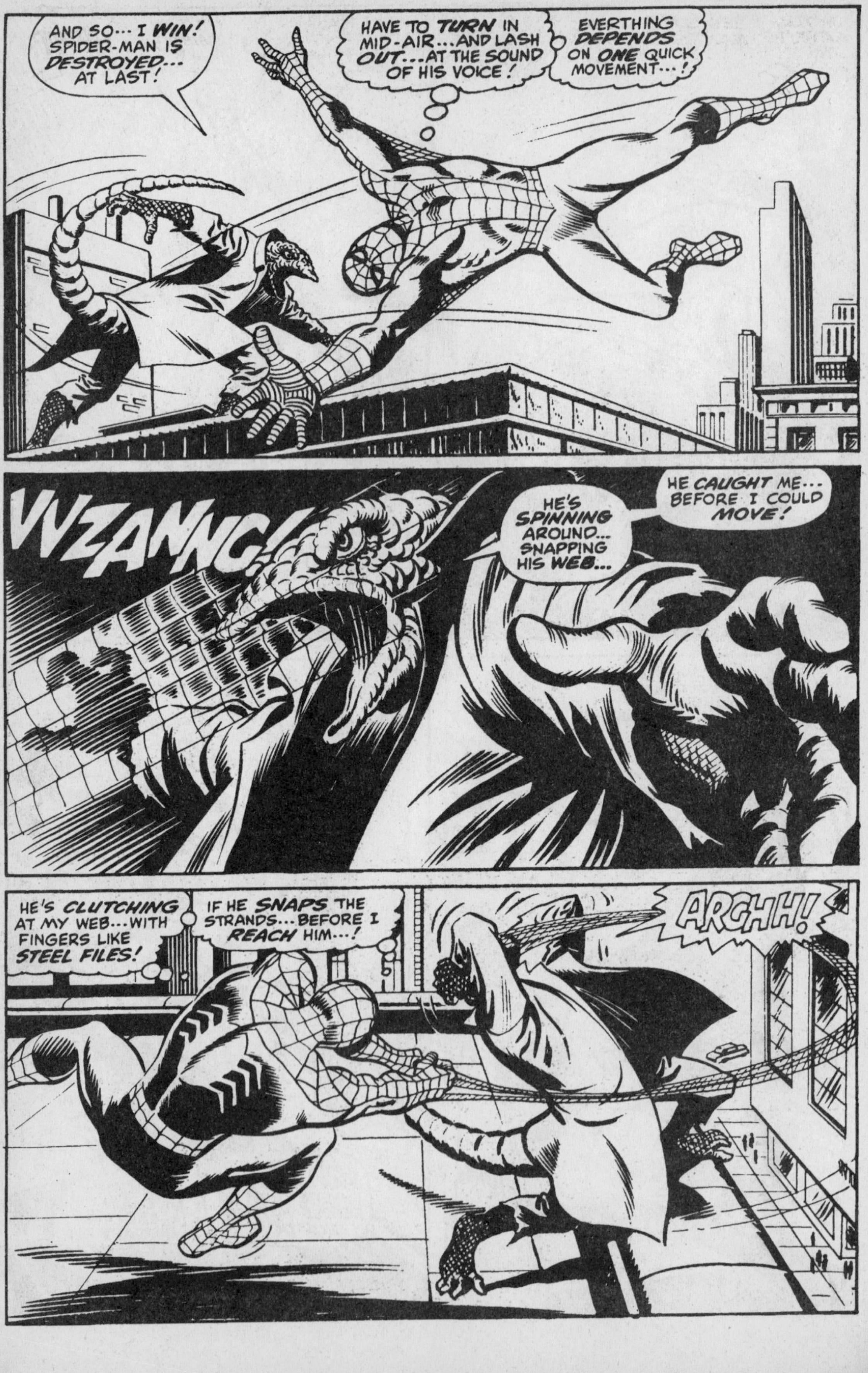
AND SO... I WIN! SPIDER-MAN IS DESTROYED... AT LAST!
HAVE TO TURN IN MID-AIR... AND LASH OUT... AT THE SOUND OF HIS VOICE!
EVERTHING DEPENDS ON ONE QUICK MOVEMENT...!
VVZANNG!
HE'S SPINNING AROUND... SNAPPING HIS WEB...
HE CAUGHT ME... BEFORE I COULD MOVE!
HE'S CLUTCHING AT MY WEB... WITH FINGERS LIKE STEEL FILES!
IF HE SNAPS THE STRANDS... BEFORE I REACH HIM...!
ARGHH!

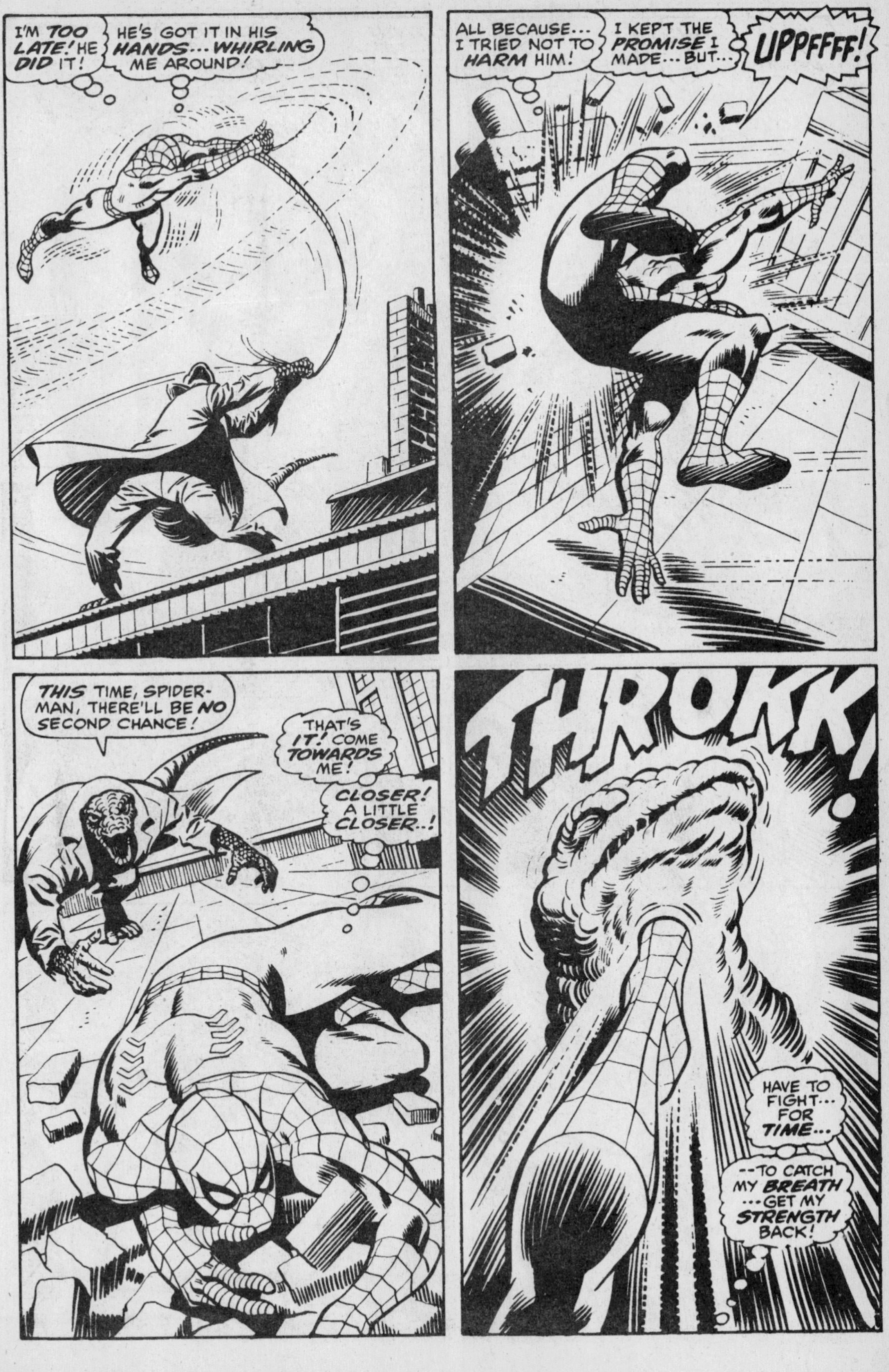

I'M TOO LATE! HE DID IT!
HE'S GOT IT IN HIS HANDS... WHIRLING ME AROUND!
ALL BECAUSE... I TRIED NOT TO HARM HIM!
I KEPT THE PROMISE I MADE... BUT...
UPPFFFF!
THIS TIME, SPIDER-MAN, THERE'LL BE NO SECOND CHANCE!
THAT'S IT! COME TOWARDS ME!
CLOSER! A LITTLE CLOSER..!
THROKK!
HAVE TO FIGHT... FOR TIME...
--TO CATCH MY BREATH ...GET MY STRENGTH BACK!

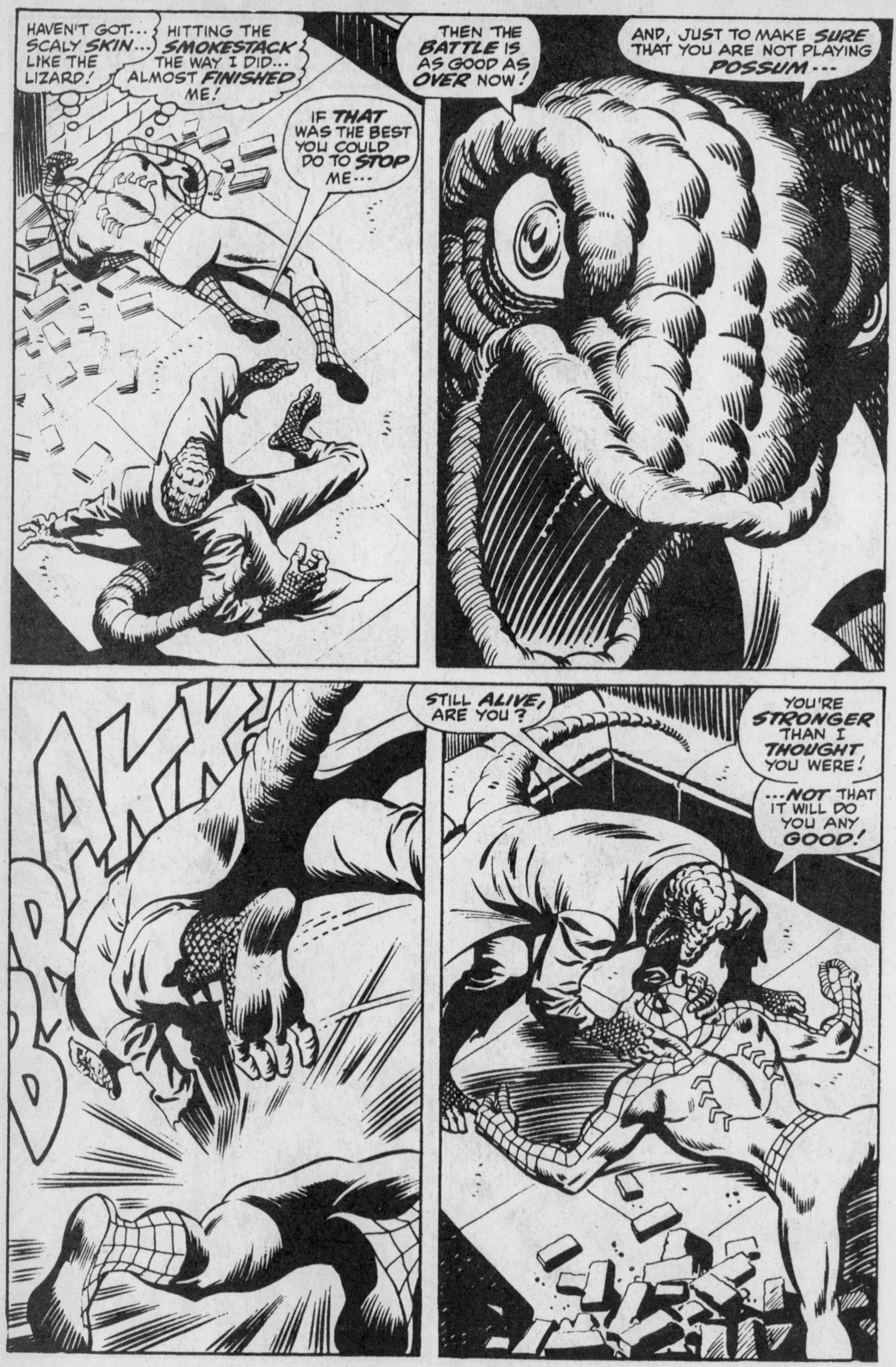
HAVEN'T GOT... SCALY SKIN... LIKE THE LIZARD!
HITTING THE SMOKESTACK THE WAY I DID... ALMOST FINISHED ME!
IF THAT WAS THE BEST YOU COULD DO TO STOP ME...
THEN THE BATTLE IS AS GOOD AS OVER NOW!
AND, JUST TO MAKE SURE THAT YOU ARE NOT PLAYING POSSUM...
BRAKK
STILL ALIVE, ARE YOU?
YOU'RE STRONGER THAN I THOUGHT YOU WERE!
...NOT THAT IT WILL DO YOU ANY GOOD!

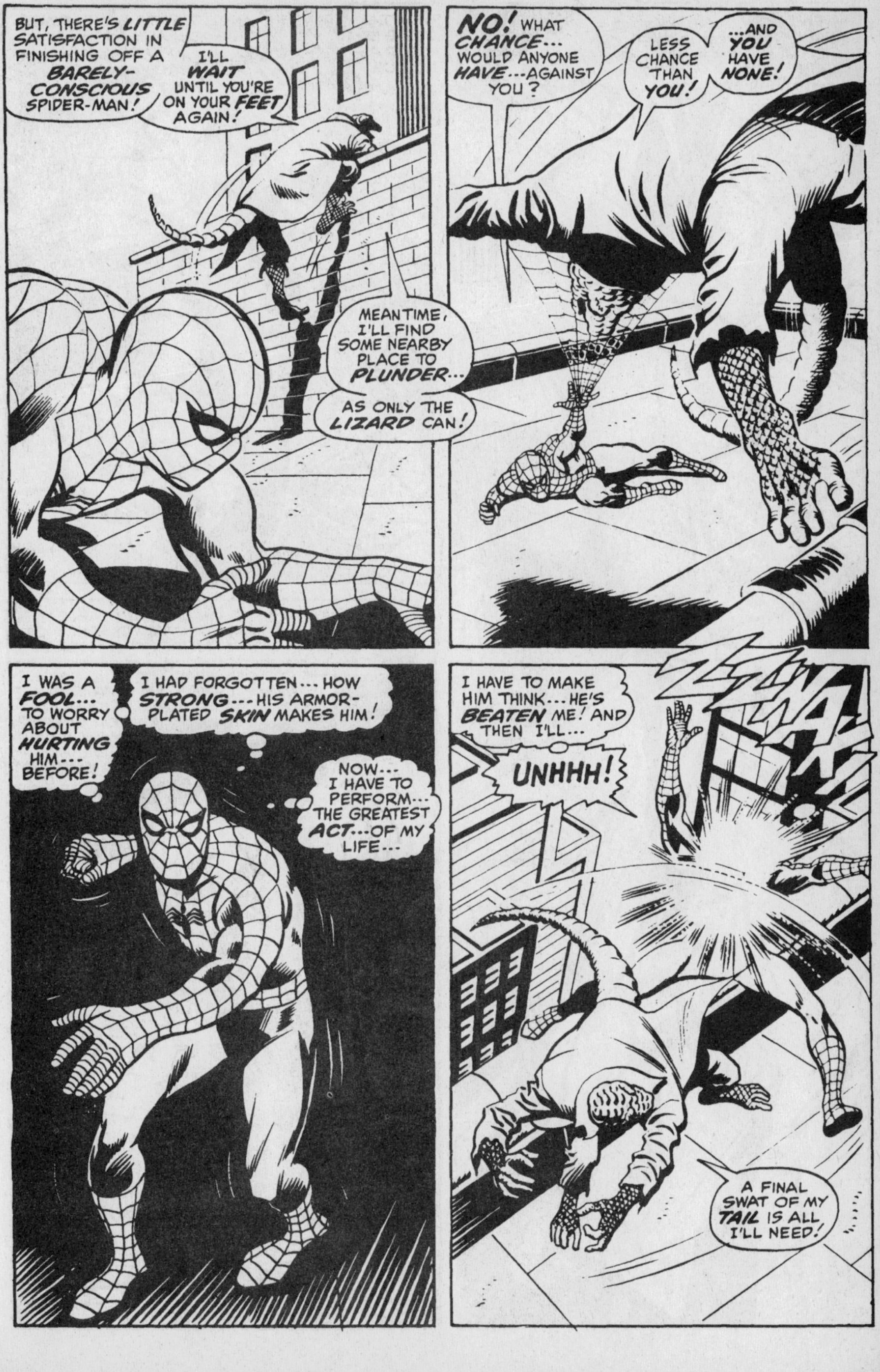
BUT, THERE'S LITTLE SATISFACTION IN FINISHING OFF A BARELY-CONSCIOUS SPIDER-MAN!
I'LL WAIT UNTIL YOU'RE ON YOUR FEET AGAIN!
MEANTIME, I'LL FIND SOME NEARBY PLACE TO PLUNDER...
AS ONLY THE LIZARD CAN!
NO! WHAT CHANCE... WOULD ANYONE HAVE...AGAINST YOU?
LESS CHANCE THAN YOU!
...AND YOU HAVE NONE!
I WAS A FOOL... TO WORRY ABOUT HURTING HIM... BEFORE!
I HAD FORGOTTEN... HOW STRONG... HIS ARMOR-PLATED SKIN MAKES HIM!
NOW... I HAVE TO PERFORM... THE GREATEST ACT...OF MY LIFE...
I HAVE TO MAKE HIM THINK... HE'S BEATEN ME! AND THEN I'LL...
UNHHH!
A FINAL SWAT OF MY TAIL IS ALL I'LL NEED!

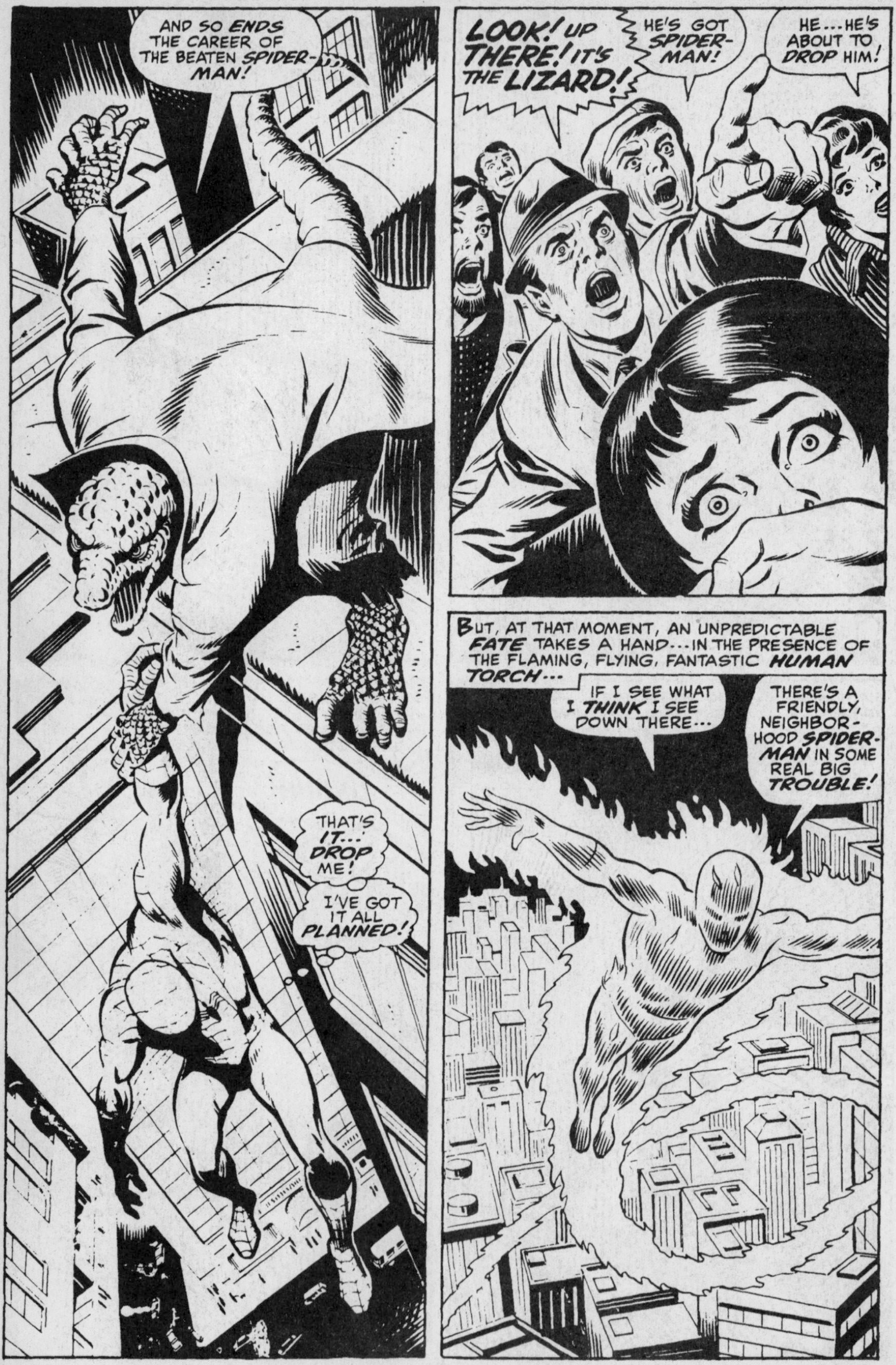
AND SO ENDS THE CAREER OF THE BEATEN SPIDER-MAN!
THAT'S IT... DROP ME!
I'VE GOT IT ALL PLANNED!
LOOK! UP THERE! IT'S THE LIZARD!
HE'S GOT SPIDER-MAN!
HE...HE'S ABOUT TO DROP HIM!
BUT, AT THAT MOMENT, AN UNPREDICTABLE FATE TAKES A HAND... IN THE PRESENCE OF THE FLAMING, FLYING, FANTASTIC HUMAN TORCH...
IF I SEE WHAT I THINK I SEE DOWN THERE...
THERE'S A FRIENDLY, NEIGHBOR-HOOD SPIDER-MAN IN SOME REAL BIG TROUBLE!

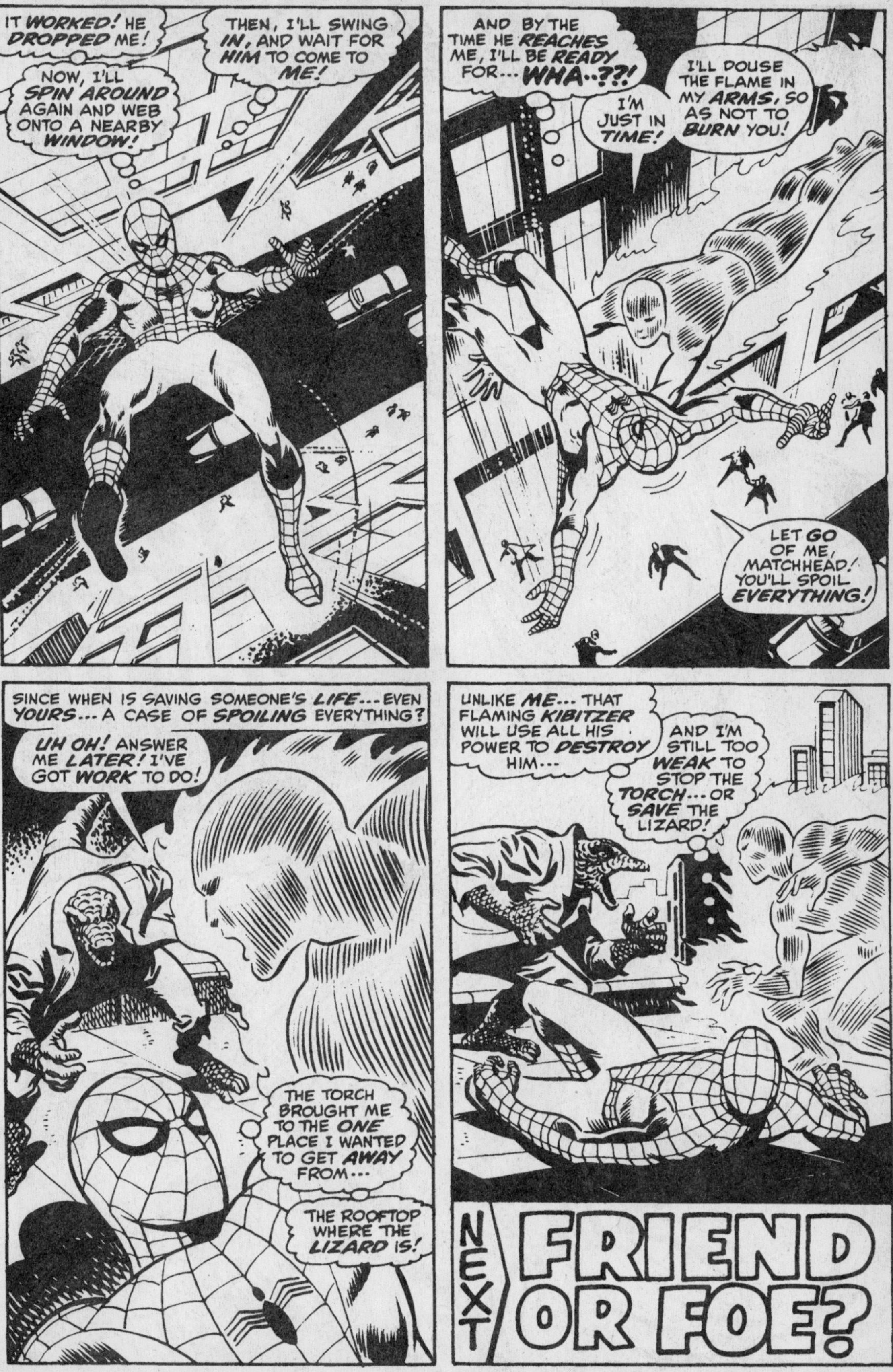
IT WORKED! HE DROPPED ME!
NOW, I'LL SPIN AROUND AGAIN AND WEB ONTO A NEARBY WINDOW!
THEN, I'LL SWING IN, AND WAIT FOR HIM TO COME TO ME!
AND BY THE TIME HE REACHES ME, I'LL BE READY FOR... WHA..??!
I'M JUST IN TIME!
I'LL DOUSE THE FLAME IN MY ARMS, SO AS NOT TO BURN YOU!
LET GO OF ME, MATCHHEAD! YOU'LL SPOIL EVERYTHING!
SINCE WHEN IS SAVING SOMEONE'S LIFE... EVEN YOURS... A CASE OF SPOILING EVERYTHING?
UH OH! ANSWER ME LATER! I'VE GOT WORK TO DO!
THE TORCH BROUGHT ME TO THE ONE PLACE I WANTED TO GET AWAY FROM...
THE ROOFTOP WHERE THE LIZARD IS!
UNLIKE ME... THAT FLAMING KIBITZER WILL USE ALL HIS POWER TO DESTROY HIM...
AND I'M STILL TOO WEAK TO STOP THE TORCH... OR SAVE THE LIZARD!
NEXT
FRIEND OR FOE?

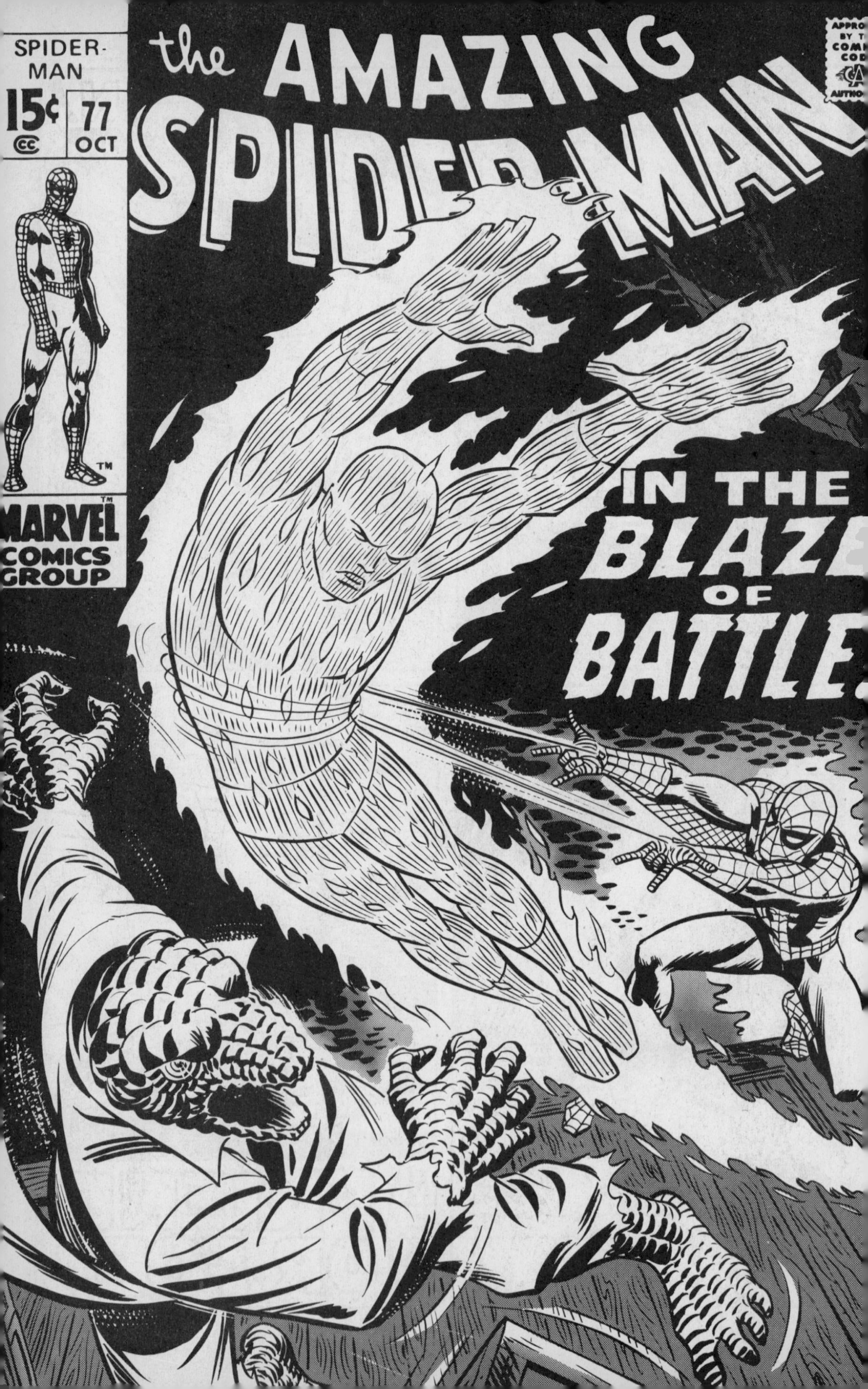
SPIDER-MAN
15¢
77
OCT
MARVEL COMICS GROUP
the AMAZING SPIDER-MAN
IN THE BLAZE OF BATTLE!

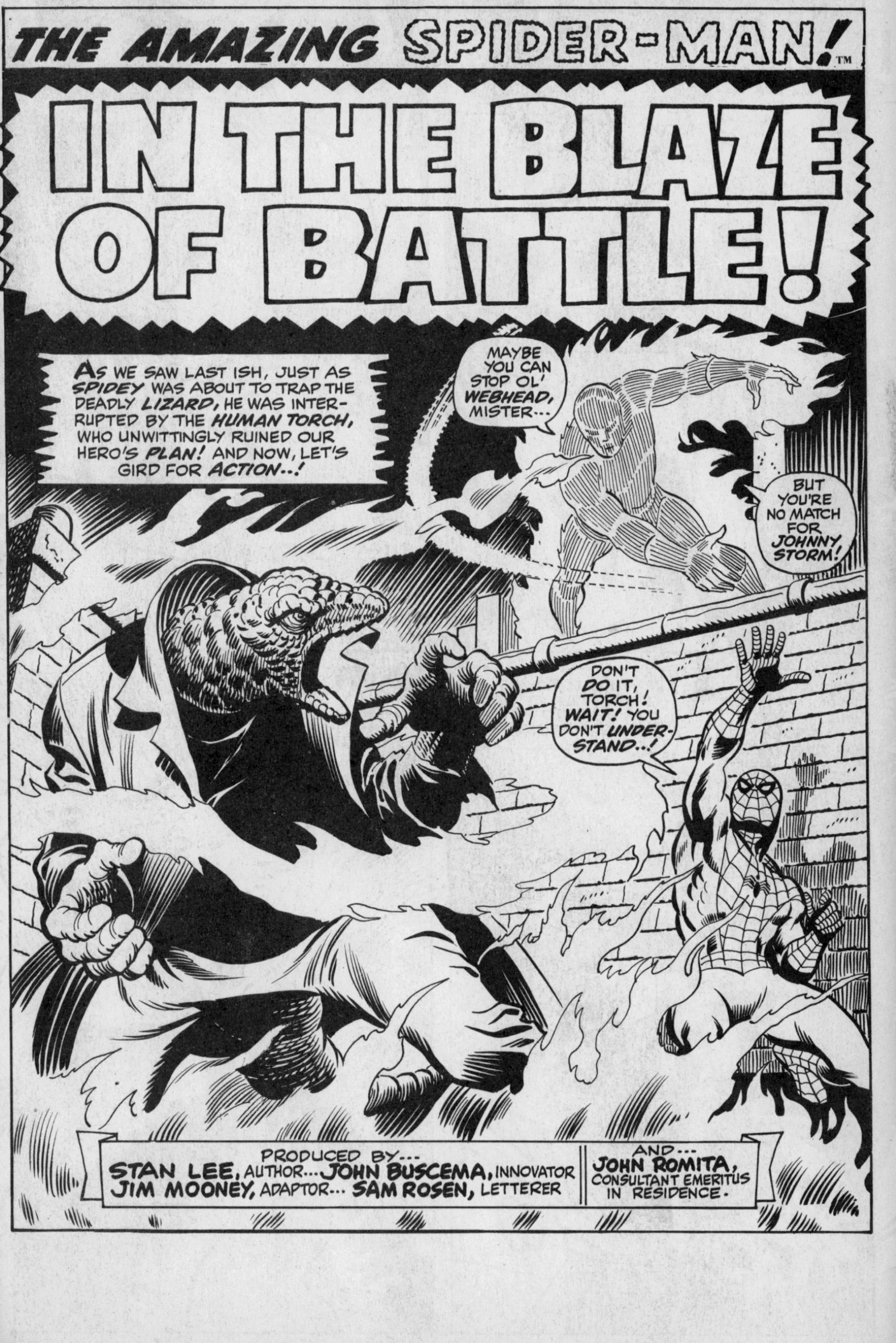
THE AMAZING SPIDER-MAN! TM
IN THE BLAZE OF BATTLE!
AS WE SAW LAST ISH, JUST AS SPIDEY WAS ABOUT TO TRAP THE DEADLY LIZARD, HE WAS INTERRUPTED BY THE HUMAN TORCH, WHO UNWITTINGLY RUINED OUR HERO'S PLAN! AND NOW, LET'S GIRD FOR ACTION..!
MAYBE YOU CAN STOP OL' WEBHEAD, MISTER...
BUT YOU'RE NO MATCH FOR JOHNNY STORM!
DON'T DO IT, TORCH! WAIT! YOU DON'T UNDERSTAND..!
PRODUCED BY... STAN LEE, AUTHOR... JOHN BUSCEMA, INNOVATOR JIM MOONEY, ADAPTOR... SAM ROSEN, LETTERER
AND... JOHN ROMITA, CONSULTANT EMERITUS IN RESIDENCE.

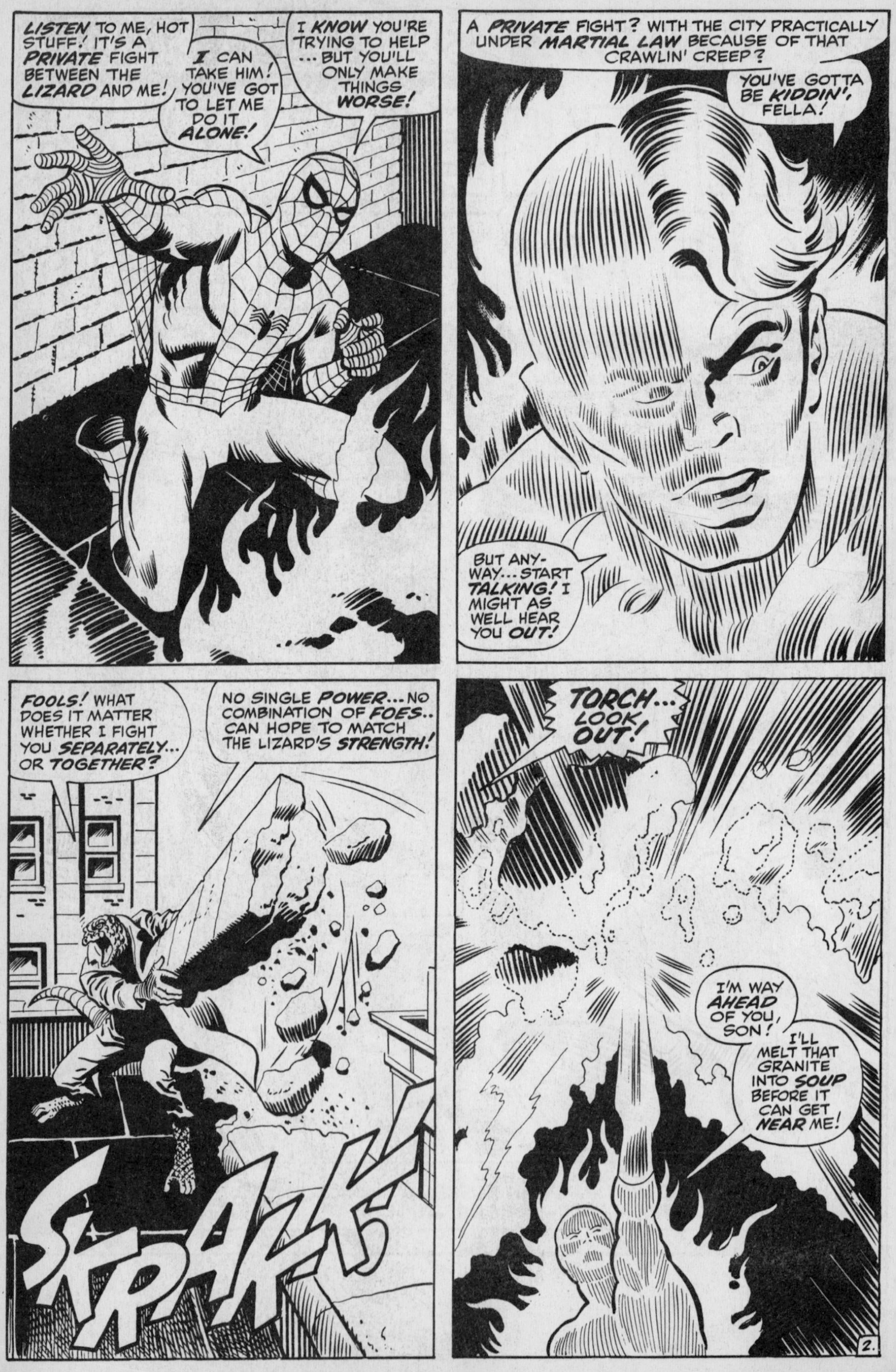
LISTEN TO ME, HOT STUFF! IT'S A PRIVATE FIGHT BETWEEN THE LIZARD AND ME!
I CAN TAKE HIM! YOU'VE GOT TO LET ME DO IT ALONE!
I KNOW YOU'RE TRYING TO HELP ... BUT YOU'LL ONLY MAKE THINGS WORSE!
A PRIVATE FIGHT? WITH THE CITY PRACTICALLY UNDER MARTIAL LAW BECAUSE OF THAT CRAWLIN' CREEP?
YOU'VE GOTTA BE KIDDIN', FELLA!
BUT ANY-WAY... START TALKING! I MIGHT AS WELL HEAR YOU OUT!
FOOLS! WHAT DOES IT MATTER WHETHER I FIGHT YOU SEPARATELY... OR TOGETHER?
NO SINGLE POWER... NO COMBINATION OF FOES.. CAN HOPE TO MATCH THE LIZARD'S STRENGTH!
SKRAKK!
TORCH... LOOK OUT!
I'M WAY AHEAD OF YOU, SON!
I'LL MELT THAT GRANITE INTO SOUP BEFORE IT CAN GET NEAR ME!
2.

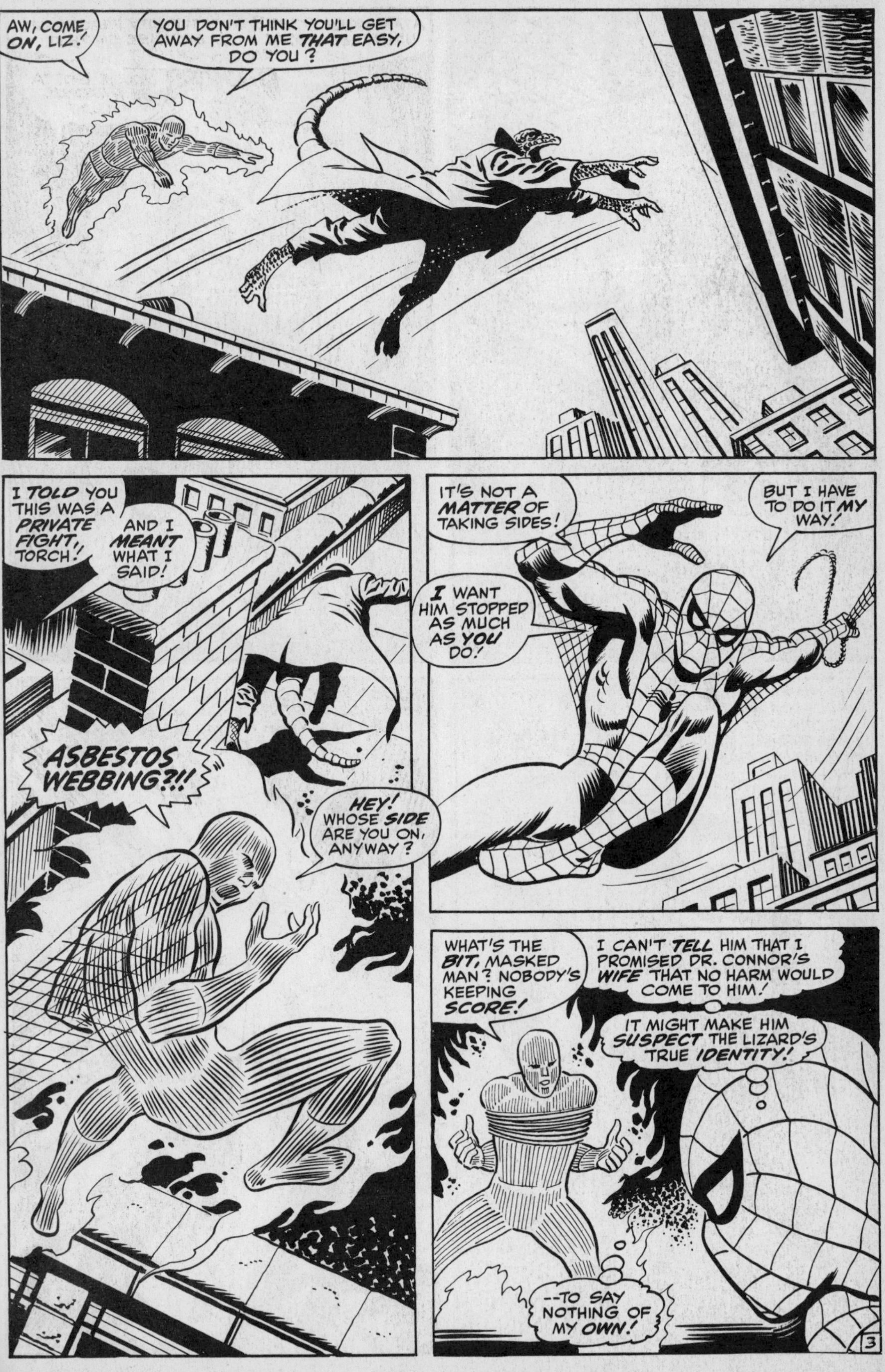
AW, COME ON, LIZ!
YOU DON'T THINK YOU'LL GET AWAY FROM ME THAT EASY, DO YOU?
I TOLD YOU THIS WAS A PRIVATE FIGHT, TORCH!
AND I MEANT WHAT I SAID!
ASBESTOS WEBBING?!!
HEY! WHOSE SIDE ARE YOU ON, ANYWAY?
IT'S NOT A MATTER OF TAKING SIDES!
I WANT HIM STOPPED AS MUCH AS YOU DO!
BUT I HAVE TO DO IT MY WAY!
WHAT'S THE BIT, MASKED MAN? NOBODY'S KEEPING SCORE!
I CAN'T TELL HIM THAT I PROMISED DR. CONNOR'S WIFE THAT NO HARM WOULD COME TO HIM!
IT MIGHT MAKE HIM SUSPECT THE LIZARD'S TRUE IDENTITY!
--TO SAY NOTHING OF MY OWN!
3

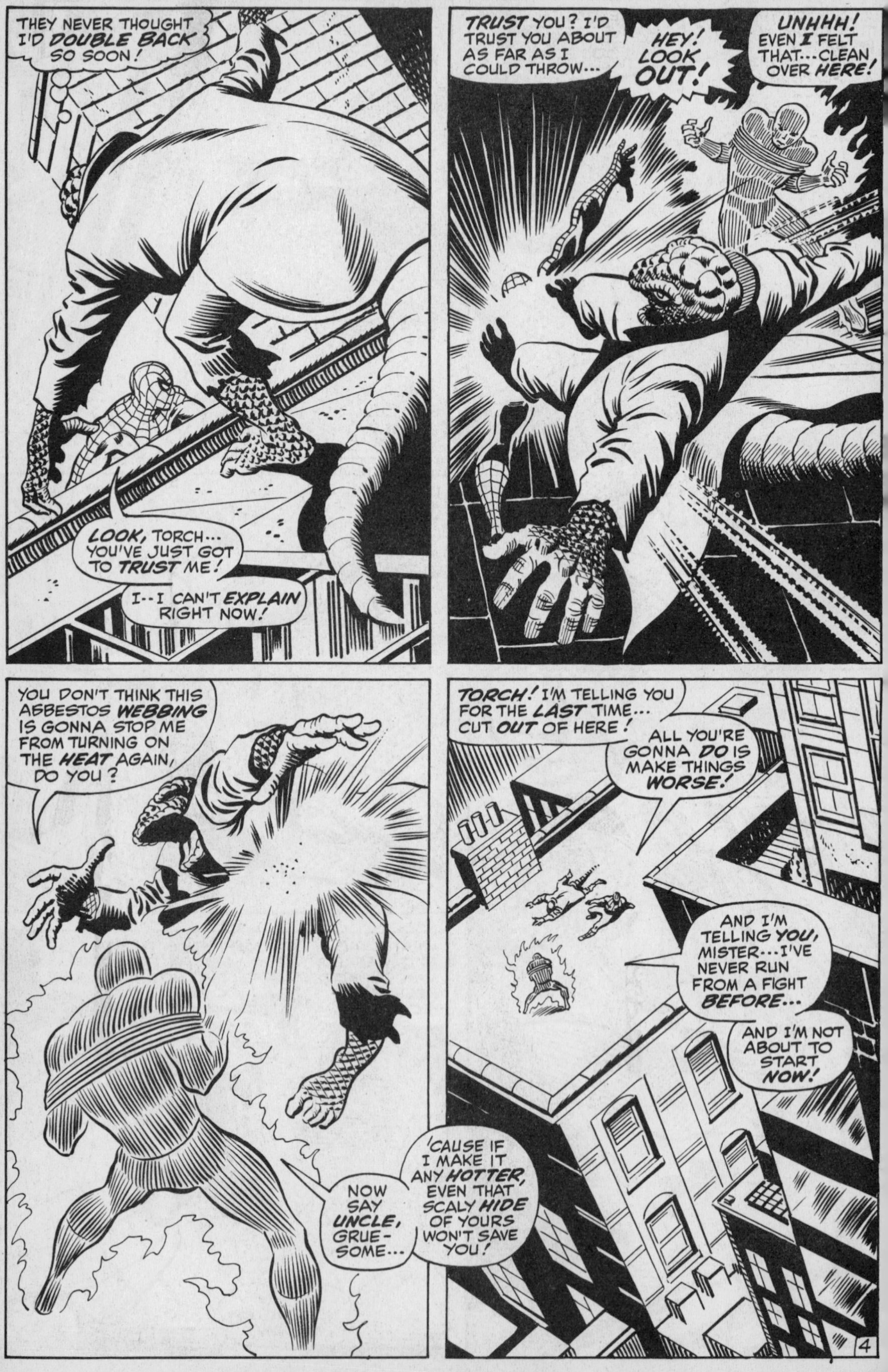
THEY NEVER THOUGHT I'D DOUBLE BACK SO SOON!
LOOK, TORCH... YOU'VE JUST GOT TO TRUST ME!
I--I CAN'T EXPLAIN RIGHT NOW!
TRUST YOU? I'D TRUST YOU ABOUT AS FAR AS I COULD THROW...
HEY! LOOK OUT!
UNHHH! EVEN I FELT THAT...CLEAN OVER HERE!
YOU DON'T THINK THIS ASBESTOS WEBBING IS GONNA STOP ME FROM TURNING ON THE HEAT AGAIN, DO YOU?
NOW SAY UNCLE, GRUE-SOME...
'CAUSE IF I MAKE IT ANY HOTTER, EVEN THAT SCALY HIDE OF YOURS WON'T SAVE YOU!
TORCH! I'M TELLING YOU FOR THE LAST TIME... CUT OUT OF HERE!
ALL YOU'RE GONNA DO IS MAKE THINGS WORSE!
AND I'M TELLING YOU, MISTER...I'VE NEVER RUN FROM A FIGHT BEFORE...
AND I'M NOT ABOUT TO START NOW!
4

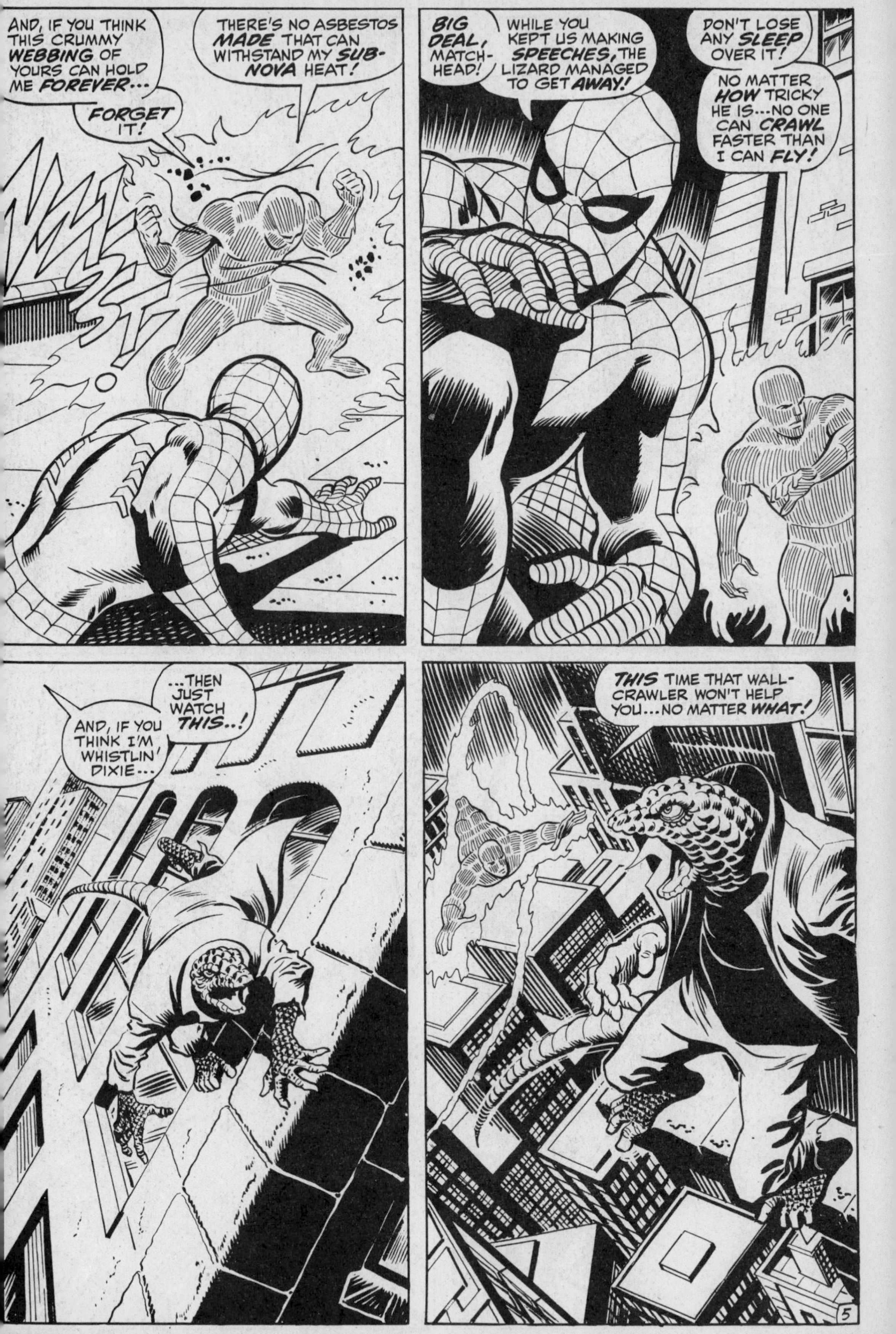
AND, IF YOU THINK THIS CRUMMY WEBBING OF YOURS CAN HOLD ME FOREVER...
FORGET IT!
THERE'S NO ASBESTOS MADE THAT CAN WITHSTAND MY SUB-NOVA HEAT!
BIG DEAL, MATCH-HEAD!
WHILE YOU KEPT US MAKING SPEECHES, THE LIZARD MANAGED TO GET AWAY!
DON'T LOSE ANY SLEEP OVER IT!
NO MATTER HOW TRICKY HE IS...NO ONE CAN CRAWL FASTER THAN I CAN FLY!
AND, IF YOU THINK I'M WHISTLIN' DIXIE...
...THEN JUST WATCH THIS..!
THIS TIME THAT WALL-CRAWLER WON'T HELP YOU...NO MATTER WHAT!

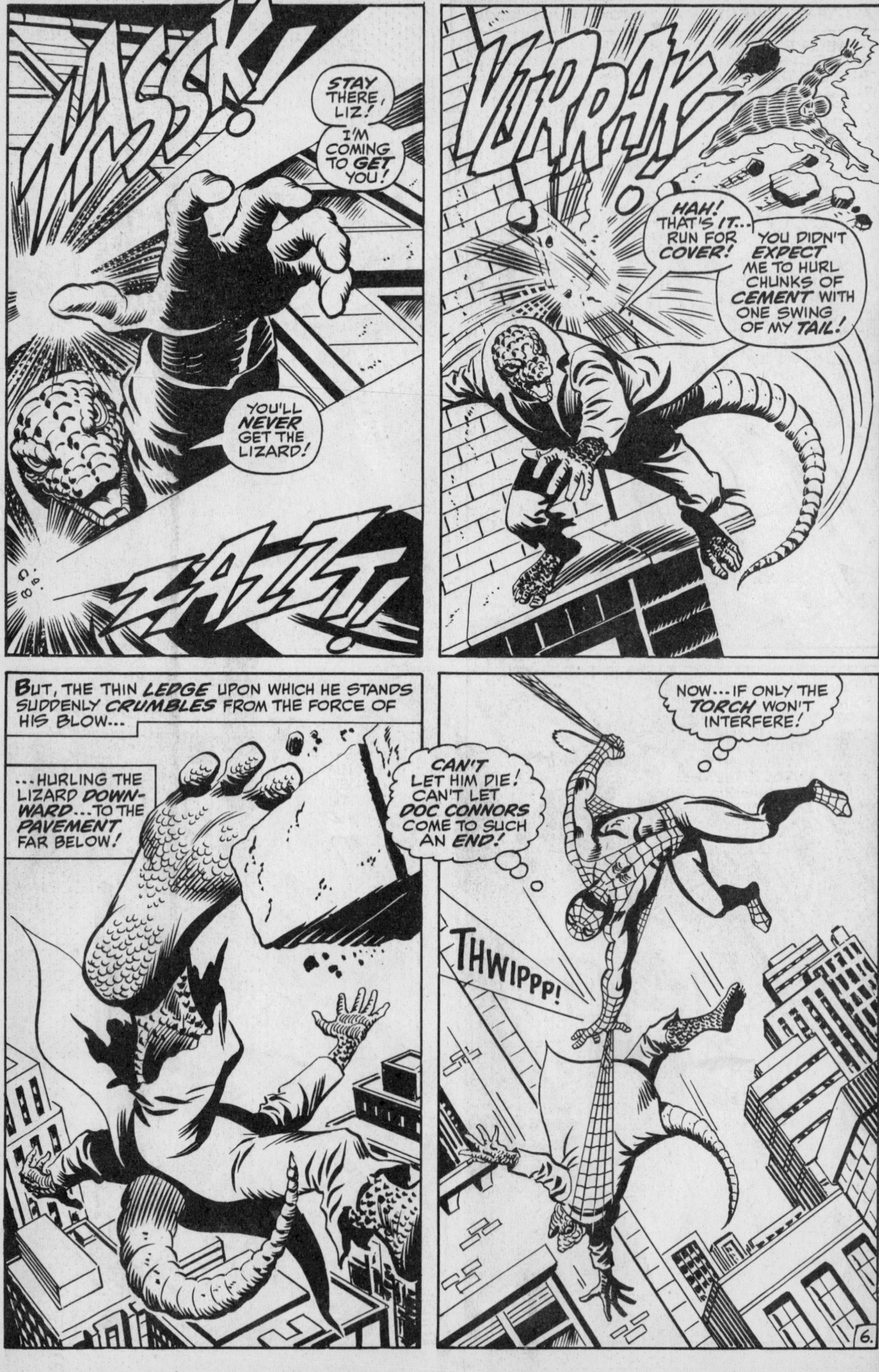

WASSK!
STAY THERE, LIZ! I'M COMING TO GET YOU!
YOU'LL NEVER GET THE LIZARD!
ZAAT!
VURRAK!
HAH! THAT'S IT... RUN FOR COVER!
YOU DIDN'T EXPECT ME TO HURL CHUNKS OF CEMENT WITH ONE SWING OF MY TAIL!
BUT, THE THIN LEDGE UPON WHICH HE STANDS SUDDENLY CRUMBLES FROM THE FORCE OF HIS BLOW...
...HURLING THE LIZARD DOWN-WARD...TO THE PAVEMENT FAR BELOW!
CAN'T LET HIM DIE! CAN'T LET DOC CONNORS COME TO SUCH AN END!
NOW... IF ONLY THE TORCH WON'T INTERFERE!
THWIPPP!

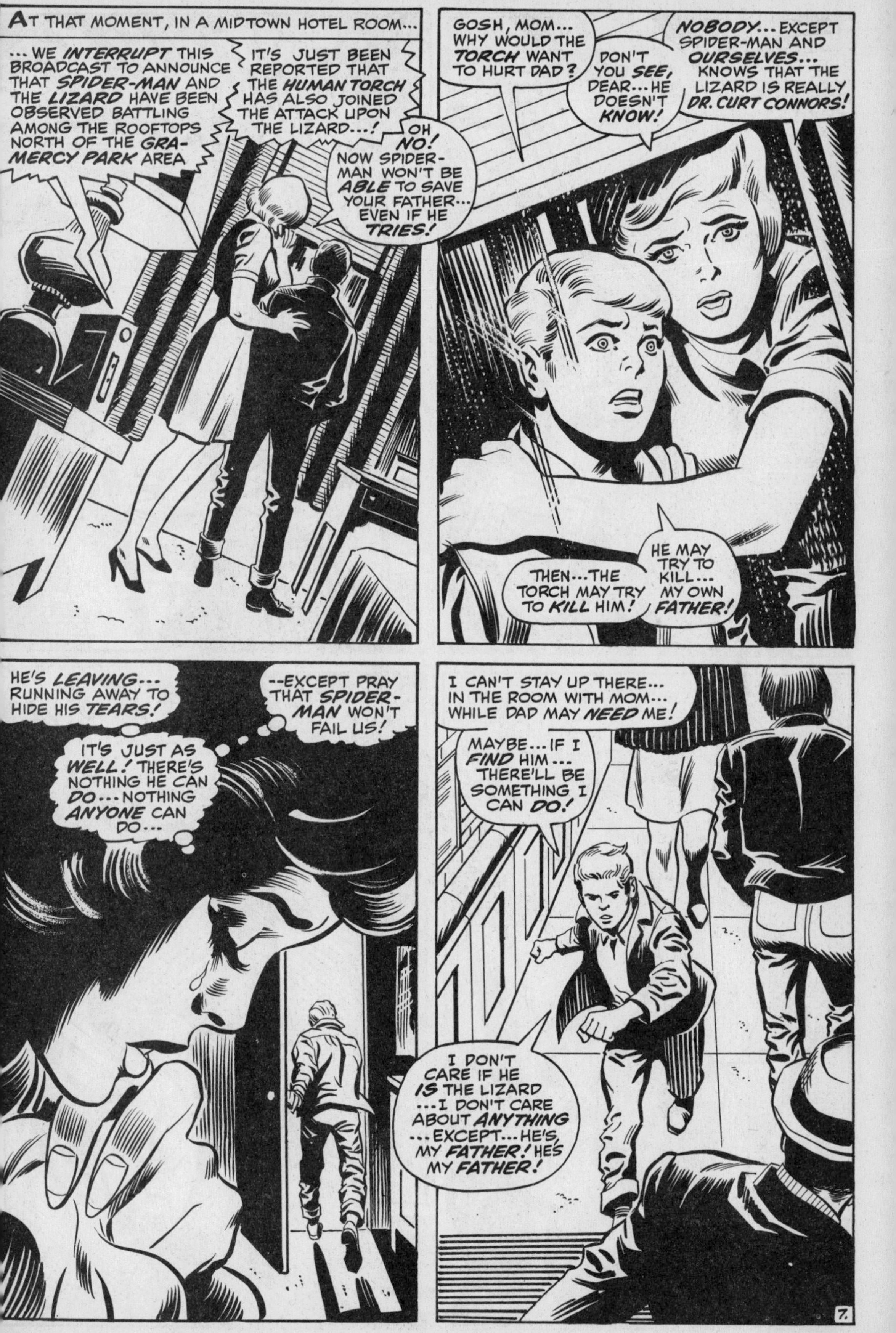
AT THAT MOMENT, IN A MIDTOWN HOTEL ROOM...
...WE INTERRUPT THIS BROADCAST TO ANNOUNCE THAT SPIDER-MAN AND THE LIZARD HAVE BEEN OBSERVED BATTLING AMONG THE ROOFTOPS NORTH OF THE GRAMERCY PARK AREA
IT'S JUST BEEN REPORTED THAT THE HUMAN TORCH HAS ALSO JOINED THE ATTACK UPON THE LIZARD...!
OH NO! NOW SPIDER-MAN WON'T BE ABLE TO SAVE YOUR FATHER... EVEN IF HE TRIES!
GOSH, MOM... WHY WOULD THE TORCH WANT TO HURT DAD?
DON'T YOU SEE, DEAR... HE DOESN'T KNOW!
NOBODY... EXCEPT SPIDER-MAN AND OURSELVES... KNOWS THAT THE LIZARD IS REALLY DR. CURT CONNORS!
THEN... THE TORCH MAY TRY TO KILL HIM!
HE MAY TRY TO KILL... MY OWN FATHER!
HE'S LEAVING... RUNNING AWAY TO HIDE HIS TEARS!
--EXCEPT PRAY THAT SPIDER-MAN WON'T FAIL US!
IT'S JUST AS WELL! THERE'S NOTHING HE CAN DO... NOTHING ANYONE CAN DO...
I CAN'T STAY UP THERE... IN THE ROOM WITH MOM... WHILE DAD MAY NEED ME!
MAYBE... IF I FIND HIM... THERE'LL BE SOMETHING I CAN DO!
I DON'T CARE IF HE IS THE LIZARD ...I DON'T CARE ABOUT ANYTHING ...EXCEPT... HE'S MY FATHER! HE'S MY FATHER!
7.

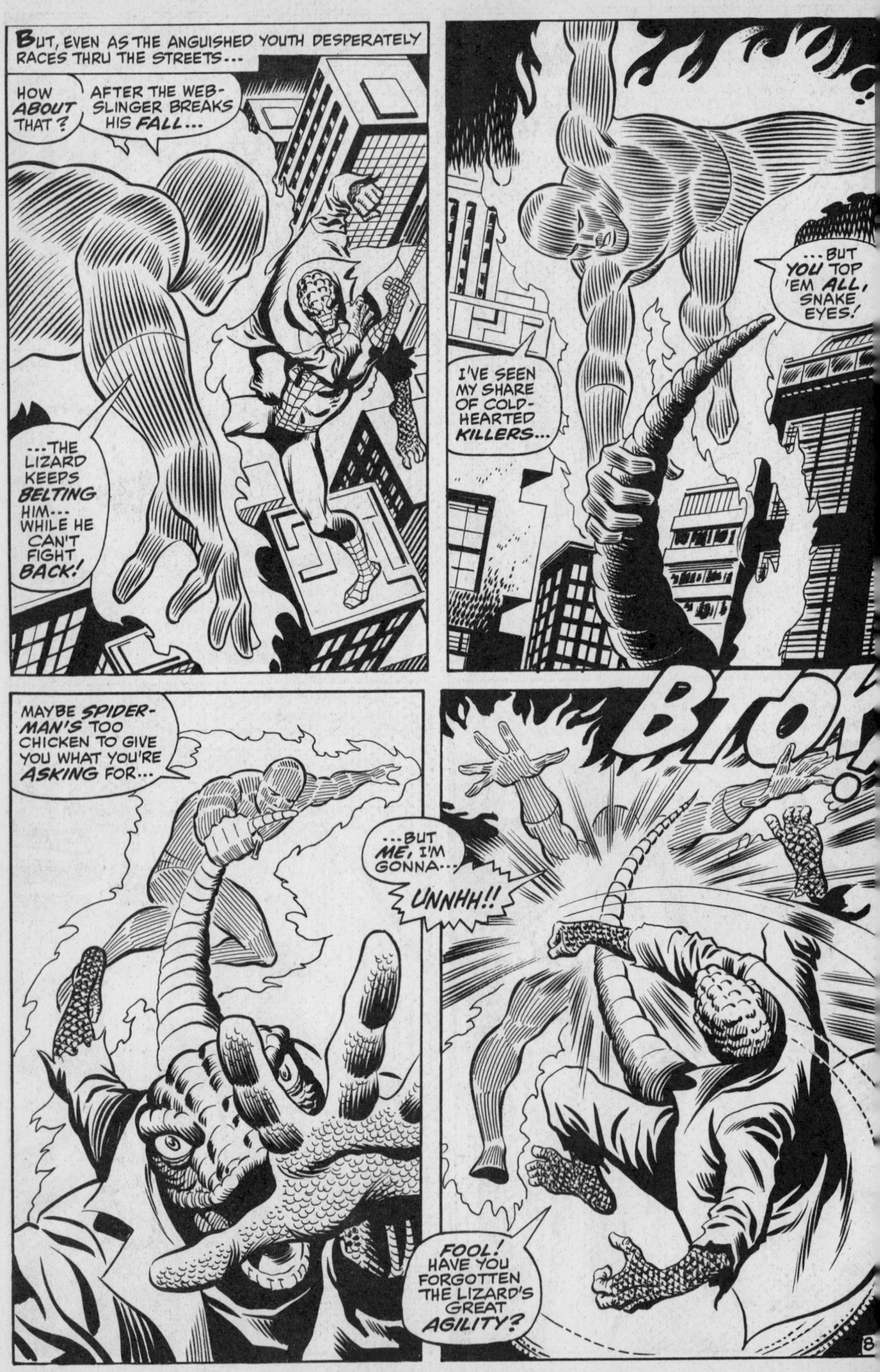
BUT, EVEN AS THE ANGUISHED YOUTH DESPERATELY RACES THRU THE STREETS...
HOW ABOUT THAT?
AFTER THE WEB-SLINGER BREAKS HIS FALL...
...THE LIZARD KEEPS BELTING HIM... WHILE HE CAN'T FIGHT BACK!
I'VE SEEN MY SHARE OF COLD-HEARTED KILLERS...
...BUT YOU TOP 'EM ALL, SNAKE EYES!
MAYBE SPIDER-MAN'S TOO CHICKEN TO GIVE YOU WHAT YOU'RE ASKING FOR...
...BUT ME, I'M GONNA...
UNNHH!!
FOOL! HAVE YOU FORGOTTEN THE LIZARD'S GREAT AGILITY?

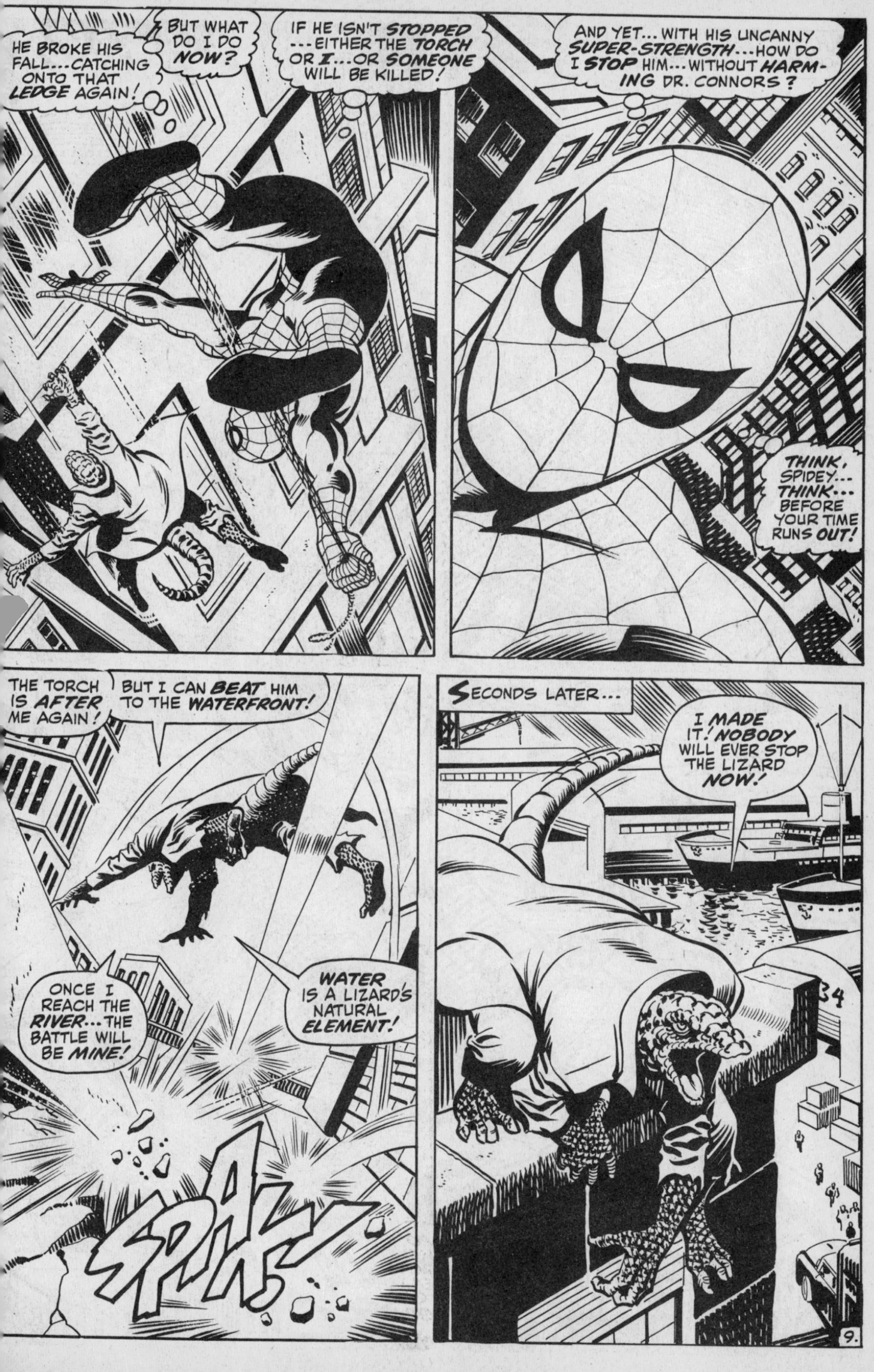
HE BROKE HIS FALL... CATCHING ONTO THAT LEDGE AGAIN!
BUT WHAT DO I DO NOW?
IF HE ISN'T STOPPED --- EITHER THE TORCH OR I... OR SOMEONE WILL BE KILLED!
AND YET... WITH HIS UNCANNY SUPER-STRENGTH... HOW DO I STOP HIM... WITHOUT HARMING DR. CONNORS?
THINK, SPIDEY... THINK... BEFORE YOUR TIME RUNS OUT!
THE TORCH IS AFTER ME AGAIN!
BUT I CAN BEAT HIM TO THE WATERFRONT!
ONCE I REACH THE RIVER... THE BATTLE WILL BE MINE!
WATER IS A LIZARD'S NATURAL ELEMENT!
SPAK
SECONDS LATER...
I MADE IT! NOBODY WILL EVER STOP THE LIZARD NOW!
34

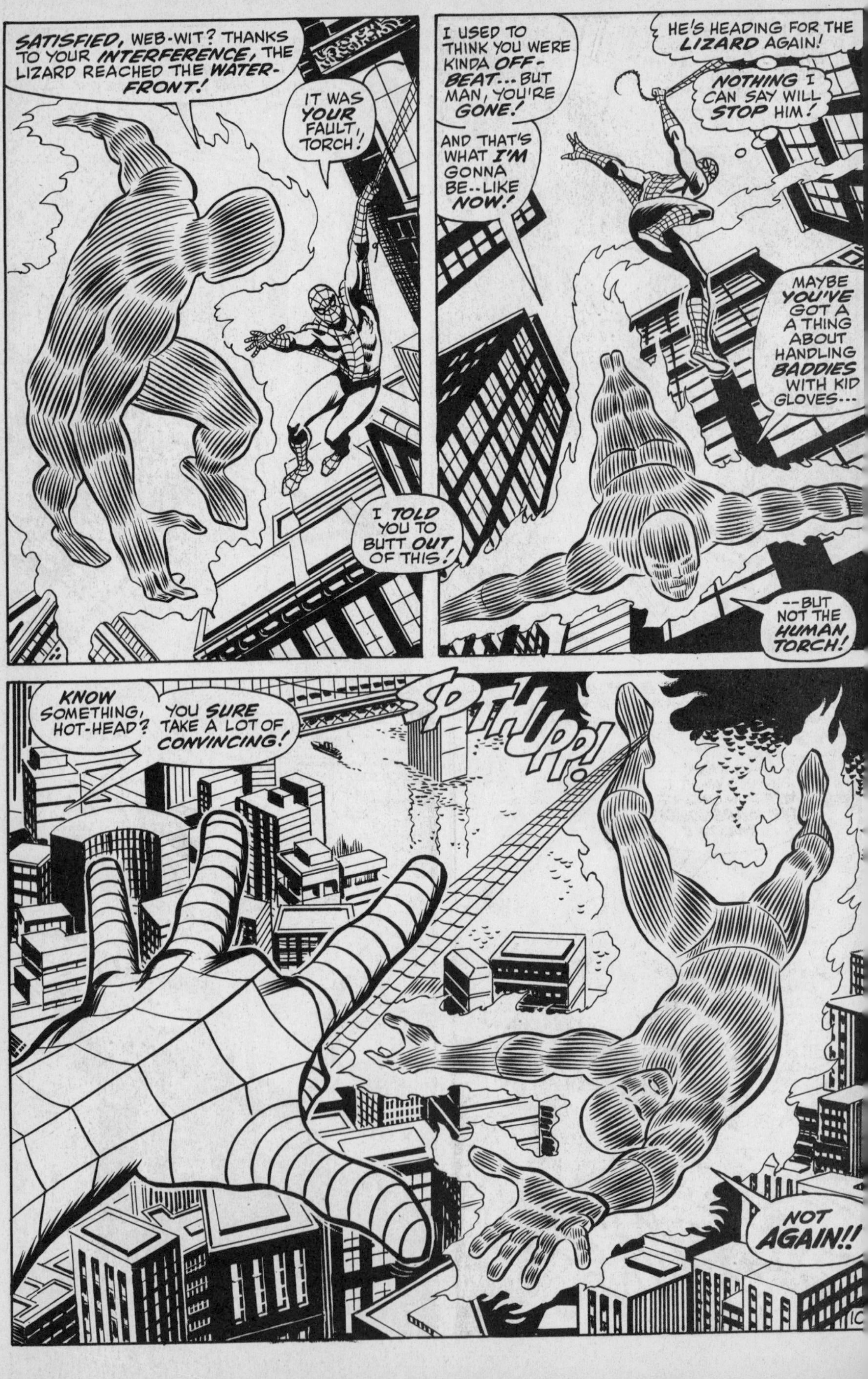

SATISFIED, WEB-WIT? THANKS TO YOUR INTERFERENCE, THE LIZARD REACHED THE WATER-FRONT!
IT WAS YOUR FAULT, TORCH!
I TOLD YOU TO BUTT OUT OF THIS!
I USED TO THINK YOU WERE KINDA OFF-BEAT... BUT MAN, YOU'RE GONE!
AND THAT'S WHAT I'M GONNA BE--LIKE NOW!
HE'S HEADING FOR THE LIZARD AGAIN!
NOTHING I CAN SAY WILL STOP HIM!
MAYBE YOU'VE GOT A THING ABOUT HANDLING BADDIES WITH KID GLOVES---
--BUT NOT THE HUMAN TORCH!
KNOW SOMETHING, HOT-HEAD?
YOU SURE TAKE A LOT OF CONVINCING!
SPTHUPP!
NOT AGAIN!!

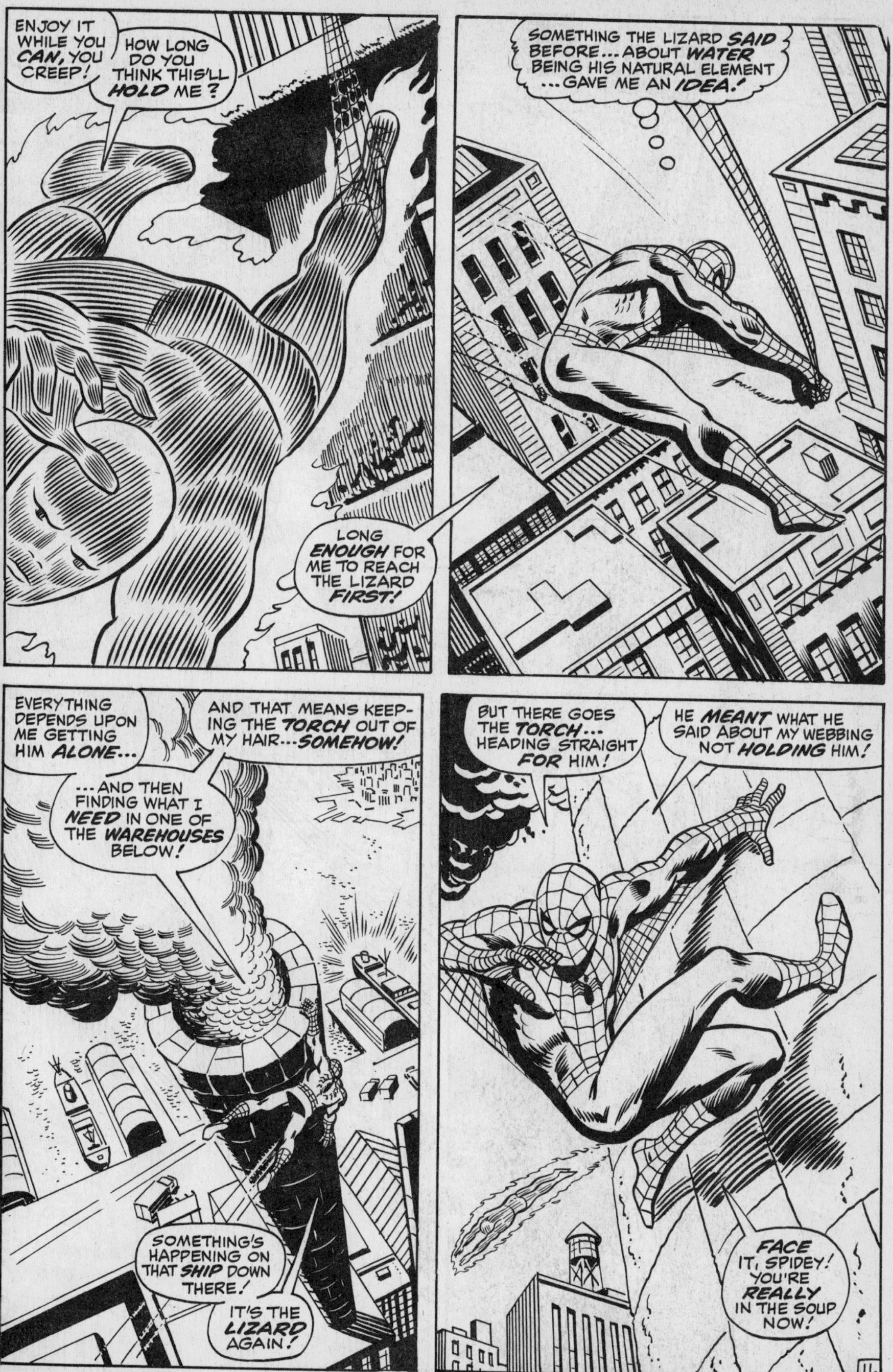

ENJOY IT WHILE YOU CAN, YOU CREEP!
HOW LONG DO YOU THINK THIS'LL HOLD ME?
LONG ENOUGH FOR ME TO REACH THE LIZARD FIRST!
SOMETHING THE LIZARD SAID BEFORE... ABOUT WATER BEING HIS NATURAL ELEMENT ...GAVE ME AN IDEA!
EVERYTHING DEPENDS UPON ME GETTING HIM ALONE...
AND THAT MEANS KEEPING THE TORCH OUT OF MY HAIR...SOMEHOW!
...AND THEN FINDING WHAT I NEED IN ONE OF THE WAREHOUSES BELOW!
SOMETHING'S HAPPENING ON THAT SHIP DOWN THERE!
IT'S THE LIZARD AGAIN!
BUT THERE GOES THE TORCH... HEADING STRAIGHT FOR HIM!
HE MEANT WHAT HE SAID ABOUT MY WEBBING NOT HOLDING HIM!
FACE IT, SPIDEY! YOU'RE REALLY IN THE SOUP NOW!
11.

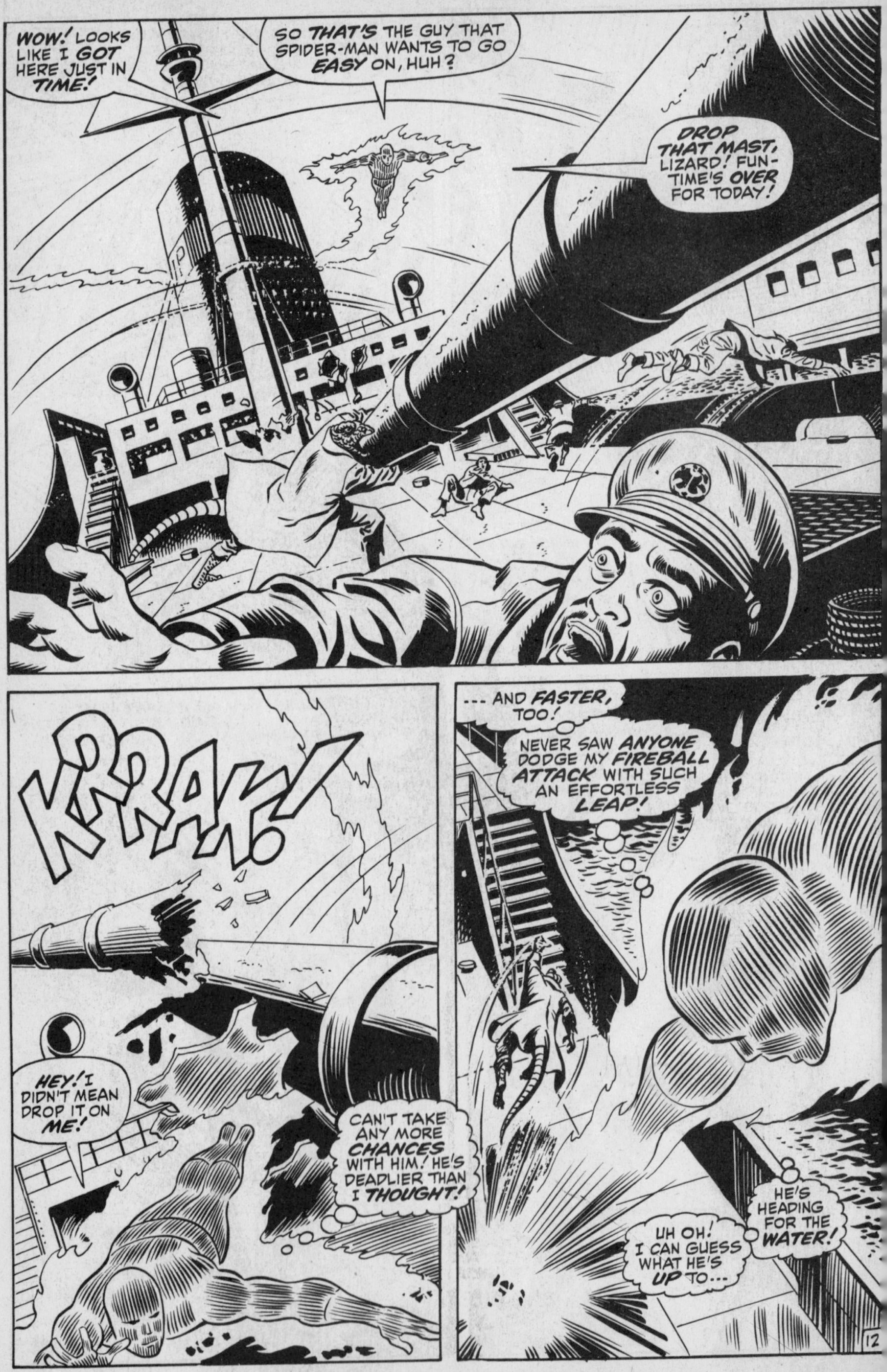
WOW! LOOKS LIKE I GOT HERE JUST IN TIME!
SO THAT'S THE GUY THAT SPIDER-MAN WANTS TO GO EASY ON, HUH?
DROP THAT MAST, LIZARD! FUN-TIME'S OVER FOR TODAY!
KRRAK!
HEY! I DIDN'T MEAN DROP IT ON ME!
CAN'T TAKE ANY MORE CHANCES WITH HIM! HE'S DEADLIER THAN I THOUGHT!
--- AND FASTER, TOO!
NEVER SAW ANYONE DODGE MY FIREBALL ATTACK WITH SUCH AN EFFORTLESS LEAP!
HE'S HEADING FOR THE WATER!
UH OH! I CAN GUESS WHAT HE'S UP TO...
12

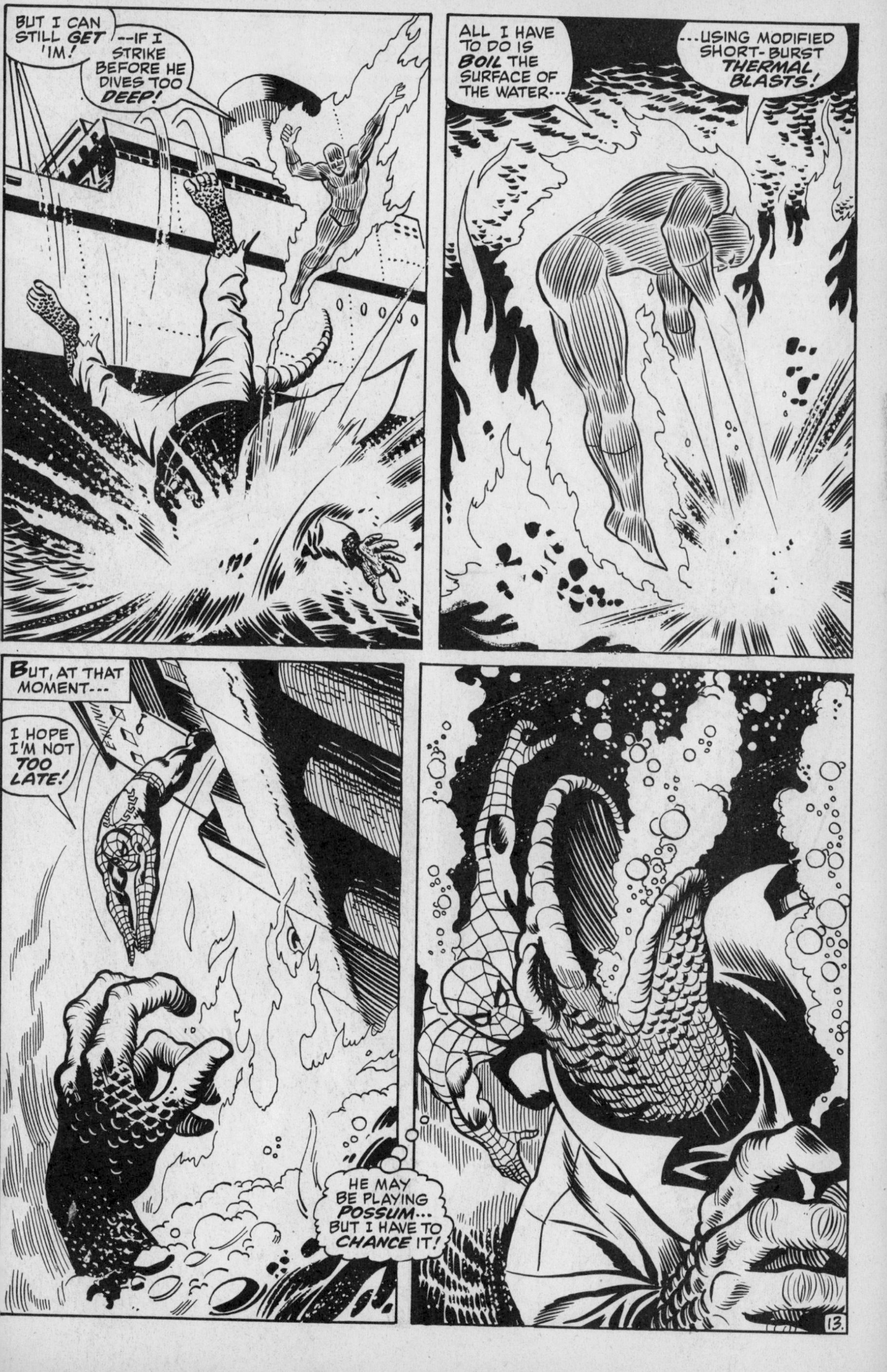
BUT I CAN STILL GET 'IM!
--IF I STRIKE BEFORE HE DIVES TOO DEEP!
ALL I HAVE TO DO IS BOIL THE SURFACE OF THE WATER---
---USING MODIFIED SHORT-BURST THERMAL BLASTS!
BUT, AT THAT MOMENT---
I HOPE I'M NOT TOO LATE!
HE MAY BE PLAYING POSSUM... BUT I HAVE TO CHANCE IT!
13.

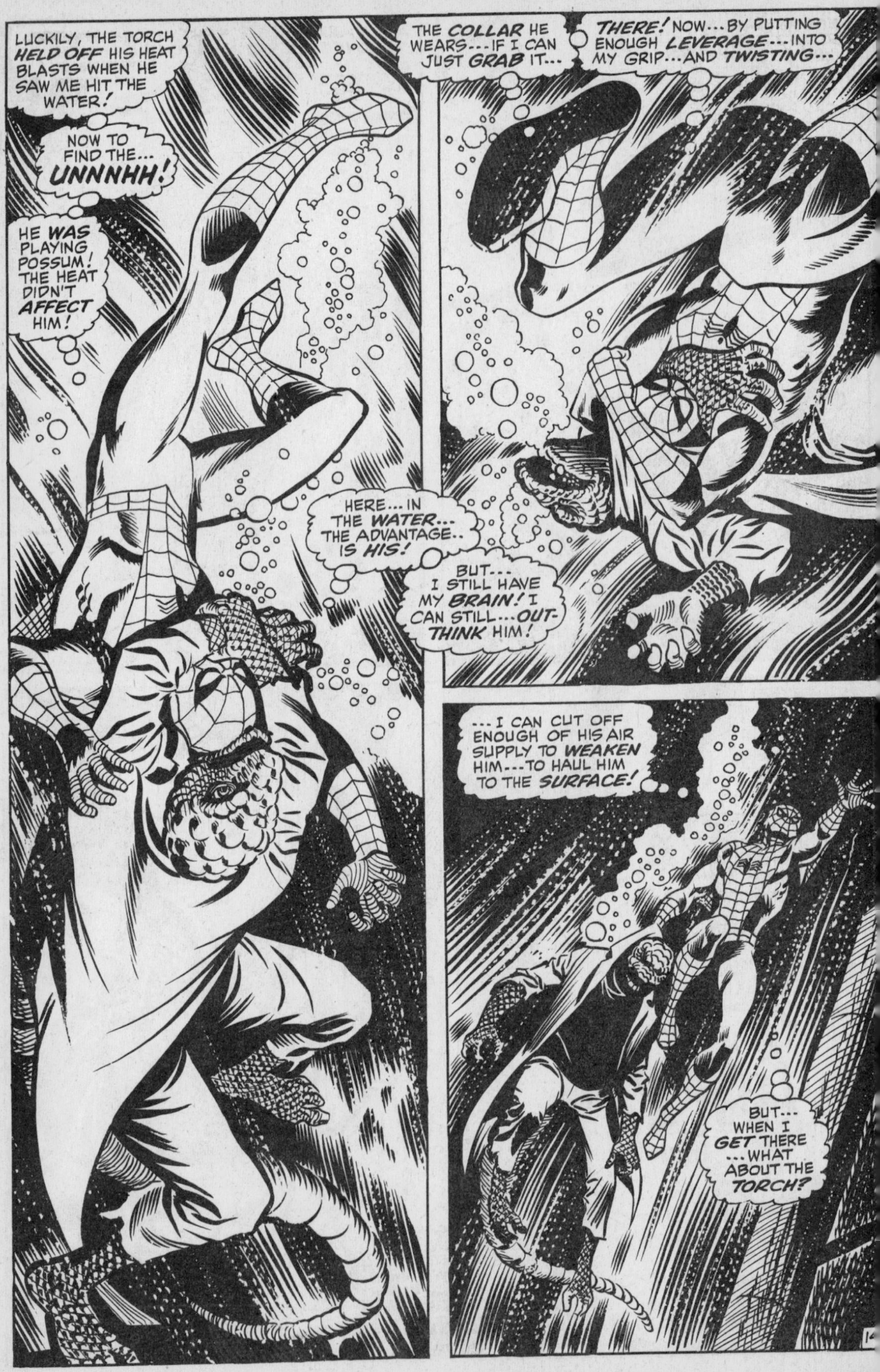

LUCKILY, THE TORCH HELD OFF HIS HEAT BLASTS WHEN HE SAW ME HIT THE WATER!
NOW TO FIND THE... UNNNHH!
HE WAS PLAYING POSSUM! THE HEAT DIDN'T AFFECT HIM!
HERE... IN THE WATER... THE ADVANTAGE.. IS HIS!
BUT--- I STILL HAVE MY BRAIN! I CAN STILL...OUT-THINK HIM!
THE COLLAR HE WEARS---IF I CAN JUST GRAB IT...
THERE! NOW...BY PUTTING ENOUGH LEVERAGE---INTO MY GRIP...AND TWISTING...
...I CAN CUT OFF ENOUGH OF HIS AIR SUPPLY TO WEAKEN HIM---TO HAUL HIM TO THE SURFACE!
BUT--- WHEN I GET THERE ...WHAT ABOUT THE TORCH?

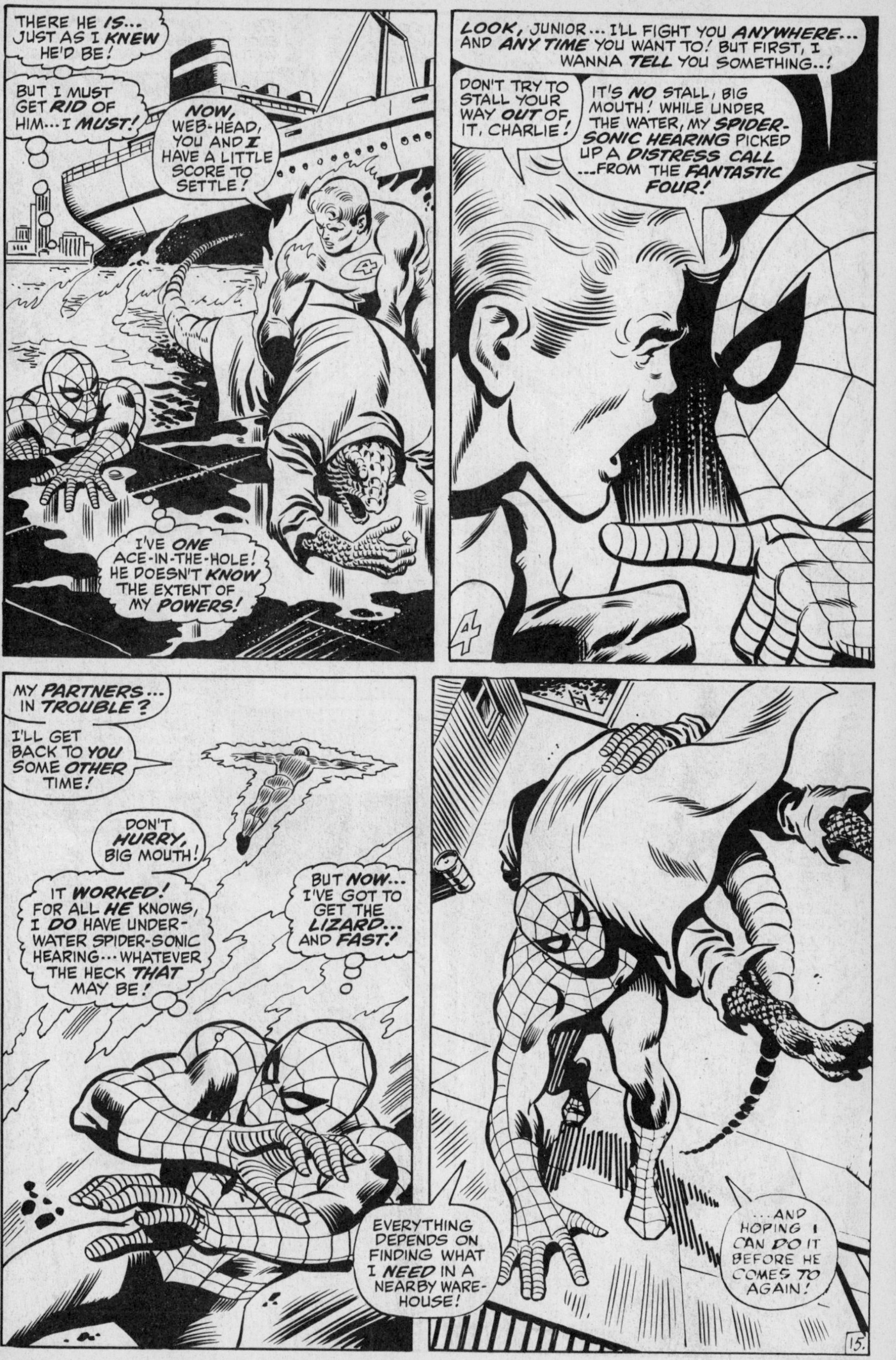
THERE HE IS... JUST AS I KNEW HE'D BE!
BUT I MUST GET RID OF HIM... I MUST!
NOW, WEB-HEAD, YOU AND I HAVE A LITTLE SCORE TO SETTLE!
I'VE ONE ACE-IN-THE-HOLE! HE DOESN'T KNOW THE EXTENT OF MY POWERS!
LOOK, JUNIOR... I'LL FIGHT YOU ANYWHERE... AND ANY TIME YOU WANT TO! BUT FIRST, I WANNA TELL YOU SOMETHING..!
DON'T TRY TO STALL YOUR WAY OUT OF IT, CHARLIE!
IT'S NO STALL, BIG MOUTH! WHILE UNDER THE WATER, MY SPIDER-SONIC HEARING PICKED UP A DISTRESS CALL ...FROM THE FANTASTIC FOUR!
MY PARTNERS... IN TROUBLE?
I'LL GET BACK TO YOU SOME OTHER TIME!
DON'T HURRY, BIG MOUTH!
IT WORKED! FOR ALL HE KNOWS, I DO HAVE UNDER-WATER SPIDER-SONIC HEARING... WHATEVER THE HECK THAT MAY BE!
BUT NOW... I'VE GOT TO GET THE LIZARD... AND FAST!
EVERYTHING DEPENDS ON FINDING WHAT I NEED IN A NEARBY WARE-HOUSE!
...AND HOPING I CAN DO IT BEFORE HE COMES TO AGAIN!
15.

BUT THEN, AS AN UNPREDICTABLE *FATE* WOULD HAVE IT...

IT'S *SPIDER-MAN!!* AND... HE HAS MY *DAD!*

BUT... WHAT *HAPPENED?* WHY IS HE... SO *STILL?*

NO TIME TO FIDDLE WITH *DOOR LOCKS* NOW!

EVEN IF THIS THREE-INCH THICK *STEEL* GIVES ME A SKINNED KNUCKLE-- IT'LL BE *WORTH* IT!

SPLANNNG

NOW! A PLACE LIKE THIS JUST *HAS* TO HAVE WHAT I'M *LOOKING* FOR!

THE ONLY *PROBLEM* IS... WHERE DO I *FIND* IT?

SECONDS LATER...

OVER *THERE!* THOSE DRUMS OF *CHEMICALS!* THAT'S *IT!*

THOUGHT I HEARD *FOOT-STEPS...* BACK ALONG THE CORRIDOR!

BUT THEY DIDN'T SOUND LIKE THE *LIZARD...*

SO I'LL *WORRY* ABOUT THEM *LATER!*

16

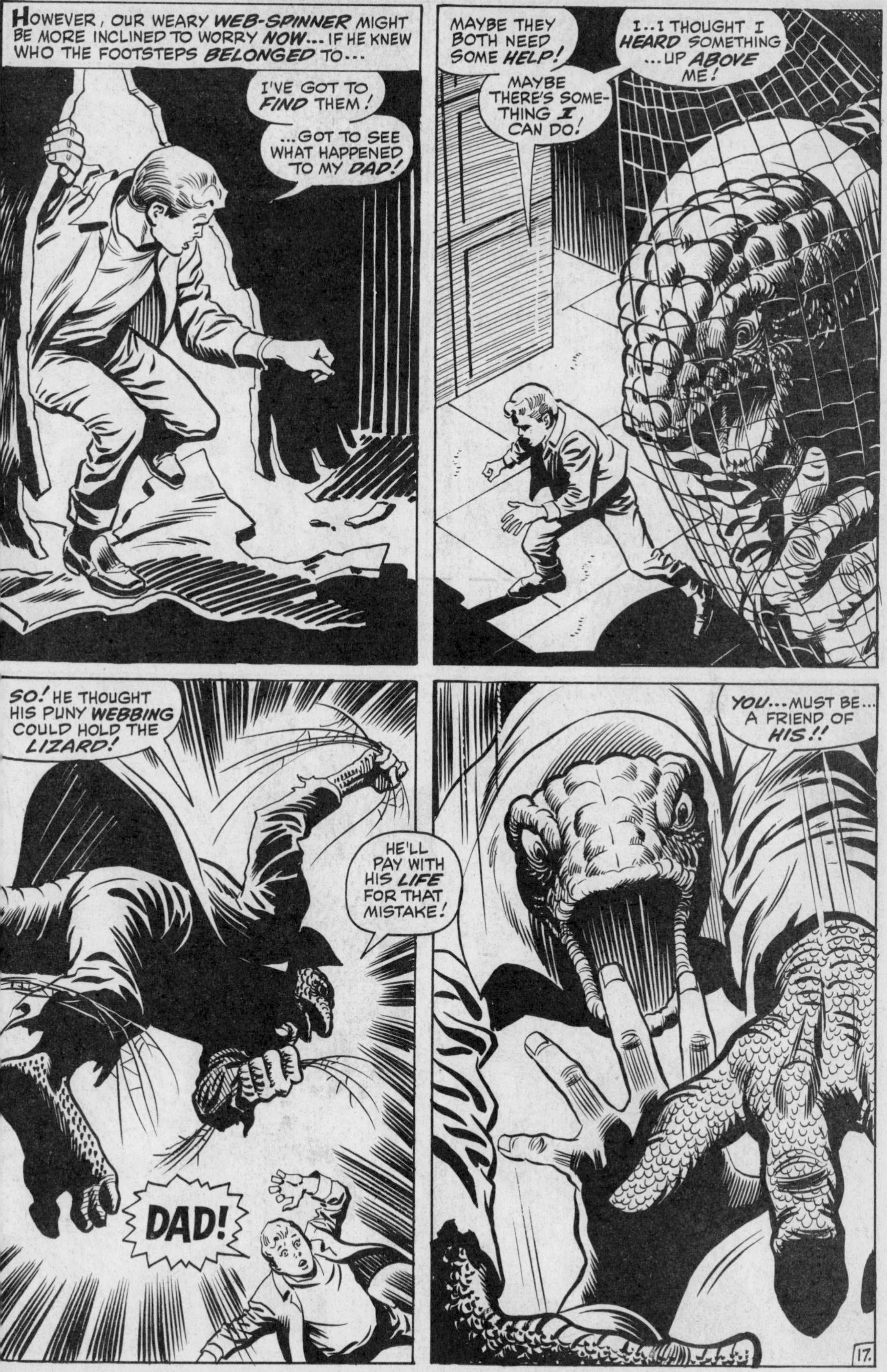
HOWEVER, OUR WEARY WEB-SPINNER MIGHT BE MORE INCLINED TO WORRY NOW... IF HE KNEW WHO THE FOOTSTEPS BELONGED TO...
I'VE GOT TO FIND THEM!
...GOT TO SEE WHAT HAPPENED TO MY DAD!
MAYBE THEY BOTH NEED SOME HELP!
MAYBE THERE'S SOMETHING I CAN DO!
I..I THOUGHT I HEARD SOMETHING ...UP ABOVE ME!
SO! HE THOUGHT HIS PUNY WEBBING COULD HOLD THE LIZARD!
HE'LL PAY WITH HIS LIFE FOR THAT MISTAKE!
DAD!
YOU...MUST BE... A FRIEND OF HIS!!
17.

SPIDER-MAN!! HELP!

THAT SOUNDED LIKE...*BOBBY CONNORS!*

If He's HERE... AND THE LIZARD HAS BROKEN FREE--!!

CaCl₂

CaCl₂

CaCl₂

CaCl₂

Ca

IT *IS* BOBBY! HE'S *FAINTED!* BUT-- THE *LIZARD...*

THE WAY HE'S *LOOKING* AT HIM...AS THOUGH, IN SOME DIM *RECESS* OF HIS *TORTURED* BRAIN... HE *REMEMBERS...* WHAT HE WAS!

CaCl₂

SPIDER-MAN! NOW I *HAVE* YOU! NOW YOU'LL *NEVER* ESCAPE ME!

I'VE SURVIVED YOUR *ATTACK*... SMASHED THRU YOUR *WEBBING*--

NOW, ALL THAT REMAINS ...IS TO *CRUSH* YOU!

NOT IF THIS *DEHYDRATING POWDER* WILL DO ITS JOB, YOU *WON'T!*

SK-RUNCH

18

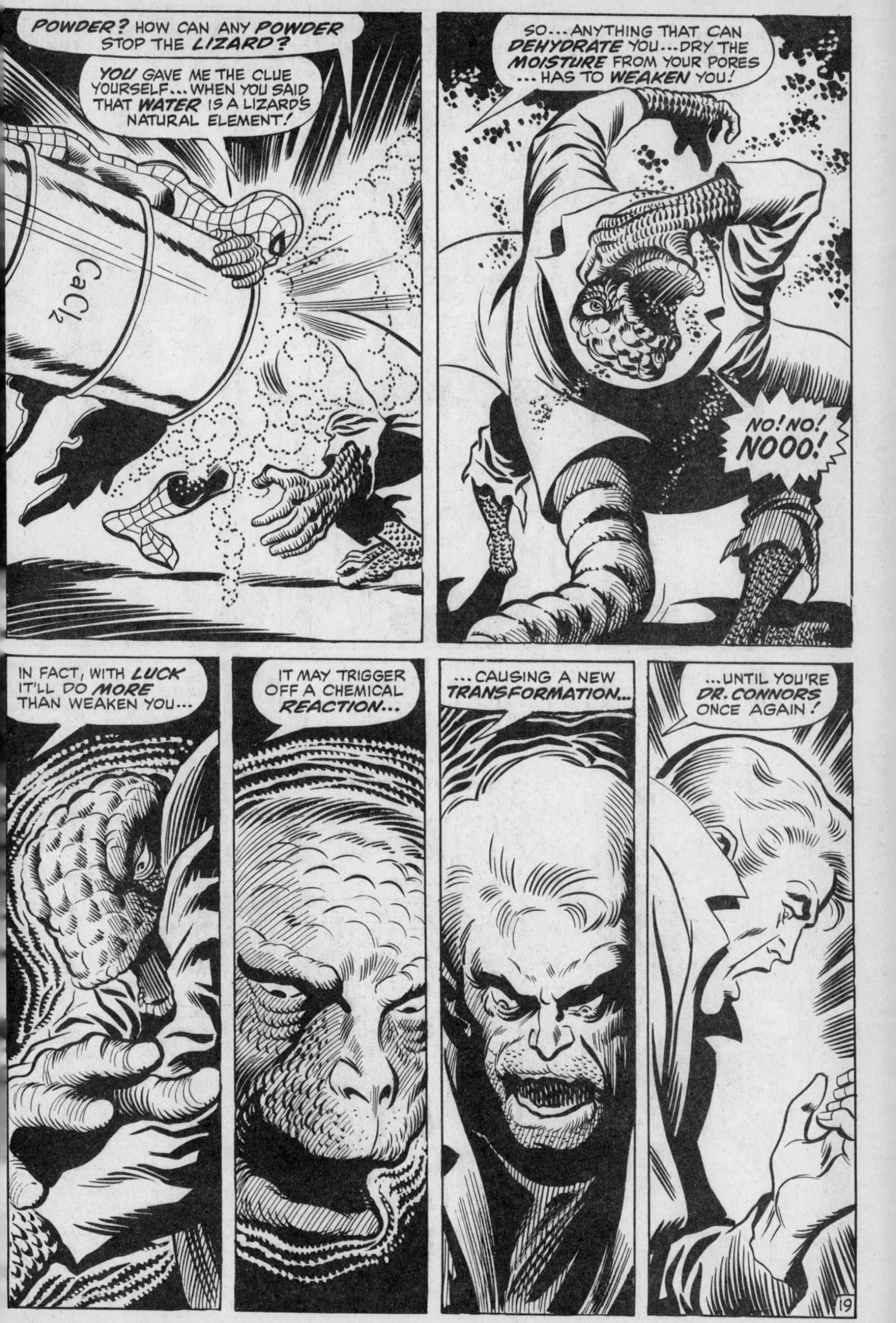
POWDER? HOW CAN ANY POWDER STOP THE LIZARD?
YOU GAVE ME THE CLUE YOURSELF... WHEN YOU SAID THAT WATER IS A LIZARD'S NATURAL ELEMENT!
CaCl2
SO... ANYTHING THAT CAN DEHYDRATE YOU... DRY THE MOISTURE FROM YOUR PORES ... HAS TO WEAKEN YOU!
NO! NO! NOOO!
IN FACT, WITH LUCK IT'LL DO MORE THAN WEAKEN YOU...
IT MAY TRIGGER OFF A CHEMICAL REACTION...
...CAUSING A NEW TRANSFORMATION...
...UNTIL YOU'RE DR. CONNORS ONCE AGAIN!
19

BOBBY! BOBBY! MY SON! ARE YOU ALL RIGHT! DID...DID THE LIZARD HURT YOU?

I'M OKAY, DAD! THE LIZARD WOULDN'T EVER HURT ME! I COULDN'T BE AFRAID...OF HIM!

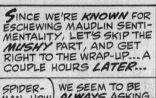

SINCE WE'RE KNOWN FOR ESCHEWING MAUDLIN SENTIMENTALITY, LET'S SKIP THE MUSHY PART, AND GET RIGHT TO THE WRAP-UP...A COUPLE HOURS LATER...

SPIDER-MAN..HOW CAN WE EVER THANK YOU?

WE SEEM TO BE ALWAYS ASKING YOU THAT QUESTION!

CAREFUL! ONE DAY I'LL COME UP WITH AN ANSWER!

BUT, TILL THEN... JUST KEEP THY WEBS UNTANGLED!

MAN! IF THERE'S ONE THING I LIKE, IT'S A HAPPY ENDING!

I CAN HARDLY BELIEVE I'M THE SAME OLD HARD-LUCK WEB-SPINNER!

THE ONLY THING I'VE GOT TO WORRY ABOUT IS...

MEETING THE TORCH--- AFTER HE REALIZES HE'S BEEN HAD!

BUT, AFTER SOME OF THE PROBLEMS I'VE BEEN LIVING WITH...

A HASSLE WITH THAT HUMAN MATCHSTICK COULD SEEM LIKE SWINGING VACATION!

AND, SPEAKING OF PROBLEMS...PERHAPS IT'S JUST AS WELL THAT SPIDEY DOESN'T SUSPECT THAT HE WILL NEXT CONFRONT...

THE PROWLER!

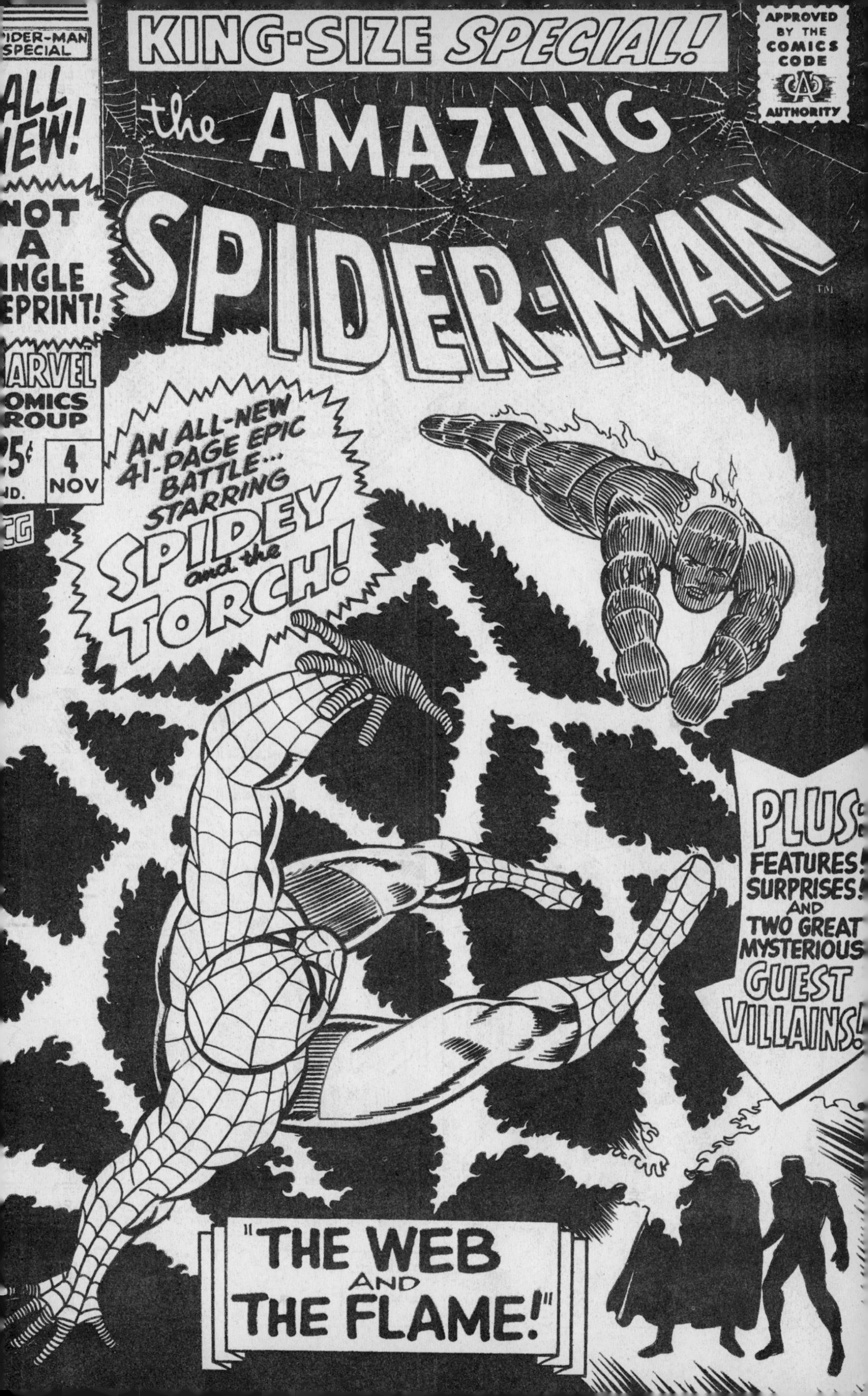
SPIDER-MAN SPECIAL
KING-SIZE SPECIAL!
APPROVED BY THE COMICS CODE AUTHORITY
ALL NEW!
NOT A SINGLE REPRINT!
the AMAZING SPIDER-MAN
MARVEL COMICS GROUP
25¢ 4 NOV
AN ALL-NEW 41-PAGE EPIC BATTLE... STARRING SPIDEY and the TORCH!
PLUS: FEATURES! SURPRISES! AND TWO GREAT MYSTERIOUS GUEST VILLAINS!
"THE WEB AND THE FLAME!"

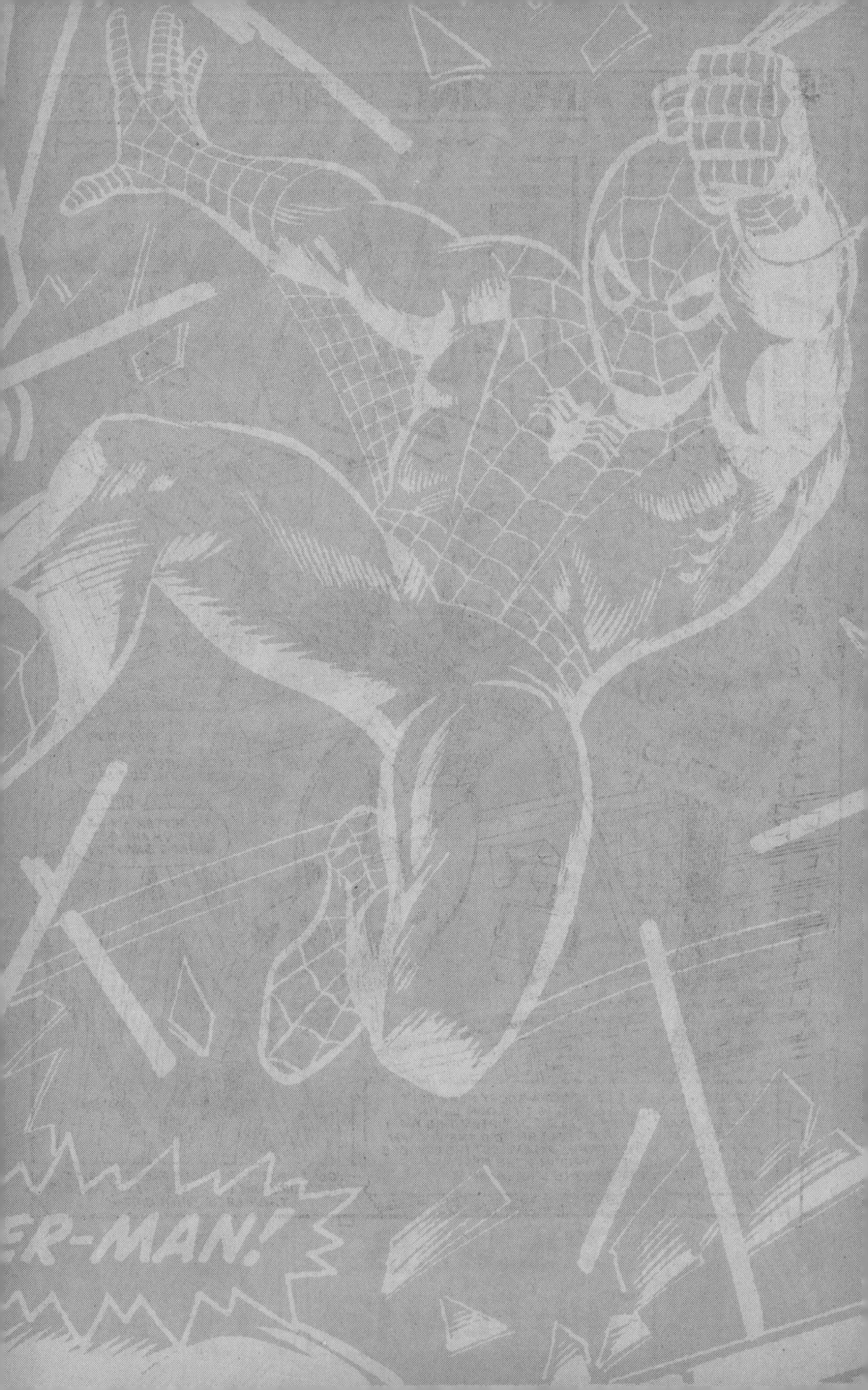
ER-MAN!

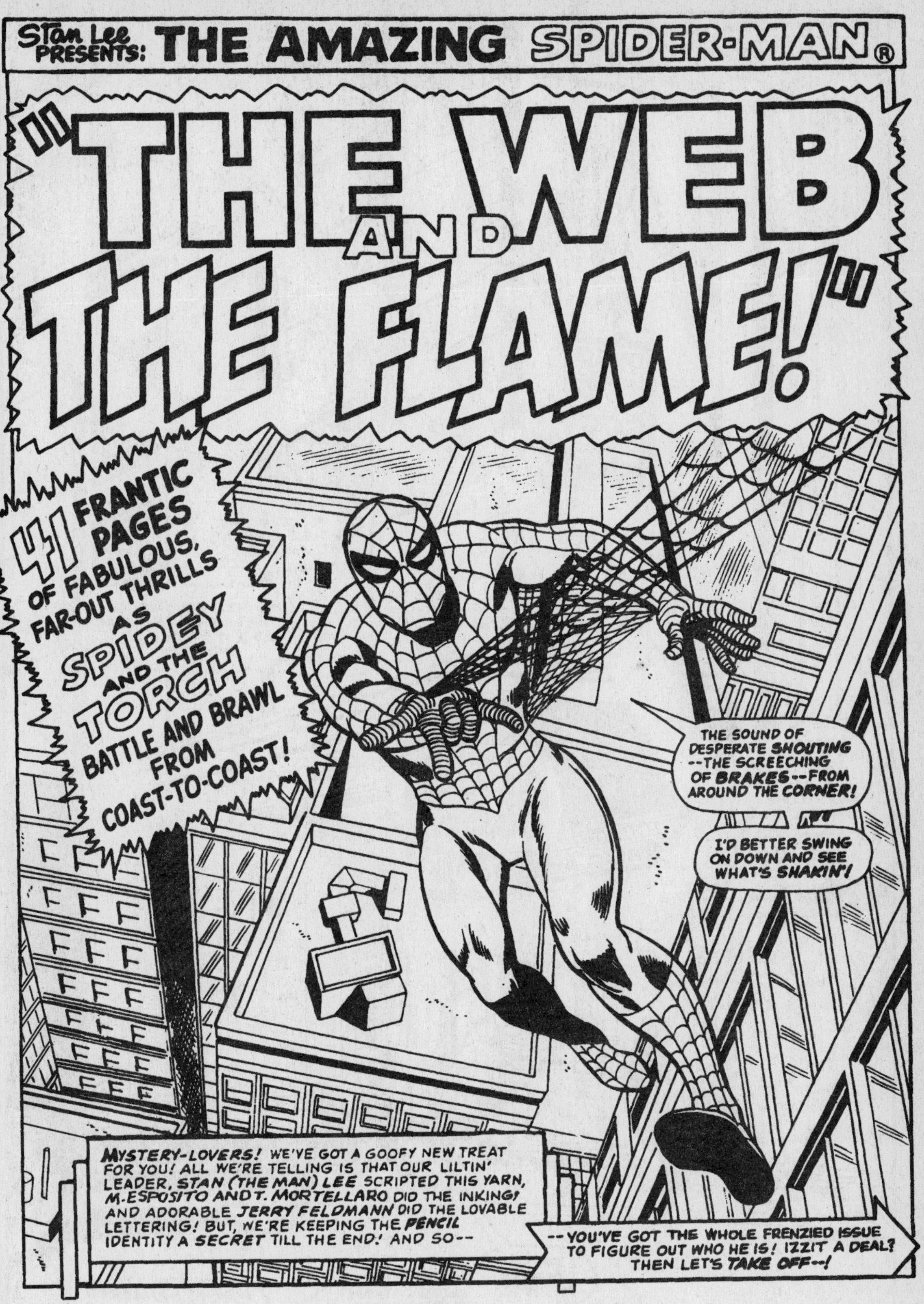
Stan Lee PRESENTS: THE AMAZING SPIDER-MAN®
"THE WEB AND THE FLAME!"
41 FRANTIC PAGES OF FABULOUS, FAR-OUT THRILLS AS SPIDEY AND THE TORCH BATTLE AND BRAWL FROM COAST-TO-COAST!
THE SOUND OF DESPERATE SHOUTING --THE SCREECHING OF BRAKES--FROM AROUND THE CORNER!
I'D BETTER SWING ON DOWN AND SEE WHAT'S SHAKIN'!
MYSTERY-LOVERS! WE'VE GOT A GOOFY NEW TREAT FOR YOU! ALL WE'RE TELLING IS THAT OUR LILTIN' LEADER, STAN (THE MAN) LEE SCRIPTED THIS YARN, M. ESPOSITO AND T. MORTELLARO DID THE INKING, AND ADORABLE JERRY FELDMANN DID THE LOVABLE LETTERING! BUT, WE'RE KEEPING THE PENCIL IDENTITY A SECRET TILL THE END! AND SO--
--YOU'VE GOT THE WHOLE FRENZIED ISSUE TO FIGURE OUT WHO HE IS! IZZIT A DEAL? THEN LET'S TAKE OFF--!

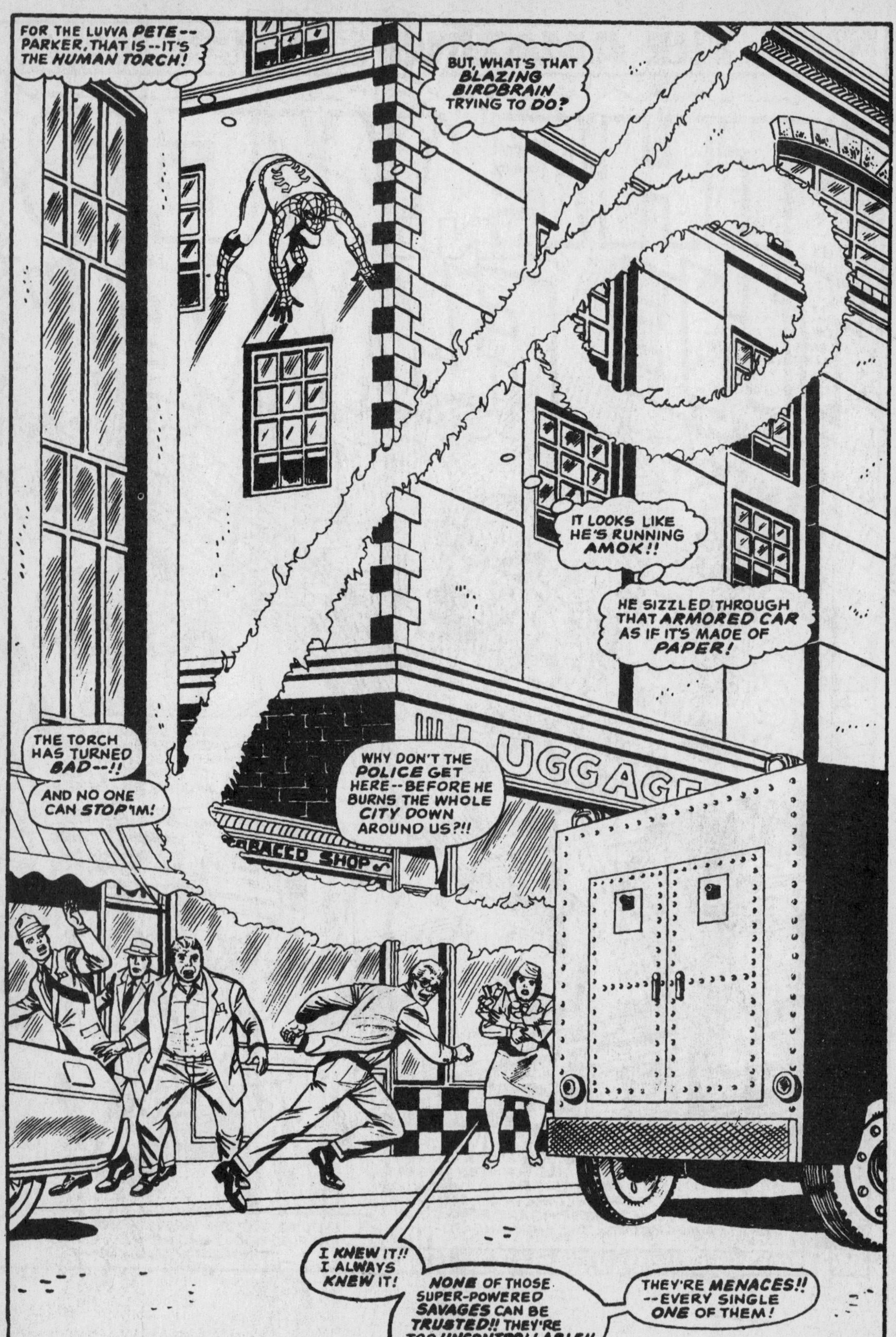

FOR THE LUVVA PETE-- PARKER, THAT IS--IT'S THE HUMAN TORCH!
BUT, WHAT'S THAT BLAZING BIRDBRAIN TRYING TO DO?
IT LOOKS LIKE HE'S RUNNING AMOK!!
HE SIZZLED THROUGH THAT ARMORED CAR AS IF IT'S MADE OF PAPER!
THE TORCH HAS TURNED BAD--!!
AND NO ONE CAN STOP 'IM!
WHY DON'T THE POLICE GET HERE--BEFORE HE BURNS THE WHOLE CITY DOWN AROUND US?!!
UGGAGE
BACCO SHOP
I KNEW IT!! I ALWAYS KNEW IT!
NONE OF THOSE SUPER-POWERED SAVAGES CAN BE TRUSTED!! THEY'RE TOO UNCONTROLLABLE!!
THEY'RE MENACES!! --EVERY SINGLE ONE OF THEM!

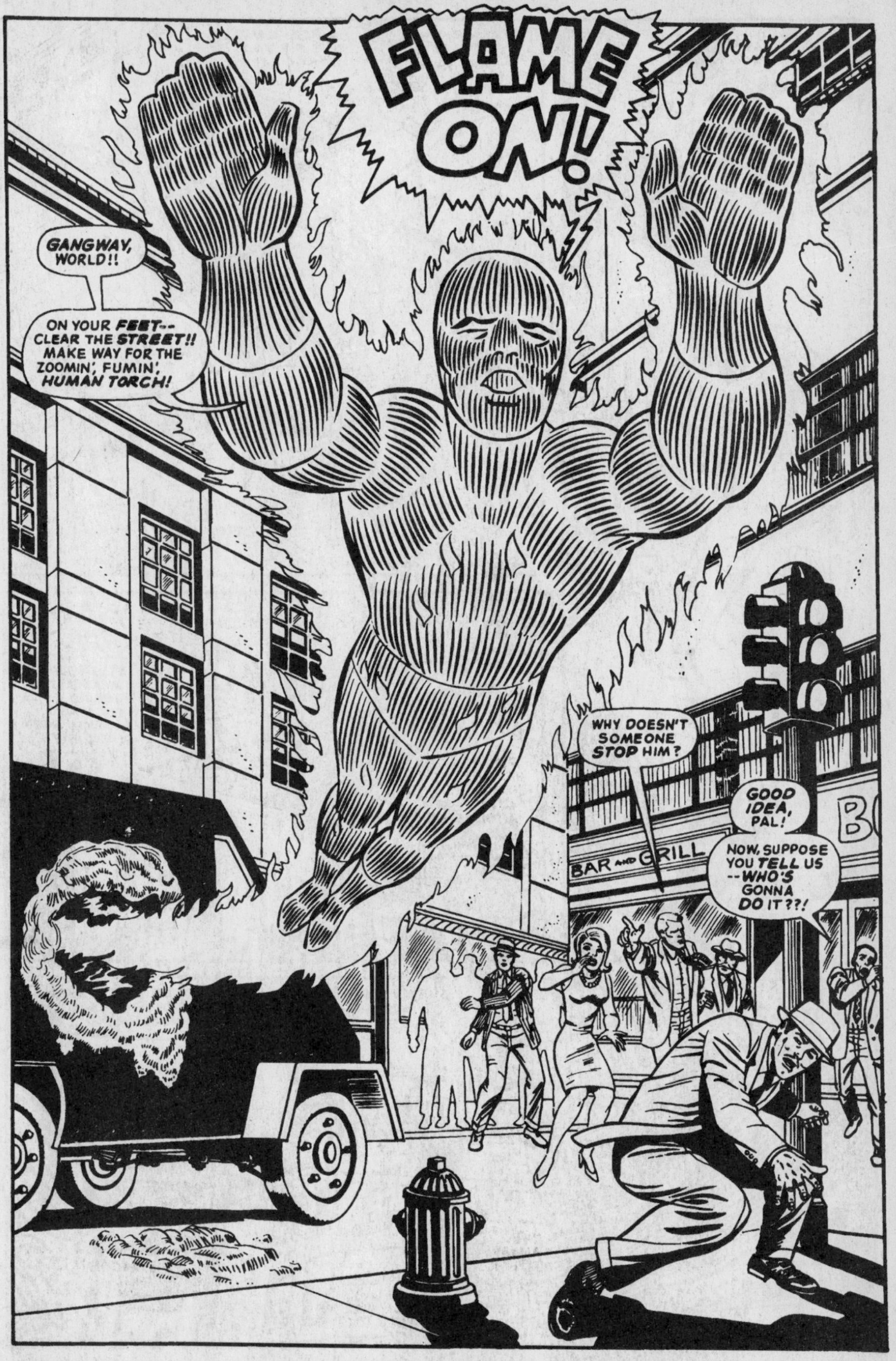
FLAME ON!
GANGWAY, WORLD!!
ON YOUR FEET-- CLEAR THE STREET!! MAKE WAY FOR THE ZOOMIN', FUMIN', HUMAN TORCH!
WHY DOESN'T SOMEONE STOP HIM?
GOOD IDEA, PAL!
NOW, SUPPOSE YOU TELL US --WHO'S GONNA DO IT??!
BAR AND GRILL

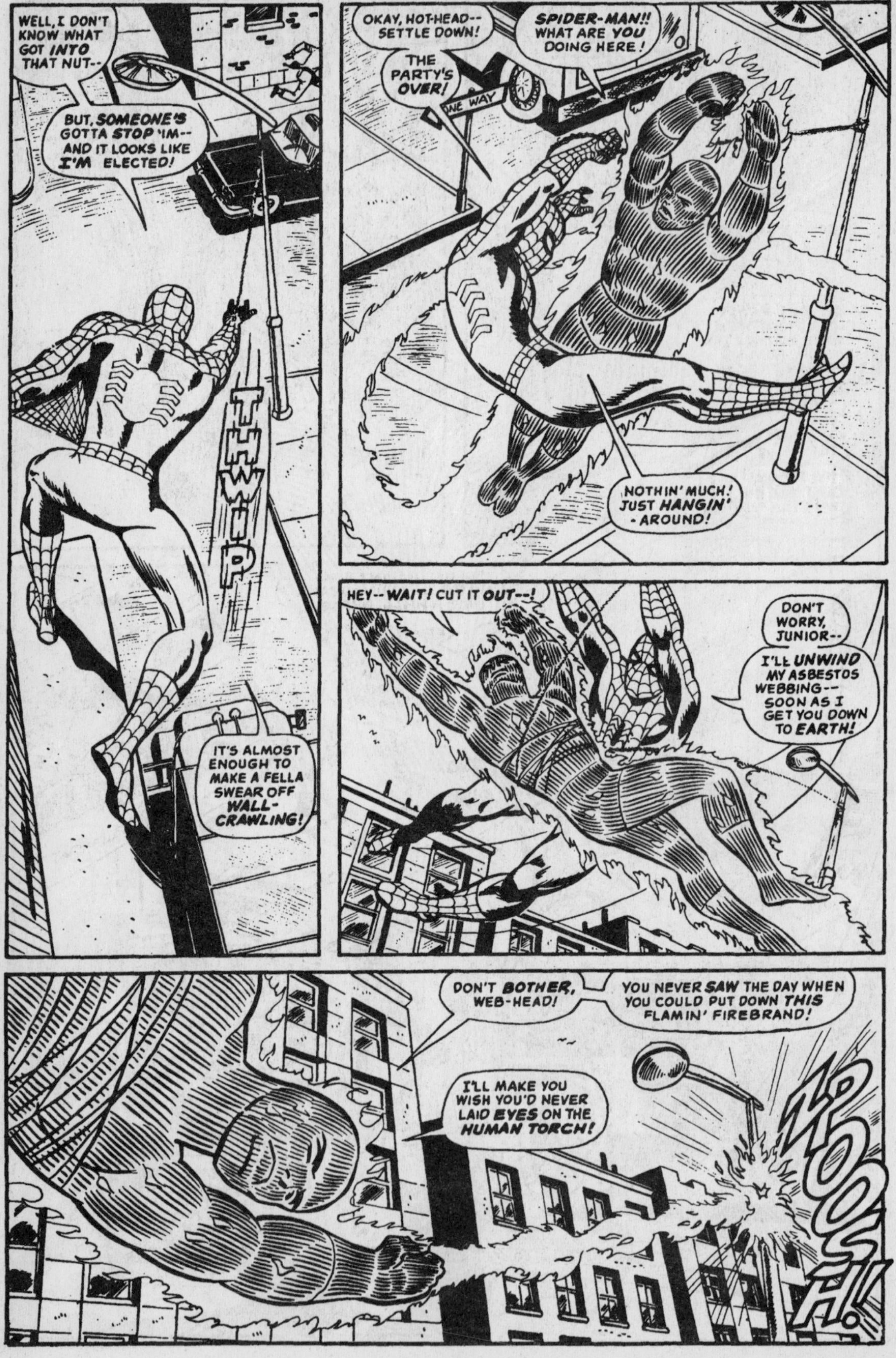

WELL, I DON'T KNOW WHAT GOT INTO THAT NUT--
BUT, SOMEONE'S GOTTA STOP 'IM-- AND IT LOOKS LIKE I'M ELECTED!
THWHIP
IT'S ALMOST ENOUGH TO MAKE A FELLA SWEAR OFF WALL-CRAWLING!
OKAY, HOT-HEAD-- SETTLE DOWN!
THE PARTY'S OVER!
SPIDER-MAN!! WHAT ARE YOU DOING HERE!
NOTHIN' MUCH! JUST HANGIN' - AROUND!
HEY-- WAIT! CUT IT OUT--!
DON'T WORRY, JUNIOR--
I'LL UNWIND MY ASBESTOS WEBBING-- SOON AS I GET YOU DOWN TO EARTH!
DON'T BOTHER, WEB-HEAD!
YOU NEVER SAW THE DAY WHEN YOU COULD PUT DOWN THIS FLAMIN' FIREBRAND!
I'LL MAKE YOU WISH YOU'D NEVER LAID EYES ON THE HUMAN TORCH!
ZROOOSH!

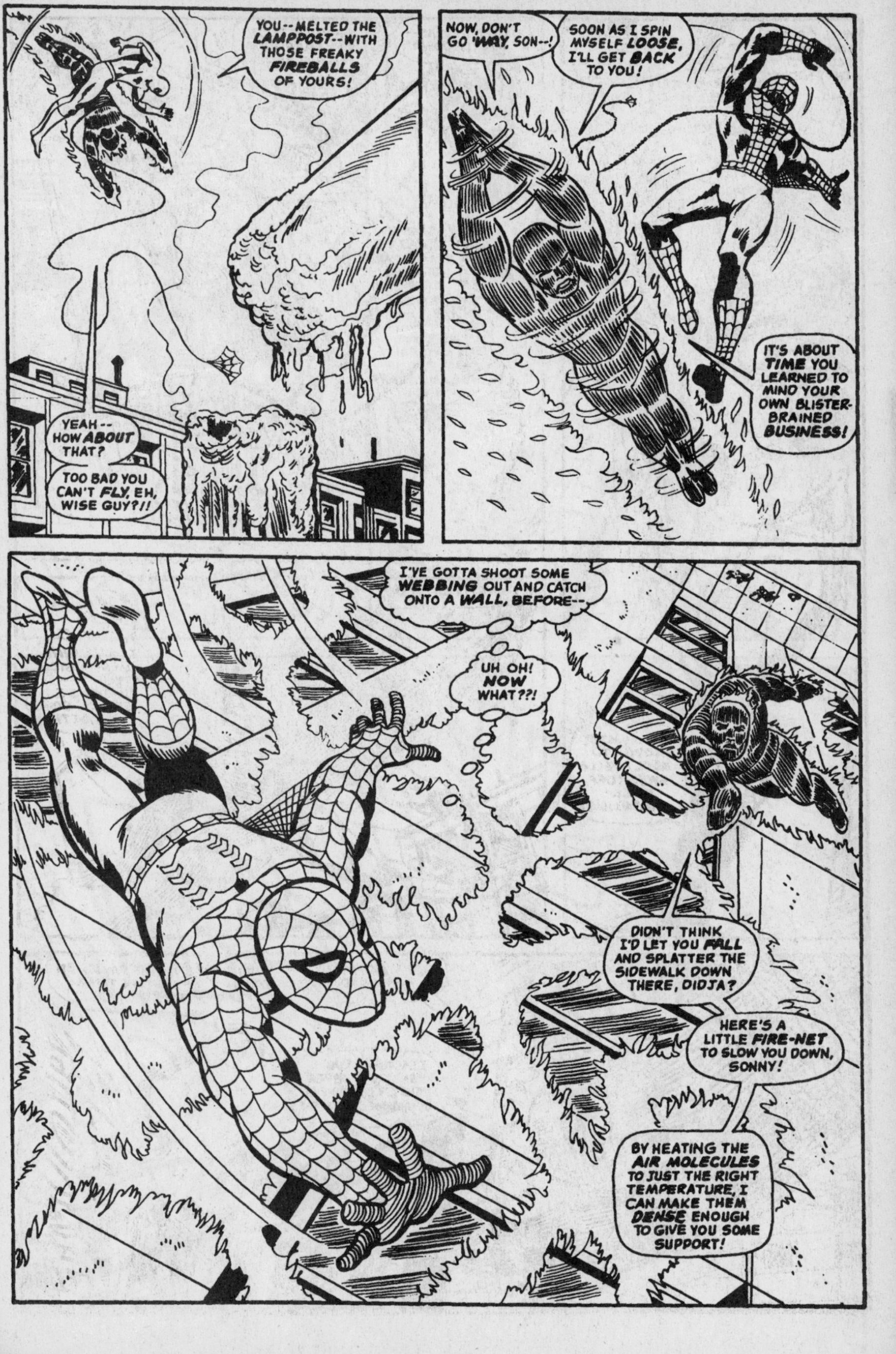

YOU--MELTED THE LAMPPOST--WITH THOSE FREAKY FIREBALLS OF YOURS!
YEAH -- HOW ABOUT THAT?
TOO BAD YOU CAN'T FLY, EH, WISE GUY?!!
NOW, DON'T GO 'WAY, SON--!
SOON AS I SPIN MYSELF LOOSE, I'LL GET BACK TO YOU!
IT'S ABOUT TIME YOU LEARNED TO MIND YOUR OWN BLISTER-BRAINED BUSINESS!
I'VE GOTTA SHOOT SOME WEBBING OUT AND CATCH ONTO A WALL, BEFORE--
UH OH! NOW WHAT??!
DIDN'T THINK I'D LET YOU FALL AND SPLATTER THE SIDEWALK DOWN THERE, DIDJA?
HERE'S A LITTLE FIRE-NET TO SLOW YOU DOWN, SONNY!
BY HEATING THE AIR MOLECULES TO JUST THE RIGHT TEMPERATURE, I CAN MAKE THEM DENSE ENOUGH TO GIVE YOU SOME SUPPORT!

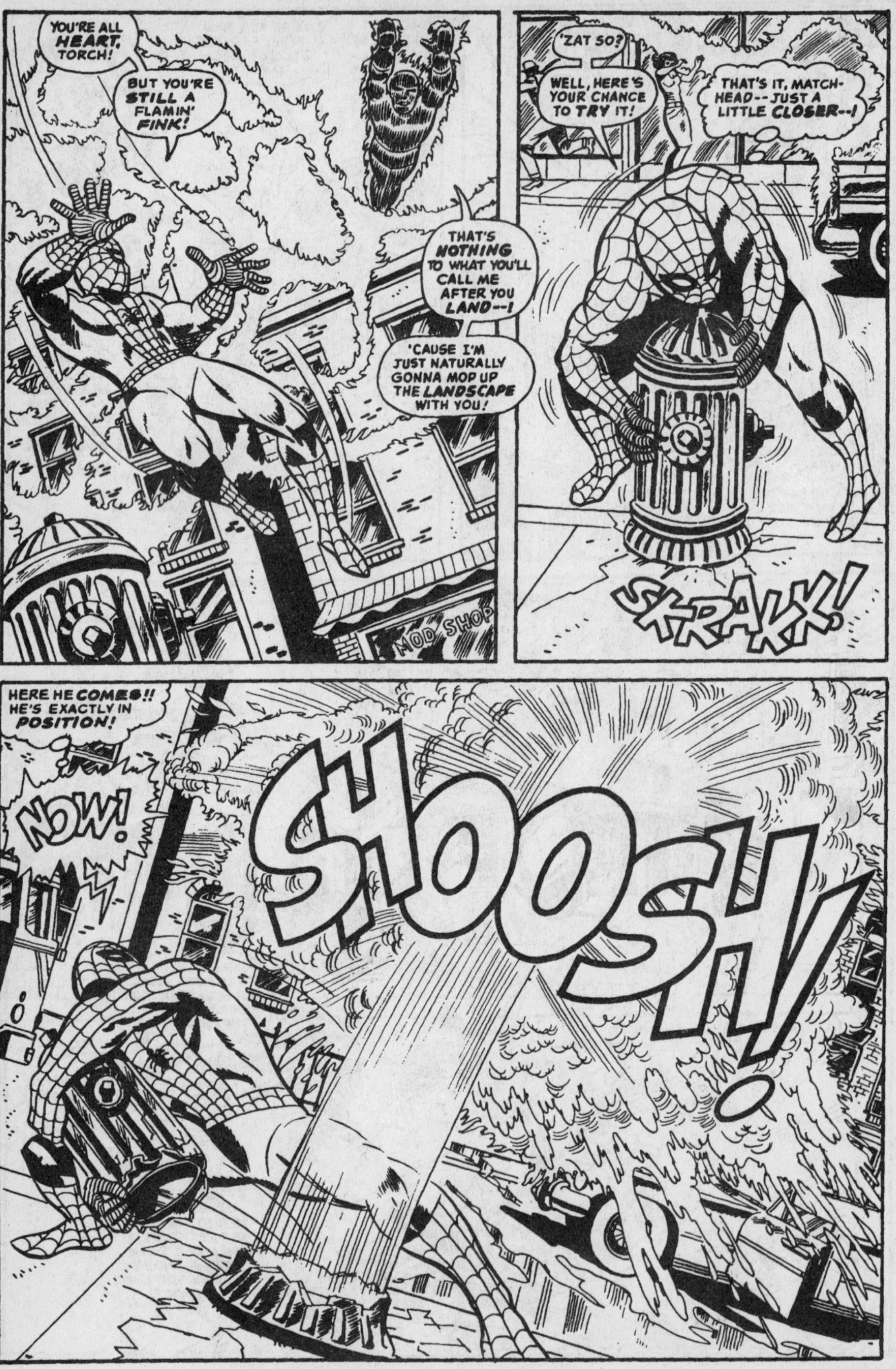
YOU'RE ALL HEART, TORCH!
BUT YOU'RE STILL A FLAMIN' FINK!
THAT'S NOTHING TO WHAT YOU'LL CALL ME AFTER YOU LAND--!
'CAUSE I'M JUST NATURALLY GONNA MOP UP THE LANDSCAPE WITH YOU!
MOD SHOP
'ZAT SO?
WELL, HERE'S YOUR CHANCE TO TRY IT!
THAT'S IT, MATCH-HEAD--JUST A LITTLE CLOSER--!
SKRAKK!
HERE HE COMES!! HE'S EXACTLY IN POSITION!
NOW!
SHOOSH!

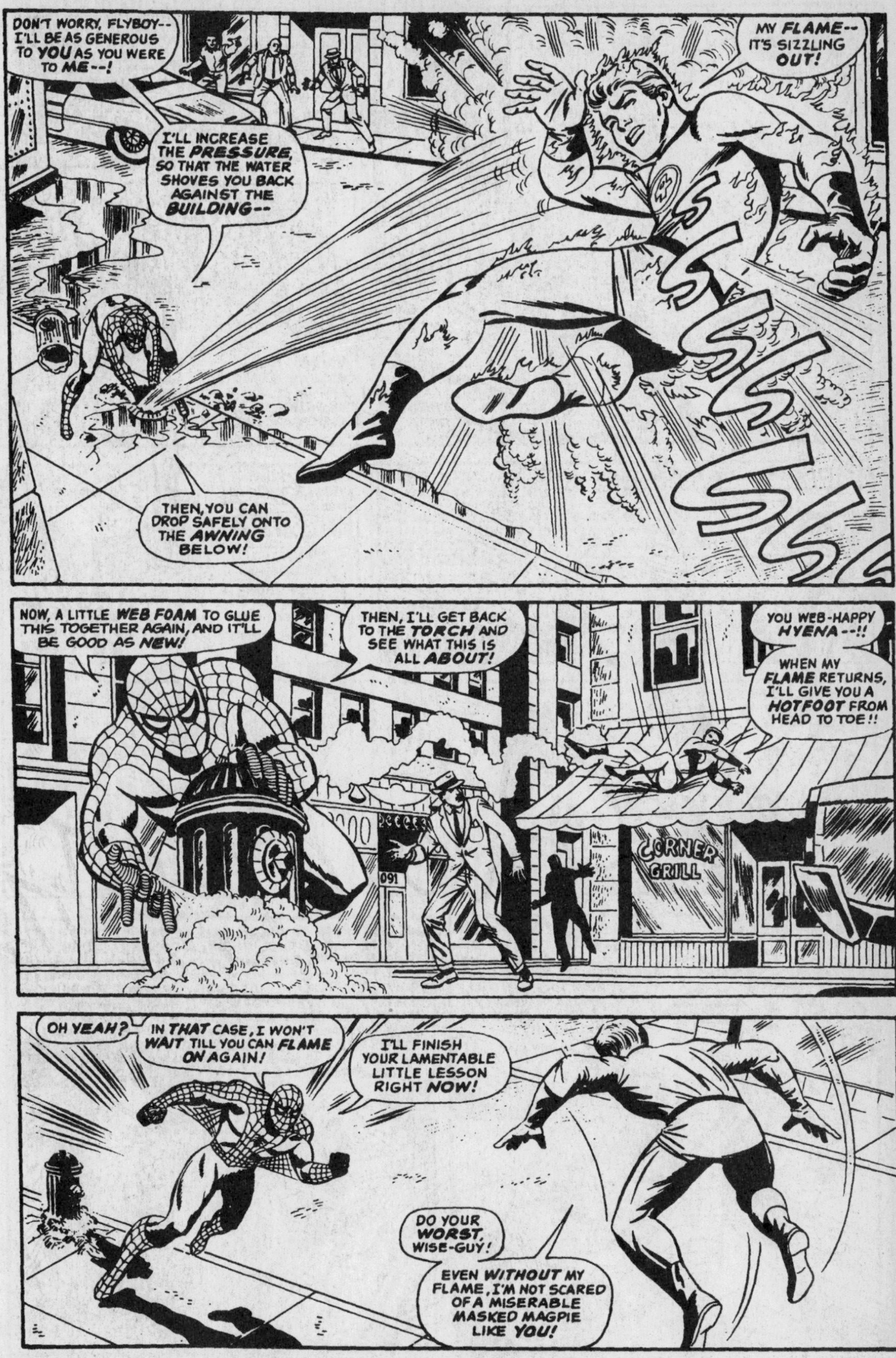
DON'T WORRY, FLYBOY-- I'LL BE AS GENEROUS TO YOU AS YOU WERE TO ME--!
MY FLAME-- IT'S SIZZLING OUT!
I'LL INCREASE THE PRESSURE, SO THAT THE WATER SHOVES YOU BACK AGAINST THE BUILDING--
SSSSSS
THEN, YOU CAN DROP SAFELY ONTO THE AWNING BELOW!
NOW, A LITTLE WEB FOAM TO GLUE THIS TOGETHER AGAIN, AND IT'LL BE GOOD AS NEW!
THEN, I'LL GET BACK TO THE TORCH AND SEE WHAT THIS IS ALL ABOUT!
YOU WEB-HAPPY HYENA--!!
WHEN MY FLAME RETURNS, I'LL GIVE YOU A HOTFOOT FROM HEAD TO TOE!!
091
CORNER GRILL
OH YEAH?
IN THAT CASE, I WON'T WAIT TILL YOU CAN FLAME ON AGAIN!
I'LL FINISH YOUR LAMENTABLE LITTLE LESSON RIGHT NOW!
DO YOUR WORST, WISE-GUY!
EVEN WITHOUT MY FLAME, I'M NOT SCARED OF A MISERABLE MASKED MAGPIE LIKE YOU!

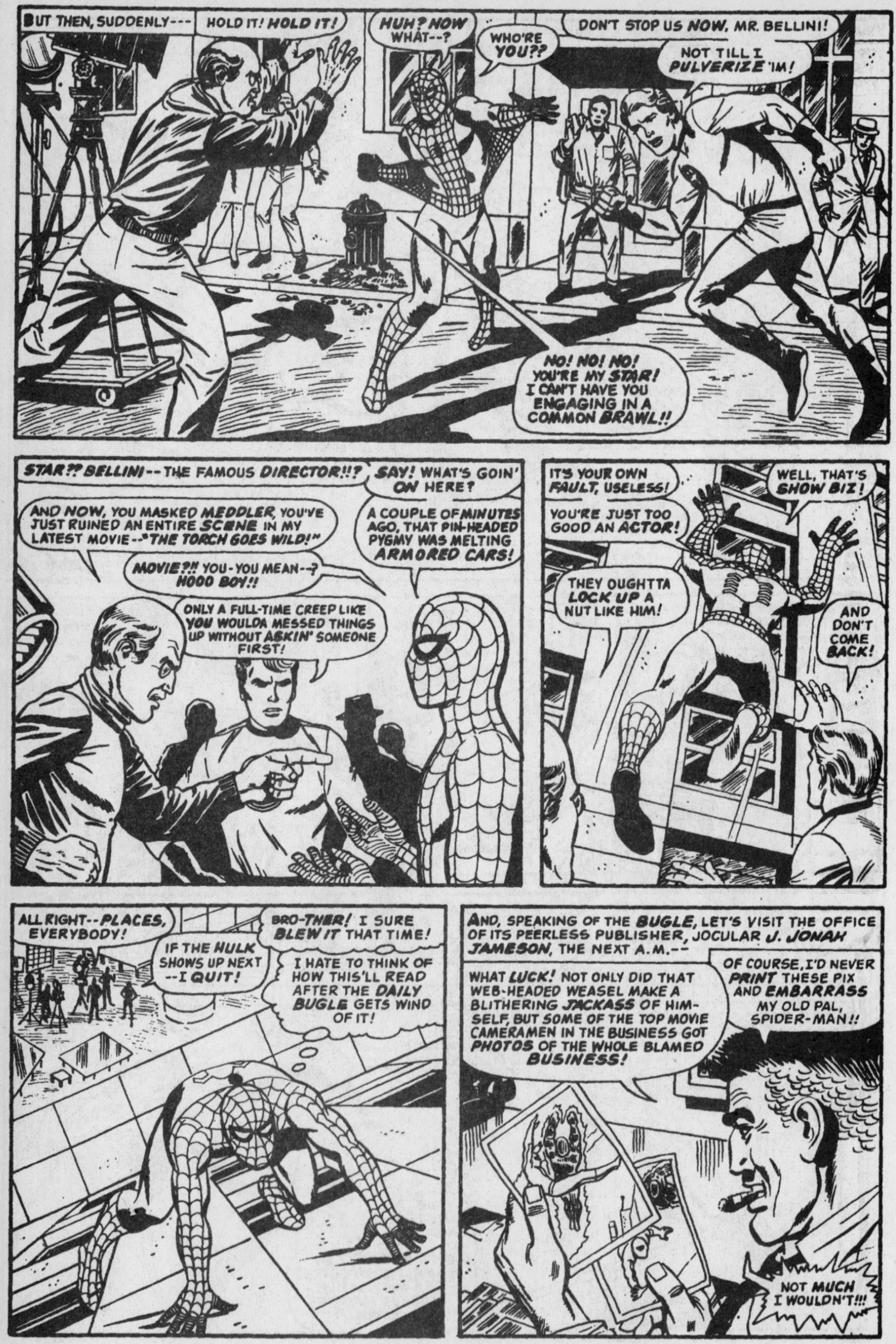

BUT THEN, SUDDENLY---
HOLD IT! HOLD IT!
HUH? NOW WHAT--?
WHO'RE YOU??
DON'T STOP US NOW, MR. BELLINI!
NOT TILL I PULVERIZE 'IM!
NO! NO! NO! YOU'RE MY STAR! I CAN'T HAVE YOU ENGAGING IN A COMMON BRAWL!!
STAR?? BELLINI--THE FAMOUS DIRECTOR!!?
SAY! WHAT'S GOIN' ON HERE?
AND NOW, YOU MASKED MEDDLER, YOU'VE JUST RUINED AN ENTIRE SCENE IN MY LATEST MOVIE--"THE TORCH GOES WILD!"
A COUPLE OF MINUTES AGO, THAT PIN-HEADED PYGMY WAS MELTING ARMORED CARS!
MOVIE?!! YOU-YOU MEAN--? HOOD BOY!!
ONLY A FULL-TIME CREEP LIKE YOU WOULDA MESSED THINGS UP WITHOUT ASKIN' SOMEONE FIRST!
IT'S YOUR OWN FAULT, USELESS!
WELL, THAT'S SHOW BIZ!
YOU'RE JUST TOO GOOD AN ACTOR!
THEY OUGHTTA LOCK UP A NUT LIKE HIM!
AND DON'T COME BACK!
ALL RIGHT--PLACES, EVERYBODY!
IF THE HULK SHOWS UP NEXT --I QUIT!
BRO-THER! I SURE BLEW IT THAT TIME!
I HATE TO THINK OF HOW THIS'LL READ AFTER THE DAILY BUGLE GETS WIND OF IT!
AND, SPEAKING OF THE BUGLE, LET'S VISIT THE OFFICE OF ITS PEERLESS PUBLISHER, JOCULAR J. JONAH JAMESON, THE NEXT A.M.--
WHAT LUCK! NOT ONLY DID THAT WEB-HEADED WEASEL MAKE A BLITHERING JACKASS OF HIM-SELF, BUT SOME OF THE TOP MOVIE CAMERAMEN IN THE BUSINESS GOT PHOTOS OF THE WHOLE BLAMED BUSINESS!
OF COURSE, I'D NEVER PRINT THESE PIX AND EMBARRASS MY OLD PAL, SPIDER-MAN!!
NOT MUCH I WOULDN'T!!!

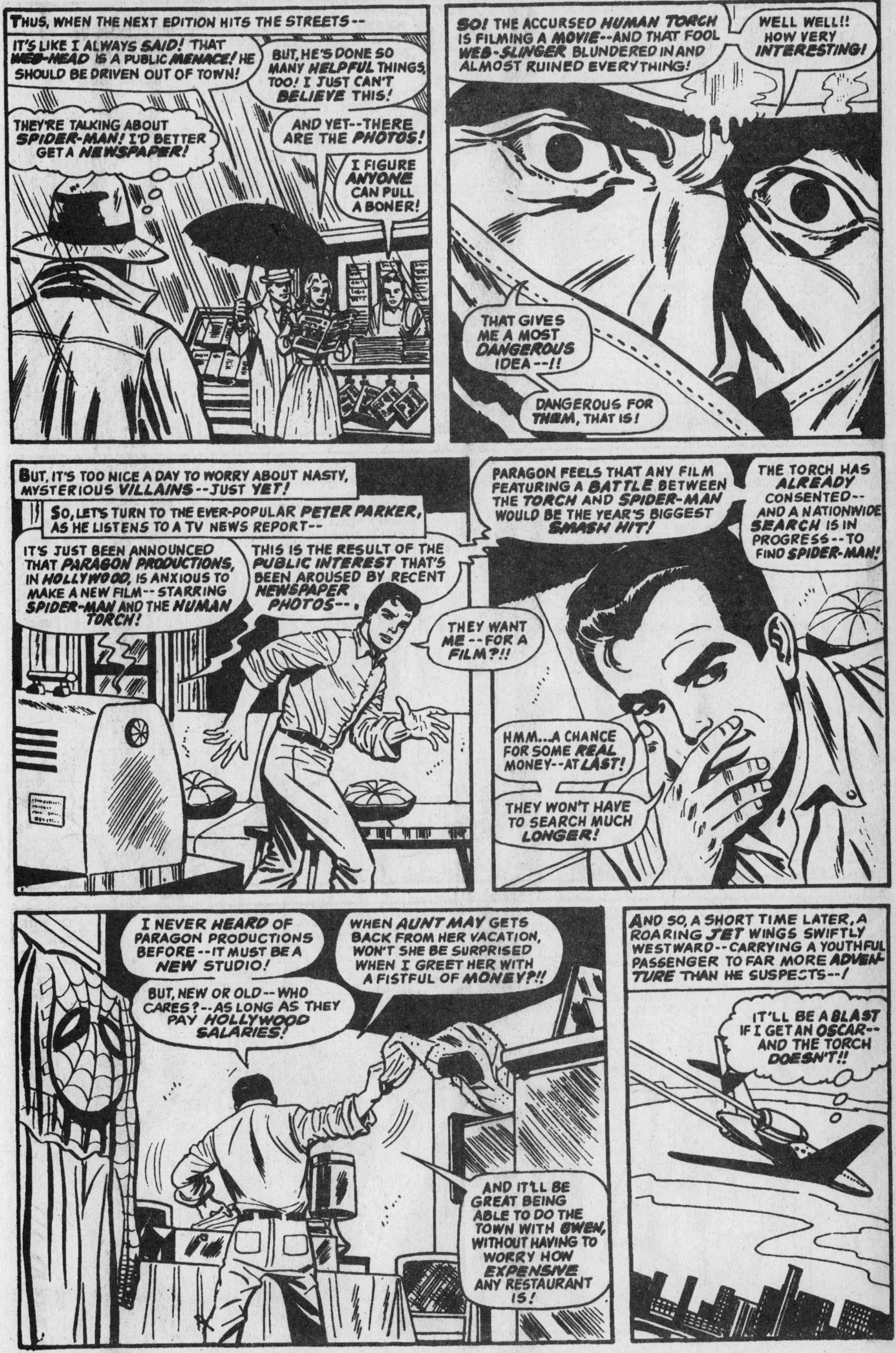
THUS, WHEN THE NEXT EDITION HITS THE STREETS--
IT'S LIKE I ALWAYS SAID! THAT WEB-HEAD IS A PUBLIC MENACE! HE SHOULD BE DRIVEN OUT OF TOWN!
BUT, HE'S DONE SO MANY HELPFUL THINGS, TOO! I JUST CAN'T BELIEVE THIS!
THEY'RE TALKING ABOUT SPIDER-MAN! I'D BETTER GET A NEWSPAPER!
AND YET--THERE ARE THE PHOTOS!
I FIGURE ANYONE CAN PULL A BONER!
SO! THE ACCURSED HUMAN TORCH IS FILMING A MOVIE--AND THAT FOOL WEB-SLINGER BLUNDERED IN AND ALMOST RUINED EVERYTHING!
WELL WELL!! HOW VERY INTERESTING!
THAT GIVES ME A MOST DANGEROUS IDEA--!!
DANGEROUS FOR THEM, THAT IS!
BUT, IT'S TOO NICE A DAY TO WORRY ABOUT NASTY, MYSTERIOUS VILLAINS--JUST YET!
SO, LET'S TURN TO THE EVER-POPULAR PETER PARKER, AS HE LISTENS TO A TV NEWS REPORT--
IT'S JUST BEEN ANNOUNCED THAT PARAGON PRODUCTIONS, IN HOLLYWOOD, IS ANXIOUS TO MAKE A NEW FILM--STARRING SPIDER-MAN AND THE HUMAN TORCH!
THIS IS THE RESULT OF THE PUBLIC INTEREST THAT'S BEEN AROUSED BY RECENT NEWSPAPER PHOTOS--.
THEY WANT ME--FOR A FILM?!!
PARAGON FEELS THAT ANY FILM FEATURING A BATTLE BETWEEN THE TORCH AND SPIDER-MAN WOULD BE THE YEAR'S BIGGEST SMASH HIT!
THE TORCH HAS ALREADY CONSENTED--AND A NATIONWIDE SEARCH IS IN PROGRESS--TO FIND SPIDER-MAN!
HMM...A CHANCE FOR SOME REAL MONEY--AT LAST!
THEY WON'T HAVE TO SEARCH MUCH LONGER!
I NEVER HEARD OF PARAGON PRODUCTIONS BEFORE--IT MUST BE A NEW STUDIO!
BUT, NEW OR OLD--WHO CARES?--AS LONG AS THEY PAY HOLLYWOOD SALARIES!
WHEN AUNT MAY GETS BACK FROM HER VACATION, WON'T SHE BE SURPRISED WHEN I GREET HER WITH A FISTFUL OF MONEY?!!
AND IT'LL BE GREAT BEING ABLE TO DO THE TOWN WITH GWEN, WITHOUT HAVING TO WORRY HOW EXPENSIVE ANY RESTAURANT IS!
AND SO, A SHORT TIME LATER, A ROARING JET WINGS SWIFTLY WESTWARD--CARRYING A YOUTHFUL PASSENGER TO FAR MORE ADVENTURE THAN HE SUSPECTS--!
IT'LL BE A BLAST IF I GET AN OSCAR--AND THE TORCH DOESN'T!!

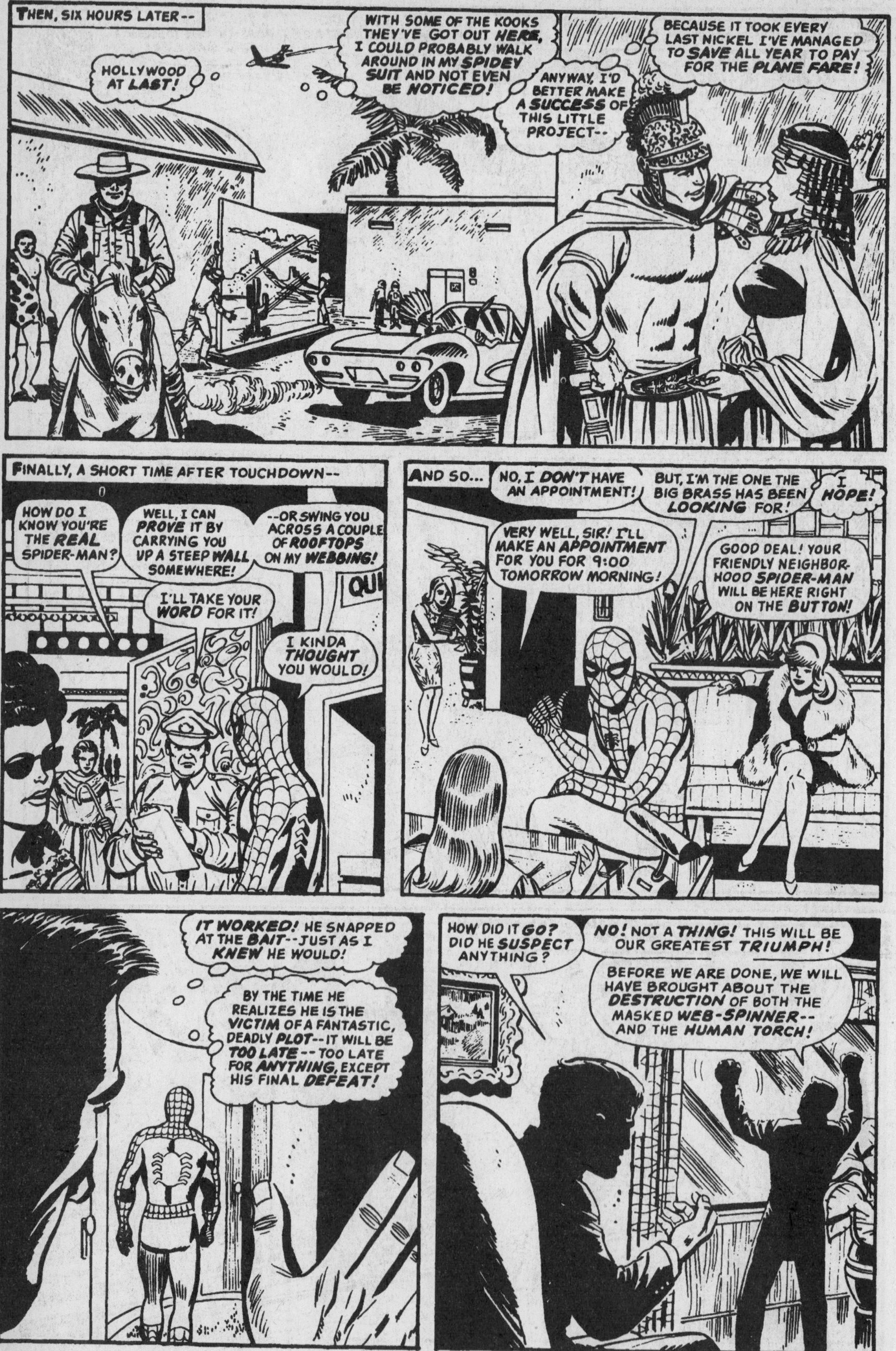

THEN, SIX HOURS LATER--
HOLLYWOOD AT LAST!
WITH SOME OF THE KOOKS THEY'VE GOT OUT HERE, I COULD PROBABLY WALK AROUND IN MY SPIDEY SUIT AND NOT EVEN BE NOTICED!
ANYWAY, I'D BETTER MAKE A SUCCESS OF THIS LITTLE PROJECT--
BECAUSE IT TOOK EVERY LAST NICKEL I'VE MANAGED TO SAVE ALL YEAR TO PAY FOR THE PLANE FARE!
FINALLY, A SHORT TIME AFTER TOUCHDOWN--
HOW DO I KNOW YOU'RE THE REAL SPIDER-MAN?
WELL, I CAN PROVE IT BY CARRYING YOU UP A STEEP WALL SOMEWHERE!
--OR SWING YOU ACROSS A COUPLE OF ROOFTOPS ON MY WEBBING!
I'LL TAKE YOUR WORD FOR IT!
I KINDA THOUGHT YOU WOULD!
AND SO...
NO, I DON'T HAVE AN APPOINTMENT!
BUT, I'M THE ONE THE BIG BRASS HAS BEEN LOOKING FOR!
I HOPE!
VERY WELL, SIR! I'LL MAKE AN APPOINTMENT FOR YOU FOR 9:00 TOMORROW MORNING!
GOOD DEAL! YOUR FRIENDLY NEIGHBOR-HOOD SPIDER-MAN WILL BE HERE RIGHT ON THE BUTTON!
IT WORKED! HE SNAPPED AT THE BAIT--JUST AS I KNEW HE WOULD!
BY THE TIME HE REALIZES HE IS THE VICTIM OF A FANTASTIC, DEADLY PLOT--IT WILL BE TOO LATE--TOO LATE FOR ANYTHING, EXCEPT HIS FINAL DEFEAT!
HOW DID IT GO? DID HE SUSPECT ANYTHING?
NO! NOT A THING! THIS WILL BE OUR GREATEST TRIUMPH!
BEFORE WE ARE DONE, WE WILL HAVE BROUGHT ABOUT THE DESTRUCTION OF BOTH THE MASKED WEB-SPINNER--AND THE HUMAN TORCH!

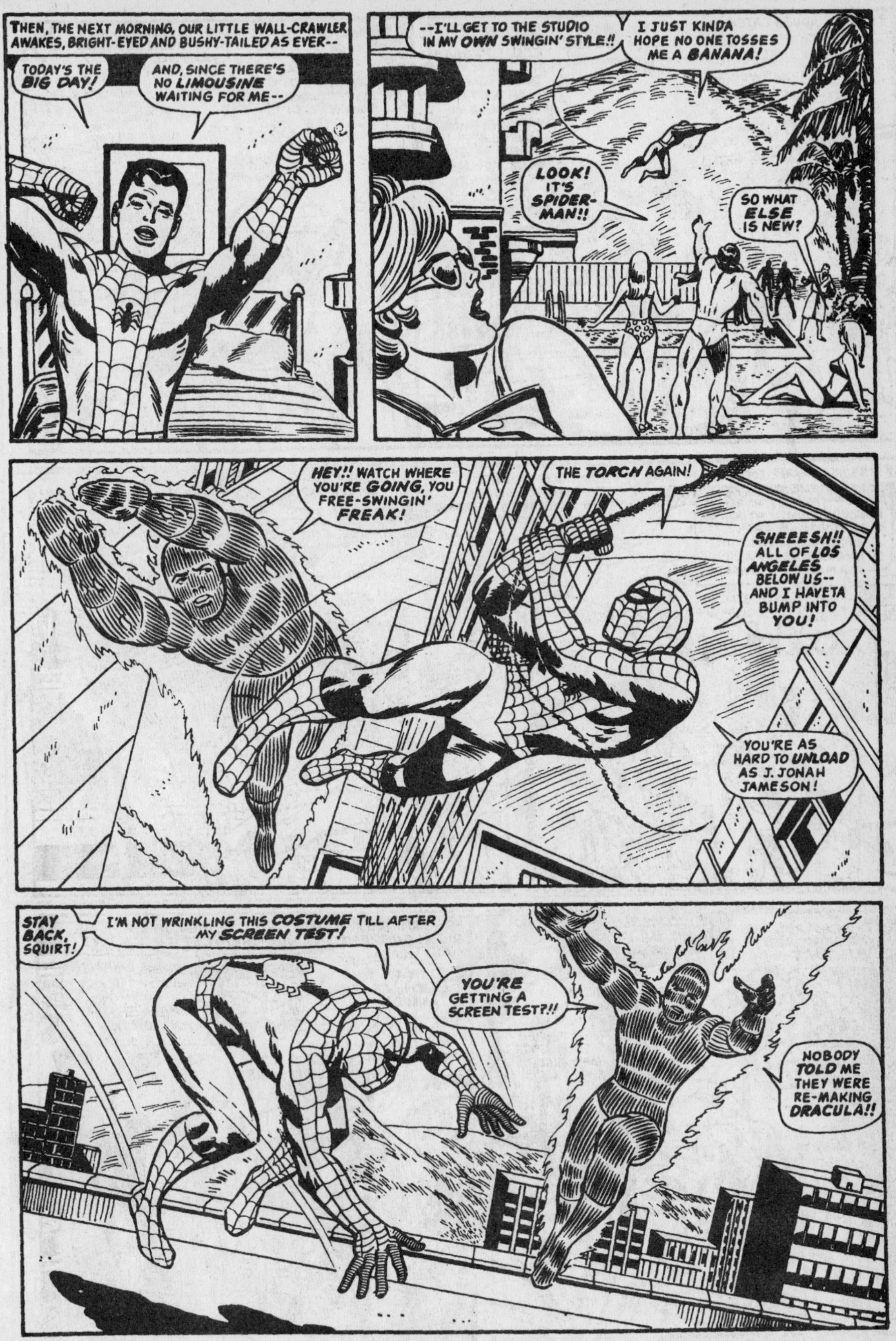
THEN, THE NEXT MORNING, OUR LITTLE WALL-CRAWLER AWAKES, BRIGHT-EYED AND BUSHY-TAILED AS EVER--
TODAY'S THE BIG DAY!
AND, SINCE THERE'S NO LIMOUSINE WAITING FOR ME--
--I'LL GET TO THE STUDIO IN MY OWN SWINGIN' STYLE!!
I JUST KINDA HOPE NO ONE TOSSES ME A BANANA!
LOOK! IT'S SPIDER-MAN!!
SO WHAT ELSE IS NEW?
HEY!! WATCH WHERE YOU'RE GOING, YOU FREE-SWINGIN' FREAK!
THE TORCH AGAIN!
SHEEESH!! ALL OF LOS ANGELES BELOW US-- AND I HAVETA BUMP INTO YOU!
YOU'RE AS HARD TO UNLOAD AS J. JONAH JAMESON!
STAY BACK, SQUIRT!
I'M NOT WRINKLING THIS COSTUME TILL AFTER MY SCREEN TEST!
YOU'RE GETTING A SCREEN TEST?!!
NOBODY TOLD ME THEY WERE RE-MAKING DRACULA!!

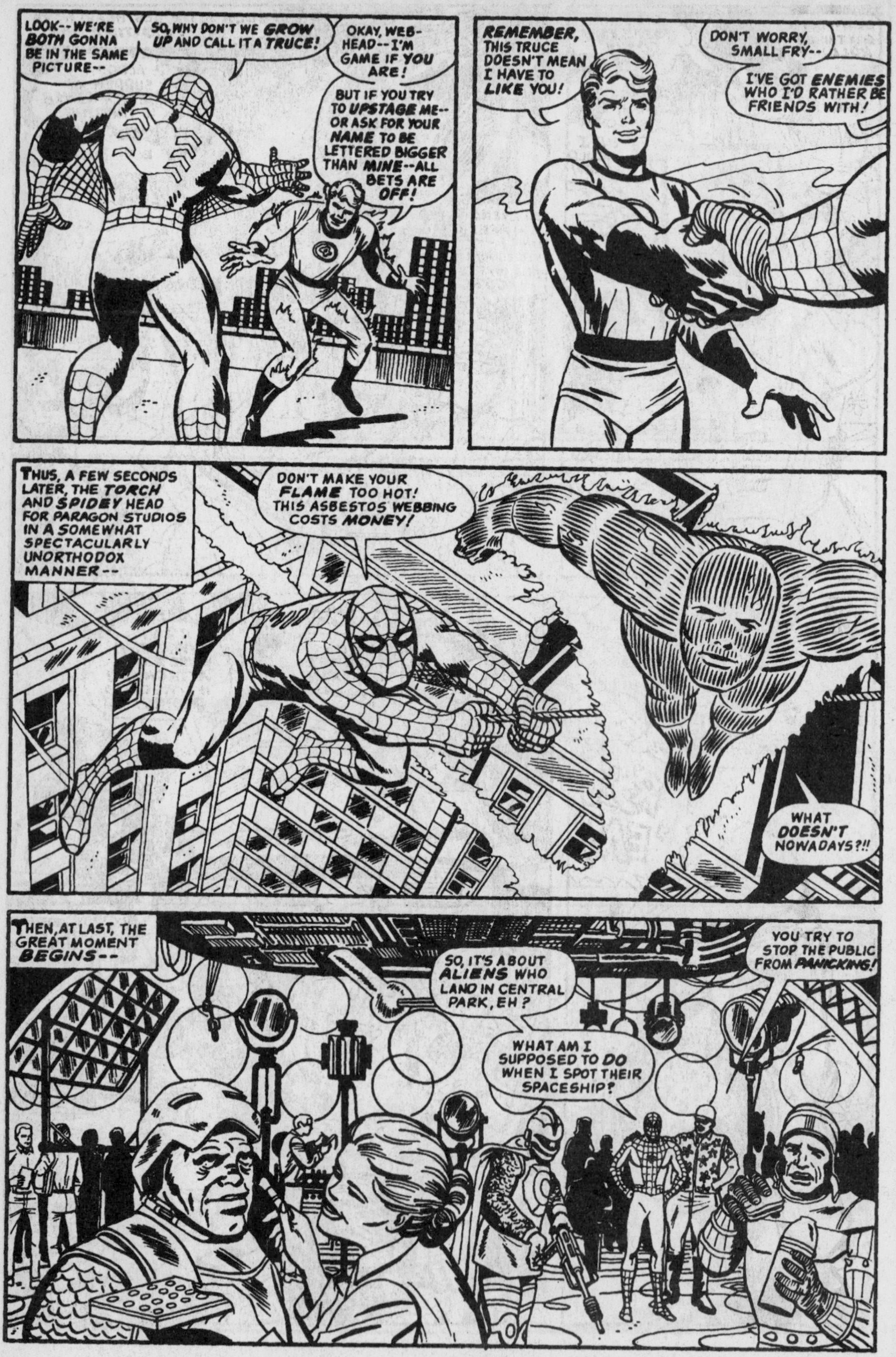
LOOK--WE'RE BOTH GONNA BE IN THE SAME PICTURE--
SO, WHY DON'T WE GROW UP AND CALL IT A TRUCE!
OKAY, WEB-HEAD--I'M GAME IF YOU ARE!
BUT IF YOU TRY TO UPSTAGE ME--OR ASK FOR YOUR NAME TO BE LETTERED BIGGER THAN MINE--ALL BETS ARE OFF!
REMEMBER, THIS TRUCE DOESN'T MEAN I HAVE TO LIKE YOU!
DON'T WORRY, SMALL FRY--
I'VE GOT ENEMIES WHO I'D RATHER BE FRIENDS WITH!
THUS, A FEW SECONDS LATER, THE TORCH AND SPIDEY HEAD FOR PARAGON STUDIOS IN A SOMEWHAT SPECTACULARLY UNORTHODOX MANNER--
DON'T MAKE YOUR FLAME TOO HOT! THIS ASBESTOS WEBBING COSTS MONEY!
WHAT DOESN'T NOWADAYS?!!
THEN, AT LAST, THE GREAT MOMENT BEGINS--
SO, IT'S ABOUT ALIENS WHO LAND IN CENTRAL PARK, EH?
YOU TRY TO STOP THE PUBLIC FROM PANICKING!
WHAT AM I SUPPOSED TO DO WHEN I SPOT THEIR SPACESHIP?

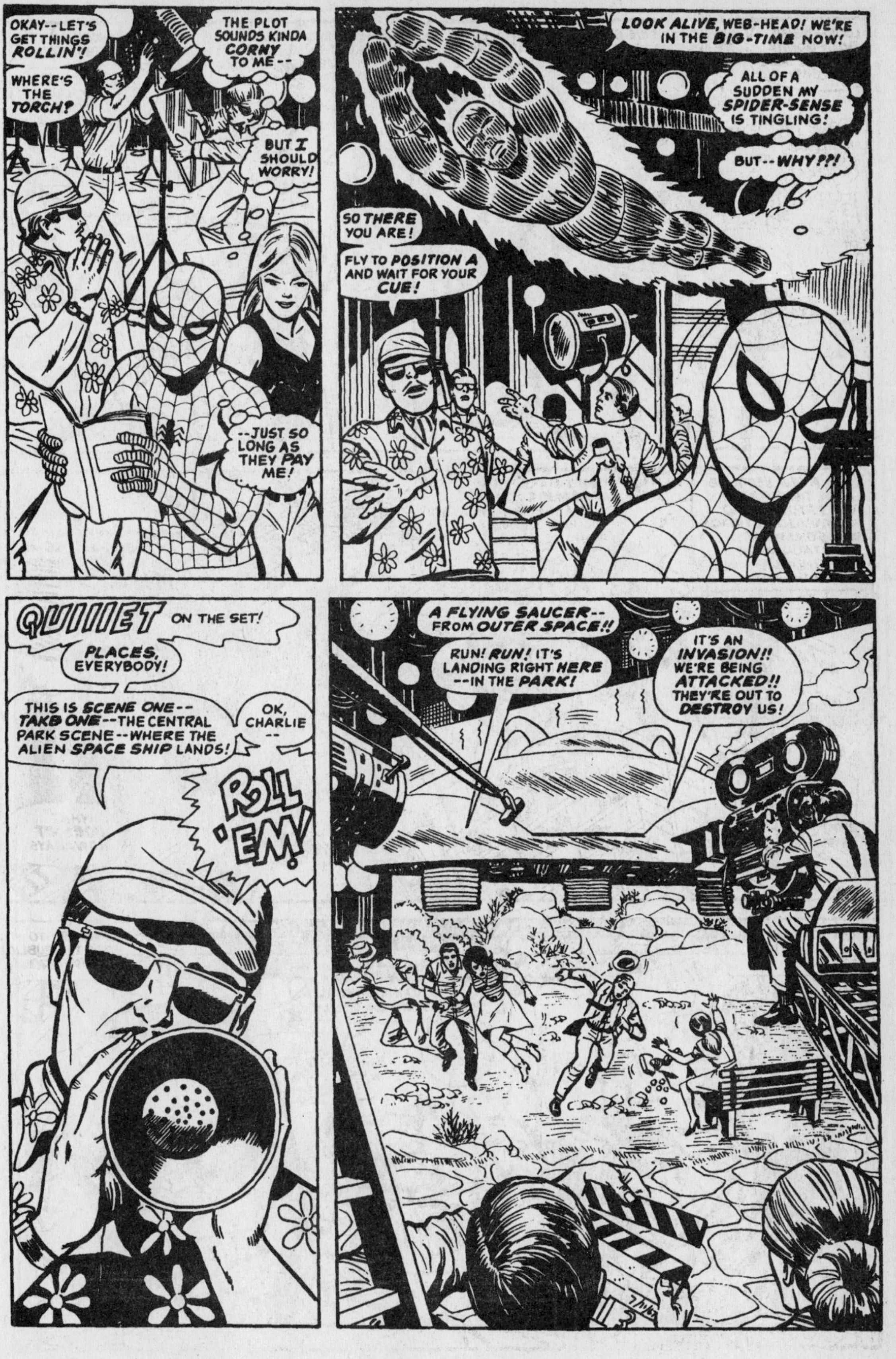
OKAY--LET'S GET THINGS ROLLIN'!
WHERE'S THE TORCH?
THE PLOT SOUNDS KINDA CORNY TO ME--
BUT I SHOULD WORRY!
--JUST SO LONG AS THEY PAY ME!
LOOK ALIVE, WEB-HEAD! WE'RE IN THE BIG-TIME NOW!
ALL OF A SUDDEN MY SPIDER-SENSE IS TINGLING!
BUT--WHY?!?
SO THERE YOU ARE!
FLY TO POSITION A AND WAIT FOR YOUR CUE!
QUIIIET ON THE SET!
PLACES, EVERYBODY!
THIS IS SCENE ONE--TAKE ONE--THE CENTRAL PARK SCENE--WHERE THE ALIEN SPACE SHIP LANDS!
OK, CHARLIE--
ROLL 'EM!
A FLYING SAUCER--FROM OUTER SPACE!!
RUN! RUN! IT'S LANDING RIGHT HERE--IN THE PARK!
IT'S AN INVASION!! WE'RE BEING ATTACKED!! THEY'RE OUT TO DESTROY US!

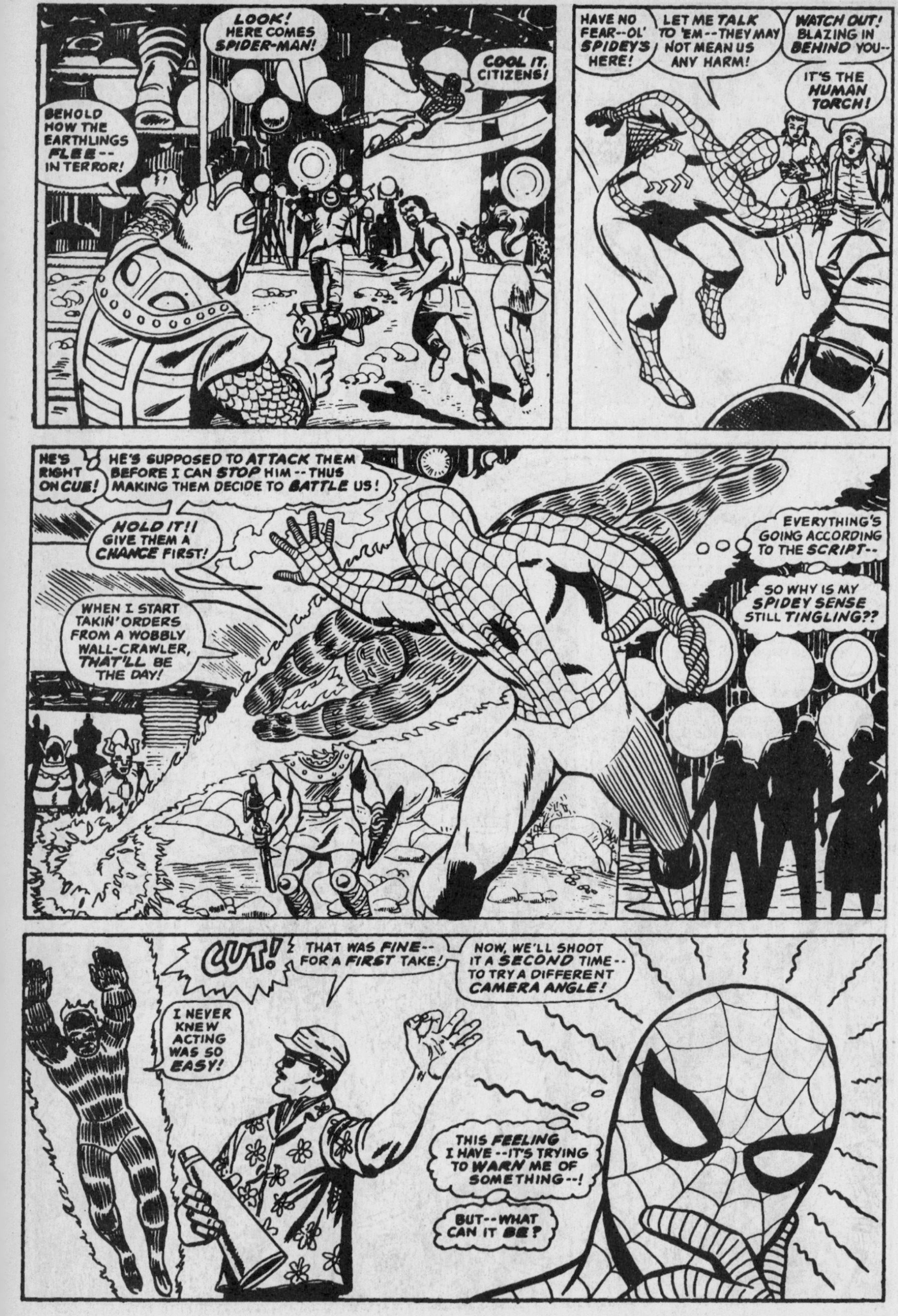
LOOK! HERE COMES SPIDER-MAN!
COOL IT, CITIZENS!
BEHOLD HOW THE EARTHLINGS FLEE-- IN TERROR!
HAVE NO FEAR--OL' SPIDEY'S HERE!
LET ME TALK TO 'EM--THEY MAY NOT MEAN US ANY HARM!
WATCH OUT! BLAZING IN BEHIND YOU--
IT'S THE HUMAN TORCH!
HE'S RIGHT ON CUE!
HE'S SUPPOSED TO ATTACK THEM BEFORE I CAN STOP HIM--THUS MAKING THEM DECIDE TO BATTLE US!
HOLD IT!! GIVE THEM A CHANCE FIRST!
WHEN I START TAKIN' ORDERS FROM A WOBBLY WALL-CRAWLER, THAT'LL BE THE DAY!
EVERYTHING'S GOING ACCORDING TO THE SCRIPT--
SO WHY IS MY SPIDEY SENSE STILL TINGLING??
CUT!
THAT WAS FINE-- FOR A FIRST TAKE!
NOW, WE'LL SHOOT IT A SECOND TIME-- TO TRY A DIFFERENT CAMERA ANGLE!
I NEVER KNEW ACTING WAS SO EASY!
THIS FEELING I HAVE--IT'S TRYING TO WARN ME OF SOMETHING--!
BUT--WHAT CAN IT BE?

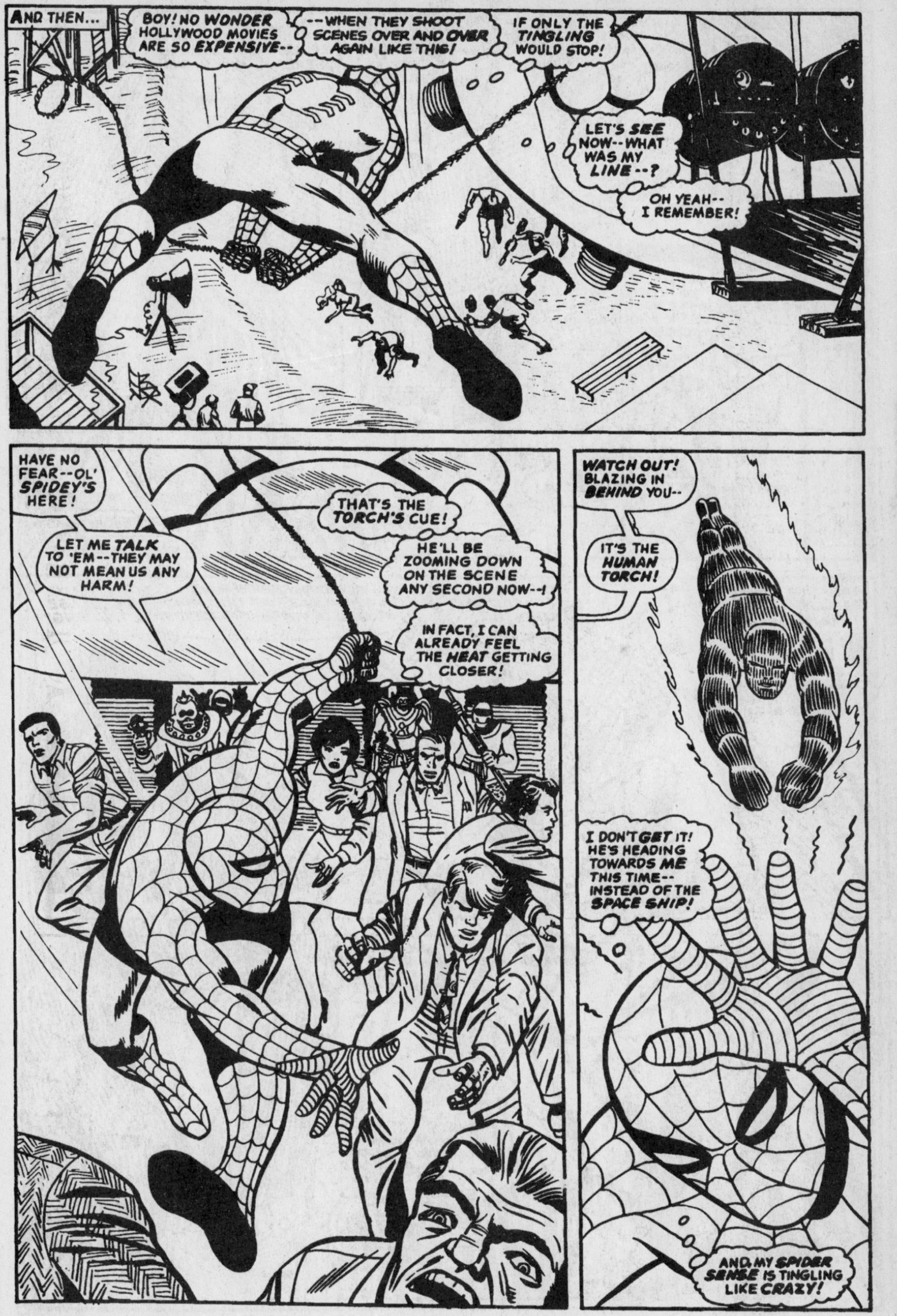
AND THEN...
BOY! NO WONDER HOLLYWOOD MOVIES ARE SO EXPENSIVE--
--WHEN THEY SHOOT SCENES OVER AND OVER AGAIN LIKE THIS!
IF ONLY THE TINGLING WOULD STOP!
LET'S SEE NOW--WHAT WAS MY LINE--?
OH YEAH-- I REMEMBER!
HAVE NO FEAR--OL' SPIDEY'S HERE!
LET ME TALK TO 'EM--THEY MAY NOT MEAN US ANY HARM!
THAT'S THE TORCH'S CUE!
HE'LL BE ZOOMING DOWN ON THE SCENE ANY SECOND NOW--!
IN FACT, I CAN ALREADY FEEL THE HEAT GETTING CLOSER!
WATCH OUT! BLAZING IN BEHIND YOU--
IT'S THE HUMAN TORCH!
I DON'T GET IT! HE'S HEADING TOWARDS ME THIS TIME--INSTEAD OF THE SPACE SHIP!
AND MY SPIDER SENSE IS TINGLING LIKE CRAZY!

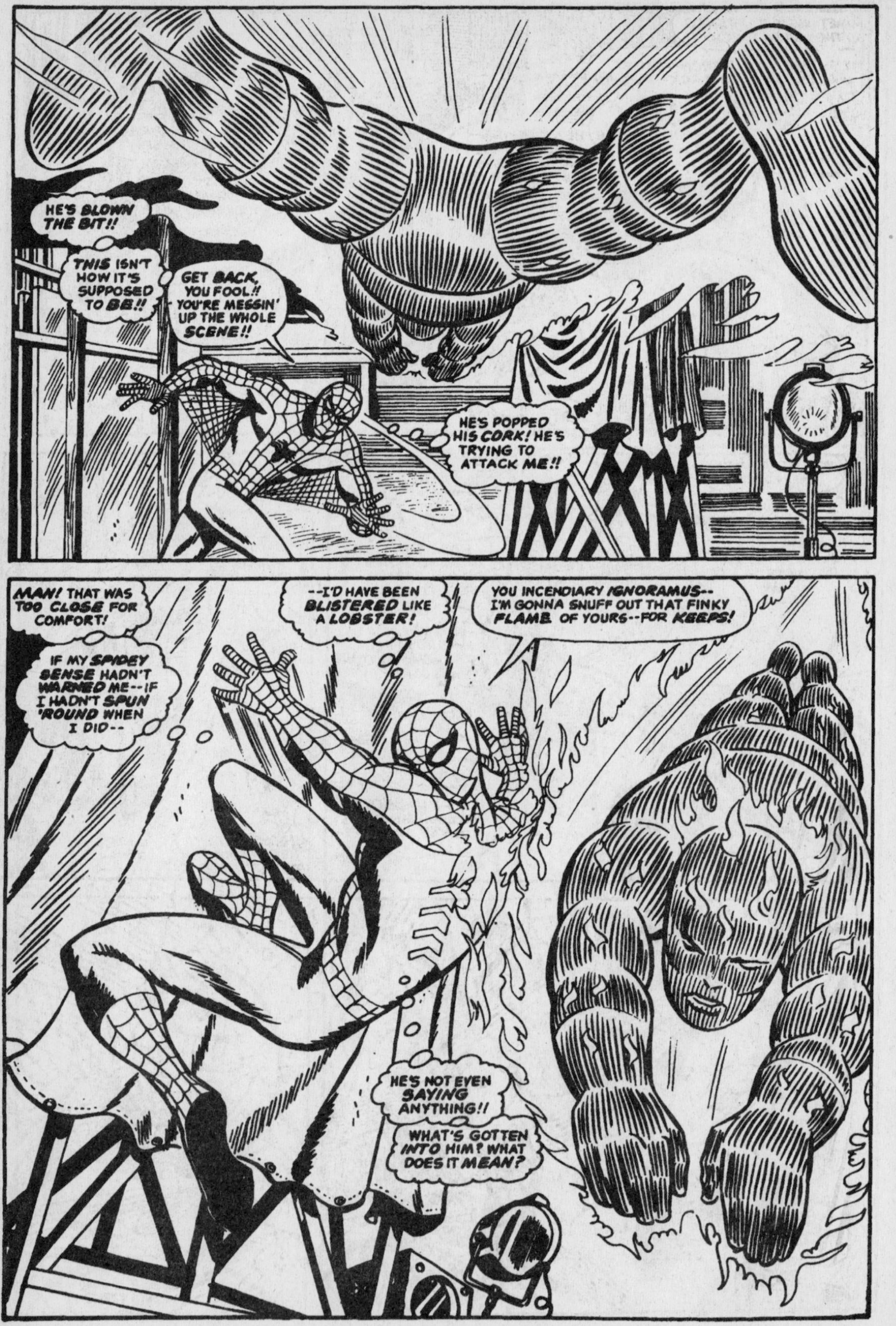
HE'S BLOWN THE BIT!!
THIS ISN'T HOW IT'S SUPPOSED TO BE!!
GET BACK, YOU FOOL!! YOU'RE MESSIN' UP THE WHOLE SCENE!!
HE'S POPPED HIS CORK! HE'S TRYING TO ATTACK ME!!
MAN! THAT WAS TOO CLOSE FOR COMFORT!
IF MY SPIDEY SENSE HADN'T WARNED ME--IF I HADN'T SPUN 'ROUND WHEN I DID--
--I'D HAVE BEEN BLISTERED LIKE A LOBSTER!
YOU INCENDIARY IGNORAMUS-- I'M GONNA SNUFF OUT THAT FINKY FLAME OF YOURS--FOR KEEPS!
HE'S NOT EVEN SAYING ANYTHING!!
WHAT'S GOTTEN INTO HIM? WHAT DOES IT MEAN?

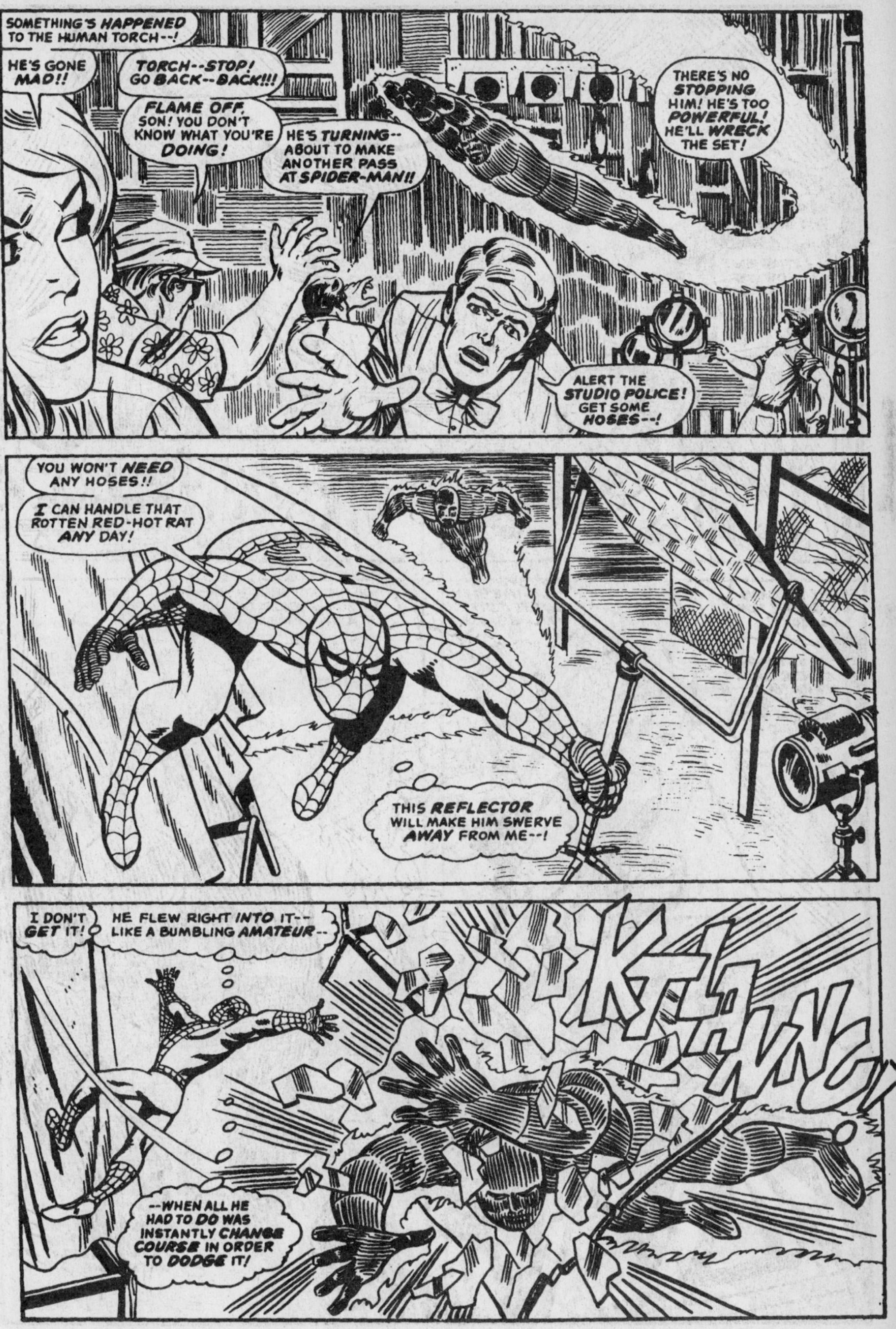
SOMETHING'S HAPPENED TO THE HUMAN TORCH--!
HE'S GONE MAD!!
TORCH--STOP! GO BACK--BACK!!!
FLAME OFF, SON! YOU DON'T KNOW WHAT YOU'RE DOING!
HE'S TURNING-- ABOUT TO MAKE ANOTHER PASS AT SPIDER-MAN!!
THERE'S NO STOPPING HIM! HE'S TOO POWERFUL! HE'LL WRECK THE SET!
ALERT THE STUDIO POLICE! GET SOME HOSES--!
YOU WON'T NEED ANY HOSES!!
I CAN HANDLE THAT ROTTEN RED-HOT RAT ANY DAY!
THIS REFLECTOR WILL MAKE HIM SWERVE AWAY FROM ME--!
I DON'T GET IT!
HE FLEW RIGHT INTO IT-- LIKE A BUMBLING AMATEUR--
KTHANNG
--WHEN ALL HE HAD TO DO WAS INSTANTLY CHANGE COURSE IN ORDER TO DODGE IT!

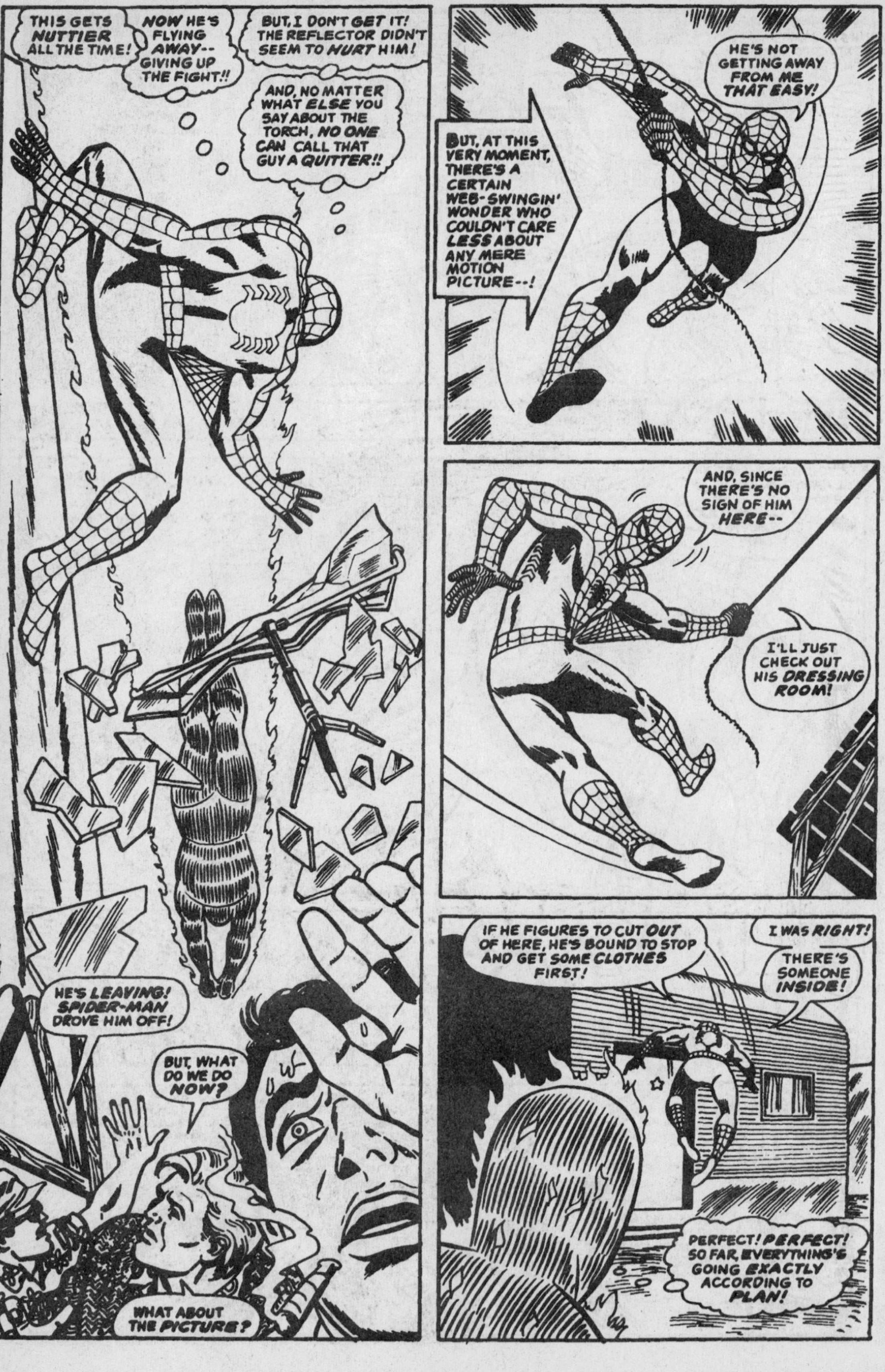

THIS GETS NUTTIER ALL THE TIME!
NOW HE'S FLYING AWAY-- GIVING UP THE FIGHT!!
BUT, I DON'T GET IT! THE REFLECTOR DIDN'T SEEM TO HURT HIM!
AND, NO MATTER WHAT ELSE YOU SAY ABOUT THE TORCH, NO ONE CAN CALL THAT GUY A QUITTER!!
HE'S LEAVING! SPIDER-MAN DROVE HIM OFF!
BUT, WHAT DO WE DO NOW?
WHAT ABOUT THE PICTURE?
BUT, AT THIS VERY MOMENT, THERE'S A CERTAIN WEB-SWINGIN' WONDER WHO COULDN'T CARE LESS ABOUT ANY MERE MOTION PICTURE--!
HE'S NOT GETTING AWAY FROM ME THAT EASY!
AND, SINCE THERE'S NO SIGN OF HIM HERE--
I'LL JUST CHECK OUT HIS DRESSING ROOM!
IF HE FIGURES TO CUT OUT OF HERE, HE'S BOUND TO STOP AND GET SOME CLOTHES FIRST!
I WAS RIGHT!
THERE'S SOMEONE INSIDE!
PERFECT! PERFECT! SO FAR, EVERYTHING'S GOING EXACTLY ACCORDING TO PLAN!

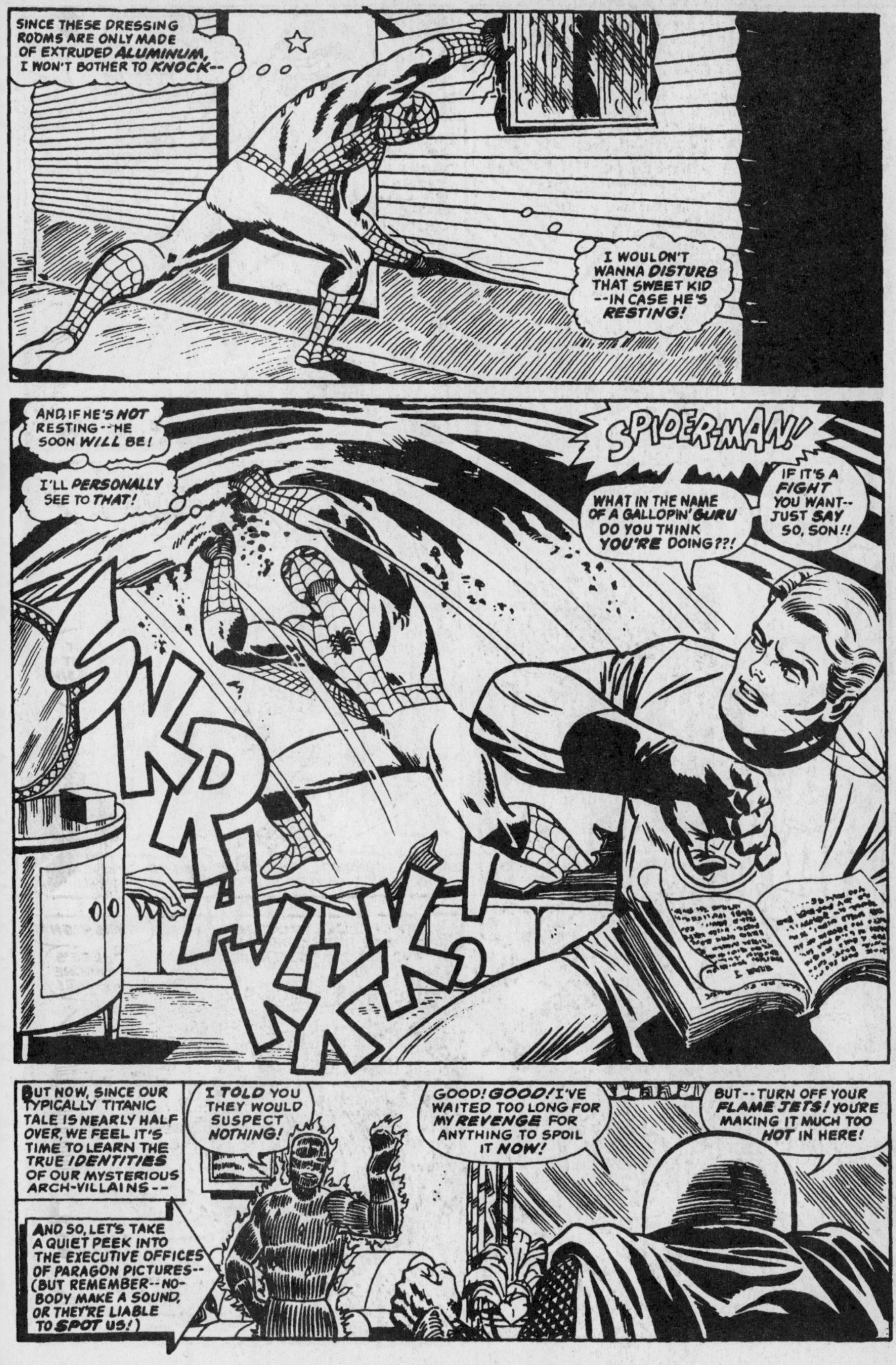

SINCE THESE DRESSING ROOMS ARE ONLY MADE OF EXTRUDED ALUMINUM, I WON'T BOTHER TO KNOCK--
I WOULDN'T WANNA DISTURB THAT SWEET KID --IN CASE HE'S RESTING!
AND, IF HE'S NOT RESTING--HE SOON WILL BE!
I'LL PERSONALLY SEE TO THAT!
SKRAKKK!
SPIDER-MAN!
WHAT IN THE NAME OF A GALLOPIN' GURU DO YOU THINK YOU'RE DOING??!
IF IT'S A FIGHT YOU WANT-- JUST SAY SO, SON!!
BUT NOW, SINCE OUR TYPICALLY TITANIC TALE IS NEARLY HALF OVER, WE FEEL IT'S TIME TO LEARN THE TRUE IDENTITIES OF OUR MYSTERIOUS ARCH-VILLAINS--
AND SO, LET'S TAKE A QUIET PEEK INTO THE EXECUTIVE OFFICES OF PARAGON PICTURES-- (BUT REMEMBER--NO-BODY MAKE A SOUND, OR THEY'RE LIABLE TO SPOT US!)
I TOLD YOU THEY WOULD SUSPECT NOTHING!
GOOD! GOOD! I'VE WAITED TOO LONG FOR MY REVENGE FOR ANYTHING TO SPOIL IT NOW!
BUT--TURN OFF YOUR FLAME JETS! YOU'RE MAKING IT MUCH TOO HOT IN HERE!

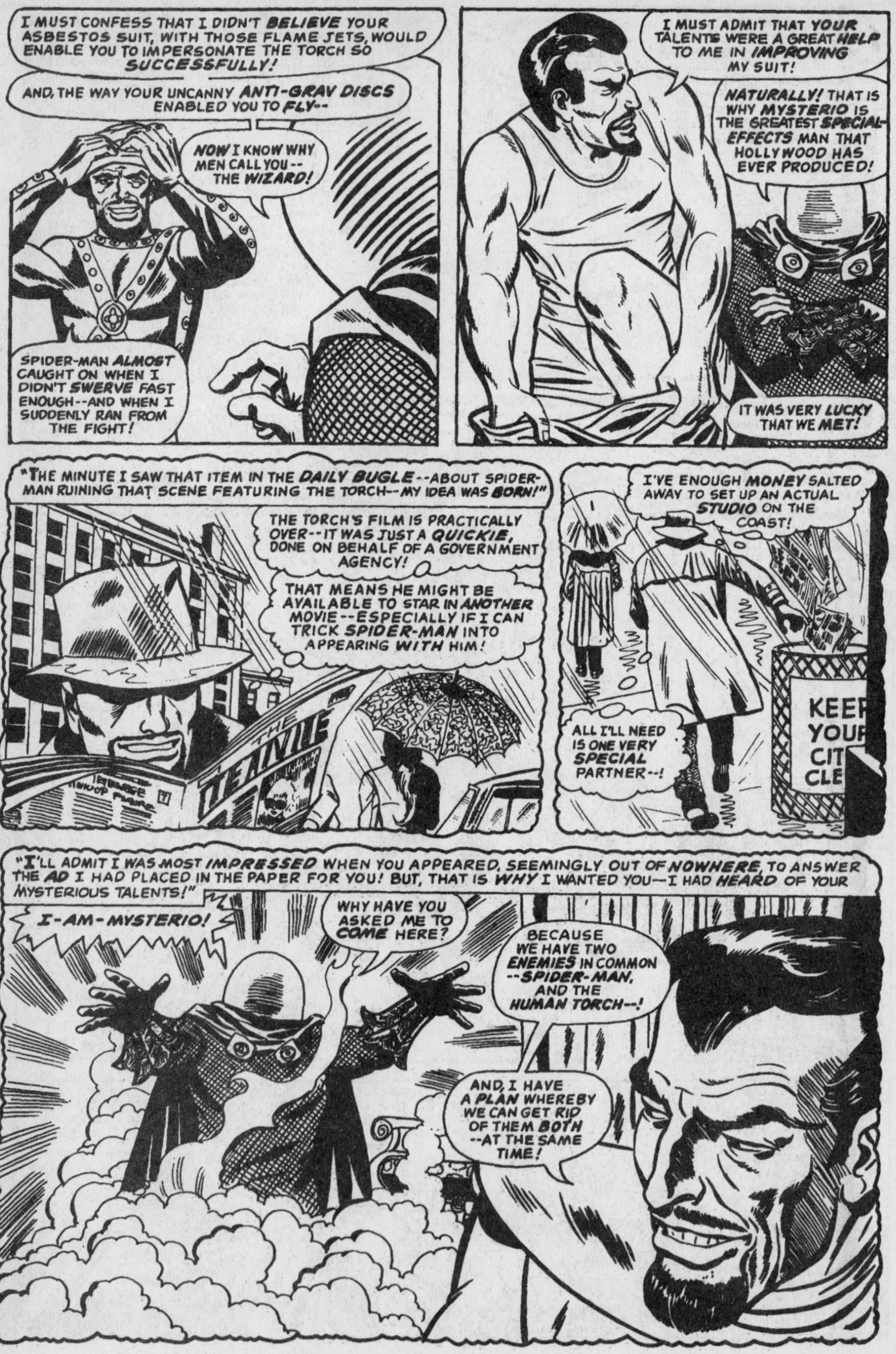
I MUST CONFESS THAT I DIDN'T BELIEVE YOUR ASBESTOS SUIT, WITH THOSE FLAME JETS, WOULD ENABLE YOU TO IMPERSONATE THE TORCH SO SUCCESSFULLY!
AND, THE WAY YOUR UNCANNY ANTI-GRAV DISCS ENABLED YOU TO FLY--
NOW I KNOW WHY MEN CALL YOU -- THE WIZARD!
SPIDER-MAN ALMOST CAUGHT ON WHEN I DIDN'T SWERVE FAST ENOUGH--AND WHEN I SUDDENLY RAN FROM THE FIGHT!
I MUST ADMIT THAT YOUR TALENTS WERE A GREAT HELP TO ME IN IMPROVING MY SUIT!
NATURALLY! THAT IS WHY MYSTERIO IS THE GREATEST SPECIAL-EFFECTS MAN THAT HOLLYWOOD HAS EVER PRODUCED!
IT WAS VERY LUCKY THAT WE MET!
"THE MINUTE I SAW THAT ITEM IN THE DAILY BUGLE--ABOUT SPIDER-MAN RUINING THAT SCENE FEATURING THE TORCH-- MY IDEA WAS BORN!"
THE TORCH'S FILM IS PRACTICALLY OVER--IT WAS JUST A QUICKIE, DONE ON BEHALF OF A GOVERNMENT AGENCY!
THAT MEANS HE MIGHT BE AVAILABLE TO STAR IN ANOTHER MOVIE --ESPECIALLY IF I CAN TRICK SPIDER-MAN INTO APPEARING WITH HIM!
I'VE ENOUGH MONEY SALTED AWAY TO SET UP AN ACTUAL STUDIO ON THE COAST!
ALL I'LL NEED IS ONE VERY SPECIAL PARTNER--!
KEEP YOUR CIT CLE
"I'LL ADMIT I WAS MOST IMPRESSED WHEN YOU APPEARED, SEEMINGLY OUT OF NOWHERE, TO ANSWER THE AD I HAD PLACED IN THE PAPER FOR YOU! BUT, THAT IS WHY I WANTED YOU--I HAD HEARD OF YOUR MYSTERIOUS TALENTS!"
I-AM-MYSTERIO!
WHY HAVE YOU ASKED ME TO COME HERE?
BECAUSE WE HAVE TWO ENEMIES IN COMMON --SPIDER-MAN, AND THE HUMAN TORCH--!
AND, I HAVE A PLAN WHEREBY WE CAN GET RID OF THEM BOTH --AT THE SAME TIME!

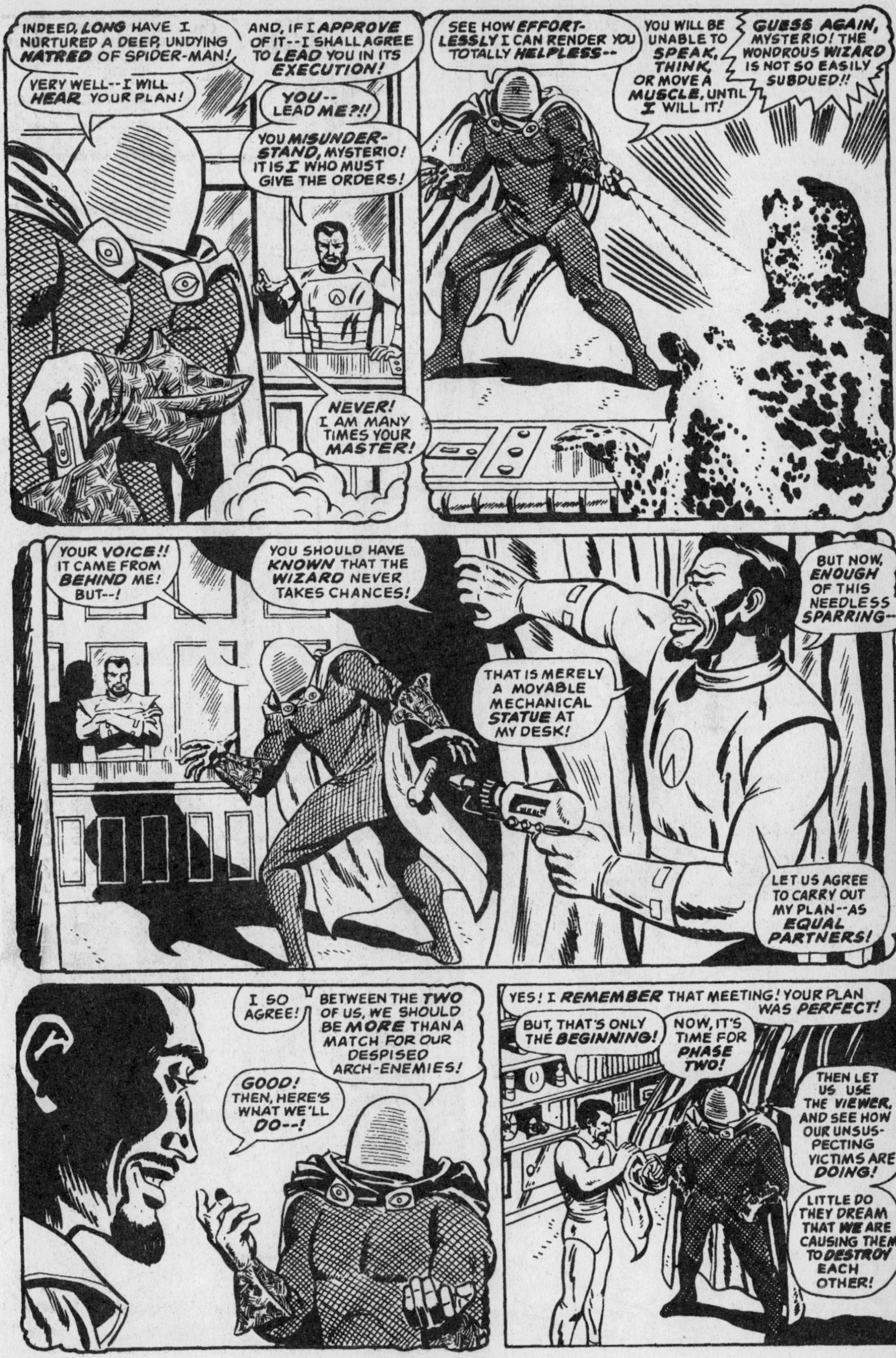
INDEED, LONG HAVE I NURTURED A DEEP, UNDYING HATRED OF SPIDER-MAN!
VERY WELL--I WILL HEAR YOUR PLAN!
AND, IF I APPROVE OF IT--I SHALL AGREE TO LEAD YOU IN ITS EXECUTION!
YOU--LEAD ME?!!
YOU MISUNDERSTAND, MYSTERIO! IT IS I WHO MUST GIVE THE ORDERS!
NEVER! I AM MANY TIMES YOUR MASTER!
SEE HOW EFFORTLESSLY I CAN RENDER YOU TOTALLY HELPLESS--
YOU WILL BE UNABLE TO SPEAK, THINK, OR MOVE A MUSCLE, UNTIL I WILL IT!
GUESS AGAIN, MYSTERIO! THE WONDROUS WIZARD IS NOT SO EASILY SUBDUED!!
YOUR VOICE!! IT CAME FROM BEHIND ME! BUT--!
YOU SHOULD HAVE KNOWN THAT THE WIZARD NEVER TAKES CHANCES!
THAT IS MERELY A MOVABLE MECHANICAL STATUE AT MY DESK!
BUT NOW, ENOUGH OF THIS NEEDLESS SPARRING--!
LET US AGREE TO CARRY OUT MY PLAN--AS EQUAL PARTNERS!
I SO AGREE!
BETWEEN THE TWO OF US, WE SHOULD BE MORE THAN A MATCH FOR OUR DESPISED ARCH-ENEMIES!
GOOD! THEN, HERE'S WHAT WE'LL DO--!
YES! I REMEMBER THAT MEETING! YOUR PLAN WAS PERFECT!
BUT, THAT'S ONLY THE BEGINNING!
NOW, IT'S TIME FOR PHASE TWO!
THEN LET US USE THE VIEWER, AND SEE HOW OUR UNSUSPECTING VICTIMS ARE DOING!
LITTLE DO THEY DREAM THAT WE ARE CAUSING THEM TO DESTROY EACH OTHER!

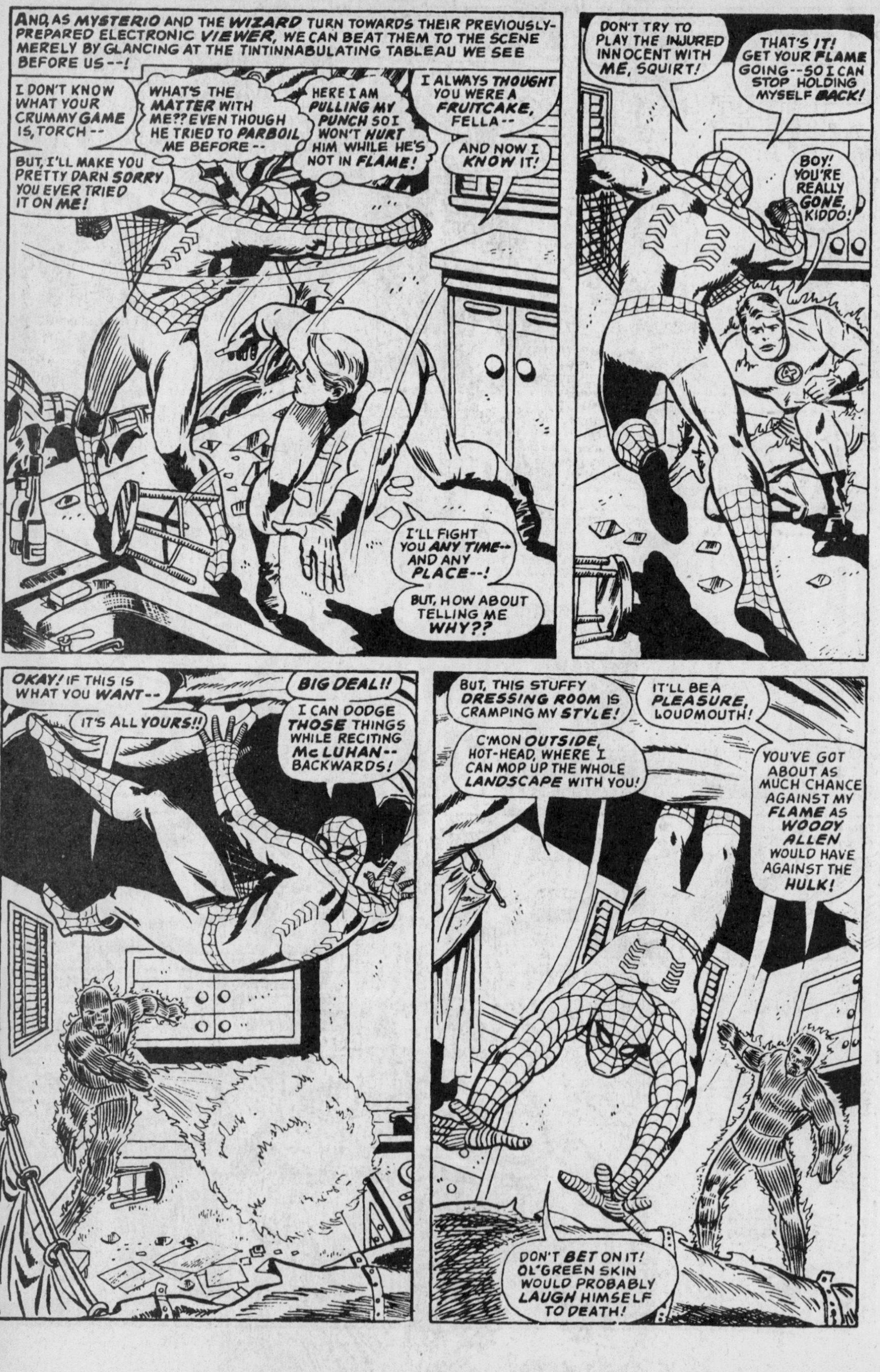
AND, AS MYSTERIO AND THE WIZARD TURN TOWARDS THEIR PREVIOUSLY-PREPARED ELECTRONIC VIEWER, WE CAN BEAT THEM TO THE SCENE MERELY BY GLANCING AT THE TINTINNABULATING TABLEAU WE SEE BEFORE US--!
I DON'T KNOW WHAT YOUR CRUMMY GAME IS, TORCH--
BUT, I'LL MAKE YOU PRETTY DARN SORRY YOU EVER TRIED IT ON ME!
WHAT'S THE MATTER WITH ME?? EVEN THOUGH HE TRIED TO PARBOIL ME BEFORE--
HERE I AM PULLING MY PUNCH SO I WON'T HURT HIM WHILE HE'S NOT IN FLAME!
I ALWAYS THOUGHT YOU WERE A FRUITCAKE, FELLA--
AND NOW I KNOW IT!
I'LL FIGHT YOU ANY TIME-- AND ANY PLACE--!
BUT, HOW ABOUT TELLING ME WHY??
DON'T TRY TO PLAY THE INJURED INNOCENT WITH ME, SQUIRT!
THAT'S IT! GET YOUR FLAME GOING--SO I CAN STOP HOLDING MYSELF BACK!
BOY! YOU'RE REALLY GONE, KIDDO!
OKAY! IF THIS IS WHAT YOU WANT--
IT'S ALL YOURS!!
BIG DEAL!!
I CAN DODGE THOSE THINGS WHILE RECITING McLUHAN-- BACKWARDS!
BUT, THIS STUFFY DRESSING ROOM IS CRAMPING MY STYLE!
C'MON OUTSIDE, HOT-HEAD, WHERE I CAN MOP UP THE WHOLE LANDSCAPE WITH YOU!
IT'LL BE A PLEASURE, LOUDMOUTH!
YOU'VE GOT ABOUT AS MUCH CHANCE AGAINST MY FLAME AS WOODY ALLEN WOULD HAVE AGAINST THE HULK!
DON'T BET ON IT! OL' GREEN SKIN WOULD PROBABLY LAUGH HIMSELF TO DEATH!

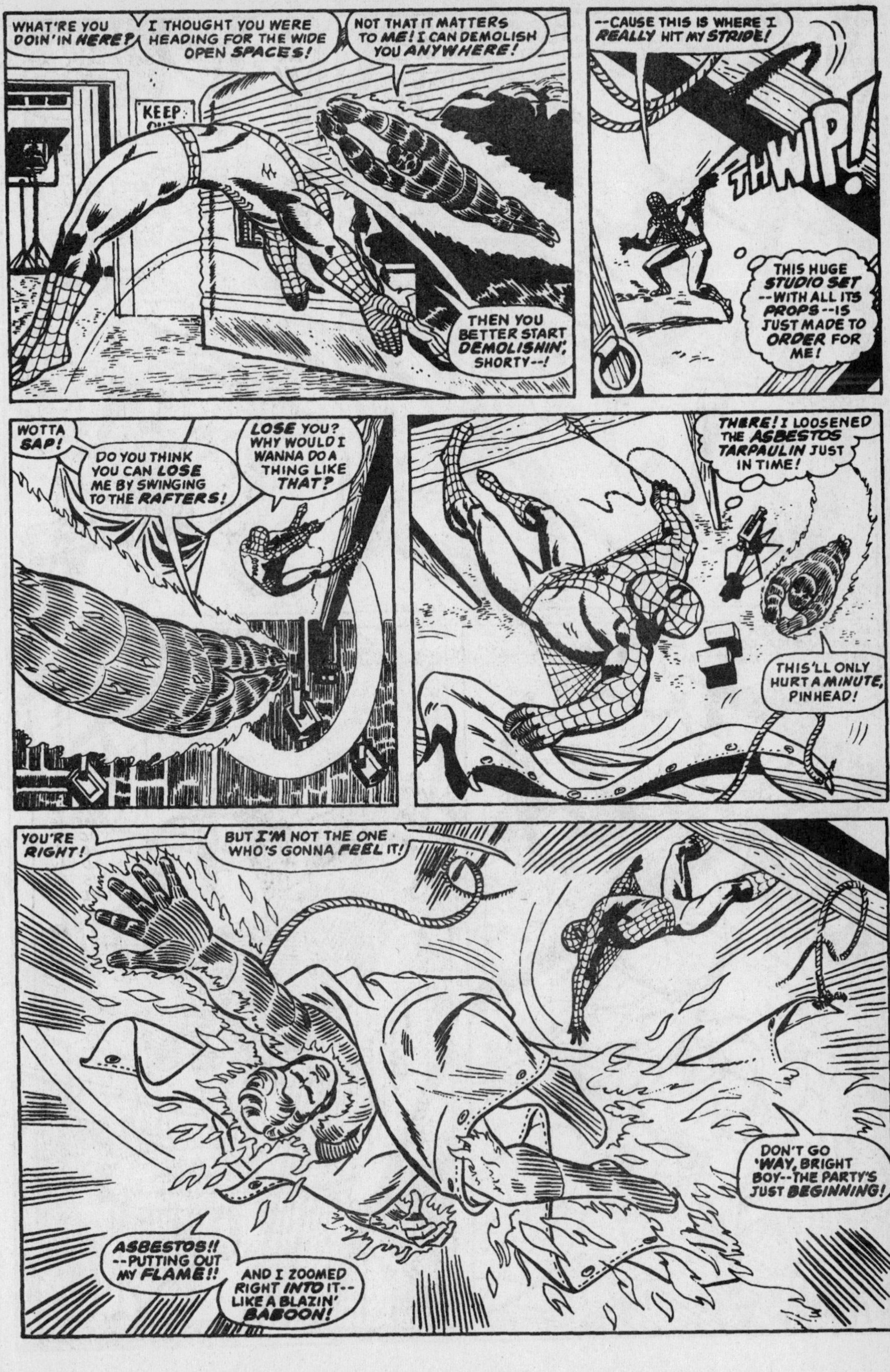
WHAT'RE YOU DOIN' IN HERE?
I THOUGHT YOU WERE HEADING FOR THE WIDE OPEN SPACES!
NOT THAT IT MATTERS TO ME! I CAN DEMOLISH YOU ANYWHERE!
KEEP
THEN YOU BETTER START DEMOLISHIN', SHORTY--!
--CAUSE THIS IS WHERE I REALLY HIT MY STRIDE!
THWIP!
THIS HUGE STUDIO SET --WITH ALL ITS PROPS--IS JUST MADE TO ORDER FOR ME!
WOTTA SAP!
DO YOU THINK YOU CAN LOSE ME BY SWINGING TO THE RAFTERS!
LOSE YOU? WHY WOULD I WANNA DO A THING LIKE THAT?
THERE! I LOOSENED THE ASBESTOS TARPAULIN JUST IN TIME!
THIS'LL ONLY HURT A MINUTE, PINHEAD!
YOU'RE RIGHT!
BUT I'M NOT THE ONE WHO'S GONNA FEEL IT!
DON'T GO 'WAY, BRIGHT BOY--THE PARTY'S JUST BEGINNING!
ASBESTOS!! --PUTTING OUT MY FLAME!!
AND I ZOOMED RIGHT INTO IT-- LIKE A BLAZIN' BABOON!

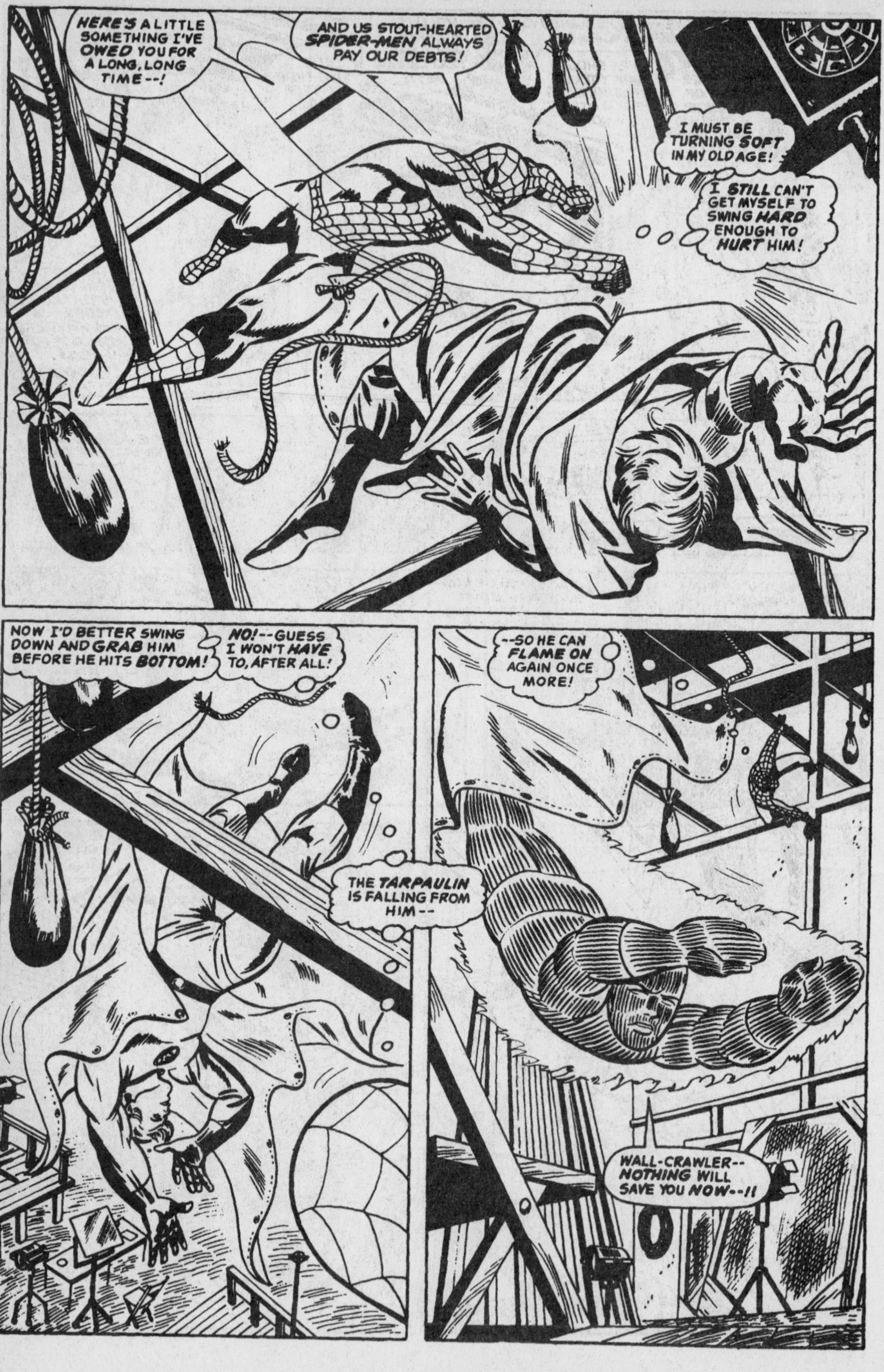
HERE'S A LITTLE SOMETHING I'VE OWED YOU FOR A LONG, LONG TIME--!
AND US STOUT-HEARTED SPIDER-MEN ALWAYS PAY OUR DEBTS!
I MUST BE TURNING SOFT IN MY OLD AGE!
I STILL CAN'T GET MYSELF TO SWING HARD ENOUGH TO HURT HIM!
NOW I'D BETTER SWING DOWN AND GRAB HIM BEFORE HE HITS BOTTOM!
NO!--GUESS I WON'T HAVE TO, AFTER ALL!
THE TARPAULIN IS FALLING FROM HIM--
--SO HE CAN FLAME ON AGAIN ONCE MORE!
WALL-CRAWLER--NOTHING WILL SAVE YOU NOW--!!

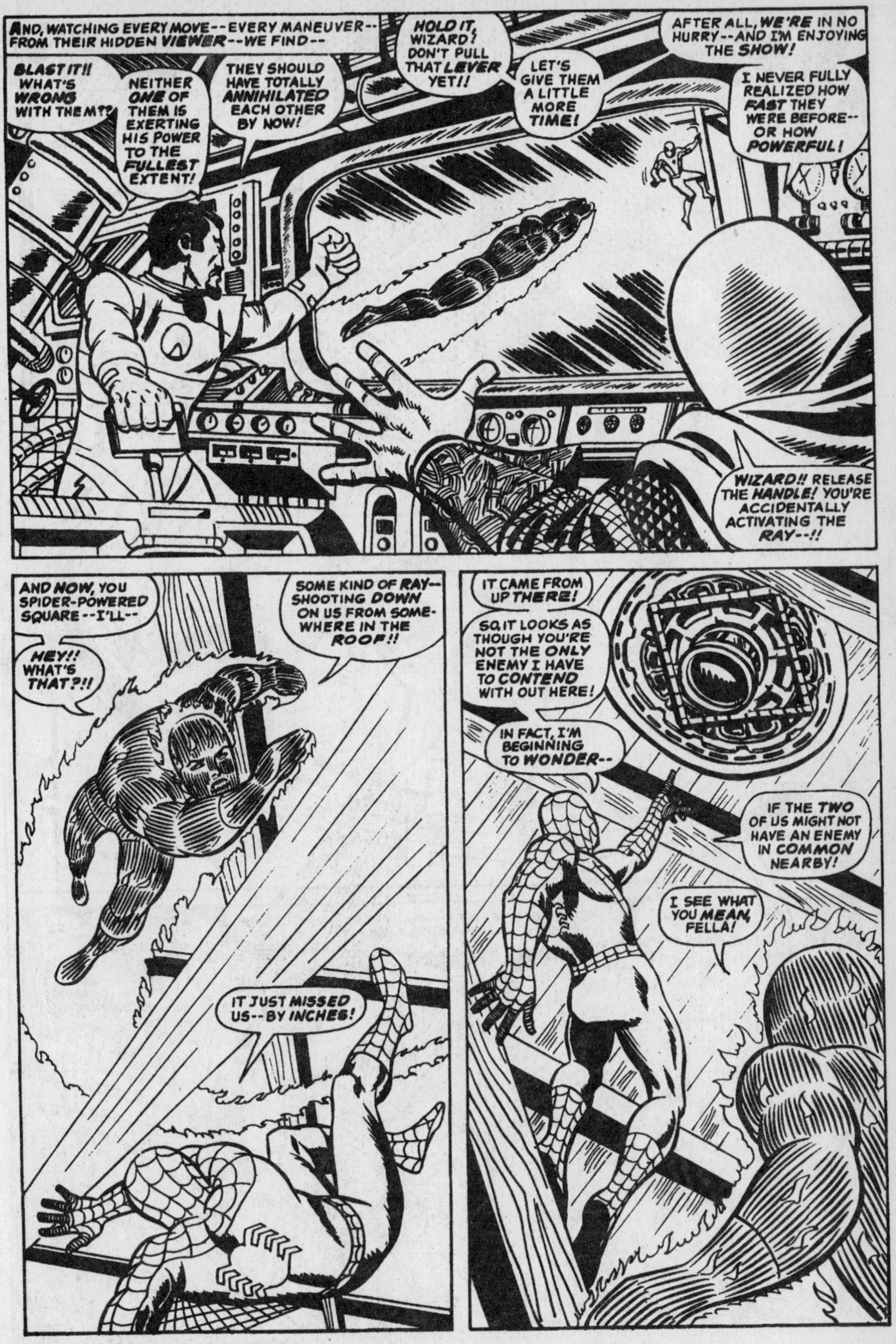

AND, WATCHING EVERY MOVE--EVERY MANEUVER--FROM THEIR HIDDEN VIEWER--WE FIND--
BLAST IT!! WHAT'S WRONG WITH THEM??
NEITHER ONE OF THEM IS EXERTING HIS POWER TO THE FULLEST EXTENT!
THEY SHOULD HAVE TOTALLY ANNIHILATED EACH OTHER BY NOW!
HOLD IT, WIZARD! DON'T PULL THAT LEVER YET!!
LET'S GIVE THEM A LITTLE MORE TIME!
AFTER ALL, WE'RE IN NO HURRY--AND I'M ENJOYING THE SHOW!
I NEVER FULLY REALIZED HOW FAST THEY WERE BEFORE--OR HOW POWERFUL!
WIZARD!! RELEASE THE HANDLE! YOU'RE ACCIDENTALLY ACTIVATING THE RAY--!!
AND NOW, YOU SPIDER-POWERED SQUARE--I'LL--
HEY!! WHAT'S THAT?!!
SOME KIND OF RAY--SHOOTING DOWN ON US FROM SOMEWHERE IN THE ROOF!!
IT JUST MISSED US--BY INCHES!
IT CAME FROM UP THERE!
SO, IT LOOKS AS THOUGH YOU'RE NOT THE ONLY ENEMY I HAVE TO CONTEND WITH OUT HERE!
IN FACT, I'M BEGINNING TO WONDER--
IF THE TWO OF US MIGHT NOT HAVE AN ENEMY IN COMMON NEARBY!
I SEE WHAT YOU MEAN, FELLA!

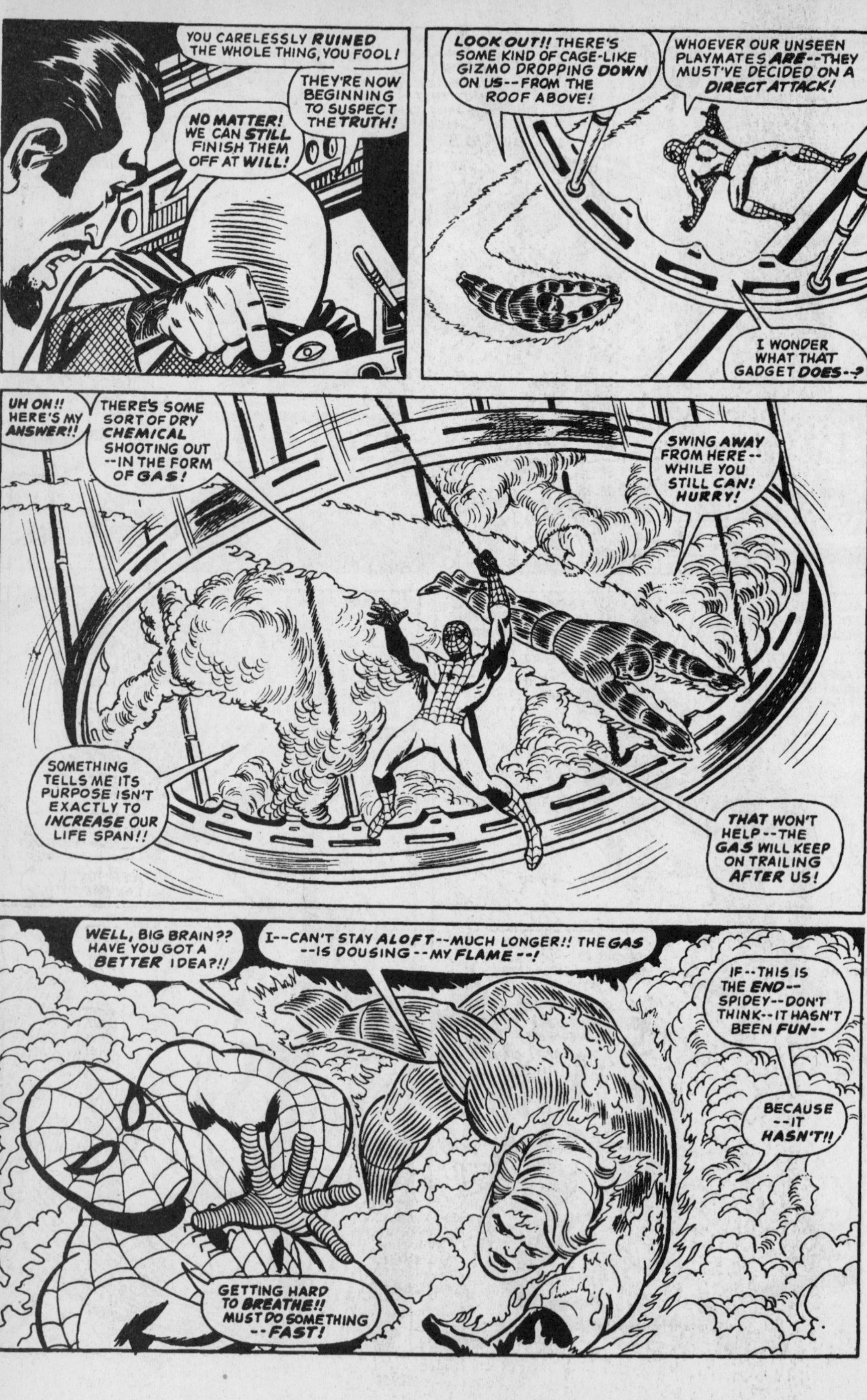
YOU CARELESSLY RUINED THE WHOLE THING, YOU FOOL!
THEY'RE NOW BEGINNING TO SUSPECT THE TRUTH!
NO MATTER! WE CAN STILL FINISH THEM OFF AT WILL!
LOOK OUT!! THERE'S SOME KIND OF CAGE-LIKE GIZMO DROPPING DOWN ON US--FROM THE ROOF ABOVE!
WHOEVER OUR UNSEEN PLAYMATES ARE--THEY MUST'VE DECIDED ON A DIRECT ATTACK!
I WONDER WHAT THAT GADGET DOES--?
UH OH!! HERE'S MY ANSWER!!
THERE'S SOME SORT OF DRY CHEMICAL SHOOTING OUT --IN THE FORM OF GAS!
SWING AWAY FROM HERE--WHILE YOU STILL CAN! HURRY!
SOMETHING TELLS ME ITS PURPOSE ISN'T EXACTLY TO INCREASE OUR LIFE SPAN!!
THAT WON'T HELP--THE GAS WILL KEEP ON TRAILING AFTER US!
WELL, BIG BRAIN?? HAVE YOU GOT A BETTER IDEA?!!
I--CAN'T STAY ALOFT--MUCH LONGER!! THE GAS --IS DOUSING--MY FLAME--!
IF--THIS IS THE END--SPIDEY--DON'T THINK--IT HASN'T BEEN FUN--
BECAUSE --IT HASN'T!!
GETTING HARD TO BREATHE!! MUST DO SOMETHING --FAST!

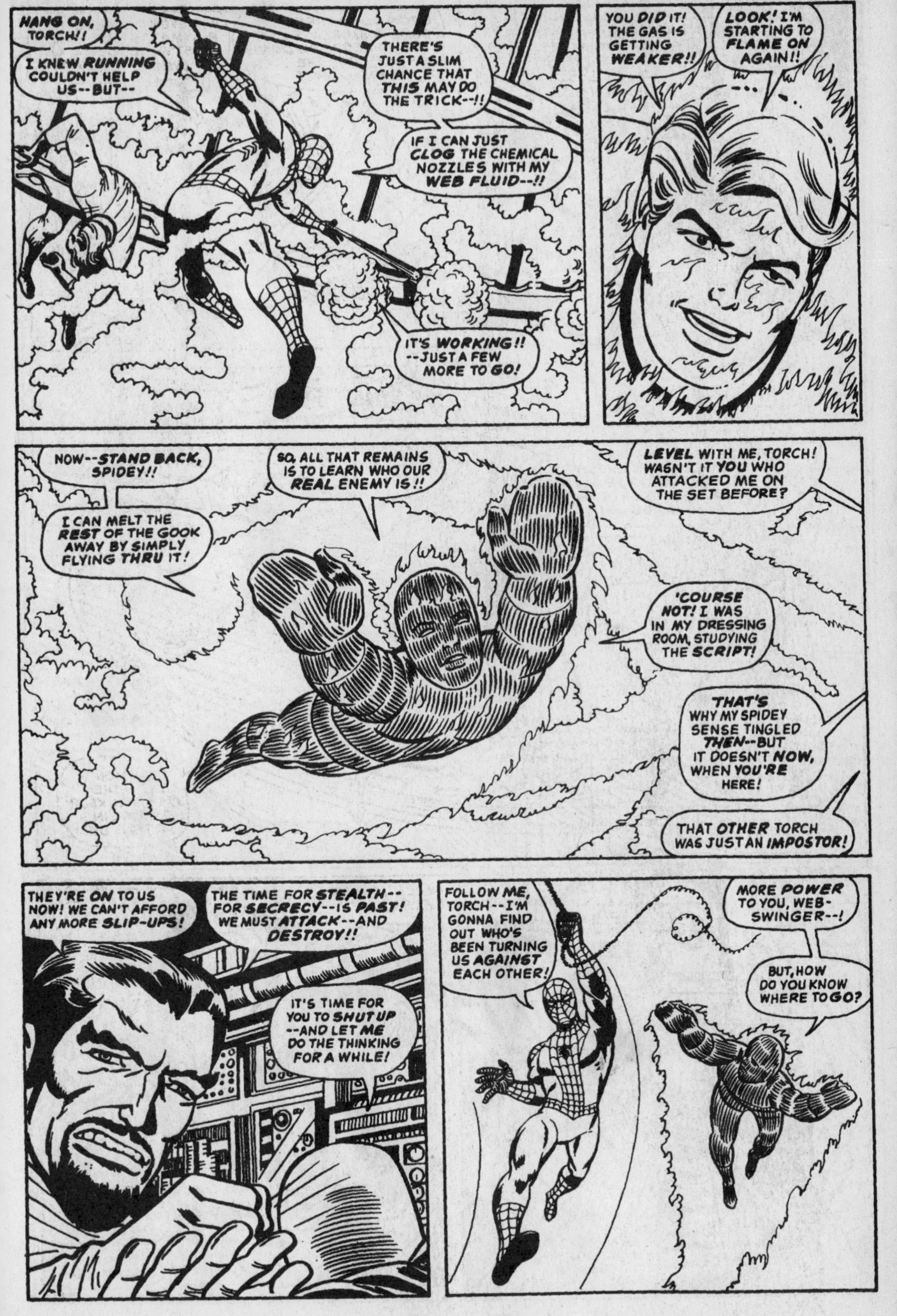

HANG ON, TORCH!!
I KNEW RUNNING COULDN'T HELP US--BUT--
THERE'S JUST A SLIM CHANCE THAT THIS MAY DO THE TRICK--!!
IF I CAN JUST CLOG THE CHEMICAL NOZZLES WITH MY WEB FLUID--!!
IT'S WORKING!! --JUST A FEW MORE TO GO!
YOU DID IT! THE GAS IS GETTING WEAKER!!
LOOK! I'M STARTING TO FLAME ON AGAIN!!
NOW--STAND BACK, SPIDEY!!
I CAN MELT THE REST OF THE GOOK AWAY BY SIMPLY FLYING THRU IT!
SO, ALL THAT REMAINS IS TO LEARN WHO OUR REAL ENEMY IS!!
LEVEL WITH ME, TORCH! WASN'T IT YOU WHO ATTACKED ME ON THE SET BEFORE?
'COURSE NOT! I WAS IN MY DRESSING ROOM, STUDYING THE SCRIPT!
THAT'S WHY MY SPIDEY SENSE TINGLED THEN--BUT IT DOESN'T NOW, WHEN YOU'RE HERE!
THAT OTHER TORCH WAS JUST AN IMPOSTOR!
THEY'RE ON TO US NOW! WE CAN'T AFFORD ANY MORE SLIP-UPS!
THE TIME FOR STEALTH--FOR SECRECY--IS PAST! WE MUST ATTACK--AND DESTROY!!
IT'S TIME FOR YOU TO SHUT UP --AND LET ME DO THE THINKING FOR A WHILE!
FOLLOW ME, TORCH--I'M GONNA FIND OUT WHO'S BEEN TURNING US AGAINST EACH OTHER!
MORE POWER TO YOU, WEB-SWINGER--!
BUT, HOW DO YOU KNOW WHERE TO GO?

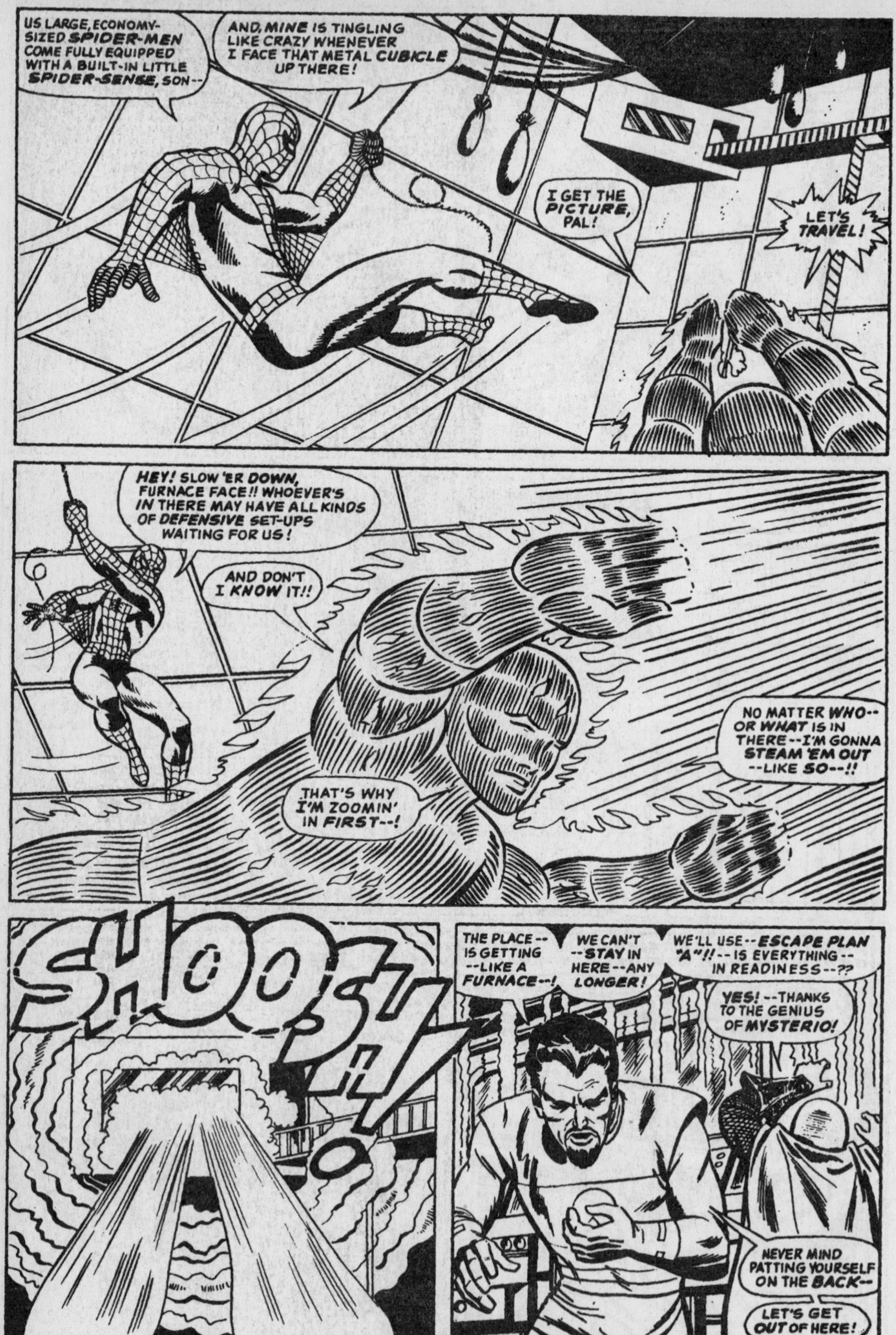
US LARGE, ECONOMY-SIZED SPIDER-MEN COME FULLY EQUIPPED WITH A BUILT-IN LITTLE SPIDER-SENSE, SON--
AND, MINE IS TINGLING LIKE CRAZY WHENEVER I FACE THAT METAL CUBICLE UP THERE!
I GET THE PICTURE, PAL!
LET'S TRAVEL!
HEY! SLOW 'ER DOWN, FURNACE FACE!! WHOEVER'S IN THERE MAY HAVE ALL KINDS OF DEFENSIVE SET-UPS WAITING FOR US!
AND DON'T I KNOW IT!!
THAT'S WHY I'M ZOOMIN' IN FIRST--!
NO MATTER WHO-- OR WHAT IS IN THERE --I'M GONNA STEAM 'EM OUT --LIKE SO--!!
SHOOSH!
THE PLACE --IS GETTING --LIKE A FURNACE--!
WE CAN'T --STAY IN HERE --ANY LONGER!
WE'LL USE --ESCAPE PLAN "A"!! --IS EVERYTHING --IN READINESS--??
YES! --THANKS TO THE GENIUS OF MYSTERIO!
NEVER MIND PATTING YOURSELF ON THE BACK--
LET'S GET OUT OF HERE!

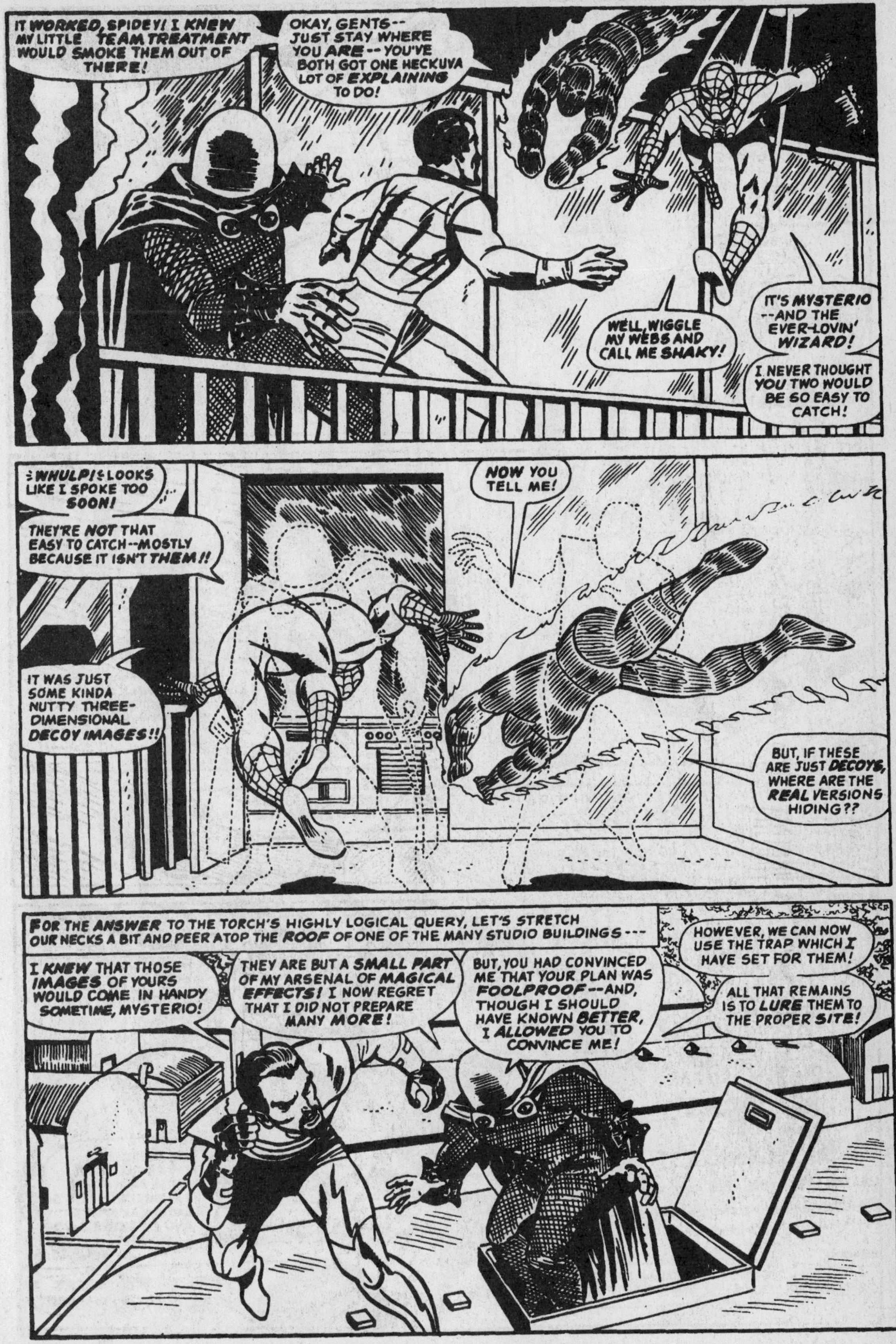

IT WORKED, SPIDEY! I KNEW MY LITTLE TEAM TREATMENT WOULD SMOKE THEM OUT OF THERE!
OKAY, GENTS-- JUST STAY WHERE YOU ARE -- YOU'VE BOTH GOT ONE HECKUVA LOT OF EXPLAINING TO DO!
WELL, WIGGLE MY WEBS AND CALL ME SHAKY!
IT'S MYSTERIO --AND THE EVER-LOVIN' WIZARD!
I NEVER THOUGHT YOU TWO WOULD BE SO EASY TO CATCH!
WHULP! LOOKS LIKE I SPOKE TOO SOON!
THEY'RE NOT THAT EASY TO CATCH--MOSTLY BECAUSE IT ISN'T THEM!!
NOW YOU TELL ME!
IT WAS JUST SOME KINDA NUTTY THREE-DIMENSIONAL DECOY IMAGES!!
BUT, IF THESE ARE JUST DECOYS, WHERE ARE THE REAL VERSIONS HIDING??
FOR THE ANSWER TO THE TORCH'S HIGHLY LOGICAL QUERY, LET'S STRETCH OUR NECKS A BIT AND PEER ATOP THE ROOF OF ONE OF THE MANY STUDIO BUILDINGS ---
I KNEW THAT THOSE IMAGES OF YOURS WOULD COME IN HANDY SOMETIME, MYSTERIO!
THEY ARE BUT A SMALL PART OF MY ARSENAL OF MAGICAL EFFECTS! I NOW REGRET THAT I DID NOT PREPARE MANY MORE!
BUT, YOU HAD CONVINCED ME THAT YOUR PLAN WAS FOOLPROOF--AND, THOUGH I SHOULD HAVE KNOWN BETTER, I ALLOWED YOU TO CONVINCE ME!
HOWEVER, WE CAN NOW USE THE TRAP WHICH I HAVE SET FOR THEM!
ALL THAT REMAINS IS TO LURE THEM TO THE PROPER SITE!

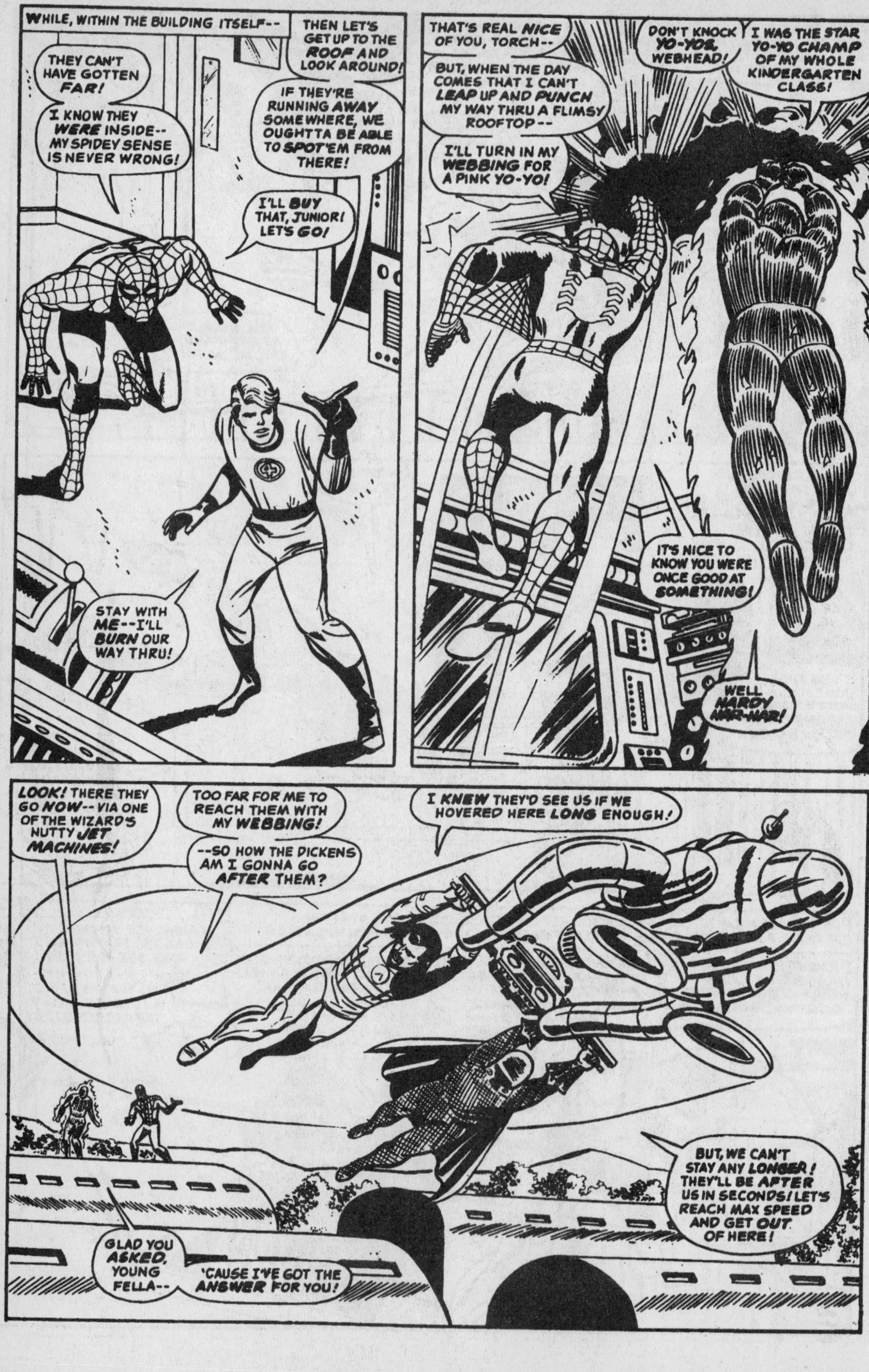
WHILE, WITHIN THE BUILDING ITSELF--
THEY CAN'T HAVE GOTTEN FAR!
I KNOW THEY WERE INSIDE-- MY SPIDEY SENSE IS NEVER WRONG!
THEN LET'S GET UP TO THE ROOF AND LOOK AROUND!
IF THEY'RE RUNNING AWAY SOMEWHERE, WE OUGHTTA BE ABLE TO SPOT'EM FROM THERE!
I'LL BUY THAT, JUNIOR! LET'S GO!
STAY WITH ME--I'LL BURN OUR WAY THRU!
THAT'S REAL NICE OF YOU, TORCH--
BUT, WHEN THE DAY COMES THAT I CAN'T LEAP UP AND PUNCH MY WAY THRU A FLIMSY ROOFTOP--
I'LL TURN IN MY WEBBING FOR A PINK YO-YO!
DON'T KNOCK YO-YOS, WEBHEAD!
I WAS THE STAR YO-YO CHAMP OF MY WHOLE KINDERGARTEN CLASS!
IT'S NICE TO KNOW YOU WERE ONCE GOOD AT SOMETHING!
WELL HARDY HAR-HAR!
LOOK! THERE THEY GO NOW--VIA ONE OF THE WIZARD'S NUTTY JET MACHINES!
TOO FAR FOR ME TO REACH THEM WITH MY WEBBING!
--SO HOW THE DICKENS AM I GONNA GO AFTER THEM?
I KNEW THEY'D SEE US IF WE HOVERED HERE LONG ENOUGH!
BUT, WE CAN'T STAY ANY LONGER! THEY'LL BE AFTER US IN SECONDS! LET'S REACH MAX SPEED AND GET OUT OF HERE!
GLAD YOU ASKED, YOUNG FELLA--
'CAUSE I'VE GOT THE ANSWER FOR YOU!

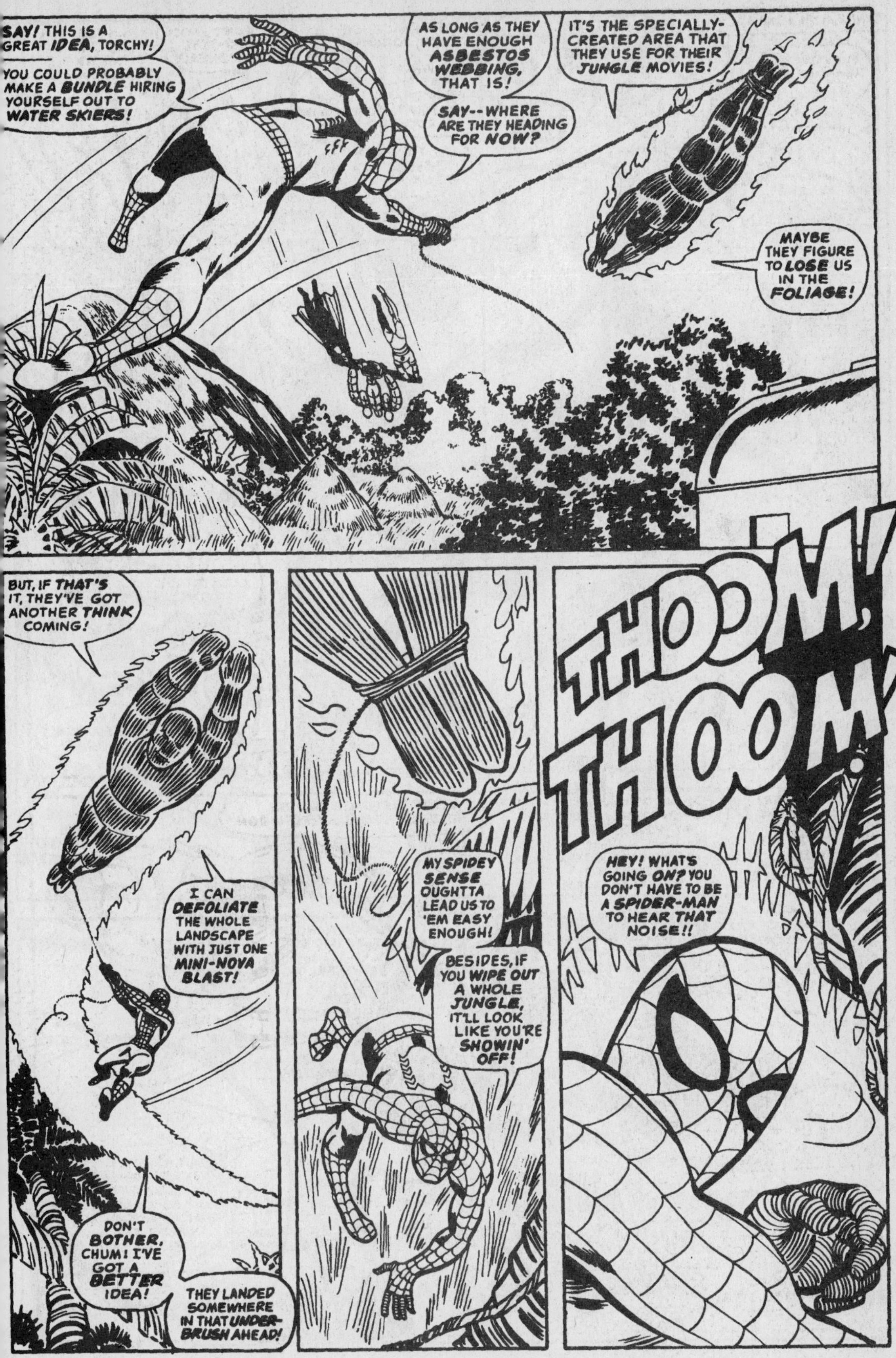
SAY! THIS IS A GREAT IDEA, TORCHY!
YOU COULD PROBABLY MAKE A BUNDLE HIRING YOURSELF OUT TO WATER SKIERS!
AS LONG AS THEY HAVE ENOUGH ASBESTOS WEBBING, THAT IS!
SAY--WHERE ARE THEY HEADING FOR NOW?
IT'S THE SPECIALLY-CREATED AREA THAT THEY USE FOR THEIR JUNGLE MOVIES!
MAYBE THEY FIGURE TO LOSE US IN THE FOLIAGE!
BUT, IF THAT'S IT, THEY'VE GOT ANOTHER THINK COMING!
I CAN DEFOLIATE THE WHOLE LANDSCAPE WITH JUST ONE MINI-NOVA BLAST!
DON'T BOTHER, CHUM! I'VE GOT A BETTER IDEA!
THEY LANDED SOMEWHERE IN THAT UNDER-BRUSH AHEAD!
MY SPIDEY SENSE OUGHTTA LEAD US TO 'EM EASY ENOUGH!
BESIDES, IF YOU WIPE OUT A WHOLE JUNGLE, IT'LL LOOK LIKE YOU'RE SHOWIN' OFF!
THOOM! THOOM!
HEY! WHAT'S GOING ON? YOU DON'T HAVE TO BE A SPIDER-MAN TO HEAR THAT NOISE!!

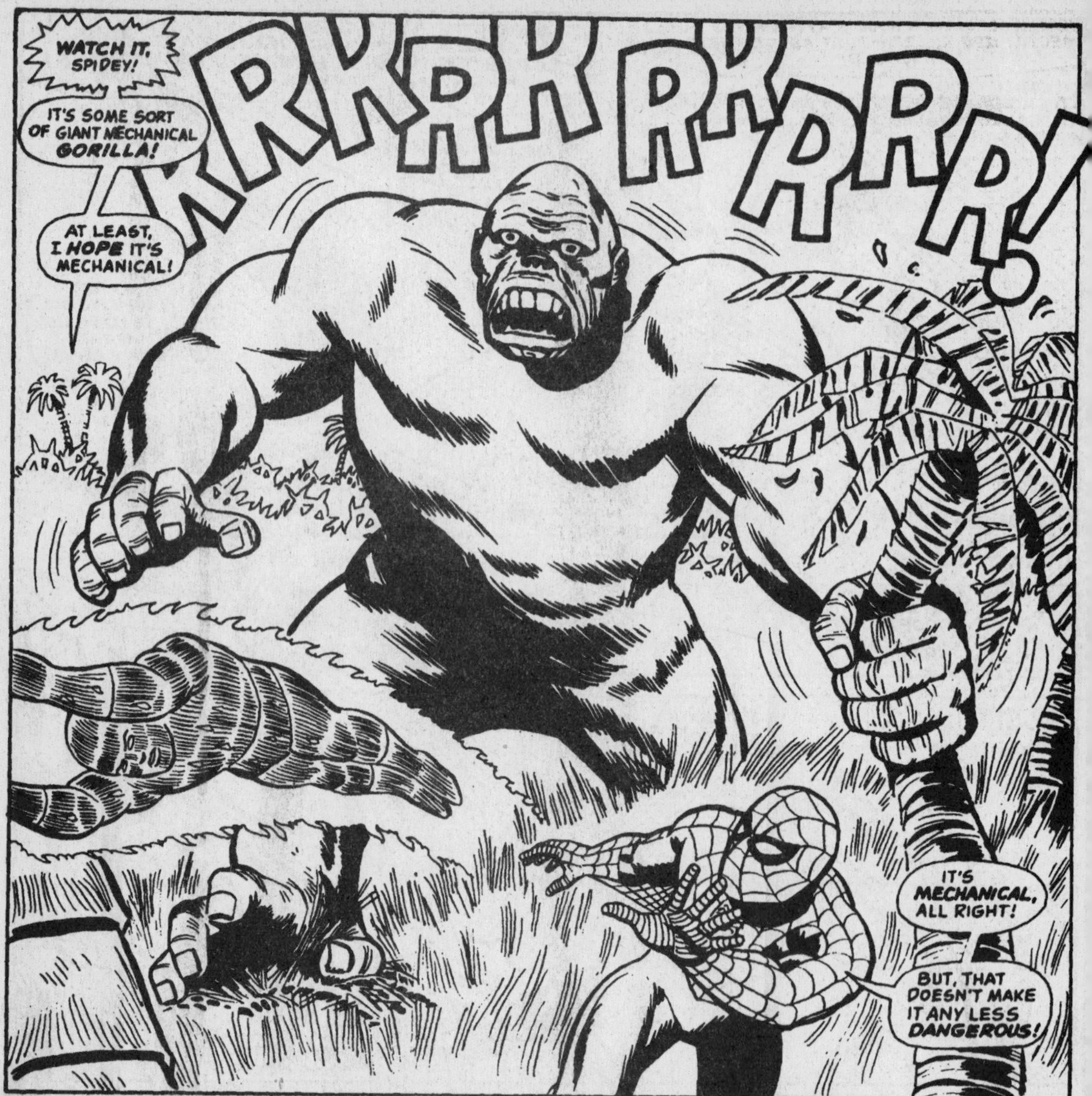
WATCH IT, SPIDEY!
KRRKRKRKRKRRRR!
IT'S SOME SORT OF GIANT MECHANICAL GORILLA!
AT LEAST, I HOPE IT'S MECHANICAL!
IT'S MECHANICAL, ALL RIGHT!
BUT, THAT DOESN'T MAKE IT ANY LESS DANGEROUS!

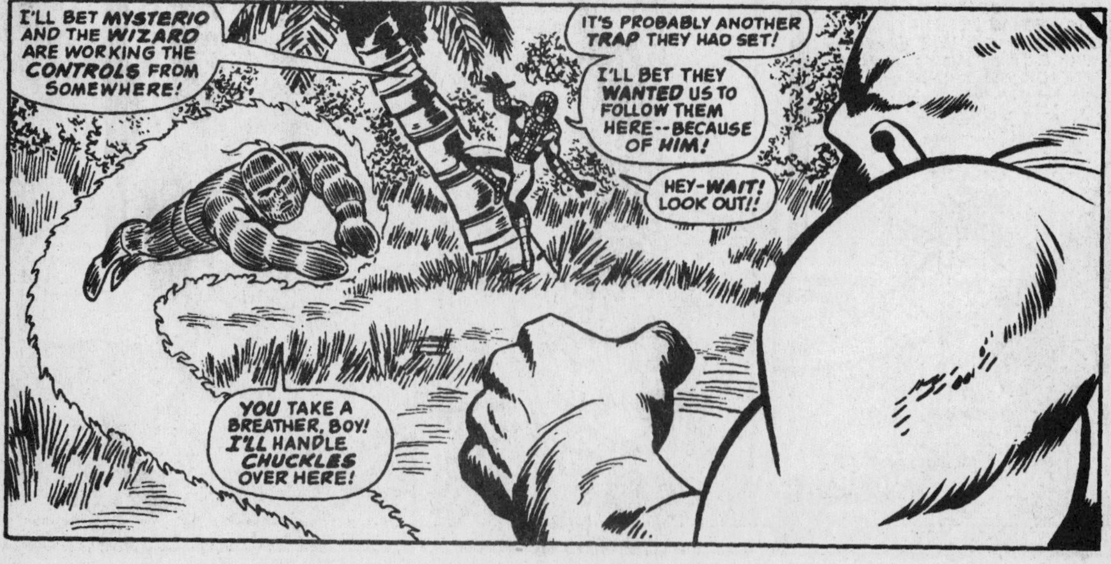
I'LL BET MYSTERIO AND THE WIZARD ARE WORKING THE CONTROLS FROM SOMEWHERE!
IT'S PROBABLY ANOTHER TRAP THEY HAD SET!
I'LL BET THEY WANTED US TO FOLLOW THEM HERE--BECAUSE OF HIM!
HEY-WAIT! LOOK OUT!!
YOU TAKE A BREATHER, BOY! I'LL HANDLE CHUCKLES OVER HERE!

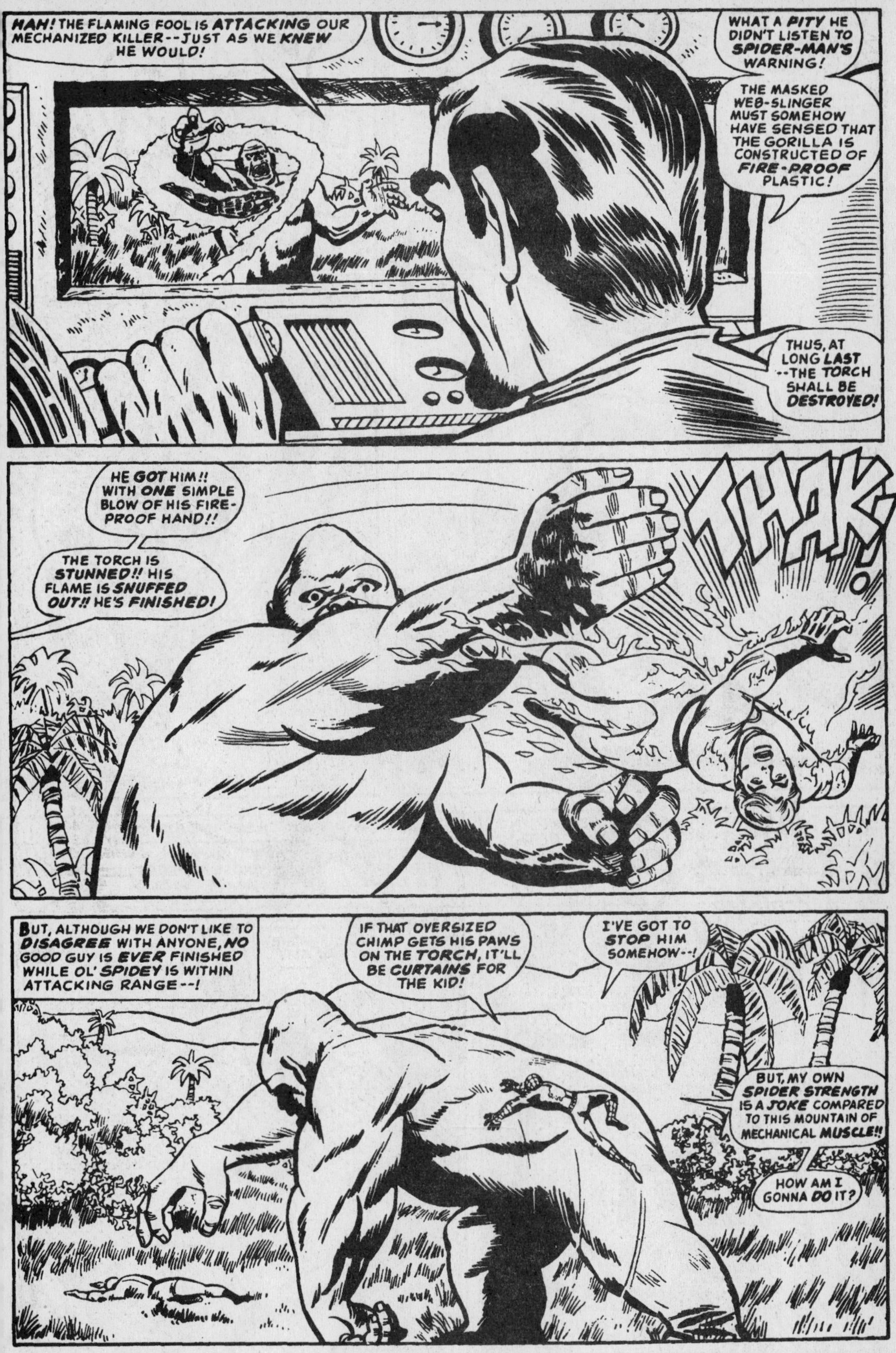
HAH! THE FLAMING FOOL IS ATTACKING OUR MECHANIZED KILLER--JUST AS WE KNEW HE WOULD!
WHAT A PITY HE DIDN'T LISTEN TO SPIDER-MAN'S WARNING!
THE MASKED WEB-SLINGER MUST SOMEHOW HAVE SENSED THAT THE GORILLA IS CONSTRUCTED OF FIRE-PROOF PLASTIC!
THUS, AT LONG LAST --THE TORCH SHALL BE DESTROYED!
HE GOT HIM!! WITH ONE SIMPLE BLOW OF HIS FIRE-PROOF HAND!!
THE TORCH IS STUNNED!! HIS FLAME IS SNUFFED OUT!! HE'S FINISHED!
THAK!
BUT, ALTHOUGH WE DON'T LIKE TO DISAGREE WITH ANYONE, NO GOOD GUY IS EVER FINISHED WHILE OL' SPIDEY IS WITHIN ATTACKING RANGE--!
IF THAT OVERSIZED CHIMP GETS HIS PAWS ON THE TORCH, IT'LL BE CURTAINS FOR THE KID!
I'VE GOT TO STOP HIM SOMEHOW--!
BUT, MY OWN SPIDER STRENGTH IS A JOKE COMPARED TO THIS MOUNTAIN OF MECHANICAL MUSCLE!!
HOW AM I GONNA DO IT?

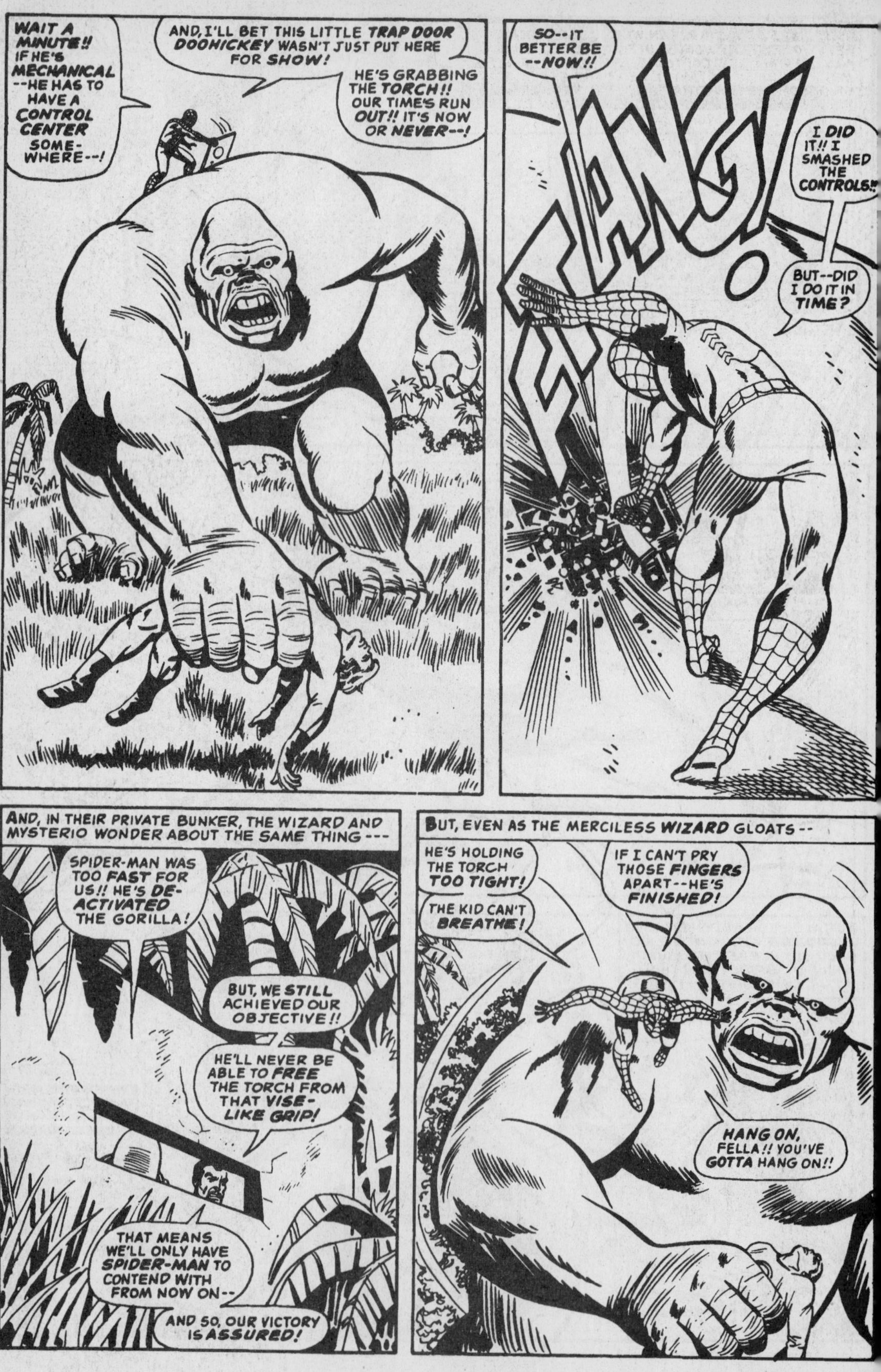
WAIT A MINUTE!! IF HE'S MECHANICAL --HE HAS TO HAVE A CONTROL CENTER SOME-WHERE--!
AND, I'LL BET THIS LITTLE TRAP DOOR DOOHICKEY WASN'T JUST PUT HERE FOR SHOW!
HE'S GRABBING THE TORCH!! OUR TIME'S RUN OUT!! IT'S NOW OR NEVER--!
SO--IT BETTER BE --NOW!!
CLANG!
I DID IT!! I SMASHED THE CONTROLS!!
BUT--DID I DO IT IN TIME?
AND, IN THEIR PRIVATE BUNKER, THE WIZARD AND MYSTERIO WONDER ABOUT THE SAME THING---
SPIDER-MAN WAS TOO FAST FOR US!! HE'S DE-ACTIVATED THE GORILLA!
BUT, WE STILL ACHIEVED OUR OBJECTIVE!!
HE'LL NEVER BE ABLE TO FREE THE TORCH FROM THAT VISE-LIKE GRIP!
THAT MEANS WE'LL ONLY HAVE SPIDER-MAN TO CONTEND WITH FROM NOW ON--
AND SO, OUR VICTORY IS ASSURED!
BUT, EVEN AS THE MERCILESS WIZARD GLOATS--
HE'S HOLDING THE TORCH TOO TIGHT!
THE KID CAN'T BREATHE!
IF I CAN'T PRY THOSE FINGERS APART--HE'S FINISHED!
HANG ON, FELLA!! YOU'VE GOTTA HANG ON!!

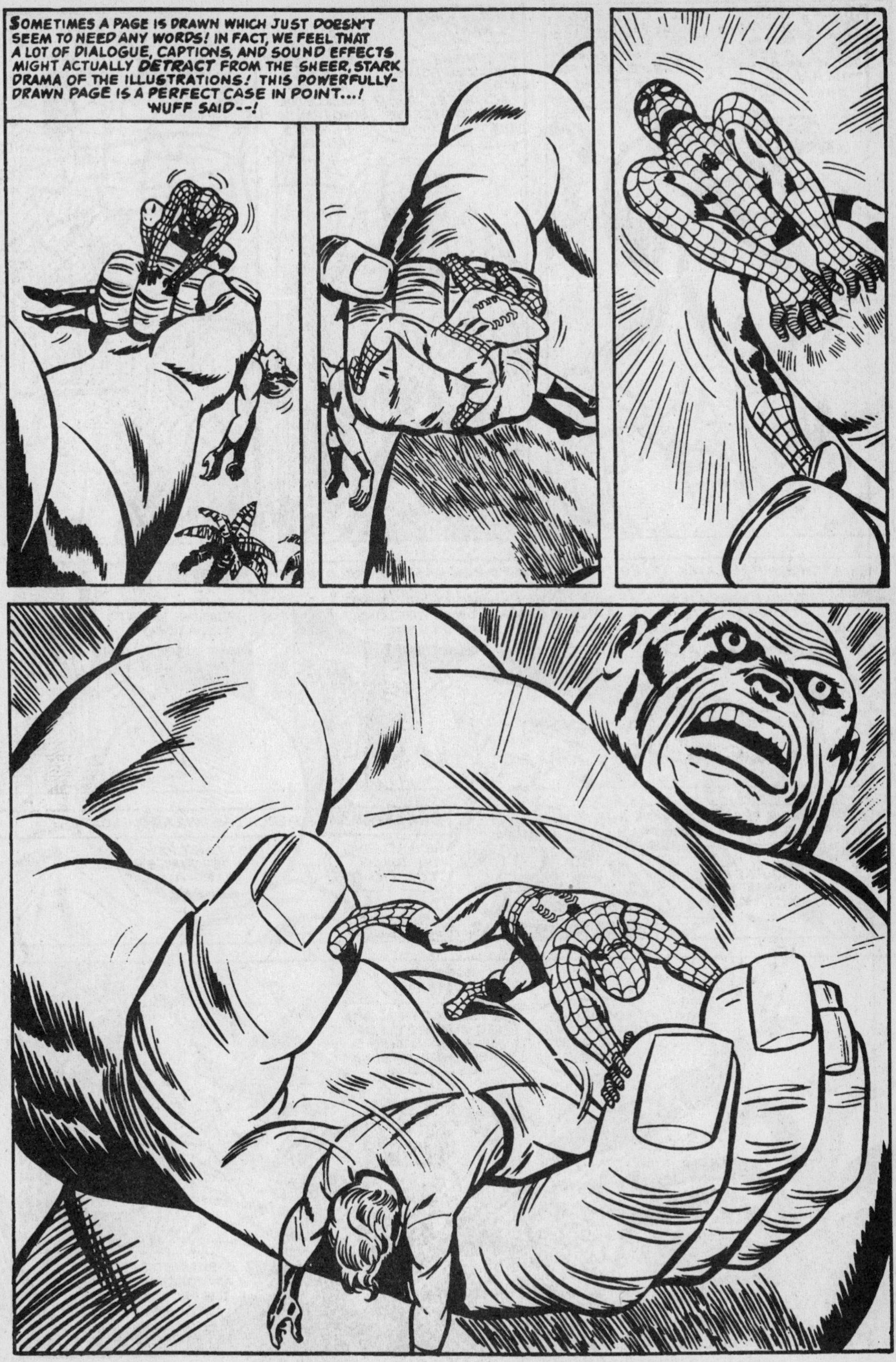
SOMETIMES A PAGE IS DRAWN WHICH JUST DOESN'T SEEM TO NEED ANY WORDS! IN FACT, WE FEEL THAT A LOT OF DIALOGUE, CAPTIONS, AND SOUND EFFECTS MIGHT ACTUALLY DETRACT FROM THE SHEER, STARK DRAMA OF THE ILLUSTRATIONS! THIS POWERFULLY-DRAWN PAGE IS A PERFECT CASE IN POINT...!
'NUFF SAID--!

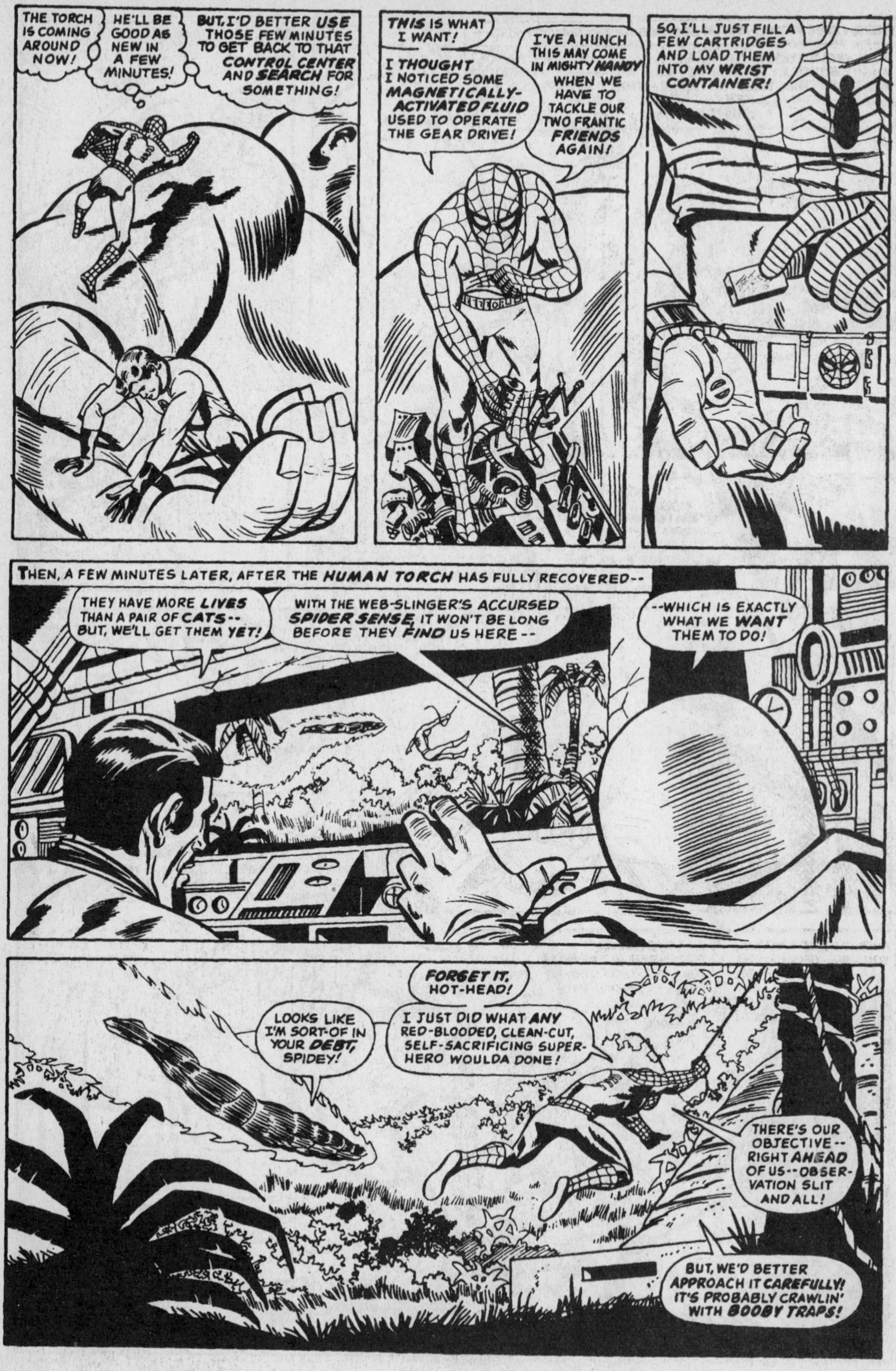
THE TORCH IS COMING AROUND NOW!
HE'LL BE GOOD AS NEW IN A FEW MINUTES!
BUT, I'D BETTER USE THOSE FEW MINUTES TO GET BACK TO THAT CONTROL CENTER AND SEARCH FOR SOMETHING!
THIS IS WHAT I WANT!
I THOUGHT I NOTICED SOME MAGNETICALLY-ACTIVATED FLUID USED TO OPERATE THE GEAR DRIVE!
I'VE A HUNCH THIS MAY COME IN MIGHTY HANDY WHEN WE HAVE TO TACKLE OUR TWO FRANTIC FRIENDS AGAIN!
SO, I'LL JUST FILL A FEW CARTRIDGES AND LOAD THEM INTO MY WRIST CONTAINER!
THEN, A FEW MINUTES LATER, AFTER THE HUMAN TORCH HAS FULLY RECOVERED--
THEY HAVE MORE LIVES THAN A PAIR OF CATS-- BUT, WE'LL GET THEM YET!
WITH THE WEB-SLINGER'S ACCURSED SPIDER SENSE, IT WON'T BE LONG BEFORE THEY FIND US HERE--
--WHICH IS EXACTLY WHAT WE WANT THEM TO DO!
LOOKS LIKE I'M SORT-OF IN YOUR DEBT, SPIDEY!
FORGET IT, HOT-HEAD!
I JUST DID WHAT ANY RED-BLOODED, CLEAN-CUT, SELF-SACRIFICING SUPER-HERO WOULDA DONE!
THERE'S OUR OBJECTIVE -- RIGHT AHEAD OF US--OBSERVATION SLIT AND ALL!
BUT, WE'D BETTER APPROACH IT CAREFULLY! IT'S PROBABLY CRAWLIN' WITH BOOBY TRAPS!

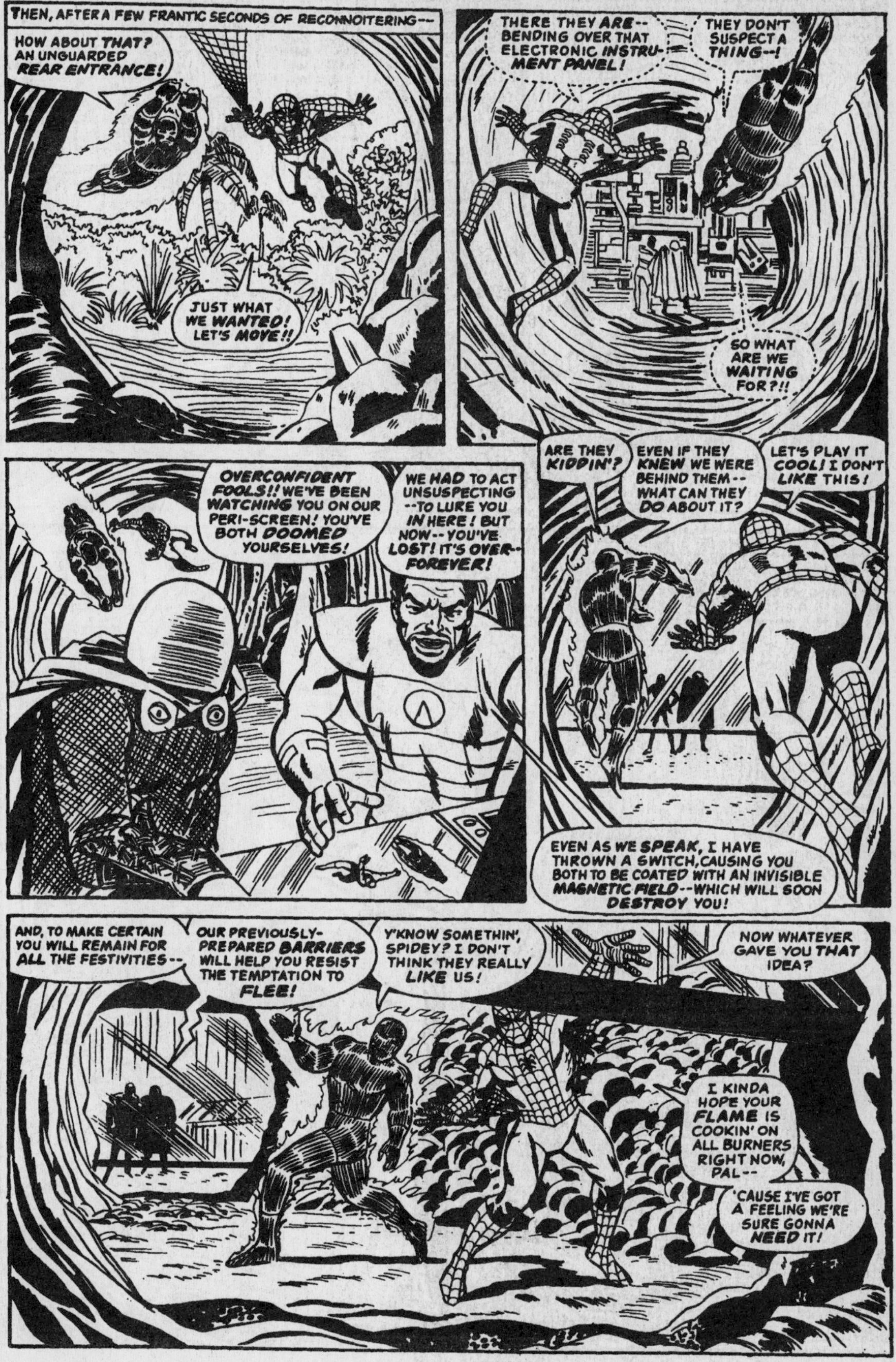
THEN, AFTER A FEW FRANTIC SECONDS OF RECONNOITERING--
HOW ABOUT THAT? AN UNGUARDED REAR ENTRANCE!
JUST WHAT WE WANTED! LET'S MOVE!!
THERE THEY ARE-- BENDING OVER THAT ELECTRONIC INSTRUMENT PANEL!
THEY DON'T SUSPECT A THING--!
SO WHAT ARE WE WAITING FOR?!!
OVERCONFIDENT FOOLS!! WE'VE BEEN WATCHING YOU ON OUR PERI-SCREEN! YOU'VE BOTH DOOMED YOURSELVES!
WE HAD TO ACT UNSUSPECTING --TO LURE YOU IN HERE! BUT NOW--YOU'VE LOST! IT'S OVER-- FOREVER!
ARE THEY KIDDIN'?
EVEN IF THEY KNEW WE WERE BEHIND THEM-- WHAT CAN THEY DO ABOUT IT?
LET'S PLAY IT COOL! I DON'T LIKE THIS!
EVEN AS WE SPEAK, I HAVE THROWN A SWITCH, CAUSING YOU BOTH TO BE COATED WITH AN INVISIBLE MAGNETIC FIELD--WHICH WILL SOON DESTROY YOU!
AND, TO MAKE CERTAIN YOU WILL REMAIN FOR ALL THE FESTIVITIES--
OUR PREVIOUSLY-PREPARED BARRIERS WILL HELP YOU RESIST THE TEMPTATION TO FLEE!
Y'KNOW SOMETHIN', SPIDEY? I DON'T THINK THEY REALLY LIKE US!
NOW WHATEVER GAVE YOU THAT IDEA?
I KINDA HOPE YOUR FLAME IS COOKIN' ON ALL BURNERS RIGHT NOW, PAL--
'CAUSE I'VE GOT A FEELING WE'RE SURE GONNA NEED IT!

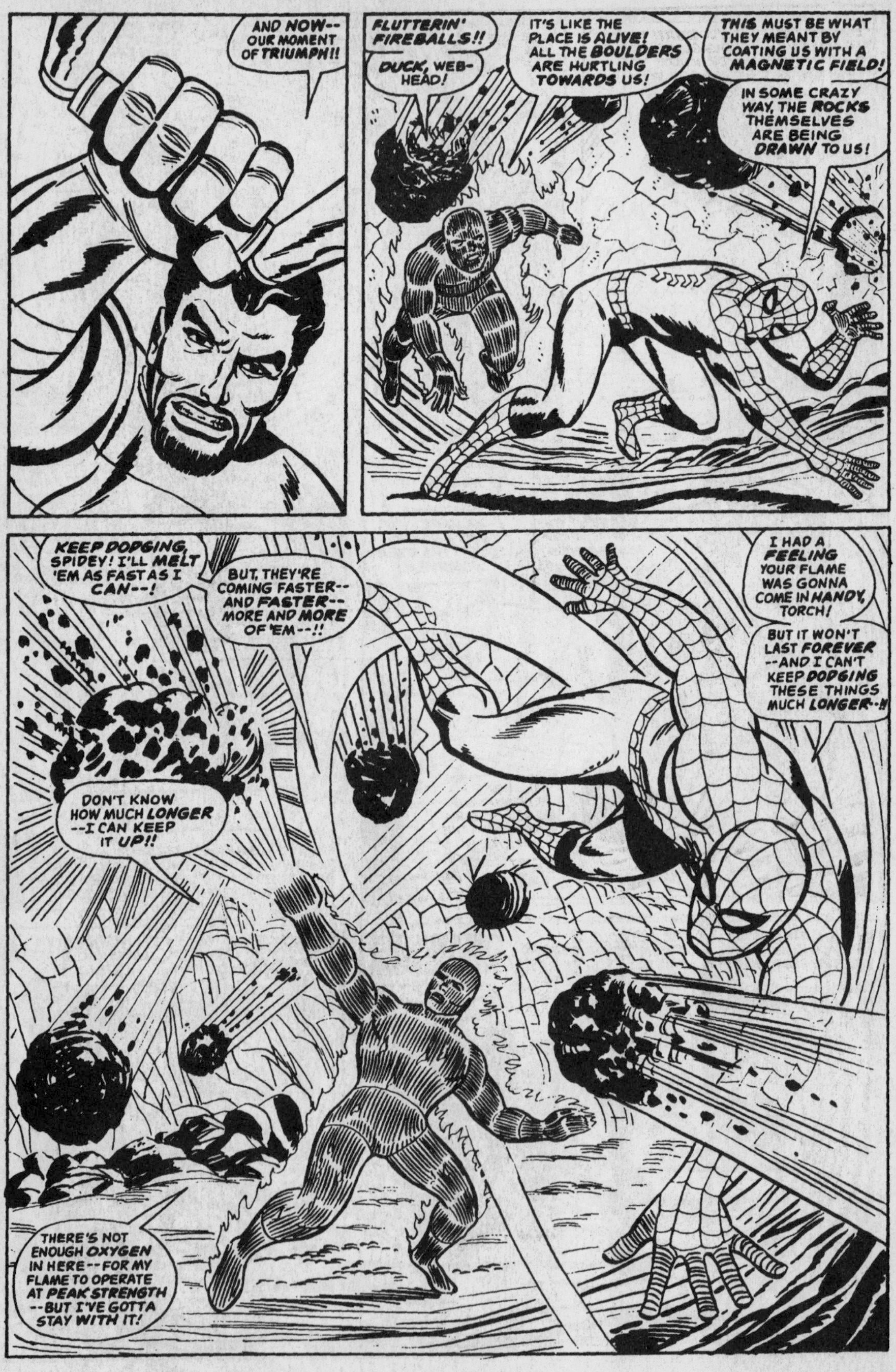
AND NOW-- OUR MOMENT OF TRIUMPH!!
FLUTTERIN' FIREBALLS!!
DUCK, WEB-HEAD!
IT'S LIKE THE PLACE IS ALIVE! ALL THE BOULDERS ARE HURTLING TOWARDS US!
THIS MUST BE WHAT THEY MEANT BY COATING US WITH A MAGNETIC FIELD!
IN SOME CRAZY WAY, THE ROCKS THEMSELVES ARE BEING DRAWN TO US!
KEEP DODGING, SPIDEY! I'LL MELT 'EM AS FAST AS I CAN--!
BUT, THEY'RE COMING FASTER--AND FASTER--MORE AND MORE OF 'EM--!!
I HAD A FEELING YOUR FLAME WAS GONNA COME IN HANDY, TORCH!
BUT IT WON'T LAST FOREVER --AND I CAN'T KEEP DODGING THESE THINGS MUCH LONGER--!!
DON'T KNOW HOW MUCH LONGER --I CAN KEEP IT UP!!
THERE'S NOT ENOUGH OXYGEN IN HERE--FOR MY FLAME TO OPERATE AT PEAK STRENGTH --BUT I'VE GOTTA STAY WITH IT!

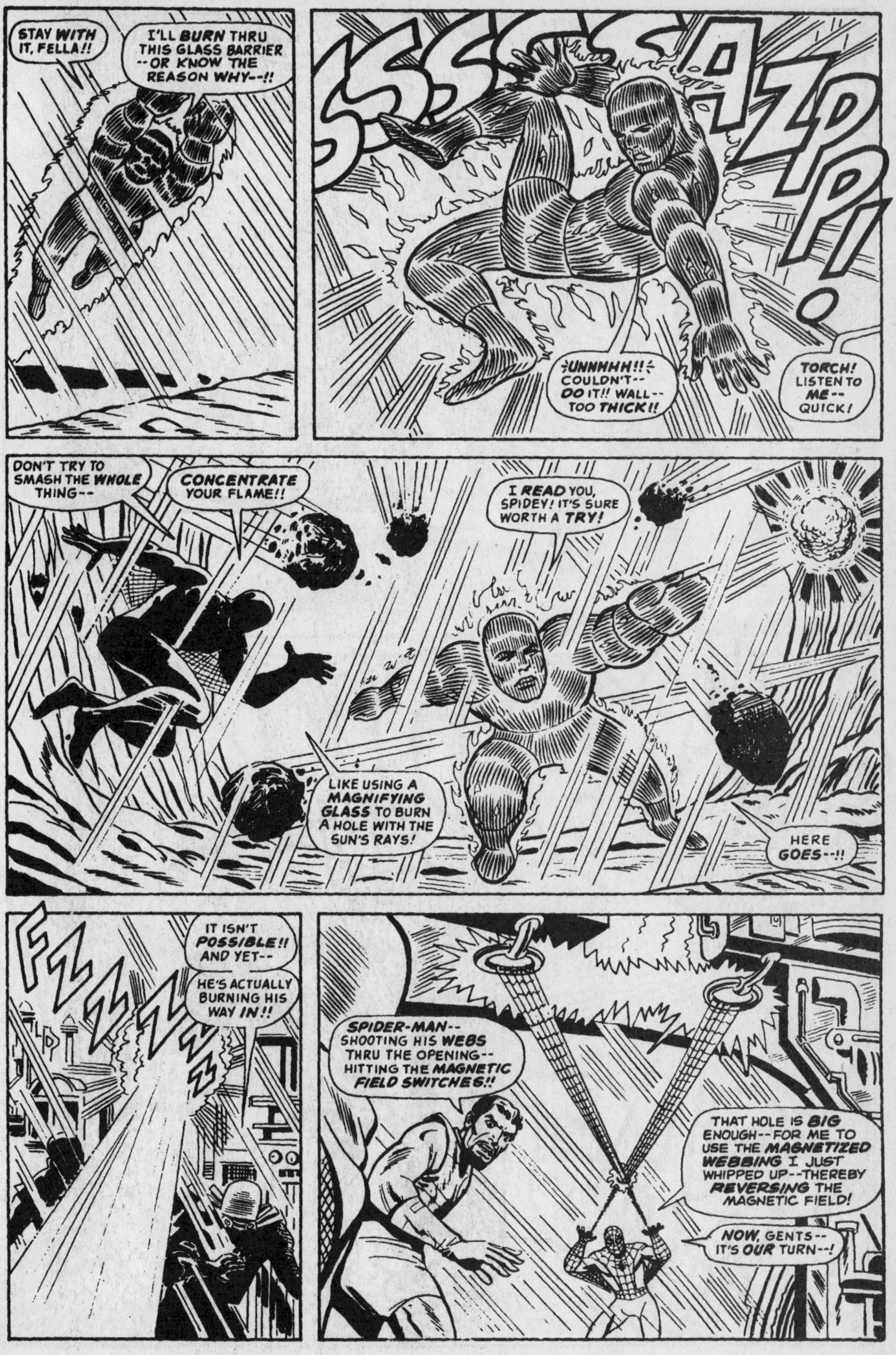
STAY WITH IT, FELLA!!
I'LL BURN THRU THIS GLASS BARRIER --OR KNOW THE REASON WHY--!!
SSSSSSAZAPP!
UNNHHH!! COULDN'T-- DO IT!! WALL-- TOO THICK!!
TORCH! LISTEN TO ME-- QUICK!
DON'T TRY TO SMASH THE WHOLE THING--
CONCENTRATE YOUR FLAME!!
I READ YOU, SPIDEY! IT'S SURE WORTH A TRY!
LIKE USING A MAGNIFYING GLASS TO BURN A HOLE WITH THE SUN'S RAYS!
HERE GOES--!!
FZZZZZZ
IT ISN'T POSSIBLE!! AND YET--
HE'S ACTUALLY BURNING HIS WAY IN!!
SPIDER-MAN-- SHOOTING HIS WEBS THRU THE OPENING-- HITTING THE MAGNETIC FIELD SWITCHES!!
THAT HOLE IS BIG ENOUGH--FOR ME TO USE THE MAGNETIZED WEBBING I JUST WHIPPED UP--THEREBY REVERSING THE MAGNETIC FIELD!
NOW, GENTS-- IT'S OUR TURN--!

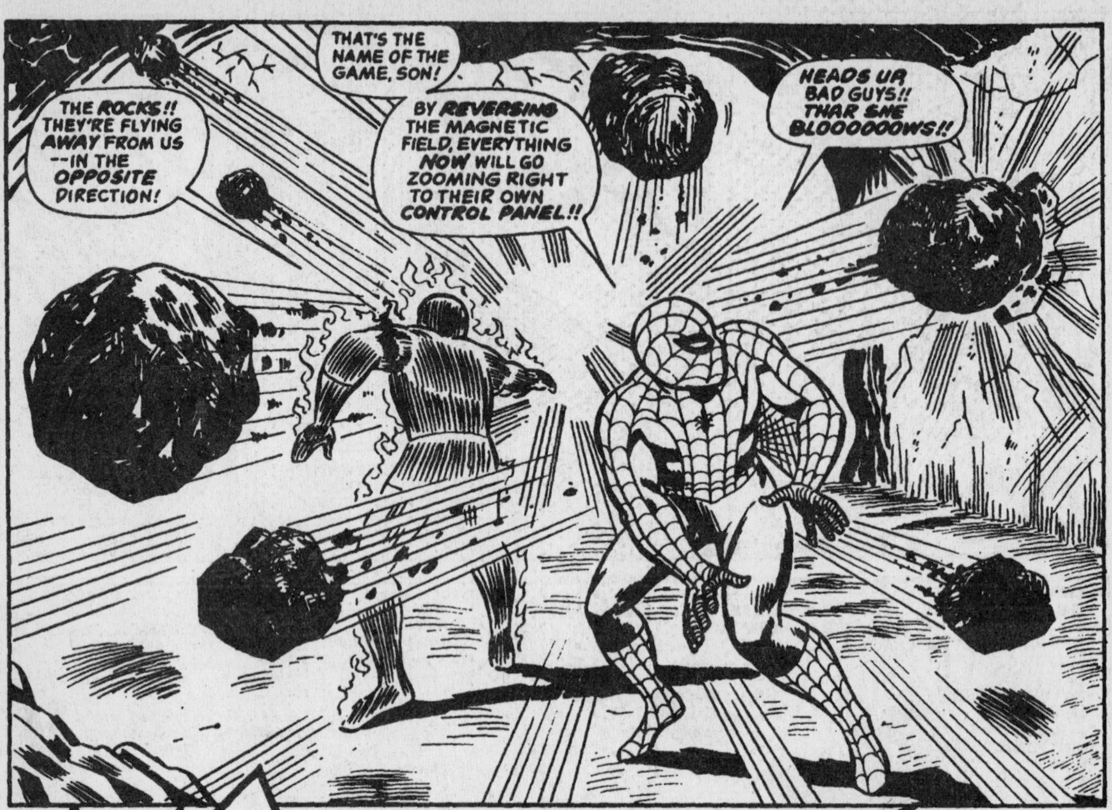
THE ROCKS!! THEY'RE FLYING AWAY FROM US --IN THE OPPOSITE DIRECTION!
THAT'S THE NAME OF THE GAME, SON!
BY REVERSING THE MAGNETIC FIELD, EVERYTHING NOW WILL GO ZOOMING RIGHT TO THEIR OWN CONTROL PANEL!!
HEADS UP, BAD GUYS!! THAR SHE BLOOOOOOWS!!

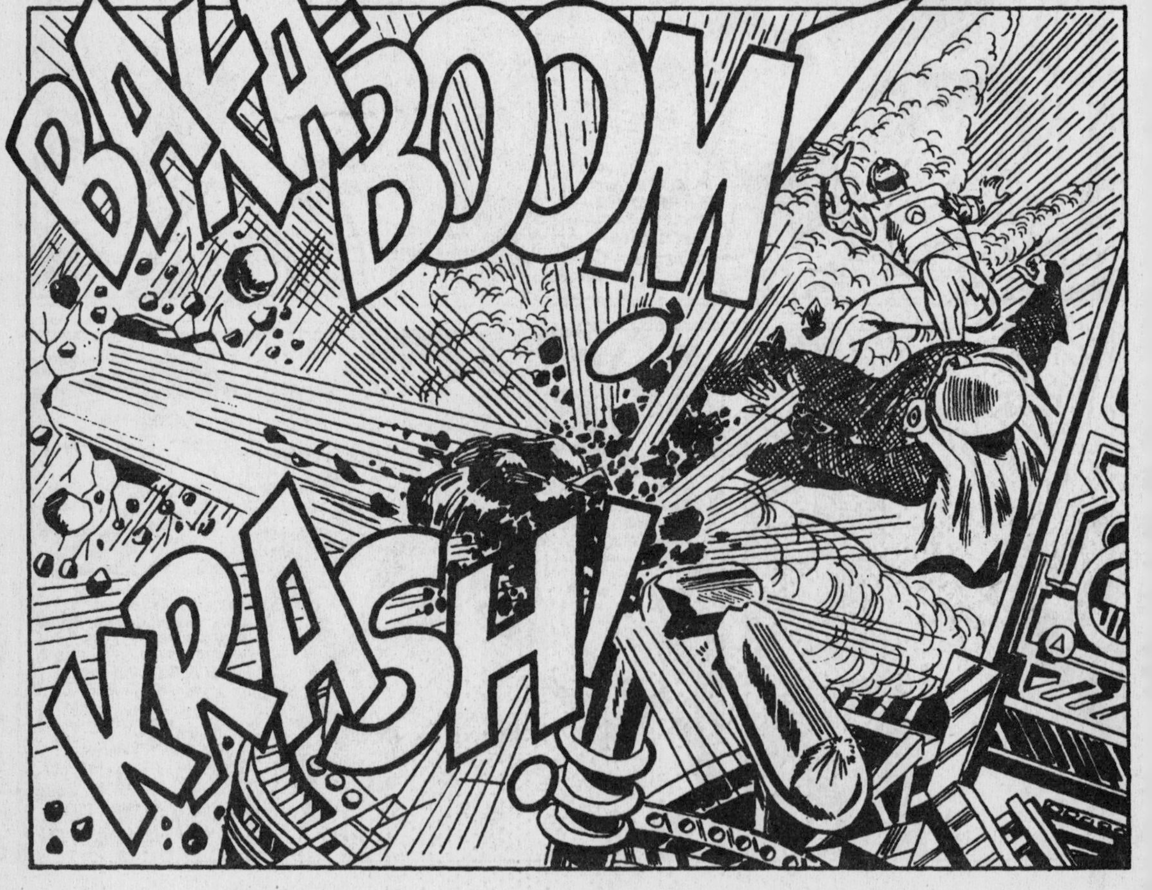
BA-KA-BOOOM
KRASH!

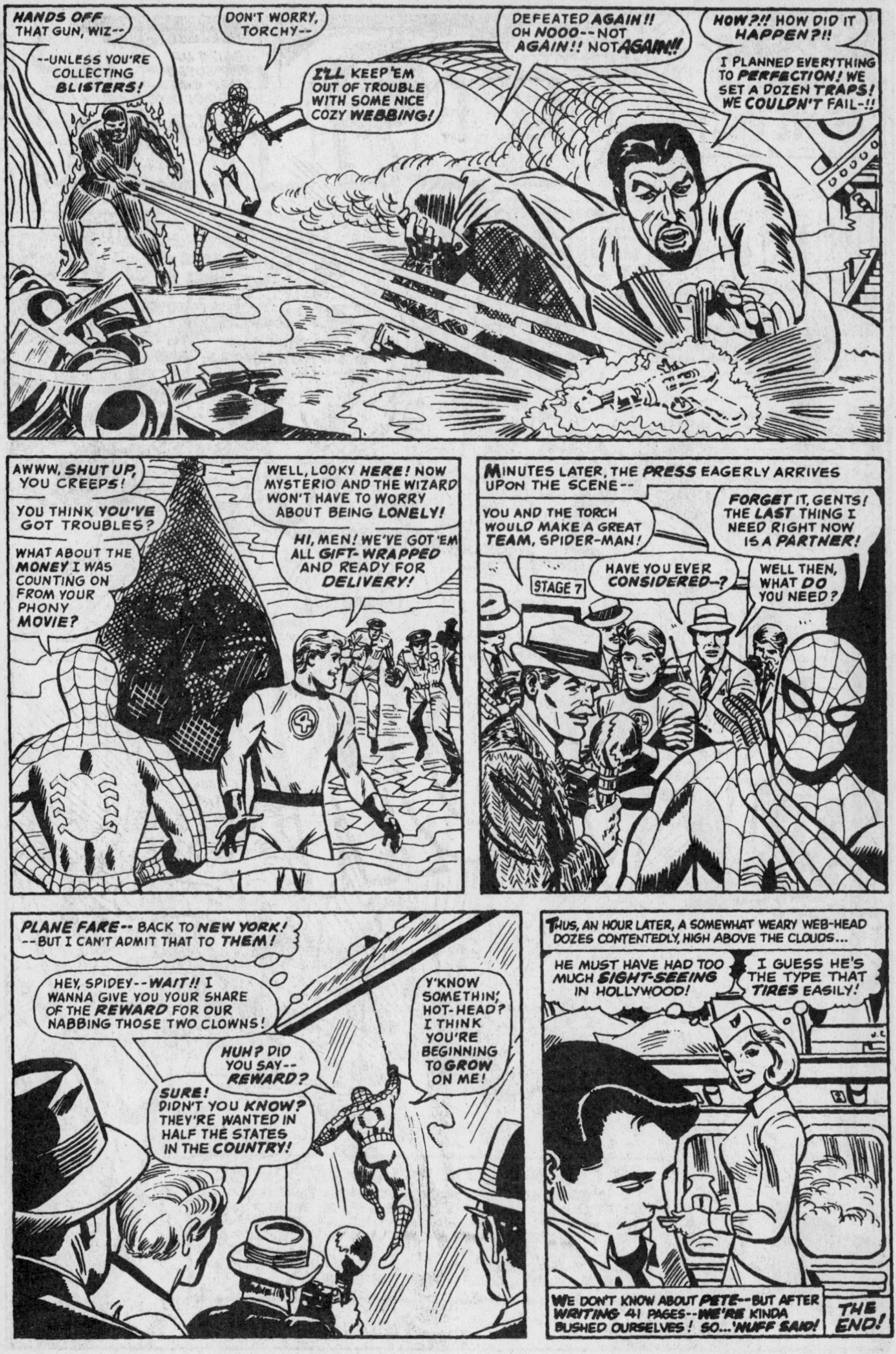
HANDS OFF THAT GUN, WIZ--
--UNLESS YOU'RE COLLECTING BLISTERS!
DON'T WORRY, TORCHY--
I'LL KEEP 'EM OUT OF TROUBLE WITH SOME NICE COZY WEBBING!
DEFEATED AGAIN!! OH NOOO--NOT AGAIN!! NOT AGAIN!!
HOW?!! HOW DID IT HAPPEN?!!
I PLANNED EVERYTHING TO PERFECTION! WE SET A DOZEN TRAPS! WE COULDN'T FAIL-!!
AWWW, SHUT UP, YOU CREEPS!
YOU THINK YOU'VE GOT TROUBLES?
WHAT ABOUT THE MONEY I WAS COUNTING ON FROM YOUR PHONY MOVIE?
WELL, LOOKY HERE! NOW MYSTERIO AND THE WIZARD WON'T HAVE TO WORRY ABOUT BEING LONELY!
HI, MEN! WE'VE GOT 'EM ALL GIFT-WRAPPED AND READY FOR DELIVERY!
MINUTES LATER, THE PRESS EAGERLY ARRIVES UPON THE SCENE--
YOU AND THE TORCH WOULD MAKE A GREAT TEAM, SPIDER-MAN!
FORGET IT, GENTS! THE LAST THING I NEED RIGHT NOW IS A PARTNER!
STAGE 7
HAVE YOU EVER CONSIDERED--?
WELL THEN, WHAT DO YOU NEED?
PLANE FARE-- BACK TO NEW YORK! --BUT I CAN'T ADMIT THAT TO THEM!
HEY, SPIDEY--WAIT!! I WANNA GIVE YOU YOUR SHARE OF THE REWARD FOR OUR NABBING THOSE TWO CLOWNS!
Y'KNOW SOMETHIN', HOT-HEAD? I THINK YOU'RE BEGINNING TO GROW ON ME!
HUH? DID YOU SAY-- REWARD?
SURE! DIDN'T YOU KNOW? THEY'RE WANTED IN HALF THE STATES IN THE COUNTRY!
THUS, AN HOUR LATER, A SOMEWHAT WEARY WEB-HEAD DOZES CONTENTEDLY, HIGH ABOVE THE CLOUDS...
HE MUST HAVE HAD TOO MUCH SIGHT-SEEING IN HOLLYWOOD!
I GUESS HE'S THE TYPE THAT TIRES EASILY!
WE DON'T KNOW ABOUT PETE--BUT AFTER WRITING 41 PAGES--WE'RE KINDA BUSHED OURSELVES! SO...'NUFF SAID!
THE END!

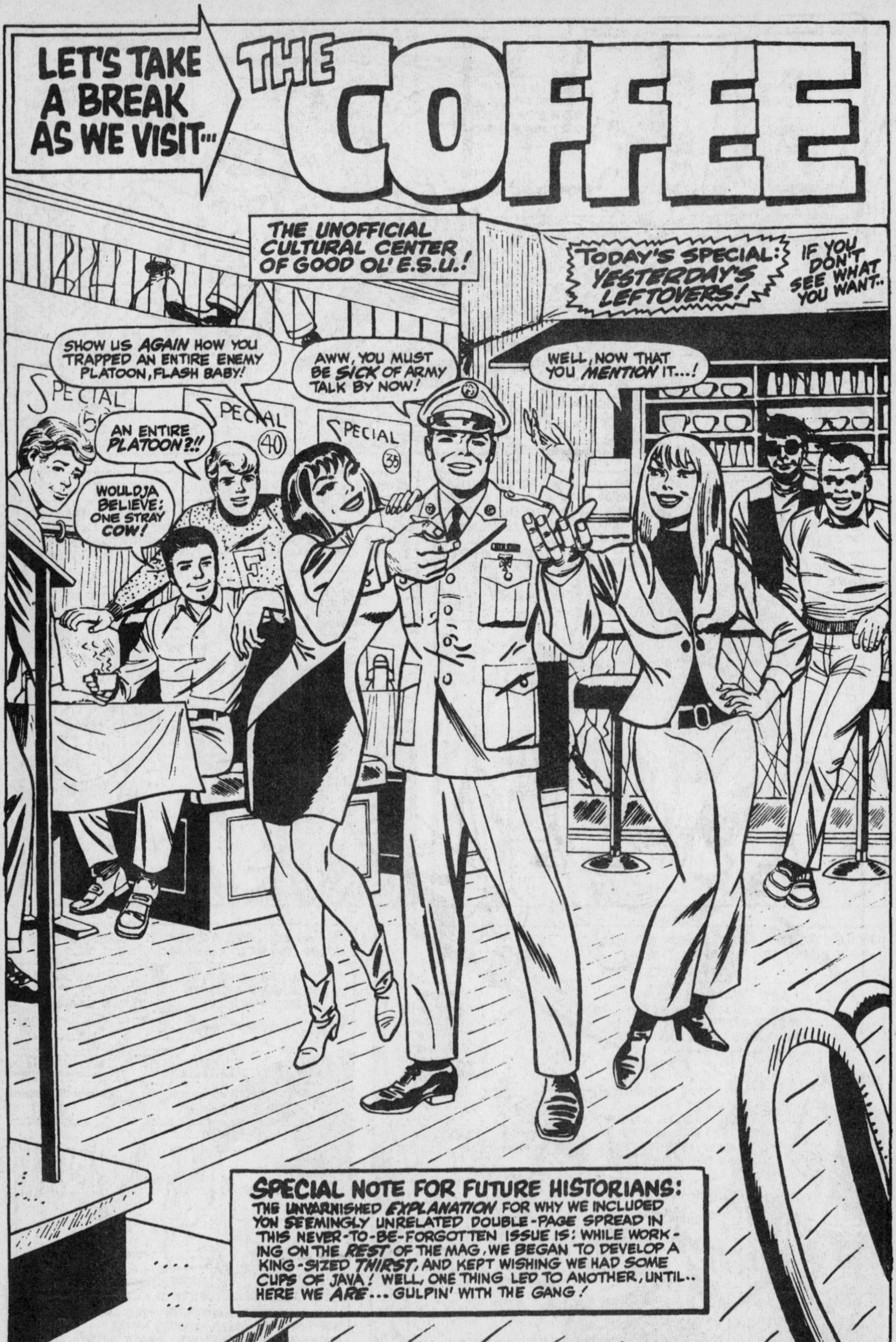
LET'S TAKE A BREAK AS WE VISIT...
THE COFFEE
THE UNOFFICIAL CULTURAL CENTER OF GOOD OL' E.S.U.!
TODAY'S SPECIAL: YESTERDAY'S LEFTOVERS!
IF YOU DON'T SEE WHAT YOU WANT..
SHOW US AGAIN HOW YOU TRAPPED AN ENTIRE ENEMY PLATOON, FLASH BABY!
AN ENTIRE PLATOON?!!
WOULDJA BELIEVE: ONE STRAY COW!
AWW, YOU MUST BE SICK OF ARMY TALK BY NOW!
WELL, NOW THAT YOU MENTION IT...!
SPECIAL 5
SPECIAL 40
SPECIAL 35
SPECIAL NOTE FOR FUTURE HISTORIANS:
THE UNVARNISHED EXPLANATION FOR WHY WE INCLUDED YON SEEMINGLY UNRELATED DOUBLE-PAGE SPREAD IN THIS NEVER-TO-BE-FORGOTTEN ISSUE IS: WHILE WORKING ON THE REST OF THE MAG, WE BEGAN TO DEVELOP A KING-SIZED THIRST, AND KEPT WISHING WE HAD SOME CUPS OF JAVA! WELL, ONE THING LED TO ANOTHER, UNTIL.. HERE WE ARE... GULPIN' WITH THE GANG!

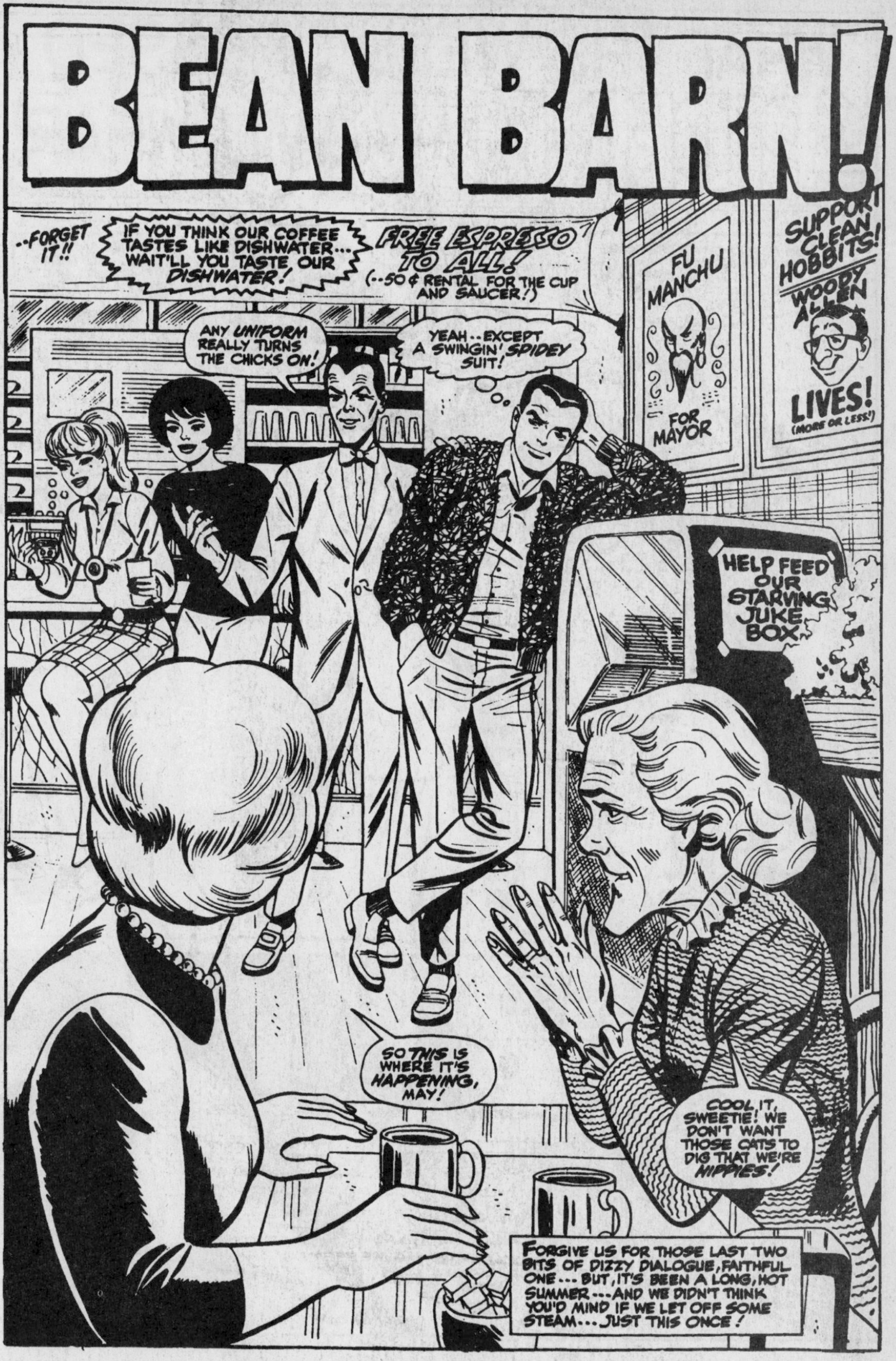
BEAN BARN!
..FORGET IT!!
IF YOU THINK OUR COFFEE TASTES LIKE DISHWATER... WAIT'LL YOU TASTE OUR DISHWATER!
FREE ESPRESSO TO ALL! (..50¢ RENTAL FOR THE CUP AND SAUCER!)
SUPPORT CLEAN HOBBITS!
FU MANCHU FOR MAYOR
WOODY ALLEN LIVES! (MORE OR LESS!)
ANY UNIFORM REALLY TURNS THE CHICKS ON!
YEAH..EXCEPT A SWINGIN' SPIDEY SUIT!
HELP FEED OUR STARVING JUKE BOX.
SO THIS IS WHERE IT'S HAPPENING, MAY!
COOL IT, SWEETIE! WE DON'T WANT THOSE CATS TO DIG THAT WE'RE HIPPIES!
FORGIVE US FOR THOSE LAST TWO BITS OF DIZZY DIALOGUE, FAITHFUL ONE... BUT, IT'S BEEN A LONG, HOT SUMMER...AND WE DIDN'T THINK YOU'D MIND IF WE LET OFF SOME STEAM... JUST THIS ONCE!

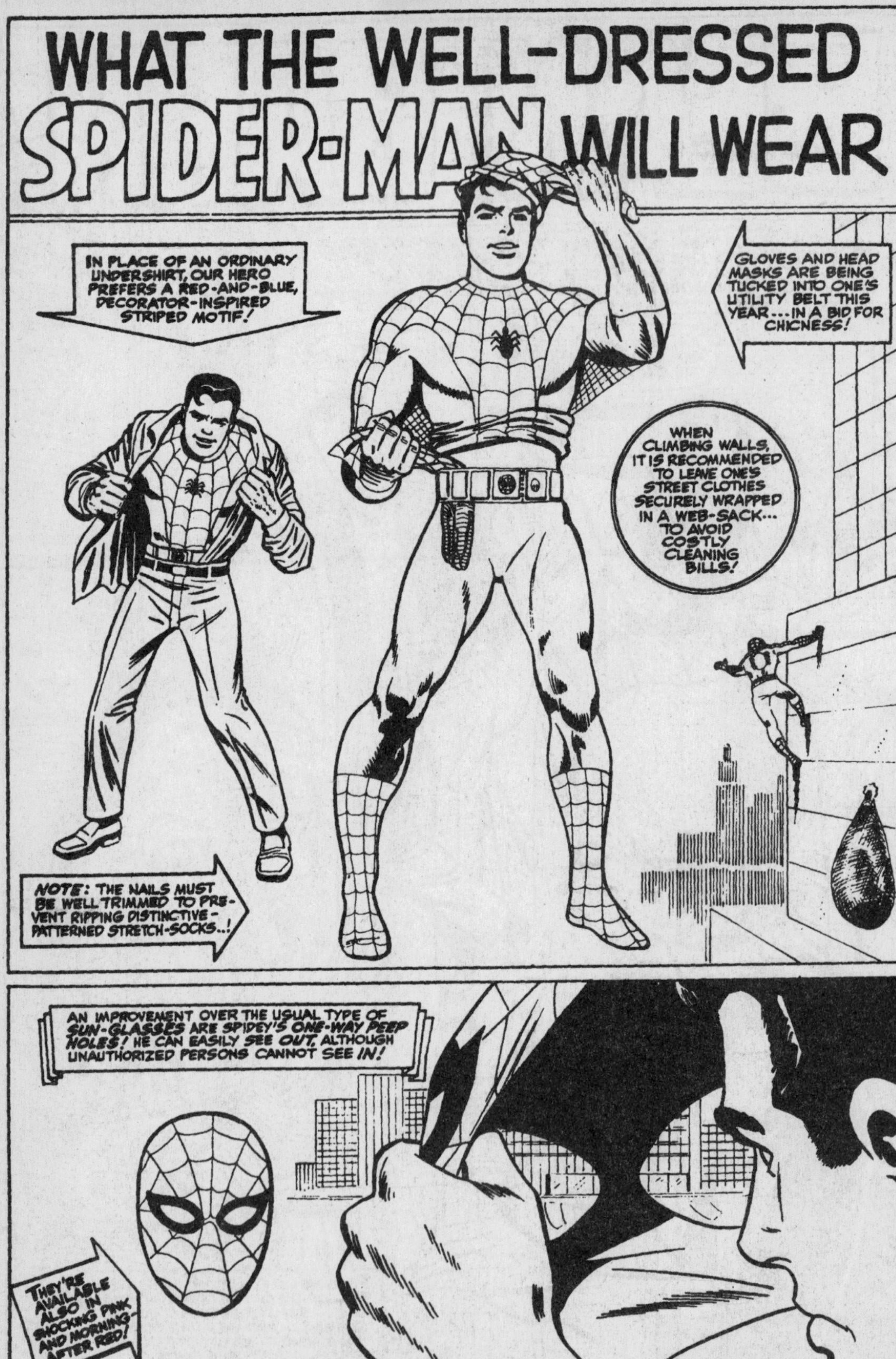
WHAT THE WELL-DRESSED SPIDER-MAN WILL WEAR
IN PLACE OF AN ORDINARY UNDERSHIRT, OUR HERO PREFERS A RED-AND-BLUE, DECORATOR-INSPIRED STRIPED MOTIF!
GLOVES AND HEAD MASKS ARE BEING TUCKED INTO ONE'S UTILITY BELT THIS YEAR... IN A BID FOR CHICNESS!
WHEN CLIMBING WALLS, IT IS RECOMMENDED TO LEAVE ONE'S STREET CLOTHES SECURELY WRAPPED IN A WEB-SACK... TO AVOID COSTLY CLEANING BILLS!
NOTE: THE NAILS MUST BE WELL TRIMMED TO PREVENT RIPPING DISTINCTIVE-PATTERNED STRETCH-SOCKS...!
AN IMPROVEMENT OVER THE USUAL TYPE OF SUN-GLASSES ARE SPIDEY'S ONE-WAY PEEP HOLES! HE CAN EASILY SEE OUT, ALTHOUGH UNAUTHORIZED PERSONS CANNOT SEE IN!
THEY'RE AVAILABLE ALSO IN SHOCKING PINK AND MORNING-AFTER RED!

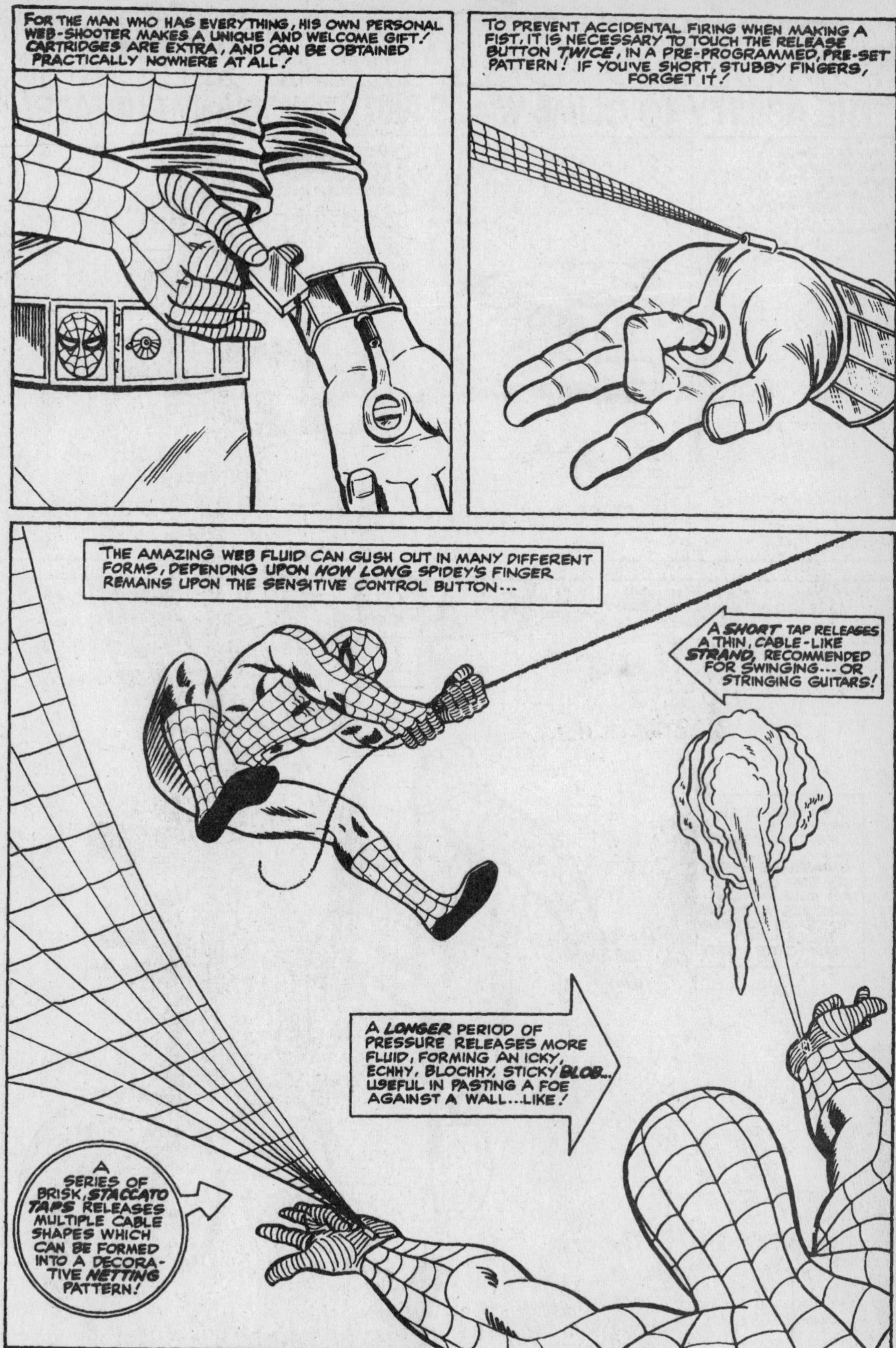
FOR THE MAN WHO HAS EVERYTHING, HIS OWN PERSONAL WEB-SHOOTER MAKES A UNIQUE AND WELCOME GIFT! CARTRIDGES ARE EXTRA, AND CAN BE OBTAINED PRACTICALLY NOWHERE AT ALL!
TO PREVENT ACCIDENTAL FIRING WHEN MAKING A FIST, IT IS NECESSARY TO TOUCH THE RELEASE BUTTON TWICE, IN A PRE-PROGRAMMED, PRE-SET PATTERN! IF YOU'VE SHORT, STUBBY FINGERS, FORGET IT!
THE AMAZING WEB FLUID CAN GUSH OUT IN MANY DIFFERENT FORMS, DEPENDING UPON HOW LONG SPIDEY'S FINGER REMAINS UPON THE SENSITIVE CONTROL BUTTON...
A SHORT TAP RELEASES A THIN, CABLE-LIKE STRAND, RECOMMENDED FOR SWINGING... OR STRINGING GUITARS!
A LONGER PERIOD OF PRESSURE RELEASES MORE FLUID, FORMING AN ICKY, ECHHY, BLOCHHY, STICKY BLOB... USEFUL IN PASTING A FOE AGAINST A WALL...LIKE!
A SERIES OF BRISK, STACCATO TAPS RELEASES MULTIPLE CABLE SHAPES WHICH CAN BE FORMED INTO A DECORATIVE NETTING PATTERN!

SPIDEY'S GREATEST TALENT

THE ABILITY TO CLIMB WALLS AND STICK TO ANY SURFACE!

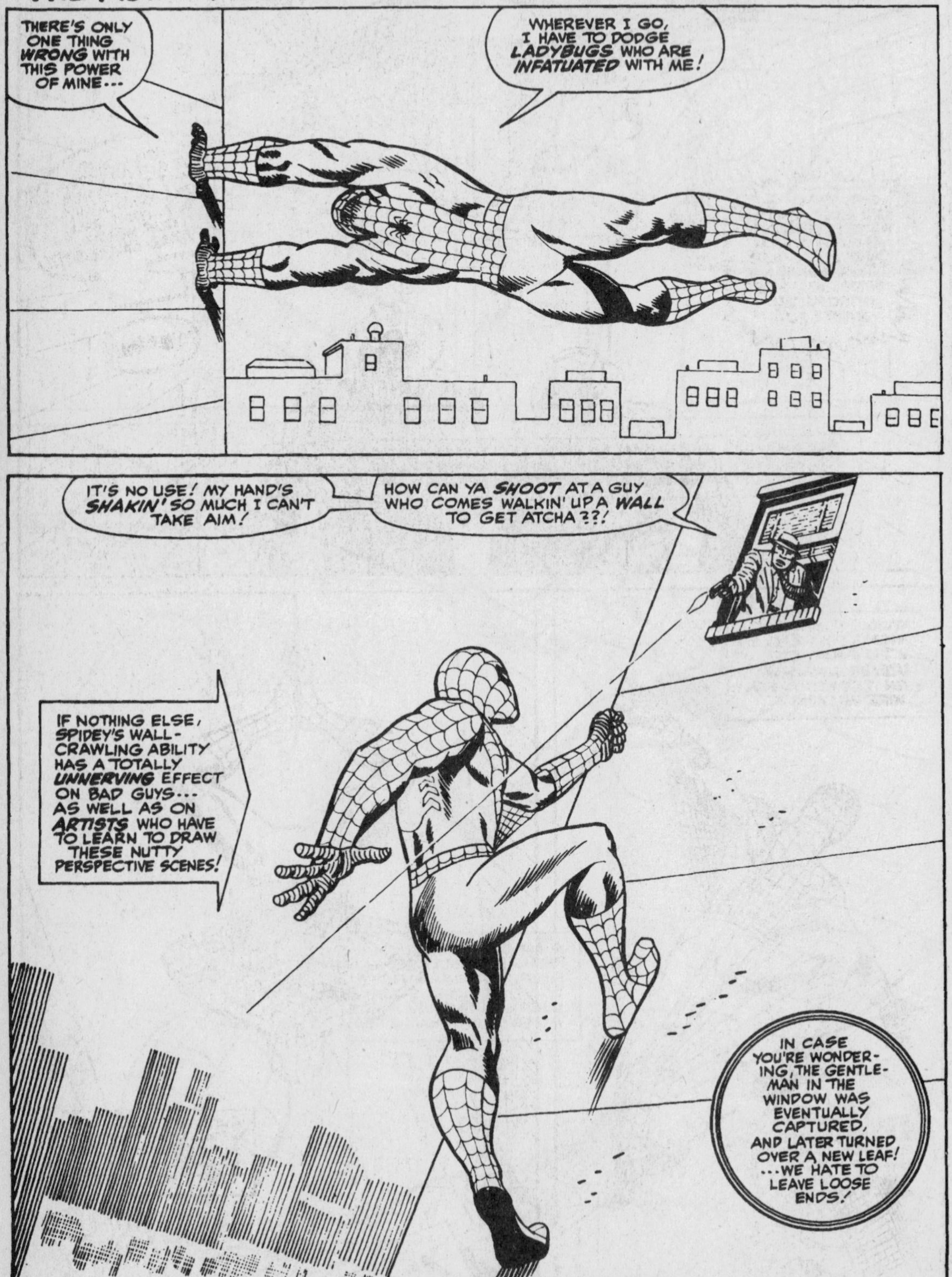
THERE'S ONLY ONE THING WRONG WITH THIS POWER OF MINE---
WHEREVER I GO, I HAVE TO DODGE LADYBUGS WHO ARE INFATUATED WITH ME!
IT'S NO USE! MY HAND'S SHAKIN' SO MUCH I CAN'T TAKE AIM!
HOW CAN YA SHOOT AT A GUY WHO COMES WALKIN' UP A WALL TO GET ATCHA??!
IF NOTHING ELSE, SPIDEY'S WALL-CRAWLING ABILITY HAS A TOTALLY UNNERVING EFFECT ON BAD GUYS... AS WELL AS ON ARTISTS WHO HAVE TO LEARN TO DRAW THESE NUTTY PERSPECTIVE SCENES!
IN CASE YOU'RE WONDERING, THE GENTLEMAN IN THE WINDOW WAS EVENTUALLY CAPTURED, AND LATER TURNED OVER A NEW LEAF! ...WE HATE TO LEAVE LOOSE ENDS!

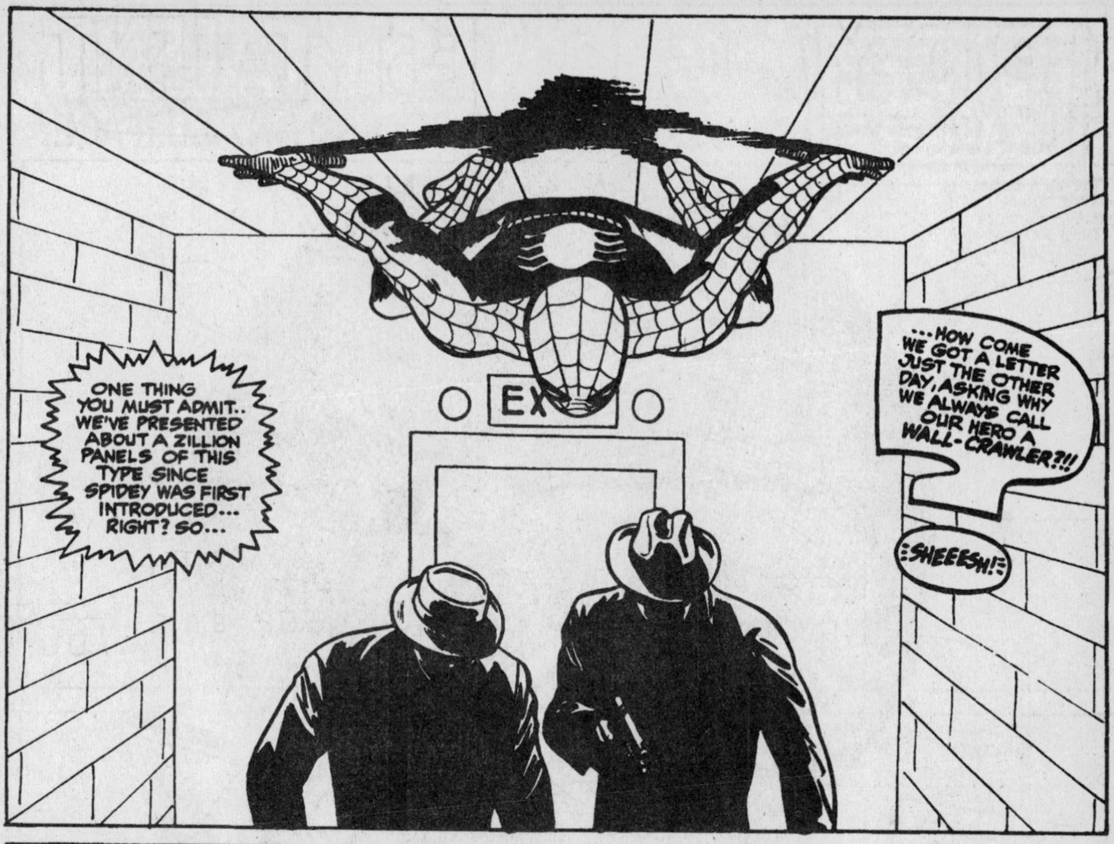
ONE THING YOU MUST ADMIT.. WE'VE PRESENTED ABOUT A ZILLION PANELS OF THIS TYPE SINCE SPIDEY WAS FIRST INTRODUCED... RIGHT? SO...
...HOW COME WE GOT A LETTER JUST THE OTHER DAY, ASKING WHY WE ALWAYS CALL OUR HERO A WALL-CRAWLER?!!
SHEEESH!
EX

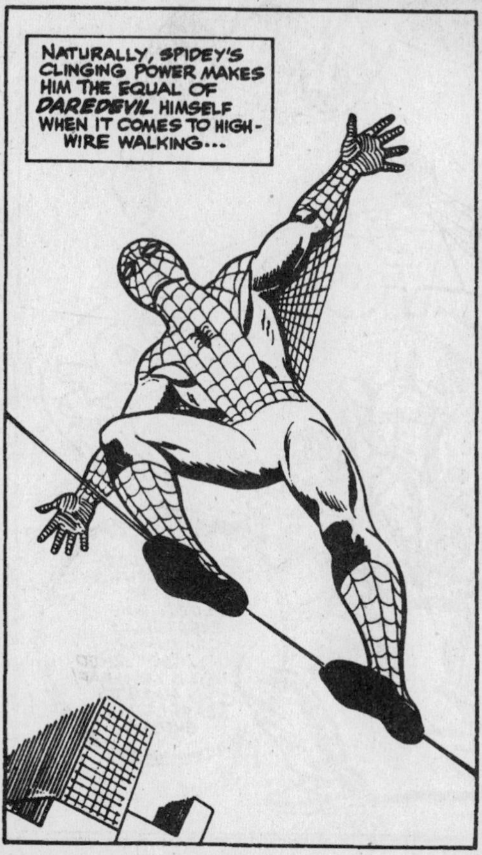
NATURALLY, SPIDEY'S CLINGING POWER MAKES HIM THE EQUAL OF DAREDEVIL HIMSELF WHEN IT COMES TO HIGH-WIRE WALKING...

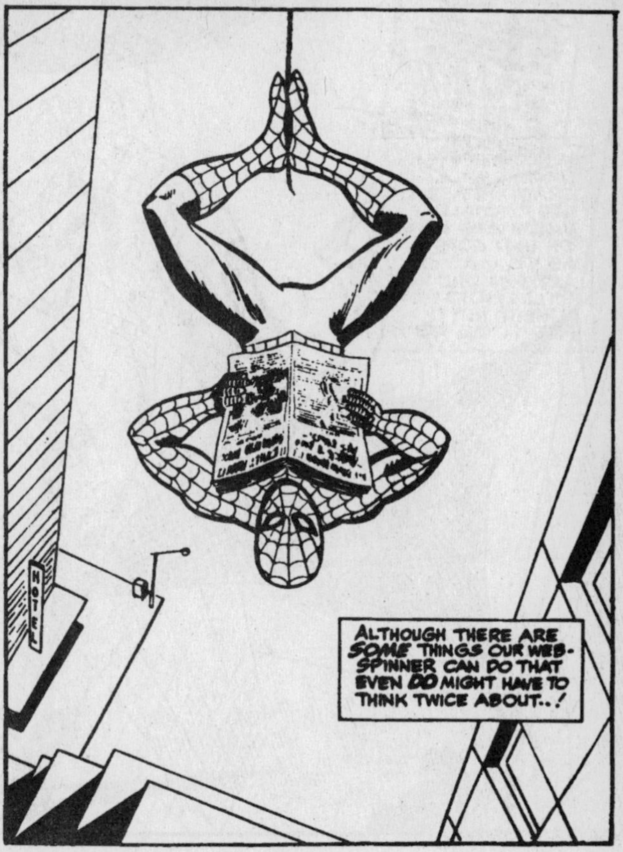
HOTEL
ALTHOUGH THERE ARE SOME THINGS OUR WEB-SPINNER CAN DO THAT EVEN DD MIGHT HAVE TO THINK TWICE ABOUT..!

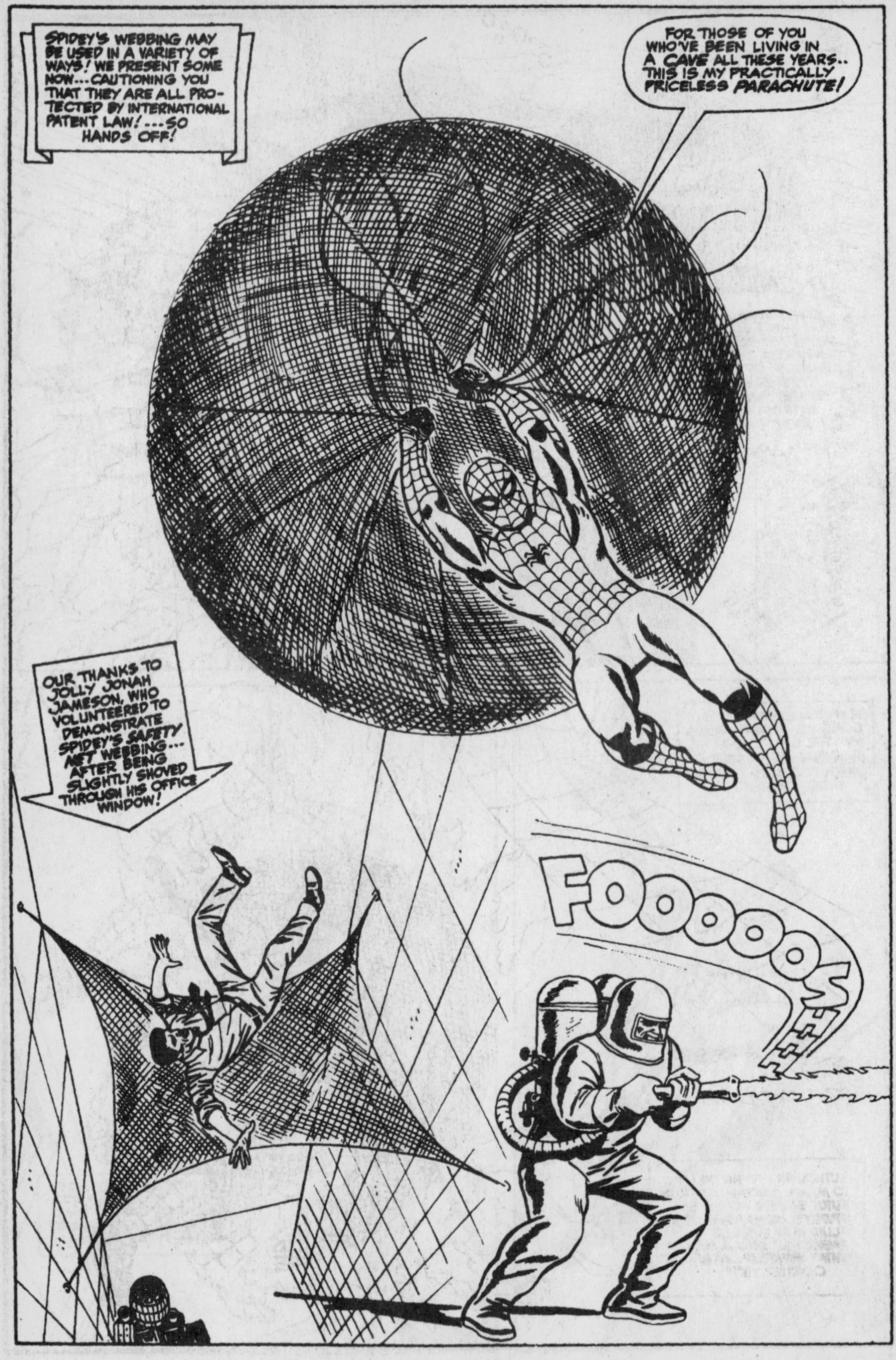
SPIDEY'S WEBBING MAY BE USED IN A VARIETY OF WAYS! WE PRESENT SOME NOW...CAUTIONING YOU THAT THEY ARE ALL PROTECTED BY INTERNATIONAL PATENT LAW! ...SO HANDS OFF!
FOR THOSE OF YOU WHO'VE BEEN LIVING IN A CAVE ALL THESE YEARS.. THIS IS MY PRACTICALLY PRICELESS PARACHUTE!
OUR THANKS TO JOLLY JONAH JAMESON, WHO VOLUNTEERED TO DEMONSTRATE SPIDEY'S SAFETY NET WEBBING... AFTER BEING SLIGHTLY SHOVED THROUGH HIS OFFICE WINDOW!
FOOOOOSHHH

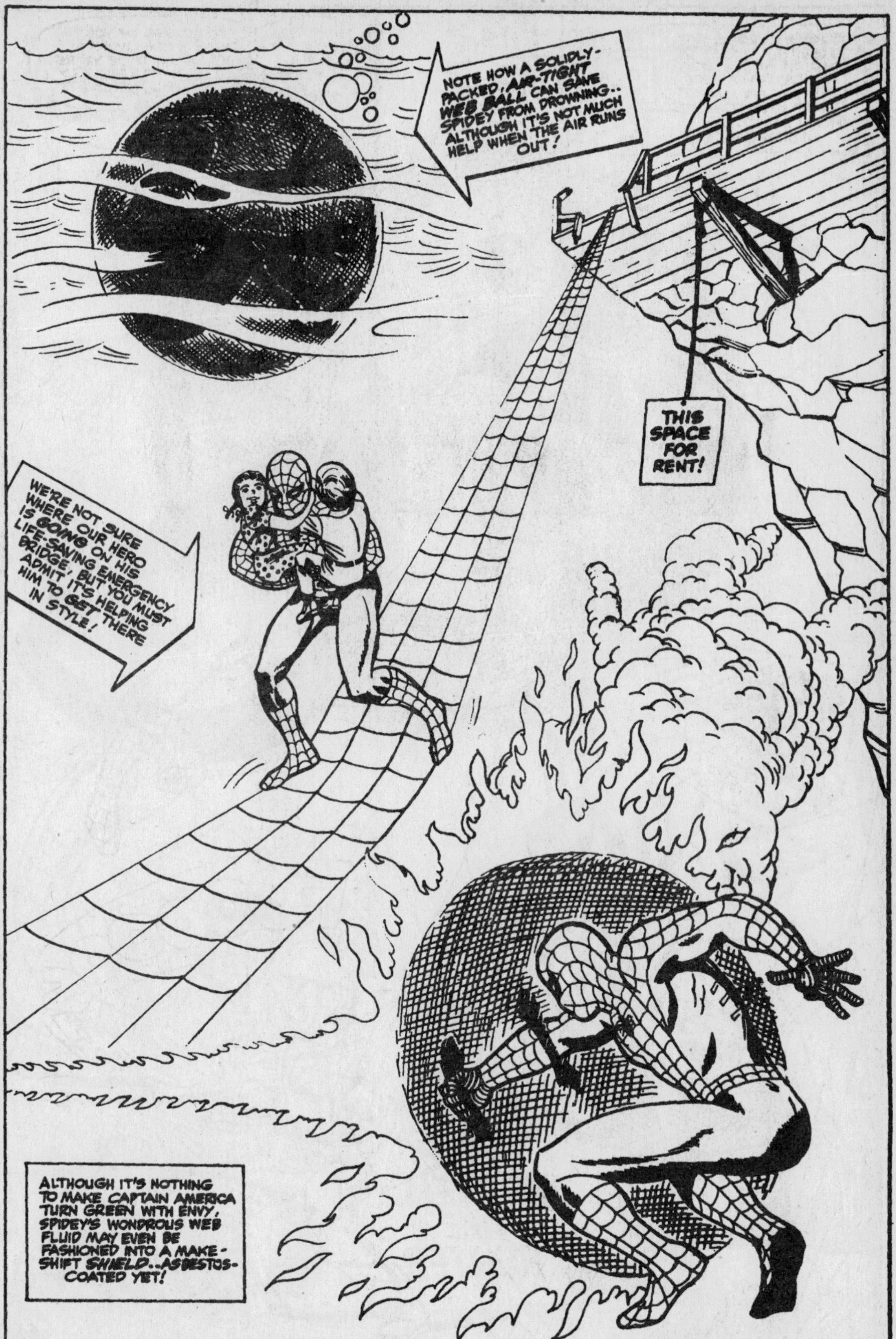
NOTE HOW A SOLIDLY-PACKED, AIR-TIGHT WEB BALL CAN SAVE SPIDEY FROM DROWNING.. ALTHOUGH IT'S NOT MUCH HELP WHEN THE AIR RUNS OUT!
THIS SPACE FOR RENT!
WE'RE NOT SURE WHERE OUR HERO IS GOING ON HIS LIFE-SAVING EMERGENCY BRIDGE, BUT YOU MUST ADMIT IT'S HELPING HIM TO GET THERE IN STYLE!
ALTHOUGH IT'S NOTHING TO MAKE CAPTAIN AMERICA TURN GREEN WITH ENVY, SPIDEY'S WONDROUS WEB FLUID MAY EVEN BE FASHIONED INTO A MAKE-SHIFT SHIELD..ASBESTOS-COATED YET!

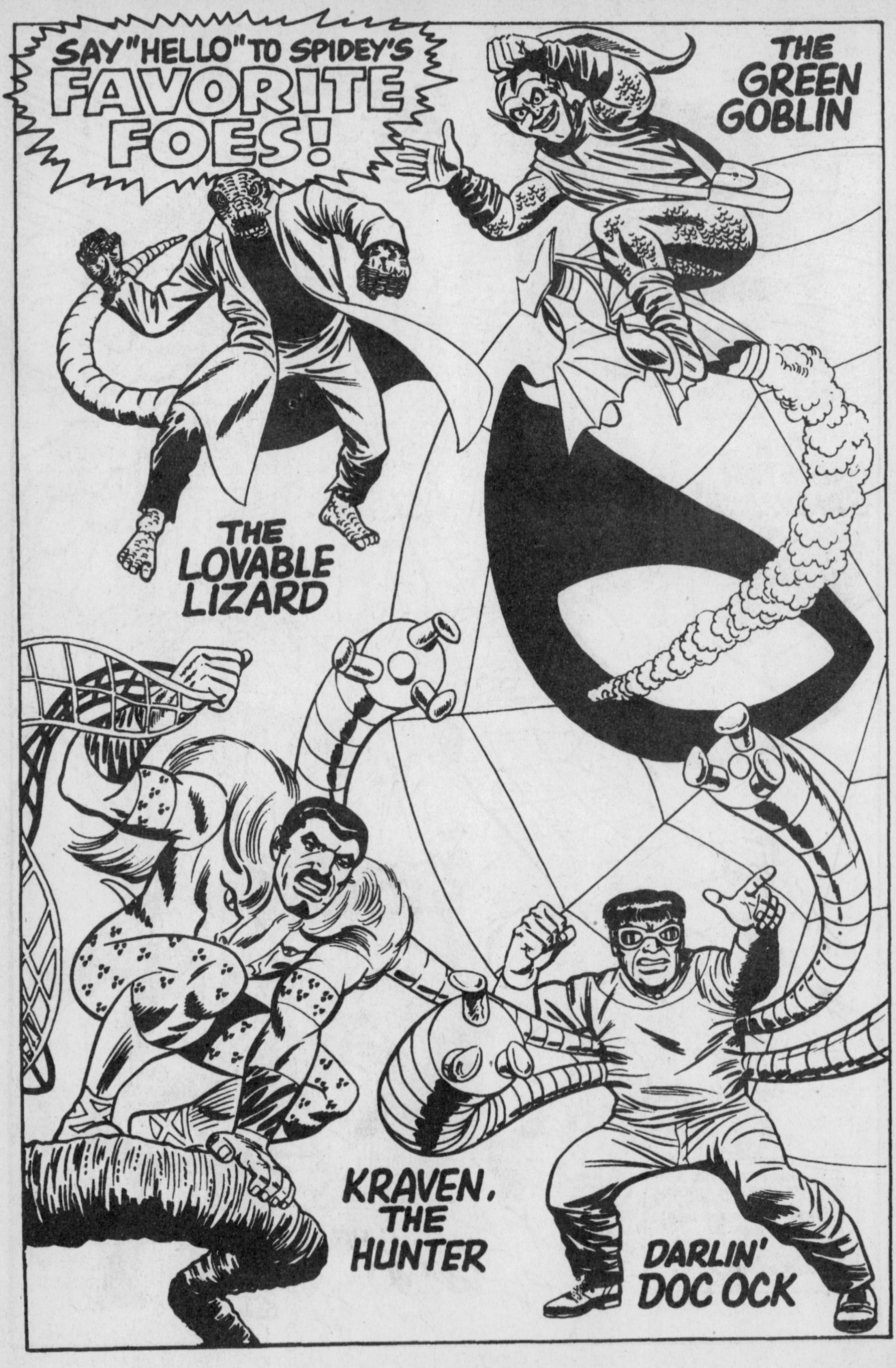
SAY "HELLO" TO SPIDEY'S FAVORITE FOES!
THE GREEN GOBLIN
THE LOVABLE LIZARD
KRAVEN, THE HUNTER
DARLIN' DOC OCK

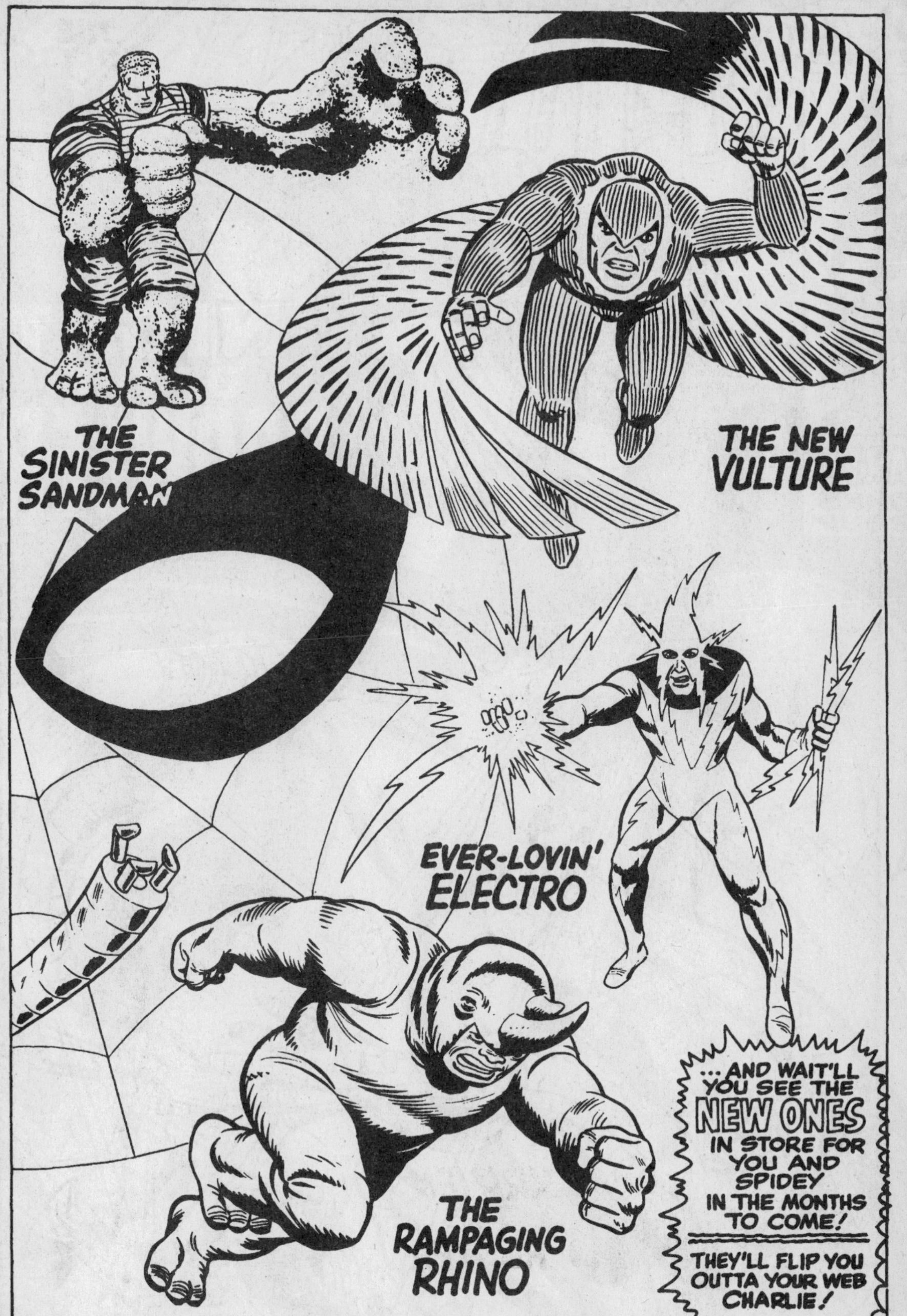
THE SINISTER SANDMAN
THE NEW VULTURE
EVER-LOVIN' ELECTRO
THE RAMPAGING RHINO
...AND WAIT'LL YOU SEE THE NEW ONES IN STORE FOR YOU AND SPIDEY IN THE MONTHS TO COME!
THEY'LL FLIP YOU OUTTA YOUR WEB CHARLIE!

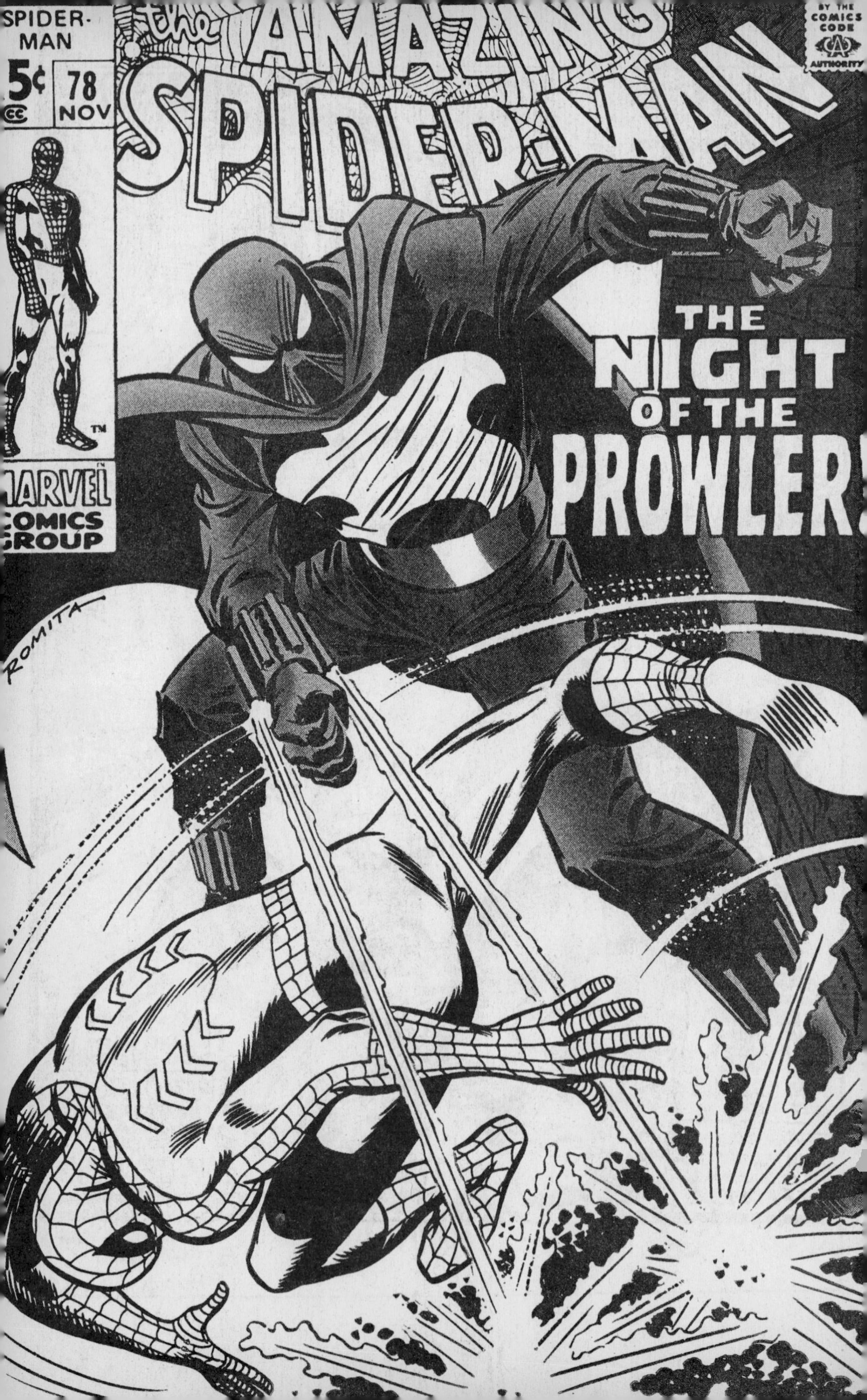
SPIDER-MAN
5¢
78
NOV
the AMAZING SPIDER-MAN
BY THE COMICS CODE AUTHORITY
MARVEL COMICS GROUP
THE NIGHT OF THE PROWLER!
ROMITA

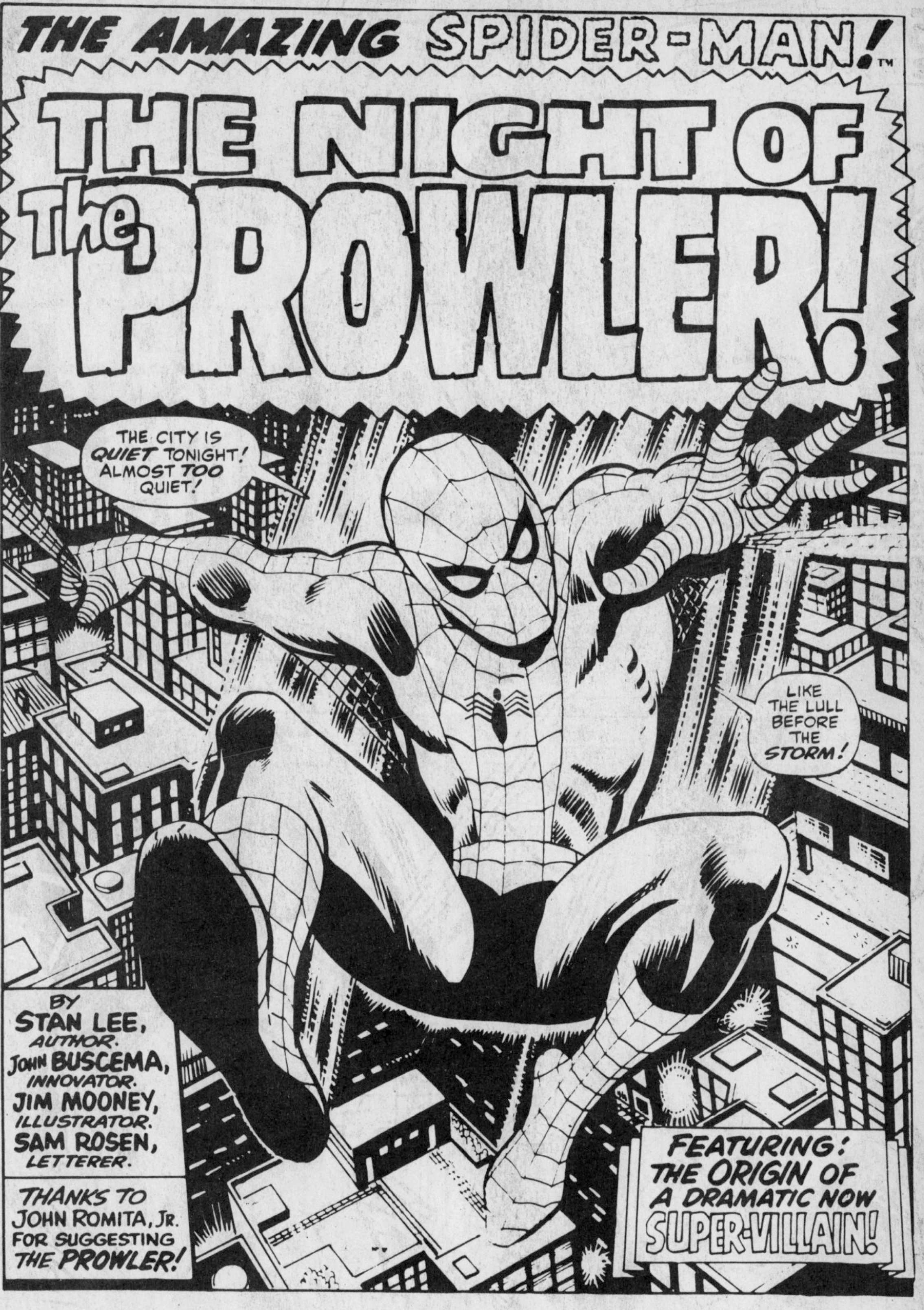
THE AMAZING SPIDER-MAN!™
THE NIGHT OF The PROWLER!
THE CITY IS QUIET TONIGHT! ALMOST TOO QUIET!
LIKE THE LULL BEFORE THE STORM!
BY STAN LEE, AUTHOR. JOHN BUSCEMA, INNOVATOR. JIM MOONEY, ILLUSTRATOR. SAM ROSEN, LETTERER.
THANKS TO JOHN ROMITA, JR. FOR SUGGESTING THE PROWLER!
FEATURING: THE ORIGIN OF A DRAMATIC NOW SUPER-VILLAIN!

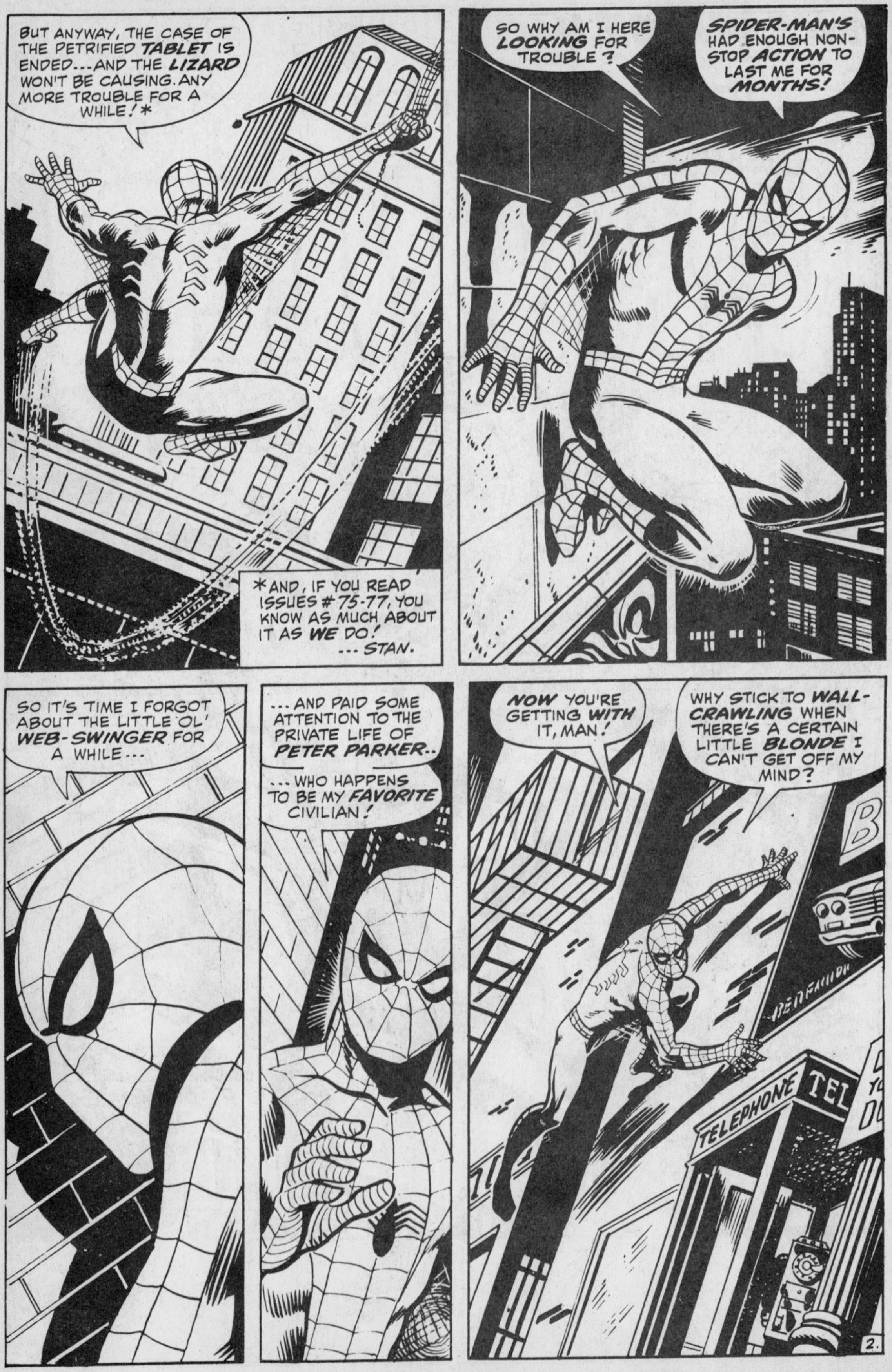
BUT ANYWAY, THE CASE OF THE PETRIFIED TABLET IS ENDED...AND THE LIZARD WON'T BE CAUSING ANY MORE TROUBLE FOR A WHILE! *
*AND, IF YOU READ ISSUES #75-77, YOU KNOW AS MUCH ABOUT IT AS WE DO! ...STAN.
SO WHY AM I HERE LOOKING FOR TROUBLE?
SPIDER-MAN'S HAD ENOUGH NON-STOP ACTION TO LAST ME FOR MONTHS!
SO IT'S TIME I FORGOT ABOUT THE LITTLE 'OL' WEB-SWINGER FOR A WHILE...
...AND PAID SOME ATTENTION TO THE PRIVATE LIFE OF PETER PARKER..
...WHO HAPPENS TO BE MY FAVORITE CIVILIAN!
NOW YOU'RE GETTING WITH IT, MAN!
WHY STICK TO WALL-CRAWLING WHEN THERE'S A CERTAIN LITTLE BLONDE I CAN'T GET OFF MY MIND?
TELEPHONE
TEL

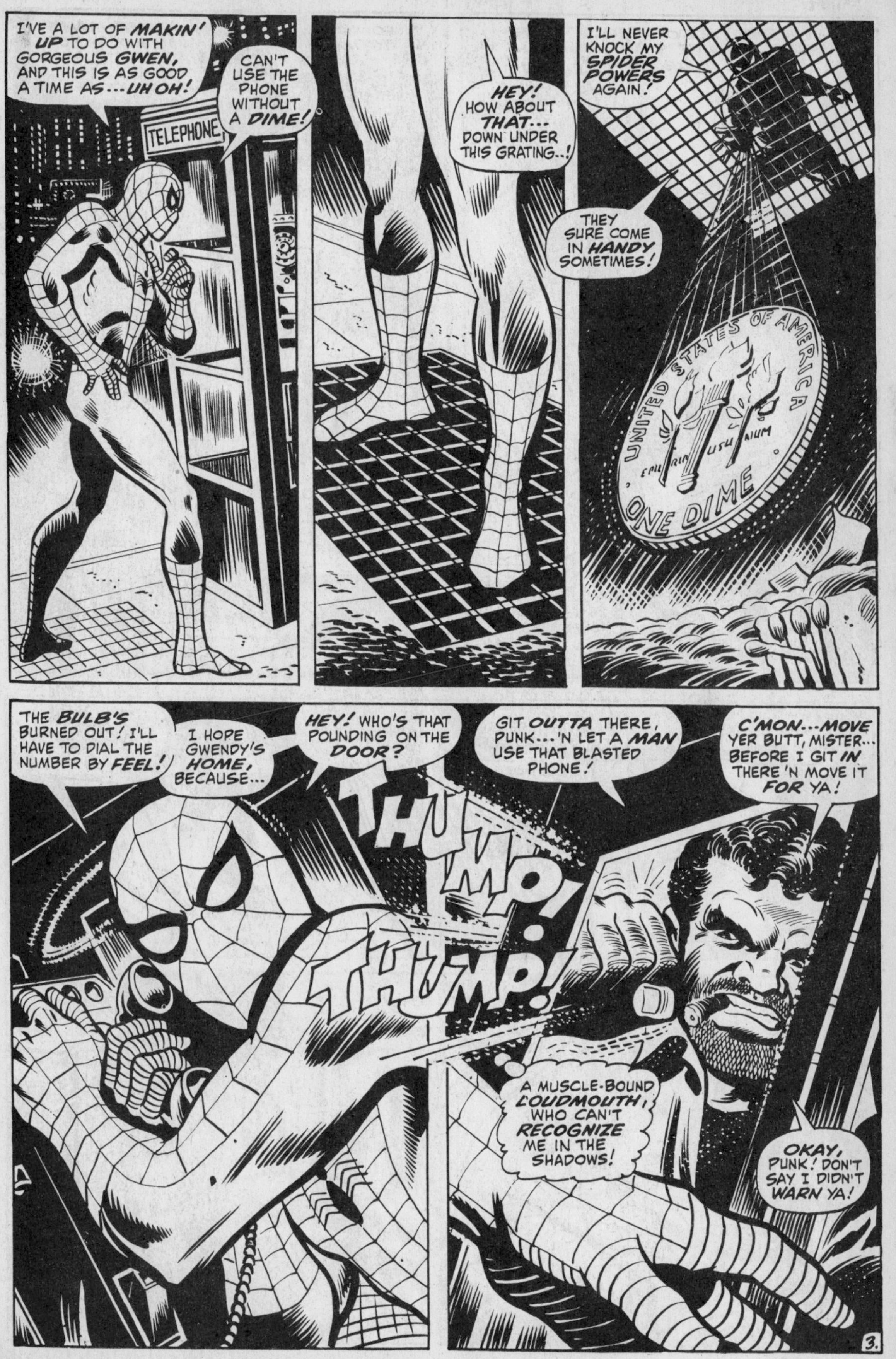
I'VE A LOT OF MAKIN' UP TO DO WITH GORGEOUS GWEN, AND THIS IS AS GOOD A TIME AS--- UH OH!
CAN'T USE THE PHONE WITHOUT A DIME!
TELEPHONE
HEY! HOW ABOUT THAT... DOWN UNDER THIS GRATING..!
I'LL NEVER KNOCK MY SPIDER POWERS AGAIN!
THEY SURE COME IN HANDY SOMETIMES!
UNITED STATES OF AMERICA
ONE DIME
THE BULB'S BURNED OUT! I'LL HAVE TO DIAL THE NUMBER BY FEEL!
I HOPE GWENDY'S HOME, BECAUSE...
HEY! WHO'S THAT POUNDING ON THE DOOR?
THUMP!
THUMP!
GIT OUTTA THERE, PUNK...'N LET A MAN USE THAT BLASTED PHONE!
C'MON...MOVE YER BUTT, MISTER... BEFORE I GIT IN THERE 'N MOVE IT FOR YA!
A MUSCLE-BOUND LOUDMOUTH, WHO CAN'T RECOGNIZE ME IN THE SHADOWS!
OKAY, PUNK! DON'T SAY I DIDN'T WARN YA!

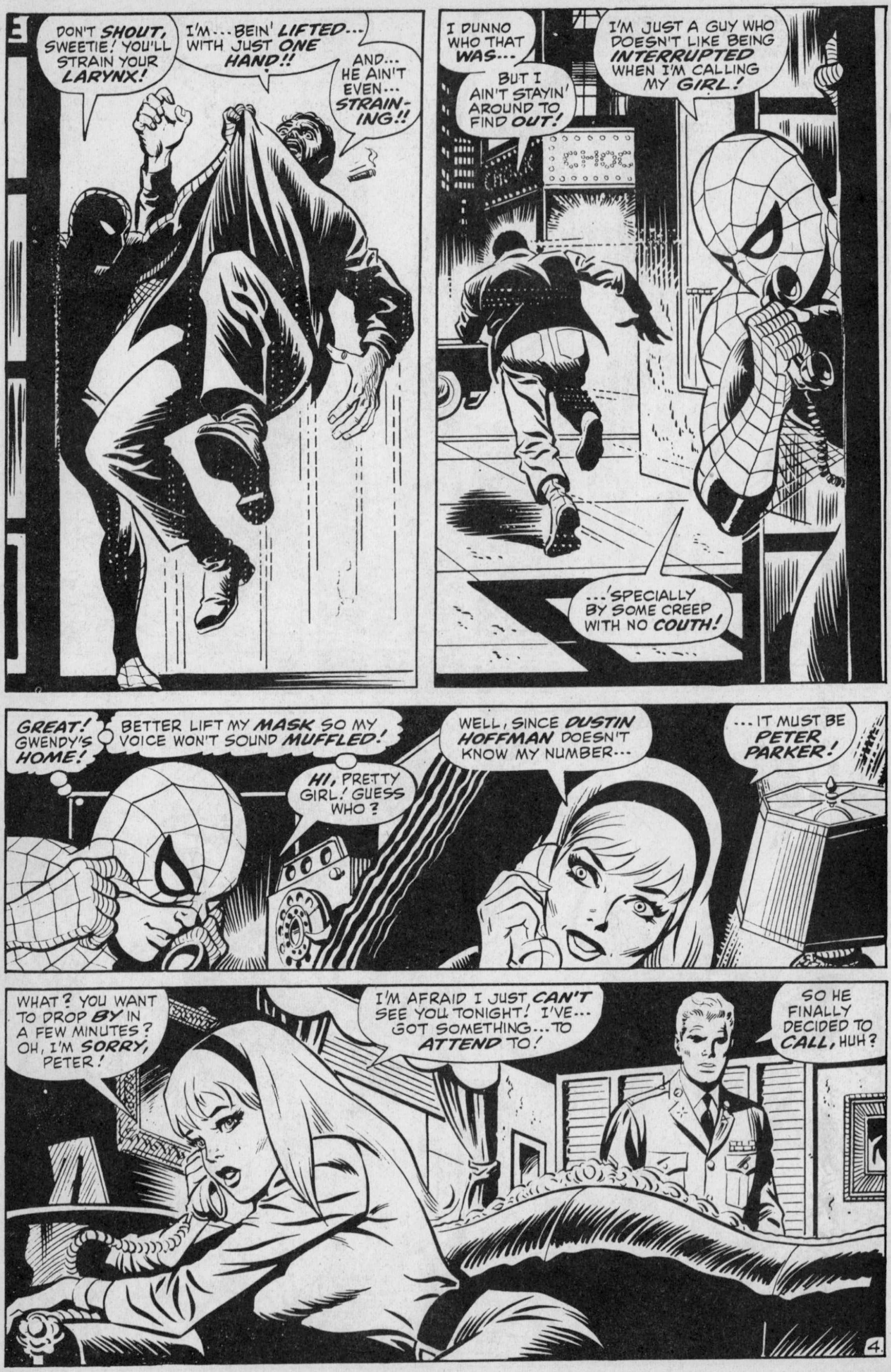
DON'T SHOUT, SWEETIE! YOU'LL STRAIN YOUR LARYNX!
I'M... BEIN' LIFTED... WITH JUST ONE HAND!!
AND... HE AIN'T EVEN... STRAIN-ING!!
I DUNNO WHO THAT WAS...
BUT I AIN'T STAYIN' AROUND TO FIND OUT!
I'M JUST A GUY WHO DOESN'T LIKE BEING INTERRUPTED WHEN I'M CALLING MY GIRL!
...'SPECIALLY BY SOME CREEP WITH NO COUTH!
GREAT! GWENDY'S HOME!
BETTER LIFT MY MASK SO MY VOICE WON'T SOUND MUFFLED!
HI, PRETTY GIRL! GUESS WHO?
WELL, SINCE DUSTIN HOFFMAN DOESN'T KNOW MY NUMBER...
...IT MUST BE PETER PARKER!
WHAT? YOU WANT TO DROP BY IN A FEW MINUTES? OH, I'M SORRY, PETER!
I'M AFRAID I JUST CAN'T SEE YOU TONIGHT! I'VE... GOT SOMETHING... TO ATTEND TO!
SO HE FINALLY DECIDED TO CALL, HUH?

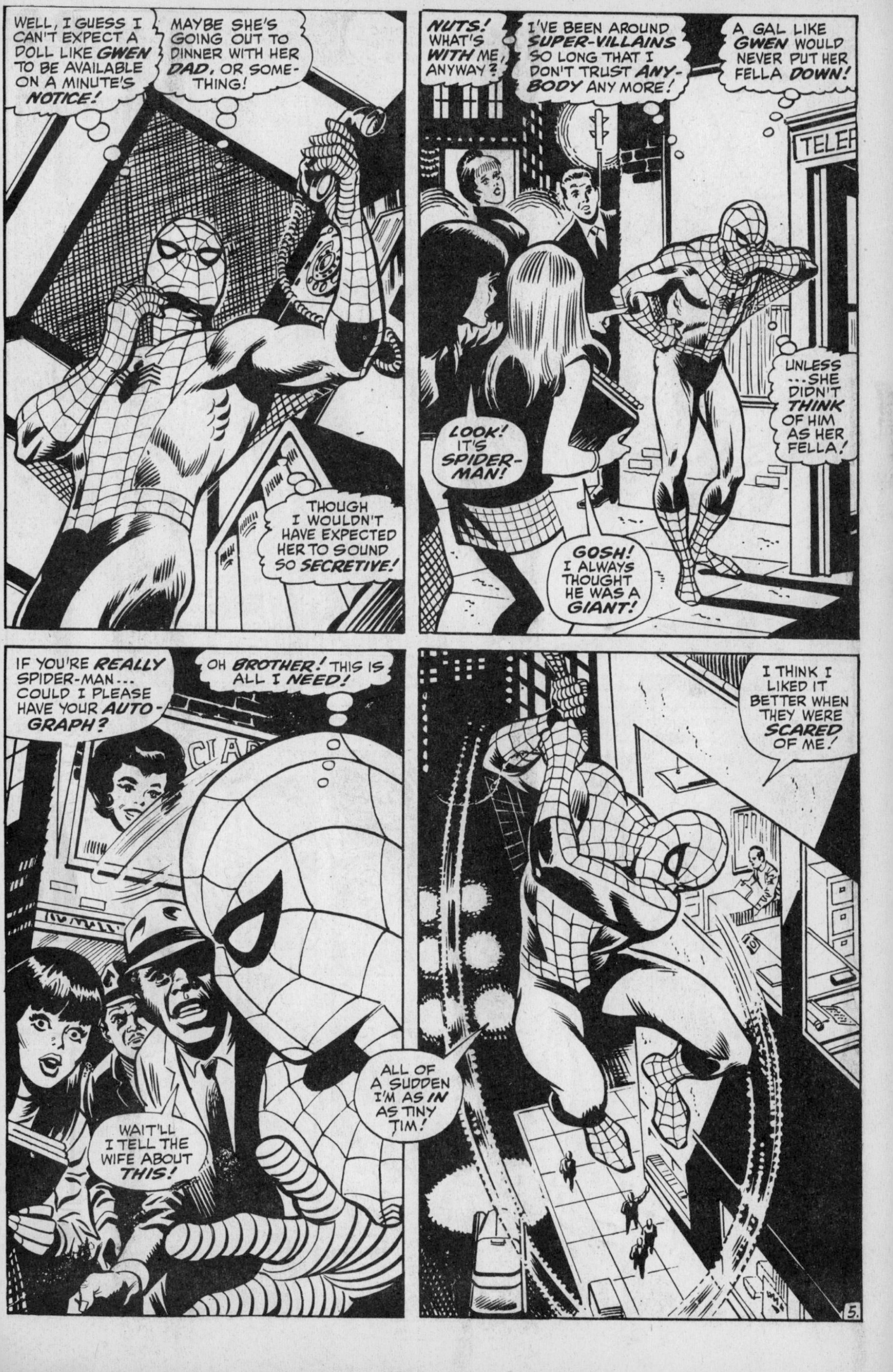

WELL, I GUESS I CAN'T EXPECT A DOLL LIKE GWEN TO BE AVAILABLE ON A MINUTE'S NOTICE!
MAYBE SHE'S GOING OUT TO DINNER WITH HER DAD, OR SOMETHING!
THOUGH I WOULDN'T HAVE EXPECTED HER TO SOUND SO SECRETIVE!
NUTS! WHAT'S WITH ME, ANYWAY?
I'VE BEEN AROUND SUPER-VILLAINS SO LONG THAT I DON'T TRUST ANYBODY ANY MORE!
A GAL LIKE GWEN WOULD NEVER PUT HER FELLA DOWN!
TELEP
UNLESS ...SHE DIDN'T THINK OF HIM AS HER FELLA!
LOOK! IT'S SPIDER-MAN!
GOSH! I ALWAYS THOUGHT HE WAS A GIANT!
IF YOU'RE REALLY SPIDER-MAN... COULD I PLEASE HAVE YOUR AUTOGRAPH?
OH BROTHER! THIS IS ALL I NEED!
ALL OF A SUDDEN I'M AS IN AS TINY TIM!
WAIT'LL I TELL THE WIFE ABOUT THIS!
I THINK I LIKED IT BETTER WHEN THEY WERE SCARED OF ME!

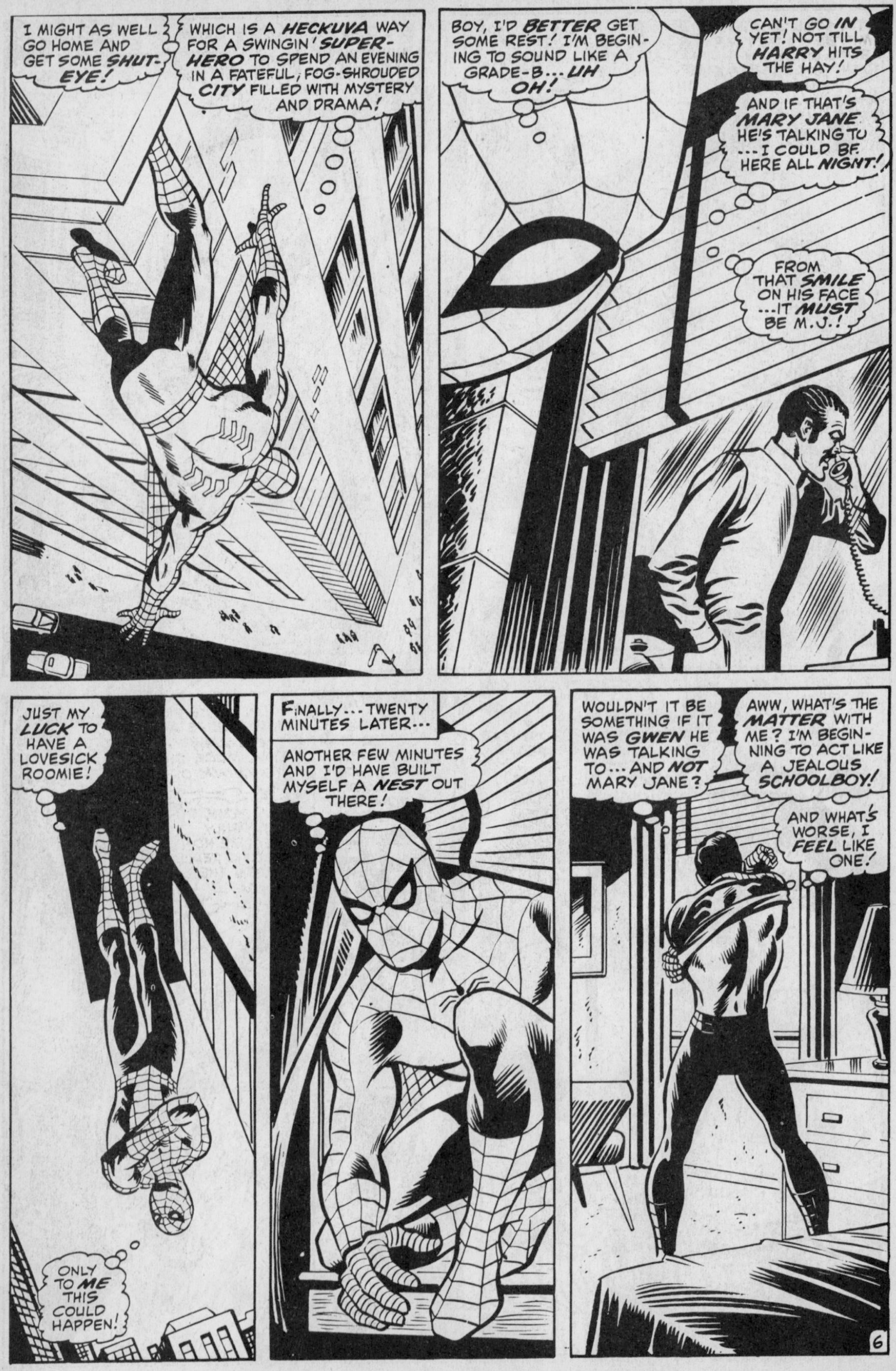
I MIGHT AS WELL GO HOME AND GET SOME SHUT-EYE!
WHICH IS A HECKUVA WAY FOR A SWINGIN' SUPER-HERO TO SPEND AN EVENING IN A FATEFUL, FOG-SHROUDED CITY FILLED WITH MYSTERY AND DRAMA!
BOY, I'D BETTER GET SOME REST! I'M BEGINING TO SOUND LIKE A GRADE-B... UH OH!
CAN'T GO IN YET! NOT TILL HARRY HITS THE HAY!
AND IF THAT'S MARY JANE HE'S TALKING TO ... I COULD BE HERE ALL NIGHT!
FROM THAT SMILE ON HIS FACE ...IT MUST BE M.J.!
JUST MY LUCK TO HAVE A LOVESICK ROOMIE!
ONLY TO ME THIS COULD HAPPEN!
FINALLY... TWENTY MINUTES LATER...
ANOTHER FEW MINUTES AND I'D HAVE BUILT MYSELF A NEST OUT THERE!
WOULDN'T IT BE SOMETHING IF IT WAS GWEN HE WAS TALKING TO... AND NOT MARY JANE?
AWW, WHAT'S THE MATTER WITH ME? I'M BEGINNING TO ACT LIKE A JEALOUS SCHOOLBOY!
AND WHAT'S WORSE, I FEEL LIKE ONE!
6

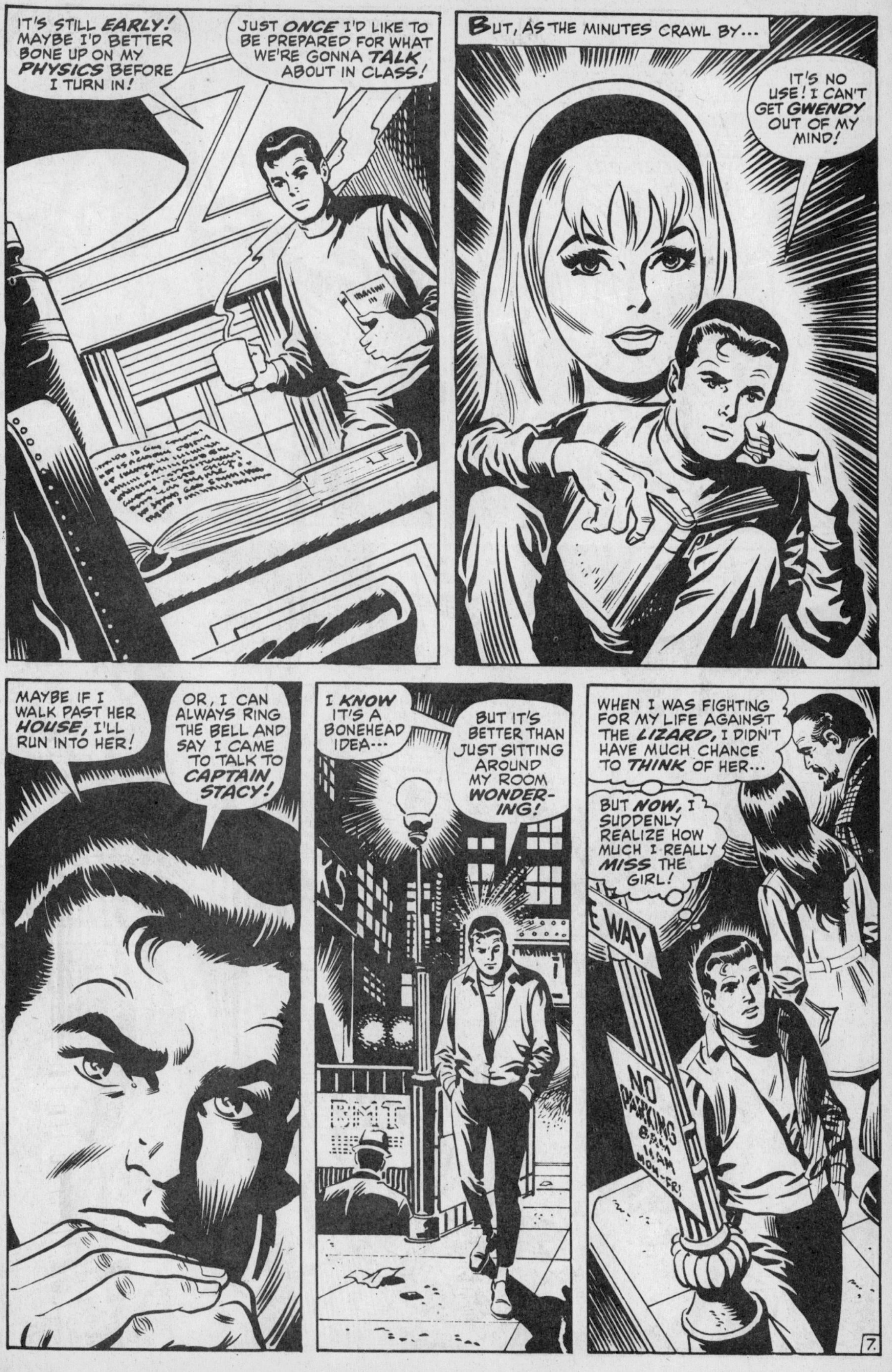
IT'S STILL EARLY! MAYBE I'D BETTER BONE UP ON MY PHYSICS BEFORE I TURN IN!
JUST ONCE I'D LIKE TO BE PREPARED FOR WHAT WE'RE GONNA TALK ABOUT IN CLASS!
BUT, AS THE MINUTES CRAWL BY...
IT'S NO USE! I CAN'T GET GWENDY OUT OF MY MIND!
MAYBE IF I WALK PAST HER HOUSE, I'LL RUN INTO HER!
OR, I CAN ALWAYS RING THE BELL AND SAY I CAME TO TALK TO CAPTAIN STACY!
I KNOW IT'S A BONEHEAD IDEA---
BUT IT'S BETTER THAN JUST SITTING AROUND MY ROOM WONDERING!
BMT
WHEN I WAS FIGHTING FOR MY LIFE AGAINST THE LIZARD, I DIDN'T HAVE MUCH CHANCE TO THINK OF HER...
BUT NOW, I SUDDENLY REALIZE HOW MUCH I REALLY MISS THE GIRL!
E WAY
NO PARKING

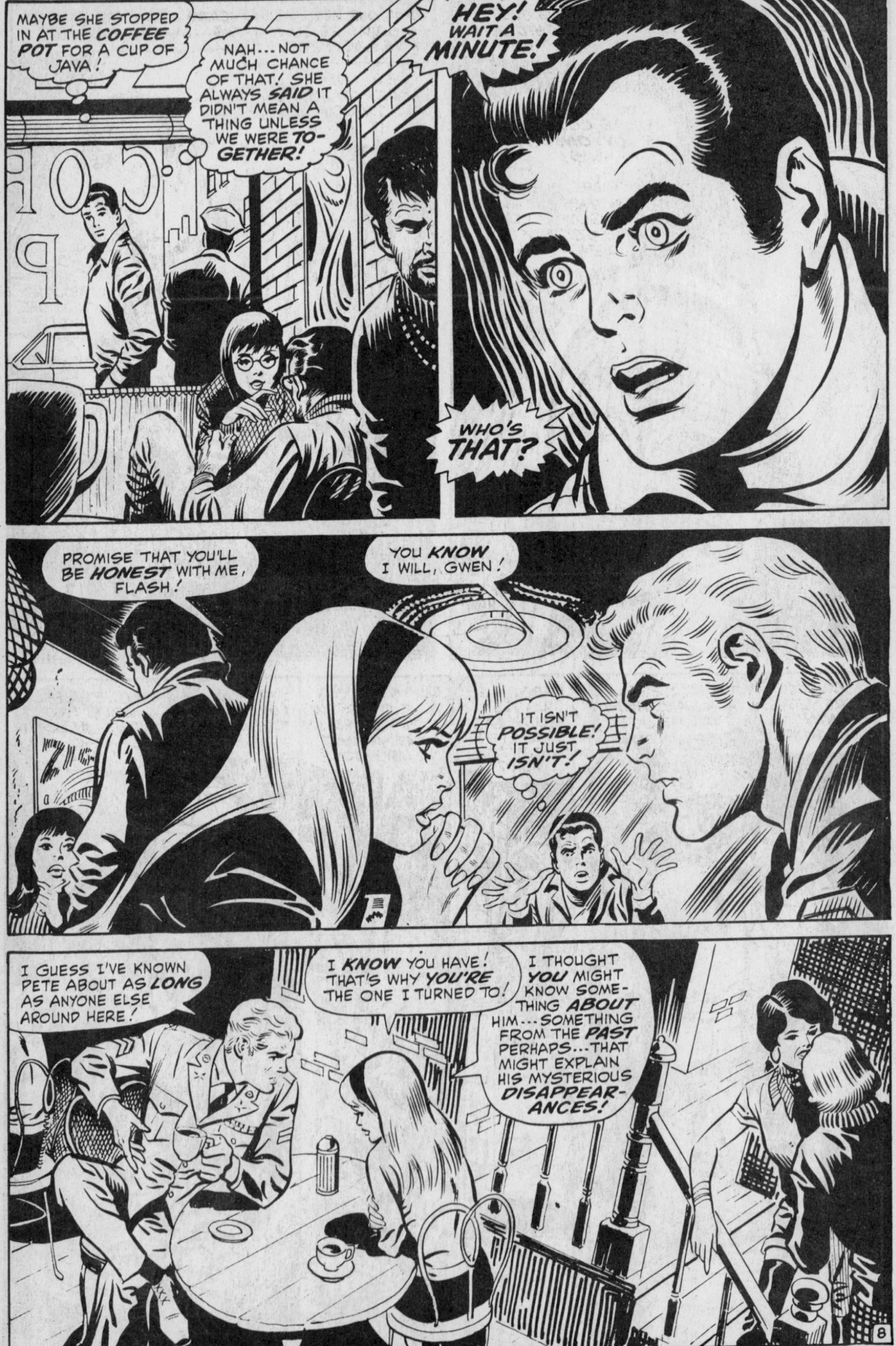
MAYBE SHE STOPPED IN AT THE COFFEE POT FOR A CUP OF JAVA!
NAH... NOT MUCH CHANCE OF THAT! SHE ALWAYS SAID IT DIDN'T MEAN A THING UNLESS WE WERE TO-GETHER!
HEY! WAIT A MINUTE!
WHO'S THAT?
PROMISE THAT YOU'LL BE HONEST WITH ME, FLASH!
YOU KNOW I WILL, GWEN!
IT ISN'T POSSIBLE! IT JUST ISN'T!
I GUESS I'VE KNOWN PETE ABOUT AS LONG AS ANYONE ELSE AROUND HERE!
I KNOW YOU HAVE! THAT'S WHY YOU'RE THE ONE I TURNED TO!
I THOUGHT YOU MIGHT KNOW SOME-THING ABOUT HIM... SOMETHING FROM THE PAST PERHAPS... THAT MIGHT EXPLAIN HIS MYSTERIOUS DISAPPEAR-ANCES!
8

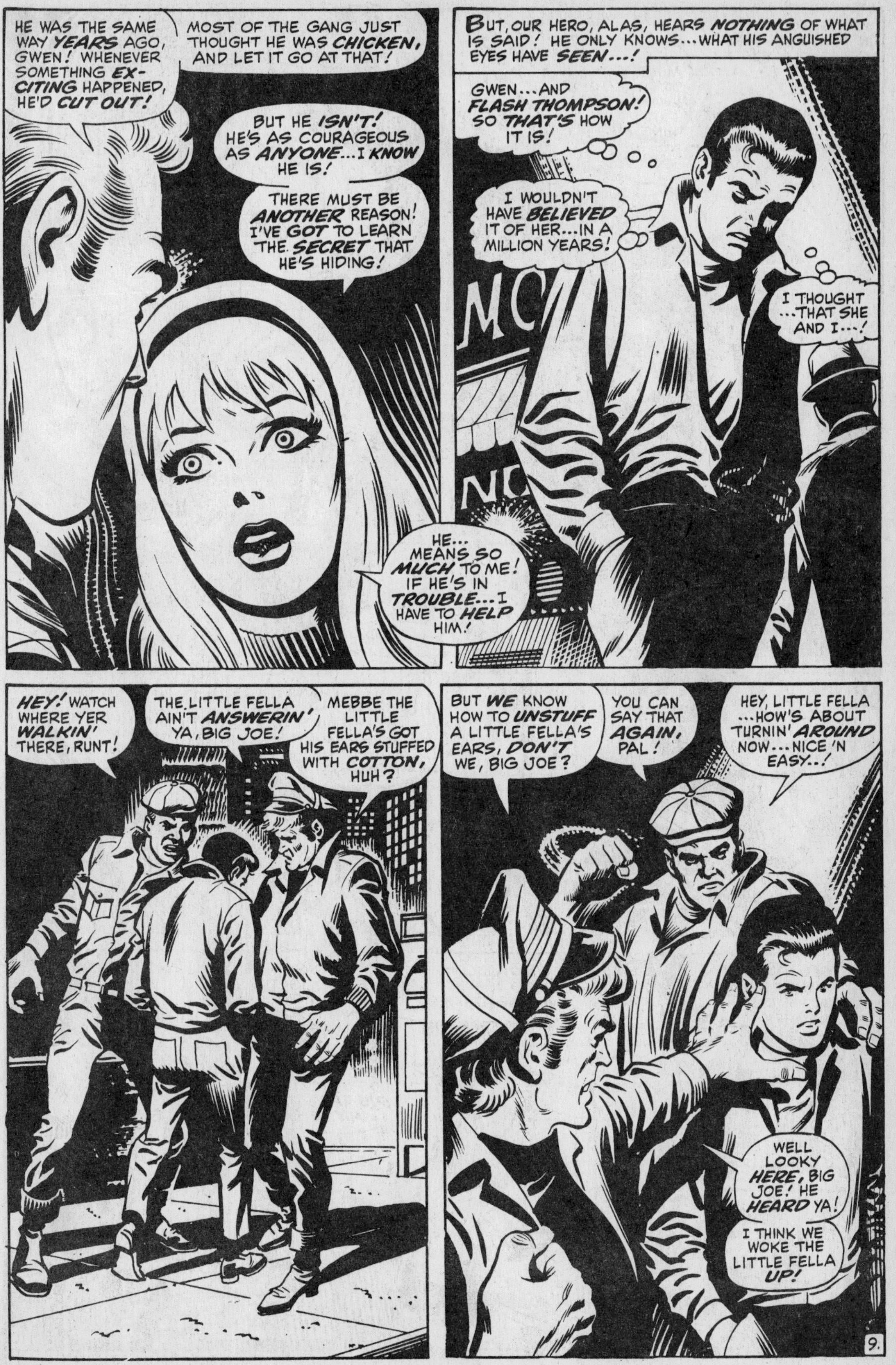

HE WAS THE SAME WAY YEARS AGO, GWEN! WHENEVER SOMETHING EXCITING HAPPENED, HE'D CUT OUT!
MOST OF THE GANG JUST THOUGHT HE WAS CHICKEN, AND LET IT GO AT THAT!
BUT HE ISN'T! HE'S AS COURAGEOUS AS ANYONE...I KNOW HE IS!
THERE MUST BE ANOTHER REASON! I'VE GOT TO LEARN THE SECRET THAT HE'S HIDING!
HE... MEANS SO MUCH TO ME! IF HE'S IN TROUBLE...I HAVE TO HELP HIM!
BUT, OUR HERO, ALAS, HEARS NOTHING OF WHAT IS SAID! HE ONLY KNOWS...WHAT HIS ANGUISHED EYES HAVE SEEN...!
GWEN...AND FLASH THOMPSON! SO THAT'S HOW IT IS!
I WOULDN'T HAVE BELIEVED IT OF HER...IN A MILLION YEARS!
I THOUGHT ...THAT SHE AND I...!
HEY! WATCH WHERE YER WALKIN' THERE, RUNT!
THE LITTLE FELLA AIN'T ANSWERIN' YA, BIG JOE!
MEBBE THE LITTLE FELLA'S GOT HIS EARS STUFFED WITH COTTON, HUH?
BUT WE KNOW HOW TO UNSTUFF A LITTLE FELLA'S EARS, DON'T WE, BIG JOE?
YOU CAN SAY THAT AGAIN, PAL!
HEY, LITTLE FELLA ...HOW'S ABOUT TURNIN' AROUND NOW...NICE 'N EASY..!
WELL LOOKY HERE, BIG JOE! HE HEARD YA!
I THINK WE WOKE THE LITTLE FELLA UP!

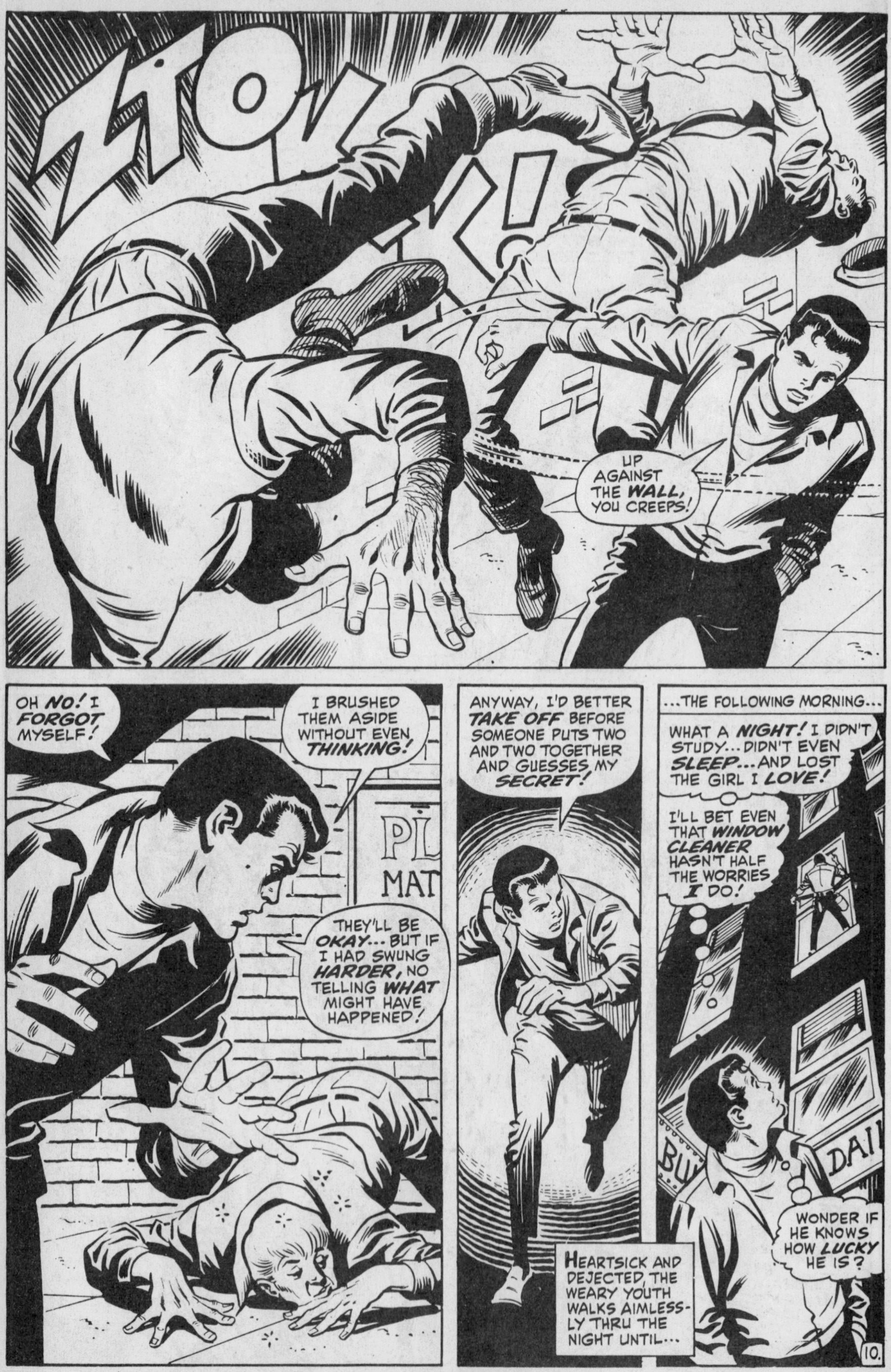

ZTOK!
UP AGAINST THE WALL, YOU CREEPS!
OH NO! I FORGOT MYSELF!
I BRUSHED THEM ASIDE WITHOUT EVEN THINKING!
PL
MAT
THEY'LL BE OKAY... BUT IF I HAD SWUNG HARDER, NO TELLING WHAT MIGHT HAVE HAPPENED!
ANYWAY, I'D BETTER TAKE OFF BEFORE SOMEONE PUTS TWO AND TWO TOGETHER AND GUESSES MY SECRET!
HEARTSICK AND DEJECTED, THE WEARY YOUTH WALKS AIMLESS-LY THRU THE NIGHT UNTIL...
...THE FOLLOWING MORNING...
WHAT A NIGHT! I DIDN'T STUDY... DIDN'T EVEN SLEEP... AND LOST THE GIRL I LOVE!
I'LL BET EVEN THAT WINDOW CLEANER HASN'T HALF THE WORRIES I DO!
BU
DAI
WONDER IF HE KNOWS HOW LUCKY HE IS?
10.

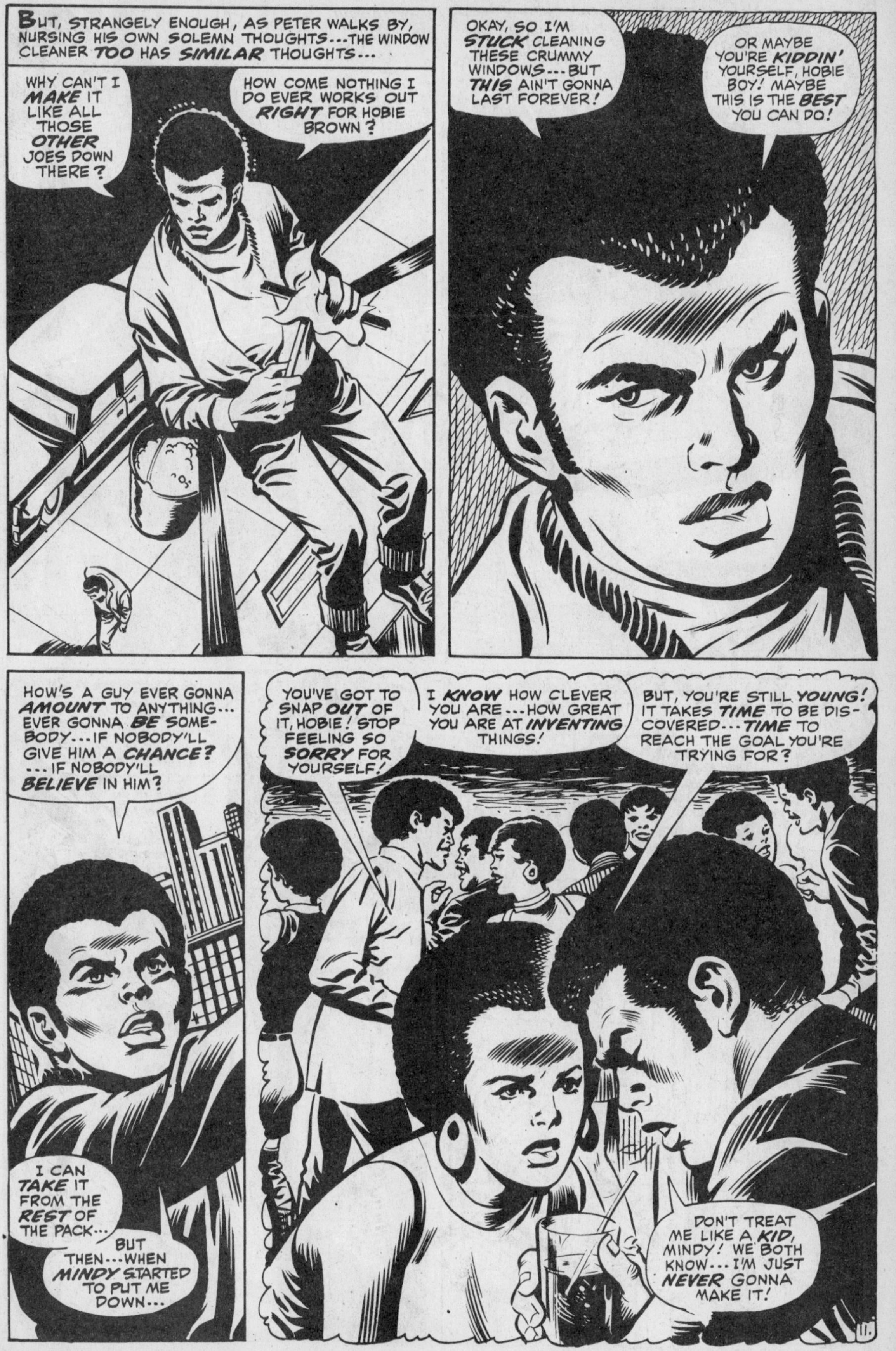
BUT, STRANGELY ENOUGH, AS PETER WALKS BY, NURSING HIS OWN SOLEMN THOUGHTS... THE WINDOW CLEANER TOO HAS SIMILAR THOUGHTS...
WHY CAN'T I MAKE IT LIKE ALL THOSE OTHER JOES DOWN THERE?
HOW COME NOTHING I DO EVER WORKS OUT RIGHT FOR HOBIE BROWN?
OKAY, SO I'M STUCK CLEANING THESE CRUMMY WINDOWS... BUT THIS AIN'T GONNA LAST FOREVER!
OR MAYBE YOU'RE KIDDIN' YOURSELF, HOBIE BOY! MAYBE THIS IS THE BEST YOU CAN DO!
HOW'S A GUY EVER GONNA AMOUNT TO ANYTHING... EVER GONNA BE SOMEBODY... IF NOBODY'LL GIVE HIM A CHANCE? ... IF NOBODY'LL BELIEVE IN HIM?
I CAN TAKE IT FROM THE REST OF THE PACK...
BUT THEN... WHEN MINDY STARTED TO PUT ME DOWN...
YOU'VE GOT TO SNAP OUT OF IT, HOBIE! STOP FEELING SO SORRY FOR YOURSELF!
I KNOW HOW CLEVER YOU ARE... HOW GREAT YOU ARE AT INVENTING THINGS!
BUT, YOU'RE STILL YOUNG! IT TAKES TIME TO BE DISCOVERED... TIME TO REACH THE GOAL YOU'RE TRYING FOR?
DON'T TREAT ME LIKE A KID, MINDY! WE BOTH KNOW... I'M JUST NEVER GONNA MAKE IT!
11.

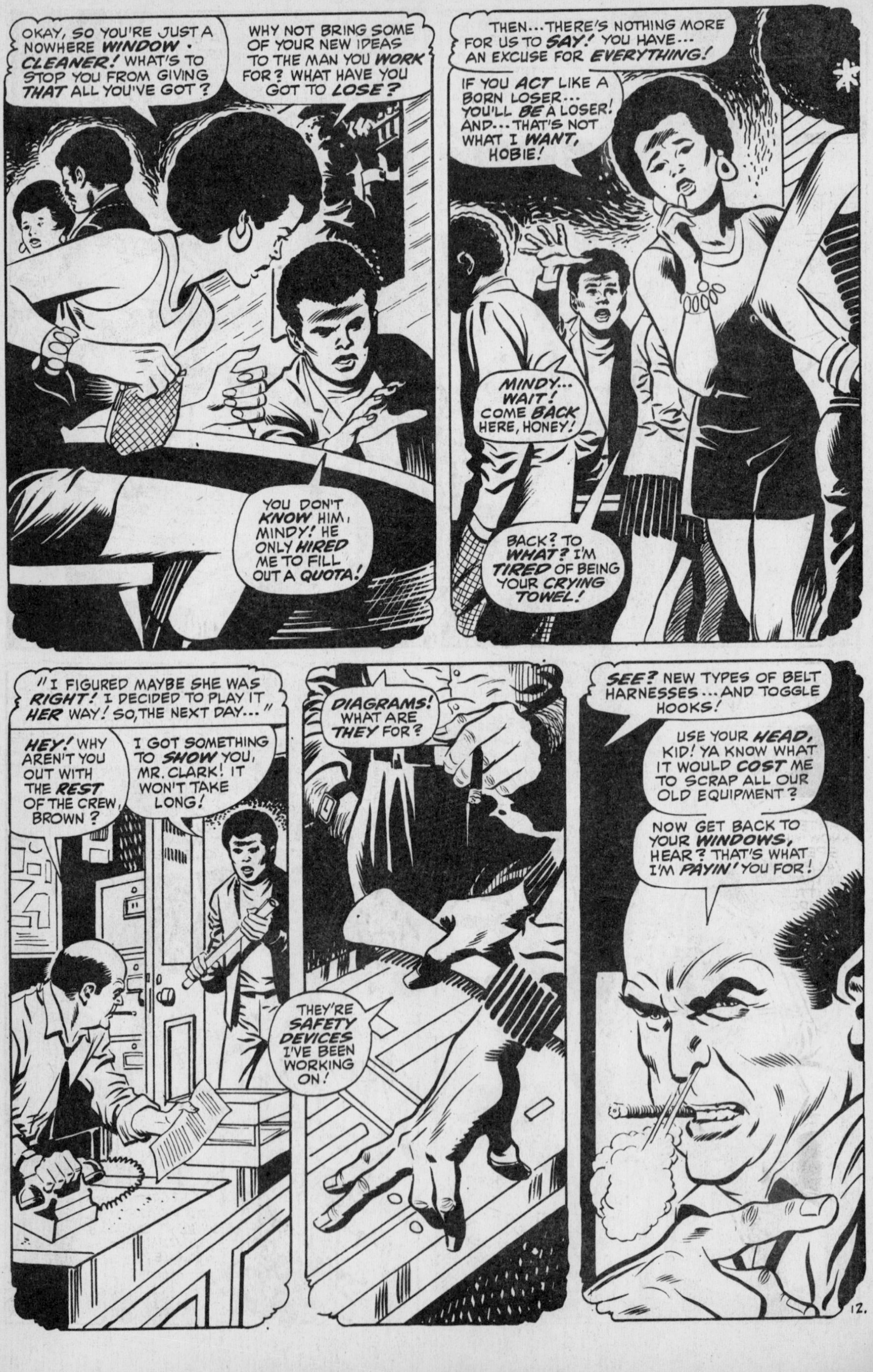

OKAY, SO YOU'RE JUST A NOWHERE WINDOW-CLEANER! WHAT'S TO STOP YOU FROM GIVING THAT ALL YOU'VE GOT?
WHY NOT BRING SOME OF YOUR NEW IDEAS TO THE MAN YOU WORK FOR? WHAT HAVE YOU GOT TO LOSE?
YOU DON'T KNOW HIM, MINDY! HE ONLY HIRED ME TO FILL OUT A QUOTA!
THEN... THERE'S NOTHING MORE FOR US TO SAY! YOU HAVE... AN EXCUSE FOR EVERYTHING!
IF YOU ACT LIKE A BORN LOSER... YOU'LL BE A LOSER! AND... THAT'S NOT WHAT I WANT, HOBIE!
MINDY... WAIT! COME BACK HERE, HONEY!
BACK? TO WHAT? I'M TIRED OF BEING YOUR CRYING TOWEL!
"I FIGURED MAYBE SHE WAS RIGHT! I DECIDED TO PLAY IT HER WAY! SO, THE NEXT DAY..."
HEY! WHY AREN'T YOU OUT WITH THE REST OF THE CREW, BROWN?
I GOT SOMETHING TO SHOW YOU, MR. CLARK! IT WON'T TAKE LONG!
DIAGRAMS! WHAT ARE THEY FOR?
THEY'RE SAFETY DEVICES I'VE BEEN WORKING ON!
SEE? NEW TYPES OF BELT HARNESSES... AND TOGGLE HOOKS!
USE YOUR HEAD, KID! YA KNOW WHAT IT WOULD COST ME TO SCRAP ALL OUR OLD EQUIPMENT?
NOW GET BACK TO YOUR WINDOWS, HEAR? THAT'S WHAT I'M PAYIN' YOU FOR!

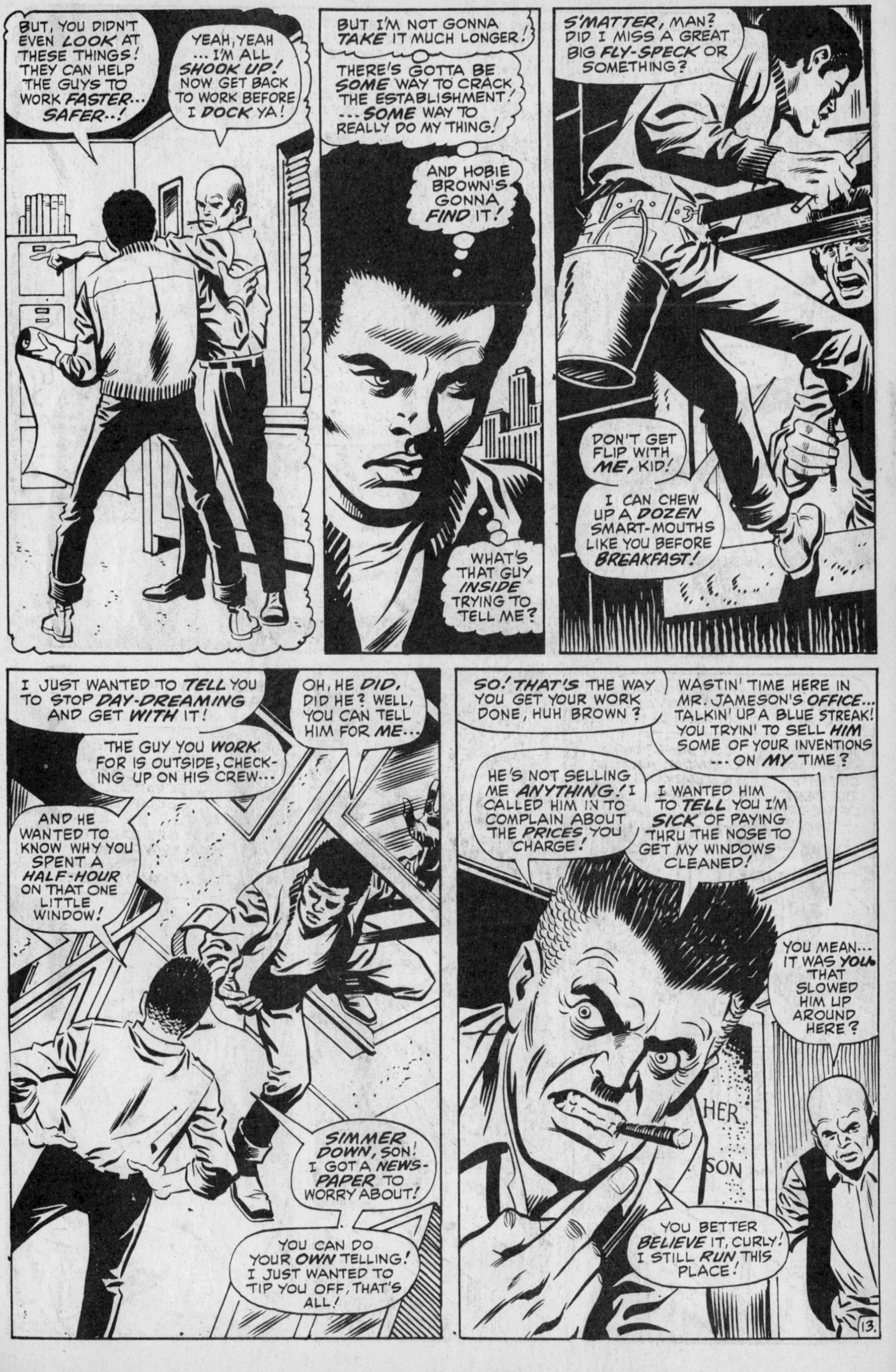
BUT, YOU DIDN'T EVEN LOOK AT THESE THINGS! THEY CAN HELP THE GUYS TO WORK FASTER... SAFER..!
YEAH, YEAH ... I'M ALL SHOOK UP! NOW GET BACK TO WORK BEFORE I DOCK YA!
BUT I'M NOT GONNA TAKE IT MUCH LONGER!
THERE'S GOTTA BE SOME WAY TO CRACK THE ESTABLISHMENT! ---SOME WAY TO REALLY DO MY THING!
AND HOBIE BROWN'S GONNA FIND IT!
WHAT'S THAT GUY INSIDE TRYING TO TELL ME?
S'MATTER, MAN? DID I MISS A GREAT BIG FLY-SPECK OR SOMETHING?
DON'T GET FLIP WITH ME, KID!
I CAN CHEW UP A DOZEN SMART-MOUTHS LIKE YOU BEFORE BREAKFAST!
I JUST WANTED TO TELL YOU TO STOP DAY-DREAMING AND GET WITH IT!
THE GUY YOU WORK FOR IS OUTSIDE, CHECKING UP ON HIS CREW...
AND HE WANTED TO KNOW WHY YOU SPENT A HALF-HOUR ON THAT ONE LITTLE WINDOW!
OH, HE DID, DID HE? WELL, YOU CAN TELL HIM FOR ME...
SIMMER DOWN, SON! I GOT A NEWSPAPER TO WORRY ABOUT!
YOU CAN DO YOUR OWN TELLING! I JUST WANTED TO TIP YOU OFF, THAT'S ALL!
SO! THAT'S THE WAY YOU GET YOUR WORK DONE, HUH BROWN?
WASTIN' TIME HERE IN MR. JAMESON'S OFFICE... TALKIN' UP A BLUE STREAK! YOU TRYIN' TO SELL HIM SOME OF YOUR INVENTIONS ... ON MY TIME?
HE'S NOT SELLING ME ANYTHING! I CALLED HIM IN TO COMPLAIN ABOUT THE PRICES YOU CHARGE!
I WANTED HIM TO TELL YOU I'M SICK OF PAYING THRU THE NOSE TO GET MY WINDOWS CLEANED!
YOU MEAN... IT WAS YOU THAT SLOWED HIM UP AROUND HERE?
HER
SON
YOU BETTER BELIEVE IT, CURLY! I STILL RUN THIS PLACE!

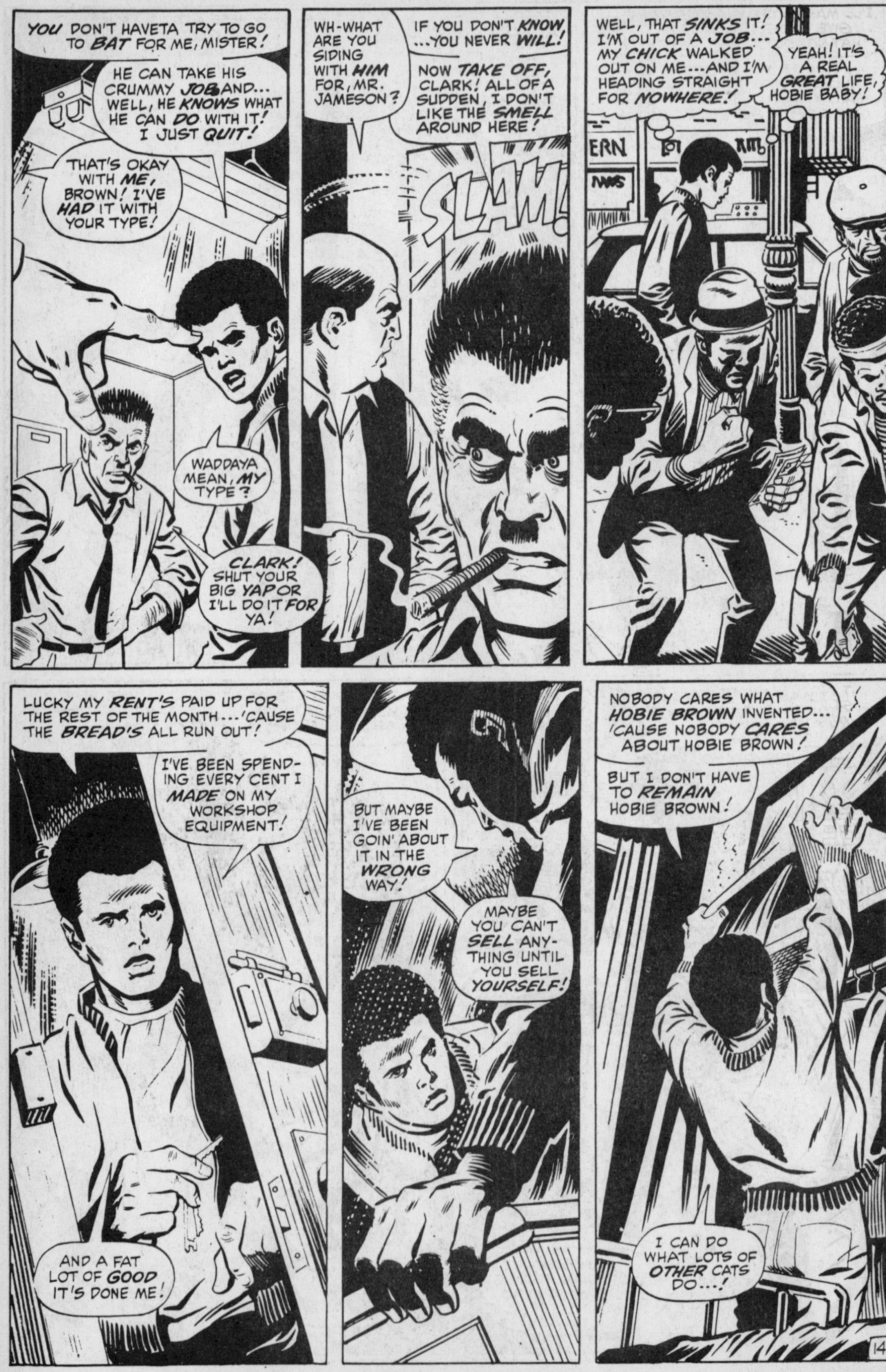
YOU DON'T HAVETA TRY TO GO TO BAT FOR ME, MISTER!
HE CAN TAKE HIS CRUMMY JOB AND... WELL, HE KNOWS WHAT HE CAN DO WITH IT! I JUST QUIT!
THAT'S OKAY WITH ME, BROWN! I'VE HAD IT WITH YOUR TYPE!
WADDAYA MEAN, MY TYPE?
CLARK! SHUT YOUR BIG YAP OR I'LL DO IT FOR YA!
WH-WHAT ARE YOU SIDING WITH HIM FOR, MR. JAMESON?
IF YOU DON'T KNOW ...YOU NEVER WILL!
NOW TAKE OFF, CLARK! ALL OF A SUDDEN, I DON'T LIKE THE SMELL AROUND HERE!
SLAM!
WELL, THAT SINKS IT! I'M OUT OF A JOB... MY CHICK WALKED OUT ON ME... AND I'M HEADING STRAIGHT FOR NOWHERE!
YEAH! IT'S A REAL GREAT LIFE, HOBIE BABY!
LUCKY MY RENT'S PAID UP FOR THE REST OF THE MONTH...'CAUSE THE BREAD'S ALL RUN OUT!
I'VE BEEN SPENDING EVERY CENT I MADE ON MY WORKSHOP EQUIPMENT!
AND A FAT LOT OF GOOD IT'S DONE ME!
BUT MAYBE I'VE BEEN GOIN' ABOUT IT IN THE WRONG WAY!
MAYBE YOU CAN'T SELL ANYTHING UNTIL YOU SELL YOURSELF!
NOBODY CARES WHAT HOBIE BROWN INVENTED... 'CAUSE NOBODY CARES ABOUT HOBIE BROWN!
BUT I DON'T HAVE TO REMAIN HOBIE BROWN!
I CAN DO WHAT LOTS OF OTHER CATS DO...!
14

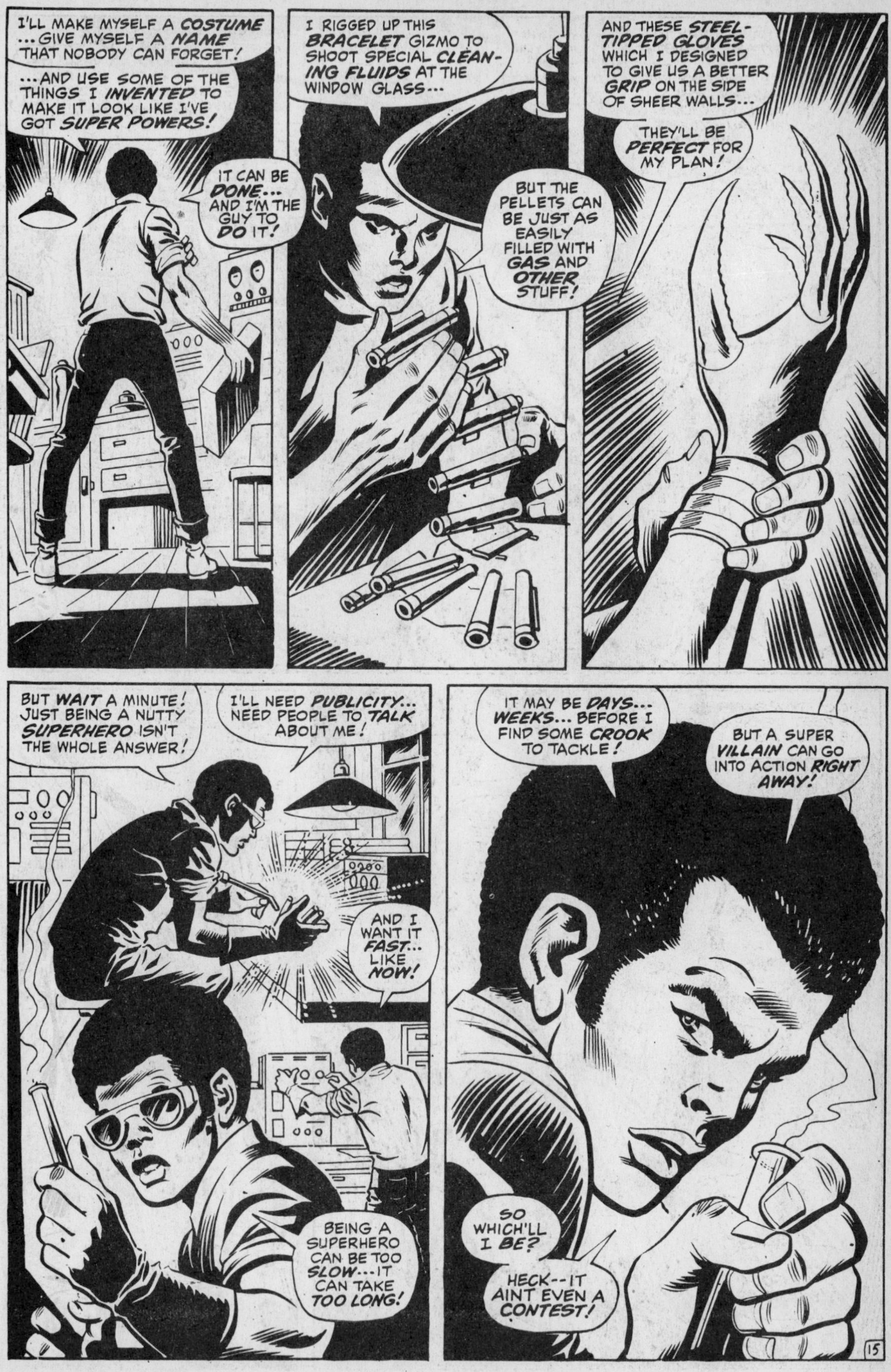
I'LL MAKE MYSELF A COSTUME ...GIVE MYSELF A NAME THAT NOBODY CAN FORGET!
...AND USE SOME OF THE THINGS I INVENTED TO MAKE IT LOOK LIKE I'VE GOT SUPER POWERS!
IT CAN BE DONE... AND I'M THE GUY TO DO IT!
I RIGGED UP THIS BRACELET GIZMO TO SHOOT SPECIAL CLEANING FLUIDS AT THE WINDOW GLASS...
BUT THE PELLETS CAN BE JUST AS EASILY FILLED WITH GAS AND OTHER STUFF!
AND THESE STEEL-TIPPED GLOVES WHICH I DESIGNED TO GIVE US A BETTER GRIP ON THE SIDE OF SHEER WALLS...
THEY'LL BE PERFECT FOR MY PLAN!
BUT WAIT A MINUTE! JUST BEING A NUTTY SUPERHERO ISN'T THE WHOLE ANSWER!
I'LL NEED PUBLICITY... NEED PEOPLE TO TALK ABOUT ME!
AND I WANT IT FAST... LIKE NOW!
BEING A SUPERHERO CAN BE TOO SLOW---IT CAN TAKE TOO LONG!
IT MAY BE DAYS... WEEKS... BEFORE I FIND SOME CROOK TO TACKLE!
BUT A SUPER VILLAIN CAN GO INTO ACTION RIGHT AWAY!
SO WHICH'LL I BE?
HECK--IT AINT EVEN A CONTEST!

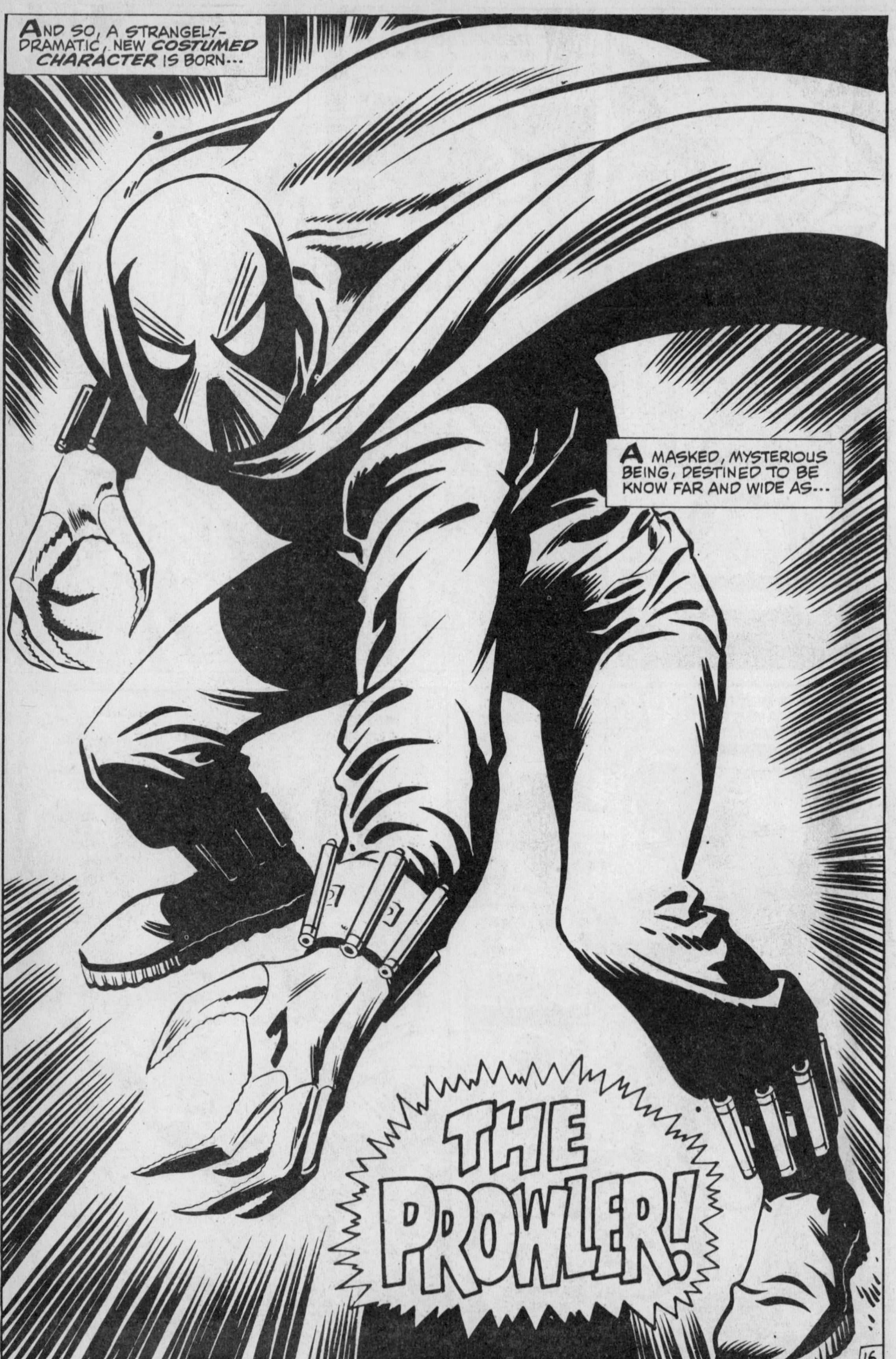
AND SO, A STRANGELY-DRAMATIC, NEW COSTUMED CHARACTER IS BORN...
A MASKED, MYSTERIOUS BEING, DESTINED TO BE KNOW FAR AND WIDE AS...
THE PROWLER!
16.

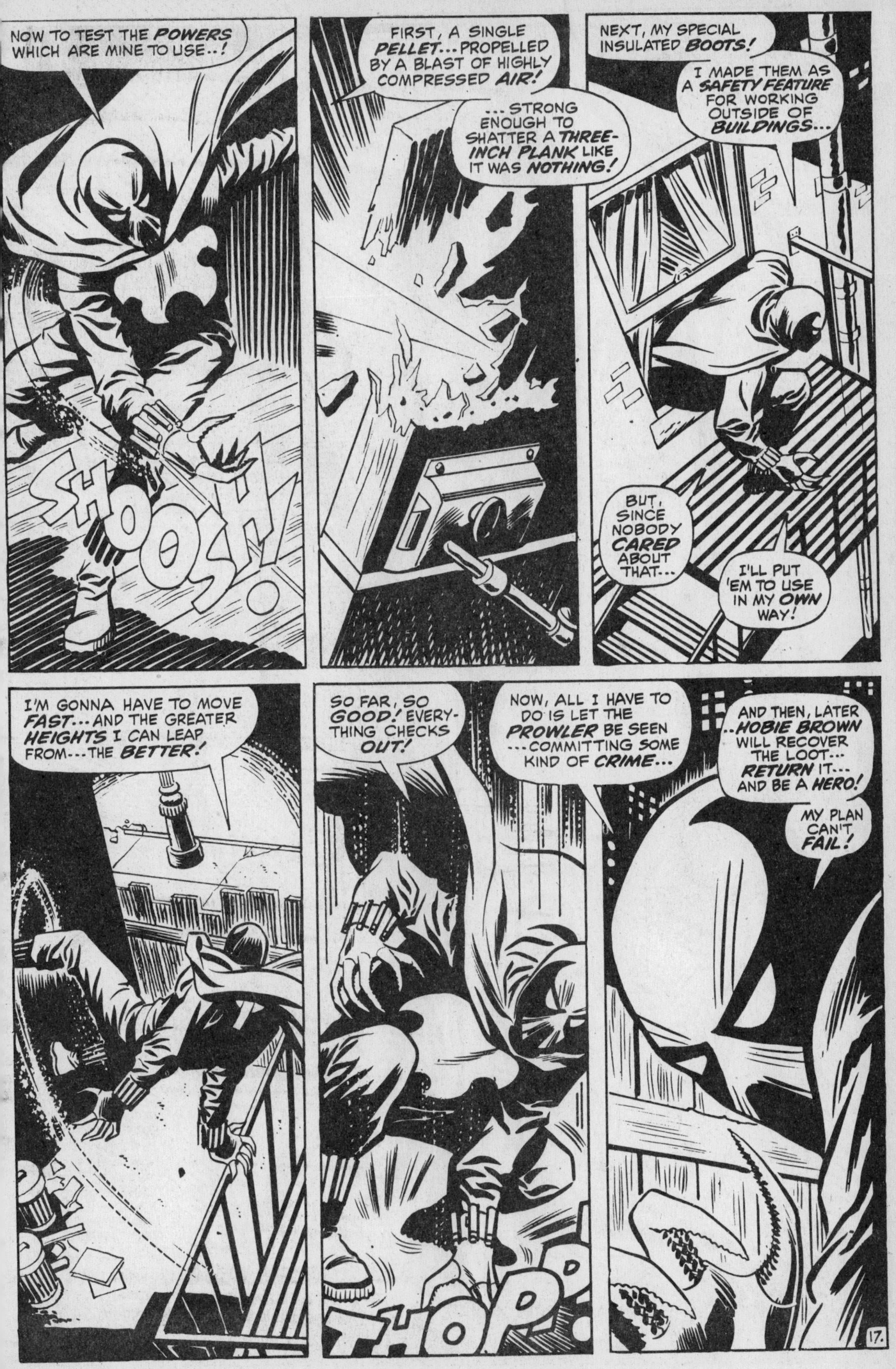
NOW TO TEST THE POWERS WHICH ARE MINE TO USE..!
SHOOOSH!
FIRST, A SINGLE PELLET... PROPELLED BY A BLAST OF HIGHLY COMPRESSED AIR!
...STRONG ENOUGH TO SHATTER A THREE-INCH PLANK LIKE IT WAS NOTHING!
NEXT, MY SPECIAL INSULATED BOOTS!
I MADE THEM AS A SAFETY FEATURE FOR WORKING OUTSIDE OF BUILDINGS...
BUT, SINCE NOBODY CARED ABOUT THAT...
I'LL PUT 'EM TO USE IN MY OWN WAY!
I'M GONNA HAVE TO MOVE FAST... AND THE GREATER HEIGHTS I CAN LEAP FROM--- THE BETTER!
SO FAR, SO GOOD! EVERY-THING CHECKS OUT!
THOPP
NOW, ALL I HAVE TO DO IS LET THE PROWLER BE SEEN ---COMMITTING SOME KIND OF CRIME...
AND THEN, LATER ..HOBIE BROWN WILL RECOVER THE LOOT... RETURN IT... AND BE A HERO!
MY PLAN CAN'T FAIL!

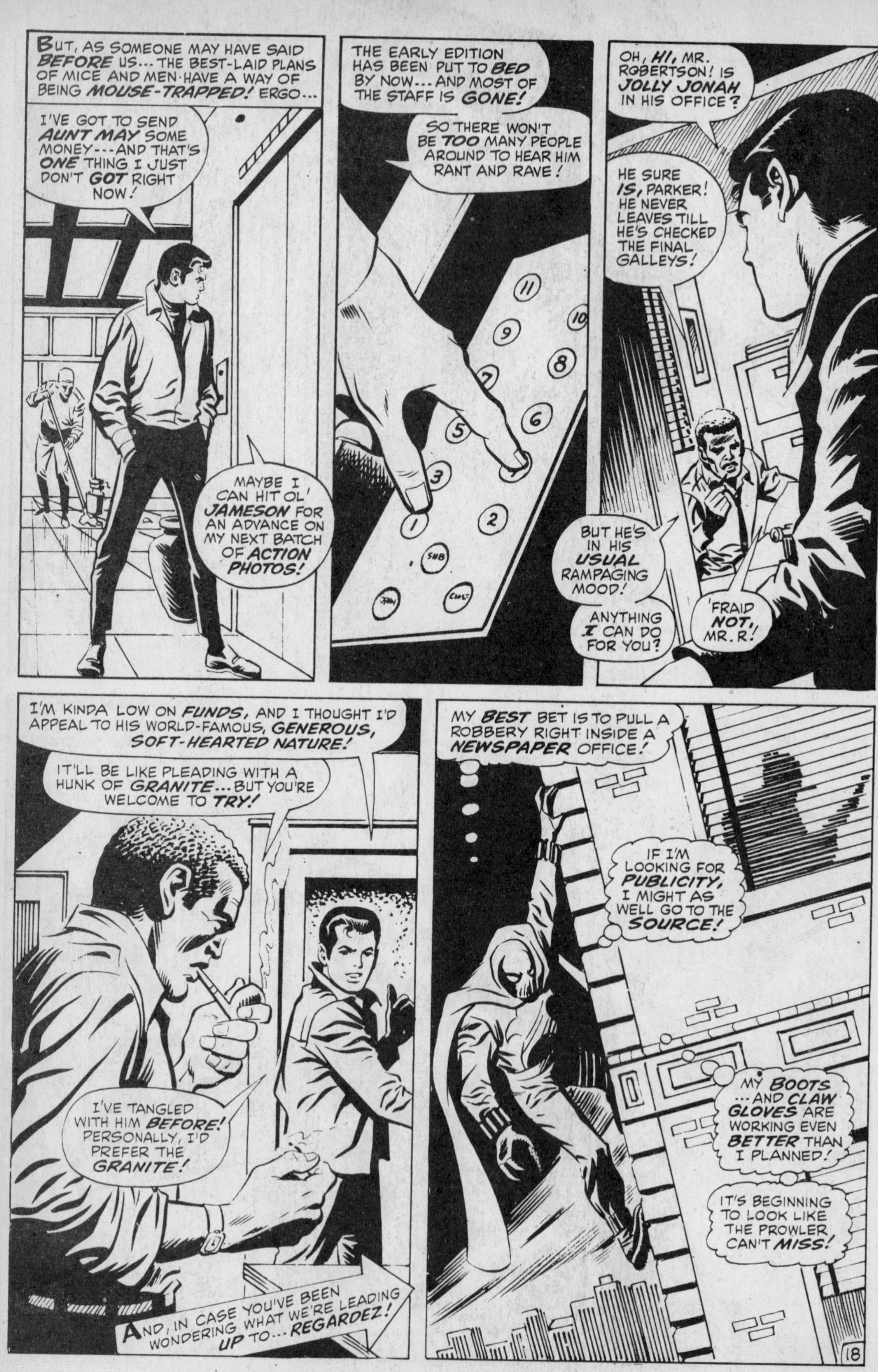
BUT, AS SOMEONE MAY HAVE SAID BEFORE US... THE BEST-LAID PLANS OF MICE AND MEN HAVE A WAY OF BEING MOUSE-TRAPPED! ERGO...
I'VE GOT TO SEND AUNT MAY SOME MONEY---AND THAT'S ONE THING I JUST DON'T GOT RIGHT NOW!
MAYBE I CAN HIT OL' JAMESON FOR AN ADVANCE ON MY NEXT BATCH OF ACTION PHOTOS!
THE EARLY EDITION HAS BEEN PUT TO BED BY NOW... AND MOST OF THE STAFF IS GONE!
SO THERE WON'T BE TOO MANY PEOPLE AROUND TO HEAR HIM RANT AND RAVE!
OH, HI, MR. ROBERTSON! IS JOLLY JONAH IN HIS OFFICE?
HE SURE IS, PARKER! HE NEVER LEAVES TILL HE'S CHECKED THE FINAL GALLEYS!
BUT HE'S IN HIS USUAL RAMPAGING MOOD!
ANYTHING I CAN DO FOR YOU?
'FRAID NOT, MR. R!
I'M KINDA LOW ON FUNDS, AND I THOUGHT I'D APPEAL TO HIS WORLD-FAMOUS, GENEROUS, SOFT-HEARTED NATURE!
IT'LL BE LIKE PLEADING WITH A HUNK OF GRANITE... BUT YOU'RE WELCOME TO TRY!
I'VE TANGLED WITH HIM BEFORE! PERSONALLY, I'D PREFER THE GRANITE!
AND, IN CASE YOU'VE BEEN WONDERING WHAT WE'RE LEADING UP TO... REGARDEZ!
MY BEST BET IS TO PULL A ROBBERY RIGHT INSIDE A NEWSPAPER OFFICE!
IF I'M LOOKING FOR PUBLICITY, I MIGHT AS WELL GO TO THE SOURCE!
MY BOOTS ...AND CLAW GLOVES ARE WORKING EVEN BETTER THAN I PLANNED!
IT'S BEGINNING TO LOOK LIKE THE PROWLER CAN'T MISS!
18

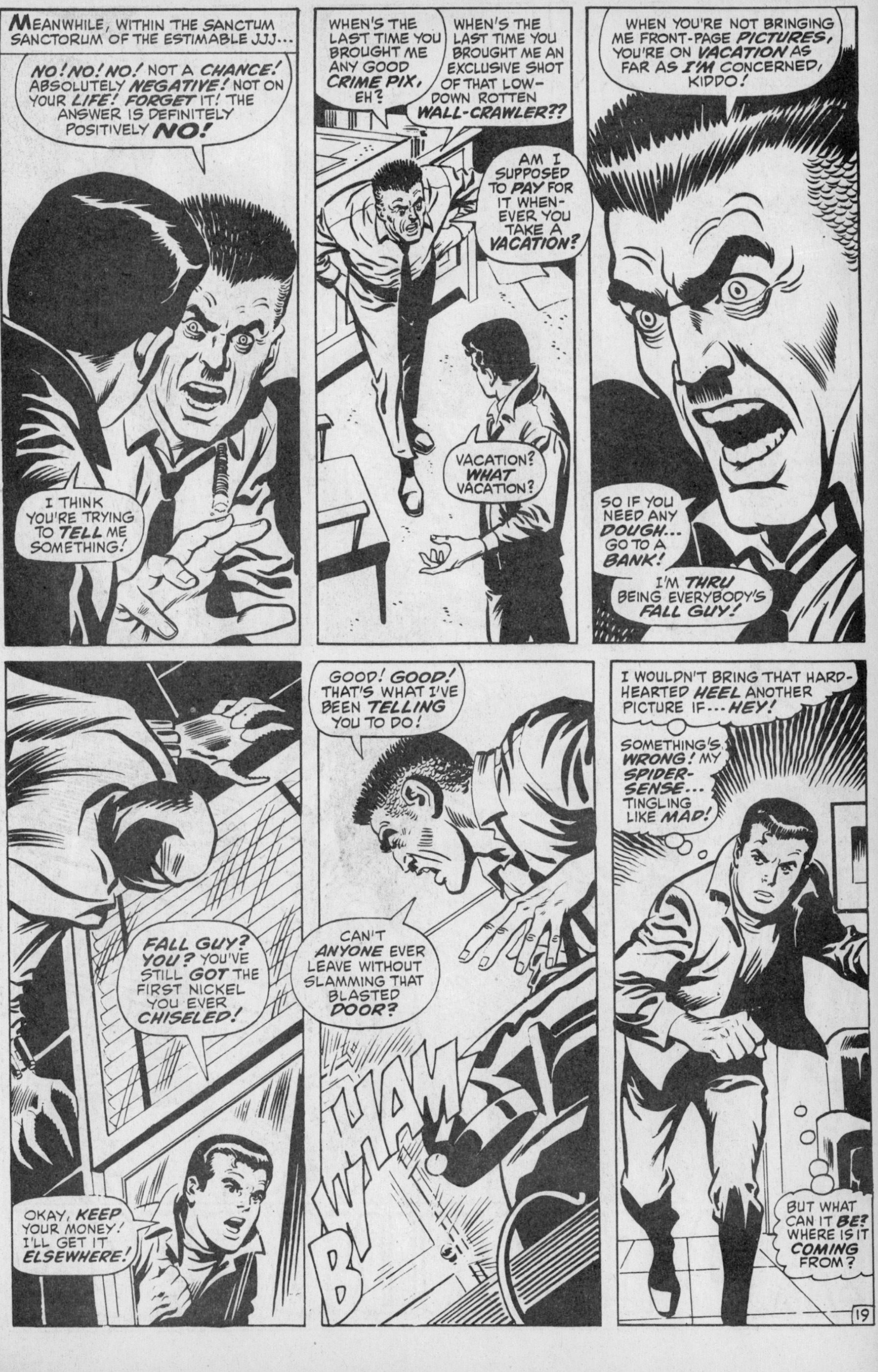
MEANWHILE, WITHIN THE SANCTUM SANCTORUM OF THE ESTIMABLE JJJ...
NO! NO! NO! NOT A CHANCE! ABSOLUTELY NEGATIVE! NOT ON YOUR LIFE! FORGET IT! THE ANSWER IS DEFINITELY POSITIVELY NO!
I THINK YOU'RE TRYING TO TELL ME SOMETHING!
WHEN'S THE LAST TIME YOU BROUGHT ME ANY GOOD CRIME PIX, EH?
WHEN'S THE LAST TIME YOU BROUGHT ME AN EXCLUSIVE SHOT OF THAT LOW-DOWN ROTTEN WALL-CRAWLER??
AM I SUPPOSED TO PAY FOR IT WHEN-EVER YOU TAKE A VACATION?
VACATION? WHAT VACATION?
WHEN YOU'RE NOT BRINGING ME FRONT-PAGE PICTURES, YOU'RE ON VACATION AS FAR AS I'M CONCERNED, KIDDO!
SO IF YOU NEED ANY DOUGH... GO TO A BANK!
I'M THRU BEING EVERYBODY'S FALL GUY!
FALL GUY? YOU? YOU'VE STILL GOT THE FIRST NICKEL YOU EVER CHISELED!
OKAY, KEEP YOUR MONEY! I'LL GET IT ELSEWHERE!
GOOD! GOOD! THAT'S WHAT I'VE BEEN TELLING YOU TO DO!
CAN'T ANYONE EVER LEAVE WITHOUT SLAMMING THAT BLASTED DOOR?
BWHAM!
I WOULDN'T BRING THAT HARD-HEARTED HEEL ANOTHER PICTURE IF--- HEY!
SOMETHING'S WRONG! MY SPIDER-SENSE... TINGLING LIKE MAD!
BUT WHAT CAN IT BE? WHERE IS IT COMING FROM?

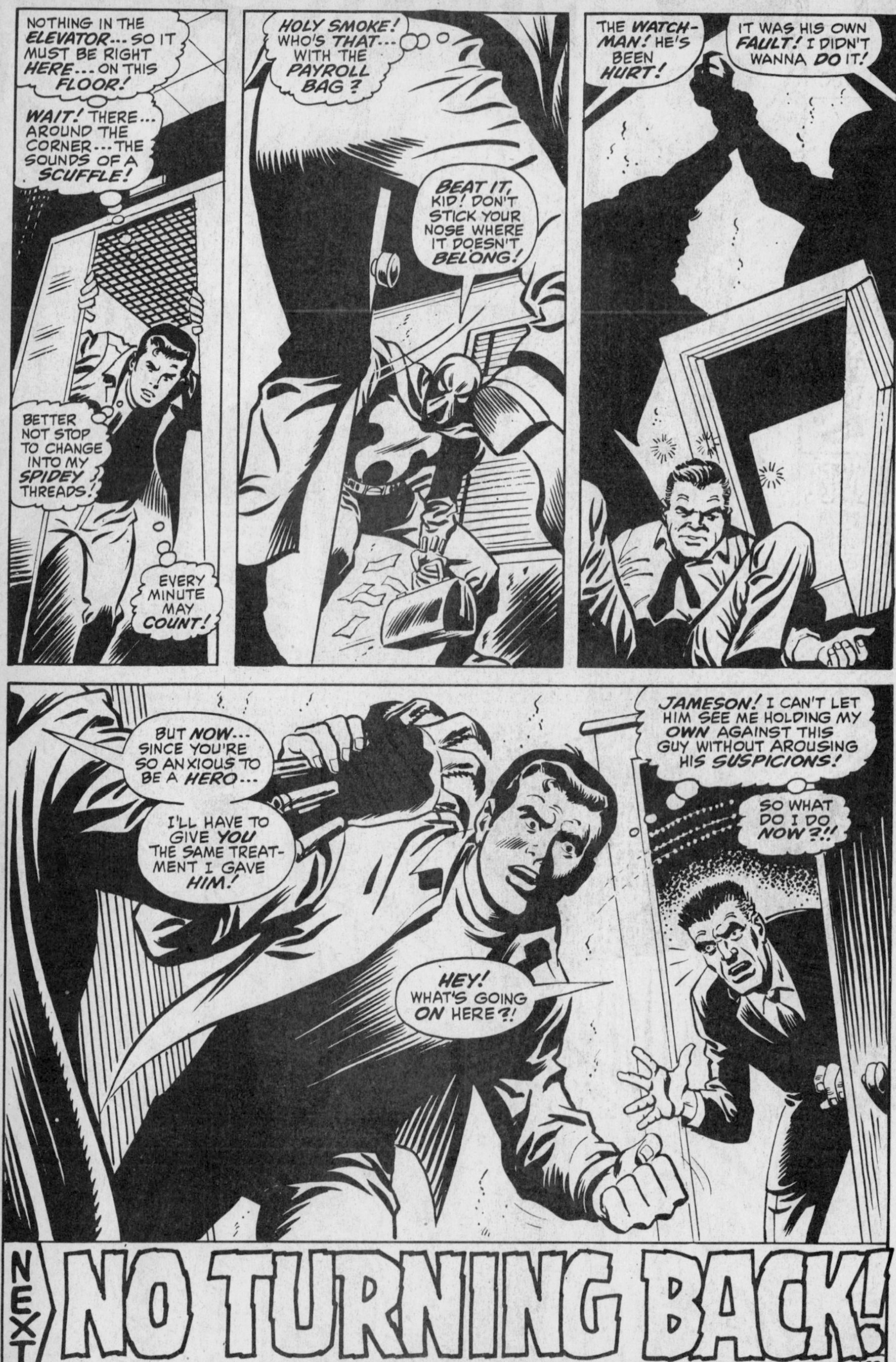
NOTHING IN THE ELEVATOR... SO IT MUST BE RIGHT HERE... ON THIS FLOOR!
WAIT! THERE... AROUND THE CORNER... THE SOUNDS OF A SCUFFLE!
BETTER NOT STOP TO CHANGE INTO MY SPIDEY THREADS!
EVERY MINUTE MAY COUNT!
HOLY SMOKE! WHO'S THAT... WITH THE PAYROLL BAG?
BEAT IT, KID! DON'T STICK YOUR NOSE WHERE IT DOESN'T BELONG!
THE WATCH-MAN! HE'S BEEN HURT!
IT WAS HIS OWN FAULT! I DIDN'T WANNA DO IT!
BUT NOW... SINCE YOU'RE SO ANXIOUS TO BE A HERO...
I'LL HAVE TO GIVE YOU THE SAME TREAT-MENT I GAVE HIM!
JAMESON! I CAN'T LET HIM SEE ME HOLDING MY OWN AGAINST THIS GUY WITHOUT AROUSING HIS SUSPICIONS!
SO WHAT DO I DO NOW?!!
HEY! WHAT'S GOING ON HERE?!
NEXT
NO TURNING BACK!
20

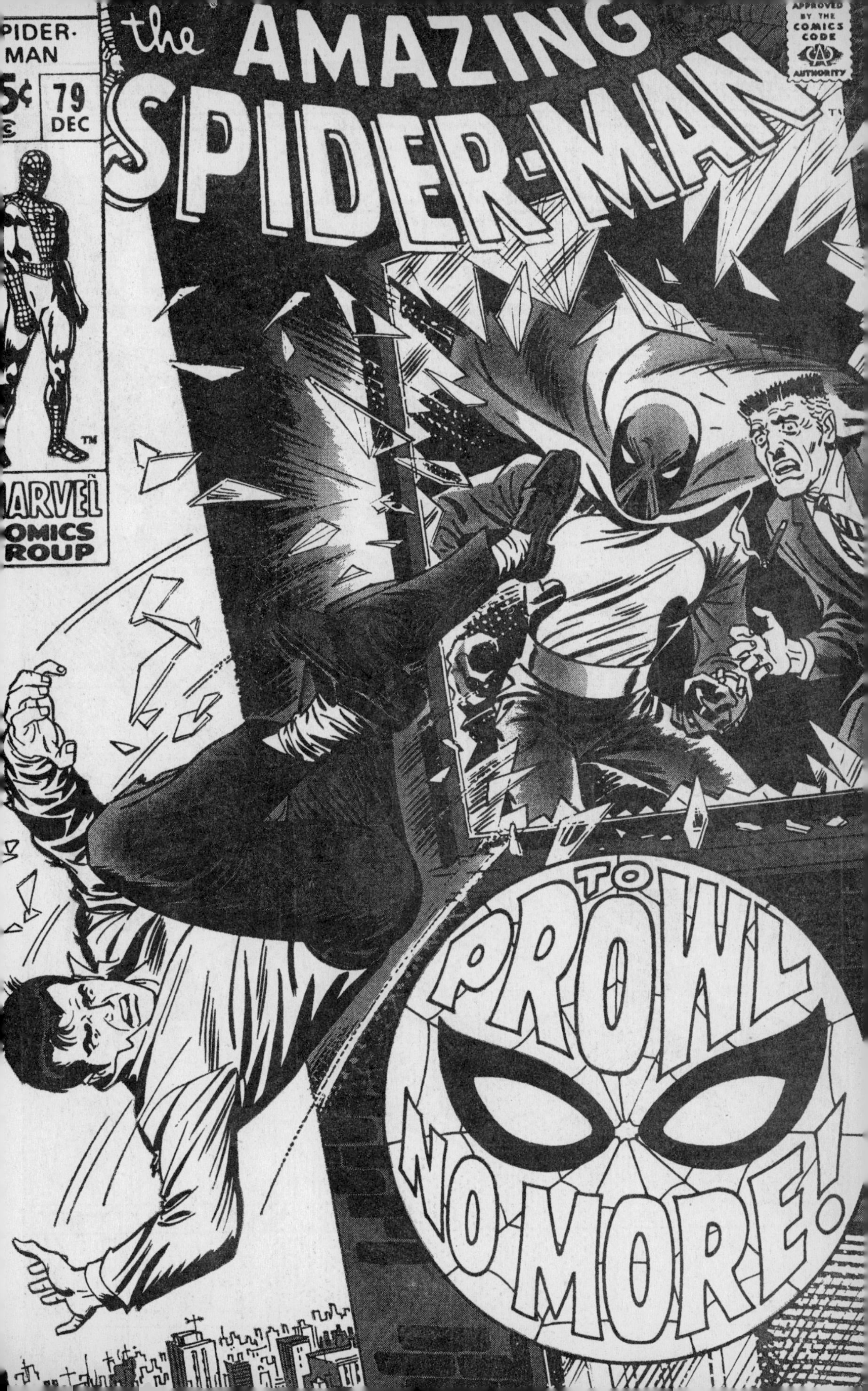
SPIDER-MAN
15¢
79
DEC
MARVEL COMICS GROUP
the AMAZING SPIDER-MAN
APPROVED BY THE COMICS CODE AUTHORITY
TO PROWL NO MORE!

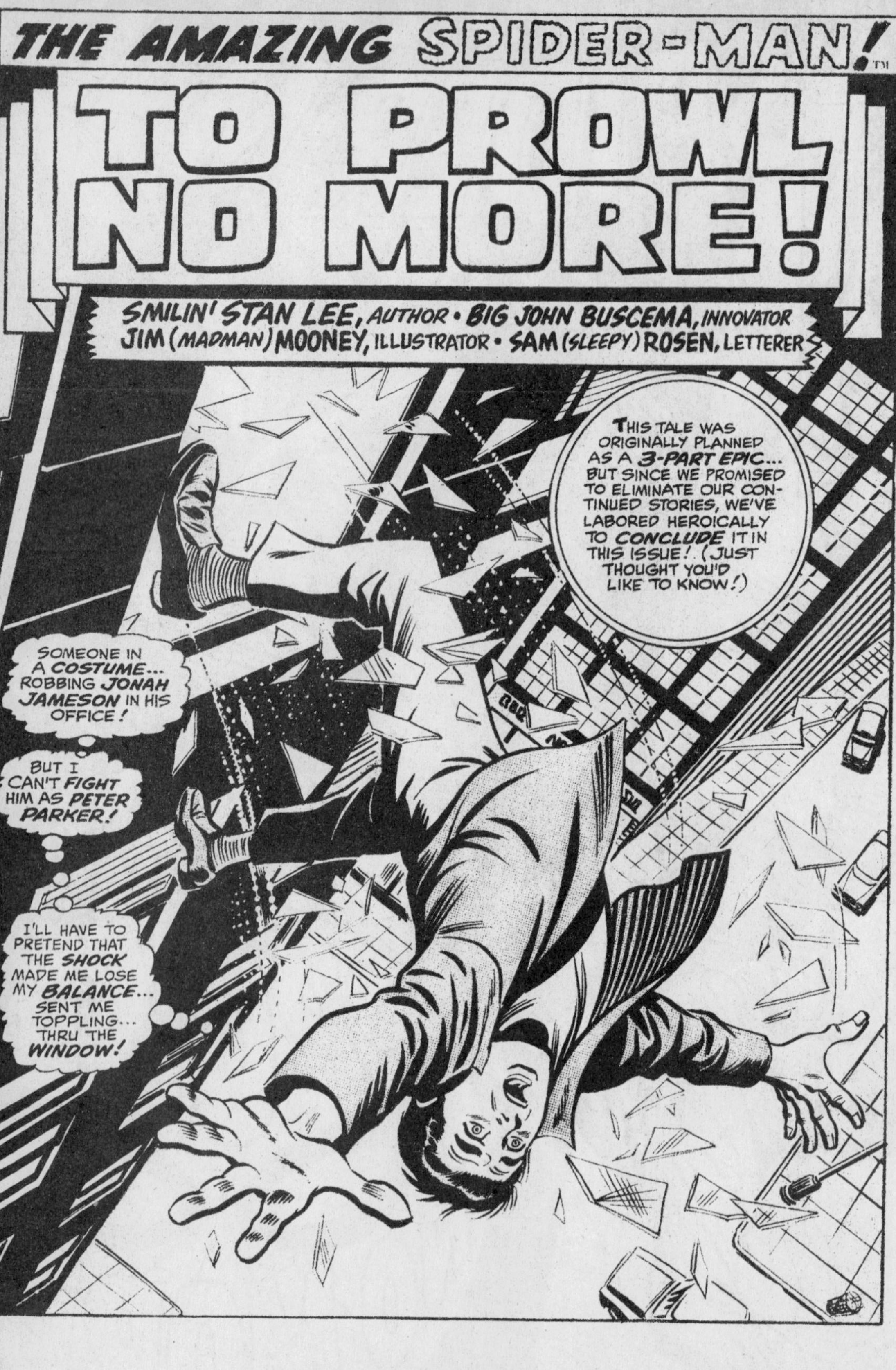

THE AMAZING SPIDER-MAN!
TO PROWL NO MORE!
SMILIN' STAN LEE, AUTHOR • BIG JOHN BUSCEMA, INNOVATOR
JIM (MADMAN) MOONEY, ILLUSTRATOR • SAM (SLEEPY) ROSEN, LETTERER
THIS TALE WAS ORIGINALLY PLANNED AS A 3-PART EPIC... BUT SINCE WE PROMISED TO ELIMINATE OUR CONTINUED STORIES, WE'VE LABORED HEROICALLY TO CONCLUDE IT IN THIS ISSUE! (JUST THOUGHT YOU'D LIKE TO KNOW!)
SOMEONE IN A COSTUME... ROBBING JONAH JAMESON IN HIS OFFICE!
BUT I CAN'T FIGHT HIM AS PETER PARKER!
I'LL HAVE TO PRETEND THAT THE SHOCK MADE ME LOSE MY BALANCE... SENT ME TOPPLING... THRU THE WINDOW!

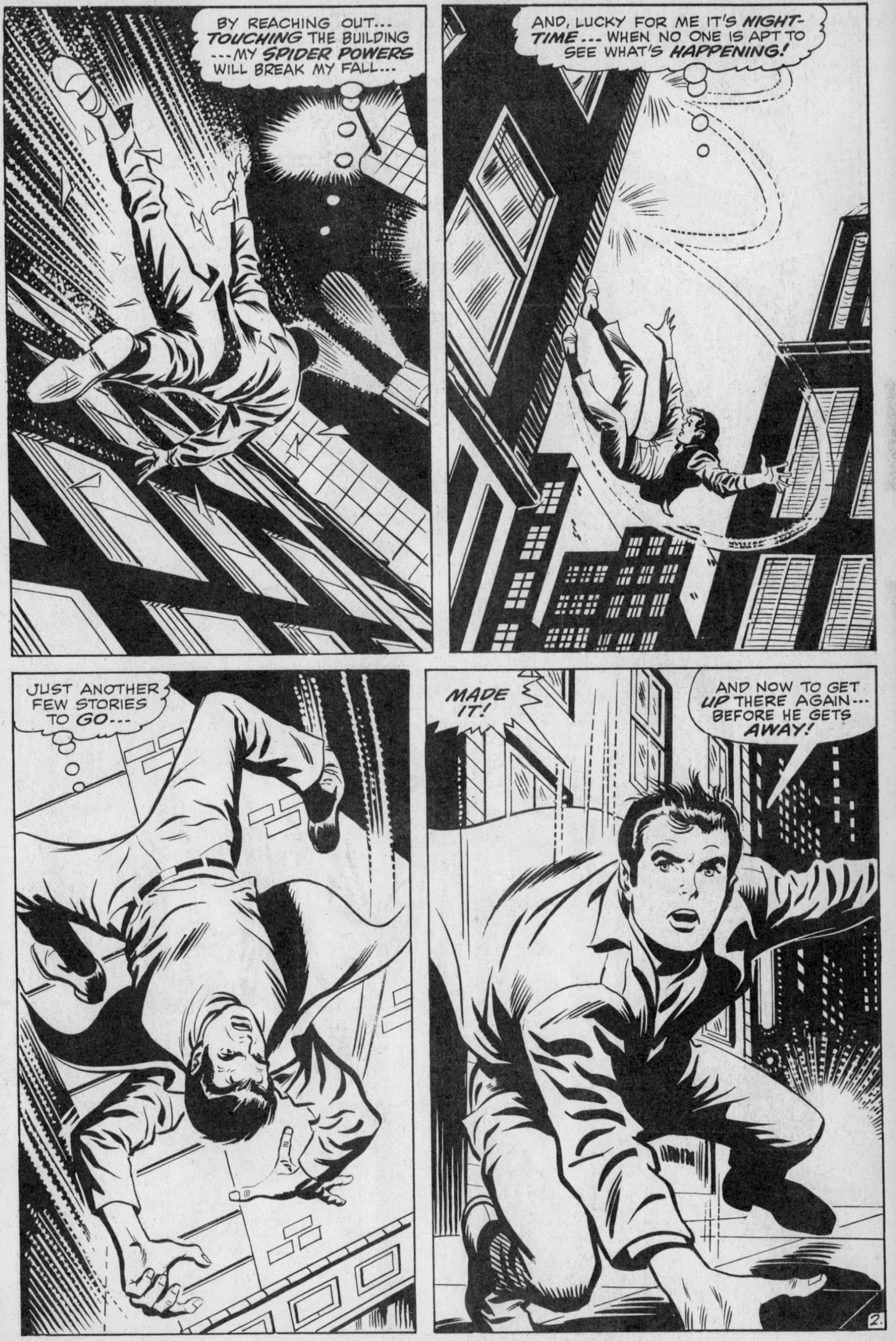
BY REACHING OUT... TOUCHING THE BUILDING ---MY SPIDER POWERS WILL BREAK MY FALL...
AND, LUCKY FOR ME IT'S NIGHT-TIME... WHEN NO ONE IS APT TO SEE WHAT'S HAPPENING!
JUST ANOTHER FEW STORIES TO GO...
MADE IT!
AND NOW TO GET UP THERE AGAIN--- BEFORE HE GETS AWAY!
2.

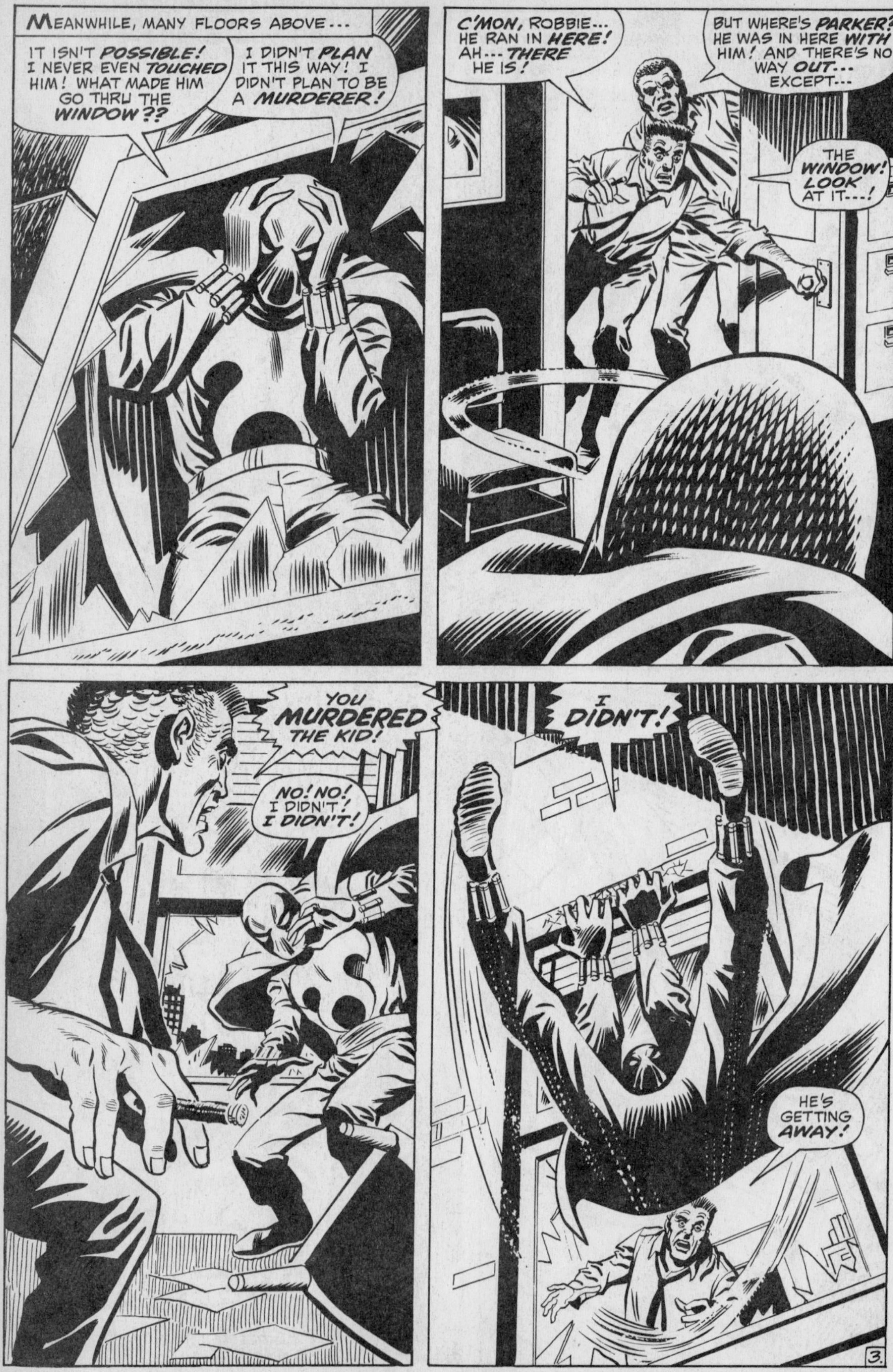
MEANWHILE, MANY FLOORS ABOVE...
IT ISN'T POSSIBLE! I NEVER EVEN TOUCHED HIM! WHAT MADE HIM GO THRU THE WINDOW??
I DIDN'T PLAN IT THIS WAY! I DIDN'T PLAN TO BE A MURDERER!
C'MON, ROBBIE... HE RAN IN HERE! AH--- THERE HE IS!
BUT WHERE'S PARKER? HE WAS IN HERE WITH HIM! AND THERE'S NO WAY OUT--- EXCEPT---
THE WINDOW! LOOK AT IT---!
YOU MURDERED THE KID!
NO! NO! I DIDN'T! I DIDN'T!
I DIDN'T!
HE'S GETTING AWAY!
3.

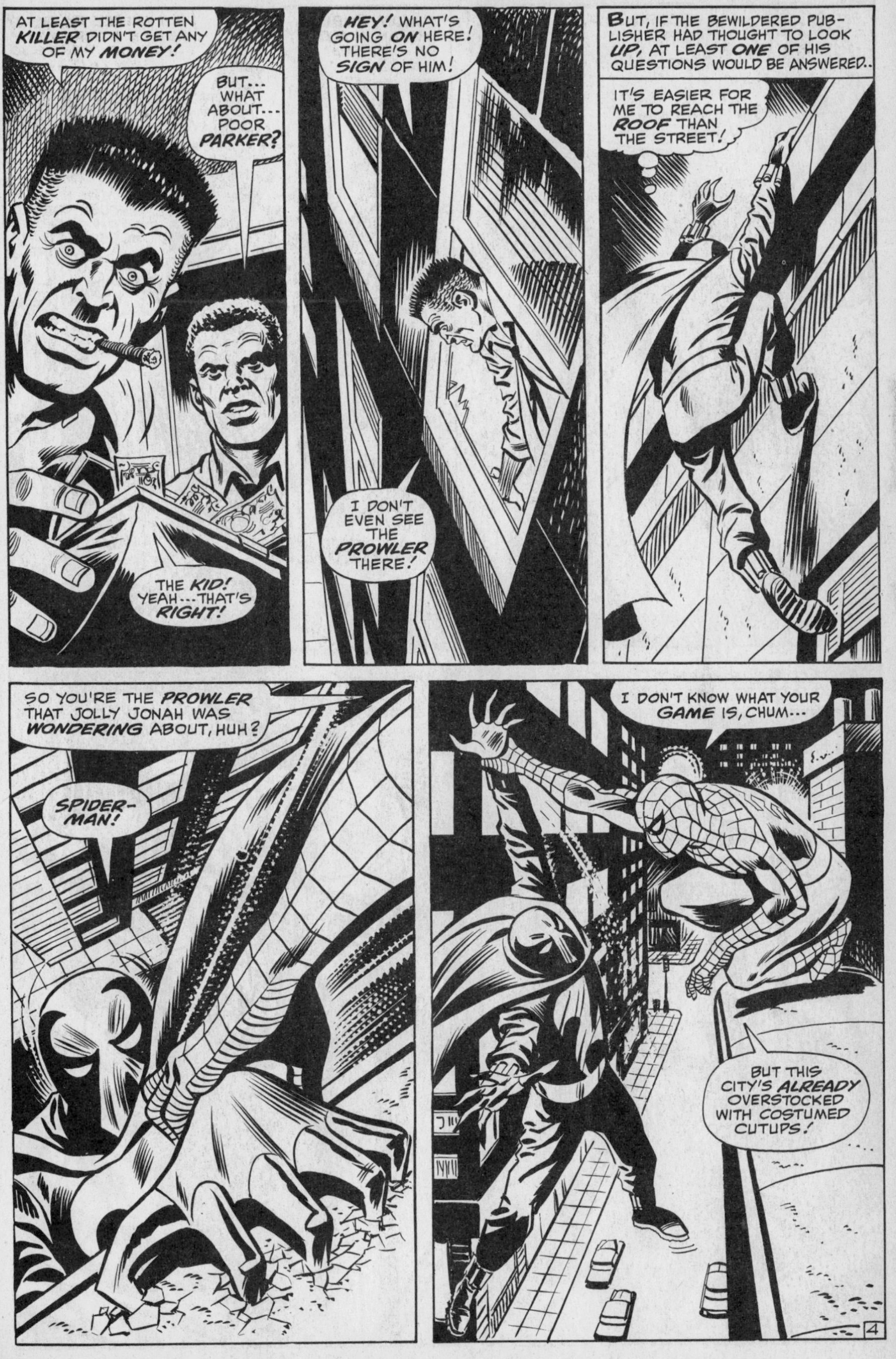

AT LEAST THE ROTTEN KILLER DIDN'T GET ANY OF MY MONEY!
BUT... WHAT ABOUT... POOR PARKER?
THE KID! YEAH---THAT'S RIGHT!
HEY! WHAT'S GOING ON HERE! THERE'S NO SIGN OF HIM!
I DON'T EVEN SEE THE PROWLER THERE!
BUT, IF THE BEWILDERED PUBLISHER HAD THOUGHT TO LOOK UP, AT LEAST ONE OF HIS QUESTIONS WOULD BE ANSWERED..
IT'S EASIER FOR ME TO REACH THE ROOF THAN THE STREET!
SO YOU'RE THE PROWLER THAT JOLLY JONAH WAS WONDERING ABOUT, HUH?
SPIDER-MAN!
I DON'T KNOW WHAT YOUR GAME IS, CHUM...
BUT THIS CITY'S ALREADY OVERSTOCKED WITH COSTUMED CUTUPS!
4

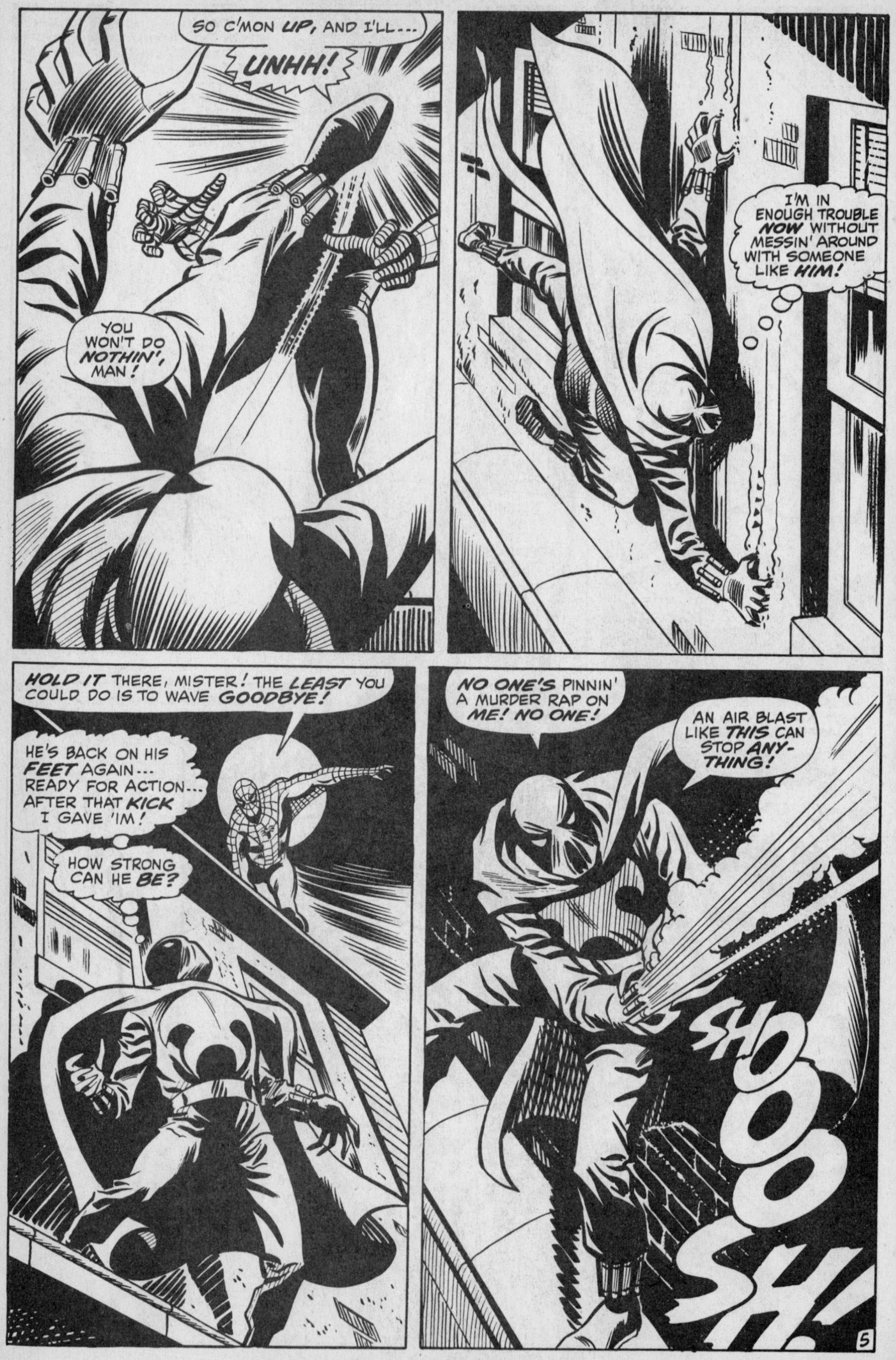
SO C'MON UP, AND I'LL...
UNHH!
YOU WON'T DO NOTHIN', MAN!
I'M IN ENOUGH TROUBLE NOW WITHOUT MESSIN' AROUND WITH SOMEONE LIKE HIM!
HOLD IT THERE, MISTER! THE LEAST YOU COULD DO IS TO WAVE GOODBYE!
HE'S BACK ON HIS FEET AGAIN... READY FOR ACTION... AFTER THAT KICK I GAVE 'IM!
HOW STRONG CAN HE BE?
NO ONE'S PINNIN' A MURDER RAP ON ME! NO ONE!
AN AIR BLAST LIKE THIS CAN STOP ANY-THING!
SHOOOSH!
5

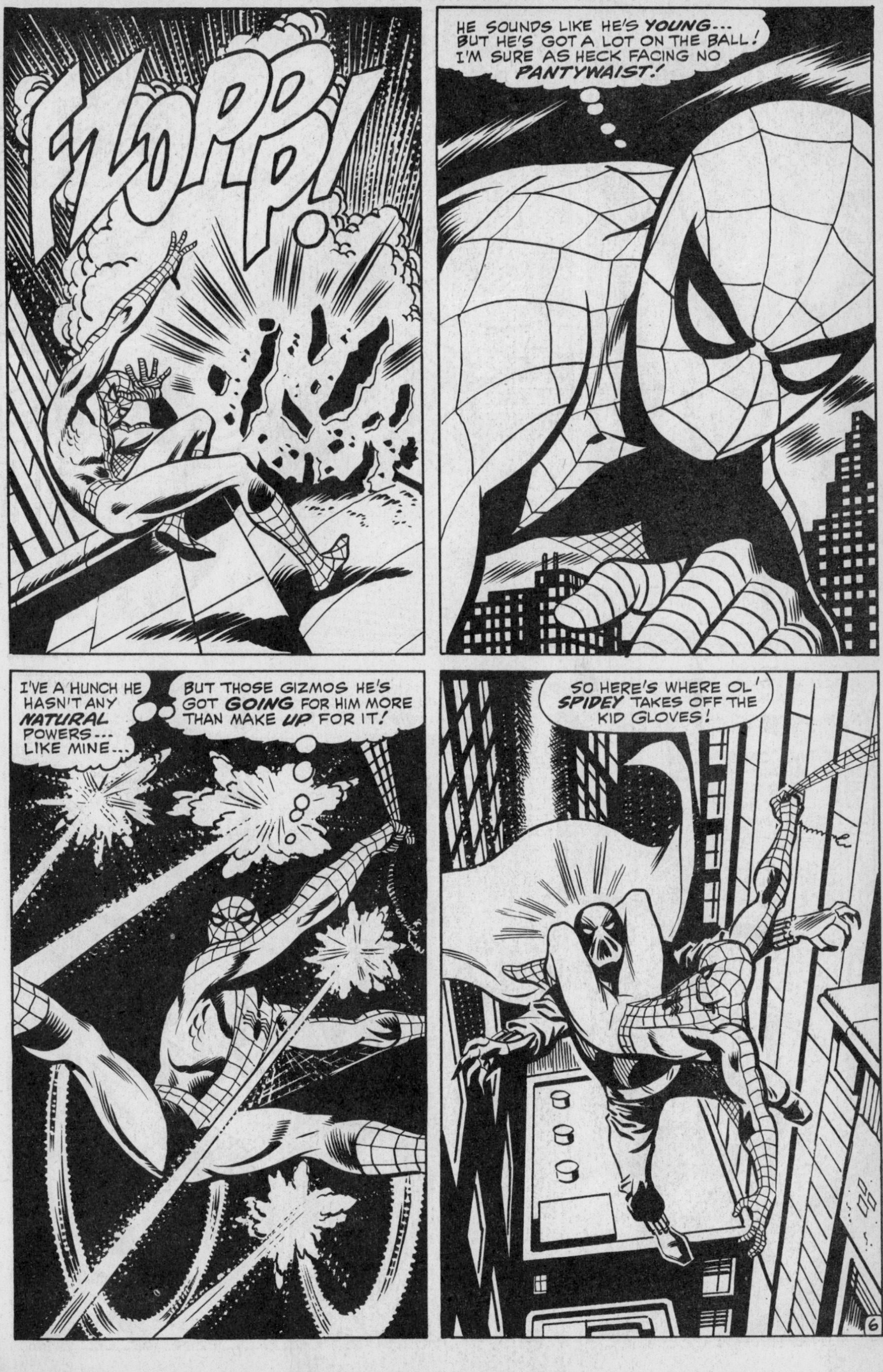
FZOPP!
HE SOUNDS LIKE HE'S YOUNG... BUT HE'S GOT A LOT ON THE BALL! I'M SURE AS HECK FACING NO PANTYWAIST!
I'VE A HUNCH HE HASN'T ANY NATURAL POWERS... LIKE MINE...
BUT THOSE GIZMOS HE'S GOT GOING FOR HIM MORE THAN MAKE UP FOR IT!
SO HERE'S WHERE OL' SPIDEY TAKES OFF THE KID GLOVES!
6

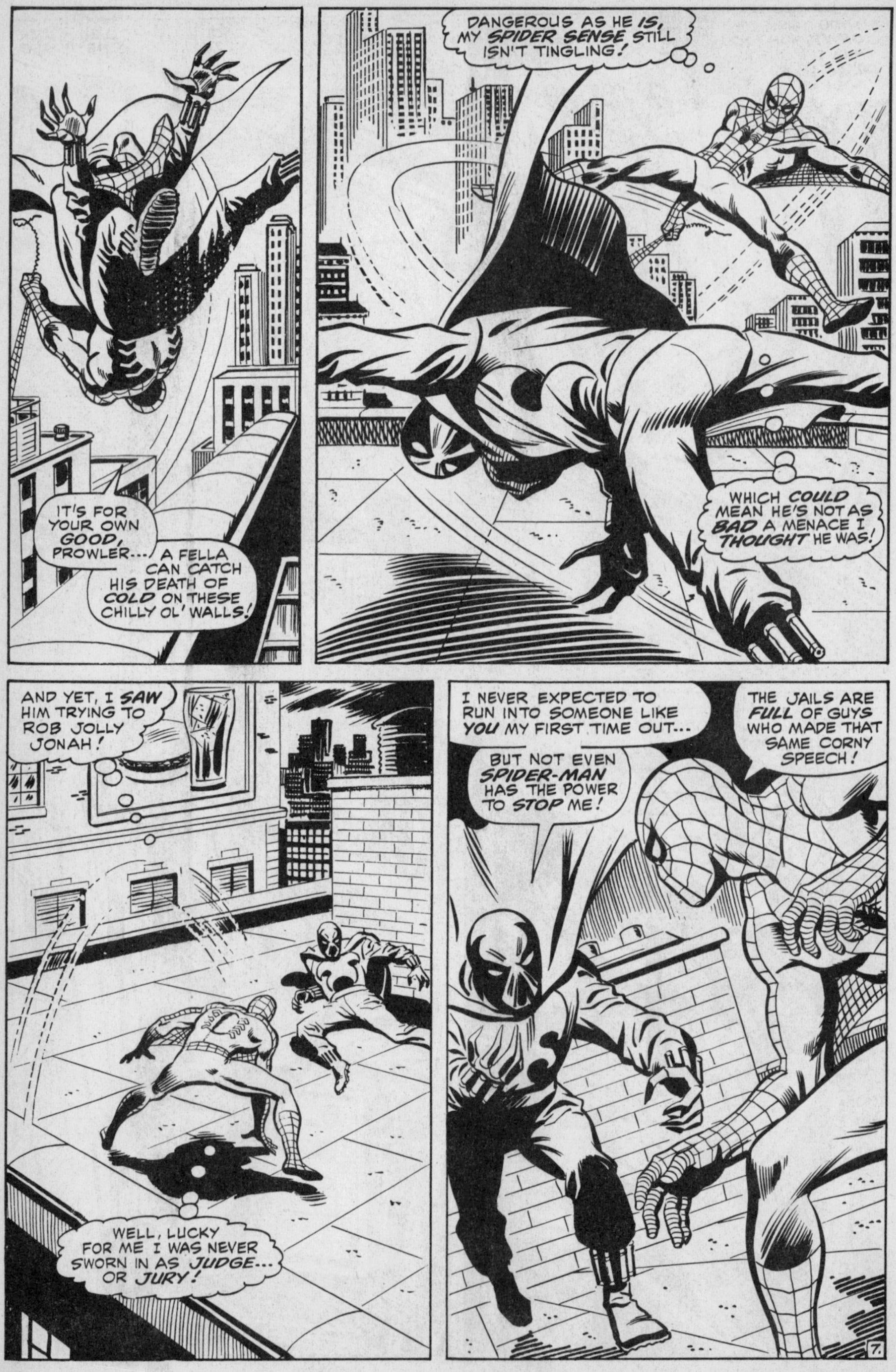
IT'S FOR YOUR OWN GOOD, PROWLER... A FELLA CAN CATCH HIS DEATH OF COLD ON THESE CHILLY OL' WALLS!
DANGEROUS AS HE IS, MY SPIDER SENSE STILL ISN'T TINGLING!
WHICH COULD MEAN HE'S NOT AS BAD A MENACE I THOUGHT HE WAS!
AND YET, I SAW HIM TRYING TO ROB JOLLY JONAH!
WELL, LUCKY FOR ME I WAS NEVER SWORN IN AS JUDGE... OR JURY!
I NEVER EXPECTED TO RUN INTO SOMEONE LIKE YOU MY FIRST TIME OUT...
BUT NOT EVEN SPIDER-MAN HAS THE POWER TO STOP ME!
THE JAILS ARE FULL OF GUYS WHO MADE THAT SAME CORNY SPEECH!
7.

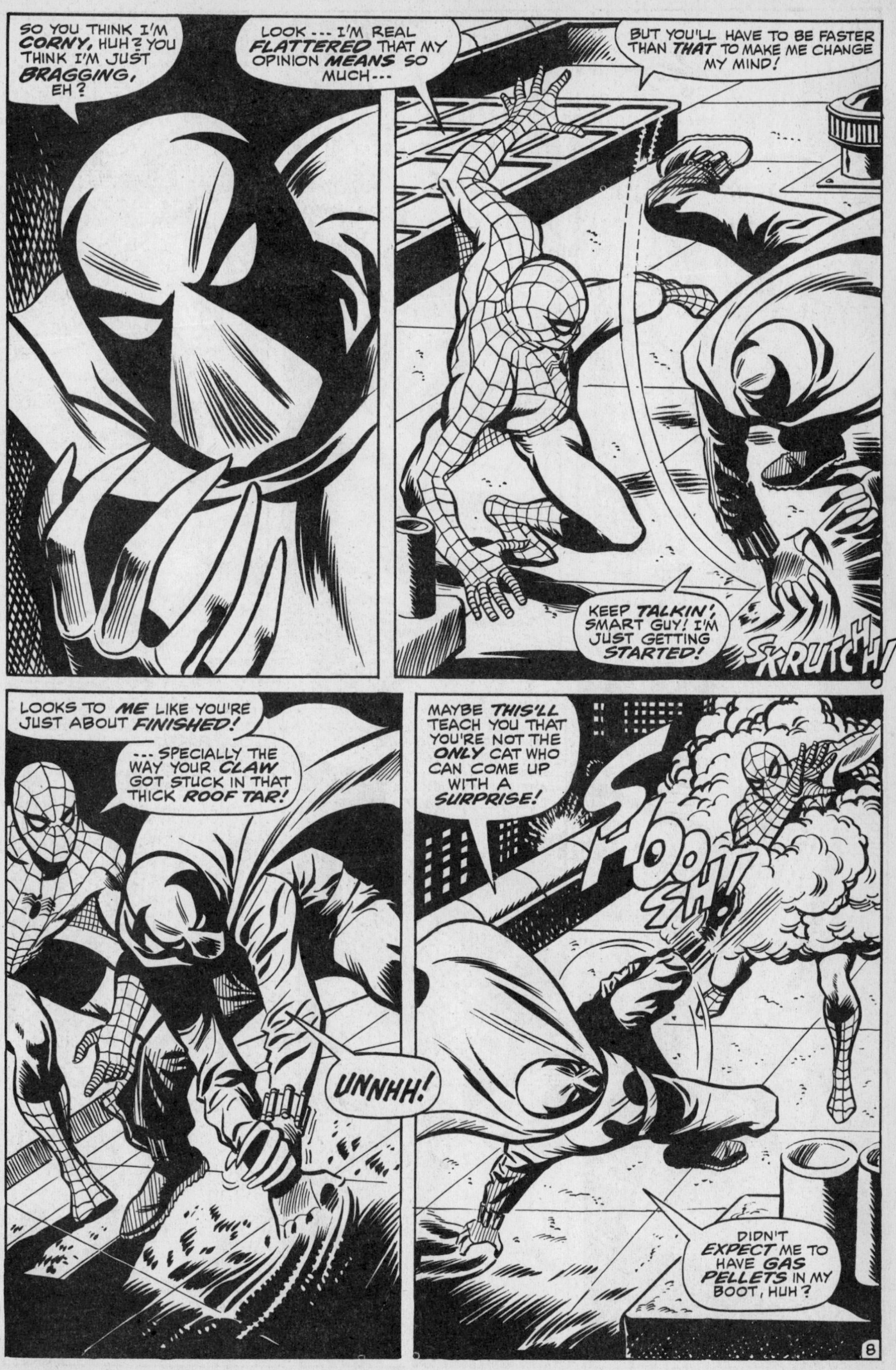

SO YOU THINK I'M CORNY, HUH? YOU THINK I'M JUST BRAGGING, EH?
LOOK --- I'M REAL FLATTERED THAT MY OPINION MEANS SO MUCH---
BUT YOU'LL HAVE TO BE FASTER THAN THAT TO MAKE ME CHANGE MY MIND!
KEEP TALKIN', SMART GUY! I'M JUST GETTING STARTED!
SKRUTCHH!
LOOKS TO ME LIKE YOU'RE JUST ABOUT FINISHED!
--- SPECIALLY THE WAY YOUR CLAW GOT STUCK IN THAT THICK ROOF TAR!
UNNHH!
MAYBE THIS'LL TEACH YOU THAT YOU'RE NOT THE ONLY CAT WHO CAN COME UP WITH A SURPRISE!
SHOOOSH!
DIDN'T EXPECT ME TO HAVE GAS PELLETS IN MY BOOT, HUH?

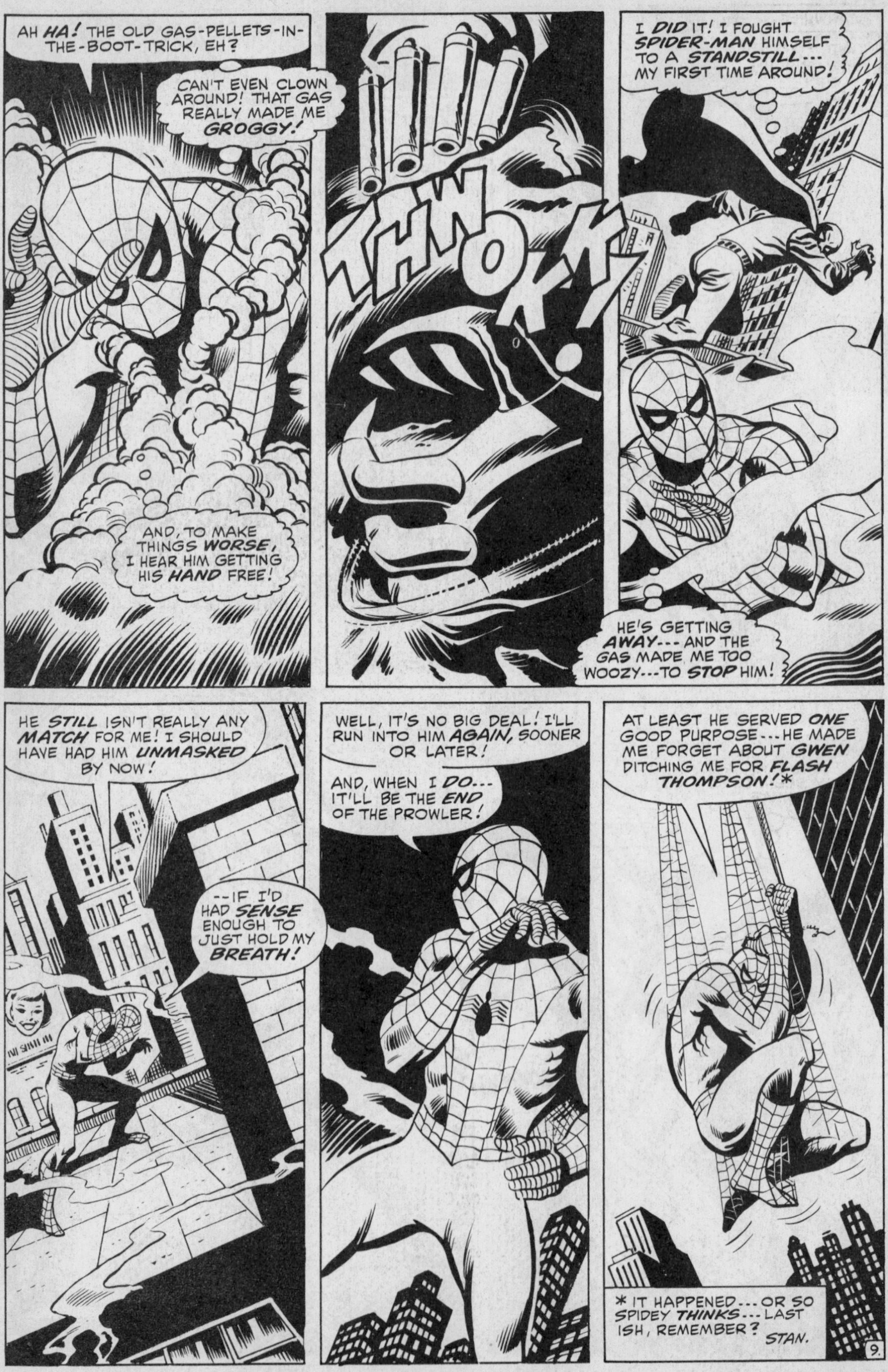
AH HA! THE OLD GAS-PELLETS-IN-THE-BOOT-TRICK, EH?
CAN'T EVEN CLOWN AROUND! THAT GAS REALLY MADE ME GROGGY!
AND, TO MAKE THINGS WORSE, I HEAR HIM GETTING HIS HAND FREE!
THWOK!
I DID IT! I FOUGHT SPIDER-MAN HIMSELF TO A STANDSTILL--- MY FIRST TIME AROUND!
HE'S GETTING AWAY--- AND THE GAS MADE ME TOO WOOZY---TO STOP HIM!
HE STILL ISN'T REALLY ANY MATCH FOR ME! I SHOULD HAVE HAD HIM UNMASKED BY NOW!
--IF I'D HAD SENSE ENOUGH TO JUST HOLD MY BREATH!
WELL, IT'S NO BIG DEAL! I'LL RUN INTO HIM AGAIN, SOONER OR LATER!
AND, WHEN I DO... IT'LL BE THE END OF THE PROWLER!
AT LEAST HE SERVED ONE GOOD PURPOSE---HE MADE ME FORGET ABOUT GWEN DITCHING ME FOR FLASH THOMPSON!*
* IT HAPPENED--- OR SO SPIDEY THINKS--- LAST ISH, REMEMBER? STAN.

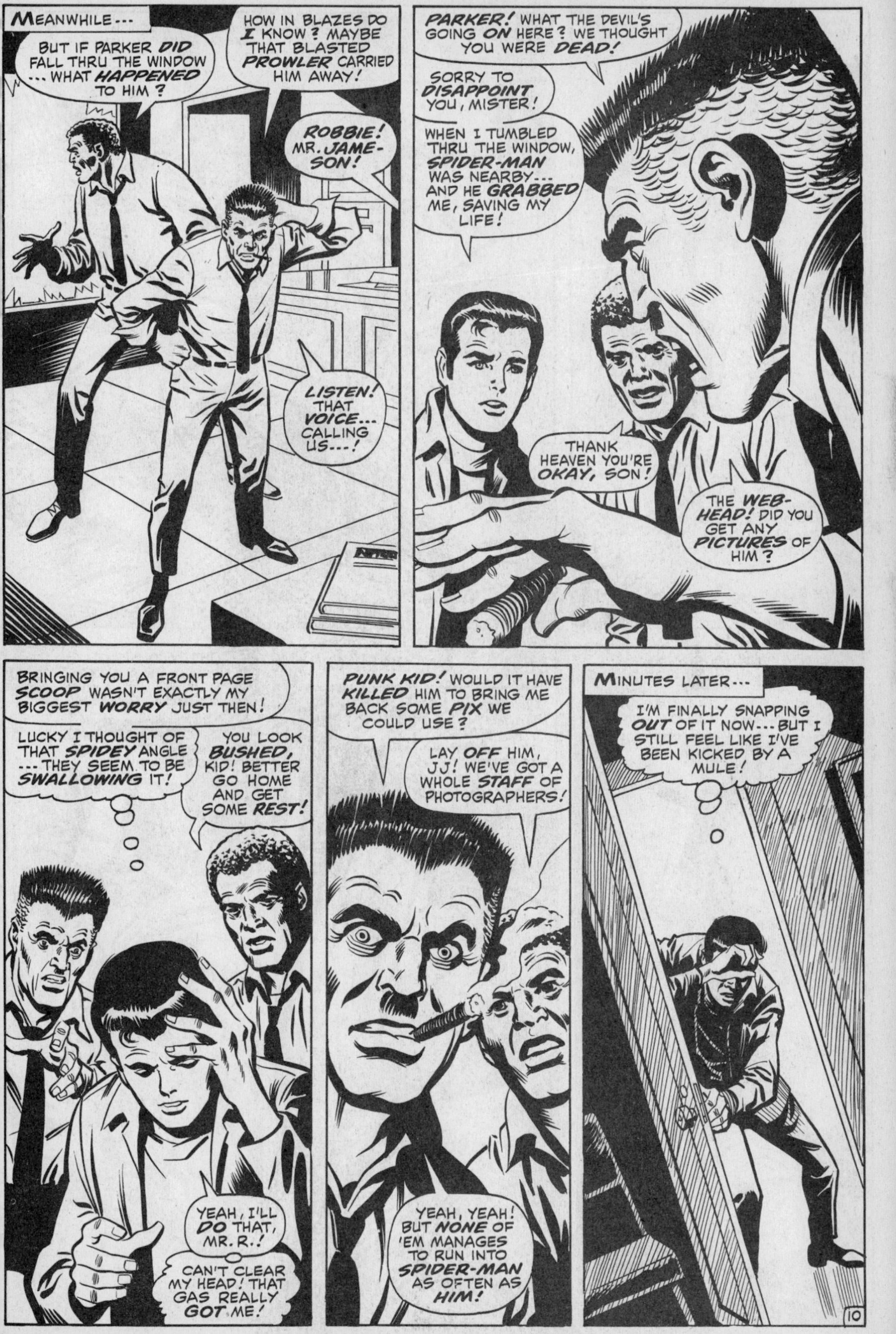
MEANWHILE...
BUT IF PARKER DID FALL THRU THE WINDOW ...WHAT HAPPENED TO HIM ?
HOW IN BLAZES DO I KNOW ? MAYBE THAT BLASTED PROWLER CARRIED HIM AWAY !
ROBBIE! MR. JAMESON!
LISTEN! THAT VOICE... CALLING US...!
PARKER! WHAT THE DEVIL'S GOING ON HERE ? WE THOUGHT YOU WERE DEAD!
SORRY TO DISAPPOINT YOU, MISTER!
WHEN I TUMBLED THRU THE WINDOW, SPIDER-MAN WAS NEARBY... AND HE GRABBED ME, SAVING MY LIFE!
THANK HEAVEN YOU'RE OKAY, SON!
THE WEB-HEAD! DID YOU GET ANY PICTURES OF HIM ?
BRINGING YOU A FRONT PAGE SCOOP WASN'T EXACTLY MY BIGGEST WORRY JUST THEN!
LUCKY I THOUGHT OF THAT SPIDEY ANGLE --- THEY SEEM TO BE SWALLOWING IT!
YOU LOOK BUSHED, KID! BETTER GO HOME AND GET SOME REST!
YEAH, I'LL DO THAT, MR. R.!
CAN'T CLEAR MY HEAD! THAT GAS REALLY GOT ME!
PUNK KID! WOULD IT HAVE KILLED HIM TO BRING ME BACK SOME PIX WE COULD USE ?
LAY OFF HIM, JJ! WE'VE GOT A WHOLE STAFF OF PHOTOGRAPHERS!
YEAH, YEAH! BUT NONE OF 'EM MANAGES TO RUN INTO SPIDER-MAN AS OFTEN AS HIM!
MINUTES LATER...
I'M FINALLY SNAPPING OUT OF IT NOW... BUT I STILL FEEL LIKE I'VE BEEN KICKED BY A MULE!
10

WHY NOT BE *HONEST* WITH YOURSELF, PARKER? WHY NOT *ADMIT* IT---?

IT HURTS LOTS *MORE*... WHEN I THINK OF *GWEN*---THAN THE *PROWLER'S GAS BLAST* COULD EVER HURT ME!

I CAN ALWAYS WAIT FOR A *REMATCH* IF SOME COSTUMED CLOWN MANAGES TO *BEAT* ME THE FIRST TIME AROUND--

BUT WHAT DOES A FELLA *DO*...WHEN HE LEARNS THAT HE GAVE HIS *HEART* TO THE WRONG GIRL?

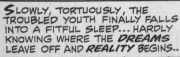

SLOWLY, TORTUOUSLY, THE TROUBLED YOUTH FINALLY FALLS INTO A FITFUL SLEEP...HARDLY KNOWING WHERE THE *DREAMS* LEAVE OFF AND *REALITY* BEGINS...

WHILE, IN ANOTHER PART OF TOWN...

I'M *HOME* AT LAST! STILL *SAFE*... STILL *UNDIS-COVERED*!

BUT, I THOUGHT IT WOULD BE A *LARK!* I THOUGHT I'D WIN *FAME--- GLORY!*

I DIDN'T KNOW I'D END UP...ACCUSED OF *MURDER!*

11.

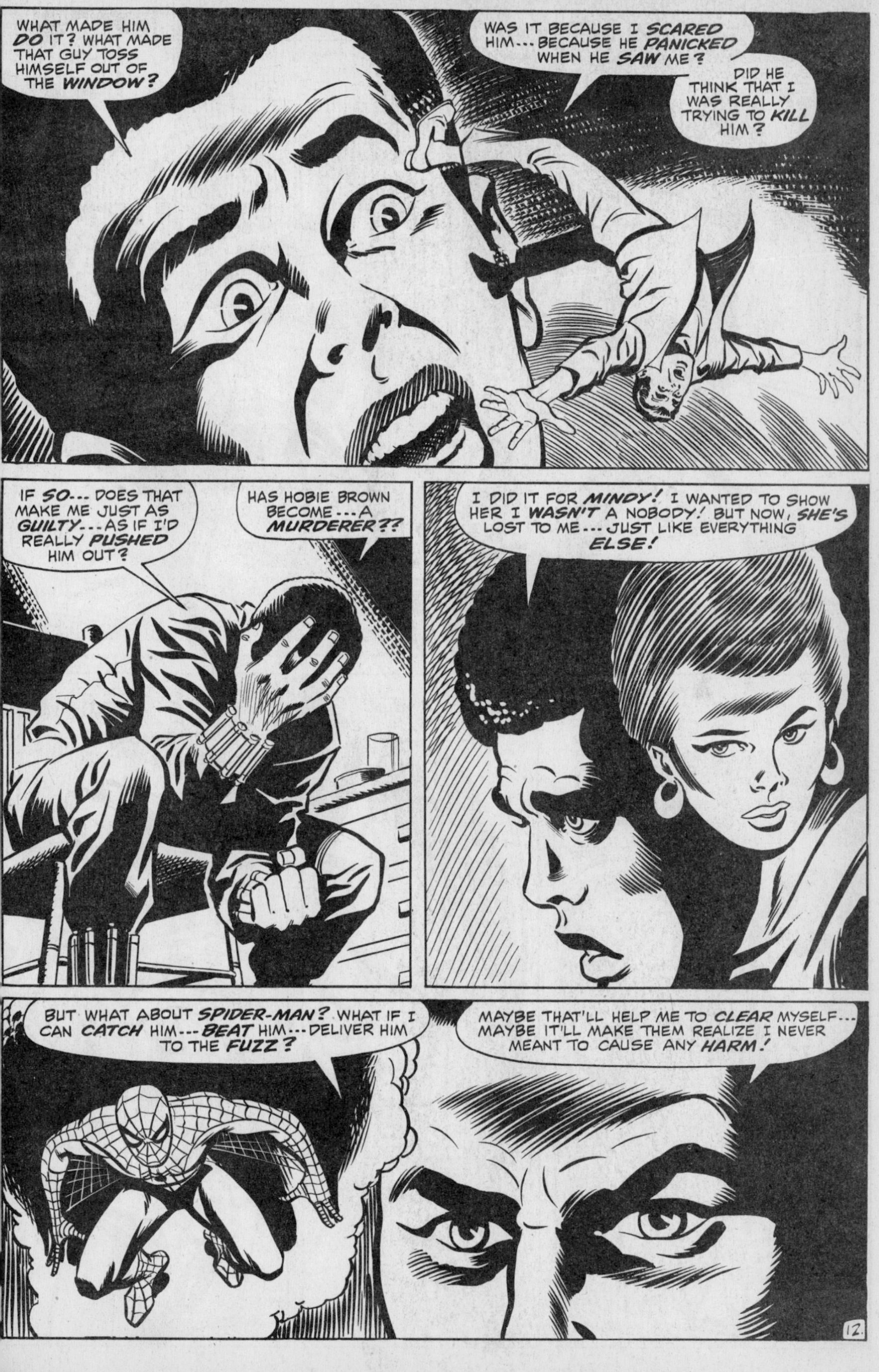
WHAT MADE HIM DO IT? WHAT MADE THAT GUY TOSS HIMSELF OUT OF THE WINDOW?
WAS IT BECAUSE I SCARED HIM--- BECAUSE HE PANICKED WHEN HE SAW ME?
DID HE THINK THAT I WAS REALLY TRYING TO KILL HIM?
IF SO--- DOES THAT MAKE ME JUST AS GUILTY---AS IF I'D REALLY PUSHED HIM OUT?
HAS HOBIE BROWN BECOME --- A MURDERER??
I DID IT FOR MINDY! I WANTED TO SHOW HER I WASN'T A NOBODY! BUT NOW, SHE'S LOST TO ME--- JUST LIKE EVERYTHING ELSE!
BUT WHAT ABOUT SPIDER-MAN? WHAT IF I CAN CATCH HIM--- BEAT HIM--- DELIVER HIM TO THE FUZZ?
MAYBE THAT'LL HELP ME TO CLEAR MYSELF--- MAYBE IT'LL MAKE THEM REALIZE I NEVER MEANT TO CAUSE ANY HARM!
12.

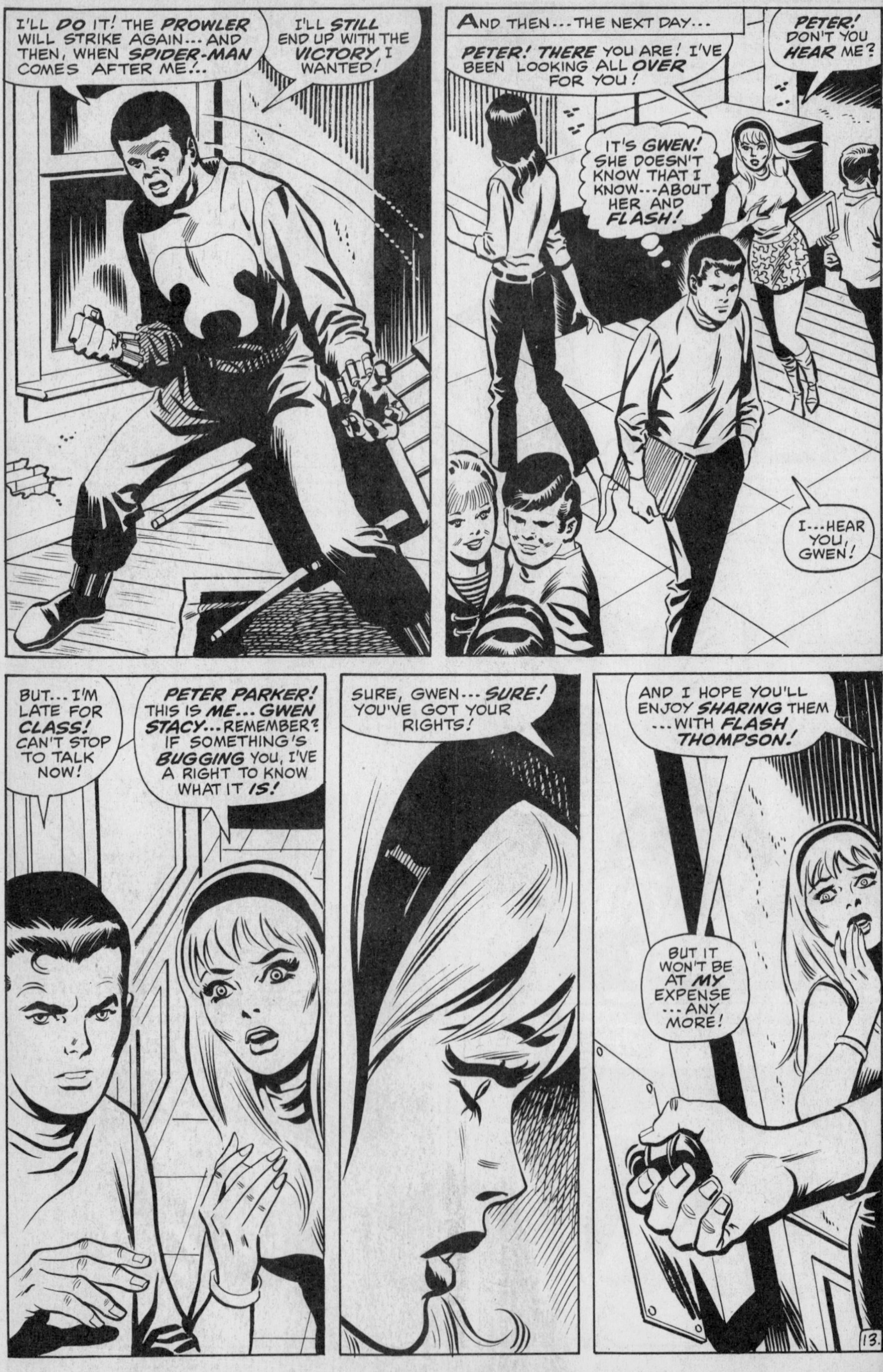
I'LL DO IT! THE PROWLER WILL STRIKE AGAIN... AND THEN, WHEN SPIDER-MAN COMES AFTER ME!...
I'LL STILL END UP WITH THE VICTORY I WANTED!
AND THEN... THE NEXT DAY...
PETER! THERE YOU ARE! I'VE BEEN LOOKING ALL OVER FOR YOU!
PETER! DON'T YOU HEAR ME?
IT'S GWEN! SHE DOESN'T KNOW THAT I KNOW... ABOUT HER AND FLASH!
I... HEAR YOU, GWEN!
BUT... I'M LATE FOR CLASS! CAN'T STOP TO TALK NOW!
PETER PARKER! THIS IS ME... GWEN STACY... REMEMBER? IF SOMETHING'S BUGGING YOU, I'VE A RIGHT TO KNOW WHAT IT IS!
SURE, GWEN... SURE! YOU'VE GOT YOUR RIGHTS!
AND I HOPE YOU'LL ENJOY SHARING THEM ...WITH FLASH THOMPSON!
BUT IT WON'T BE AT MY EXPENSE ... ANY MORE!
13.

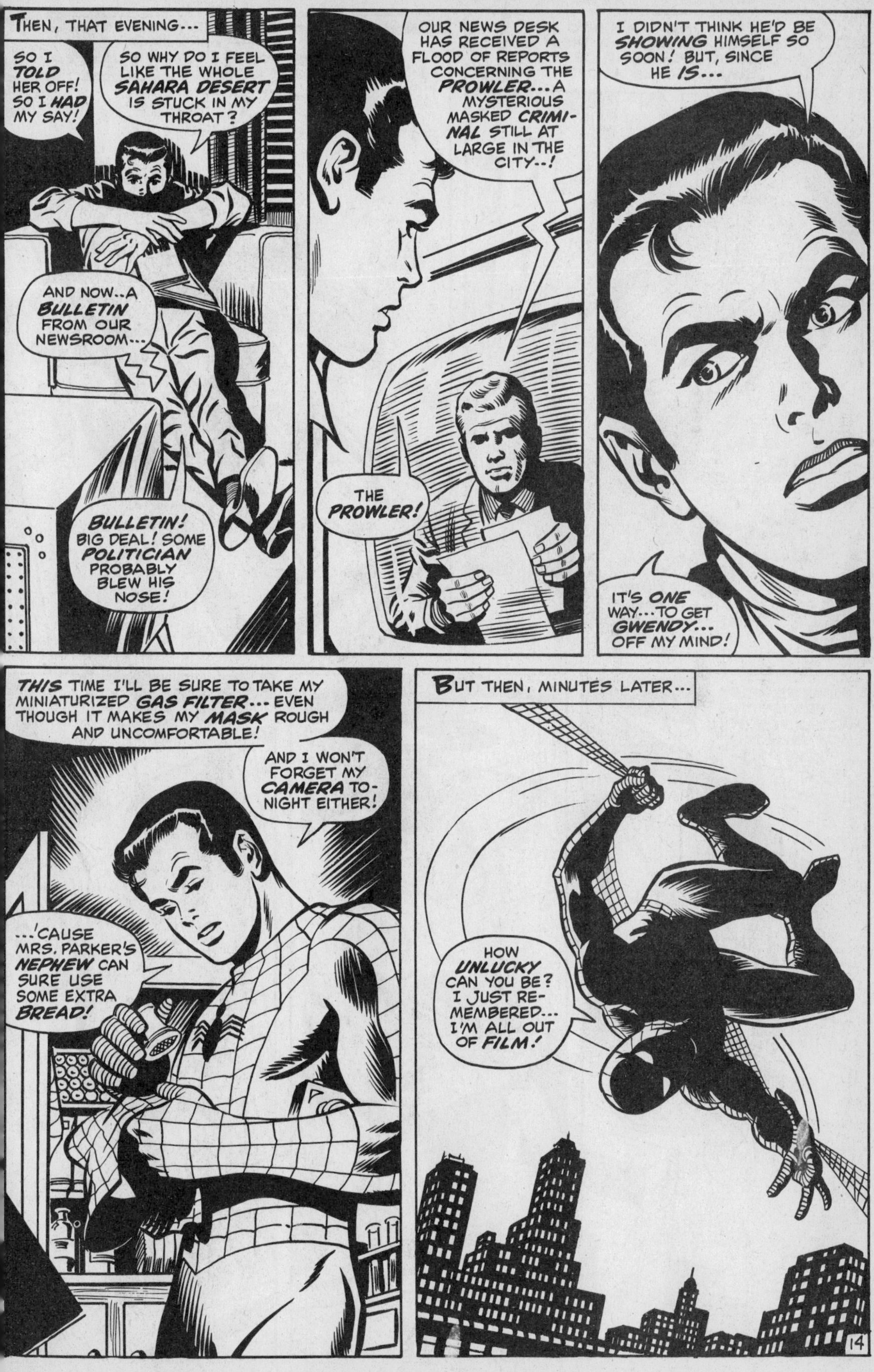
THEN, THAT EVENING...
SO I TOLD HER OFF! SO I HAD MY SAY!
SO WHY DO I FEEL LIKE THE WHOLE SAHARA DESERT IS STUCK IN MY THROAT?
AND NOW..A BULLETIN FROM OUR NEWSROOM...
BULLETIN! BIG DEAL! SOME POLITICIAN PROBABLY BLEW HIS NOSE!
OUR NEWS DESK HAS RECEIVED A FLOOD OF REPORTS CONCERNING THE PROWLER...A MYSTERIOUS MASKED CRIMINAL STILL AT LARGE IN THE CITY--!
THE PROWLER!
I DIDN'T THINK HE'D BE SHOWING HIMSELF SO SOON! BUT, SINCE HE IS...
IT'S ONE WAY...TO GET GWENDY... OFF MY MIND!
THIS TIME I'LL BE SURE TO TAKE MY MINIATURIZED GAS FILTER... EVEN THOUGH IT MAKES MY MASK ROUGH AND UNCOMFORTABLE!
AND I WON'T FORGET MY CAMERA TONIGHT EITHER!
...'CAUSE MRS. PARKER'S NEPHEW CAN SURE USE SOME EXTRA BREAD!
BUT THEN, MINUTES LATER...
HOW UNLUCKY CAN YOU BE? I JUST REMEMBERED... I'M ALL OUT OF FILM!
14

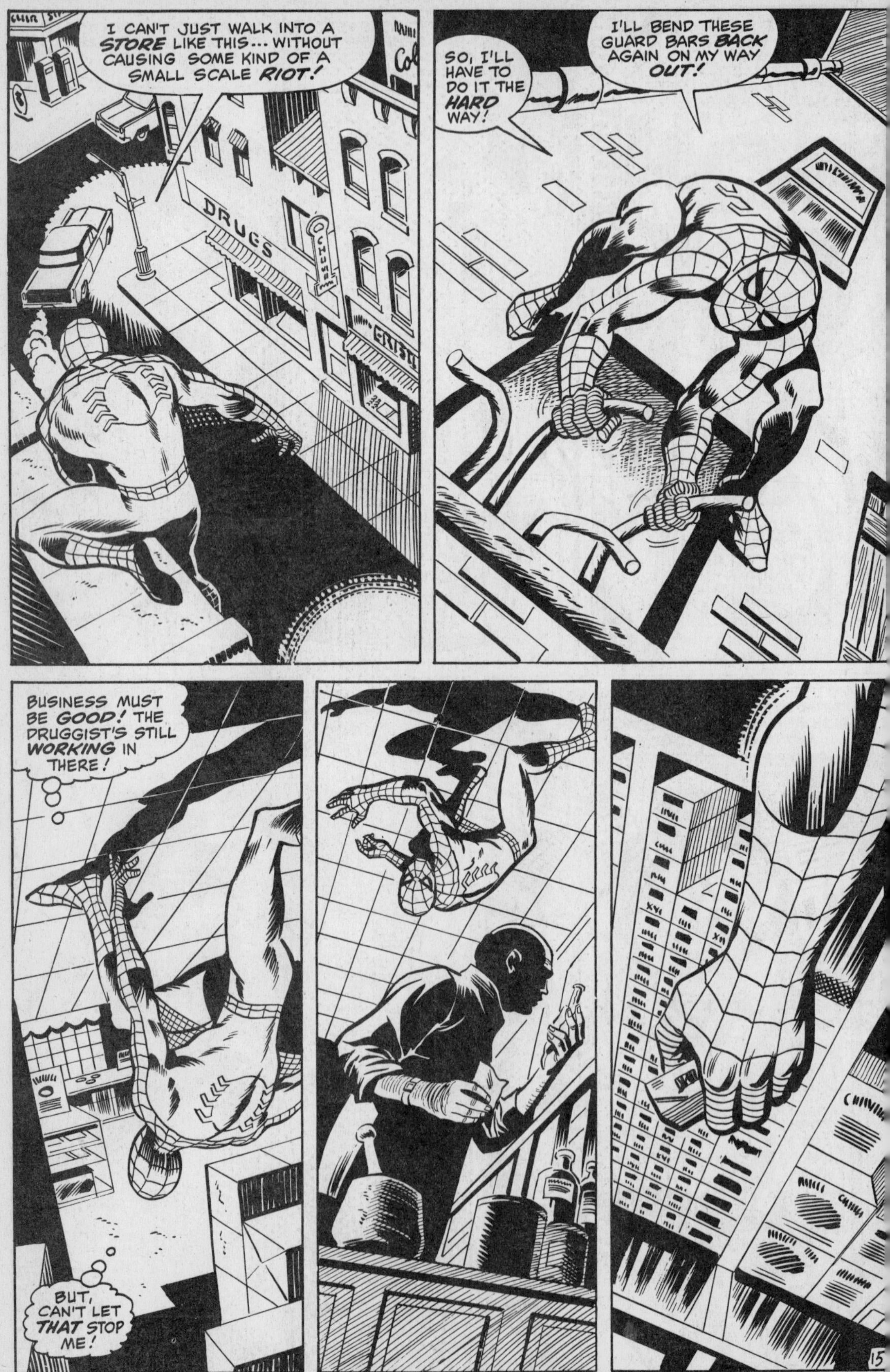
I CAN'T JUST WALK INTO A STORE LIKE THIS... WITHOUT CAUSING SOME KIND OF A SMALL SCALE RIOT!
DRUGS
SO, I'LL HAVE TO DO IT THE HARD WAY!
I'LL BEND THESE GUARD BARS BACK AGAIN ON MY WAY OUT!
BUSINESS MUST BE GOOD! THE DRUGGIST'S STILL WORKING IN THERE!
BUT, CAN'T LET THAT STOP ME!

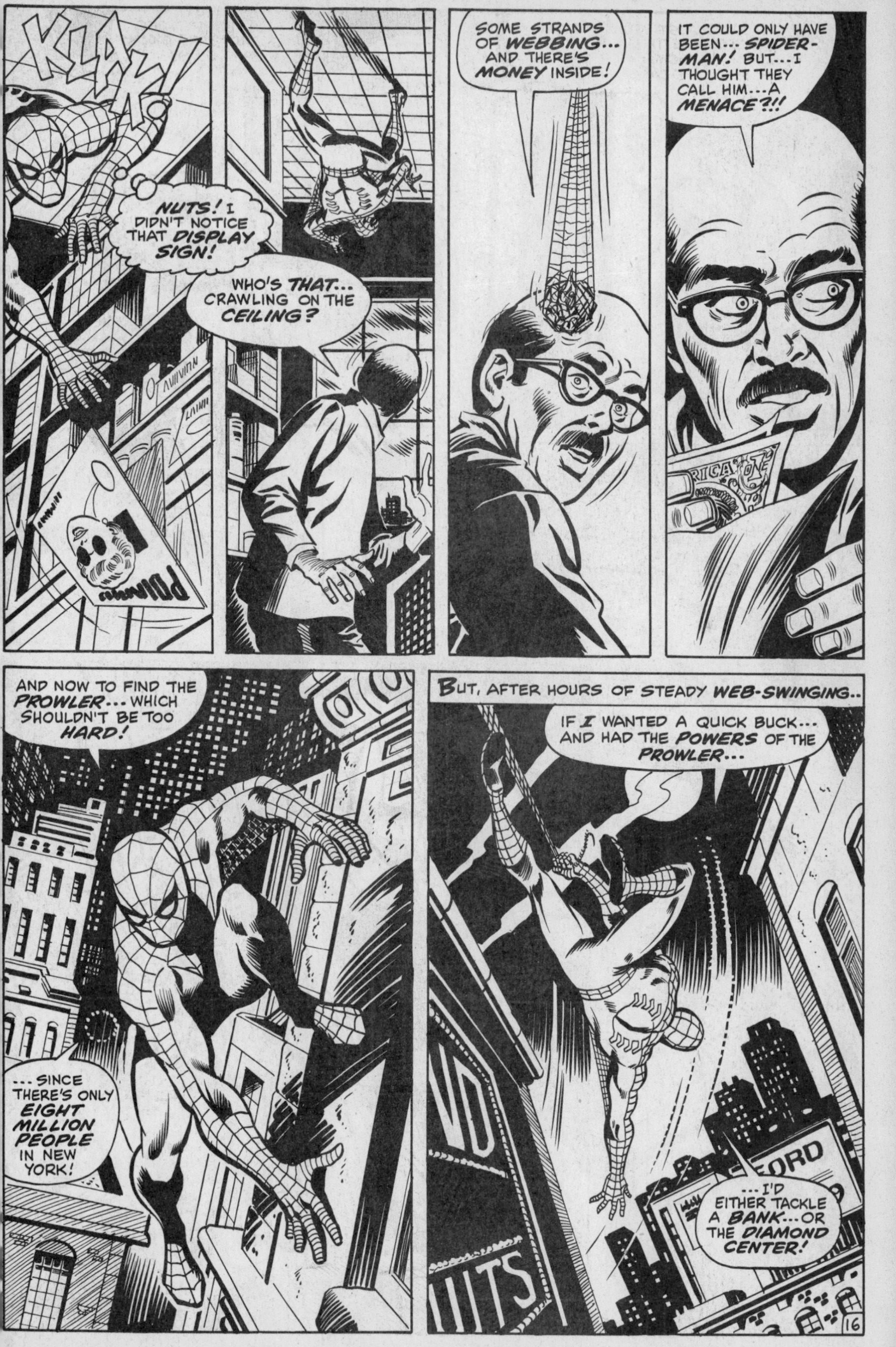
KLAK!
NUTS! I DIDN'T NOTICE THAT DISPLAY SIGN!
WHO'S THAT... CRAWLING ON THE CEILING?
SOME STRANDS OF WEBBING... AND THERE'S MONEY INSIDE!
IT COULD ONLY HAVE BEEN... SPIDER-MAN! BUT... I THOUGHT THEY CALL HIM... A MENACE?!!
AND NOW TO FIND THE PROWLER... WHICH SHOULDN'T BE TOO HARD!
...SINCE THERE'S ONLY EIGHT MILLION PEOPLE IN NEW YORK!
BUT, AFTER HOURS OF STEADY WEB-SWINGING..
IF I WANTED A QUICK BUCK... AND HAD THE POWERS OF THE PROWLER...
...I'D EITHER TACKLE A BANK... OR THE DIAMOND CENTER!
16

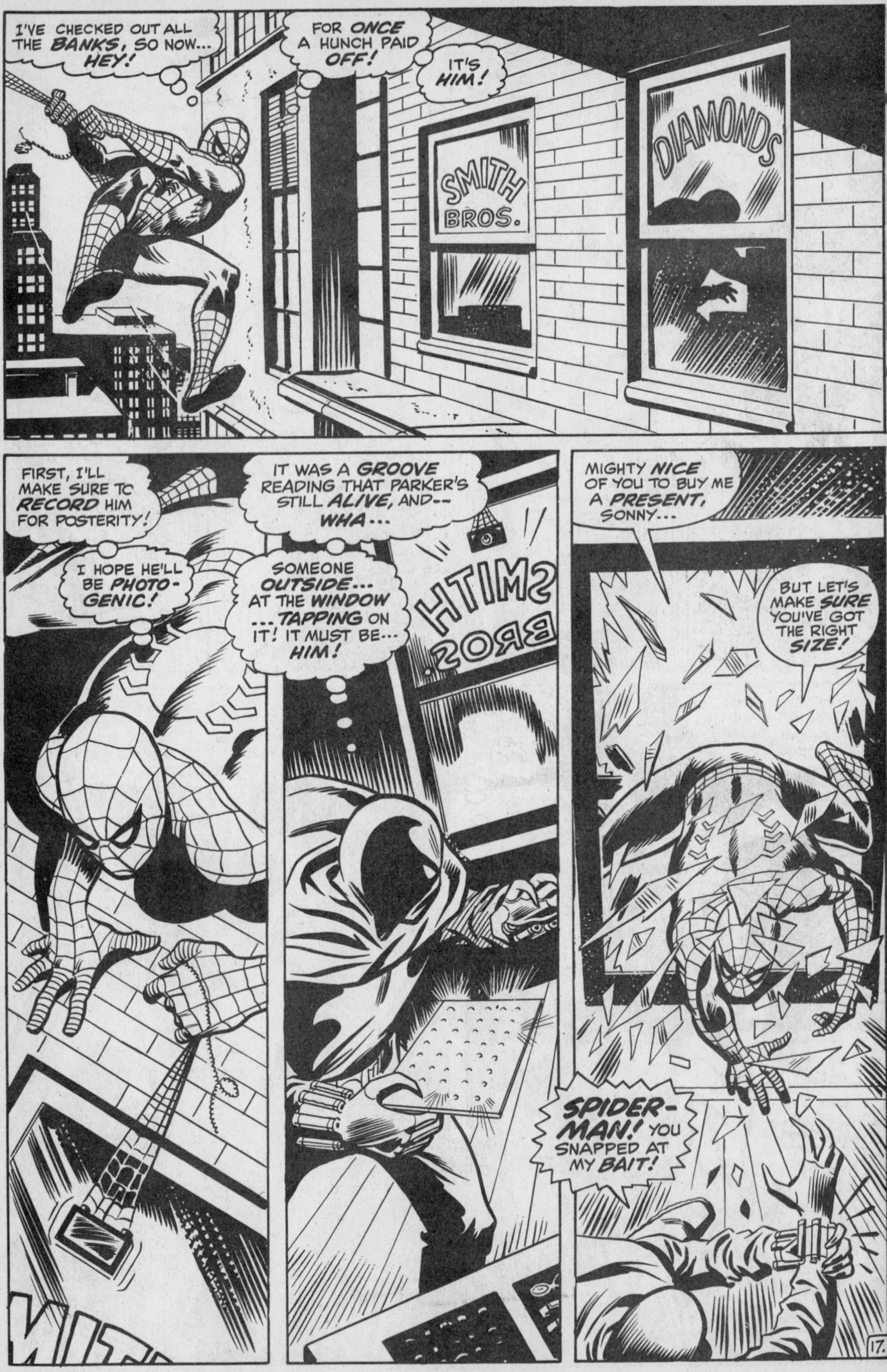
I'VE CHECKED OUT ALL THE BANKS, SO NOW... HEY!
FOR ONCE A HUNCH PAID OFF!
IT'S HIM!
SMITH BROS.
DIAMONDS
FIRST, I'LL MAKE SURE TO RECORD HIM FOR POSTERITY!
I HOPE HE'LL BE PHOTO-GENIC!
IT WAS A GROOVE READING THAT PARKER'S STILL ALIVE, AND-- WHA...
SOMEONE OUTSIDE... AT THE WINDOW ...TAPPING ON IT! IT MUST BE... HIM!
MIGHTY NICE OF YOU TO BUY ME A PRESENT, SONNY...
BUT LET'S MAKE SURE YOU'VE GOT THE RIGHT SIZE!
SPIDER-MAN! YOU SNAPPED AT MY BAIT!
17.

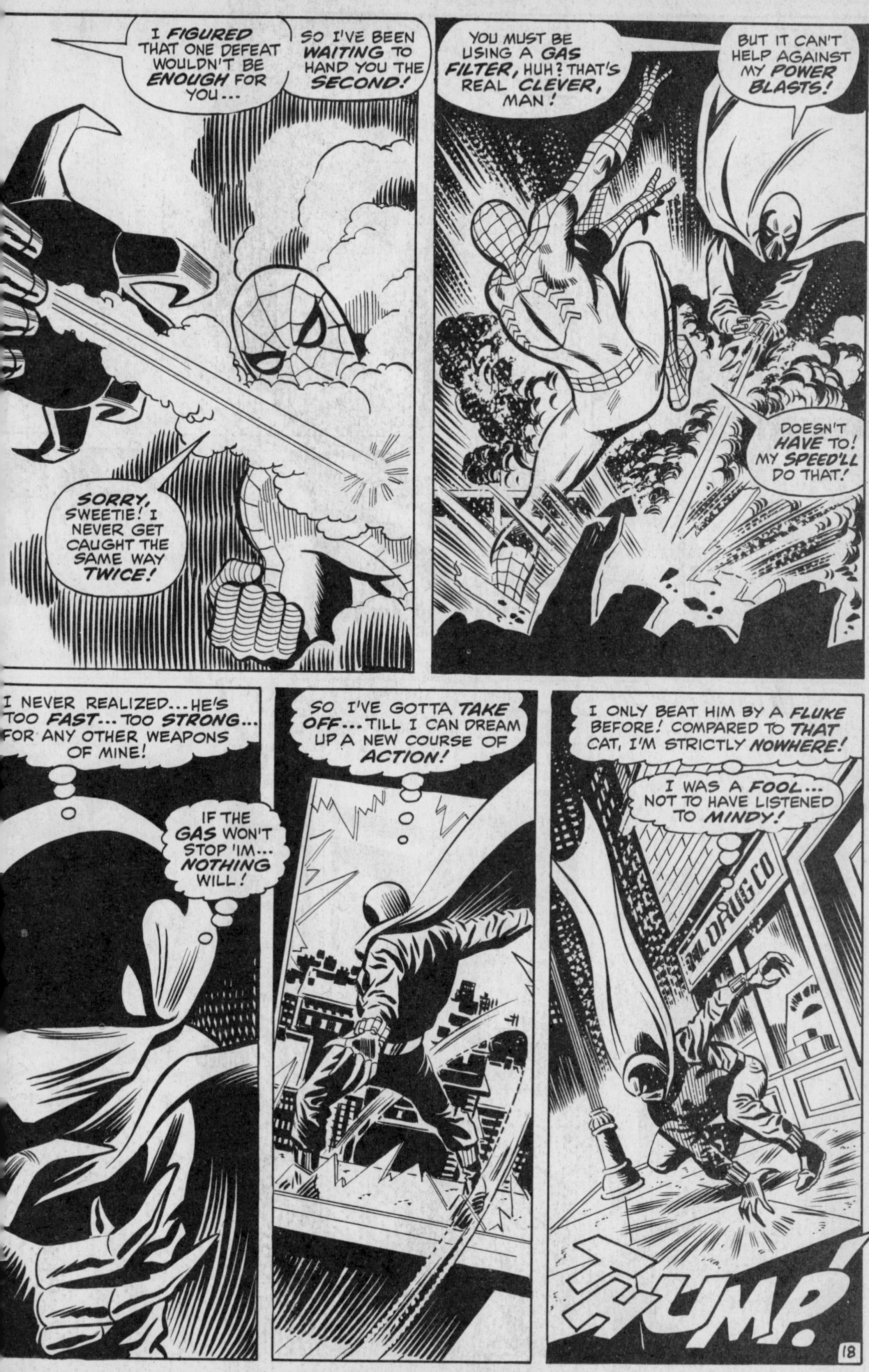

I FIGURED THAT ONE DEFEAT WOULDN'T BE ENOUGH FOR YOU...
SO I'VE BEEN WAITING TO HAND YOU THE SECOND!
SORRY, SWEETIE! I NEVER GET CAUGHT THE SAME WAY TWICE!
YOU MUST BE USING A GAS FILTER, HUH? THAT'S REAL CLEVER, MAN!
BUT IT CAN'T HELP AGAINST MY POWER BLASTS!
DOESN'T HAVE TO! MY SPEED'LL DO THAT!
I NEVER REALIZED... HE'S TOO FAST... TOO STRONG... FOR ANY OTHER WEAPONS OF MINE!
IF THE GAS WON'T STOP 'IM... NOTHING WILL!
SO I'VE GOTTA TAKE OFF... TILL I CAN DREAM UP A NEW COURSE OF ACTION!
I ONLY BEAT HIM BY A FLUKE BEFORE! COMPARED TO THAT CAT, I'M STRICTLY NOWHERE!
I WAS A FOOL... NOT TO HAVE LISTENED TO MINDY!
DRUG CO
THUMP!
18

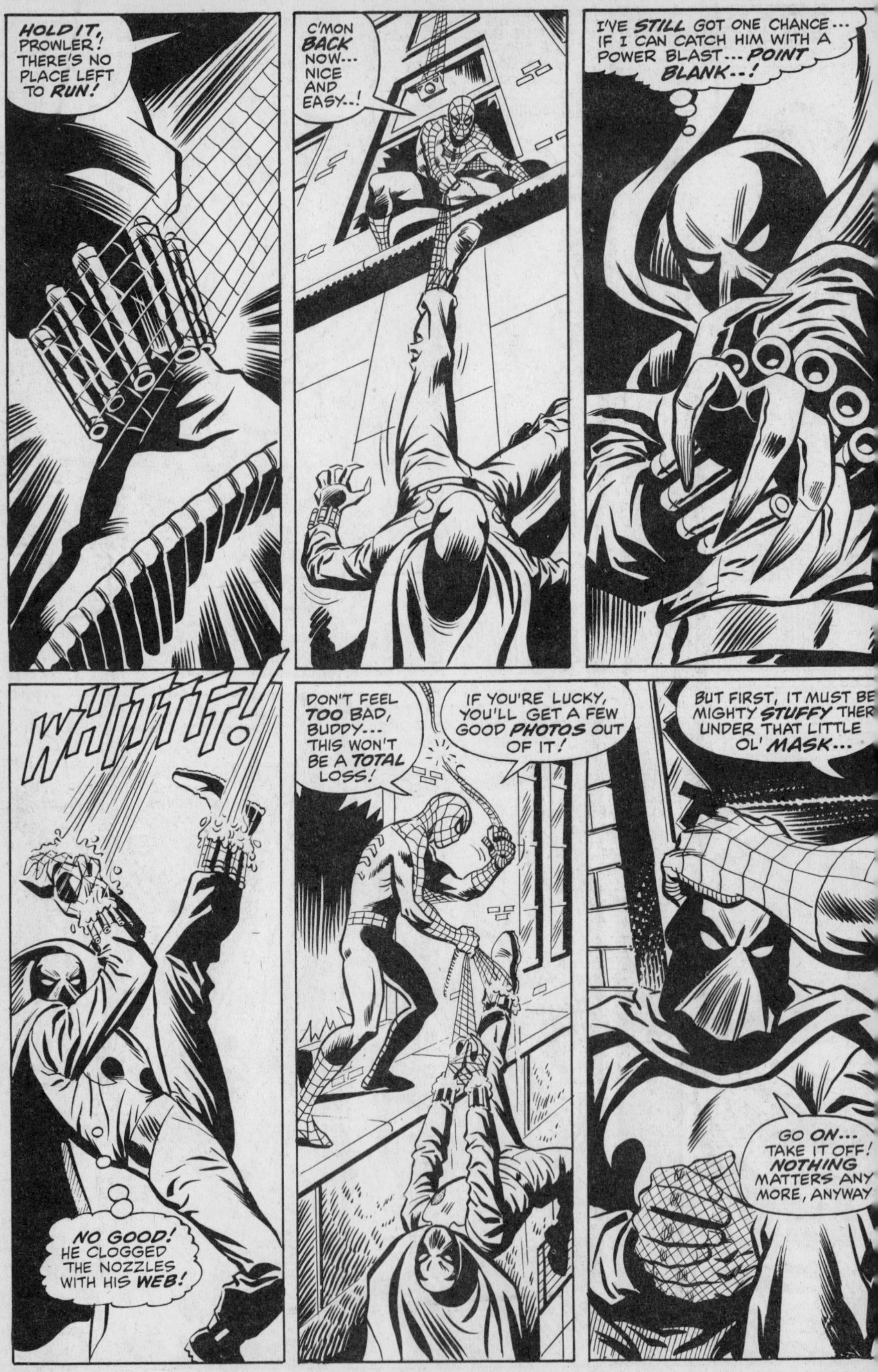
HOLD IT, PROWLER! THERE'S NO PLACE LEFT TO RUN!
C'MON BACK NOW... NICE AND EASY..!
I'VE STILL GOT ONE CHANCE... IF I CAN CATCH HIM WITH A POWER BLAST... POINT BLANK..!
WHIIITT!
NO GOOD! HE CLOGGED THE NOZZLES WITH HIS WEB!
DON'T FEEL TOO BAD, BUDDY--- THIS WON'T BE A TOTAL LOSS!
IF YOU'RE LUCKY, YOU'LL GET A FEW GOOD PHOTOS OUT OF IT!
BUT FIRST, IT MUST BE MIGHTY STUFFY THER UNDER THAT LITTLE OL' MASK...
GO ON... TAKE IT OFF! NOTHING MATTERS ANY MORE, ANYWAY

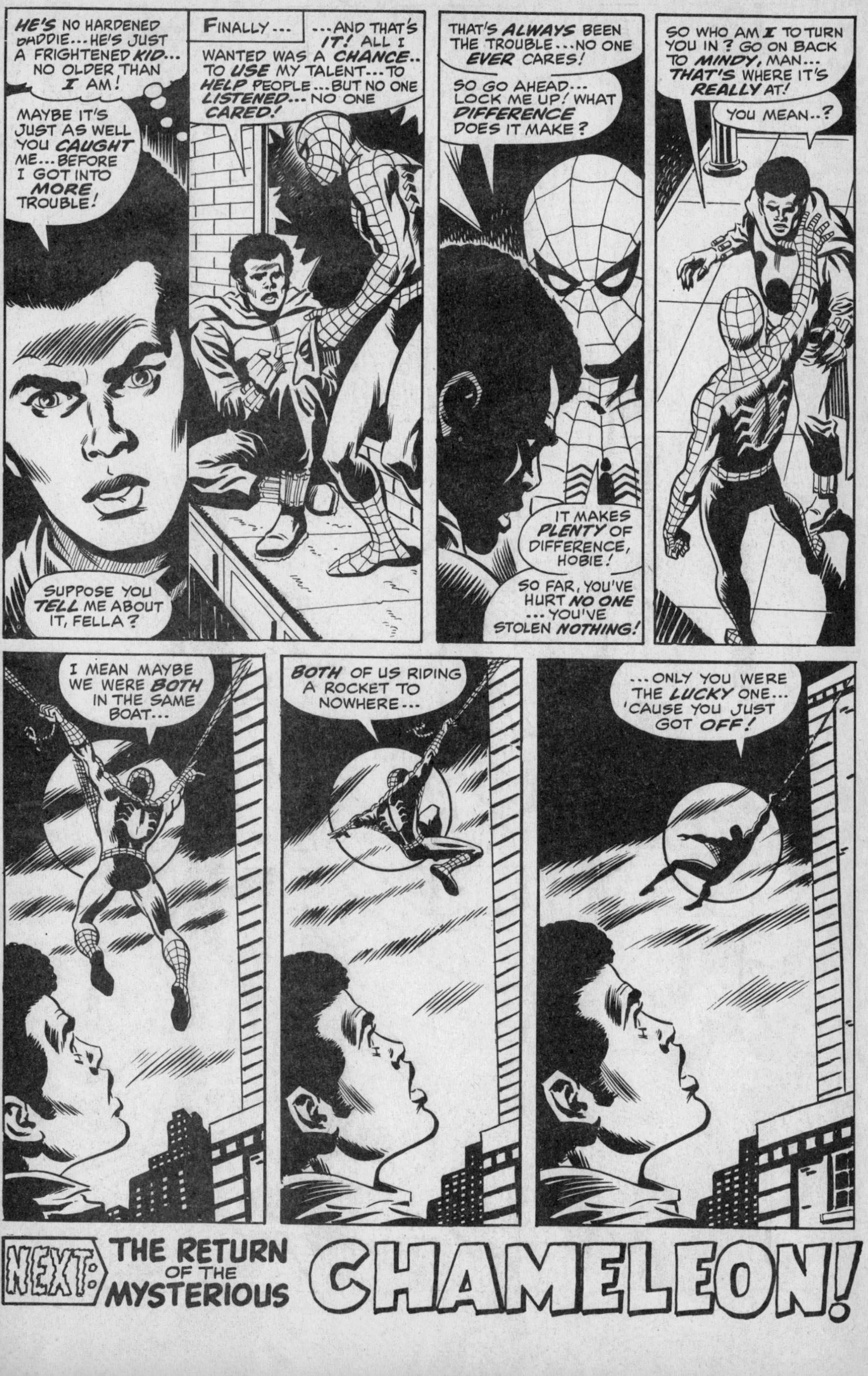
HE'S NO HARDENED BADDIE... HE'S JUST A FRIGHTENED KID... NO OLDER THAN I AM!
MAYBE IT'S JUST AS WELL YOU CAUGHT ME... BEFORE I GOT INTO MORE TROUBLE!
SUPPOSE YOU TELL ME ABOUT IT, FELLA?
FINALLY...
...AND THAT'S IT! ALL I WANTED WAS A CHANCE.. TO USE MY TALENT... TO HELP PEOPLE... BUT NO ONE LISTENED... NO ONE CARED!
THAT'S ALWAYS BEEN THE TROUBLE... NO ONE EVER CARES!
SO GO AHEAD... LOCK ME UP! WHAT DIFFERENCE DOES IT MAKE?
IT MAKES PLENTY OF DIFFERENCE, HOBIE!
SO FAR, YOU'VE HURT NO ONE ...YOU'VE STOLEN NOTHING!
SO WHO AM I TO TURN YOU IN? GO ON BACK TO MINDY, MAN... THAT'S WHERE IT'S REALLY AT!
YOU MEAN..?
I MEAN MAYBE WE WERE BOTH IN THE SAME BOAT...
BOTH OF US RIDING A ROCKET TO NOWHERE...
...ONLY YOU WERE THE LUCKY ONE... 'CAUSE YOU JUST GOT OFF!
NEXT: THE RETURN OF THE MYSTERIOUS CHAMELEON!

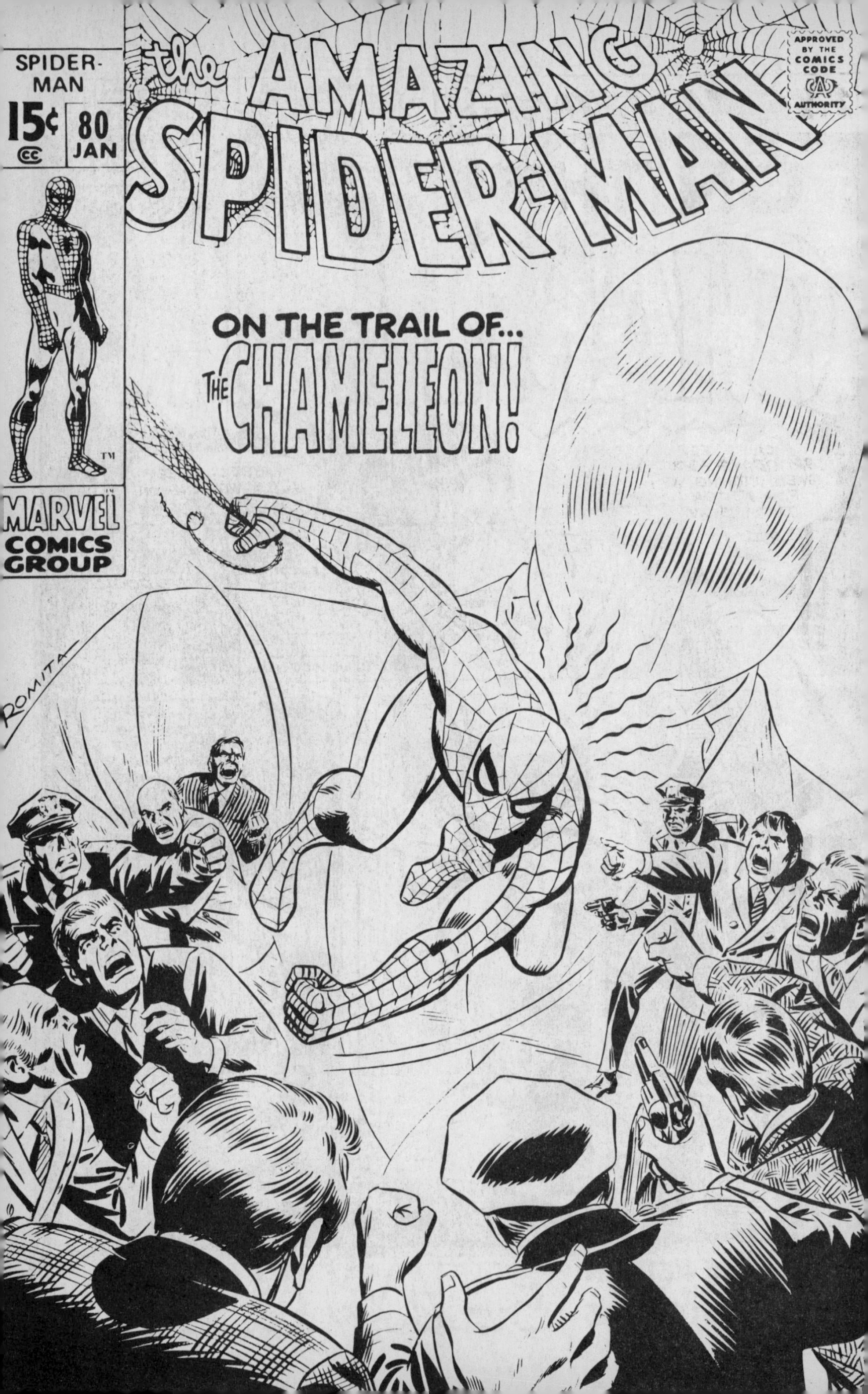
SPIDER-MAN
15¢
CC
80
JAN
the AMAZING SPIDER-MAN
APPROVED BY THE COMICS CODE AUTHORITY
MARVEL COMICS GROUP
ON THE TRAIL OF...
THE CHAMELEON!
ROMITA

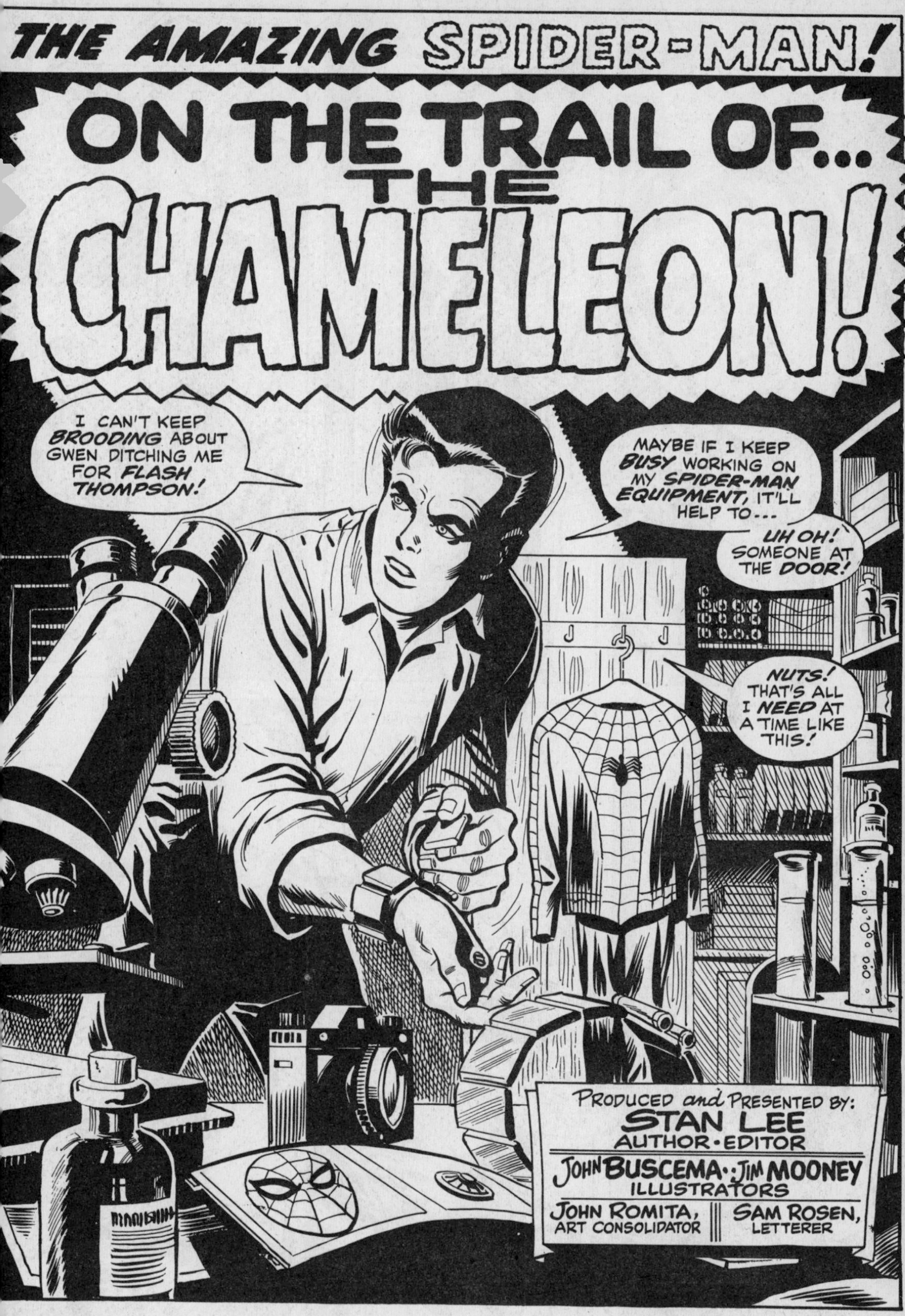
THE AMAZING SPIDER-MAN!
ON THE TRAIL OF... THE CHAMELEON!
I CAN'T KEEP BROODING ABOUT GWEN DITCHING ME FOR FLASH THOMPSON!
MAYBE IF I KEEP BUSY WORKING ON MY SPIDER-MAN EQUIPMENT, IT'LL HELP TO...
UH OH! SOMEONE AT THE DOOR!
NUTS! THAT'S ALL I NEED AT A TIME LIKE THIS!
PRODUCED and PRESENTED BY: STAN LEE AUTHOR • EDITOR
JOHN BUSCEMA • JIM MOONEY ILLUSTRATORS
JOHN ROMITA, ART CONSOLIDATOR
SAM ROSEN, LETTERER

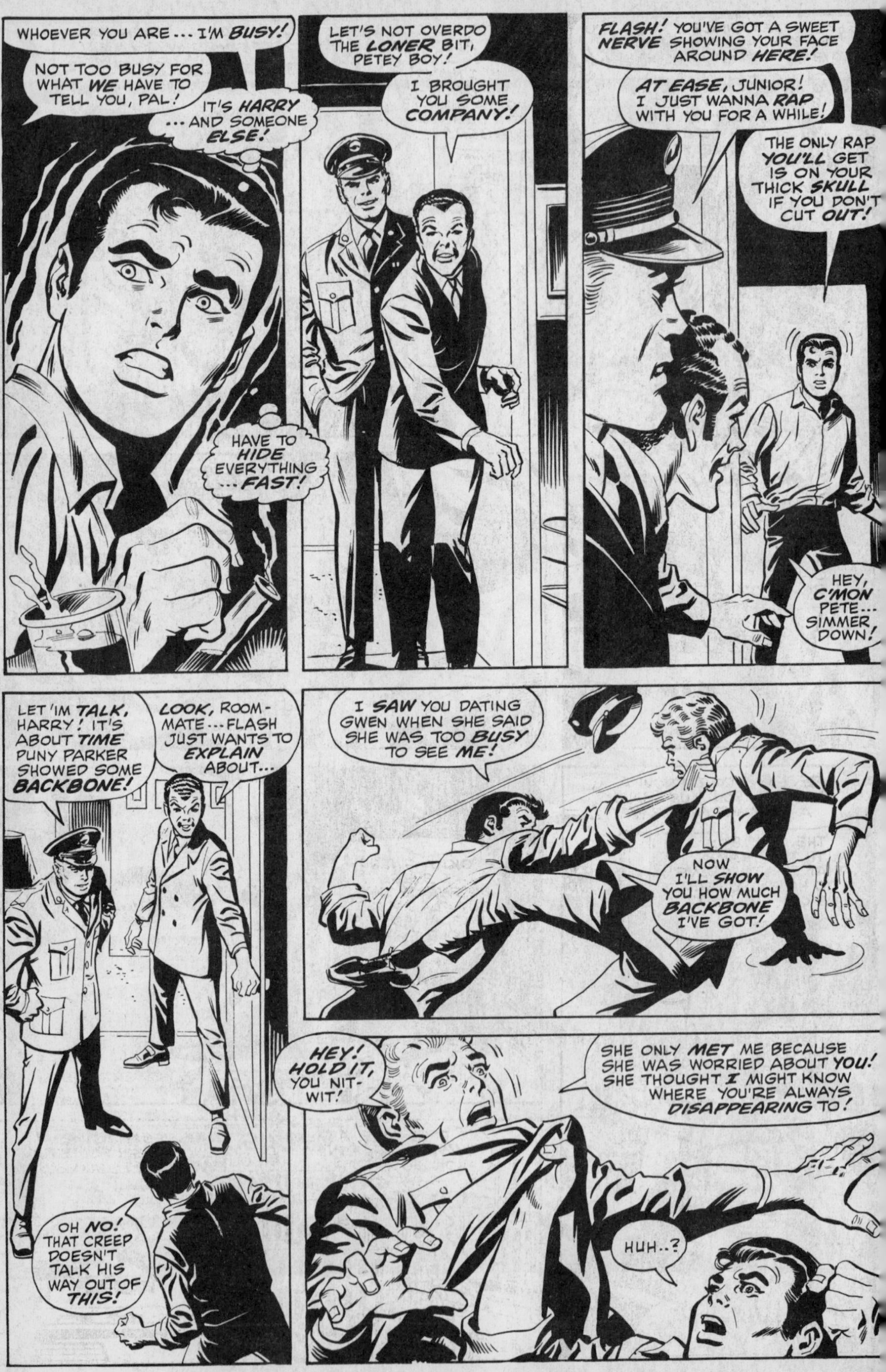
WHOEVER YOU ARE... I'M BUSY!
NOT TOO BUSY FOR WHAT WE HAVE TO TELL YOU, PAL!
IT'S HARRY ...AND SOMEONE ELSE!
HAVE TO HIDE EVERYTHING ...FAST!
LET'S NOT OVERDO THE LONER BIT, PETEY BOY!
I BROUGHT YOU SOME COMPANY!
FLASH! YOU'VE GOT A SWEET NERVE SHOWING YOUR FACE AROUND HERE!
AT EASE, JUNIOR! I JUST WANNA RAP WITH YOU FOR A WHILE!
THE ONLY RAP YOU'LL GET IS ON YOUR THICK SKULL IF YOU DON'T CUT OUT!
HEY, C'MON PETE... SIMMER DOWN!
LET 'IM TALK, HARRY! IT'S ABOUT TIME PUNY PARKER SHOWED SOME BACKBONE!
LOOK, ROOM-MATE... FLASH JUST WANTS TO EXPLAIN ABOUT...
I SAW YOU DATING GWEN WHEN SHE SAID SHE WAS TOO BUSY TO SEE ME!
NOW I'LL SHOW YOU HOW MUCH BACKBONE I'VE GOT!
OH NO! THAT CREEP DOESN'T TALK HIS WAY OUT OF THIS!
HEY! HOLD IT, YOU NIT-WIT!
SHE ONLY MET ME BECAUSE SHE WAS WORRIED ABOUT YOU! SHE THOUGHT I MIGHT KNOW WHERE YOU'RE ALWAYS DISAPPEARING TO!
HUH..?

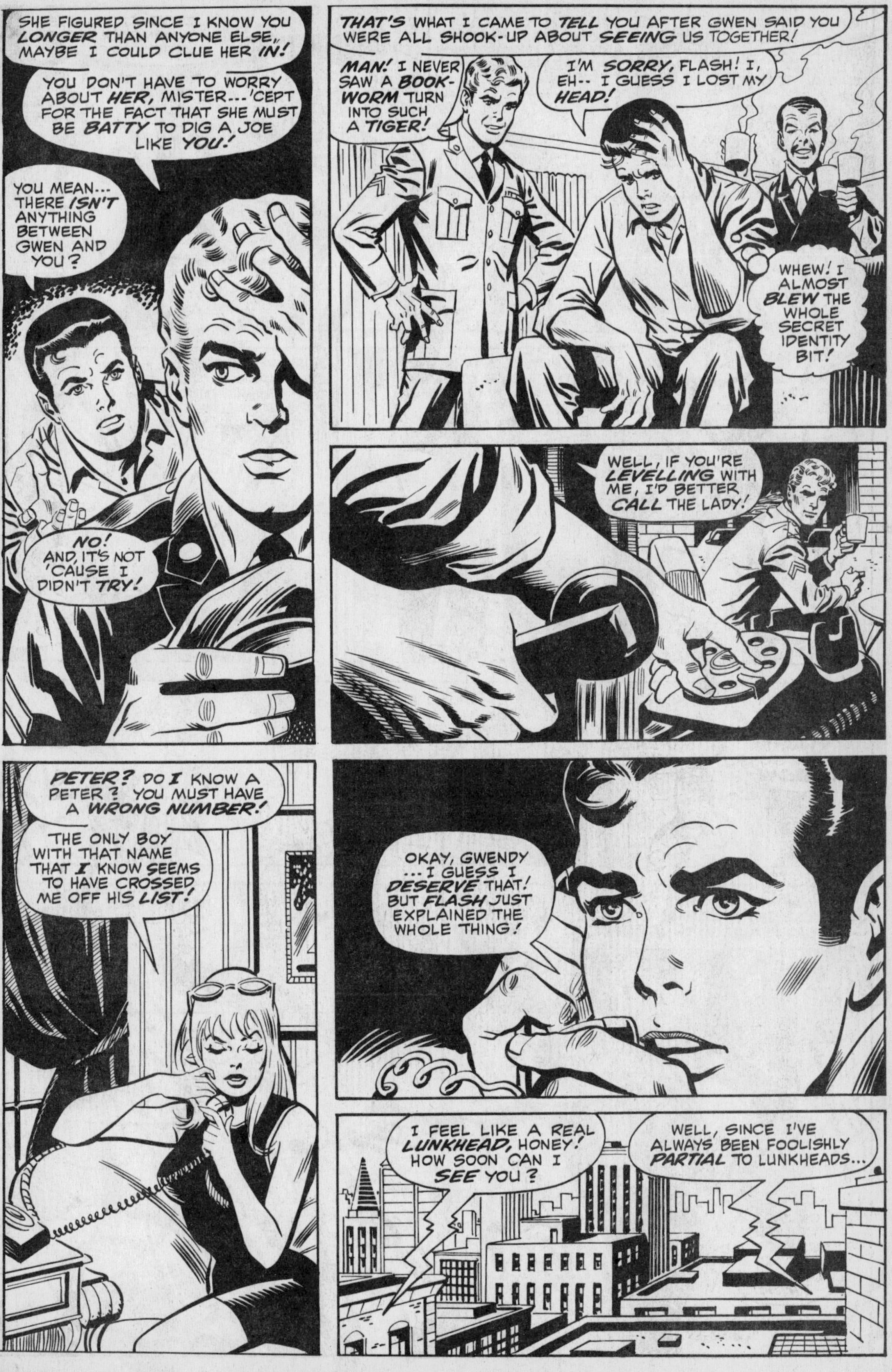
SHE FIGURED SINCE I KNOW YOU LONGER THAN ANYONE ELSE, MAYBE I COULD CLUE HER IN!
YOU DON'T HAVE TO WORRY ABOUT HER, MISTER...'CEPT FOR THE FACT THAT SHE MUST BE BATTY TO DIG A JOE LIKE YOU!
YOU MEAN... THERE ISN'T ANYTHING BETWEEN GWEN AND YOU?
NO! AND, IT'S NOT 'CAUSE I DIDN'T TRY!
THAT'S WHAT I CAME TO TELL YOU AFTER GWEN SAID YOU WERE ALL SHOOK-UP ABOUT SEEING US TOGETHER!
MAN! I NEVER SAW A BOOK-WORM TURN INTO SUCH A TIGER!
I'M SORRY, FLASH! I, EH-- I GUESS I LOST MY HEAD!
WHEW! I ALMOST BLEW THE WHOLE SECRET IDENTITY BIT!
WELL, IF YOU'RE LEVELLING WITH ME, I'D BETTER CALL THE LADY!
PETER? DO I KNOW A PETER? YOU MUST HAVE A WRONG NUMBER!
THE ONLY BOY WITH THAT NAME THAT I KNOW SEEMS TO HAVE CROSSED ME OFF HIS LIST!
OKAY, GWENDY ...I GUESS I DESERVE THAT! BUT FLASH JUST EXPLAINED THE WHOLE THING!
I FEEL LIKE A REAL LUNKHEAD, HONEY! HOW SOON CAN I SEE YOU?
WELL, SINCE I'VE ALWAYS BEEN FOOLISHLY PARTIAL TO LUNKHEADS...

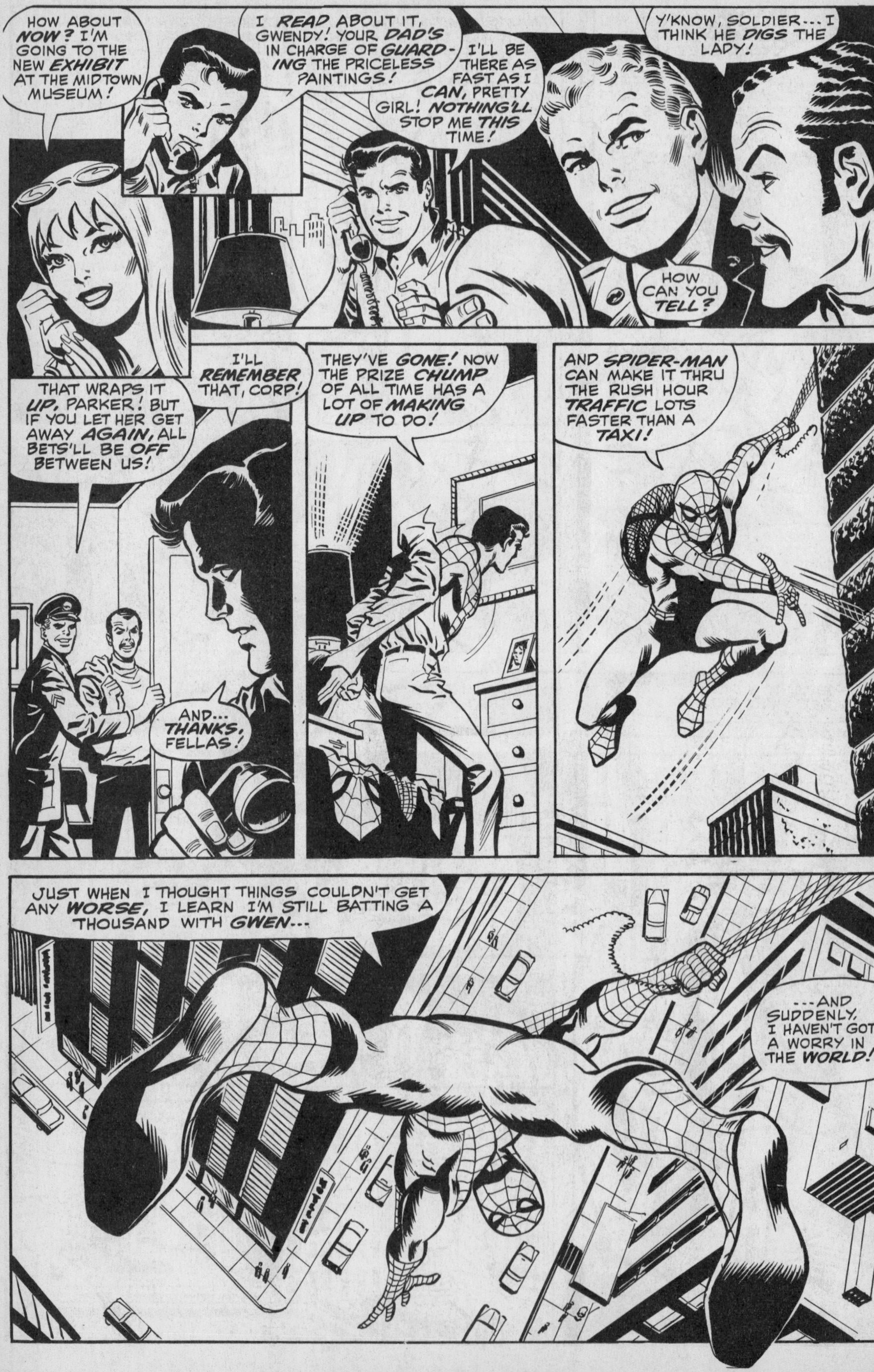

HOW ABOUT NOW? I'M GOING TO THE NEW EXHIBIT AT THE MIDTOWN MUSEUM!
I READ ABOUT IT, GWENDY! YOUR DAD'S IN CHARGE OF GUARDING THE PRICELESS PAINTINGS!
I'LL BE THERE AS FAST AS I CAN, PRETTY GIRL! NOTHING'LL STOP ME THIS TIME!
Y'KNOW, SOLDIER... I THINK HE DIGS THE LADY!
HOW CAN YOU TELL?
THAT WRAPS IT UP, PARKER! BUT IF YOU LET HER GET AWAY AGAIN, ALL BETS'LL BE OFF BETWEEN US!
I'LL REMEMBER THAT, CORP!
AND... THANKS, FELLAS!
THEY'VE GONE! NOW THE PRIZE CHUMP OF ALL TIME HAS A LOT OF MAKING UP TO DO!
AND SPIDER-MAN CAN MAKE IT THRU THE RUSH HOUR TRAFFIC LOTS FASTER THAN A TAXI!
JUST WHEN I THOUGHT THINGS COULDN'T GET ANY WORSE, I LEARN I'M STILL BATTING A THOUSAND WITH GWEN...
...AND SUDDENLY, I HAVEN'T GOT A WORRY IN THE WORLD!

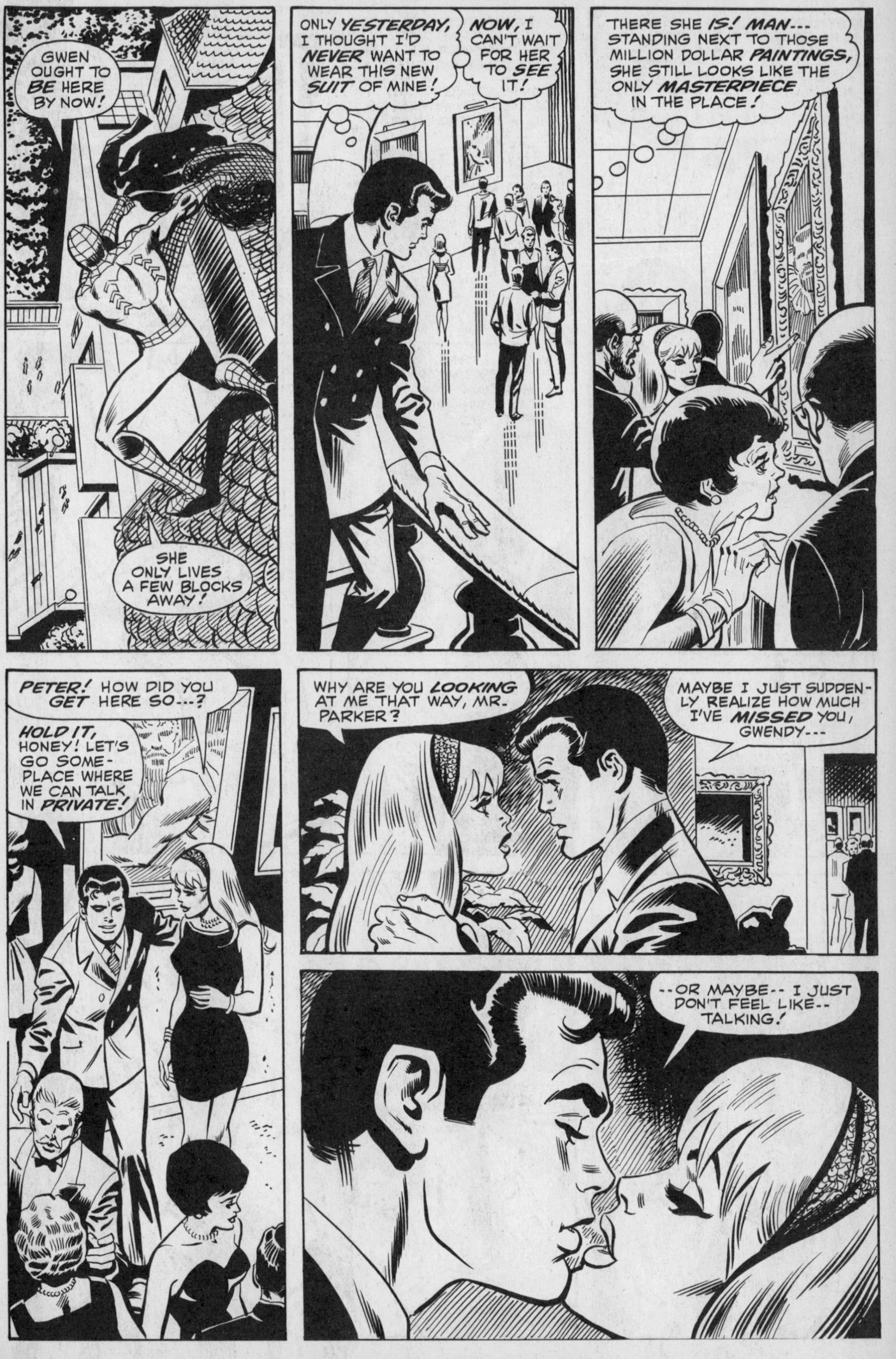
GWEN OUGHT TO BE HERE BY NOW!
SHE ONLY LIVES A FEW BLOCKS AWAY!
ONLY YESTERDAY, I THOUGHT I'D NEVER WANT TO WEAR THIS NEW SUIT OF MINE!
NOW, I CAN'T WAIT FOR HER TO SEE IT!
THERE SHE IS! MAN--- STANDING NEXT TO THOSE MILLION DOLLAR PAINTINGS, SHE STILL LOOKS LIKE THE ONLY MASTERPIECE IN THE PLACE!
PETER! HOW DID YOU GET HERE SO--?
HOLD IT, HONEY! LET'S GO SOME-PLACE WHERE WE CAN TALK IN PRIVATE!
WHY ARE YOU LOOKING AT ME THAT WAY, MR. PARKER?
MAYBE I JUST SUDDEN-LY REALIZE HOW MUCH I'VE MISSED YOU, GWENDY---
--OR MAYBE-- I JUST DON'T FEEL LIKE-- TALKING!

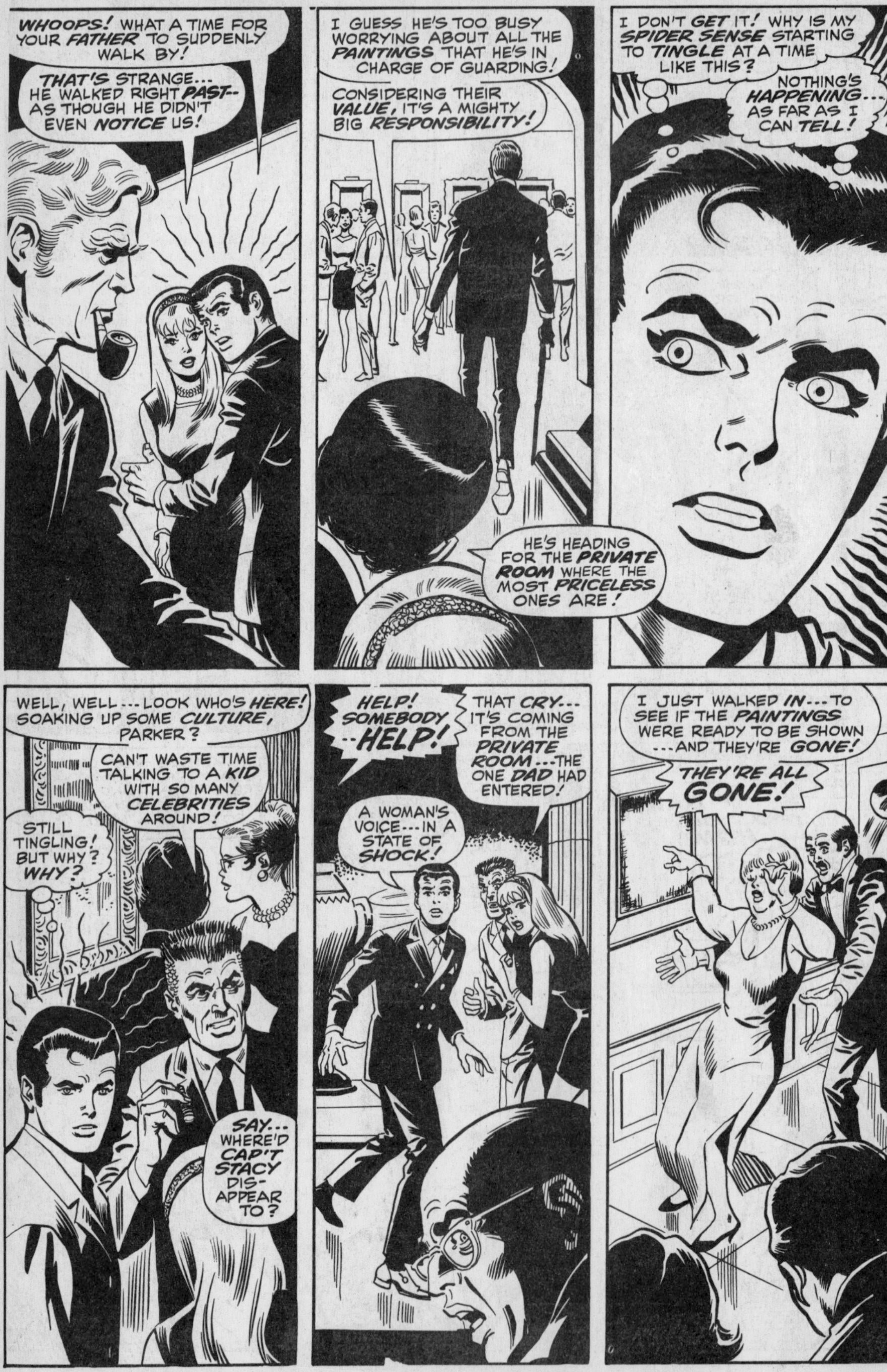
WHOOPS! WHAT A TIME FOR YOUR FATHER TO SUDDENLY WALK BY!
THAT'S STRANGE... HE WALKED RIGHT PAST--AS THOUGH HE DIDN'T EVEN NOTICE US!
I GUESS HE'S TOO BUSY WORRYING ABOUT ALL THE PAINTINGS THAT HE'S IN CHARGE OF GUARDING!
CONSIDERING THEIR VALUE, IT'S A MIGHTY BIG RESPONSIBILITY!
HE'S HEADING FOR THE PRIVATE ROOM WHERE THE MOST PRICELESS ONES ARE!
I DON'T GET IT! WHY IS MY SPIDER SENSE STARTING TO TINGLE AT A TIME LIKE THIS?
NOTHING'S HAPPENING... AS FAR AS I CAN TELL!
WELL, WELL --- LOOK WHO'S HERE! SOAKING UP SOME CULTURE, PARKER?
CAN'T WASTE TIME TALKING TO A KID WITH SO MANY CELEBRITIES AROUND!
STILL TINGLING! BUT WHY? WHY?
SAY... WHERE'D CAP'T STACY DIS-APPEAR TO?
HELP! SOMEBODY --HELP!
THAT CRY--- IT'S COMING FROM THE PRIVATE ROOM---THE ONE DAD HAD ENTERED!
A WOMAN'S VOICE--- IN A STATE OF SHOCK!
I JUST WALKED IN---TO SEE IF THE PAINTINGS WERE READY TO BE SHOWN ---AND THEY'RE GONE!
THEY'RE ALL GONE!

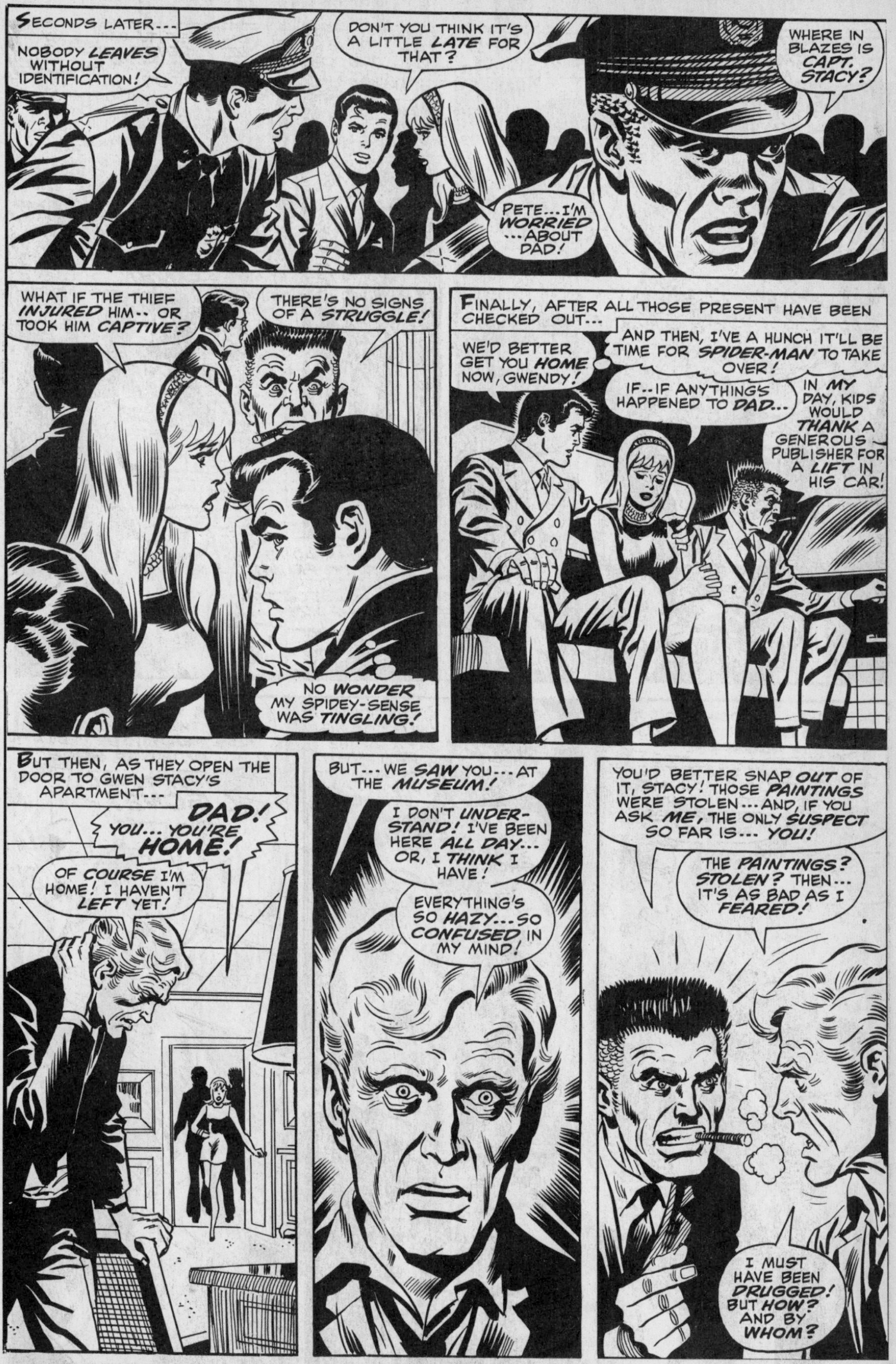
SECONDS LATER---
NOBODY LEAVES WITHOUT IDENTIFICATION!
DON'T YOU THINK IT'S A LITTLE LATE FOR THAT?
PETE...I'M WORRIED ...ABOUT DAD!
WHERE IN BLAZES IS CAPT. STACY?
WHAT IF THE THIEF INJURED HIM-- OR TOOK HIM CAPTIVE?
THERE'S NO SIGNS OF A STRUGGLE!
NO WONDER MY SPIDEY-SENSE WAS TINGLING!
FINALLY, AFTER ALL THOSE PRESENT HAVE BEEN CHECKED OUT...
WE'D BETTER GET YOU HOME NOW, GWENDY!
AND THEN, I'VE A HUNCH IT'LL BE TIME FOR SPIDER-MAN TO TAKE OVER!
IF--IF ANYTHING'S HAPPENED TO DAD...
IN MY DAY, KIDS WOULD THANK A GENEROUS PUBLISHER FOR A LIFT IN HIS CAR!
BUT THEN, AS THEY OPEN THE DOOR TO GWEN STACY'S APARTMENT---
DAD! YOU... YOU'RE HOME!
OF COURSE I'M HOME! I HAVEN'T LEFT YET!
BUT... WE SAW YOU... AT THE MUSEUM!
I DON'T UNDERSTAND! I'VE BEEN HERE ALL DAY... OR, I THINK I HAVE!
EVERYTHING'S SO HAZY... SO CONFUSED IN MY MIND!
YOU'D BETTER SNAP OUT OF IT, STACY! THOSE PAINTINGS WERE STOLEN... AND, IF YOU ASK ME, THE ONLY SUSPECT SO FAR IS... YOU!
THE PAINTINGS? STOLEN? THEN... IT'S AS BAD AS I FEARED!
I MUST HAVE BEEN DRUGGED! BUT HOW? AND BY WHOM?

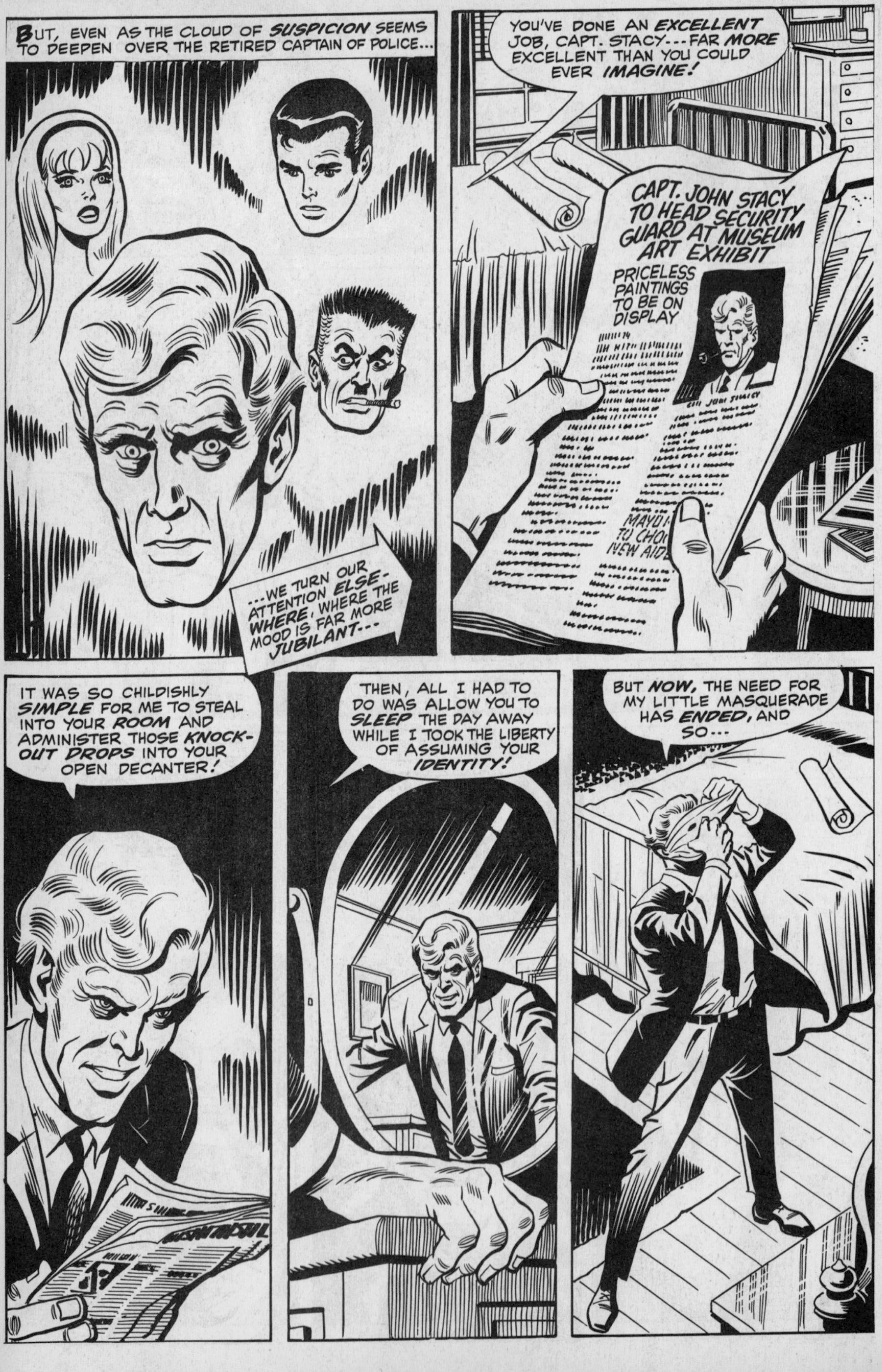
BUT, EVEN AS THE CLOUD OF SUSPICION SEEMS TO DEEPEN OVER THE RETIRED CAPTAIN OF POLICE...
...WE TURN OUR ATTENTION ELSEWHERE, WHERE THE MOOD IS FAR MORE JUBILANT---
YOU'VE DONE AN EXCELLENT JOB, CAPT. STACY---FAR MORE EXCELLENT THAN YOU COULD EVER IMAGINE!
CAPT. JOHN STACY TO HEAD SECURITY GUARD AT MUSEUM ART EXHIBIT
PRICELESS PAINTINGS TO BE ON DISPLAY
IT WAS SO CHILDISHLY SIMPLE FOR ME TO STEAL INTO YOUR ROOM AND ADMINISTER THOSE KNOCK-OUT DROPS INTO YOUR OPEN DECANTER!
THEN, ALL I HAD TO DO WAS ALLOW YOU TO SLEEP THE DAY AWAY WHILE I TOOK THE LIBERTY OF ASSUMING YOUR IDENTITY!
BUT NOW, THE NEED FOR MY LITTLE MASQUERADE HAS ENDED, AND SO...

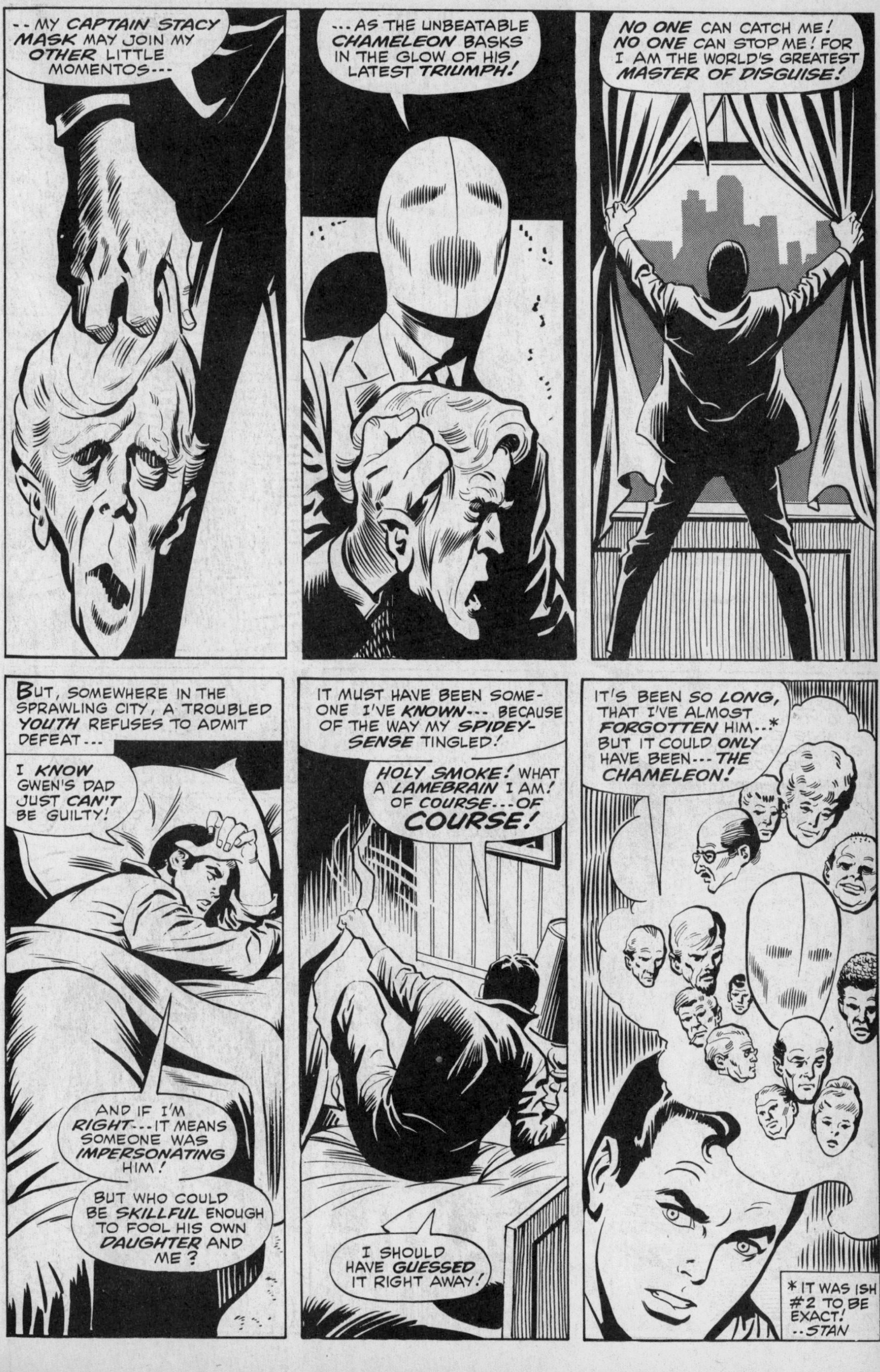

-- MY CAPTAIN STACY MASK MAY JOIN MY OTHER LITTLE MOMENTOS---
...AS THE UNBEATABLE CHAMELEON BASKS IN THE GLOW OF HIS LATEST TRIUMPH!
NO ONE CAN CATCH ME! NO ONE CAN STOP ME! FOR I AM THE WORLD'S GREATEST MASTER OF DISGUISE!
BUT, SOMEWHERE IN THE SPRAWLING CITY, A TROUBLED YOUTH REFUSES TO ADMIT DEFEAT...
I KNOW GWEN'S DAD JUST CAN'T BE GUILTY!
AND IF I'M RIGHT---IT MEANS SOMEONE WAS IMPERSONATING HIM!
BUT WHO COULD BE SKILLFUL ENOUGH TO FOOL HIS OWN DAUGHTER AND ME?
IT MUST HAVE BEEN SOME-ONE I'VE KNOWN--- BECAUSE OF THE WAY MY SPIDEY-SENSE TINGLED!
HOLY SMOKE! WHAT A LAMEBRAIN I AM! OF COURSE---OF COURSE!
I SHOULD HAVE GUESSED IT RIGHT AWAY!
IT'S BEEN SO LONG, THAT I'VE ALMOST FORGOTTEN HIM...* BUT IT COULD ONLY HAVE BEEN--- THE CHAMELEON!
*IT WAS ISH #2 TO BE EXACT! ..STAN

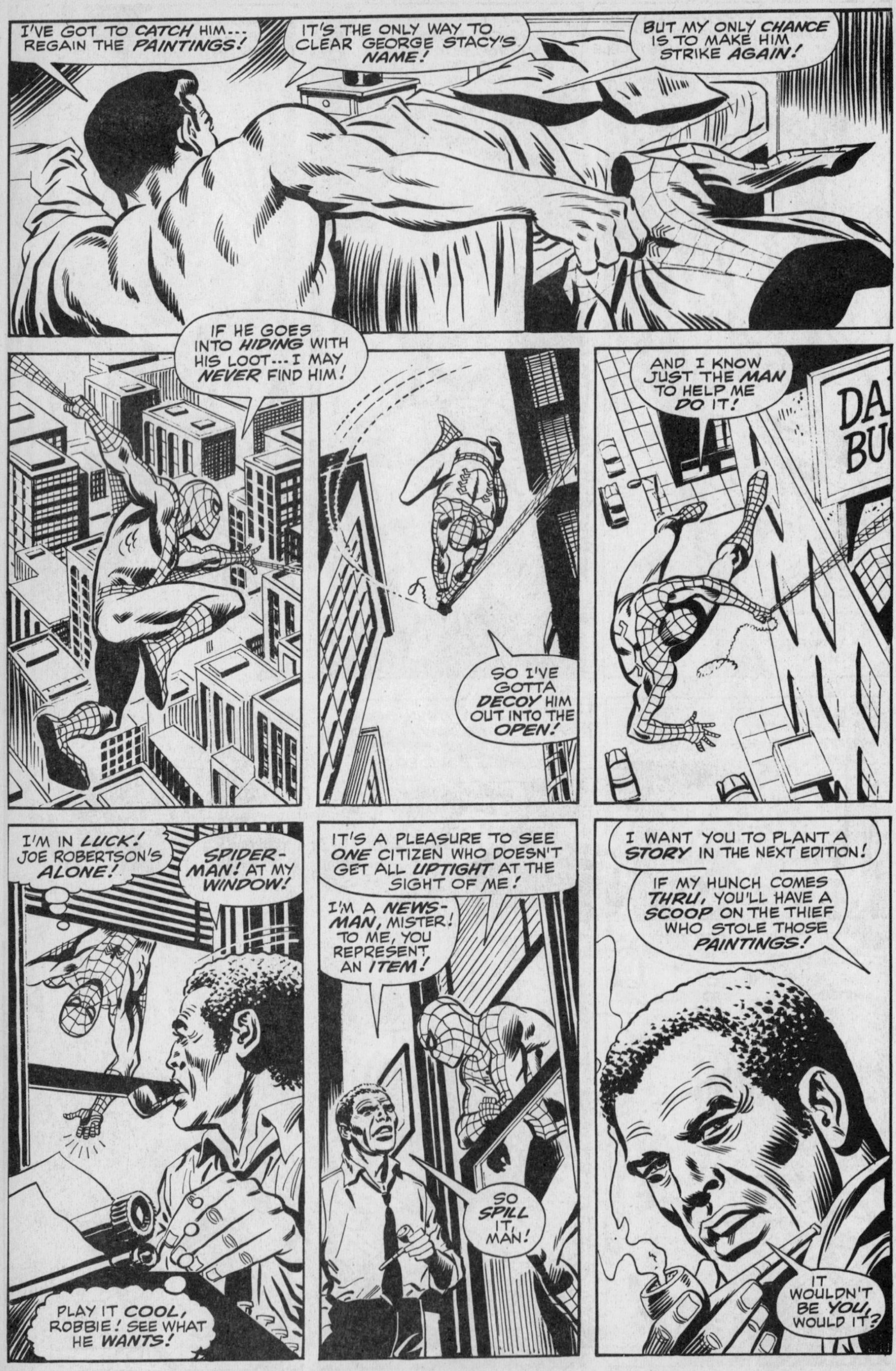
I'VE GOT TO CATCH HIM... REGAIN THE PAINTINGS!
IT'S THE ONLY WAY TO CLEAR GEORGE STACY'S NAME!
BUT MY ONLY CHANCE IS TO MAKE HIM STRIKE AGAIN!
IF HE GOES INTO HIDING WITH HIS LOOT... I MAY NEVER FIND HIM!
SO I'VE GOTTA DECOY HIM OUT INTO THE OPEN!
AND I KNOW JUST THE MAN TO HELP ME DO IT!
DA
BU
I'M IN LUCK! JOE ROBERTSON'S ALONE!
SPIDER-MAN! AT MY WINDOW!
PLAY IT COOL, ROBBIE! SEE WHAT HE WANTS!
IT'S A PLEASURE TO SEE ONE CITIZEN WHO DOESN'T GET ALL UPTIGHT AT THE SIGHT OF ME!
I'M A NEWS-MAN, MISTER! TO ME, YOU REPRESENT AN ITEM!
SO SPILL IT, MAN!
I WANT YOU TO PLANT A STORY IN THE NEXT EDITION!
IF MY HUNCH COMES THRU, YOU'LL HAVE A SCOOP ON THE THIEF WHO STOLE THOSE PAINTINGS!
IT WOULDN'T BE YOU, WOULD IT?

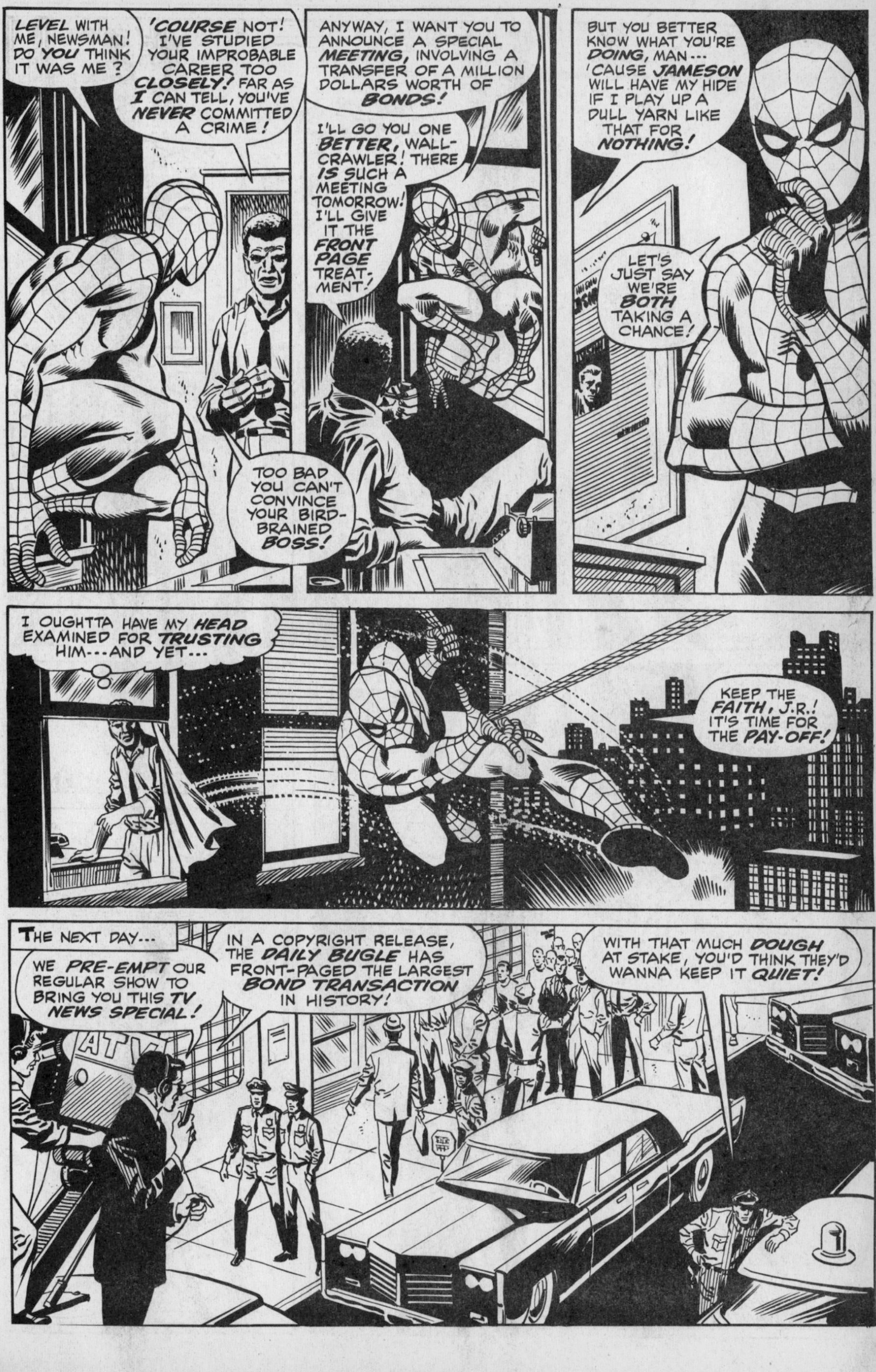
LEVEL WITH ME, NEWSMAN! DO YOU THINK IT WAS ME?
'COURSE NOT! I'VE STUDIED YOUR IMPROBABLE CAREER TOO CLOSELY! FAR AS I CAN TELL, YOU'VE NEVER COMMITTED A CRIME!
TOO BAD YOU CAN'T CONVINCE YOUR BIRD-BRAINED BOSS!
ANYWAY, I WANT YOU TO ANNOUNCE A SPECIAL MEETING, INVOLVING A TRANSFER OF A MILLION DOLLARS WORTH OF BONDS!
I'LL GO YOU ONE BETTER, WALL-CRAWLER! THERE IS SUCH A MEETING TOMORROW! I'LL GIVE IT THE FRONT PAGE TREATMENT!
BUT YOU BETTER KNOW WHAT YOU'RE DOING, MAN--- 'CAUSE JAMESON WILL HAVE MY HIDE IF I PLAY UP A DULL YARN LIKE THAT FOR NOTHING!
LET'S JUST SAY WE'RE BOTH TAKING A CHANCE!
I OUGHTTA HAVE MY HEAD EXAMINED FOR TRUSTING HIM---AND YET---
KEEP THE FAITH, J.R.! IT'S TIME FOR THE PAY-OFF!
THE NEXT DAY---
WE PRE-EMPT OUR REGULAR SHOW TO BRING YOU THIS TV NEWS SPECIAL!
IN A COPYRIGHT RELEASE, THE DAILY BUGLE HAS FRONT-PAGED THE LARGEST BOND TRANSACTION IN HISTORY!
WITH THAT MUCH DOUGH AT STAKE, YOU'D THINK THEY'D WANNA KEEP IT QUIET!

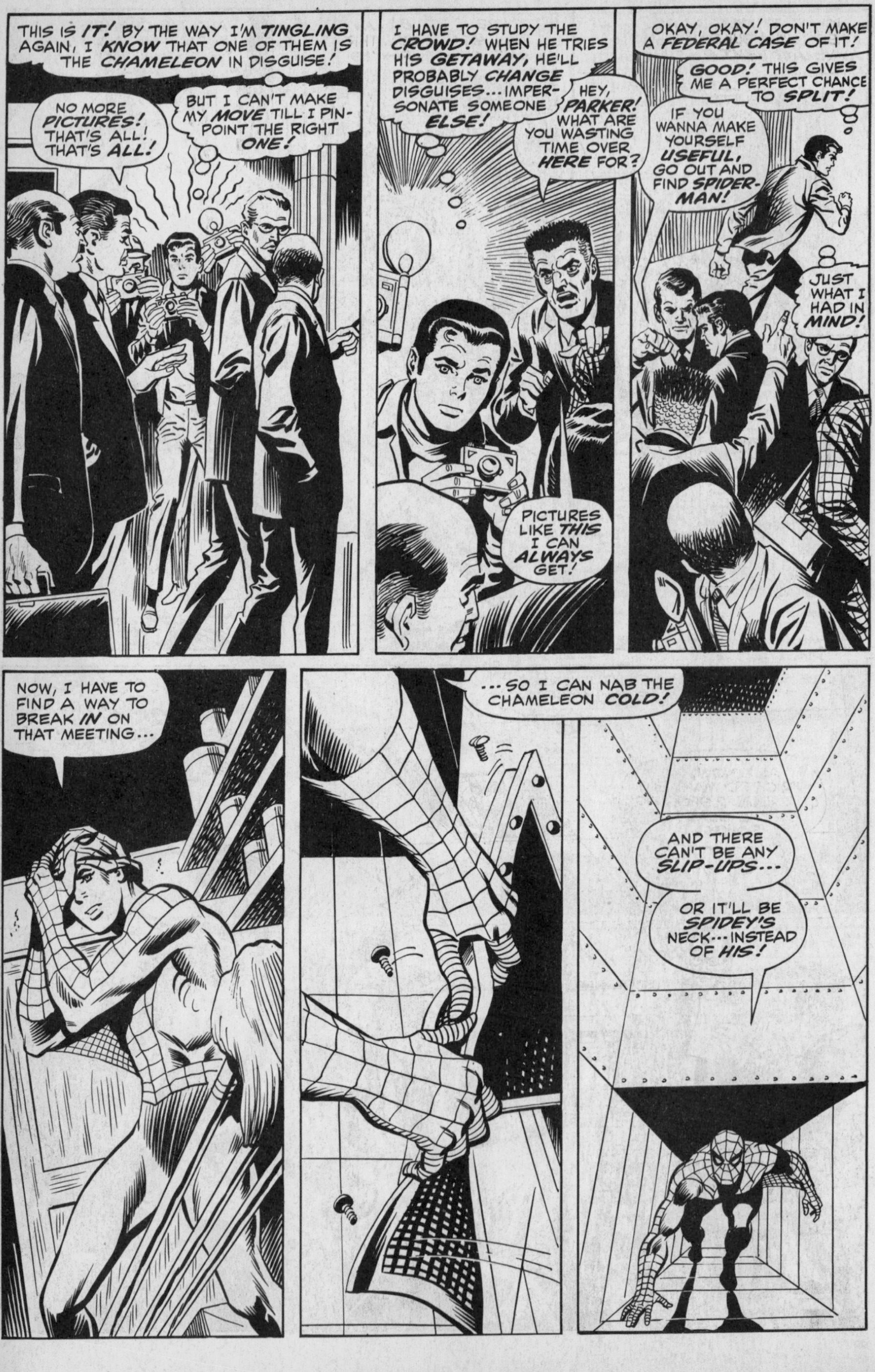
THIS IS IT! BY THE WAY I'M TINGLING AGAIN, I KNOW THAT ONE OF THEM IS THE CHAMELEON IN DISGUISE!
NO MORE PICTURES! THAT'S ALL! THAT'S ALL!
BUT I CAN'T MAKE MY MOVE TILL I PIN-POINT THE RIGHT ONE!
I HAVE TO STUDY THE CROWD! WHEN HE TRIES HIS GETAWAY, HE'LL PROBABLY CHANGE DISGUISES... IMPER-SONATE SOMEONE ELSE!
HEY, PARKER! WHAT ARE YOU WASTING TIME OVER HERE FOR?
PICTURES LIKE THIS I CAN ALWAYS GET!
OKAY, OKAY! DON'T MAKE A FEDERAL CASE OF IT!
GOOD! THIS GIVES ME A PERFECT CHANCE TO SPLIT!
IF YOU WANNA MAKE YOURSELF USEFUL, GO OUT AND FIND SPIDER-MAN!
JUST WHAT I HAD IN MIND!
NOW, I HAVE TO FIND A WAY TO BREAK IN ON THAT MEETING...
...SO I CAN NAB THE CHAMELEON COLD!
AND THERE CAN'T BE ANY SLIP-UPS...
OR IT'LL BE SPIDEY'S NECK... INSTEAD OF HIS!

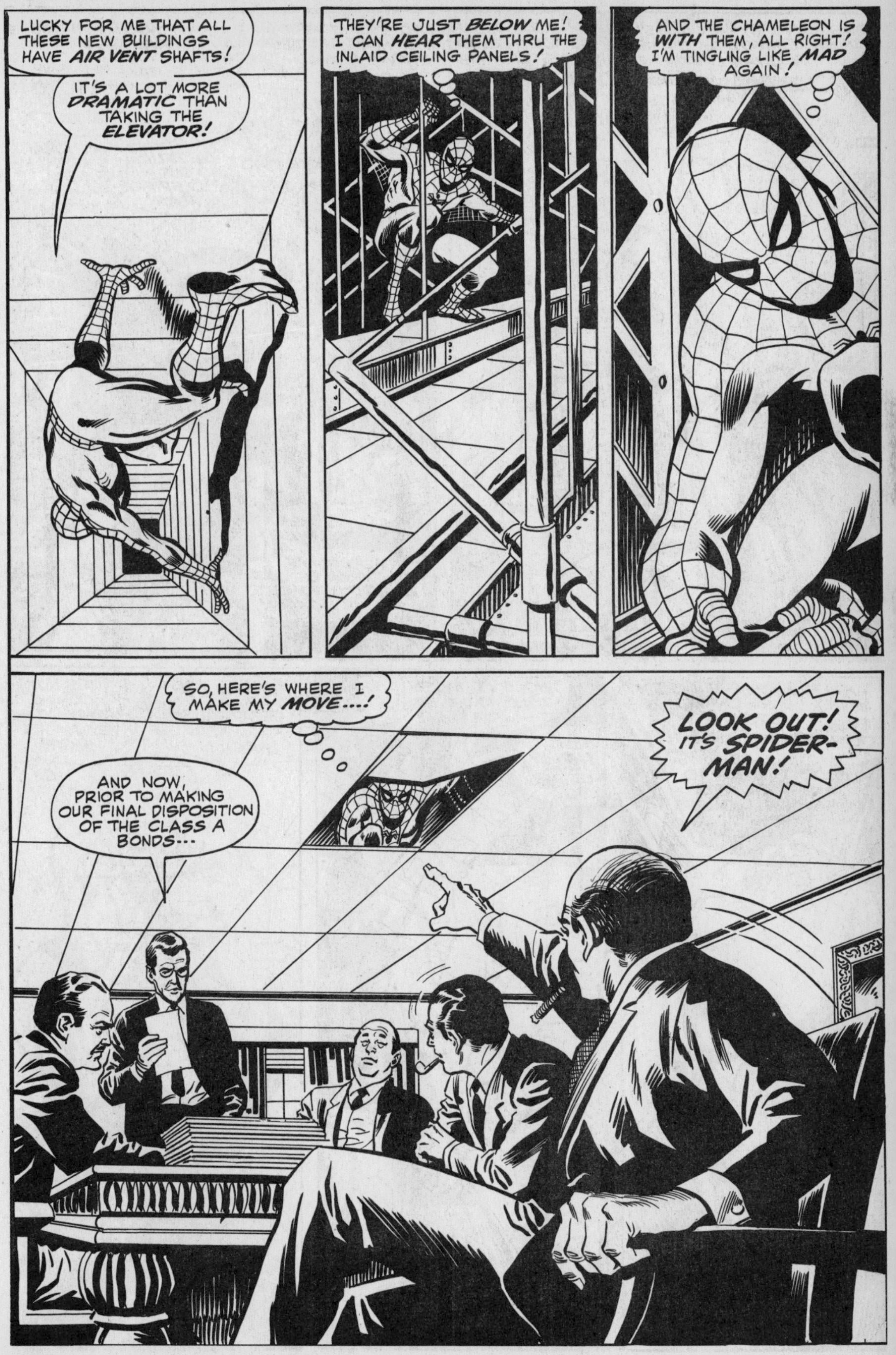
LUCKY FOR ME THAT ALL THESE NEW BUILDINGS HAVE AIR VENT SHAFTS!
IT'S A LOT MORE DRAMATIC THAN TAKING THE ELEVATOR!
THEY'RE JUST BELOW ME! I CAN HEAR THEM THRU THE INLAID CEILING PANELS!
AND THE CHAMELEON IS WITH THEM, ALL RIGHT! I'M TINGLING LIKE MAD AGAIN!
SO, HERE'S WHERE I MAKE MY MOVE...!
AND NOW, PRIOR TO MAKING OUR FINAL DISPOSITION OF THE CLASS A BONDS...
LOOK OUT! IT'S SPIDER-MAN!

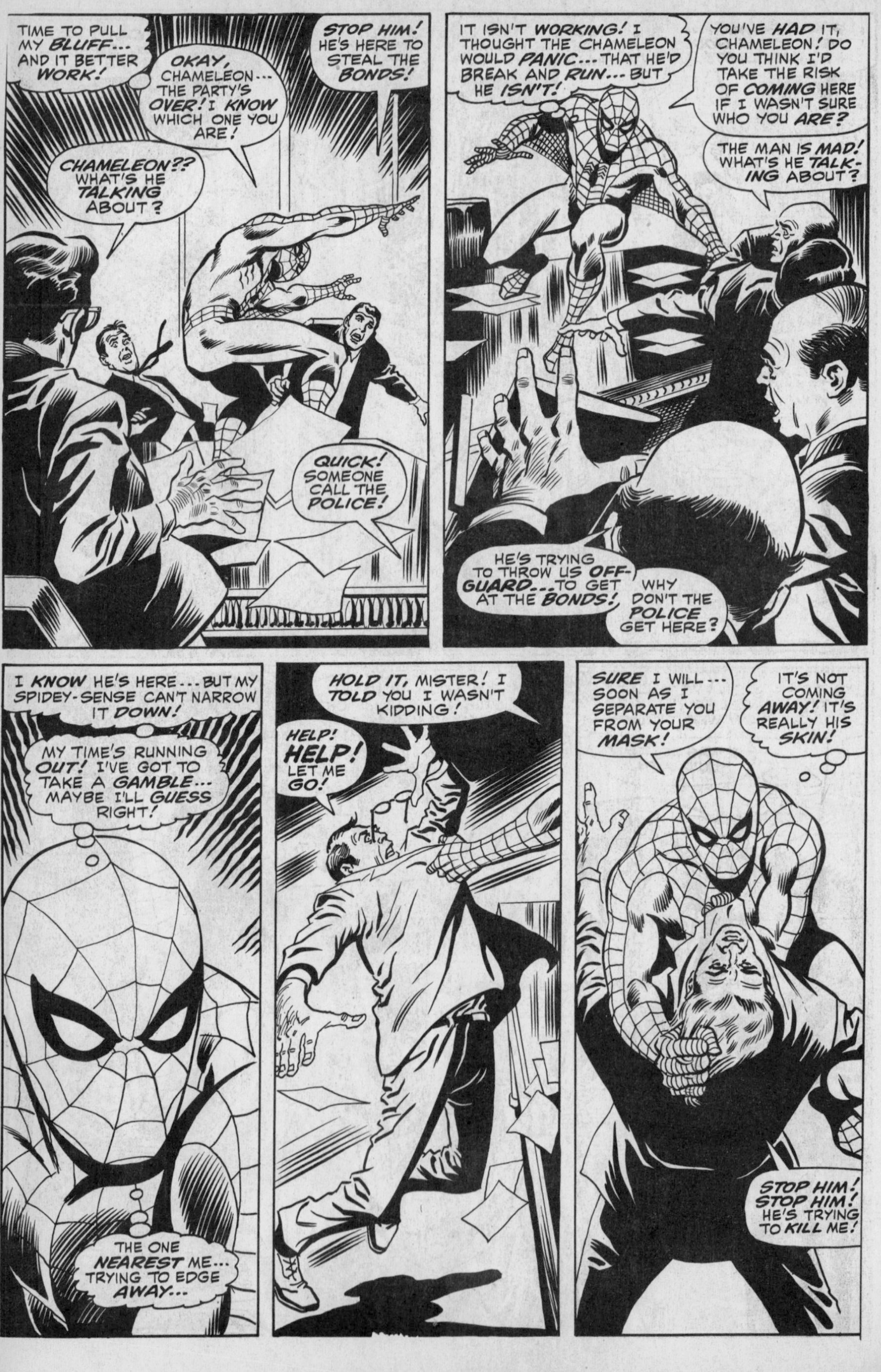
TIME TO PULL MY BLUFF... AND IT BETTER WORK!
OKAY, CHAMELEON... THE PARTY'S OVER! I KNOW WHICH ONE YOU ARE!
STOP HIM! HE'S HERE TO STEAL THE BONDS!
CHAMELEON?? WHAT'S HE TALKING ABOUT?
QUICK! SOMEONE CALL THE POLICE!
IT ISN'T WORKING! I THOUGHT THE CHAMELEON WOULD PANIC... THAT HE'D BREAK AND RUN... BUT HE ISN'T!
YOU'VE HAD IT, CHAMELEON! DO YOU THINK I'D TAKE THE RISK OF COMING HERE IF I WASN'T SURE WHO YOU ARE?
THE MAN IS MAD! WHAT'S HE TALKING ABOUT?
HE'S TRYING TO THROW US OFF-GUARD... TO GET AT THE BONDS!
WHY DON'T THE POLICE GET HERE?
I KNOW HE'S HERE... BUT MY SPIDEY-SENSE CAN'T NARROW IT DOWN!
MY TIME'S RUNNING OUT! I'VE GOT TO TAKE A GAMBLE... MAYBE I'LL GUESS RIGHT!
THE ONE NEAREST ME... TRYING TO EDGE AWAY...
HOLD IT, MISTER! I TOLD YOU I WASN'T KIDDING!
HELP! HELP! LET ME GO!
SURE I WILL... SOON AS I SEPARATE YOU FROM YOUR MASK!
IT'S NOT COMING AWAY! IT'S REALLY HIS SKIN!
STOP HIM! STOP HIM! HE'S TRYING TO KILL ME!

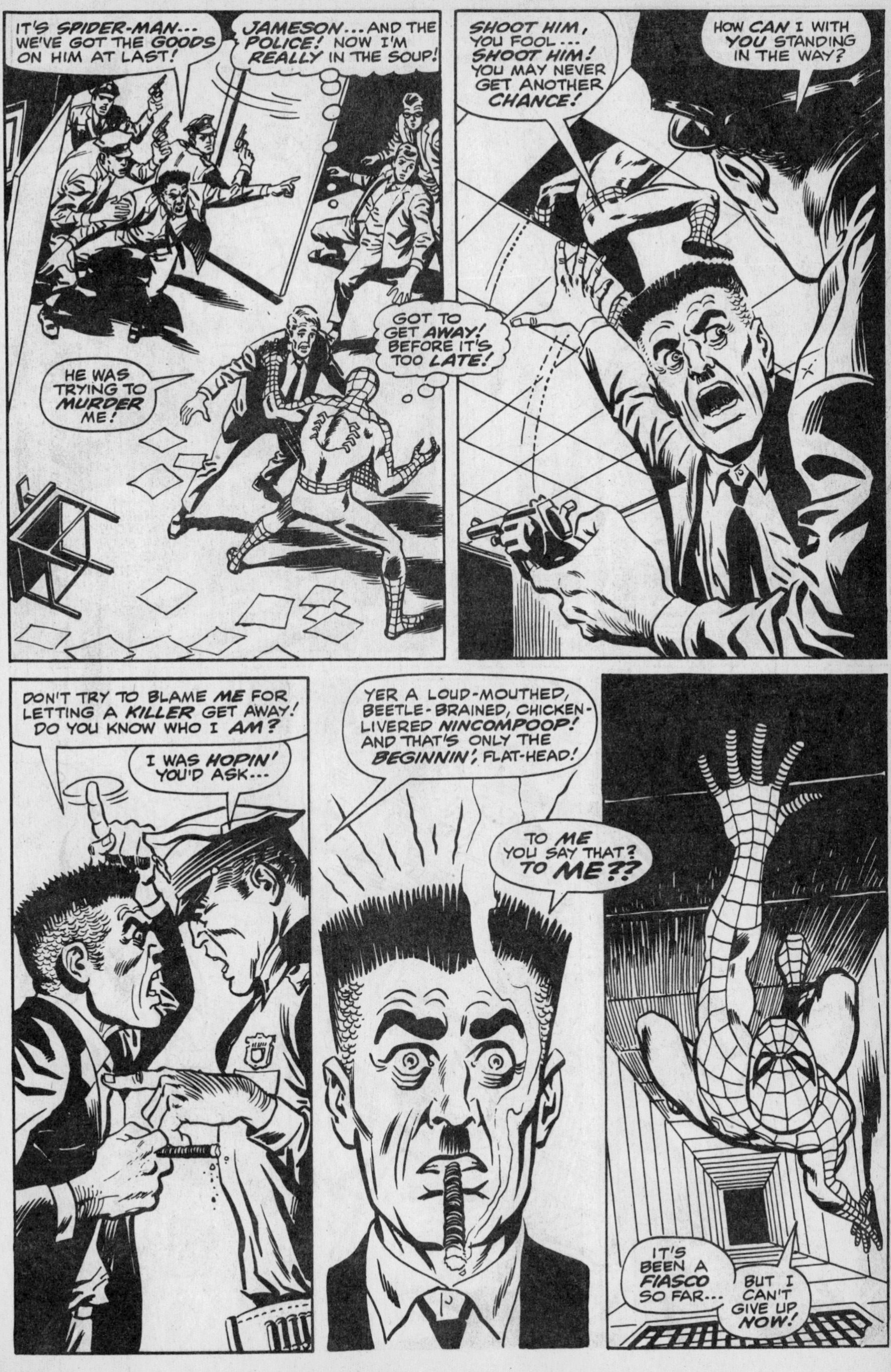
IT'S SPIDER-MAN... WE'VE GOT THE GOODS ON HIM AT LAST!
JAMESON... AND THE POLICE! NOW I'M REALLY IN THE SOUP!
HE WAS TRYING TO MURDER ME!
GOT TO GET AWAY! BEFORE IT'S TOO LATE!
SHOOT HIM, YOU FOOL... SHOOT HIM! YOU MAY NEVER GET ANOTHER CHANCE!
HOW CAN I WITH YOU STANDING IN THE WAY?
DON'T TRY TO BLAME ME FOR LETTING A KILLER GET AWAY! DO YOU KNOW WHO I AM?
I WAS HOPIN' YOU'D ASK...
YER A LOUD-MOUTHED, BEETLE-BRAINED, CHICKEN-LIVERED NINCOMPOOP! AND THAT'S ONLY THE BEGINNIN', FLAT-HEAD!
TO ME YOU SAY THAT? TO ME??
IT'S BEEN A FIASCO SO FAR...
BUT I CAN'T GIVE UP NOW!

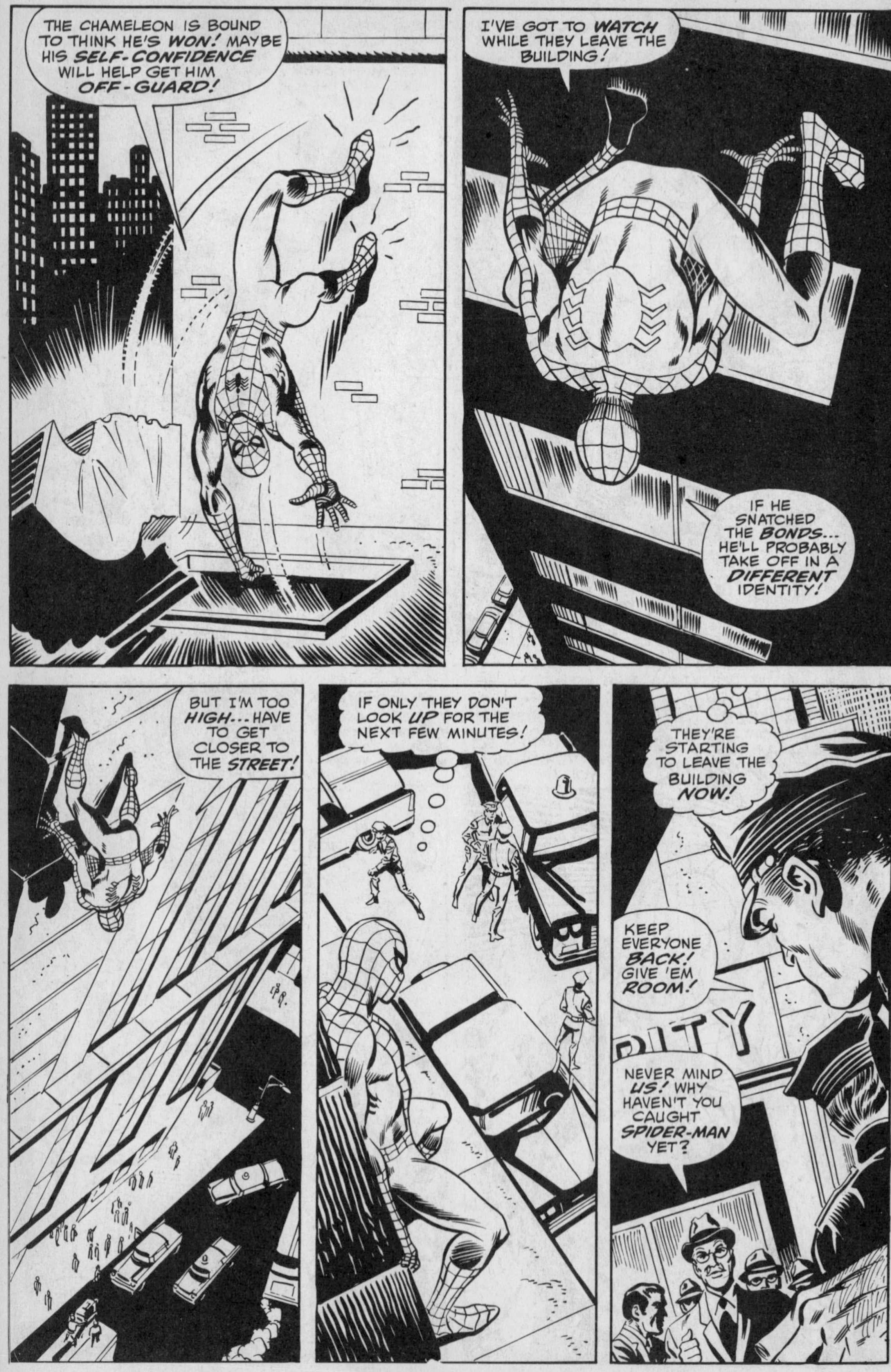
THE CHAMELEON IS BOUND TO THINK HE'S WON! MAYBE HIS SELF-CONFIDENCE WILL HELP GET HIM OFF-GUARD!
I'VE GOT TO WATCH WHILE THEY LEAVE THE BUILDING!
IF HE SNATCHED THE BONDS... HE'LL PROBABLY TAKE OFF IN A DIFFERENT IDENTITY!
BUT I'M TOO HIGH... HAVE TO GET CLOSER TO THE STREET!
IF ONLY THEY DON'T LOOK UP FOR THE NEXT FEW MINUTES!
THEY'RE STARTING TO LEAVE THE BUILDING NOW!
KEEP EVERYONE BACK! GIVE 'EM ROOM!
NEVER MIND US! WHY HAVEN'T YOU CAUGHT SPIDER-MAN YET?

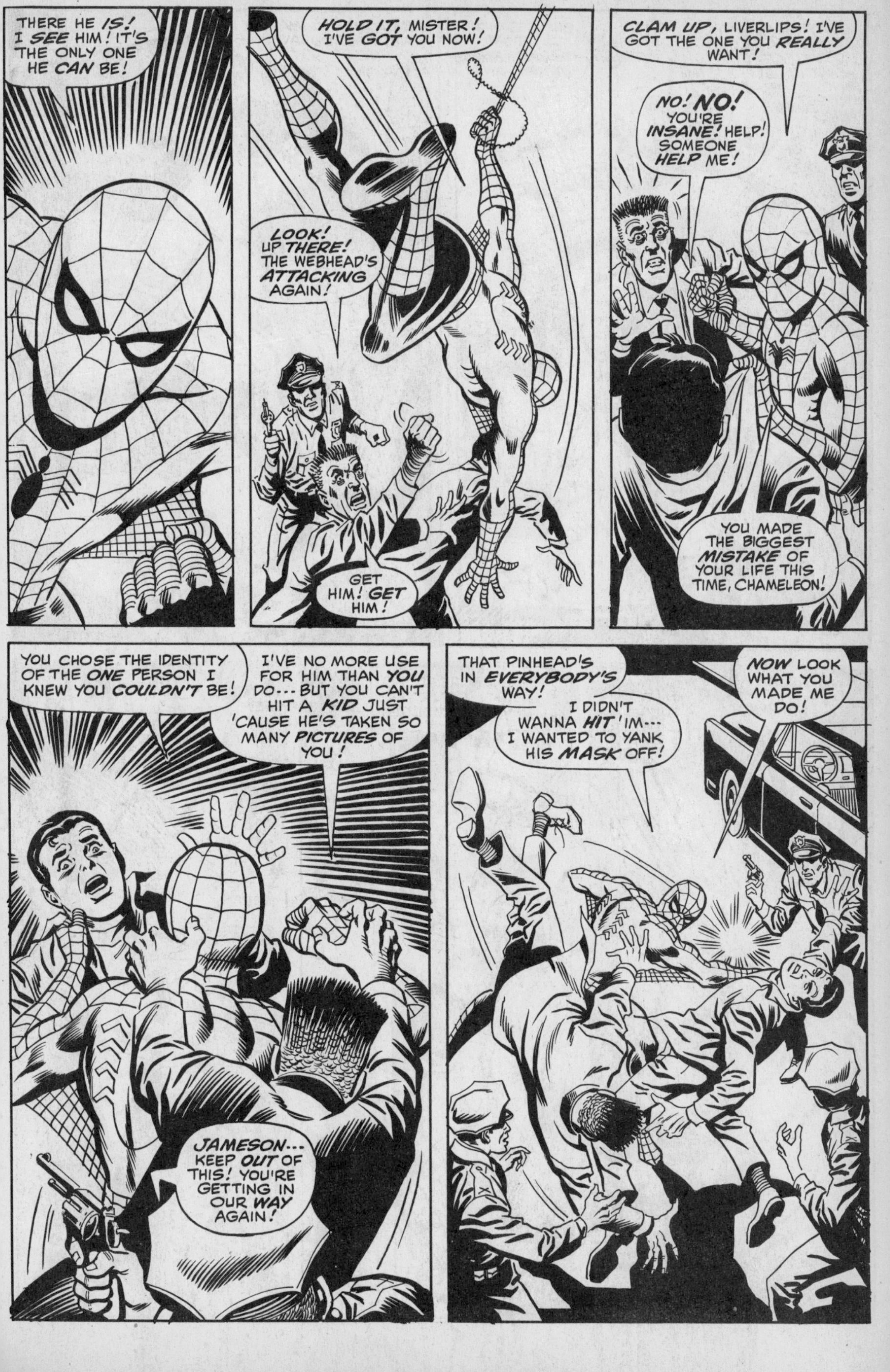
THERE HE IS! I SEE HIM! IT'S THE ONLY ONE HE CAN BE!
HOLD IT, MISTER! I'VE GOT YOU NOW!
LOOK! UP THERE! THE WEBHEAD'S ATTACKING AGAIN!
GET HIM! GET HIM!
CLAM UP, LIVERLIPS! I'VE GOT THE ONE YOU REALLY WANT!
NO! NO! YOU'RE INSANE! HELP! SOMEONE HELP ME!
YOU MADE THE BIGGEST MISTAKE OF YOUR LIFE THIS TIME, CHAMELEON!
YOU CHOSE THE IDENTITY OF THE ONE PERSON I KNEW YOU COULDN'T BE!
I'VE NO MORE USE FOR HIM THAN YOU DO--- BUT YOU CAN'T HIT A KID JUST 'CAUSE HE'S TAKEN SO MANY PICTURES OF YOU!
JAMESON--- KEEP OUT OF THIS! YOU'RE GETTING IN OUR WAY AGAIN!
THAT PINHEAD'S IN EVERYBODY'S WAY!
I DIDN'T WANNA HIT 'IM--- I WANTED TO YANK HIS MASK OFF!
NOW LOOK WHAT YOU MADE ME DO!

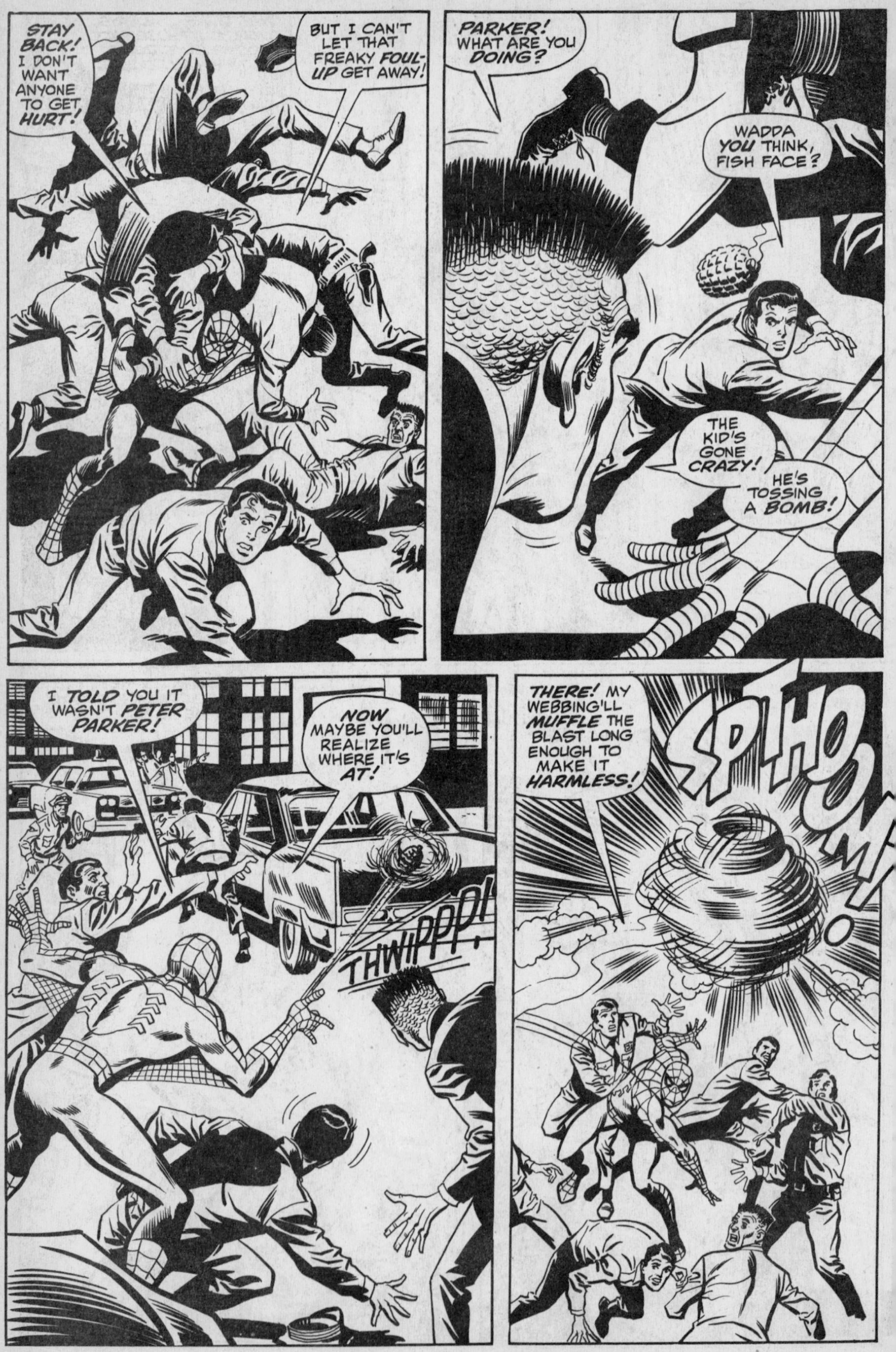
STAY BACK! I DON'T WANT ANYONE TO GET HURT!
BUT I CAN'T LET THAT FREAKY FOUL-UP GET AWAY!
PARKER! WHAT ARE YOU DOING?
WADDA YOU THINK, FISH FACE?
THE KID'S GONE CRAZY!
HE'S TOSSING A BOMB!
I TOLD YOU IT WASN'T PETER PARKER!
NOW MAYBE YOU'LL REALIZE WHERE IT'S AT!
THWIPPP!
THERE! MY WEBBING'LL MUFFLE THE BLAST LONG ENOUGH TO MAKE IT HARMLESS!
SPTHOOM!

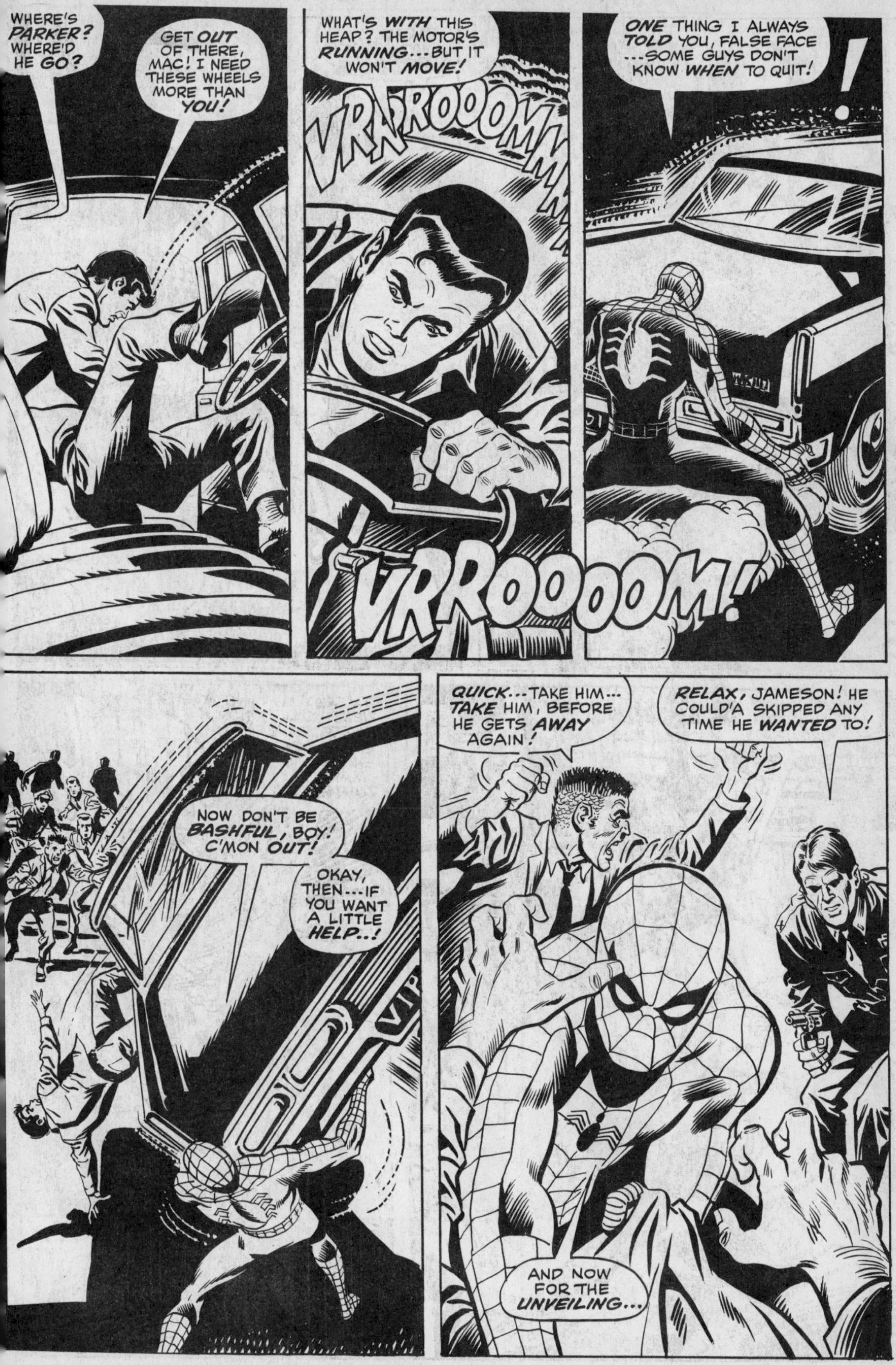
WHERE'S PARKER? WHERE'D HE GO?
GET OUT OF THERE, MAC! I NEED THESE WHEELS MORE THAN YOU!
WHAT'S WITH THIS HEAP? THE MOTOR'S RUNNING... BUT IT WON'T MOVE!
VRAROOOMMM
VRROOOOM!
ONE THING I ALWAYS TOLD YOU, FALSE FACE ...SOME GUYS DON'T KNOW WHEN TO QUIT!
!
NOW DON'T BE BASHFUL, BOY! C'MON OUT!
OKAY, THEN... IF YOU WANT A LITTLE HELP..!
QUICK...TAKE HIM... TAKE HIM, BEFORE HE GETS AWAY AGAIN!
RELAX, JAMESON! HE COULD'A SKIPPED ANY TIME HE WANTED TO!
AND NOW FOR THE UNVEILING...

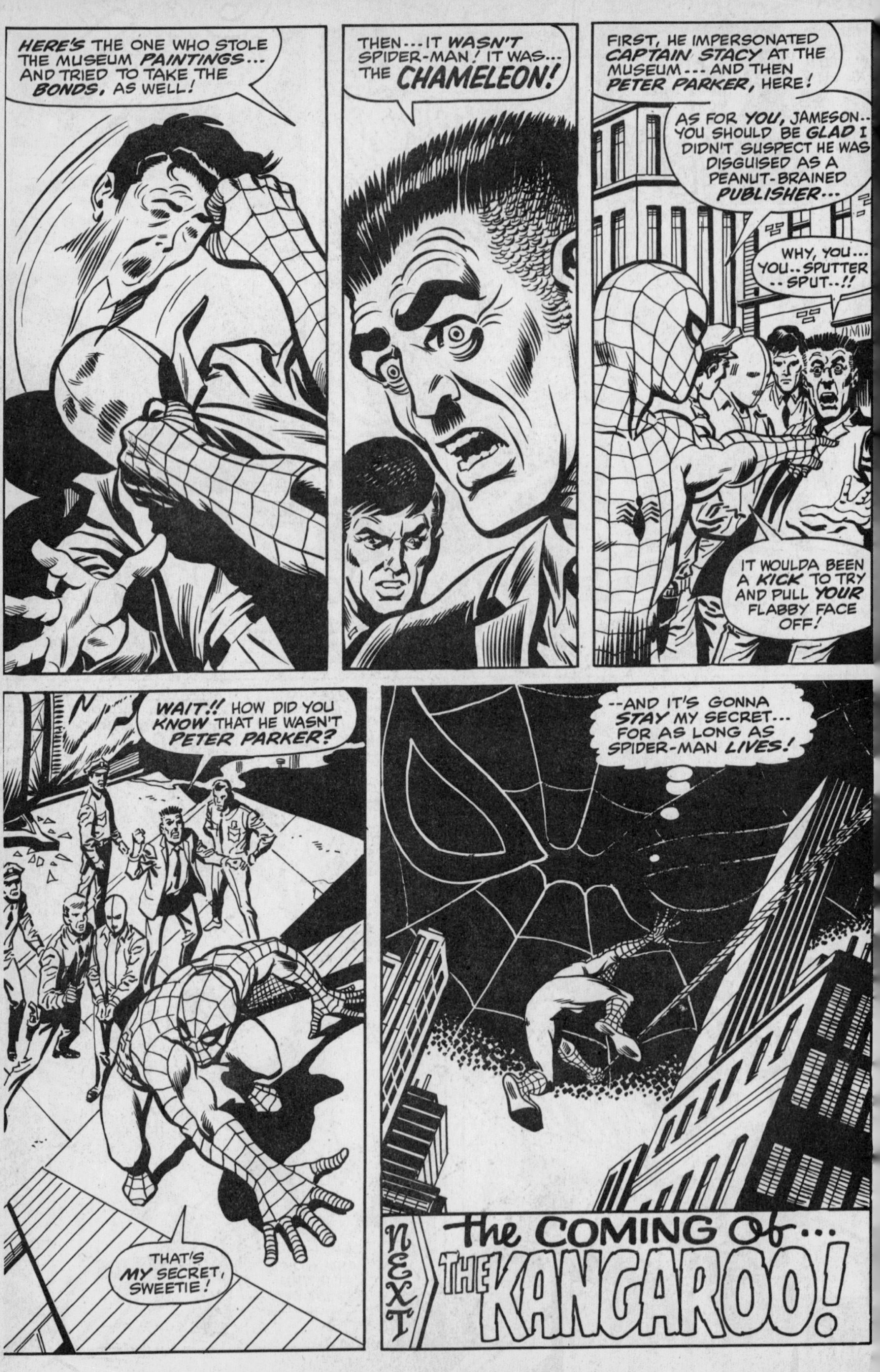
HERE'S THE ONE WHO STOLE THE MUSEUM PAINTINGS... AND TRIED TO TAKE THE BONDS, AS WELL!
THEN... IT WASN'T SPIDER-MAN! IT WAS... THE CHAMELEON!
FIRST, HE IMPERSONATED CAPTAIN STACY AT THE MUSEUM... AND THEN PETER PARKER, HERE!
AS FOR YOU, JAMESON... YOU SHOULD BE GLAD I DIDN'T SUSPECT HE WAS DISGUISED AS A PEANUT-BRAINED PUBLISHER...
WHY, YOU... YOU.. SPUTTER -- SPUT--!!
IT WOULDA BEEN A KICK TO TRY AND PULL YOUR FLABBY FACE OFF!
WAIT!! HOW DID YOU KNOW THAT HE WASN'T PETER PARKER?
THAT'S MY SECRET, SWEETIE!
--AND IT'S GONNA STAY MY SECRET... FOR AS LONG AS SPIDER-MAN LIVES!
NEXT
the COMING Of... THE KANGAROO!

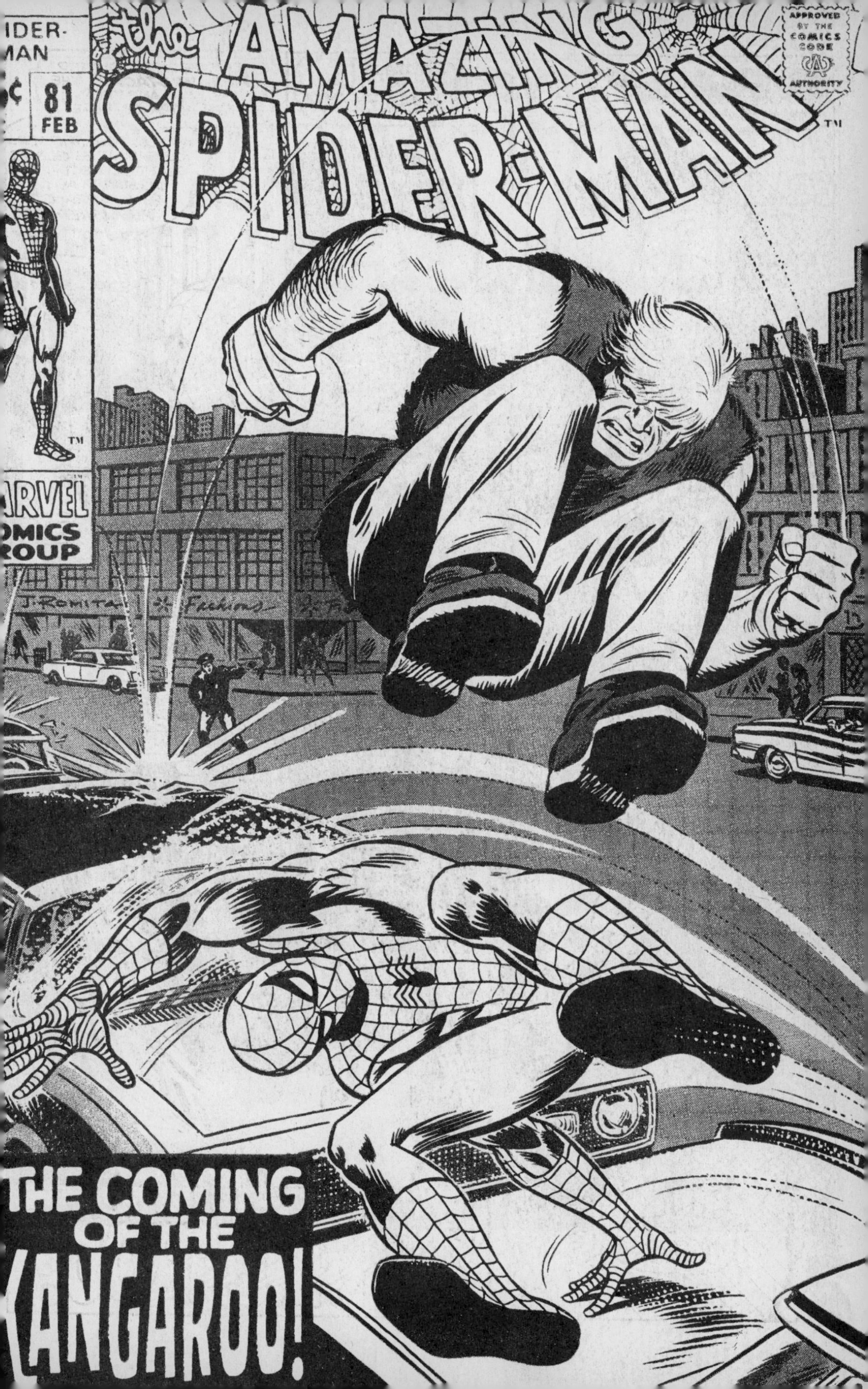

the AMAZING SPIDER-MAN
81
FEB
APPROVED BY THE COMICS CODE AUTHORITY
ARVEL
OMICS
ROUP
J. ROMITA
Fashions
THE COMING OF THE
ANGAROO!

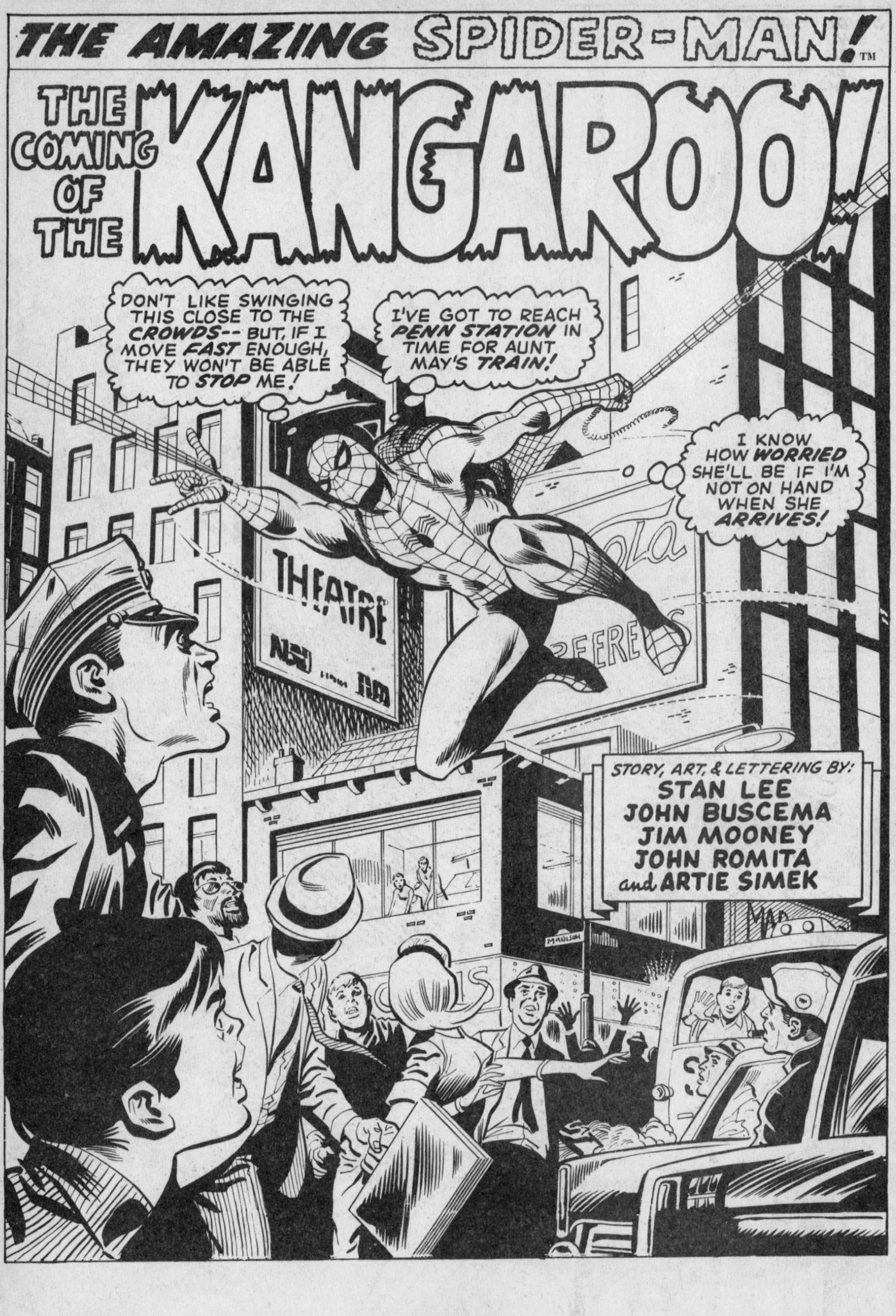
THE AMAZING SPIDER-MAN!™
THE COMING OF THE KANGAROO!
DON'T LIKE SWINGING THIS CLOSE TO THE CROWDS-- BUT, IF I MOVE FAST ENOUGH, THEY WON'T BE ABLE TO STOP ME!
I'VE GOT TO REACH PENN STATION IN TIME FOR AUNT MAY'S TRAIN!
I KNOW HOW WORRIED SHE'LL BE IF I'M NOT ON HAND WHEN SHE ARRIVES!
THEATRE
STORY, ART, & LETTERING BY:
STAN LEE
JOHN BUSCEMA
JIM MOONEY
JOHN ROMITA
and ARTIE SIMEK

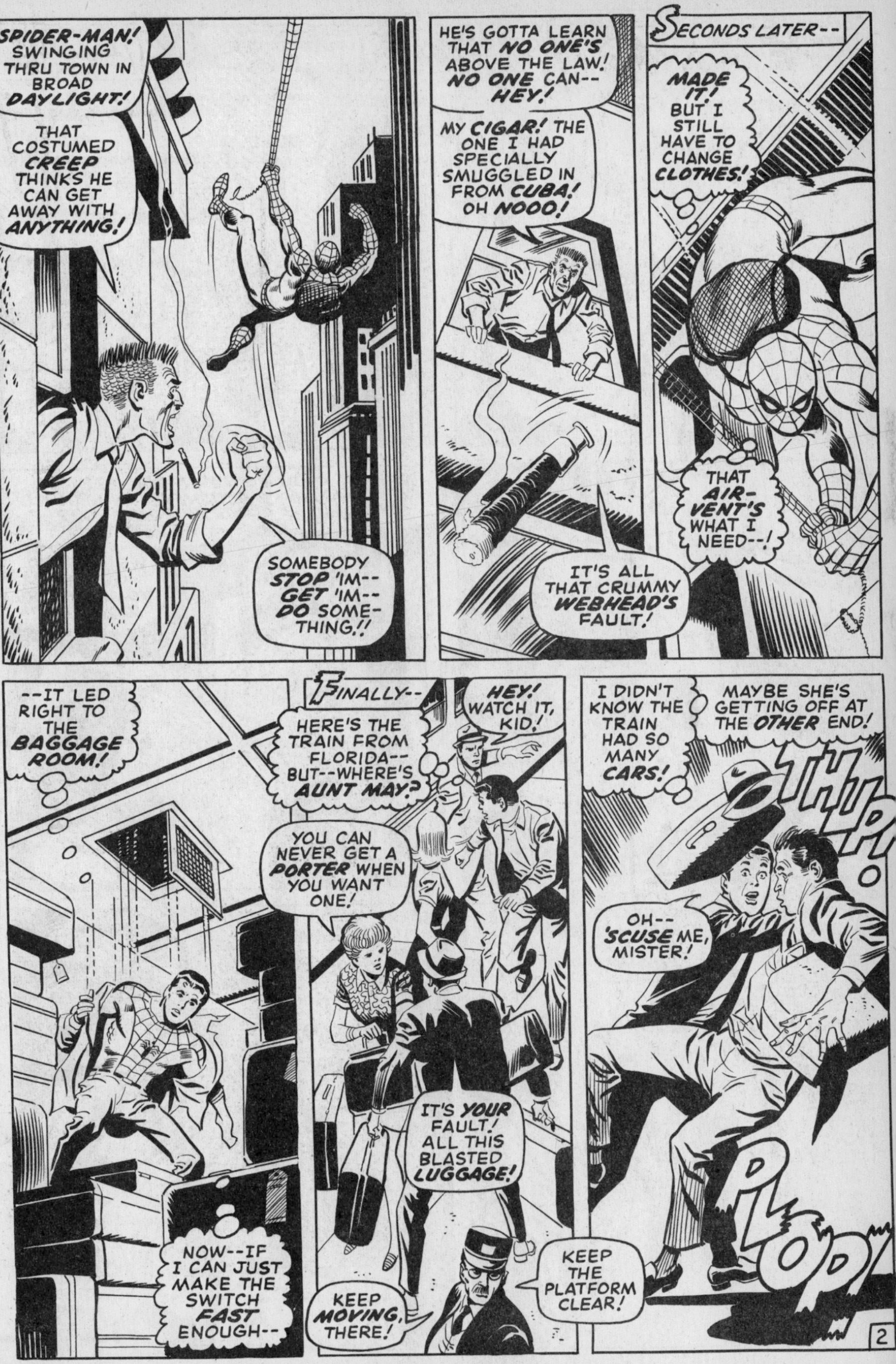
SPIDER-MAN! SWINGING THRU TOWN IN BROAD DAYLIGHT!
THAT COSTUMED CREEP THINKS HE CAN GET AWAY WITH ANYTHING!
SOMEBODY STOP 'IM-- GET 'IM-- DO SOMETHING.!!
HE'S GOTTA LEARN THAT NO ONE'S ABOVE THE LAW! NO ONE CAN-- HEY!
MY CIGAR! THE ONE I HAD SPECIALLY SMUGGLED IN FROM CUBA! OH NOOO!
IT'S ALL THAT CRUMMY WEBHEAD'S FAULT!
SECONDS LATER--
MADE IT! BUT I STILL HAVE TO CHANGE CLOTHES!
THAT AIR-VENT'S WHAT I NEED--!
--IT LED RIGHT TO THE BAGGAGE ROOM!
NOW--IF I CAN JUST MAKE THE SWITCH FAST ENOUGH--
FINALLY--
HERE'S THE TRAIN FROM FLORIDA-- BUT--WHERE'S AUNT MAY?
HEY! WATCH IT, KID!
YOU CAN NEVER GET A PORTER WHEN YOU WANT ONE!
IT'S YOUR FAULT! ALL THIS BLASTED LUGGAGE!
KEEP MOVING, THERE!
KEEP THE PLATFORM CLEAR!
I DIDN'T KNOW THE TRAIN HAD SO MANY CARS!
MAYBE SHE'S GETTING OFF AT THE OTHER END!
THUMP
OH-- 'SCUSE ME, MISTER!
PLOP!

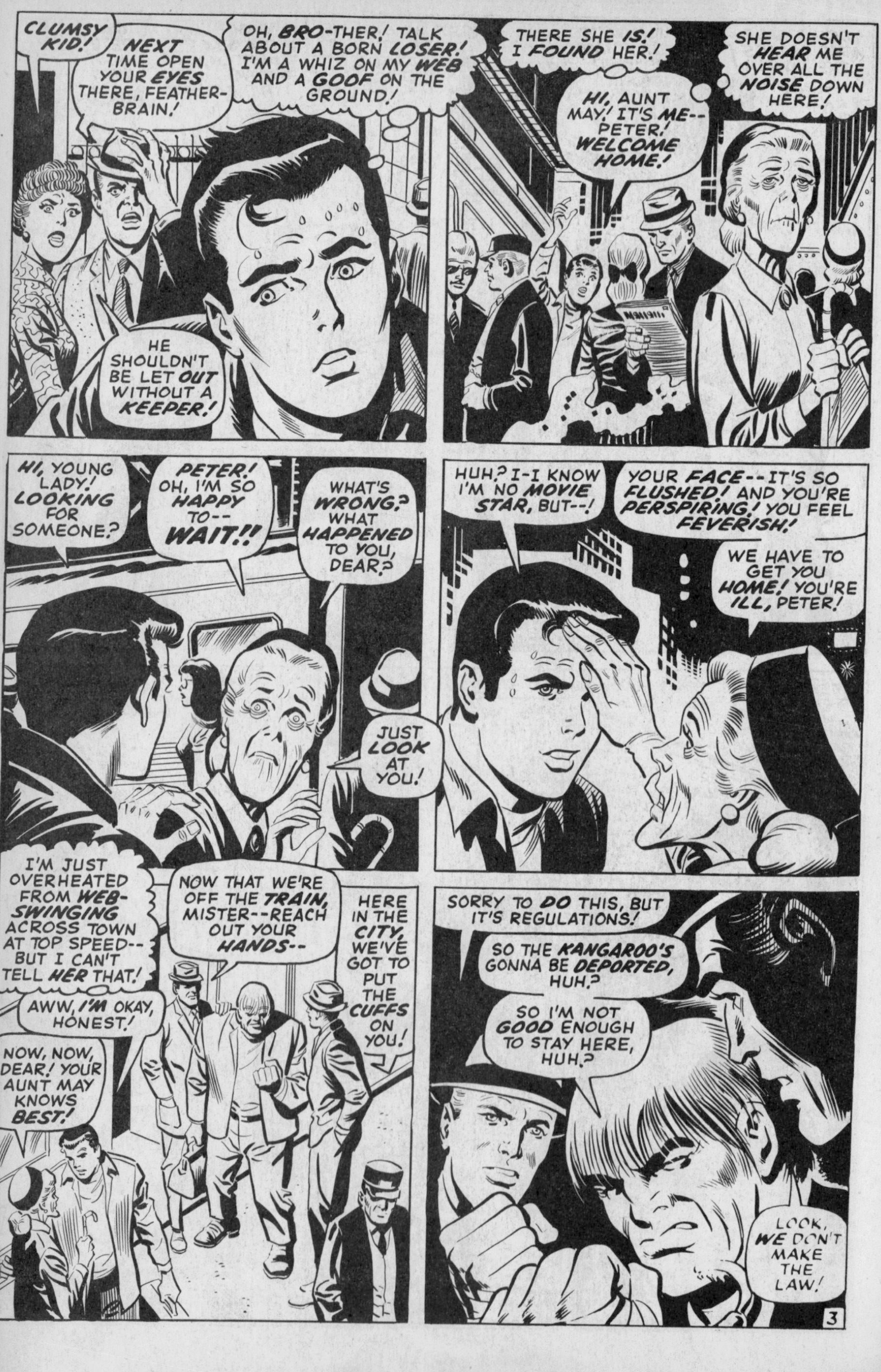
CLUMSY KID!
NEXT TIME OPEN YOUR EYES THERE, FEATHER-BRAIN!
OH, BRO-THER! TALK ABOUT A BORN LOSER! I'M A WHIZ ON MY WEB AND A GOOF ON THE GROUND!
HE SHOULDN'T BE LET OUT WITHOUT A KEEPER!
THERE SHE IS! I FOUND HER!
SHE DOESN'T HEAR ME OVER ALL THE NOISE DOWN HERE!
HI, AUNT MAY! IT'S ME-- PETER! WELCOME HOME!
HI, YOUNG LADY! LOOKING FOR SOMEONE?
PETER! OH, I'M SO HAPPY TO-- WAIT!!
WHAT'S WRONG? WHAT HAPPENED TO YOU, DEAR?
JUST LOOK AT YOU!
HUH? I-I KNOW I'M NO MOVIE STAR, BUT--!
YOUR FACE--IT'S SO FLUSHED! AND YOU'RE PERSPIRING! YOU FEEL FEVERISH!
WE HAVE TO GET YOU HOME! YOU'RE ILL, PETER!
I'M JUST OVERHEATED FROM WEB-SWINGING ACROSS TOWN AT TOP SPEED-- BUT I CAN'T TELL HER THAT!
AWW, I'M OKAY, HONEST!
NOW, NOW, DEAR! YOUR AUNT MAY KNOWS BEST!
NOW THAT WE'RE OFF THE TRAIN, MISTER--REACH OUT YOUR HANDS--
HERE IN THE CITY, WE'VE GOT TO PUT THE CUFFS ON YOU!
SORRY TO DO THIS, BUT IT'S REGULATIONS!
SO THE KANGAROO'S GONNA BE DEPORTED, HUH?
SO I'M NOT GOOD ENOUGH TO STAY HERE, HUH?
LOOK, WE DON'T MAKE THE LAW!
3

Panel 1 (top left):

"I DON'T CARE *WHO* MAKES THE LAW!"

"NO ONE'S PUSHING *ME* AROUND AGAIN!"

"YOU *FOOL!* YOU'LL NEVER GET *AWAY* WITH THIS!"

"*NO?* JUST TRY'N *STOP* ME!"

Panel 2 (top right):

"GET 'IM, CHARLIE! DON'T LET THE KANGAROO GET *LOOSE!*"

"HE'S GOT TOO BIG A *START!* CAN'T CHANCE *FIRING*--IN ALL THIS *CROWD!*"

"*QUICKLY*, PETER! YOU MUST COME *AWAY* FROM HERE!"

Panel 3 (bottom left):

"THEY SHOULD BE *ASHAMED* OF THEMSELVES--*FRIGHTENING* LAW-ABIDING PEOPLE LIKE THAT!"

"*SPIDER-MAN* COULD PROBABLY NAIL THAT CHARACTER--BUT NOT WHILE *AUNT MAY* IS HERE!"

"*HEY!* SO THAT'S WHY THEY CALL HIM *KANGAROO!*"

Panel 4 (bottom middle):

"*CROWDS* CAN'T STOP A MAN WHO CAN LEAP RIGHT OVER THEIR *HEADS!*"

Panel 5 (bottom right):

"*AND* NOW THAT I'M *FREE*--"

"NO ONE'S EVER MAKING A FALL GUY OF THE *KANGAROO* AGAIN!"

4

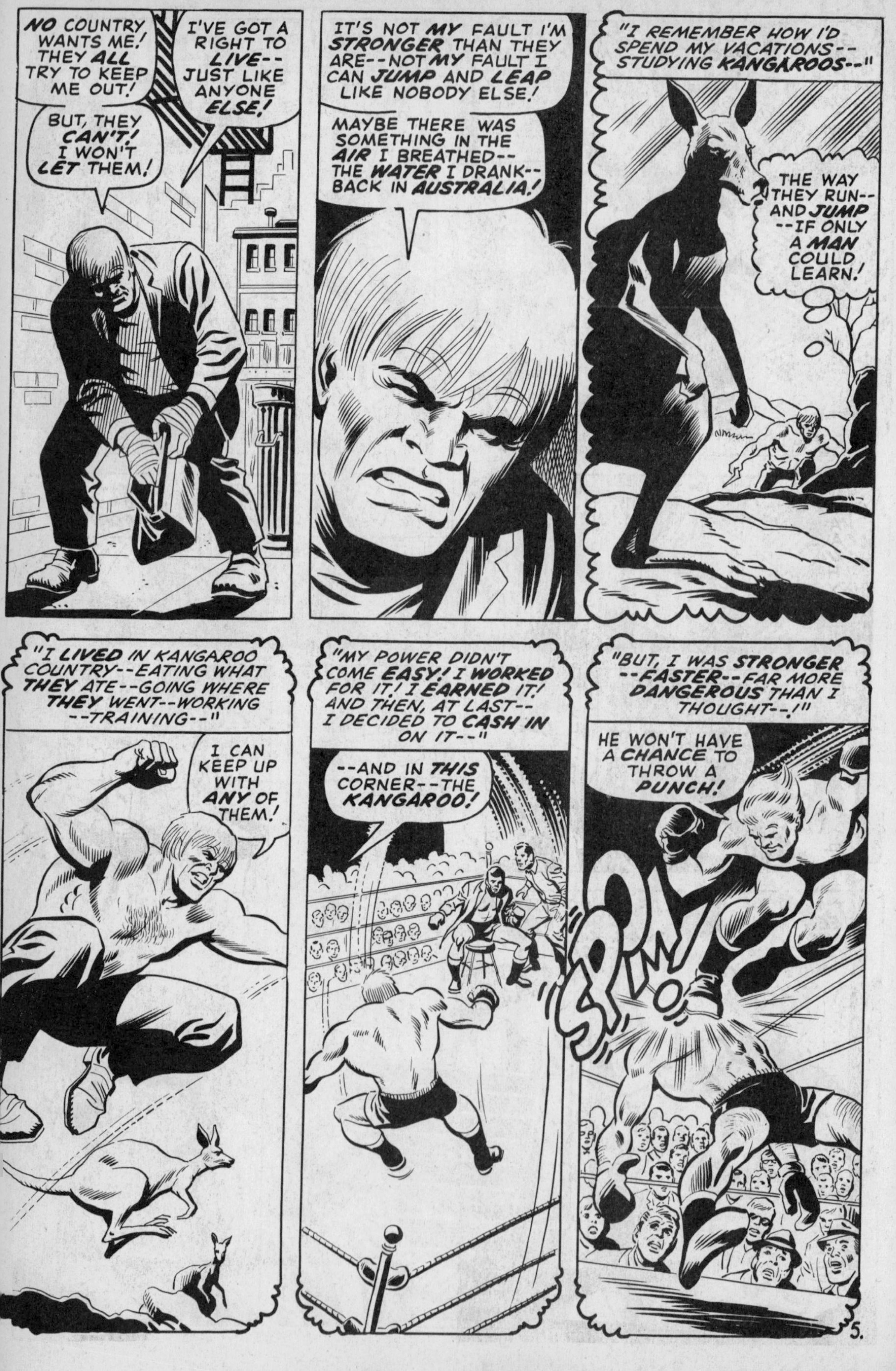
NO COUNTRY WANTS ME! THEY ALL TRY TO KEEP ME OUT!
I'VE GOT A RIGHT TO LIVE-- JUST LIKE ANYONE ELSE!
BUT, THEY CAN'T! I WON'T LET THEM!
IT'S NOT MY FAULT I'M STRONGER THAN THEY ARE--NOT MY FAULT I CAN JUMP AND LEAP LIKE NOBODY ELSE!
MAYBE THERE WAS SOMETHING IN THE AIR I BREATHED-- THE WATER I DRANK-- BACK IN AUSTRALIA!
"I REMEMBER HOW I'D SPEND MY VACATIONS-- STUDYING KANGAROOS--"
THE WAY THEY RUN-- AND JUMP --IF ONLY A MAN COULD LEARN!
"I LIVED IN KANGAROO COUNTRY--EATING WHAT THEY ATE--GOING WHERE THEY WENT--WORKING --TRAINING--"
I CAN KEEP UP WITH ANY OF THEM!
"MY POWER DIDN'T COME EASY! I WORKED FOR IT! I EARNED IT! AND THEN, AT LAST-- I DECIDED TO CASH IN ON IT--"
--AND IN THIS CORNER--THE KANGAROO!
"BUT, I WAS STRONGER --FASTER--FAR MORE DANGEROUS THAN I THOUGHT--!"
HE WON'T HAVE A CHANCE TO THROW A PUNCH!
SPWOOM
5.

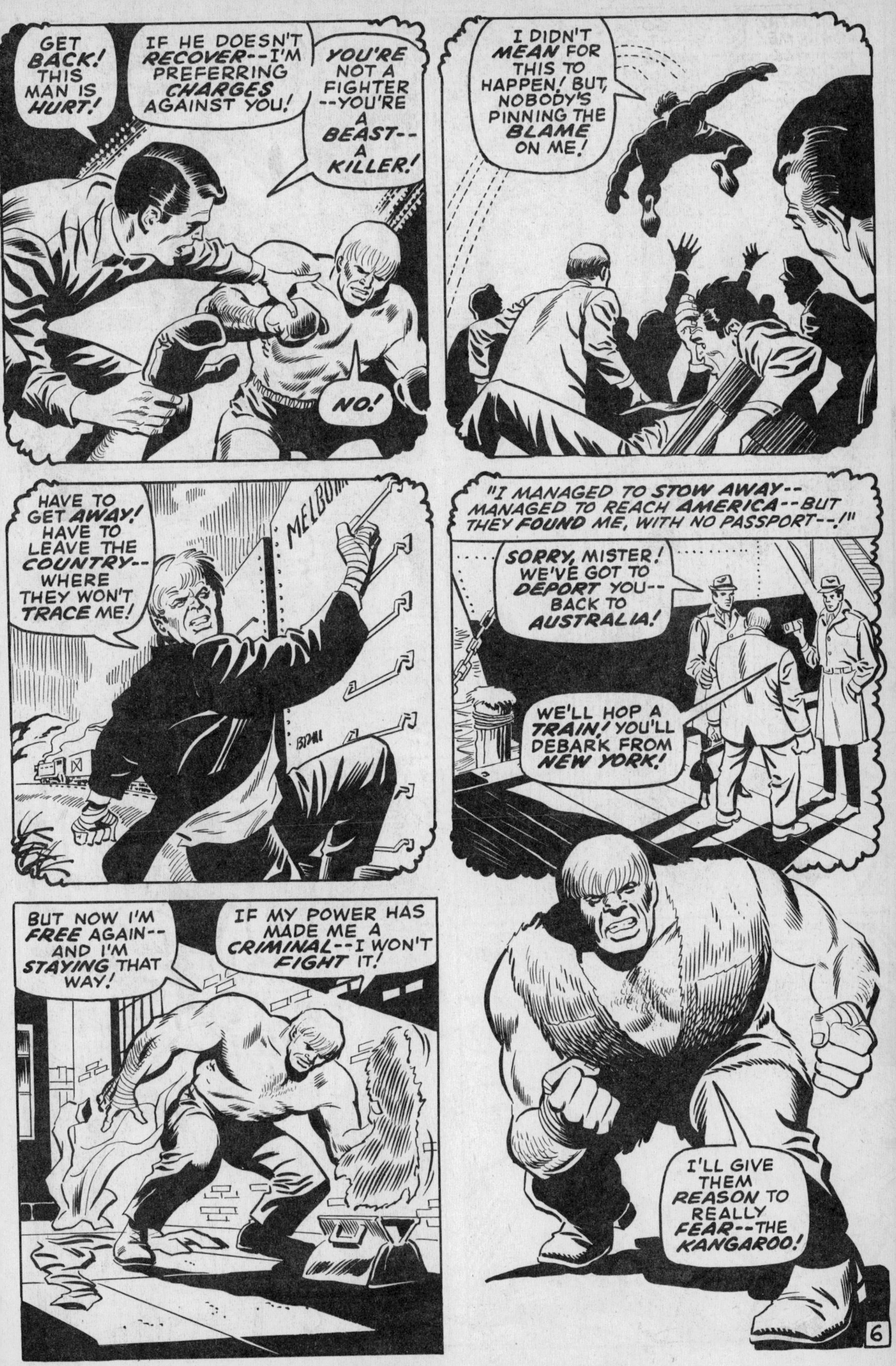
GET BACK! THIS MAN IS HURT!
IF HE DOESN'T RECOVER--I'M PREFERRING CHARGES AGAINST YOU!
YOU'RE NOT A FIGHTER --YOU'RE A BEAST-- A KILLER!
NO!
I DIDN'T MEAN FOR THIS TO HAPPEN! BUT, NOBODY'S PINNING THE BLAME ON ME!
HAVE TO GET AWAY! HAVE TO LEAVE THE COUNTRY-- WHERE THEY WON'T TRACE ME!
"I MANAGED TO STOW AWAY-- MANAGED TO REACH AMERICA--BUT THEY FOUND ME, WITH NO PASSPORT--!"
SORRY, MISTER! WE'VE GOT TO DEPORT YOU-- BACK TO AUSTRALIA!
WE'LL HOP A TRAIN! YOU'LL DEBARK FROM NEW YORK!
BUT NOW I'M FREE AGAIN-- AND I'M STAYING THAT WAY!
IF MY POWER HAS MADE ME A CRIMINAL--I WON'T FIGHT IT!
I'LL GIVE THEM REASON TO REALLY FEAR--THE KANGAROO!
6

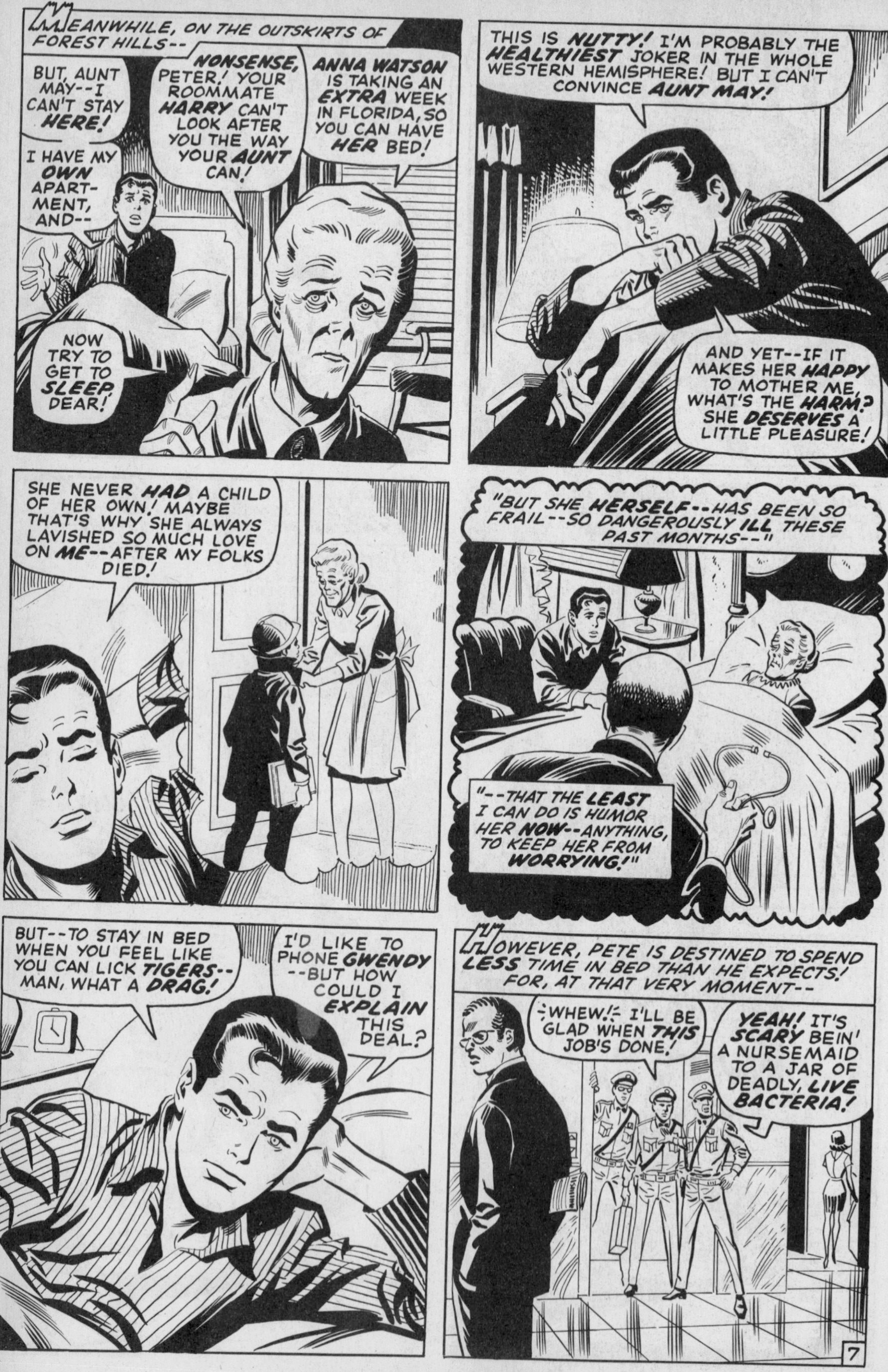
MEANWHILE, ON THE OUTSKIRTS OF FOREST HILLS--
BUT, AUNT MAY--I CAN'T STAY HERE!
I HAVE MY OWN APARTMENT, AND--
NONSENSE, PETER! YOUR ROOMMATE HARRY CAN'T LOOK AFTER YOU THE WAY YOUR AUNT CAN!
ANNA WATSON IS TAKING AN EXTRA WEEK IN FLORIDA, SO YOU CAN HAVE HER BED!
NOW TRY TO GET TO SLEEP, DEAR!
THIS IS NUTTY! I'M PROBABLY THE HEALTHIEST JOKER IN THE WHOLE WESTERN HEMISPHERE! BUT I CAN'T CONVINCE AUNT MAY!
AND YET--IF IT MAKES HER HAPPY TO MOTHER ME, WHAT'S THE HARM? SHE DESERVES A LITTLE PLEASURE!
SHE NEVER HAD A CHILD OF HER OWN! MAYBE THAT'S WHY SHE ALWAYS LAVISHED SO MUCH LOVE ON ME--AFTER MY FOLKS DIED!
"BUT SHE HERSELF--HAS BEEN SO FRAIL--SO DANGEROUSLY ILL THESE PAST MONTHS--"
"--THAT THE LEAST I CAN DO IS HUMOR HER NOW--ANYTHING, TO KEEP HER FROM WORRYING!"
BUT--TO STAY IN BED WHEN YOU FEEL LIKE YOU CAN LICK TIGERS--MAN, WHAT A DRAG!
I'D LIKE TO PHONE GWENDY--BUT HOW COULD I EXPLAIN THIS DEAL?
HOWEVER, PETE IS DESTINED TO SPEND LESS TIME IN BED THAN HE EXPECTS! FOR, AT THAT VERY MOMENT--
WHEW! I'LL BE GLAD WHEN THIS JOB'S DONE!
YEAH! IT'S SCARY BEIN' A NURSEMAID TO A JAR OF DEADLY, LIVE BACTERIA!
7

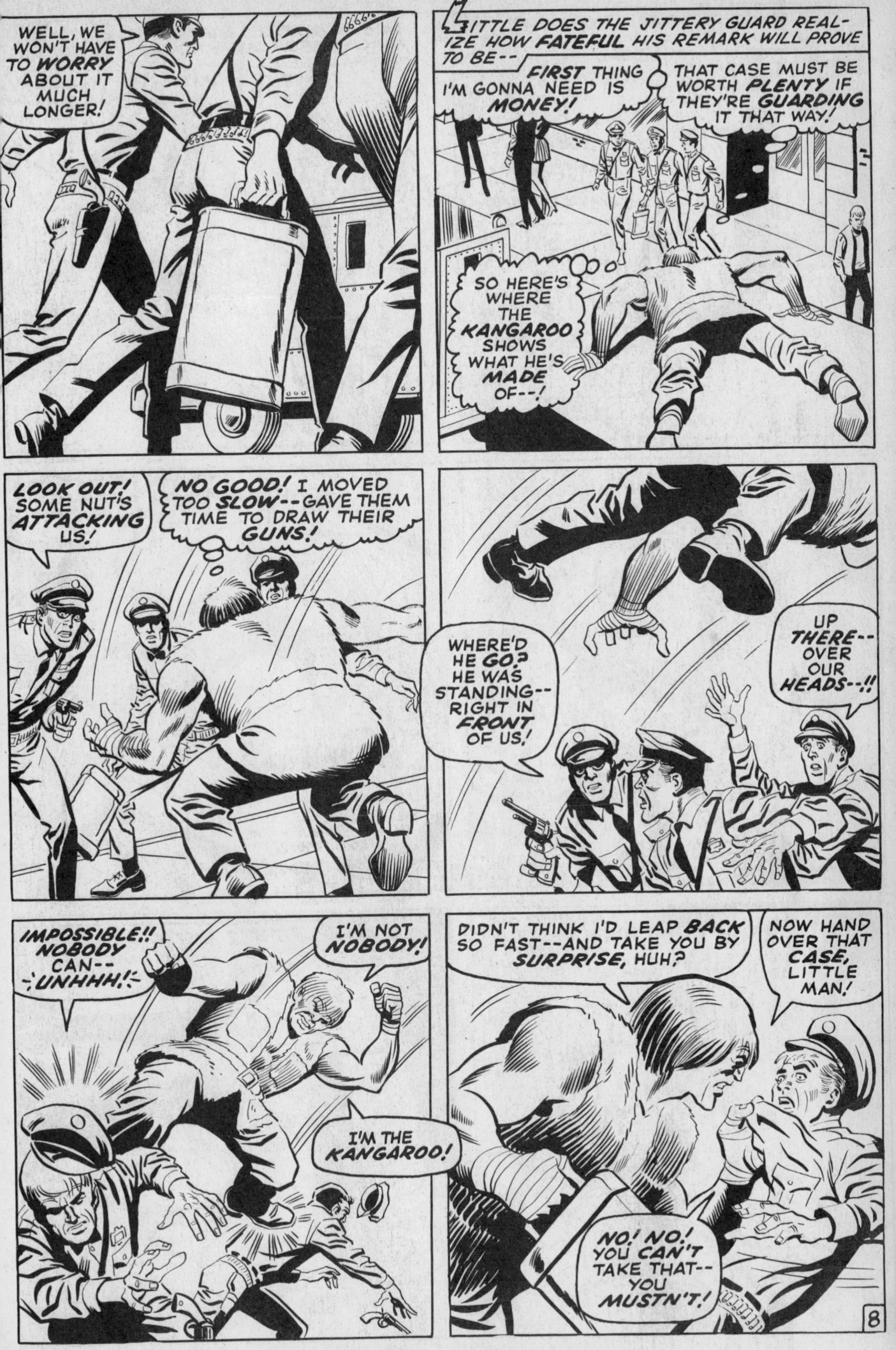

WELL, WE WON'T HAVE TO WORRY ABOUT IT MUCH LONGER!
LITTLE DOES THE JITTERY GUARD REALIZE HOW FATEFUL HIS REMARK WILL PROVE TO BE--
FIRST THING I'M GONNA NEED IS MONEY!
THAT CASE MUST BE WORTH PLENTY IF THEY'RE GUARDING IT THAT WAY!
SO HERE'S WHERE THE KANGAROO SHOWS WHAT HE'S MADE OF--!
LOOK OUT! SOME NUT'S ATTACKING US!
NO GOOD! I MOVED TOO SLOW--GAVE THEM TIME TO DRAW THEIR GUNS!
WHERE'D HE GO? HE WAS STANDING-- RIGHT IN FRONT OF US!
UP THERE-- OVER OUR HEADS--!!
IMPOSSIBLE!! NOBODY CAN-- -UNHHH!-
I'M NOT NOBODY!
I'M THE KANGAROO!
DIDN'T THINK I'D LEAP BACK SO FAST--AND TAKE YOU BY SURPRISE, HUH?
NOW HAND OVER THAT CASE, LITTLE MAN!
NO! NO! YOU CAN'T TAKE THAT-- YOU MUSTN'T!
8

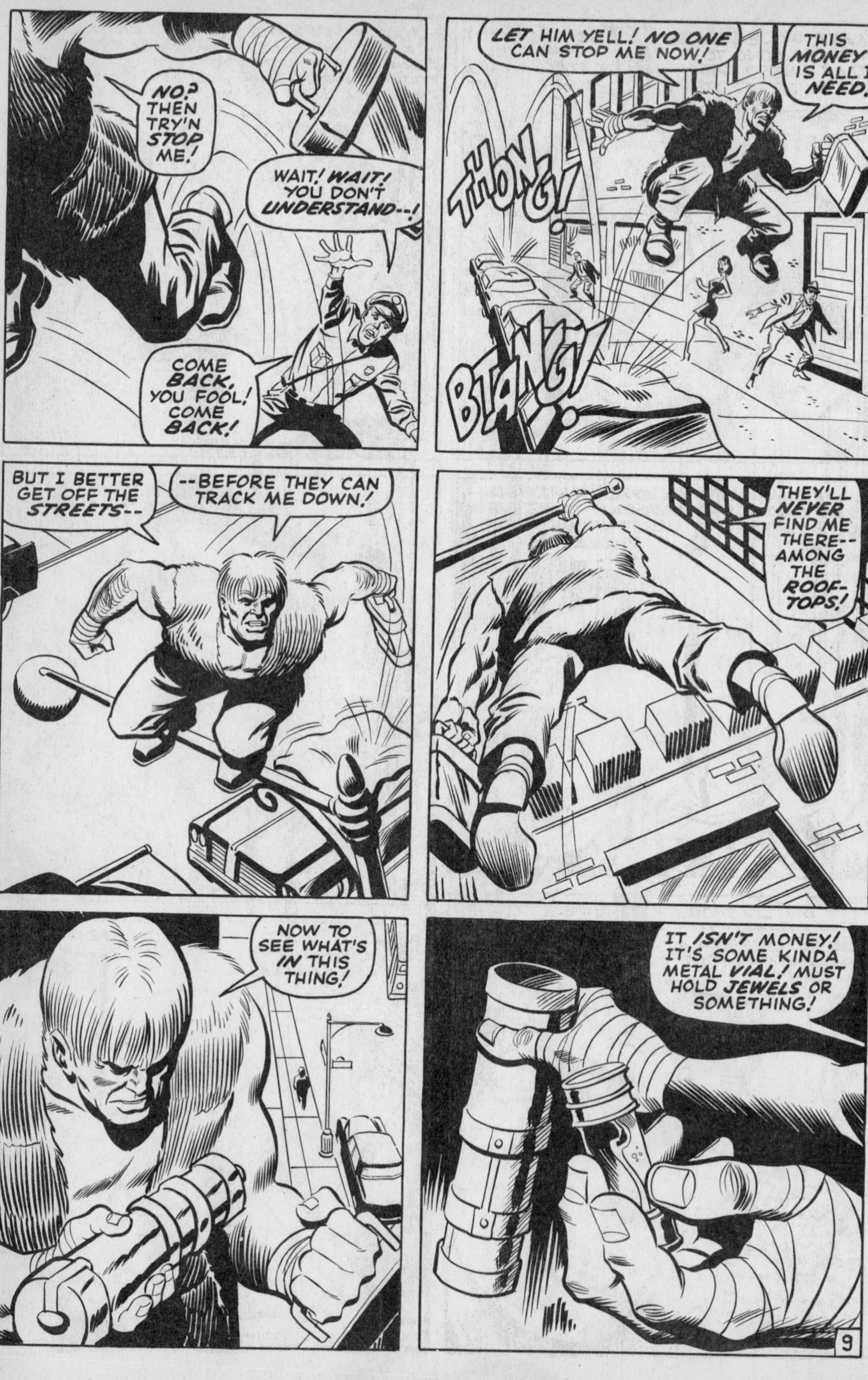
NO? THEN TRY'N STOP ME.!
WAIT! WAIT! YOU DON'T UNDERSTAND--!
COME BACK, YOU FOOL! COME BACK!
LET HIM YELL! NO ONE CAN STOP ME NOW!
THIS MONEY IS ALL I NEED!
THONG!
BTANG!
BUT I BETTER GET OFF THE STREETS--
--BEFORE THEY CAN TRACK ME DOWN!
THEY'LL NEVER FIND ME THERE--AMONG THE ROOF-TOPS!
NOW TO SEE WHAT'S IN THIS THING!
IT ISN'T MONEY! IT'S SOME KINDA METAL VIAL! MUST HOLD JEWELS OR SOMETHING!
9

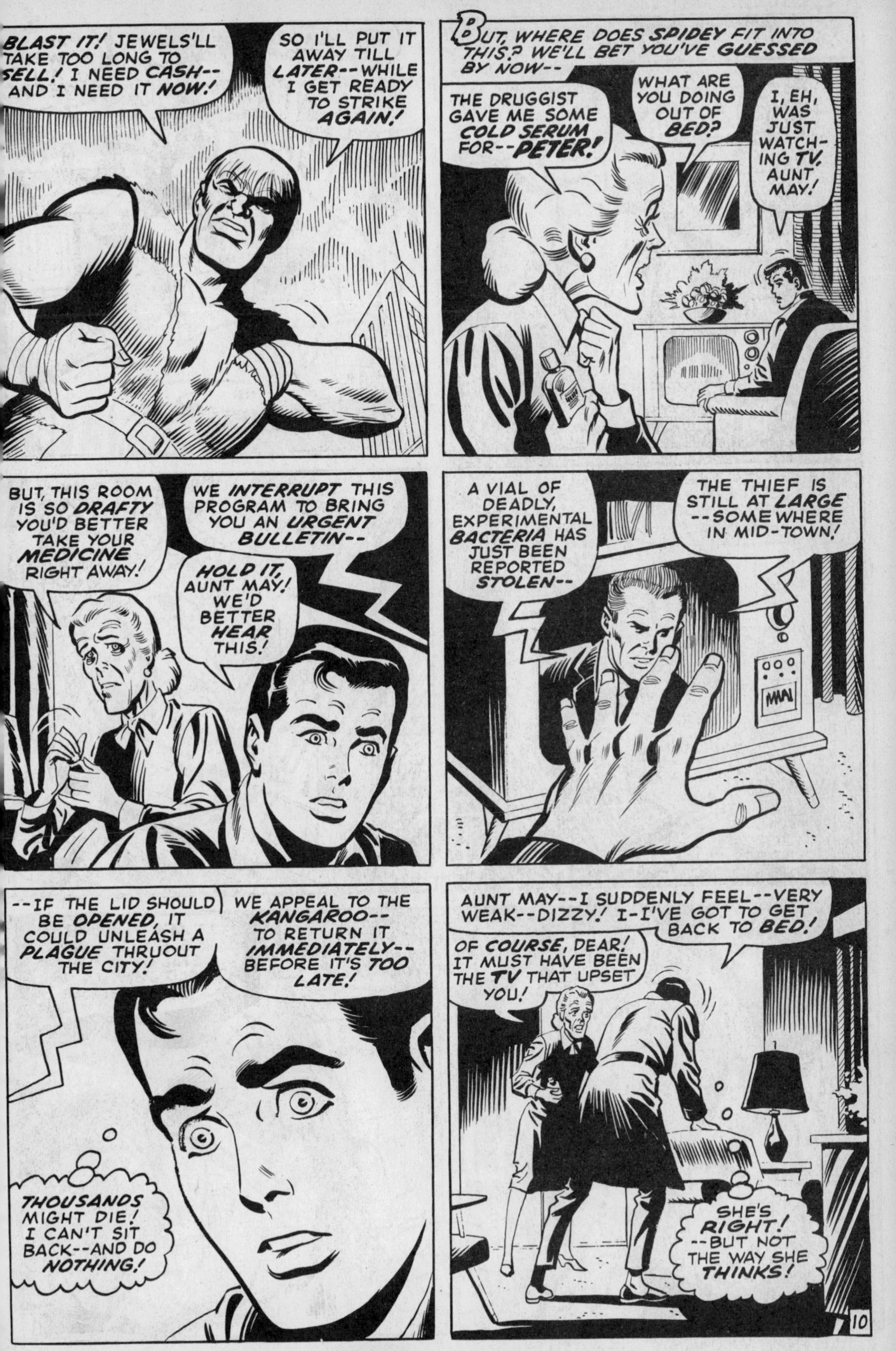
BLAST IT! JEWELS'LL TAKE TOO LONG TO SELL! I NEED CASH-- AND I NEED IT NOW!
SO I'LL PUT IT AWAY TILL LATER--WHILE I GET READY TO STRIKE AGAIN!
BUT, WHERE DOES SPIDEY FIT INTO THIS? WE'LL BET YOU'VE GUESSED BY NOW--
THE DRUGGIST GAVE ME SOME COLD SERUM FOR--PETER!
WHAT ARE YOU DOING OUT OF BED?
I, EH, WAS JUST WATCHING TV, AUNT MAY!
BUT, THIS ROOM IS SO DRAFTY YOU'D BETTER TAKE YOUR MEDICINE RIGHT AWAY!
WE INTERRUPT THIS PROGRAM TO BRING YOU AN URGENT BULLETIN--
HOLD IT, AUNT MAY! WE'D BETTER HEAR THIS!
A VIAL OF DEADLY, EXPERIMENTAL BACTERIA HAS JUST BEEN REPORTED STOLEN--
THE THIEF IS STILL AT LARGE --SOME WHERE IN MID-TOWN!
--IF THE LID SHOULD BE OPENED, IT COULD UNLEASH A PLAGUE THRUOUT THE CITY!
WE APPEAL TO THE KANGAROO-- TO RETURN IT IMMEDIATELY-- BEFORE IT'S TOO LATE!
THOUSANDS MIGHT DIE! I CAN'T SIT BACK--AND DO NOTHING!
AUNT MAY--I SUDDENLY FEEL--VERY WEAK--DIZZY! I-I'VE GOT TO GET BACK TO BED!
OF COURSE, DEAR! IT MUST HAVE BEEN THE TV THAT UPSET YOU!
SHE'S RIGHT! --BUT NOT THE WAY SHE THINKS!
10

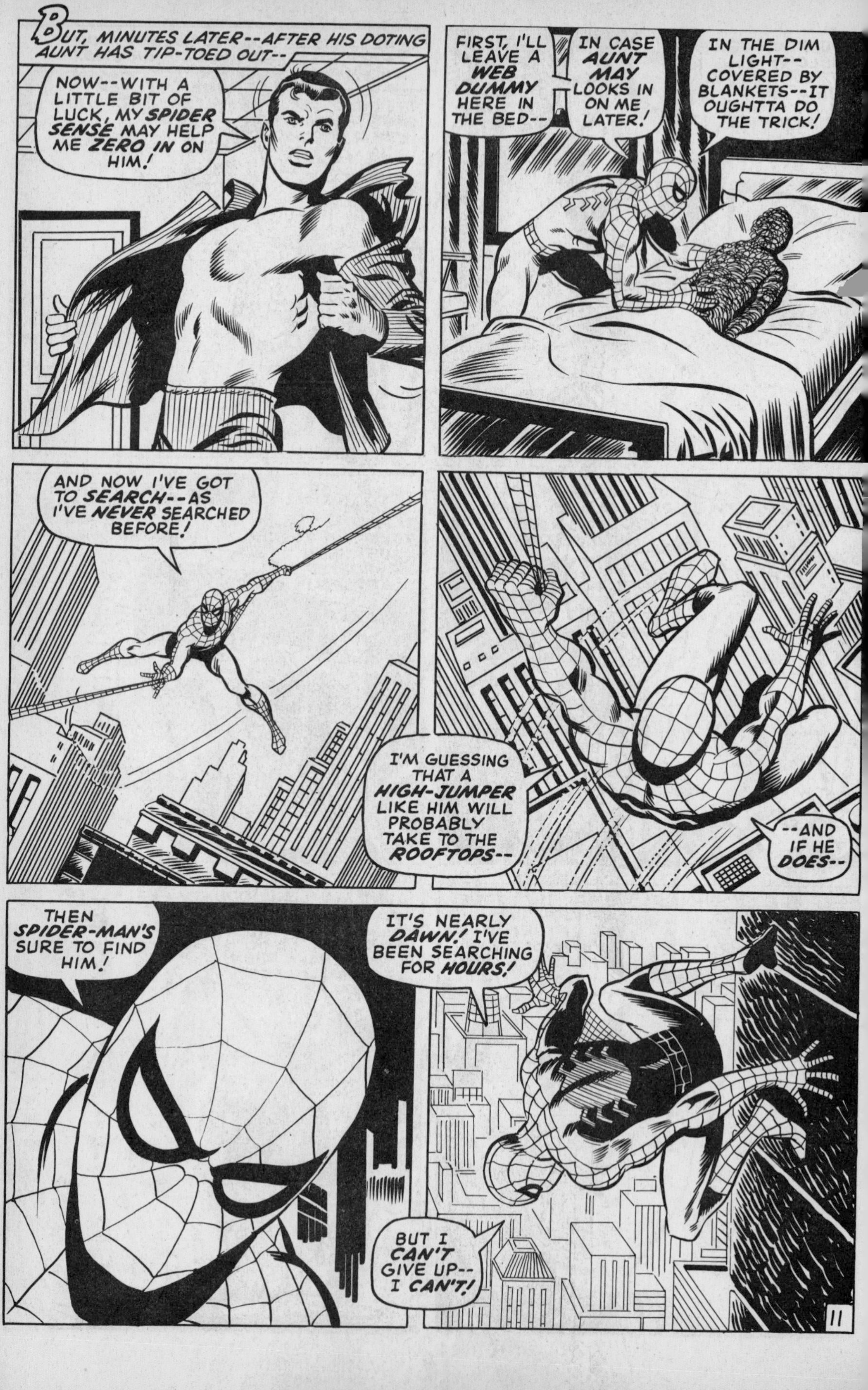
BUT, MINUTES LATER--AFTER HIS DOTING AUNT HAS TIP-TOED OUT--
NOW--WITH A LITTLE BIT OF LUCK, MY SPIDER SENSE MAY HELP ME ZERO IN ON HIM!
FIRST, I'LL LEAVE A WEB DUMMY HERE IN THE BED--
IN CASE AUNT MAY LOOKS IN ON ME LATER!
IN THE DIM LIGHT--COVERED BY BLANKETS--IT OUGHTTA DO THE TRICK!
AND NOW I'VE GOT TO SEARCH--AS I'VE NEVER SEARCHED BEFORE!
I'M GUESSING THAT A HIGH-JUMPER LIKE HIM WILL PROBABLY TAKE TO THE ROOFTOPS--
--AND IF HE DOES--
THEN SPIDER-MAN'S SURE TO FIND HIM!
IT'S NEARLY DAWN! I'VE BEEN SEARCHING FOR HOURS!
BUT I CAN'T GIVE UP--I CAN'T!

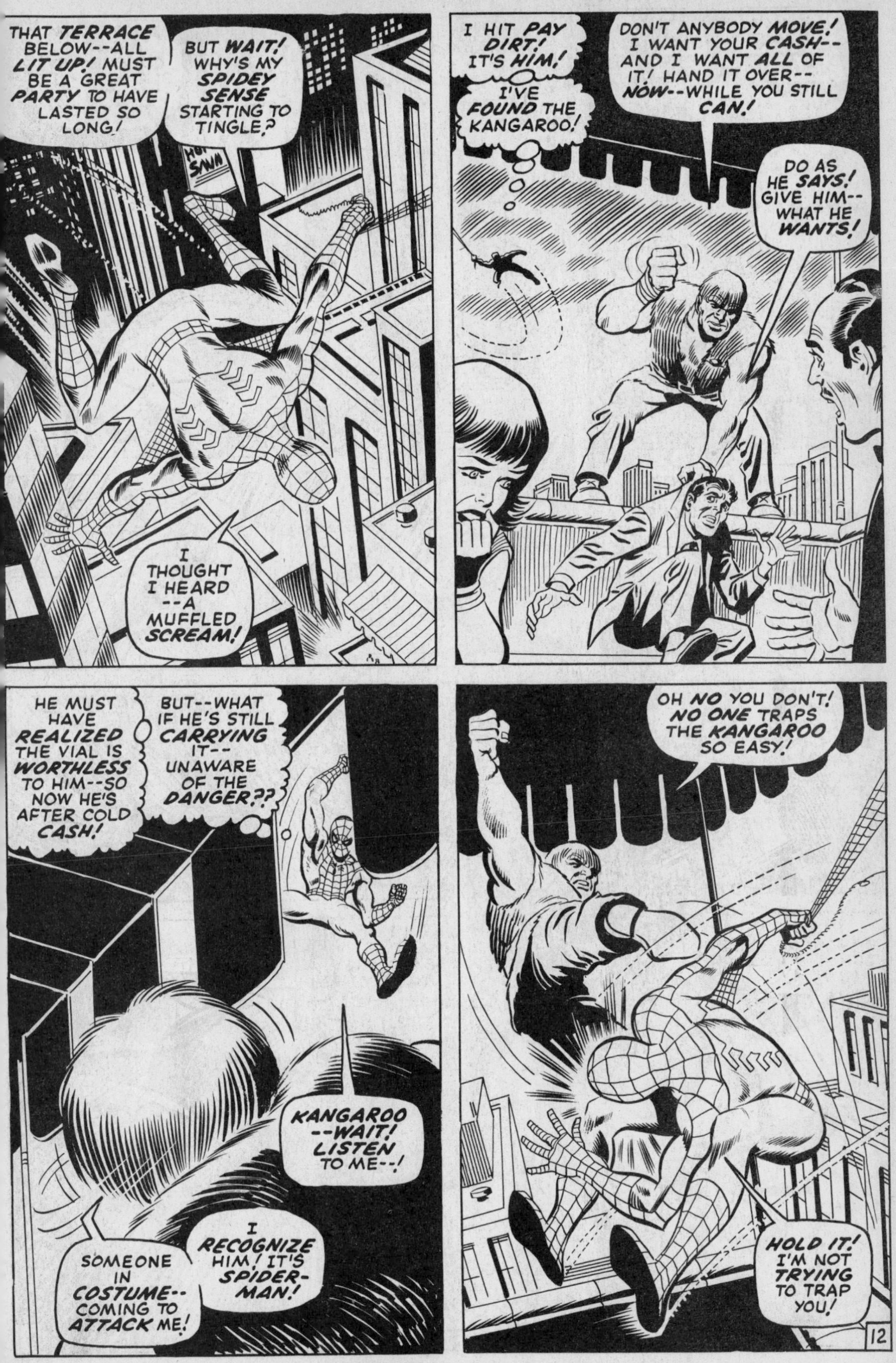
THAT TERRACE BELOW--ALL LIT UP! MUST BE A GREAT PARTY TO HAVE LASTED SO LONG!
BUT WAIT! WHY'S MY SPIDEY SENSE STARTING TO TINGLE?
I THOUGHT I HEARD --A MUFFLED SCREAM!
I HIT PAY DIRT! IT'S HIM! I'VE FOUND THE KANGAROO!
DON'T ANYBODY MOVE! I WANT YOUR CASH-- AND I WANT ALL OF IT! HAND IT OVER-- NOW--WHILE YOU STILL CAN!
DO AS HE SAYS! GIVE HIM-- WHAT HE WANTS!
HE MUST HAVE REALIZED THE VIAL IS WORTHLESS TO HIM--SO NOW HE'S AFTER COLD CASH!
BUT--WHAT IF HE'S STILL CARRYING IT-- UNAWARE OF THE DANGER??
KANGAROO --WAIT! LISTEN TO ME--!
SOMEONE IN COSTUME-- COMING TO ATTACK ME!
I RECOGNIZE HIM! IT'S SPIDER-MAN!
OH NO YOU DON'T! NO ONE TRAPS THE KANGAROO SO EASY!
HOLD IT! I'M NOT TRYING TO TRAP YOU!
12

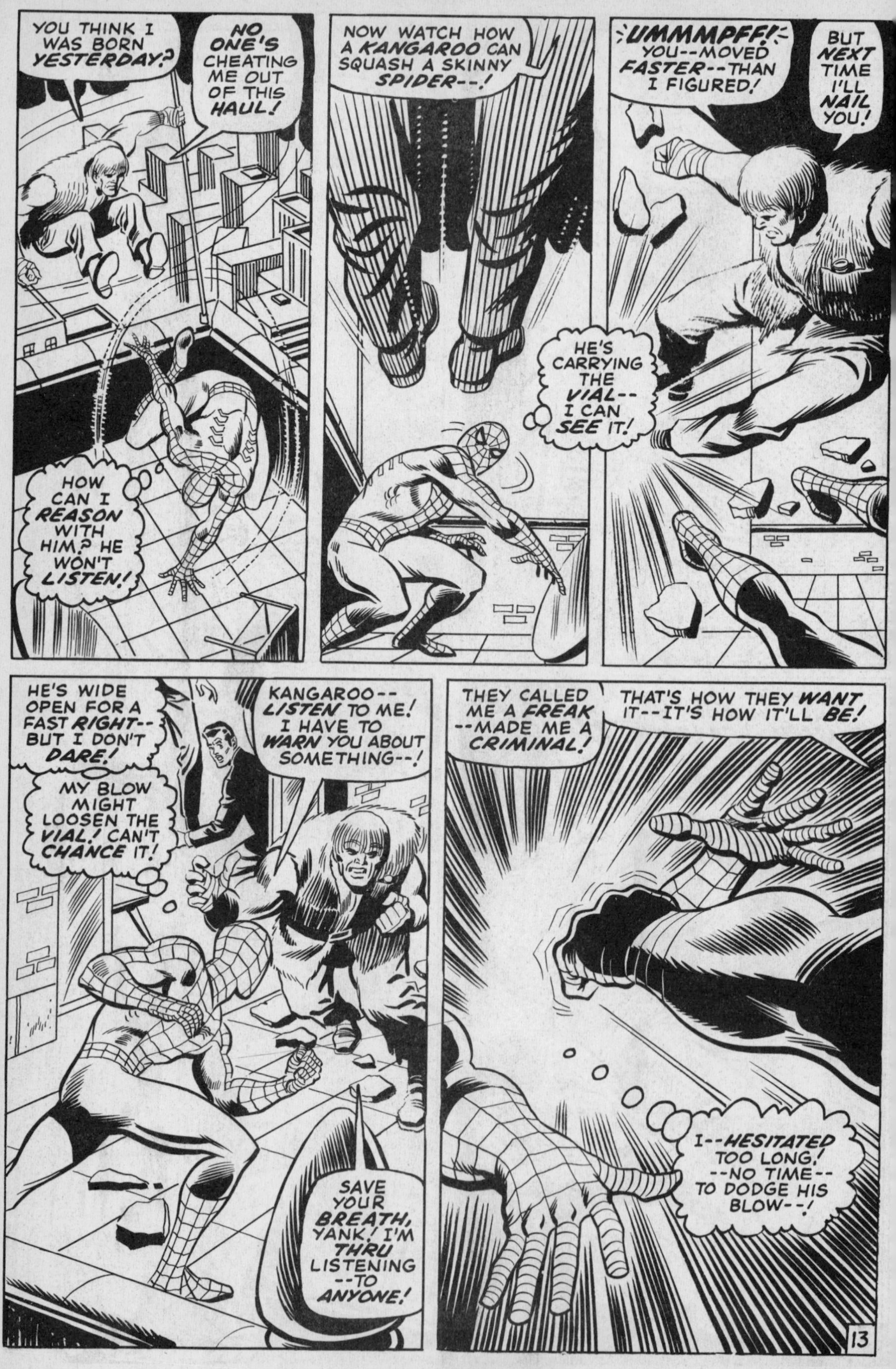
YOU THINK I WAS BORN YESTERDAY?
NO ONE'S CHEATING ME OUT OF THIS HAUL!
HOW CAN I REASON WITH HIM? HE WON'T LISTEN!
NOW WATCH HOW A KANGAROO CAN SQUASH A SKINNY SPIDER--!
HE'S CARRYING THE VIAL-- I CAN SEE IT!
UMMMPFF! YOU--MOVED FASTER--THAN I FIGURED!
BUT NEXT TIME I'LL NAIL YOU!
HE'S WIDE OPEN FOR A FAST RIGHT-- BUT I DON'T DARE!
MY BLOW MIGHT LOOSEN THE VIAL! CAN'T CHANCE IT!
KANGAROO-- LISTEN TO ME! I HAVE TO WARN YOU ABOUT SOMETHING--!
SAVE YOUR BREATH, YANK! I'M THRU LISTENING --TO ANYONE!
THEY CALLED ME A FREAK --MADE ME A CRIMINAL!
THAT'S HOW THEY WANT IT--IT'S HOW IT'LL BE!
I--HESITATED TOO LONG! --NO TIME-- TO DODGE HIS BLOW--!
13

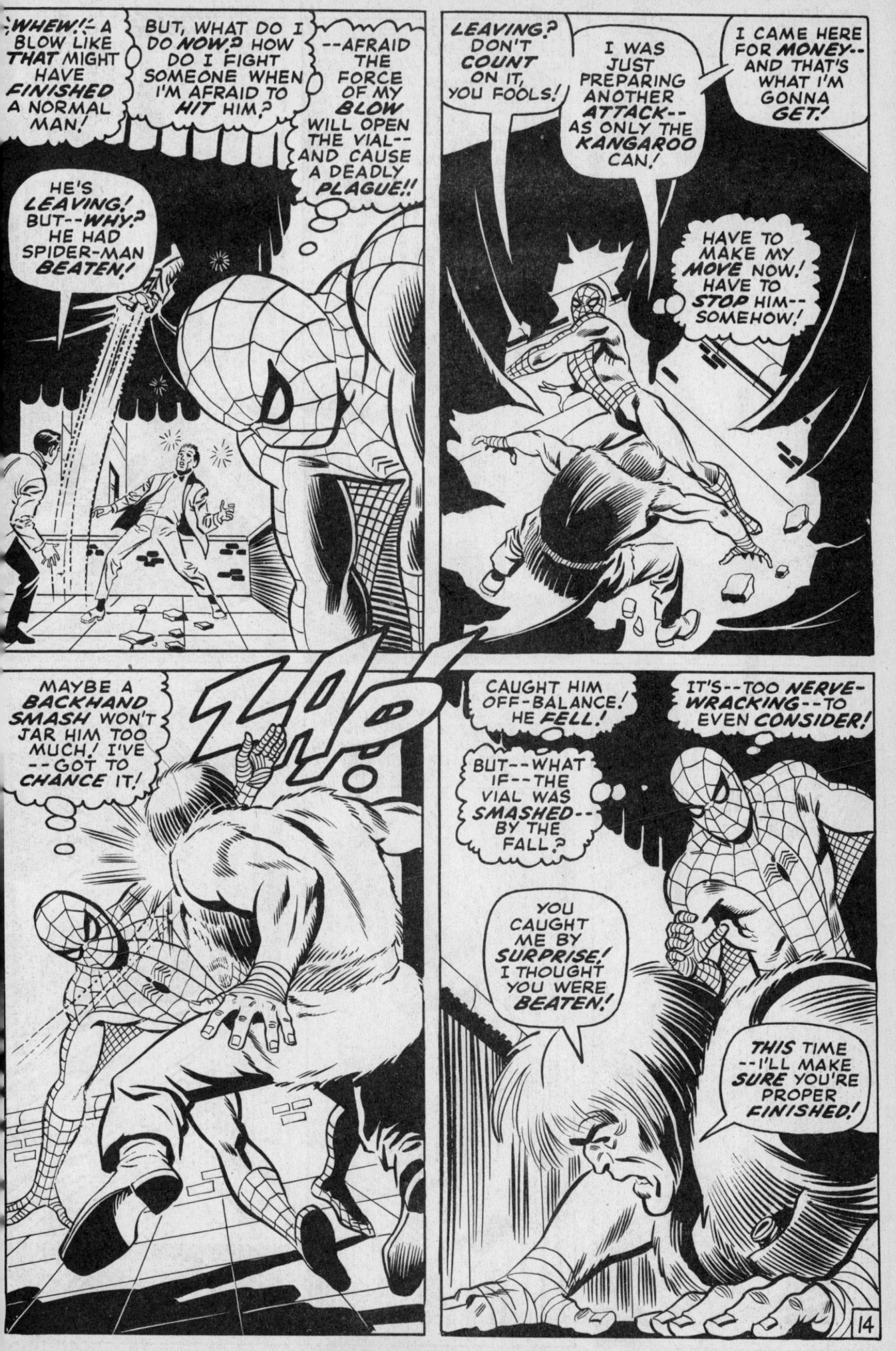
WHEW!--A BLOW LIKE THAT MIGHT HAVE FINISHED A NORMAL MAN!
BUT, WHAT DO I DO NOW? HOW DO I FIGHT SOMEONE WHEN I'M AFRAID TO HIT HIM?
--AFRAID THE FORCE OF MY BLOW WILL OPEN THE VIAL--AND CAUSE A DEADLY PLAGUE!!
HE'S LEAVING! BUT--WHY? HE HAD SPIDER-MAN BEATEN!
LEAVING? DON'T COUNT ON IT, YOU FOOLS!
I WAS JUST PREPARING ANOTHER ATTACK--AS ONLY THE KANGAROO CAN!
I CAME HERE FOR MONEY--AND THAT'S WHAT I'M GONNA GET!
HAVE TO MAKE MY MOVE NOW! HAVE TO STOP HIM--SOMEHOW!
MAYBE A BACKHAND SMASH WON'T JAR HIM TOO MUCH! I'VE--GOT TO CHANCE IT!
ZAP!
CAUGHT HIM OFF-BALANCE! HE FELL!
IT'S--TOO NERVE-WRACKING--TO EVEN CONSIDER!
BUT--WHAT IF--THE VIAL WAS SMASHED--BY THE FALL?
YOU CAUGHT ME BY SURPRISE! I THOUGHT YOU WERE BEATEN!
THIS TIME--I'LL MAKE SURE YOU'RE PROPER FINISHED!
14

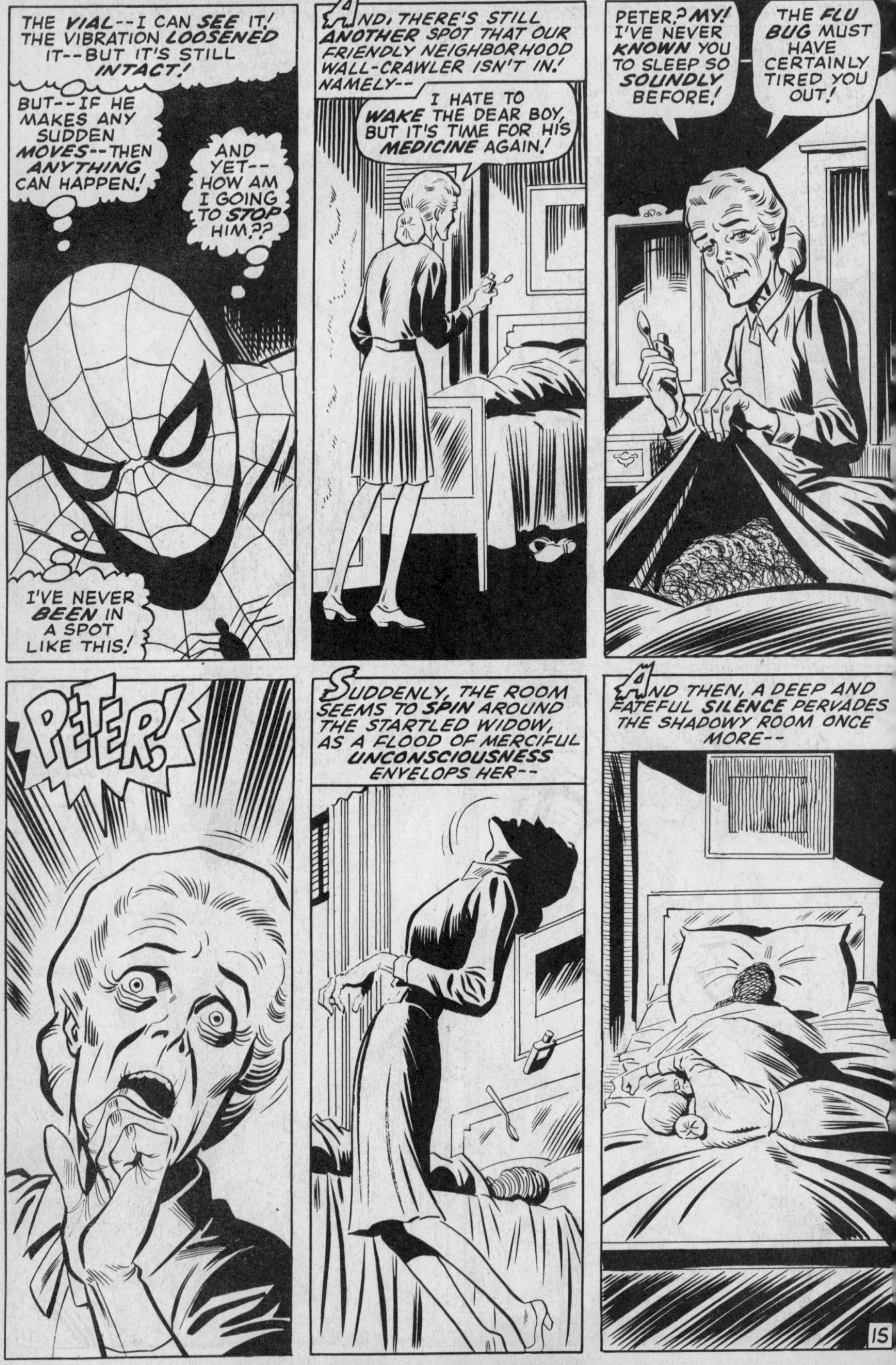
THE VIAL--I CAN SEE IT! THE VIBRATION LOOSENED IT--BUT IT'S STILL INTACT!
BUT--IF HE MAKES ANY SUDDEN MOVES--THEN ANYTHING CAN HAPPEN!
AND YET--HOW AM I GOING TO STOP HIM??
I'VE NEVER BEEN IN A SPOT LIKE THIS!
AND, THERE'S STILL ANOTHER SPOT THAT OUR FRIENDLY NEIGHBORHOOD WALL-CRAWLER ISN'T IN! NAMELY--
I HATE TO WAKE THE DEAR BOY, BUT IT'S TIME FOR HIS MEDICINE AGAIN!
PETER? MY! I'VE NEVER KNOWN YOU TO SLEEP SO SOUNDLY BEFORE!
THE FLU BUG MUST HAVE CERTAINLY TIRED YOU OUT!
PETER!
SUDDENLY, THE ROOM SEEMS TO SPIN AROUND THE STARTLED WIDOW, AS A FLOOD OF MERCIFUL UNCONSCIOUSNESS ENVELOPS HER--
AND THEN, A DEEP AND FATEFUL SILENCE PERVADES THE SHADOWY ROOM ONCE MORE--
15

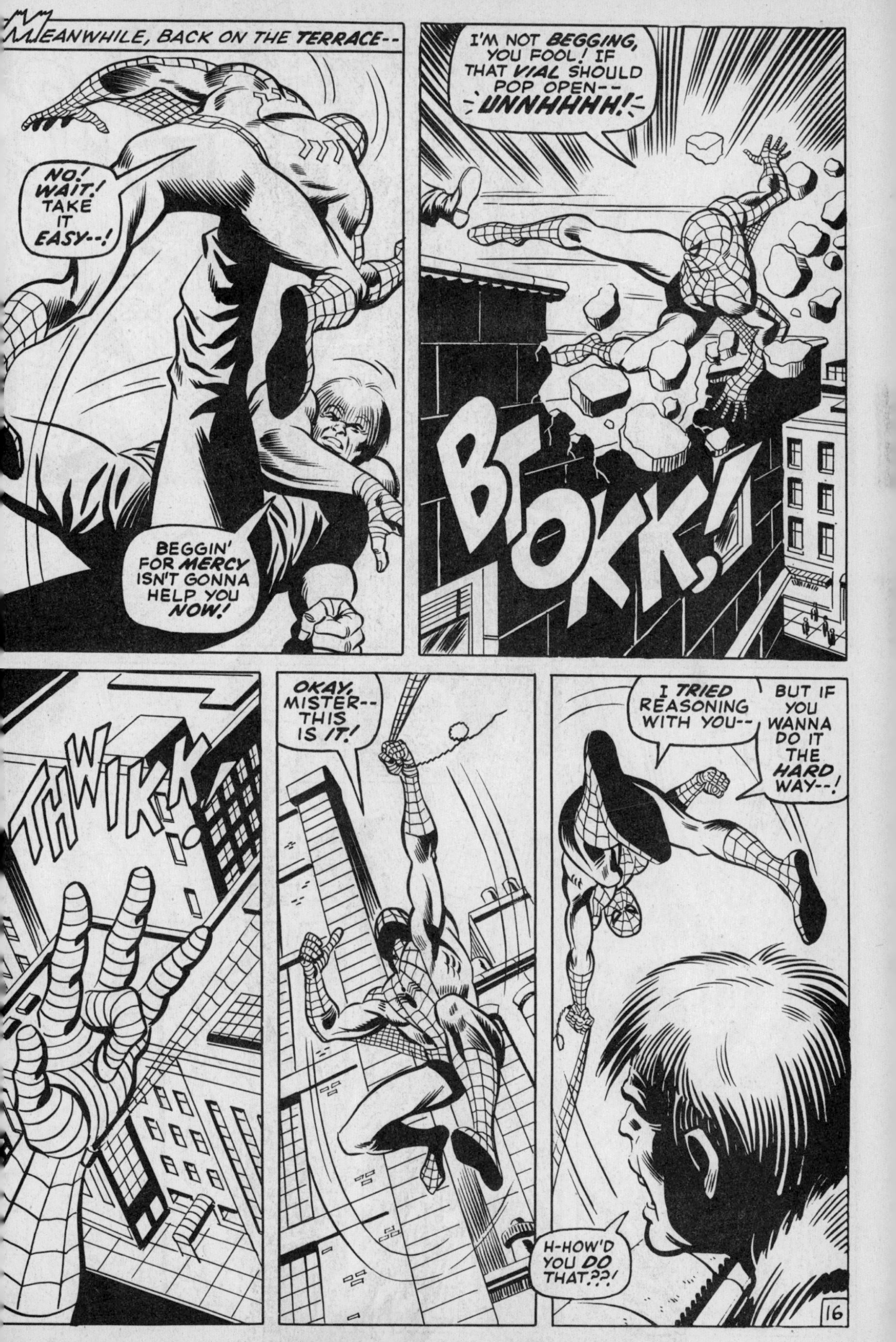
MEANWHILE, BACK ON THE TERRACE--
NO! WAIT! TAKE IT EASY--!
BEGGIN' FOR MERCY ISN'T GONNA HELP YOU NOW!
I'M NOT BEGGING, YOU FOOL! IF THAT VIAL SHOULD POP OPEN-- UNNHHHH!
BT OKK!
THWIKK
OKAY, MISTER-- THIS IS IT!
I TRIED REASONING WITH YOU--
BUT IF YOU WANNA DO IT THE HARD WAY--!
H-HOW'D YOU DO THAT??!
16

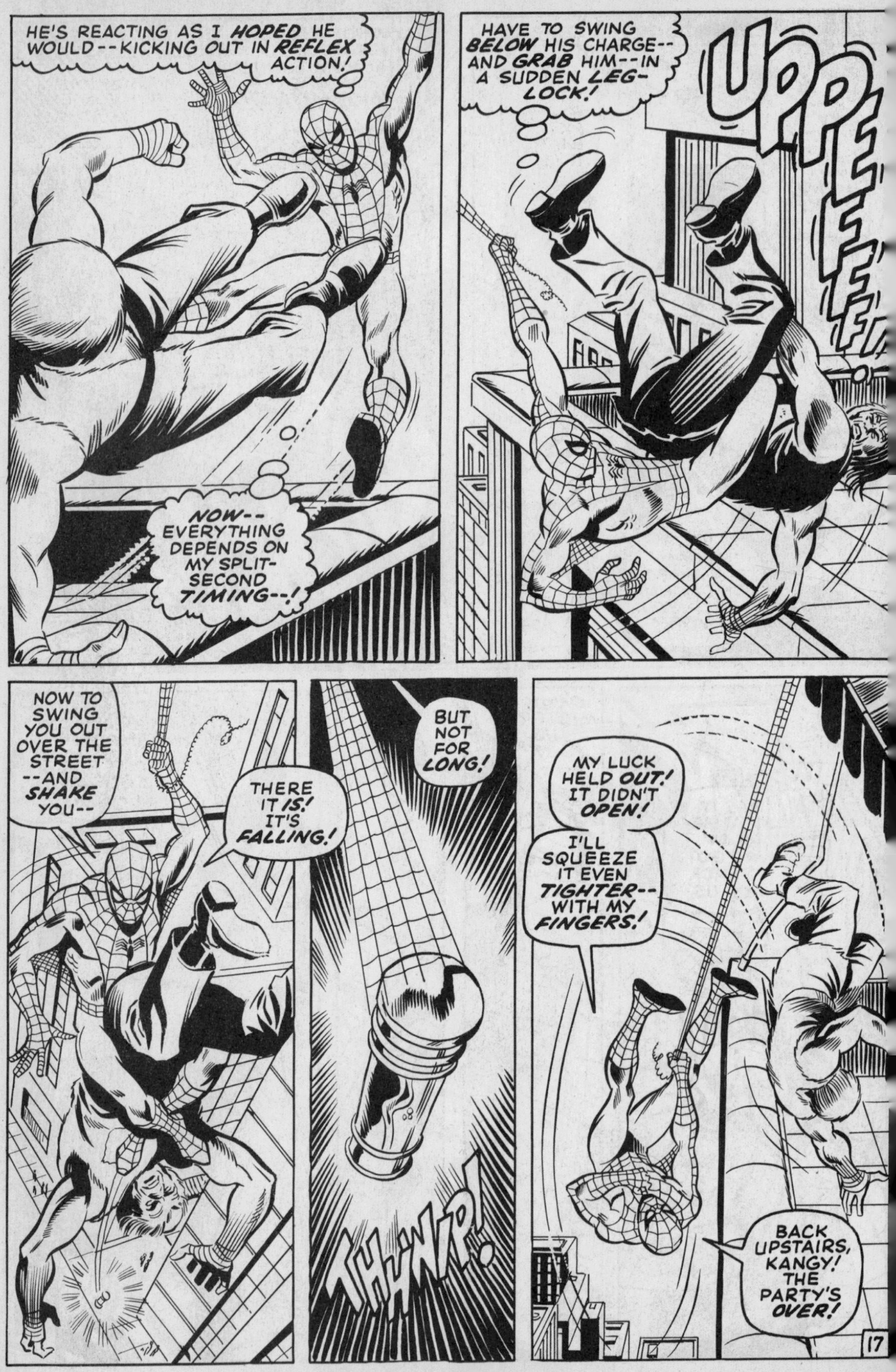
HE'S REACTING AS I HOPED HE WOULD--KICKING OUT IN REFLEX ACTION!
NOW--EVERYTHING DEPENDS ON MY SPLIT-SECOND TIMING--!
HAVE TO SWING BELOW HIS CHARGE--AND GRAB HIM--IN A SUDDEN LEG-LOCK!
UPPEEFFF
NOW TO SWING YOU OUT OVER THE STREET--AND SHAKE YOU--
THERE IT IS! IT'S FALLING!
BUT NOT FOR LONG!
KHUNP!
MY LUCK HELD OUT! IT DIDN'T OPEN!
I'LL SQUEEZE IT EVEN TIGHTER--WITH MY FINGERS!
BACK UPSTAIRS, KANGY! THE PARTY'S OVER!
17

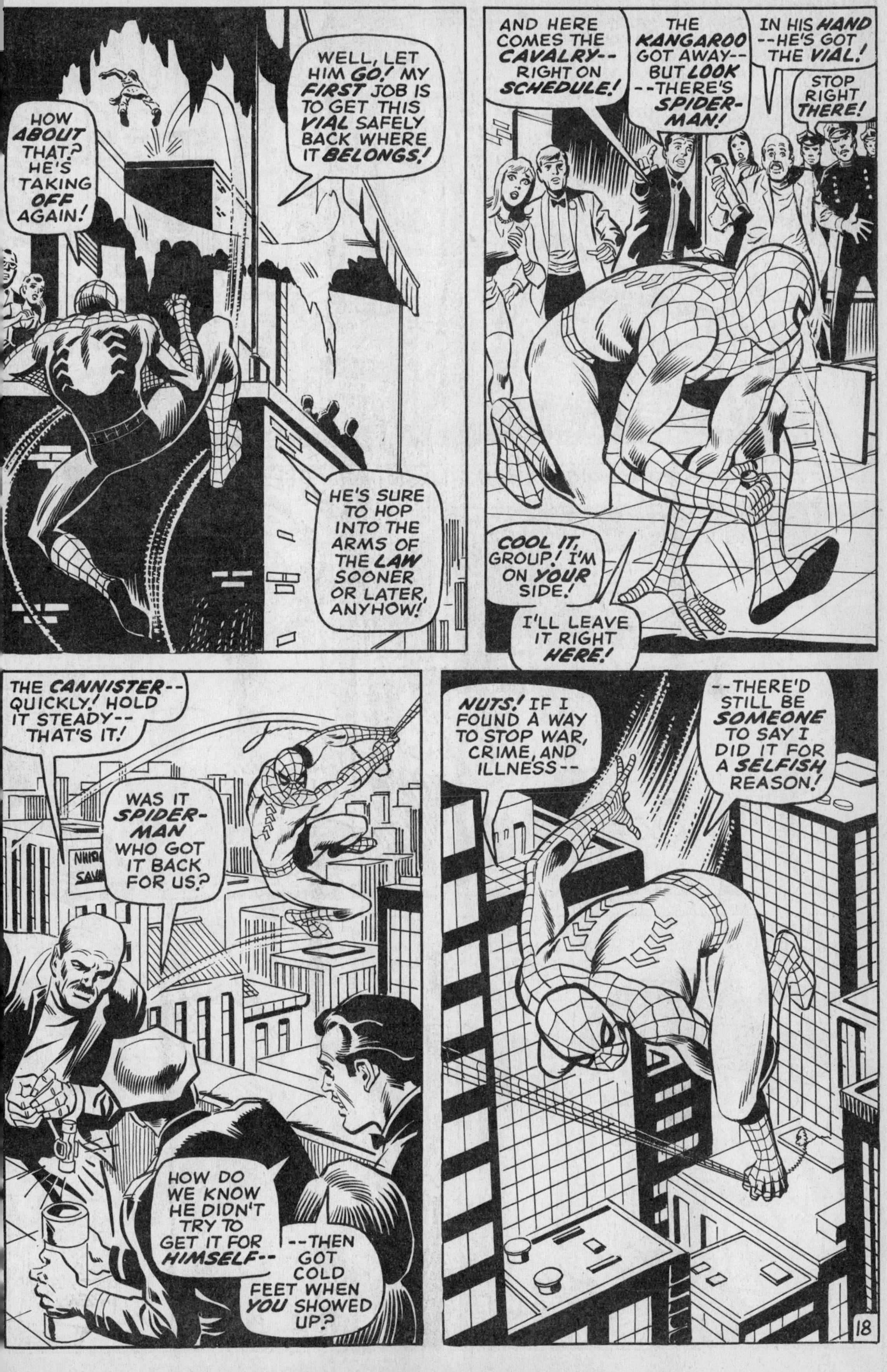
HOW ABOUT THAT? HE'S TAKING OFF AGAIN!
WELL, LET HIM GO! MY FIRST JOB IS TO GET THIS VIAL SAFELY BACK WHERE IT BELONGS!
HE'S SURE TO HOP INTO THE ARMS OF THE LAW SOONER OR LATER, ANYHOW!
AND HERE COMES THE CAVALRY-- RIGHT ON SCHEDULE!
THE KANGAROO GOT AWAY-- BUT LOOK --THERE'S SPIDER-MAN!
IN HIS HAND --HE'S GOT THE VIAL!
STOP RIGHT THERE!
COOL IT, GROUP! I'M ON YOUR SIDE!
I'LL LEAVE IT RIGHT HERE!
THE CANNISTER-- QUICKLY! HOLD IT STEADY-- THAT'S IT!
WAS IT SPIDER-MAN WHO GOT IT BACK FOR US?
HOW DO WE KNOW HE DIDN'T TRY TO GET IT FOR HIMSELF--
--THEN GOT COLD FEET WHEN YOU SHOWED UP?
NUTS! IF I FOUND A WAY TO STOP WAR, CRIME, AND ILLNESS--
--THERE'D STILL BE SOMEONE TO SAY I DID IT FOR A SELFISH REASON!
18

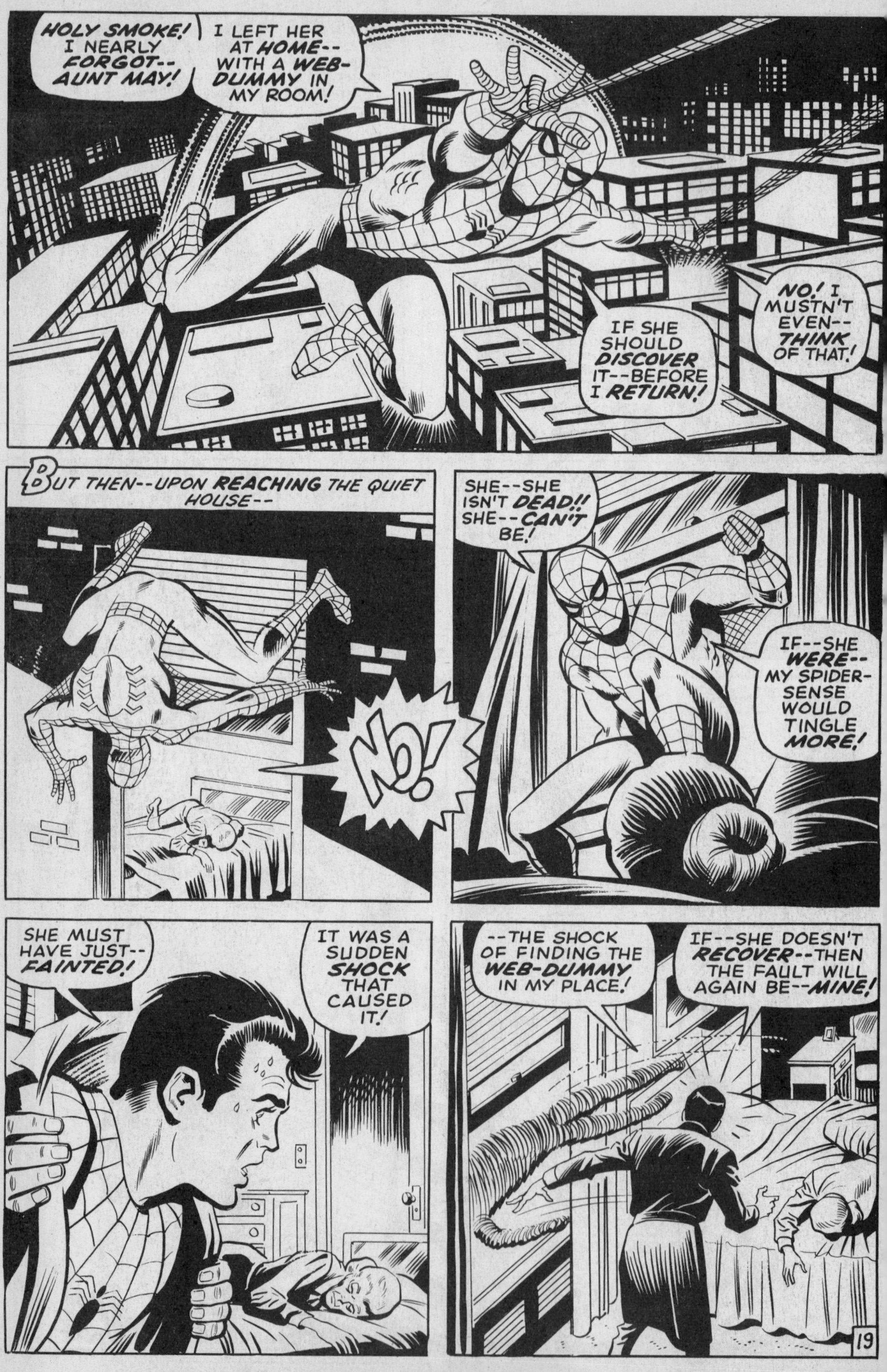

HOLY SMOKE! I NEARLY FORGOT-- AUNT MAY!
I LEFT HER AT HOME-- WITH A WEB-DUMMY IN MY ROOM!
IF SHE SHOULD DISCOVER IT--BEFORE I RETURN!
NO! I MUSTN'T EVEN-- THINK OF THAT!
BUT THEN--UPON REACHING THE QUIET HOUSE--
NO!
SHE--SHE ISN'T DEAD!! SHE--CAN'T BE!
IF--SHE WERE-- MY SPIDER-SENSE WOULD TINGLE MORE!
SHE MUST HAVE JUST-- FAINTED!
IT WAS A SUDDEN SHOCK THAT CAUSED IT!
--THE SHOCK OF FINDING THE WEB-DUMMY IN MY PLACE!
IF--SHE DOESN'T RECOVER--THEN THE FAULT WILL AGAIN BE--MINE!

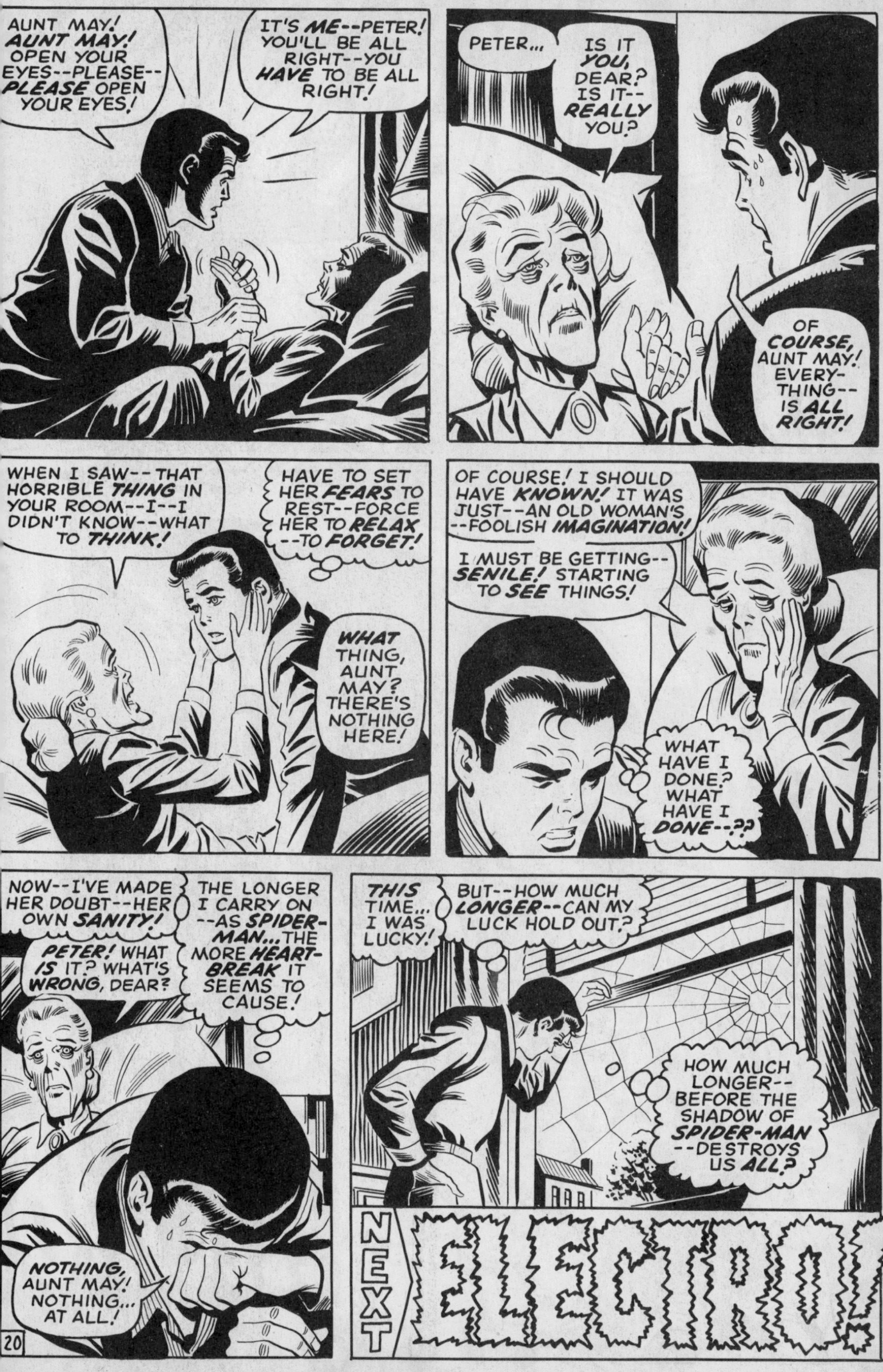
AUNT MAY! AUNT MAY! OPEN YOUR EYES--PLEASE--PLEASE OPEN YOUR EYES!
IT'S ME--PETER! YOU'LL BE ALL RIGHT--YOU HAVE TO BE ALL RIGHT!
PETER...
IS IT YOU, DEAR? IS IT--REALLY YOU?
OF COURSE, AUNT MAY! EVERY-THING--IS ALL RIGHT!
WHEN I SAW--THAT HORRIBLE THING IN YOUR ROOM--I--I DIDN'T KNOW--WHAT TO THINK!
HAVE TO SET HER FEARS TO REST--FORCE HER TO RELAX--TO FORGET!
WHAT THING, AUNT MAY? THERE'S NOTHING HERE!
OF COURSE! I SHOULD HAVE KNOWN! IT WAS JUST--AN OLD WOMAN'S--FOOLISH IMAGINATION!
I MUST BE GETTING--SENILE! STARTING TO SEE THINGS!
WHAT HAVE I DONE? WHAT HAVE I DONE--??
NOW--I'VE MADE HER DOUBT--HER OWN SANITY!
THE LONGER I CARRY ON--AS SPIDER-MAN...THE MORE HEART-BREAK IT SEEMS TO CAUSE!
PETER! WHAT IS IT? WHAT'S WRONG, DEAR?
NOTHING, AUNT MAY! NOTHING... AT ALL!
20
THIS TIME... I WAS LUCKY!
BUT--HOW MUCH LONGER--CAN MY LUCK HOLD OUT?
HOW MUCH LONGER--BEFORE THE SHADOW OF SPIDER-MAN--DESTROYS US ALL?
NEXT
ELECTRO!

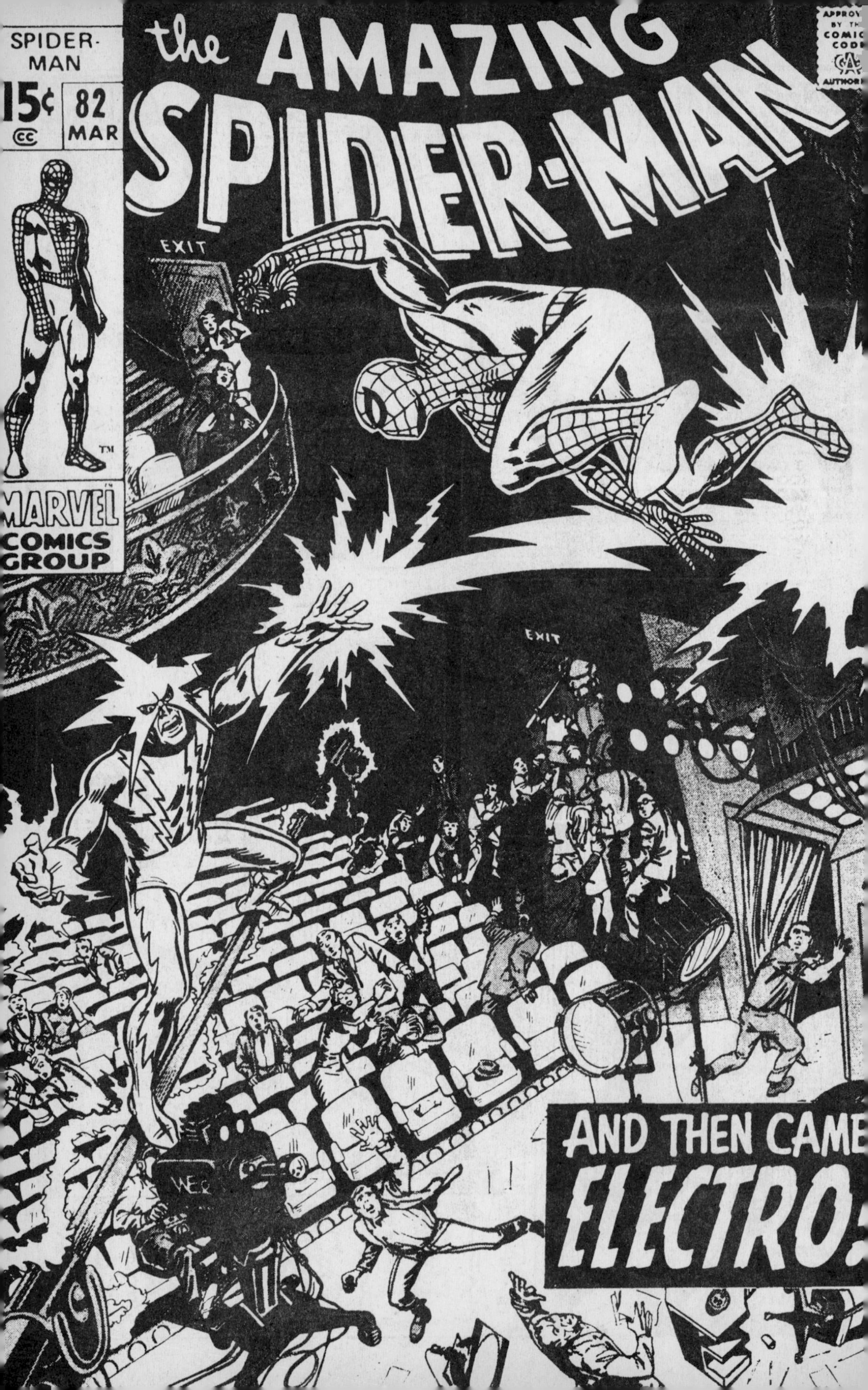

SPIDER-MAN
15¢
CC
82
MAR
MARVEL COMICS GROUP
the AMAZING SPIDER-MAN
APPROVED BY THE COMICS CODE AUTHORITY
EXIT
EXIT
AND THEN CAME ELECTRO!

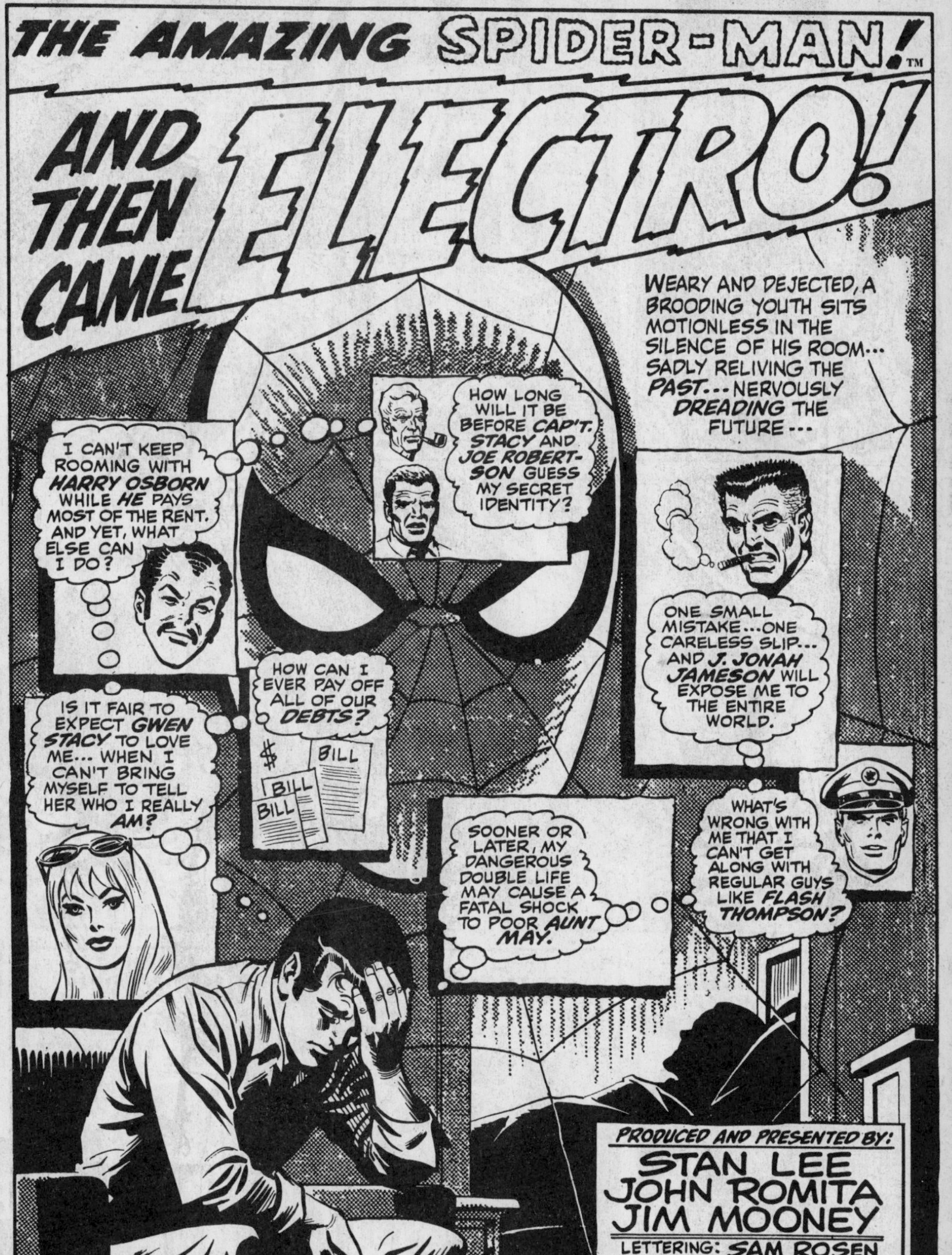
THE AMAZING SPIDER-MAN!™
AND THEN CAME ELECTRO!
WEARY AND DEJECTED, A BROODING YOUTH SITS MOTIONLESS IN THE SILENCE OF HIS ROOM... SADLY RELIVING THE PAST... NERVOUSLY DREADING THE FUTURE...
I CAN'T KEEP ROOMING WITH HARRY OSBORN WHILE HE PAYS MOST OF THE RENT. AND YET, WHAT ELSE CAN I DO?
HOW LONG WILL IT BE BEFORE CAP'T. STACY AND JOE ROBERTSON GUESS MY SECRET IDENTITY?
ONE SMALL MISTAKE...ONE CARELESS SLIP... AND J. JONAH JAMESON WILL EXPOSE ME TO THE ENTIRE WORLD.
IS IT FAIR TO EXPECT GWEN STACY TO LOVE ME... WHEN I CAN'T BRING MYSELF TO TELL HER WHO I REALLY AM?
HOW CAN I EVER PAY OFF ALL OF OUR DEBTS?
$
BILL
BILL
BILL
SOONER OR LATER, MY DANGEROUS DOUBLE LIFE MAY CAUSE A FATAL SHOCK TO POOR AUNT MAY.
WHAT'S WRONG WITH ME THAT I CAN'T GET ALONG WITH REGULAR GUYS LIKE FLASH THOMPSON?
PRODUCED AND PRESENTED BY:
STAN LEE
JOHN ROMITA
JIM MOONEY
LETTERING: SAM ROSEN

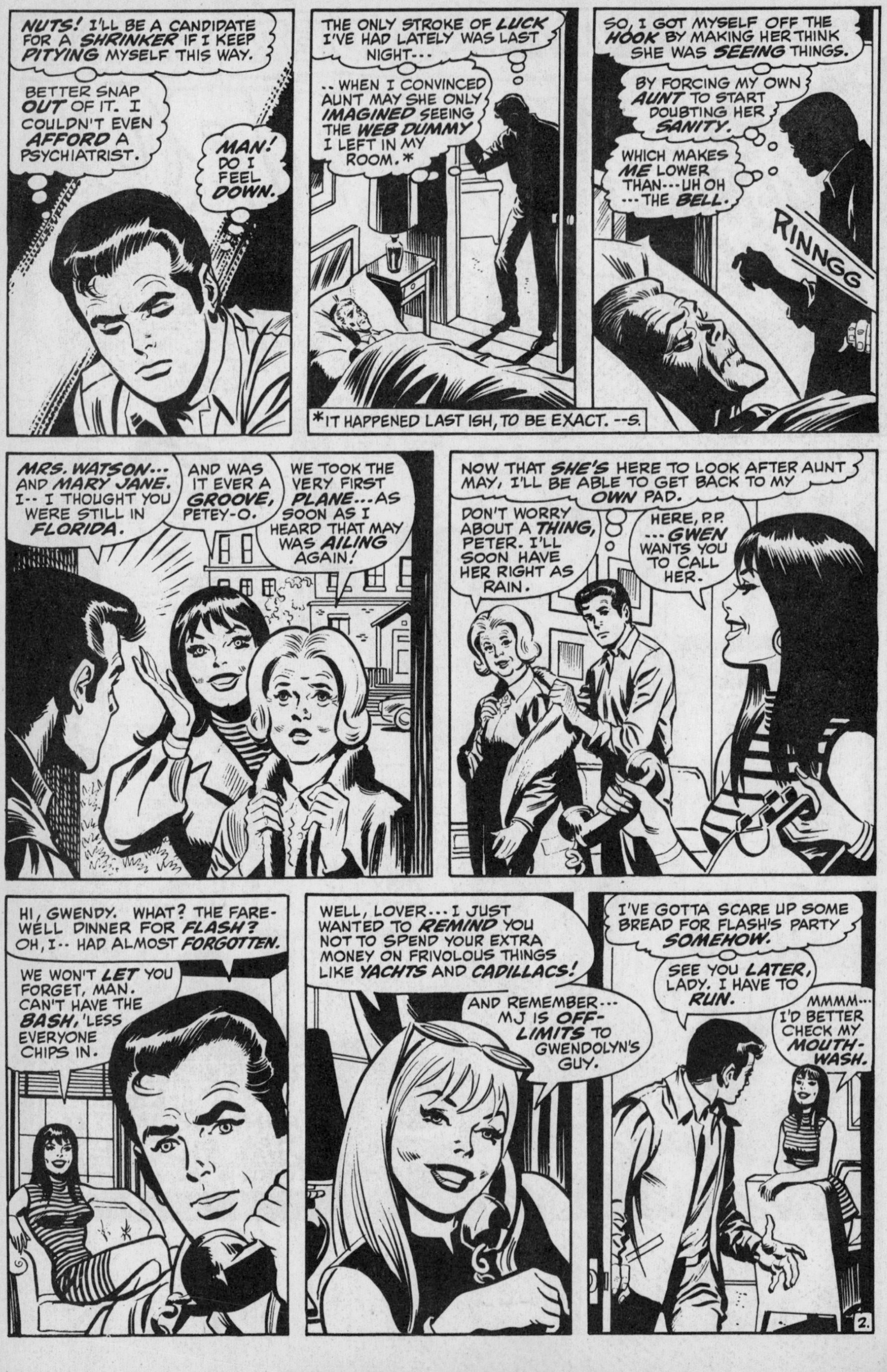
NUTS! I'LL BE A CANDIDATE FOR A SHRINKER IF I KEEP PITYING MYSELF THIS WAY.
BETTER SNAP OUT OF IT. I COULDN'T EVEN AFFORD A PSYCHIATRIST.
MAN! DO I FEEL DOWN.
THE ONLY STROKE OF LUCK I'VE HAD LATELY WAS LAST NIGHT---
.. WHEN I CONVINCED AUNT MAY SHE ONLY IMAGINED SEEING THE WEB DUMMY I LEFT IN MY ROOM.*
*IT HAPPENED LAST ISH, TO BE EXACT. --S.
SO, I GOT MYSELF OFF THE HOOK BY MAKING HER THINK SHE WAS SEEING THINGS.
BY FORCING MY OWN AUNT TO START DOUBTING HER SANITY.
WHICH MAKES ME LOWER THAN---UH OH ---THE BELL.
RINNGG
MRS. WATSON... AND MARY JANE. I-- I THOUGHT YOU WERE STILL IN FLORIDA.
AND WAS IT EVER A GROOVE, PETEY-O.
WE TOOK THE VERY FIRST PLANE...AS SOON AS I HEARD THAT MAY WAS AILING AGAIN!
NOW THAT SHE'S HERE TO LOOK AFTER AUNT MAY, I'LL BE ABLE TO GET BACK TO MY OWN PAD.
DON'T WORRY ABOUT A THING, PETER. I'LL SOON HAVE HER RIGHT AS RAIN.
HERE, P.P. ...GWEN WANTS YOU TO CALL HER.
HI, GWENDY. WHAT? THE FARE-WELL DINNER FOR FLASH? OH, I-- HAD ALMOST FORGOTTEN.
WE WON'T LET YOU FORGET, MAN. CAN'T HAVE THE BASH, 'LESS EVERYONE CHIPS IN.
WELL, LOVER... I JUST WANTED TO REMIND YOU NOT TO SPEND YOUR EXTRA MONEY ON FRIVOLOUS THINGS LIKE YACHTS AND CADILLACS!
AND REMEMBER--- MJ IS OFF-LIMITS TO GWENDOLYN'S GUY.
I'VE GOTTA SCARE UP SOME BREAD FOR FLASH'S PARTY SOMEHOW.
SEE YOU LATER, LADY. I HAVE TO RUN.
MMMM... I'D BETTER CHECK MY MOUTH-WASH.
2.

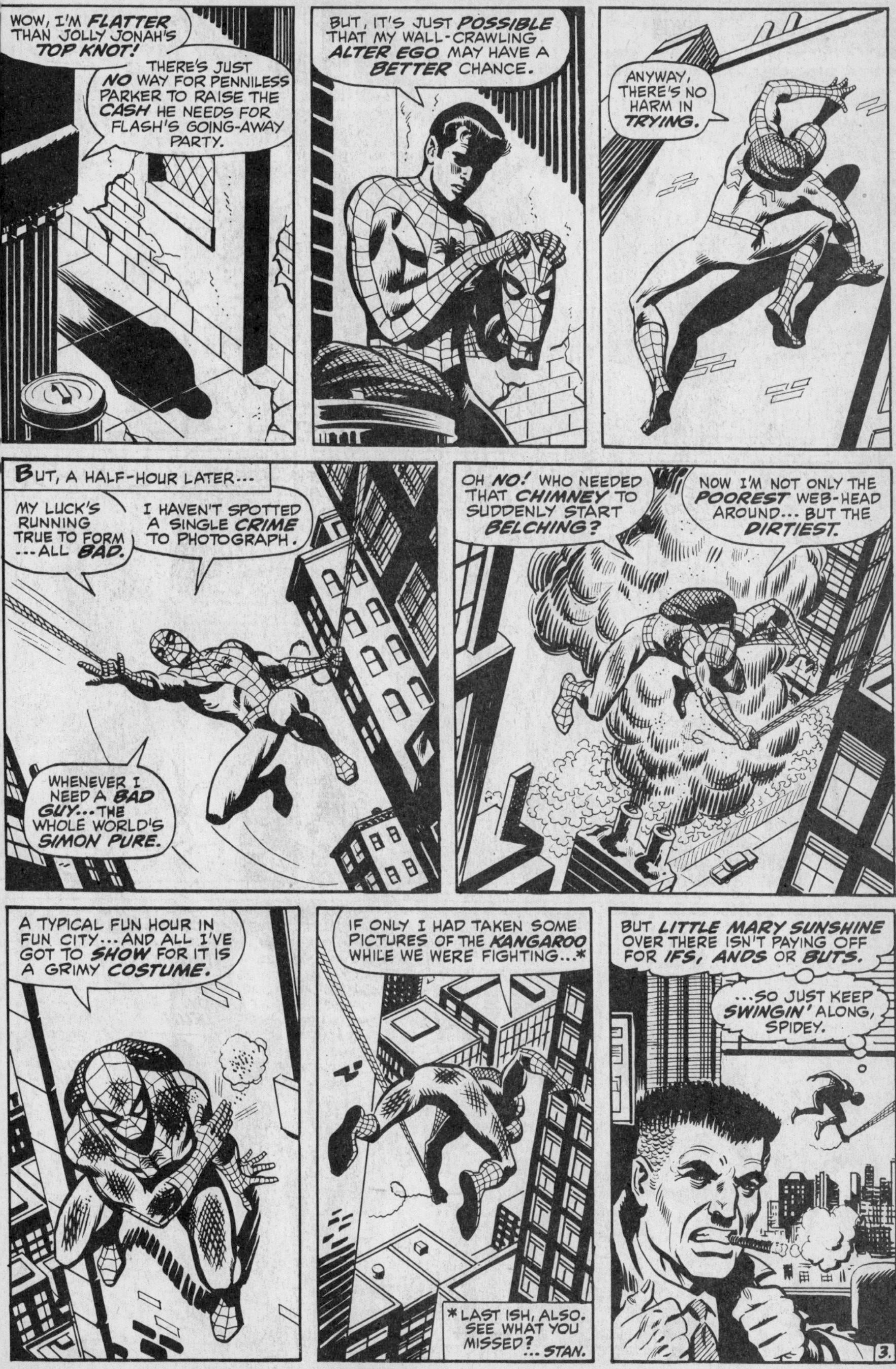
WOW, I'M FLATTER THAN JOLLY JONAH'S TOP KNOT!
THERE'S JUST NO WAY FOR PENNILESS PARKER TO RAISE THE CASH HE NEEDS FOR FLASH'S GOING-AWAY PARTY.
BUT, IT'S JUST POSSIBLE THAT MY WALL-CRAWLING ALTER EGO MAY HAVE A BETTER CHANCE.
ANYWAY, THERE'S NO HARM IN TRYING.
BUT, A HALF-HOUR LATER...
MY LUCK'S RUNNING TRUE TO FORM ---ALL BAD.
I HAVEN'T SPOTTED A SINGLE CRIME TO PHOTOGRAPH.
WHENEVER I NEED A BAD GUY... THE WHOLE WORLD'S SIMON PURE.
OH NO! WHO NEEDED THAT CHIMNEY TO SUDDENLY START BELCHING?
NOW I'M NOT ONLY THE POOREST WEB-HEAD AROUND... BUT THE DIRTIEST.
A TYPICAL FUN HOUR IN FUN CITY... AND ALL I'VE GOT TO SHOW FOR IT IS A GRIMY COSTUME.
IF ONLY I HAD TAKEN SOME PICTURES OF THE KANGAROO WHILE WE WERE FIGHTING...*
*LAST ISH, ALSO. SEE WHAT YOU MISSED? ... STAN.
BUT LITTLE MARY SUNSHINE OVER THERE ISN'T PAYING OFF FOR IFS, ANDS OR BUTS.
...SO JUST KEEP SWINGIN' ALONG, SPIDEY.
3.

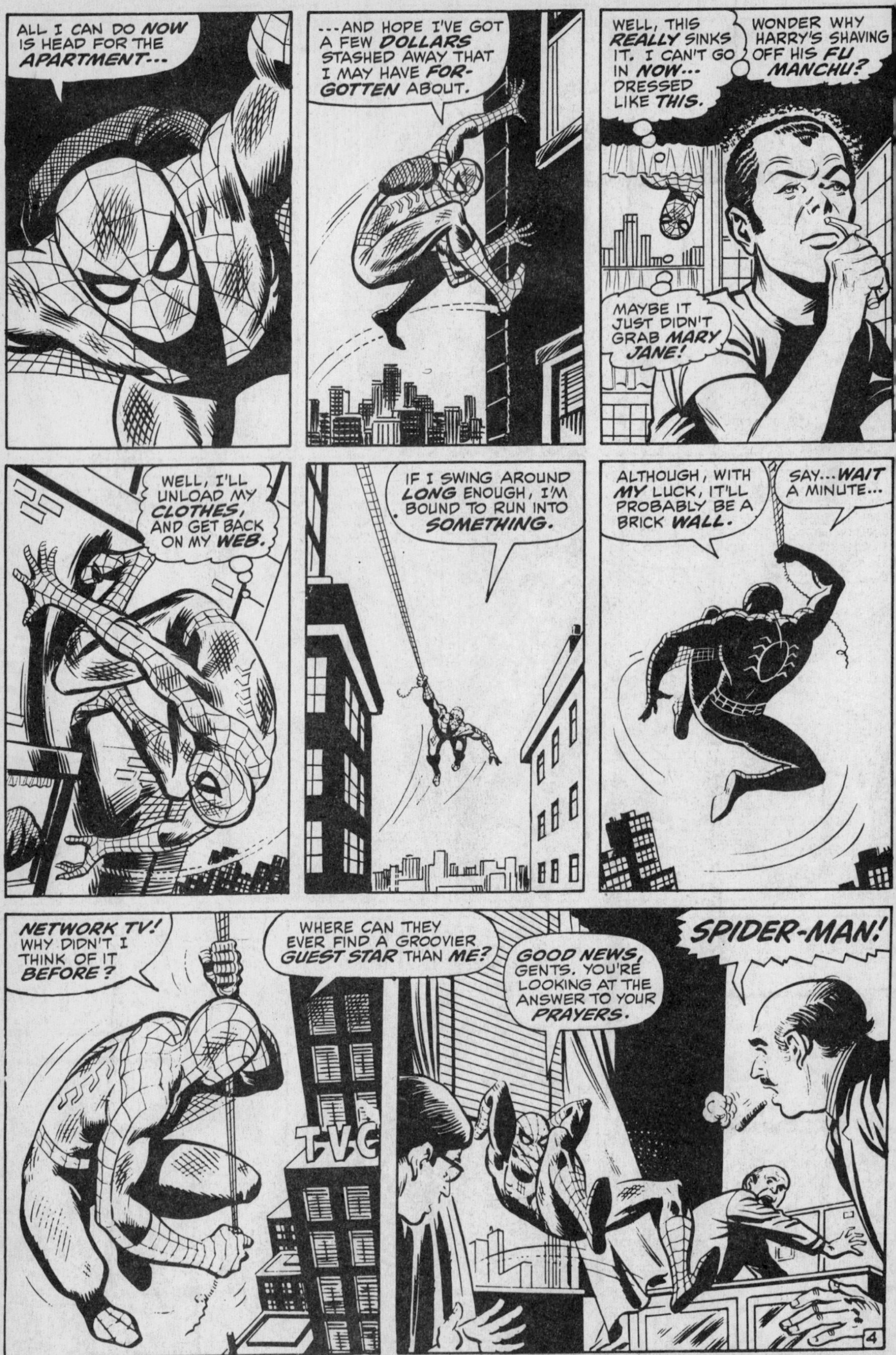
ALL I CAN DO NOW IS HEAD FOR THE APARTMENT---
---AND HOPE I'VE GOT A FEW DOLLARS STASHED AWAY THAT I MAY HAVE FORGOTTEN ABOUT.
WELL, THIS REALLY SINKS IT. I CAN'T GO IN NOW... DRESSED LIKE THIS.
WONDER WHY HARRY'S SHAVING OFF HIS FU MANCHU?
MAYBE IT JUST DIDN'T GRAB MARY JANE!
WELL, I'LL UNLOAD MY CLOTHES, AND GET BACK ON MY WEB.
IF I SWING AROUND LONG ENOUGH, I'M BOUND TO RUN INTO SOMETHING.
ALTHOUGH, WITH MY LUCK, IT'LL PROBABLY BE A BRICK WALL.
SAY...WAIT A MINUTE...
NETWORK TV! WHY DIDN'T I THINK OF IT BEFORE?
WHERE CAN THEY EVER FIND A GROOVIER GUEST STAR THAN ME?
TVC
GOOD NEWS, GENTS. YOU'RE LOOKING AT THE ANSWER TO YOUR PRAYERS.
SPIDER-MAN!
4

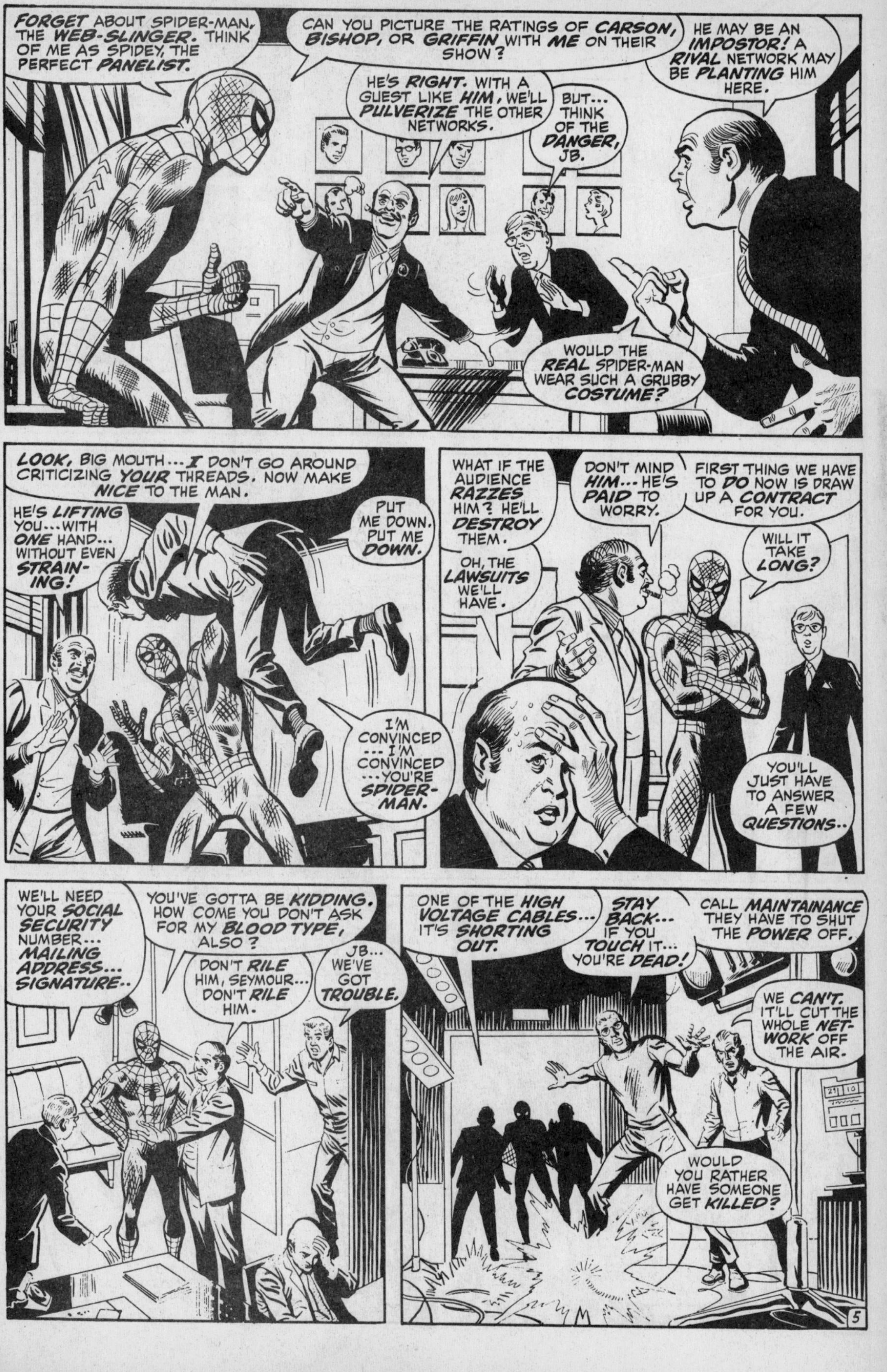
FORGET ABOUT SPIDER-MAN, THE WEB-SLINGER. THINK OF ME AS SPIDEY, THE PERFECT PANELIST.
CAN YOU PICTURE THE RATINGS OF CARSON, BISHOP, OR GRIFFIN WITH ME ON THEIR SHOW?
HE MAY BE AN IMPOSTOR! A RIVAL NETWORK MAY BE PLANTING HIM HERE.
HE'S RIGHT. WITH A GUEST LIKE HIM, WE'LL PULVERIZE THE OTHER NETWORKS.
BUT... THINK OF THE DANGER, JB.
WOULD THE REAL SPIDER-MAN WEAR SUCH A GRUBBY COSTUME?
LOOK, BIG MOUTH... I DON'T GO AROUND CRITICIZING YOUR THREADS. NOW MAKE NICE TO THE MAN.
HE'S LIFTING YOU... WITH ONE HAND... WITHOUT EVEN STRAIN-ING!
PUT ME DOWN. PUT ME DOWN.
I'M CONVINCED... I'M CONVINCED... YOU'RE SPIDER-MAN.
WHAT IF THE AUDIENCE RAZZES HIM? HE'LL DESTROY THEM.
OH, THE LAWSUITS WE'LL HAVE.
DON'T MIND HIM... HE'S PAID TO WORRY.
FIRST THING WE HAVE TO DO NOW IS DRAW UP A CONTRACT FOR YOU.
WILL IT TAKE LONG?
YOU'LL JUST HAVE TO ANSWER A FEW QUESTIONS..
WE'LL NEED YOUR SOCIAL SECURITY NUMBER... MAILING ADDRESS... SIGNATURE..
YOU'VE GOTTA BE KIDDING. HOW COME YOU DON'T ASK FOR MY BLOOD TYPE, ALSO?
DON'T RILE HIM, SEYMOUR... DON'T RILE HIM.
JB... WE'VE GOT TROUBLE.
ONE OF THE HIGH VOLTAGE CABLES... IT'S SHORTING OUT.
STAY BACK... IF YOU TOUCH IT... YOU'RE DEAD!
CALL MAINTAINANCE THEY HAVE TO SHUT THE POWER OFF.
WE CAN'T. IT'LL CUT THE WHOLE NET-WORK OFF THE AIR.
WOULD YOU RATHER HAVE SOMEONE GET KILLED?
5

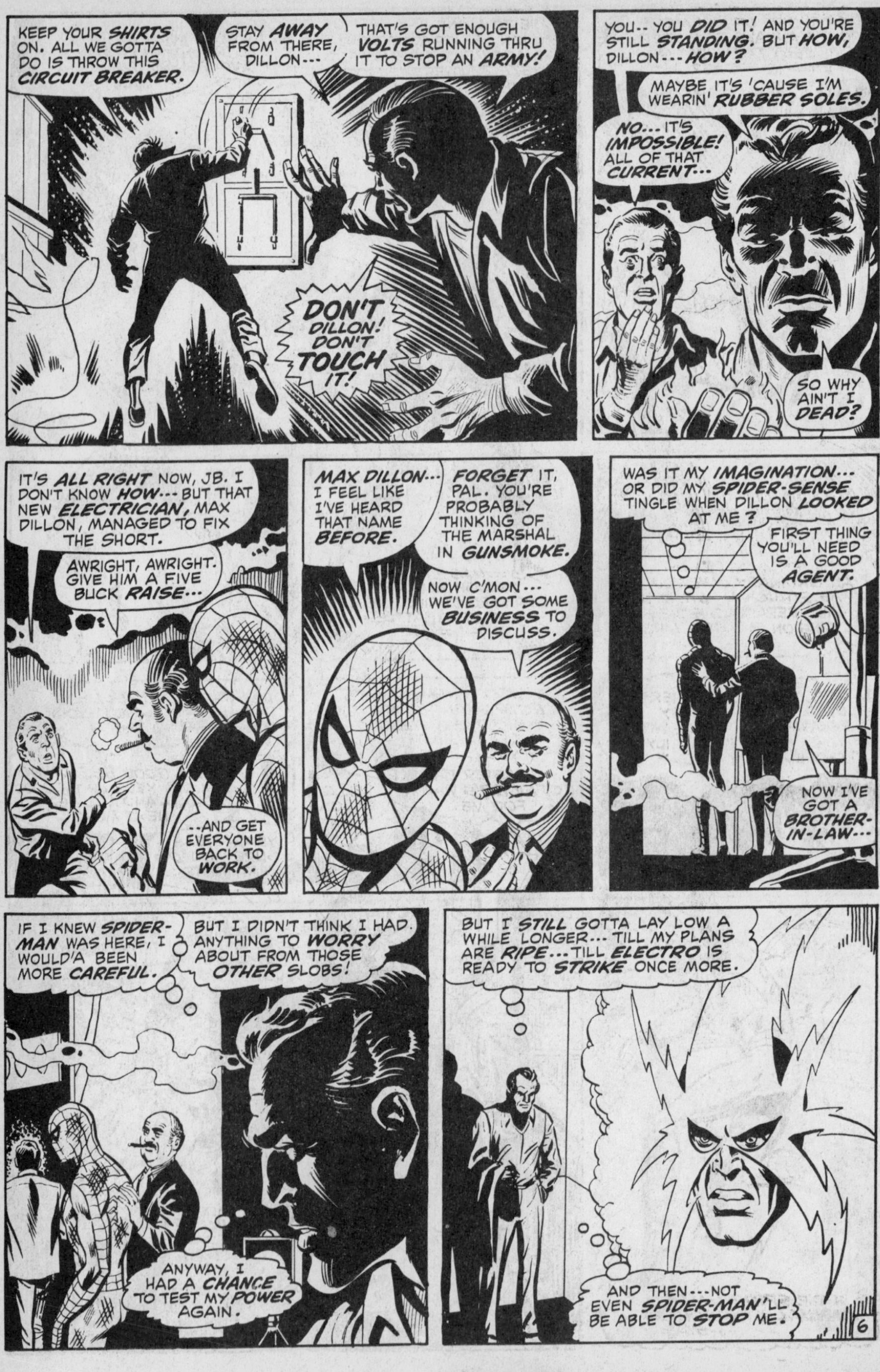

KEEP YOUR SHIRTS ON. ALL WE GOTTA DO IS THROW THIS CIRCUIT BREAKER.
STAY AWAY FROM THERE, DILLON---
THAT'S GOT ENOUGH VOLTS RUNNING THRU IT TO STOP AN ARMY!
DON'T DILLON! DON'T TOUCH IT!
YOU-- YOU DID IT! AND YOU'RE STILL STANDING. BUT HOW, DILLON---HOW?
MAYBE IT'S 'CAUSE I'M WEARIN' RUBBER SOLES.
NO... IT'S IMPOSSIBLE! ALL OF THAT CURRENT...
SO WHY AIN'T I DEAD?
IT'S ALL RIGHT NOW, JB. I DON'T KNOW HOW--- BUT THAT NEW ELECTRICIAN, MAX DILLON, MANAGED TO FIX THE SHORT.
AWRIGHT, AWRIGHT. GIVE HIM A FIVE BUCK RAISE...
..AND GET EVERYONE BACK TO WORK.
MAX DILLON... I FEEL LIKE I'VE HEARD THAT NAME BEFORE.
FORGET IT, PAL. YOU'RE PROBABLY THINKING OF THE MARSHAL IN GUNSMOKE.
NOW C'MON... WE'VE GOT SOME BUSINESS TO DISCUSS.
WAS IT MY IMAGINATION... OR DID MY SPIDER-SENSE TINGLE WHEN DILLON LOOKED AT ME?
FIRST THING YOU'LL NEED IS A GOOD AGENT.
NOW I'VE GOT A BROTHER-IN-LAW...
IF I KNEW SPIDER-MAN WAS HERE, I WOULD'A BEEN MORE CAREFUL.
BUT I DIDN'T THINK I HAD ANYTHING TO WORRY ABOUT FROM THOSE OTHER SLOBS!
ANYWAY, I HAD A CHANCE TO TEST MY POWER AGAIN.
BUT I STILL GOTTA LAY LOW A WHILE LONGER--- TILL MY PLANS ARE RIPE... TILL ELECTRO IS READY TO STRIKE ONCE MORE.
AND THEN---NOT EVEN SPIDER-MAN'LL BE ABLE TO STOP ME.
6

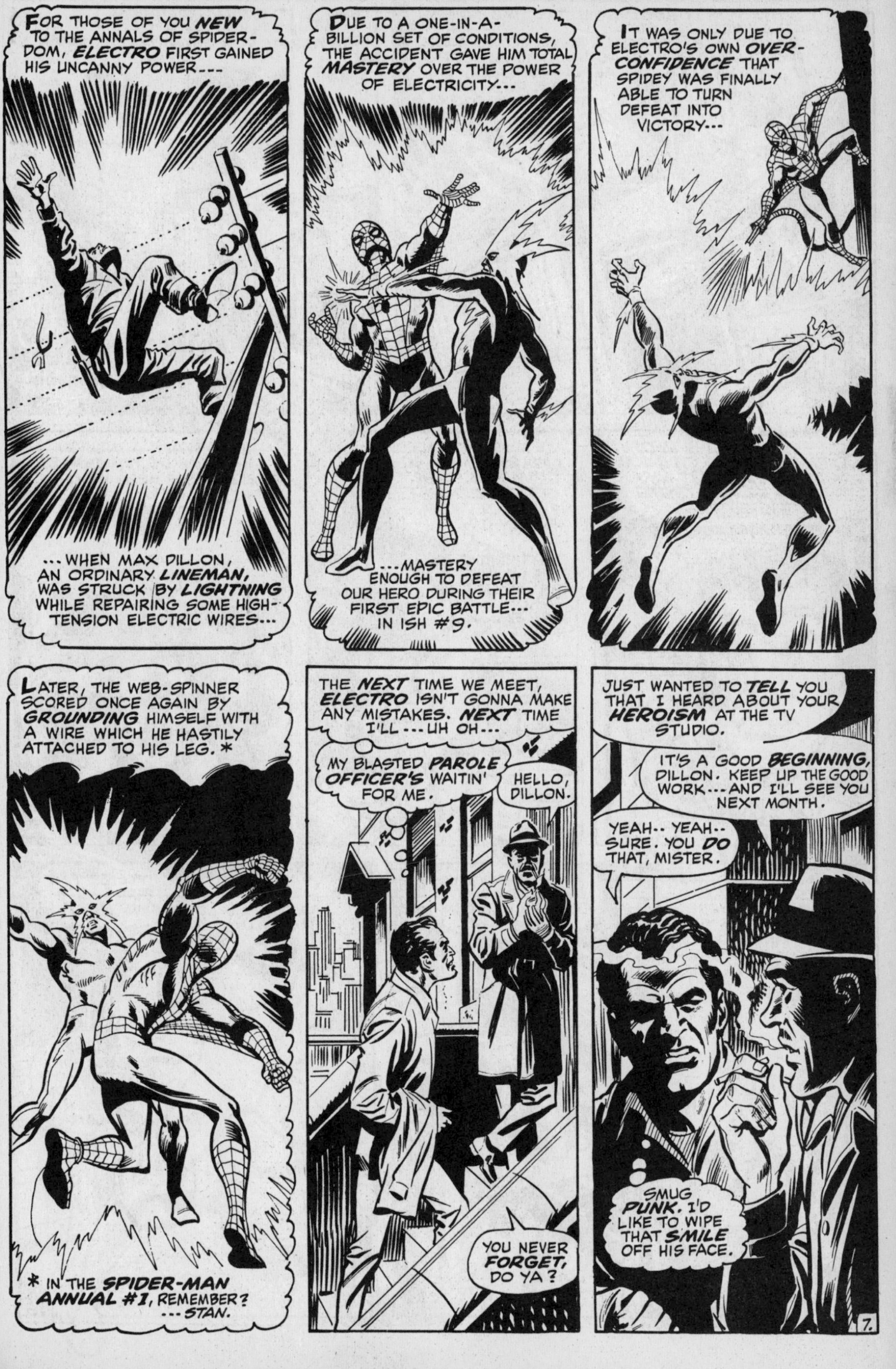
FOR THOSE OF YOU NEW TO THE ANNALS OF SPIDER-DOM, ELECTRO FIRST GAINED HIS UNCANNY POWER---
...WHEN MAX DILLON, AN ORDINARY LINEMAN, WAS STRUCK BY LIGHTNING WHILE REPAIRING SOME HIGH-TENSION ELECTRIC WIRES...
DUE TO A ONE-IN-A-BILLION SET OF CONDITIONS, THE ACCIDENT GAVE HIM TOTAL MASTERY OVER THE POWER OF ELECTRICITY...
...MASTERY ENOUGH TO DEFEAT OUR HERO DURING THEIR FIRST EPIC BATTLE... IN ISH #9.
IT WAS ONLY DUE TO ELECTRO'S OWN OVER-CONFIDENCE THAT SPIDEY WAS FINALLY ABLE TO TURN DEFEAT INTO VICTORY...
LATER, THE WEB-SPINNER SCORED ONCE AGAIN BY GROUNDING HIMSELF WITH A WIRE WHICH HE HASTILY ATTACHED TO HIS LEG. *
* IN THE SPIDER-MAN ANNUAL #1, REMEMBER? ...STAN.
THE NEXT TIME WE MEET, ELECTRO ISN'T GONNA MAKE ANY MISTAKES. NEXT TIME I'LL ---UH OH---
MY BLASTED PAROLE OFFICER'S WAITIN' FOR ME.
HELLO, DILLON.
YOU NEVER FORGET, DO YA?
JUST WANTED TO TELL YOU THAT I HEARD ABOUT YOUR HEROISM AT THE TV STUDIO.
IT'S A GOOD BEGINNING, DILLON. KEEP UP THE GOOD WORK--- AND I'LL SEE YOU NEXT MONTH.
YEAH-- YEAH-- SURE. YOU DO THAT, MISTER.
SMUG PUNK. I'D LIKE TO WIPE THAT SMILE OFF HIS FACE.
7.

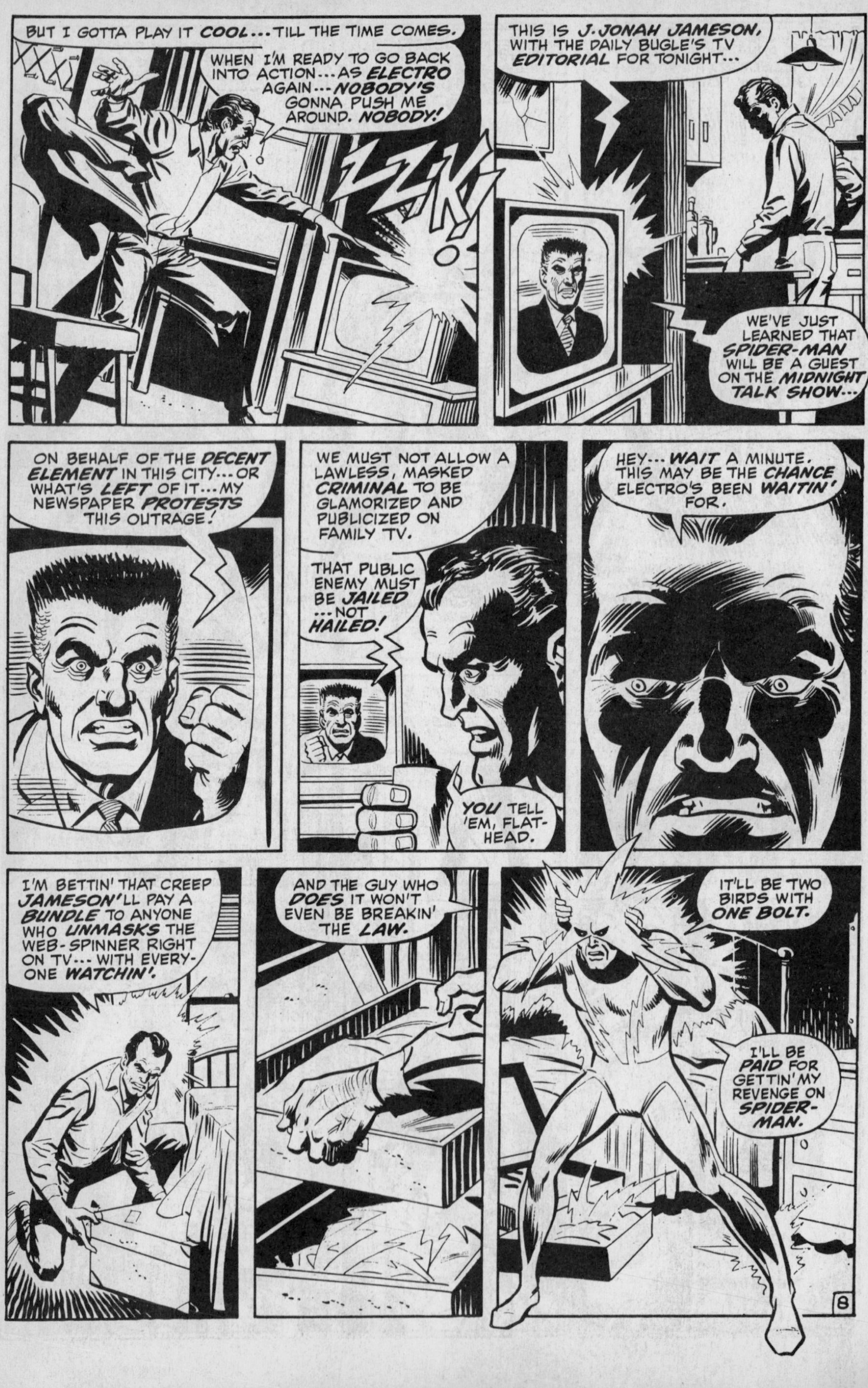

BUT I GOTTA PLAY IT COOL... TILL THE TIME COMES.
WHEN I'M READY TO GO BACK INTO ACTION... AS ELECTRO AGAIN... NOBODY'S GONNA PUSH ME AROUND. NOBODY!
ZZZK!
THIS IS J. JONAH JAMESON, WITH THE DAILY BUGLE'S TV EDITORIAL FOR TONIGHT...
WE'VE JUST LEARNED THAT SPIDER-MAN WILL BE A GUEST ON THE MIDNIGHT TALK SHOW...
ON BEHALF OF THE DECENT ELEMENT IN THIS CITY... OR WHAT'S LEFT OF IT... MY NEWSPAPER PROTESTS THIS OUTRAGE!
WE MUST NOT ALLOW A LAWLESS, MASKED CRIMINAL TO BE GLAMORIZED AND PUBLICIZED ON FAMILY TV.
THAT PUBLIC ENEMY MUST BE JAILED ...NOT HAILED!
YOU TELL 'EM, FLAT-HEAD.
HEY... WAIT A MINUTE. THIS MAY BE THE CHANCE ELECTRO'S BEEN WAITIN' FOR.
I'M BETTIN' THAT CREEP JAMESON'LL PAY A BUNDLE TO ANYONE WHO UNMASKS THE WEB-SPINNER RIGHT ON TV... WITH EVERYONE WATCHIN'.
AND THE GUY WHO DOES IT WON'T EVEN BE BREAKIN' THE LAW.
IT'LL BE TWO BIRDS WITH ONE BOLT.
I'LL BE PAID FOR GETTIN' MY REVENGE ON SPIDER-MAN.
8

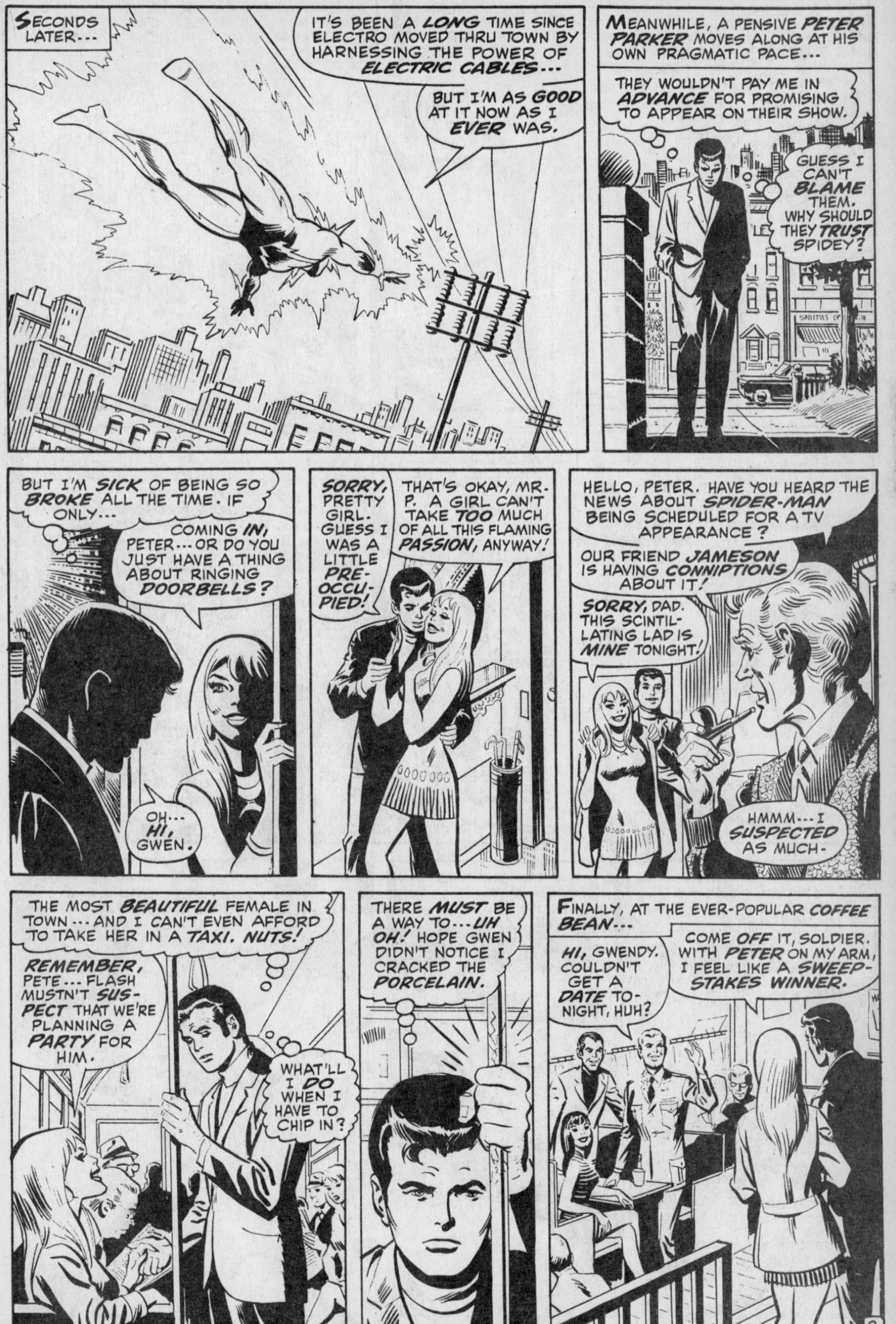
SECONDS LATER...
IT'S BEEN A LONG TIME SINCE ELECTRO MOVED THRU TOWN BY HARNESSING THE POWER OF ELECTRIC CABLES...
BUT I'M AS GOOD AT IT NOW AS I EVER WAS.
MEANWHILE, A PENSIVE PETER PARKER MOVES ALONG AT HIS OWN PRAGMATIC PACE...
THEY WOULDN'T PAY ME IN ADVANCE FOR PROMISING TO APPEAR ON THEIR SHOW.
GUESS I CAN'T BLAME THEM. WHY SHOULD THEY TRUST SPIDEY?
BUT I'M SICK OF BEING SO BROKE ALL THE TIME. IF ONLY...
COMING IN, PETER... OR DO YOU JUST HAVE A THING ABOUT RINGING DOORBELLS?
OH... HI, GWEN.
SORRY, PRETTY GIRL. GUESS I WAS A LITTLE PRE-OCCU-PIED!
THAT'S OKAY, MR. P. A GIRL CAN'T TAKE TOO MUCH OF ALL THIS FLAMING PASSION, ANYWAY!
HELLO, PETER. HAVE YOU HEARD THE NEWS ABOUT SPIDER-MAN BEING SCHEDULED FOR A TV APPEARANCE?
OUR FRIEND JAMESON IS HAVING CONNIPTIONS ABOUT IT!
SORRY, DAD. THIS SCINTIL-LATING LAD IS MINE TONIGHT!
HMMM... I SUSPECTED AS MUCH-
THE MOST BEAUTIFUL FEMALE IN TOWN... AND I CAN'T EVEN AFFORD TO TAKE HER IN A TAXI. NUTS!
REMEMBER, PETE... FLASH MUSTN'T SUS-PECT THAT WE'RE PLANNING A PARTY FOR HIM.
WHAT'LL I DO WHEN I HAVE TO CHIP IN?
THERE MUST BE A WAY TO... UH OH! HOPE GWEN DIDN'T NOTICE I CRACKED THE PORCELAIN.
FINALLY, AT THE EVER-POPULAR COFFEE BEAN...
HI, GWENDY. COULDN'T GET A DATE TO-NIGHT, HUH?
COME OFF IT, SOLDIER. WITH PETER ON MY ARM, I FEEL LIKE A SWEEP-STAKES WINNER.
9.

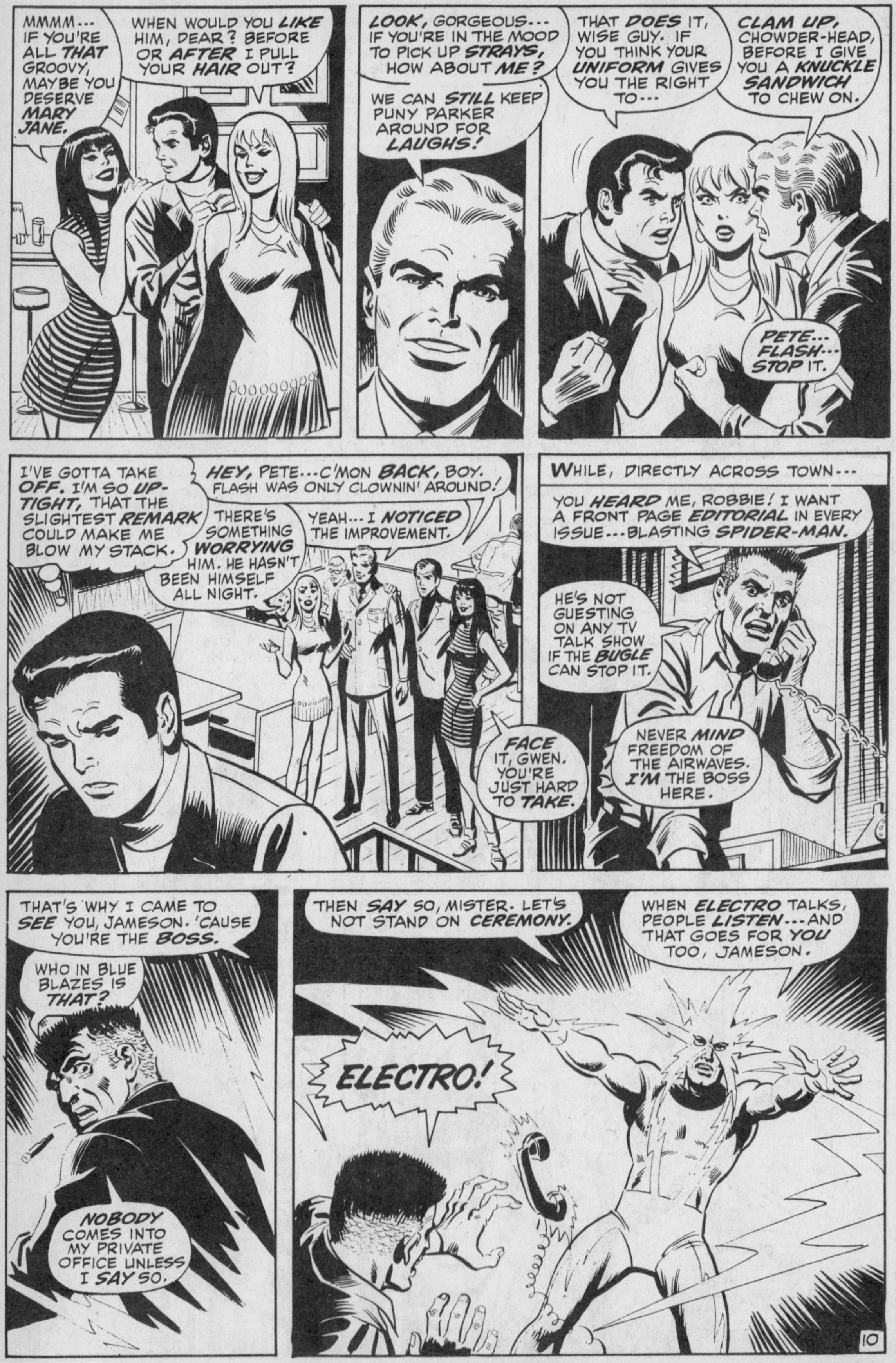
MMMM... IF YOU'RE ALL THAT GROOVY, MAYBE YOU DESERVE MARY JANE.
WHEN WOULD YOU LIKE HIM, DEAR? BEFORE OR AFTER I PULL YOUR HAIR OUT?
LOOK, GORGEOUS... IF YOU'RE IN THE MOOD TO PICK UP STRAYS, HOW ABOUT ME?
WE CAN STILL KEEP PUNY PARKER AROUND FOR LAUGHS!
THAT DOES IT, WISE GUY. IF YOU THINK YOUR UNIFORM GIVES YOU THE RIGHT TO...
CLAM UP, CHOWDER-HEAD, BEFORE I GIVE YOU A KNUCKLE SANDWICH TO CHEW ON.
PETE... FLASH... STOP IT.
I'VE GOTTA TAKE OFF. I'M SO UP-TIGHT, THAT THE SLIGHTEST REMARK COULD MAKE ME BLOW MY STACK.
HEY, PETE...C'MON BACK, BOY. FLASH WAS ONLY CLOWNIN' AROUND!
THERE'S SOMETHING WORRYING HIM. HE HASN'T BEEN HIMSELF ALL NIGHT.
YEAH... I NOTICED THE IMPROVEMENT.
FACE IT, GWEN. YOU'RE JUST HARD TO TAKE.
WHILE, DIRECTLY ACROSS TOWN...
YOU HEARD ME, ROBBIE! I WANT A FRONT PAGE EDITORIAL IN EVERY ISSUE...BLASTING SPIDER-MAN.
HE'S NOT GUESTING ON ANY TV TALK SHOW IF THE BUGLE CAN STOP IT.
NEVER MIND FREEDOM OF THE AIRWAVES. I'M THE BOSS HERE.
THAT'S WHY I CAME TO SEE YOU, JAMESON. 'CAUSE YOU'RE THE BOSS.
WHO IN BLUE BLAZES IS THAT?
NOBODY COMES INTO MY PRIVATE OFFICE UNLESS I SAY SO.
THEN SAY SO, MISTER. LET'S NOT STAND ON CEREMONY.
WHEN ELECTRO TALKS, PEOPLE LISTEN...AND THAT GOES FOR YOU TOO, JAMESON.
ELECTRO!
10

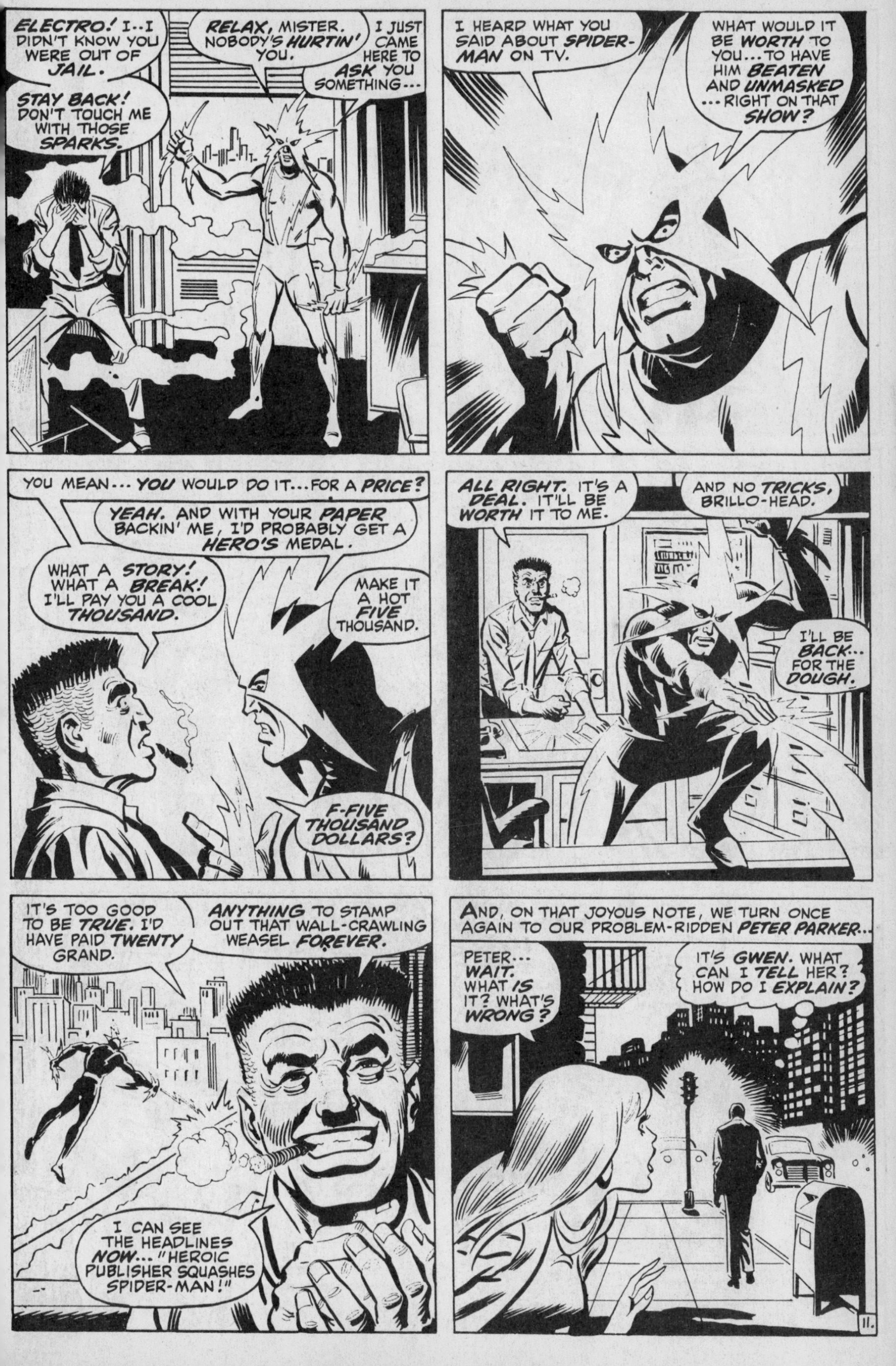

ELECTRO! I..I DIDN'T KNOW YOU WERE OUT OF JAIL.
STAY BACK! DON'T TOUCH ME WITH THOSE SPARKS.
RELAX, MISTER. NOBODY'S HURTIN' YOU.
I JUST CAME HERE TO ASK YOU SOMETHING...
I HEARD WHAT YOU SAID ABOUT SPIDER-MAN ON TV.
WHAT WOULD IT BE WORTH TO YOU...TO HAVE HIM BEATEN AND UNMASKED ...RIGHT ON THAT SHOW?
YOU MEAN...YOU WOULD DO IT...FOR A PRICE?
YEAH. AND WITH YOUR PAPER BACKIN' ME, I'D PROBABLY GET A HERO'S MEDAL.
WHAT A STORY! WHAT A BREAK! I'LL PAY YOU A COOL THOUSAND.
MAKE IT A HOT FIVE THOUSAND.
F-FIVE THOUSAND DOLLARS?
ALL RIGHT. IT'S A DEAL. IT'LL BE WORTH IT TO ME.
AND NO TRICKS, BRILLO-HEAD.
I'LL BE BACK... FOR THE DOUGH.
IT'S TOO GOOD TO BE TRUE. I'D HAVE PAID TWENTY GRAND.
ANYTHING TO STAMP OUT THAT WALL-CRAWLING WEASEL FOREVER.
I CAN SEE THE HEADLINES NOW... "HEROIC PUBLISHER SQUASHES SPIDER-MAN!"
AND, ON THAT JOYOUS NOTE, WE TURN ONCE AGAIN TO OUR PROBLEM-RIDDEN PETER PARKER...
PETER... WAIT. WHAT IS IT? WHAT'S WRONG?
IT'S GWEN. WHAT CAN I TELL HER? HOW DO I EXPLAIN?
11.

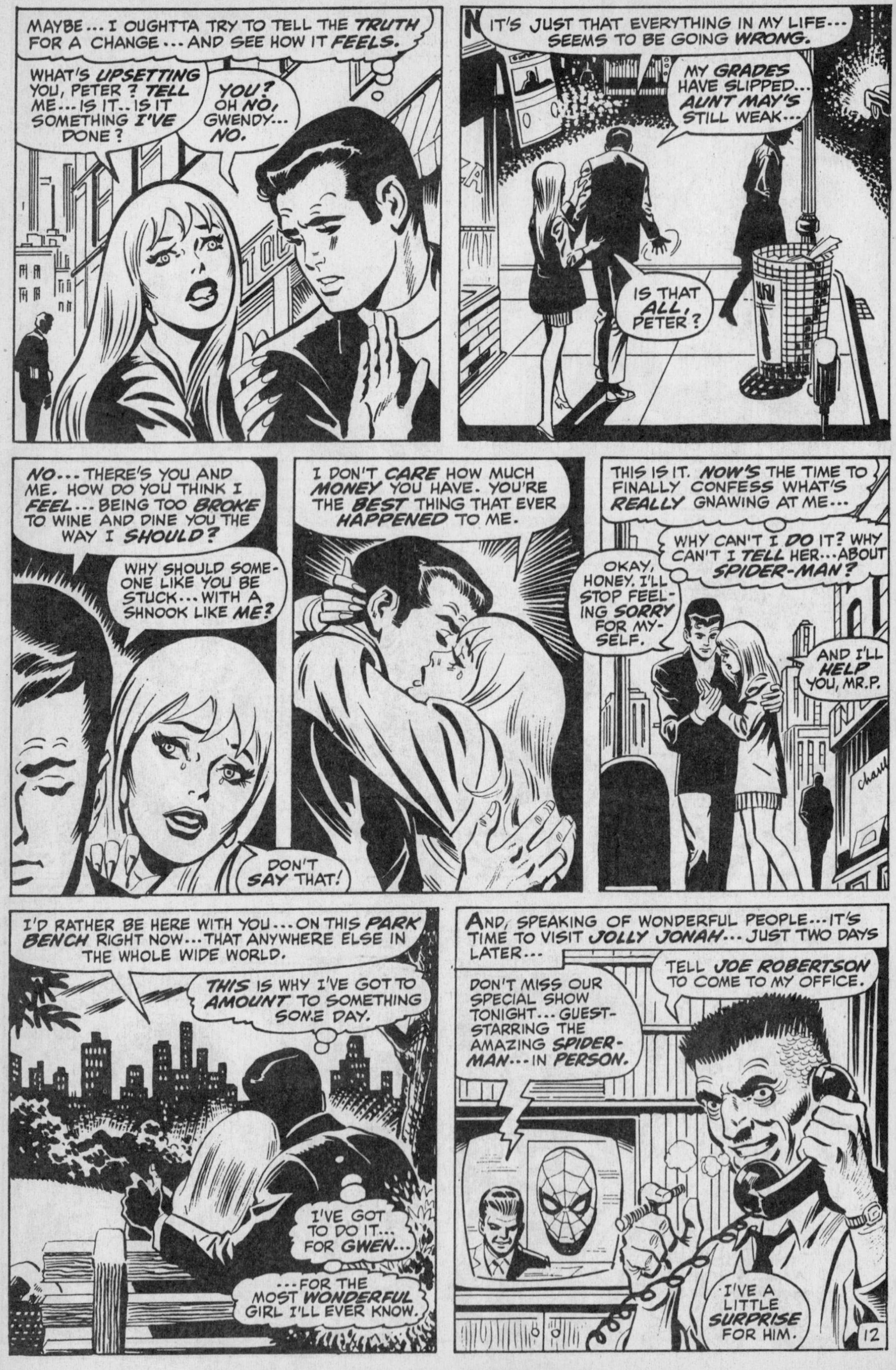

MAYBE... I OUGHTTA TRY TO TELL THE TRUTH FOR A CHANGE... AND SEE HOW IT FEELS.
WHAT'S UPSETTING YOU, PETER? TELL ME... IS IT.. IS IT SOMETHING I'VE DONE?
YOU? OH NO, GWENDY... NO.
IT'S JUST THAT EVERYTHING IN MY LIFE... SEEMS TO BE GOING WRONG.
MY GRADES HAVE SLIPPED... AUNT MAY'S STILL WEAK...
IS THAT ALL, PETER?
NO... THERE'S YOU AND ME. HOW DO YOU THINK I FEEL... BEING TOO BROKE TO WINE AND DINE YOU THE WAY I SHOULD?
WHY SHOULD SOME-ONE LIKE YOU BE STUCK... WITH A SHNOOK LIKE ME?
DON'T SAY THAT!
I DON'T CARE HOW MUCH MONEY YOU HAVE. YOU'RE THE BEST THING THAT EVER HAPPENED TO ME.
THIS IS IT. NOW'S THE TIME TO FINALLY CONFESS WHAT'S REALLY GNAWING AT ME...
WHY CAN'T I DO IT? WHY CAN'T I TELL HER... ABOUT SPIDER-MAN?
OKAY, HONEY. I'LL STOP FEEL-ING SORRY FOR MY-SELF.
AND I'LL HELP YOU, MR.P.
I'D RATHER BE HERE WITH YOU... ON THIS PARK BENCH RIGHT NOW... THAT ANYWHERE ELSE IN THE WHOLE WIDE WORLD.
THIS IS WHY I'VE GOT TO AMOUNT TO SOMETHING SOME DAY.
I'VE GOT TO DO IT... FOR GWEN...
...FOR THE MOST WONDERFUL GIRL I'LL EVER KNOW.
AND, SPEAKING OF WONDERFUL PEOPLE... IT'S TIME TO VISIT JOLLY JONAH... JUST TWO DAYS LATER...
TELL JOE ROBERTSON TO COME TO MY OFFICE.
DON'T MISS OUR SPECIAL SHOW TONIGHT... GUEST-STARRING THE AMAZING SPIDER-MAN... IN PERSON.
I'VE A LITTLE SURPRISE FOR HIM.
12

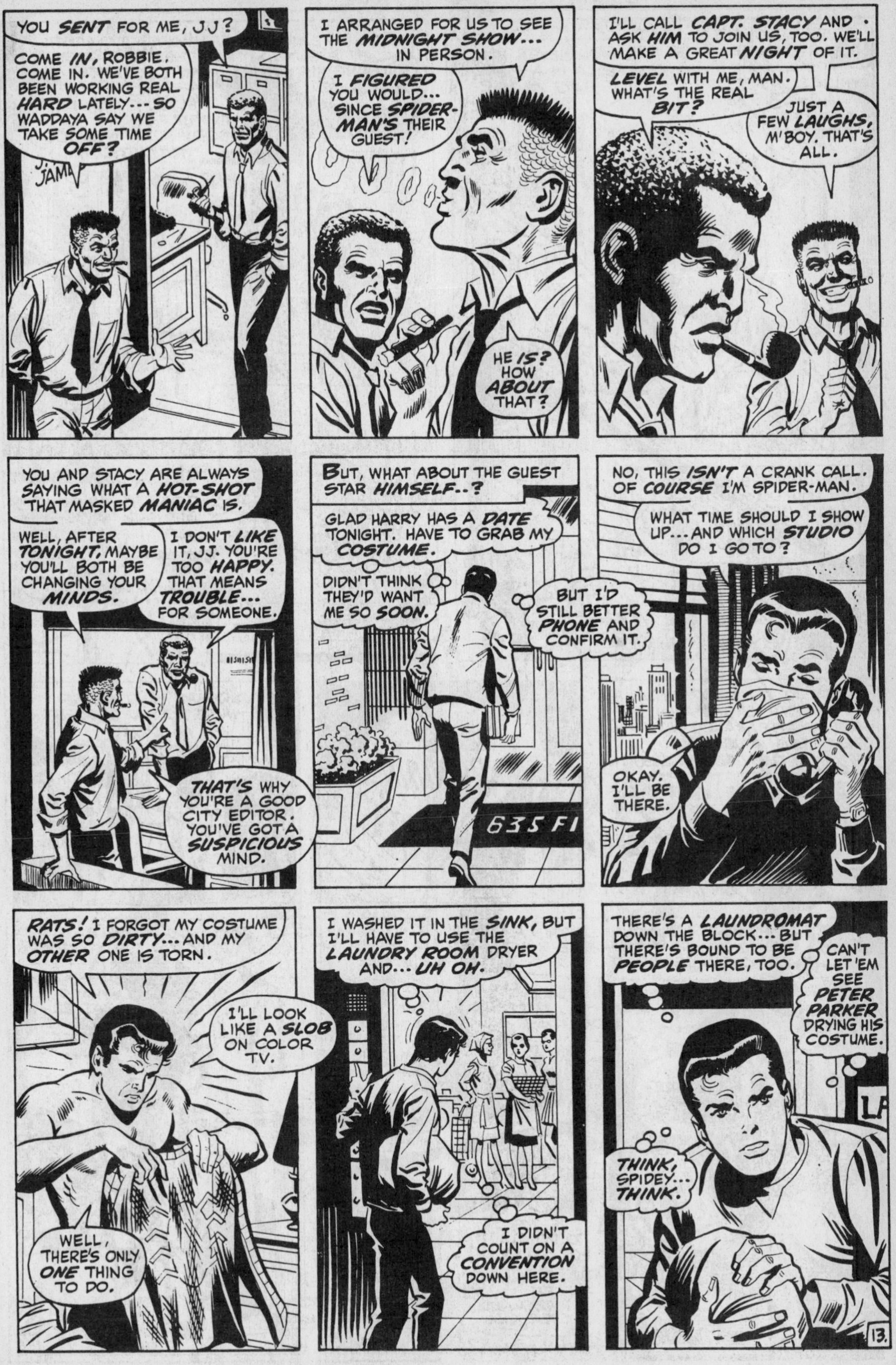
YOU SENT FOR ME, JJ?
COME IN, ROBBIE. COME IN. WE'VE BOTH BEEN WORKING REAL HARD LATELY... SO WADDAYA SAY WE TAKE SOME TIME OFF?
I ARRANGED FOR US TO SEE THE MIDNIGHT SHOW... IN PERSON.
I FIGURED YOU WOULD... SINCE SPIDER-MAN'S THEIR GUEST!
HE IS? HOW ABOUT THAT?
I'LL CALL CAPT. STACY AND ASK HIM TO JOIN US, TOO. WE'LL MAKE A GREAT NIGHT OF IT.
LEVEL WITH ME, MAN. WHAT'S THE REAL BIT?
JUST A FEW LAUGHS, M'BOY. THAT'S ALL.
YOU AND STACY ARE ALWAYS SAYING WHAT A HOT-SHOT THAT MASKED MANIAC IS.
WELL, AFTER TONIGHT, MAYBE YOU'LL BOTH BE CHANGING YOUR MINDS.
I DON'T LIKE IT, JJ. YOU'RE TOO HAPPY. THAT MEANS TROUBLE... FOR SOMEONE.
THAT'S WHY YOU'RE A GOOD CITY EDITOR. YOU'VE GOT A SUSPICIOUS MIND.
BUT, WHAT ABOUT THE GUEST STAR HIMSELF..?
GLAD HARRY HAS A DATE TONIGHT. HAVE TO GRAB MY COSTUME.
DIDN'T THINK THEY'D WANT ME SO SOON.
BUT I'D STILL BETTER PHONE AND CONFIRM IT.
635 FI
NO, THIS ISN'T A CRANK CALL. OF COURSE I'M SPIDER-MAN.
WHAT TIME SHOULD I SHOW UP... AND WHICH STUDIO DO I GO TO?
OKAY. I'LL BE THERE.
RATS! I FORGOT MY COSTUME WAS SO DIRTY... AND MY OTHER ONE IS TORN.
I'LL LOOK LIKE A SLOB ON COLOR TV.
WELL, THERE'S ONLY ONE THING TO DO.
I WASHED IT IN THE SINK, BUT I'LL HAVE TO USE THE LAUNDRY ROOM DRYER AND... UH OH.
I DIDN'T COUNT ON A CONVENTION DOWN HERE.
THERE'S A LAUNDROMAT DOWN THE BLOCK... BUT THERE'S BOUND TO BE PEOPLE THERE, TOO.
CAN'T LET 'EM SEE PETER PARKER DRYING HIS COSTUME.
THINK, SPIDEY... THINK.
13.

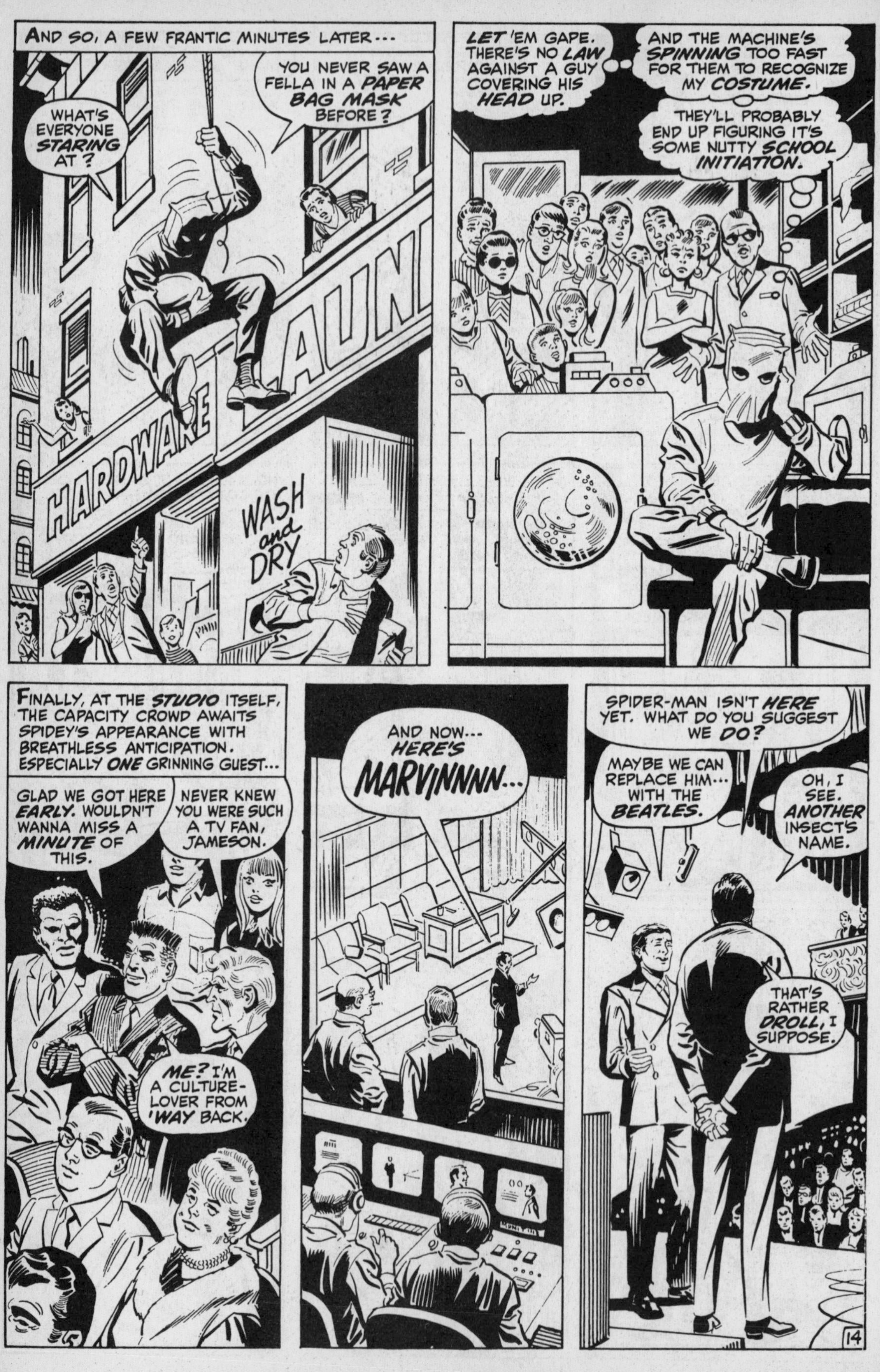

AND SO, A FEW FRANTIC MINUTES LATER---
WHAT'S EVERYONE STARING AT?
YOU NEVER SAW A FELLA IN A PAPER BAG MASK BEFORE?
HARDWARE
LAUN
WASH and DRY
LET 'EM GAPE. THERE'S NO LAW AGAINST A GUY COVERING HIS HEAD UP.
AND THE MACHINE'S SPINNING TOO FAST FOR THEM TO RECOGNIZE MY COSTUME.
THEY'LL PROBABLY END UP FIGURING IT'S SOME NUTTY SCHOOL INITIATION.
FINALLY, AT THE STUDIO ITSELF, THE CAPACITY CROWD AWAITS SPIDEY'S APPEARANCE WITH BREATHLESS ANTICIPATION. ESPECIALLY ONE GRINNING GUEST...
GLAD WE GOT HERE EARLY. WOULDN'T WANNA MISS A MINUTE OF THIS.
NEVER KNEW YOU WERE SUCH A TV FAN, JAMESON.
ME? I'M A CULTURE-LOVER FROM 'WAY BACK.
AND NOW... HERE'S MARVINNNN...
SPIDER-MAN ISN'T HERE YET. WHAT DO YOU SUGGEST WE DO?
MAYBE WE CAN REPLACE HIM... WITH THE BEATLES.
OH, I SEE. ANOTHER INSECT'S NAME.
THAT'S RATHER DROLL, I SUPPOSE.
14

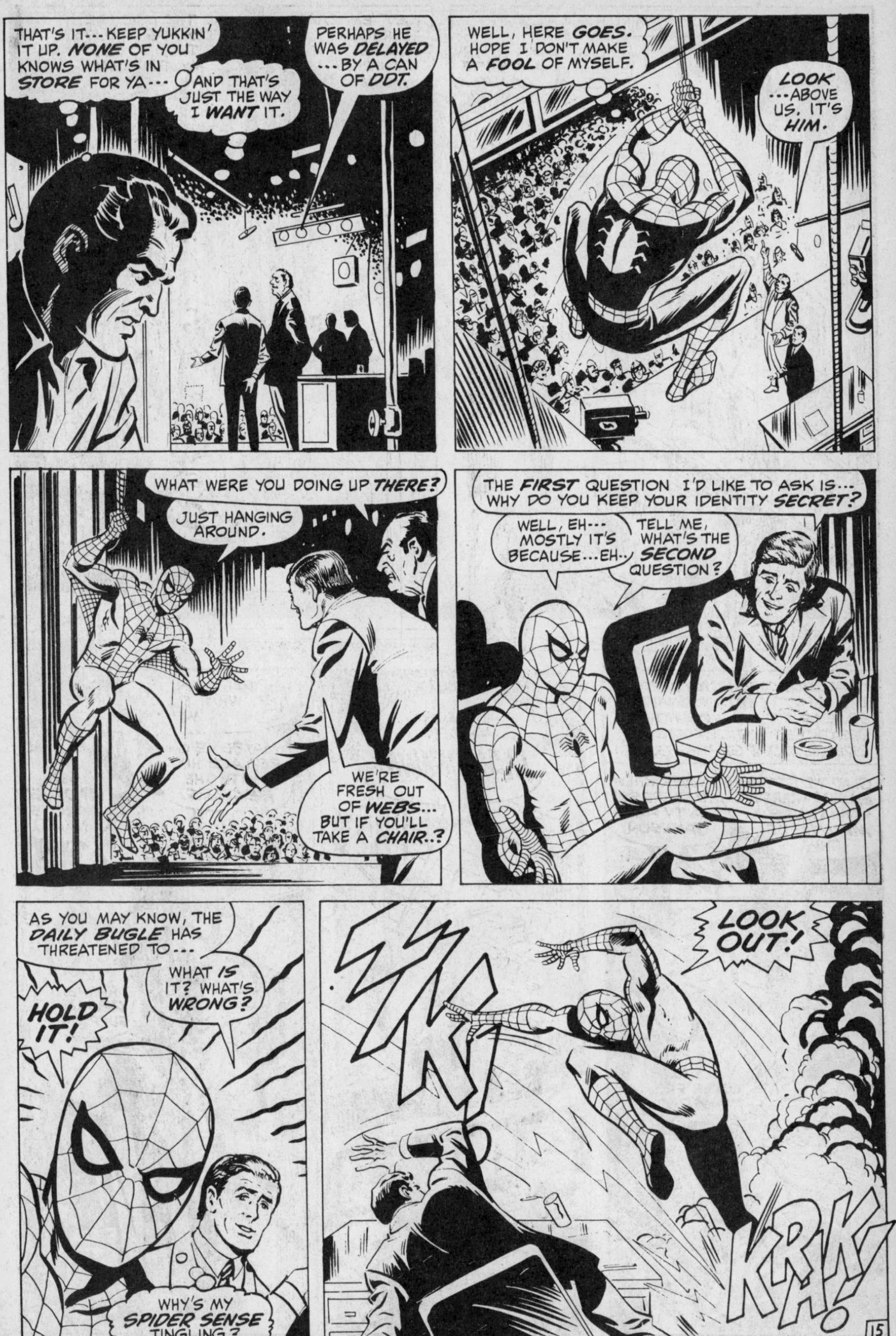
THAT'S IT--- KEEP YUKKIN' IT UP. NONE OF YOU KNOWS WHAT'S IN STORE FOR YA---
AND THAT'S JUST THE WAY I WANT IT.
PERHAPS HE WAS DELAYED ---BY A CAN OF DDT.
WELL, HERE GOES. HOPE I DON'T MAKE A FOOL OF MYSELF.
LOOK ---ABOVE US. IT'S HIM.
WHAT WERE YOU DOING UP THERE?
JUST HANGING AROUND.
WE'RE FRESH OUT OF WEBS... BUT IF YOU'LL TAKE A CHAIR..?
THE FIRST QUESTION I'D LIKE TO ASK IS... WHY DO YOU KEEP YOUR IDENTITY SECRET?
WELL, EH--- MOSTLY IT'S BECAUSE---EH--
TELL ME, WHAT'S THE SECOND QUESTION?
AS YOU MAY KNOW, THE DAILY BUGLE HAS THREATENED TO ---
HOLD IT!
WHAT IS IT? WHAT'S WRONG?
WHY'S MY SPIDER SENSE TINGLING?
ZAK
LOOK OUT!
KRAK!
15

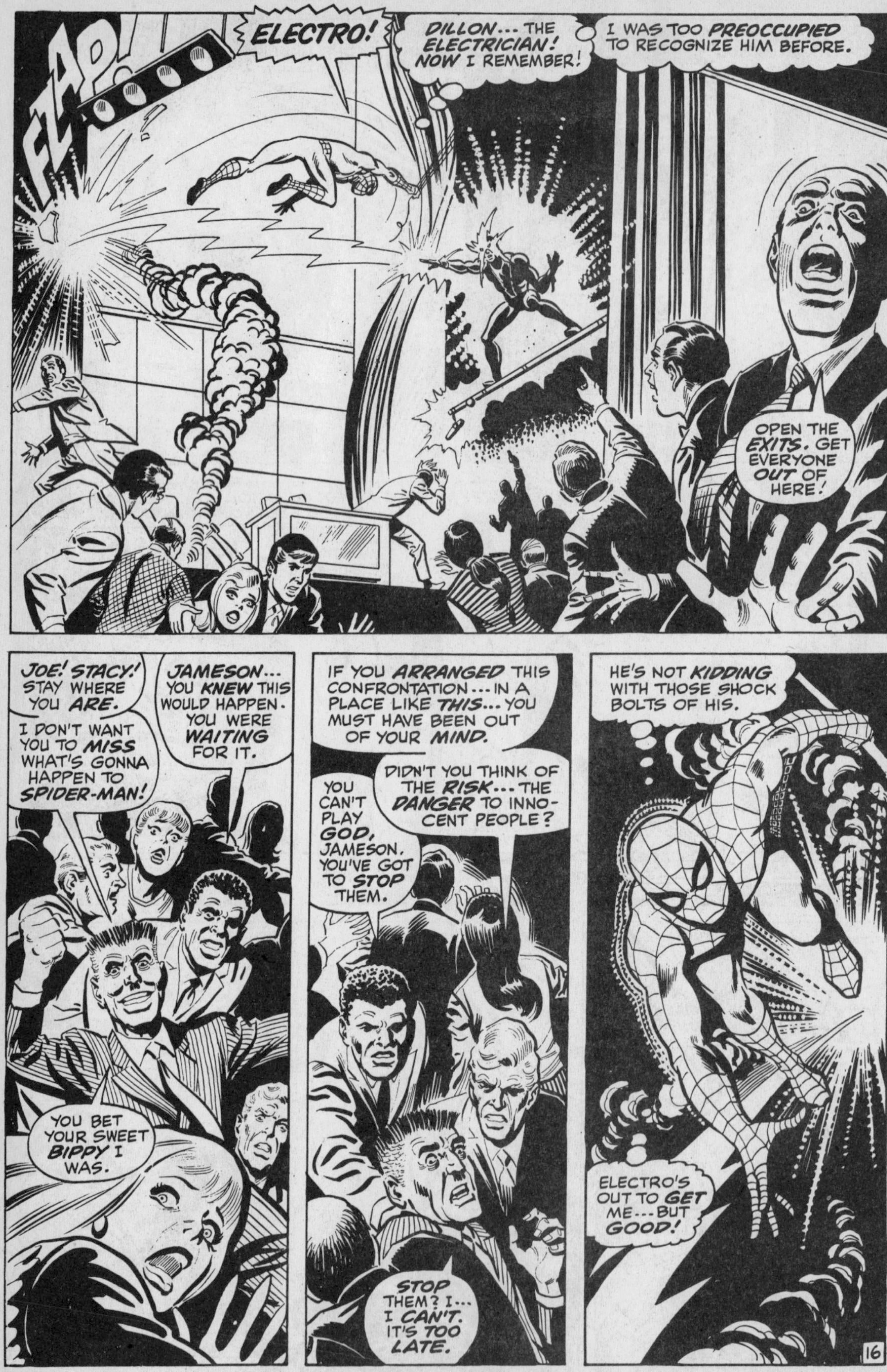
FZAP!
ELECTRO!
DILLON... THE ELECTRICIAN! NOW I REMEMBER!
I WAS TOO PREOCCUPIED TO RECOGNIZE HIM BEFORE.
OPEN THE EXITS. GET EVERYONE OUT OF HERE!
JOE! STACY! STAY WHERE YOU ARE.
I DON'T WANT YOU TO MISS WHAT'S GONNA HAPPEN TO SPIDER-MAN!
JAMESON... YOU KNEW THIS WOULD HAPPEN. YOU WERE WAITING FOR IT.
YOU BET YOUR SWEET BIPPY I WAS.
IF YOU ARRANGED THIS CONFRONTATION... IN A PLACE LIKE THIS... YOU MUST HAVE BEEN OUT OF YOUR MIND.
DIDN'T YOU THINK OF THE RISK... THE DANGER TO INNOCENT PEOPLE?
YOU CAN'T PLAY GOD, JAMESON. YOU'VE GOT TO STOP THEM.
STOP THEM? I... I CAN'T. IT'S TOO LATE.
HE'S NOT KIDDING WITH THOSE SHOCK BOLTS OF HIS.
ELECTRO'S OUT TO GET ME... BUT GOOD!
16

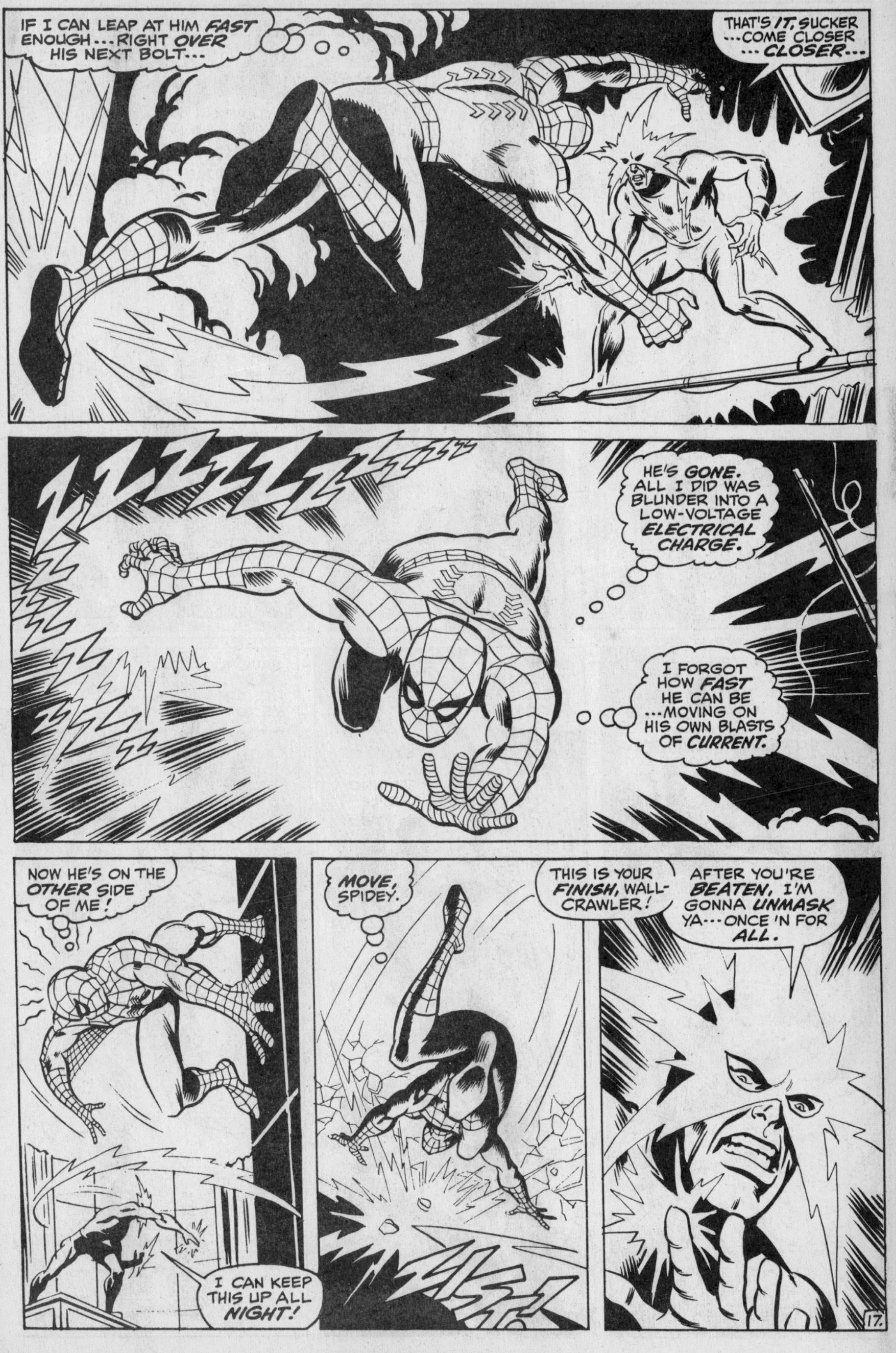
IF I CAN LEAP AT HIM FAST ENOUGH... RIGHT OVER HIS NEXT BOLT...
THAT'S IT, SUCKER ...COME CLOSER ...CLOSER...
HE'S GONE. ALL I DID WAS BLUNDER INTO A LOW-VOLTAGE ELECTRICAL CHARGE.
I FORGOT HOW FAST HE CAN BE ...MOVING ON HIS OWN BLASTS OF CURRENT.
NOW HE'S ON THE OTHER SIDE OF ME!
I CAN KEEP THIS UP ALL NIGHT!
MOVE, SPIDEY.
THIS IS YOUR FINISH, WALL-CRAWLER!
AFTER YOU'RE BEATEN, I'M GONNA UNMASK YA... ONCE 'N FOR ALL.
17.

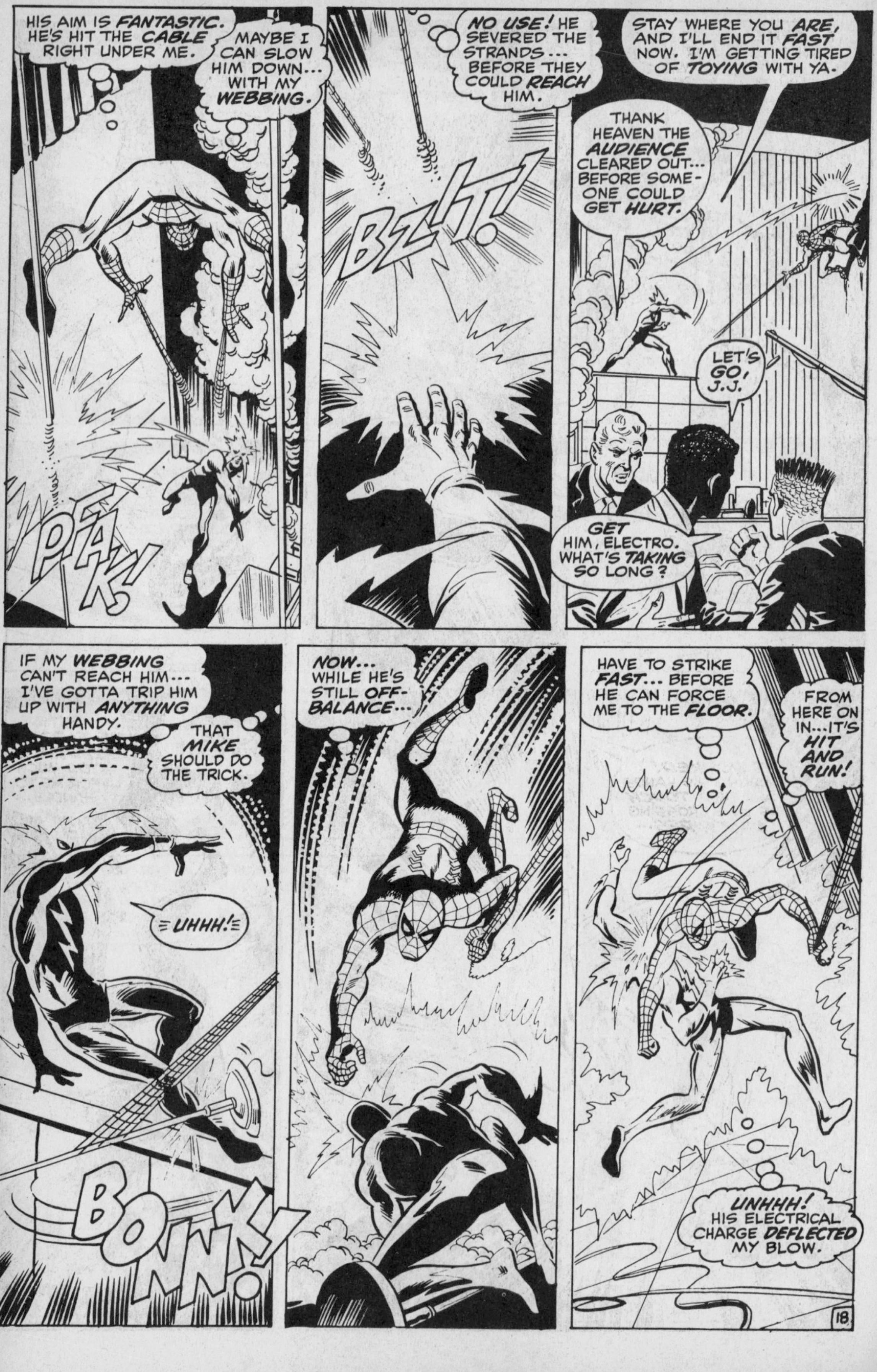
HIS AIM IS FANTASTIC. HE'S HIT THE CABLE RIGHT UNDER ME.
MAYBE I CAN SLOW HIM DOWN... WITH MY WEBBING.
PFAK!
NO USE! HE SEVERED THE STRANDS... BEFORE THEY COULD REACH HIM.
BZZT!
STAY WHERE YOU ARE, AND I'LL END IT FAST NOW. I'M GETTING TIRED OF TOYING WITH YA.
THANK HEAVEN THE AUDIENCE CLEARED OUT... BEFORE SOME-ONE COULD GET HURT.
LET'S GO, J.J.
GET HIM, ELECTRO. WHAT'S TAKING SO LONG?
IF MY WEBBING CAN'T REACH HIM... I'VE GOTTA TRIP HIM UP WITH ANYTHING HANDY.
THAT MIKE SHOULD DO THE TRICK.
UHHH!
BONNK!
NOW... WHILE HE'S STILL OFF-BALANCE...
HAVE TO STRIKE FAST... BEFORE HE CAN FORCE ME TO THE FLOOR.
FROM HERE ON IN... IT'S HIT AND RUN!
UNHHH! HIS ELECTRICAL CHARGE DEFLECTED MY BLOW.
18

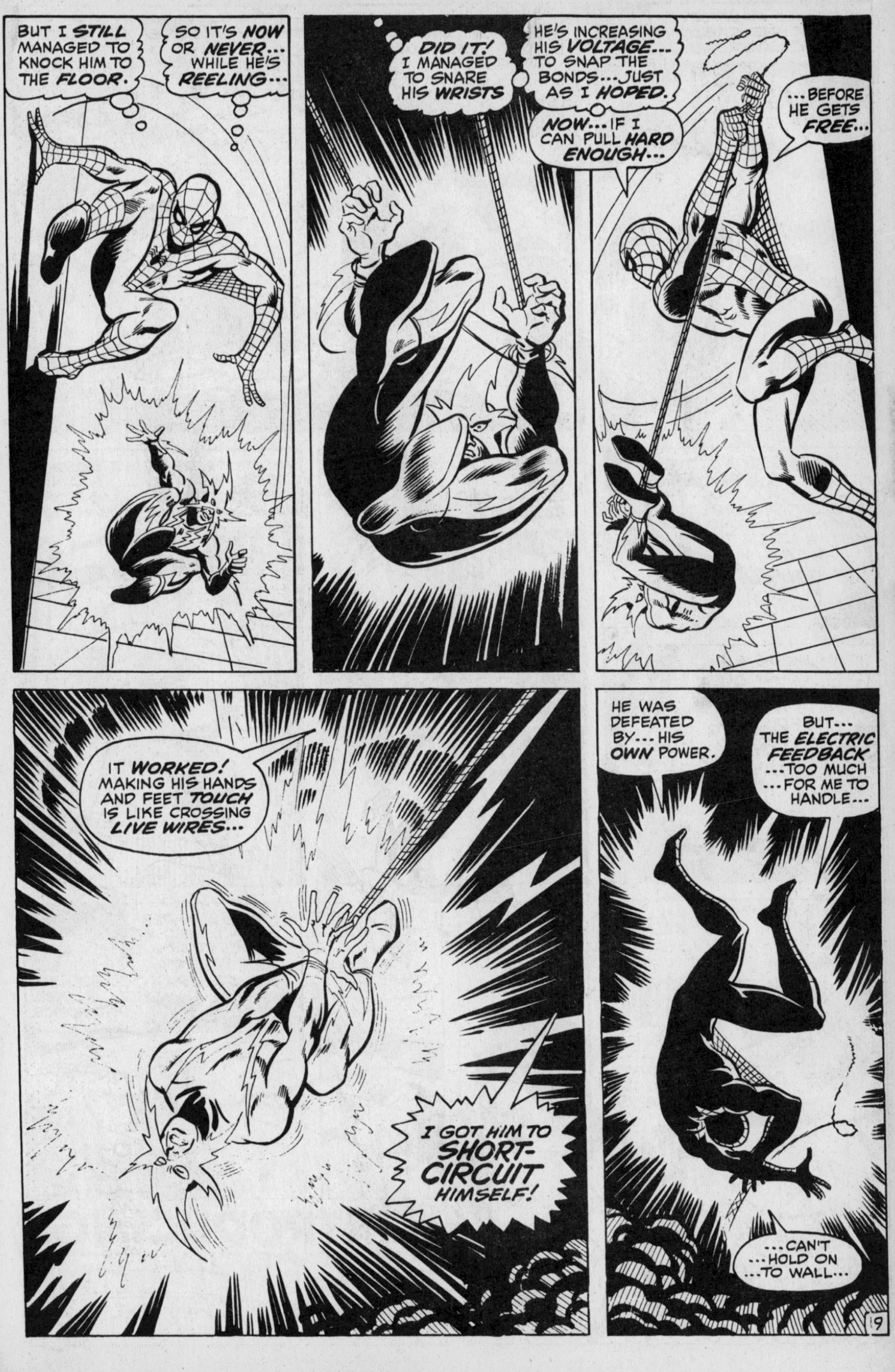

BUT I STILL MANAGED TO KNOCK HIM TO THE FLOOR.
SO IT'S NOW OR NEVER... WHILE HE'S REELING...
DID IT! I MANAGED TO SNARE HIS WRISTS
HE'S INCREASING HIS VOLTAGE... TO SNAP THE BONDS... JUST AS I HOPED.
NOW... IF I CAN PULL HARD ENOUGH...
...BEFORE HE GETS FREE...
IT WORKED! MAKING HIS HANDS AND FEET TOUCH IS LIKE CROSSING LIVE WIRES...
I GOT HIM TO SHORT-CIRCUIT HIMSELF!
HE WAS DEFEATED BY... HIS OWN POWER.
BUT... THE ELECTRIC FEEDBACK ...TOO MUCH ...FOR ME TO HANDLE...
...CAN'T ...HOLD ON ...TO WALL...

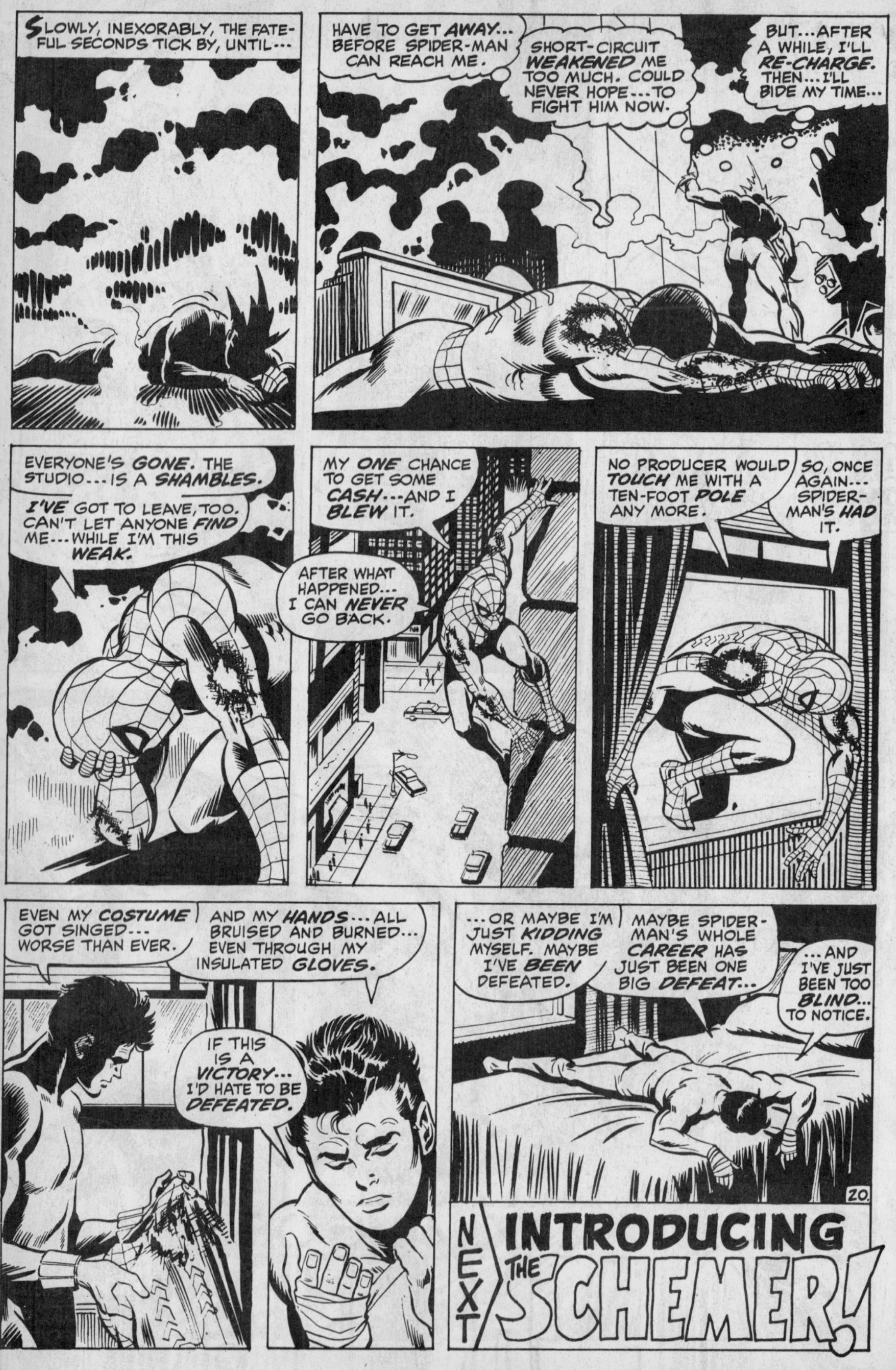
SLOWLY, INEXORABLY, THE FATE-FUL SECONDS TICK BY, UNTIL---
HAVE TO GET AWAY... BEFORE SPIDER-MAN CAN REACH ME.
SHORT-CIRCUIT WEAKENED ME TOO MUCH. COULD NEVER HOPE---TO FIGHT HIM NOW.
BUT...AFTER A WHILE, I'LL RE-CHARGE. THEN...I'LL BIDE MY TIME...
EVERYONE'S GONE. THE STUDIO---IS A SHAMBLES.
I'VE GOT TO LEAVE, TOO. CAN'T LET ANYONE FIND ME---WHILE I'M THIS WEAK.
MY ONE CHANCE TO GET SOME CASH---AND I BLEW IT.
AFTER WHAT HAPPENED... I CAN NEVER GO BACK.
NO PRODUCER WOULD TOUCH ME WITH A TEN-FOOT POLE ANY MORE.
SO, ONCE AGAIN--- SPIDER-MAN'S HAD IT.
EVEN MY COSTUME GOT SINGED--- WORSE THAN EVER.
AND MY HANDS...ALL BRUISED AND BURNED... EVEN THROUGH MY INSULATED GLOVES.
IF THIS IS A VICTORY... I'D HATE TO BE DEFEATED.
...OR MAYBE I'M JUST KIDDING MYSELF. MAYBE I'VE BEEN DEFEATED.
MAYBE SPIDER-MAN'S WHOLE CAREER HAS JUST BEEN ONE BIG DEFEAT...
...AND I'VE JUST BEEN TOO BLIND... TO NOTICE.
20.
NEXT
INTRODUCING THE SCHEMER!

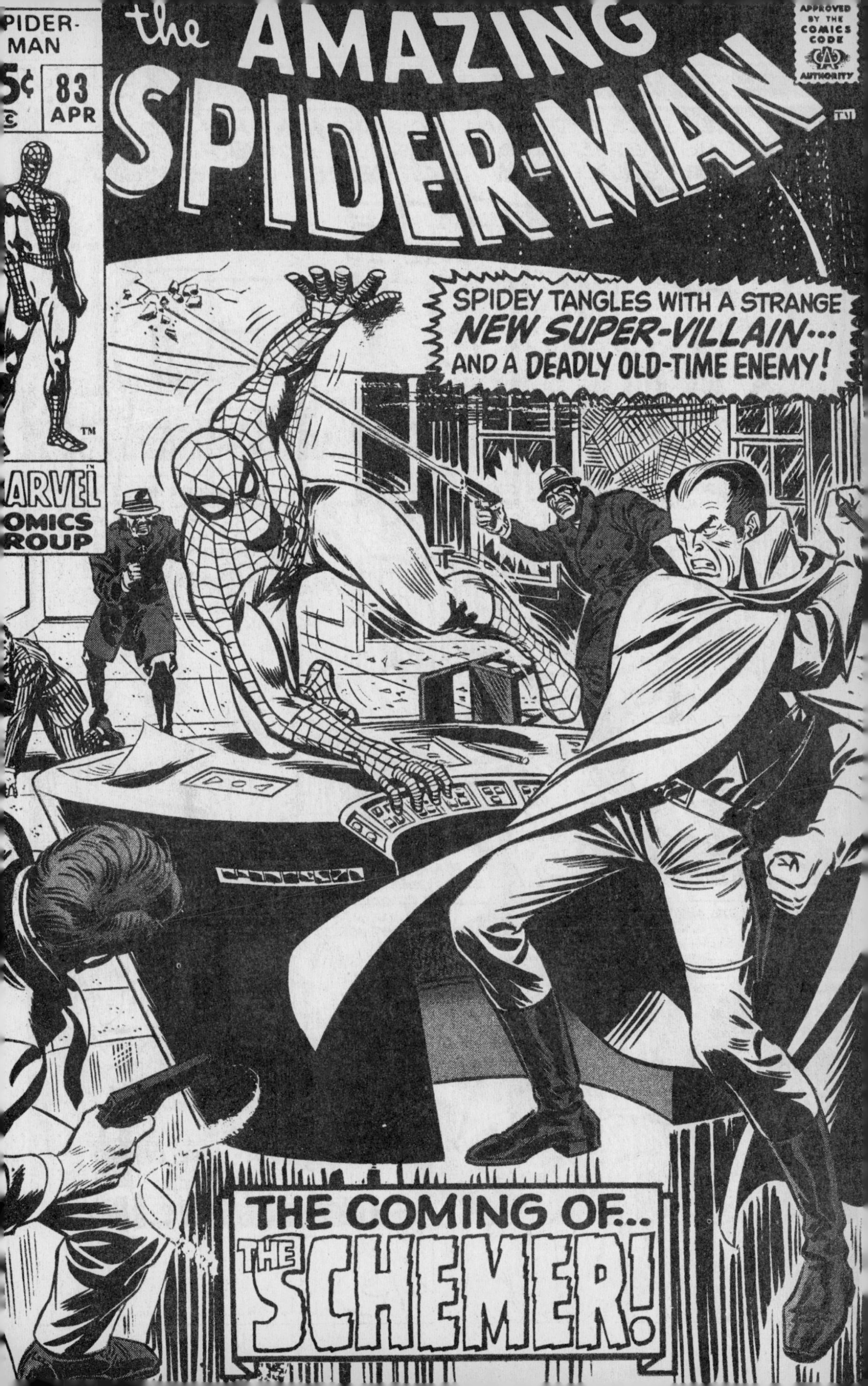

SPIDER-MAN
15¢
83
APR
the AMAZING SPIDER-MAN
APPROVED BY THE COMICS CODE AUTHORITY
MARVEL COMICS GROUP
SPIDEY TANGLES WITH A STRANGE NEW SUPER-VILLAIN... AND A DEADLY OLD-TIME ENEMY!
THE COMING OF... THE SCHEMER!

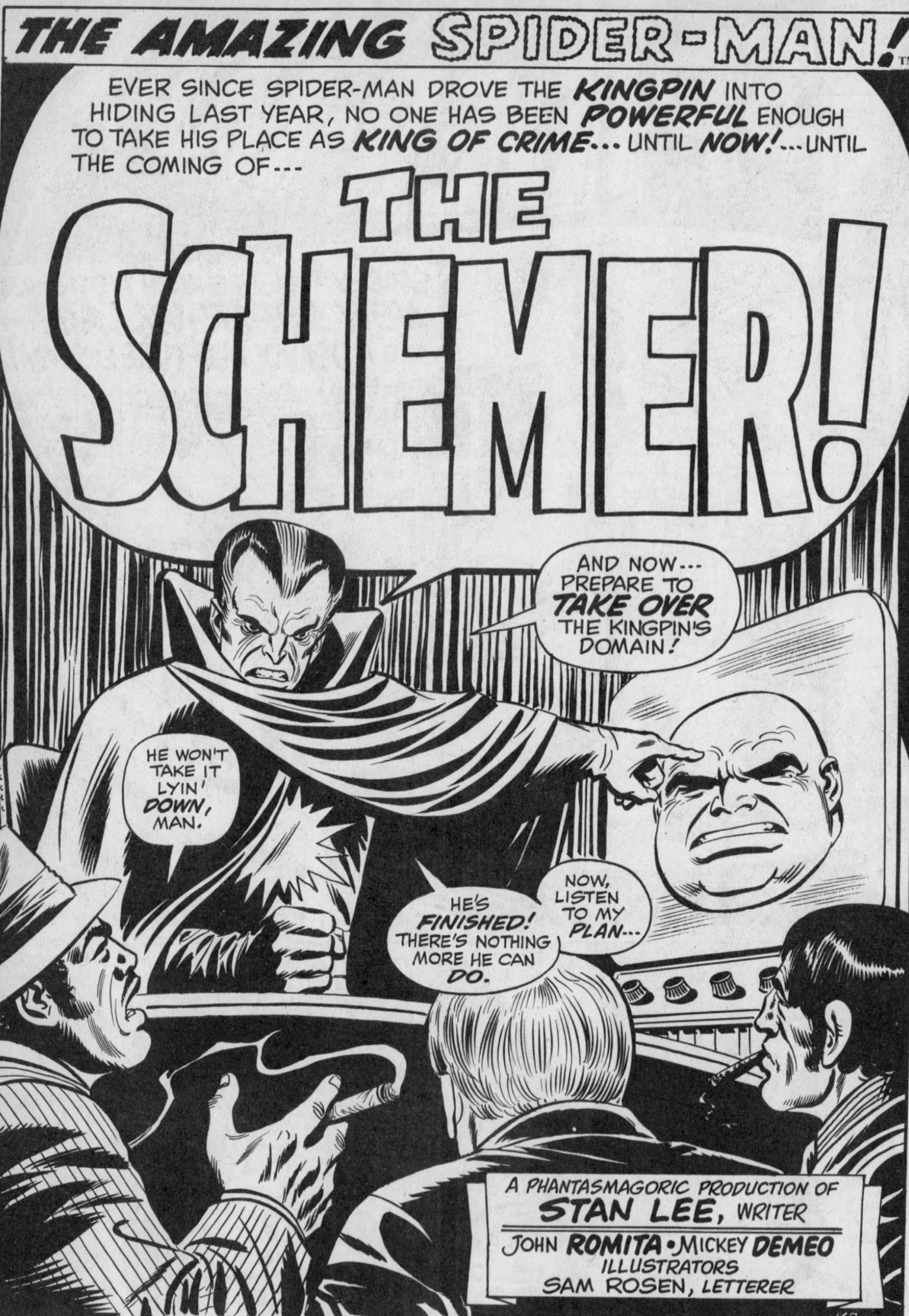
THE AMAZING SPIDER-MAN!™
EVER SINCE SPIDER-MAN DROVE THE KINGPIN INTO HIDING LAST YEAR, NO ONE HAS BEEN POWERFUL ENOUGH TO TAKE HIS PLACE AS KING OF CRIME... UNTIL NOW!... UNTIL THE COMING OF---
THE SCHEMER!
AND NOW--- PREPARE TO TAKE OVER THE KINGPIN'S DOMAIN!
HE WON'T TAKE IT LYIN' DOWN, MAN.
HE'S FINISHED! THERE'S NOTHING MORE HE CAN DO.
NOW, LISTEN TO MY PLAN...
A PHANTASMAGORIC PRODUCTION OF STAN LEE, WRITER
JOHN ROMITA • MICKEY DEMEO ILLUSTRATORS
SAM ROSEN, LETTERER

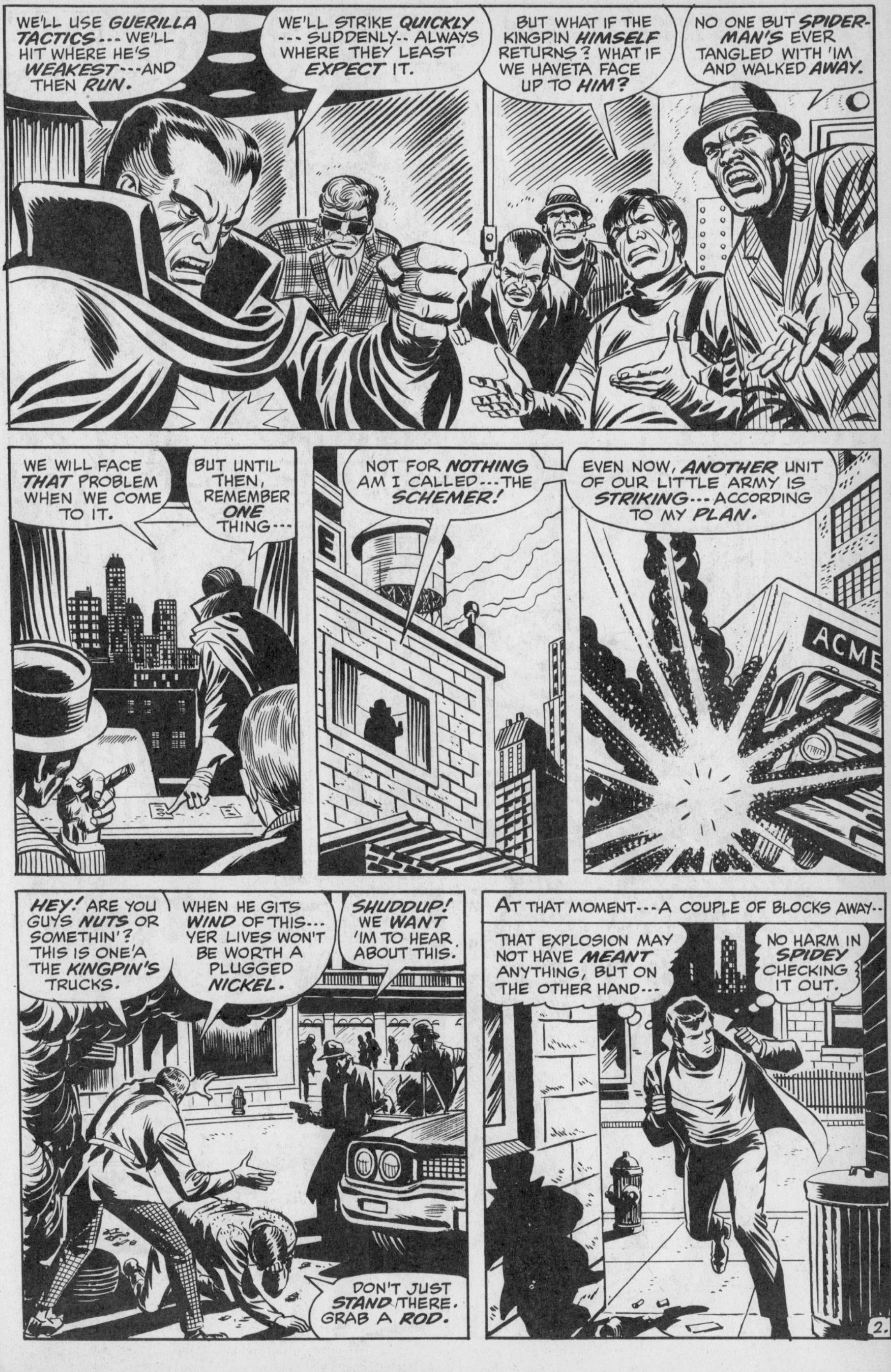
WE'LL USE GUERILLA TACTICS--- WE'LL HIT WHERE HE'S WEAKEST---AND THEN RUN.
WE'LL STRIKE QUICKLY --- SUDDENLY-- ALWAYS WHERE THEY LEAST EXPECT IT.
BUT WHAT IF THE KINGPIN HIMSELF RETURNS? WHAT IF WE HAVETA FACE UP TO HIM?
NO ONE BUT SPIDER-MAN'S EVER TANGLED WITH 'IM AND WALKED AWAY.
WE WILL FACE THAT PROBLEM WHEN WE COME TO IT.
BUT UNTIL THEN, REMEMBER ONE THING---
NOT FOR NOTHING AM I CALLED---THE SCHEMER!
EVEN NOW, ANOTHER UNIT OF OUR LITTLE ARMY IS STRIKING--- ACCORDING TO MY PLAN.
ACME
HEY! ARE YOU GUYS NUTS OR SOMETHIN'? THIS IS ONE'A THE KINGPIN'S TRUCKS.
WHEN HE GITS WIND OF THIS... YER LIVES WON'T BE WORTH A PLUGGED NICKEL.
SHUDDUP! WE WANT 'IM TO HEAR ABOUT THIS.
DON'T JUST STAND THERE. GRAB A ROD.
AT THAT MOMENT---A COUPLE OF BLOCKS AWAY--
THAT EXPLOSION MAY NOT HAVE MEANT ANYTHING, BUT ON THE OTHER HAND---
NO HARM IN SPIDEY CHECKING IT OUT.

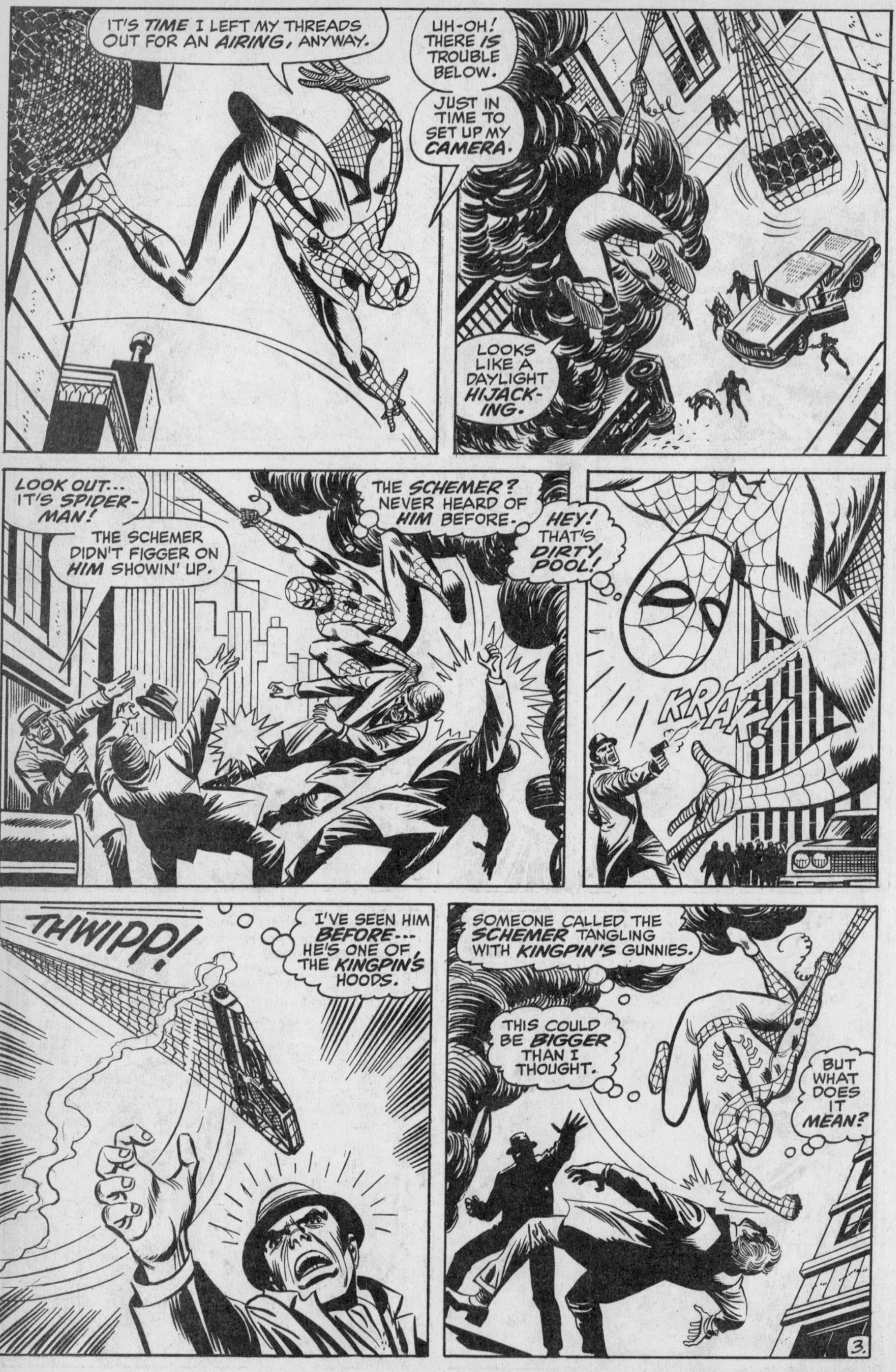
IT'S TIME I LEFT MY THREADS OUT FOR AN AIRING, ANYWAY.
UH-OH! THERE IS TROUBLE BELOW.
JUST IN TIME TO SET UP MY CAMERA.
LOOKS LIKE A DAYLIGHT HIJACKING.
LOOK OUT... IT'S SPIDER-MAN!
THE SCHEMER DIDN'T FIGGER ON HIM SHOWIN' UP.
THE SCHEMER? NEVER HEARD OF HIM BEFORE.
HEY! THAT'S DIRTY POOL!
KRAK!
THWIPP!
I'VE SEEN HIM BEFORE--- HE'S ONE OF THE KINGPIN'S HOODS.
SOMEONE CALLED THE SCHEMER TANGLING WITH KINGPIN'S GUNNIES.
THIS COULD BE BIGGER THAN I THOUGHT.
BUT WHAT DOES IT MEAN?
3.

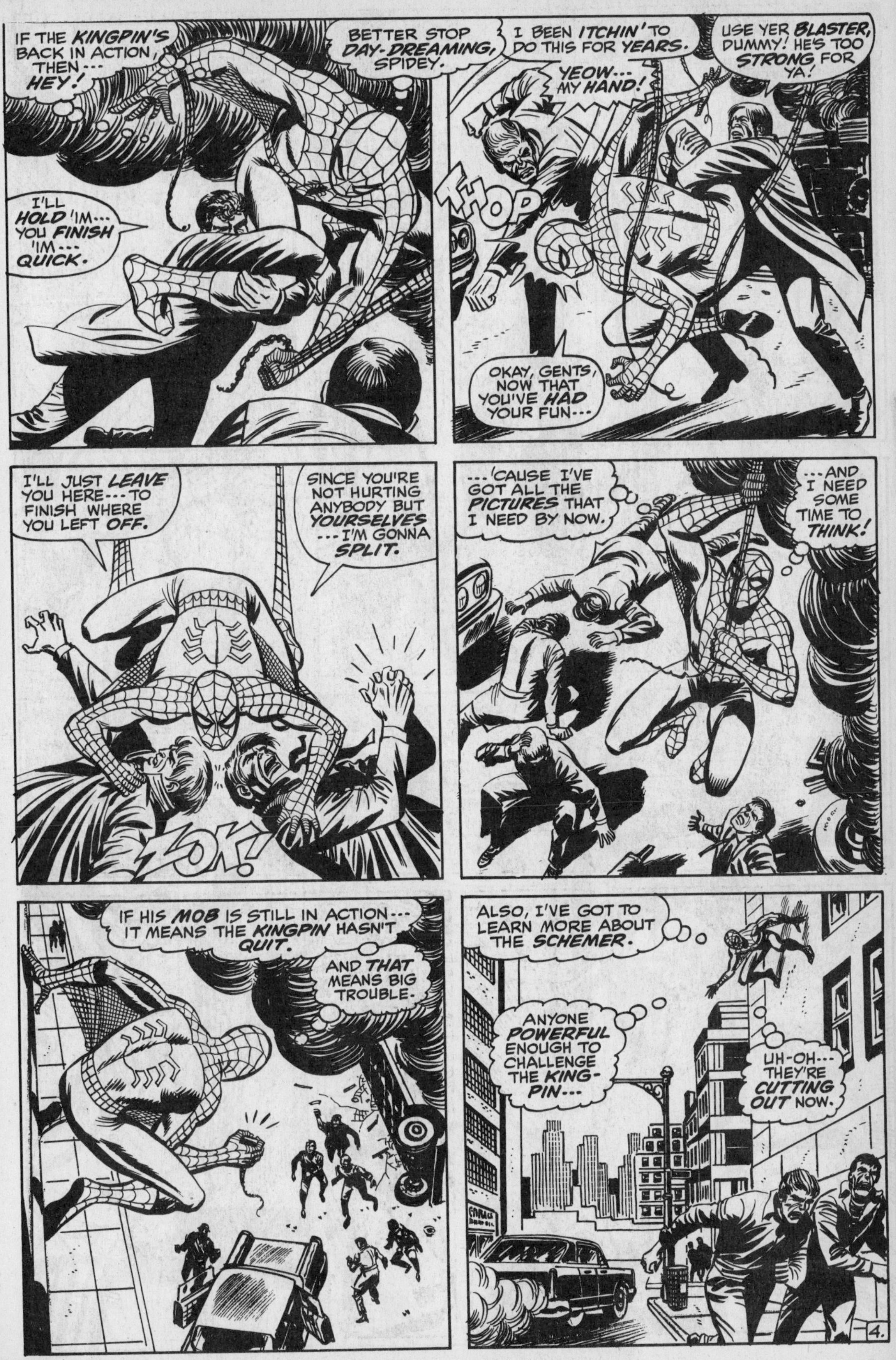
IF THE KINGPIN'S BACK IN ACTION, THEN--- HEY!
BETTER STOP DAY-DREAMING, SPIDEY.
I'LL HOLD 'IM... YOU FINISH 'IM... QUICK.
I BEEN ITCHIN' TO DO THIS FOR YEARS.
YEOW... MY HAND!
USE YER BLASTER, DUMMY! HE'S TOO STRONG FOR YA!
THOP
OKAY, GENTS, NOW THAT YOU'VE HAD YOUR FUN---
I'LL JUST LEAVE YOU HERE---TO FINISH WHERE YOU LEFT OFF.
SINCE YOU'RE NOT HURTING ANYBODY BUT YOURSELVES ---I'M GONNA SPLIT.
ZOK!
---'CAUSE I'VE GOT ALL THE PICTURES THAT I NEED BY NOW.
---AND I NEED SOME TIME TO THINK!
IF HIS MOB IS STILL IN ACTION--- IT MEANS THE KINGPIN HASN'T QUIT.
AND THAT MEANS BIG TROUBLE.
ALSO, I'VE GOT TO LEARN MORE ABOUT THE SCHEMER.
ANYONE POWERFUL ENOUGH TO CHALLENGE THE KING-PIN---
UH-OH--- THEY'RE CUTTING OUT NOW.
4.

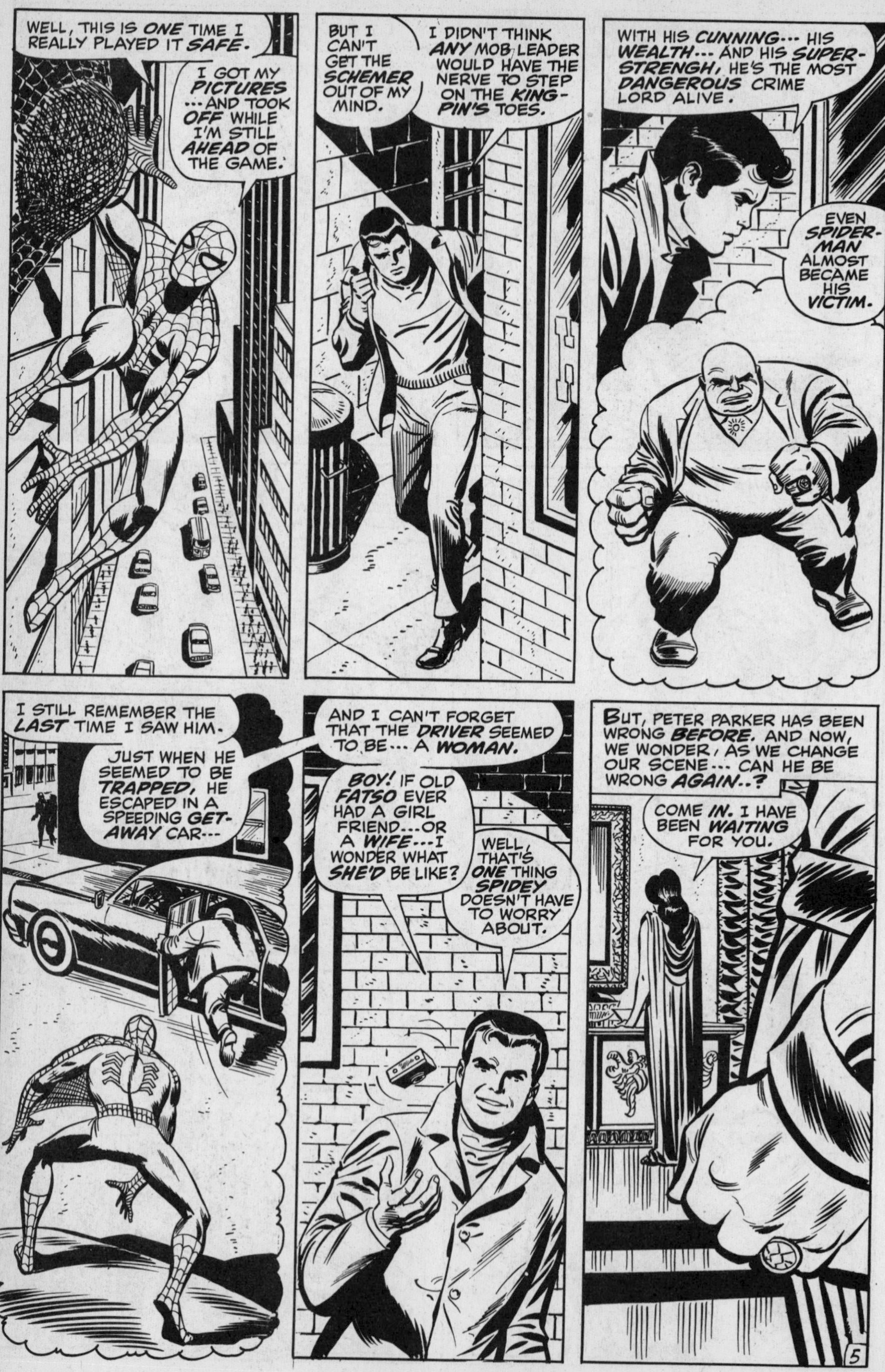
WELL, THIS IS ONE TIME I REALLY PLAYED IT SAFE.
I GOT MY PICTURES ...AND TOOK OFF WHILE I'M STILL AHEAD OF THE GAME.
BUT I CAN'T GET THE SCHEMER OUT OF MY MIND.
I DIDN'T THINK ANY MOB LEADER WOULD HAVE THE NERVE TO STEP ON THE KING-PIN'S TOES.
WITH HIS CUNNING... HIS WEALTH... AND HIS SUPER-STRENGH, HE'S THE MOST DANGEROUS CRIME LORD ALIVE.
EVEN SPIDER-MAN ALMOST BECAME HIS VICTIM.
I STILL REMEMBER THE LAST TIME I SAW HIM.
JUST WHEN HE SEEMED TO BE TRAPPED, HE ESCAPED IN A SPEEDING GET-AWAY CAR---
AND I CAN'T FORGET THAT THE DRIVER SEEMED TO BE... A WOMAN.
BOY! IF OLD FATSO EVER HAD A GIRL FRIEND...OR A WIFE...I WONDER WHAT SHE'D BE LIKE?
WELL, THAT'S ONE THING SPIDEY DOESN'T HAVE TO WORRY ABOUT.
BUT, PETER PARKER HAS BEEN WRONG BEFORE. AND NOW, WE WONDER, AS WE CHANGE OUR SCENE... CAN HE BE WRONG AGAIN..?
COME IN. I HAVE BEEN WAITING FOR YOU.
5

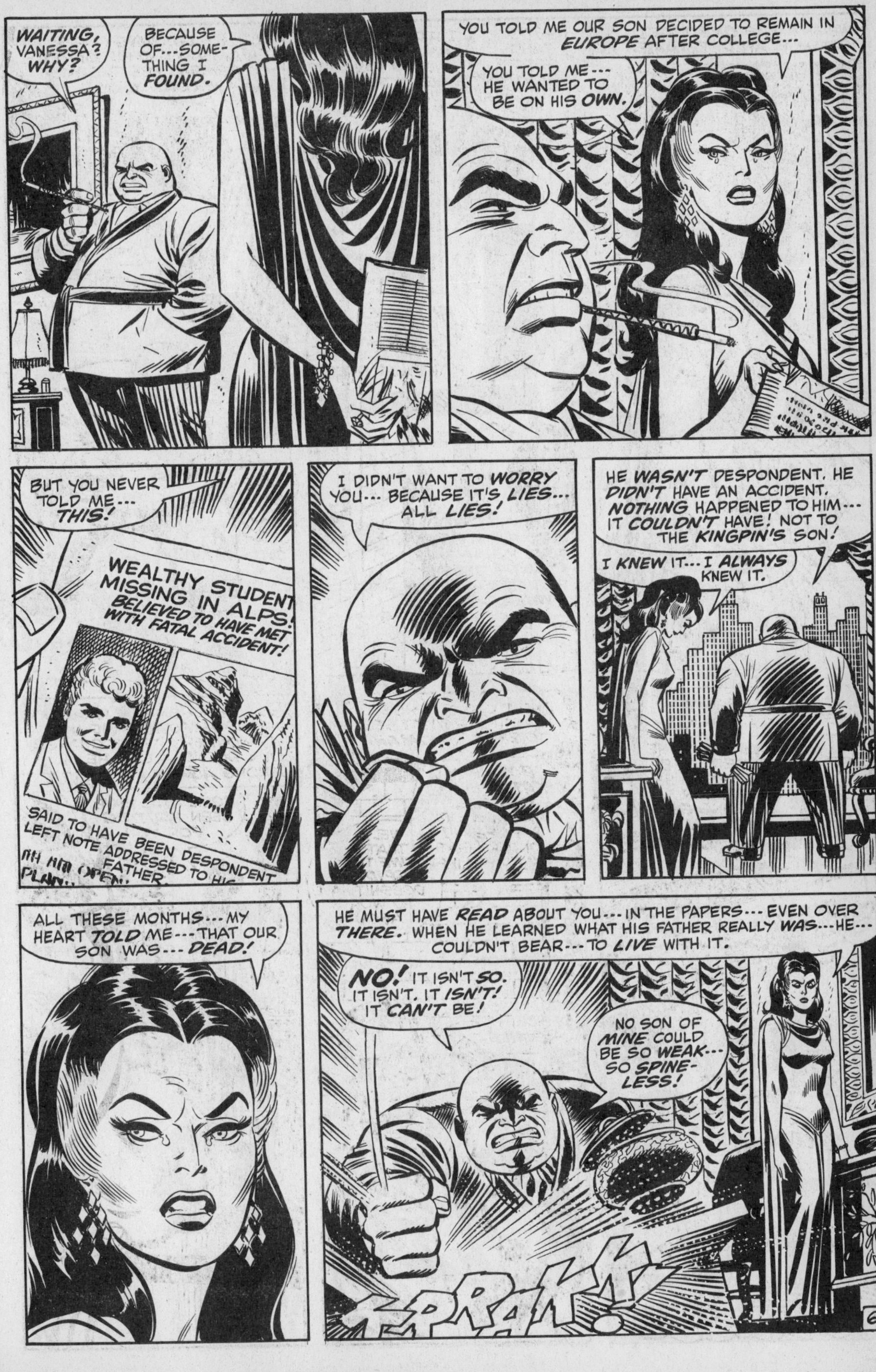

WAITING, VANESSA? WHY?
BECAUSE OF---SOME-THING I FOUND.
YOU TOLD ME OUR SON DECIDED TO REMAIN IN EUROPE AFTER COLLEGE---
YOU TOLD ME--- HE WANTED TO BE ON HIS OWN.
BUT YOU NEVER TOLD ME--- THIS!
WEALTHY STUDENT MISSING IN ALPS! BELIEVED TO HAVE MET WITH FATAL ACCIDENT!
SAID TO HAVE BEEN DESPONDENT LEFT NOTE ADDRESSED TO HIS FATHER
I DIDN'T WANT TO WORRY YOU--- BECAUSE IT'S LIES... ALL LIES!
HE WASN'T DESPONDENT. HE DIDN'T HAVE AN ACCIDENT. NOTHING HAPPENED TO HIM--- IT COULDN'T HAVE! NOT TO THE KINGPIN'S SON!
I KNEW IT... I ALWAYS KNEW IT.
ALL THESE MONTHS--- MY HEART TOLD ME---THAT OUR SON WAS--- DEAD!
HE MUST HAVE READ ABOUT YOU--- IN THE PAPERS--- EVEN OVER THERE. WHEN HE LEARNED WHAT HIS FATHER REALLY WAS---HE--- COULDN'T BEAR--- TO LIVE WITH IT.
NO! IT ISN'T SO. IT ISN'T. IT ISN'T! IT CAN'T BE!
NO SON OF MINE COULD BE SO WEAK--- SO SPINE-LESS!
KRAKK!
6

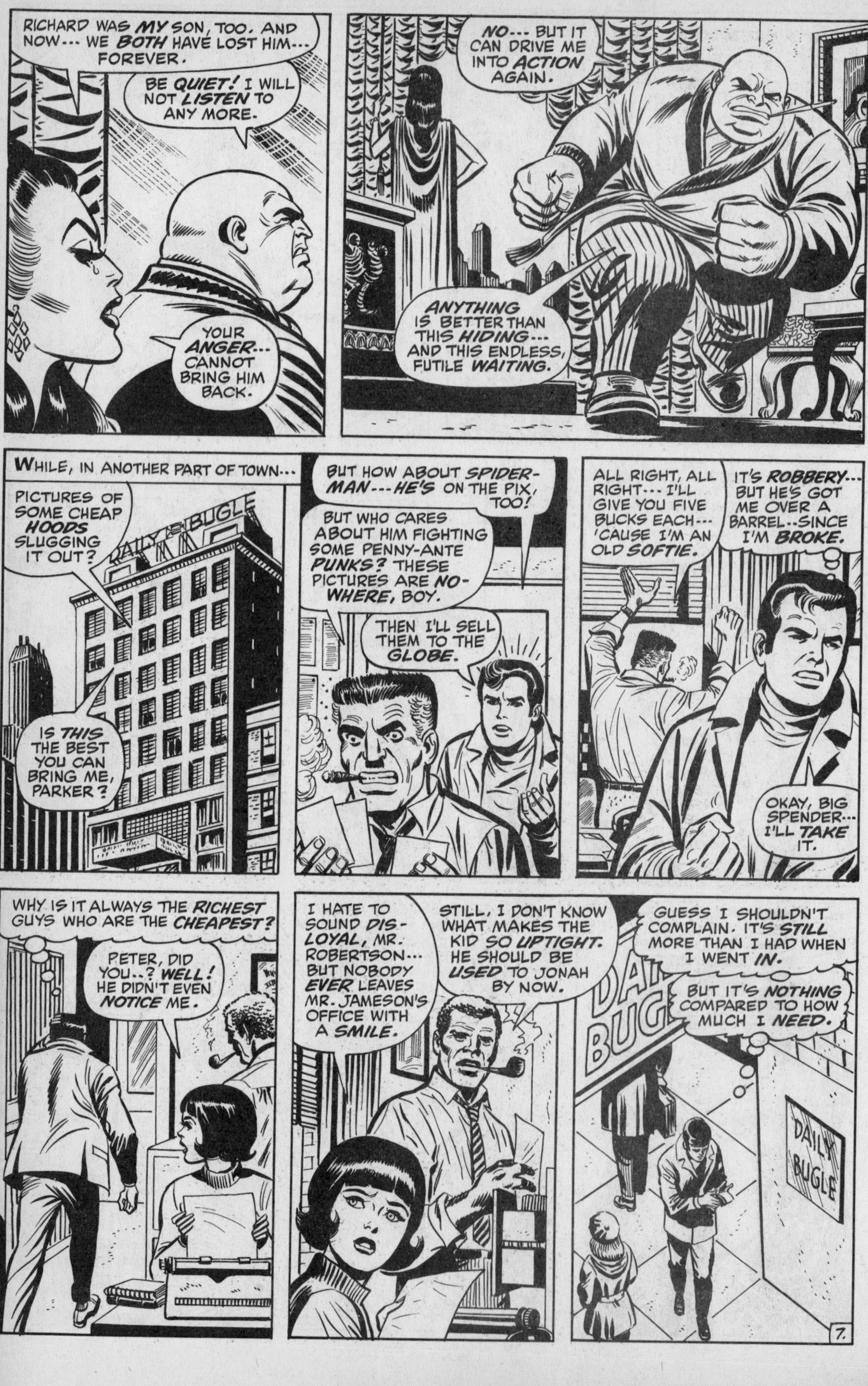
RICHARD WAS MY SON, TOO. AND NOW--- WE BOTH HAVE LOST HIM--- FOREVER.
BE QUIET! I WILL NOT LISTEN TO ANY MORE.
YOUR ANGER--- CANNOT BRING HIM BACK.
NO--- BUT IT CAN DRIVE ME INTO ACTION AGAIN.
ANYTHING IS BETTER THAN THIS HIDING--- AND THIS ENDLESS, FUTILE WAITING.
WHILE, IN ANOTHER PART OF TOWN---
PICTURES OF SOME CHEAP HOODS SLUGGING IT OUT?
IS THIS THE BEST YOU CAN BRING ME, PARKER?
BUT HOW ABOUT SPIDER-MAN---HE'S ON THE PIX, TOO!
BUT WHO CARES ABOUT HIM FIGHTING SOME PENNY-ANTE PUNKS? THESE PICTURES ARE NO-WHERE, BOY.
THEN I'LL SELL THEM TO THE GLOBE.
ALL RIGHT, ALL RIGHT--- I'LL GIVE YOU FIVE BUCKS EACH--- 'CAUSE I'M AN OLD SOFTIE.
IT'S ROBBERY--- BUT HE'S GOT ME OVER A BARREL--SINCE I'M BROKE.
OKAY, BIG SPENDER--- I'LL TAKE IT.
WHY IS IT ALWAYS THE RICHEST GUYS WHO ARE THE CHEAPEST?
PETER, DID YOU--? WELL! HE DIDN'T EVEN NOTICE ME.
I HATE TO SOUND DIS-LOYAL, MR. ROBERTSON--- BUT NOBODY EVER LEAVES MR. JAMESON'S OFFICE WITH A SMILE.
STILL, I DON'T KNOW WHAT MAKES THE KID SO UPTIGHT. HE SHOULD BE USED TO JONAH BY NOW.
GUESS I SHOULDN'T COMPLAIN. IT'S STILL MORE THAN I HAD WHEN I WENT IN.
BUT IT'S NOTHING COMPARED TO HOW MUCH I NEED.
DAILY BUGLE
7.

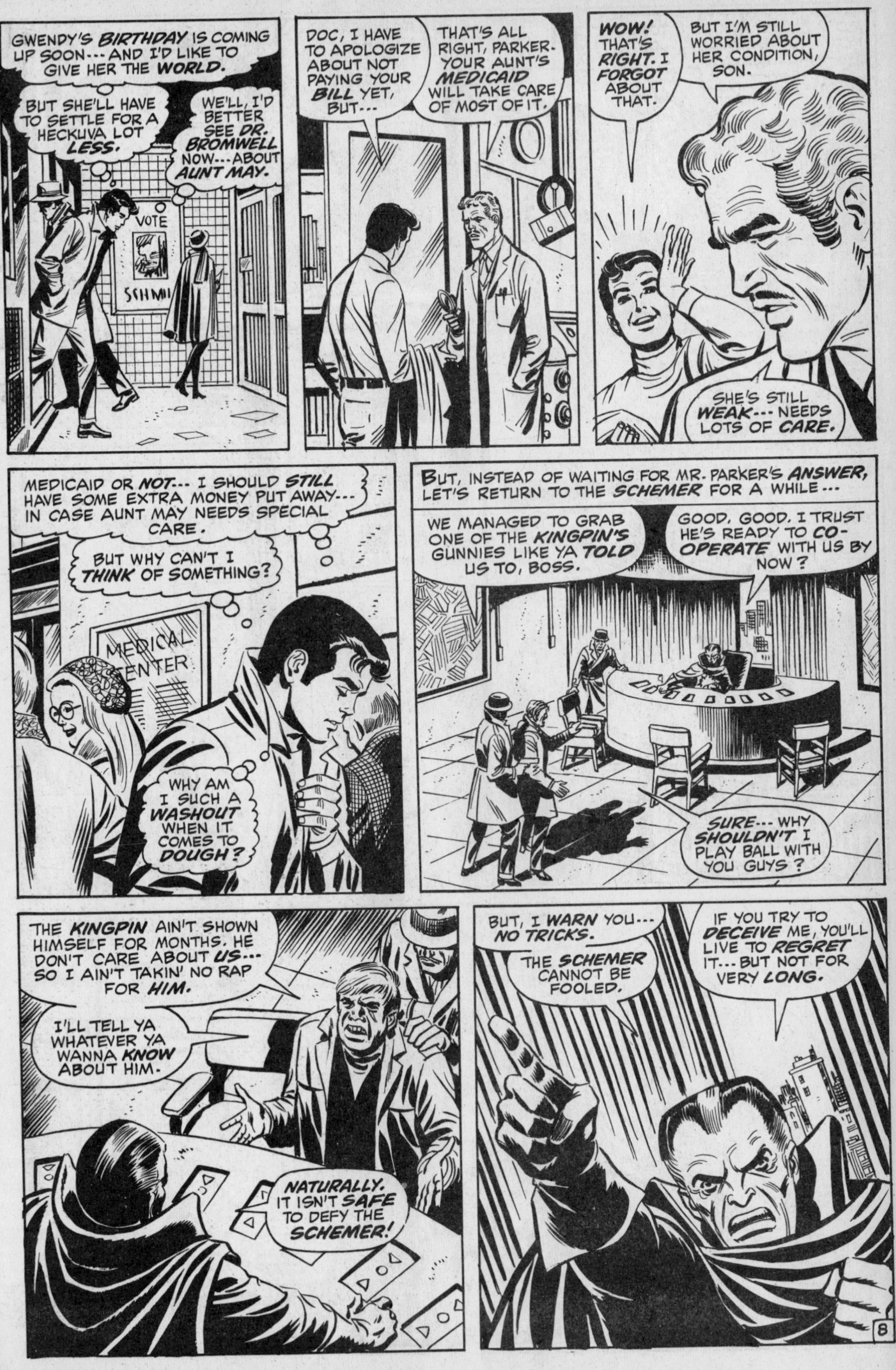
GWENDY'S BIRTHDAY IS COMING UP SOON--- AND I'D LIKE TO GIVE HER THE WORLD.
BUT SHE'LL HAVE TO SETTLE FOR A HECKUVA LOT LESS.
WE'LL, I'D BETTER SEE DR. BROMWELL NOW--- ABOUT AUNT MAY.
VOTE
SCHMI
DOC, I HAVE TO APOLOGIZE ABOUT NOT PAYING YOUR BILL YET, BUT---
THAT'S ALL RIGHT, PARKER-YOUR AUNT'S MEDICAID WILL TAKE CARE OF MOST OF IT.
WOW! THAT'S RIGHT. I FORGOT ABOUT THAT.
BUT I'M STILL WORRIED ABOUT HER CONDITION, SON.
SHE'S STILL WEAK--- NEEDS LOTS OF CARE.
MEDICAID OR NOT--- I SHOULD STILL HAVE SOME EXTRA MONEY PUT AWAY--- IN CASE AUNT MAY NEEDS SPECIAL CARE.
BUT WHY CAN'T I THINK OF SOMETHING?
MEDICAL CENTER
WHY AM I SUCH A WASHOUT WHEN IT COMES TO DOUGH?
BUT, INSTEAD OF WAITING FOR MR. PARKER'S ANSWER, LET'S RETURN TO THE SCHEMER FOR A WHILE---
WE MANAGED TO GRAB ONE OF THE KINGPIN'S GUNNIES LIKE YA TOLD US TO, BOSS.
GOOD, GOOD. I TRUST HE'S READY TO CO-OPERATE WITH US BY NOW?
SURE--- WHY SHOULDN'T I PLAY BALL WITH YOU GUYS?
THE KINGPIN AIN'T SHOWN HIMSELF FOR MONTHS. HE DON'T CARE ABOUT US--- SO I AIN'T TAKIN' NO RAP FOR HIM.
I'LL TELL YA WHATEVER YA WANNA KNOW ABOUT HIM.
NATURALLY. IT ISN'T SAFE TO DEFY THE SCHEMER!
BUT, I WARN YOU--- NO TRICKS.
THE SCHEMER CANNOT BE FOOLED.
IF YOU TRY TO DECEIVE ME, YOU'LL LIVE TO REGRET IT--- BUT NOT FOR VERY LONG.
8

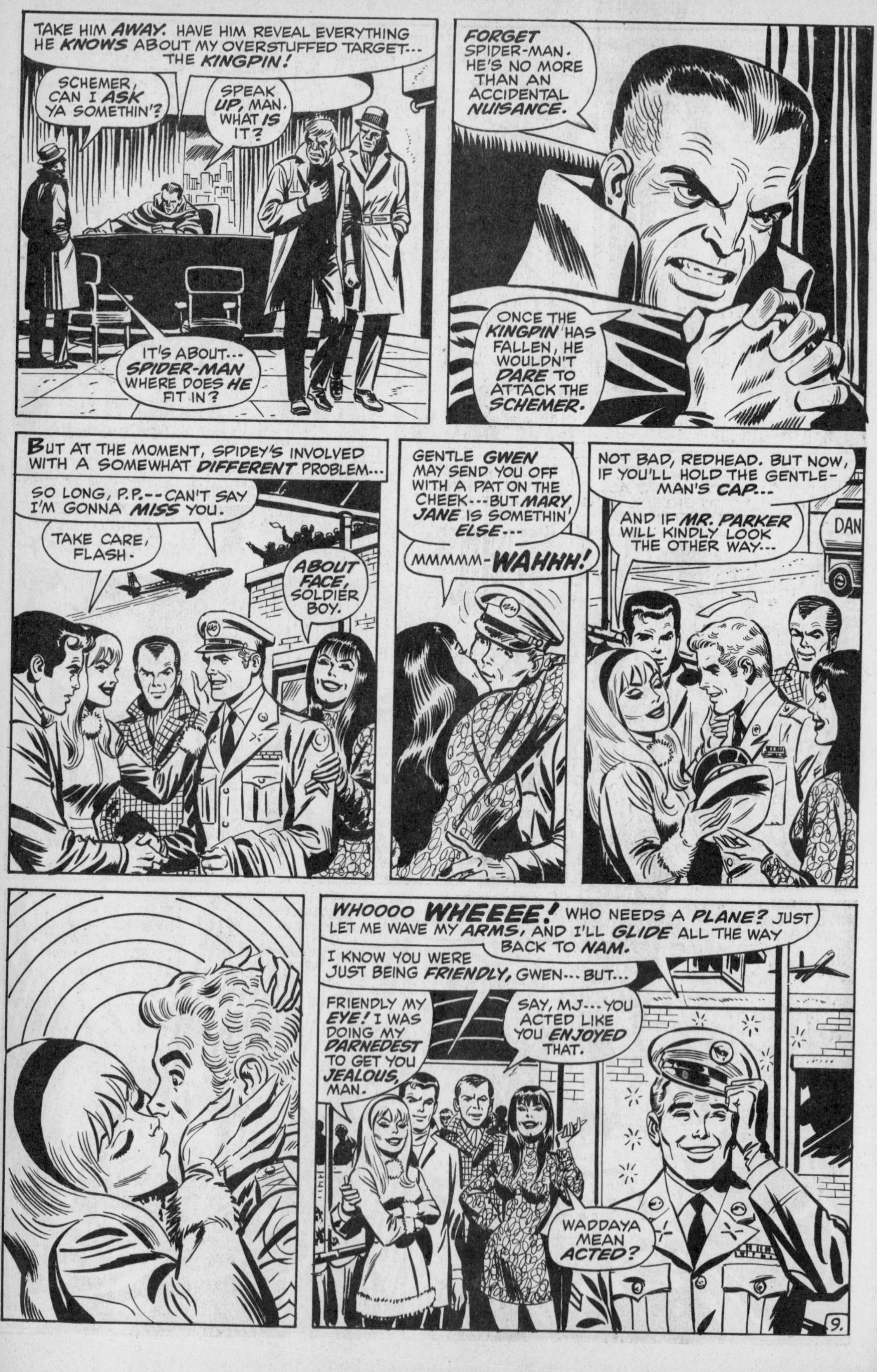

TAKE HIM AWAY. HAVE HIM REVEAL EVERYTHING HE KNOWS ABOUT MY OVERSTUFFED TARGET--- THE KINGPIN!
SCHEMER, CAN I ASK YA SOMETHIN'?
SPEAK UP, MAN. WHAT IS IT?
IT'S ABOUT--- SPIDER-MAN WHERE DOES HE FIT IN?
FORGET SPIDER-MAN. HE'S NO MORE THAN AN ACCIDENTAL NUISANCE.
ONCE THE KINGPIN HAS FALLEN, HE WOULDN'T DARE TO ATTACK THE SCHEMER.
BUT AT THE MOMENT, SPIDEY'S INVOLVED WITH A SOMEWHAT DIFFERENT PROBLEM...
SO LONG, P.P.--CAN'T SAY I'M GONNA MISS YOU.
TAKE CARE, FLASH.
ABOUT FACE, SOLDIER BOY.
GENTLE GWEN MAY SEND YOU OFF WITH A PAT ON THE CHEEK---BUT MARY JANE IS SOMETHIN' ELSE---
MMMMM-WAHHH!
NOT BAD, REDHEAD. BUT NOW, IF YOU'LL HOLD THE GENTLE-MAN'S CAP...
AND IF MR. PARKER WILL KINDLY LOOK THE OTHER WAY---
WHOOOO WHEEEE! WHO NEEDS A PLANE? JUST LET ME WAVE MY ARMS, AND I'LL GLIDE ALL THE WAY BACK TO NAM.
I KNOW YOU WERE JUST BEING FRIENDLY, GWEN--- BUT...
FRIENDLY MY EYE! I WAS DOING MY DARNEDEST TO GET YOU JEALOUS, MAN.
SAY, MJ--- YOU ACTED LIKE YOU ENJOYED THAT.
WADDAYA MEAN ACTED?

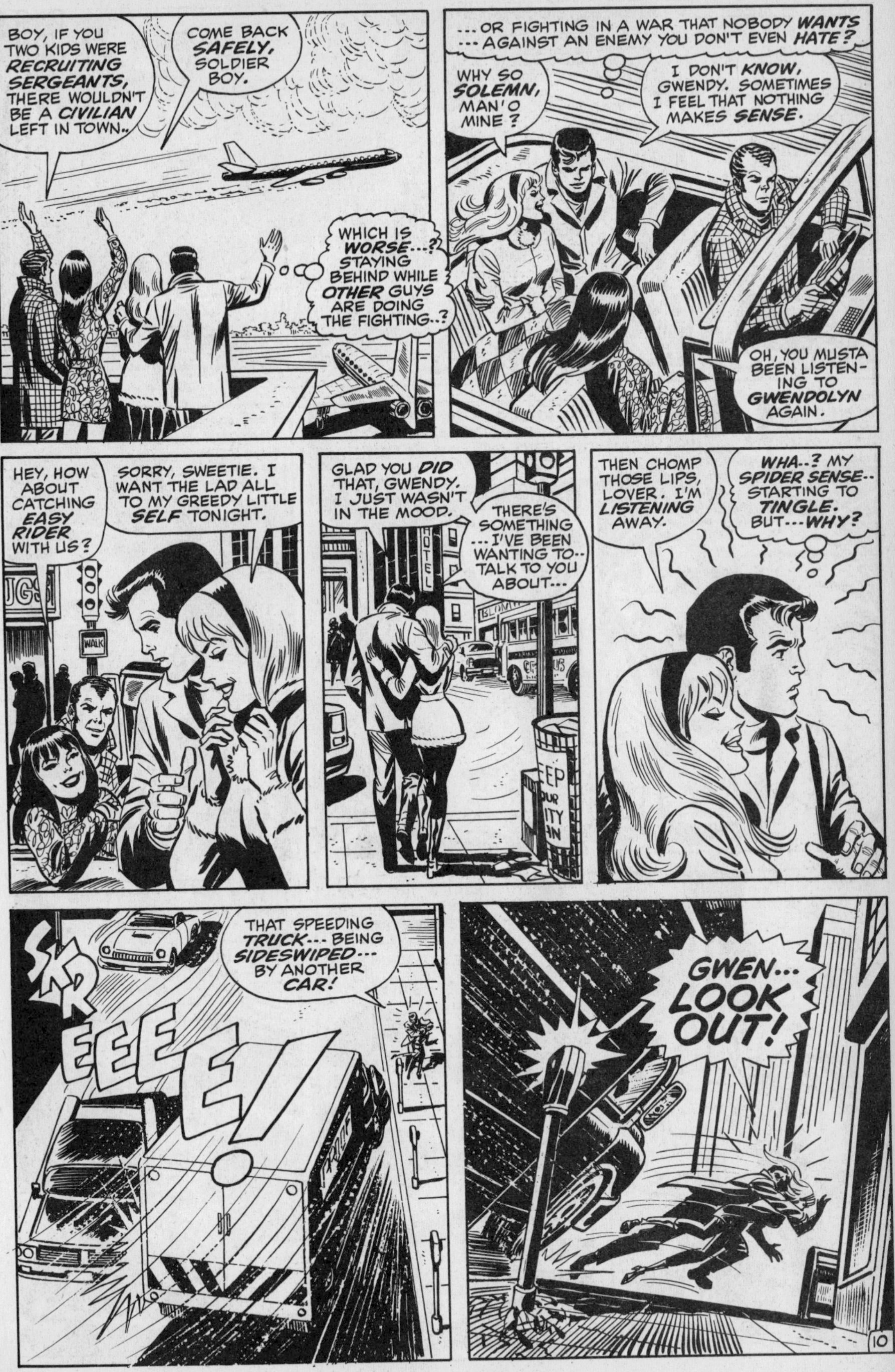
BOY, IF YOU TWO KIDS WERE RECRUITING SERGEANTS, THERE WOULDN'T BE A CIVILIAN LEFT IN TOWN..
COME BACK SAFELY, SOLDIER BOY.
WHICH IS WORSE...? STAYING BEHIND WHILE OTHER GUYS ARE DOING THE FIGHTING..?
...OR FIGHTING IN A WAR THAT NOBODY WANTS ---AGAINST AN ENEMY YOU DON'T EVEN HATE?
WHY SO SOLEMN, MAN'O MINE?
I DON'T KNOW, GWENDY. SOMETIMES I FEEL THAT NOTHING MAKES SENSE.
OH, YOU MUSTA BEEN LISTEN-ING TO GWENDOLYN AGAIN.
HEY, HOW ABOUT CATCHING EASY RIDER WITH US?
SORRY, SWEETIE. I WANT THE LAD ALL TO MY GREEDY LITTLE SELF TONIGHT.
WALK
GLAD YOU DID THAT, GWENDY. I JUST WASN'T IN THE MOOD.
THERE'S SOMETHING ...I'VE BEEN WANTING TO.. TALK TO YOU ABOUT...
HOTEL
THEN CHOMP THOSE LIPS, LOVER. I'M LISTENING AWAY.
WHA..? MY SPIDER SENSE.. STARTING TO TINGLE. BUT---WHY?
SKREEEEE!
THAT SPEEDING TRUCK--- BEING SIDESWIPED--- BY ANOTHER CAR!
GWEN... LOOK OUT!

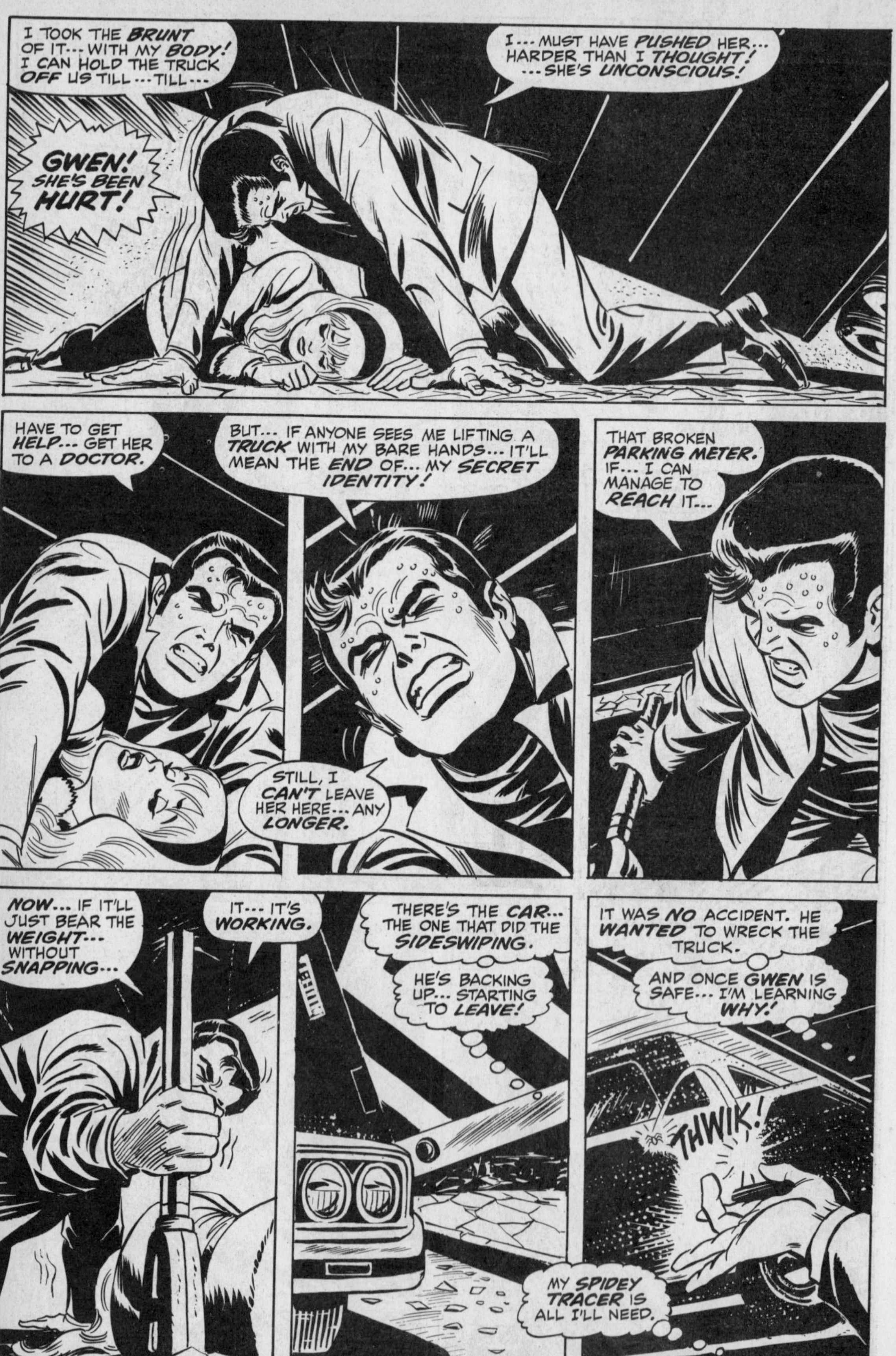

I TOOK THE BRUNT OF IT--- WITH MY BODY! I CAN HOLD THE TRUCK OFF US TILL --- TILL ---
GWEN! SHE'S BEEN HURT!
I --- MUST HAVE PUSHED HER... HARDER THAN I THOUGHT! --- SHE'S UNCONSCIOUS!
HAVE TO GET HELP... GET HER TO A DOCTOR.
BUT... IF ANYONE SEES ME LIFTING A TRUCK WITH MY BARE HANDS... IT'LL MEAN THE END OF... MY SECRET IDENTITY!
STILL, I CAN'T LEAVE HER HERE... ANY LONGER.
THAT BROKEN PARKING METER. IF... I CAN MANAGE TO REACH IT...
NOW... IF IT'LL JUST BEAR THE WEIGHT... WITHOUT SNAPPING...
IT--- IT'S WORKING.
THERE'S THE CAR... THE ONE THAT DID THE SIDESWIPING.
HE'S BACKING UP... STARTING TO LEAVE!
IT WAS NO ACCIDENT. HE WANTED TO WRECK THE TRUCK.
AND ONCE GWEN IS SAFE... I'M LEARNING WHY!
THWIK!
MY SPIDEY TRACER IS ALL I'LL NEED.

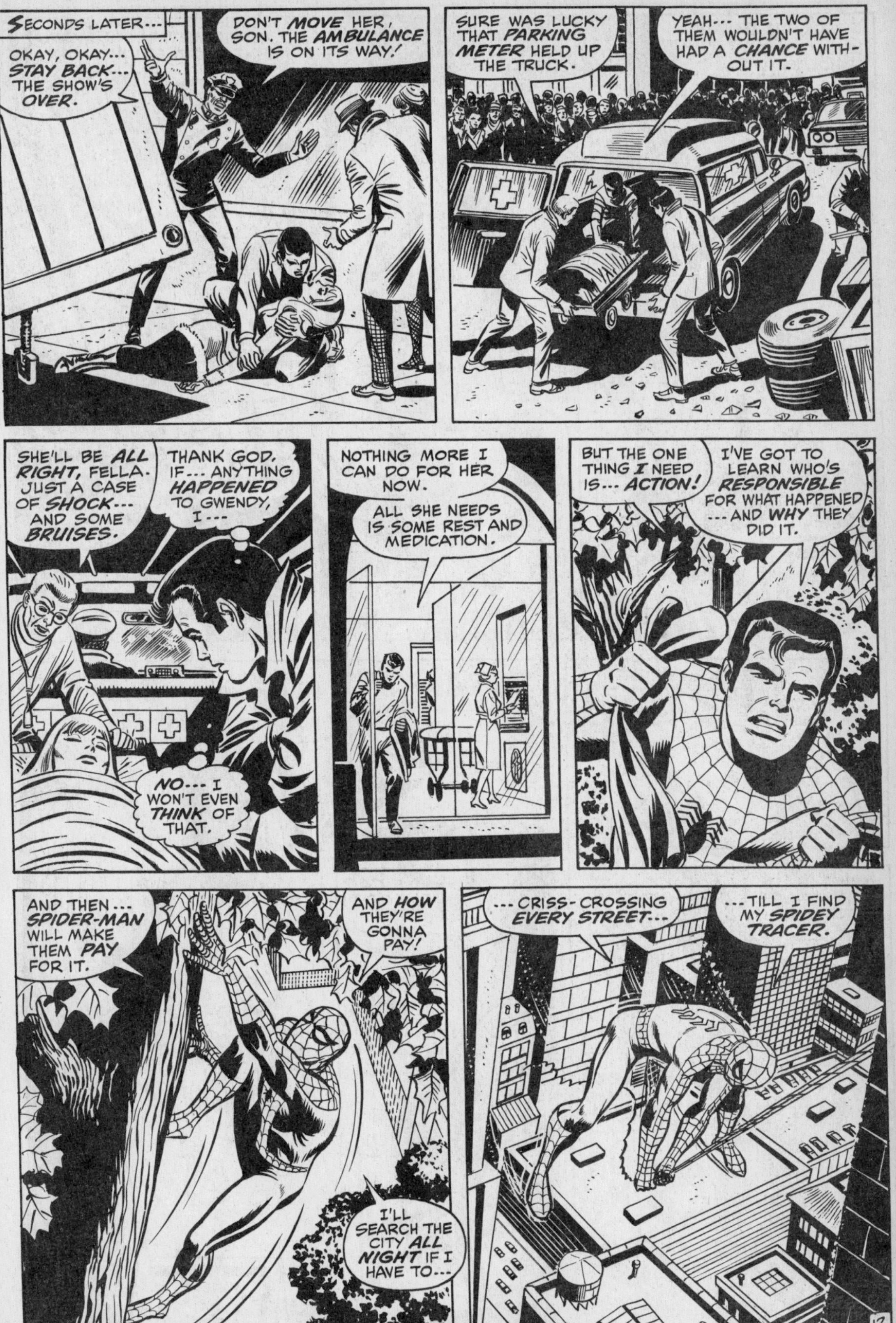
SECONDS LATER...
DON'T MOVE HER, SON. THE AMBULANCE IS ON ITS WAY!
OKAY, OKAY... STAY BACK... THE SHOW'S OVER.
SURE WAS LUCKY THAT PARKING METER HELD UP THE TRUCK.
YEAH--- THE TWO OF THEM WOULDN'T HAVE HAD A CHANCE WITH-OUT IT.
SHE'LL BE ALL RIGHT, FELLA. JUST A CASE OF SHOCK--- AND SOME BRUISES.
THANK GOD. IF--- ANYTHING HAPPENED TO GWENDY, I---
NO--- I WON'T EVEN THINK OF THAT.
NOTHING MORE I CAN DO FOR HER NOW.
ALL SHE NEEDS IS SOME REST AND MEDICATION.
BUT THE ONE THING I NEED IS--- ACTION!
I'VE GOT TO LEARN WHO'S RESPONSIBLE FOR WHAT HAPPENED ---AND WHY THEY DID IT.
AND THEN... SPIDER-MAN WILL MAKE THEM PAY FOR IT.
AND HOW THEY'RE GONNA PAY!
I'LL SEARCH THE CITY ALL NIGHT IF I HAVE TO---
---CRISS-CROSSING EVERY STREET---
---TILL I FIND MY SPIDEY TRACER.
12

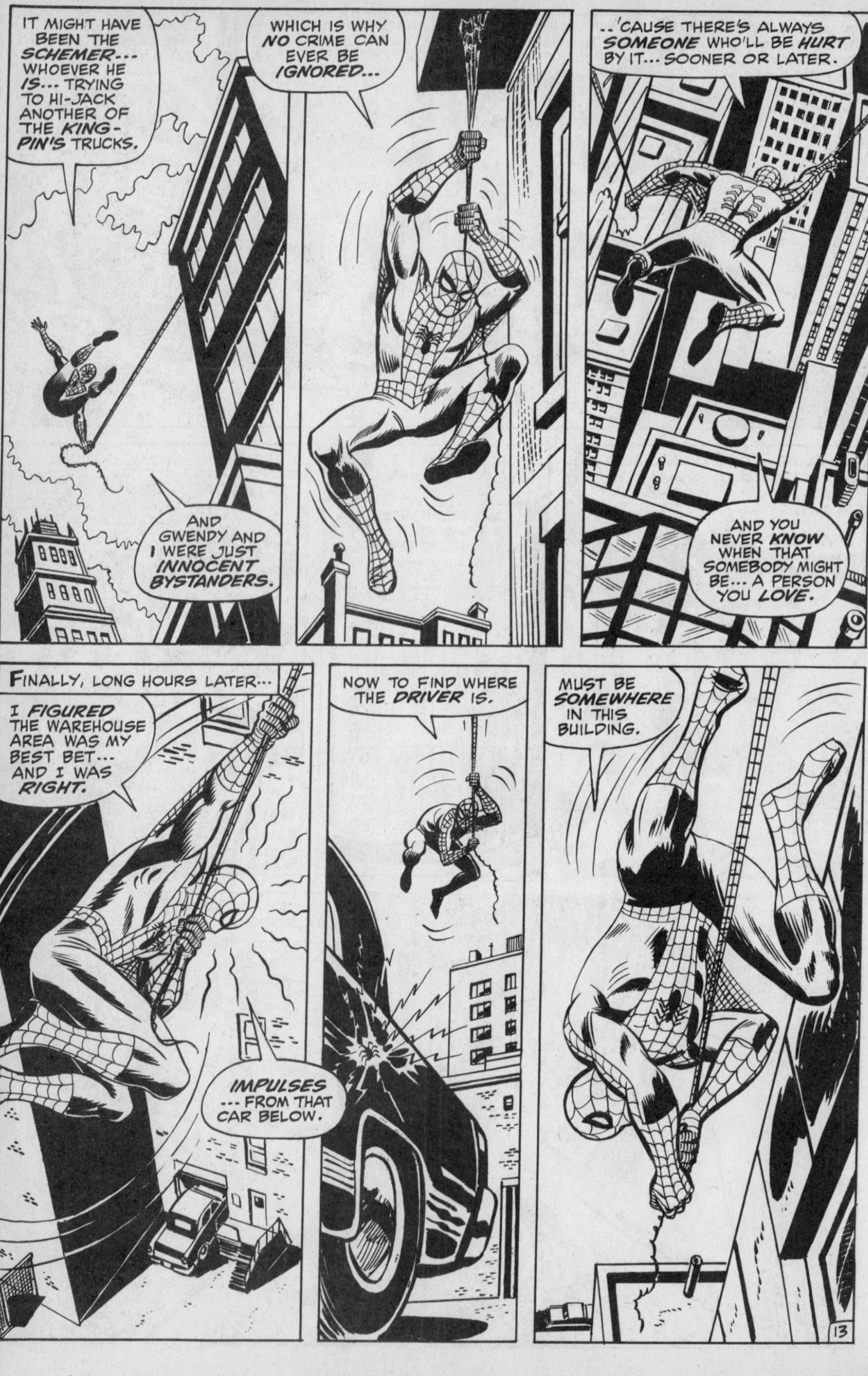
IT MIGHT HAVE BEEN THE SCHEMER... WHOEVER HE IS... TRYING TO HI-JACK ANOTHER OF THE KING-PIN'S TRUCKS.
AND GWENDY AND I WERE JUST INNOCENT BYSTANDERS.
WHICH IS WHY NO CRIME CAN EVER BE IGNORED...
..'CAUSE THERE'S ALWAYS SOMEONE WHO'LL BE HURT BY IT... SOONER OR LATER.
AND YOU NEVER KNOW WHEN THAT SOMEBODY MIGHT BE... A PERSON YOU LOVE.
FINALLY, LONG HOURS LATER...
I FIGURED THE WAREHOUSE AREA WAS MY BEST BET... AND I WAS RIGHT.
IMPULSES ... FROM THAT CAR BELOW.
NOW TO FIND WHERE THE DRIVER IS.
MUST BE SOMEWHERE IN THIS BUILDING.

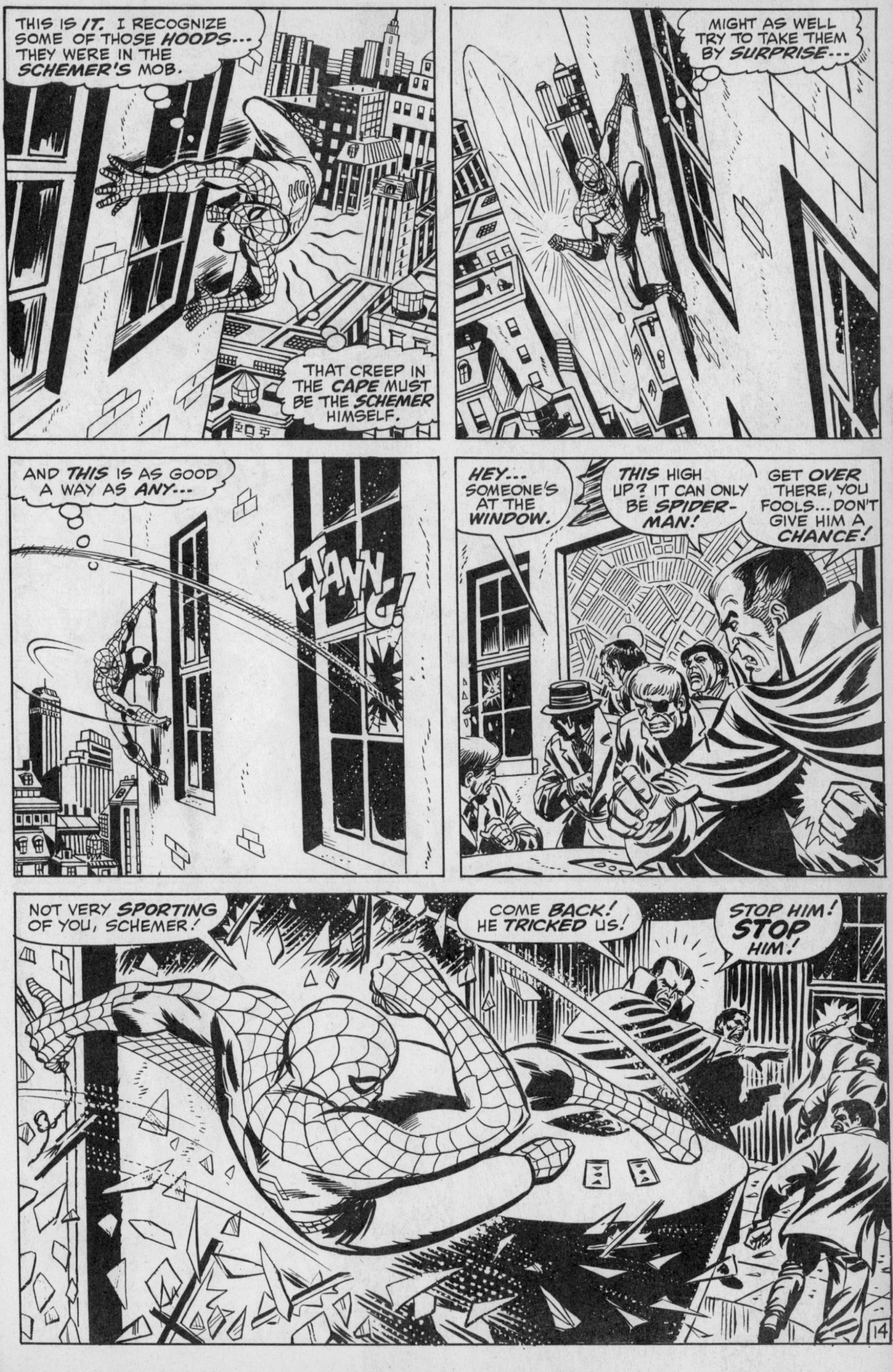
THIS IS IT. I RECOGNIZE SOME OF THOSE HOODS... THEY WERE IN THE SCHEMER'S MOB.
THAT CREEP IN THE CAPE MUST BE THE SCHEMER HIMSELF.
MIGHT AS WELL TRY TO TAKE THEM BY SURPRISE...
AND THIS IS AS GOOD A WAY AS ANY...
FTANNG!
HEY... SOMEONE'S AT THE WINDOW.
THIS HIGH UP? IT CAN ONLY BE SPIDER-MAN!
GET OVER THERE, YOU FOOLS... DON'T GIVE HIM A CHANCE!
NOT VERY SPORTING OF YOU, SCHEMER!
COME BACK! HE TRICKED US!
STOP HIM! STOP HIM!
14

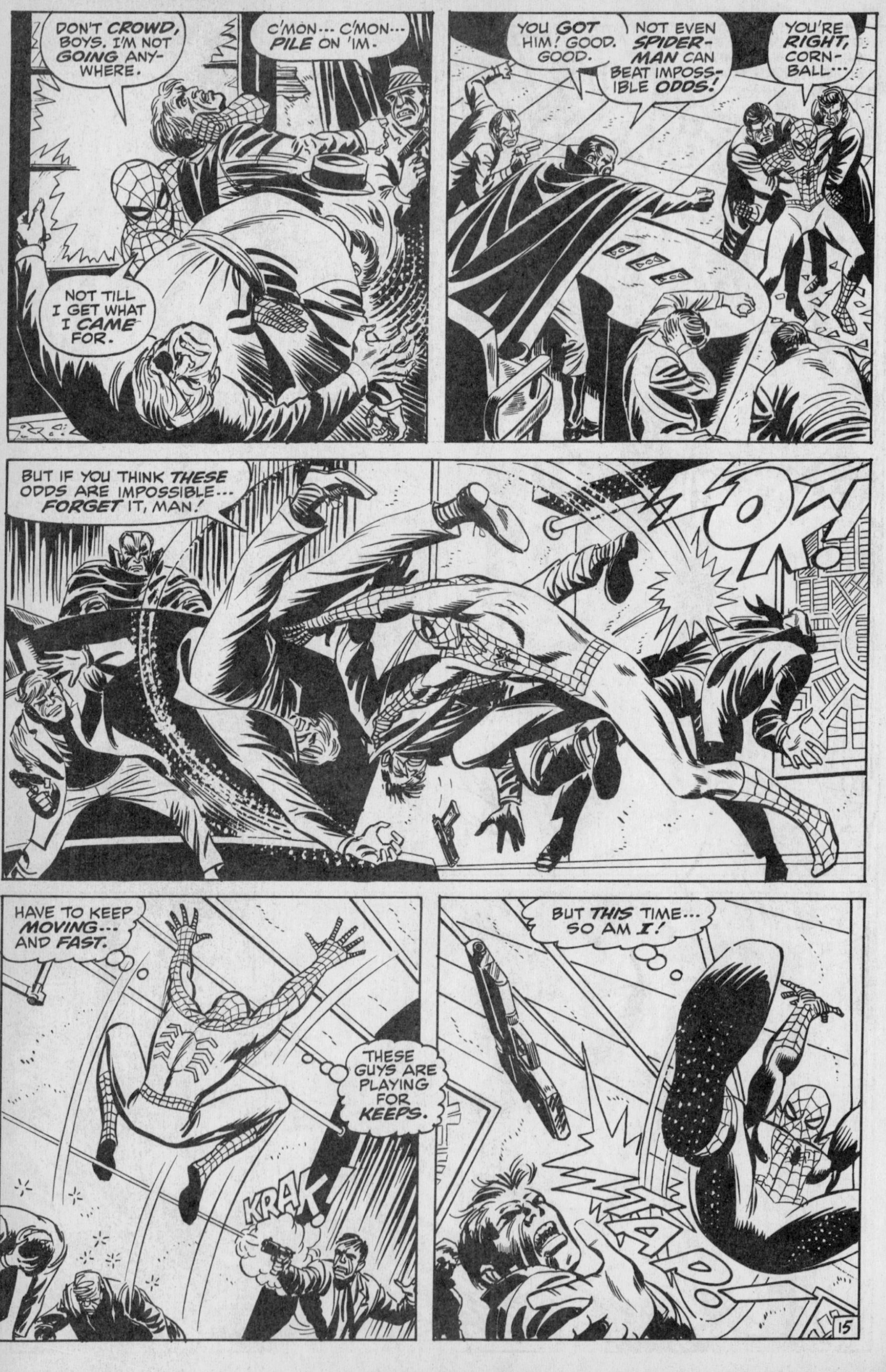
DON'T CROWD, BOYS. I'M NOT GOING ANYWHERE.
C'MON... C'MON... PILE ON 'IM.
NOT TILL I GET WHAT I CAME FOR.
YOU GOT HIM! GOOD. GOOD.
NOT EVEN SPIDER-MAN CAN BEAT IMPOSSIBLE ODDS!
YOU'RE RIGHT, CORNBALL...
BUT IF YOU THINK THESE ODDS ARE IMPOSSIBLE... FORGET IT, MAN!
SOK!
HAVE TO KEEP MOVING... AND FAST.
THESE GUYS ARE PLAYING FOR KEEPS.
KRAK!
BUT THIS TIME... SO AM I!
THAP!
15

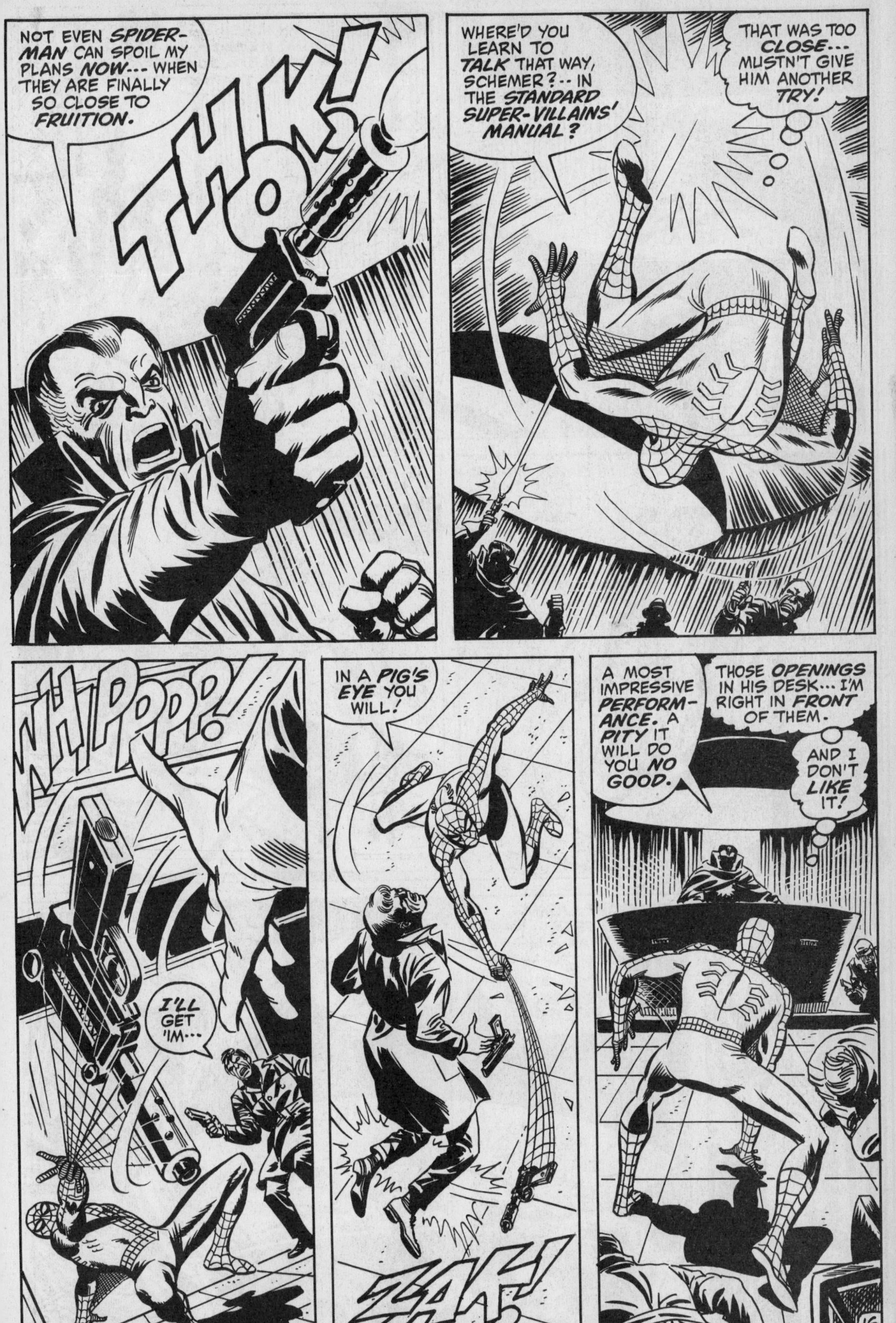
NOT EVEN SPIDER-MAN CAN SPOIL MY PLANS NOW--- WHEN THEY ARE FINALLY SO CLOSE TO FRUITION.
THK!
WHERE'D YOU LEARN TO TALK THAT WAY, SCHEMER?-- IN THE STANDARD SUPER-VILLAINS' MANUAL?
THAT WAS TOO CLOSE... MUSTN'T GIVE HIM ANOTHER TRY!
WHIPPPP!
I'LL GET 'IM...
IN A PIG'S EYE YOU WILL!
ZAK!
A MOST IMPRESSIVE PERFORMANCE. A PITY IT WILL DO YOU NO GOOD.
THOSE OPENINGS IN HIS DESK... I'M RIGHT IN FRONT OF THEM.
AND I DON'T LIKE IT!
16

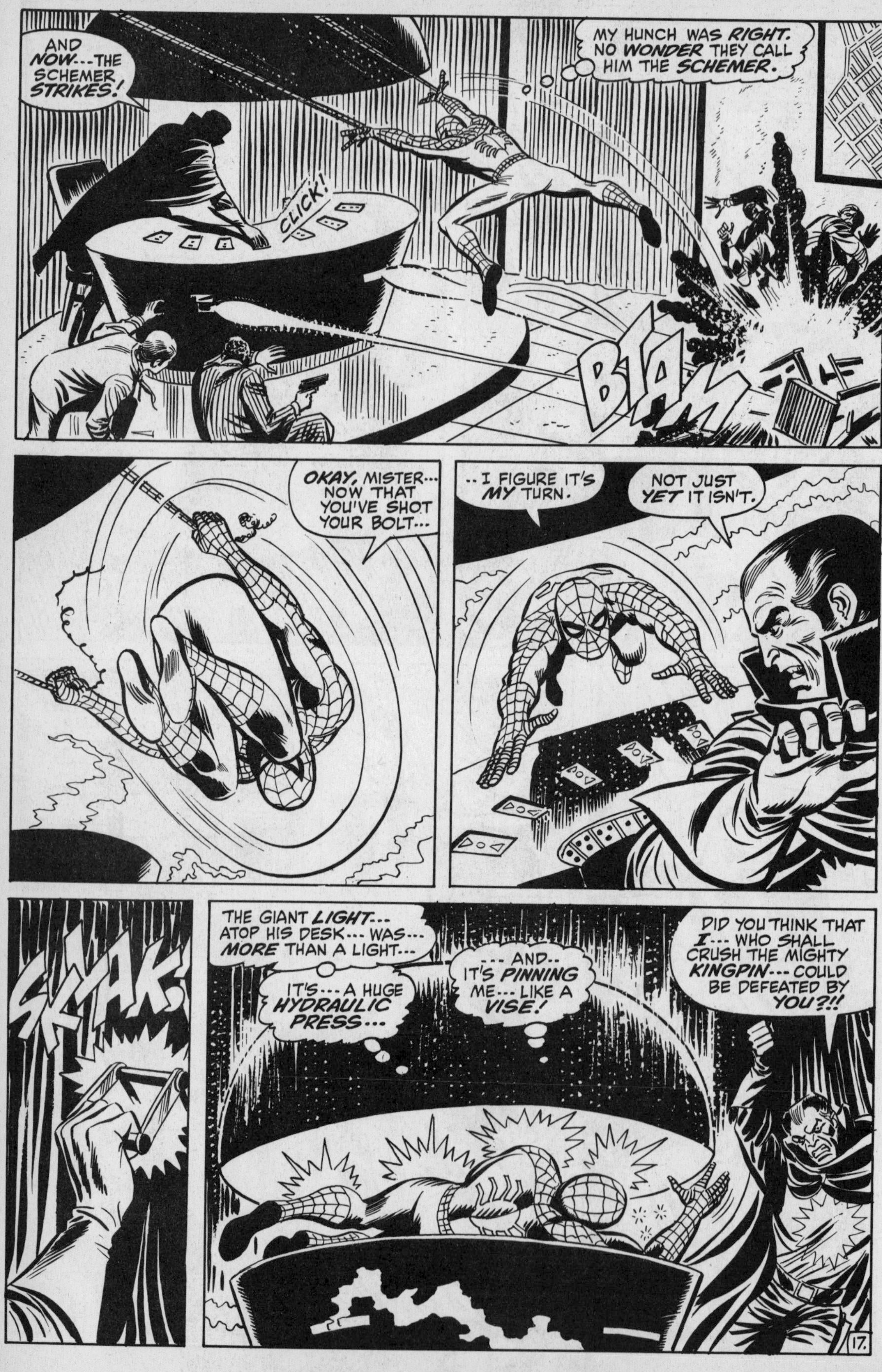

AND NOW---THE SCHEMER STRIKES!
CLICK!
MY HUNCH WAS RIGHT. NO WONDER THEY CALL HIM THE SCHEMER.
BLAM
OKAY, MISTER--- NOW THAT YOU'VE SHOT YOUR BOLT---
--I FIGURE IT'S MY TURN.
NOT JUST YET IT ISN'T.
SKLAK!
THE GIANT LIGHT--- ATOP HIS DESK--- WAS--- MORE THAN A LIGHT---
IT'S--- A HUGE HYDRAULIC PRESS---
--- AND-- IT'S PINNING ME--- LIKE A VISE!
DID YOU THINK THAT I--- WHO SHALL CRUSH THE MIGHTY KINGPIN--- COULD BE DEFEATED BY YOU?!!
17.

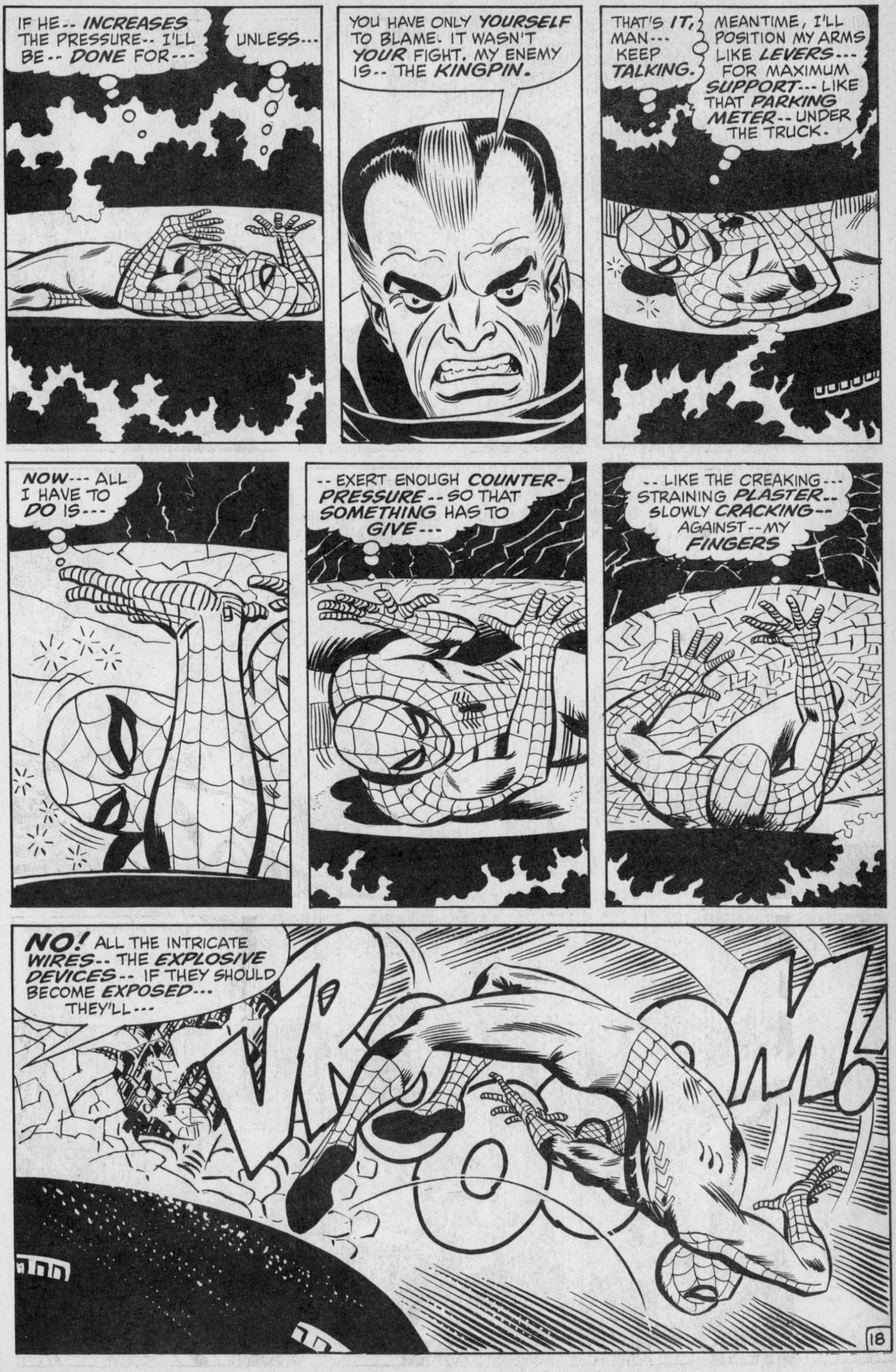

IF HE-- INCREASES THE PRESSURE-- I'LL BE-- DONE FOR---
UNLESS---
YOU HAVE ONLY YOURSELF TO BLAME. IT WASN'T YOUR FIGHT. MY ENEMY IS-- THE KINGPIN.
THAT'S IT, MAN--- KEEP TALKING.
MEANTIME, I'LL POSITION MY ARMS LIKE LEVERS--- FOR MAXIMUM SUPPORT--- LIKE THAT PARKING METER-- UNDER THE TRUCK.
NOW--- ALL I HAVE TO DO IS---
--EXERT ENOUGH COUNTER-PRESSURE-- SO THAT SOMETHING HAS TO GIVE---
--LIKE THE CREAKING--- STRAINING PLASTER-- SLOWLY CRACKING-- AGAINST--MY FINGERS
NO! ALL THE INTRICATE WIRES-- THE EXPLOSIVE DEVICES-- IF THEY SHOULD BECOME EXPOSED--- THEY'LL---
VAROOM!
18

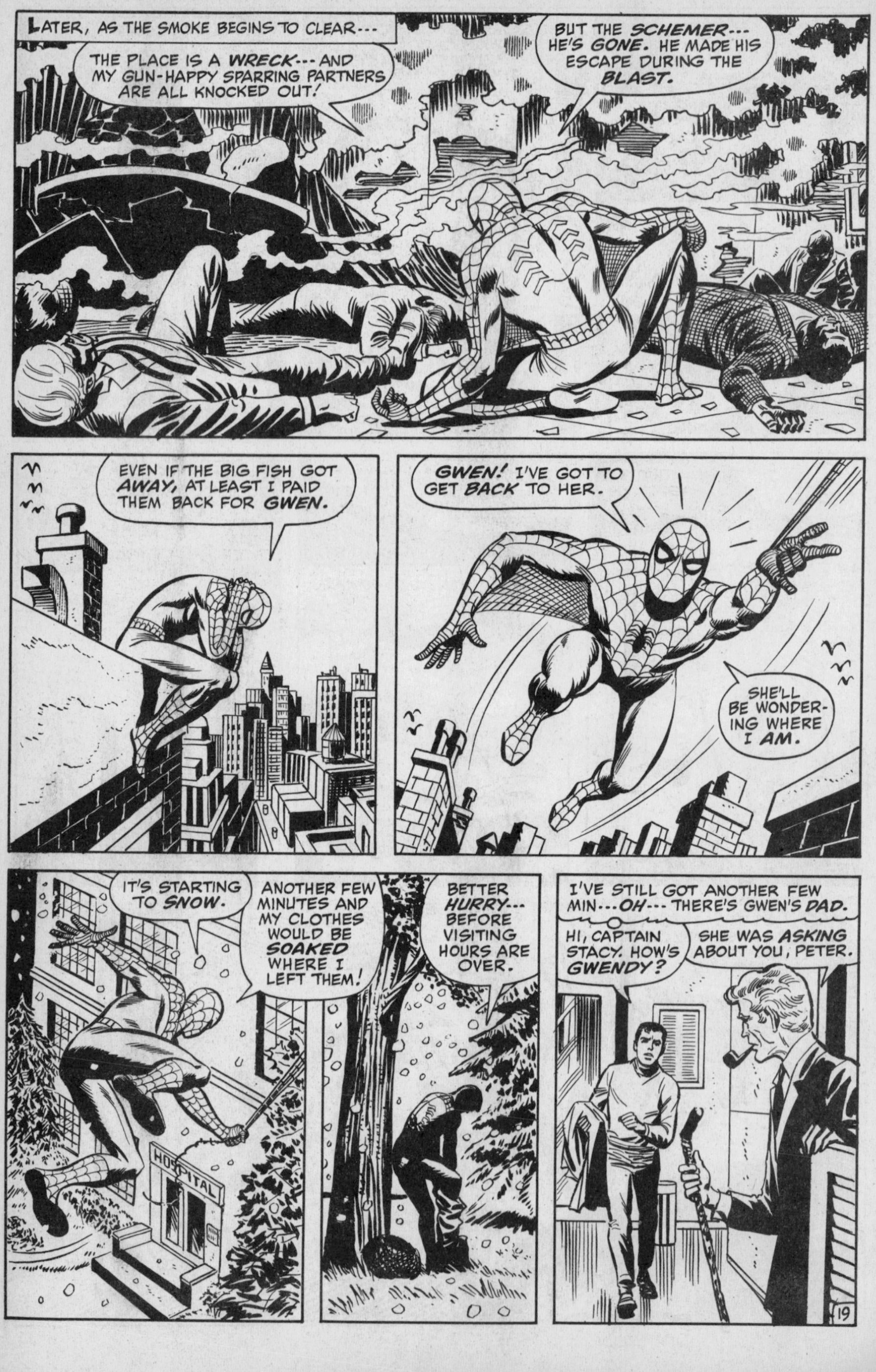
LATER, AS THE SMOKE BEGINS TO CLEAR---
THE PLACE IS A WRECK--- AND MY GUN-HAPPY SPARRING PARTNERS ARE ALL KNOCKED OUT!
BUT THE SCHEMER--- HE'S GONE. HE MADE HIS ESCAPE DURING THE BLAST.
EVEN IF THE BIG FISH GOT AWAY, AT LEAST I PAID THEM BACK FOR GWEN.
GWEN! I'VE GOT TO GET BACK TO HER.
SHE'LL BE WONDERING WHERE I AM.
IT'S STARTING TO SNOW.
ANOTHER FEW MINUTES AND MY CLOTHES WOULD BE SOAKED WHERE I LEFT THEM!
HOSPITAL
BETTER HURRY--- BEFORE VISITING HOURS ARE OVER.
I'VE STILL GOT ANOTHER FEW MIN---OH--- THERE'S GWEN'S DAD.
HI, CAPTAIN STACY. HOW'S GWENDY?
SHE WAS ASKING ABOUT YOU, PETER.
19

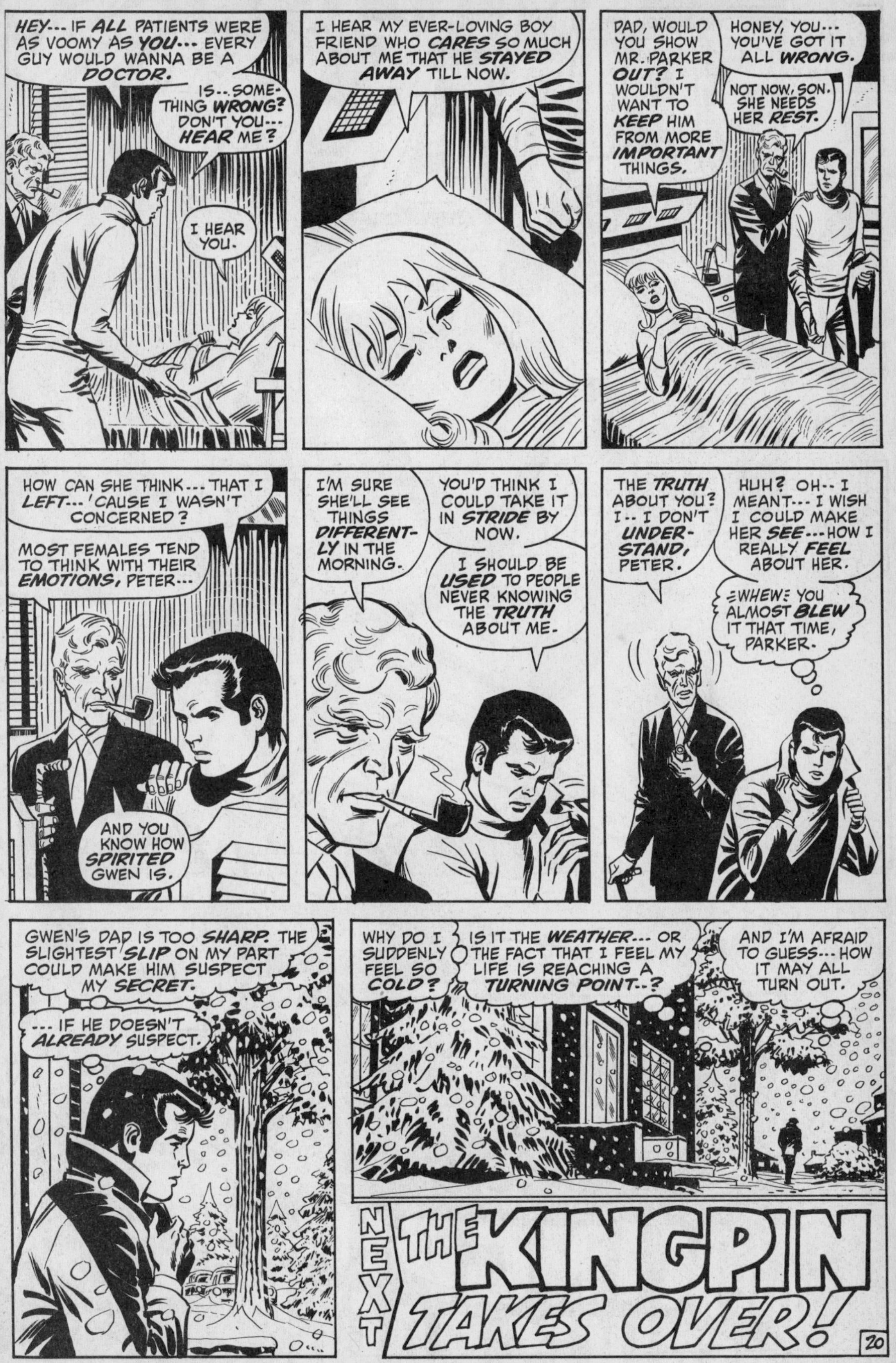

HEY--- IF ALL PATIENTS WERE AS VOOMY AS YOU--- EVERY GUY WOULD WANNA BE A DOCTOR.
IS-- SOME-THING WRONG? DON'T YOU--- HEAR ME?
I HEAR YOU.
I HEAR MY EVER-LOVING BOY FRIEND WHO CARES SO MUCH ABOUT ME THAT HE STAYED AWAY TILL NOW.
DAD, WOULD YOU SHOW MR. PARKER OUT? I WOULDN'T WANT TO KEEP HIM FROM MORE IMPORTANT THINGS.
HONEY, YOU--- YOU'VE GOT IT ALL WRONG.
NOT NOW, SON. SHE NEEDS HER REST.
HOW CAN SHE THINK--- THAT I LEFT--- 'CAUSE I WASN'T CONCERNED?
MOST FEMALES TEND TO THINK WITH THEIR EMOTIONS, PETER---
AND YOU KNOW HOW SPIRITED GWEN IS.
I'M SURE SHE'LL SEE THINGS DIFFERENTLY IN THE MORNING.
YOU'D THINK I COULD TAKE IT IN STRIDE BY NOW.
I SHOULD BE USED TO PEOPLE NEVER KNOWING THE TRUTH ABOUT ME.
THE TRUTH ABOUT YOU? I-- I DON'T UNDERSTAND, PETER.
HUH? OH-- I MEANT--- I WISH I COULD MAKE HER SEE---HOW I REALLY FEEL ABOUT HER.
WHEW! YOU ALMOST BLEW IT THAT TIME, PARKER.
GWEN'S DAD IS TOO SHARP. THE SLIGHTEST SLIP ON MY PART COULD MAKE HIM SUSPECT MY SECRET.
--- IF HE DOESN'T ALREADY SUSPECT.
WHY DO I SUDDENLY FEEL SO COLD?
IS IT THE WEATHER--- OR THE FACT THAT I FEEL MY LIFE IS REACHING A TURNING POINT--?
AND I'M AFRAID TO GUESS--- HOW IT MAY ALL TURN OUT.
NEXT
THE KINGPIN TAKES OVER!
20

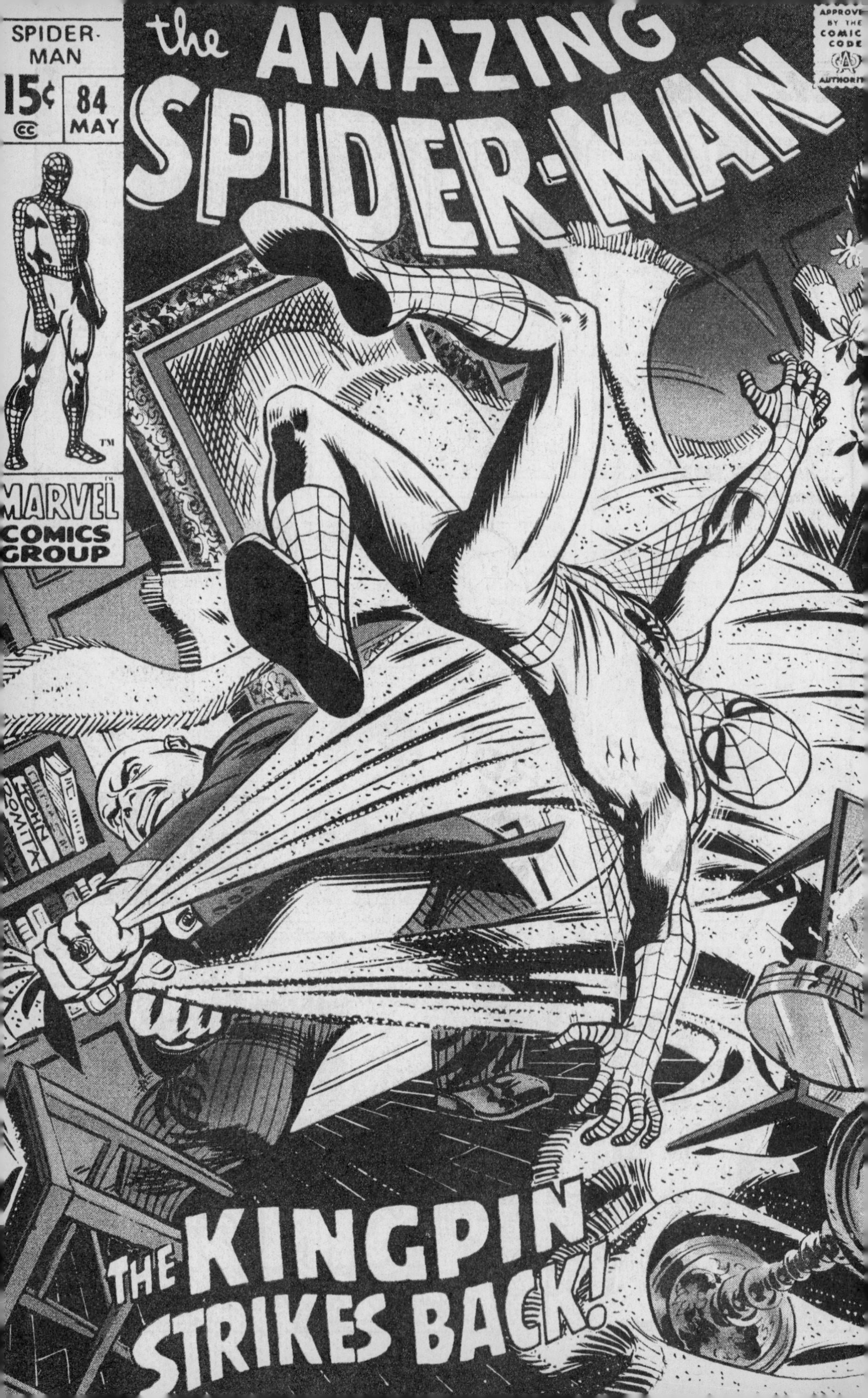
SPIDER-MAN
15¢
CC
84
MAY
the AMAZING SPIDER-MAN
APPROVED BY THE COMIC CODE AUTHORITY
MARVEL COMICS GROUP
JOHN ROMITA
THE KINGPIN STRIKES BACK!

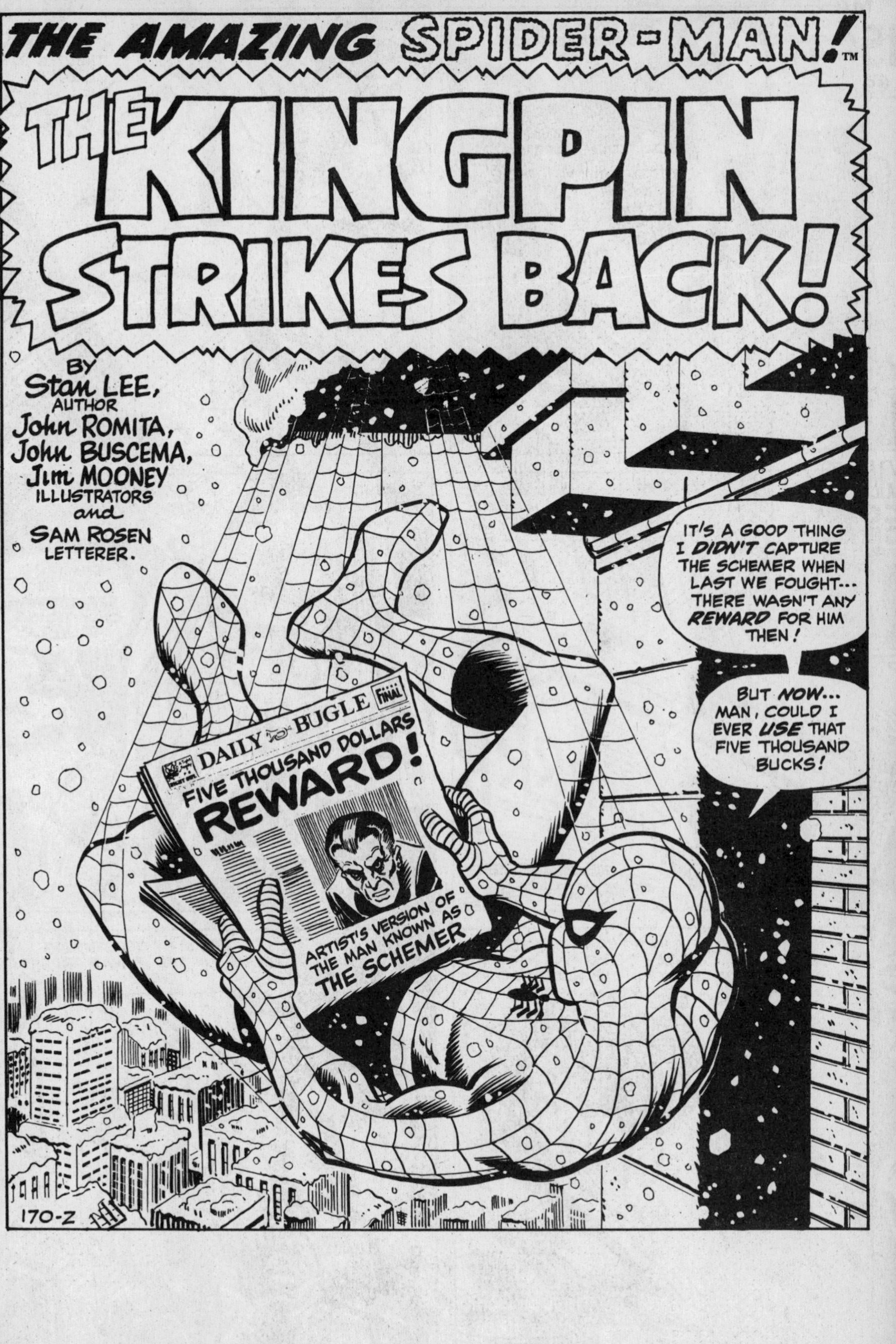
THE AMAZING SPIDER-MAN! ™
THE KINGPIN STRIKES BACK!
BY Stan LEE, AUTHOR John ROMITA, John BUSCEMA, Jim MOONEY ILLUSTRATORS and SAM ROSEN LETTERER.
IT'S A GOOD THING I DIDN'T CAPTURE THE SCHEMER WHEN LAST WE FOUGHT... THERE WASN'T ANY REWARD FOR HIM THEN!
BUT NOW... MAN, COULD I EVER USE THAT FIVE THOUSAND BUCKS!
DAILY BUGLE FINAL
FIVE THOUSAND DOLLARS REWARD!
ARTIST'S VERSION OF THE MAN KNOWN AS THE SCHEMER
170-2

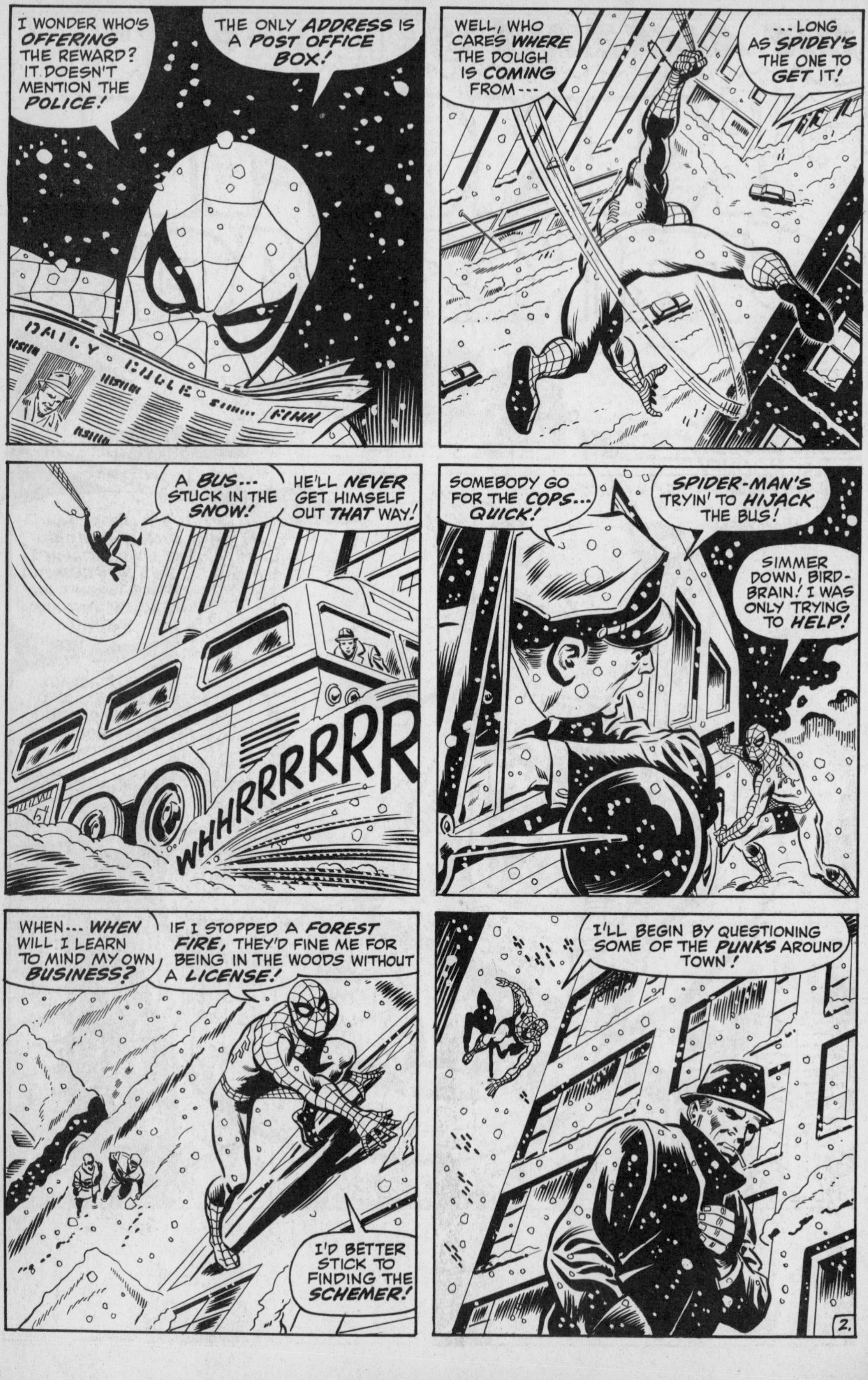
I WONDER WHO'S OFFERING THE REWARD? IT DOESN'T MENTION THE POLICE!
THE ONLY ADDRESS IS A POST OFFICE BOX!
WELL, WHO CARES WHERE THE DOUGH IS COMING FROM---
...LONG AS SPIDEY'S THE ONE TO GET IT!
A BUS... STUCK IN THE SNOW!
HE'LL NEVER GET HIMSELF OUT THAT WAY!
WHHRRRRRRR
SOMEBODY GO FOR THE COPS... QUICK!
SPIDER-MAN'S TRYIN' TO HIJACK THE BUS!
SIMMER DOWN, BIRD-BRAIN! I WAS ONLY TRYING TO HELP!
WHEN... WHEN WILL I LEARN TO MIND MY OWN BUSINESS?
IF I STOPPED A FOREST FIRE, THEY'D FINE ME FOR BEING IN THE WOODS WITHOUT A LICENSE!
I'D BETTER STICK TO FINDING THE SCHEMER!
I'LL BEGIN BY QUESTIONING SOME OF THE PUNKS AROUND TOWN!
2.

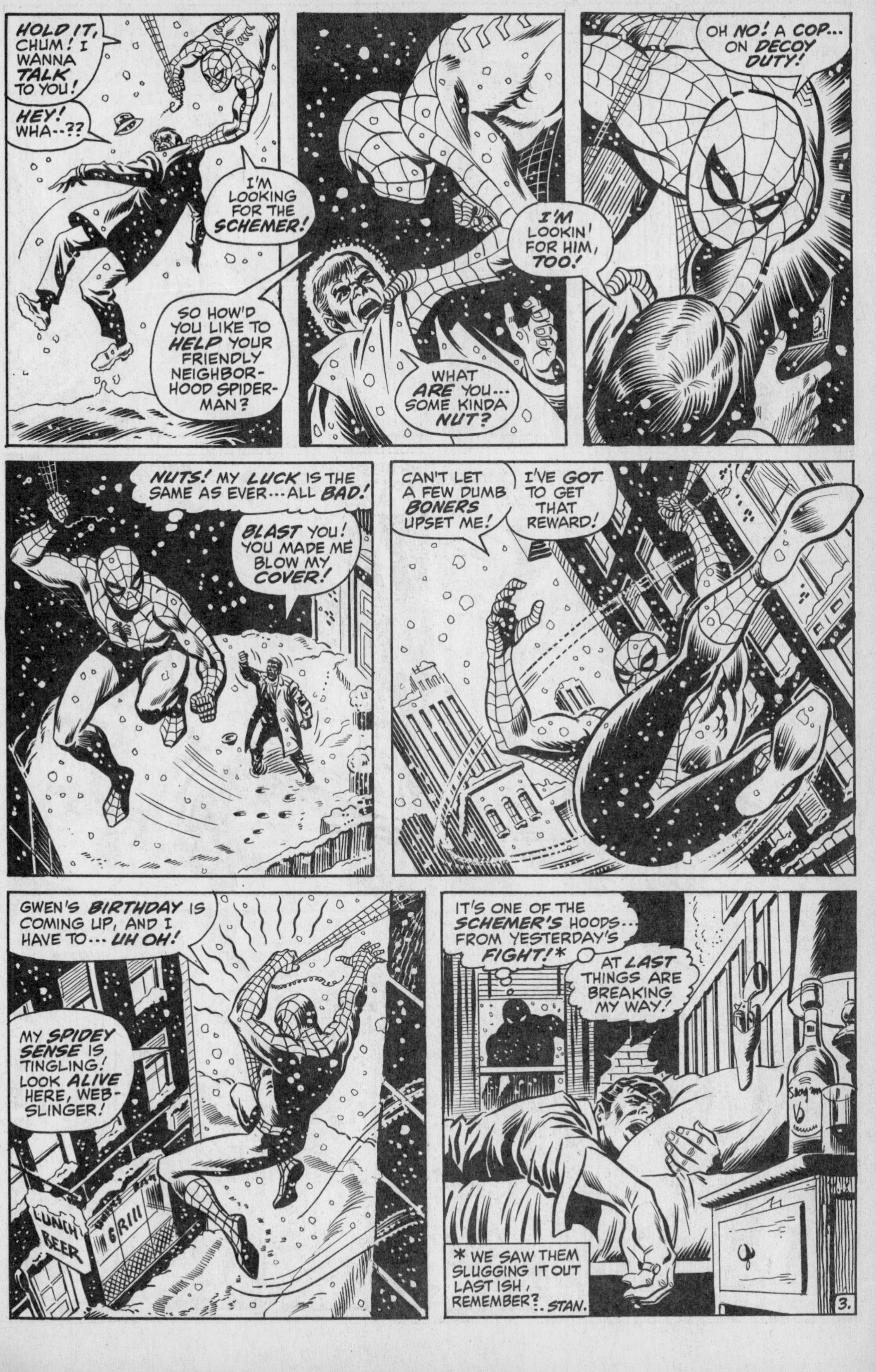
HOLD IT, CHUM! I WANNA TALK TO YOU!
HEY! WHA--??
I'M LOOKING FOR THE SCHEMER!
SO HOW'D YOU LIKE TO HELP YOUR FRIENDLY NEIGHBOR-HOOD SPIDER-MAN?
WHAT ARE YOU... SOME KINDA NUT?
I'M LOOKIN' FOR HIM, TOO!
OH NO! A COP... ON DECOY DUTY!
NUTS! MY LUCK IS THE SAME AS EVER... ALL BAD!
BLAST YOU! YOU MADE ME BLOW MY COVER!
CAN'T LET A FEW DUMB BONERS UPSET ME!
I'VE GOT TO GET THAT REWARD!
GWEN'S BIRTHDAY IS COMING UP, AND I HAVE TO... UH OH!
MY SPIDEY SENSE IS TINGLING! LOOK ALIVE HERE, WEB-SLINGER!
LUNCH BEER
GRILL
IT'S ONE OF THE SCHEMER'S HOODS... FROM YESTERDAY'S FIGHT!*
AT LAST THINGS ARE BREAKING MY WAY!
* WE SAW THEM SLUGGING IT OUT LAST ISH, REMEMBER? -- STAN.

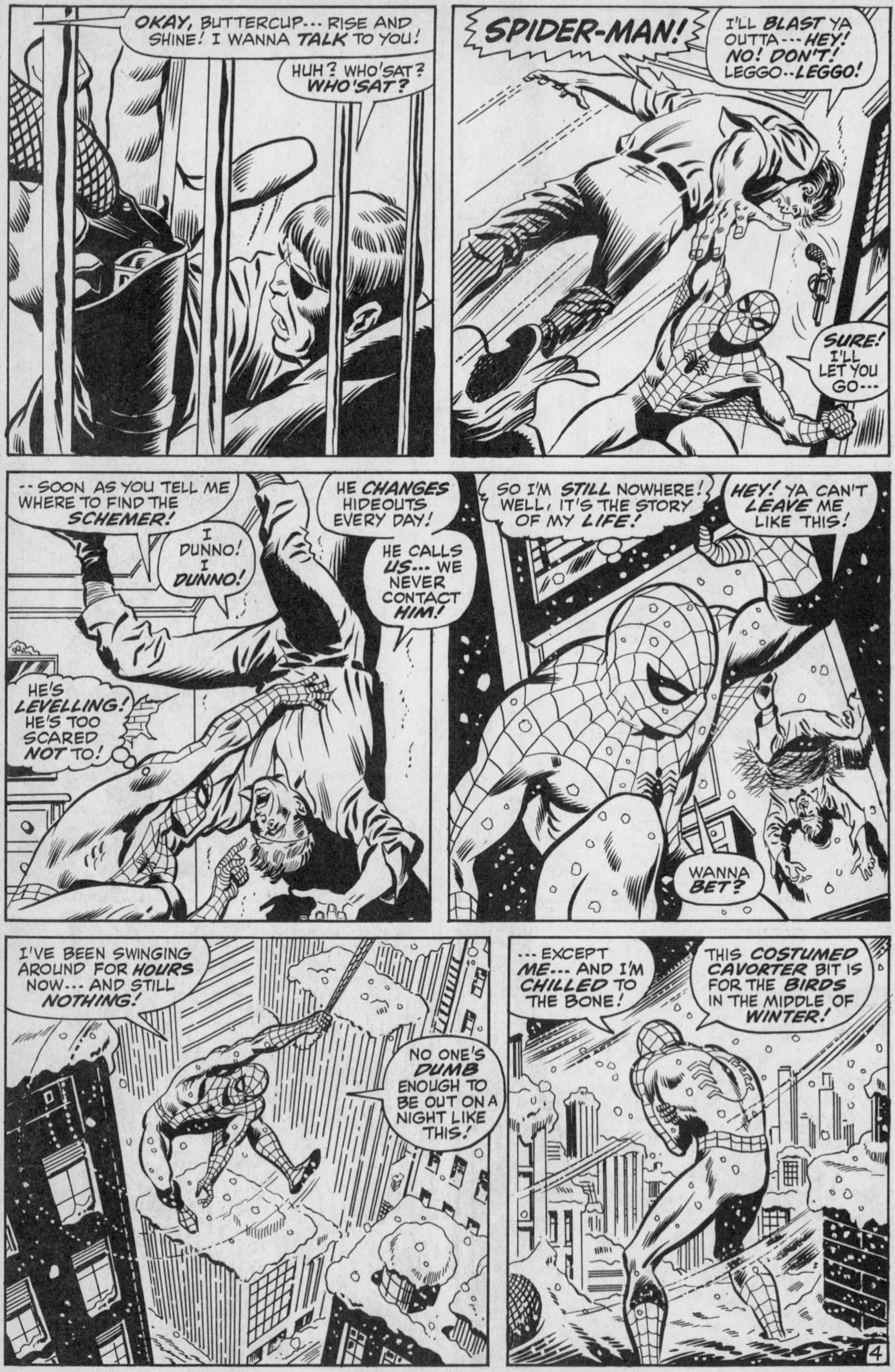
OKAY, BUTTERCUP... RISE AND SHINE! I WANNA TALK TO YOU!
HUH? WHO'SAT? WHO'SAT?
SPIDER-MAN!
I'LL BLAST YA OUTTA--- HEY! NO! DON'T! LEGGO--LEGGO!
SURE! I'LL LET YOU GO---
--SOON AS YOU TELL ME WHERE TO FIND THE SCHEMER!
I DUNNO! I DUNNO!
HE CHANGES HIDEOUTS EVERY DAY!
HE CALLS US... WE NEVER CONTACT HIM!
HE'S LEVELLING! HE'S TOO SCARED NOT TO!
SO I'M STILL NOWHERE! WELL, IT'S THE STORY OF MY LIFE!
HEY! YA CAN'T LEAVE ME LIKE THIS!
WANNA BET?
I'VE BEEN SWINGING AROUND FOR HOURS NOW... AND STILL NOTHING!
NO ONE'S DUMB ENOUGH TO BE OUT ON A NIGHT LIKE THIS!
...EXCEPT ME... AND I'M CHILLED TO THE BONE!
THIS COSTUMED CAVORTER BIT IS FOR THE BIRDS IN THE MIDDLE OF WINTER!
4

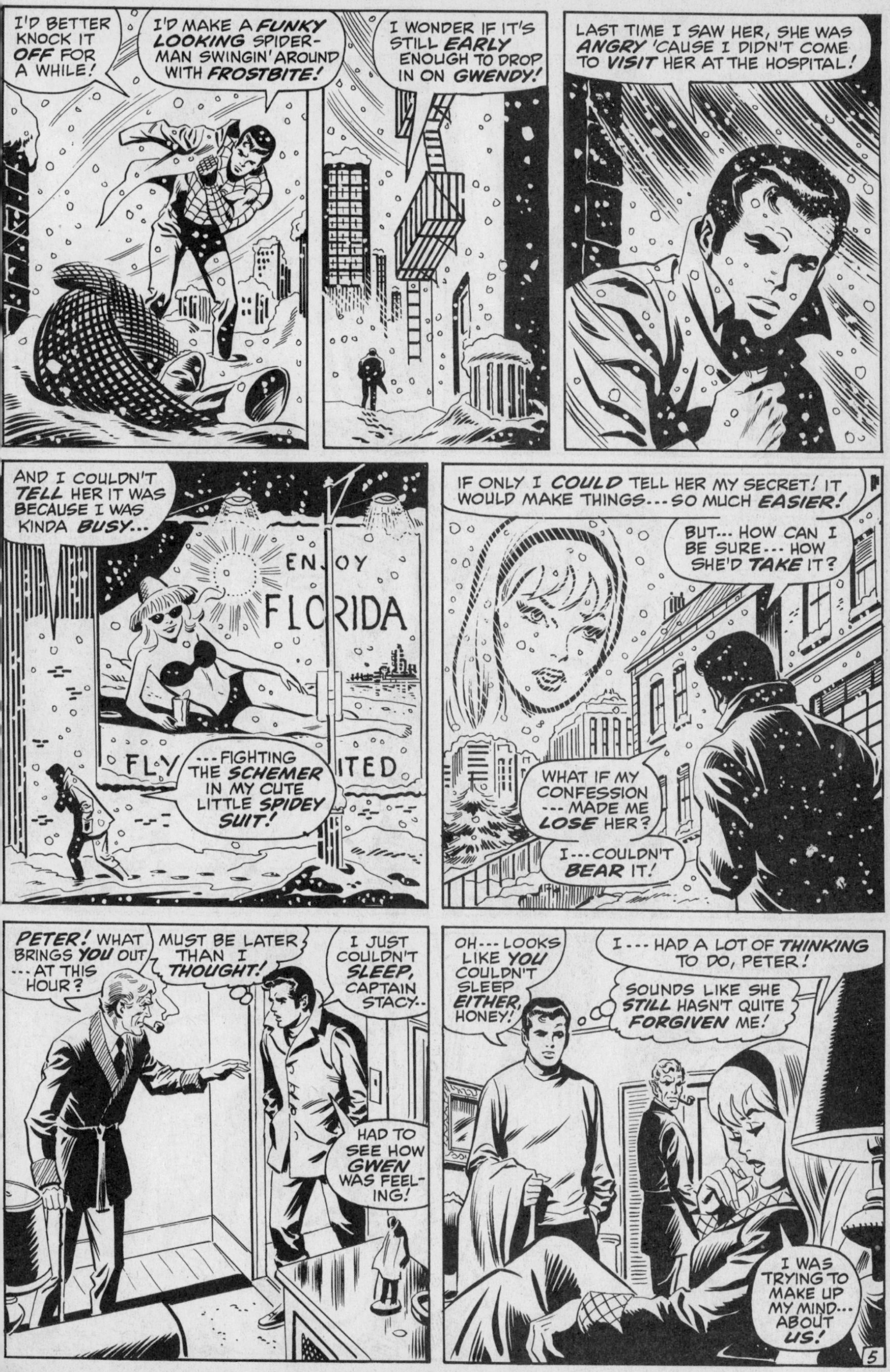

I'D BETTER KNOCK IT OFF FOR A WHILE!
I'D MAKE A FUNKY LOOKING SPIDER-MAN SWINGIN' AROUND WITH FROSTBITE!
I WONDER IF IT'S STILL EARLY ENOUGH TO DROP IN ON GWENDY!
LAST TIME I SAW HER, SHE WAS ANGRY 'CAUSE I DIDN'T COME TO VISIT HER AT THE HOSPITAL!
AND I COULDN'T TELL HER IT WAS BECAUSE I WAS KINDA BUSY...
ENJOY
FLORIDA
FLY
ITED
...FIGHTING THE SCHEMER IN MY CUTE LITTLE SPIDEY SUIT!
IF ONLY I COULD TELL HER MY SECRET! IT WOULD MAKE THINGS... SO MUCH EASIER!
BUT... HOW CAN I BE SURE... HOW SHE'D TAKE IT?
WHAT IF MY CONFESSION ... MADE ME LOSE HER?
I... COULDN'T BEAR IT!
PETER! WHAT BRINGS YOU OUT ... AT THIS HOUR?
MUST BE LATER THAN I THOUGHT!
I JUST COULDN'T SLEEP, CAPTAIN STACY..
HAD TO SEE HOW GWEN WAS FEELING!
OH... LOOKS LIKE YOU COULDN'T SLEEP EITHER, HONEY!
I... HAD A LOT OF THINKING TO DO, PETER!
SOUNDS LIKE SHE STILL HASN'T QUITE FORGIVEN ME!
I WAS TRYING TO MAKE UP MY MIND... ABOUT US!

THERE'S SO MUCH *ABOUT* YOU, PETER... SO MUCH I DON'T *UNDERSTAND!*

...SO MANY THINGS ...YOU'RE SO *SECRETIVE* ABOUT!

THIS IS THE MOMENT... I'VE BEEN *DREADING!*

BUT THERE'S *ONE* THING YOU NEVER NEED HAVE ANY *DOUBTS* ABOUT, GWEN...

AND THAT'S THE WAY THAT I FEEL... ABOUT *YOU!*

IT WOULD SEEM I PICKED AN AWKWARD MOMENT TO BRING IN SOME *COCOA!*

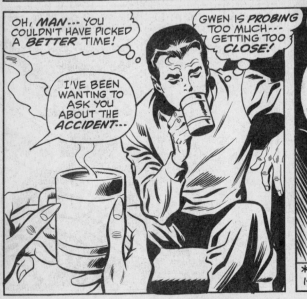

OH, *MAN*... YOU COULDN'T HAVE PICKED A *BETTER* TIME!

GWEN IS *PROBING* TOO MUCH... GETTING TOO *CLOSE!*

I'VE BEEN WANTING TO ASK YOU ABOUT THE *ACCIDENT*...

WHEN THAT CAR SIDE-SWIPED THE *TRUCK*, AND IT FELL *OVER* ON US... YOU WEREN'T EVEN *SCRATCHED!* *

BUT WASN'T THAT BECAUSE THE *PARKING METER* ACTED AS A *WEDGE* WHEN IT SNAPPED OFF?

* AS SEEN LAST ISH ALSO...S.

YES, DAD... BUT I'VE BEEN *WONDERING*...

HAVE TO GET MYSELF *OUT* OF THIS... SOMEHOW!

PETER! WHAT'S *WRONG?*

GOSH, I... I'M *SORRY!* ALL OF A SUDDEN... I'VE GOT THE *SHAKES!*

MUST HAVE CAUGHT A *CHILL*... OUT IN THE *SNOW!* I'D BETTER GET *HOME*... AND INTO BED!

I *THOUGHT* YOU DIDN'T SEEM TO BE *YOURSELF!*

OH, GWENDY ...YOU DON'T KNOW THE *HALF* OF IT!

6

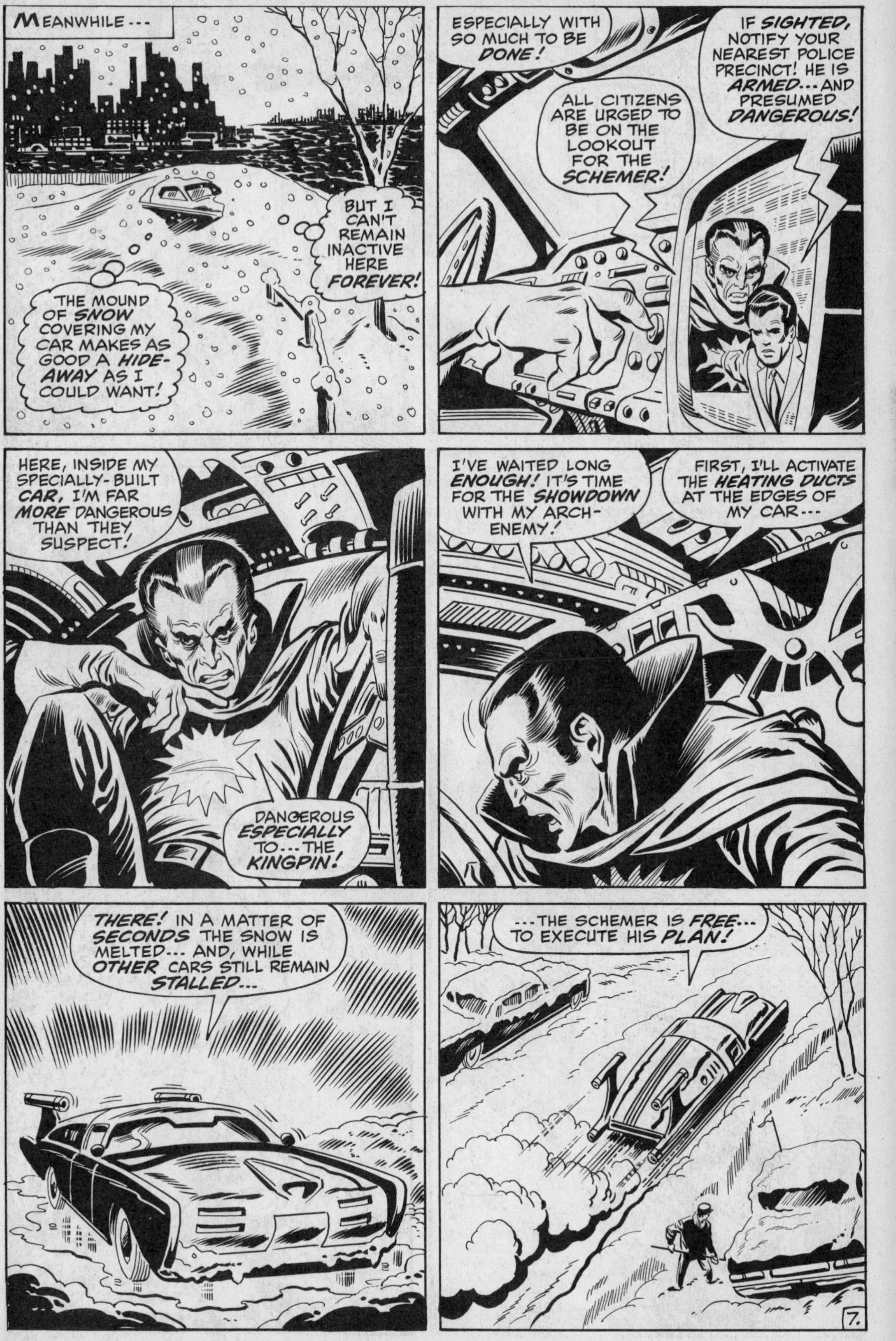
MEANWHILE---
BUT I CAN'T REMAIN INACTIVE HERE FOREVER!
THE MOUND OF SNOW COVERING MY CAR MAKES AS GOOD A HIDE-AWAY AS I COULD WANT!
ESPECIALLY WITH SO MUCH TO BE DONE!
ALL CITIZENS ARE URGED TO BE ON THE LOOKOUT FOR THE SCHEMER!
IF SIGHTED, NOTIFY YOUR NEAREST POLICE PRECINCT! HE IS ARMED... AND PRESUMED DANGEROUS!
HERE, INSIDE MY SPECIALLY-BUILT CAR, I'M FAR MORE DANGEROUS THAN THEY SUSPECT!
DANGEROUS ESPECIALLY TO---THE KINGPIN!
I'VE WAITED LONG ENOUGH! IT'S TIME FOR THE SHOWDOWN WITH MY ARCH-ENEMY!
FIRST, I'LL ACTIVATE THE HEATING DUCTS AT THE EDGES OF MY CAR---
THERE! IN A MATTER OF SECONDS THE SNOW IS MELTED... AND, WHILE OTHER CARS STILL REMAIN STALLED...
---THE SCHEMER IS FREE... TO EXECUTE HIS PLAN!
7.

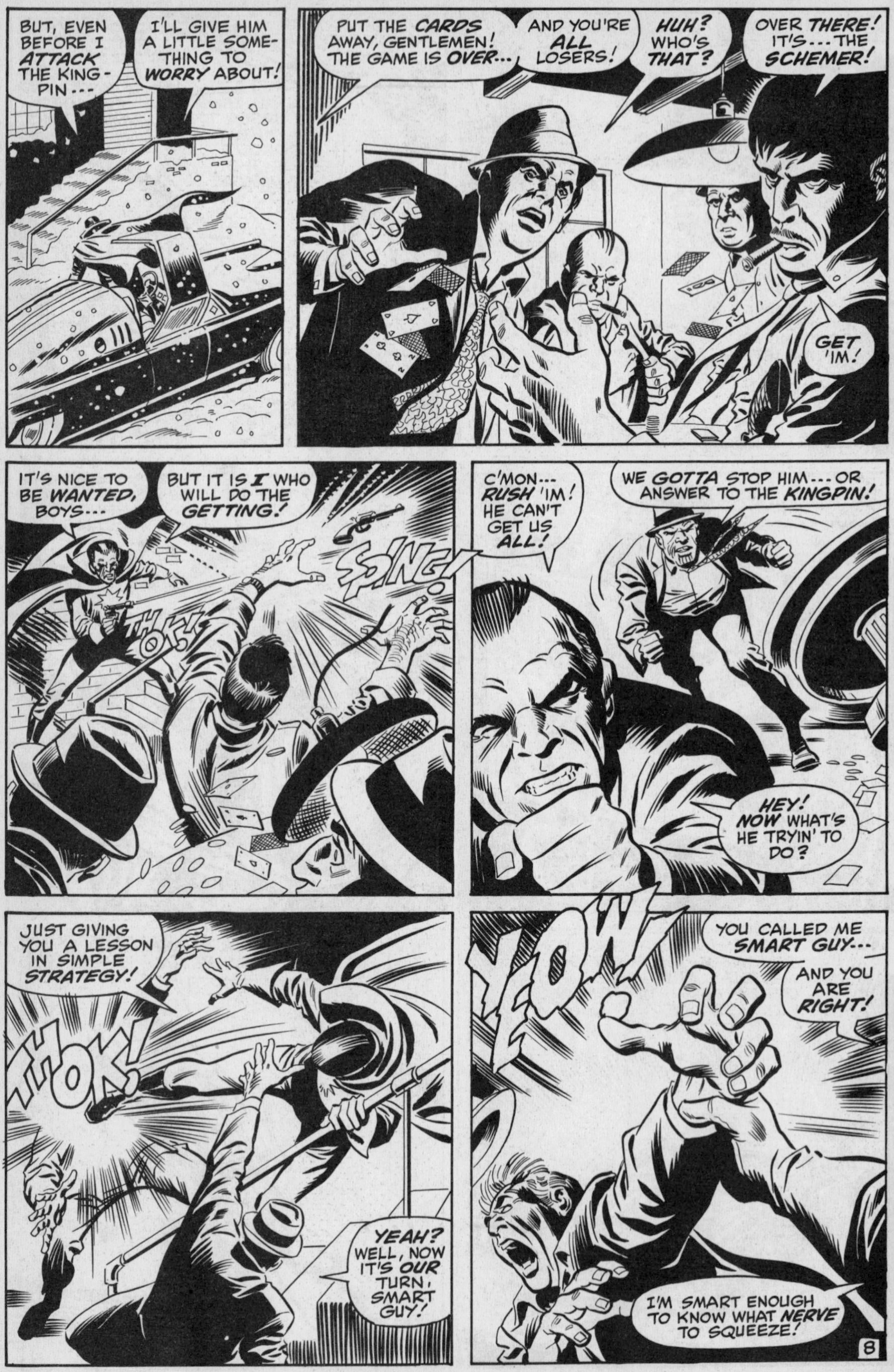
BUT, EVEN BEFORE I ATTACK THE KING-PIN---
I'LL GIVE HIM A LITTLE SOMETHING TO WORRY ABOUT!
PUT THE CARDS AWAY, GENTLEMEN! THE GAME IS OVER...
AND YOU'RE ALL LOSERS!
HUH? WHO'S THAT?
OVER THERE! IT'S---THE SCHEMER!
GET 'IM!
IT'S NICE TO BE WANTED, BOYS---
BUT IT IS I WHO WILL DO THE GETTING!
SPANG!
THOK!
C'MON--- RUSH 'IM! HE CAN'T GET US ALL!
WE GOTTA STOP HIM---OR ANSWER TO THE KINGPIN!
HEY! NOW WHAT'S HE TRYIN' TO DO?
JUST GIVING YOU A LESSON IN SIMPLE STRATEGY!
THOK!
YEAH? WELL, NOW IT'S OUR TURN, SMART GUY!
YOW
YOU CALLED ME SMART GUY...
AND YOU ARE RIGHT!
I'M SMART ENOUGH TO KNOW WHAT NERVE TO SQUEEZE!
8

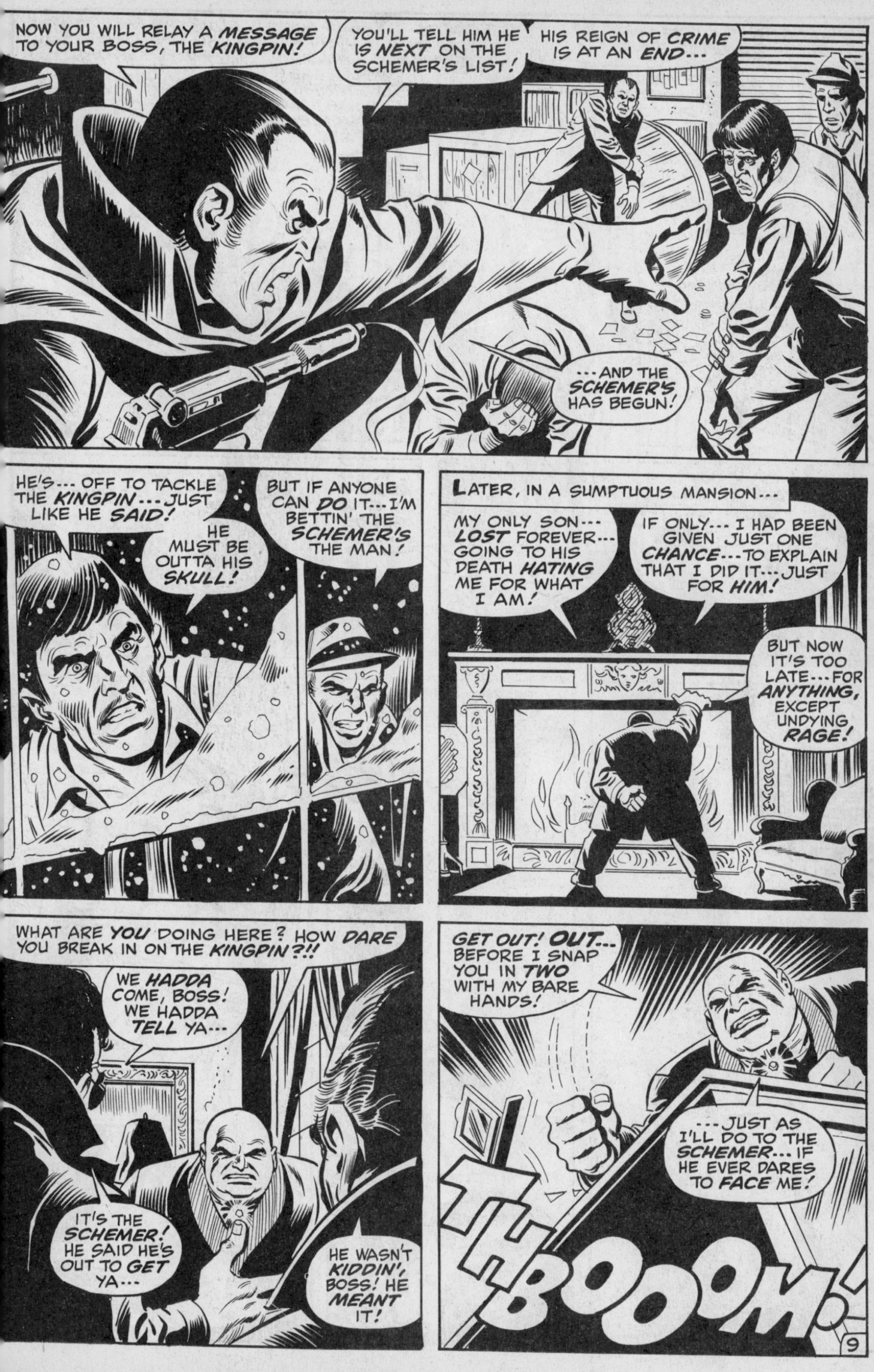
NOW YOU WILL RELAY A MESSAGE TO YOUR BOSS, THE KINGPIN!
YOU'LL TELL HIM HE IS NEXT ON THE SCHEMER'S LIST!
HIS REIGN OF CRIME IS AT AN END...
...AND THE SCHEMER'S HAS BEGUN!
HE'S... OFF TO TACKLE THE KINGPIN... JUST LIKE HE SAID!
HE MUST BE OUTTA HIS SKULL!
BUT IF ANYONE CAN DO IT... I'M BETTIN' THE SCHEMER'S THE MAN!
LATER, IN A SUMPTUOUS MANSION...
MY ONLY SON... LOST FOREVER... GOING TO HIS DEATH HATING ME FOR WHAT I AM!
IF ONLY... I HAD BEEN GIVEN JUST ONE CHANCE... TO EXPLAIN THAT I DID IT... JUST FOR HIM!
BUT NOW IT'S TOO LATE... FOR ANYTHING, EXCEPT UNDYING RAGE!
WHAT ARE YOU DOING HERE? HOW DARE YOU BREAK IN ON THE KINGPIN?!!
WE HADDA COME, BOSS! WE HADDA TELL YA...
IT'S THE SCHEMER! HE SAID HE'S OUT TO GET YA...
HE WASN'T KIDDIN', BOSS! HE MEANT IT!
GET OUT! OUT... BEFORE I SNAP YOU IN TWO WITH MY BARE HANDS!
...JUST AS I'LL DO TO THE SCHEMER... IF HE EVER DARES TO FACE ME!
THBOOOM!

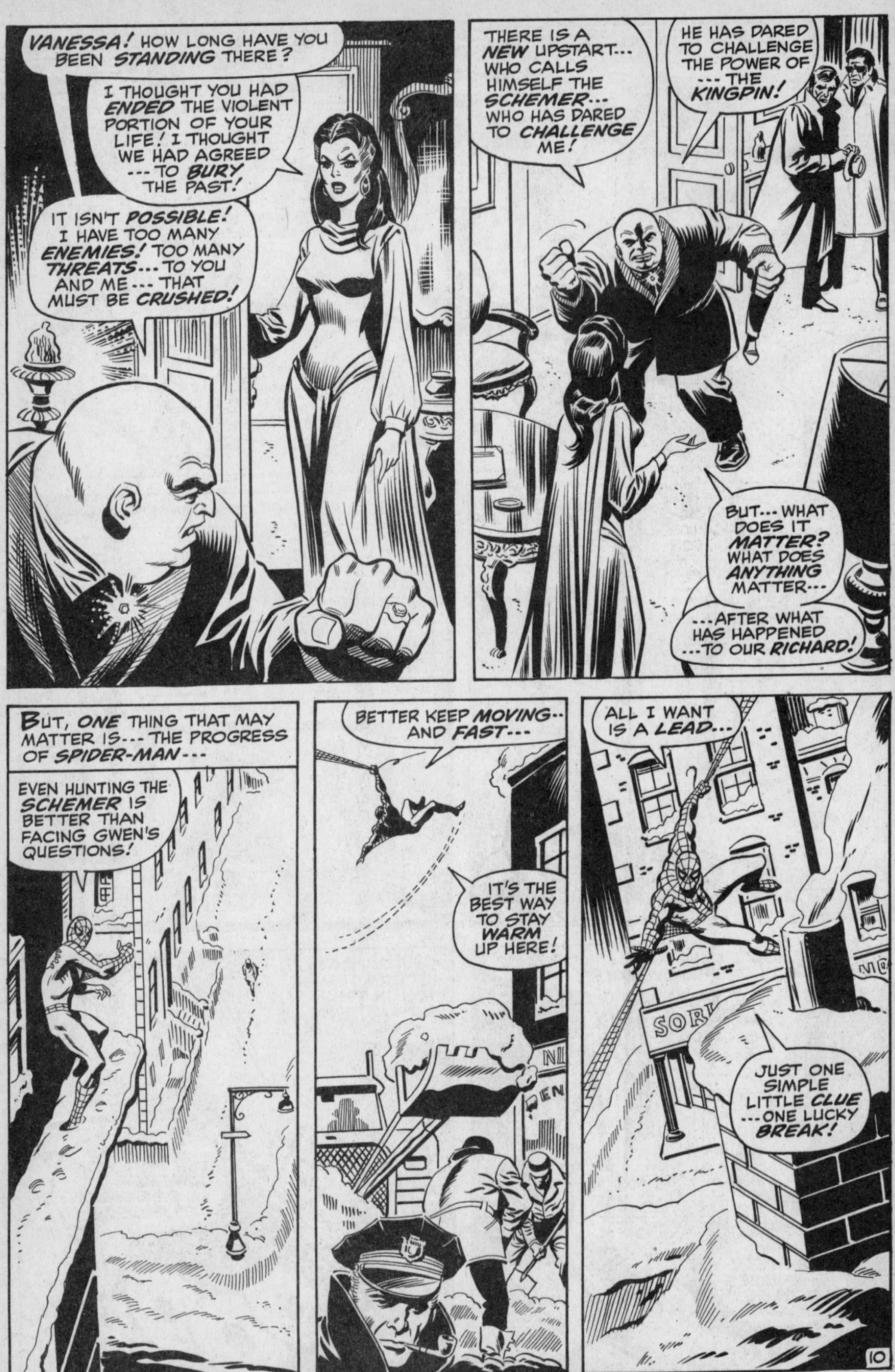
VANESSA! HOW LONG HAVE YOU BEEN STANDING THERE?
I THOUGHT YOU HAD ENDED THE VIOLENT PORTION OF YOUR LIFE! I THOUGHT WE HAD AGREED --- TO BURY THE PAST!
IT ISN'T POSSIBLE! I HAVE TOO MANY ENEMIES! TOO MANY THREATS--- TO YOU AND ME--- THAT MUST BE CRUSHED!
THERE IS A NEW UPSTART--- WHO CALLS HIMSELF THE SCHEMER--- WHO HAS DARED TO CHALLENGE ME!
HE HAS DARED TO CHALLENGE THE POWER OF --- THE KINGPIN!
BUT--- WHAT DOES IT MATTER? WHAT DOES ANYTHING MATTER---
---AFTER WHAT HAS HAPPENED ---TO OUR RICHARD!
BUT, ONE THING THAT MAY MATTER IS--- THE PROGRESS OF SPIDER-MAN---
EVEN HUNTING THE SCHEMER IS BETTER THAN FACING GWEN'S QUESTIONS!
BETTER KEEP MOVING-- AND FAST---
IT'S THE BEST WAY TO STAY WARM UP HERE!
ALL I WANT IS A LEAD---
JUST ONE SIMPLE LITTLE CLUE ---ONE LUCKY BREAK!
10

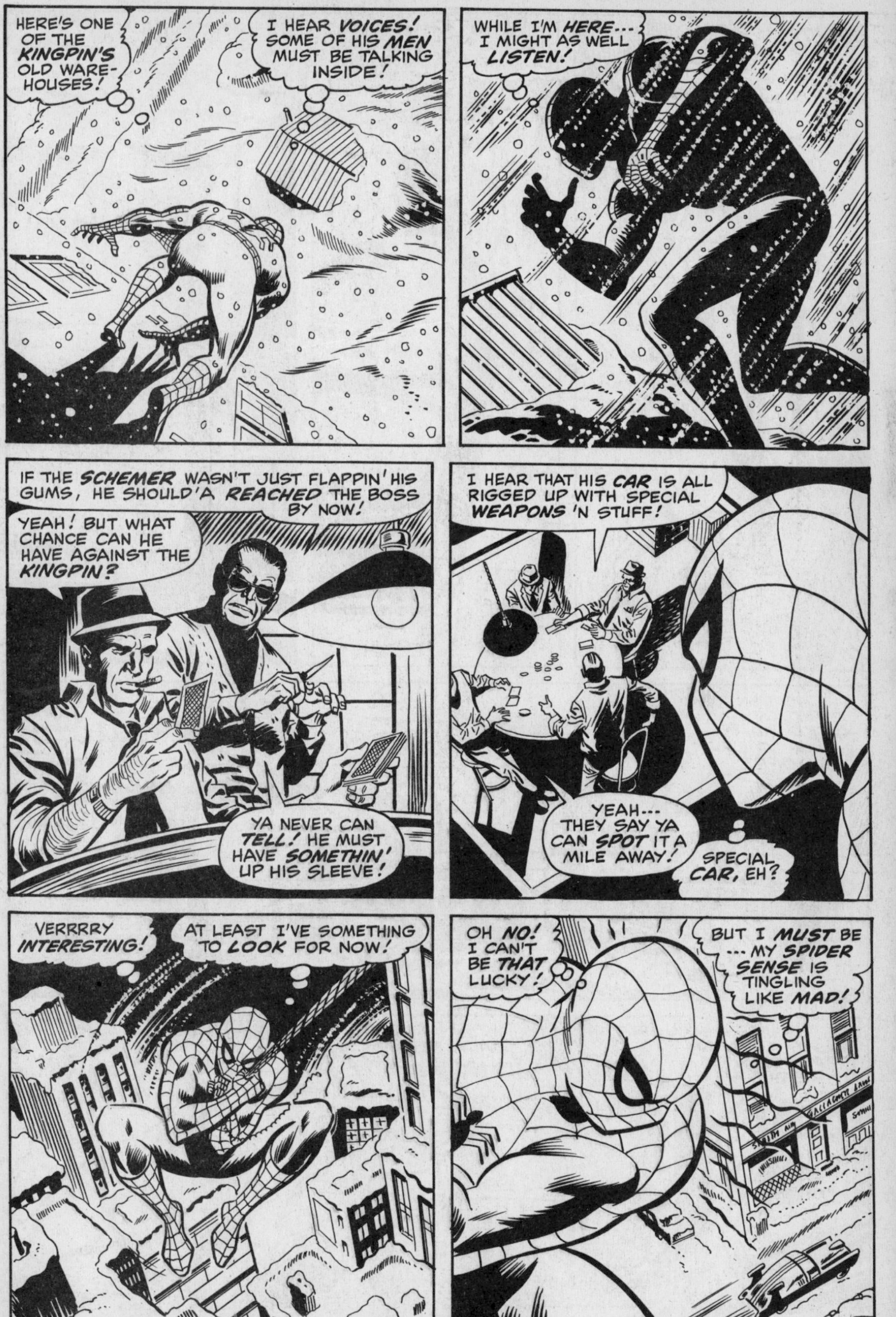

HERE'S ONE OF THE KINGPIN'S OLD WARE-HOUSES!
I HEAR VOICES! SOME OF HIS MEN MUST BE TALKING INSIDE!
WHILE I'M HERE... I MIGHT AS WELL LISTEN!
IF THE SCHEMER WASN'T JUST FLAPPIN' HIS GUMS, HE SHOULD'A REACHED THE BOSS BY NOW!
YEAH! BUT WHAT CHANCE CAN HE HAVE AGAINST THE KINGPIN?
YA NEVER CAN TELL! HE MUST HAVE SOMETHIN' UP HIS SLEEVE!
I HEAR THAT HIS CAR IS ALL RIGGED UP WITH SPECIAL WEAPONS 'N STUFF!
YEAH--- THEY SAY YA CAN SPOT IT A MILE AWAY!
SPECIAL CAR, EH?
VERRRRY INTERESTING!
AT LEAST I'VE SOMETHING TO LOOK FOR NOW!
OH NO! I CAN'T BE THAT LUCKY!
BUT I MUST BE --- MY SPIDER SENSE IS TINGLING LIKE MAD!

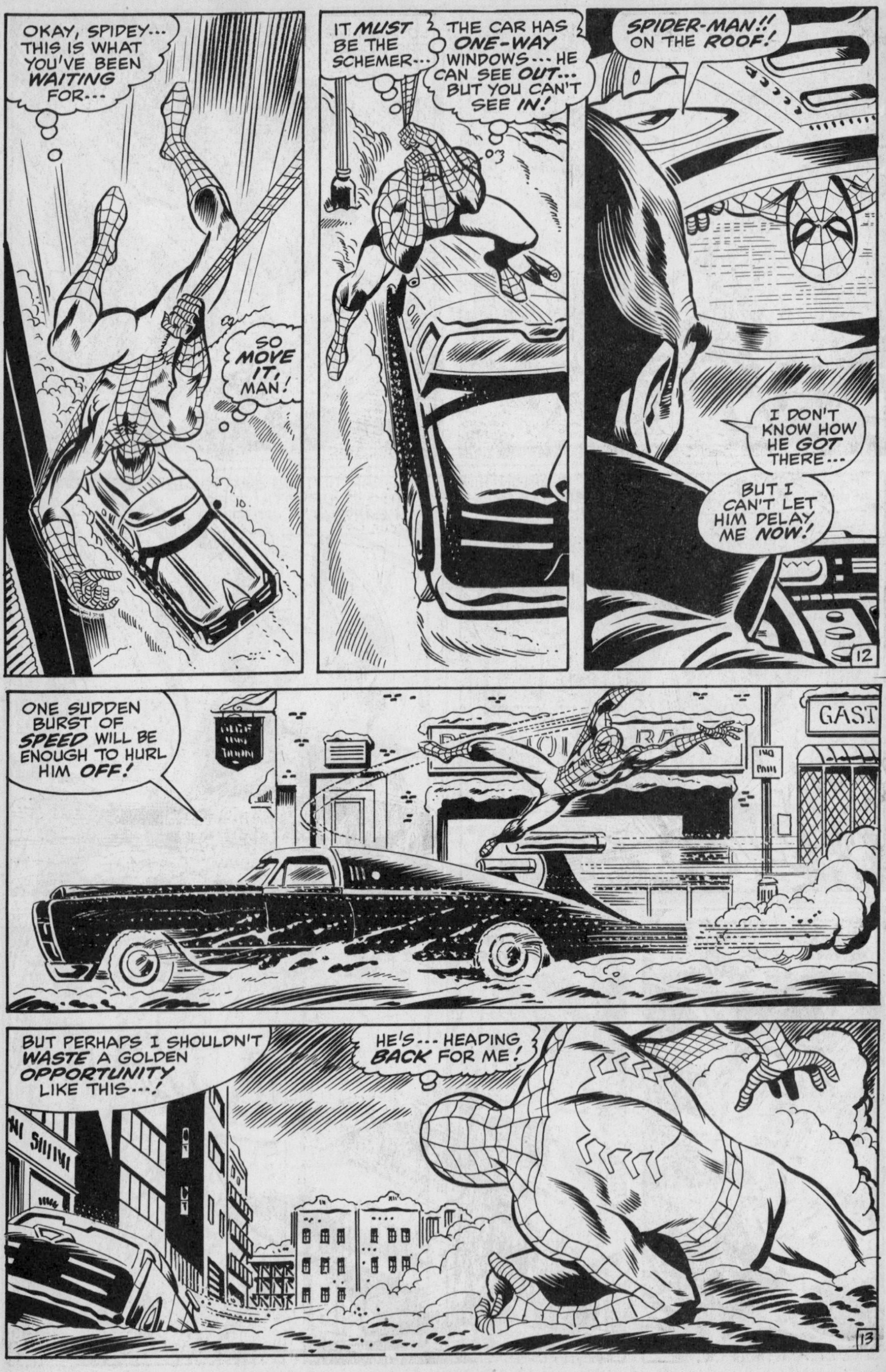

OKAY, SPIDEY... THIS IS WHAT YOU'VE BEEN WAITING FOR...
SO MOVE IT, MAN!
IT MUST BE THE SCHEMER...
THE CAR HAS ONE-WAY WINDOWS... HE CAN SEE OUT... BUT YOU CAN'T SEE IN!
SPIDER-MAN!! ON THE ROOF!
I DON'T KNOW HOW HE GOT THERE...
BUT I CAN'T LET HIM DELAY ME NOW!
12
ONE SUDDEN BURST OF SPEED WILL BE ENOUGH TO HURL HIM OFF!
GAST
BUT PERHAPS I SHOULDN'T WASTE A GOLDEN OPPORTUNITY LIKE THIS...!
HE'S... HEADING BACK FOR ME!
13

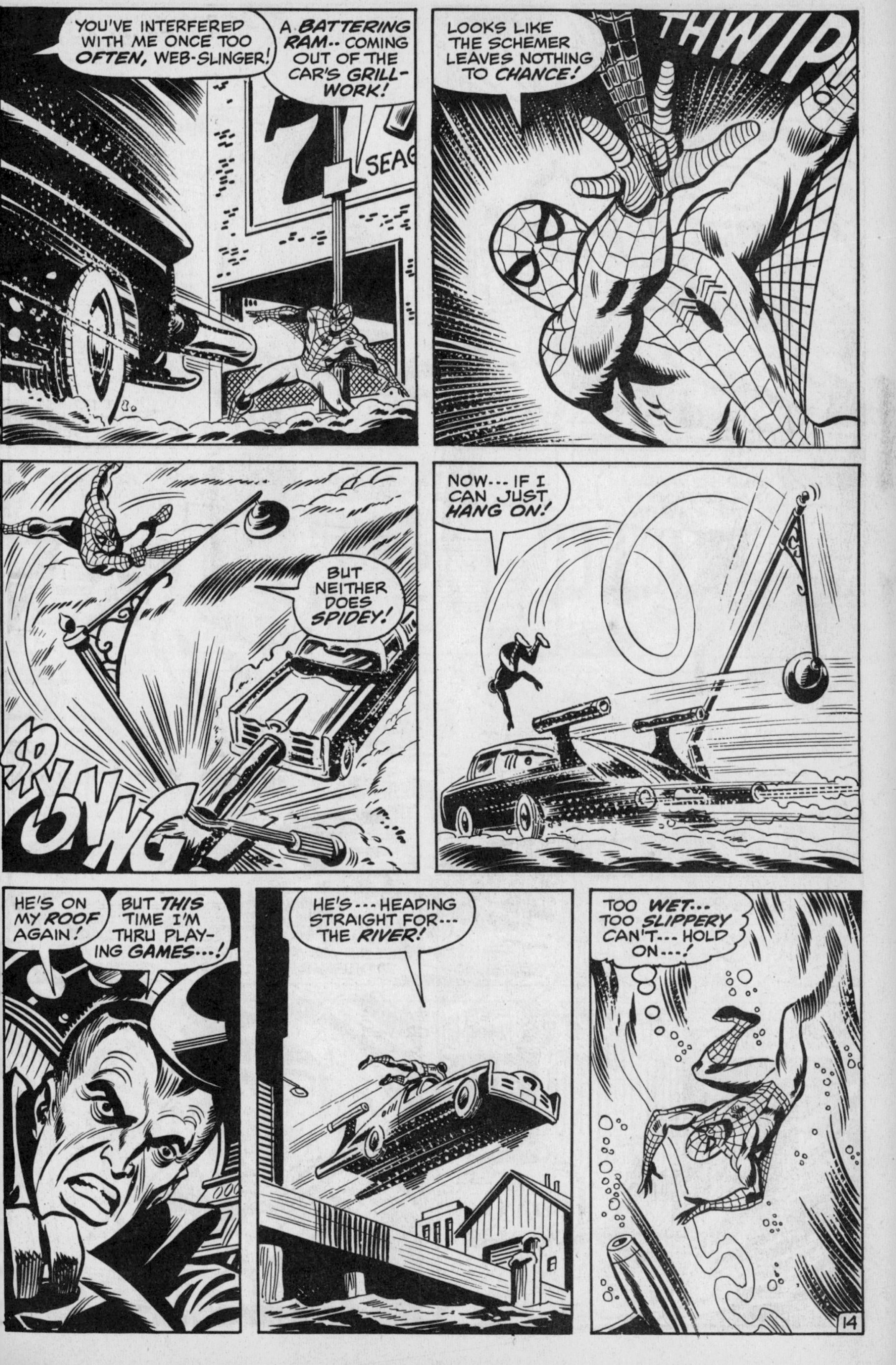
YOU'VE INTERFERED WITH ME ONCE TOO OFTEN, WEB-SLINGER!
A BATTERING RAM.. COMING OUT OF THE CAR'S GRILL-WORK!
SEAG
LOOKS LIKE THE SCHEMER LEAVES NOTHING TO CHANCE!
THWIP!
BUT NEITHER DOES SPIDEY!
SPANNNG!
NOW--- IF I CAN JUST HANG ON!
HE'S ON MY ROOF AGAIN!
BUT THIS TIME I'M THRU PLAYING GAMES...!
HE'S--- HEADING STRAIGHT FOR--- THE RIVER!
TOO WET... TOO SLIPPERY CAN'T--- HOLD ON---!
14

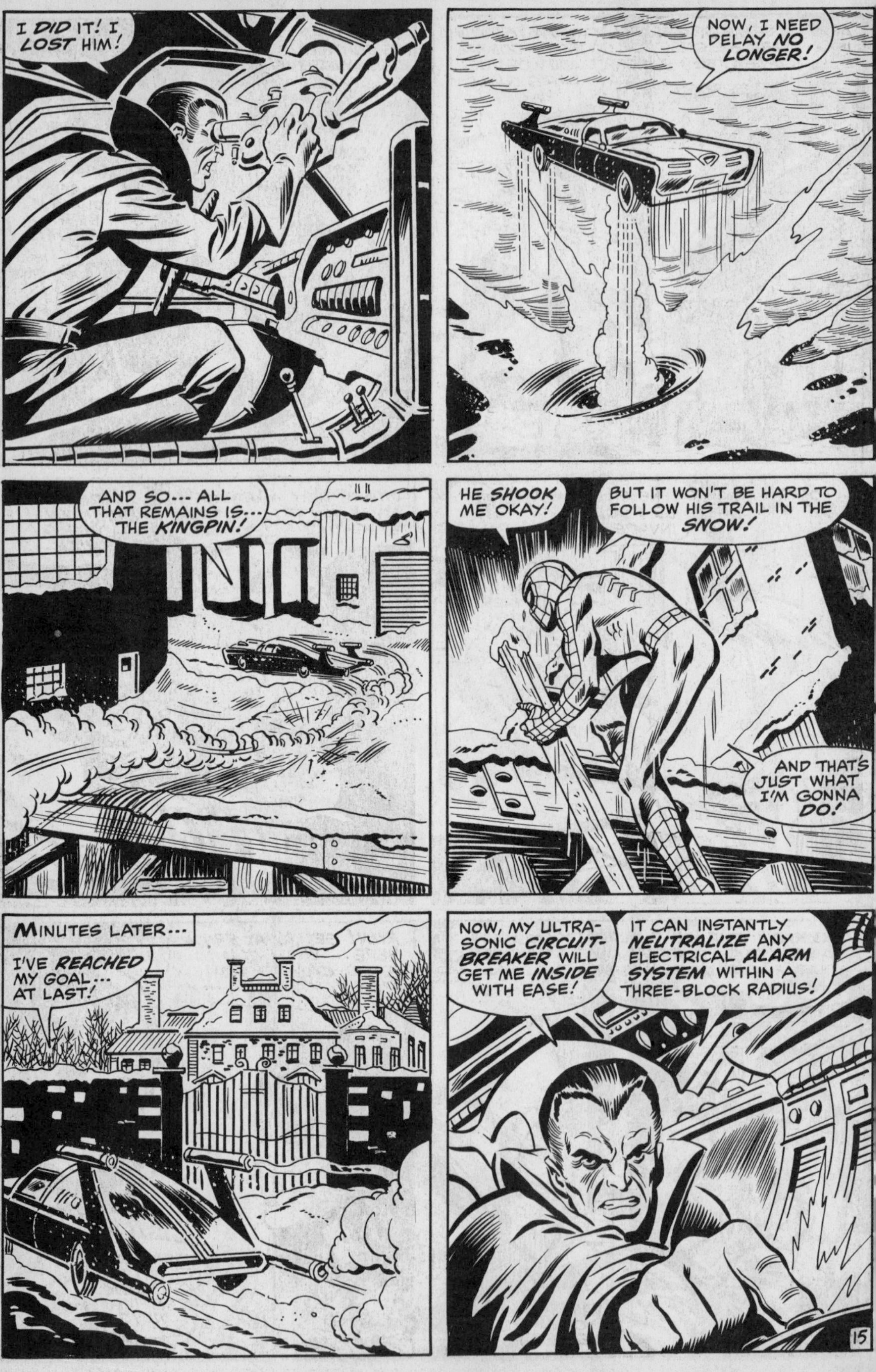
I DID IT! I LOST HIM!
NOW, I NEED DELAY NO LONGER!
AND SO... ALL THAT REMAINS IS... THE KINGPIN!
HE SHOOK ME OKAY!
BUT IT WON'T BE HARD TO FOLLOW HIS TRAIL IN THE SNOW!
AND THAT'S JUST WHAT I'M GONNA DO!
MINUTES LATER...
I'VE REACHED MY GOAL... AT LAST!
NOW, MY ULTRA-SONIC CIRCUIT-BREAKER WILL GET ME INSIDE WITH EASE!
IT CAN INSTANTLY NEUTRALIZE ANY ELECTRICAL ALARM SYSTEM WITHIN A THREE-BLOCK RADIUS!
15

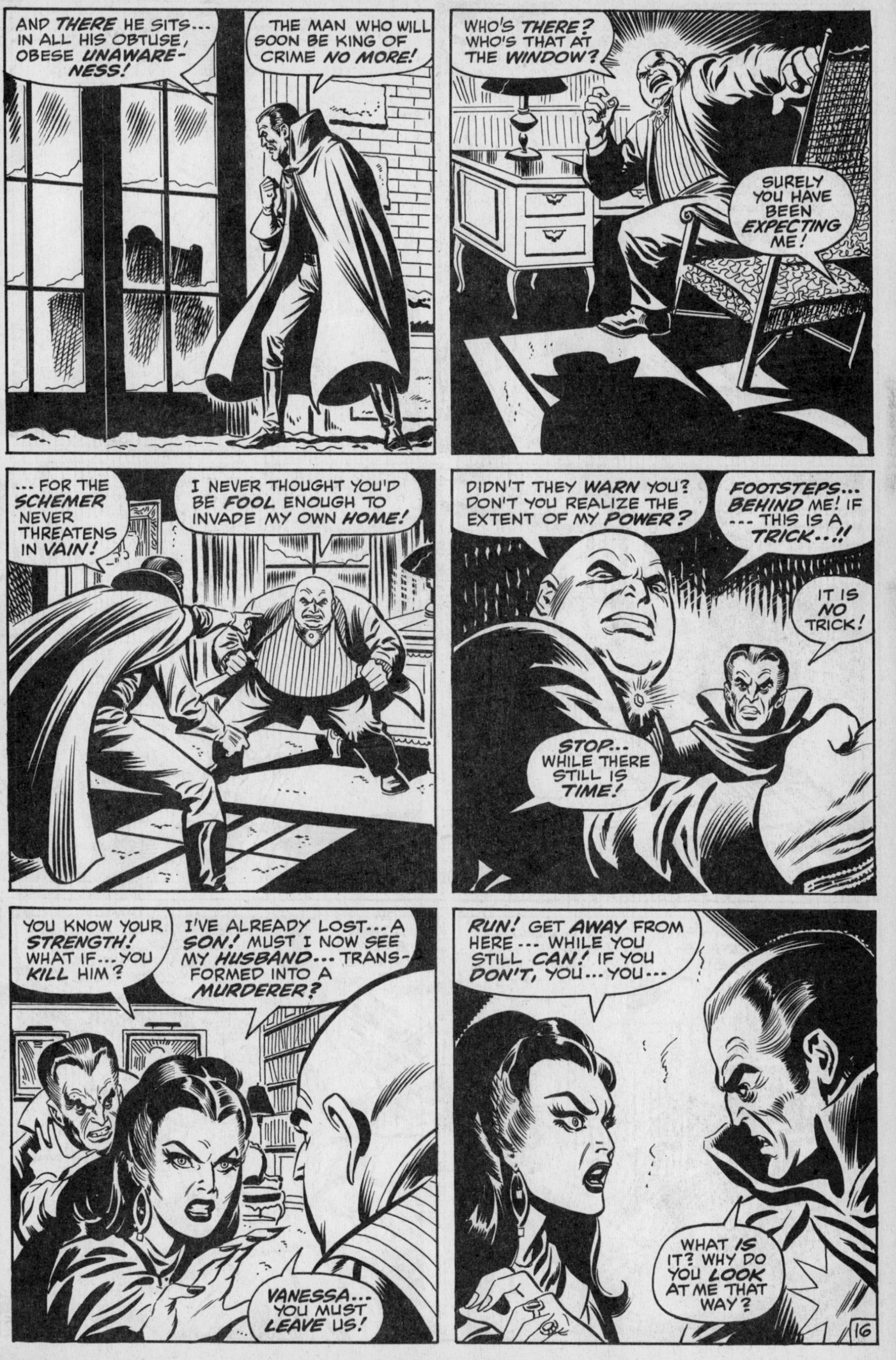
AND THERE HE SITS... IN ALL HIS OBTUSE, OBESE UNAWARENESS!
THE MAN WHO WILL SOON BE KING OF CRIME NO MORE!
WHO'S THERE? WHO'S THAT AT THE WINDOW?
SURELY YOU HAVE BEEN EXPECTING ME!
... FOR THE SCHEMER NEVER THREATENS IN VAIN!
I NEVER THOUGHT YOU'D BE FOOL ENOUGH TO INVADE MY OWN HOME!
DIDN'T THEY WARN YOU? DON'T YOU REALIZE THE EXTENT OF MY POWER?
FOOTSTEPS... BEHIND ME! IF --- THIS IS A TRICK--!!
IT IS NO TRICK!
STOP... WHILE THERE STILL IS TIME!
YOU KNOW YOUR STRENGTH! WHAT IF... YOU KILL HIM?
I'VE ALREADY LOST... A SON! MUST I NOW SEE MY HUSBAND... TRANSFORMED INTO A MURDERER?
VANESSA... YOU MUST LEAVE US!
RUN! GET AWAY FROM HERE --- WHILE YOU STILL CAN! IF YOU DON'T, YOU... YOU...
WHAT IS IT? WHY DO YOU LOOK AT ME THAT WAY?
16

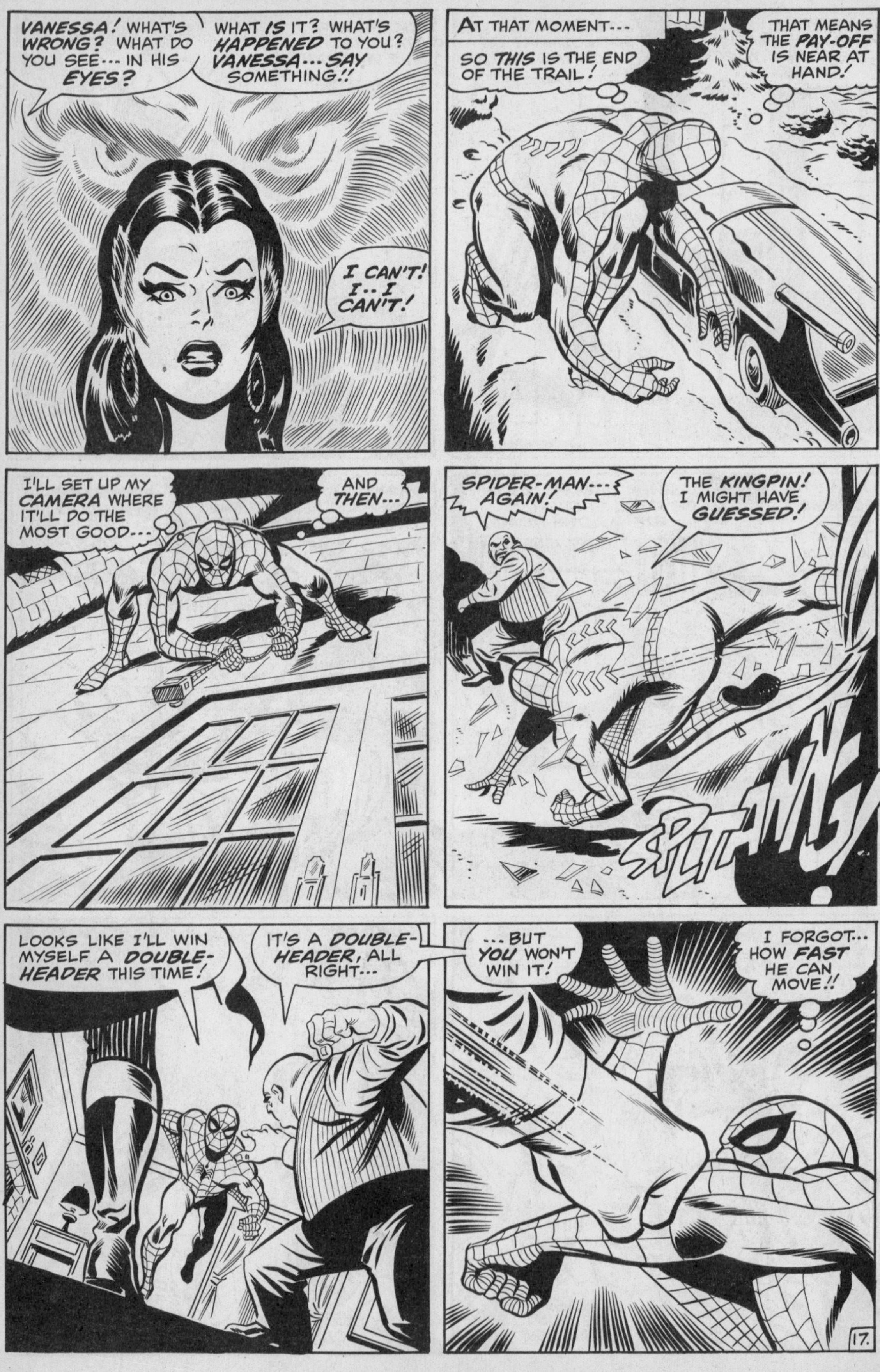
VANESSA! WHAT'S WRONG? WHAT DO YOU SEE--- IN HIS EYES?
WHAT IS IT? WHAT'S HAPPENED TO YOU? VANESSA... SAY SOMETHING!!
I CAN'T! I.. I CAN'T!
AT THAT MOMENT---
SO THIS IS THE END OF THE TRAIL!
THAT MEANS THE PAY-OFF IS NEAR AT HAND!
I'LL SET UP MY CAMERA WHERE IT'LL DO THE MOST GOOD---
AND THEN...
SPIDER-MAN--- AGAIN!
THE KINGPIN! I MIGHT HAVE GUESSED!
SPLTANNG!
LOOKS LIKE I'LL WIN MYSELF A DOUBLE-HEADER THIS TIME!
IT'S A DOUBLE-HEADER, ALL RIGHT...
... BUT YOU WON'T WIN IT!
I FORGOT... HOW FAST HE CAN MOVE!!
17.

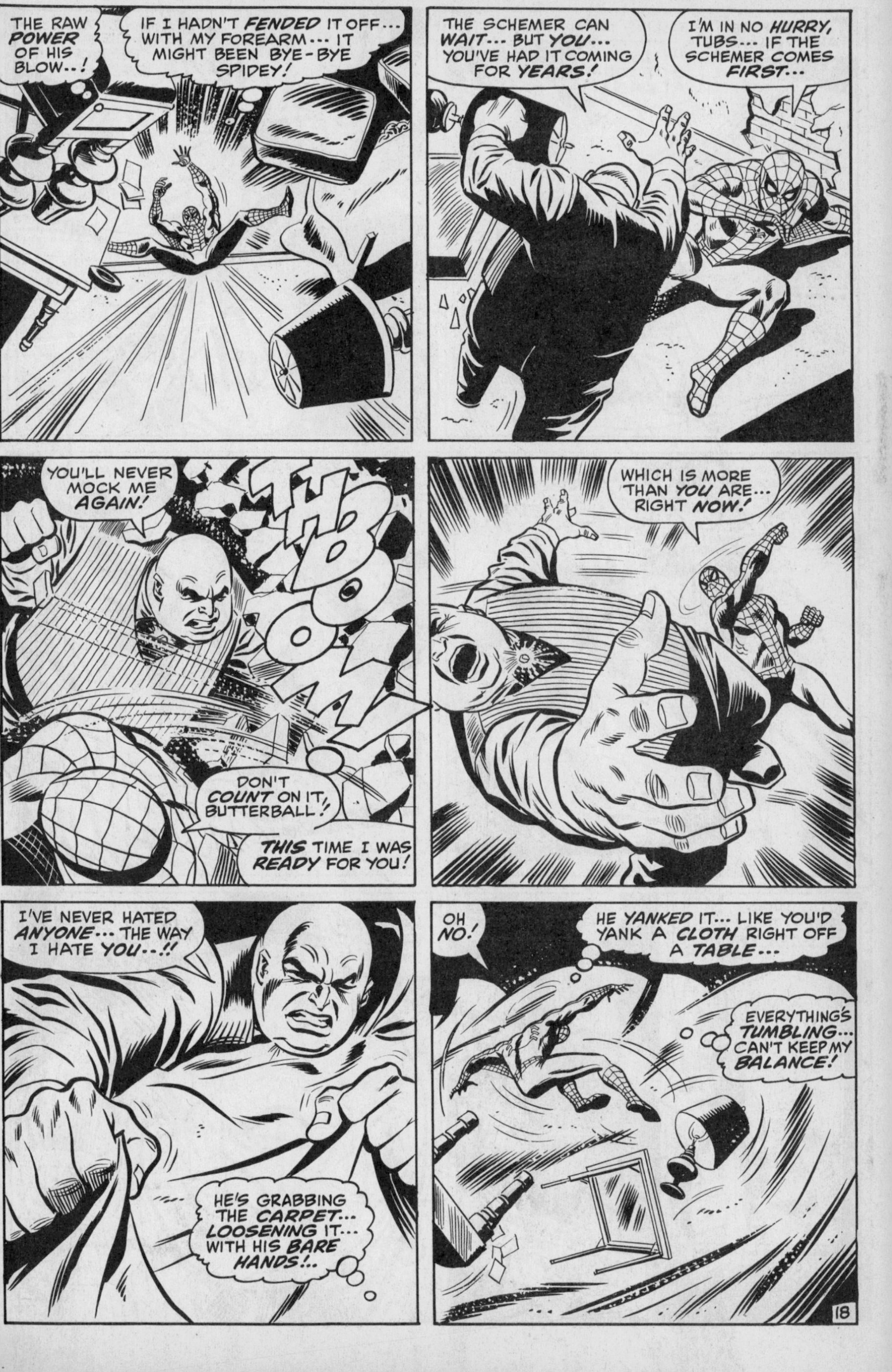
THE RAW POWER OF HIS BLOW..!
IF I HADN'T FENDED IT OFF... WITH MY FOREARM... IT MIGHT BEEN BYE-BYE SPIDEY!
THE SCHEMER CAN WAIT... BUT YOU... YOU'VE HAD IT COMING FOR YEARS!
I'M IN NO HURRY, TUBS... IF THE SCHEMER COMES FIRST...
YOU'LL NEVER MOCK ME AGAIN!
THOOOM!
DON'T COUNT ON IT, BUTTERBALL!
THIS TIME I WAS READY FOR YOU!
WHICH IS MORE THAN YOU ARE... RIGHT NOW!
I'VE NEVER HATED ANYONE... THE WAY I HATE YOU..!!
HE'S GRABBING THE CARPET... LOOSENING IT... WITH HIS BARE HANDS!..
OH NO!
HE YANKED IT... LIKE YOU'D YANK A CLOTH RIGHT OFF A TABLE...
EVERYTHING'S TUMBLING... CAN'T KEEP MY BALANCE!

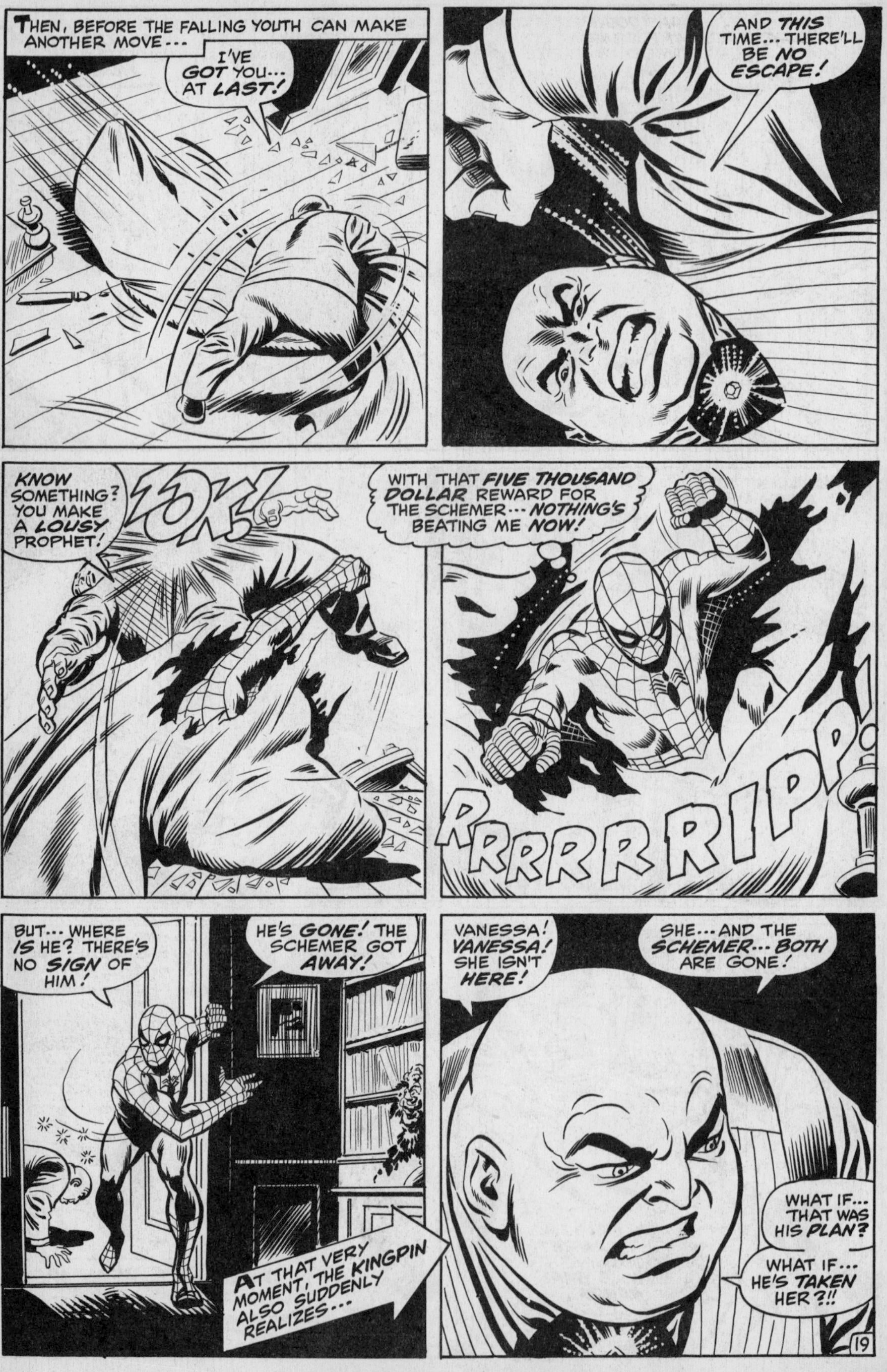
THEN, BEFORE THE FALLING YOUTH CAN MAKE ANOTHER MOVE...
I'VE GOT YOU... AT LAST!
AND THIS TIME... THERE'LL BE NO ESCAPE!
KNOW SOMETHING? YOU MAKE A LOUSY PROPHET!
SOK!
WITH THAT FIVE THOUSAND DOLLAR REWARD FOR THE SCHEMER... NOTHING'S BEATING ME NOW!
RRRRRRIPP!
BUT... WHERE IS HE? THERE'S NO SIGN OF HIM!
HE'S GONE! THE SCHEMER GOT AWAY!
AT THAT VERY MOMENT, THE KINGPIN ALSO SUDDENLY REALIZES...
VANESSA! VANESSA! SHE ISN'T HERE!
SHE... AND THE SCHEMER... BOTH ARE GONE!
WHAT IF... THAT WAS HIS PLAN?
WHAT IF... HE'S TAKEN HER?!!
19

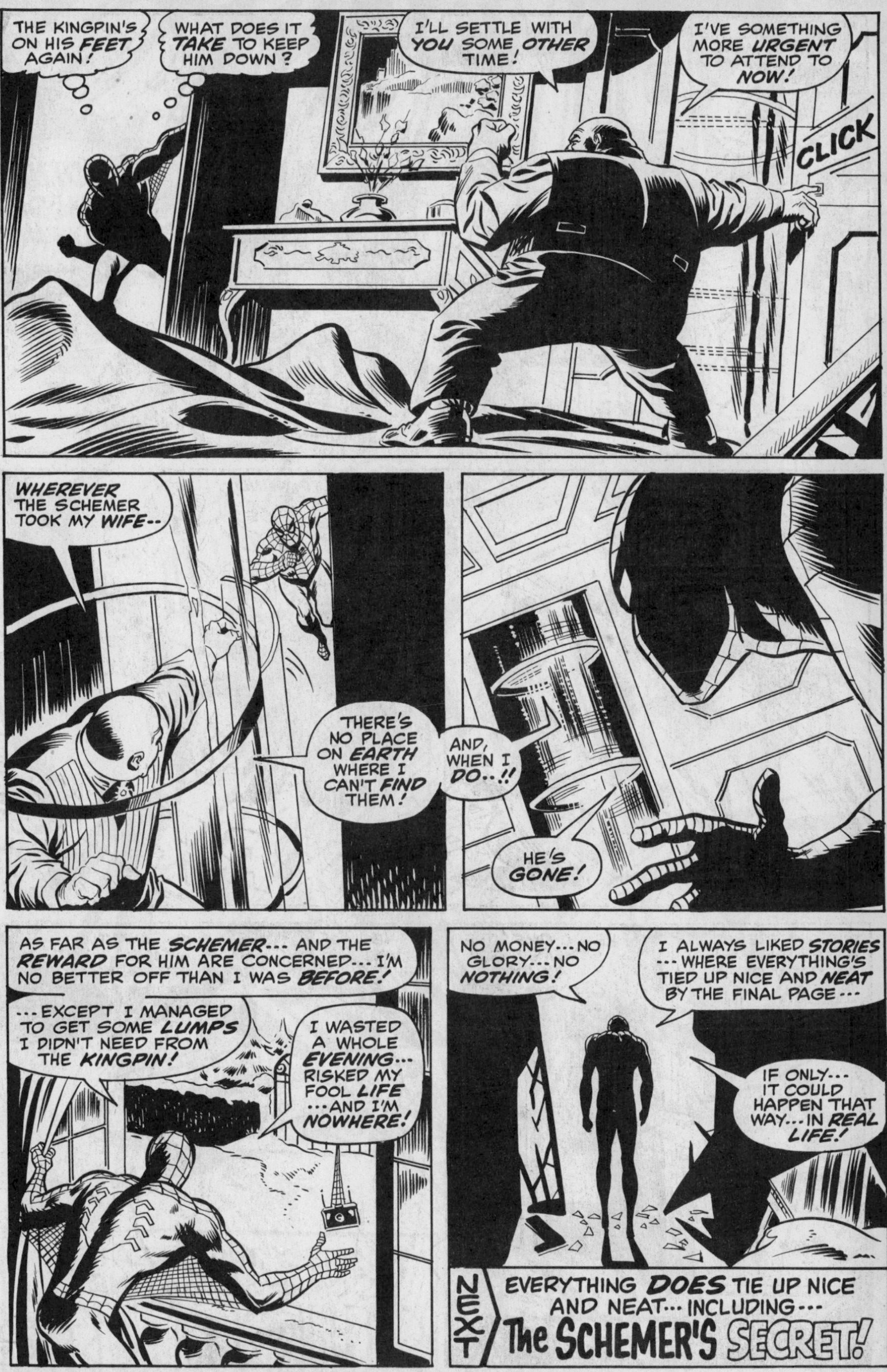
THE KINGPIN'S ON HIS FEET AGAIN!
WHAT DOES IT TAKE TO KEEP HIM DOWN?
I'LL SETTLE WITH YOU SOME OTHER TIME!
I'VE SOMETHING MORE URGENT TO ATTEND TO NOW!
CLICK
WHEREVER THE SCHEMER TOOK MY WIFE--
THERE'S NO PLACE ON EARTH WHERE I CAN'T FIND THEM!
AND, WHEN I DO..!!
HE'S GONE!
AS FAR AS THE SCHEMER--- AND THE REWARD FOR HIM ARE CONCERNED--- I'M NO BETTER OFF THAN I WAS BEFORE!
---EXCEPT I MANAGED TO GET SOME LUMPS I DIDN'T NEED FROM THE KINGPIN!
I WASTED A WHOLE EVENING... RISKED MY FOOL LIFE ---AND I'M NOWHERE!
NO MONEY---NO GLORY---NO NOTHING!
I ALWAYS LIKED STORIES ---WHERE EVERYTHING'S TIED UP NICE AND NEAT BY THE FINAL PAGE---
IF ONLY--- IT COULD HAPPEN THAT WAY... IN REAL LIFE!
NEXT
EVERYTHING DOES TIE UP NICE AND NEAT--- INCLUDING---
The SCHEMER'S SECRET!

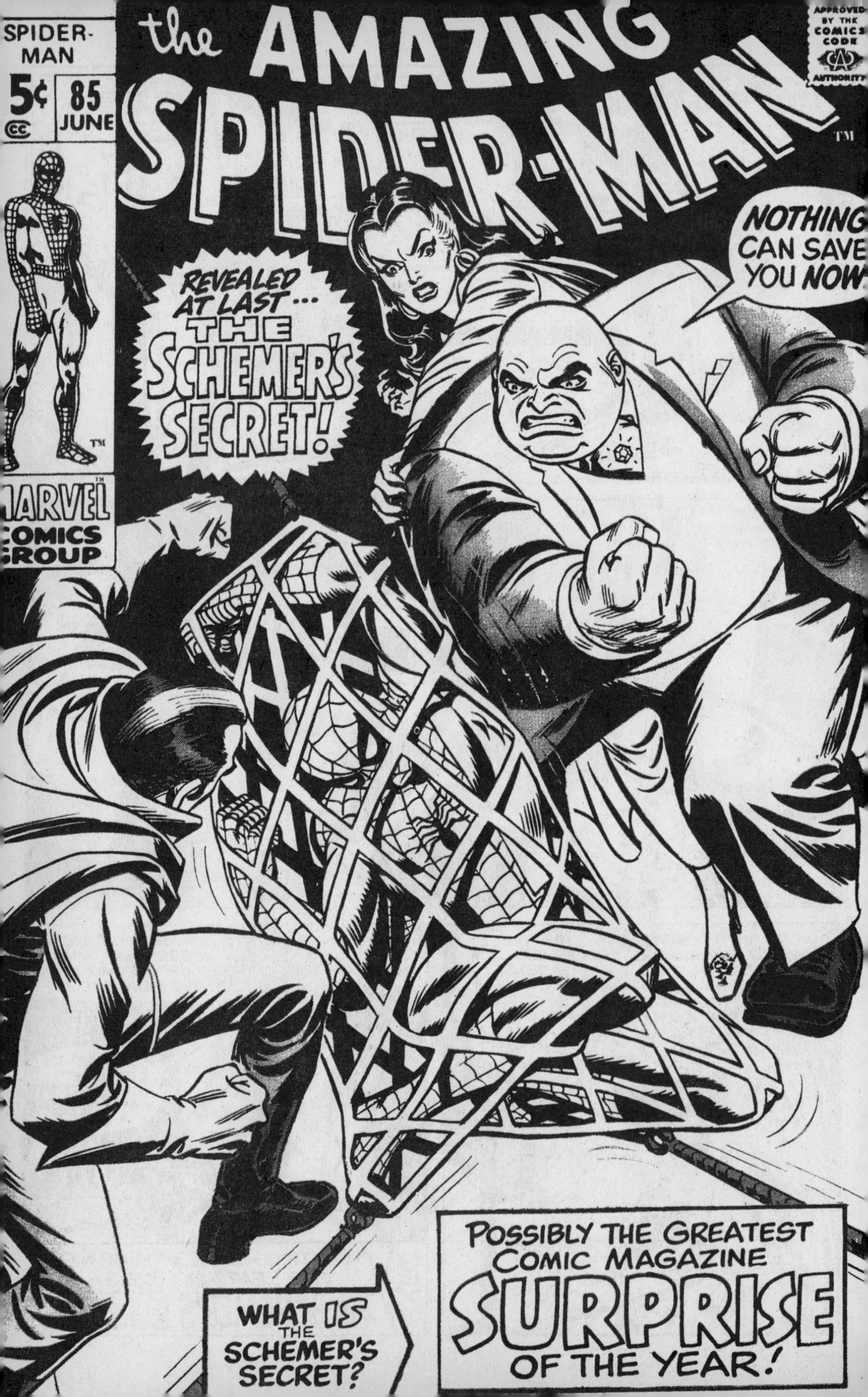

SPIDER-MAN
5¢
85
JUNE
APPROVED BY THE COMICS CODE AUTHORITY
the AMAZING SPIDER-MAN
MARVEL COMICS GROUP
REVEALED AT LAST... THE SCHEMER'S SECRET!
NOTHING CAN SAVE YOU NOW
POSSIBLY THE GREATEST COMIC MAGAZINE SURPRISE OF THE YEAR!
WHAT IS THE SCHEMER'S SECRET?

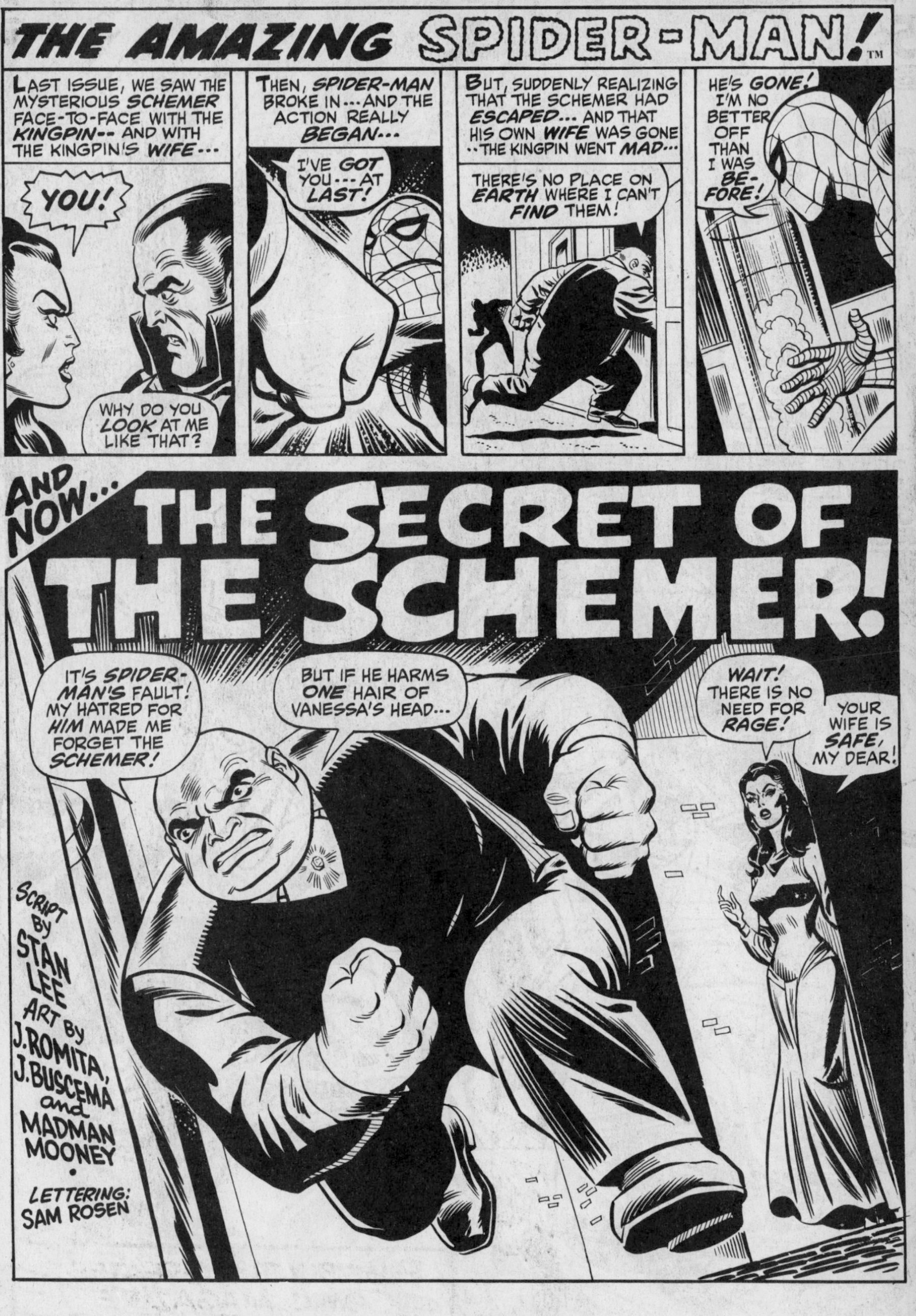
THE AMAZING SPIDER-MAN! TM
LAST ISSUE, WE SAW THE MYSTERIOUS SCHEMER FACE-TO-FACE WITH THE KINGPIN-- AND WITH THE KINGPIN'S WIFE...
YOU!
WHY DO YOU LOOK AT ME LIKE THAT?
THEN, SPIDER-MAN BROKE IN... AND THE ACTION REALLY BEGAN...
I'VE GOT YOU--- AT LAST!
BUT, SUDDENLY REALIZING THAT THE SCHEMER HAD ESCAPED... AND THAT HIS OWN WIFE WAS GONE --THE KINGPIN WENT MAD...
THERE'S NO PLACE ON EARTH WHERE I CAN'T FIND THEM!
HE'S GONE! I'M NO BETTER OFF THAN I WAS BE-FORE!
AND NOW... THE SECRET OF THE SCHEMER!
IT'S SPIDER-MAN'S FAULT! MY HATRED FOR HIM MADE ME FORGET THE SCHEMER!
BUT IF HE HARMS ONE HAIR OF VANESSA'S HEAD...
WAIT! THERE IS NO NEED FOR RAGE!
YOUR WIFE IS SAFE, MY DEAR!
SCRIPT BY STAN LEE
ART BY J. ROMITA, J. BUSCEMA and MADMAN MOONEY
LETTERING: SAM ROSEN

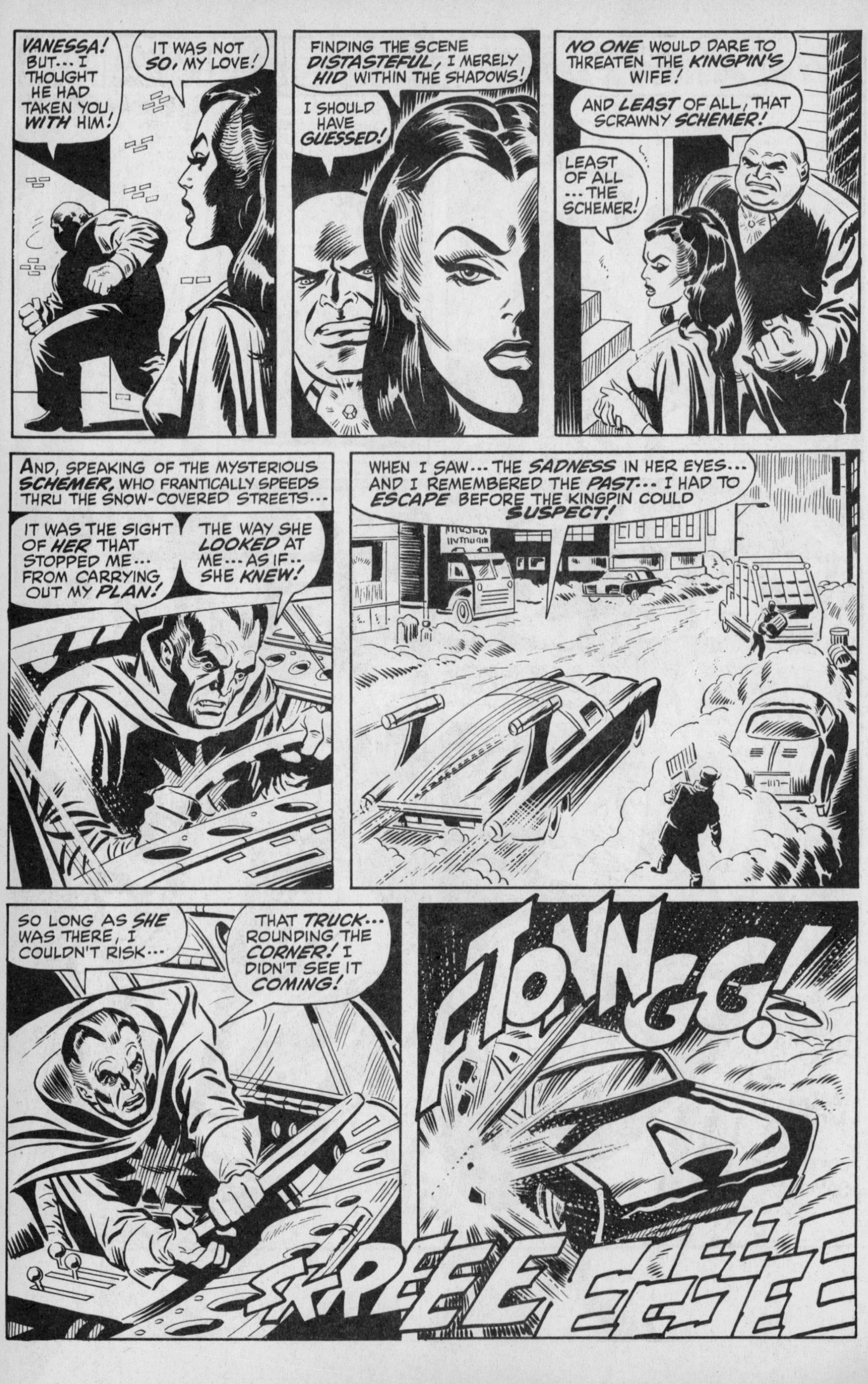
VANESSA! BUT... I THOUGHT HE HAD TAKEN YOU WITH HIM!
IT WAS NOT SO, MY LOVE!
FINDING THE SCENE DISTASTEFUL, I MERELY HID WITHIN THE SHADOWS!
I SHOULD HAVE GUESSED!
NO ONE WOULD DARE TO THREATEN THE KINGPIN'S WIFE!
AND LEAST OF ALL, THAT SCRAWNY SCHEMER!
LEAST OF ALL ... THE SCHEMER!
AND, SPEAKING OF THE MYSTERIOUS SCHEMER, WHO FRANTICALLY SPEEDS THRU THE SNOW-COVERED STREETS...
IT WAS THE SIGHT OF HER THAT STOPPED ME... FROM CARRYING OUT MY PLAN!
THE WAY SHE LOOKED AT ME... AS IF.. SHE KNEW!
WHEN I SAW... THE SADNESS IN HER EYES... AND I REMEMBERED THE PAST... I HAD TO ESCAPE BEFORE THE KINGPIN COULD SUSPECT!
SO LONG AS SHE WAS THERE, I COULDN'T RISK...
THAT TRUCK... ROUNDING THE CORNER! I DIDN'T SEE IT COMING!
TONNGG!
SKREEEEEEEE

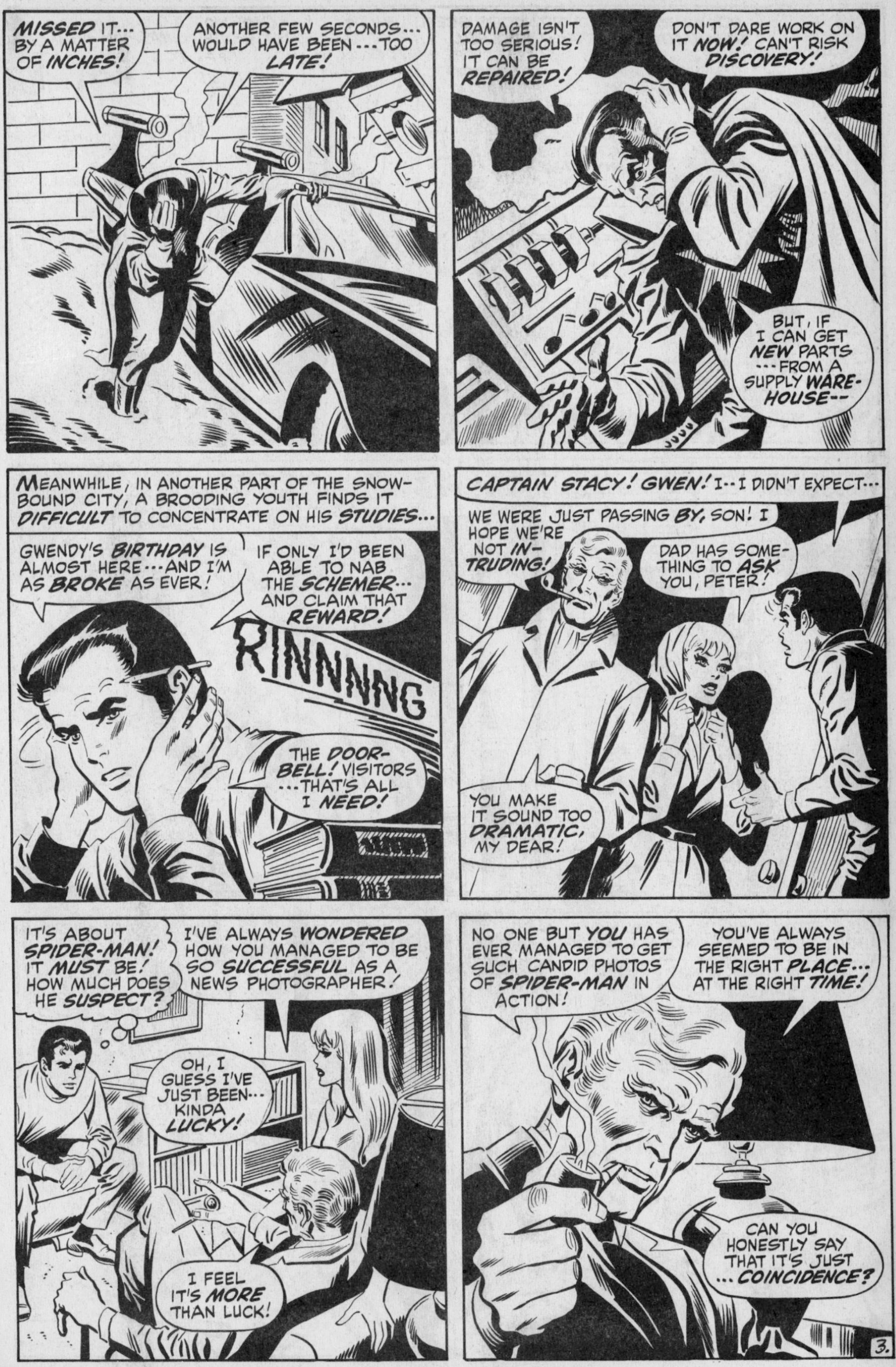
MISSED IT... BY A MATTER OF INCHES!
ANOTHER FEW SECONDS... WOULD HAVE BEEN---TOO LATE!
DAMAGE ISN'T TOO SERIOUS! IT CAN BE REPAIRED!
DON'T DARE WORK ON IT NOW! CAN'T RISK DISCOVERY!
BUT, IF I CAN GET NEW PARTS---FROM A SUPPLY WARE-HOUSE--
MEANWHILE, IN ANOTHER PART OF THE SNOW-BOUND CITY, A BROODING YOUTH FINDS IT DIFFICULT TO CONCENTRATE ON HIS STUDIES...
GWENDY'S BIRTHDAY IS ALMOST HERE---AND I'M AS BROKE AS EVER!
IF ONLY I'D BEEN ABLE TO NAB THE SCHEMER... AND CLAIM THAT REWARD!
RINNNNG
THE DOOR-BELL! VISITORS...THAT'S ALL I NEED!
CAPTAIN STACY! GWEN! I--I DIDN'T EXPECT...
WE WERE JUST PASSING BY, SON! I HOPE WE'RE NOT IN-TRUDING!
DAD HAS SOME-THING TO ASK YOU, PETER!
YOU MAKE IT SOUND TOO DRAMATIC, MY DEAR!
IT'S ABOUT SPIDER-MAN! IT MUST BE! HOW MUCH DOES HE SUSPECT?
I'VE ALWAYS WONDERED HOW YOU MANAGED TO BE SO SUCCESSFUL AS A NEWS PHOTOGRAPHER!
OH, I GUESS I'VE JUST BEEN--- KINDA LUCKY!
I FEEL IT'S MORE THAN LUCK!
NO ONE BUT YOU HAS EVER MANAGED TO GET SUCH CANDID PHOTOS OF SPIDER-MAN IN ACTION!
YOU'VE ALWAYS SEEMED TO BE IN THE RIGHT PLACE... AT THE RIGHT TIME!
CAN YOU HONESTLY SAY THAT IT'S JUST ...COINCIDENCE?
3.

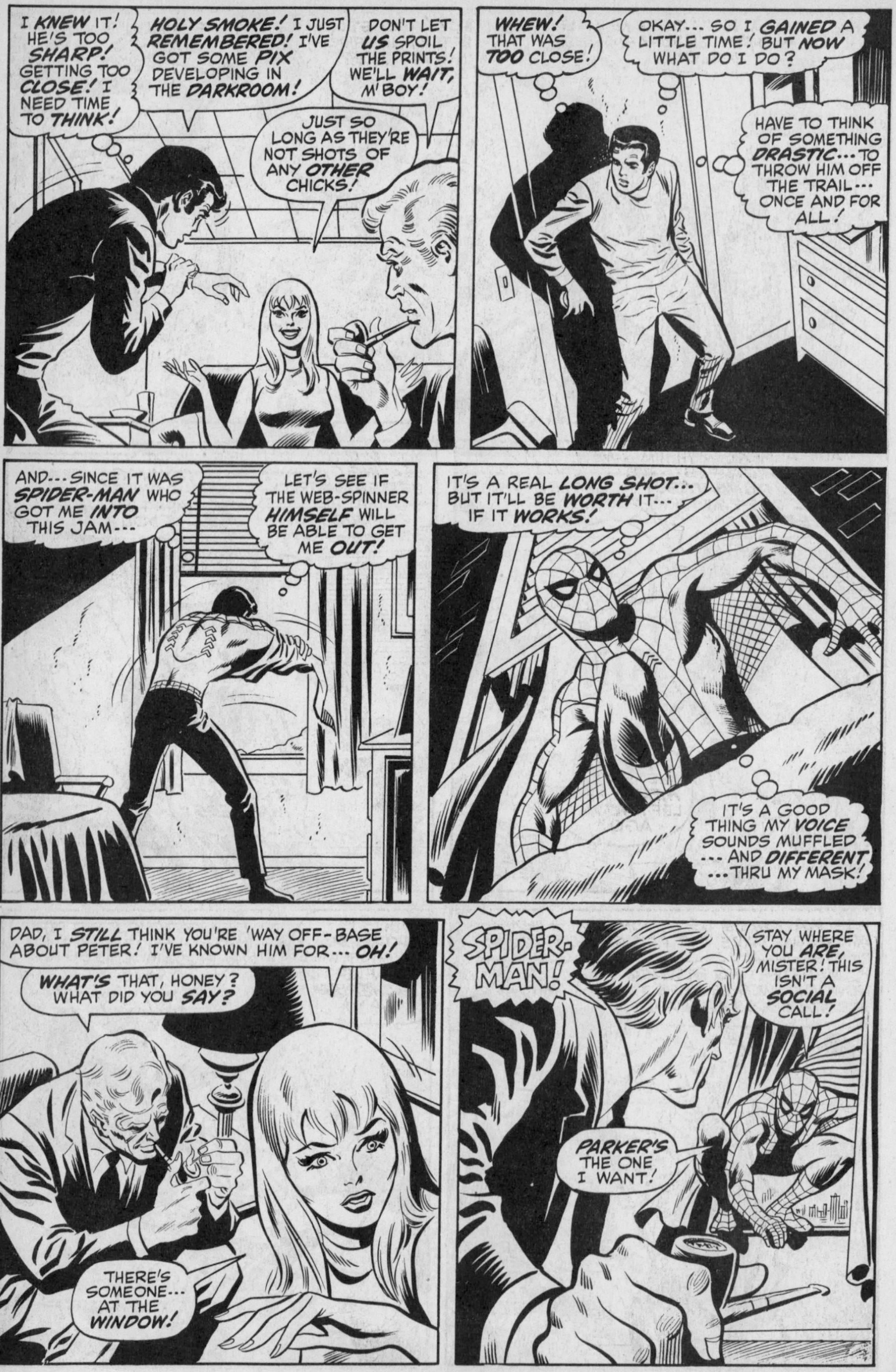

I KNEW IT! HE'S TOO SHARP! GETTING TOO CLOSE! I NEED TIME TO THINK!
HOLY SMOKE! I JUST REMEMBERED! I'VE GOT SOME PIX DEVELOPING IN THE DARKROOM!
DON'T LET US SPOIL THE PRINTS! WE'LL WAIT, M'BOY!
JUST SO LONG AS THEY'RE NOT SHOTS OF ANY OTHER CHICKS!
WHEW! THAT WAS TOO CLOSE!
OKAY... SO I GAINED A LITTLE TIME! BUT NOW WHAT DO I DO?
HAVE TO THINK OF SOMETHING DRASTIC... TO THROW HIM OFF THE TRAIL... ONCE AND FOR ALL!
AND... SINCE IT WAS SPIDER-MAN WHO GOT ME INTO THIS JAM...
LET'S SEE IF THE WEB-SPINNER HIMSELF WILL BE ABLE TO GET ME OUT!
IT'S A REAL LONG SHOT... BUT IT'LL BE WORTH IT... IF IT WORKS!
IT'S A GOOD THING MY VOICE SOUNDS MUFFLED... AND DIFFERENT ...THRU MY MASK!
DAD, I STILL THINK YOU'RE 'WAY OFF-BASE ABOUT PETER! I'VE KNOWN HIM FOR... OH!
WHAT'S THAT, HONEY? WHAT DID YOU SAY?
THERE'S SOMEONE... AT THE WINDOW!
SPIDER-MAN!
STAY WHERE YOU ARE, MISTER! THIS ISN'T A SOCIAL CALL!
PARKER'S THE ONE I WANT!

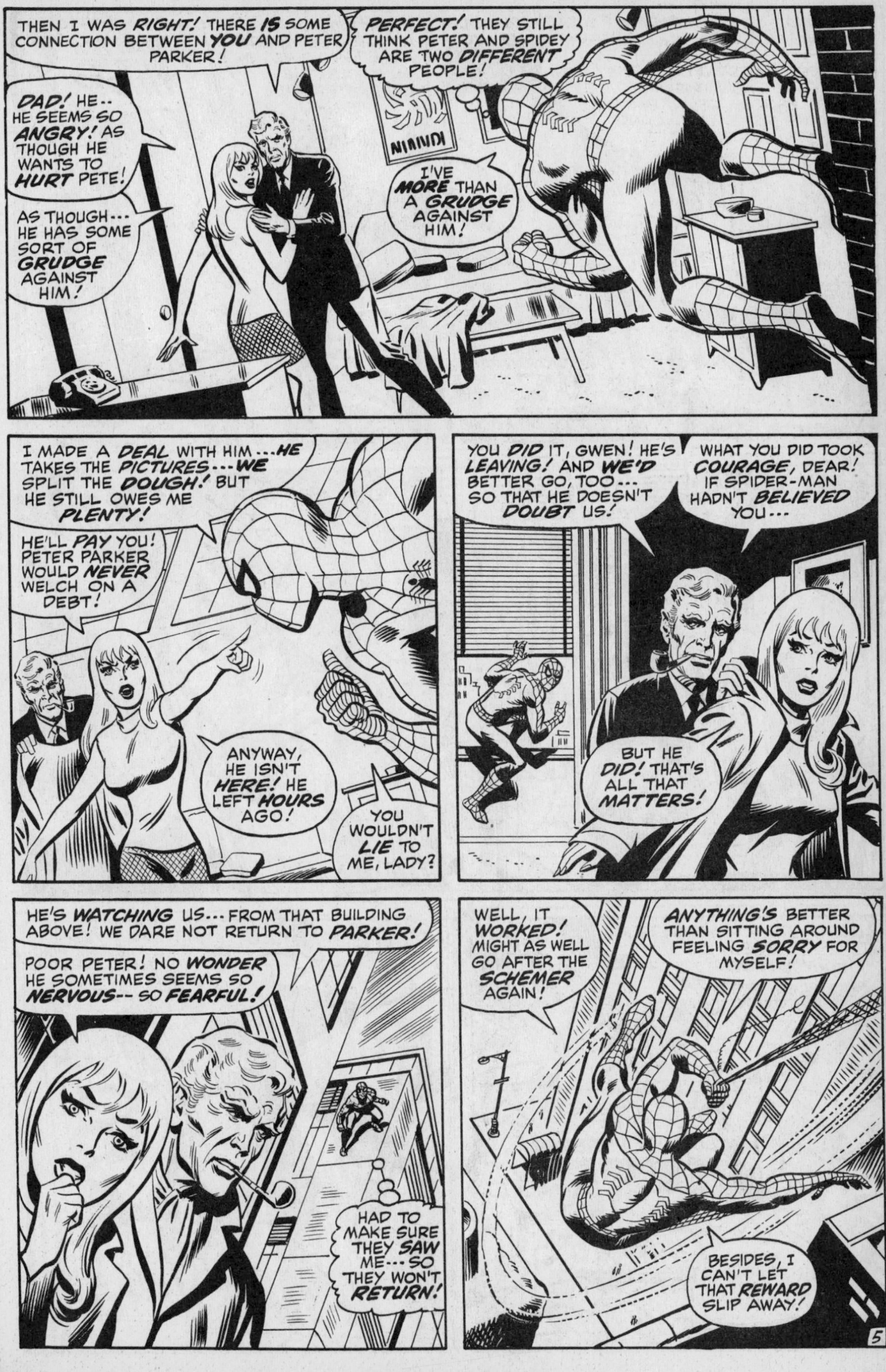
THEN I WAS RIGHT! THERE IS SOME CONNECTION BETWEEN YOU AND PETER PARKER!
PERFECT! THEY STILL THINK PETER AND SPIDEY ARE TWO DIFFERENT PEOPLE!
DAD! HE.. HE SEEMS SO ANGRY! AS THOUGH HE WANTS TO HURT PETE!
AS THOUGH... HE HAS SOME SORT OF GRUDGE AGAINST HIM!
I'VE MORE THAN A GRUDGE AGAINST HIM!
I MADE A DEAL WITH HIM ...HE TAKES THE PICTURES---WE SPLIT THE DOUGH! BUT HE STILL OWES ME PLENTY!
HE'LL PAY YOU! PETER PARKER WOULD NEVER WELCH ON A DEBT!
ANYWAY, HE ISN'T HERE! HE LEFT HOURS AGO!
YOU WOULDN'T LIE TO ME, LADY?
YOU DID IT, GWEN! HE'S LEAVING! AND WE'D BETTER GO, TOO... SO THAT HE DOESN'T DOUBT US!
WHAT YOU DID TOOK COURAGE, DEAR! IF SPIDER-MAN HADN'T BELIEVED YOU...
BUT HE DID! THAT'S ALL THAT MATTERS!
HE'S WATCHING US... FROM THAT BUILDING ABOVE! WE DARE NOT RETURN TO PARKER!
POOR PETER! NO WONDER HE SOMETIMES SEEMS SO NERVOUS-- SO FEARFUL!
HAD TO MAKE SURE THEY SAW ME--- SO THEY WON'T RETURN!
WELL, IT WORKED! MIGHT AS WELL GO AFTER THE SCHEMER AGAIN!
ANYTHING'S BETTER THAN SITTING AROUND FEELING SORRY FOR MYSELF!
BESIDES, I CAN'T LET THAT REWARD SLIP AWAY!
5

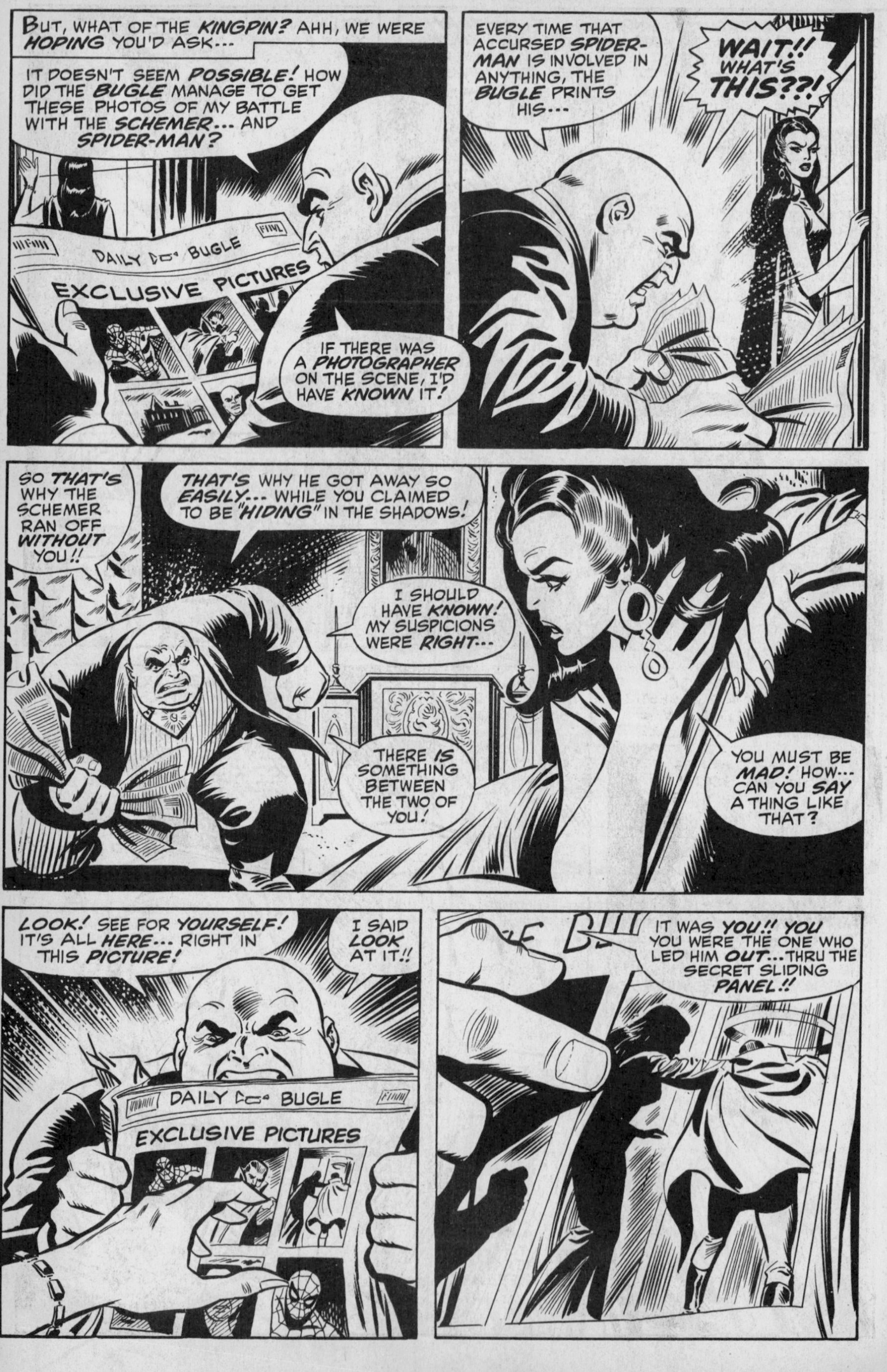

BUT, WHAT OF THE KINGPIN? AHH, WE WERE HOPING YOU'D ASK---
IT DOESN'T SEEM POSSIBLE! HOW DID THE BUGLE MANAGE TO GET THESE PHOTOS OF MY BATTLE WITH THE SCHEMER--- AND SPIDER-MAN?
DAILY BUGLE
EXCLUSIVE PICTURES
IF THERE WAS A PHOTOGRAPHER ON THE SCENE, I'D HAVE KNOWN IT!
EVERY TIME THAT ACCURSED SPIDER-MAN IS INVOLVED IN ANYTHING, THE BUGLE PRINTS HIS---
WAIT!! WHAT'S THIS??!
SO THAT'S WHY THE SCHEMER RAN OFF WITHOUT YOU!!
THAT'S WHY HE GOT AWAY SO EASILY--- WHILE YOU CLAIMED TO BE "HIDING" IN THE SHADOWS!
I SHOULD HAVE KNOWN! MY SUSPICIONS WERE RIGHT---
THERE IS SOMETHING BETWEEN THE TWO OF YOU!
YOU MUST BE MAD! HOW--- CAN YOU SAY A THING LIKE THAT?
LOOK! SEE FOR YOURSELF! IT'S ALL HERE--- RIGHT IN THIS PICTURE!
I SAID LOOK AT IT!!
DAILY BUGLE
EXCLUSIVE PICTURES
IT WAS YOU!! YOU YOU WERE THE ONE WHO LED HIM OUT---THRU THE SECRET SLIDING PANEL!!

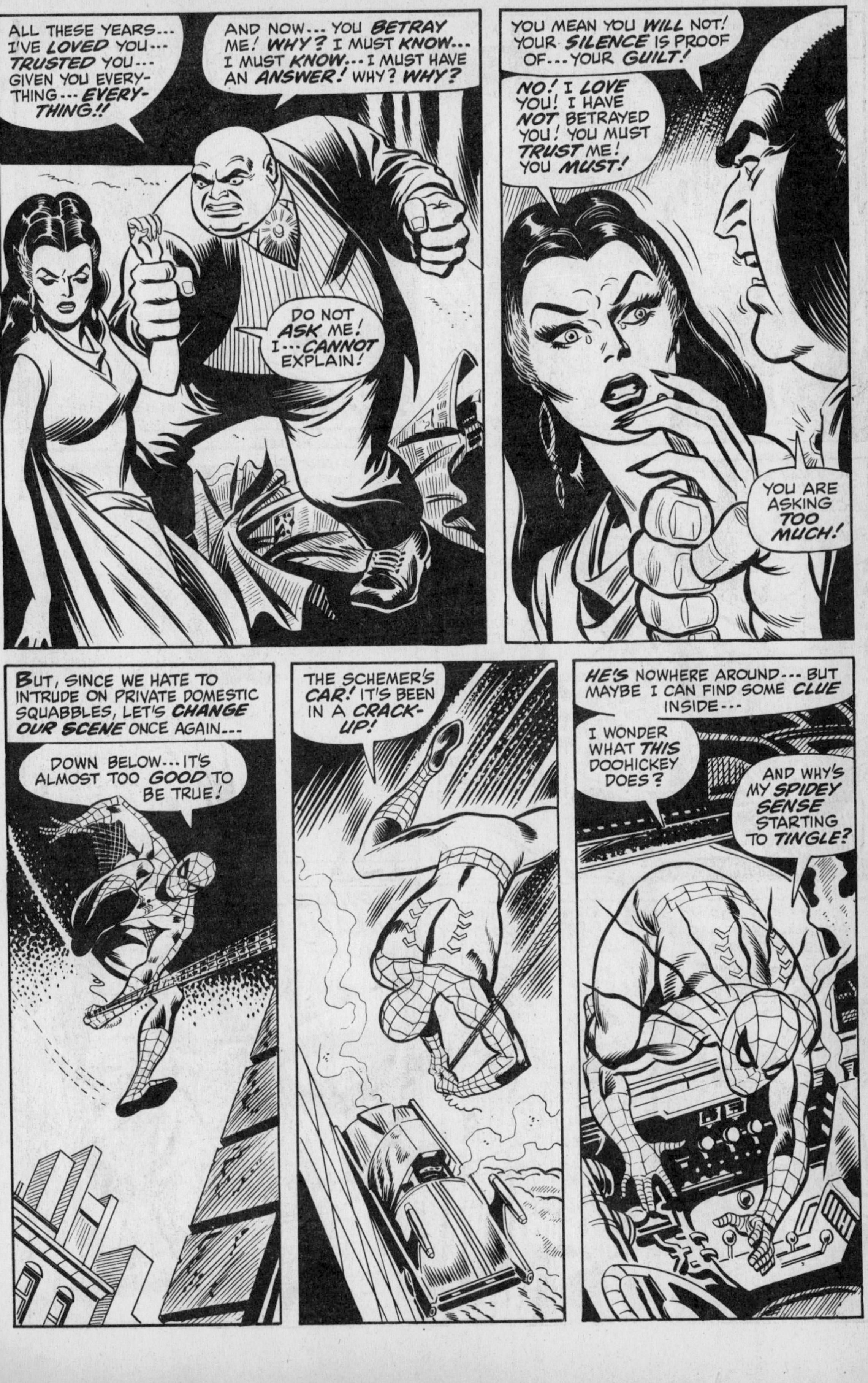

ALL THESE YEARS... I'VE LOVED YOU... TRUSTED YOU... GIVEN YOU EVERYTHING... EVERYTHING!!
AND NOW... YOU BETRAY ME! WHY? I MUST KNOW... I MUST KNOW... I MUST HAVE AN ANSWER! WHY? WHY?
DO NOT ASK ME! I... CANNOT EXPLAIN!
YOU MEAN YOU WILL NOT! YOUR SILENCE IS PROOF OF... YOUR GUILT!
NO! I LOVE YOU! I HAVE NOT BETRAYED YOU! YOU MUST TRUST ME! YOU MUST!
YOU ARE ASKING TOO MUCH!
BUT, SINCE WE HATE TO INTRUDE ON PRIVATE DOMESTIC SQUABBLES, LET'S CHANGE OUR SCENE ONCE AGAIN...
DOWN BELOW... IT'S ALMOST TOO GOOD TO BE TRUE!
THE SCHEMER'S CAR! IT'S BEEN IN A CRACK-UP!
HE'S NOWHERE AROUND... BUT MAYBE I CAN FIND SOME CLUE INSIDE...
I WONDER WHAT THIS DOOHICKEY DOES?
AND WHY'S MY SPIDEY SENSE STARTING TO TINGLE?

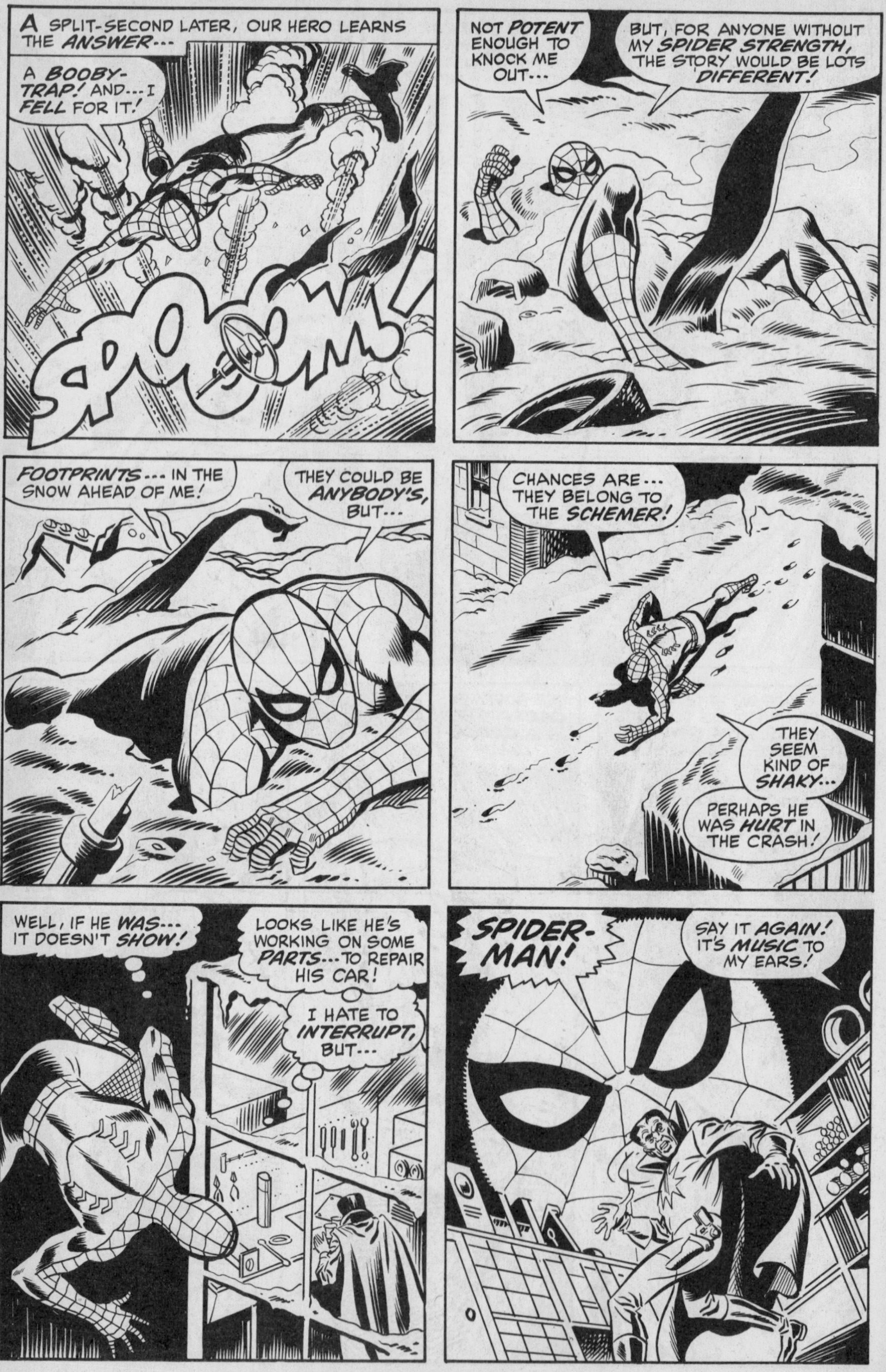
A SPLIT-SECOND LATER, OUR HERO LEARNS THE ANSWER...
A BOOBY-TRAP! AND...I FELL FOR IT!
SPOOM
NOT POTENT ENOUGH TO KNOCK ME OUT...
BUT, FOR ANYONE WITHOUT MY SPIDER STRENGTH, THE STORY WOULD BE LOTS DIFFERENT!
FOOTPRINTS... IN THE SNOW AHEAD OF ME!
THEY COULD BE ANYBODY'S, BUT...
CHANCES ARE... THEY BELONG TO THE SCHEMER!
THEY SEEM KIND OF SHAKY...
PERHAPS HE WAS HURT IN THE CRASH!
WELL, IF HE WAS... IT DOESN'T SHOW!
LOOKS LIKE HE'S WORKING ON SOME PARTS...TO REPAIR HIS CAR!
I HATE TO INTERRUPT, BUT...
SPIDER-MAN!
SAY IT AGAIN! IT'S MUSIC TO MY EARS!

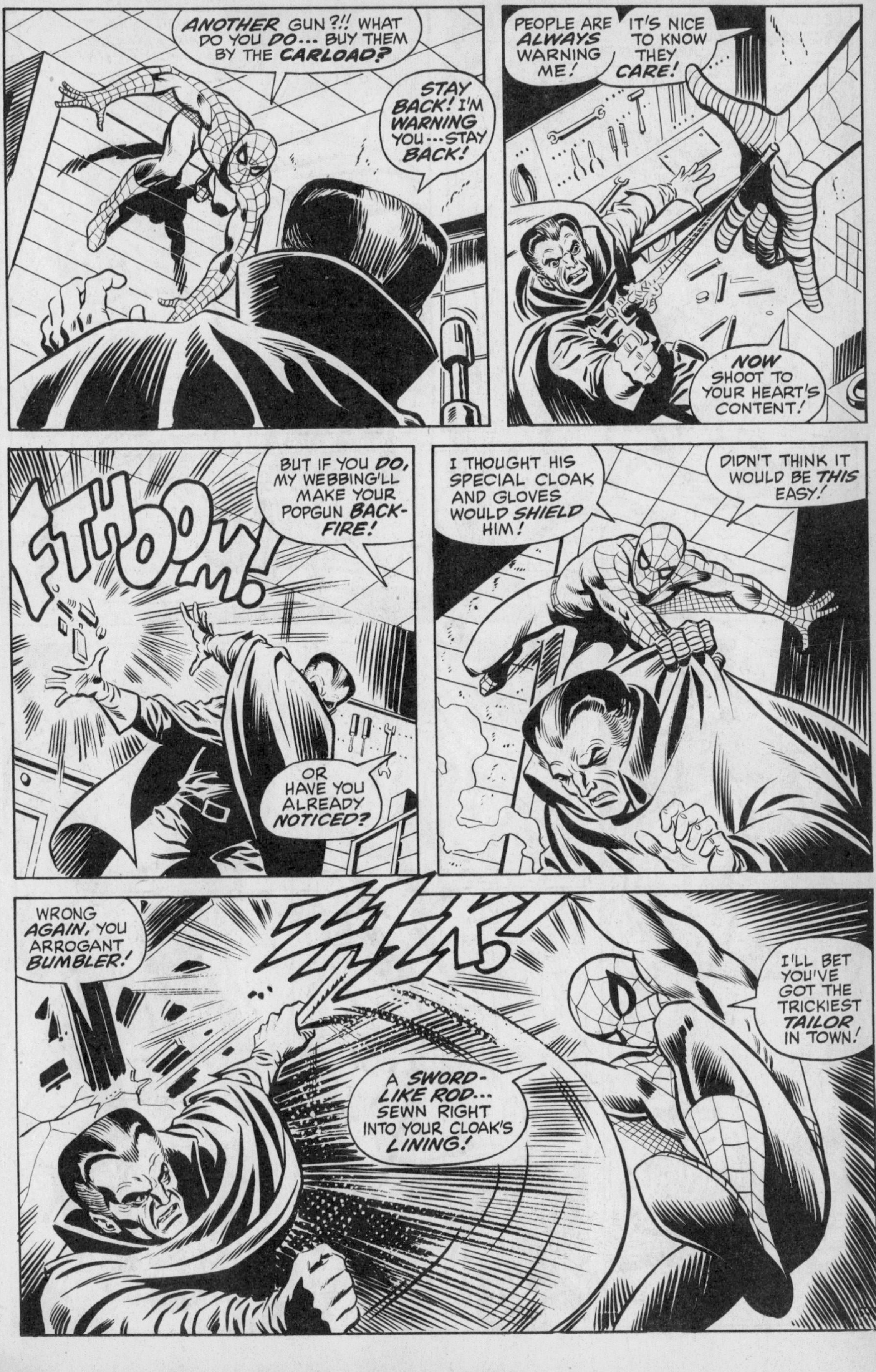
ANOTHER GUN?!! WHAT DO YOU DO... BUY THEM BY THE CARLOAD?
STAY BACK! I'M WARNING YOU---STAY BACK!
PEOPLE ARE ALWAYS WARNING ME!
IT'S NICE TO KNOW THEY CARE!
NOW SHOOT TO YOUR HEART'S CONTENT!
BUT IF YOU DO, MY WEBBING'LL MAKE YOUR POPGUN BACK-FIRE!
FTHOOM!
OR HAVE YOU ALREADY NOTICED?
I THOUGHT HIS SPECIAL CLOAK AND GLOVES WOULD SHIELD HIM!
DIDN'T THINK IT WOULD BE THIS EASY!
WRONG AGAIN, YOU ARROGANT BUMBLER!
ZZIK!
I'LL BET YOU'VE GOT THE TRICKIEST TAILOR IN TOWN!
A SWORD-LIKE ROD... SEWN RIGHT INTO YOUR CLOAK'S LINING!

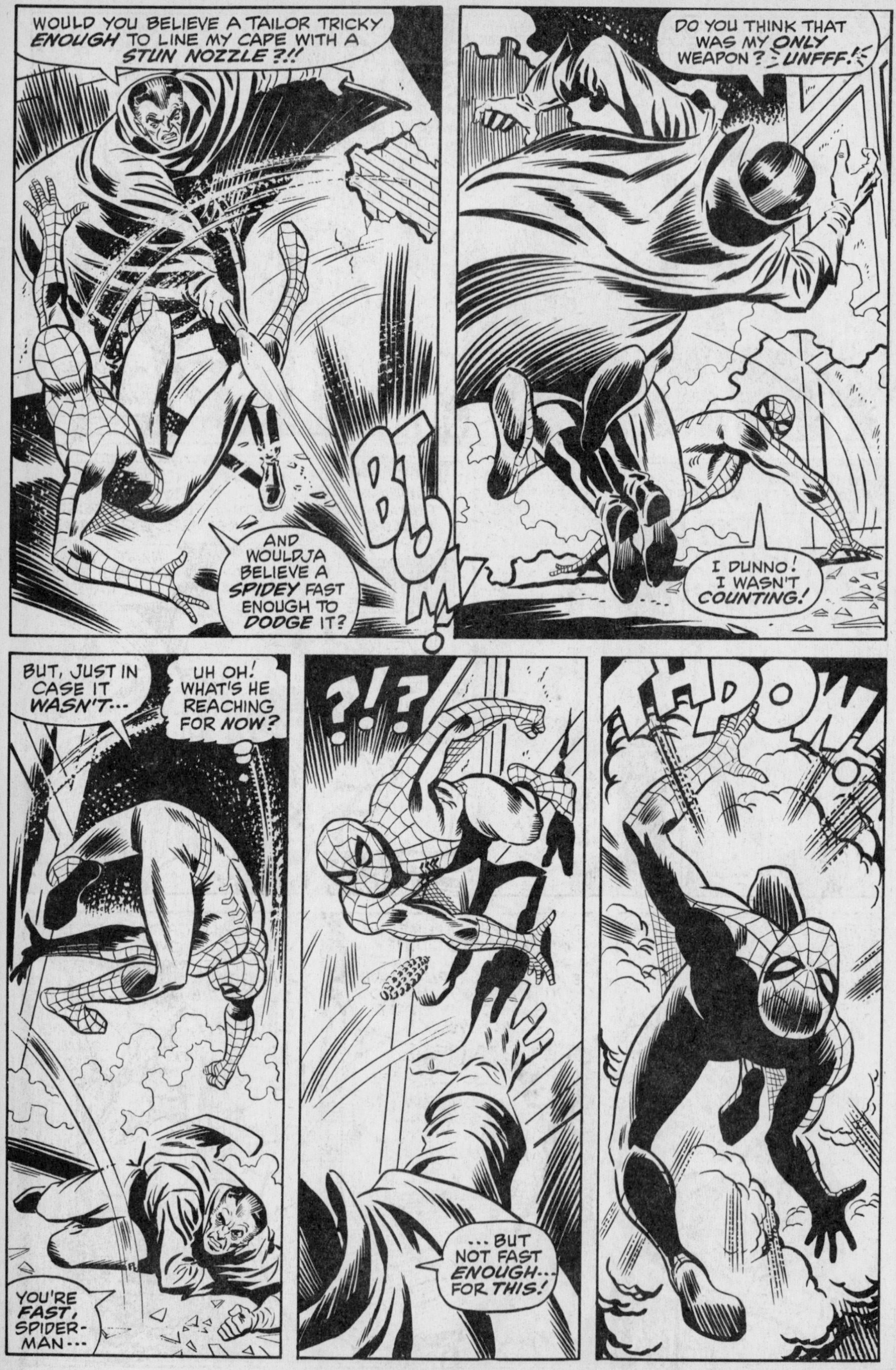
WOULD YOU BELIEVE A TAILOR TRICKY ENOUGH TO LINE MY CAPE WITH A STUN NOZZLE ?!!
AND WOULDJA BELIEVE A SPIDEY FAST ENOUGH TO DODGE IT?
BTOWM!
DO YOU THINK THAT WAS MY ONLY WEAPON? UNFFF!
I DUNNO! I WASN'T COUNTING!
BUT, JUST IN CASE IT WASN'T...
UH OH! WHAT'S HE REACHING FOR NOW?
YOU'RE FAST, SPIDER-MAN...
?!?
...BUT NOT FAST ENOUGH... FOR THIS!
THDOW!

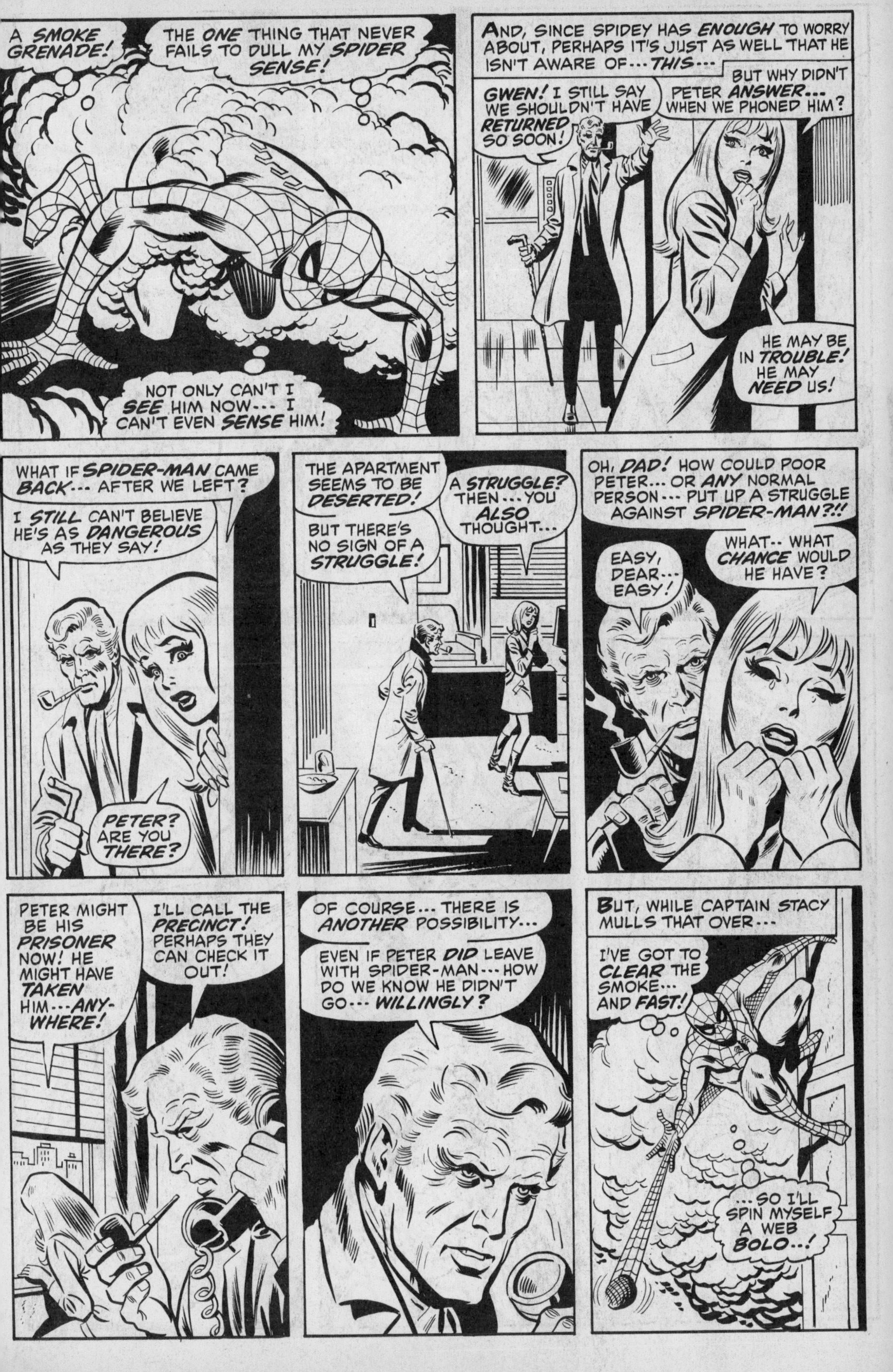
A SMOKE GRENADE!
THE ONE THING THAT NEVER FAILS TO DULL MY SPIDER SENSE!
NOT ONLY CAN'T I SEE HIM NOW--- I CAN'T EVEN SENSE HIM!
AND, SINCE SPIDEY HAS ENOUGH TO WORRY ABOUT, PERHAPS IT'S JUST AS WELL THAT HE ISN'T AWARE OF--- THIS---
GWEN! I STILL SAY WE SHOULDN'T HAVE RETURNED SO SOON!
BUT WHY DIDN'T PETER ANSWER... WHEN WE PHONED HIM?
HE MAY BE IN TROUBLE! HE MAY NEED US!
WHAT IF SPIDER-MAN CAME BACK--- AFTER WE LEFT?
I STILL CAN'T BELIEVE HE'S AS DANGEROUS AS THEY SAY!
PETER? ARE YOU THERE?
THE APARTMENT SEEMS TO BE DESERTED!
BUT THERE'S NO SIGN OF A STRUGGLE!
A STRUGGLE? THEN--- YOU ALSO THOUGHT---
OH, DAD! HOW COULD POOR PETER--- OR ANY NORMAL PERSON--- PUT UP A STRUGGLE AGAINST SPIDER-MAN?!!
EASY, DEAR--- EASY!
WHAT-- WHAT CHANCE WOULD HE HAVE?
PETER MIGHT BE HIS PRISONER NOW! HE MIGHT HAVE TAKEN HIM---ANY-WHERE!
I'LL CALL THE PRECINCT! PERHAPS THEY CAN CHECK IT OUT!
OF COURSE--- THERE IS ANOTHER POSSIBILITY---
EVEN IF PETER DID LEAVE WITH SPIDER-MAN--- HOW DO WE KNOW HE DIDN'T GO--- WILLINGLY?
BUT, WHILE CAPTAIN STACY MULLS THAT OVER---
I'VE GOT TO CLEAR THE SMOKE--- AND FAST!
---SO I'LL SPIN MYSELF A WEB BOLO--!

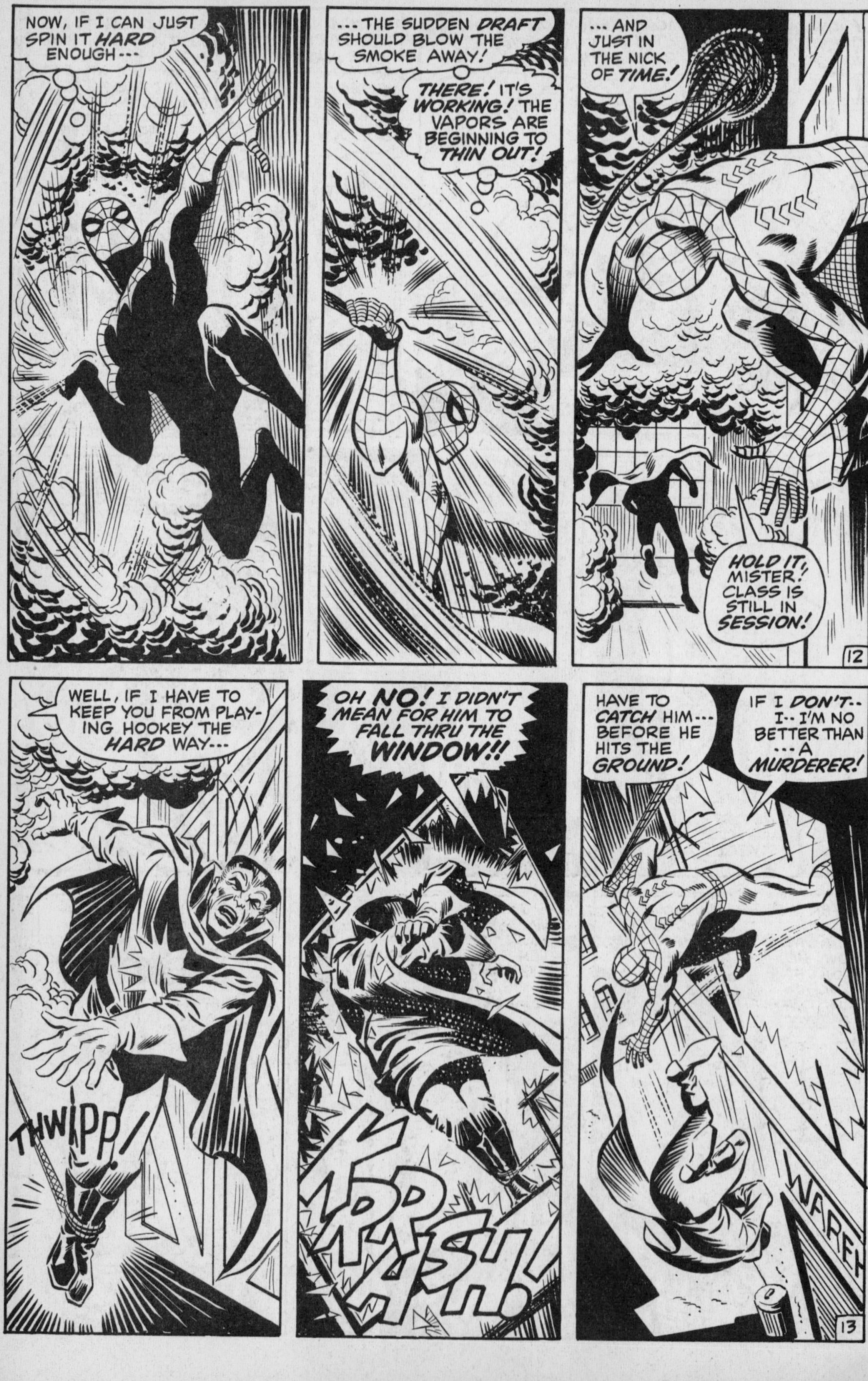
NOW, IF I CAN JUST SPIN IT HARD ENOUGH---
---THE SUDDEN DRAFT SHOULD BLOW THE SMOKE AWAY!
THERE! IT'S WORKING! THE VAPORS ARE BEGINNING TO THIN OUT!
---AND JUST IN THE NICK OF TIME!
HOLD IT, MISTER! CLASS IS STILL IN SESSION!
12
WELL, IF I HAVE TO KEEP YOU FROM PLAYING HOOKEY THE HARD WAY---
THWIPP!
OH NO! I DIDN'T MEAN FOR HIM TO FALL THRU THE WINDOW!!
KRRASH!
HAVE TO CATCH HIM--- BEFORE HE HITS THE GROUND!
IF I DON'T-- I-- I'M NO BETTER THAN ---A MURDERER!
WAREH
13

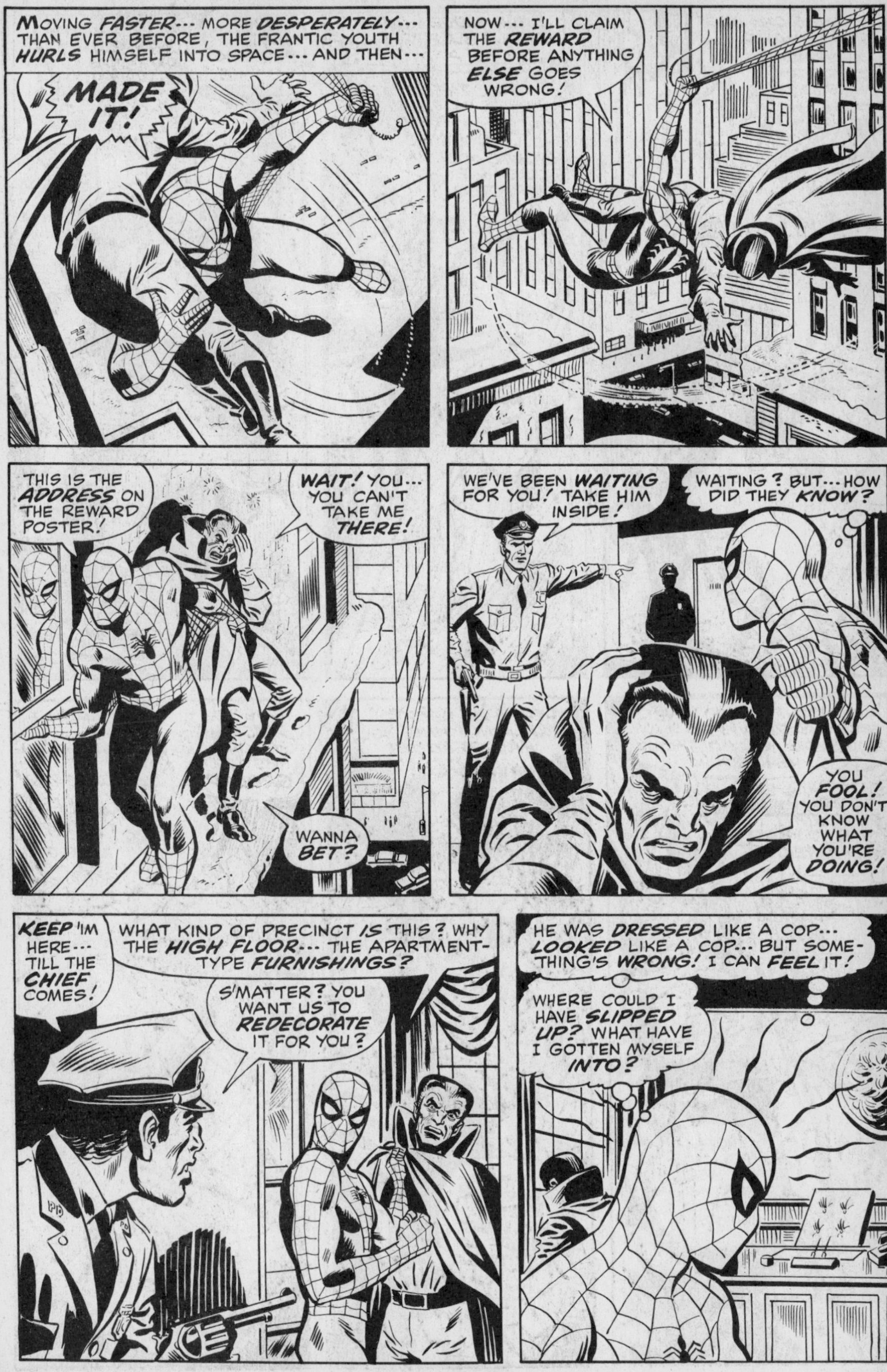
MOVING FASTER... MORE DESPERATELY... THAN EVER BEFORE, THE FRANTIC YOUTH HURLS HIMSELF INTO SPACE... AND THEN...
MADE IT!
NOW... I'LL CLAIM THE REWARD BEFORE ANYTHING ELSE GOES WRONG!
THIS IS THE ADDRESS ON THE REWARD POSTER!
WAIT! YOU... YOU CAN'T TAKE ME THERE!
WANNA BET?
WE'VE BEEN WAITING FOR YOU! TAKE HIM INSIDE!
WAITING? BUT... HOW DID THEY KNOW?
YOU FOOL! YOU DON'T KNOW WHAT YOU'RE DOING!
KEEP 'IM HERE--- TILL THE CHIEF COMES!
WHAT KIND OF PRECINCT IS THIS? WHY THE HIGH FLOOR... THE APARTMENT-TYPE FURNISHINGS?
S'MATTER? YOU WANT US TO REDECORATE IT FOR YOU?
HE WAS DRESSED LIKE A COP... LOOKED LIKE A COP... BUT SOMETHING'S WRONG! I CAN FEEL IT!
WHERE COULD I HAVE SLIPPED UP? WHAT HAVE I GOTTEN MYSELF INTO?

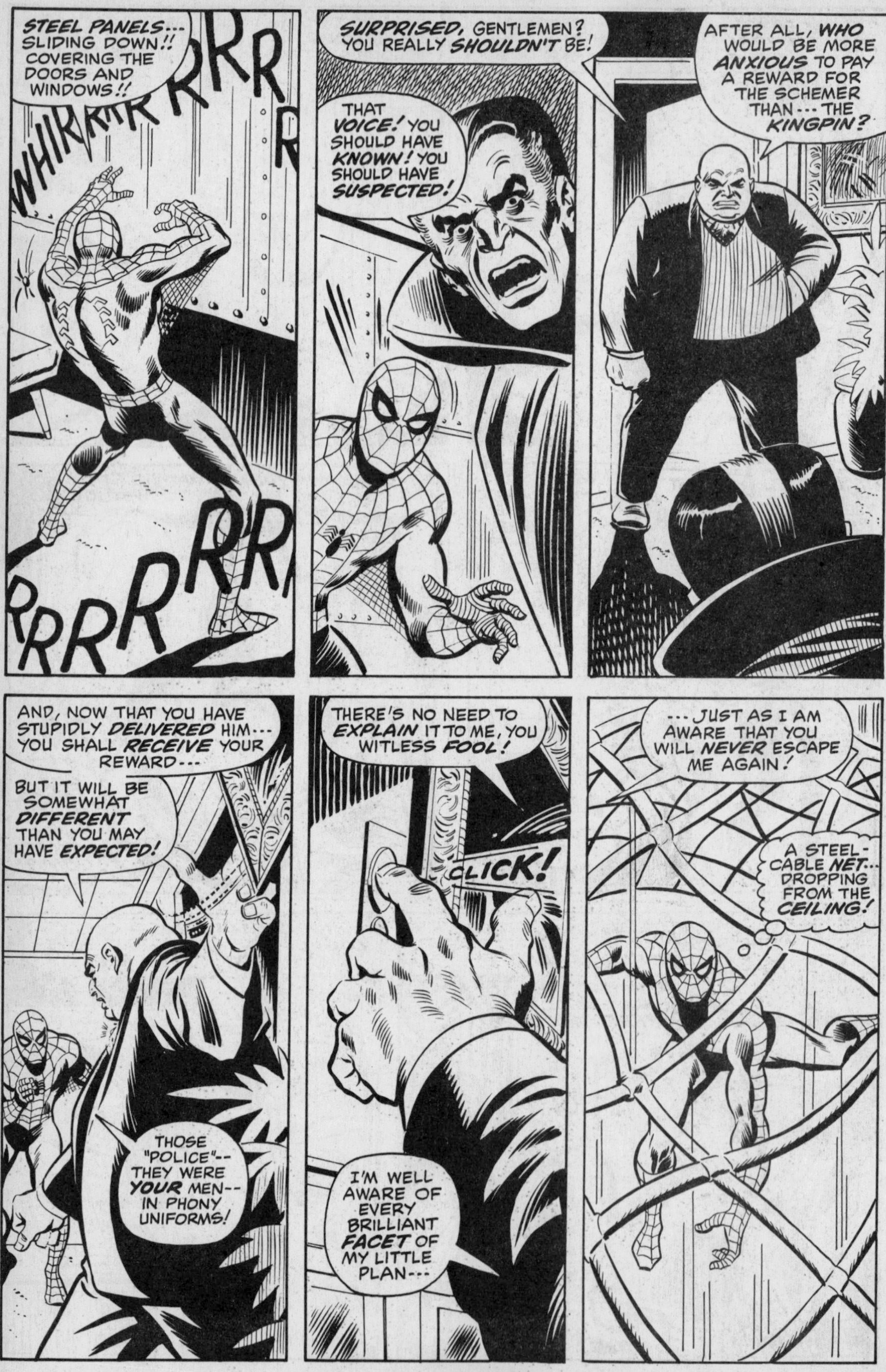
STEEL PANELS... SLIDING DOWN!! COVERING THE DOORS AND WINDOWS!!
WHIRRRRR RRRR
RRRRRRRRR
SURPRISED, GENTLEMEN? YOU REALLY SHOULDN'T BE!
THAT VOICE! YOU SHOULD HAVE KNOWN! YOU SHOULD HAVE SUSPECTED!
AFTER ALL, WHO WOULD BE MORE ANXIOUS TO PAY A REWARD FOR THE SCHEMER THAN--- THE KINGPIN?
AND, NOW THAT YOU HAVE STUPIDLY DELIVERED HIM--- YOU SHALL RECEIVE YOUR REWARD---
BUT IT WILL BE SOMEWHAT DIFFERENT THAN YOU MAY HAVE EXPECTED!
THOSE "POLICE"-- THEY WERE YOUR MEN-- IN PHONY UNIFORMS!
THERE'S NO NEED TO EXPLAIN IT TO ME, YOU WITLESS FOOL!
CLICK!
I'M WELL AWARE OF EVERY BRILLIANT FACET OF MY LITTLE PLAN---
---JUST AS I AM AWARE THAT YOU WILL NEVER ESCAPE ME AGAIN!
A STEEL-CABLE NET... DROPPING FROM THE CEILING!

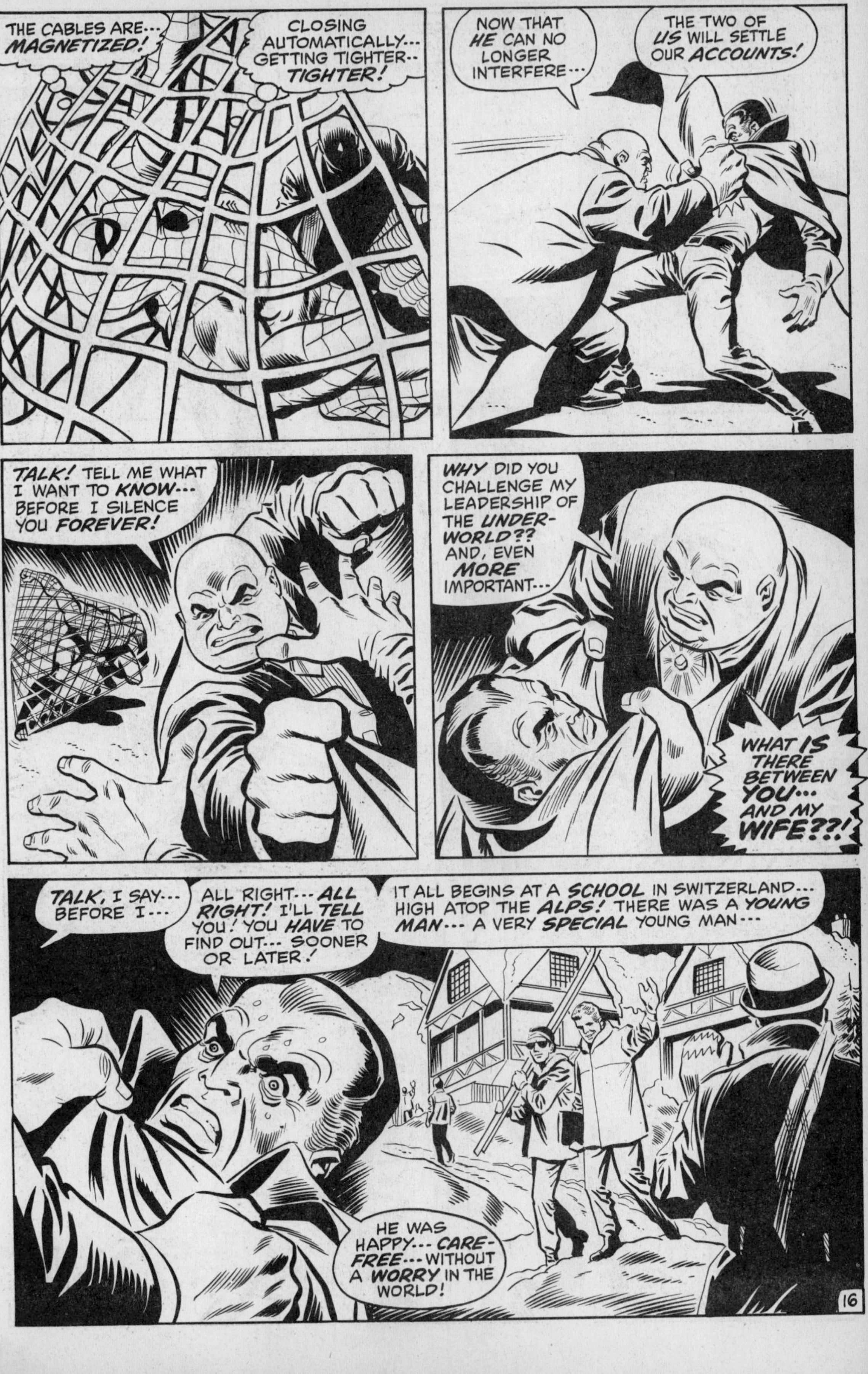
THE CABLES ARE... MAGNETIZED!
CLOSING AUTOMATICALLY... GETTING TIGHTER-- TIGHTER!
NOW THAT HE CAN NO LONGER INTERFERE...
THE TWO OF US WILL SETTLE OUR ACCOUNTS!
TALK! TELL ME WHAT I WANT TO KNOW... BEFORE I SILENCE YOU FOREVER!
WHY DID YOU CHALLENGE MY LEADERSHIP OF THE UNDER-WORLD?? AND, EVEN MORE IMPORTANT...
WHAT IS THERE BETWEEN YOU... AND MY WIFE??!
TALK, I SAY... BEFORE I...
ALL RIGHT... ALL RIGHT! I'LL TELL YOU! YOU HAVE TO FIND OUT... SOONER OR LATER!
IT ALL BEGINS AT A SCHOOL IN SWITZERLAND... HIGH ATOP THE ALPS! THERE WAS A YOUNG MAN... A VERY SPECIAL YOUNG MAN...
HE WAS HAPPY... CARE-FREE... WITHOUT A WORRY IN THE WORLD!
16

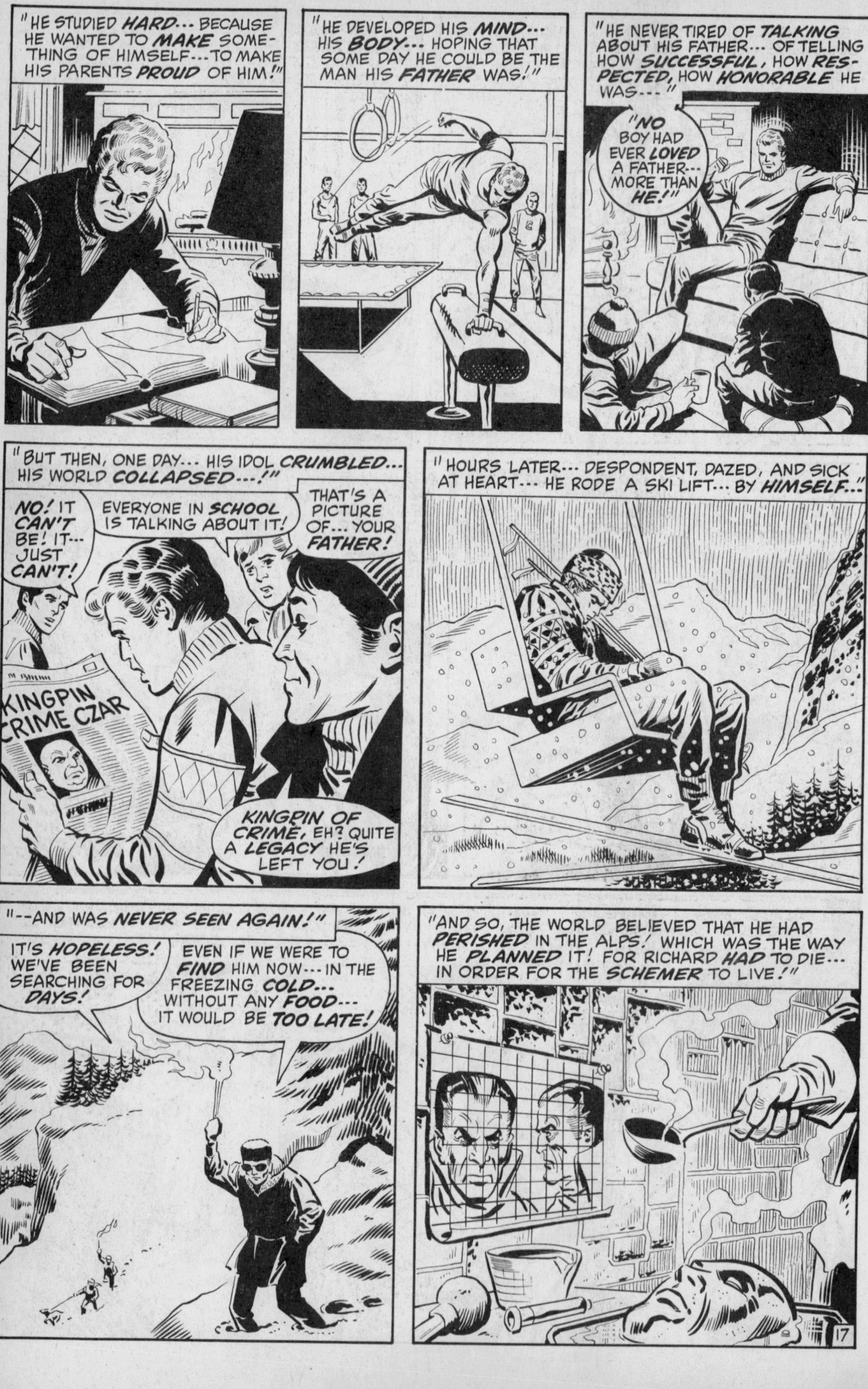
"HE STUDIED HARD... BECAUSE HE WANTED TO MAKE SOMETHING OF HIMSELF...TO MAKE HIS PARENTS PROUD OF HIM!"
"HE DEVELOPED HIS MIND... HIS BODY... HOPING THAT SOME DAY HE COULD BE THE MAN HIS FATHER WAS!"
"HE NEVER TIRED OF TALKING ABOUT HIS FATHER... OF TELLING HOW SUCCESSFUL, HOW RESPECTED, HOW HONORABLE HE WAS..."
"NO BOY HAD EVER LOVED A FATHER... MORE THAN HE!"
"BUT THEN, ONE DAY... HIS IDOL CRUMBLED... HIS WORLD COLLAPSED...!"
NO! IT CAN'T BE! IT... JUST CAN'T!
EVERYONE IN SCHOOL IS TALKING ABOUT IT!
THAT'S A PICTURE OF... YOUR FATHER!
KINGPIN CRIME CZAR
KINGPIN OF CRIME, EH? QUITE A LEGACY HE'S LEFT YOU!
"HOURS LATER... DESPONDENT, DAZED, AND SICK AT HEART... HE RODE A SKI LIFT... BY HIMSELF..."
"--AND WAS NEVER SEEN AGAIN!"
IT'S HOPELESS! WE'VE BEEN SEARCHING FOR DAYS!
EVEN IF WE WERE TO FIND HIM NOW... IN THE FREEZING COLD... WITHOUT ANY FOOD... IT WOULD BE TOO LATE!
"AND SO, THE WORLD BELIEVED THAT HE HAD PERISHED IN THE ALPS! WHICH WAS THE WAY HE PLANNED IT! FOR RICHARD HAD TO DIE... IN ORDER FOR THE SCHEMER TO LIVE!"

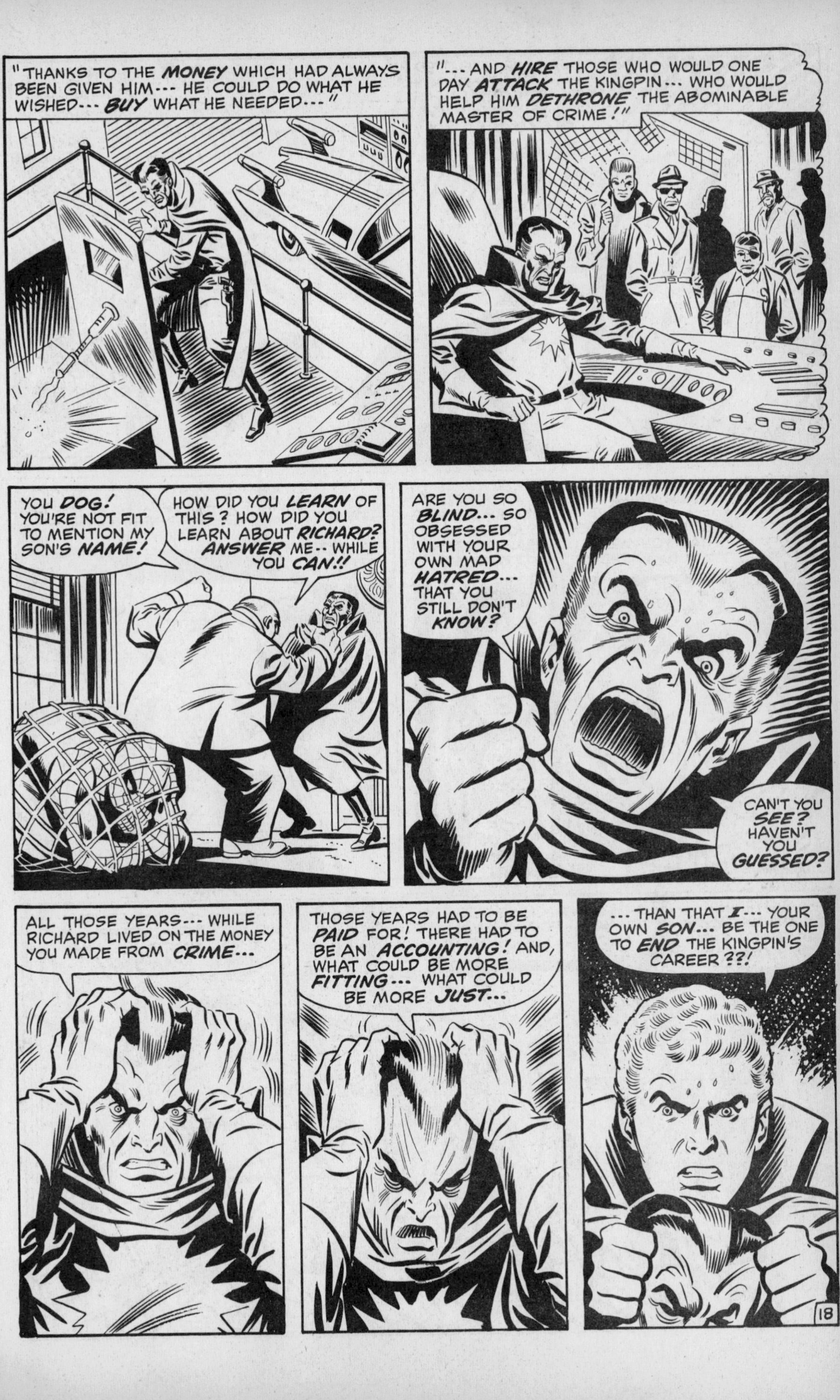
"THANKS TO THE MONEY WHICH HAD ALWAYS BEEN GIVEN HIM--- HE COULD DO WHAT HE WISHED--- BUY WHAT HE NEEDED---"
"... AND HIRE THOSE WHO WOULD ONE DAY ATTACK THE KINGPIN... WHO WOULD HELP HIM DETHRONE THE ABOMINABLE MASTER OF CRIME!"
YOU DOG! YOU'RE NOT FIT TO MENTION MY SON'S NAME!
HOW DID YOU LEARN OF THIS? HOW DID YOU LEARN ABOUT RICHARD? ANSWER ME-- WHILE YOU CAN!!
ARE YOU SO BLIND... SO OBSESSED WITH YOUR OWN MAD HATRED... THAT YOU STILL DON'T KNOW?
CAN'T YOU SEE? HAVEN'T YOU GUESSED?
ALL THOSE YEARS--- WHILE RICHARD LIVED ON THE MONEY YOU MADE FROM CRIME...
THOSE YEARS HAD TO BE PAID FOR! THERE HAD TO BE AN ACCOUNTING! AND, WHAT COULD BE MORE FITTING... WHAT COULD BE MORE JUST...
... THAN THAT I--- YOUR OWN SON... BE THE ONE TO END THE KINGPIN'S CAREER??!
18

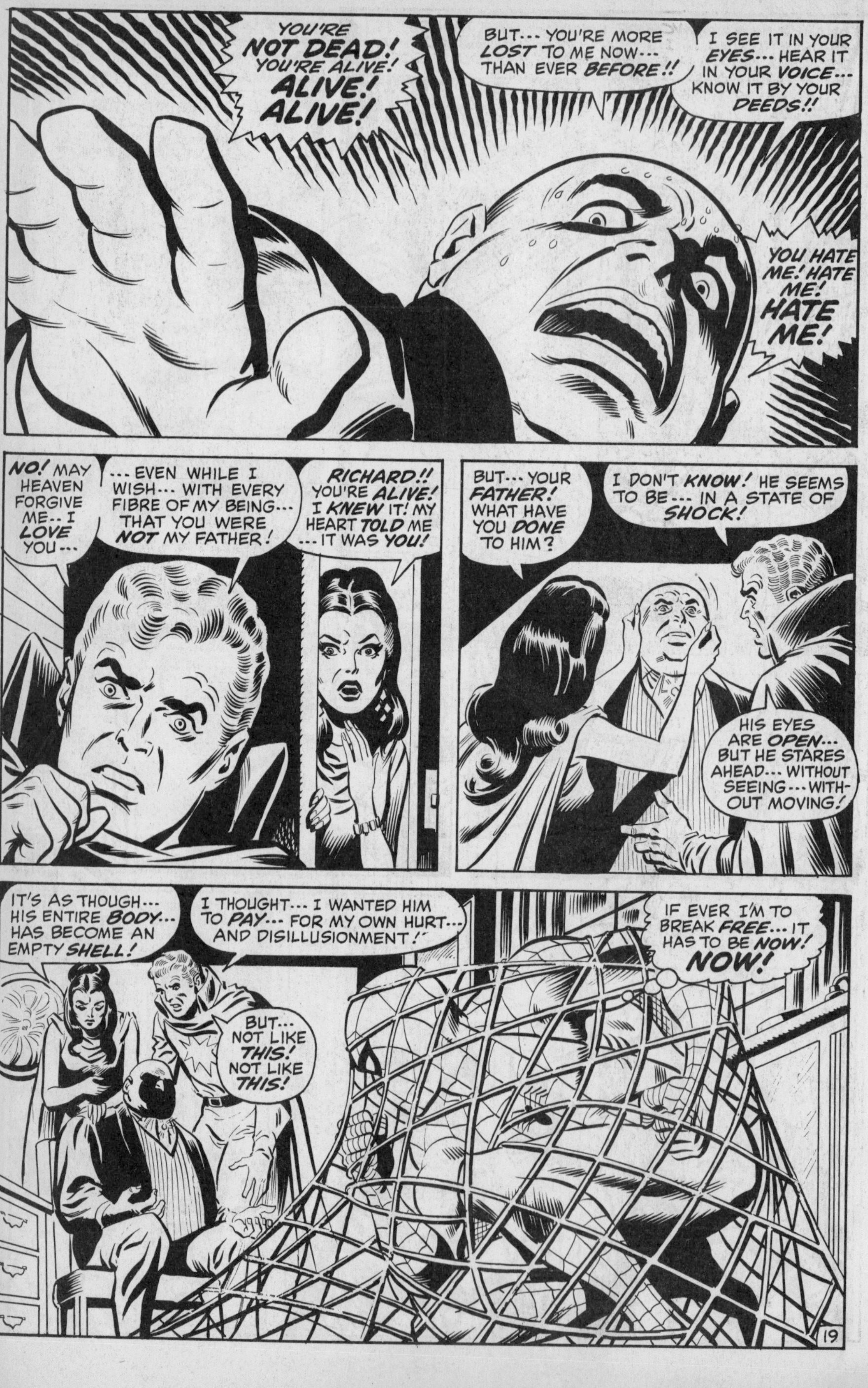

YOU'RE NOT DEAD! YOU'RE ALIVE! ALIVE! ALIVE!
BUT... YOU'RE MORE LOST TO ME NOW... THAN EVER BEFORE!!
I SEE IT IN YOUR EYES... HEAR IT IN YOUR VOICE... KNOW IT BY YOUR DEEDS!!
YOU HATE ME! HATE ME! HATE ME!
NO! MAY HEAVEN FORGIVE ME.. I LOVE YOU...
...EVEN WHILE I WISH... WITH EVERY FIBRE OF MY BEING... THAT YOU WERE NOT MY FATHER!
RICHARD!! YOU'RE ALIVE! I KNEW IT! MY HEART TOLD ME ...IT WAS YOU!
BUT... YOUR FATHER! WHAT HAVE YOU DONE TO HIM?
I DON'T KNOW! HE SEEMS TO BE... IN A STATE OF SHOCK!
HIS EYES ARE OPEN... BUT HE STARES AHEAD... WITHOUT SEEING... WITH-OUT MOVING!
IT'S AS THOUGH... HIS ENTIRE BODY... HAS BECOME AN EMPTY SHELL!
I THOUGHT... I WANTED HIM TO PAY... FOR MY OWN HURT... AND DISILLUSIONMENT!
BUT... NOT LIKE THIS! NOT LIKE THIS!
IF EVER I'M TO BREAK FREE... IT HAS TO BE NOW! NOW!

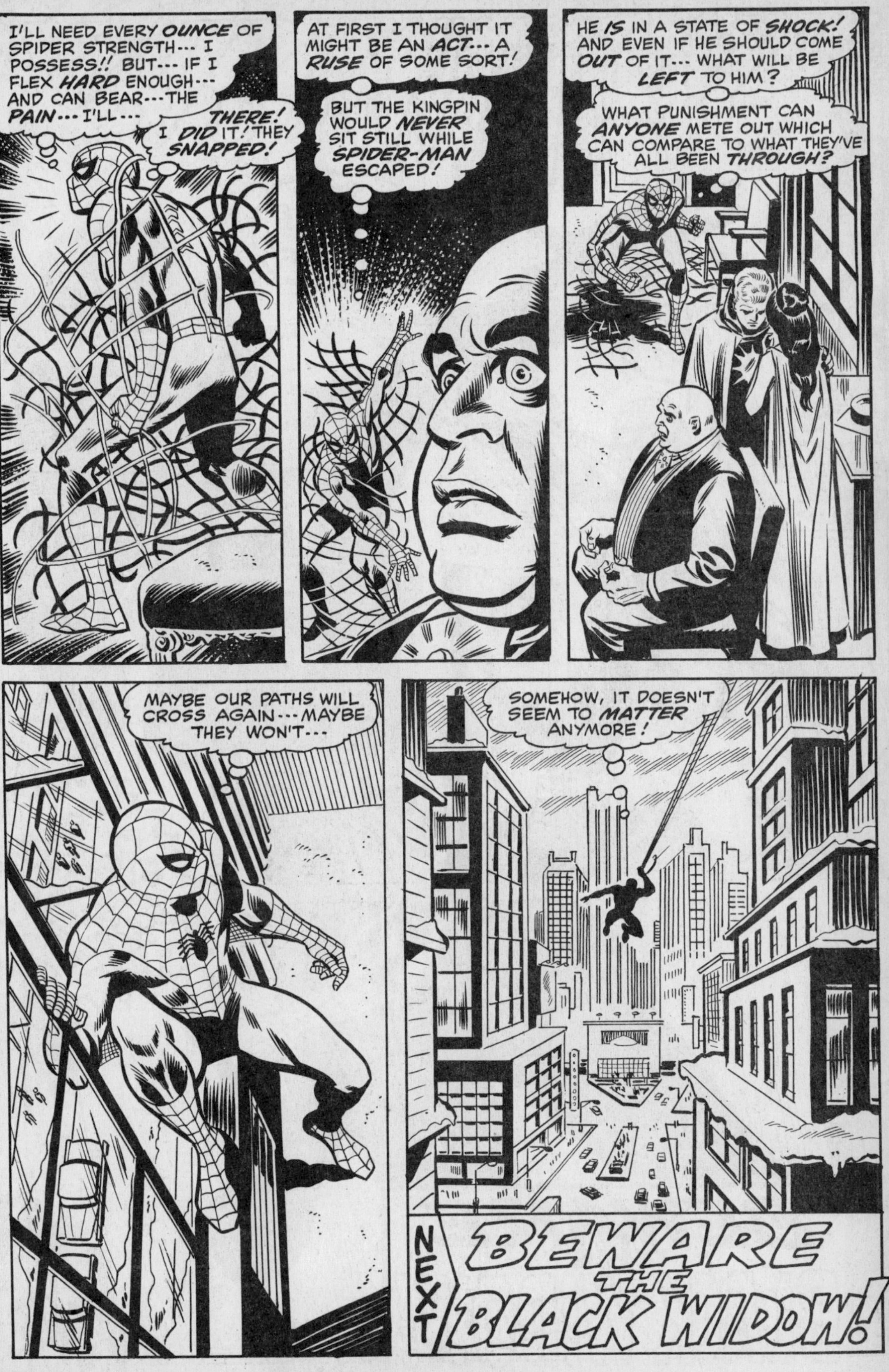
I'LL NEED EVERY OUNCE OF SPIDER STRENGTH--- I POSSESS!! BUT--- IF I FLEX HARD ENOUGH--- AND CAN BEAR---THE PAIN--- I'LL---
THERE! I DID IT! THEY SNAPPED!
AT FIRST I THOUGHT IT MIGHT BE AN ACT--- A RUSE OF SOME SORT!
BUT THE KINGPIN WOULD NEVER SIT STILL WHILE SPIDER-MAN ESCAPED!
HE IS IN A STATE OF SHOCK! AND EVEN IF HE SHOULD COME OUT OF IT--- WHAT WILL BE LEFT TO HIM?
WHAT PUNISHMENT CAN ANYONE METE OUT WHICH CAN COMPARE TO WHAT THEY'VE ALL BEEN THROUGH?
MAYBE OUR PATHS WILL CROSS AGAIN---MAYBE THEY WON'T---
SOMEHOW, IT DOESN'T SEEM TO MATTER ANYMORE!
NEXT
BEWARE THE BLACK WIDOW!

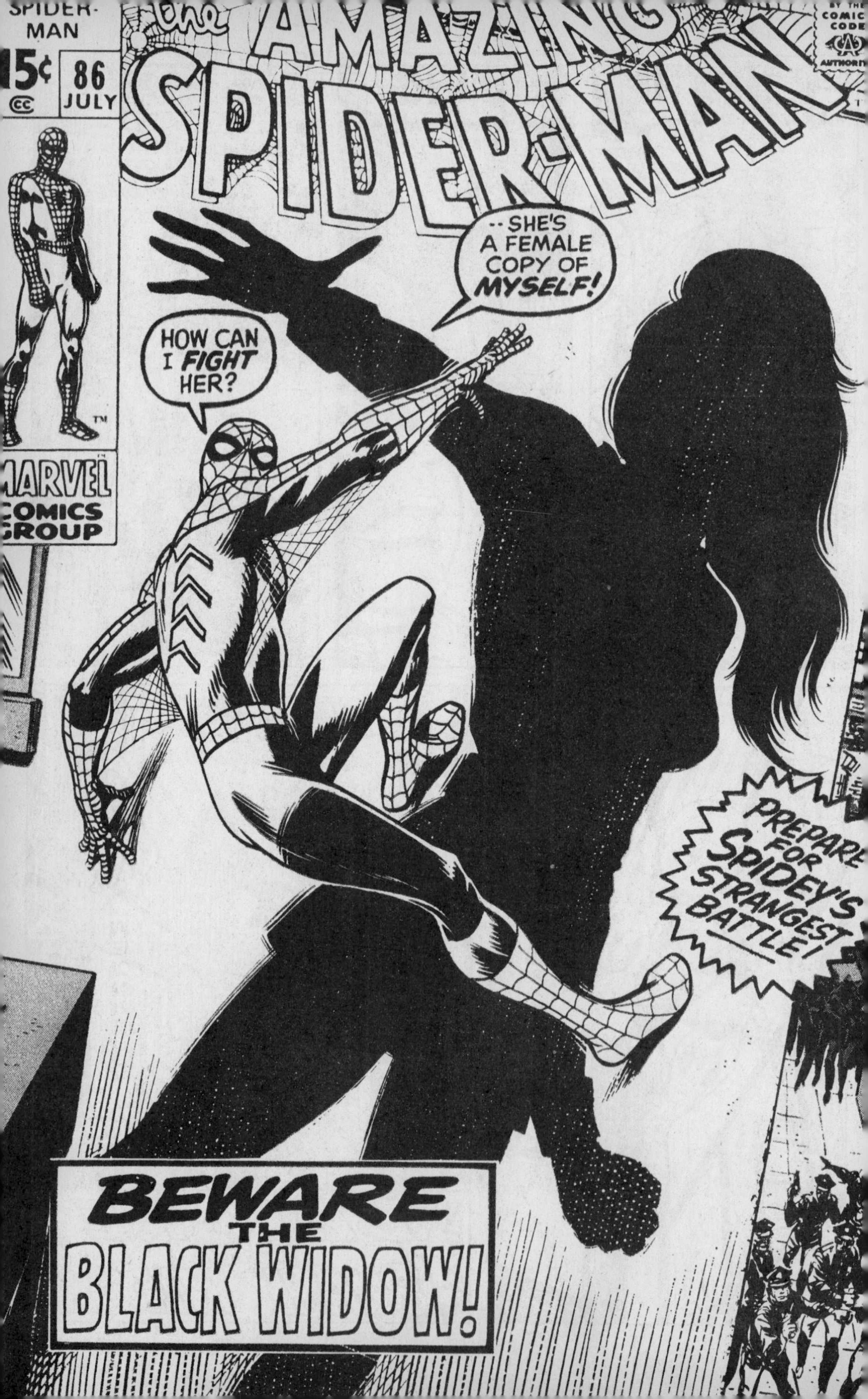
SPIDER-MAN
15¢
86
JULY
the AMAZING SPIDER-MAN
MARVEL COMICS GROUP
--SHE'S A FEMALE COPY OF MYSELF!
HOW CAN I FIGHT HER?
PREPARE FOR SPIDEY'S STRANGEST BATTLE!
BEWARE THE BLACK WIDOW!

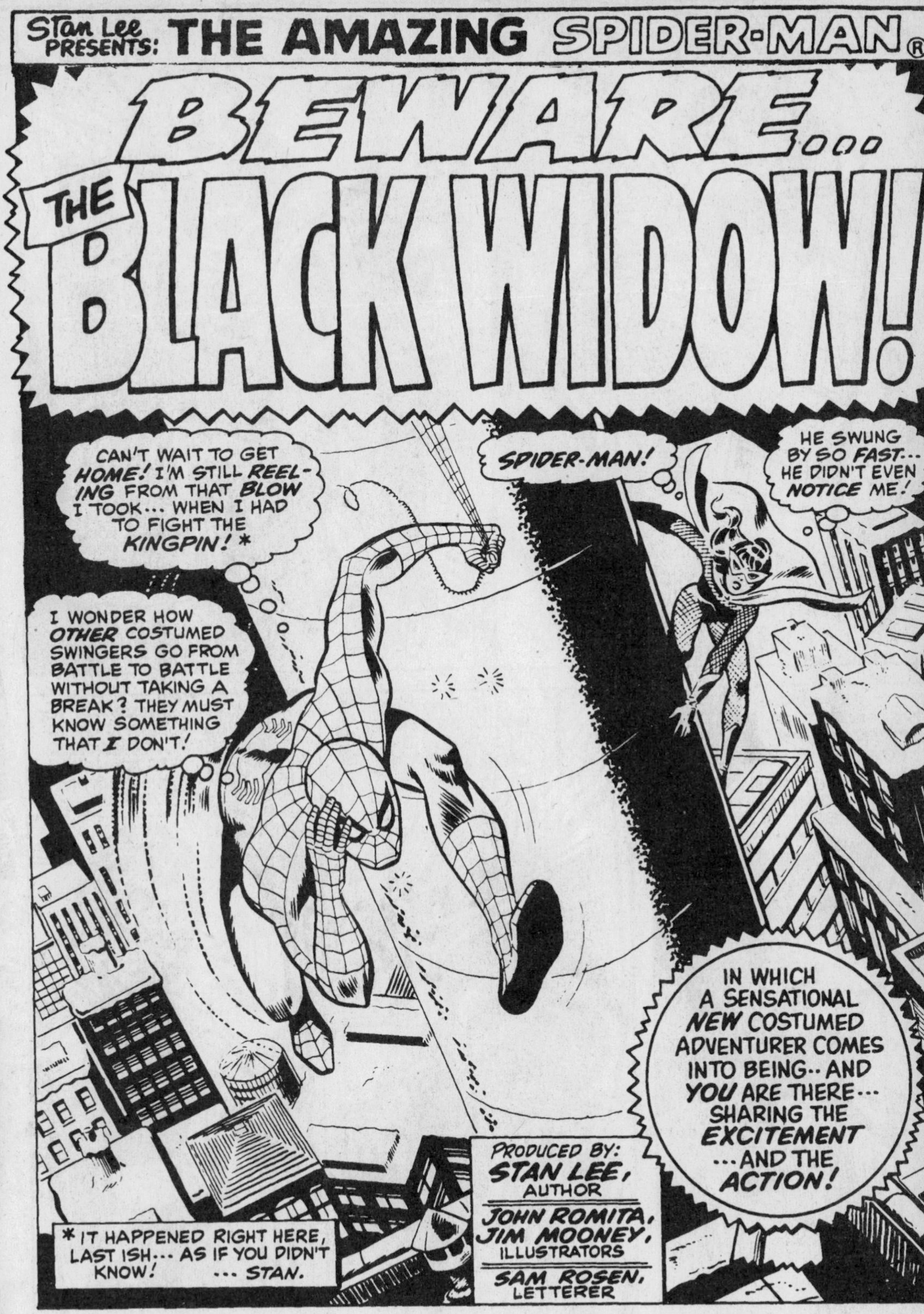

Stan Lee PRESENTS: THE AMAZING SPIDER-MAN®
BEWARE... THE BLACK WIDOW!
CAN'T WAIT TO GET HOME! I'M STILL REELING FROM THAT BLOW I TOOK... WHEN I HAD TO FIGHT THE KINGPIN! *
I WONDER HOW OTHER COSTUMED SWINGERS GO FROM BATTLE TO BATTLE WITHOUT TAKING A BREAK? THEY MUST KNOW SOMETHING THAT I DON'T!
SPIDER-MAN!
HE SWUNG BY SO FAST... HE DIDN'T EVEN NOTICE ME!
IN WHICH A SENSATIONAL NEW COSTUMED ADVENTURER COMES INTO BEING.. AND YOU ARE THERE... SHARING THE EXCITEMENT ...AND THE ACTION!
* IT HAPPENED RIGHT HERE, LAST ISH... AS IF YOU DIDN'T KNOW! ...STAN.
PRODUCED BY: STAN LEE, AUTHOR
JOHN ROMITA, JIM MOONEY, ILLUSTRATORS
SAM ROSEN, LETTERER

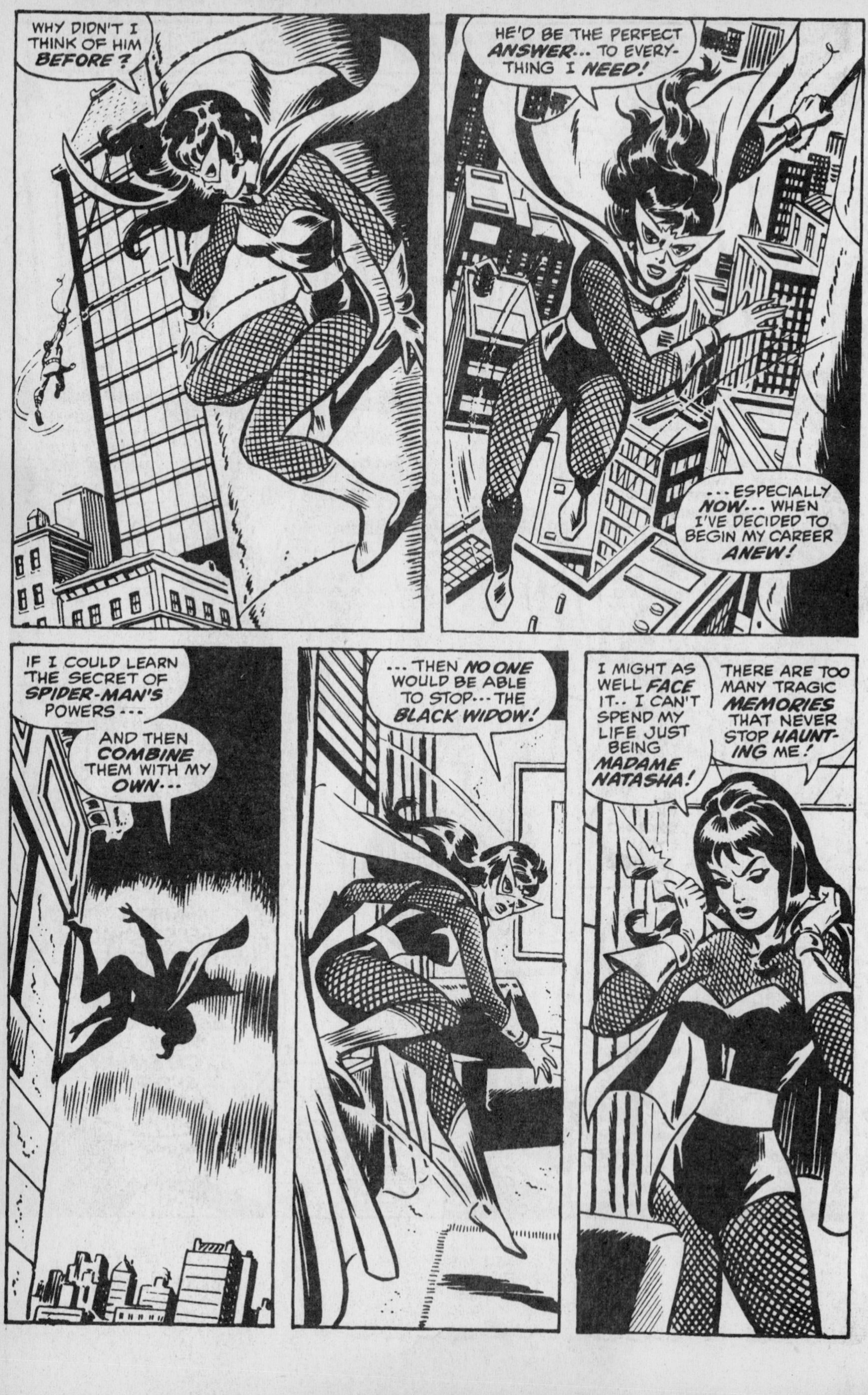

WHY DIDN'T I THINK OF HIM BEFORE?
HE'D BE THE PERFECT ANSWER... TO EVERYTHING I NEED!
...ESPECIALLY NOW... WHEN I'VE DECIDED TO BEGIN MY CAREER ANEW!
IF I COULD LEARN THE SECRET OF SPIDER-MAN'S POWERS---
AND THEN COMBINE THEM WITH MY OWN---
---THEN NO ONE WOULD BE ABLE TO STOP--- THE BLACK WIDOW!
I MIGHT AS WELL FACE IT.. I CAN'T SPEND MY LIFE JUST BEING MADAME NATASHA!
THERE ARE TOO MANY TRAGIC MEMORIES THAT NEVER STOP HAUNTING ME!

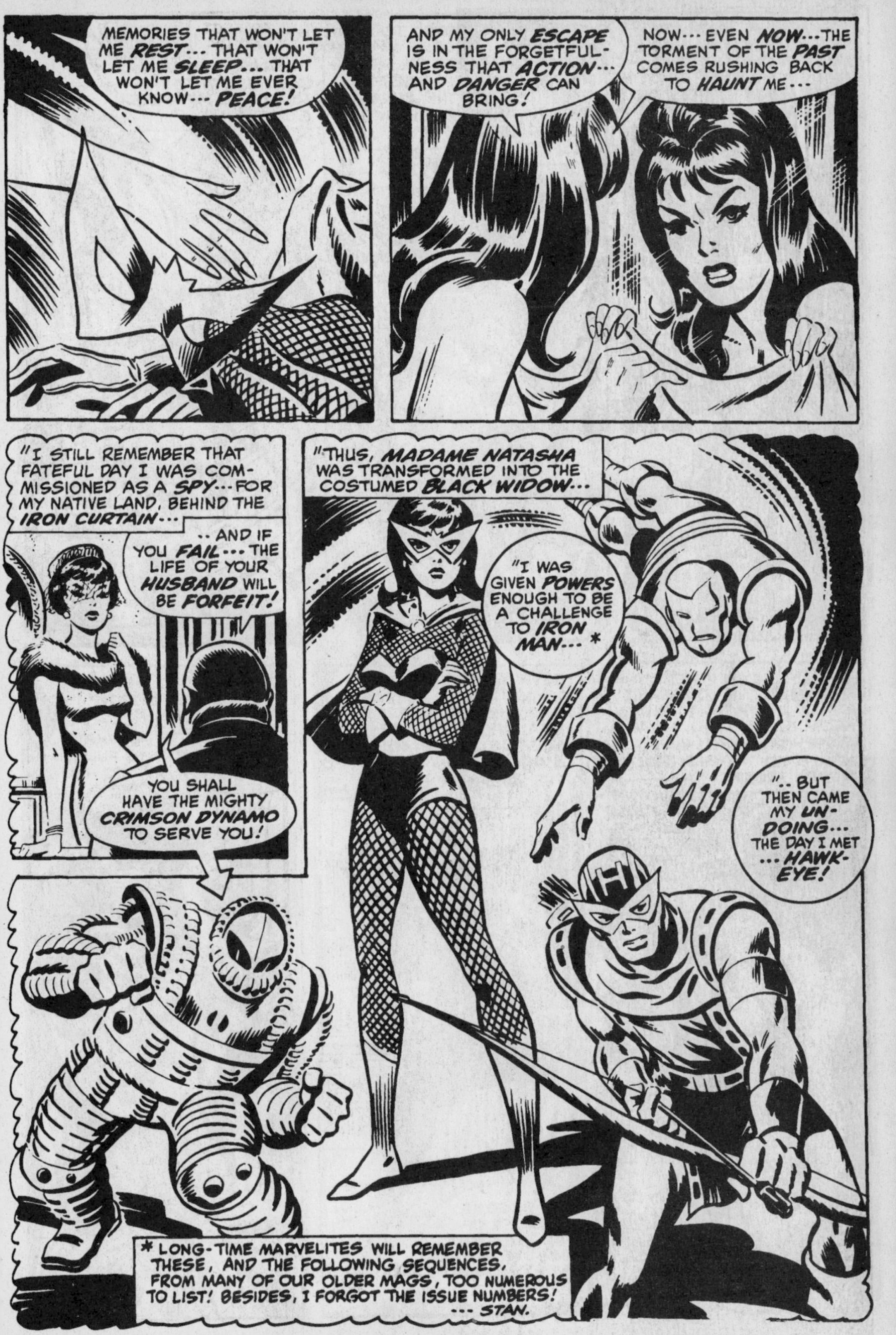
MEMORIES THAT WON'T LET ME REST... THAT WON'T LET ME SLEEP... THAT WON'T LET ME EVER KNOW... PEACE!
AND MY ONLY ESCAPE IS IN THE FORGETFULNESS THAT ACTION... AND DANGER CAN BRING!
NOW... EVEN NOW... THE TORMENT OF THE PAST COMES RUSHING BACK TO HAUNT ME...
"I STILL REMEMBER THAT FATEFUL DAY I WAS COMMISSIONED AS A SPY... FOR MY NATIVE LAND, BEHIND THE IRON CURTAIN...
..AND IF YOU FAIL... THE LIFE OF YOUR HUSBAND WILL BE FORFEIT!
YOU SHALL HAVE THE MIGHTY CRIMSON DYNAMO TO SERVE YOU!
"THUS, MADAME NATASHA WAS TRANSFORMED INTO THE COSTUMED BLACK WIDOW...
"I WAS GIVEN POWERS ENOUGH TO BE A CHALLENGE TO IRON MAN... *
"..BUT THEN CAME MY UN-DOING... THE DAY I MET ...HAWK-EYE!
* LONG-TIME MARVELITES WILL REMEMBER THESE, AND THE FOLLOWING SEQUENCES, FROM MANY OF OUR OLDER MAGS, TOO NUMEROUS TO LIST! BESIDES, I FORGOT THE ISSUE NUMBERS! --- STAN.

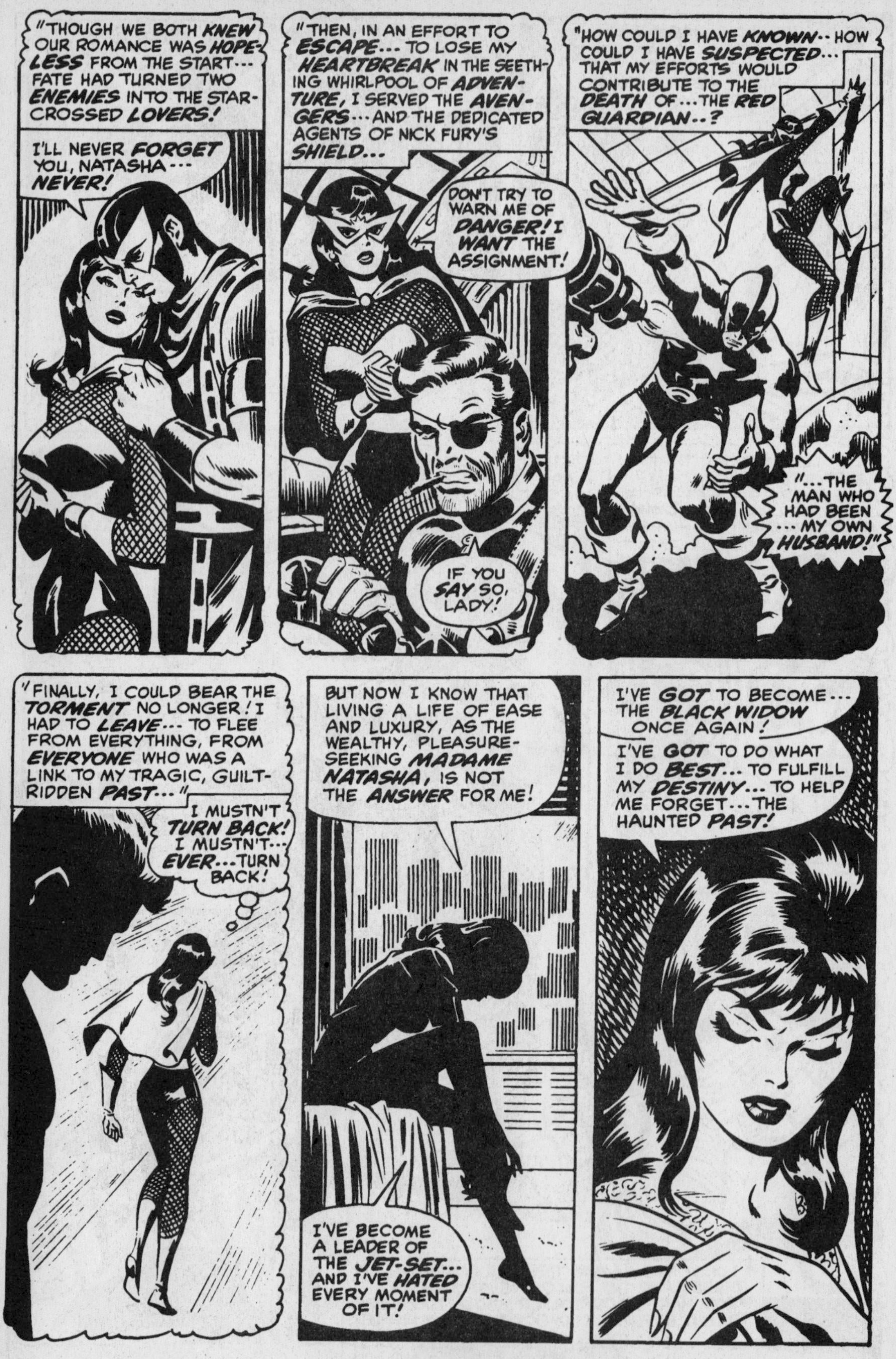
"THOUGH WE BOTH KNEW OUR ROMANCE WAS HOPELESS FROM THE START--- FATE HAD TURNED TWO ENEMIES INTO THE STAR-CROSSED LOVERS!
I'LL NEVER FORGET YOU, NATASHA--- NEVER!
"THEN, IN AN EFFORT TO ESCAPE... TO LOSE MY HEARTBREAK IN THE SEETHING WHIRLPOOL OF ADVENTURE, I SERVED THE AVENGERS... AND THE DEDICATED AGENTS OF NICK FURY'S SHIELD...
DON'T TRY TO WARN ME OF DANGER! I WANT THE ASSIGNMENT!
IF YOU SAY SO, LADY!
"HOW COULD I HAVE KNOWN-- HOW COULD I HAVE SUSPECTED... THAT MY EFFORTS WOULD CONTRIBUTE TO THE DEATH OF... THE RED GUARDIAN..?
"...THE MAN WHO HAD BEEN ...MY OWN HUSBAND!"
"FINALLY, I COULD BEAR THE TORMENT NO LONGER! I HAD TO LEAVE--- TO FLEE FROM EVERYTHING, FROM EVERYONE WHO WAS A LINK TO MY TRAGIC, GUILT-RIDDEN PAST---"
I MUSTN'T TURN BACK! I MUSTN'T... EVER...TURN BACK!
BUT NOW I KNOW THAT LIVING A LIFE OF EASE AND LUXURY, AS THE WEALTHY, PLEASURE-SEEKING MADAME NATASHA, IS NOT THE ANSWER FOR ME!
I'VE BECOME A LEADER OF THE JET-SET... AND I'VE HATED EVERY MOMENT OF IT!
I'VE GOT TO BECOME... THE BLACK WIDOW ONCE AGAIN!
I'VE GOT TO DO WHAT I DO BEST... TO FULFILL MY DESTINY... TO HELP ME FORGET... THE HAUNTED PAST!

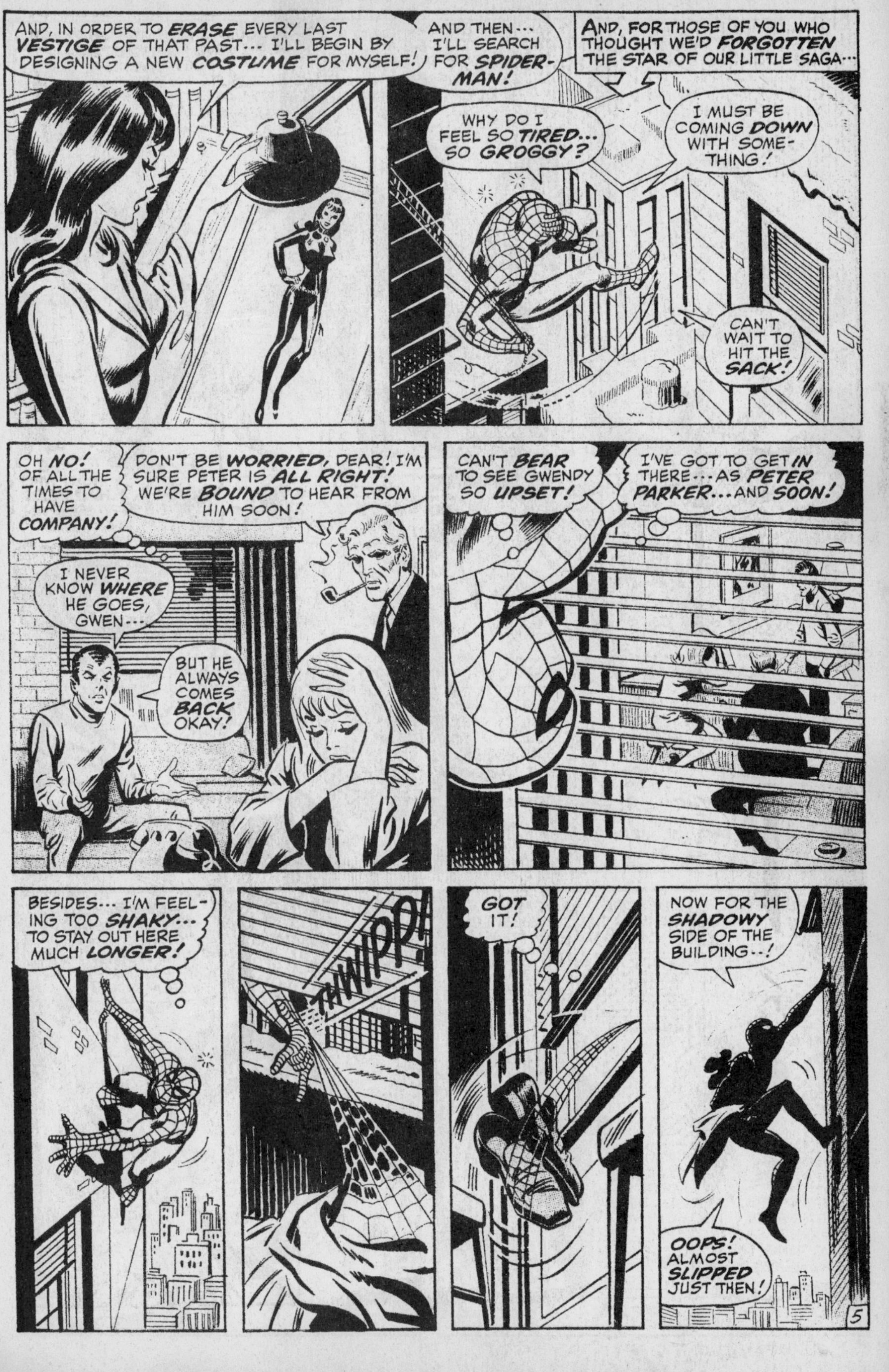
AND, IN ORDER TO ERASE EVERY LAST VESTIGE OF THAT PAST... I'LL BEGIN BY DESIGNING A NEW COSTUME FOR MYSELF!
AND THEN... I'LL SEARCH FOR SPIDER-MAN!
AND, FOR THOSE OF YOU WHO THOUGHT WE'D FORGOTTEN THE STAR OF OUR LITTLE SAGA...
WHY DO I FEEL SO TIRED... SO GROGGY?
I MUST BE COMING DOWN WITH SOME-THING!
CAN'T WAIT TO HIT THE SACK!
OH NO! OF ALL THE TIMES TO HAVE COMPANY!
DON'T BE WORRIED, DEAR! I'M SURE PETER IS ALL RIGHT! WE'RE BOUND TO HEAR FROM HIM SOON!
I NEVER KNOW WHERE HE GOES, GWEN...
BUT HE ALWAYS COMES BACK OKAY!
CAN'T BEAR TO SEE GWENDY SO UPSET!
I'VE GOT TO GET IN THERE... AS PETER PARKER... AND SOON!
BESIDES... I'M FEEL-ING TOO SHAKY... TO STAY OUT HERE MUCH LONGER!
THWIPP!
GOT IT!
NOW FOR THE SHADOWY SIDE OF THE BUILDING..!
OOPS! ALMOST SLIPPED JUST THEN!
5

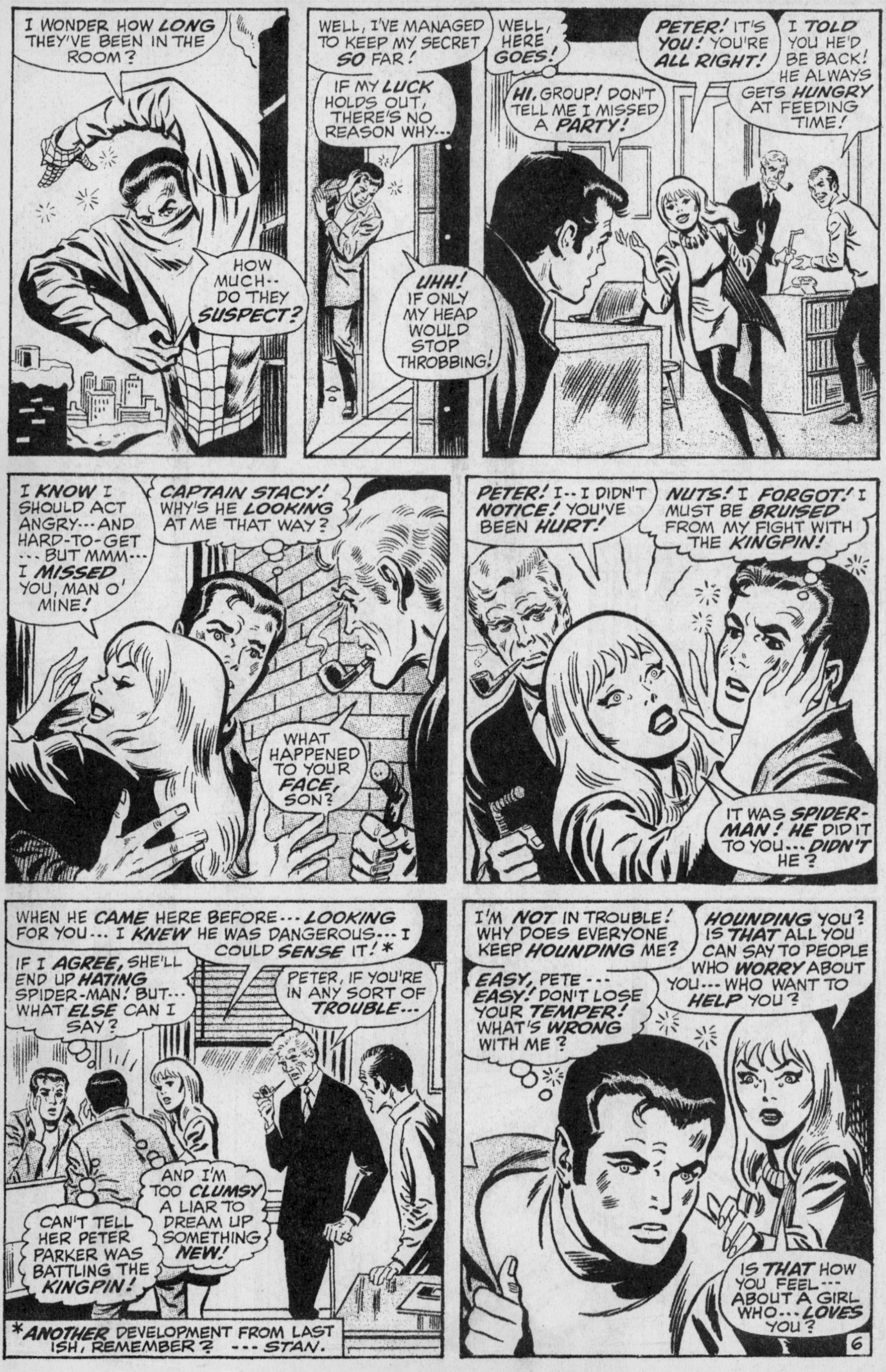
I WONDER HOW LONG THEY'VE BEEN IN THE ROOM?
HOW MUCH-- DO THEY SUSPECT?
WELL, I'VE MANAGED TO KEEP MY SECRET SO FAR!
IF MY LUCK HOLDS OUT, THERE'S NO REASON WHY...
UHH! IF ONLY MY HEAD WOULD STOP THROBBING!
WELL, HERE GOES!
HI, GROUP! DON'T TELL ME I MISSED A PARTY!
PETER! IT'S YOU! YOU'RE ALL RIGHT!
I TOLD YOU HE'D BE BACK! HE ALWAYS GETS HUNGRY AT FEEDING TIME!
I KNOW I SHOULD ACT ANGRY--- AND HARD-TO-GET --- BUT MMM--- I MISSED YOU, MAN O' MINE!
CAPTAIN STACY! WHY'S HE LOOKING AT ME THAT WAY?
WHAT HAPPENED TO YOUR FACE, SON?
PETER! I-- I DIDN'T NOTICE! YOU'VE BEEN HURT!
NUTS! I FORGOT! I MUST BE BRUISED FROM MY FIGHT WITH THE KINGPIN!
IT WAS SPIDER-MAN! HE DID IT TO YOU... DIDN'T HE?
WHEN HE CAME HERE BEFORE... LOOKING FOR YOU... I KNEW HE WAS DANGEROUS--- I COULD SENSE IT! *
IF I AGREE, SHE'LL END UP HATING SPIDER-MAN! BUT--- WHAT ELSE CAN I SAY?
PETER, IF YOU'RE IN ANY SORT OF TROUBLE...
AND I'M TOO CLUMSY A LIAR TO DREAM UP SOMETHING NEW!
CAN'T TELL HER PETER PARKER WAS BATTLING THE KINGPIN!
*ANOTHER DEVELOPMENT FROM LAST ISH, REMEMBER? --- STAN.
I'M NOT IN TROUBLE! WHY DOES EVERYONE KEEP HOUNDING ME?
EASY, PETE --- EASY! DON'T LOSE YOUR TEMPER! WHAT'S WRONG WITH ME?
HOUNDING YOU? IS THAT ALL YOU CAN SAY TO PEOPLE WHO WORRY ABOUT YOU--- WHO WANT TO HELP YOU?
IS THAT HOW YOU FEEL--- ABOUT A GIRL WHO... LOVES YOU?
6

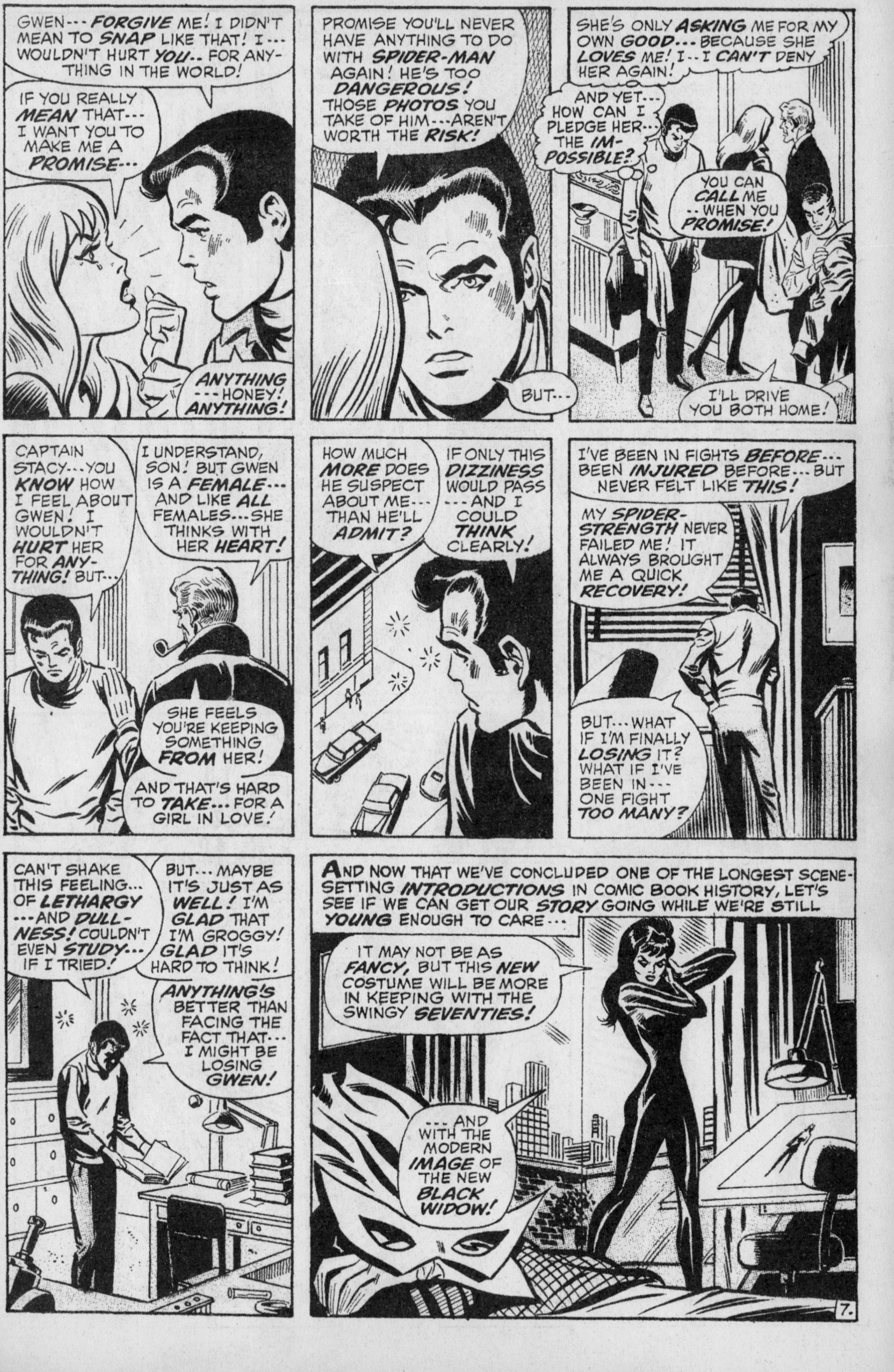
GWEN--- FORGIVE ME! I DIDN'T MEAN TO SNAP LIKE THAT! I--- WOULDN'T HURT YOU-- FOR ANYTHING IN THE WORLD!
IF YOU REALLY MEAN THAT--- I WANT YOU TO MAKE ME A PROMISE---
ANYTHING ---HONEY! ANYTHING!
PROMISE YOU'LL NEVER HAVE ANYTHING TO DO WITH SPIDER-MAN AGAIN! HE'S TOO DANGEROUS! THOSE PHOTOS YOU TAKE OF HIM---AREN'T WORTH THE RISK!
BUT---
SHE'S ONLY ASKING ME FOR MY OWN GOOD--- BECAUSE SHE LOVES ME! I--I CAN'T DENY HER AGAIN!
AND YET--- HOW CAN I PLEDGE HER--- THE IM-POSSIBLE?
YOU CAN CALL ME --WHEN YOU PROMISE!
I'LL DRIVE YOU BOTH HOME!
CAPTAIN STACY---YOU KNOW HOW I FEEL ABOUT GWEN! I WOULDN'T HURT HER FOR ANY-THING! BUT---
I UNDERSTAND, SON! BUT GWEN IS A FEMALE--- AND LIKE ALL FEMALES---SHE THINKS WITH HER HEART!
SHE FEELS YOU'RE KEEPING SOMETHING FROM HER!
AND THAT'S HARD TO TAKE--- FOR A GIRL IN LOVE!
HOW MUCH MORE DOES HE SUSPECT ABOUT ME--- THAN HE'LL ADMIT?
IF ONLY THIS DIZZINESS WOULD PASS ---AND I COULD THINK CLEARLY!
I'VE BEEN IN FIGHTS BEFORE--- BEEN INJURED BEFORE--- BUT NEVER FELT LIKE THIS!
MY SPIDER-STRENGTH NEVER FAILED ME! IT ALWAYS BROUGHT ME A QUICK RECOVERY!
BUT---WHAT IF I'M FINALLY LOSING IT? WHAT IF I'VE BEEN IN--- ONE FIGHT TOO MANY?
CAN'T SHAKE THIS FEELING... OF LETHARGY ---AND DULL-NESS! COULDN'T EVEN STUDY--- IF I TRIED!
BUT--- MAYBE IT'S JUST AS WELL! I'M GLAD THAT I'M GROGGY! GLAD IT'S HARD TO THINK!
ANYTHING'S BETTER THAN FACING THE FACT THAT--- I MIGHT BE LOSING GWEN!
AND NOW THAT WE'VE CONCLUDED ONE OF THE LONGEST SCENE-SETTING INTRODUCTIONS IN COMIC BOOK HISTORY, LET'S SEE IF WE CAN GET OUR STORY GOING WHILE WE'RE STILL YOUNG ENOUGH TO CARE---
IT MAY NOT BE AS FANCY, BUT THIS NEW COSTUME WILL BE MORE IN KEEPING WITH THE SWINGY SEVENTIES!
---AND WITH THE MODERN IMAGE OF THE NEW BLACK WIDOW!
7.

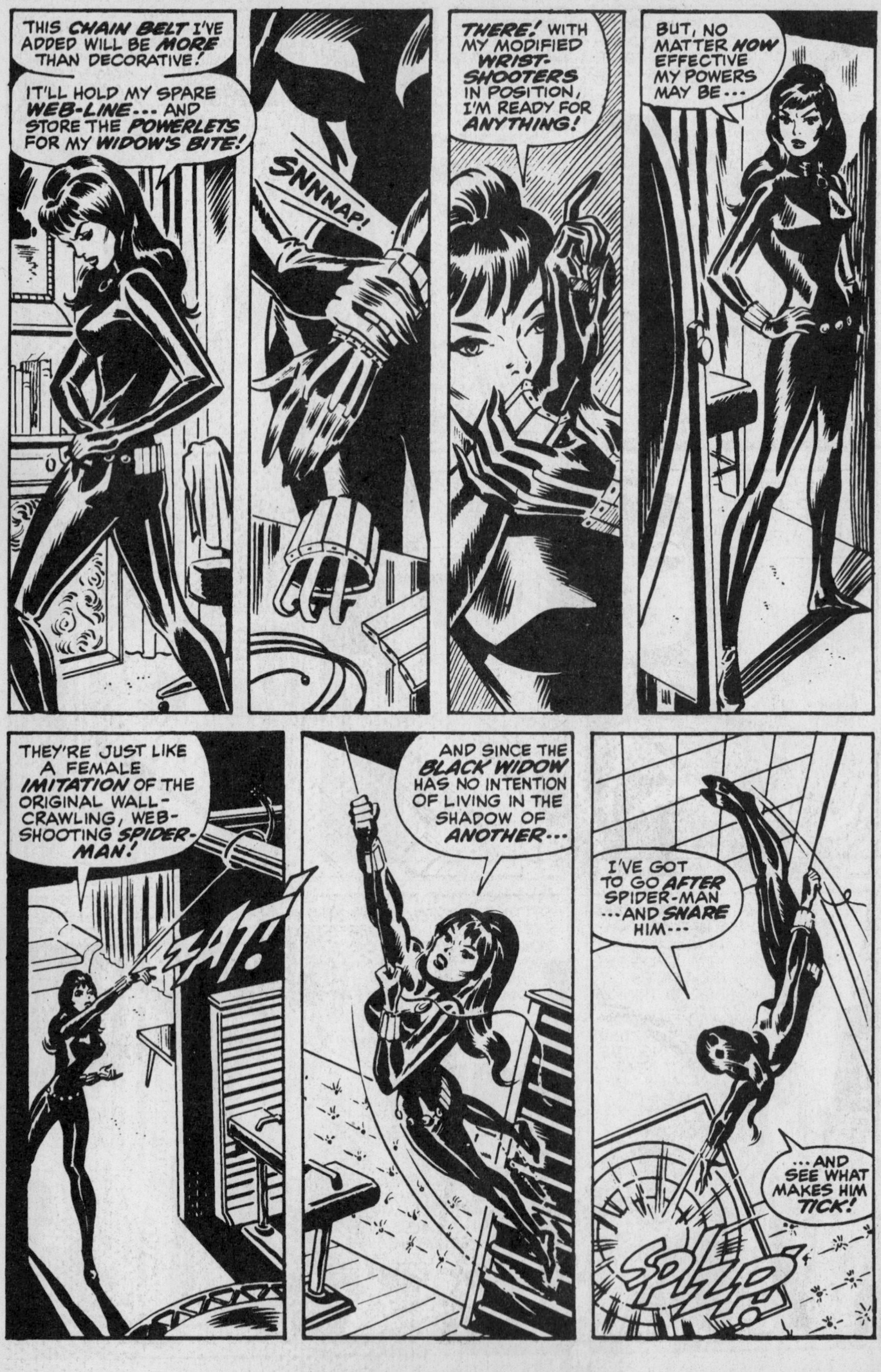
THIS CHAIN BELT I'VE ADDED WILL BE MORE THAN DECORATIVE!
IT'LL HOLD MY SPARE WEB-LINE... AND STORE THE POWERLETS FOR MY WIDOW'S BITE!
SNNNAP!
THERE! WITH MY MODIFIED WRIST-SHOOTERS IN POSITION, I'M READY FOR ANYTHING!
BUT, NO MATTER NOW EFFECTIVE MY POWERS MAY BE...
THEY'RE JUST LIKE A FEMALE IMITATION OF THE ORIGINAL WALL-CRAWLING, WEB-SHOOTING SPIDER-MAN!
AND SINCE THE BLACK WIDOW HAS NO INTENTION OF LIVING IN THE SHADOW OF ANOTHER...
I'VE GOT TO GO AFTER SPIDER-MAN ...AND SNARE HIM...
...AND SEE WHAT MAKES HIM TICK!

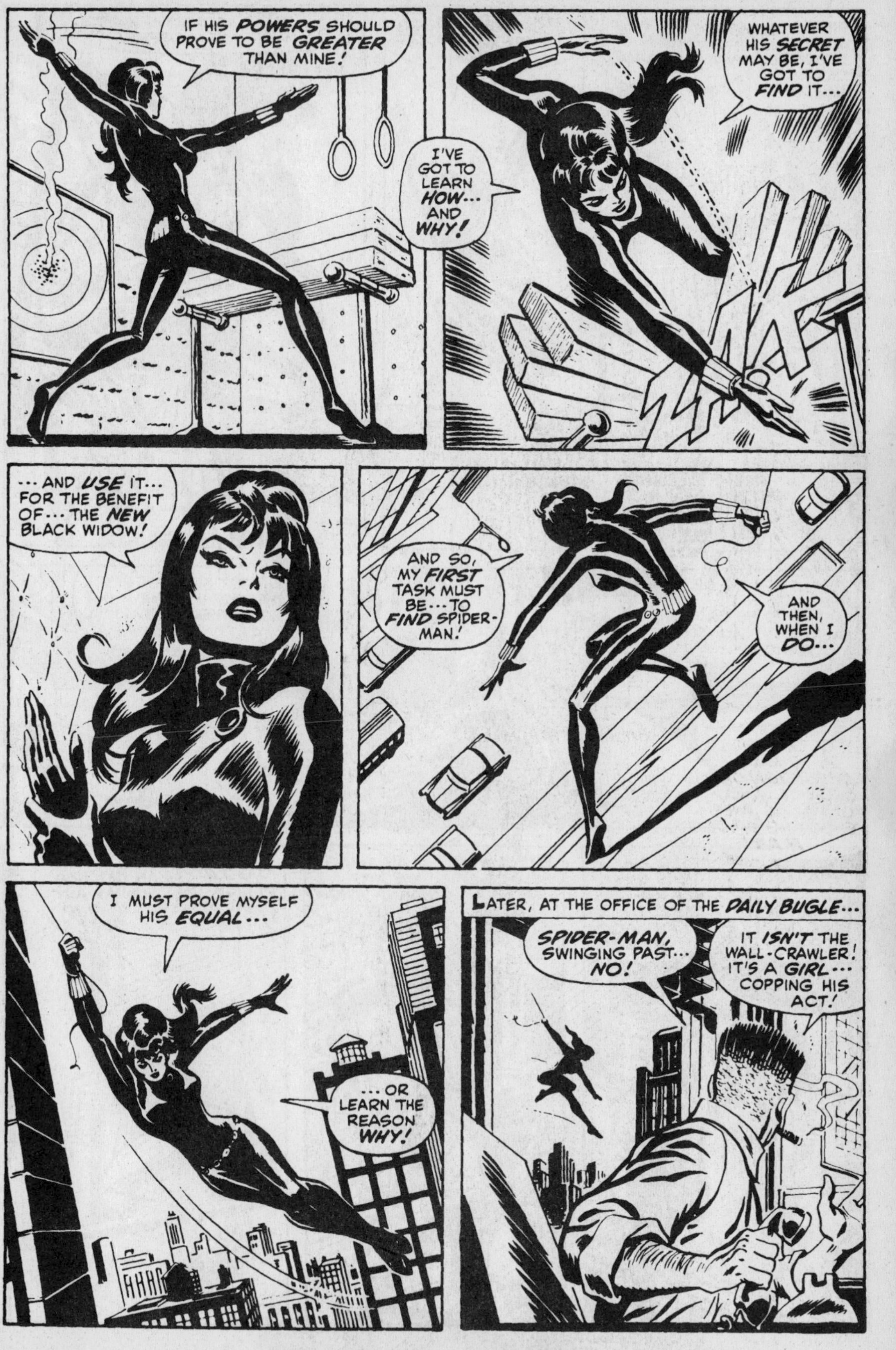

IF HIS POWERS SHOULD PROVE TO BE GREATER THAN MINE!
I'VE GOT TO LEARN HOW... AND WHY!
WHATEVER HIS SECRET MAY BE, I'VE GOT TO FIND IT...
... AND USE IT... FOR THE BENEFIT OF... THE NEW BLACK WIDOW!
AND SO, MY FIRST TASK MUST BE... TO FIND SPIDER-MAN!
AND THEN, WHEN I DO...
I MUST PROVE MYSELF HIS EQUAL...
...OR LEARN THE REASON WHY!
LATER, AT THE OFFICE OF THE DAILY BUGLE...
SPIDER-MAN, SWINGING PAST... NO!
IT ISN'T THE WALL-CRAWLER! IT'S A GIRL... COPPING HIS ACT!

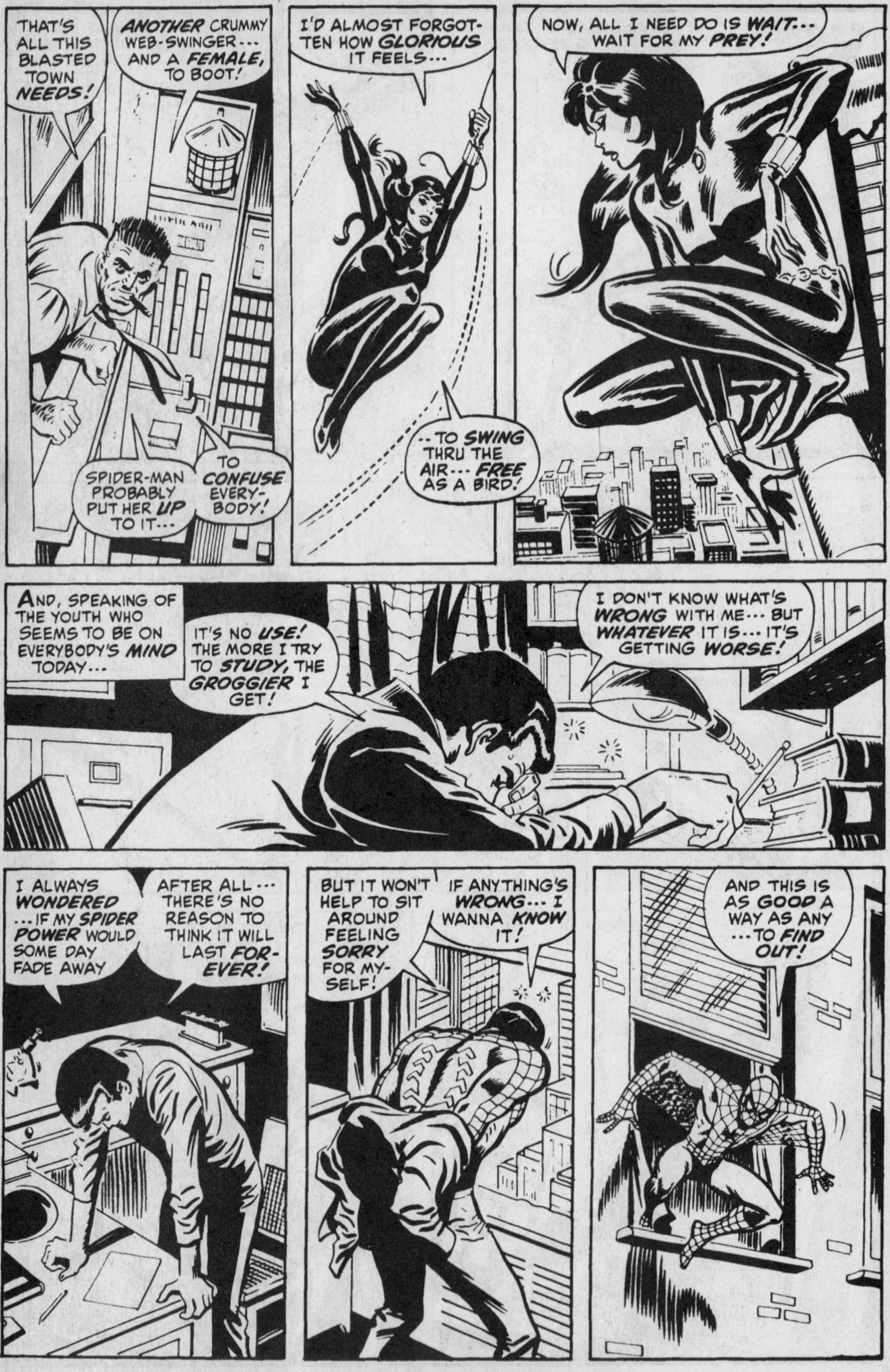

THAT'S ALL THIS BLASTED TOWN NEEDS!
ANOTHER CRUMMY WEB-SWINGER--- AND A FEMALE, TO BOOT!
SPIDER-MAN PROBABLY PUT HER UP TO IT---
TO CONFUSE EVERY-BODY!
I'D ALMOST FORGOT-TEN HOW GLORIOUS IT FEELS---
--TO SWING THRU THE AIR--- FREE AS A BIRD!
NOW, ALL I NEED DO IS WAIT--- WAIT FOR MY PREY!
AND, SPEAKING OF THE YOUTH WHO SEEMS TO BE ON EVERYBODY'S MIND TODAY---
IT'S NO USE! THE MORE I TRY TO STUDY, THE GROGGIER I GET!
I DON'T KNOW WHAT'S WRONG WITH ME--- BUT WHATEVER IT IS--- IT'S GETTING WORSE!
I ALWAYS WONDERED ---IF MY SPIDER POWER WOULD SOME DAY FADE AWAY
AFTER ALL--- THERE'S NO REASON TO THINK IT WILL LAST FOR-EVER!
BUT IT WON'T HELP TO SIT AROUND FEELING SORRY FOR MY-SELF!
IF ANYTHING'S WRONG--- I WANNA KNOW IT!
AND THIS IS AS GOOD A WAY AS ANY ---TO FIND OUT!

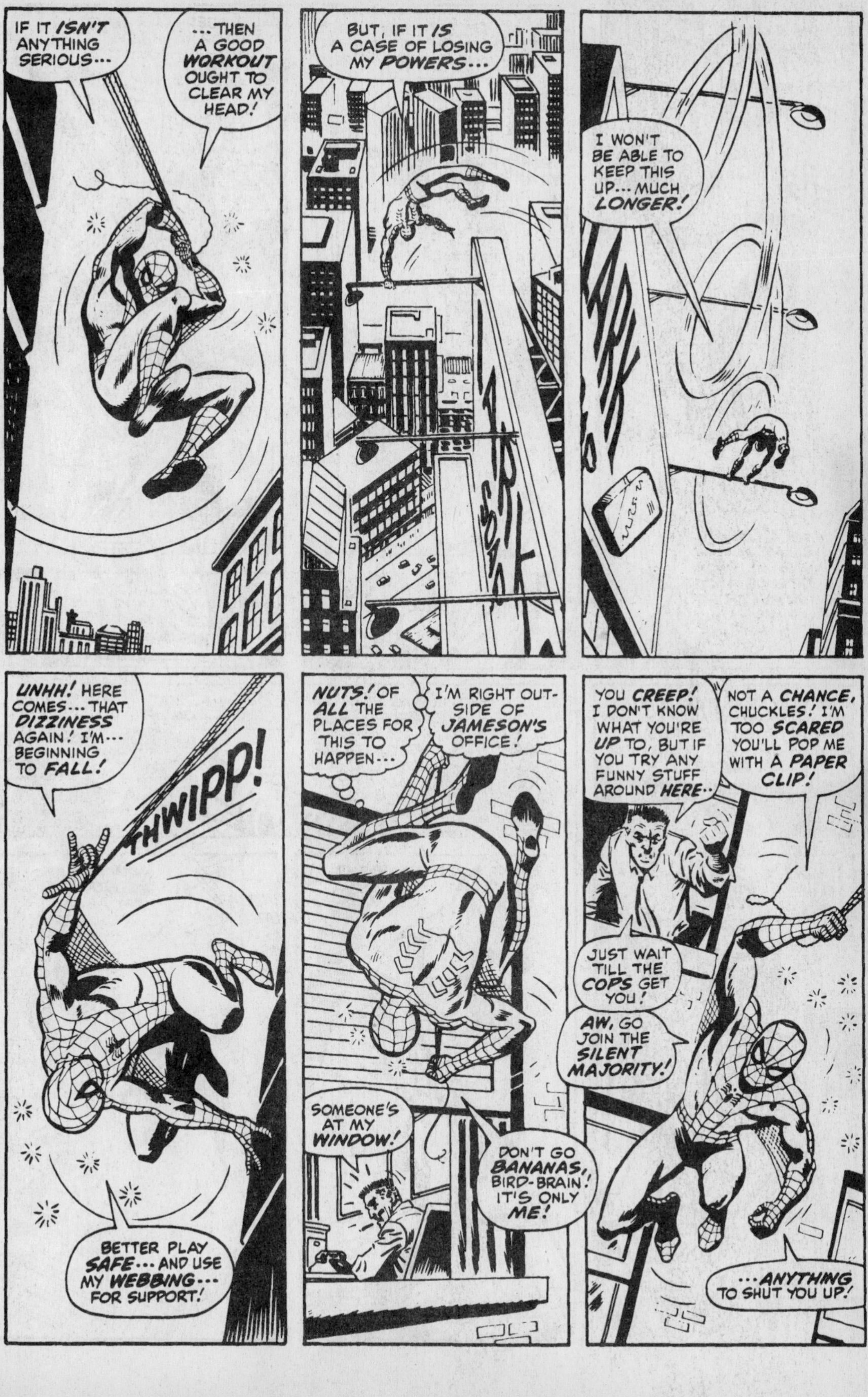
IF IT ISN'T ANYTHING SERIOUS...
...THEN A GOOD WORKOUT OUGHT TO CLEAR MY HEAD!
BUT, IF IT IS A CASE OF LOSING MY POWERS...
I WON'T BE ABLE TO KEEP THIS UP... MUCH LONGER!
UNHH! HERE COMES... THAT DIZZINESS AGAIN! I'M... BEGINNING TO FALL!
THWIPP!
BETTER PLAY SAFE... AND USE MY WEBBING... FOR SUPPORT!
NUTS! OF ALL THE PLACES FOR THIS TO HAPPEN...
I'M RIGHT OUTSIDE OF JAMESON'S OFFICE!
SOMEONE'S AT MY WINDOW!
DON'T GO BANANAS, BIRD-BRAIN! IT'S ONLY ME!
YOU CREEP! I DON'T KNOW WHAT YOU'RE UP TO, BUT IF YOU TRY ANY FUNNY STUFF AROUND HERE..
NOT A CHANCE, CHUCKLES! I'M TOO SCARED YOU'LL POP ME WITH A PAPER CLIP!
JUST WAIT TILL THE COPS GET YOU!
AW, GO JOIN THE SILENT MAJORITY!
...ANYTHING TO SHUT YOU UP!

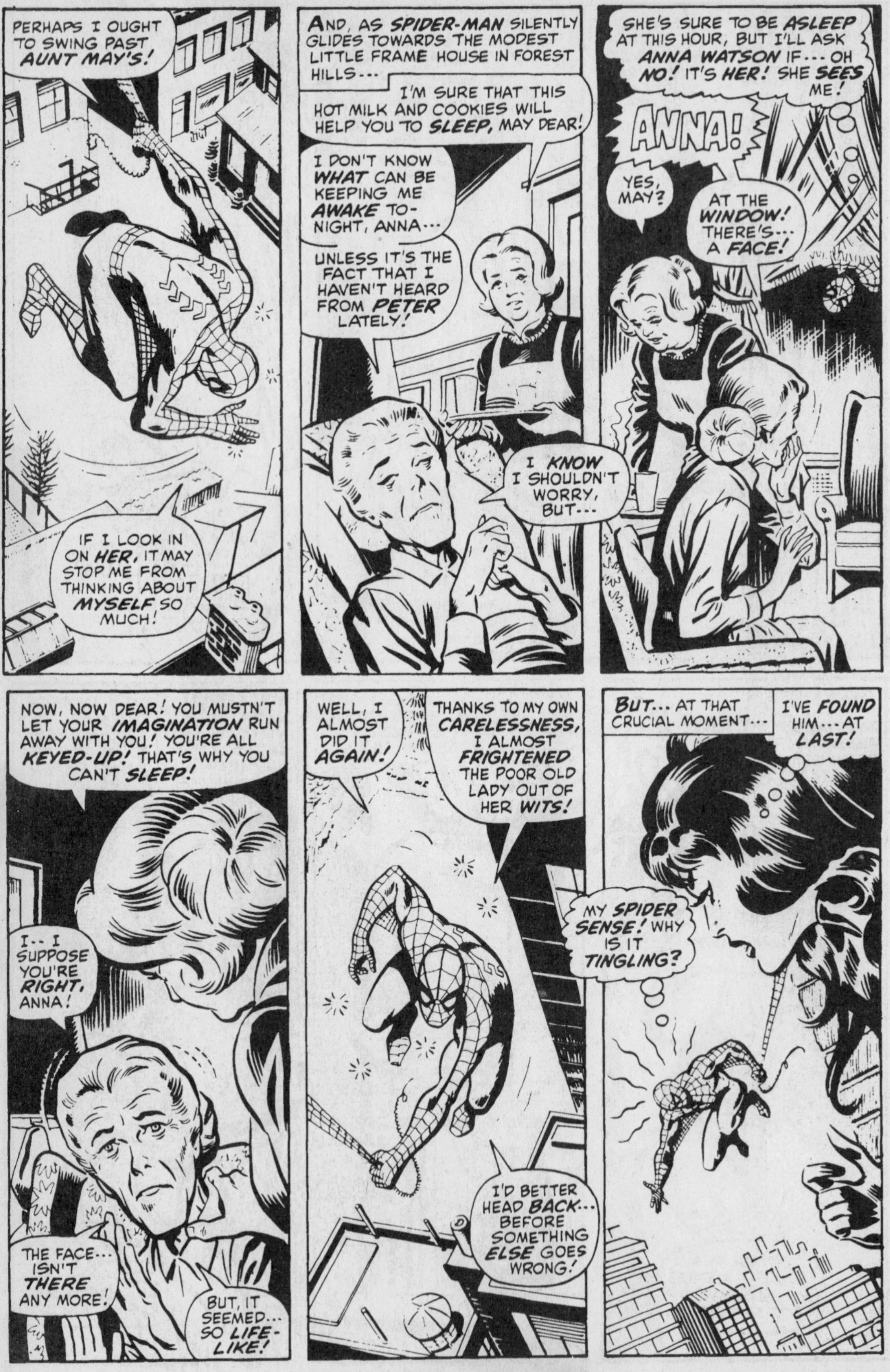
PERHAPS I OUGHT TO SWING PAST AUNT MAY'S!
IF I LOOK IN ON HER, IT MAY STOP ME FROM THINKING ABOUT MYSELF SO MUCH!
AND, AS SPIDER-MAN SILENTLY GLIDES TOWARDS THE MODEST LITTLE FRAME HOUSE IN FOREST HILLS...
I'M SURE THAT THIS HOT MILK AND COOKIES WILL HELP YOU TO SLEEP, MAY DEAR!
I DON'T KNOW WHAT CAN BE KEEPING ME AWAKE TO-NIGHT, ANNA...
UNLESS IT'S THE FACT THAT I HAVEN'T HEARD FROM PETER LATELY!
I KNOW I SHOULDN'T WORRY, BUT...
SHE'S SURE TO BE ASLEEP AT THIS HOUR, BUT I'LL ASK ANNA WATSON IF... OH NO! IT'S HER! SHE SEES ME!
ANNA!
YES, MAY?
AT THE WINDOW! THERE'S... A FACE!
NOW, NOW DEAR! YOU MUSTN'T LET YOUR IMAGINATION RUN AWAY WITH YOU! YOU'RE ALL KEYED-UP! THAT'S WHY YOU CAN'T SLEEP!
I-- I SUPPOSE YOU'RE RIGHT, ANNA!
THE FACE... ISN'T THERE ANY MORE!
BUT, IT SEEMED... SO LIFE-LIKE!
WELL, I ALMOST DID IT AGAIN!
THANKS TO MY OWN CARELESSNESS, I ALMOST FRIGHTENED THE POOR OLD LADY OUT OF HER WITS!
I'D BETTER HEAD BACK... BEFORE SOMETHING ELSE GOES WRONG!
BUT... AT THAT CRUCIAL MOMENT...
I'VE FOUND HIM... AT LAST!
MY SPIDER SENSE! WHY IS IT TINGLING?

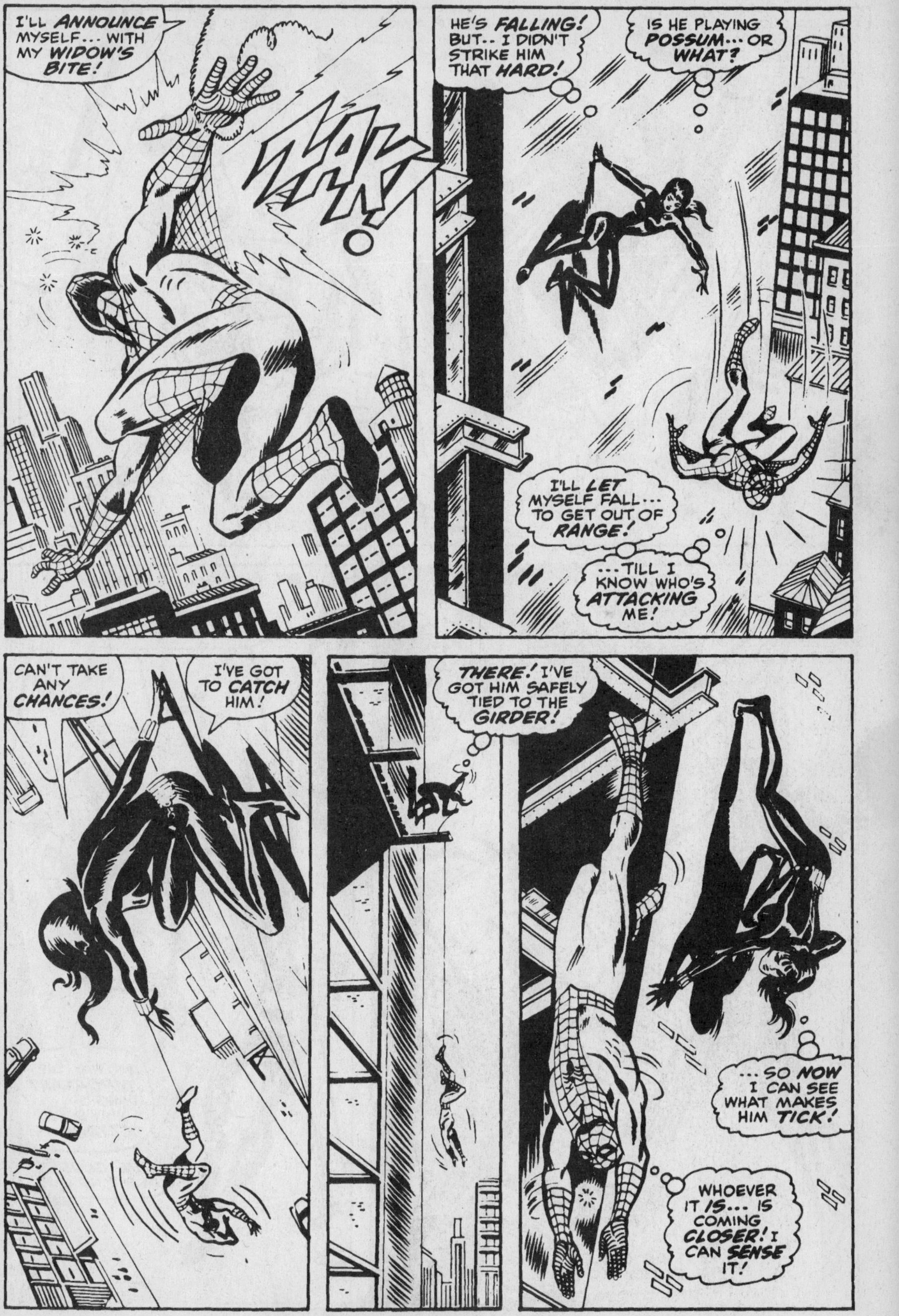
I'LL ANNOUNCE MYSELF... WITH MY WIDOW'S BITE!
ZZAK
HE'S FALLING! BUT.. I DIDN'T STRIKE HIM THAT HARD!
IS HE PLAYING POSSUM... OR WHAT?
I'LL LET MYSELF FALL... TO GET OUT OF RANGE!
...TILL I KNOW WHO'S ATTACKING ME!
CAN'T TAKE ANY CHANCES!
I'VE GOT TO CATCH HIM!
THERE! I'VE GOT HIM SAFELY TIED TO THE GIRDER!
...SO NOW I CAN SEE WHAT MAKES HIM TICK!
WHOEVER IT IS... IS COMING CLOSER! I CAN SENSE IT!

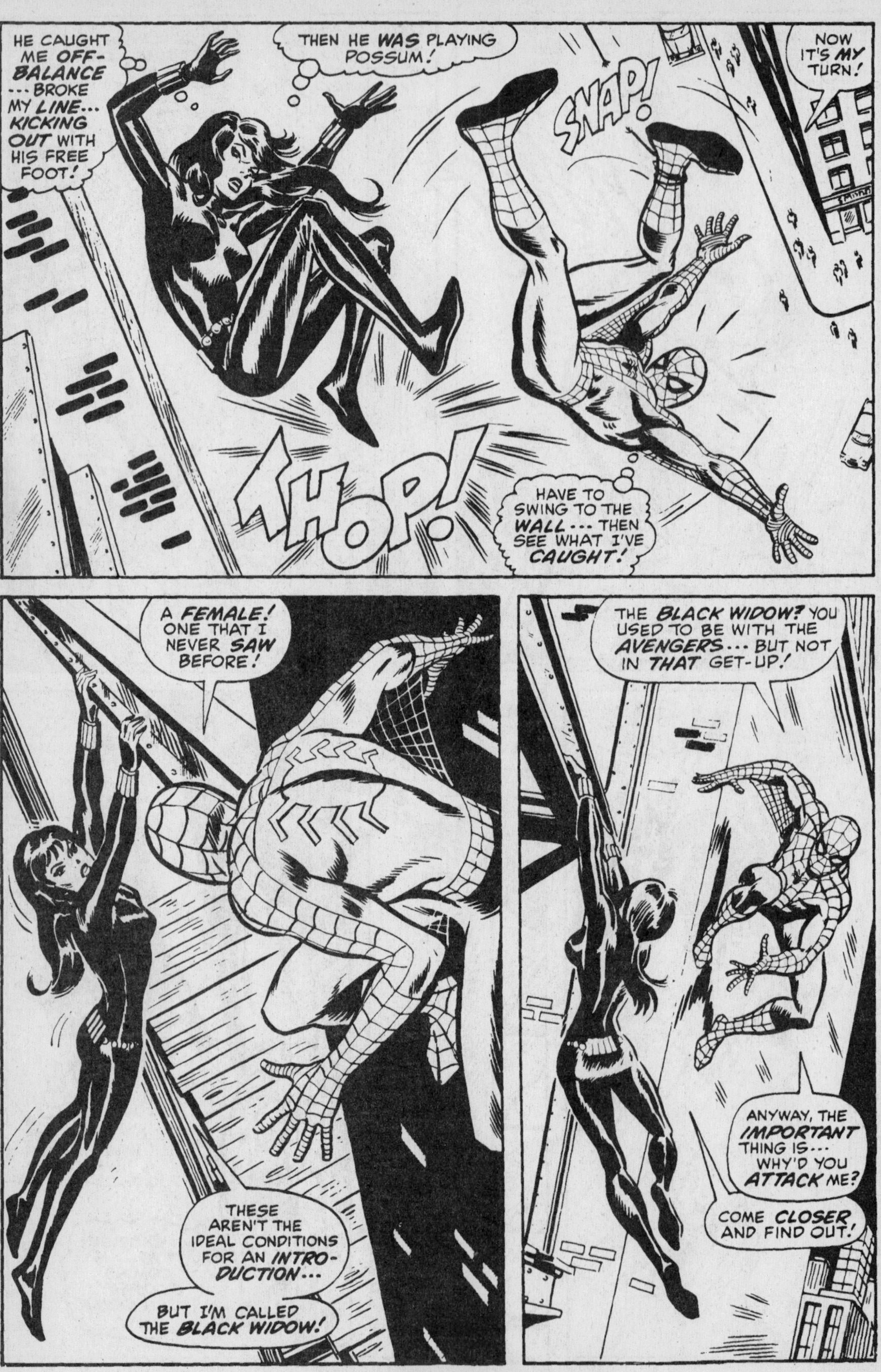
HE CAUGHT ME OFF-BALANCE --- BROKE MY LINE... KICKING OUT WITH HIS FREE FOOT!
THEN HE WAS PLAYING POSSUM!
SNAP!
NOW IT'S MY TURN!
THOP!
HAVE TO SWING TO THE WALL --- THEN SEE WHAT I'VE CAUGHT!
A FEMALE! ONE THAT I NEVER SAW BEFORE!
THESE AREN'T THE IDEAL CONDITIONS FOR AN INTRO-DUCTION...
BUT I'M CALLED THE BLACK WIDOW!
THE BLACK WIDOW? YOU USED TO BE WITH THE AVENGERS... BUT NOT IN THAT GET-UP!
ANYWAY, THE IMPORTANT THING IS--- WHY'D YOU ATTACK ME?
COME CLOSER AND FIND OUT!

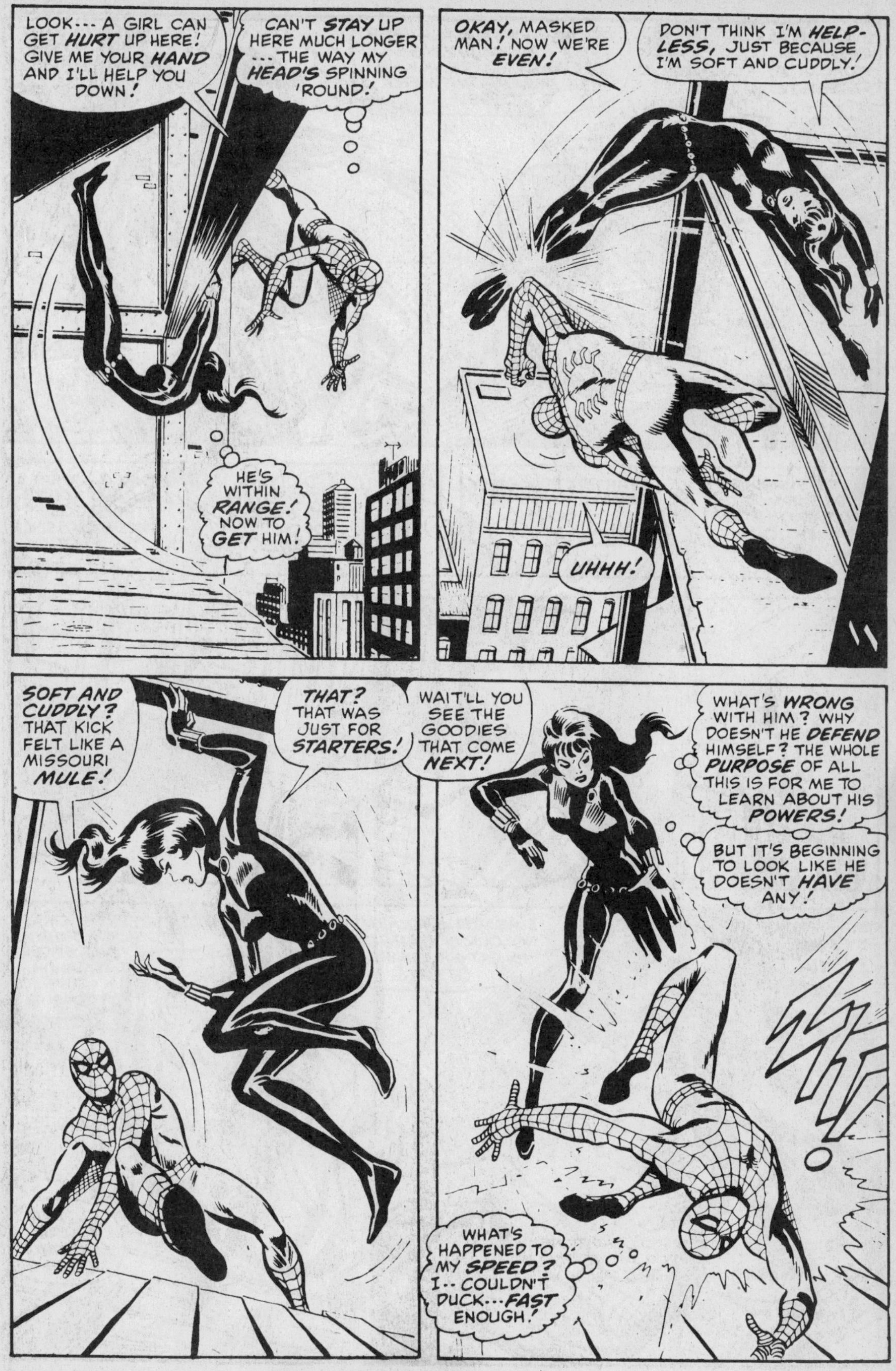
LOOK... A GIRL CAN GET HURT UP HERE! GIVE ME YOUR HAND AND I'LL HELP YOU DOWN!
CAN'T STAY UP HERE MUCH LONGER ... THE WAY MY HEAD'S SPINNING 'ROUND!
HE'S WITHIN RANGE! NOW TO GET HIM!
OKAY, MASKED MAN! NOW WE'RE EVEN!
DON'T THINK I'M HELP-LESS, JUST BECAUSE I'M SOFT AND CUDDLY!
UHHH!
SOFT AND CUDDLY? THAT KICK FELT LIKE A MISSOURI MULE!
THAT? THAT WAS JUST FOR STARTERS!
WAIT'LL YOU SEE THE GOODIES THAT COME NEXT!
WHAT'S WRONG WITH HIM? WHY DOESN'T HE DEFEND HIMSELF? THE WHOLE PURPOSE OF ALL THIS IS FOR ME TO LEARN ABOUT HIS POWERS!
BUT IT'S BEGINNING TO LOOK LIKE HE DOESN'T HAVE ANY!
WHAT'S HAPPENED TO MY SPEED? I-- COULDN'T DUCK... FAST ENOUGH!

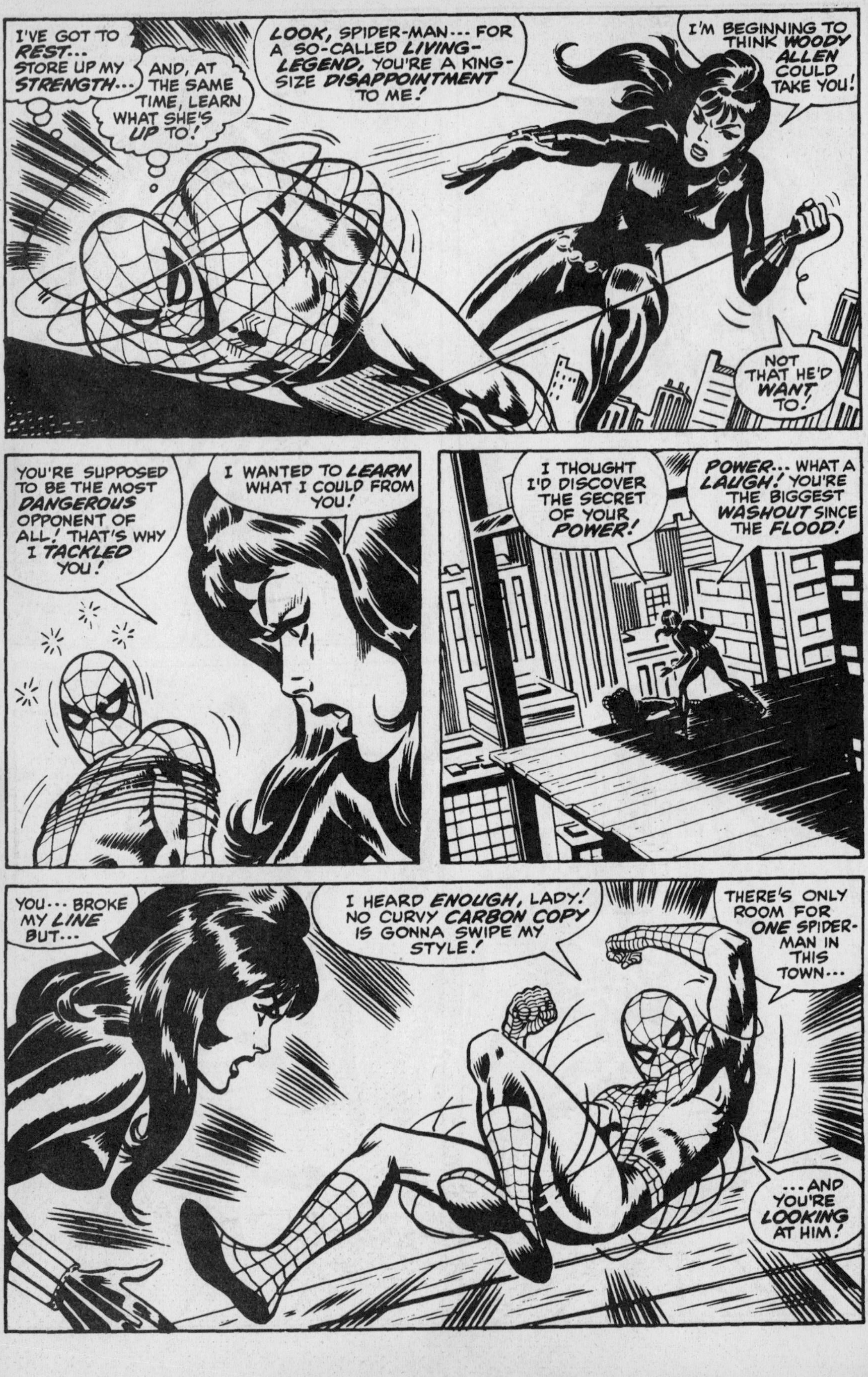
I'VE GOT TO REST... STORE UP MY STRENGTH...
AND, AT THE SAME TIME, LEARN WHAT SHE'S UP TO!
LOOK, SPIDER-MAN--- FOR A SO-CALLED LIVING-LEGEND, YOU'RE A KING-SIZE DISAPPOINTMENT TO ME!
I'M BEGINNING TO THINK WOODY ALLEN COULD TAKE YOU!
NOT THAT HE'D WANT TO!
YOU'RE SUPPOSED TO BE THE MOST DANGEROUS OPPONENT OF ALL! THAT'S WHY I TACKLED YOU!
I WANTED TO LEARN WHAT I COULD FROM YOU!
I THOUGHT I'D DISCOVER THE SECRET OF YOUR POWER!
POWER... WHAT A LAUGH! YOU'RE THE BIGGEST WASHOUT SINCE THE FLOOD!
YOU--- BROKE MY LINE BUT---
I HEARD ENOUGH, LADY! NO CURVY CARBON COPY IS GONNA SWIPE MY STYLE!
THERE'S ONLY ROOM FOR ONE SPIDER-MAN IN THIS TOWN---
...AND YOU'RE LOOKING AT HIM!

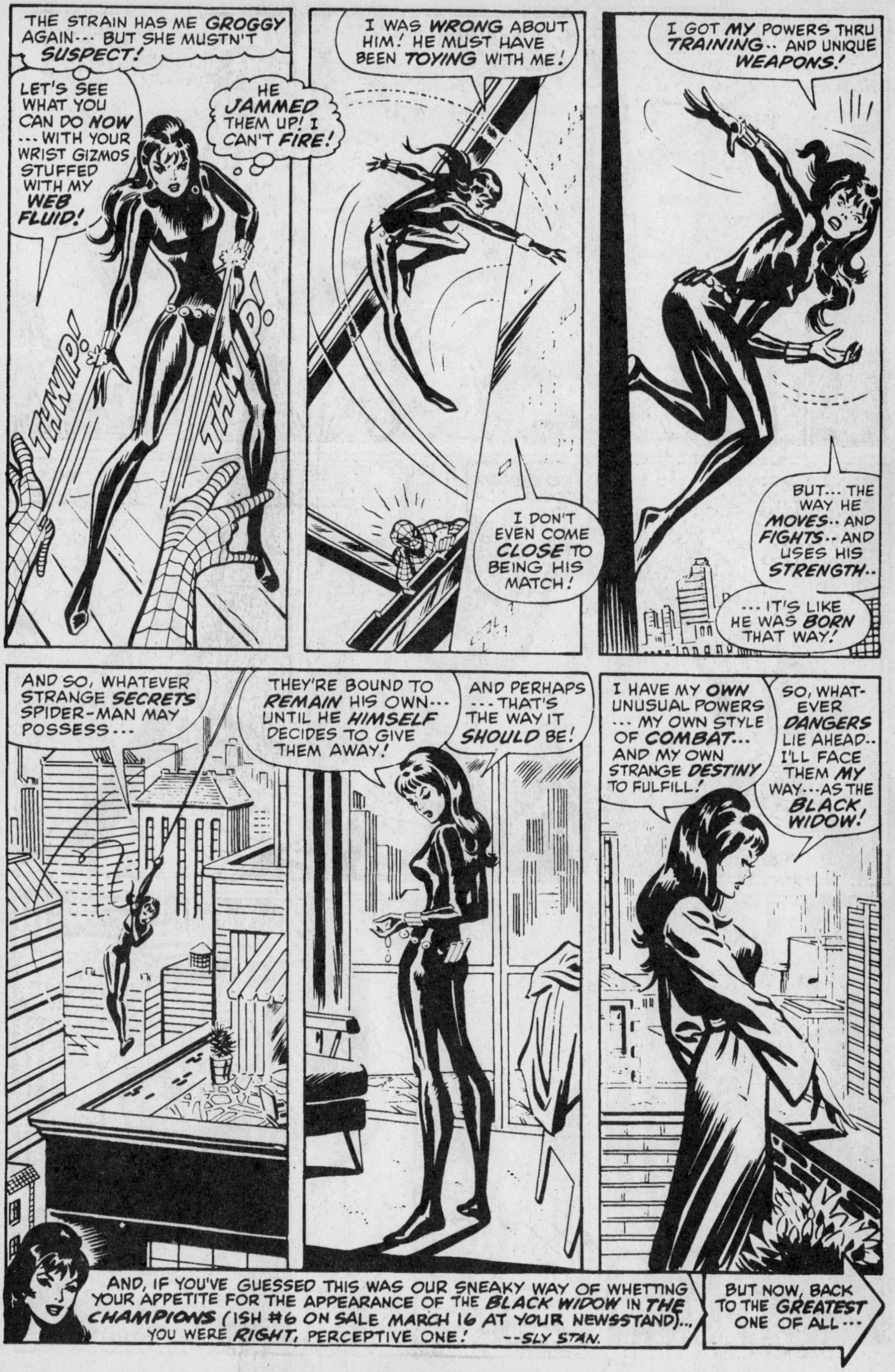
THE STRAIN HAS ME GROGGY AGAIN--- BUT SHE MUSTN'T SUSPECT!
LET'S SEE WHAT YOU CAN DO NOW --- WITH YOUR WRIST GIZMOS STUFFED WITH MY WEB FLUID!
HE JAMMED THEM UP! I CAN'T FIRE!
THWIP!
THWIP!
I WAS WRONG ABOUT HIM! HE MUST HAVE BEEN TOYING WITH ME!
I DON'T EVEN COME CLOSE TO BEING HIS MATCH!
I GOT MY POWERS THRU TRAINING.. AND UNIQUE WEAPONS!
BUT... THE WAY HE MOVES.. AND FIGHTS.. AND USES HIS STRENGTH..
... IT'S LIKE HE WAS BORN THAT WAY!
AND SO, WHATEVER STRANGE SECRETS SPIDER-MAN MAY POSSESS---
THEY'RE BOUND TO REMAIN HIS OWN--- UNTIL HE HIMSELF DECIDES TO GIVE THEM AWAY!
AND PERHAPS --- THAT'S THE WAY IT SHOULD BE!
I HAVE MY OWN UNUSUAL POWERS --- MY OWN STYLE OF COMBAT... AND MY OWN STRANGE DESTINY TO FULFILL!
SO, WHAT-EVER DANGERS LIE AHEAD.. I'LL FACE THEM MY WAY---AS THE BLACK WIDOW!
AND, IF YOU'VE GUESSED THIS WAS OUR SNEAKY WAY OF WHETTING YOUR APPETITE FOR THE APPEARANCE OF THE BLACK WIDOW IN THE CHAMPIONS (ISH #6 ON SALE MARCH 16 AT YOUR NEWSSTAND)... YOU WERE RIGHT, PERCEPTIVE ONE! --SLY STAN.
BUT NOW, BACK TO THE GREATEST ONE OF ALL---

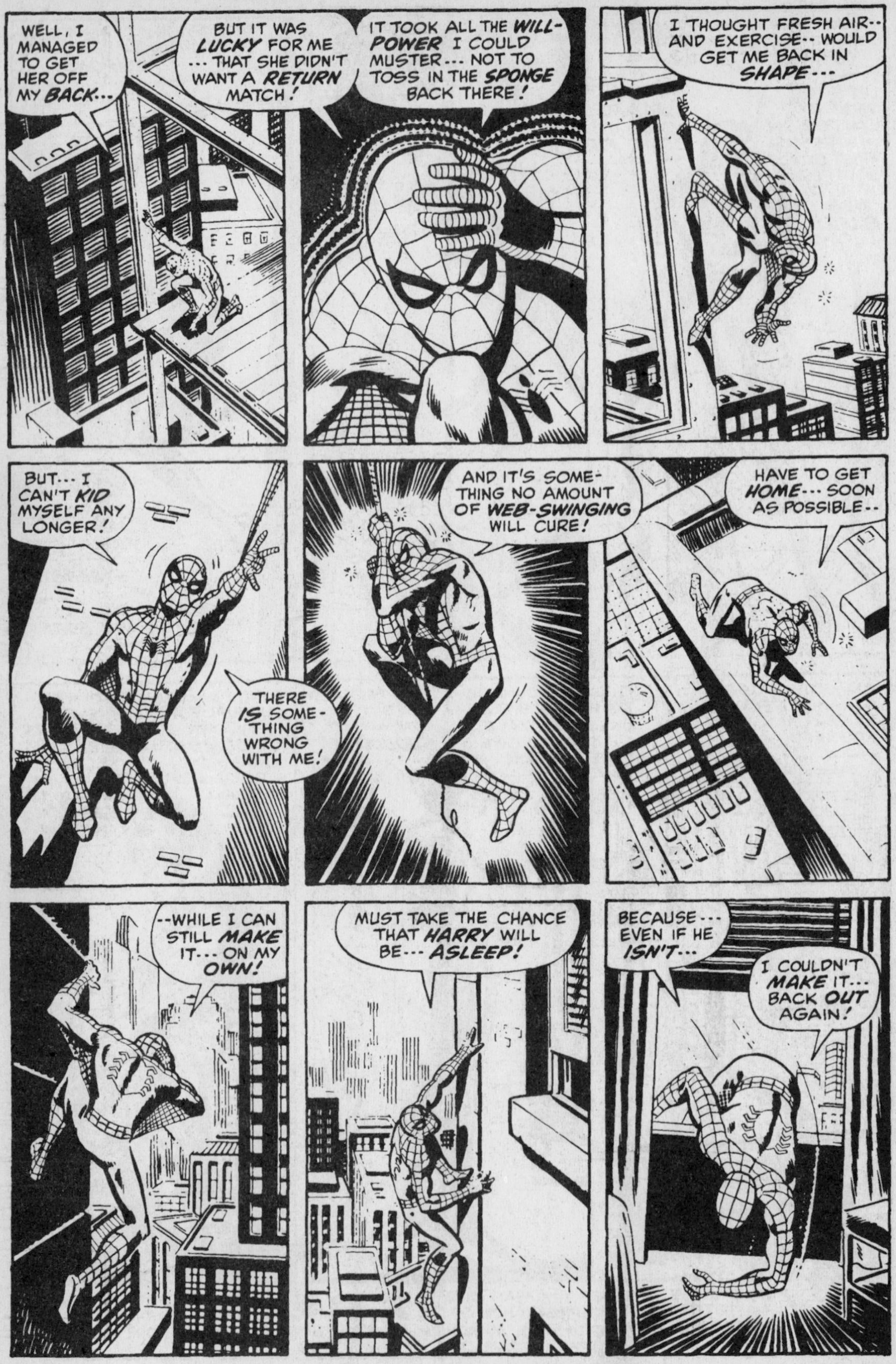
WELL, I MANAGED TO GET HER OFF MY BACK...
BUT IT WAS LUCKY FOR ME ... THAT SHE DIDN'T WANT A RETURN MATCH!
IT TOOK ALL THE WILL-POWER I COULD MUSTER... NOT TO TOSS IN THE SPONGE BACK THERE!
I THOUGHT FRESH AIR-- AND EXERCISE-- WOULD GET ME BACK IN SHAPE---
BUT--- I CAN'T KID MYSELF ANY LONGER!
THERE IS SOMETHING WRONG WITH ME!
AND IT'S SOMETHING NO AMOUNT OF WEB-SWINGING WILL CURE!
HAVE TO GET HOME--- SOON AS POSSIBLE--
--WHILE I CAN STILL MAKE IT--- ON MY OWN!
MUST TAKE THE CHANCE THAT HARRY WILL BE--- ASLEEP!
BECAUSE--- EVEN IF HE ISN'T---
I COULDN'T MAKE IT... BACK OUT AGAIN!

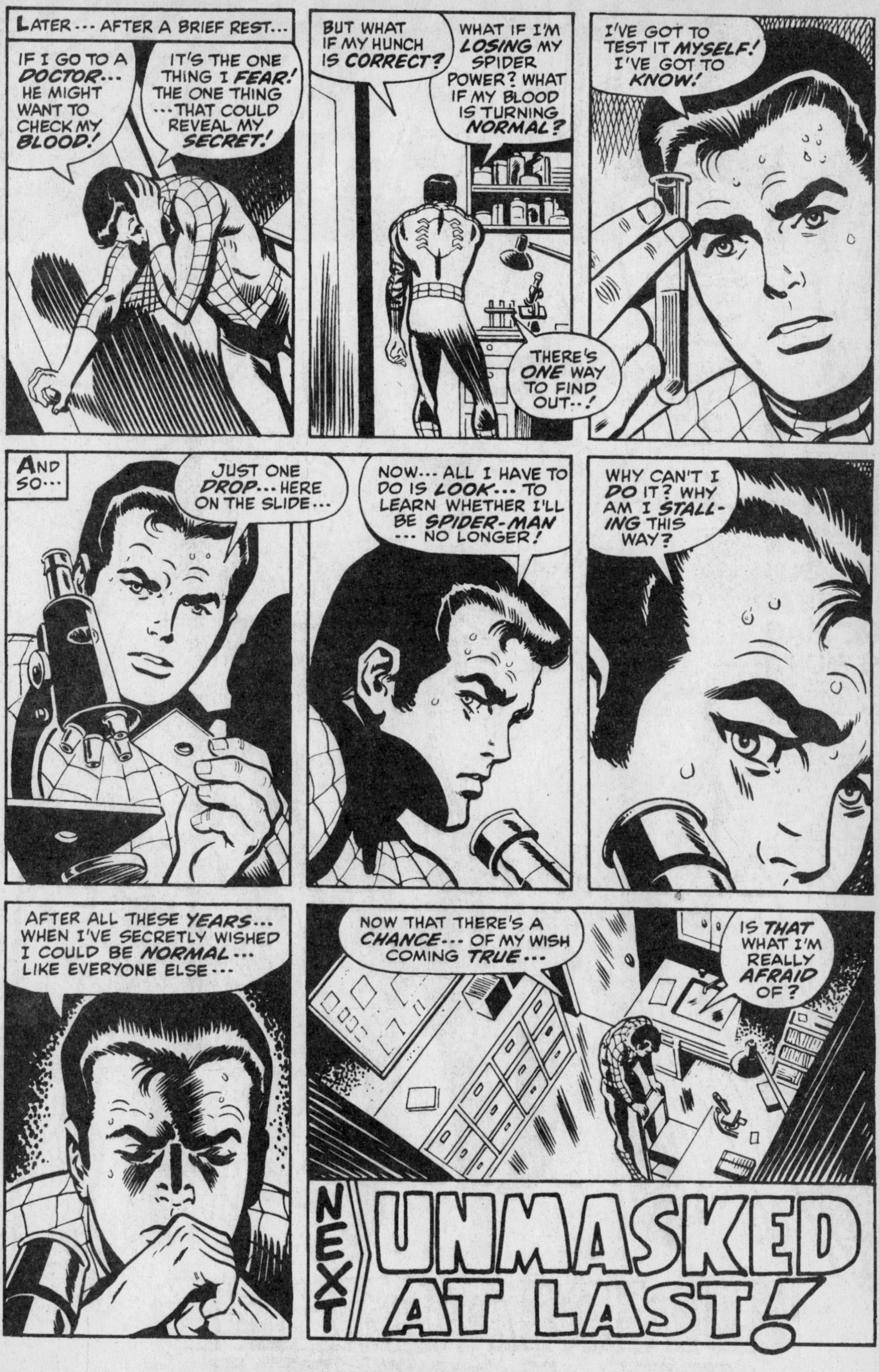
LATER... AFTER A BRIEF REST...
IF I GO TO A DOCTOR... HE MIGHT WANT TO CHECK MY BLOOD!
IT'S THE ONE THING I FEAR! THE ONE THING ...THAT COULD REVEAL MY SECRET!
BUT WHAT IF MY HUNCH IS CORRECT?
WHAT IF I'M LOSING MY SPIDER POWER? WHAT IF MY BLOOD IS TURNING NORMAL?
THERE'S ONE WAY TO FIND OUT..!
I'VE GOT TO TEST IT MYSELF! I'VE GOT TO KNOW!
AND SO...
JUST ONE DROP... HERE ON THE SLIDE...
NOW... ALL I HAVE TO DO IS LOOK... TO LEARN WHETHER I'LL BE SPIDER-MAN ... NO LONGER!
WHY CAN'T I DO IT? WHY AM I STALLING THIS WAY?
AFTER ALL THESE YEARS... WHEN I'VE SECRETLY WISHED I COULD BE NORMAL... LIKE EVERYONE ELSE...
NOW THAT THERE'S A CHANCE... OF MY WISH COMING TRUE...
IS THAT WHAT I'M REALLY AFRAID OF?
NEXT
UNMASKED AT LAST!

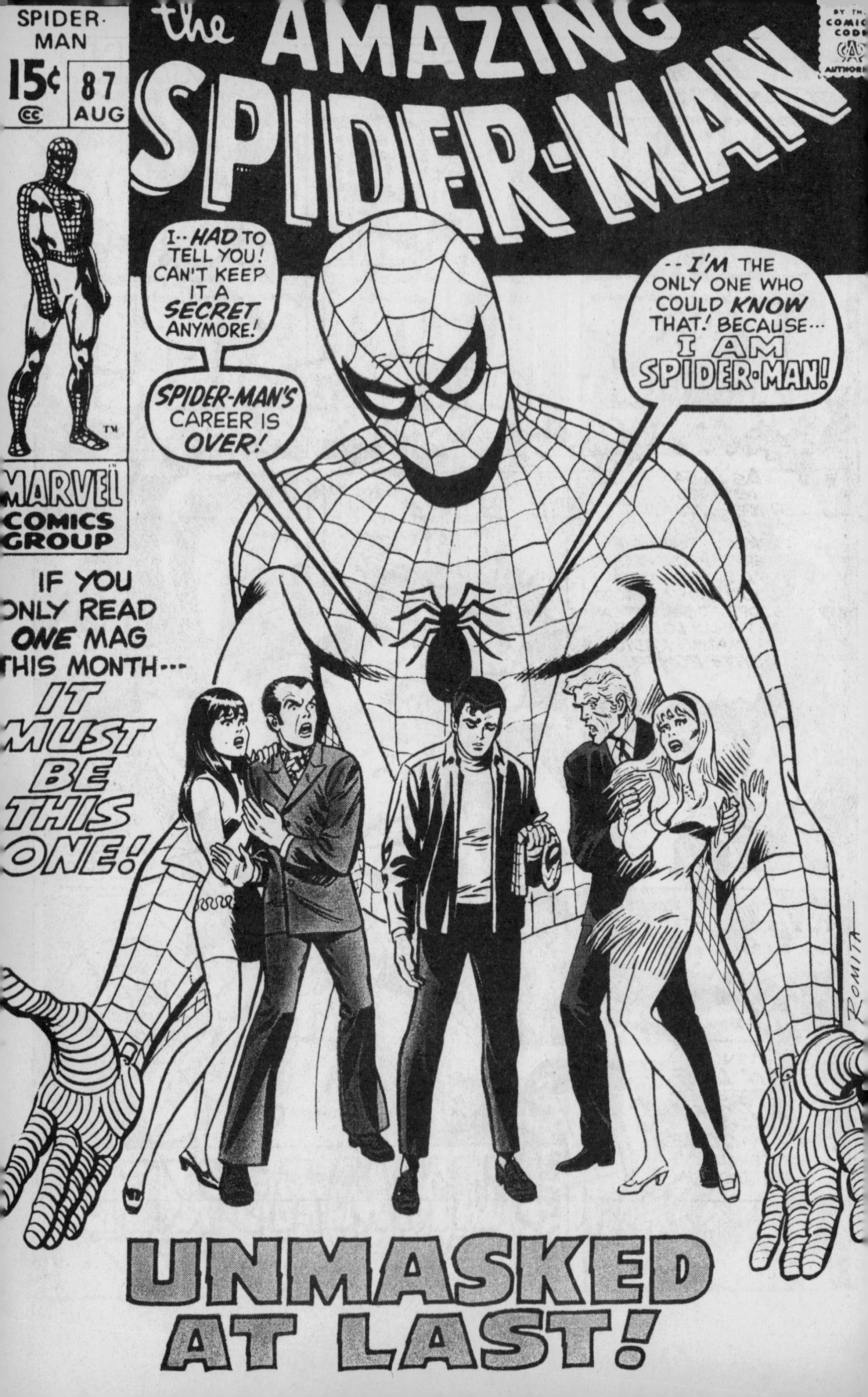
SPIDER-MAN
15¢
87
AUG
the AMAZING SPIDER-MAN
MARVEL COMICS GROUP
IF YOU ONLY READ ONE MAG THIS MONTH--- IT MUST BE THIS ONE!
I-- HAD TO TELL YOU! CAN'T KEEP IT A SECRET ANYMORE!
SPIDER-MAN'S CAREER IS OVER!
--I'M THE ONLY ONE WHO COULD KNOW THAT! BECAUSE--- I AM SPIDER-MAN!
ROMITA
UNMASKED AT LAST!

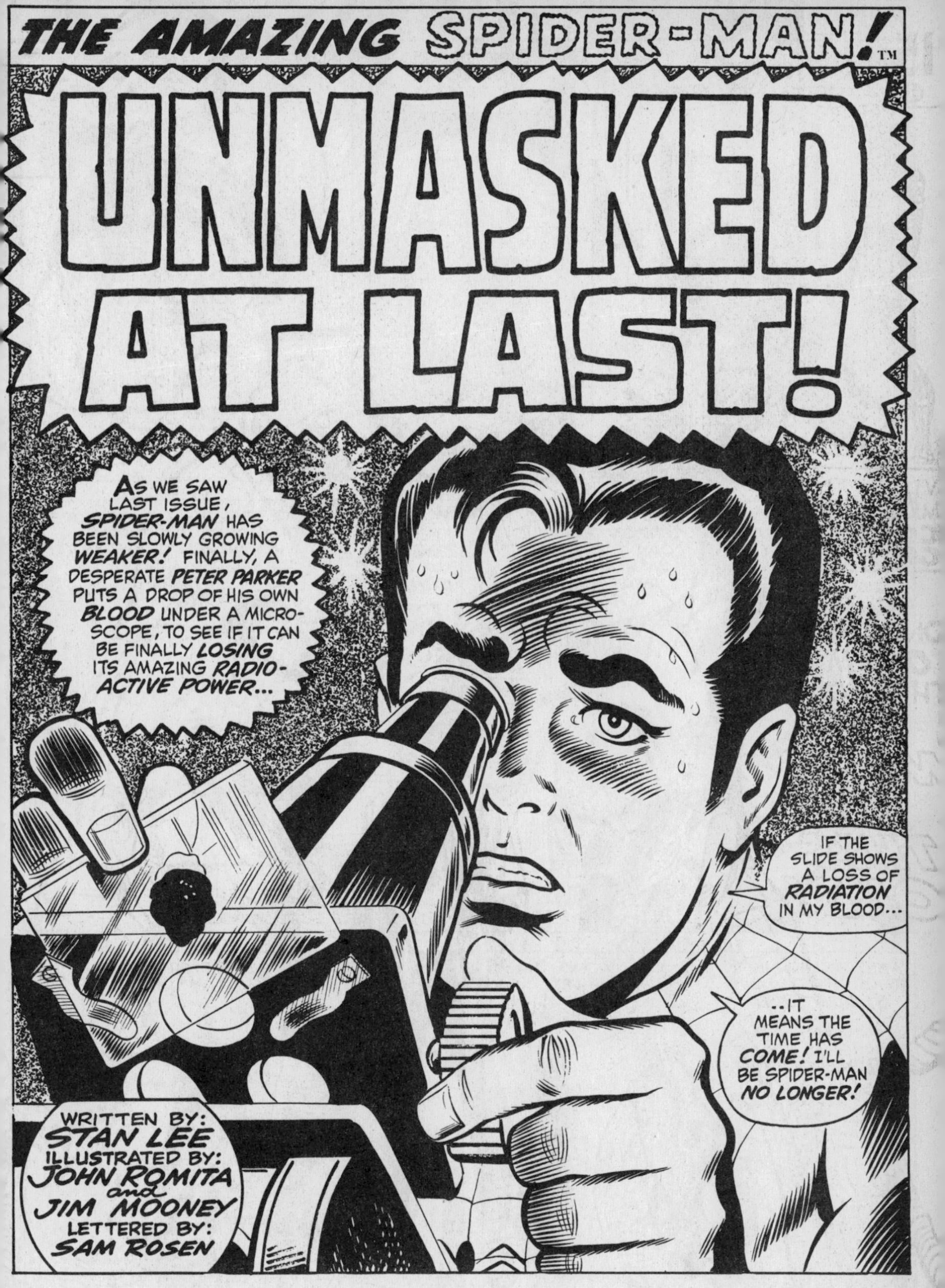

THE AMAZING SPIDER-MAN!™
UNMASKED AT LAST!
AS WE SAW LAST ISSUE, SPIDER-MAN HAS BEEN SLOWLY GROWING WEAKER! FINALLY, A DESPERATE PETER PARKER PUTS A DROP OF HIS OWN BLOOD UNDER A MICRO-SCOPE, TO SEE IF IT CAN BE FINALLY LOSING ITS AMAZING RADIO-ACTIVE POWER...
IF THE SLIDE SHOWS A LOSS OF RADIATION IN MY BLOOD...
..IT MEANS THE TIME HAS COME! I'LL BE SPIDER-MAN NO LONGER!
WRITTEN BY: STAN LEE ILLUSTRATED BY: JOHN ROMITA and JIM MOONEY LETTERED BY: SAM ROSEN

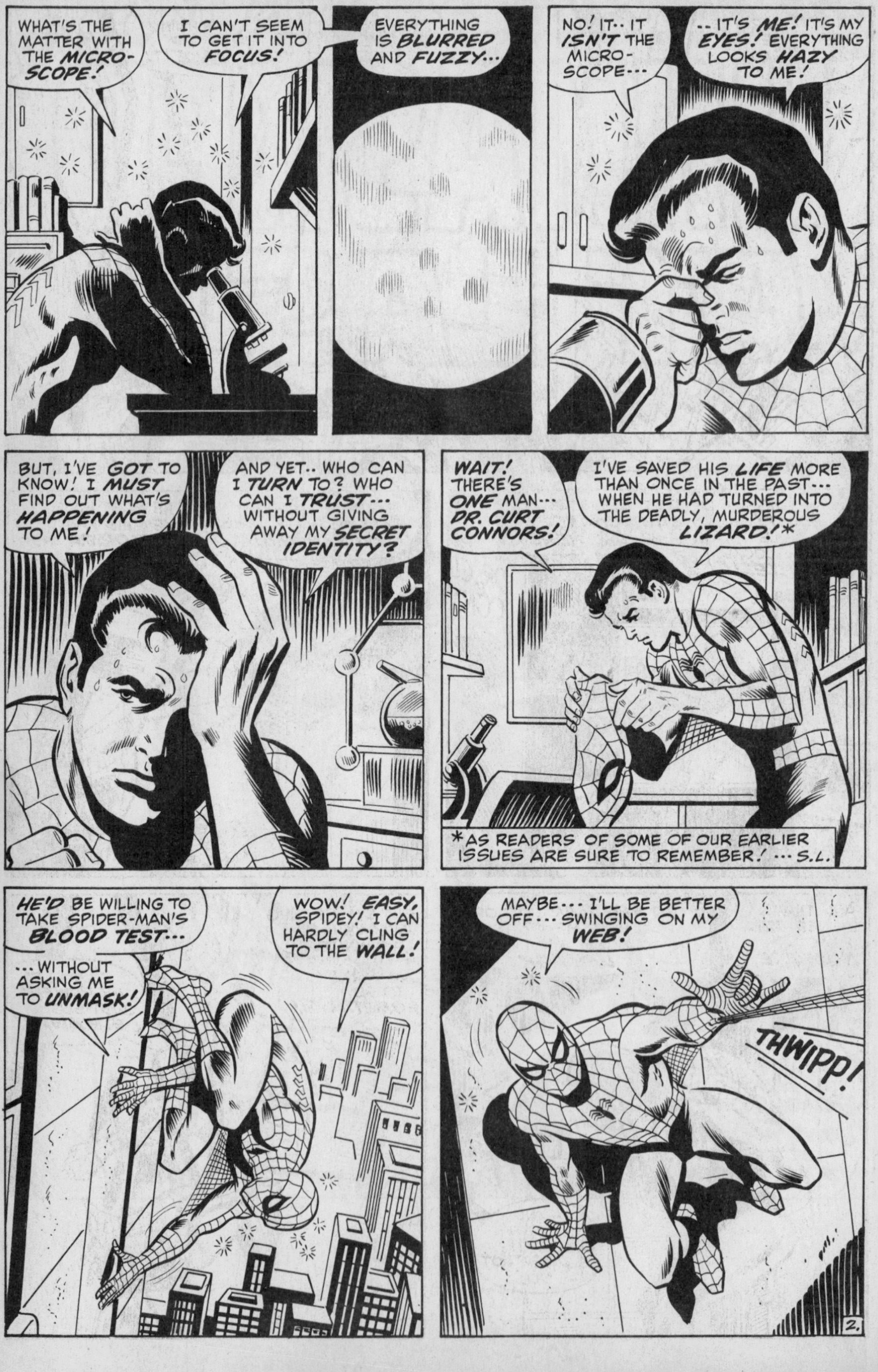
WHAT'S THE MATTER WITH THE MICRO-SCOPE!
I CAN'T SEEM TO GET IT INTO FOCUS!
EVERYTHING IS BLURRED AND FUZZY...
NO! IT.. IT ISN'T THE MICRO-SCOPE---
..IT'S ME! IT'S MY EYES! EVERYTHING LOOKS HAZY TO ME!
BUT, I'VE GOT TO KNOW! I MUST FIND OUT WHAT'S HAPPENING TO ME!
AND YET.. WHO CAN I TURN TO? WHO CAN I TRUST--- WITHOUT GIVING AWAY MY SECRET IDENTITY?
WAIT! THERE'S ONE MAN--- DR. CURT CONNORS!
I'VE SAVED HIS LIFE MORE THAN ONCE IN THE PAST--- WHEN HE HAD TURNED INTO THE DEADLY, MURDEROUS LIZARD!*
*AS READERS OF SOME OF OUR EARLIER ISSUES ARE SURE TO REMEMBER! --- S.L.
HE'D BE WILLING TO TAKE SPIDER-MAN'S BLOOD TEST---
...WITHOUT ASKING ME TO UNMASK!
WOW! EASY, SPIDEY! I CAN HARDLY CLING TO THE WALL!
MAYBE--- I'LL BE BETTER OFF--- SWINGING ON MY WEB!
THWIPP!
2.

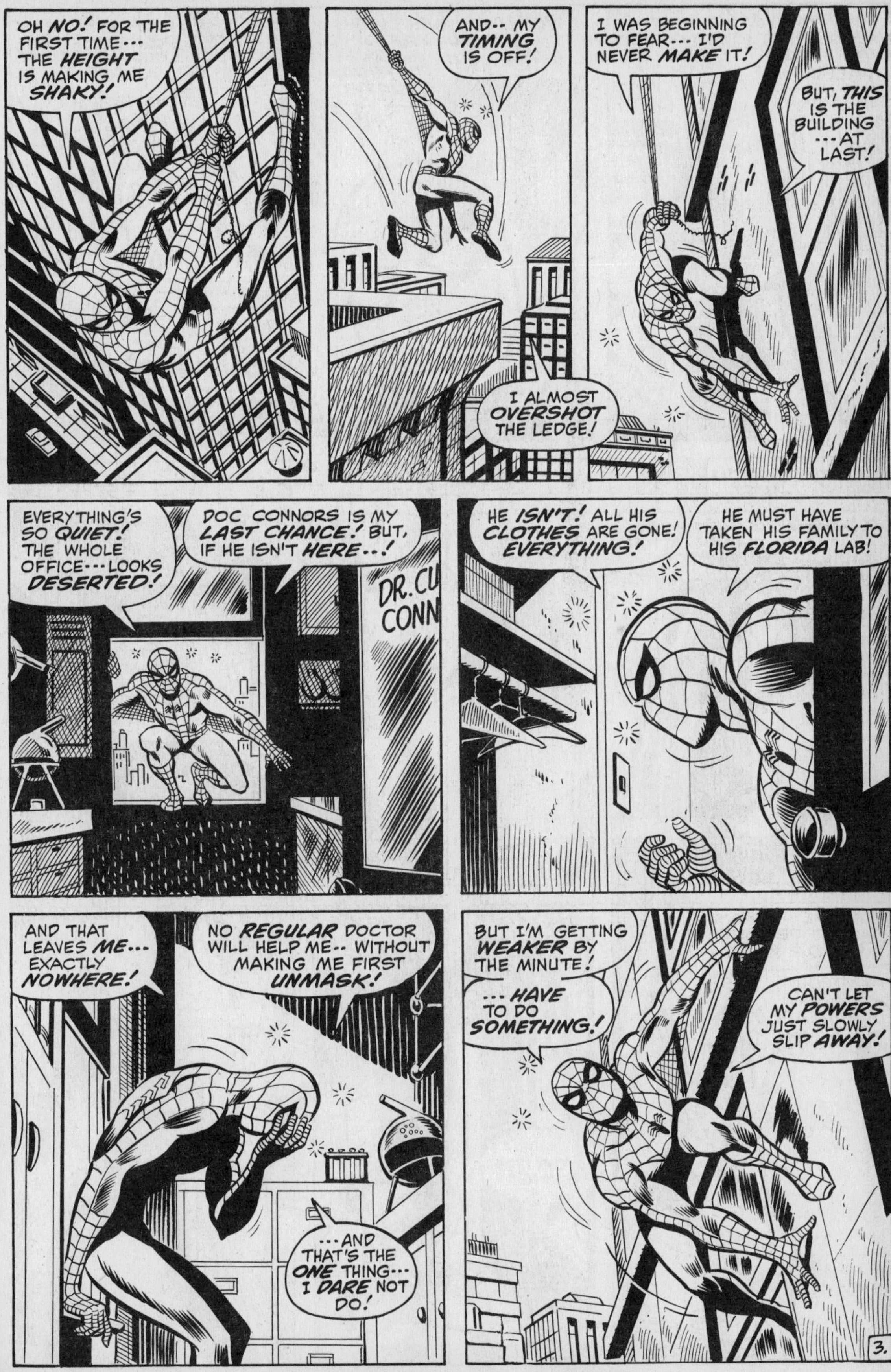
OH NO! FOR THE FIRST TIME--- THE HEIGHT IS MAKING ME SHAKY!
AND-- MY TIMING IS OFF!
I ALMOST OVERSHOT THE LEDGE!
I WAS BEGINNING TO FEAR--- I'D NEVER MAKE IT!
BUT, THIS IS THE BUILDING ---AT LAST!
EVERYTHING'S SO QUIET! THE WHOLE OFFICE---LOOKS DESERTED!
DOC CONNORS IS MY LAST CHANCE! BUT, IF HE ISN'T HERE--!
DR. CU
CONN
HE ISN'T! ALL HIS CLOTHES ARE GONE! EVERYTHING!
HE MUST HAVE TAKEN HIS FAMILY TO HIS FLORIDA LAB!
AND THAT LEAVES ME--- EXACTLY NOWHERE!
NO REGULAR DOCTOR WILL HELP ME-- WITHOUT MAKING ME FIRST UNMASK!
---AND THAT'S THE ONE THING--- I DARE NOT DO!
BUT I'M GETTING WEAKER BY THE MINUTE!
---HAVE TO DO SOMETHING!
CAN'T LET MY POWERS JUST SLOWLY SLIP AWAY!
3.

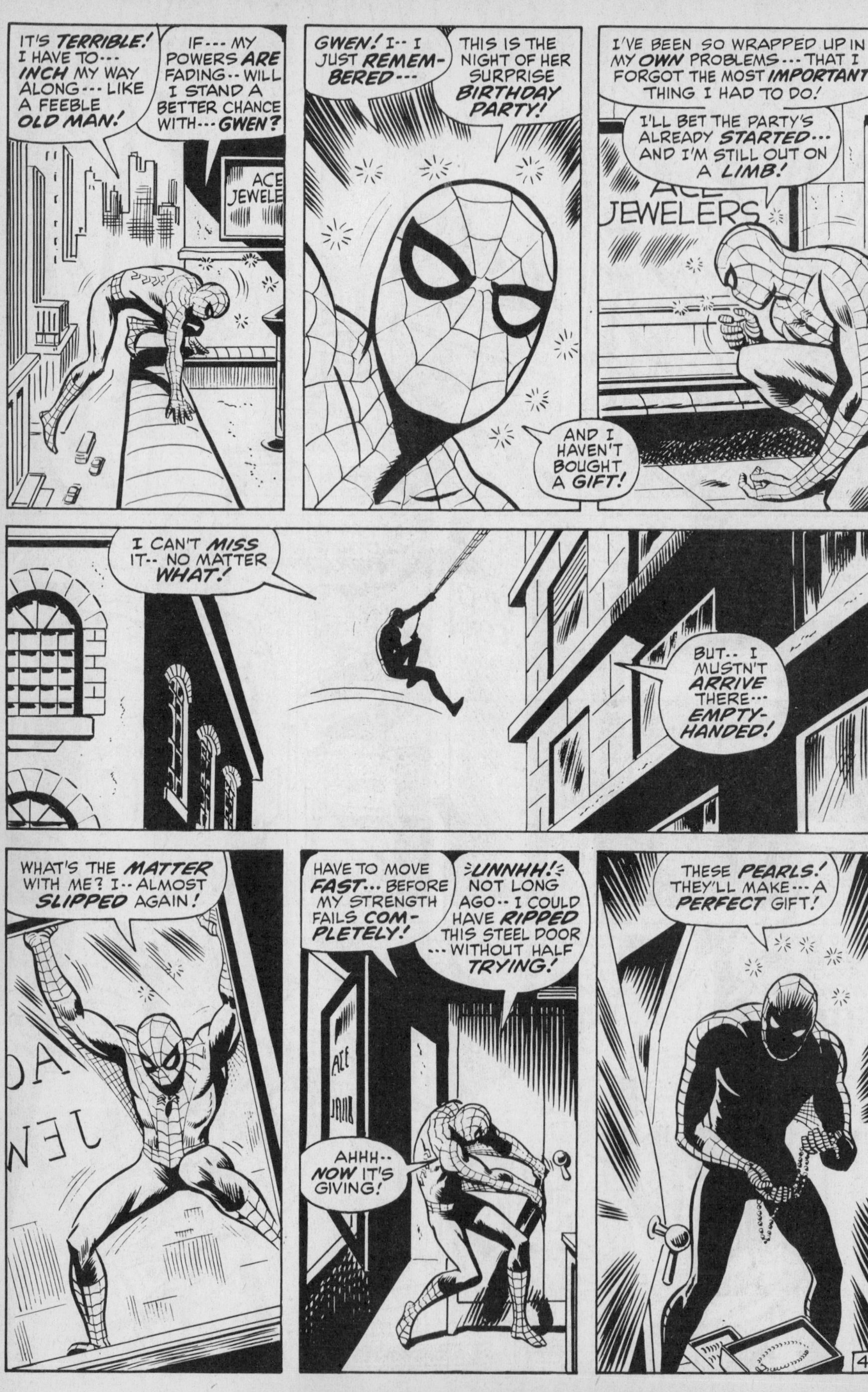

IT'S TERRIBLE! I HAVE TO--- INCH MY WAY ALONG--- LIKE A FEEBLE OLD MAN!
IF--- MY POWERS ARE FADING-- WILL I STAND A BETTER CHANCE WITH--- GWEN?
ACE JEWELE
GWEN! I-- I JUST REMEMBERED---
THIS IS THE NIGHT OF HER SURPRISE BIRTHDAY PARTY!
AND I HAVEN'T BOUGHT A GIFT!
I'VE BEEN SO WRAPPED UP IN MY OWN PROBLEMS--- THAT I FORGOT THE MOST IMPORTANT THING I HAD TO DO!
I'LL BET THE PARTY'S ALREADY STARTED--- AND I'M STILL OUT ON A LIMB!
ACE JEWELERS
I CAN'T MISS IT-- NO MATTER WHAT!
BUT-- I MUSTN'T ARRIVE THERE--- EMPTY-HANDED!
WHAT'S THE MATTER WITH ME? I-- ALMOST SLIPPED AGAIN!
HAVE TO MOVE FAST--- BEFORE MY STRENGTH FAILS COMPLETELY!
UNNHH! NOT LONG AGO-- I COULD HAVE RIPPED THIS STEEL DOOR --- WITHOUT HALF TRYING!
AHHH-- NOW IT'S GIVING!
THESE PEARLS! THEY'LL MAKE--- A PERFECT GIFT!
4

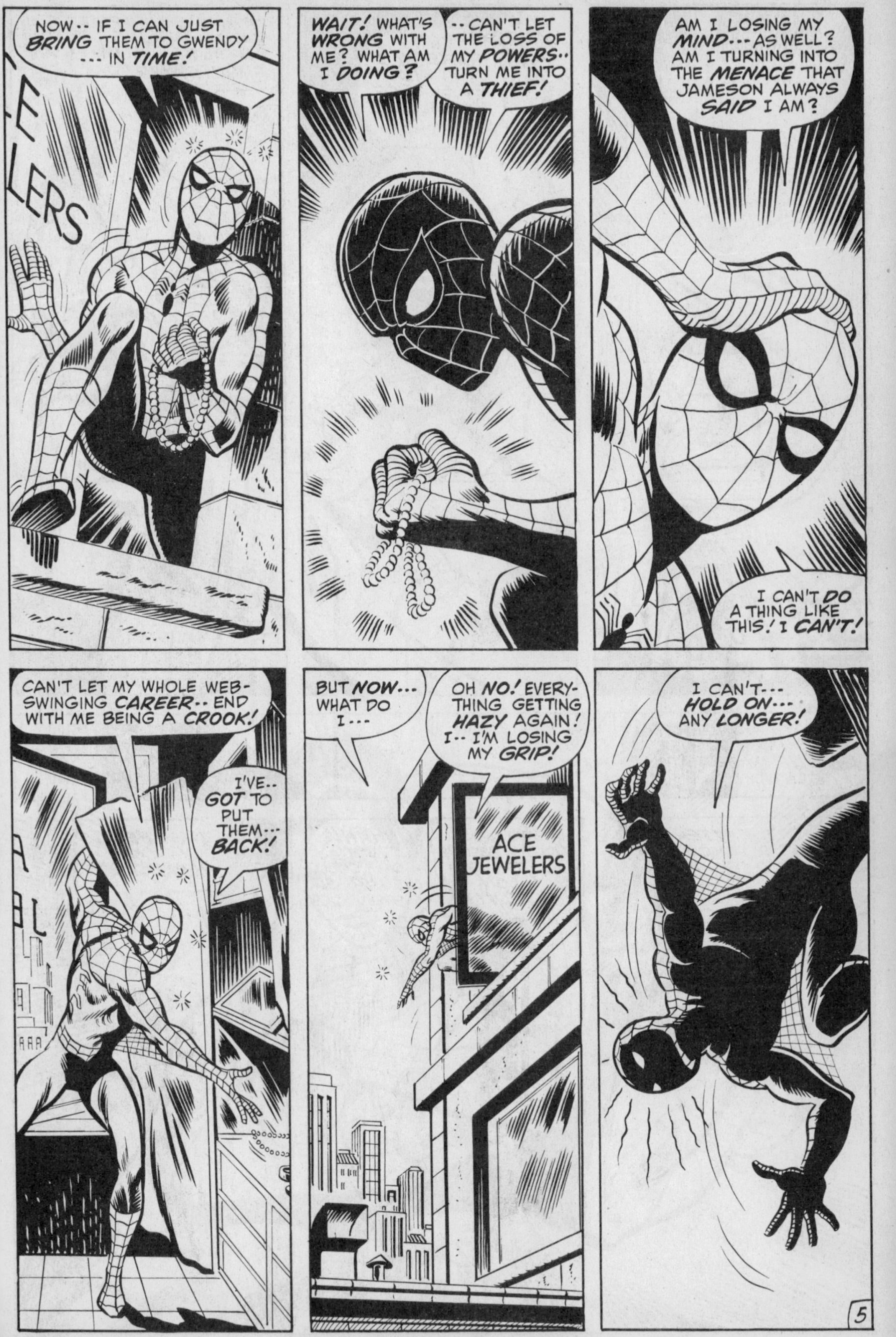
NOW-- IF I CAN JUST BRING THEM TO GWENDY --- IN TIME!
WAIT! WHAT'S WRONG WITH ME? WHAT AM I DOING?
--CAN'T LET THE LOSS OF MY POWERS-- TURN ME INTO A THIEF!
AM I LOSING MY MIND--- AS WELL? AM I TURNING INTO THE MENACE THAT JAMESON ALWAYS SAID I AM?
I CAN'T DO A THING LIKE THIS! I CAN'T!
CAN'T LET MY WHOLE WEB-SWINGING CAREER-- END WITH ME BEING A CROOK!
I'VE-- GOT TO PUT THEM--- BACK!
BUT NOW--- WHAT DO I---
OH NO! EVERYTHING GETTING HAZY AGAIN! I-- I'M LOSING MY GRIP!
ACE JEWELERS
I CAN'T--- HOLD ON--- ANY LONGER!
5

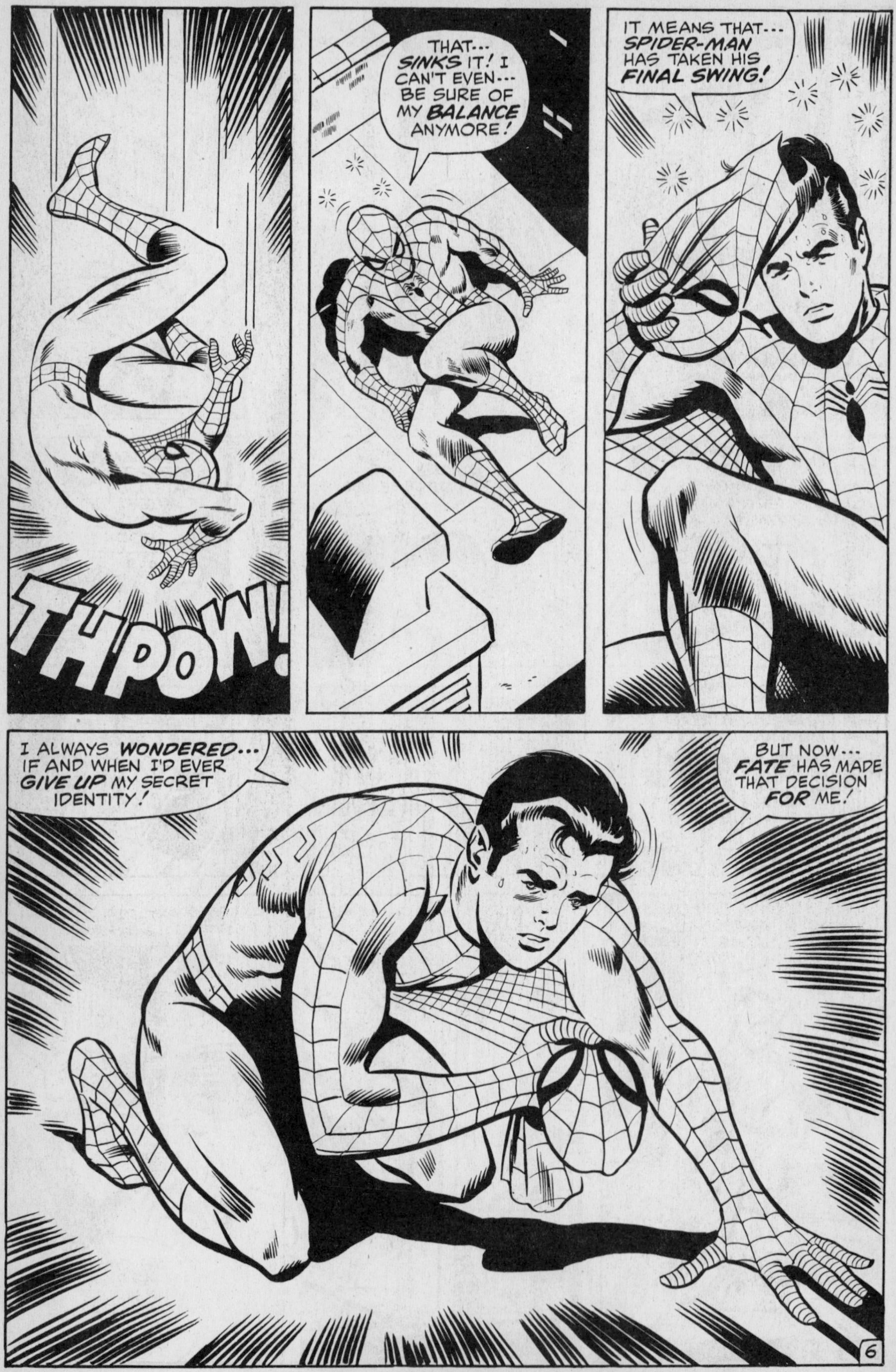

THPOW!
THAT--- SINKS IT! I CAN'T EVEN--- BE SURE OF MY BALANCE ANYMORE!
IT MEANS THAT--- SPIDER-MAN HAS TAKEN HIS FINAL SWING!
I ALWAYS WONDERED... IF AND WHEN I'D EVER GIVE UP MY SECRET IDENTITY!
BUT NOW... FATE HAS MADE THAT DECISION FOR ME!
6

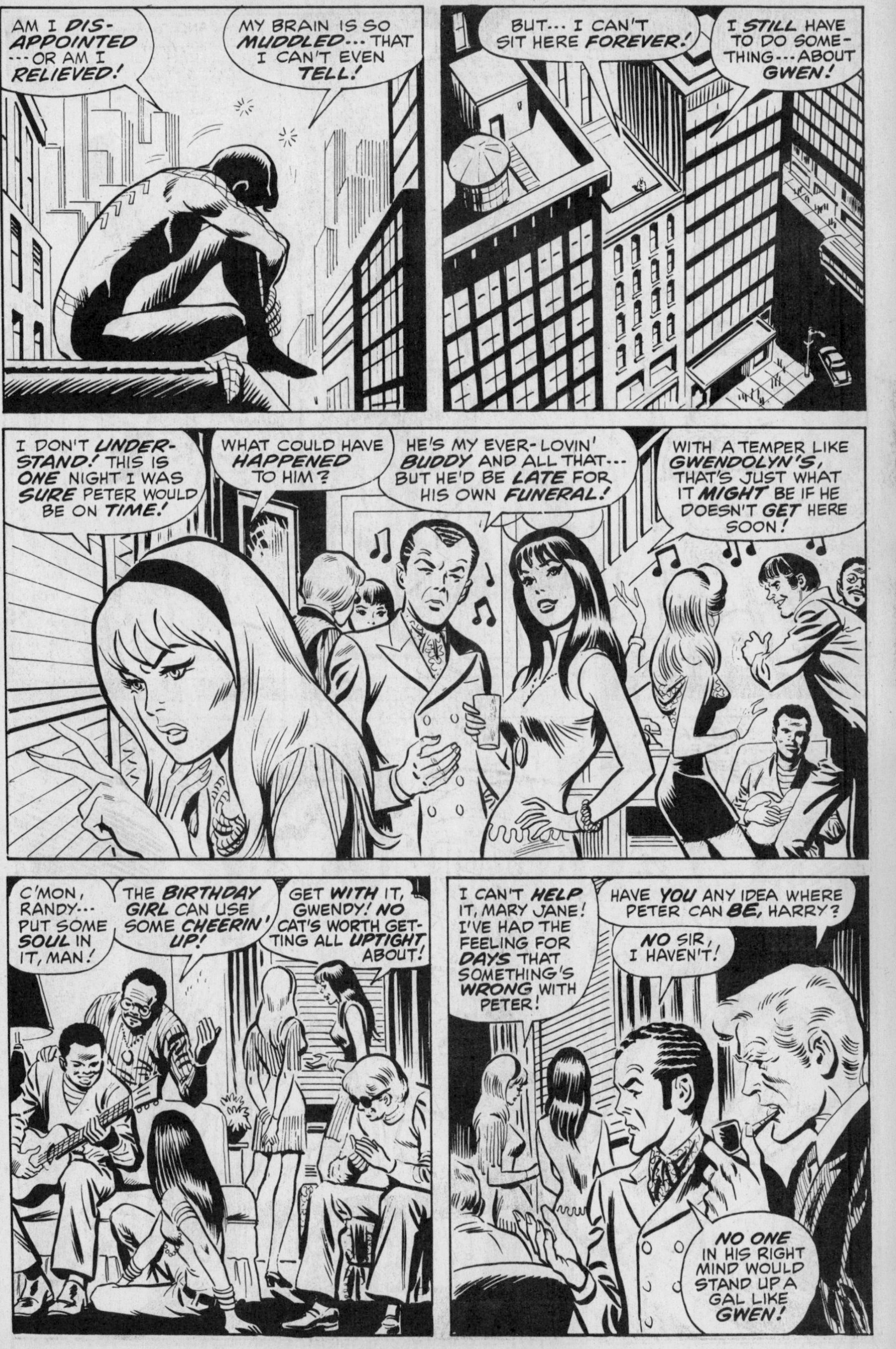
AM I DIS-APPOINTED ---OR AM I RELIEVED!
MY BRAIN IS SO MUDDLED... THAT I CAN'T EVEN TELL!
BUT... I CAN'T SIT HERE FOREVER!
I STILL HAVE TO DO SOME-THING---ABOUT GWEN!
I DON'T UNDER-STAND! THIS IS ONE NIGHT I WAS SURE PETER WOULD BE ON TIME!
WHAT COULD HAVE HAPPENED TO HIM?
HE'S MY EVER-LOVIN' BUDDY AND ALL THAT--- BUT HE'D BE LATE FOR HIS OWN FUNERAL!
WITH A TEMPER LIKE GWENDOLYN'S, THAT'S JUST WHAT IT MIGHT BE IF HE DOESN'T GET HERE SOON!
C'MON, RANDY... PUT SOME SOUL IN IT, MAN!
THE BIRTHDAY GIRL CAN USE SOME CHEERIN' UP!
GET WITH IT, GWENDY! NO CAT'S WORTH GET-TING ALL UPTIGHT ABOUT!
I CAN'T HELP IT, MARY JANE! I'VE HAD THE FEELING FOR DAYS THAT SOMETHING'S WRONG WITH PETER!
HAVE YOU ANY IDEA WHERE PETER CAN BE, HARRY?
NO SIR, I HAVEN'T!
NO ONE IN HIS RIGHT MIND WOULD STAND UP A GAL LIKE GWEN!

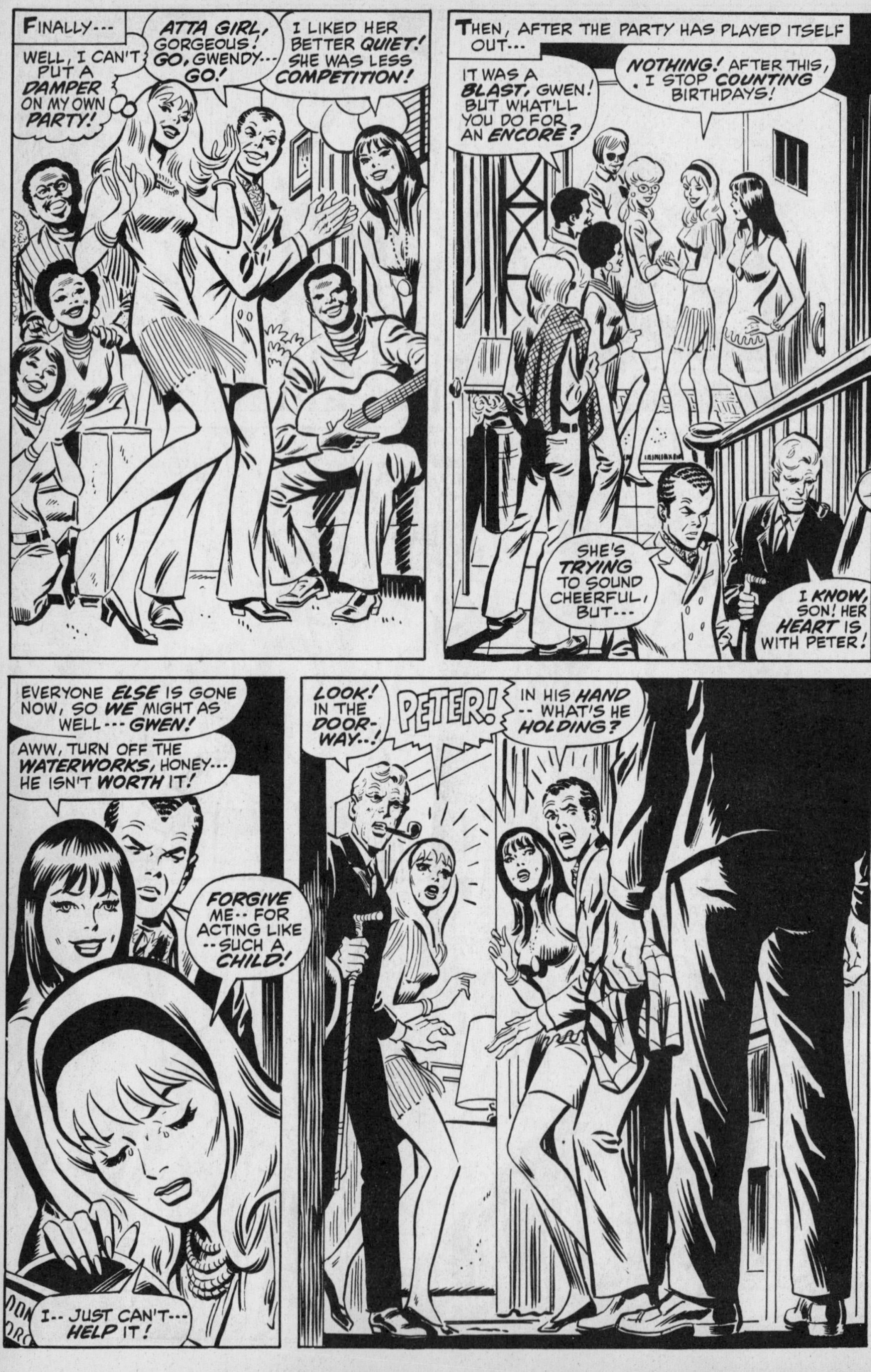
FINALLY---
WELL, I CAN'T PUT A DAMPER ON MY OWN PARTY!
ATTA GIRL, GORGEOUS! GO, GWENDY--- GO!
I LIKED HER BETTER QUIET! SHE WAS LESS COMPETITION!
THEN, AFTER THE PARTY HAS PLAYED ITSELF OUT---
IT WAS A BLAST, GWEN! BUT WHAT'LL YOU DO FOR AN ENCORE?
NOTHING! AFTER THIS, I STOP COUNTING BIRTHDAYS!
SHE'S TRYING TO SOUND CHEERFUL, BUT---
I KNOW, SON! HER HEART IS WITH PETER!
EVERYONE ELSE IS GONE NOW, SO WE MIGHT AS WELL--- GWEN!
AWW, TURN OFF THE WATERWORKS, HONEY... HE ISN'T WORTH IT!
FORGIVE ME-- FOR ACTING LIKE --SUCH A CHILD!
I-- JUST CAN'T--- HELP IT!
LOOK! IN THE DOORWAY--!
PETER!
IN HIS HAND -- WHAT'S HE HOLDING?

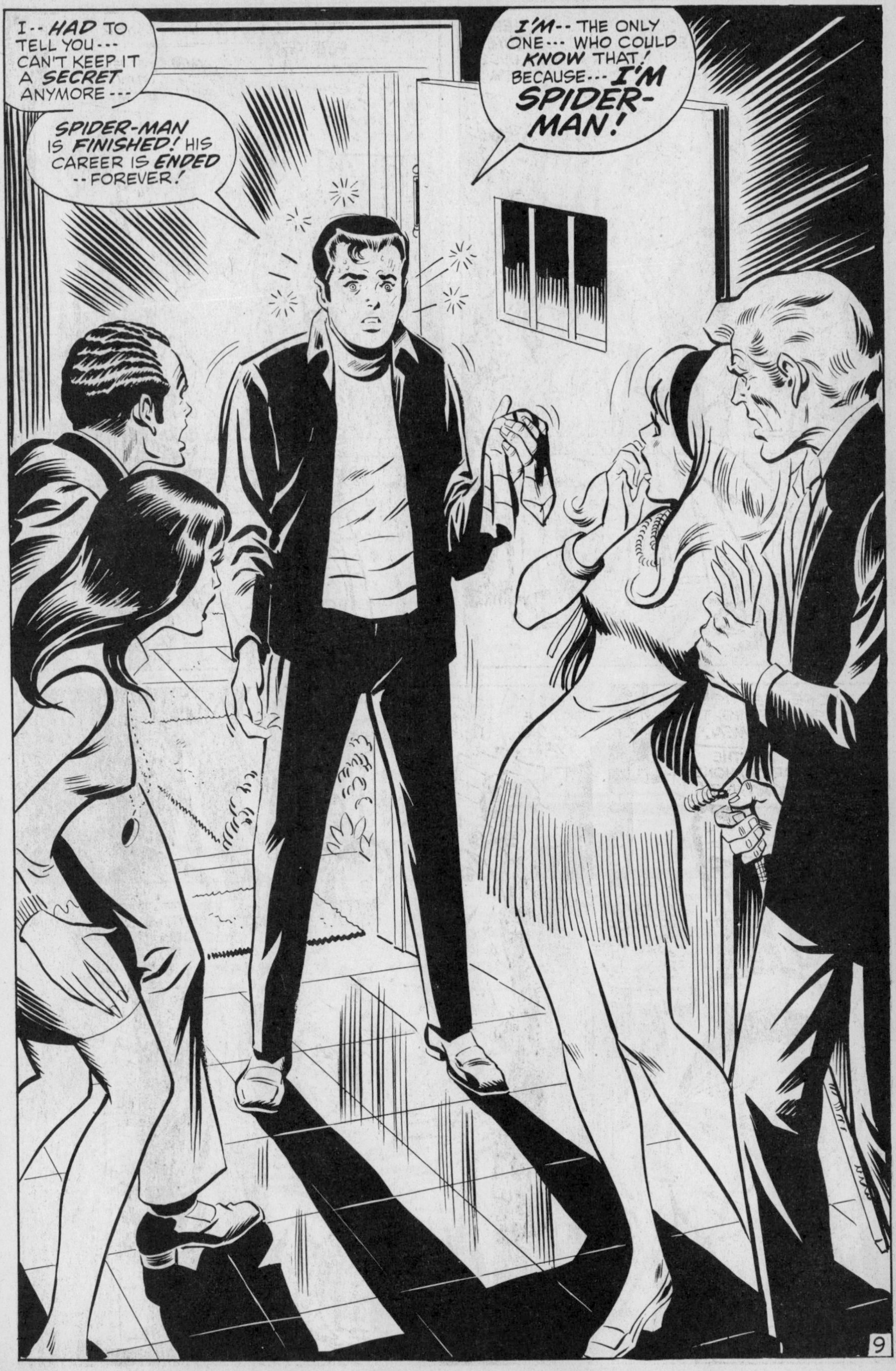
I-- HAD TO TELL YOU--- CAN'T KEEP IT A SECRET ANYMORE---
SPIDER-MAN IS FINISHED! HIS CAREER IS ENDED --FOREVER!
I'M-- THE ONLY ONE--- WHO COULD KNOW THAT! BECAUSE--- I'M SPIDER-MAN!

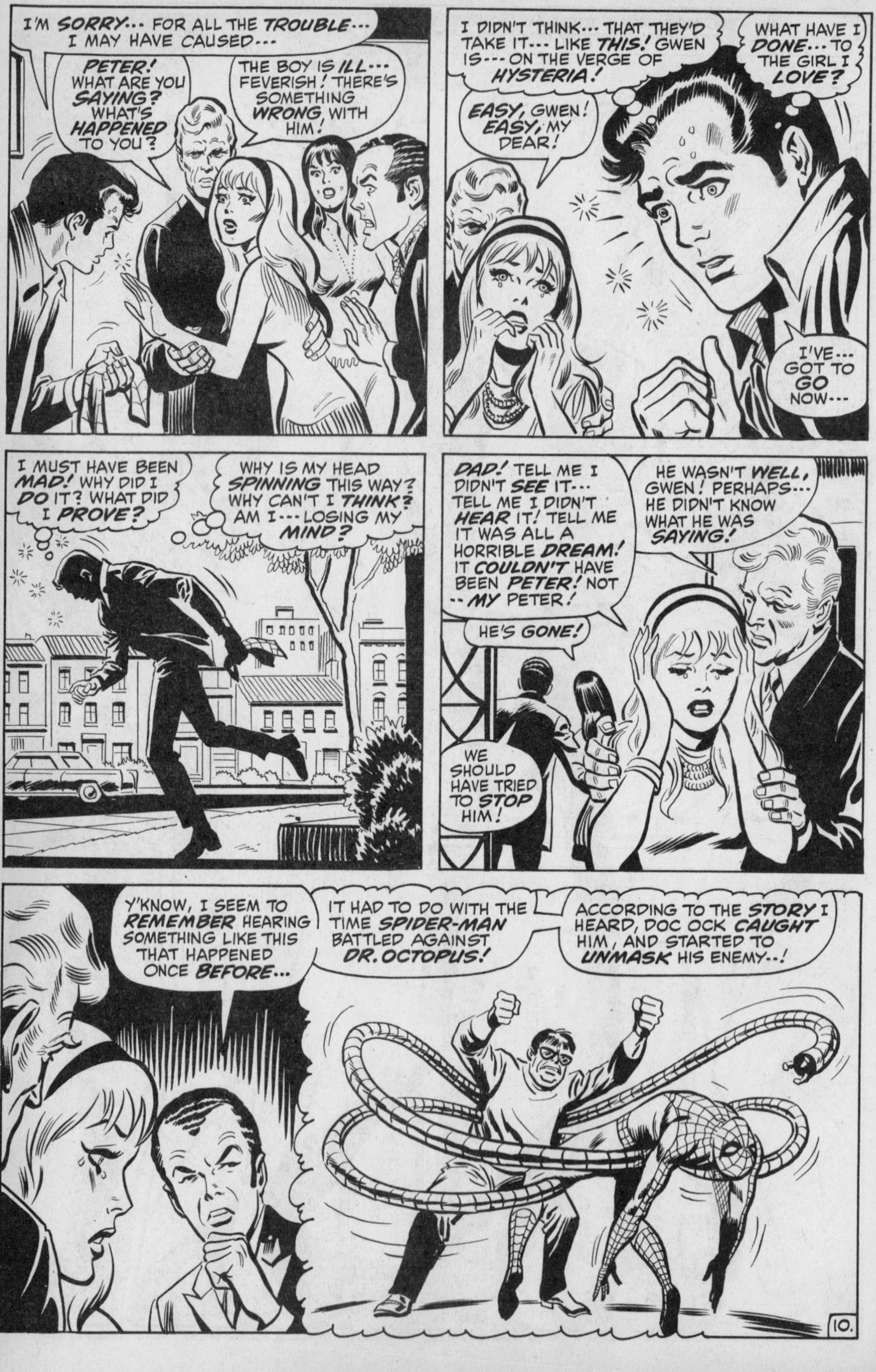
I'M SORRY... FOR ALL THE TROUBLE... I MAY HAVE CAUSED...
PETER! WHAT ARE YOU SAYING? WHAT'S HAPPENED TO YOU?
THE BOY IS ILL... FEVERISH! THERE'S SOMETHING WRONG WITH HIM!
I DIDN'T THINK... THAT THEY'D TAKE IT... LIKE THIS! GWEN IS... ON THE VERGE OF HYSTERIA!
WHAT HAVE I DONE... TO THE GIRL I LOVE?
EASY, GWEN! EASY, MY DEAR!
I'VE... GOT TO GO NOW...
I MUST HAVE BEEN MAD! WHY DID I DO IT? WHAT DID I PROVE?
WHY IS MY HEAD SPINNING THIS WAY? WHY CAN'T I THINK? AM I... LOSING MY MIND?
DAD! TELL ME I DIDN'T SEE IT... TELL ME I DIDN'T HEAR IT! TELL ME IT WAS ALL A HORRIBLE DREAM! IT COULDN'T HAVE BEEN PETER! NOT -- MY PETER!
HE WASN'T WELL, GWEN! PERHAPS... HE DIDN'T KNOW WHAT HE WAS SAYING!
HE'S GONE!
WE SHOULD HAVE TRIED TO STOP HIM!
Y'KNOW, I SEEM TO REMEMBER HEARING SOMETHING LIKE THIS THAT HAPPENED ONCE BEFORE...
IT HAD TO DO WITH THE TIME SPIDER-MAN BATTLED AGAINST DR. OCTOPUS!
ACCORDING TO THE STORY I HEARD, DOC OCK CAUGHT HIM, AND STARTED TO UNMASK HIS ENEMY..!
10.

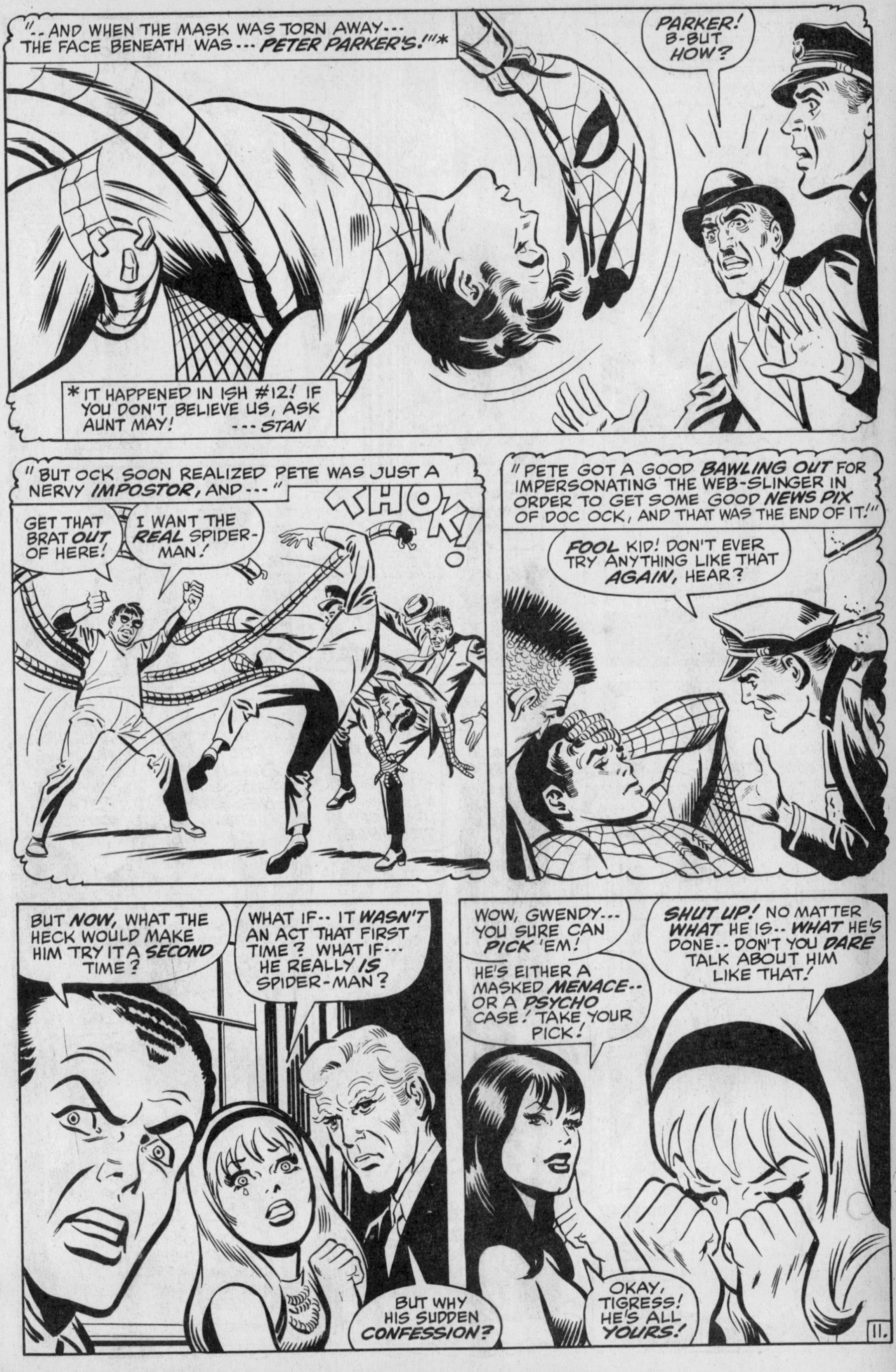
"..AND WHEN THE MASK WAS TORN AWAY... THE FACE BENEATH WAS... PETER PARKER'S!"*
PARKER! B-BUT HOW?
* IT HAPPENED IN ISH #12! IF YOU DON'T BELIEVE US, ASK AUNT MAY! ---STAN
"BUT OCK SOON REALIZED PETE WAS JUST A NERVY IMPOSTOR, AND..."
GET THAT BRAT OUT OF HERE!
I WANT THE REAL SPIDER-MAN!
THOK!
"PETE GOT A GOOD BAWLING OUT FOR IMPERSONATING THE WEB-SLINGER IN ORDER TO GET SOME GOOD NEWS PIX OF DOC OCK, AND THAT WAS THE END OF IT!"
FOOL KID! DON'T EVER TRY ANYTHING LIKE THAT AGAIN, HEAR?
BUT NOW, WHAT THE HECK WOULD MAKE HIM TRY IT A SECOND TIME?
WHAT IF.. IT WASN'T AN ACT THAT FIRST TIME? WHAT IF... HE REALLY IS SPIDER-MAN?
BUT WHY HIS SUDDEN CONFESSION?
WOW, GWENDY... YOU SURE CAN PICK 'EM!
HE'S EITHER A MASKED MENACE.. OR A PSYCHO CASE! TAKE YOUR PICK!
SHUT UP! NO MATTER WHAT HE IS.. WHAT HE'S DONE.. DON'T YOU DARE TALK ABOUT HIM LIKE THAT!
OKAY, TIGRESS! HE'S ALL YOURS!
11.

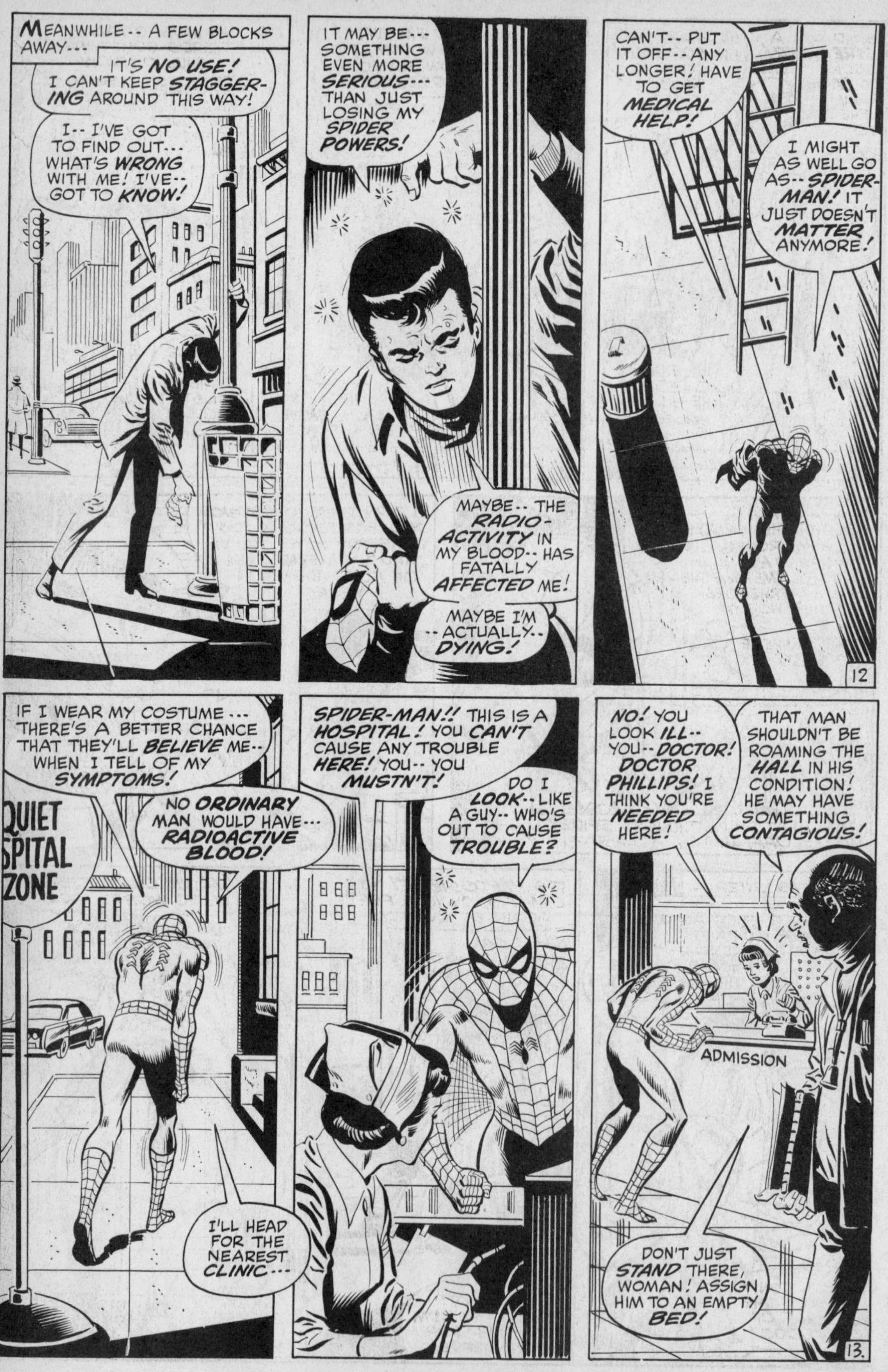
MEANWHILE -- A FEW BLOCKS AWAY ---
IT'S NO USE! I CAN'T KEEP STAGGER-ING AROUND THIS WAY!
I-- I'VE GOT TO FIND OUT--- WHAT'S WRONG WITH ME! I'VE-- GOT TO KNOW!
IT MAY BE--- SOMETHING EVEN MORE SERIOUS--- THAN JUST LOSING MY SPIDER POWERS!
MAYBE-- THE RADIO-ACTIVITY IN MY BLOOD-- HAS FATALLY AFFECTED ME!
MAYBE I'M --ACTUALLY-- DYING!
CAN'T-- PUT IT OFF-- ANY LONGER! HAVE TO GET MEDICAL HELP!
I MIGHT AS WELL GO AS-- SPIDER-MAN! IT JUST DOESN'T MATTER ANYMORE!
12
IF I WEAR MY COSTUME --- THERE'S A BETTER CHANCE THAT THEY'LL BELIEVE ME-- WHEN I TELL OF MY SYMPTOMS!
QUIET
SPITAL
ZONE
NO ORDINARY MAN WOULD HAVE--- RADIOACTIVE BLOOD!
I'LL HEAD FOR THE NEAREST CLINIC---
SPIDER-MAN!! THIS IS A HOSPITAL! YOU CAN'T CAUSE ANY TROUBLE HERE! YOU-- YOU MUSTN'T!
DO I LOOK-- LIKE A GUY-- WHO'S OUT TO CAUSE TROUBLE?
NO! YOU LOOK ILL-- YOU-- DOCTOR! DOCTOR PHILLIPS! I THINK YOU'RE NEEDED HERE!
THAT MAN SHOULDN'T BE ROAMING THE HALL IN HIS CONDITION! HE MAY HAVE SOMETHING CONTAGIOUS!
ADMISSION
DON'T JUST STAND THERE, WOMAN! ASSIGN HIM TO AN EMPTY BED!
13.

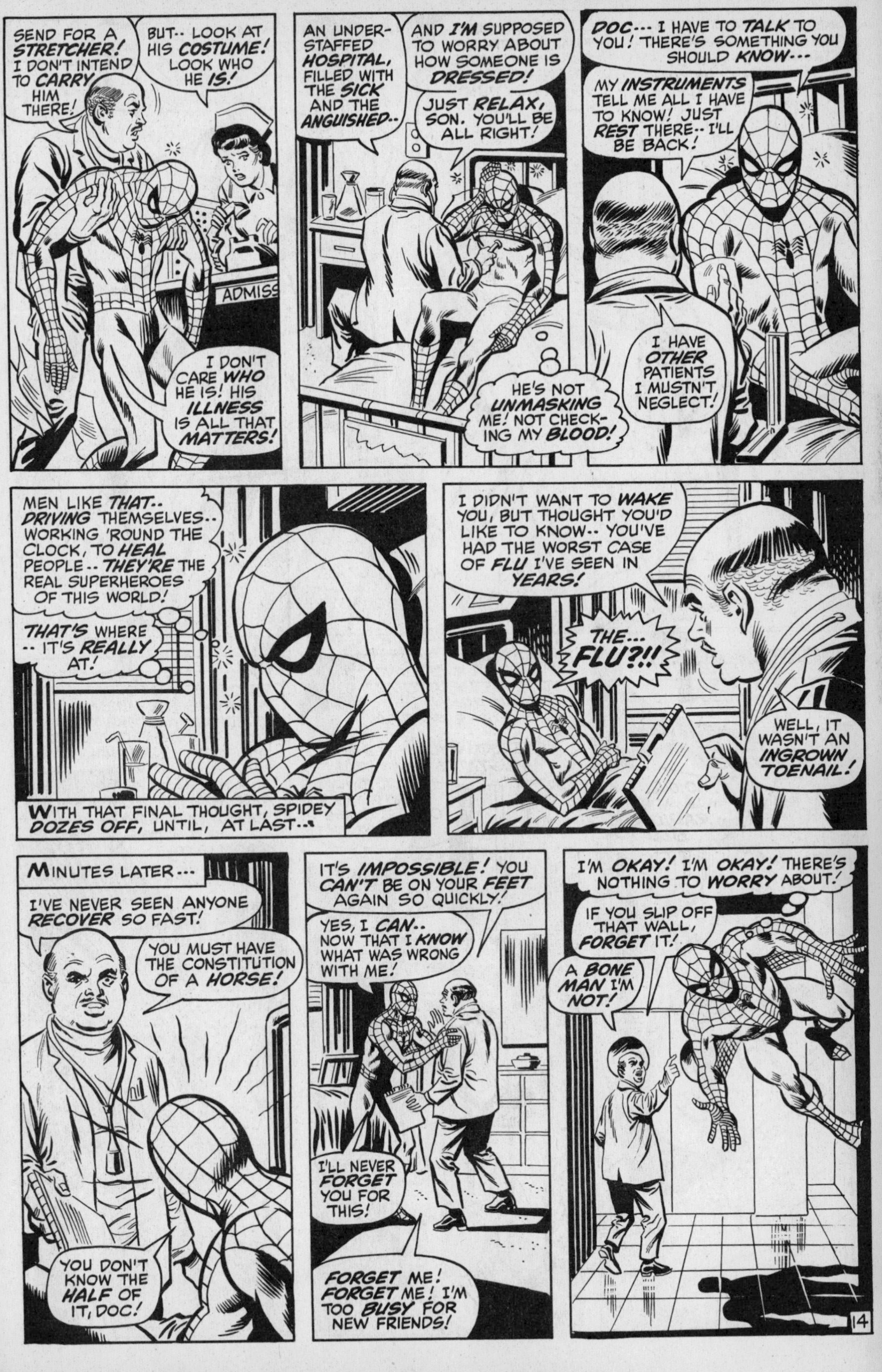
SEND FOR A STRETCHER! I DON'T INTEND TO CARRY HIM THERE!
BUT.. LOOK AT HIS COSTUME! LOOK WHO HE IS!
ADMISS
I DON'T CARE WHO HE IS! HIS ILLNESS IS ALL THAT MATTERS!
AN UNDER-STAFFED HOSPITAL, FILLED WITH THE SICK AND THE ANGUISHED..
AND I'M SUPPOSED TO WORRY ABOUT HOW SOMEONE IS DRESSED!
JUST RELAX, SON. YOU'LL BE ALL RIGHT!
HE'S NOT UNMASKING ME! NOT CHECKING MY BLOOD!
DOC... I HAVE TO TALK TO YOU! THERE'S SOMETHING YOU SHOULD KNOW...
MY INSTRUMENTS TELL ME ALL I HAVE TO KNOW! JUST REST THERE.. I'LL BE BACK!
I HAVE OTHER PATIENTS I MUSTN'T NEGLECT!
MEN LIKE THAT.. DRIVING THEMSELVES.. WORKING 'ROUND THE CLOCK, TO HEAL PEOPLE.. THEY'RE THE REAL SUPERHEROES OF THIS WORLD!
THAT'S WHERE -- IT'S REALLY AT!
WITH THAT FINAL THOUGHT, SPIDEY DOZES OFF, UNTIL, AT LAST..
I DIDN'T WANT TO WAKE YOU, BUT THOUGHT YOU'D LIKE TO KNOW.. YOU'VE HAD THE WORST CASE OF FLU I'VE SEEN IN YEARS!
THE... FLU?!!
WELL, IT WASN'T AN INGROWN TOENAIL!
MINUTES LATER...
I'VE NEVER SEEN ANYONE RECOVER SO FAST!
YOU MUST HAVE THE CONSTITUTION OF A HORSE!
YOU DON'T KNOW THE HALF OF IT, DOC!
IT'S IMPOSSIBLE! YOU CAN'T BE ON YOUR FEET AGAIN SO QUICKLY!
YES, I CAN.. NOW THAT I KNOW WHAT WAS WRONG WITH ME!
I'LL NEVER FORGET YOU FOR THIS!
FORGET ME! FORGET ME! I'M TOO BUSY FOR NEW FRIENDS!
I'M OKAY! I'M OKAY! THERE'S NOTHING TO WORRY ABOUT!
IF YOU SLIP OFF THAT WALL, FORGET IT!
A BONE MAN I'M NOT!
14

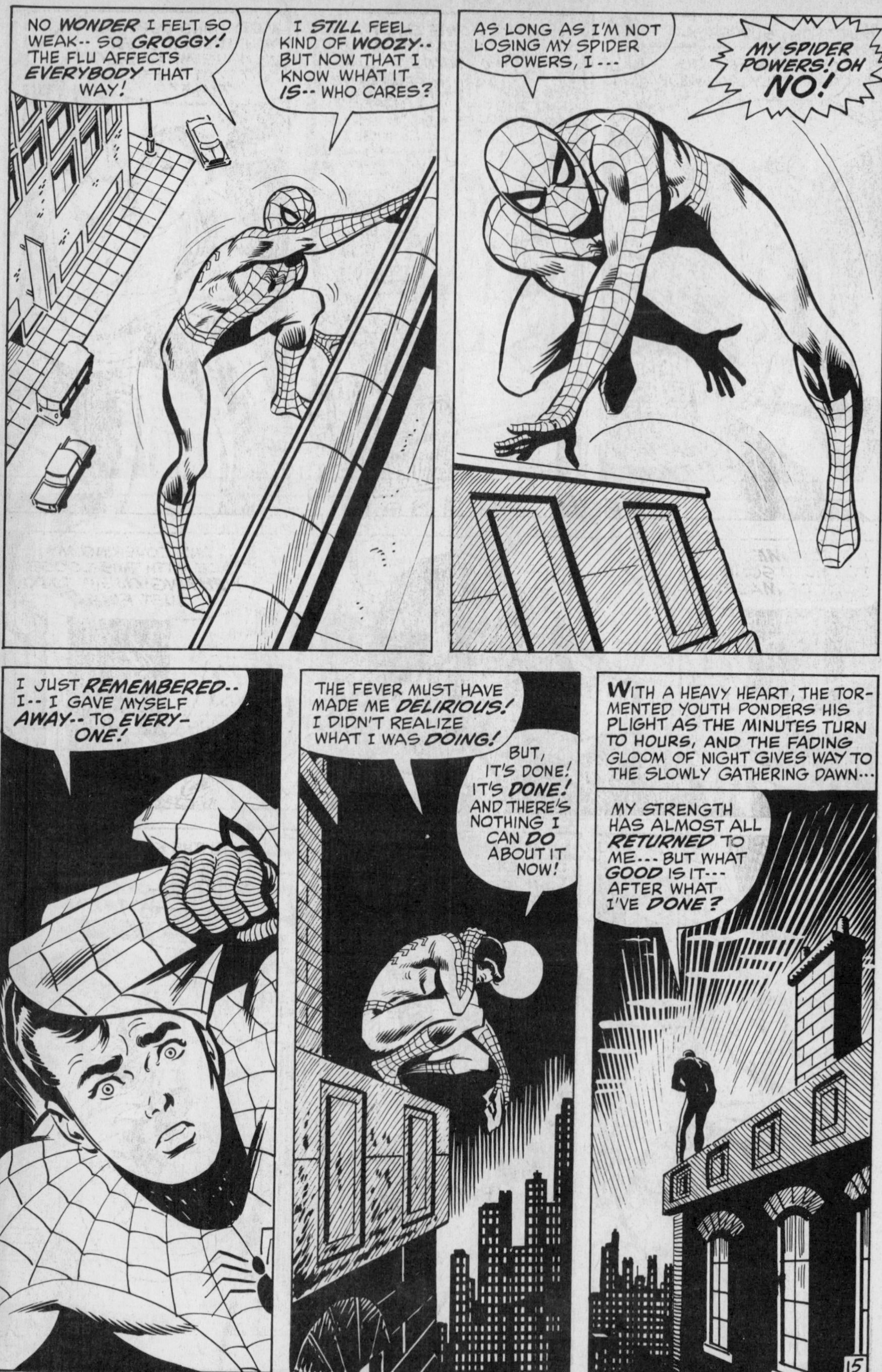
NO WONDER I FELT SO WEAK-- SO GROGGY! THE FLU AFFECTS EVERYBODY THAT WAY!
I STILL FEEL KIND OF WOOZY.. BUT NOW THAT I KNOW WHAT IT IS-- WHO CARES?
AS LONG AS I'M NOT LOSING MY SPIDER POWERS, I---
MY SPIDER POWERS! OH NO!
I JUST REMEMBERED.. I-- I GAVE MYSELF AWAY-- TO EVERY-ONE!
THE FEVER MUST HAVE MADE ME DELIRIOUS! I DIDN'T REALIZE WHAT I WAS DOING!
BUT, IT'S DONE! IT'S DONE! AND THERE'S NOTHING I CAN DO ABOUT IT NOW!
WITH A HEAVY HEART, THE TORMENTED YOUTH PONDERS HIS PLIGHT AS THE MINUTES TURN TO HOURS, AND THE FADING GLOOM OF NIGHT GIVES WAY TO THE SLOWLY GATHERING DAWN...
MY STRENGTH HAS ALMOST ALL RETURNED TO ME--- BUT WHAT GOOD IS IT--- AFTER WHAT I'VE DONE?
15

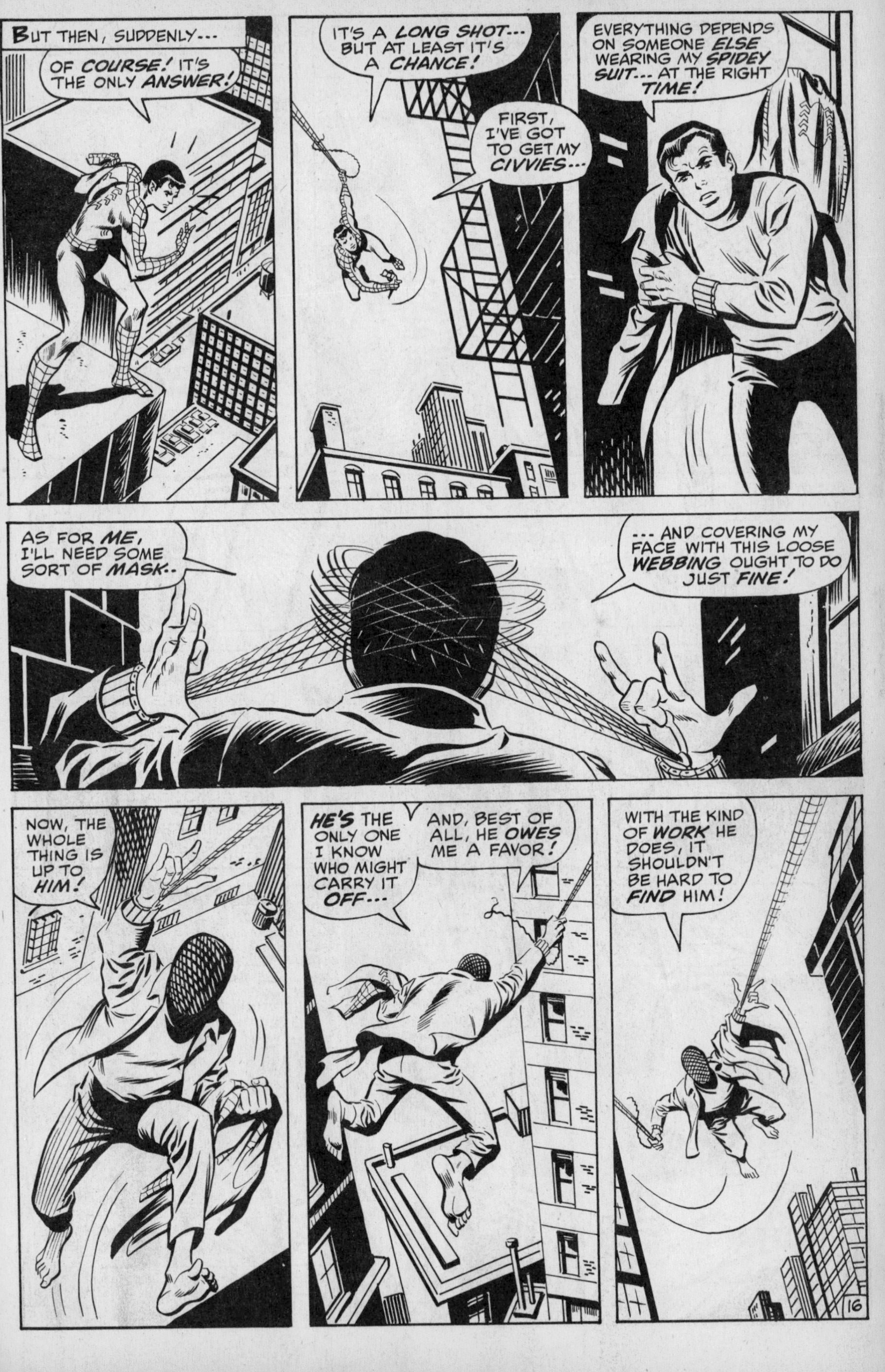

BUT THEN, SUDDENLY...
OF COURSE! IT'S THE ONLY ANSWER!
IT'S A LONG SHOT... BUT AT LEAST IT'S A CHANCE!
FIRST, I'VE GOT TO GET MY CIVVIES...
EVERYTHING DEPENDS ON SOMEONE ELSE WEARING MY SPIDEY SUIT... AT THE RIGHT TIME!
AS FOR ME, I'LL NEED SOME SORT OF MASK..
... AND COVERING MY FACE WITH THIS LOOSE WEBBING OUGHT TO DO JUST FINE!
NOW, THE WHOLE THING IS UP TO HIM!
HE'S THE ONLY ONE I KNOW WHO MIGHT CARRY IT OFF...
AND, BEST OF ALL, HE OWES ME A FAVOR!
WITH THE KIND OF WORK HE DOES, IT SHOULDN'T BE HARD TO FIND HIM!
16

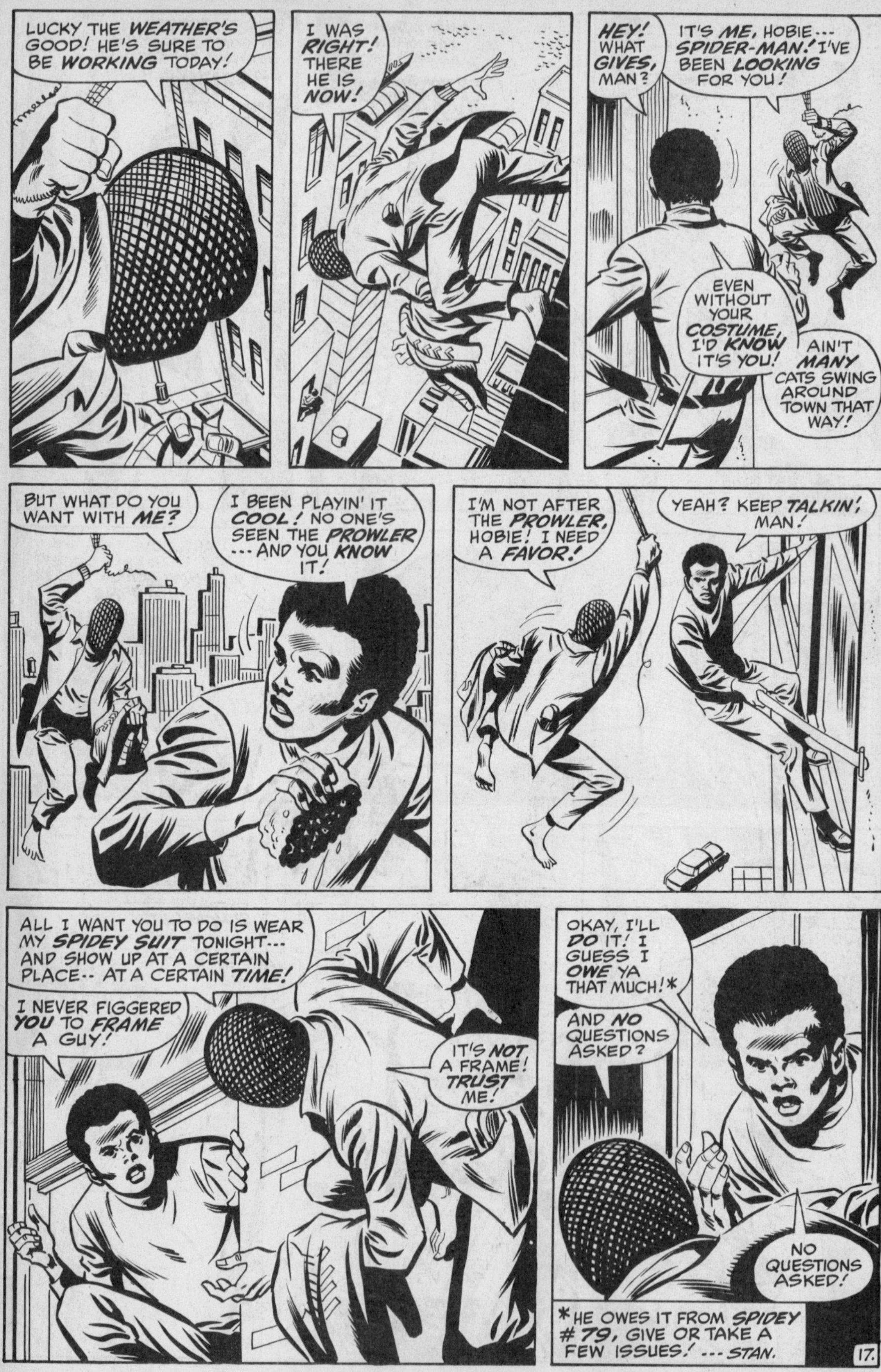
LUCKY THE WEATHER'S GOOD! HE'S SURE TO BE WORKING TODAY!
I WAS RIGHT! THERE HE IS NOW!
HEY! WHAT GIVES, MAN?
IT'S ME, HOBIE--- SPIDER-MAN! I'VE BEEN LOOKING FOR YOU!
EVEN WITHOUT YOUR COSTUME, I'D KNOW IT'S YOU!
AIN'T MANY CATS SWING AROUND TOWN THAT WAY!
BUT WHAT DO YOU WANT WITH ME?
I BEEN PLAYIN' IT COOL! NO ONE'S SEEN THE PROWLER --- AND YOU KNOW IT!
I'M NOT AFTER THE PROWLER, HOBIE! I NEED A FAVOR!
YEAH? KEEP TALKIN', MAN!
ALL I WANT YOU TO DO IS WEAR MY SPIDEY SUIT TONIGHT--- AND SHOW UP AT A CERTAIN PLACE-- AT A CERTAIN TIME!
I NEVER FIGGERED YOU TO FRAME A GUY!
IT'S NOT A FRAME! TRUST ME!
OKAY, I'LL DO IT! I GUESS I OWE YA THAT MUCH!*
AND NO QUESTIONS ASKED?
NO QUESTIONS ASKED!
*HE OWES IT FROM SPIDEY #79, GIVE OR TAKE A FEW ISSUES! --- STAN.

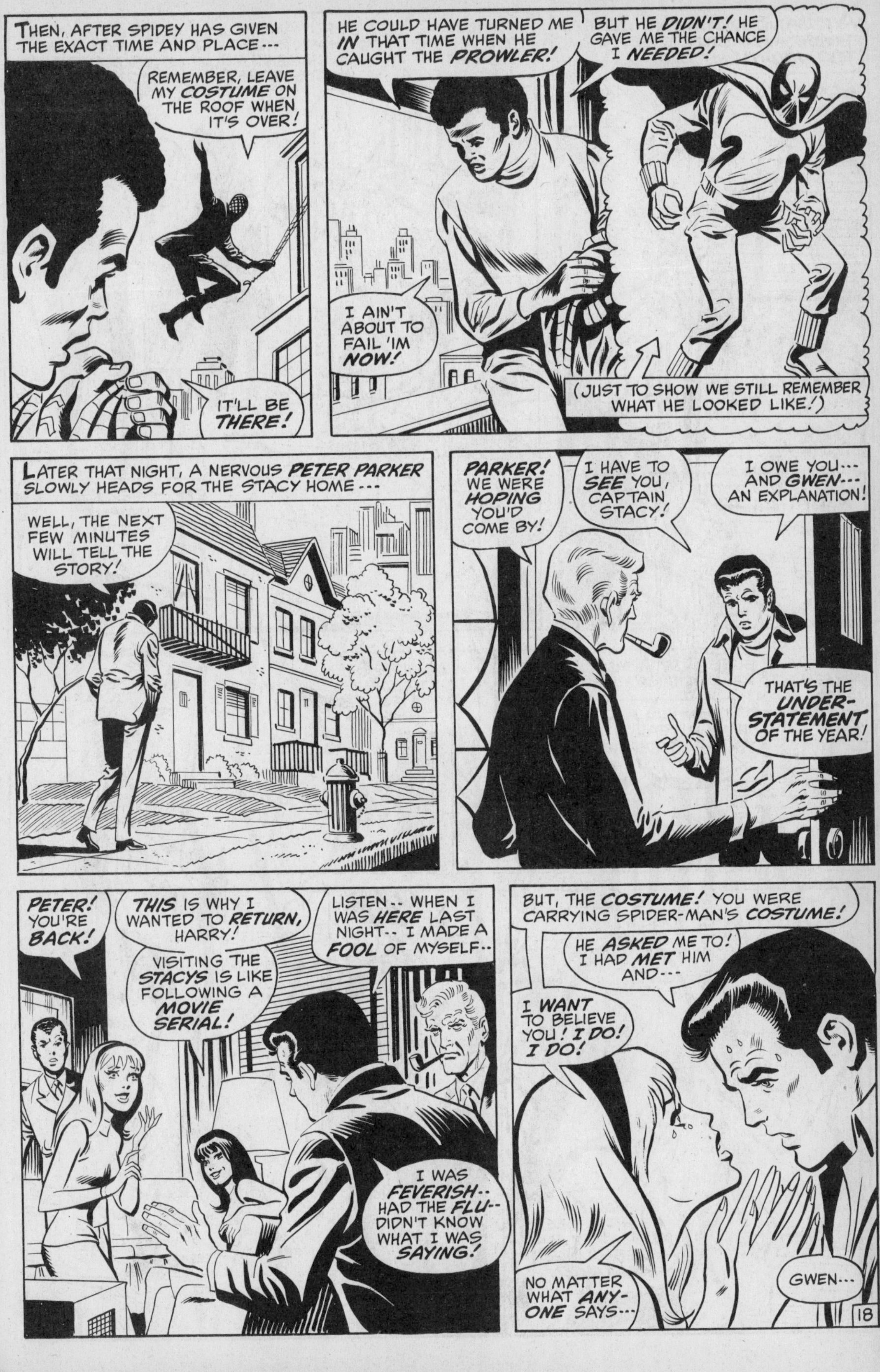

THEN, AFTER SPIDEY HAS GIVEN THE EXACT TIME AND PLACE---
REMEMBER, LEAVE MY COSTUME ON THE ROOF WHEN IT'S OVER!
IT'LL BE THERE!
HE COULD HAVE TURNED ME IN THAT TIME WHEN HE CAUGHT THE PROWLER!
BUT HE DIDN'T! HE GAVE ME THE CHANCE I NEEDED!
I AIN'T ABOUT TO FAIL 'IM NOW!
(JUST TO SHOW WE STILL REMEMBER WHAT HE LOOKED LIKE!)
LATER THAT NIGHT, A NERVOUS PETER PARKER SLOWLY HEADS FOR THE STACY HOME---
WELL, THE NEXT FEW MINUTES WILL TELL THE STORY!
PARKER! WE WERE HOPING YOU'D COME BY!
I HAVE TO SEE YOU, CAPTAIN STACY!
I OWE YOU--- AND GWEN--- AN EXPLANATION!
THAT'S THE UNDER-STATEMENT OF THE YEAR!
PETER! YOU'RE BACK!
THIS IS WHY I WANTED TO RETURN, HARRY!
VISITING THE STACYS IS LIKE FOLLOWING A MOVIE SERIAL!
LISTEN-- WHEN I WAS HERE LAST NIGHT-- I MADE A FOOL OF MYSELF--
I WAS FEVERISH-- HAD THE FLU-- DIDN'T KNOW WHAT I WAS SAYING!
BUT, THE COSTUME! YOU WERE CARRYING SPIDER-MAN'S COSTUME!
HE ASKED ME TO! I HAD MET HIM AND---
I WANT TO BELIEVE YOU! I DO! I DO!
NO MATTER WHAT ANY-ONE SAYS---
GWEN---
18

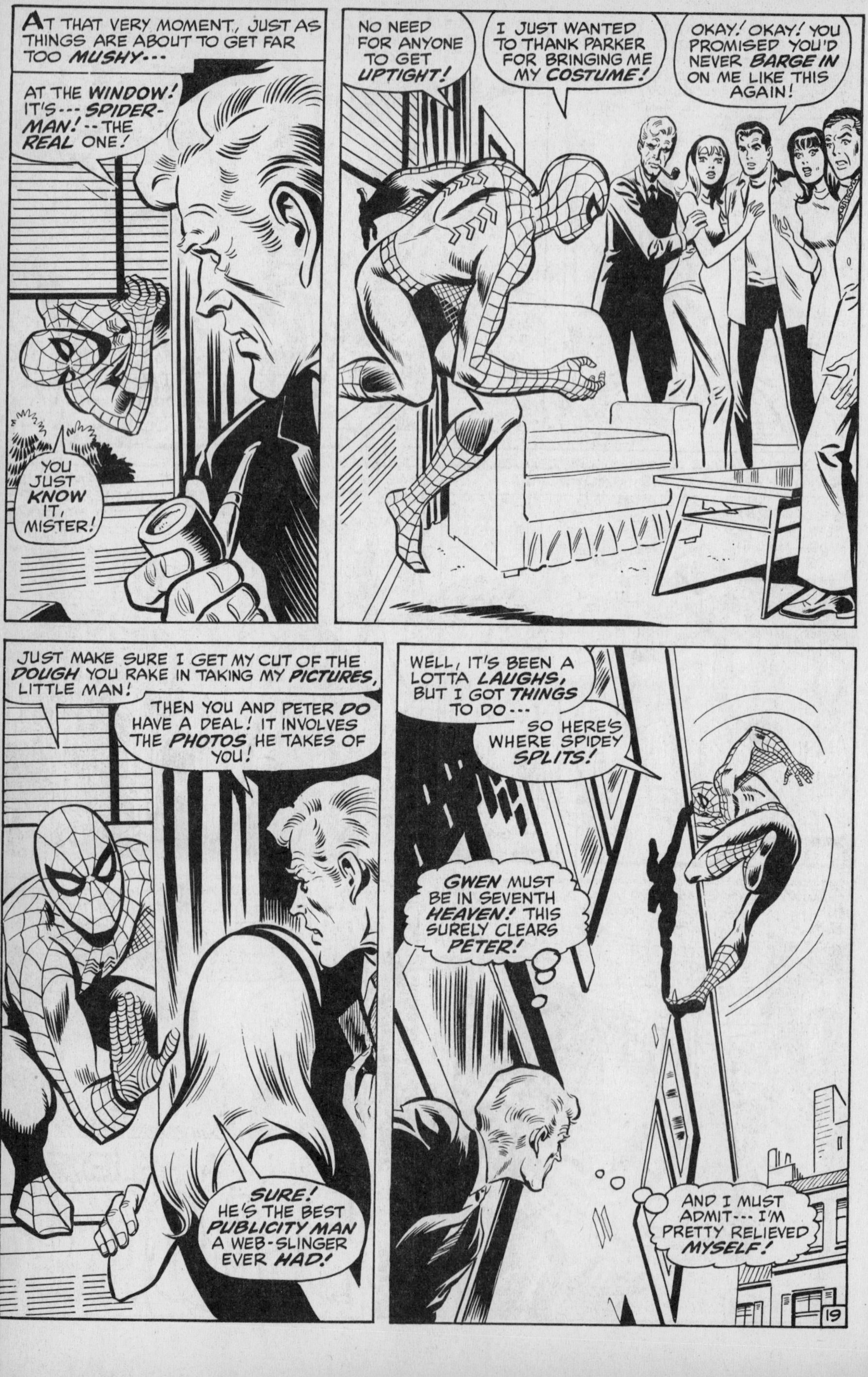
AT THAT VERY MOMENT, JUST AS THINGS ARE ABOUT TO GET FAR TOO MUSHY---
AT THE WINDOW! IT'S--- SPIDER-MAN! -- THE REAL ONE!
YOU JUST KNOW IT, MISTER!
NO NEED FOR ANYONE TO GET UPTIGHT!
I JUST WANTED TO THANK PARKER FOR BRINGING ME MY COSTUME!
OKAY! OKAY! YOU PROMISED YOU'D NEVER BARGE IN ON ME LIKE THIS AGAIN!
JUST MAKE SURE I GET MY CUT OF THE DOUGH YOU RAKE IN TAKING MY PICTURES, LITTLE MAN!
THEN YOU AND PETER DO HAVE A DEAL! IT INVOLVES THE PHOTOS HE TAKES OF YOU!
SURE! HE'S THE BEST PUBLICITY MAN A WEB-SLINGER EVER HAD!
WELL, IT'S BEEN A LOTTA LAUGHS, BUT I GOT THINGS TO DO---
SO HERE'S WHERE SPIDEY SPLITS!
GWEN MUST BE IN SEVENTH HEAVEN! THIS SURELY CLEARS PETER!
AND I MUST ADMIT--- I'M PRETTY RELIEVED MYSELF!
19

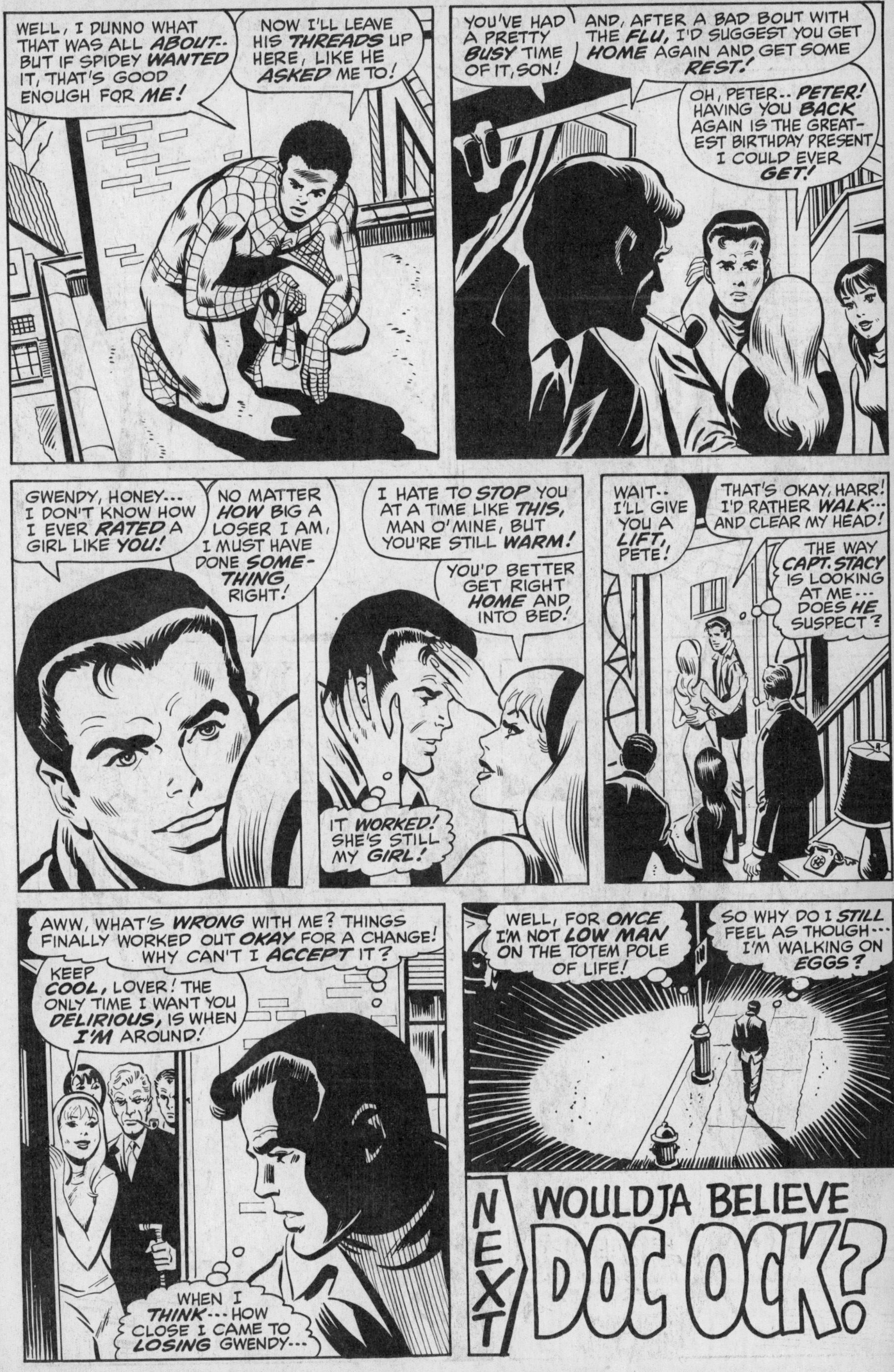
WELL, I DUNNO WHAT THAT WAS ALL ABOUT.. BUT IF SPIDEY WANTED IT, THAT'S GOOD ENOUGH FOR ME!
NOW I'LL LEAVE HIS THREADS UP HERE, LIKE HE ASKED ME TO!
YOU'VE HAD A PRETTY BUSY TIME OF IT, SON!
AND, AFTER A BAD BOUT WITH THE FLU, I'D SUGGEST YOU GET HOME AGAIN AND GET SOME REST!
OH, PETER.. PETER! HAVING YOU BACK AGAIN IS THE GREATEST BIRTHDAY PRESENT I COULD EVER GET!
GWENDY, HONEY... I DON'T KNOW HOW I EVER RATED A GIRL LIKE YOU!
NO MATTER HOW BIG A LOSER I AM, I MUST HAVE DONE SOMETHING RIGHT!
I HATE TO STOP YOU AT A TIME LIKE THIS, MAN O'MINE, BUT YOU'RE STILL WARM!
YOU'D BETTER GET RIGHT HOME AND INTO BED!
IT WORKED! SHE'S STILL MY GIRL!
WAIT.. I'LL GIVE YOU A LIFT, PETE!
THAT'S OKAY, HARR! I'D RATHER WALK... AND CLEAR MY HEAD!
THE WAY CAPT. STACY IS LOOKING AT ME... DOES HE SUSPECT?
AWW, WHAT'S WRONG WITH ME? THINGS FINALLY WORKED OUT OKAY FOR A CHANGE! WHY CAN'T I ACCEPT IT?
KEEP COOL, LOVER! THE ONLY TIME I WANT YOU DELIRIOUS, IS WHEN I'M AROUND!
WHEN I THINK... HOW CLOSE I CAME TO LOSING GWENDY...
WELL, FOR ONCE I'M NOT LOW MAN ON THE TOTEM POLE OF LIFE!
SO WHY DO I STILL FEEL AS THOUGH... I'M WALKING ON EGGS?
NEXT
WOULDJA BELIEVE
DOC OCK?

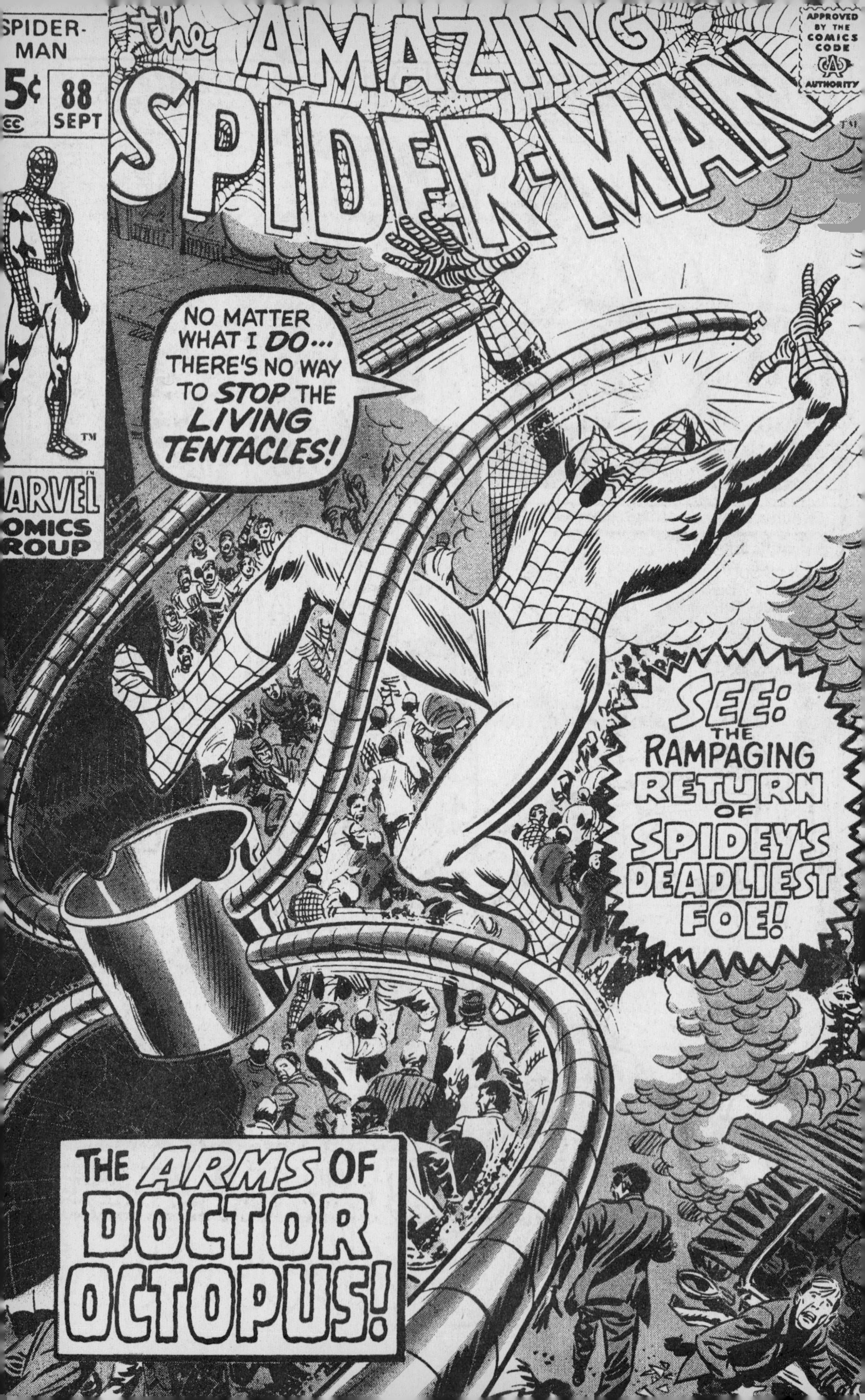
SPIDER-MAN
15¢
88
SEPT
the AMAZING SPIDER-MAN
APPROVED BY THE COMICS CODE AUTHORITY
MARVEL COMICS GROUP
NO MATTER WHAT I DO... THERE'S NO WAY TO STOP THE LIVING TENTACLES!
SEE: THE RAMPAGING RETURN OF SPIDEY'S DEADLIEST FOE!
THE ARMS OF DOCTOR OCTOPUS!

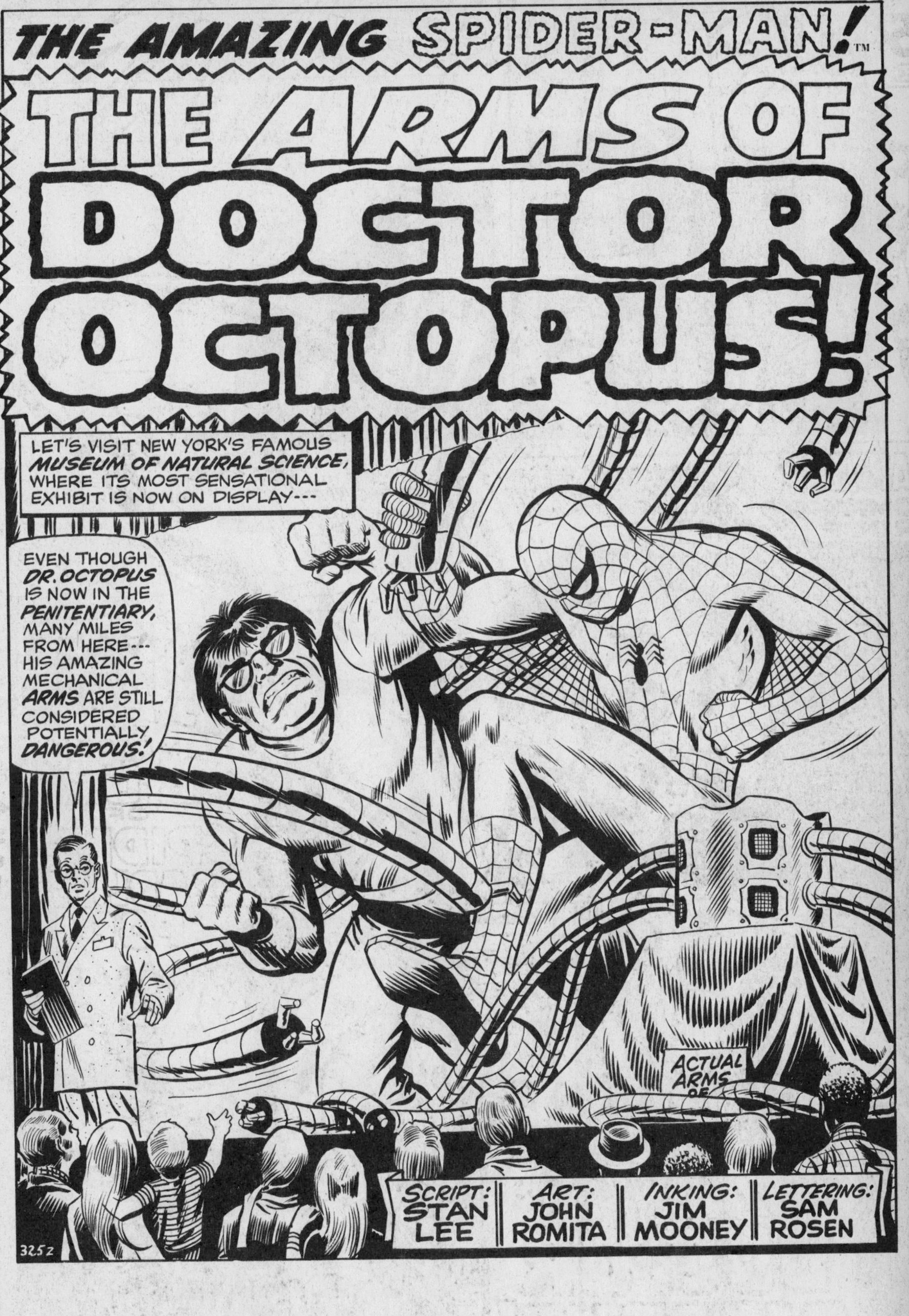
THE AMAZING SPIDER-MAN!™
THE ARMS OF DOCTOR OCTOPUS!
LET'S VISIT NEW YORK'S FAMOUS MUSEUM OF NATURAL SCIENCE, WHERE ITS MOST SENSATIONAL EXHIBIT IS NOW ON DISPLAY---
EVEN THOUGH DR. OCTOPUS IS NOW IN THE PENITENTIARY, MANY MILES FROM HERE--- HIS AMAZING MECHANICAL ARMS ARE STILL CONSIDERED POTENTIALLY DANGEROUS!
ACTUAL ARMS OF
SCRIPT: STAN LEE
ART: JOHN ROMITA
INKING: JIM MOONEY
LETTERING: SAM ROSEN
325z

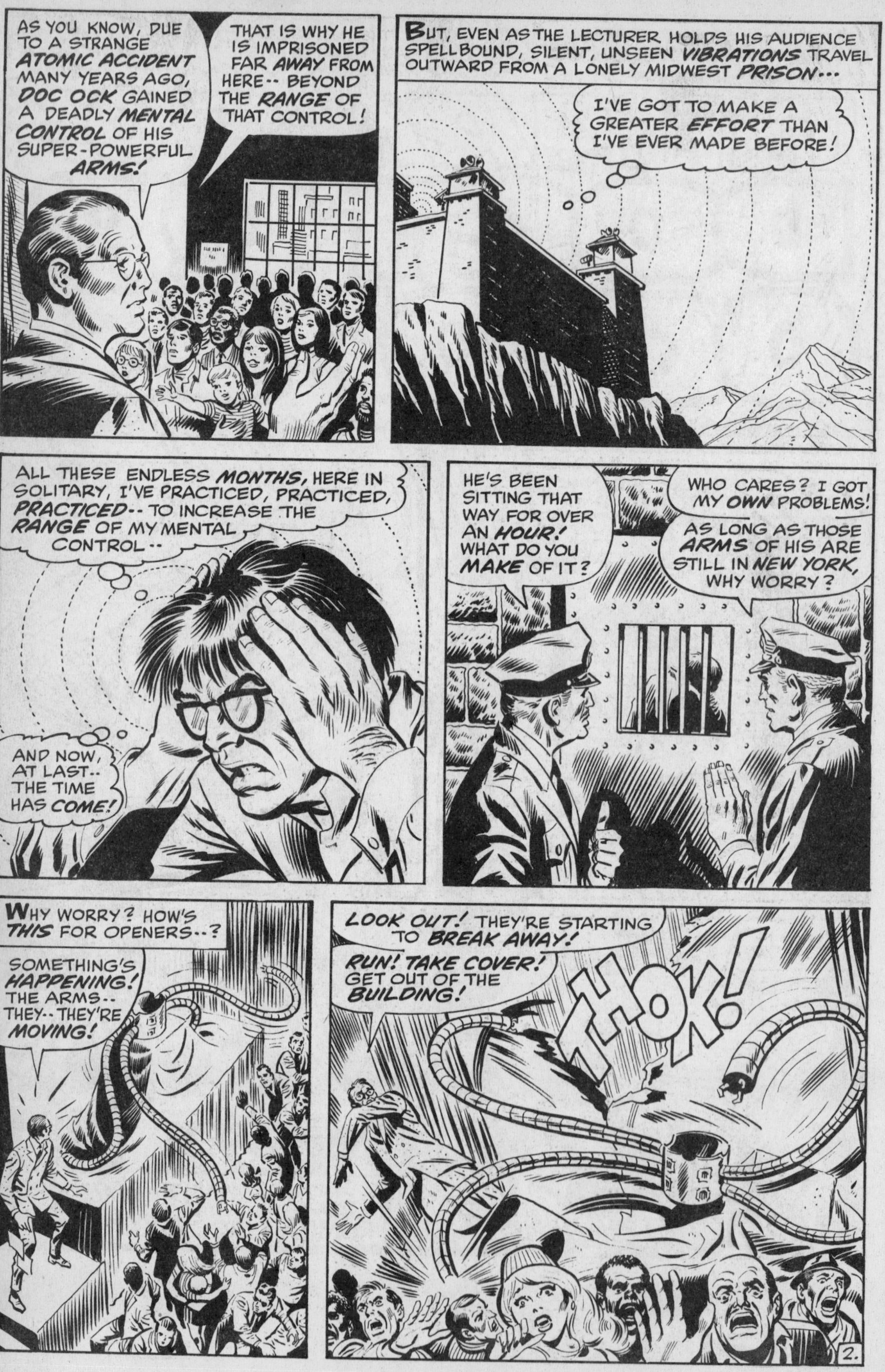

AS YOU KNOW, DUE TO A STRANGE ATOMIC ACCIDENT MANY YEARS AGO, DOC OCK GAINED A DEADLY MENTAL CONTROL OF HIS SUPER-POWERFUL ARMS!
THAT IS WHY HE IS IMPRISONED FAR AWAY FROM HERE-- BEYOND THE RANGE OF THAT CONTROL!
BUT, EVEN AS THE LECTURER HOLDS HIS AUDIENCE SPELLBOUND, SILENT, UNSEEN VIBRATIONS TRAVEL OUTWARD FROM A LONELY MIDWEST PRISON...
I'VE GOT TO MAKE A GREATER EFFORT THAN I'VE EVER MADE BEFORE!
ALL THESE ENDLESS MONTHS, HERE IN SOLITARY, I'VE PRACTICED, PRACTICED, PRACTICED-- TO INCREASE THE RANGE OF MY MENTAL CONTROL--
AND NOW, AT LAST.. THE TIME HAS COME!
HE'S BEEN SITTING THAT WAY FOR OVER AN HOUR! WHAT DO YOU MAKE OF IT?
WHO CARES? I GOT MY OWN PROBLEMS!
AS LONG AS THOSE ARMS OF HIS ARE STILL IN NEW YORK, WHY WORRY?
WHY WORRY? HOW'S THIS FOR OPENERS--?
SOMETHING'S HAPPENING! THE ARMS-- THEY-- THEY'RE MOVING!
LOOK OUT! THEY'RE STARTING TO BREAK AWAY!
RUN! TAKE COVER! GET OUT OF THE BUILDING!
THOK!
2.

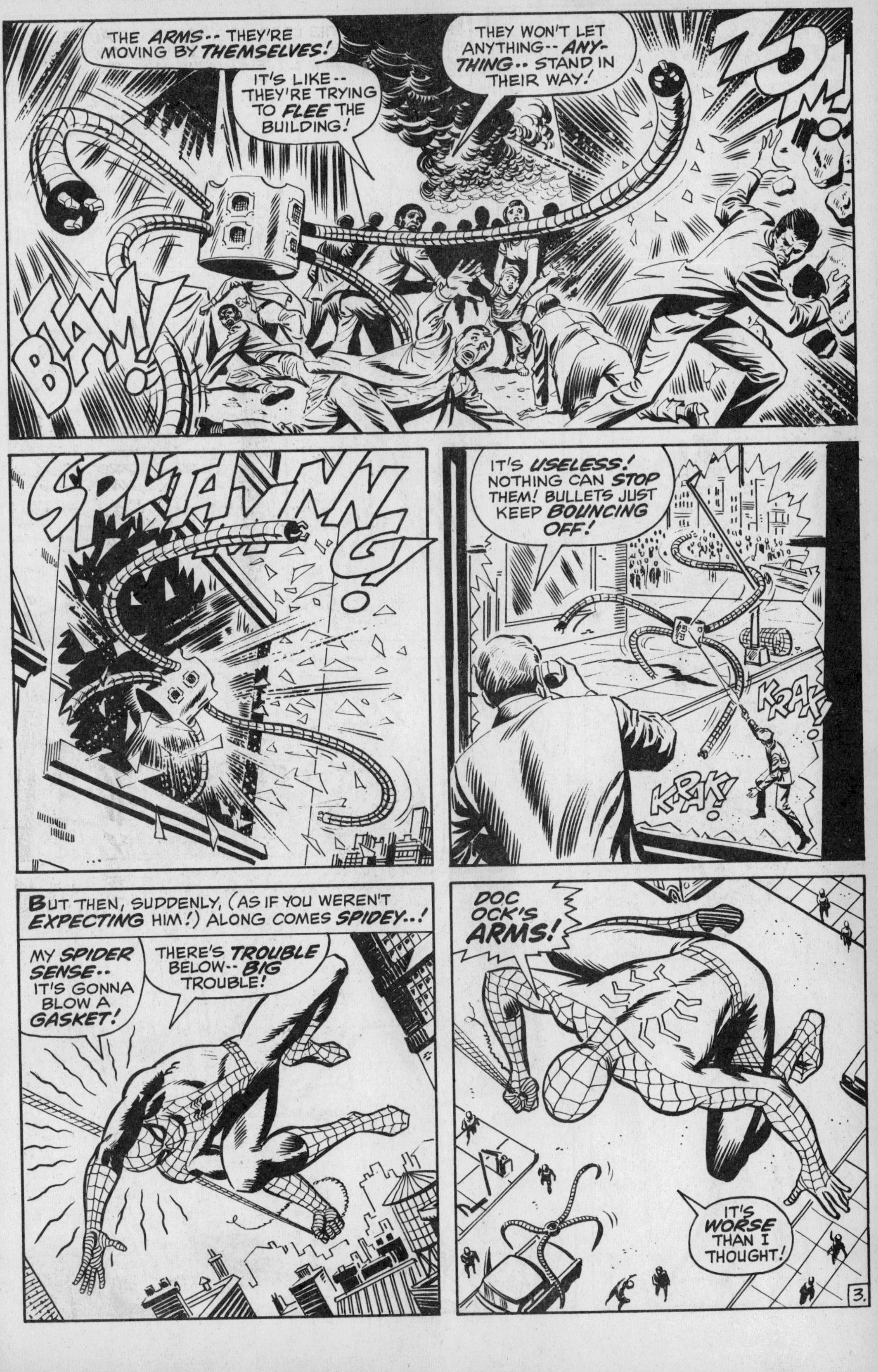
THE ARMS-- THEY'RE MOVING BY THEMSELVES!
IT'S LIKE-- THEY'RE TRYING TO FLEE THE BUILDING!
THEY WON'T LET ANYTHING-- ANY-THING-- STAND IN THEIR WAY!
BLAM!
SPLANNG!
IT'S USELESS! NOTHING CAN STOP THEM! BULLETS JUST KEEP BOUNCING OFF!
KRAK!
KRAK!
BUT THEN, SUDDENLY, (AS IF YOU WEREN'T EXPECTING HIM!) ALONG COMES SPIDEY..!
MY SPIDER SENSE.. IT'S GONNA BLOW A GASKET!
THERE'S TROUBLE BELOW-- BIG TROUBLE!
DOC OCK'S ARMS!
IT'S WORSE THAN I THOUGHT!

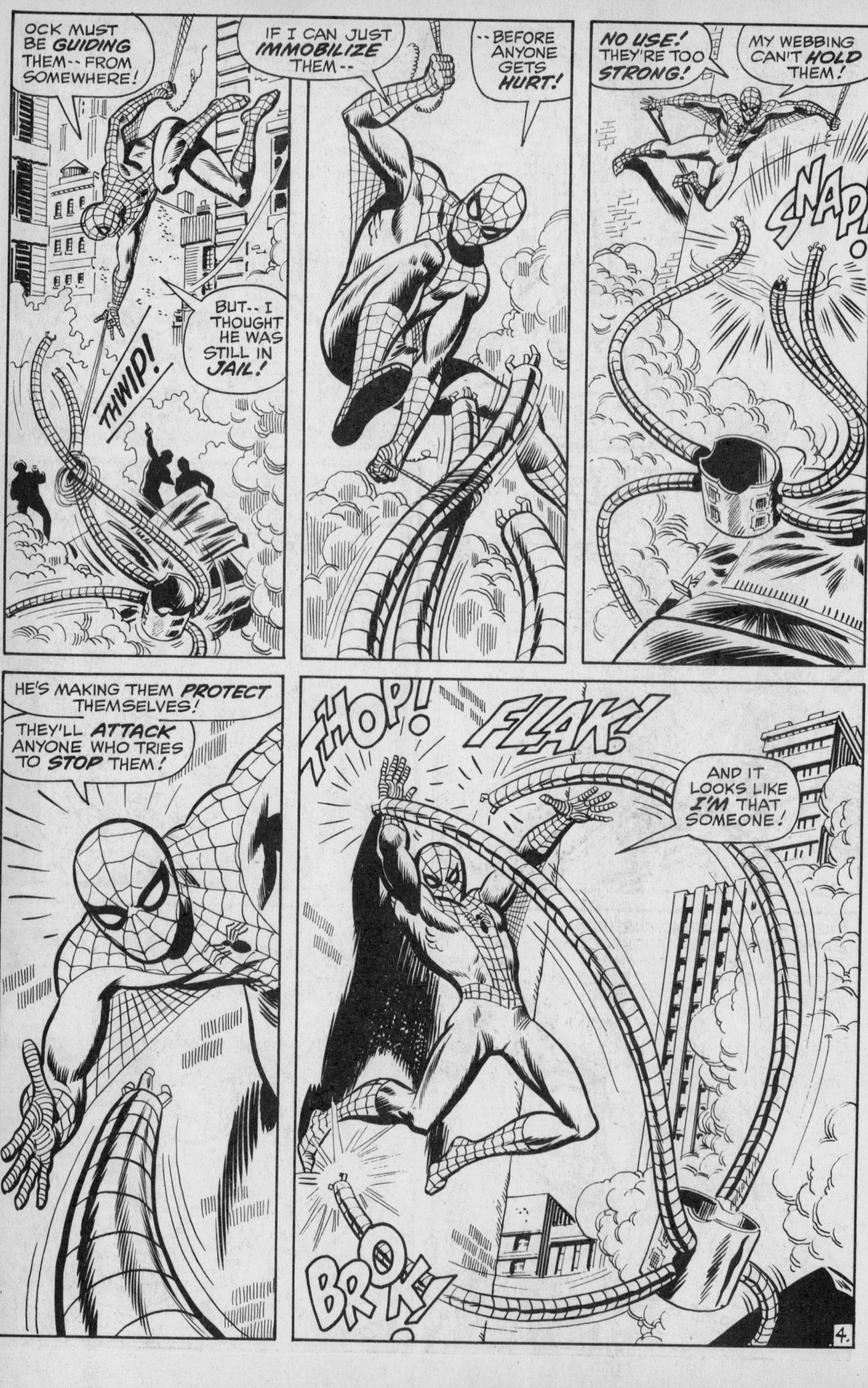
OCK MUST BE GUIDING THEM-- FROM SOMEWHERE!
BUT-- I THOUGHT HE WAS STILL IN JAIL!
THWIP!
IF I CAN JUST IMMOBILIZE THEM--
--BEFORE ANYONE GETS HURT!
NO USE! THEY'RE TOO STRONG!
MY WEBBING CAN'T HOLD THEM!
SNAP!
HE'S MAKING THEM PROTECT THEMSELVES!
THEY'LL ATTACK ANYONE WHO TRIES TO STOP THEM!
THOP!
FLAK!
AND IT LOOKS LIKE I'M THAT SOMEONE!
BROK!
4.

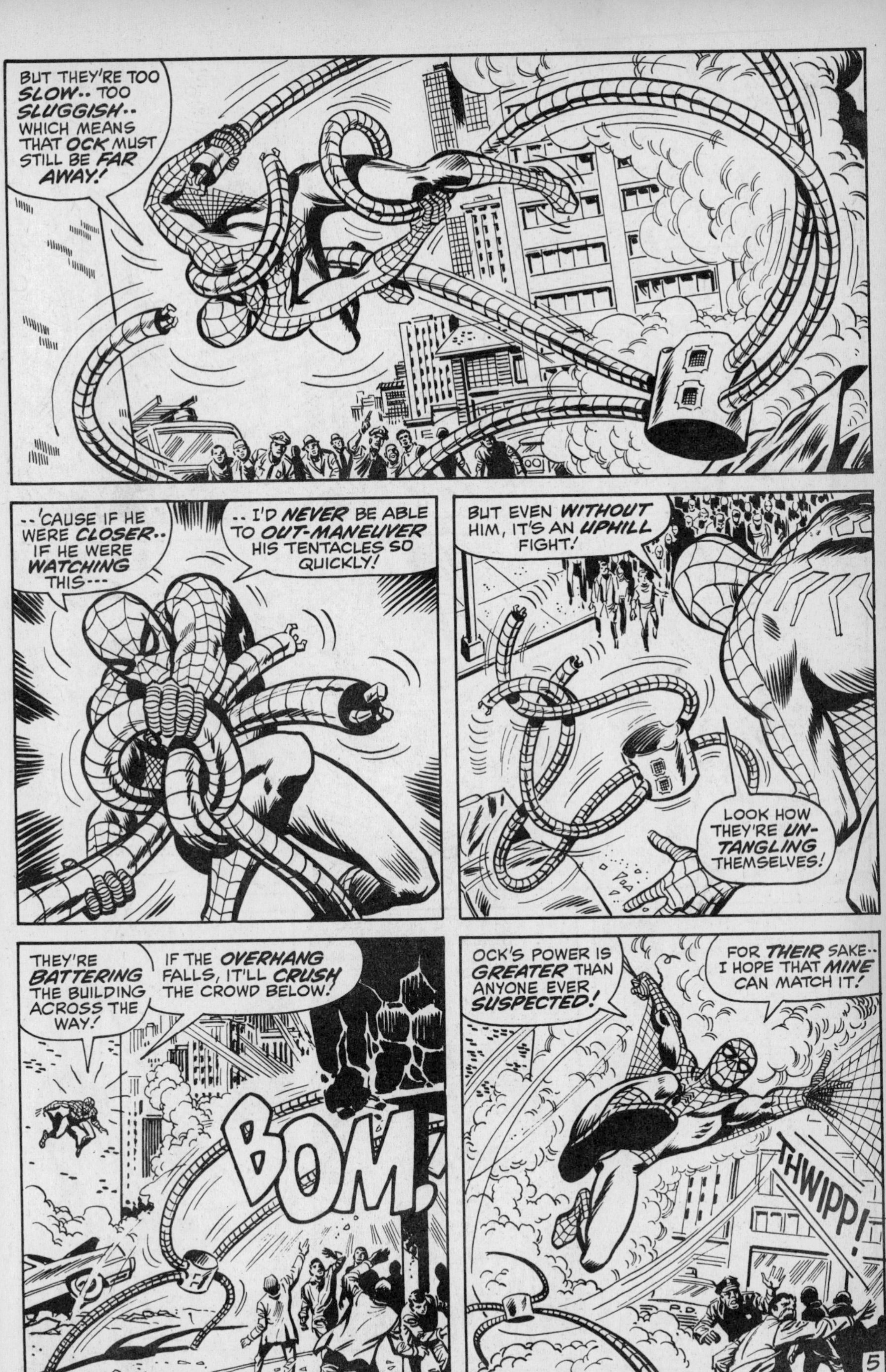
BUT THEY'RE TOO SLOW.. TOO SLUGGISH.. WHICH MEANS THAT OCK MUST STILL BE FAR AWAY!
..'CAUSE IF HE WERE CLOSER.. IF HE WERE WATCHING THIS---
..I'D NEVER BE ABLE TO OUT-MANEUVER HIS TENTACLES SO QUICKLY!
BUT EVEN WITHOUT HIM, IT'S AN UPHILL FIGHT!
LOOK HOW THEY'RE UN-TANGLING THEMSELVES!
THEY'RE BATTERING THE BUILDING ACROSS THE WAY!
IF THE OVERHANG FALLS, IT'LL CRUSH THE CROWD BELOW!
BOM
OCK'S POWER IS GREATER THAN ANYONE EVER SUSPECTED!
FOR THEIR SAKE.. I HOPE THAT MINE CAN MATCH IT!
THWIPP!
P.D.
5

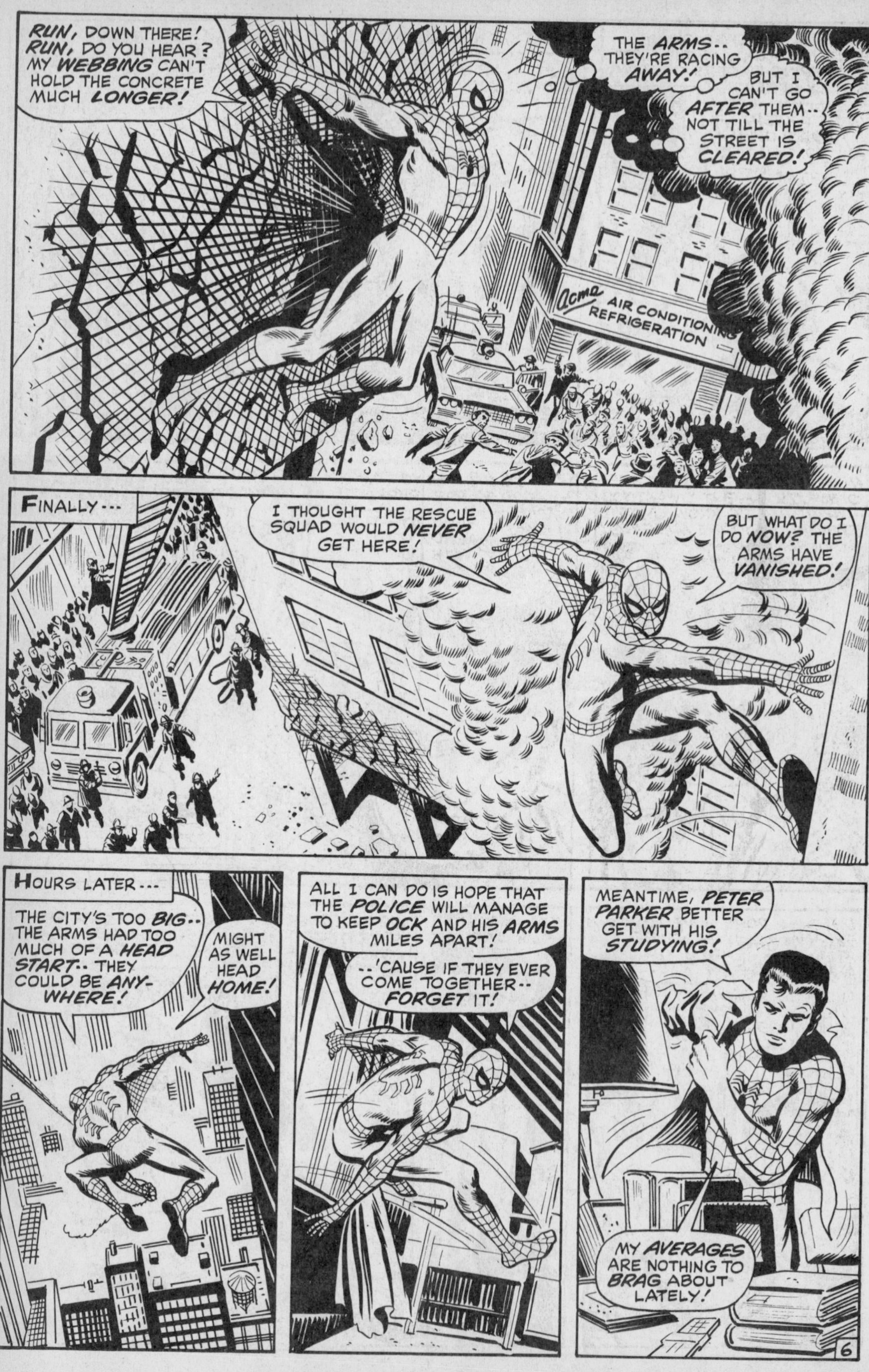
RUN, DOWN THERE! RUN, DO YOU HEAR? MY WEBBING CAN'T HOLD THE CONCRETE MUCH LONGER!
THE ARMS.. THEY'RE RACING AWAY!
BUT I CAN'T GO AFTER THEM.. NOT TILL THE STREET IS CLEARED!
Acme AIR CONDITIONING REFRIGERATION
FINALLY...
I THOUGHT THE RESCUE SQUAD WOULD NEVER GET HERE!
BUT WHAT DO I DO NOW? THE ARMS HAVE VANISHED!
HOURS LATER...
THE CITY'S TOO BIG.. THE ARMS HAD TOO MUCH OF A HEAD START.. THEY COULD BE ANYWHERE!
MIGHT AS WELL HEAD HOME!
ALL I CAN DO IS HOPE THAT THE POLICE WILL MANAGE TO KEEP OCK AND HIS ARMS MILES APART!
..'CAUSE IF THEY EVER COME TOGETHER-- FORGET IT!
MEANTIME, PETER PARKER BETTER GET WITH HIS STUDYING!
MY AVERAGES ARE NOTHING TO BRAG ABOUT LATELY!
6

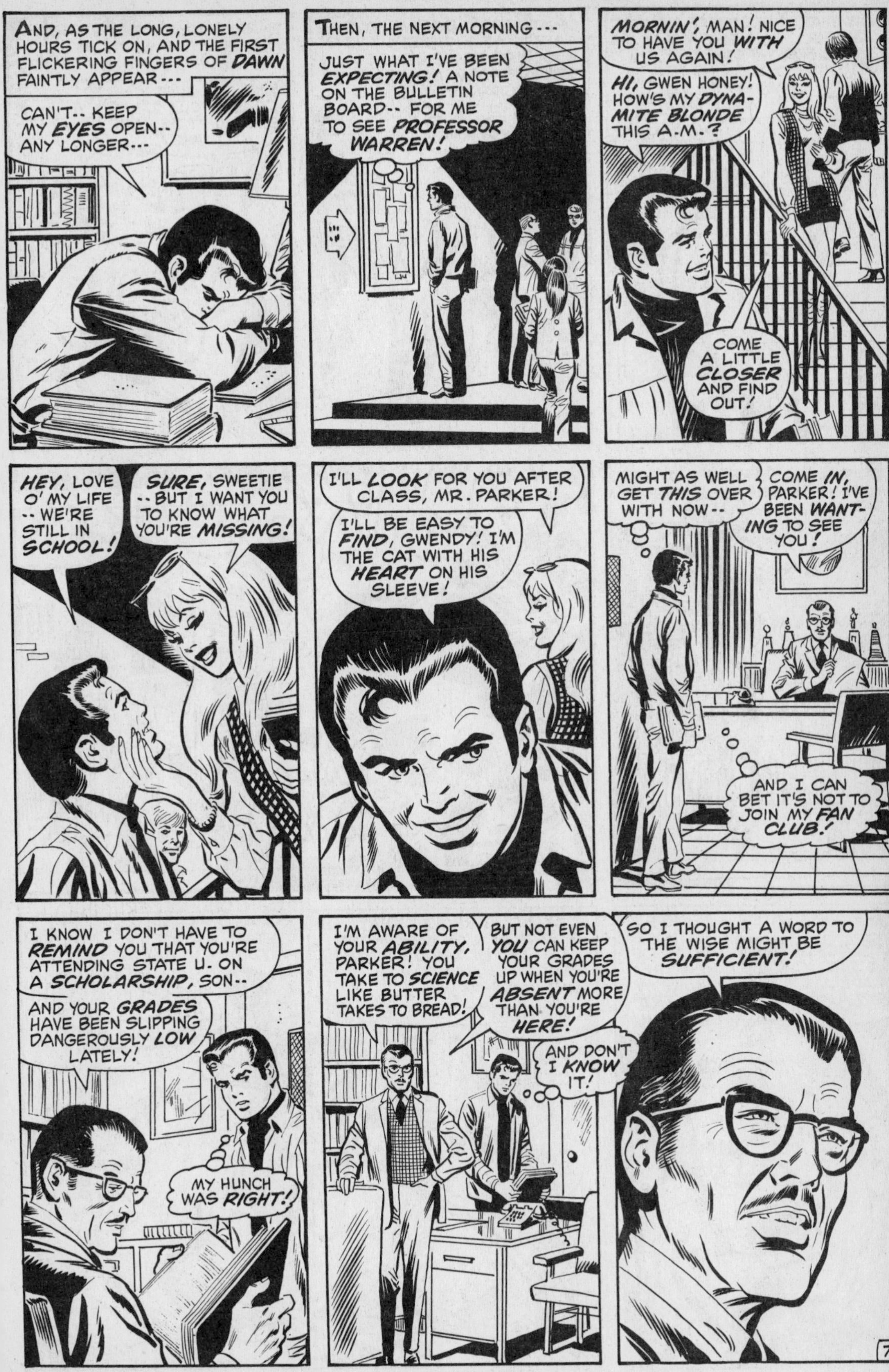
AND, AS THE LONG, LONELY HOURS TICK ON, AND THE FIRST FLICKERING FINGERS OF DAWN FAINTLY APPEAR---
CAN'T-- KEEP MY EYES OPEN-- ANY LONGER---
THEN, THE NEXT MORNING---
JUST WHAT I'VE BEEN EXPECTING! A NOTE ON THE BULLETIN BOARD-- FOR ME TO SEE PROFESSOR WARREN!
MORNIN'! MAN! NICE TO HAVE YOU WITH US AGAIN!
HI, GWEN HONEY! HOW'S MY DYNAMITE BLONDE THIS A.M.?
COME A LITTLE CLOSER AND FIND OUT!
HEY, LOVE O' MY LIFE -- WE'RE STILL IN SCHOOL!
SURE, SWEETIE -- BUT I WANT YOU TO KNOW WHAT YOU'RE MISSING!
I'LL LOOK FOR YOU AFTER CLASS, MR. PARKER!
I'LL BE EASY TO FIND, GWENDY! I'M THE CAT WITH HIS HEART ON HIS SLEEVE!
MIGHT AS WELL GET THIS OVER WITH NOW--
COME IN, PARKER! I'VE BEEN WANTING TO SEE YOU!
AND I CAN BET IT'S NOT TO JOIN MY FAN CLUB!
I KNOW I DON'T HAVE TO REMIND YOU THAT YOU'RE ATTENDING STATE U. ON A SCHOLARSHIP, SON--
AND YOUR GRADES HAVE BEEN SLIPPING DANGEROUSLY LOW LATELY!
MY HUNCH WAS RIGHT!
I'M AWARE OF YOUR ABILITY, PARKER! YOU TAKE TO SCIENCE LIKE BUTTER TAKES TO BREAD!
BUT NOT EVEN YOU CAN KEEP YOUR GRADES UP WHEN YOU'RE ABSENT MORE THAN YOU'RE HERE!
AND DON'T I KNOW IT!
SO I THOUGHT A WORD TO THE WISE MIGHT BE SUFFICIENT!
7.

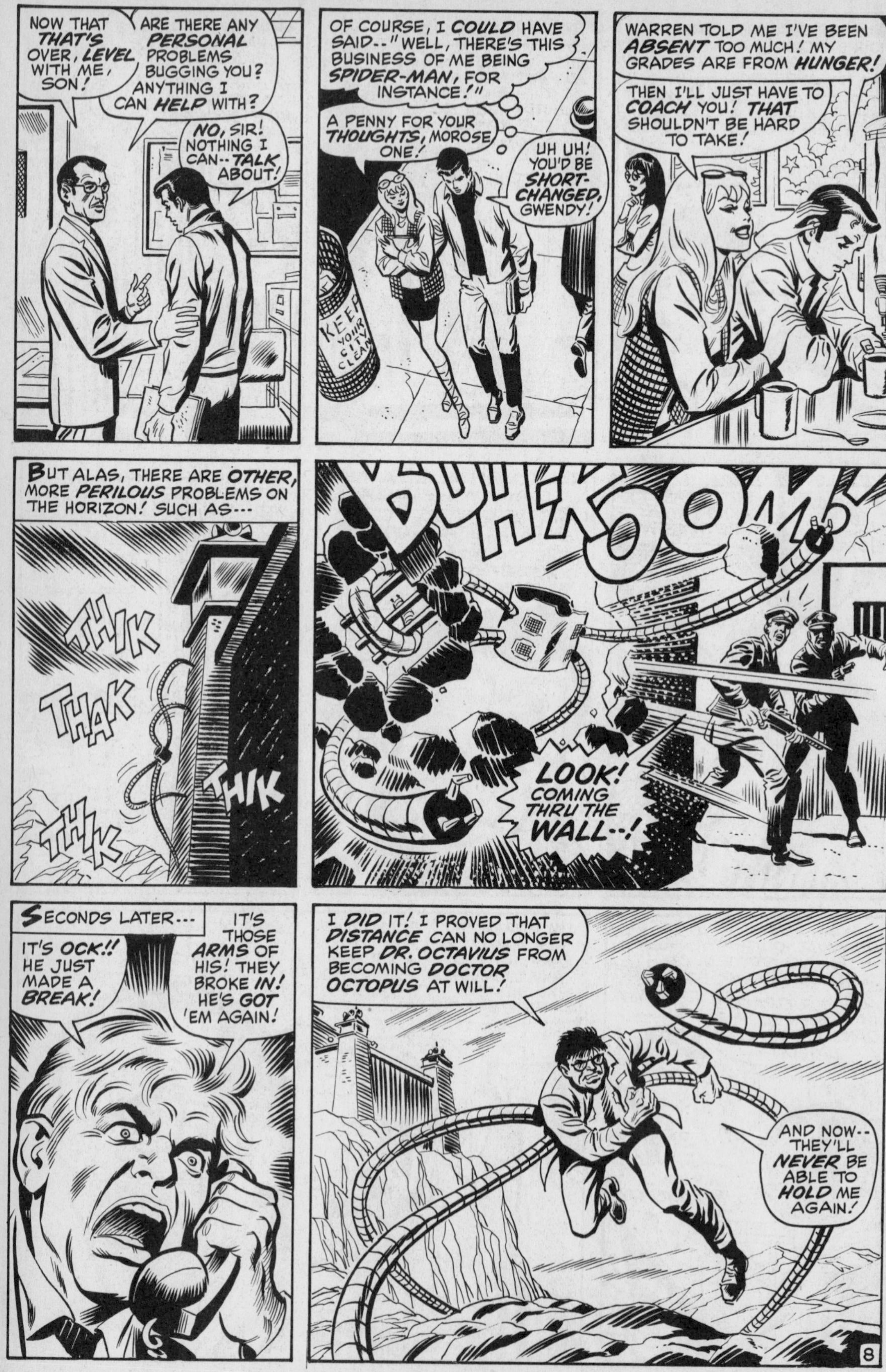
NOW THAT THAT'S OVER, LEVEL WITH ME, SON!
ARE THERE ANY PERSONAL PROBLEMS BUGGING YOU? ANYTHING I CAN HELP WITH?
NO, SIR! NOTHING I CAN--TALK ABOUT!
OF COURSE, I COULD HAVE SAID--"WELL, THERE'S THIS BUSINESS OF ME BEING SPIDER-MAN, FOR INSTANCE!"
A PENNY FOR YOUR THOUGHTS, MOROSE ONE!
UH UH! YOU'D BE SHORT-CHANGED, GWENDY!
KEEP YOUR CITY CLEAN
WARREN TOLD ME I'VE BEEN ABSENT TOO MUCH! MY GRADES ARE FROM HUNGER!
THEN I'LL JUST HAVE TO COACH YOU! THAT SHOULDN'T BE HARD TO TAKE!
BUT ALAS, THERE ARE OTHER, MORE PERILOUS PROBLEMS ON THE HORIZON! SUCH AS---
THIK
THAK
THIK
THIK
BUH-KOOM!
LOOK! COMING THRU THE WALL--!
SECONDS LATER...
IT'S OCK!! HE JUST MADE A BREAK!
IT'S THOSE ARMS OF HIS! THEY BROKE IN! HE'S GOT 'EM AGAIN!
I DID IT! I PROVED THAT DISTANCE CAN NO LONGER KEEP DR. OCTAVIUS FROM BECOMING DOCTOR OCTOPUS AT WILL!
AND NOW--THEY'LL NEVER BE ABLE TO HOLD ME AGAIN!
8

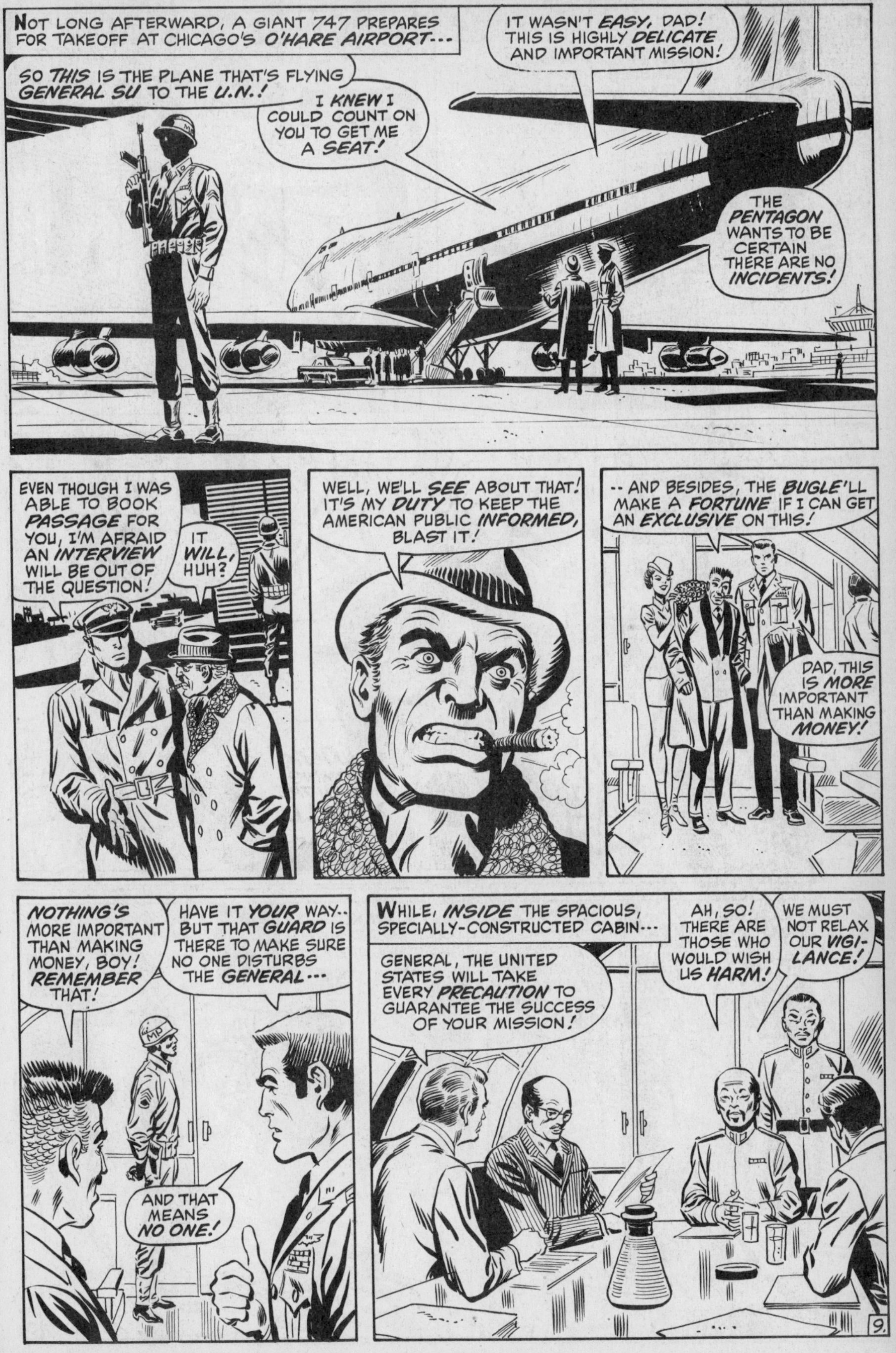

NOT LONG AFTERWARD, A GIANT 747 PREPARES FOR TAKEOFF AT CHICAGO'S O'HARE AIRPORT---
SO THIS IS THE PLANE THAT'S FLYING GENERAL SU TO THE U.N.!
I KNEW I COULD COUNT ON YOU TO GET ME A SEAT!
IT WASN'T EASY, DAD! THIS IS HIGHLY DELICATE AND IMPORTANT MISSION!
THE PENTAGON WANTS TO BE CERTAIN THERE ARE NO INCIDENTS!
EVEN THOUGH I WAS ABLE TO BOOK PASSAGE FOR YOU, I'M AFRAID AN INTERVIEW WILL BE OUT OF THE QUESTION!
IT WILL, HUH?
WELL, WE'LL SEE ABOUT THAT! IT'S MY DUTY TO KEEP THE AMERICAN PUBLIC INFORMED, BLAST IT!
-- AND BESIDES, THE BUGLE'LL MAKE A FORTUNE IF I CAN GET AN EXCLUSIVE ON THIS!
DAD, THIS IS MORE IMPORTANT THAN MAKING MONEY!
NOTHING'S MORE IMPORTANT THAN MAKING MONEY, BOY! REMEMBER THAT!
HAVE IT YOUR WAY.. BUT THAT GUARD IS THERE TO MAKE SURE NO ONE DISTURBS THE GENERAL---
AND THAT MEANS NO ONE!
WHILE, INSIDE THE SPACIOUS, SPECIALLY-CONSTRUCTED CABIN---
GENERAL, THE UNITED STATES WILL TAKE EVERY PRECAUTION TO GUARANTEE THE SUCCESS OF YOUR MISSION!
AH, SO! THERE ARE THOSE WHO WOULD WISH US HARM!
WE MUST NOT RELAX OUR VIGI-LANCE!
9.

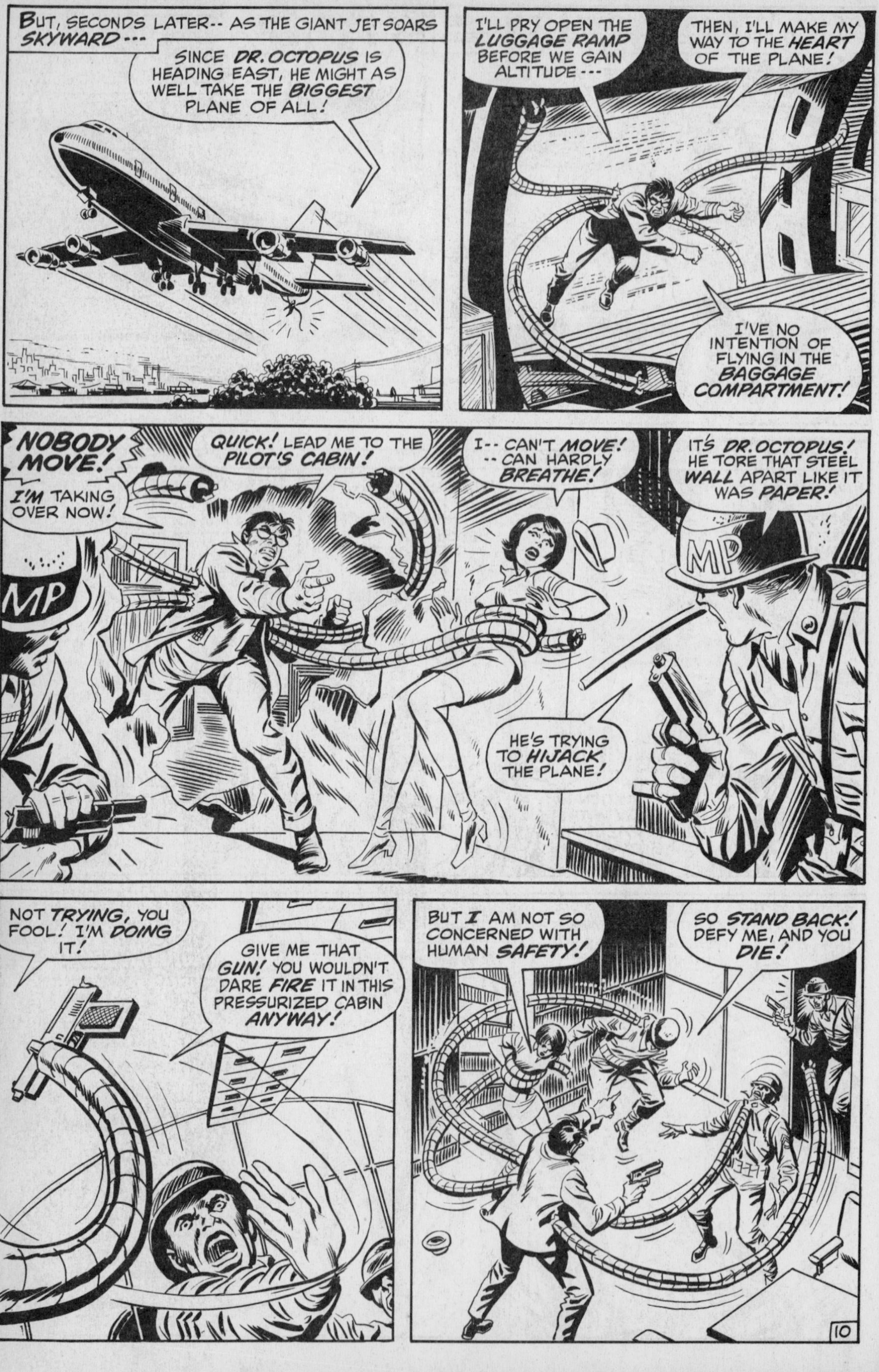

BUT, SECONDS LATER-- AS THE GIANT JET SOARS SKYWARD---
SINCE DR. OCTOPUS IS HEADING EAST, HE MIGHT AS WELL TAKE THE BIGGEST PLANE OF ALL!
I'LL PRY OPEN THE LUGGAGE RAMP BEFORE WE GAIN ALTITUDE---
THEN, I'LL MAKE MY WAY TO THE HEART OF THE PLANE!
I'VE NO INTENTION OF FLYING IN THE BAGGAGE COMPARTMENT!
NOBODY MOVE!
I'M TAKING OVER NOW!
QUICK! LEAD ME TO THE PILOT'S CABIN!
I-- CAN'T MOVE! --CAN HARDLY BREATHE!
IT'S DR. OCTOPUS! HE TORE THAT STEEL WALL APART LIKE IT WAS PAPER!
HE'S TRYING TO HIJACK THE PLANE!
MP
MP
NOT TRYING, YOU FOOL! I'M DOING IT!
GIVE ME THAT GUN! YOU WOULDN'T DARE FIRE IT IN THIS PRESSURIZED CABIN ANYWAY!
BUT I AM NOT SO CONCERNED WITH HUMAN SAFETY!
SO STAND BACK! DEFY ME, AND YOU DIE!
10

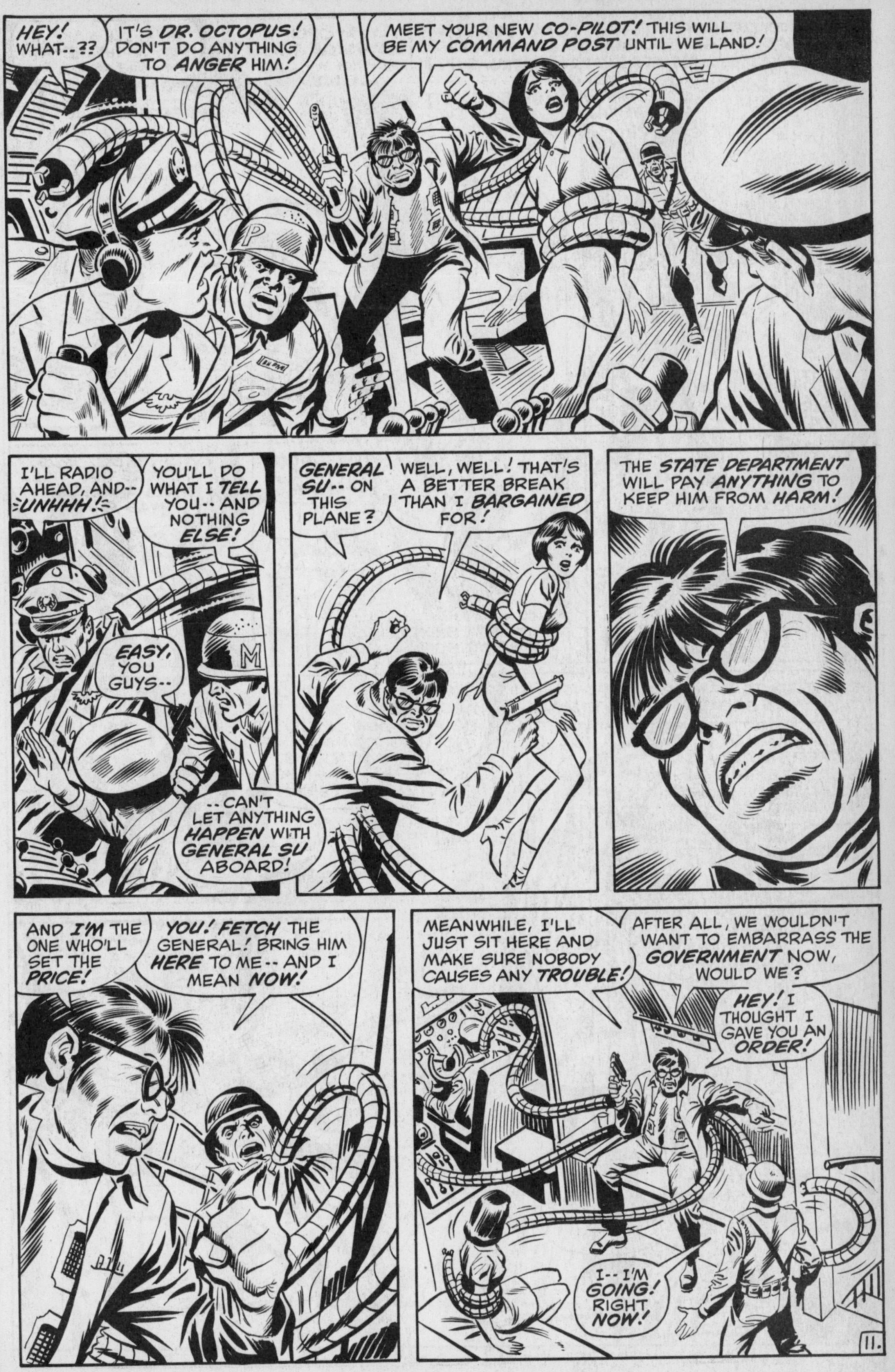
HEY! WHAT--??
IT'S DR. OCTOPUS! DON'T DO ANYTHING TO ANGER HIM!
MEET YOUR NEW CO-PILOT! THIS WILL BE MY COMMAND POST UNTIL WE LAND!
I'LL RADIO AHEAD, AND-- UNHHH!
YOU'LL DO WHAT I TELL YOU-- AND NOTHING ELSE!
EASY, YOU GUYS--
--CAN'T LET ANYTHING HAPPEN WITH GENERAL SU ABOARD!
GENERAL SU-- ON THIS PLANE?
WELL, WELL! THAT'S A BETTER BREAK THAN I BARGAINED FOR!
THE STATE DEPARTMENT WILL PAY ANYTHING TO KEEP HIM FROM HARM!
AND I'M THE ONE WHO'LL SET THE PRICE!
YOU! FETCH THE GENERAL! BRING HIM HERE TO ME-- AND I MEAN NOW!
MEANWHILE, I'LL JUST SIT HERE AND MAKE SURE NOBODY CAUSES ANY TROUBLE!
AFTER ALL, WE WOULDN'T WANT TO EMBARRASS THE GOVERNMENT NOW, WOULD WE?
HEY! I THOUGHT I GAVE YOU AN ORDER!
I-- I'M GOING! RIGHT NOW!
11.

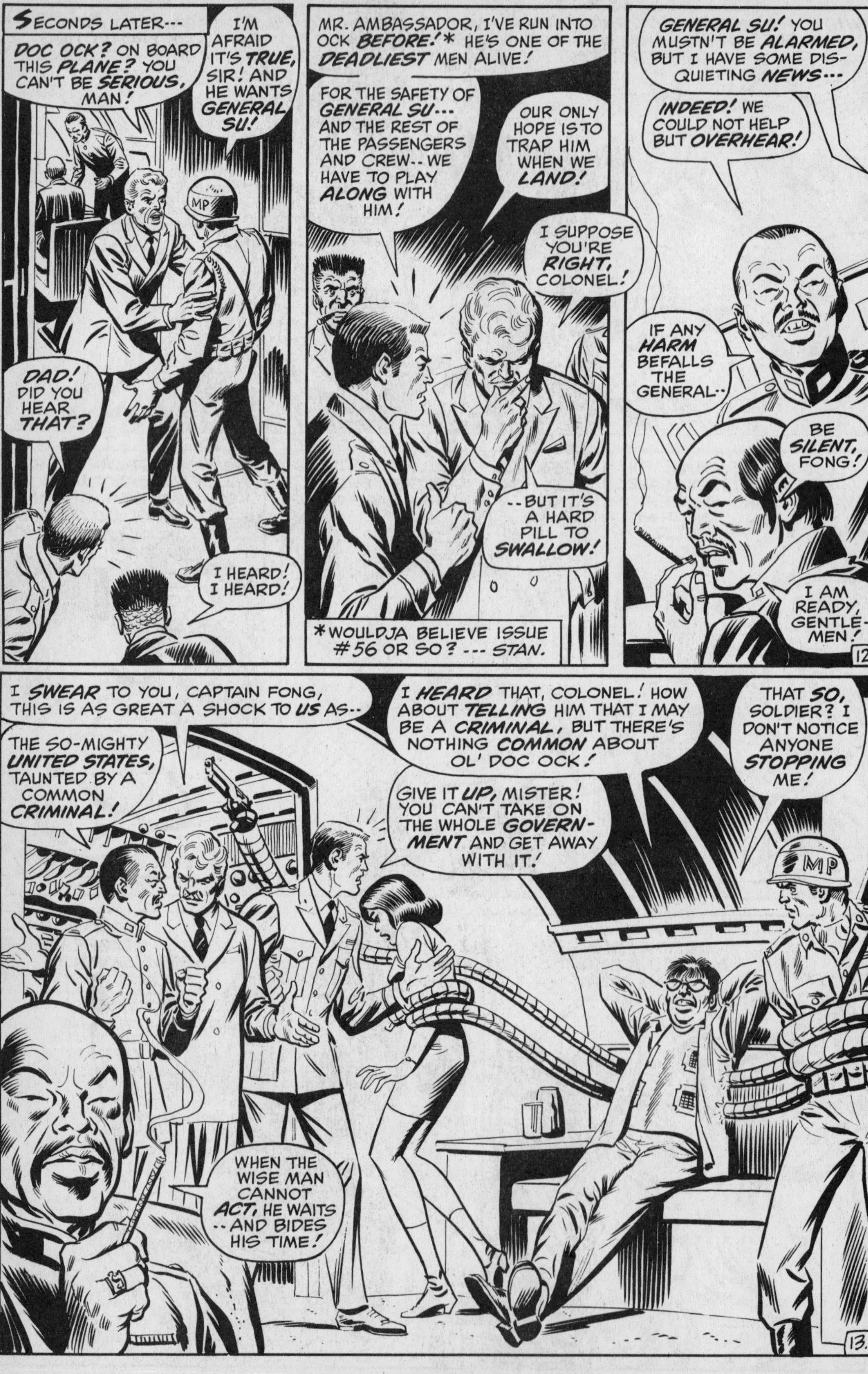
SECONDS LATER---
DOC OCK? ON BOARD THIS PLANE? YOU CAN'T BE SERIOUS, MAN!
I'M AFRAID IT'S TRUE, SIR! AND HE WANTS GENERAL SU!
DAD! DID YOU HEAR THAT?
I HEARD! I HEARD!
MR. AMBASSADOR, I'VE RUN INTO OCK BEFORE!* HE'S ONE OF THE DEADLIEST MEN ALIVE!
FOR THE SAFETY OF GENERAL SU... AND THE REST OF THE PASSENGERS AND CREW-- WE HAVE TO PLAY ALONG WITH HIM!
OUR ONLY HOPE IS TO TRAP HIM WHEN WE LAND!
I SUPPOSE YOU'RE RIGHT, COLONEL!
--BUT IT'S A HARD PILL TO SWALLOW!
*WOULDJA BELIEVE ISSUE #56 OR SO? --- STAN.
GENERAL SU! YOU MUSTN'T BE ALARMED, BUT I HAVE SOME DISQUIETING NEWS...
INDEED! WE COULD NOT HELP BUT OVERHEAR!
IF ANY HARM BEFALLS THE GENERAL--
BE SILENT, FONG!
I AM READY, GENTLEMEN!
12
I SWEAR TO YOU, CAPTAIN FONG, THIS IS AS GREAT A SHOCK TO US AS--
THE SO-MIGHTY UNITED STATES, TAUNTED BY A COMMON CRIMINAL!
I HEARD THAT, COLONEL! HOW ABOUT TELLING HIM THAT I MAY BE A CRIMINAL, BUT THERE'S NOTHING COMMON ABOUT OL' DOC OCK!
GIVE IT UP, MISTER! YOU CAN'T TAKE ON THE WHOLE GOVERNMENT AND GET AWAY WITH IT!
THAT SO, SOLDIER? I DON'T NOTICE ANYONE STOPPING ME!
WHEN THE WISE MAN CANNOT ACT, HE WAITS --AND BIDES HIS TIME!
13.

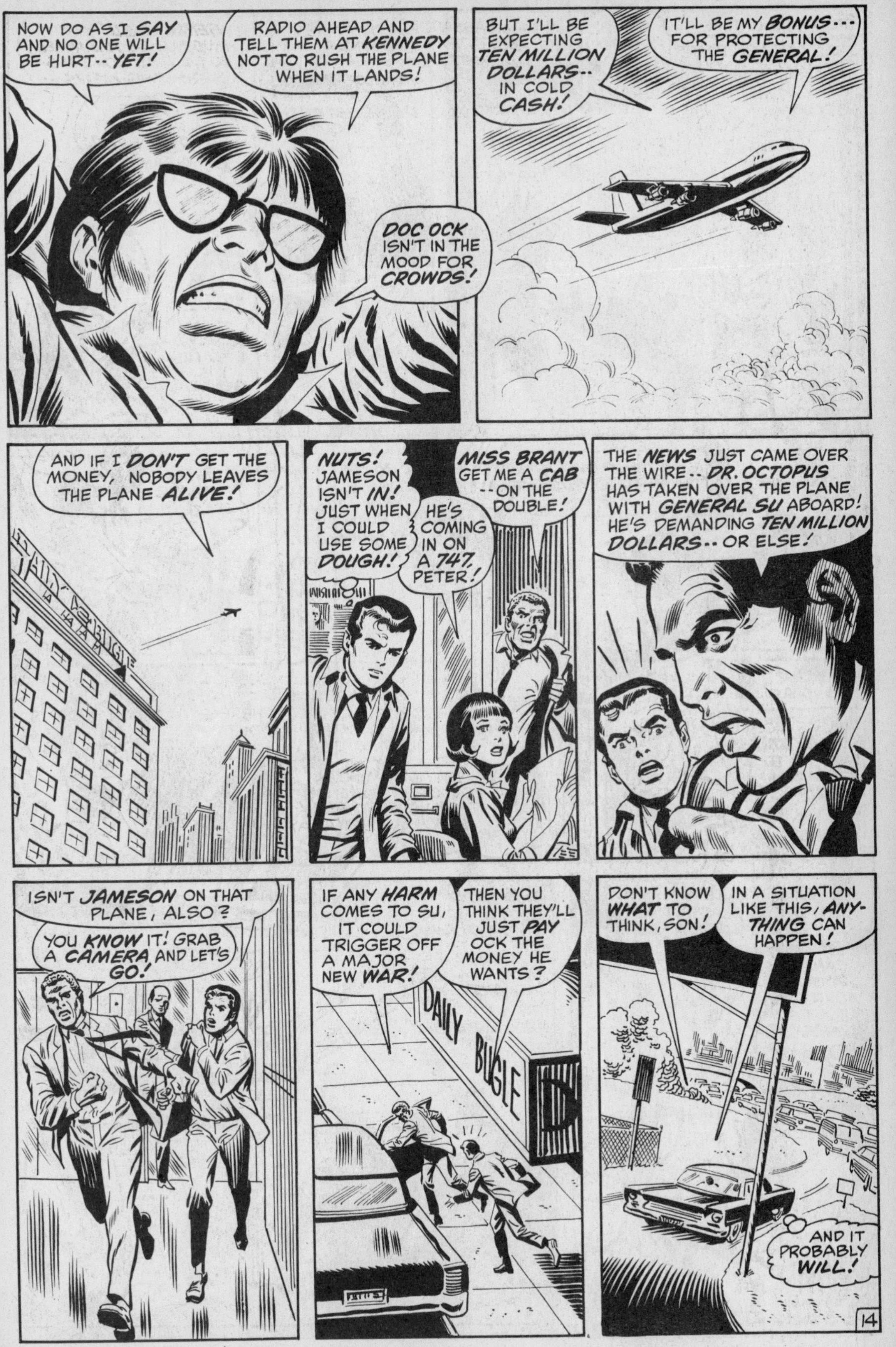
NOW DO AS I SAY AND NO ONE WILL BE HURT-- YET!
RADIO AHEAD AND TELL THEM AT KENNEDY NOT TO RUSH THE PLANE WHEN IT LANDS!
DOC OCK ISN'T IN THE MOOD FOR CROWDS!
BUT I'LL BE EXPECTING TEN MILLION DOLLARS-- IN COLD CASH!
IT'LL BE MY BONUS--- FOR PROTECTING THE GENERAL!
AND IF I DON'T GET THE MONEY, NOBODY LEAVES THE PLANE ALIVE!
NUTS! JAMESON ISN'T IN! JUST WHEN I COULD USE SOME DOUGH!
MISS BRANT GET ME A CAB --ON THE DOUBLE!
HE'S COMING IN ON A 747, PETER!
THE NEWS JUST CAME OVER THE WIRE-- DR. OCTOPUS HAS TAKEN OVER THE PLANE WITH GENERAL SU ABOARD! HE'S DEMANDING TEN MILLION DOLLARS-- OR ELSE!
ISN'T JAMESON ON THAT PLANE, ALSO?
YOU KNOW IT! GRAB A CAMERA, AND LET'S GO!
IF ANY HARM COMES TO SU, IT COULD TRIGGER OFF A MAJOR NEW WAR!
THEN YOU THINK THEY'LL JUST PAY OCK THE MONEY HE WANTS?
DAILY BUGLE
DON'T KNOW WHAT TO THINK, SON!
IN A SITUATION LIKE THIS, ANY-THING CAN HAPPEN!
AND IT PROBABLY WILL!
14

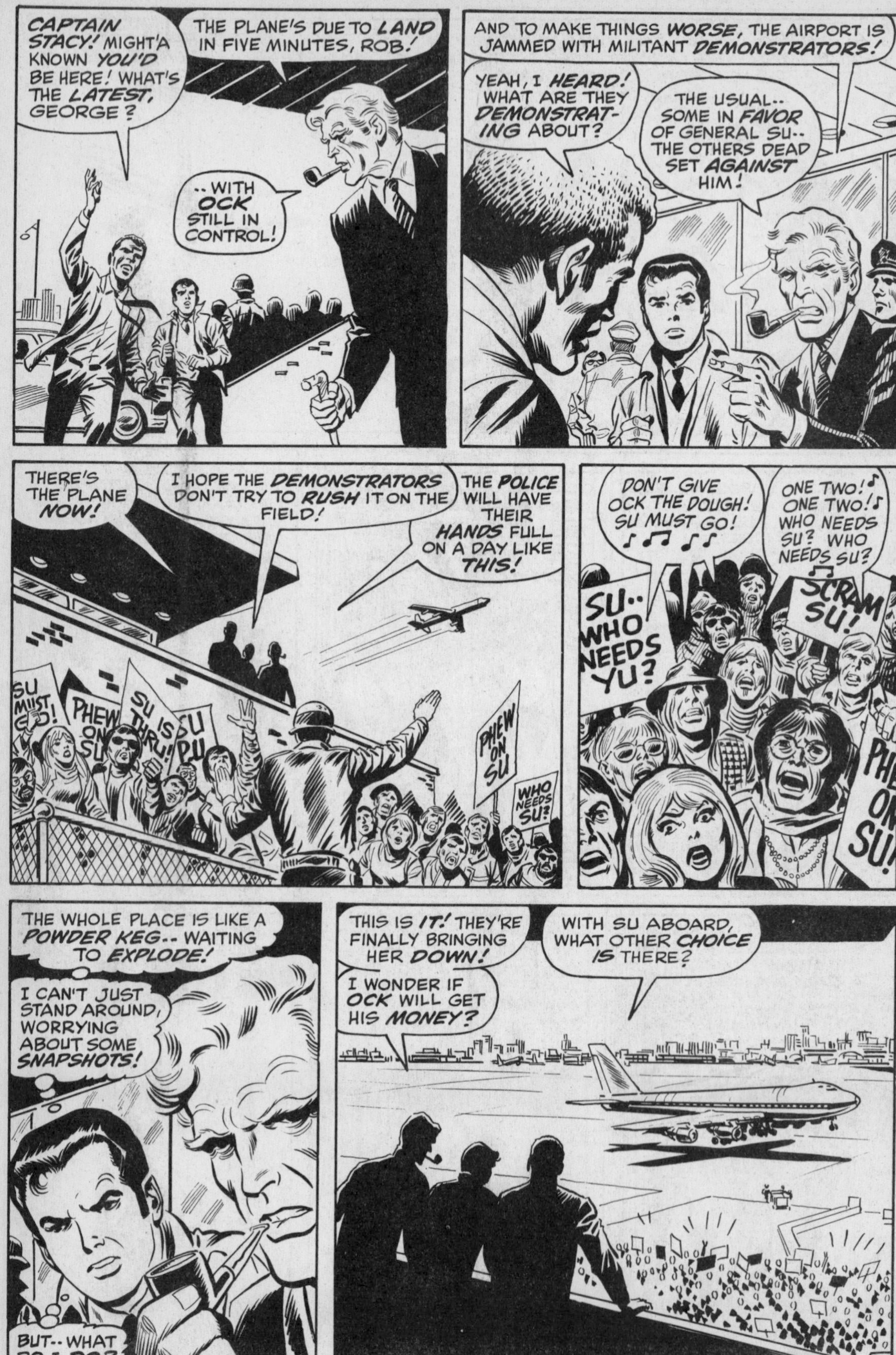

CAPTAIN STACY! MIGHT'A KNOWN YOU'D BE HERE! WHAT'S THE LATEST, GEORGE?
THE PLANE'S DUE TO LAND IN FIVE MINUTES, ROB!
..WITH OCK STILL IN CONTROL!
AND TO MAKE THINGS WORSE, THE AIRPORT IS JAMMED WITH MILITANT DEMONSTRATORS!
YEAH, I HEARD! WHAT ARE THEY DEMONSTRATING ABOUT?
THE USUAL.. SOME IN FAVOR OF GENERAL SU.. THE OTHERS DEAD SET AGAINST HIM!
THERE'S THE PLANE NOW!
I HOPE THE DEMONSTRATORS DON'T TRY TO RUSH IT ON THE FIELD!
THE POLICE WILL HAVE THEIR HANDS FULL ON A DAY LIKE THIS!
SU MUST GO!
PHEW ON SU
SU IS THRU!
SU P.U.
PHEW ON SU
WHO NEEDS SU?
DON'T GIVE OCK THE DOUGH! SU MUST GO!
ONE TWO! ONE TWO! WHO NEEDS SU? WHO NEEDS SU?
SU.. WHO NEEDS YU?
SCRAM SU!
PHEW ON SU!
THE WHOLE PLACE IS LIKE A POWDER KEG.. WAITING TO EXPLODE!
I CAN'T JUST STAND AROUND, WORRYING ABOUT SOME SNAPSHOTS!
BUT.. WHAT DO I DO?
THIS IS IT! THEY'RE FINALLY BRINGING HER DOWN!
I WONDER IF OCK WILL GET HIS MONEY?
WITH SU ABOARD, WHAT OTHER CHOICE IS THERE?

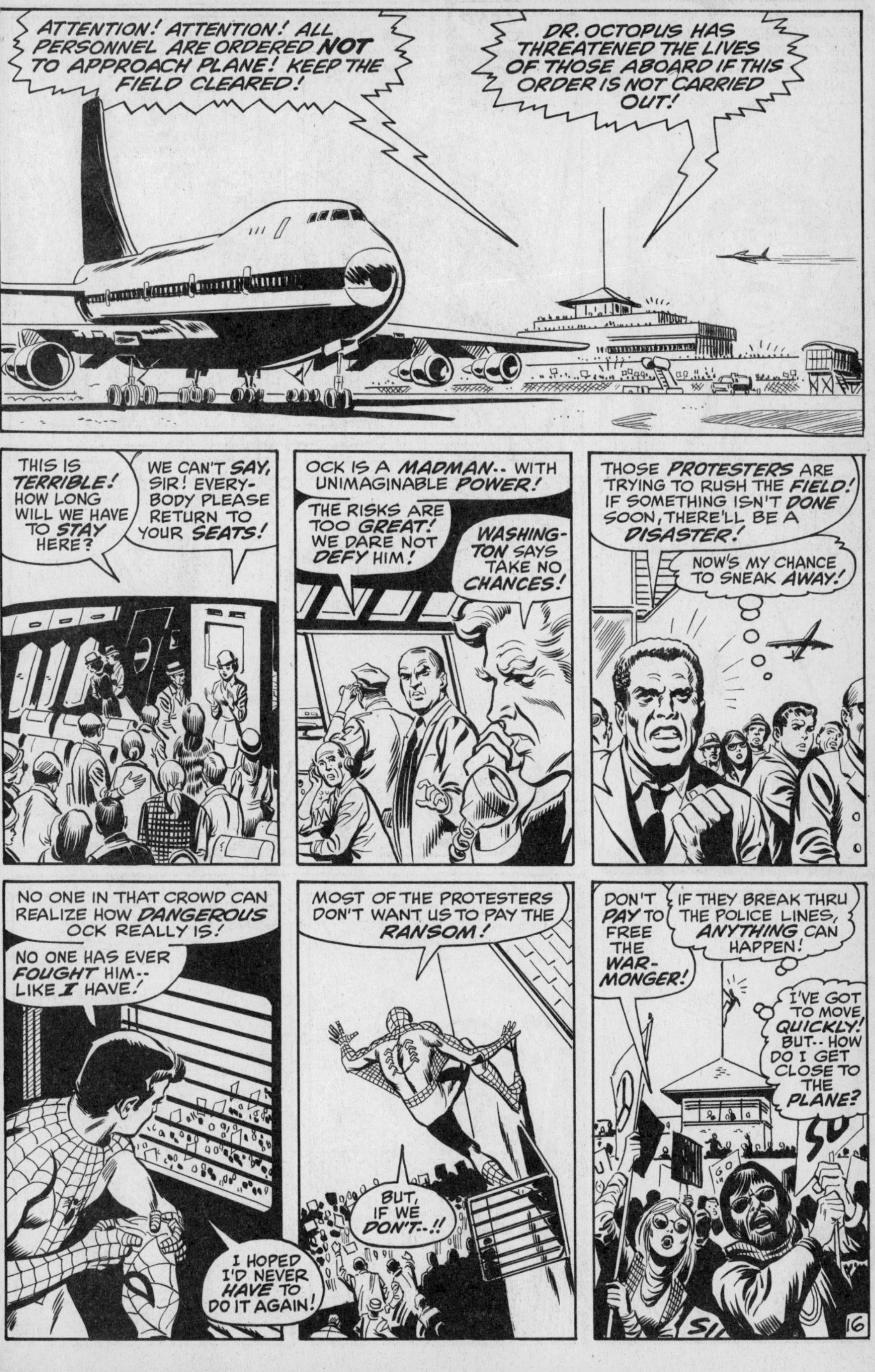

ATTENTION! ATTENTION! ALL PERSONNEL ARE ORDERED NOT TO APPROACH PLANE! KEEP THE FIELD CLEARED!
DR. OCTOPUS HAS THREATENED THE LIVES OF THOSE ABOARD IF THIS ORDER IS NOT CARRIED OUT!
THIS IS TERRIBLE! HOW LONG WILL WE HAVE TO STAY HERE?
WE CAN'T SAY, SIR! EVERYBODY PLEASE RETURN TO YOUR SEATS!
OCK IS A MADMAN.. WITH UNIMAGINABLE POWER!
THE RISKS ARE TOO GREAT! WE DARE NOT DEFY HIM!
WASHINGTON SAYS TAKE NO CHANCES!
THOSE PROTESTERS ARE TRYING TO RUSH THE FIELD! IF SOMETHING ISN'T DONE SOON, THERE'LL BE A DISASTER!
NOW'S MY CHANCE TO SNEAK AWAY!
NO ONE IN THAT CROWD CAN REALIZE HOW DANGEROUS OCK REALLY IS!
NO ONE HAS EVER FOUGHT HIM-- LIKE I HAVE.!
I HOPED I'D NEVER HAVE TO DO IT AGAIN!
MOST OF THE PROTESTERS DON'T WANT US TO PAY THE RANSOM!
BUT, IF WE DON'T..!!
DON'T PAY TO FREE THE WAR-MONGER!
IF THEY BREAK THRU THE POLICE LINES, ANYTHING CAN HAPPEN!
I'VE GOT TO MOVE QUICKLY! BUT.. HOW DO I GET CLOSE TO THE PLANE?

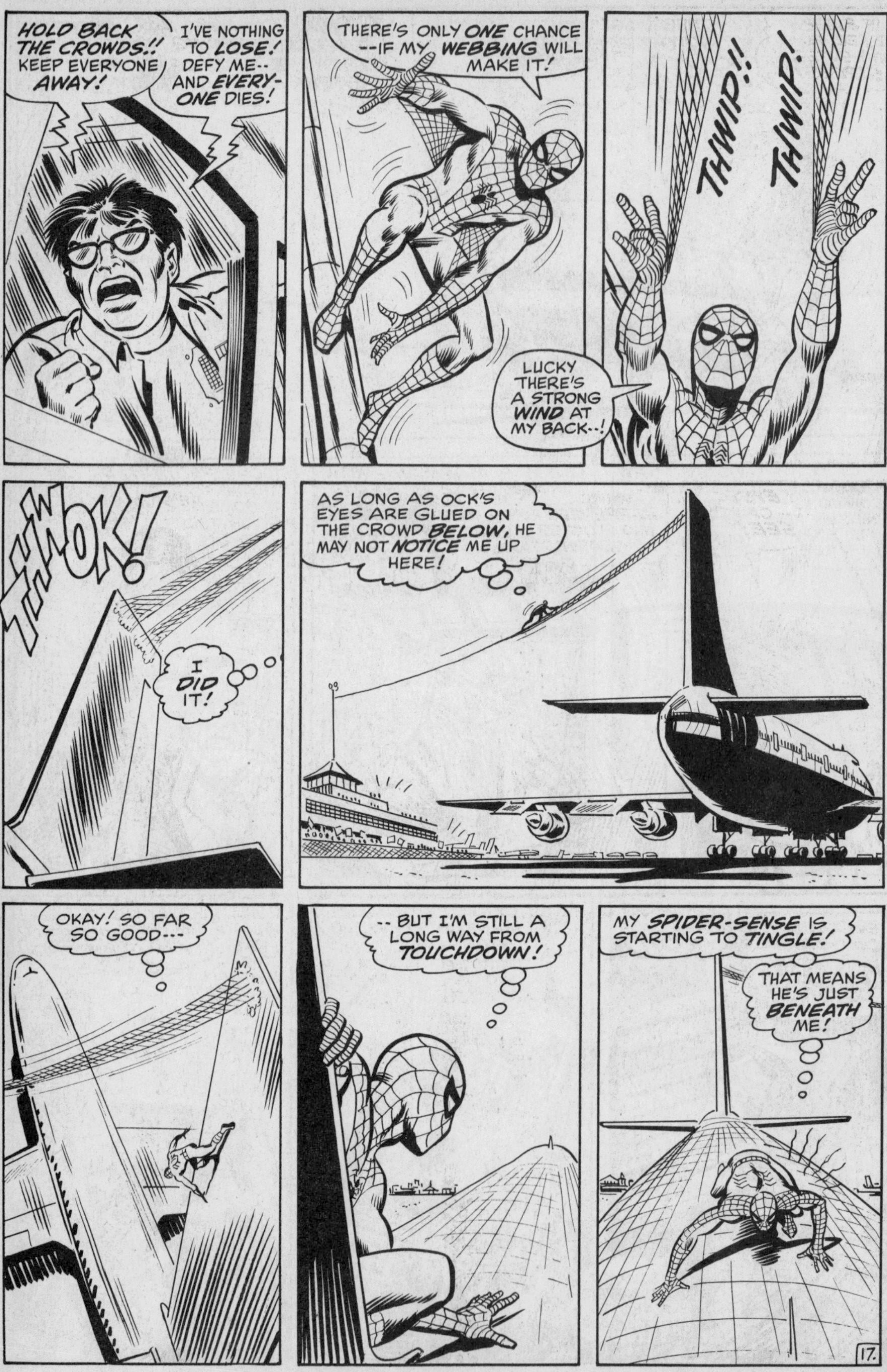
HOLD BACK THE CROWDS!! KEEP EVERYONE AWAY!
I'VE NOTHING TO LOSE! DEFY ME-- AND EVERYONE DIES!
THERE'S ONLY ONE CHANCE --IF MY WEBBING WILL MAKE IT!
THWIP!!
THWIP!
LUCKY THERE'S A STRONG WIND AT MY BACK--!
THWOK!
I DID IT!
AS LONG AS OCK'S EYES ARE GLUED ON THE CROWD BELOW, HE MAY NOT NOTICE ME UP HERE!
OKAY! SO FAR SO GOOD---
-- BUT I'M STILL A LONG WAY FROM TOUCHDOWN!
MY SPIDER-SENSE IS STARTING TO TINGLE!
THAT MEANS HE'S JUST BENEATH ME!

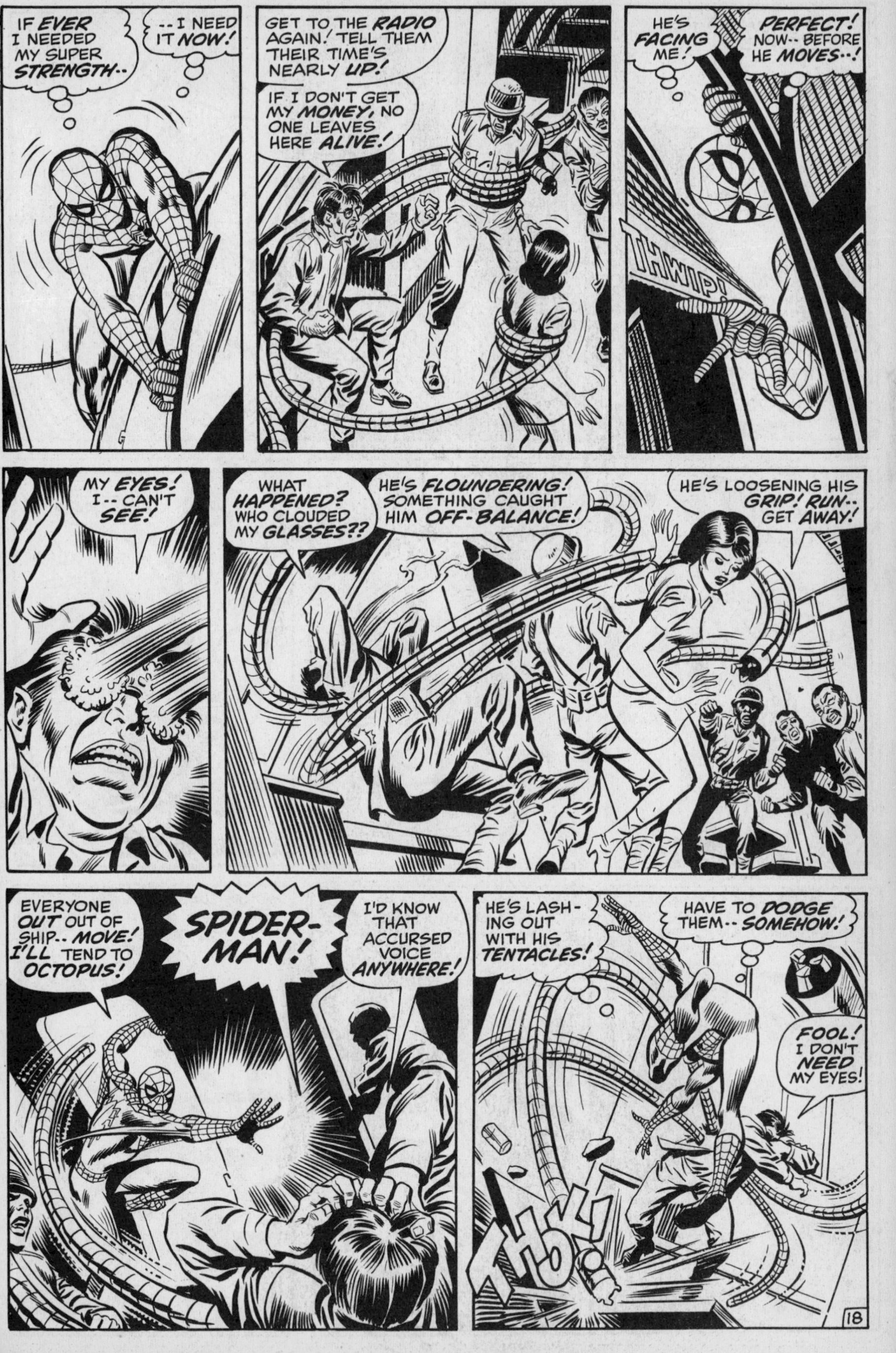

IF EVER I NEEDED MY SUPER STRENGTH--
--I NEED IT NOW!
GET TO THE RADIO AGAIN! TELL THEM THEIR TIME'S NEARLY UP!
IF I DON'T GET MY MONEY, NO ONE LEAVES HERE ALIVE!
HE'S FACING ME!
PERFECT! NOW-- BEFORE HE MOVES--!
THWIP!
MY EYES! I-- CAN'T SEE!
WHAT HAPPENED? WHO CLOUDED MY GLASSES??
HE'S FLOUNDERING! SOMETHING CAUGHT HIM OFF-BALANCE!
HE'S LOOSENING HIS GRIP! RUN-- GET AWAY!
EVERYONE OUT OUT OF SHIP-- MOVE! I'LL TEND TO OCTOPUS!
SPIDER-MAN!
I'D KNOW THAT ACCURSED VOICE ANYWHERE!
HE'S LASHING OUT WITH HIS TENTACLES!
HAVE TO DODGE THEM-- SOMEHOW!
FOOL! I DON'T NEED MY EYES!
WHOK!
18

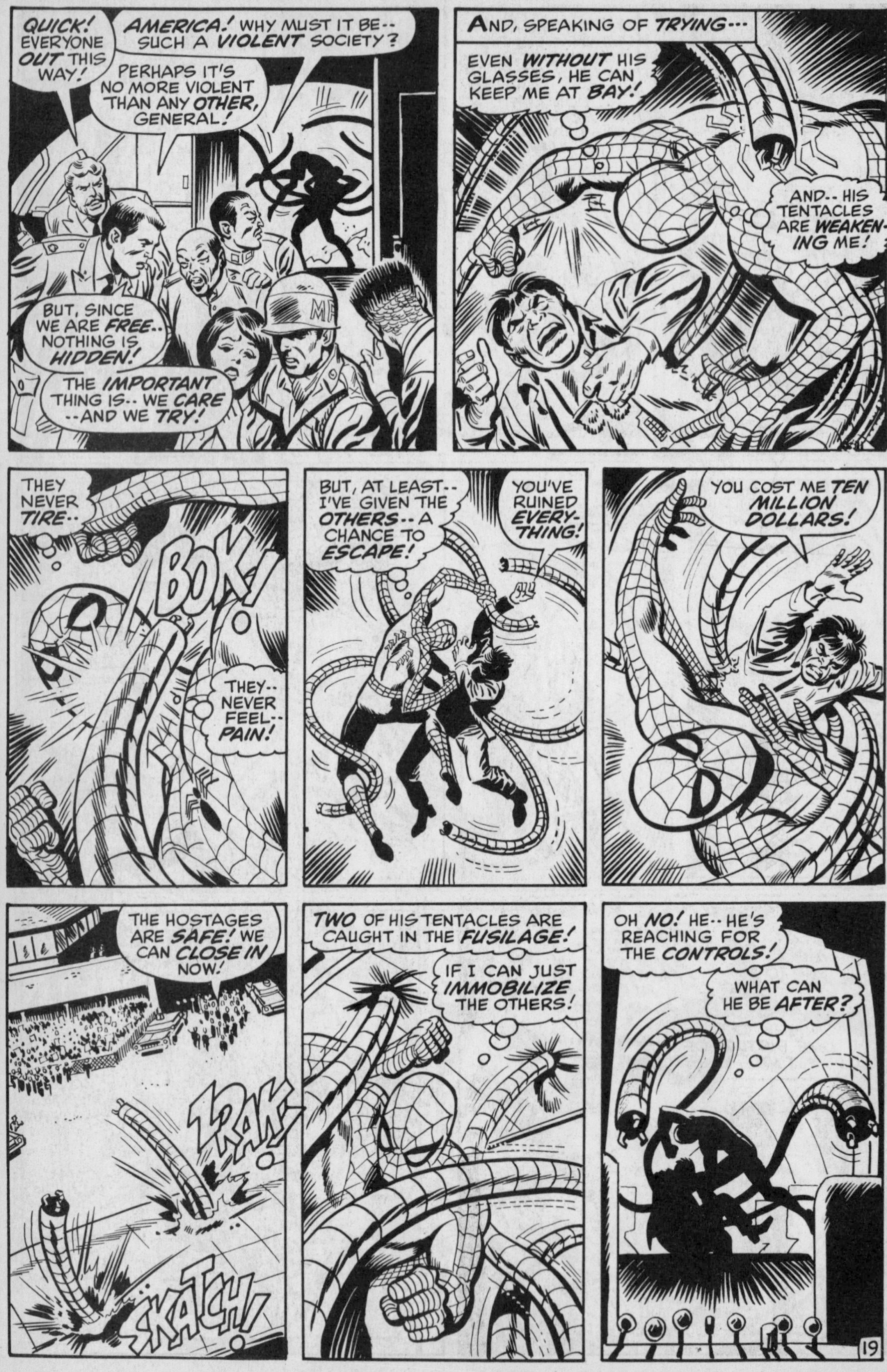
QUICK! EVERYONE OUT THIS WAY!
AMERICA! WHY MUST IT BE-- SUCH A VIOLENT SOCIETY?
PERHAPS IT'S NO MORE VIOLENT THAN ANY OTHER, GENERAL!
BUT, SINCE WE ARE FREE.. NOTHING IS HIDDEN!
THE IMPORTANT THING IS-- WE CARE --AND WE TRY!
AND, SPEAKING OF TRYING---
EVEN WITHOUT HIS GLASSES, HE CAN KEEP ME AT BAY!
AND-- HIS TENTACLES ARE WEAKEN-ING ME!
THEY NEVER TIRE--
BOK!
THEY-- NEVER FEEL-- PAIN!
BUT, AT LEAST-- I'VE GIVEN THE OTHERS-- A CHANCE TO ESCAPE!
YOU'VE RUINED EVERY-THING!
YOU COST ME TEN MILLION DOLLARS!
THE HOSTAGES ARE SAFE! WE CAN CLOSE IN NOW!
TRAK
SKATCH!
TWO OF HIS TENTACLES ARE CAUGHT IN THE FUSILAGE!
IF I CAN JUST IMMOBILIZE THE OTHERS!
OH NO! HE-- HE'S REACHING FOR THE CONTROLS!
WHAT CAN HE BE AFTER?

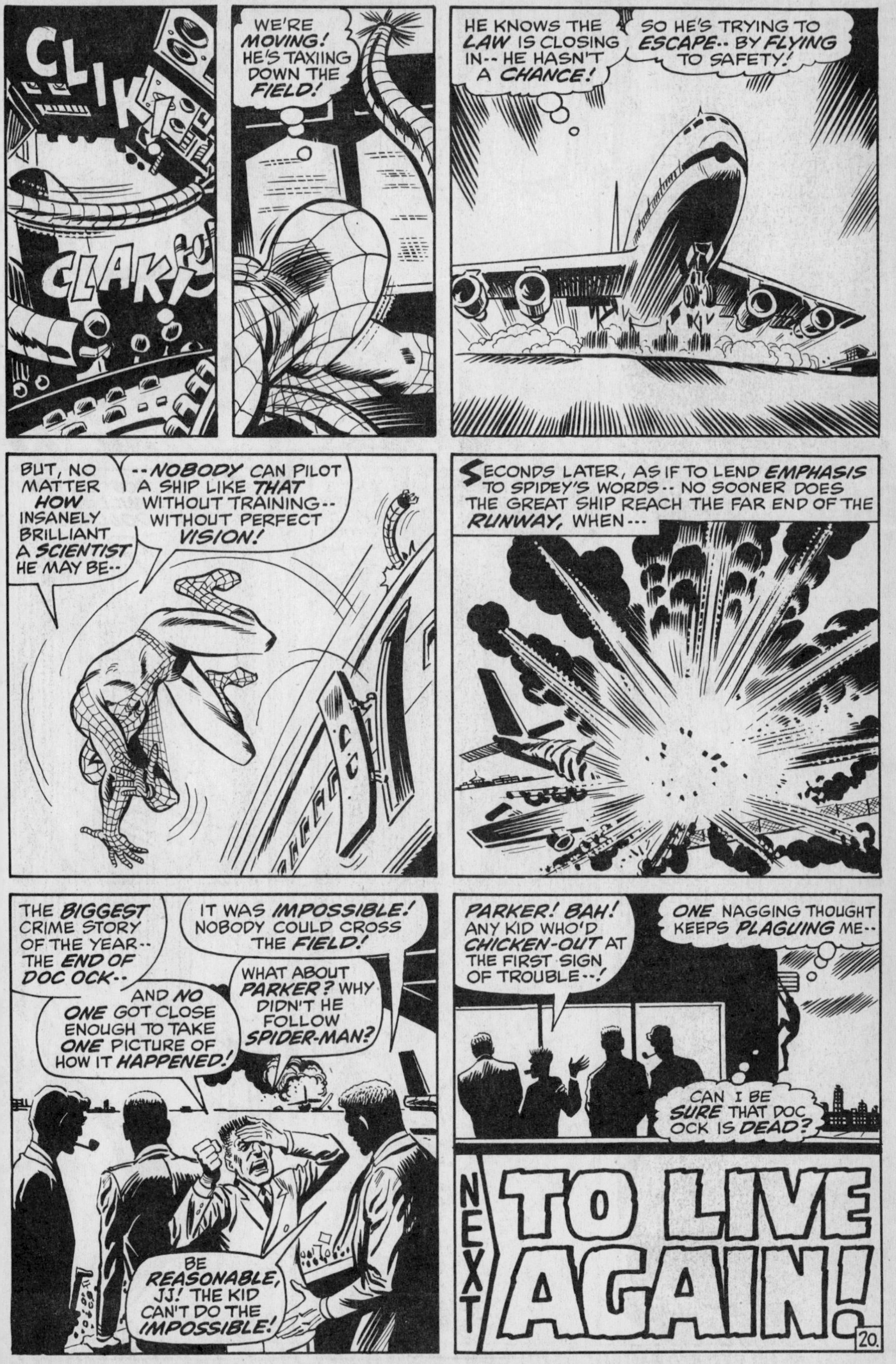
CLIK!
CLAK!
WE'RE MOVING! HE'S TAXIING DOWN THE FIELD!
HE KNOWS THE LAW IS CLOSING IN-- HE HASN'T A CHANCE!
SO HE'S TRYING TO ESCAPE-- BY FLYING TO SAFETY!
BUT, NO MATTER HOW INSANELY BRILLIANT A SCIENTIST HE MAY BE--
--NOBODY CAN PILOT A SHIP LIKE THAT WITHOUT TRAINING-- WITHOUT PERFECT VISION!
SECONDS LATER, AS IF TO LEND EMPHASIS TO SPIDEY'S WORDS-- NO SOONER DOES THE GREAT SHIP REACH THE FAR END OF THE RUNWAY, WHEN---
THE BIGGEST CRIME STORY OF THE YEAR-- THE END OF DOC OCK--
IT WAS IMPOSSIBLE! NOBODY COULD CROSS THE FIELD!
AND NO ONE GOT CLOSE ENOUGH TO TAKE ONE PICTURE OF HOW IT HAPPENED!
WHAT ABOUT PARKER? WHY DIDN'T HE FOLLOW SPIDER-MAN?
BE REASONABLE, JJ! THE KID CAN'T DO THE IMPOSSIBLE!
PARKER! BAH! ANY KID WHO'D CHICKEN-OUT AT THE FIRST SIGN OF TROUBLE--!
ONE NAGGING THOUGHT KEEPS PLAGUING ME--
CAN I BE SURE THAT DOC OCK IS DEAD?
NEXT
TO LIVE AGAIN!
20.

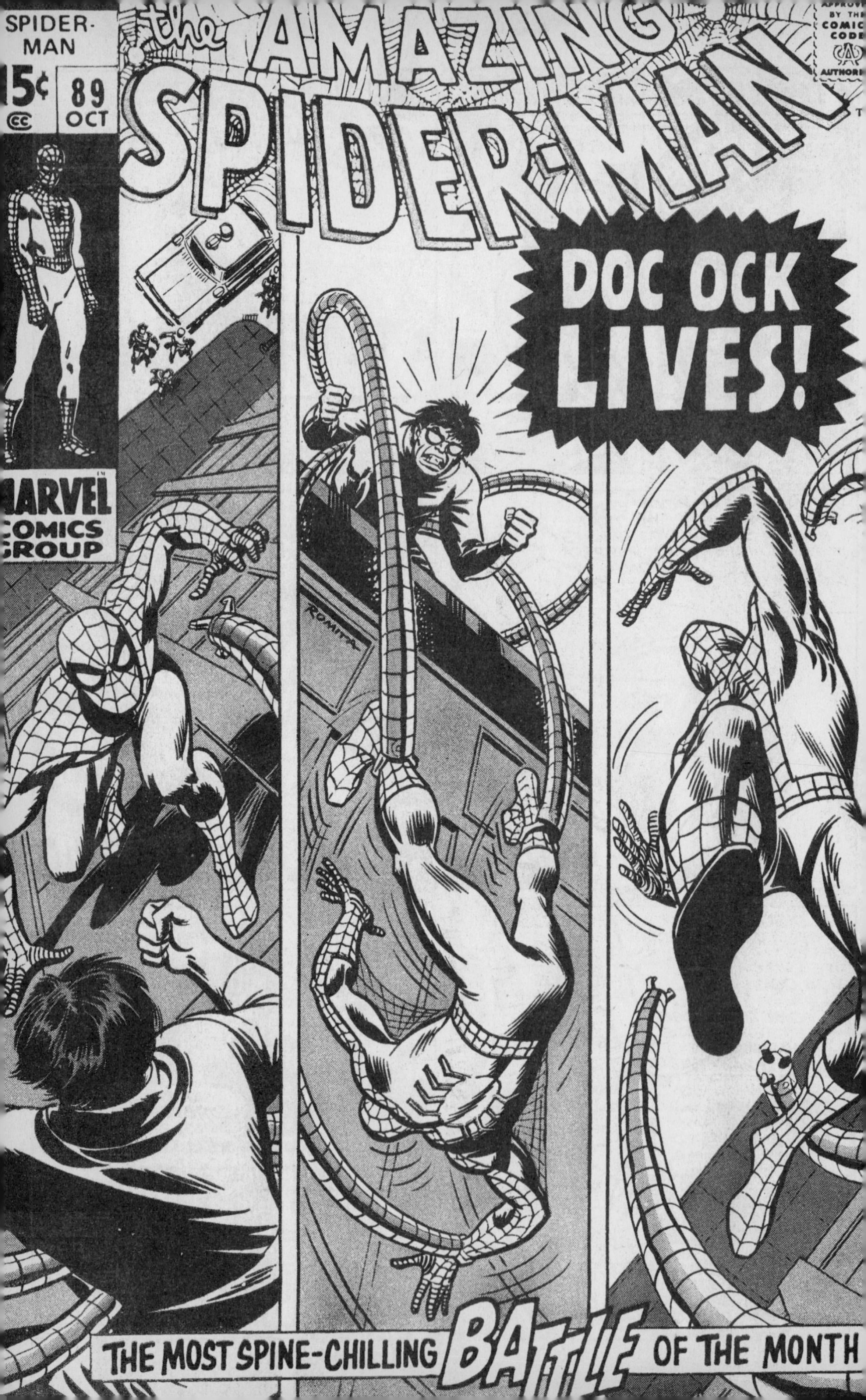

SPIDER-MAN
15¢
89
OCT
the AMAZING SPIDER-MAN
DOC OCK LIVES!
ROMITA
THE MOST SPINE-CHILLING BATTLE OF THE MONTH

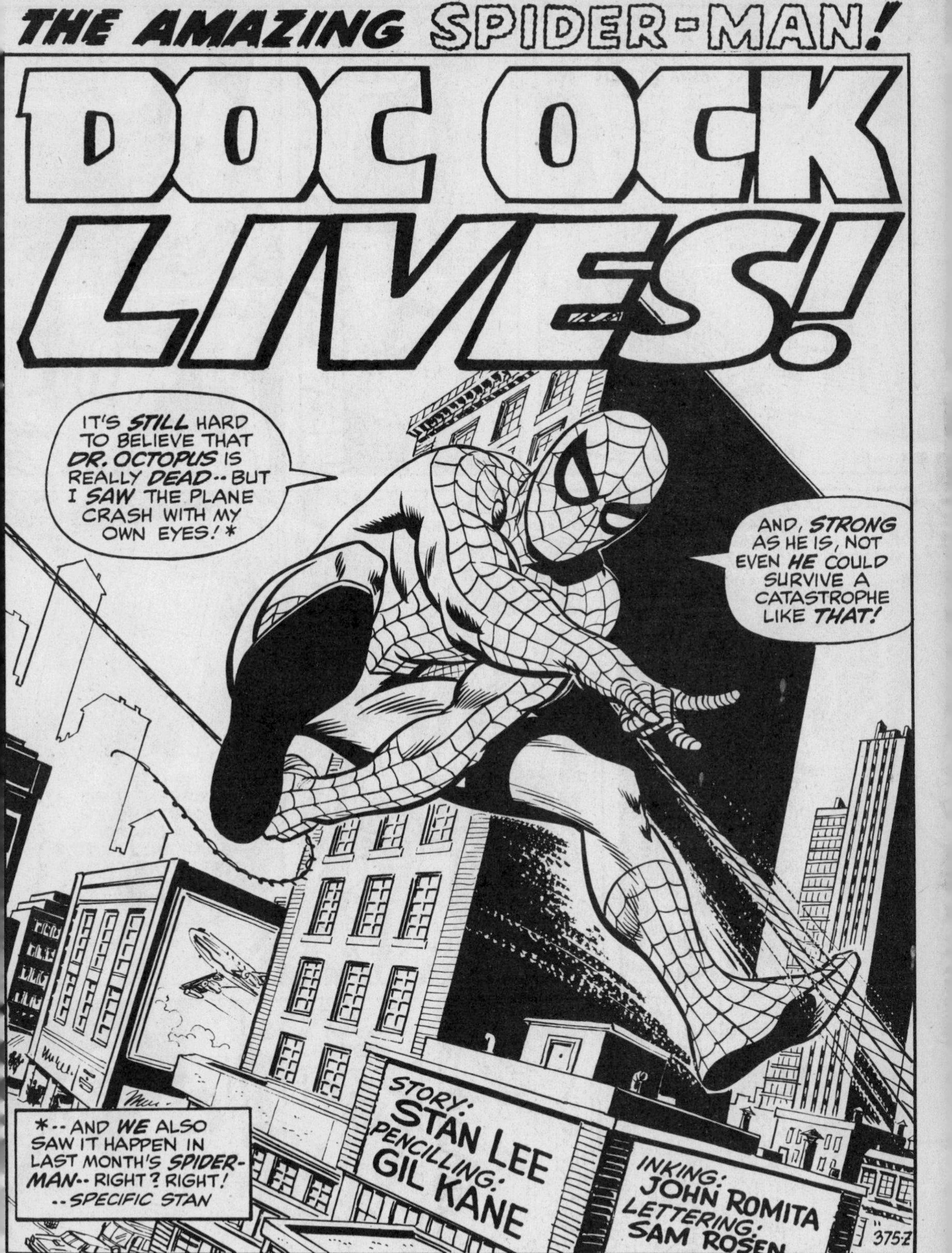
THE AMAZING SPIDER-MAN!
DOC OCK LIVES!
IT'S STILL HARD TO BELIEVE THAT DR. OCTOPUS IS REALLY DEAD-- BUT I SAW THE PLANE CRASH WITH MY OWN EYES! *
AND, STRONG AS HE IS, NOT EVEN HE COULD SURVIVE A CATASTROPHE LIKE THAT!
* -- AND WE ALSO SAW IT HAPPEN IN LAST MONTH'S SPIDER-MAN-- RIGHT? RIGHT! --SPECIFIC STAN
STORY: STAN LEE PENCILLING: GIL KANE
INKING: JOHN ROMITA LETTERING: SAM ROSEN
375-2

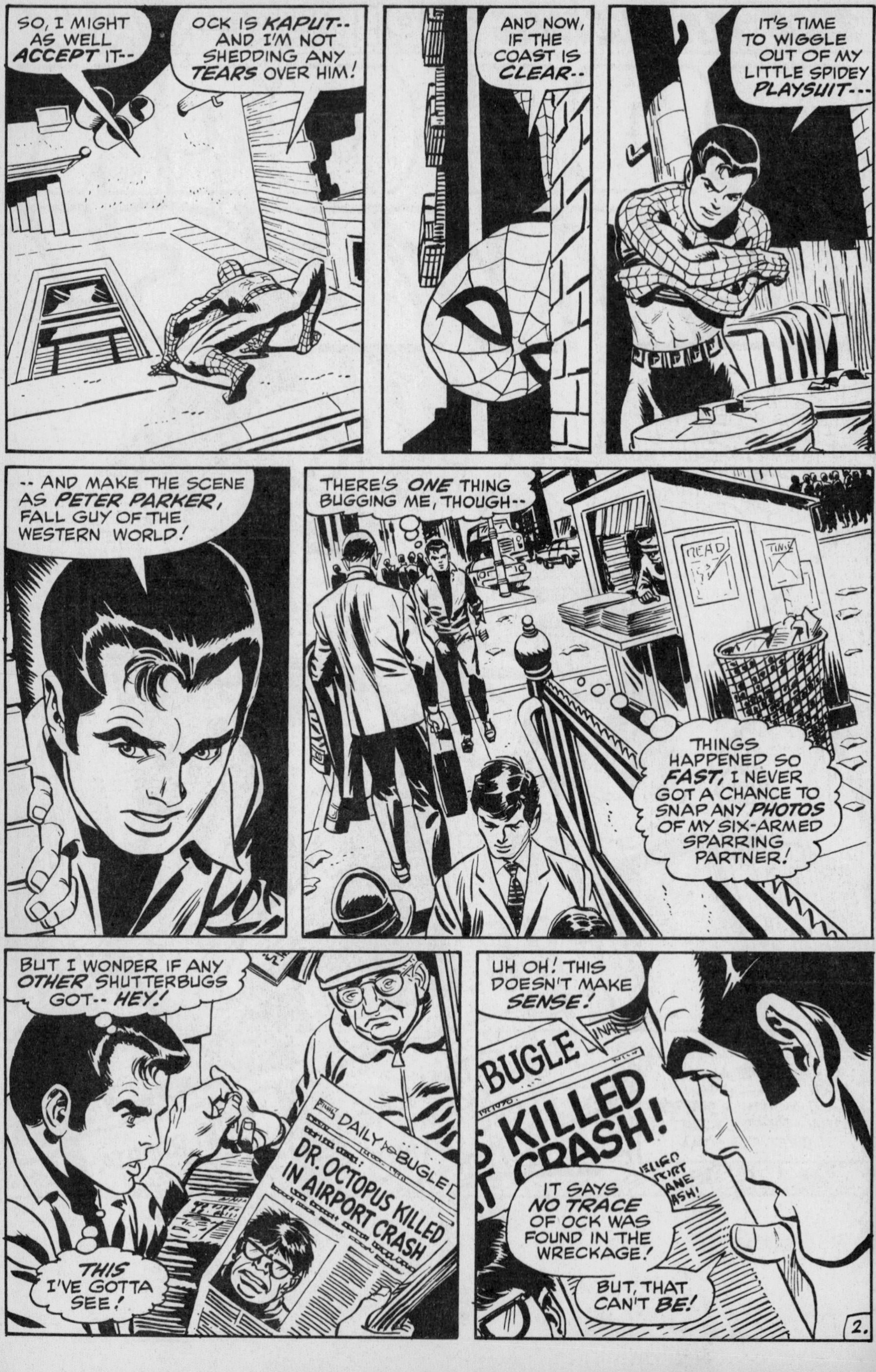

SO, I MIGHT AS WELL ACCEPT IT--
OCK IS KAPUT-- AND I'M NOT SHEDDING ANY TEARS OVER HIM!
AND NOW, IF THE COAST IS CLEAR--
IT'S TIME TO WIGGLE OUT OF MY LITTLE SPIDEY PLAYSUIT---
-- AND MAKE THE SCENE AS PETER PARKER, FALL GUY OF THE WESTERN WORLD!
THERE'S ONE THING BUGGING ME, THOUGH--
THINGS HAPPENED SO FAST, I NEVER GOT A CHANCE TO SNAP ANY PHOTOS OF MY SIX-ARMED SPARRING PARTNER!
BUT I WONDER IF ANY OTHER SHUTTERBUGS GOT-- HEY!
DAILY BUGLE
DR. OCTOPUS KILLED IN AIRPORT CRASH
THIS I'VE GOTTA SEE!
UH OH! THIS DOESN'T MAKE SENSE!
BUGLE
KILLED
CRASH!
IT SAYS NO TRACE OF OCK WAS FOUND IN THE WRECKAGE!
BUT, THAT CAN'T BE!
2.

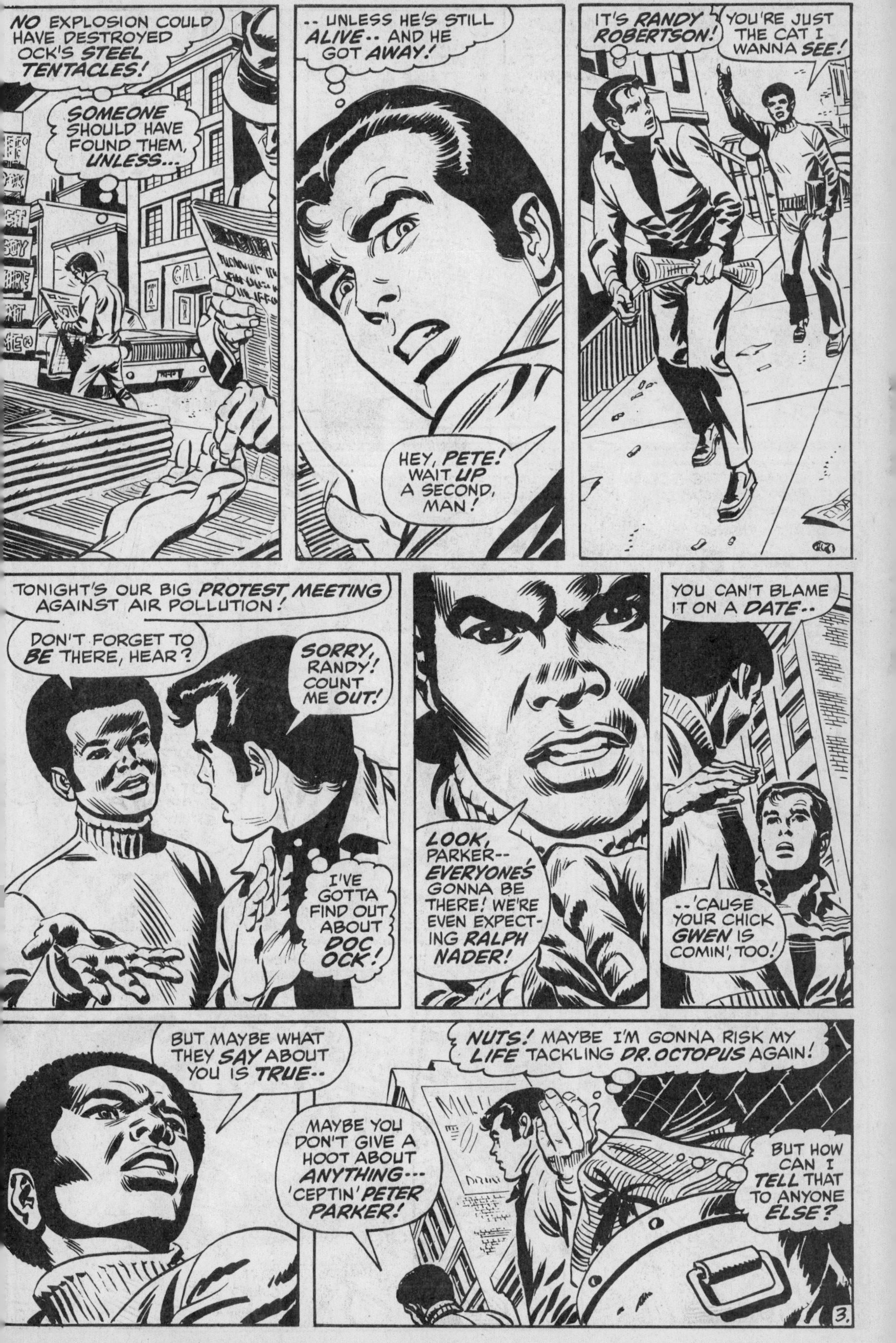
NO EXPLOSION COULD HAVE DESTROYED OCK'S STEEL TENTACLES!
SOMEONE SHOULD HAVE FOUND THEM, UNLESS...
-- UNLESS HE'S STILL ALIVE -- AND HE GOT AWAY!
HEY, PETE! WAIT UP A SECOND, MAN!
IT'S RANDY ROBERTSON!
YOU'RE JUST THE CAT I WANNA SEE!
TONIGHT'S OUR BIG PROTEST MEETING AGAINST AIR POLLUTION!
DON'T FORGET TO BE THERE, HEAR?
SORRY, RANDY! COUNT ME OUT!
I'VE GOTTA FIND OUT ABOUT DOC OCK!
LOOK, PARKER-- EVERYONE'S GONNA BE THERE! WE'RE EVEN EXPECTING RALPH NADER!
YOU CAN'T BLAME IT ON A DATE--
--'CAUSE YOUR CHICK GWEN IS COMIN', TOO!
BUT MAYBE WHAT THEY SAY ABOUT YOU IS TRUE--
MAYBE YOU DON'T GIVE A HOOT ABOUT ANYTHING--- 'CEPTIN' PETER PARKER!
NUTS! MAYBE I'M GONNA RISK MY LIFE TACKLING DR. OCTOPUS AGAIN!
BUT HOW CAN I TELL THAT TO ANYONE ELSE?
3.

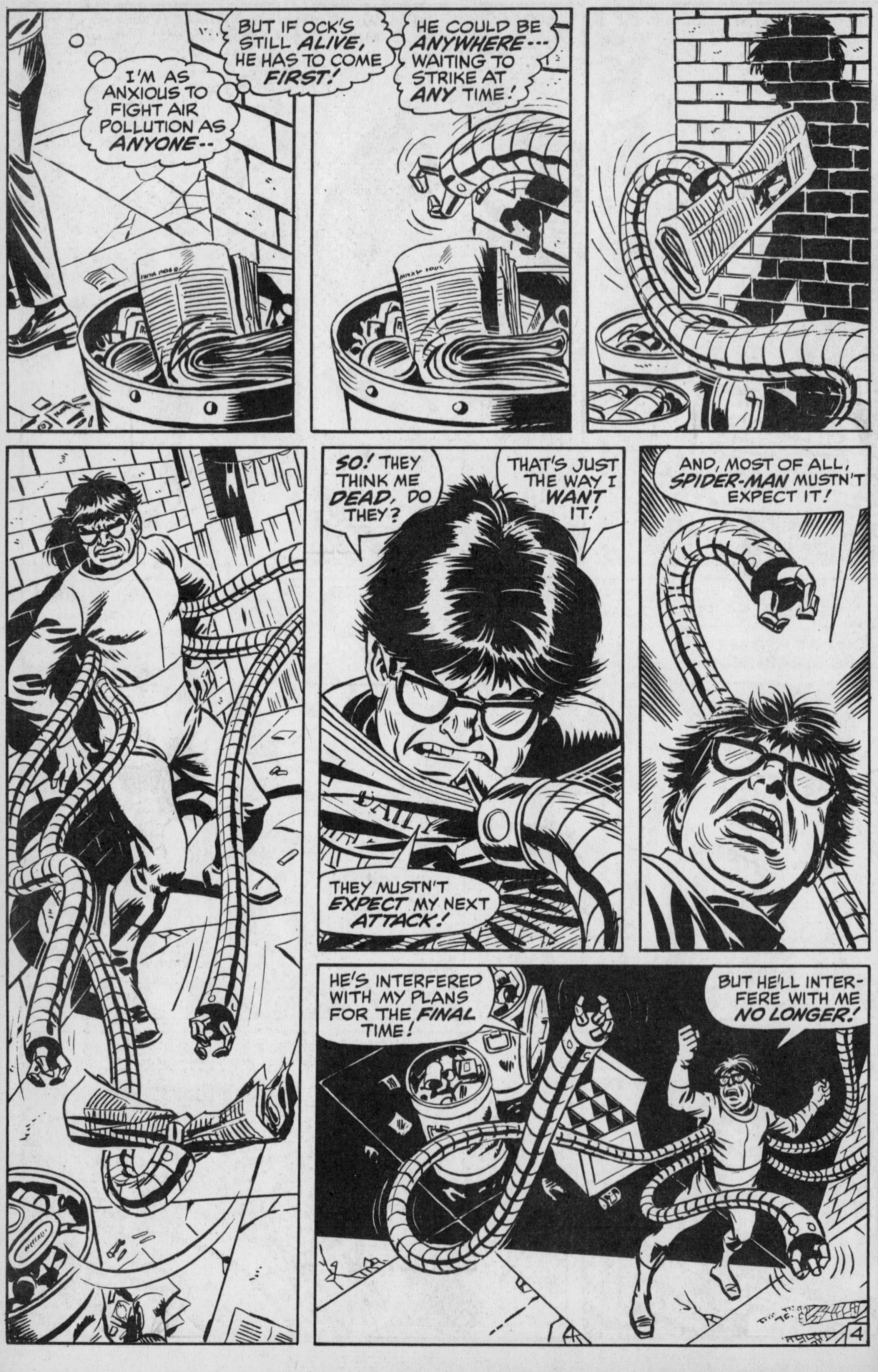

I'M AS ANXIOUS TO FIGHT AIR POLLUTION AS ANYONE--
BUT IF OCK'S STILL ALIVE, HE HAS TO COME FIRST!
HE COULD BE ANYWHERE--- WAITING TO STRIKE AT ANY TIME!
SO! THEY THINK ME DEAD, DO THEY?
THAT'S JUST THE WAY I WANT IT!
THEY MUSTN'T EXPECT MY NEXT ATTACK!
AND, MOST OF ALL, SPIDER-MAN MUSTN'T EXPECT IT!
HE'S INTERFERED WITH MY PLANS FOR THE FINAL TIME!
BUT HE'LL INTERFERE WITH ME NO LONGER!
4

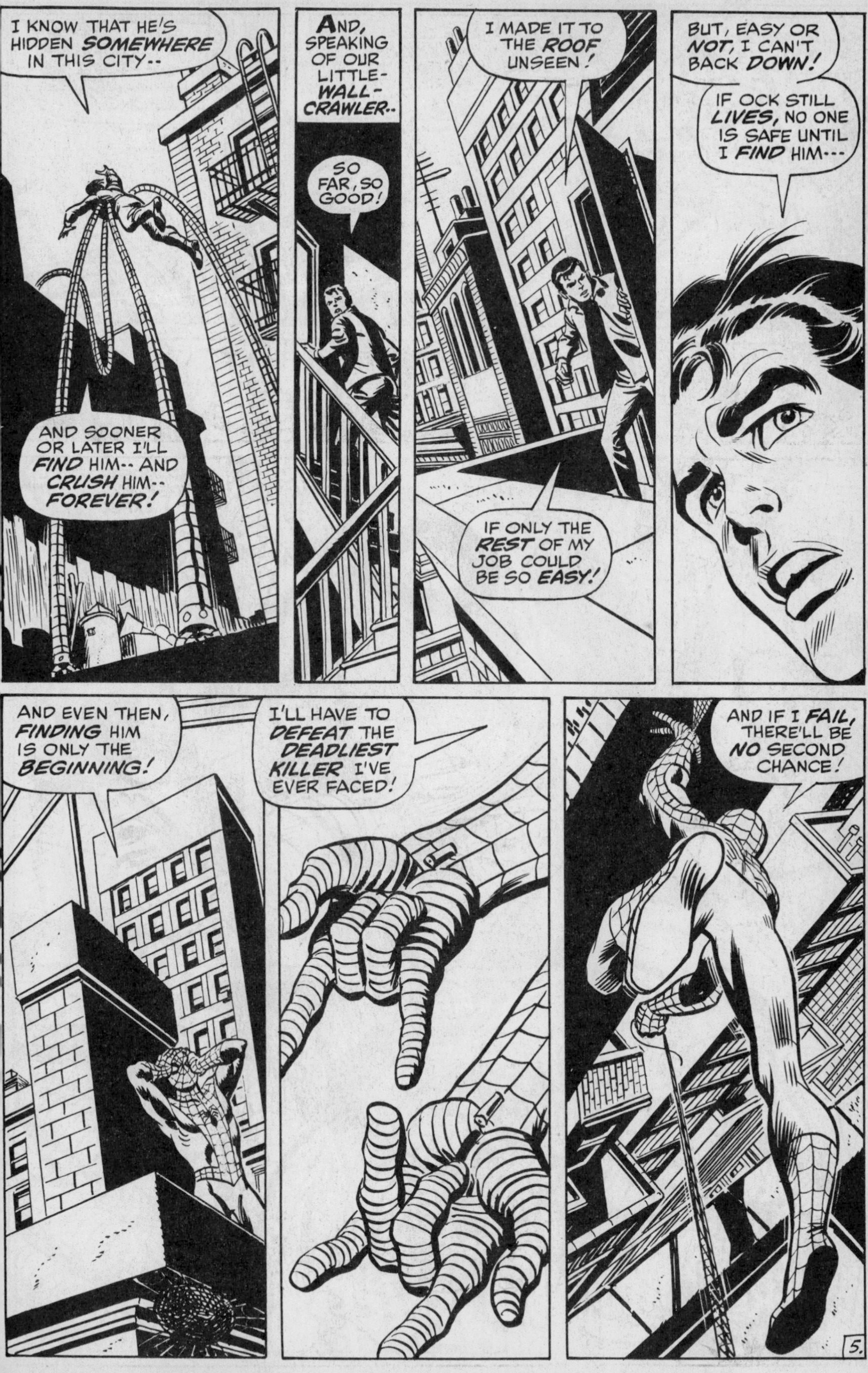

I KNOW THAT HE'S HIDDEN SOMEWHERE IN THIS CITY--
AND SOONER OR LATER I'LL FIND HIM-- AND CRUSH HIM-- FOREVER!
AND, SPEAKING OF OUR LITTLE- WALL-CRAWLER--
SO FAR, SO GOOD!
I MADE IT TO THE ROOF UNSEEN!
IF ONLY THE REST OF MY JOB COULD BE SO EASY!
BUT, EASY OR NOT, I CAN'T BACK DOWN!
IF OCK STILL LIVES, NO ONE IS SAFE UNTIL I FIND HIM---
AND EVEN THEN, FINDING HIM IS ONLY THE BEGINNING!
I'LL HAVE TO DEFEAT THE DEADLIEST KILLER I'VE EVER FACED!
AND IF I FAIL, THERE'LL BE NO SECOND CHANCE!
5.

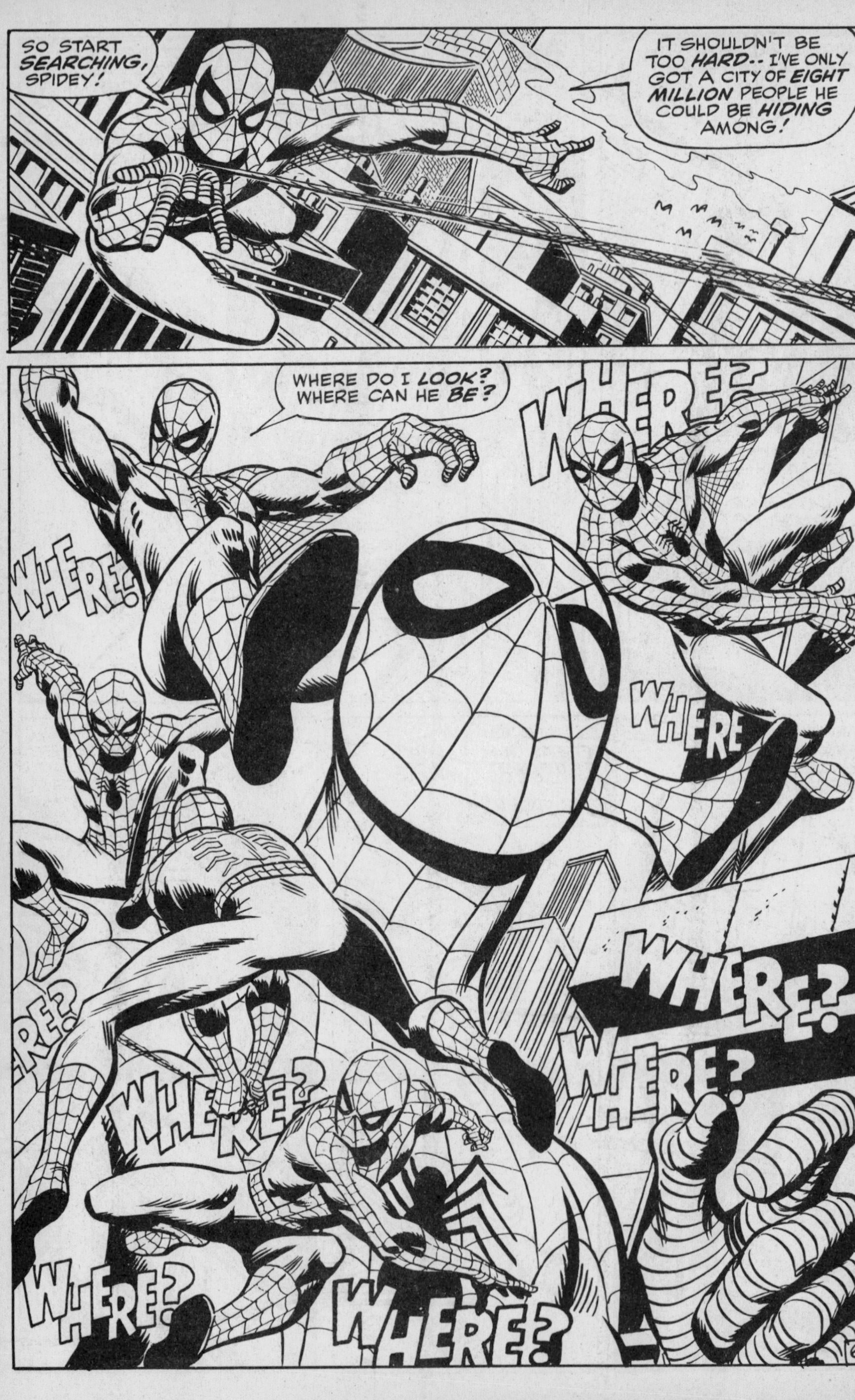

SO START SEARCHING, SPIDEY!
IT SHOULDN'T BE TOO HARD-- I'VE ONLY GOT A CITY OF EIGHT MILLION PEOPLE HE COULD BE HIDING AMONG!
WHERE DO I LOOK? WHERE CAN HE BE?
WHERE?
WHERE?
WHERE
WHERE?
WHERE?
WHERE?
WHERE?
WHERE?

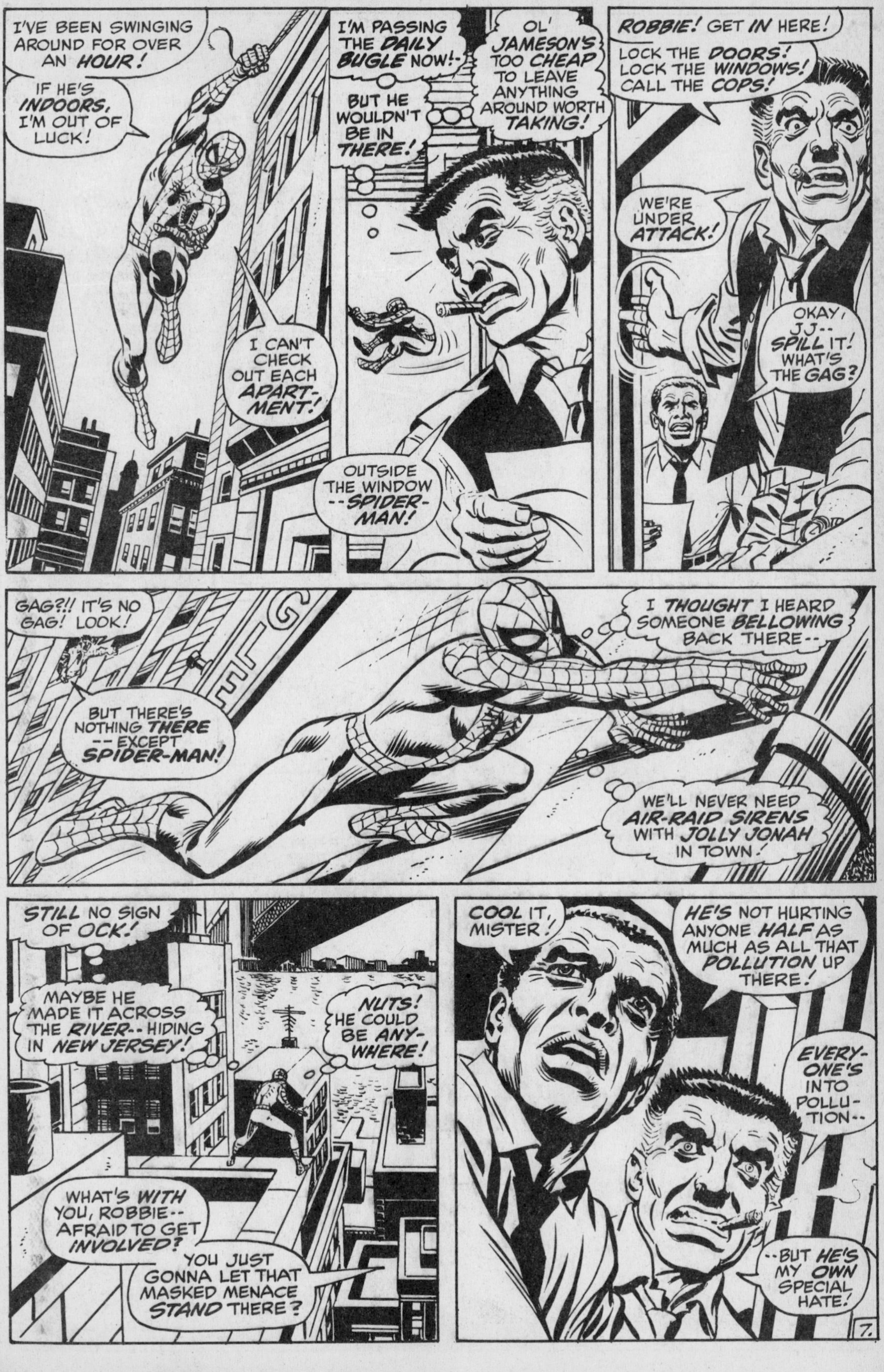
I'VE BEEN SWINGING AROUND FOR OVER AN HOUR!
IF HE'S INDOORS, I'M OUT OF LUCK!
I CAN'T CHECK OUT EACH APARTMENT!
I'M PASSING THE DAILY BUGLE NOW!-
BUT HE WOULDN'T BE IN THERE!
OL' JAMESON'S TOO CHEAP TO LEAVE ANYTHING AROUND WORTH TAKING!
OUTSIDE THE WINDOW --SPIDER-MAN!
ROBBIE! GET IN HERE!
LOCK THE DOORS! LOCK THE WINDOWS! CALL THE COPS!
WE'RE UNDER ATTACK!
OKAY, JJ-- SPILL IT! WHAT'S THE GAG?
GAG?!! IT'S NO GAG! LOOK!
BUT THERE'S NOTHING THERE -- EXCEPT SPIDER-MAN!
I THOUGHT I HEARD SOMEONE BELLOWING BACK THERE--
WE'LL NEVER NEED AIR-RAID SIRENS WITH JOLLY JONAH IN TOWN!
STILL NO SIGN OF OCK!
MAYBE HE MADE IT ACROSS THE RIVER-- HIDING IN NEW JERSEY!
NUTS! HE COULD BE ANYWHERE!
WHAT'S WITH YOU, ROBBIE-- AFRAID TO GET INVOLVED?
YOU JUST GONNA LET THAT MASKED MENACE STAND THERE?
COOL IT, MISTER!
HE'S NOT HURTING ANYONE HALF AS MUCH AS ALL THAT POLLUTION UP THERE!
EVERYONE'S INTO POLLUTION--
--BUT HE'S MY OWN SPECIAL HATE!
7.

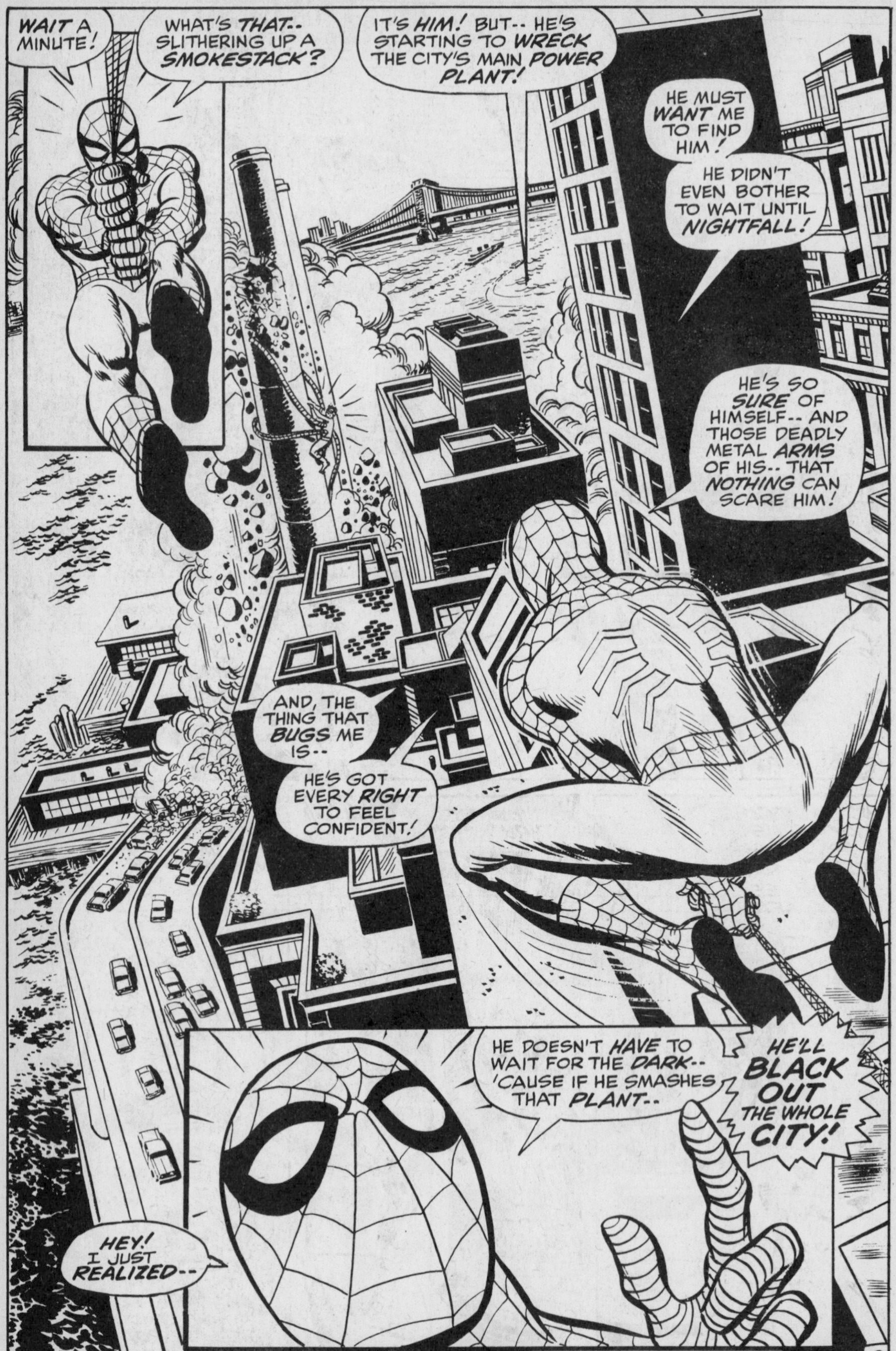

WAIT A MINUTE!
WHAT'S THAT-- SLITHERING UP A SMOKESTACK?
IT'S HIM! BUT-- HE'S STARTING TO WRECK THE CITY'S MAIN POWER PLANT!
HE MUST WANT ME TO FIND HIM!
HE DIDN'T EVEN BOTHER TO WAIT UNTIL NIGHTFALL!
HE'S SO SURE OF HIMSELF-- AND THOSE DEADLY METAL ARMS OF HIS-- THAT NOTHING CAN SCARE HIM!
AND, THE THING THAT BUGS ME IS--
HE'S GOT EVERY RIGHT TO FEEL CONFIDENT!
HEY! I JUST REALIZED--
HE DOESN'T HAVE TO WAIT FOR THE DARK-- 'CAUSE IF HE SMASHES THAT PLANT--
HE'LL BLACK OUT THE WHOLE CITY!

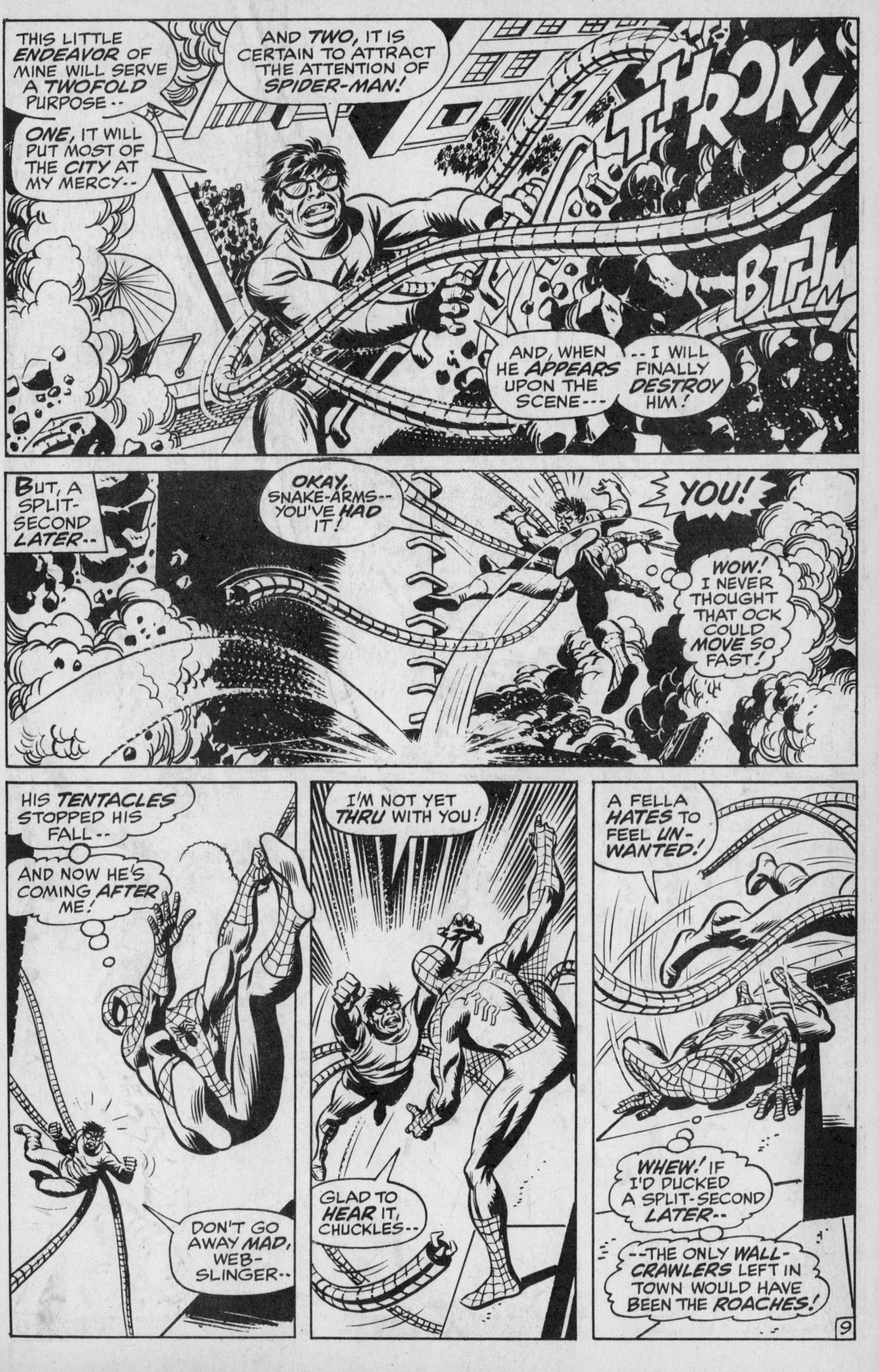
THIS LITTLE ENDEAVOR OF MINE WILL SERVE A TWOFOLD PURPOSE--
ONE, IT WILL PUT MOST OF THE CITY AT MY MERCY--
AND TWO, IT IS CERTAIN TO ATTRACT THE ATTENTION OF SPIDER-MAN!
THROK!
BTHM
AND, WHEN HE APPEARS UPON THE SCENE---
--I WILL FINALLY DESTROY HIM!
BUT, A SPLIT-SECOND LATER--
OKAY. SNAKE-ARMS-- YOU'VE HAD IT!
YOU!
WOW! I NEVER THOUGHT THAT OCK COULD MOVE SO FAST!
HIS TENTACLES STOPPED HIS FALL--
AND NOW HE'S COMING AFTER ME!
DON'T GO AWAY MAD, WEB-SLINGER--
I'M NOT YET THRU WITH YOU!
GLAD TO HEAR IT, CHUCKLES--
A FELLA HATES TO FEEL UN-WANTED!
WHEW! IF I'D DUCKED A SPLIT-SECOND LATER--
--THE ONLY WALL-CRAWLERS LEFT IN TOWN WOULD HAVE BEEN THE ROACHES!
9

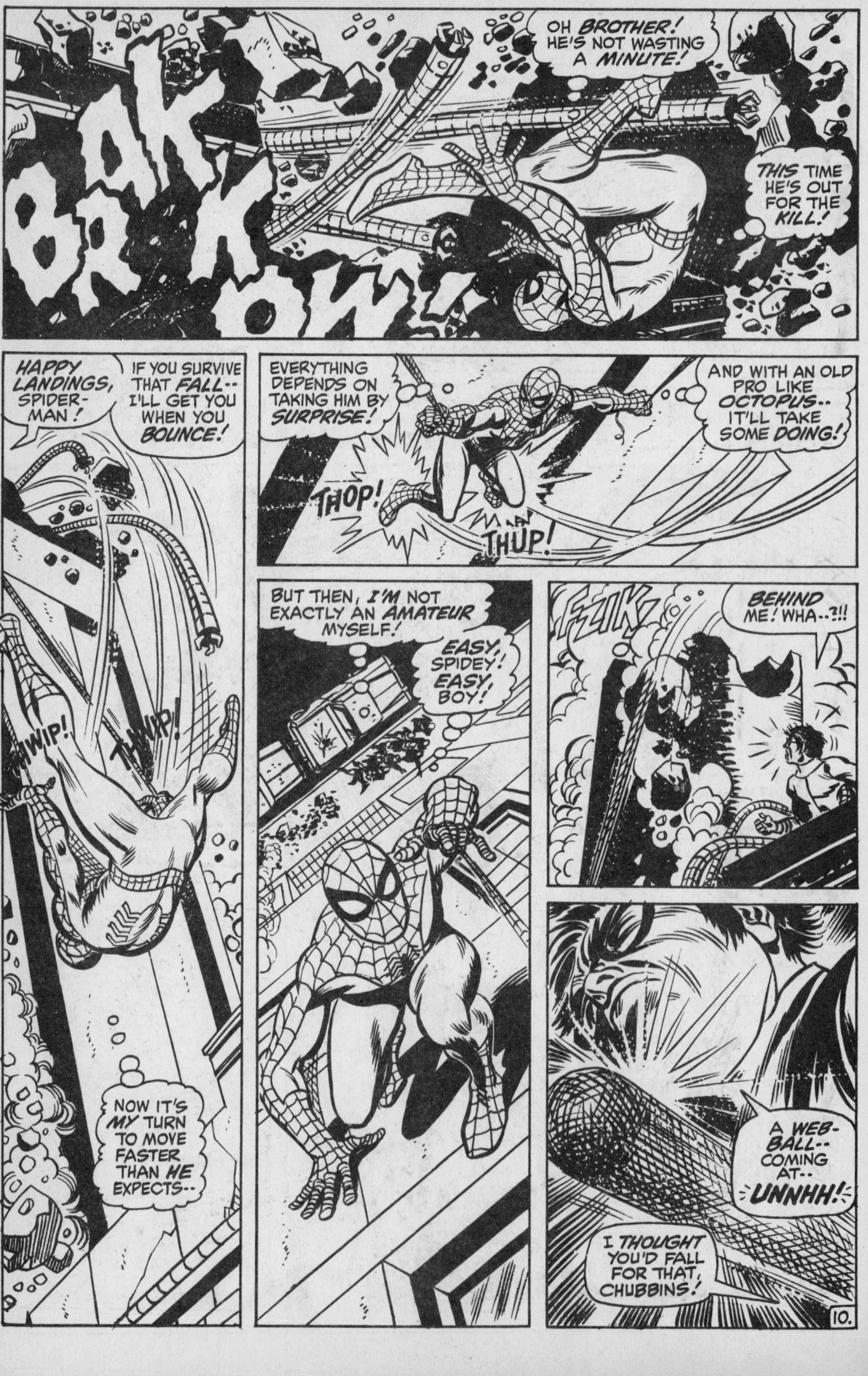
BAKOOM!
OH BROTHER! HE'S NOT WASTING A MINUTE!
THIS TIME HE'S OUT FOR THE KILL!
HAPPY LANDINGS, SPIDER-MAN!
IF YOU SURVIVE THAT FALL-- I'LL GET YOU WHEN YOU BOUNCE!
THWIP!
THWIP!
NOW IT'S MY TURN TO MOVE FASTER THAN HE EXPECTS--
EVERYTHING DEPENDS ON TAKING HIM BY SURPRISE!
AND WITH AN OLD PRO LIKE OCTOPUS.. IT'LL TAKE SOME DOING!
THOP!
THUP!
BUT THEN, I'M NOT EXACTLY AN AMATEUR MYSELF!
EASY, SPIDEY! EASY, BOY!
FZZIK
BEHIND ME! WHA--?!!
A WEB-BALL-- COMING AT-- UNNHH!
I THOUGHT YOU'D FALL FOR THAT, CHUBBINS!
10.

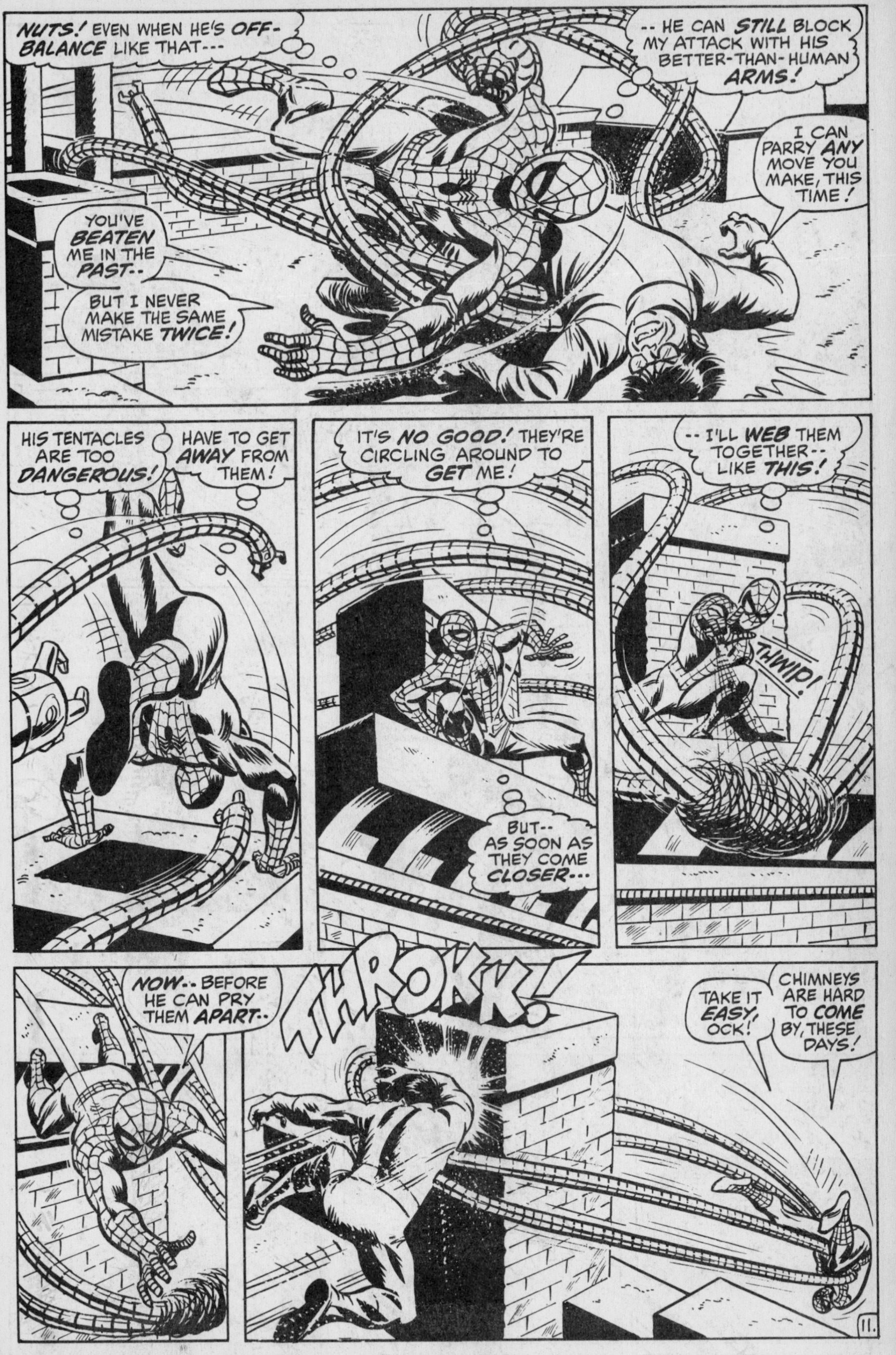
NUTS! EVEN WHEN HE'S OFF-BALANCE LIKE THAT---
-- HE CAN STILL BLOCK MY ATTACK WITH HIS BETTER-THAN-HUMAN ARMS!
I CAN PARRY ANY MOVE YOU MAKE, THIS TIME!
YOU'VE BEATEN ME IN THE PAST--
BUT I NEVER MAKE THE SAME MISTAKE TWICE!
HIS TENTACLES ARE TOO DANGEROUS!
HAVE TO GET AWAY FROM THEM!
IT'S NO GOOD! THEY'RE CIRCLING AROUND TO GET ME!
BUT-- AS SOON AS THEY COME CLOSER---
-- I'LL WEB THEM TOGETHER-- LIKE THIS!
THWIP!
NOW-- BEFORE HE CAN PRY THEM APART--
THROKK!
TAKE IT EASY, OCK!
CHIMNEYS ARE HARD TO COME BY, THESE DAYS!
11.

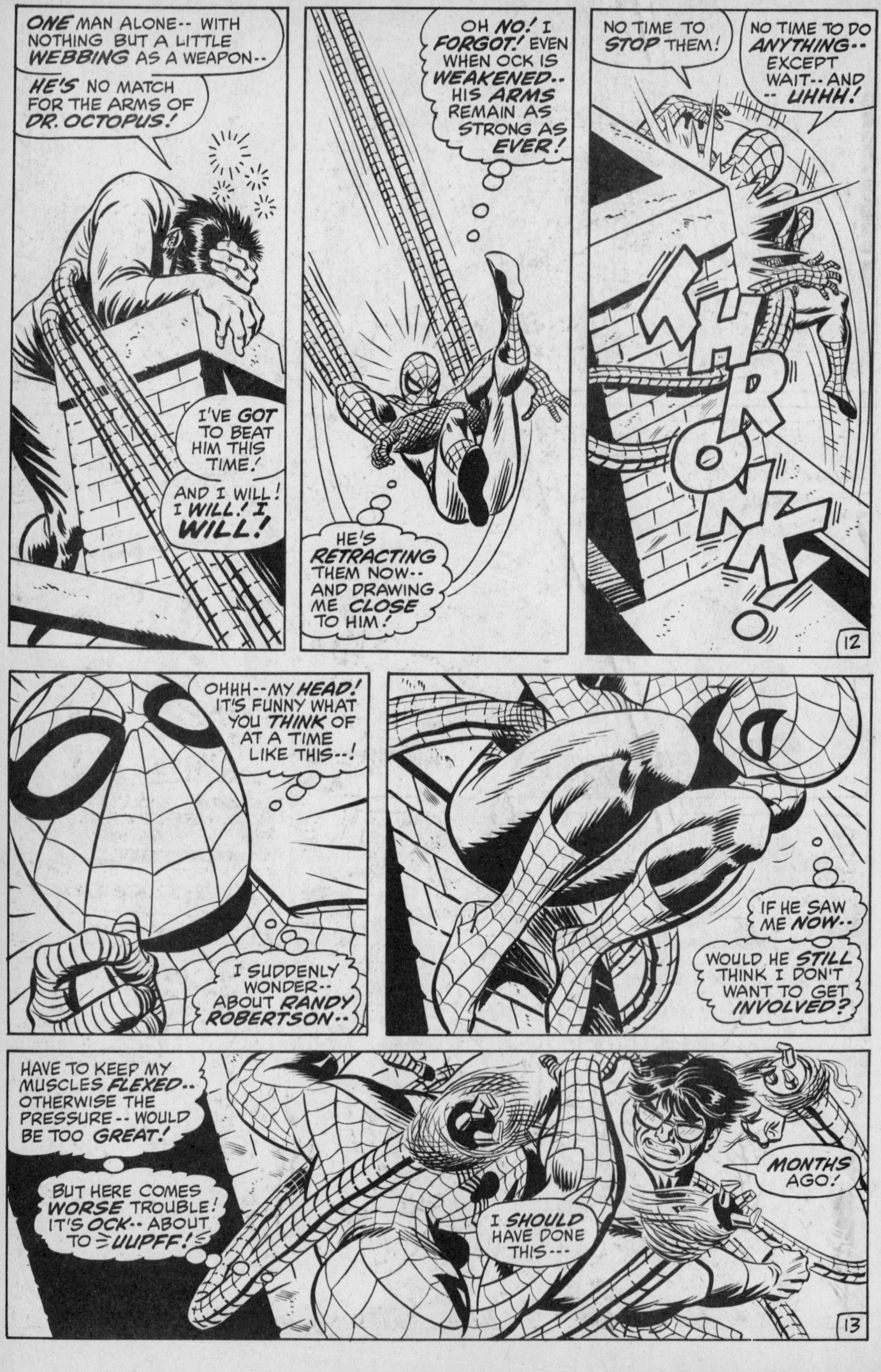
ONE MAN ALONE-- WITH NOTHING BUT A LITTLE WEBBING AS A WEAPON--
HE'S NO MATCH FOR THE ARMS OF DR. OCTOPUS!
I'VE GOT TO BEAT HIM THIS TIME!
AND I WILL! I WILL! I WILL!
OH NO! I FORGOT! EVEN WHEN OCK IS WEAKENED-- HIS ARMS REMAIN AS STRONG AS EVER!
HE'S RETRACTING THEM NOW-- AND DRAWING ME CLOSE TO HIM!
NO TIME TO STOP THEM!
NO TIME TO DO ANYTHING-- EXCEPT WAIT-- AND -- UHHH!
THRONK!
12
OHHH--MY HEAD! IT'S FUNNY WHAT YOU THINK OF AT A TIME LIKE THIS--!
I SUDDENLY WONDER-- ABOUT RANDY ROBERTSON--
IF HE SAW ME NOW--
WOULD HE STILL THINK I DON'T WANT TO GET INVOLVED?
HAVE TO KEEP MY MUSCLES FLEXED-- OTHERWISE THE PRESSURE -- WOULD BE TOO GREAT!
BUT HERE COMES WORSE TROUBLE! IT'S OCK-- ABOUT TO UUPFF!
I SHOULD HAVE DONE THIS---
MONTHS AGO!
13

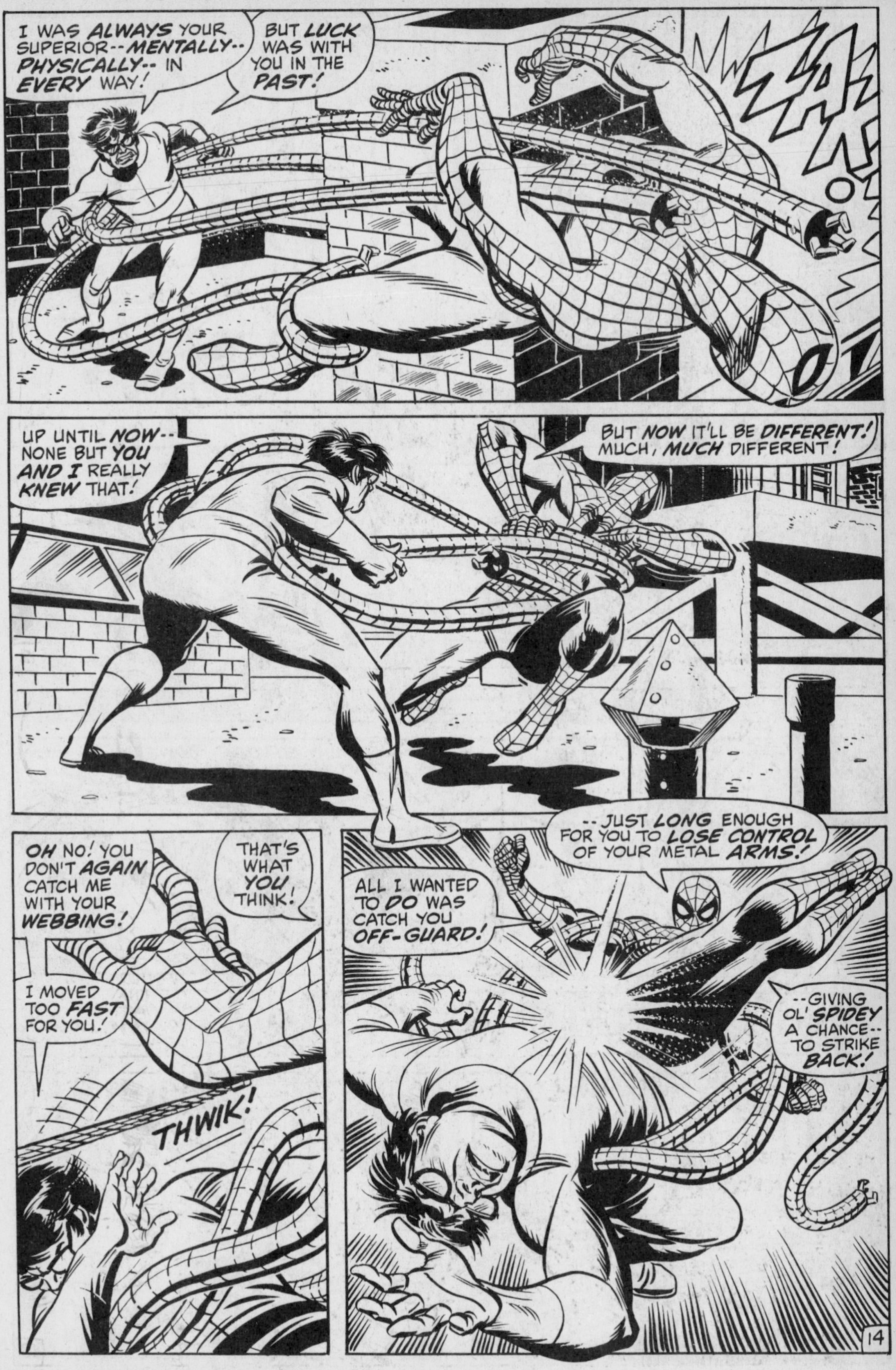
I WAS ALWAYS YOUR SUPERIOR--MENTALLY.. PHYSICALLY-- IN EVERY WAY!
BUT LUCK WAS WITH YOU IN THE PAST!
ZAK
UP UNTIL NOW-- NONE BUT YOU AND I REALLY KNEW THAT!
BUT NOW IT'LL BE DIFFERENT! MUCH, MUCH DIFFERENT!
OH NO! YOU DON'T AGAIN CATCH ME WITH YOUR WEBBING!
THAT'S WHAT YOU THINK!
I MOVED TOO FAST FOR YOU!
THWIK!
ALL I WANTED TO DO WAS CATCH YOU OFF-GUARD!
--JUST LONG ENOUGH FOR YOU TO LOSE CONTROL OF YOUR METAL ARMS!
--GIVING OL' SPIDEY A CHANCE--TO STRIKE BACK!
14

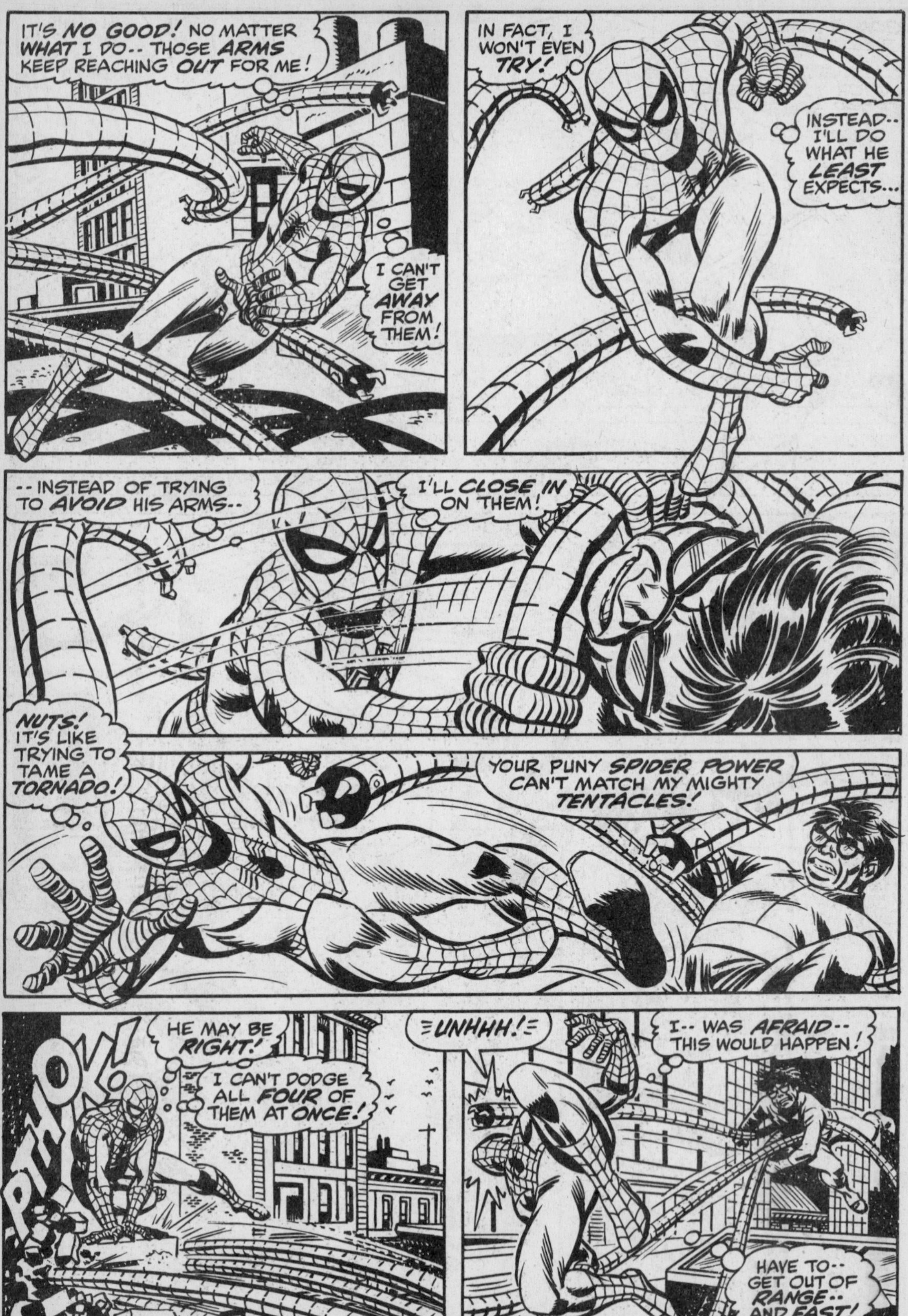
IT'S NO GOOD! NO MATTER WHAT I DO-- THOSE ARMS KEEP REACHING OUT FOR ME!
I CAN'T GET AWAY FROM THEM!
IN FACT, I WON'T EVEN TRY!
INSTEAD-- I'LL DO WHAT HE LEAST EXPECTS...
--INSTEAD OF TRYING TO AVOID HIS ARMS--
I'LL CLOSE IN ON THEM!
NUTS! IT'S LIKE TRYING TO TAME A TORNADO!
YOUR PUNY SPIDER POWER CAN'T MATCH MY MIGHTY TENTACLES!
PTHOK!
HE MAY BE RIGHT!
I CAN'T DODGE ALL FOUR OF THEM AT ONCE!
UNHHH!
I-- WAS AFRAID-- THIS WOULD HAPPEN!
HAVE TO-- GET OUT OF RANGE-- AND FAST!
15

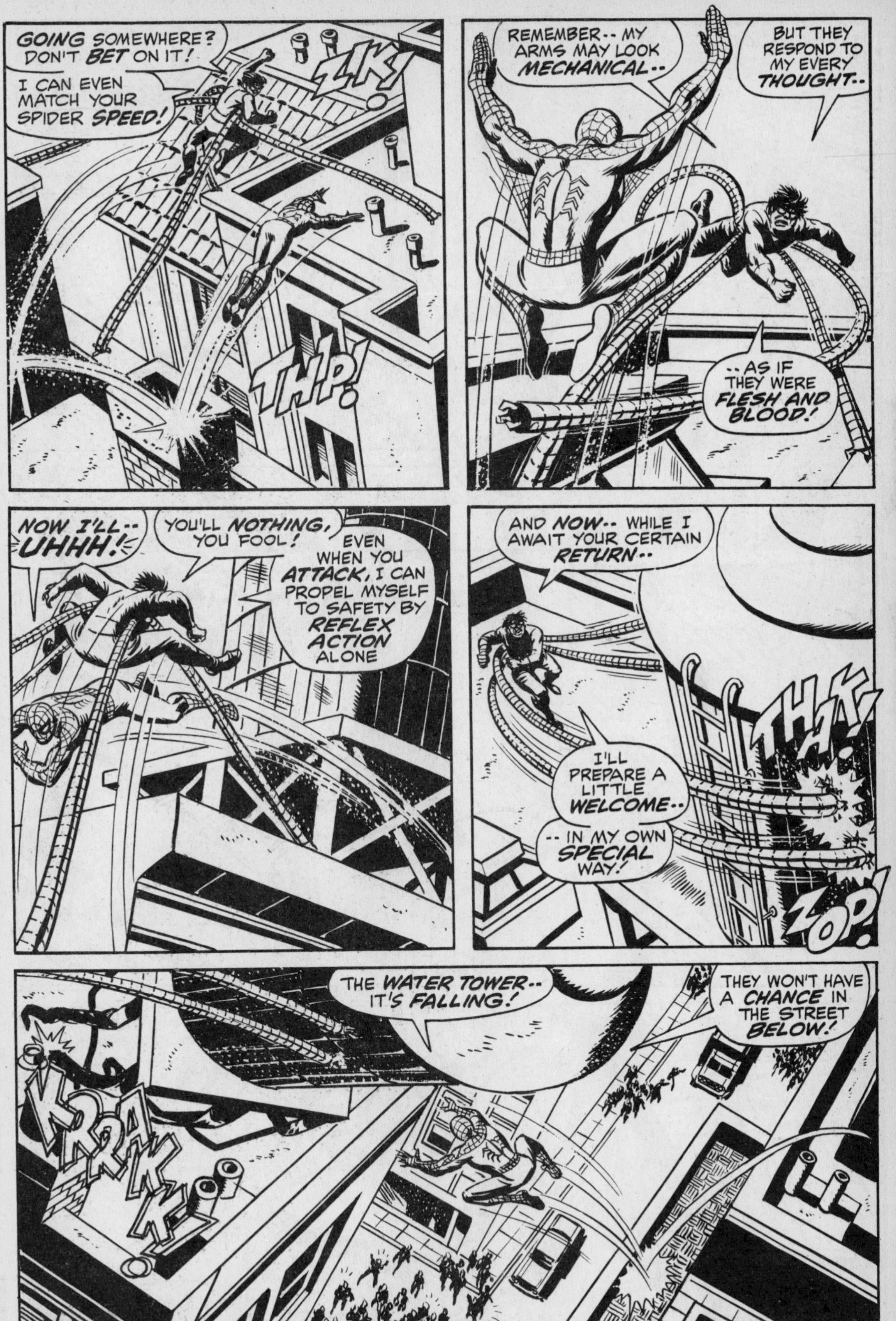
GOING SOMEWHERE? DON'T BET ON IT!
I CAN EVEN MATCH YOUR SPIDER SPEED!
ZKK!
THP!
REMEMBER-- MY ARMS MAY LOOK MECHANICAL--
BUT THEY RESPOND TO MY EVERY THOUGHT--
--AS IF THEY WERE FLESH AND BLOOD!
NOW I'LL-- UHHH!
YOU'LL NOTHING, YOU FOOL!
EVEN WHEN YOU ATTACK, I CAN PROPEL MYSELF TO SAFETY BY REFLEX ACTION ALONE
AND NOW-- WHILE I AWAIT YOUR CERTAIN RETURN--
I'LL PREPARE A LITTLE WELCOME--
--IN MY OWN SPECIAL WAY!
THAK!
ZOP!
THE WATER TOWER-- IT'S FALLING!
THEY WON'T HAVE A CHANCE IN THE STREET BELOW!
KRRAKK!

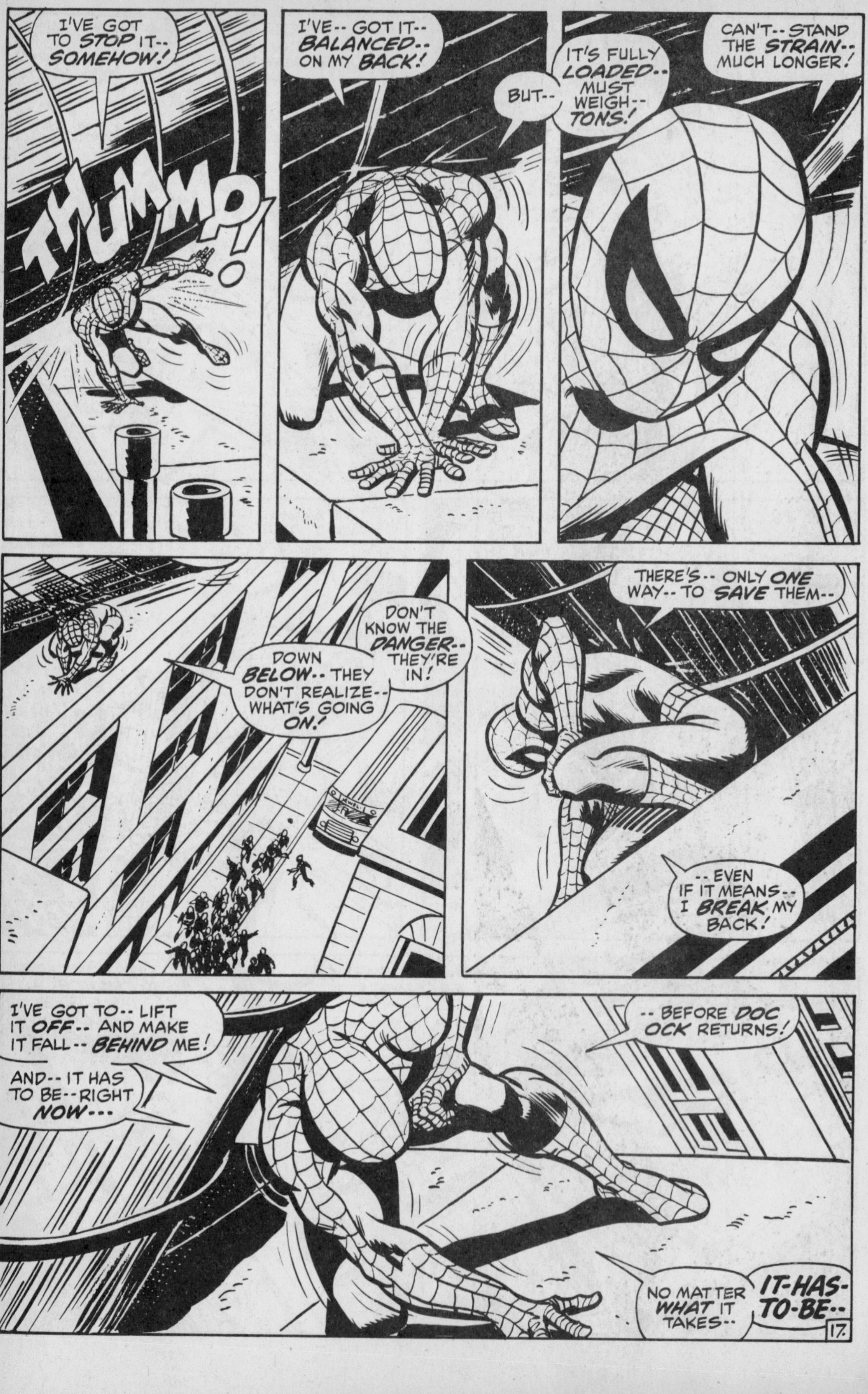
I'VE GOT TO STOP IT-- SOMEHOW!
THUMMP!
I'VE-- GOT IT-- BALANCED-- ON MY BACK!
BUT--
IT'S FULLY LOADED-- MUST WEIGH-- TONS!
CAN'T-- STAND THE STRAIN-- MUCH LONGER!
DOWN BELOW-- THEY DON'T REALIZE-- WHAT'S GOING ON!
DON'T KNOW THE DANGER-- THEY'RE IN!
THERE'S-- ONLY ONE WAY-- TO SAVE THEM--
-- EVEN IF IT MEANS-- I BREAK MY BACK!
I'VE GOT TO-- LIFT IT OFF-- AND MAKE IT FALL-- BEHIND ME!
AND-- IT HAS TO BE--RIGHT NOW---
-- BEFORE DOC OCK RETURNS!
NO MATTER WHAT IT TAKES--
IT-HAS-TO-BE--

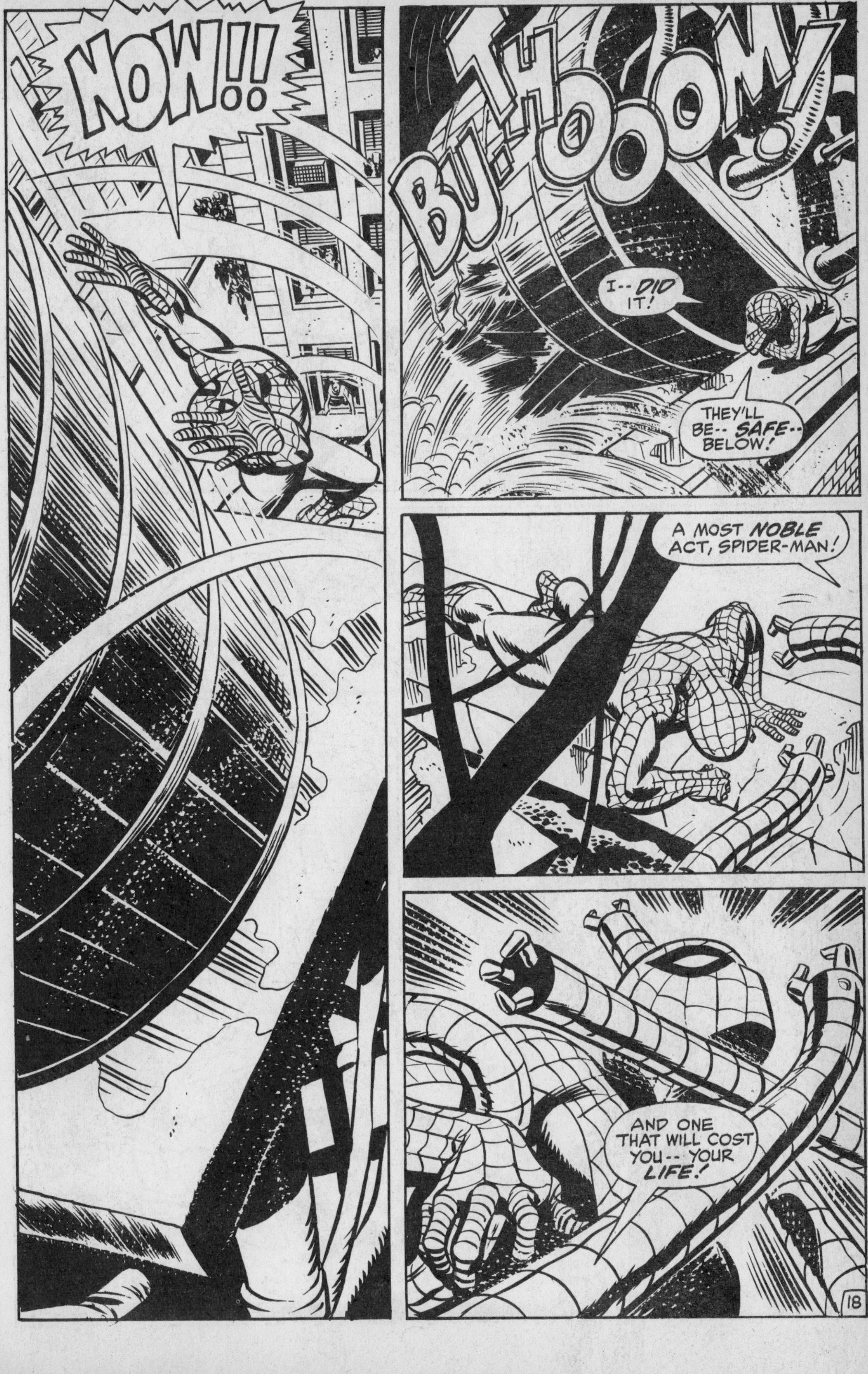
NOW!!
BU-THOOOOM!
I--DID IT!
THEY'LL BE-- SAFE-- BELOW!
A MOST NOBLE ACT, SPIDER-MAN!
AND ONE THAT WILL COST YOU-- YOUR LIFE!
18

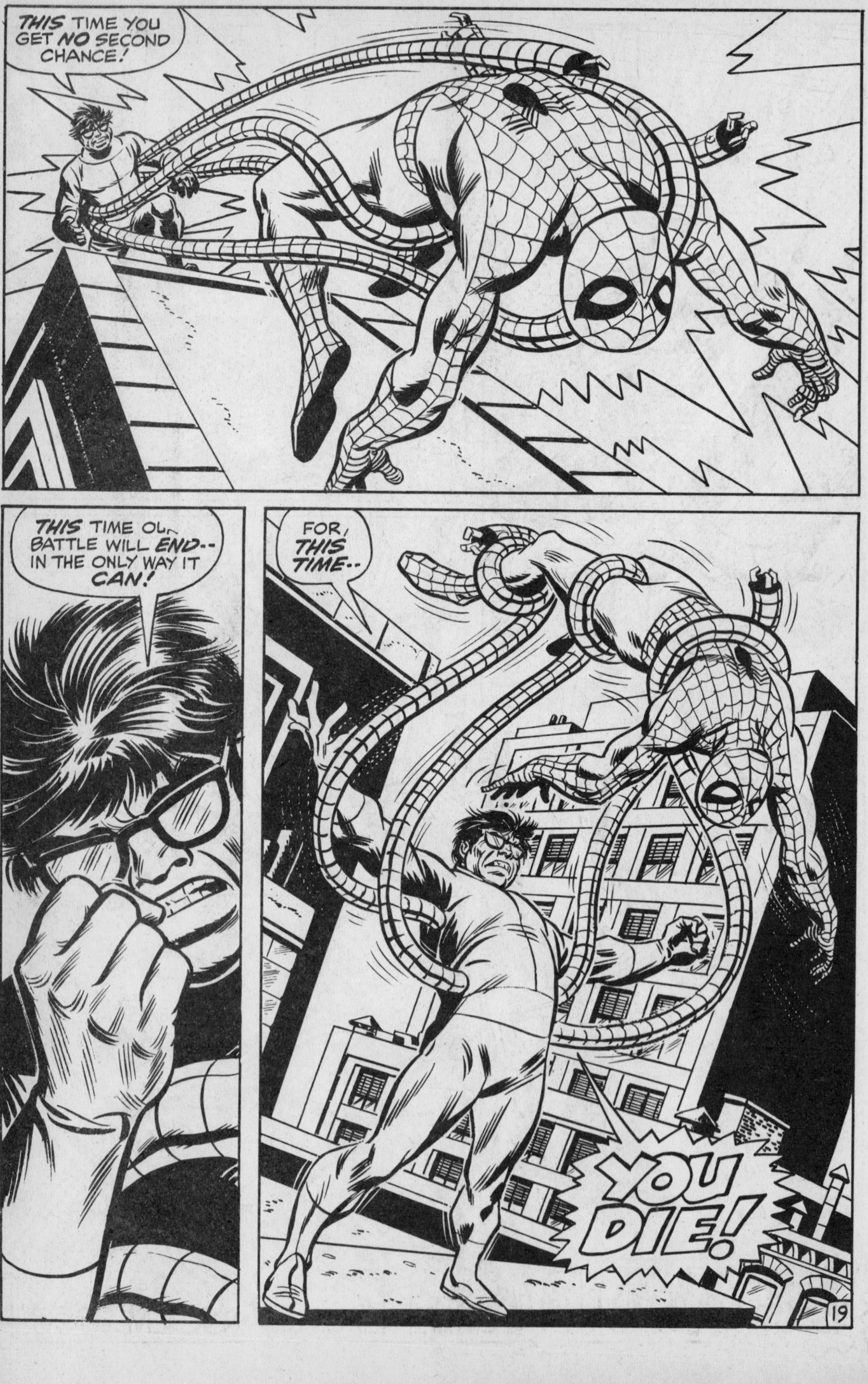
THIS TIME YOU GET NO SECOND CHANCE!
THIS TIME OU BATTLE WILL END-- IN THE ONLY WAY IT CAN!
FOR, THIS TIME--
YOU DIE!

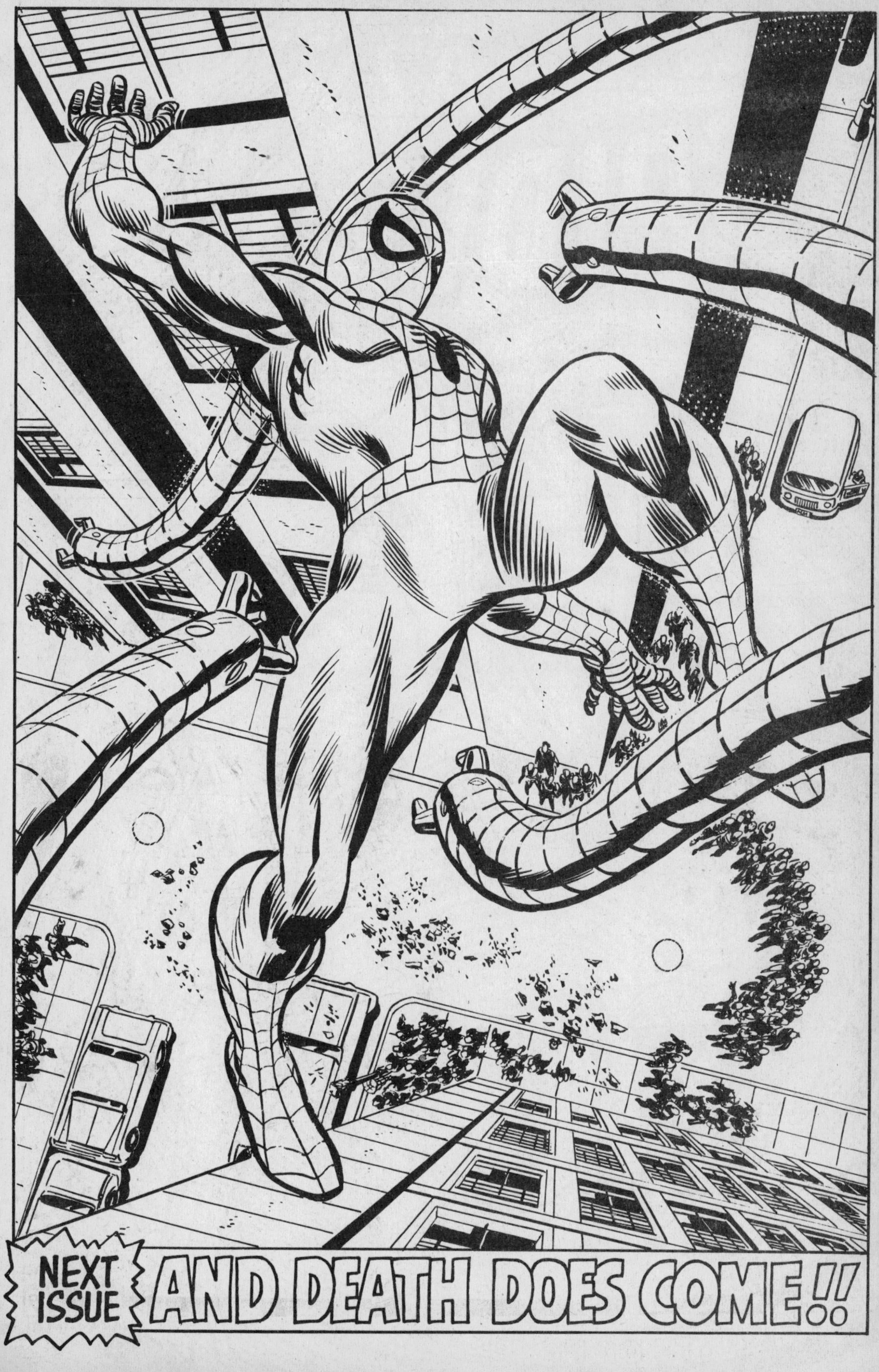
NEXT ISSUE
AND DEATH DOES COME!!

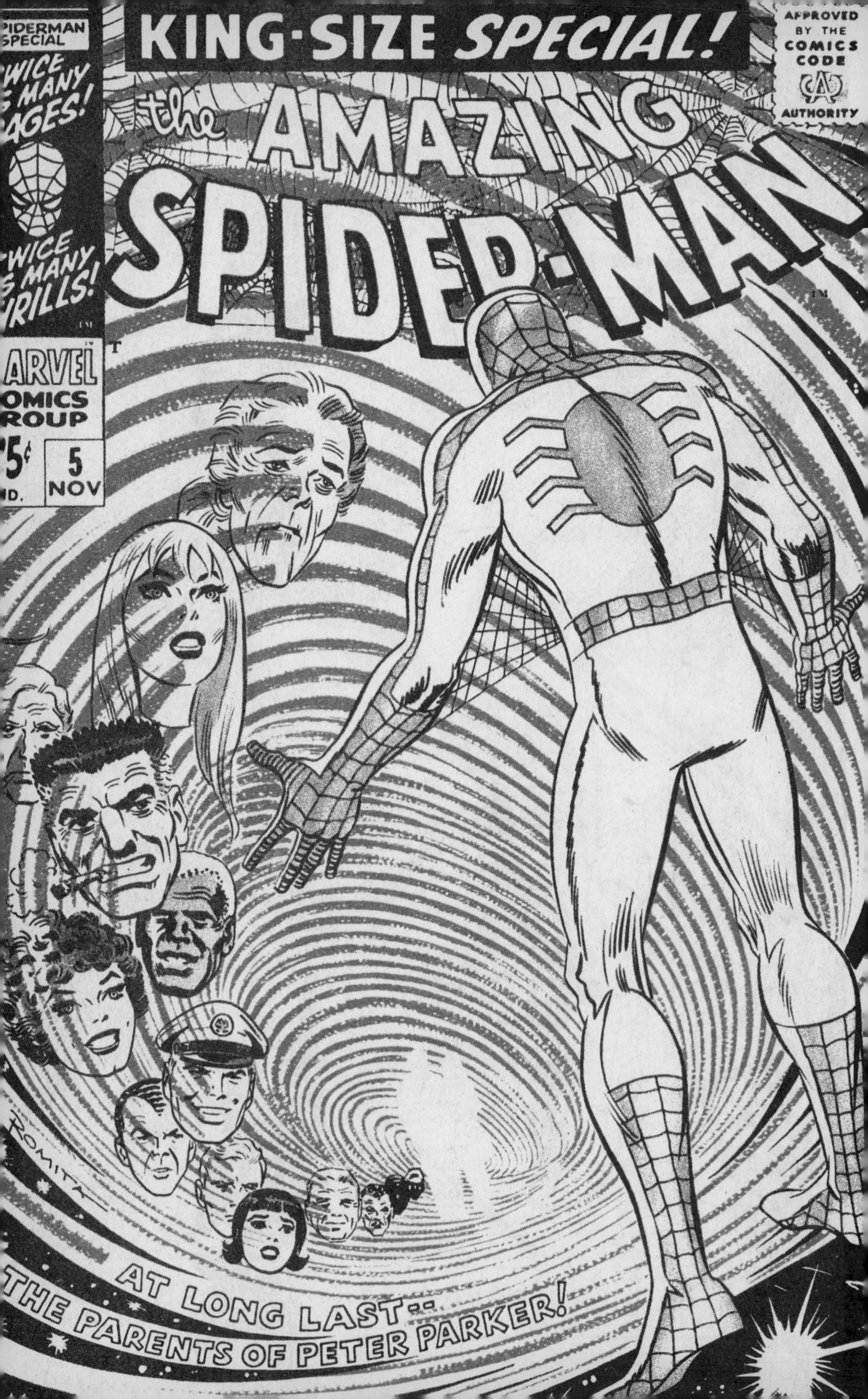

SPIDERMAN SPECIAL
KING-SIZE SPECIAL!
APPROVED BY THE COMICS CODE AUTHORITY
TWICE AS MANY PAGES!
TWICE AS MANY THRILLS!
the AMAZING SPIDER-MAN
MARVEL COMICS GROUP
25¢
5 NOV
ROMITA
AT LONG LAST--
THE PARENTS OF PETER PARKER!

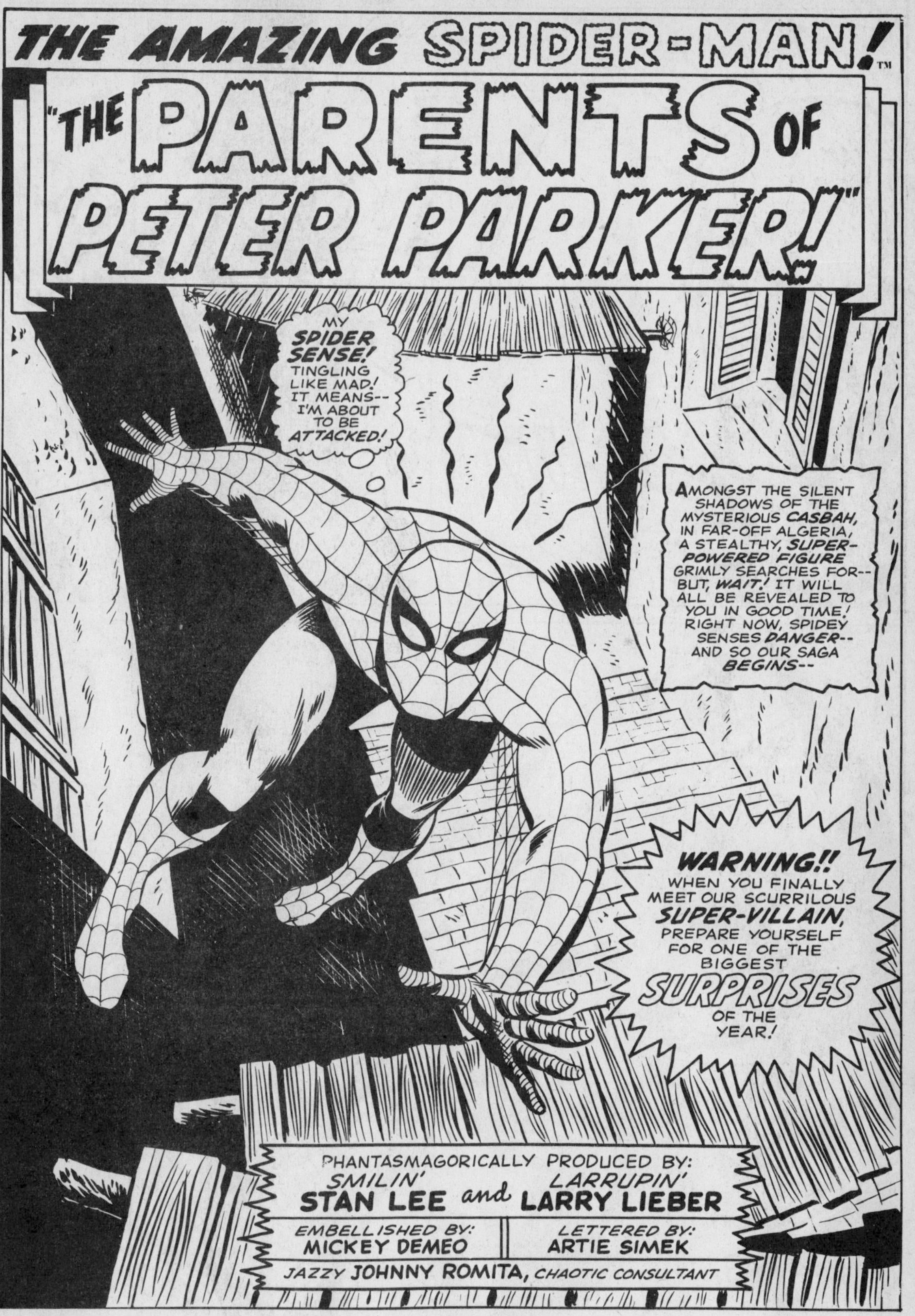
THE AMAZING SPIDER-MAN!™
"THE PARENTS OF PETER PARKER!"
MY SPIDER SENSE! TINGLING LIKE MAD! IT MEANS-- I'M ABOUT TO BE ATTACKED!
AMONGST THE SILENT SHADOWS OF THE MYSTERIOUS CASBAH, IN FAR-OFF ALGERIA, A STEALTHY, SUPER-POWERED FIGURE GRIMLY SEARCHES FOR-- BUT, WAIT! IT WILL ALL BE REVEALED TO YOU IN GOOD TIME! RIGHT NOW, SPIDEY SENSES DANGER-- AND SO OUR SAGA BEGINS--
WARNING!! WHEN YOU FINALLY MEET OUR SCURRILOUS SUPER-VILLAIN, PREPARE YOURSELF FOR ONE OF THE BIGGEST SURPRISES OF THE YEAR!
PHANTASMAGORICALLY PRODUCED BY: SMILIN' STAN LEE and LARRUPIN' LARRY LIEBER
EMBELLISHED BY: MICKEY DEMEO
LETTERED BY: ARTIE SIMEK
JAZZY JOHNNY ROMITA, CHAOTIC CONSULTANT

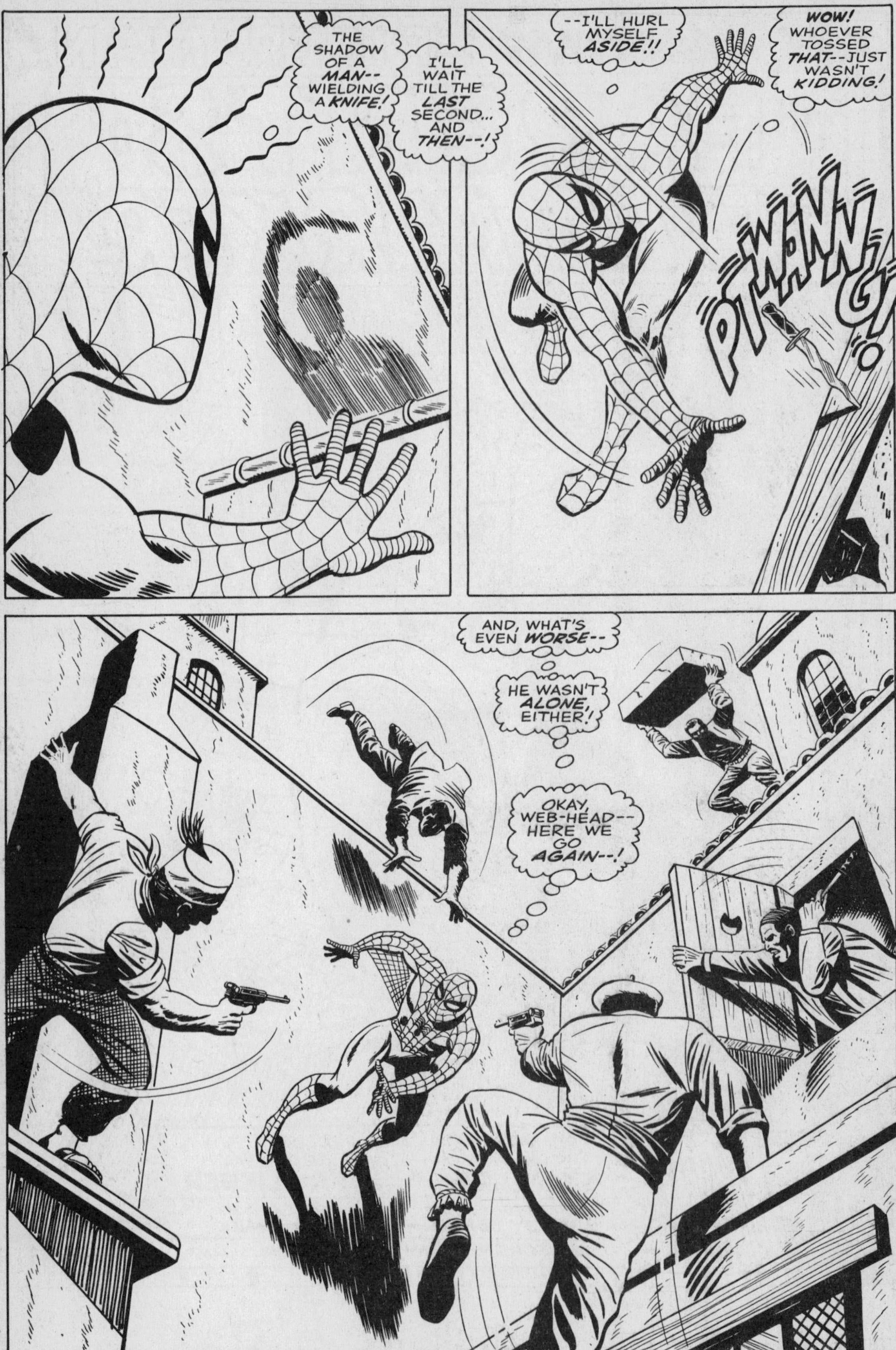
THE SHADOW OF A MAN-- WIELDING A KNIFE!
I'LL WAIT TILL THE LAST SECOND... AND THEN--!
--I'LL HURL MYSELF ASIDE!!
WOW! WHOEVER TOSSED THAT--JUST WASN'T KIDDING!
PTWANNG!
AND, WHAT'S EVEN WORSE--
HE WASN'T ALONE, EITHER!
OKAY, WEB-HEAD-- HERE WE GO AGAIN--!

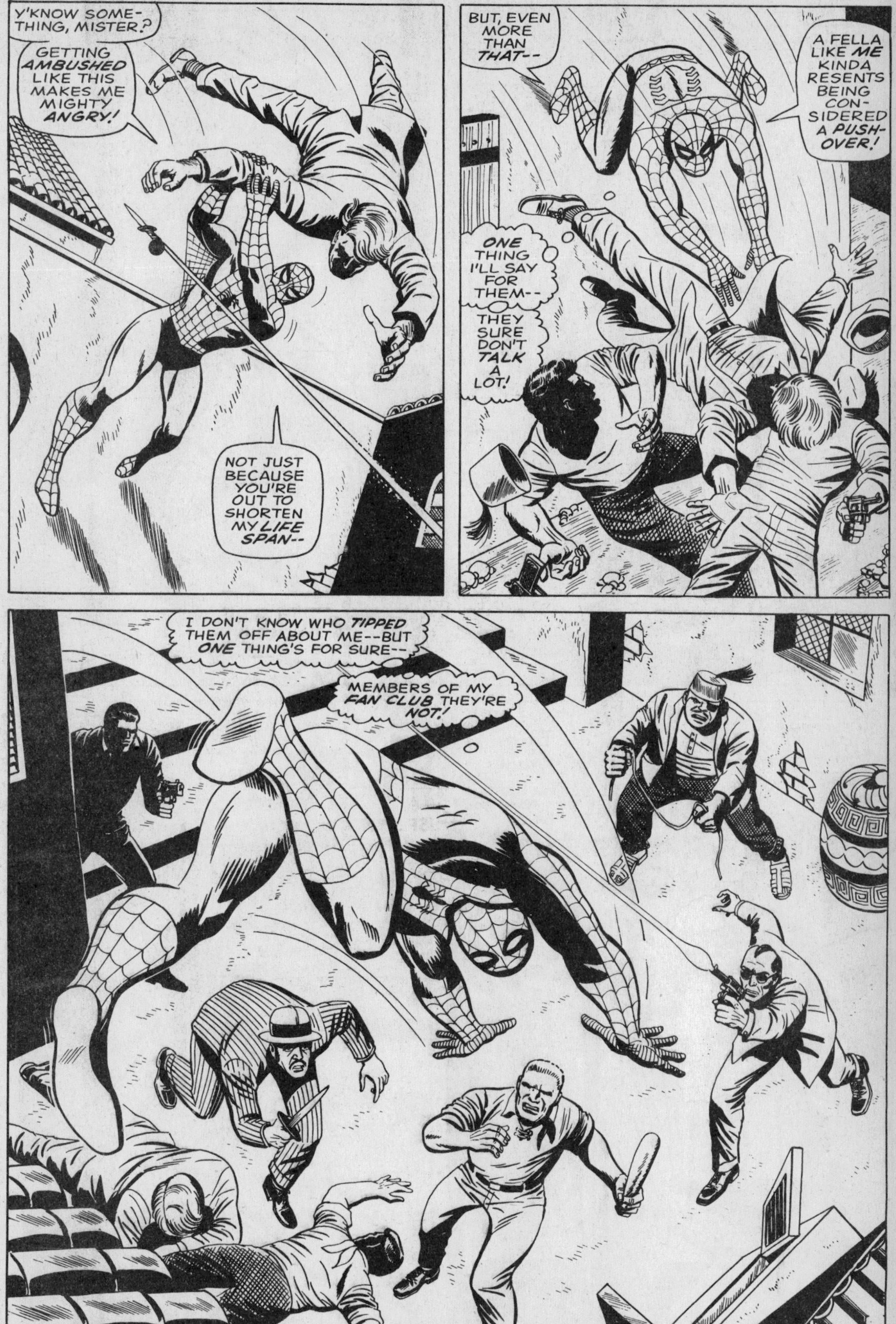
Y'KNOW SOME-THING, MISTER?
GETTING AMBUSHED LIKE THIS MAKES ME MIGHTY ANGRY!
NOT JUST BECAUSE YOU'RE OUT TO SHORTEN MY LIFE SPAN--
BUT, EVEN MORE THAN THAT--
A FELLA LIKE ME KINDA RESENTS BEING CON-SIDERED A PUSH-OVER!
ONE THING I'LL SAY FOR THEM--
THEY SURE DON'T TALK A LOT!
I DON'T KNOW WHO TIPPED THEM OFF ABOUT ME--BUT ONE THING'S FOR SURE--
MEMBERS OF MY FAN CLUB THEY'RE NOT!

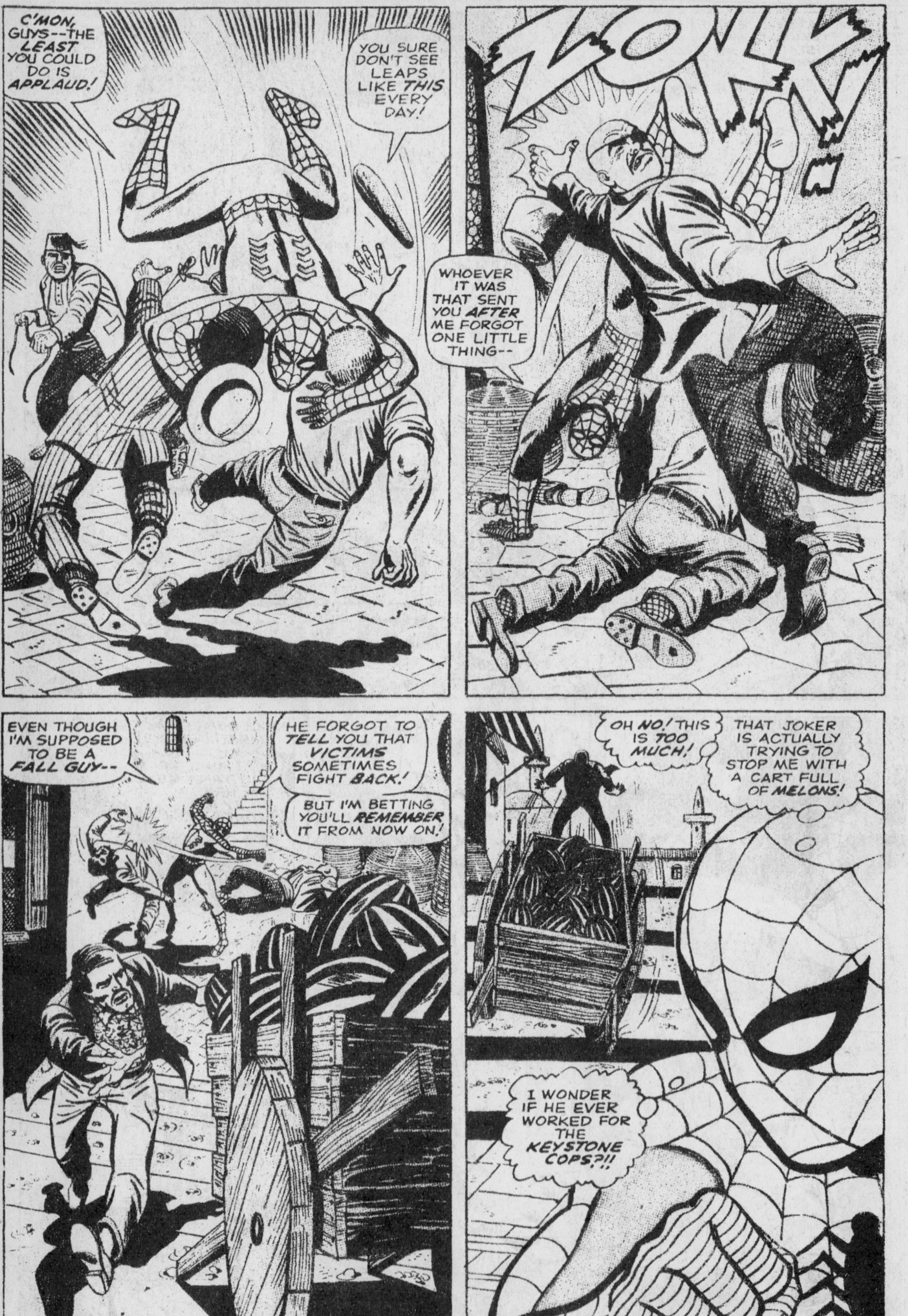
C'MON, GUYS--THE LEAST YOU COULD DO IS APPLAUD!
YOU SURE DON'T SEE LEAPS LIKE THIS EVERY DAY!
ZOKK!
WHOEVER IT WAS THAT SENT YOU AFTER ME FORGOT ONE LITTLE THING--
EVEN THOUGH I'M SUPPOSED TO BE A FALL GUY--
HE FORGOT TO TELL YOU THAT VICTIMS SOMETIMES FIGHT BACK!
BUT I'M BETTING YOU'LL REMEMBER IT FROM NOW ON!
OH NO! THIS IS TOO MUCH!
THAT JOKER IS ACTUALLY TRYING TO STOP ME WITH A CART FULL OF MELONS!
I WONDER IF HE EVER WORKED FOR THE KEYSTONE COPS?!!
4

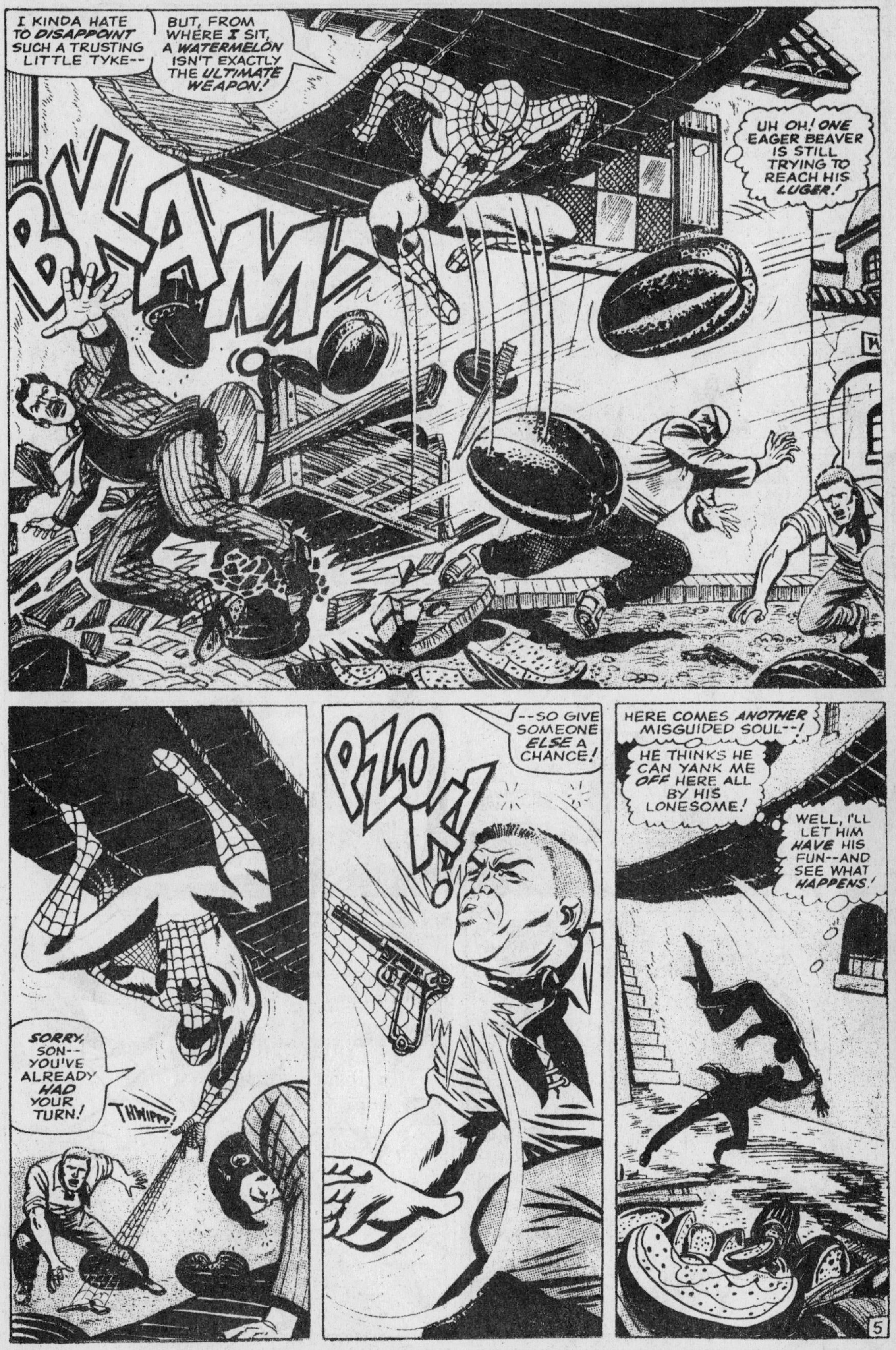
I KINDA HATE TO DISAPPOINT SUCH A TRUSTING LITTLE TYKE--
BUT, FROM WHERE I SIT, A WATERMELON ISN'T EXACTLY THE ULTIMATE WEAPON!
BKAM!
UH OH! ONE EAGER BEAVER IS STILL TRYING TO REACH HIS LUGER!
SORRY, SON-- YOU'VE ALREADY HAD YOUR TURN!
THWIPPP!
PZOK!
--SO GIVE SOMEONE ELSE A CHANCE!
HERE COMES ANOTHER MISGUIDED SOUL--!
HE THINKS HE CAN YANK ME OFF HERE ALL BY HIS LONESOME!
WELL, I'LL LET HIM HAVE HIS FUN--AND SEE WHAT HAPPENS!

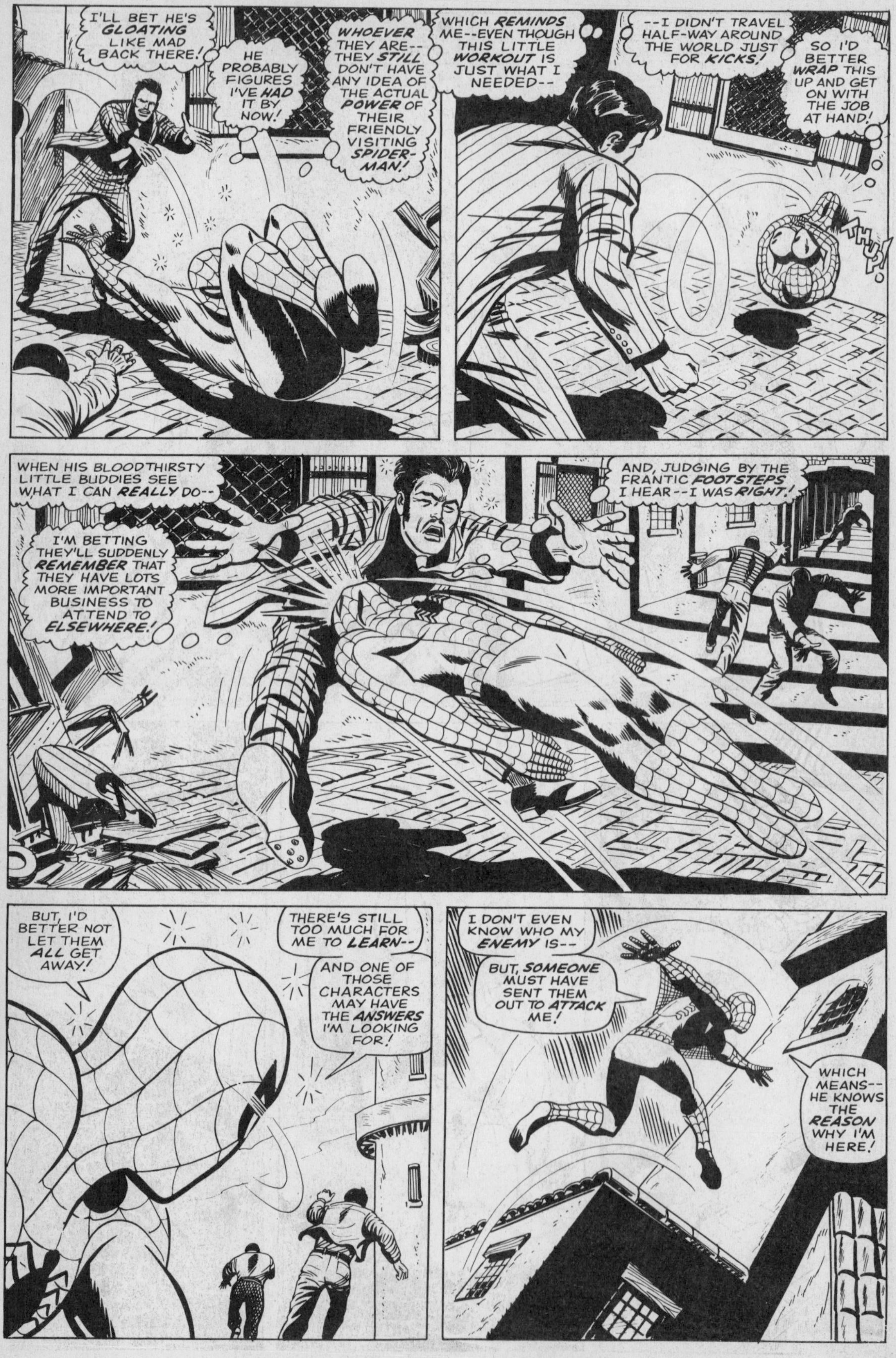
I'LL BET HE'S GLOATING LIKE MAD BACK THERE!
HE PROBABLY FIGURES I'VE HAD IT BY NOW!
WHOEVER THEY ARE-- THEY STILL DON'T HAVE ANY IDEA OF THE ACTUAL POWER OF THEIR FRIENDLY VISITING SPIDER-MAN!
WHICH REMINDS ME--EVEN THOUGH THIS LITTLE WORKOUT IS JUST WHAT I NEEDED--
--I DIDN'T TRAVEL HALF-WAY AROUND THE WORLD JUST FOR KICKS!
SO I'D BETTER WRAP THIS UP AND GET ON WITH THE JOB AT HAND!
THWUP!
WHEN HIS BLOODTHIRSTY LITTLE BUDDIES SEE WHAT I CAN REALLY DO--
I'M BETTING THEY'LL SUDDENLY REMEMBER THAT THEY HAVE LOTS MORE IMPORTANT BUSINESS TO ATTEND TO ELSEWHERE!
AND, JUDGING BY THE FRANTIC FOOTSTEPS I HEAR--I WAS RIGHT!
BUT, I'D BETTER NOT LET THEM ALL GET AWAY!
THERE'S STILL TOO MUCH FOR ME TO LEARN--
AND ONE OF THOSE CHARACTERS MAY HAVE THE ANSWERS I'M LOOKING FOR!
I DON'T EVEN KNOW WHO MY ENEMY IS--
BUT, SOMEONE MUST HAVE SENT THEM OUT TO ATTACK ME!
WHICH MEANS-- HE KNOWS THE REASON WHY I'M HERE!

BUT, FOR ONE BRIEF SECOND, THE YOUTHFUL WEB-SLINGER LOSES HIS OWN NATURAL *CAUTION*, AS HE FAILS TO NOTICE THE DEADLY *PISTOL* BEING WITHDRAWN FROM BENEATH A SILKEN WAIST SASH--!

ALL I HAVE TO DO IS KEEP THEM IN *SIGHT*--!

A SPLIT-SECOND LATER, REALIZING THE DANGER-- THE STARTLED *SPIDER-MAN* BARELY HAS TIME TO AVERT HIS HEAD ENOUGH TO SAVE HIS *LIFE*--AND THEN--

HE HAS A GUN!

ABOUT TO *SHOOT*.!!

I'VE GOT TO *SPIN* AROUND AND-- *UNHHH!*

KRAK

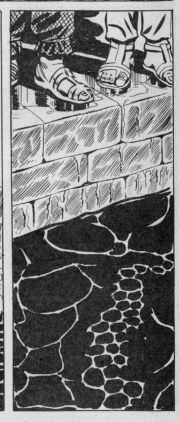

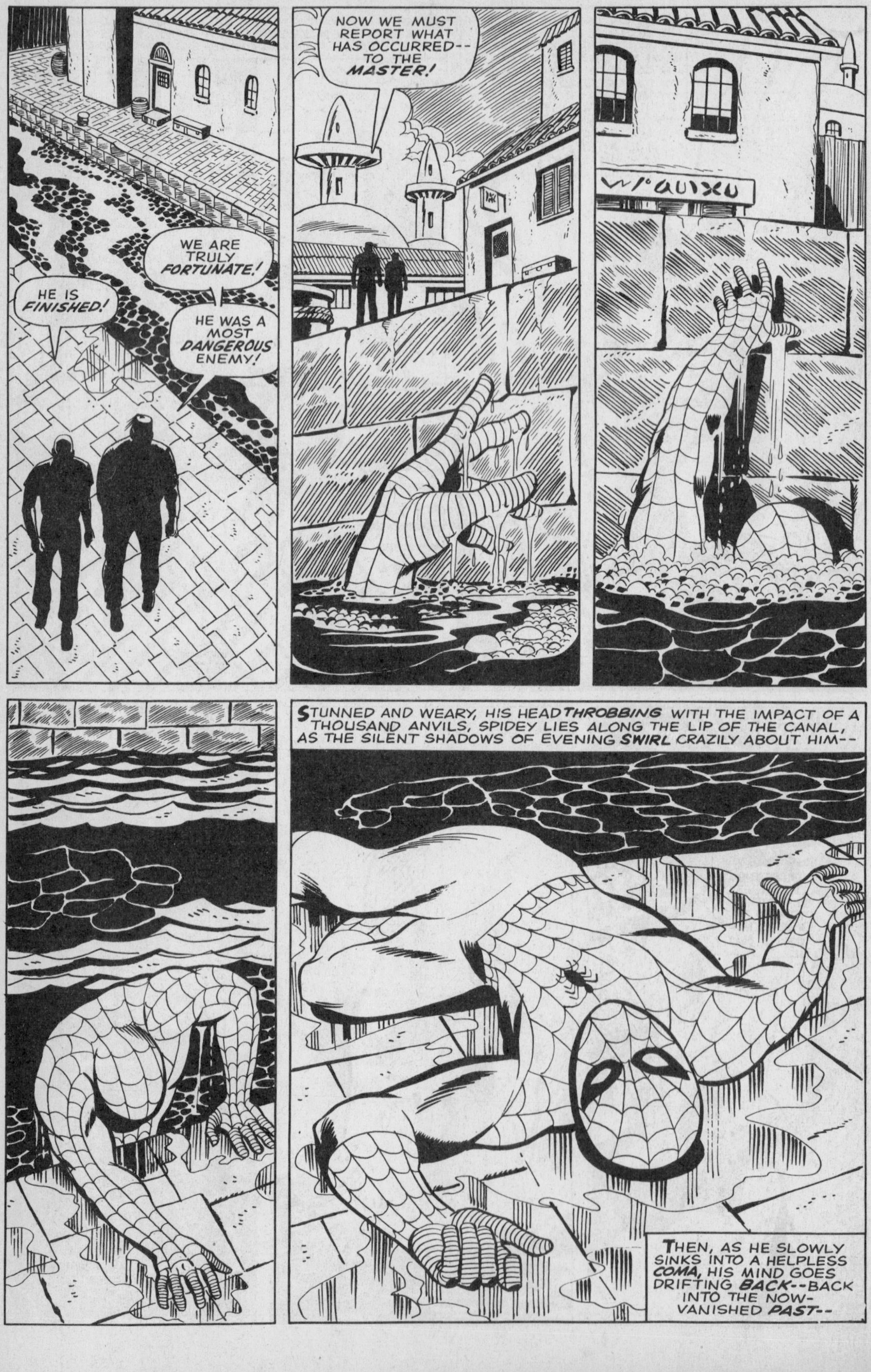

HE IS *FINISHED!*
WE ARE TRULY *FORTUNATE!*
HE WAS A MOST *DANGEROUS* ENEMY!
NOW WE MUST REPORT WHAT HAS OCCURRED-- TO THE *MASTER!*
STUNNED AND WEARY, HIS HEAD *THROBBING* WITH THE IMPACT OF A THOUSAND ANVILS, SPIDEY LIES ALONG THE LIP OF THE CANAL, AS THE SILENT SHADOWS OF EVENING *SWIRL* CRAZILY ABOUT HIM--
THEN, AS HE SLOWLY SINKS INTO A HELPLESS *COMA*, HIS MIND GOES DRIFTING *BACK*--BACK INTO THE NOW-VANISHED *PAST*--

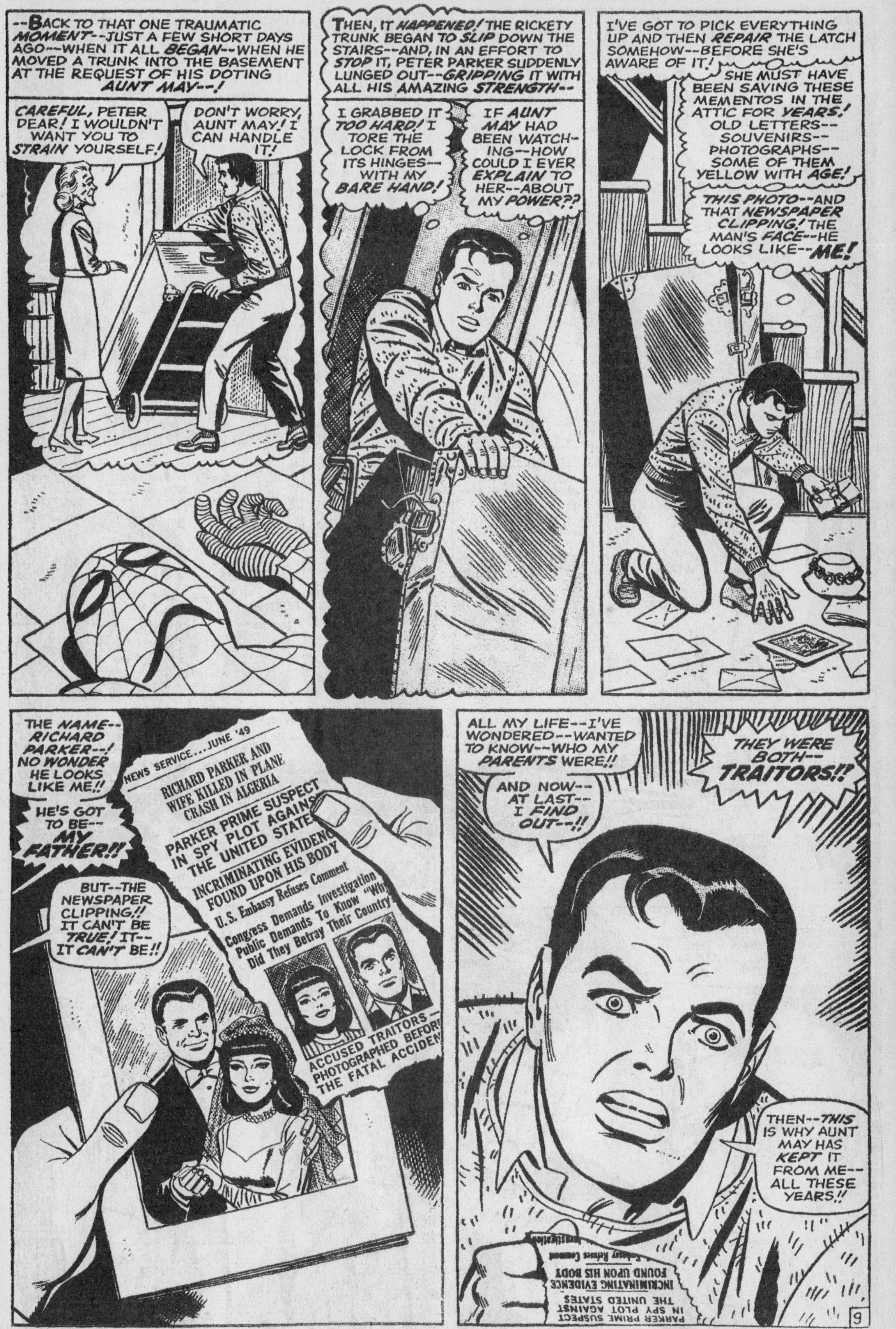
--BACK TO THAT ONE TRAUMATIC MOMENT--JUST A FEW SHORT DAYS AGO--WHEN IT ALL BEGAN--WHEN HE MOVED A TRUNK INTO THE BASEMENT AT THE REQUEST OF HIS DOTING AUNT MAY--!
CAREFUL, PETER DEAR! I WOULDN'T WANT YOU TO STRAIN YOURSELF!
DON'T WORRY, AUNT MAY! I CAN HANDLE IT!
THEN, IT HAPPENED! THE RICKETY TRUNK BEGAN TO SLIP DOWN THE STAIRS--AND, IN AN EFFORT TO STOP IT, PETER PARKER SUDDENLY LUNGED OUT--GRIPPING IT WITH ALL HIS AMAZING STRENGTH--
I GRABBED IT TOO HARD! I TORE THE LOCK FROM ITS HINGES--WITH MY BARE HAND!
IF AUNT MAY HAD BEEN WATCHING--HOW COULD I EVER EXPLAIN TO HER--ABOUT MY POWER??
I'VE GOT TO PICK EVERYTHING UP AND THEN REPAIR THE LATCH SOMEHOW--BEFORE SHE'S AWARE OF IT!
SHE MUST HAVE BEEN SAVING THESE MEMENTOS IN THE ATTIC FOR YEARS! OLD LETTERS--SOUVENIRS--PHOTOGRAPHS--SOME OF THEM YELLOW WITH AGE!
THIS PHOTO--AND THAT NEWSPAPER CLIPPING! THE MAN'S FACE--HE LOOKS LIKE--ME!
THE NAME--RICHARD PARKER--! NO WONDER HE LOOKS LIKE ME!!
HE'S GOT TO BE--MY FATHER!!
NEWS SERVICE... JUNE '49
RICHARD PARKER AND WIFE KILLED IN PLANE CRASH IN ALGERIA
PARKER PRIME SUSPECT IN SPY PLOT AGAINS THE UNITED STATE
INCRIMINATING EVIDENC FOUND UPON HIS BODY
U.S. Embassy Refuses Comment
Congress Demands Investigation
Public Demands To Know "Wh Did They Betray Their Country
ACCUSED TRAITORS PHOTOGRAPHED BEFOR THE FATAL ACCIDEN
BUT--THE NEWSPAPER CLIPPING!! IT CAN'T BE TRUE! IT--IT CAN'T BE!!
ALL MY LIFE--I'VE WONDERED--WANTED TO KNOW--WHO MY PARENTS WERE!!
AND NOW--AT LAST--I FIND OUT--!!
THEY WERE BOTH--TRAITORS!!
THEN--THIS IS WHY AUNT MAY HAS KEPT IT FROM ME--ALL THESE YEARS!!
PARKER PRIME SUSPECT IN SPY PLOT AGAINST THE UNITED STATES
INCRIMINATING EVIDENCE FOUND UPON HIS BODY

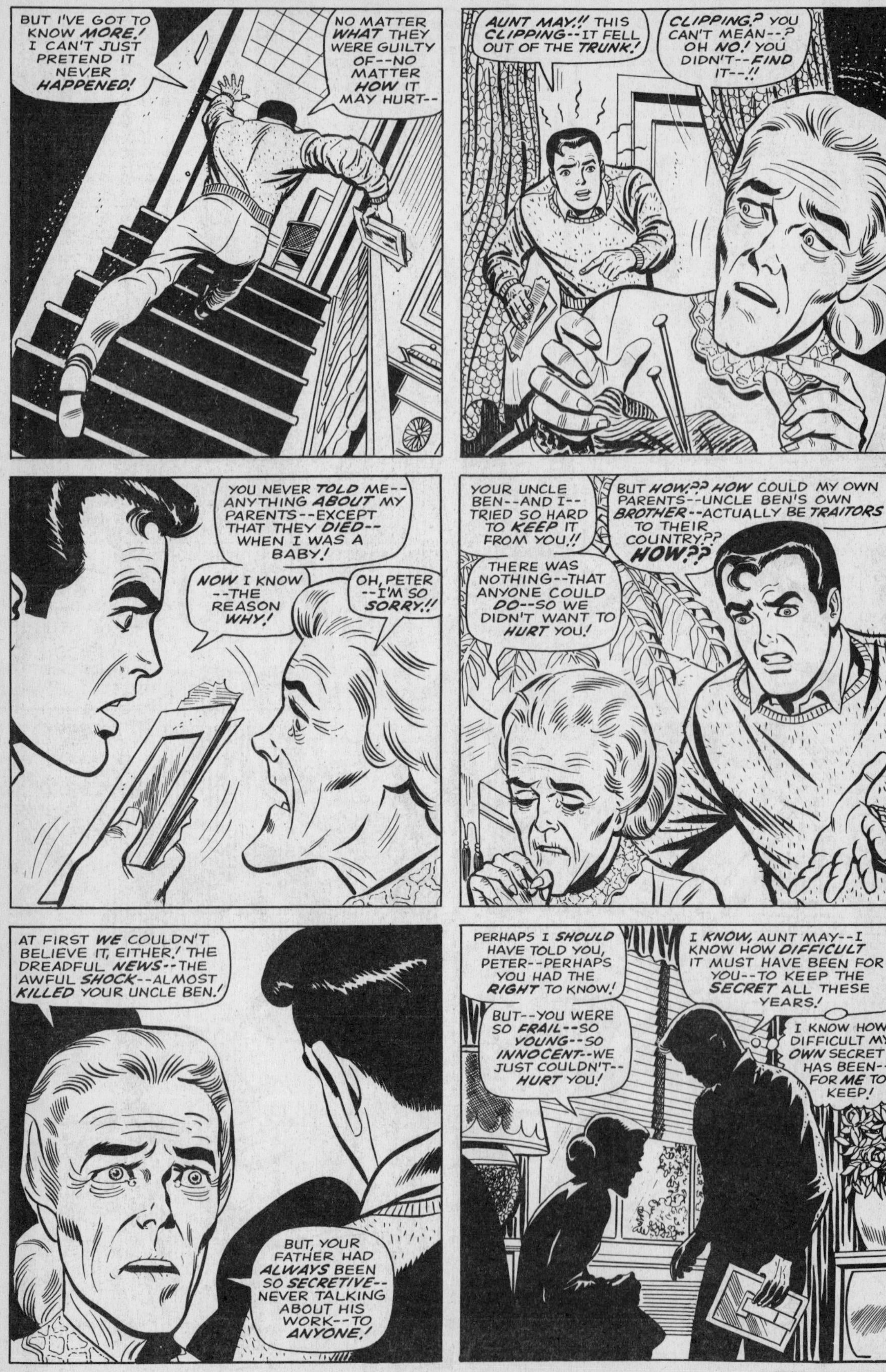
BUT I'VE GOT TO KNOW MORE! I CAN'T JUST PRETEND IT NEVER HAPPENED!
NO MATTER WHAT THEY WERE GUILTY OF--NO MATTER HOW IT MAY HURT--
AUNT MAY!! THIS CLIPPING--IT FELL OUT OF THE TRUNK!
CLIPPING? YOU CAN'T MEAN--? OH NO! YOU DIDN'T--FIND IT--!!
YOU NEVER TOLD ME--ANYTHING ABOUT MY PARENTS--EXCEPT THAT THEY DIED--WHEN I WAS A BABY!
NOW I KNOW--THE REASON WHY!
OH, PETER--I'M SO SORRY!!
YOUR UNCLE BEN--AND I--TRIED SO HARD TO KEEP IT FROM YOU!!
THERE WAS NOTHING--THAT ANYONE COULD DO--SO WE DIDN'T WANT TO HURT YOU!
BUT HOW?? HOW COULD MY OWN PARENTS--UNCLE BEN'S OWN BROTHER--ACTUALLY BE TRAITORS TO THEIR COUNTRY?? HOW??
AT FIRST WE COULDN'T BELIEVE IT, EITHER! THE DREADFUL NEWS--THE AWFUL SHOCK--ALMOST KILLED YOUR UNCLE BEN!
BUT, YOUR FATHER HAD ALWAYS BEEN SO SECRETIVE--NEVER TALKING ABOUT HIS WORK--TO ANYONE!
PERHAPS I SHOULD HAVE TOLD YOU, PETER--PERHAPS YOU HAD THE RIGHT TO KNOW!
BUT--YOU WERE SO FRAIL--SO YOUNG--SO INNOCENT--WE JUST COULDN'T--HURT YOU!
I KNOW, AUNT MAY--I KNOW HOW DIFFICULT IT MUST HAVE BEEN FOR YOU--TO KEEP THE SECRET ALL THESE YEARS!
I KNOW HOW DIFFICULT MY OWN SECRET HAS BEEN--FOR ME TO KEEP!

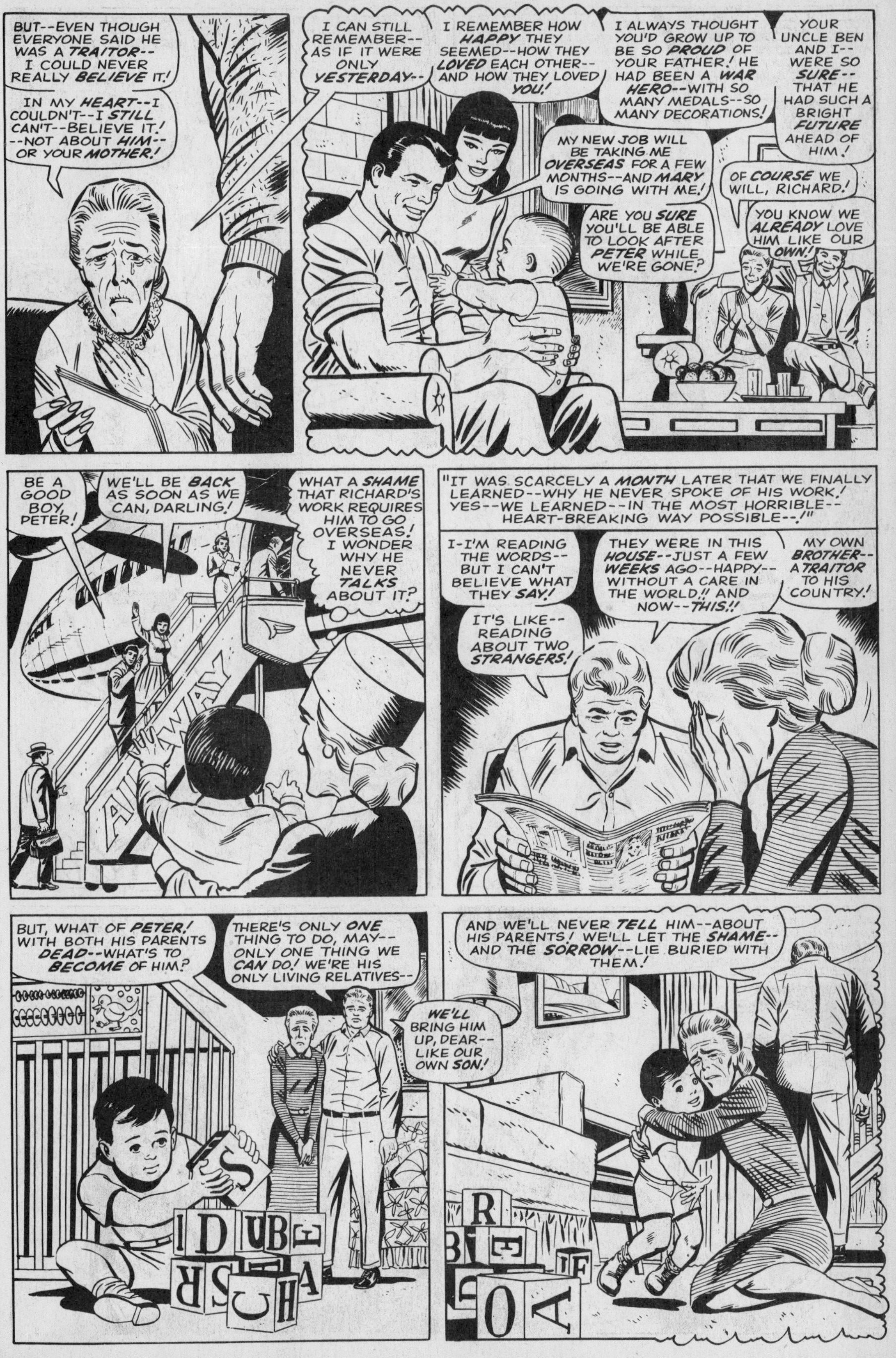
BUT--EVEN THOUGH EVERYONE SAID HE WAS A TRAITOR--I COULD NEVER REALLY BELIEVE IT!
IN MY HEART--I COULDN'T--I STILL CAN'T--BELIEVE IT! --NOT ABOUT HIM--OR YOUR MOTHER!
I CAN STILL REMEMBER--AS IF IT WERE ONLY YESTERDAY--
I REMEMBER HOW HAPPY THEY SEEMED--HOW THEY LOVED EACH OTHER--AND HOW THEY LOVED YOU!
I ALWAYS THOUGHT YOU'D GROW UP TO BE SO PROUD OF YOUR FATHER! HE HAD BEEN A WAR HERO--WITH SO MANY MEDALS--SO MANY DECORATIONS!
YOUR UNCLE BEN AND I--WERE SO SURE--THAT HE HAD SUCH A BRIGHT FUTURE AHEAD OF HIM!
MY NEW JOB WILL BE TAKING ME OVERSEAS FOR A FEW MONTHS--AND MARY IS GOING WITH ME!
ARE YOU SURE YOU'LL BE ABLE TO LOOK AFTER PETER WHILE WE'RE GONE?
OF COURSE WE WILL, RICHARD!
YOU KNOW WE ALREADY LOVE HIM LIKE OUR OWN!
BE A GOOD BOY, PETER!
WE'LL BE BACK AS SOON AS WE CAN, DARLING!
WHAT A SHAME THAT RICHARD'S WORK REQUIRES HIM TO GO OVERSEAS! I WONDER WHY HE NEVER TALKS ABOUT IT?
"IT WAS SCARCELY A MONTH LATER THAT WE FINALLY LEARNED--WHY HE NEVER SPOKE OF HIS WORK! YES--WE LEARNED--IN THE MOST HORRIBLE--HEART-BREAKING WAY POSSIBLE--!"
I-I'M READING THE WORDS--BUT I CAN'T BELIEVE WHAT THEY SAY!
IT'S LIKE--READING ABOUT TWO STRANGERS!
THEY WERE IN THIS HOUSE--JUST A FEW WEEKS AGO--HAPPY--WITHOUT A CARE IN THE WORLD!! AND NOW--THIS!!
MY OWN BROTHER--A TRAITOR TO HIS COUNTRY!
BUT, WHAT OF PETER! WITH BOTH HIS PARENTS DEAD--WHAT'S TO BECOME OF HIM?
THERE'S ONLY ONE THING TO DO, MAY--ONLY ONE THING WE CAN DO! WE'RE HIS ONLY LIVING RELATIVES--
WE'LL BRING HIM UP, DEAR--LIKE OUR OWN SON!
AND WE'LL NEVER TELL HIM--ABOUT HIS PARENTS! WE'LL LET THE SHAME--AND THE SORROW--LIE BURIED WITH THEM!

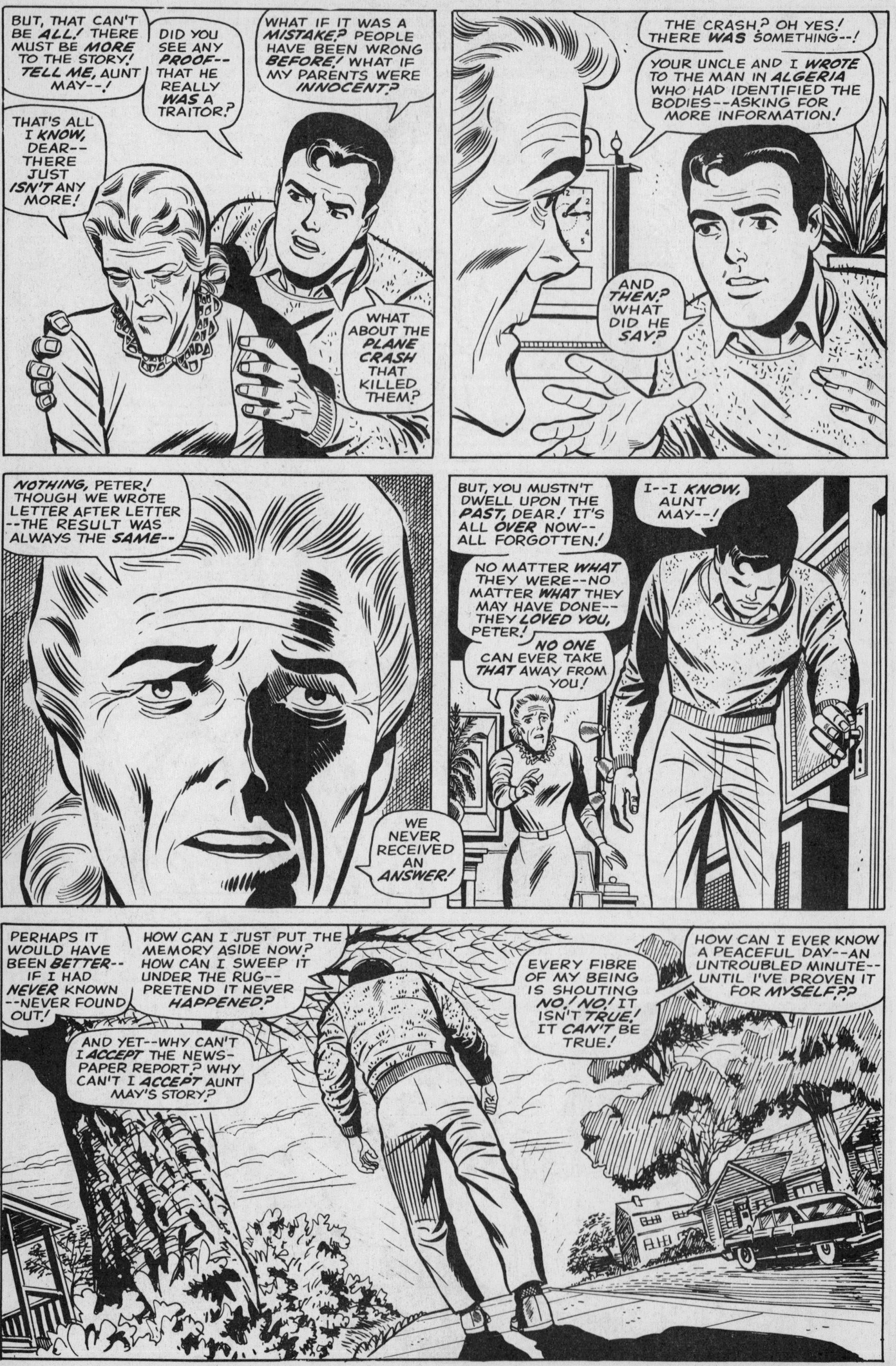

BUT, THAT CAN'T BE ALL! THERE MUST BE MORE TO THE STORY! TELL ME, AUNT MAY--!
DID YOU SEE ANY PROOF-- THAT HE REALLY WAS A TRAITOR?
WHAT IF IT WAS A MISTAKE? PEOPLE HAVE BEEN WRONG BEFORE! WHAT IF MY PARENTS WERE INNOCENT?
THAT'S ALL I KNOW, DEAR-- THERE JUST ISN'T ANY MORE!
WHAT ABOUT THE PLANE CRASH THAT KILLED THEM?
THE CRASH? OH YES! THERE WAS SOMETHING--!
YOUR UNCLE AND I WROTE TO THE MAN IN ALGERIA WHO HAD IDENTIFIED THE BODIES--ASKING FOR MORE INFORMATION!
AND THEN? WHAT DID HE SAY?
NOTHING, PETER! THOUGH WE WROTE LETTER AFTER LETTER --THE RESULT WAS ALWAYS THE SAME--
WE NEVER RECEIVED AN ANSWER!
BUT, YOU MUSTN'T DWELL UPON THE PAST, DEAR! IT'S ALL OVER NOW-- ALL FORGOTTEN!
I--I KNOW, AUNT MAY--!
NO MATTER WHAT THEY WERE--NO MATTER WHAT THEY MAY HAVE DONE-- THEY LOVED YOU, PETER!
NO ONE CAN EVER TAKE THAT AWAY FROM YOU!
PERHAPS IT WOULD HAVE BEEN BETTER-- IF I HAD NEVER KNOWN --NEVER FOUND OUT!
HOW CAN I JUST PUT THE MEMORY ASIDE NOW? HOW CAN I SWEEP IT UNDER THE RUG-- PRETEND IT NEVER HAPPENED?
AND YET--WHY CAN'T I ACCEPT THE NEWS-PAPER REPORT? WHY CAN'T I ACCEPT AUNT MAY'S STORY?
EVERY FIBRE OF MY BEING IS SHOUTING NO! NO! IT ISN'T TRUE! IT CAN'T BE TRUE!
HOW CAN I EVER KNOW A PEACEFUL DAY--AN UNTROUBLED MINUTE-- UNTIL I'VE PROVEN IT FOR MYSELF??

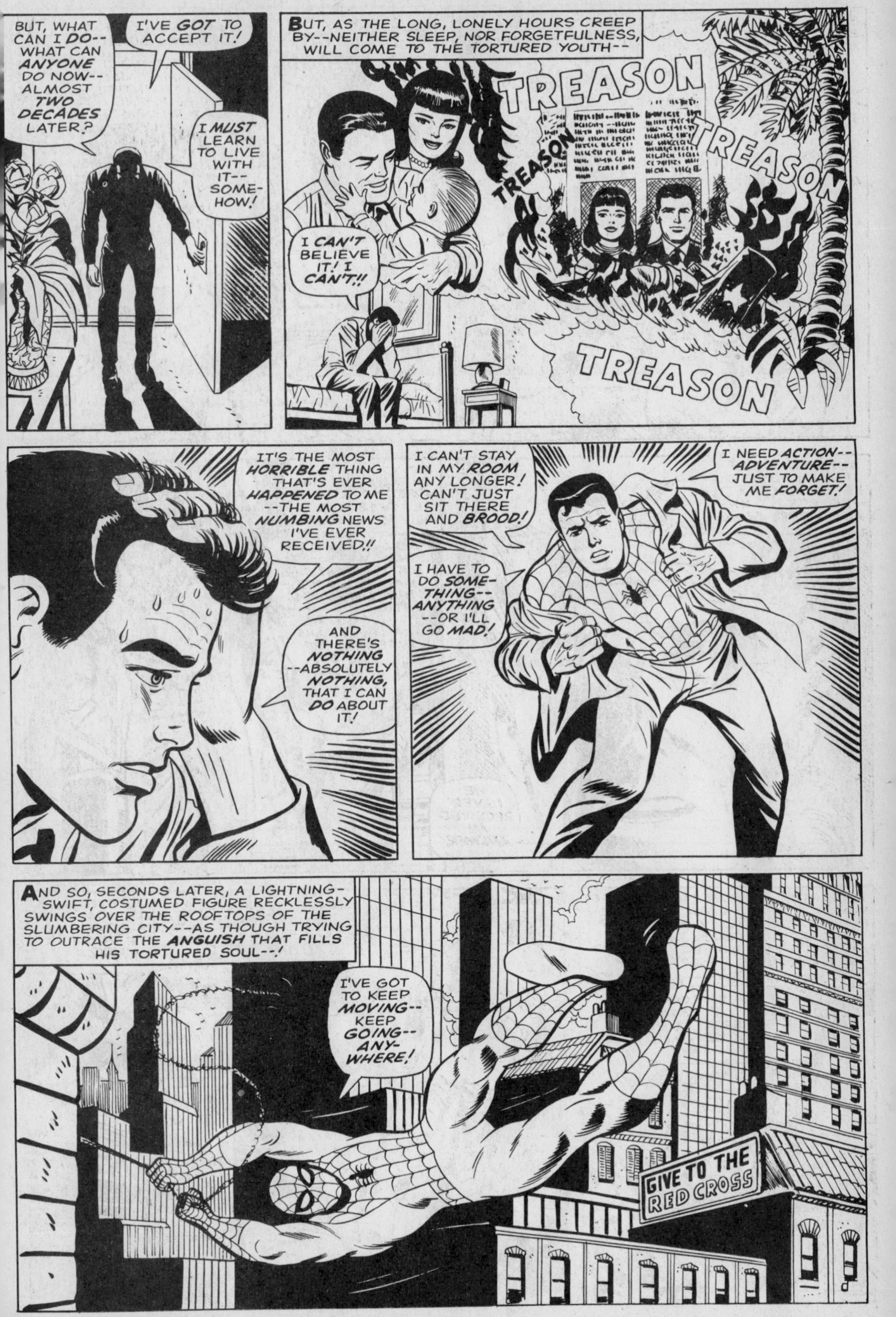
BUT, WHAT CAN I DO-- WHAT CAN ANYONE DO NOW-- ALMOST TWO DECADES LATER?
I'VE GOT TO ACCEPT IT!
I MUST LEARN TO LIVE WITH IT-- SOMEHOW!
BUT, AS THE LONG, LONELY HOURS CREEP BY--NEITHER SLEEP, NOR FORGETFULNESS, WILL COME TO THE TORTURED YOUTH--
TREASON
TREASON
TREASON
TREASON
I CAN'T BELIEVE IT! I CAN'T!!
IT'S THE MOST HORRIBLE THING THAT'S EVER HAPPENED TO ME --THE MOST NUMBING NEWS I'VE EVER RECEIVED!!
AND THERE'S NOTHING --ABSOLUTELY NOTHING, THAT I CAN DO ABOUT IT!
I CAN'T STAY IN MY ROOM ANY LONGER! CAN'T JUST SIT THERE AND BROOD!
I NEED ACTION-- ADVENTURE-- JUST TO MAKE ME FORGET!
I HAVE TO DO SOME-THING-- ANYTHING --OR I'LL GO MAD!
AND SO, SECONDS LATER, A LIGHTNING-SWIFT, COSTUMED FIGURE RECKLESSLY SWINGS OVER THE ROOFTOPS OF THE SLUMBERING CITY--AS THOUGH TRYING TO OUTRACE THE ANGUISH THAT FILLS HIS TORTURED SOUL--!
I'VE GOT TO KEEP MOVING-- KEEP GOING-- ANY-WHERE!
GIVE TO THE RED CROSS

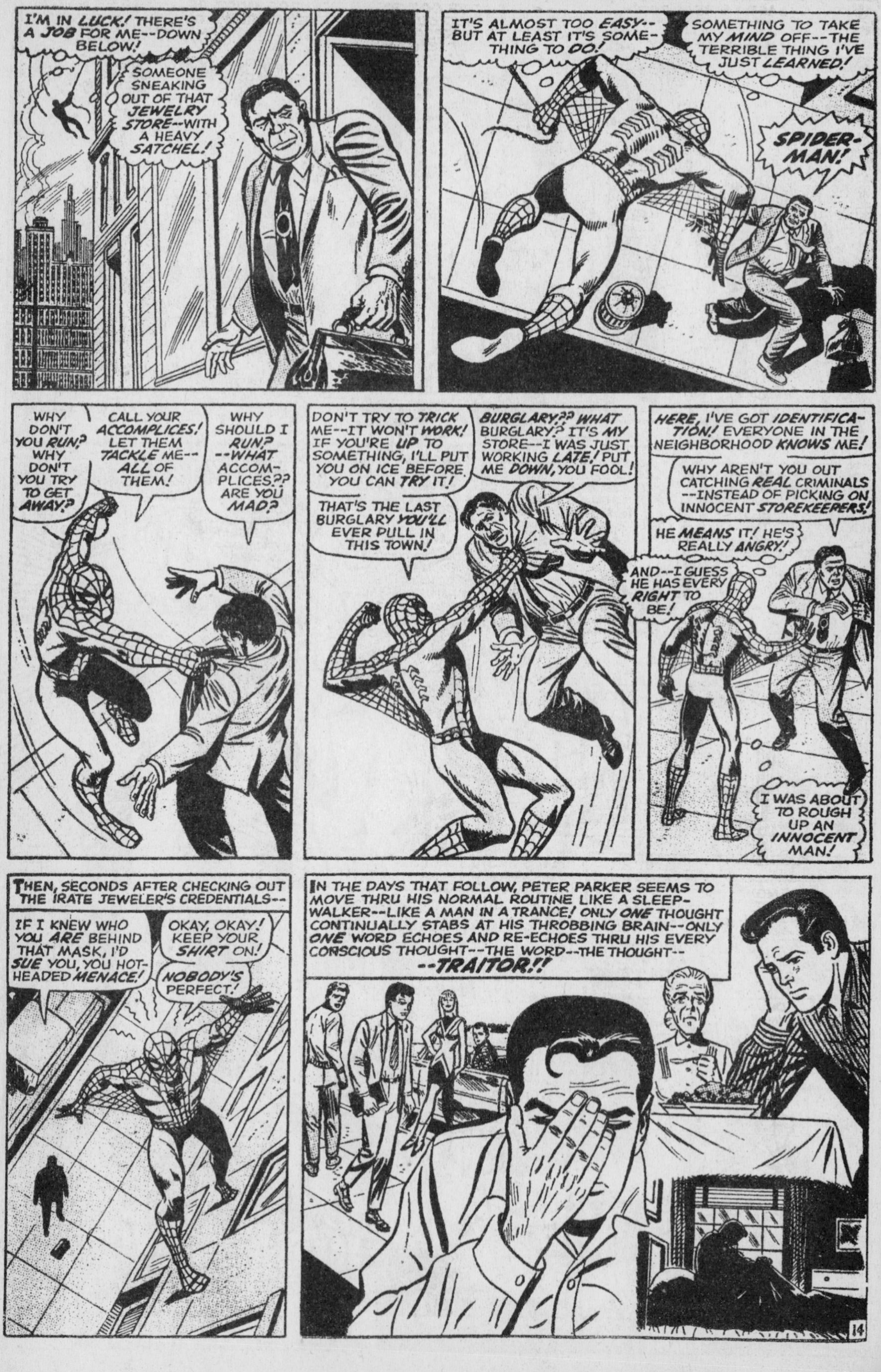

I'M IN LUCK! THERE'S A JOB FOR ME--DOWN BELOW!
SOMEONE SNEAKING OUT OF THAT JEWELRY STORE--WITH A HEAVY SATCHEL!
IT'S ALMOST TOO EASY--BUT AT LEAST IT'S SOMETHING TO DO!
SOMETHING TO TAKE MY MIND OFF--THE TERRIBLE THING I'VE JUST LEARNED!
SPIDER-MAN!
WHY DON'T YOU RUN? WHY DON'T YOU TRY TO GET AWAY?
CALL YOUR ACCOMPLICES! LET THEM TACKLE ME--ALL OF THEM!
WHY SHOULD I RUN? --WHAT ACCOMPLICES?? ARE YOU MAD?
DON'T TRY TO TRICK ME--IT WON'T WORK! IF YOU'RE UP TO SOMETHING, I'LL PUT YOU ON ICE BEFORE YOU CAN TRY IT!
BURGLARY?? WHAT BURGLARY? IT'S MY STORE--I WAS JUST WORKING LATE! PUT ME DOWN, YOU FOOL!
THAT'S THE LAST BURGLARY YOU'LL EVER PULL IN THIS TOWN!
HERE, I'VE GOT IDENTIFICATION! EVERYONE IN THE NEIGHBORHOOD KNOWS ME!
WHY AREN'T YOU OUT CATCHING REAL CRIMINALS --INSTEAD OF PICKING ON INNOCENT STOREKEEPERS!
HE MEANS IT! HE'S REALLY ANGRY!
AND--I GUESS HE HAS EVERY RIGHT TO BE!
I WAS ABOUT TO ROUGH UP AN INNOCENT MAN!
THEN, SECONDS AFTER CHECKING OUT THE IRATE JEWELER'S CREDENTIALS--
IF I KNEW WHO YOU ARE BEHIND THAT MASK, I'D SUE YOU, YOU HOT-HEADED MENACE!
OKAY, OKAY! KEEP YOUR SHIRT ON!
NOBODY'S PERFECT!
IN THE DAYS THAT FOLLOW, PETER PARKER SEEMS TO MOVE THRU HIS NORMAL ROUTINE LIKE A SLEEP-WALKER--LIKE A MAN IN A TRANCE! ONLY ONE THOUGHT CONTINUALLY STABS AT HIS THROBBING BRAIN--ONLY ONE WORD ECHOES AND RE-ECHOES THRU HIS EVERY CONSCIOUS THOUGHT--THE WORD--THE THOUGHT--
--TRAITOR!!
14

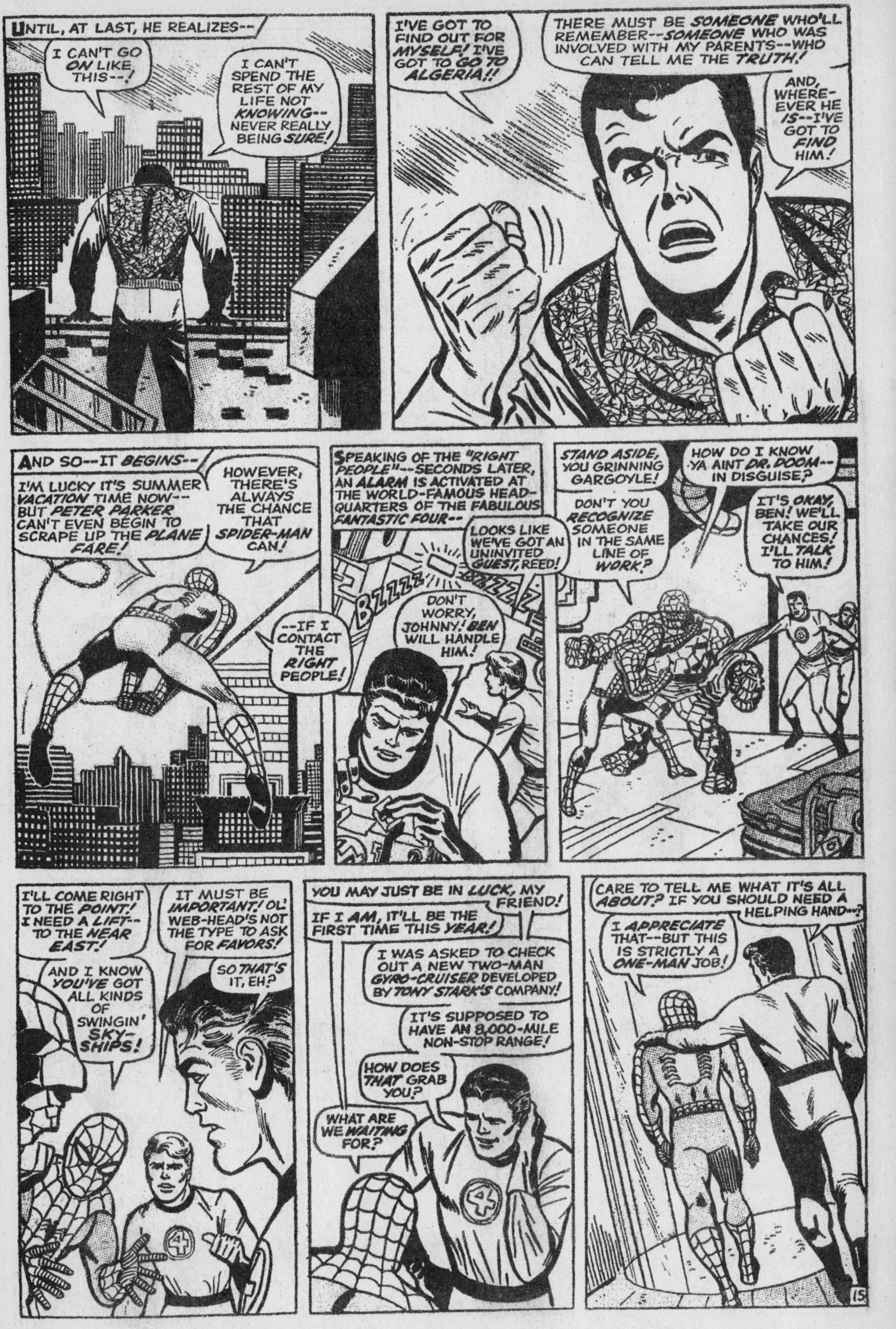
UNTIL, AT LAST, HE REALIZES--
I CAN'T GO ON LIKE THIS--!
I CAN'T SPEND THE REST OF MY LIFE NOT KNOWING-- NEVER REALLY BEING SURE!
I'VE GOT TO FIND OUT FOR MYSELF! I'VE GOT TO GO TO ALGERIA!!
THERE MUST BE SOMEONE WHO'LL REMEMBER--SOMEONE WHO WAS INVOLVED WITH MY PARENTS--WHO CAN TELL ME THE TRUTH!
AND, WHEREEVER HE IS--I'VE GOT TO FIND HIM!
AND SO--IT BEGINS--
I'M LUCKY IT'S SUMMER VACATION TIME NOW-- BUT PETER PARKER CAN'T EVEN BEGIN TO SCRAPE UP THE PLANE FARE!
HOWEVER, THERE'S ALWAYS THE CHANCE THAT SPIDER-MAN CAN!
--IF I CONTACT THE RIGHT PEOPLE!
SPEAKING OF THE "RIGHT PEOPLE"--SECONDS LATER, AN ALARM IS ACTIVATED AT THE WORLD-FAMOUS HEADQUARTERS OF THE FABULOUS FANTASTIC FOUR--
BZZZZZ
LOOKS LIKE WE'VE GOT AN UNINVITED GUEST, REED!
DON'T WORRY, JOHNNY! BEN WILL HANDLE HIM!
STAND ASIDE, YOU GRINNING GARGOYLE!
HOW DO I KNOW YA AINT DR. DOOM-- IN DISGUISE?
DON'T YOU RECOGNIZE SOMEONE IN THE SAME LINE OF WORK?
IT'S OKAY, BEN! WE'LL TAKE OUR CHANCES! I'LL TALK TO HIM!
I'LL COME RIGHT TO THE POINT! I NEED A LIFT-- TO THE NEAR EAST!
IT MUST BE IMPORTANT! OL' WEB-HEAD'S NOT THE TYPE TO ASK FOR FAVORS!
AND I KNOW YOU'VE GOT ALL KINDS OF SWINGIN' SKY-SHIPS!
SO THAT'S IT, EH?
YOU MAY JUST BE IN LUCK, MY FRIEND!
IF I AM, IT'LL BE THE FIRST TIME THIS YEAR!
I WAS ASKED TO CHECK OUT A NEW TWO-MAN GYRO-CRUISER DEVELOPED BY TONY STARK'S COMPANY!
IT'S SUPPOSED TO HAVE AN 8,000-MILE NON-STOP RANGE!
HOW DOES THAT GRAB YOU?
WHAT ARE WE WAITING FOR?
CARE TO TELL ME WHAT IT'S ALL ABOUT? IF YOU SHOULD NEED A HELPING HAND--?
I APPRECIATE THAT--BUT THIS IS STRICTLY A ONE-MAN JOB!
15

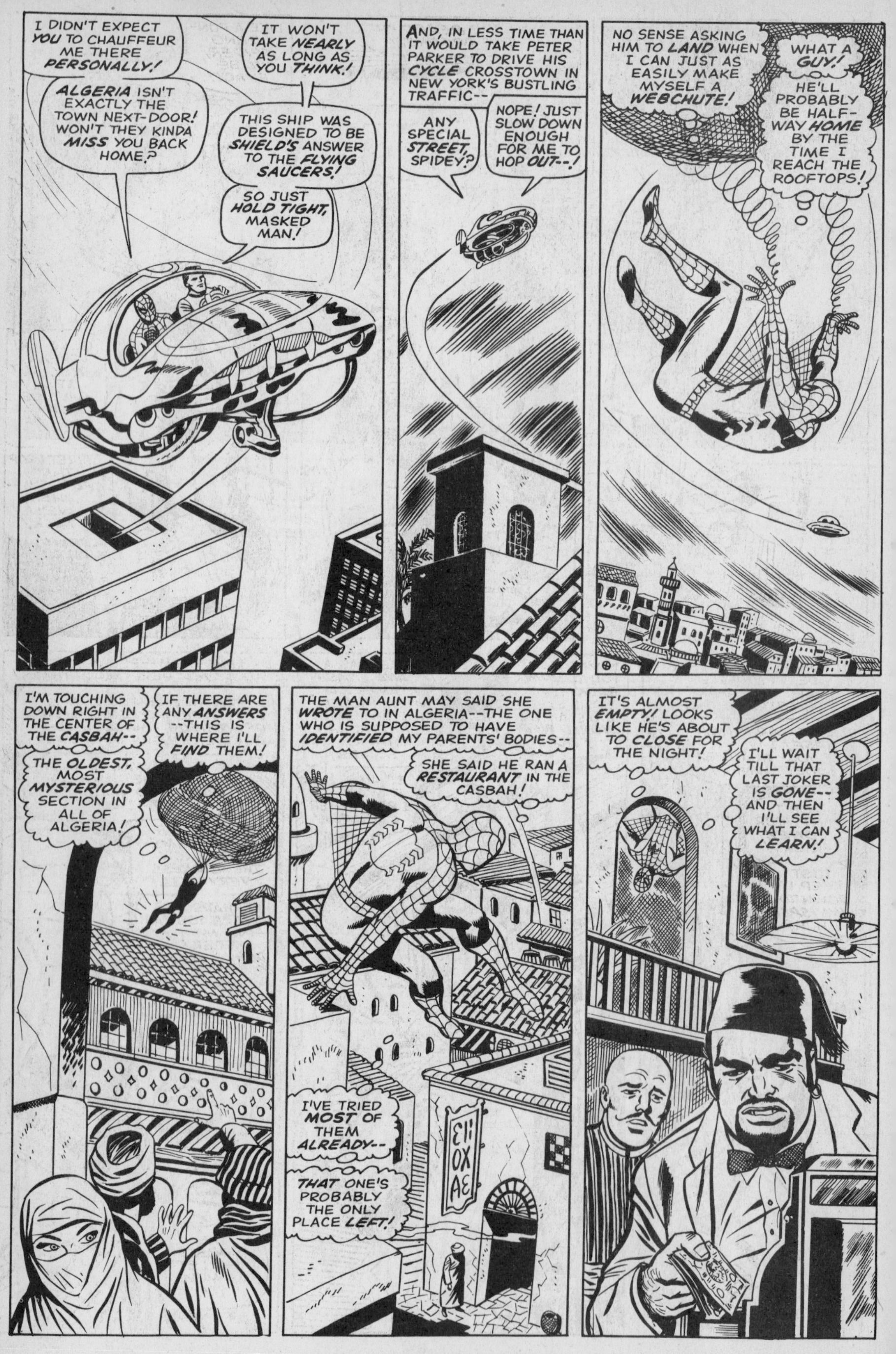

I DIDN'T EXPECT *YOU* TO CHAUFFEUR ME THERE *PERSONALLY!*
ALGERIA ISN'T EXACTLY THE TOWN NEXT-DOOR! WON'T THEY KINDA *MISS* YOU BACK HOME?
IT WON'T TAKE *NEARLY* AS LONG AS YOU *THINK!*
THIS SHIP WAS DESIGNED TO BE *SHIELD'S* ANSWER TO THE *FLYING SAUCERS!*
SO JUST *HOLD TIGHT,* MASKED MAN!
AND, IN LESS TIME THAN IT WOULD TAKE PETER PARKER TO DRIVE HIS *CYCLE* CROSSTOWN IN NEW YORK'S BUSTLING TRAFFIC--
ANY SPECIAL *STREET,* SPIDEY?
NOPE! JUST SLOW DOWN ENOUGH FOR ME TO HOP *OUT*--!
NO SENSE ASKING HIM TO *LAND* WHEN I CAN JUST AS EASILY MAKE MYSELF A *WEBCHUTE!*
WHAT A *GUY!*
HE'LL PROBABLY BE HALF-WAY *HOME* BY THE TIME I REACH THE ROOFTOPS!
I'M TOUCHING DOWN RIGHT IN THE CENTER OF THE *CASBAH*--
THE *OLDEST,* MOST *MYSTERIOUS* SECTION IN ALL OF ALGERIA!
IF THERE ARE ANY *ANSWERS* --THIS IS WHERE I'LL *FIND* THEM!
THE MAN AUNT MAY SAID SHE *WROTE* TO IN ALGERIA--THE ONE WHO IS SUPPOSED TO HAVE *IDENTIFIED* MY PARENTS' BODIES--
SHE SAID HE RAN A *RESTAURANT* IN THE CASBAH!
I'VE TRIED *MOST* OF THEM *ALREADY*--
THAT ONE'S PROBABLY THE ONLY PLACE *LEFT!*
IT'S ALMOST *EMPTY!* LOOKS LIKE HE'S ABOUT TO *CLOSE* FOR THE NIGHT!
I'LL WAIT TILL THAT LAST JOKER IS *GONE*-- AND THEN I'LL SEE WHAT I CAN *LEARN!*

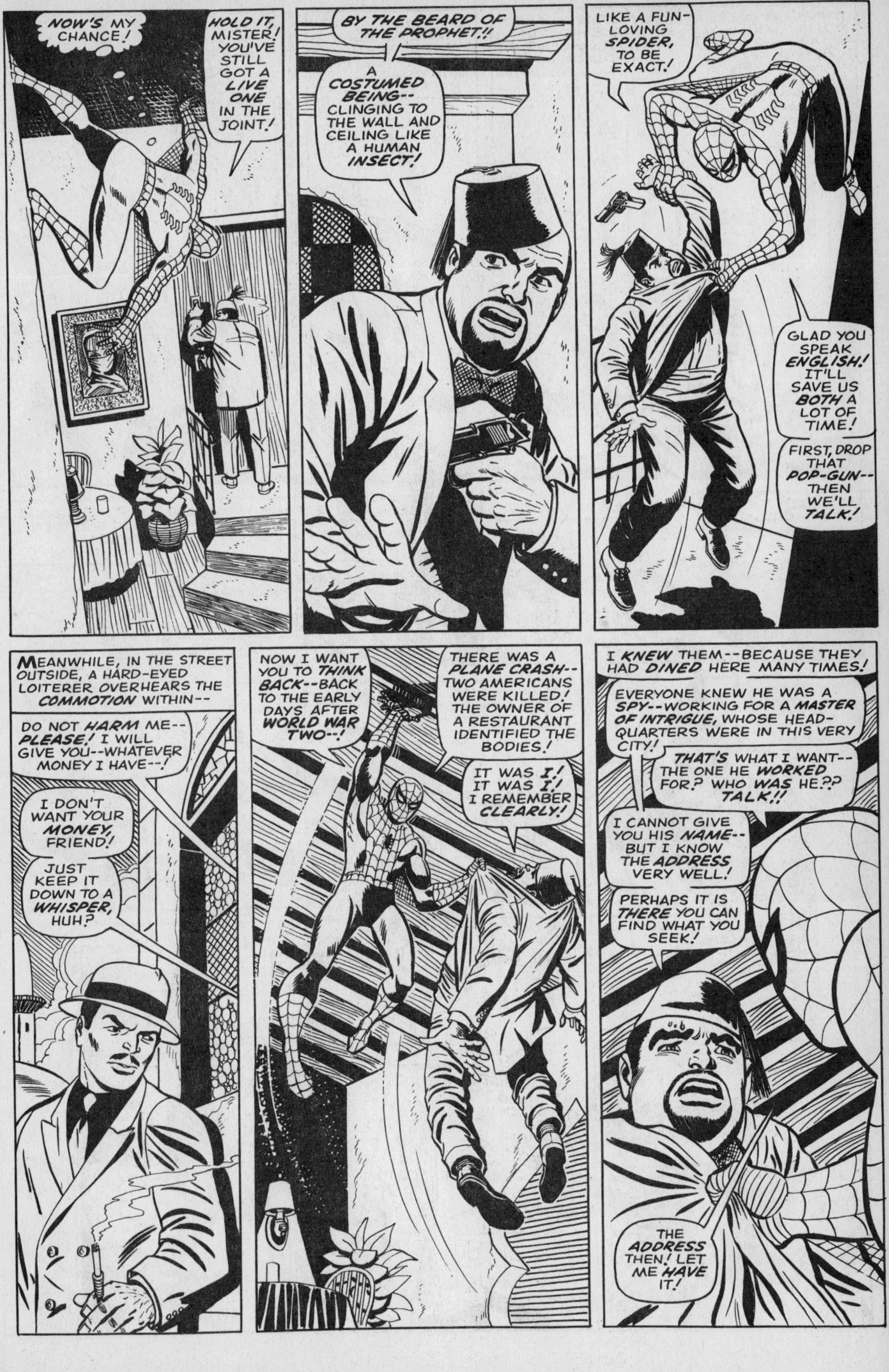

NOW'S MY CHANCE!
HOLD IT, MISTER! YOU'VE STILL GOT A LIVE ONE IN THE JOINT!
BY THE BEARD OF THE PROPHET!!
A COSTUMED BEING-- CLINGING TO THE WALL AND CEILING LIKE A HUMAN INSECT!
LIKE A FUN-LOVING SPIDER, TO BE EXACT!
GLAD YOU SPEAK ENGLISH! IT'LL SAVE US BOTH A LOT OF TIME!
FIRST, DROP THAT POP-GUN-- THEN WE'LL TALK!
MEANWHILE, IN THE STREET OUTSIDE, A HARD-EYED LOITERER OVERHEARS THE COMMOTION WITHIN--
DO NOT HARM ME-- PLEASE! I WILL GIVE YOU--WHATEVER MONEY I HAVE--!
I DON'T WANT YOUR MONEY, FRIEND!
JUST KEEP IT DOWN TO A WHISPER, HUH?
NOW I WANT YOU TO THINK BACK--BACK TO THE EARLY DAYS AFTER WORLD WAR TWO--!
THERE WAS A PLANE CRASH-- TWO AMERICANS WERE KILLED! THE OWNER OF A RESTAURANT IDENTIFIED THE BODIES!
IT WAS I! IT WAS I! I REMEMBER CLEARLY!
I KNEW THEM--BECAUSE THEY HAD DINED HERE MANY TIMES!
EVERYONE KNEW HE WAS A SPY--WORKING FOR A MASTER OF INTRIGUE, WHOSE HEAD-QUARTERS WERE IN THIS VERY CITY!
THAT'S WHAT I WANT-- THE ONE HE WORKED FOR? WHO WAS HE?? TALK!!
I CANNOT GIVE YOU HIS NAME-- BUT I KNOW THE ADDRESS VERY WELL!
PERHAPS IT IS THERE YOU CAN FIND WHAT YOU SEEK!
THE ADDRESS THEN! LET ME HAVE IT!

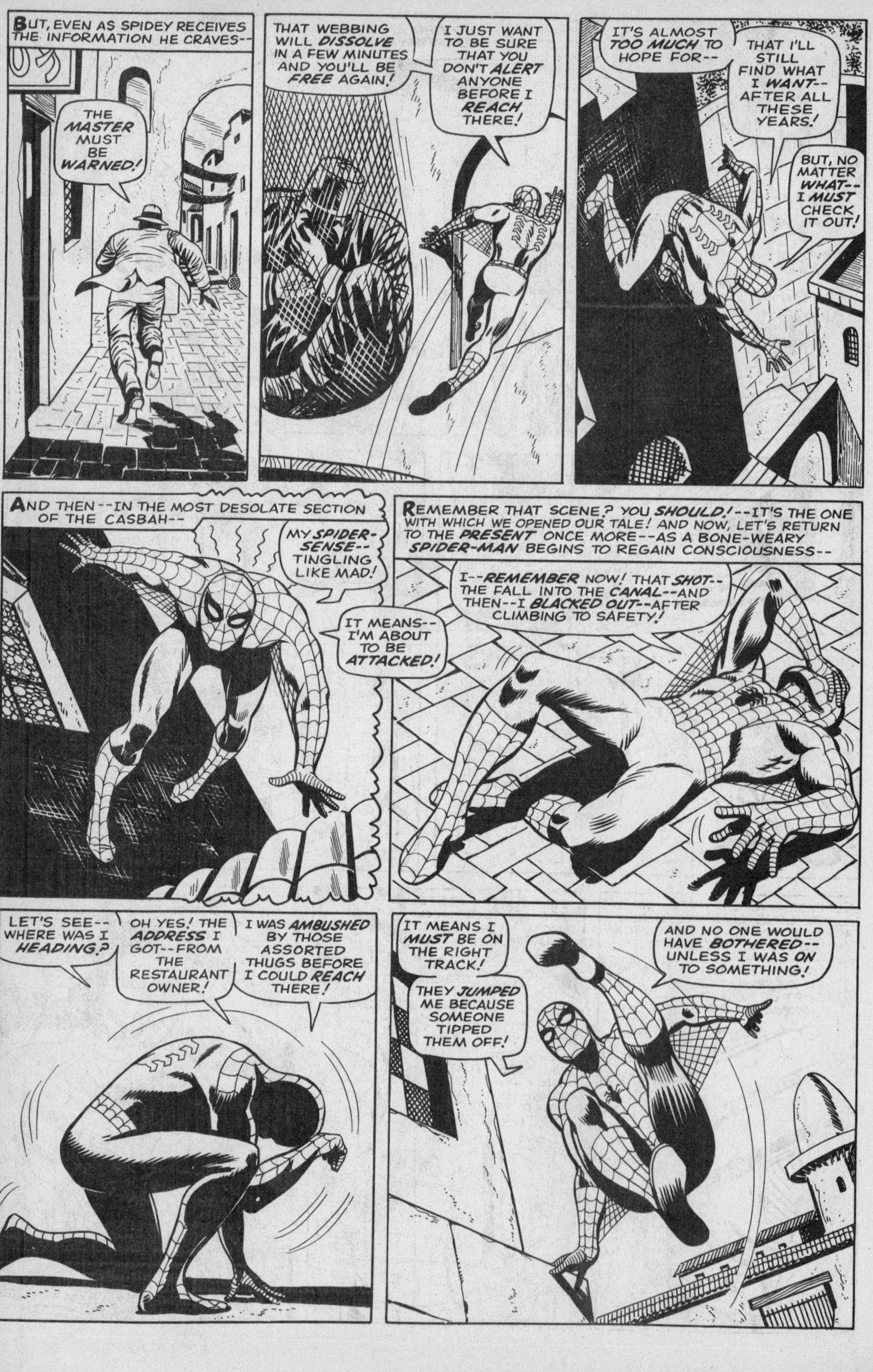
BUT, EVEN AS SPIDEY RECEIVES THE INFORMATION HE CRAVES--
THE MASTER MUST BE WARNED!
THAT WEBBING WILL DISSOLVE IN A FEW MINUTES AND YOU'LL BE FREE AGAIN!
I JUST WANT TO BE SURE THAT YOU DON'T ALERT ANYONE BEFORE I REACH THERE!
IT'S ALMOST TOO MUCH TO HOPE FOR--
THAT I'LL STILL FIND WHAT I WANT-- AFTER ALL THESE YEARS!
BUT, NO MATTER WHAT-- I MUST CHECK IT OUT!
AND THEN--IN THE MOST DESOLATE SECTION OF THE CASBAH--
MY SPIDER-SENSE-- TINGLING LIKE MAD!
IT MEANS-- I'M ABOUT TO BE ATTACKED!
REMEMBER THAT SCENE? YOU SHOULD!--IT'S THE ONE WITH WHICH WE OPENED OUR TALE! AND NOW, LET'S RETURN TO THE PRESENT ONCE MORE--AS A BONE-WEARY SPIDER-MAN BEGINS TO REGAIN CONSCIOUSNESS--
I--REMEMBER NOW! THAT SHOT-- THE FALL INTO THE CANAL--AND THEN--I BLACKED OUT--AFTER CLIMBING TO SAFETY!
LET'S SEE-- WHERE WAS I HEADING?
OH YES! THE ADDRESS I GOT--FROM THE RESTAURANT OWNER!
I WAS AMBUSHED BY THOSE ASSORTED THUGS BEFORE I COULD REACH THERE!
IT MEANS I MUST BE ON THE RIGHT TRACK!
THEY JUMPED ME BECAUSE SOMEONE TIPPED THEM OFF!
AND NO ONE WOULD HAVE BOTHERED-- UNLESS I WAS ON TO SOMETHING!

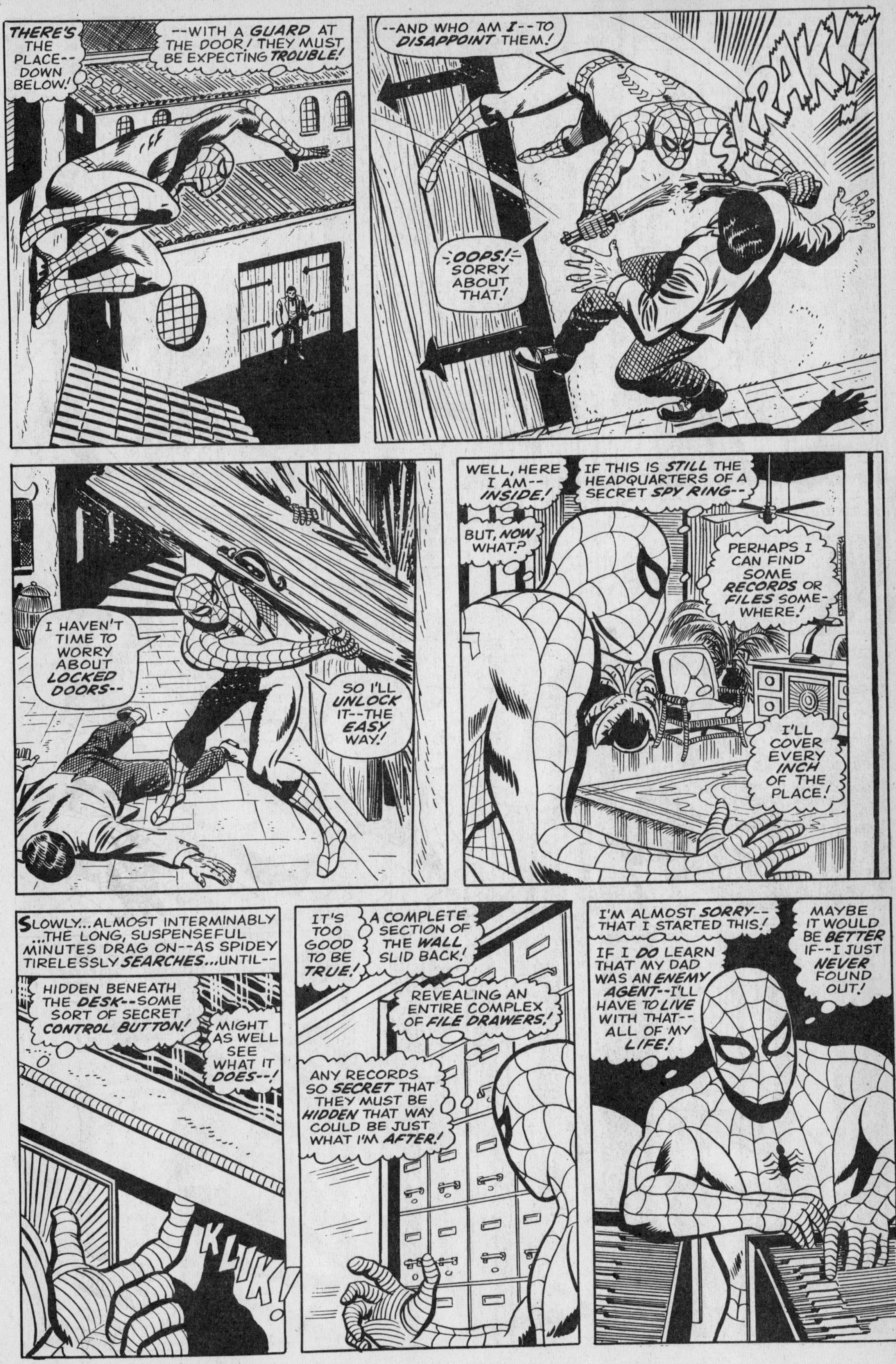
THERE'S THE PLACE--DOWN BELOW!
--WITH A GUARD AT THE DOOR! THEY MUST BE EXPECTING TROUBLE!
--AND WHO AM I--TO DISAPPOINT THEM!
SKRAKK!
OOPS! SORRY ABOUT THAT!
I HAVEN'T TIME TO WORRY ABOUT LOCKED DOORS--
SO I'LL UNLOCK IT--THE EASY WAY!
WELL, HERE I AM--INSIDE!
BUT, NOW WHAT?
IF THIS IS STILL THE HEADQUARTERS OF A SECRET SPY RING--
PERHAPS I CAN FIND SOME RECORDS OR FILES SOMEWHERE!
I'LL COVER EVERY INCH OF THE PLACE!
SLOWLY...ALMOST INTERMINABLY ...THE LONG, SUSPENSEFUL MINUTES DRAG ON--AS SPIDEY TIRELESSLY SEARCHES...UNTIL--
HIDDEN BENEATH THE DESK--SOME SORT OF SECRET CONTROL BUTTON!
MIGHT AS WELL SEE WHAT IT DOES--!
KLIK!
IT'S TOO GOOD TO BE TRUE!
A COMPLETE SECTION OF THE WALL SLID BACK!
REVEALING AN ENTIRE COMPLEX OF FILE DRAWERS!
ANY RECORDS SO SECRET THAT THEY MUST BE HIDDEN THAT WAY COULD BE JUST WHAT I'M AFTER!
I'M ALMOST SORRY--THAT I STARTED THIS!
IF I DO LEARN THAT MY DAD WAS AN ENEMY AGENT--I'LL HAVE TO LIVE WITH THAT--ALL OF MY LIFE!
MAYBE IT WOULD BE BETTER IF--I JUST NEVER FOUND OUT!

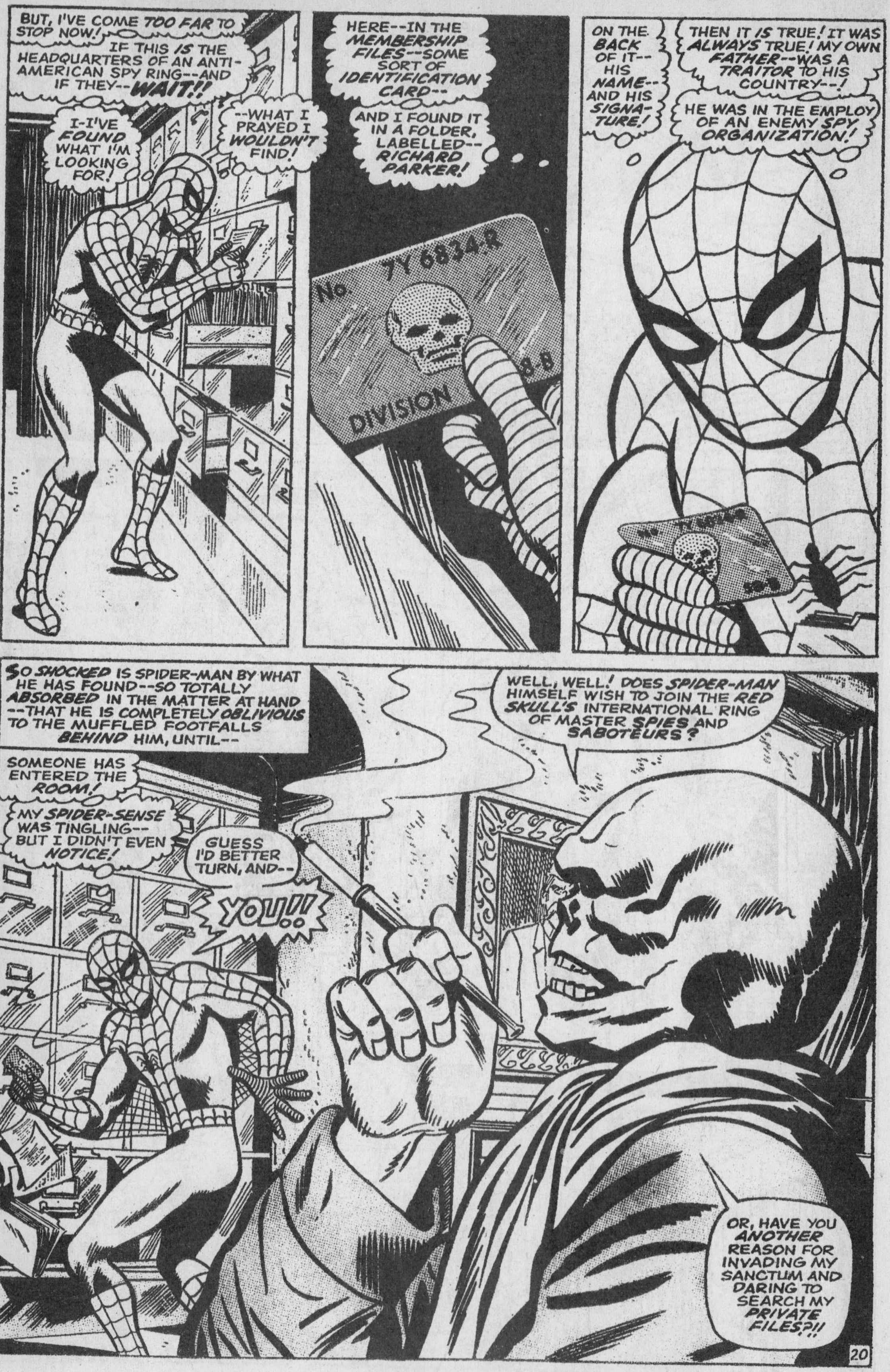
BUT, I'VE COME TOO FAR TO STOP NOW! IF THIS IS THE HEADQUARTERS OF AN ANTI-AMERICAN SPY RING--AND IF THEY--WAIT!!
I-I'VE FOUND WHAT I'M LOOKING FOR!
--WHAT I PRAYED I WOULDN'T FIND!
HERE--IN THE MEMBERSHIP FILES--SOME SORT OF IDENTIFICATION CARD--
AND I FOUND IT IN A FOLDER, LABELLED--RICHARD PARKER!
No. 7Y 6834-R
B-8
DIVISION
ON THE BACK OF IT--HIS NAME--AND HIS SIGNATURE!
THEN IT IS TRUE! IT WAS ALWAYS TRUE! MY OWN FATHER--WAS A TRAITOR TO HIS COUNTRY--!
HE WAS IN THE EMPLOY OF AN ENEMY SPY ORGANIZATION!
SO SHOCKED IS SPIDER-MAN BY WHAT HE HAS FOUND--SO TOTALLY ABSORBED IN THE MATTER AT HAND--THAT HE IS COMPLETELY OBLIVIOUS TO THE MUFFLED FOOTFALLS BEHIND HIM, UNTIL--
WELL, WELL! DOES SPIDER-MAN HIMSELF WISH TO JOIN THE RED SKULL'S INTERNATIONAL RING OF MASTER SPIES AND SABOTEURS?
SOMEONE HAS ENTERED THE ROOM!
MY SPIDER-SENSE WAS TINGLING--BUT I DIDN'T EVEN NOTICE!
GUESS I'D BETTER TURN, AND--
YOU!!
OR, HAVE YOU ANOTHER REASON FOR INVADING MY SANCTUM AND DARING TO SEARCH MY PRIVATE FILES?!!
20

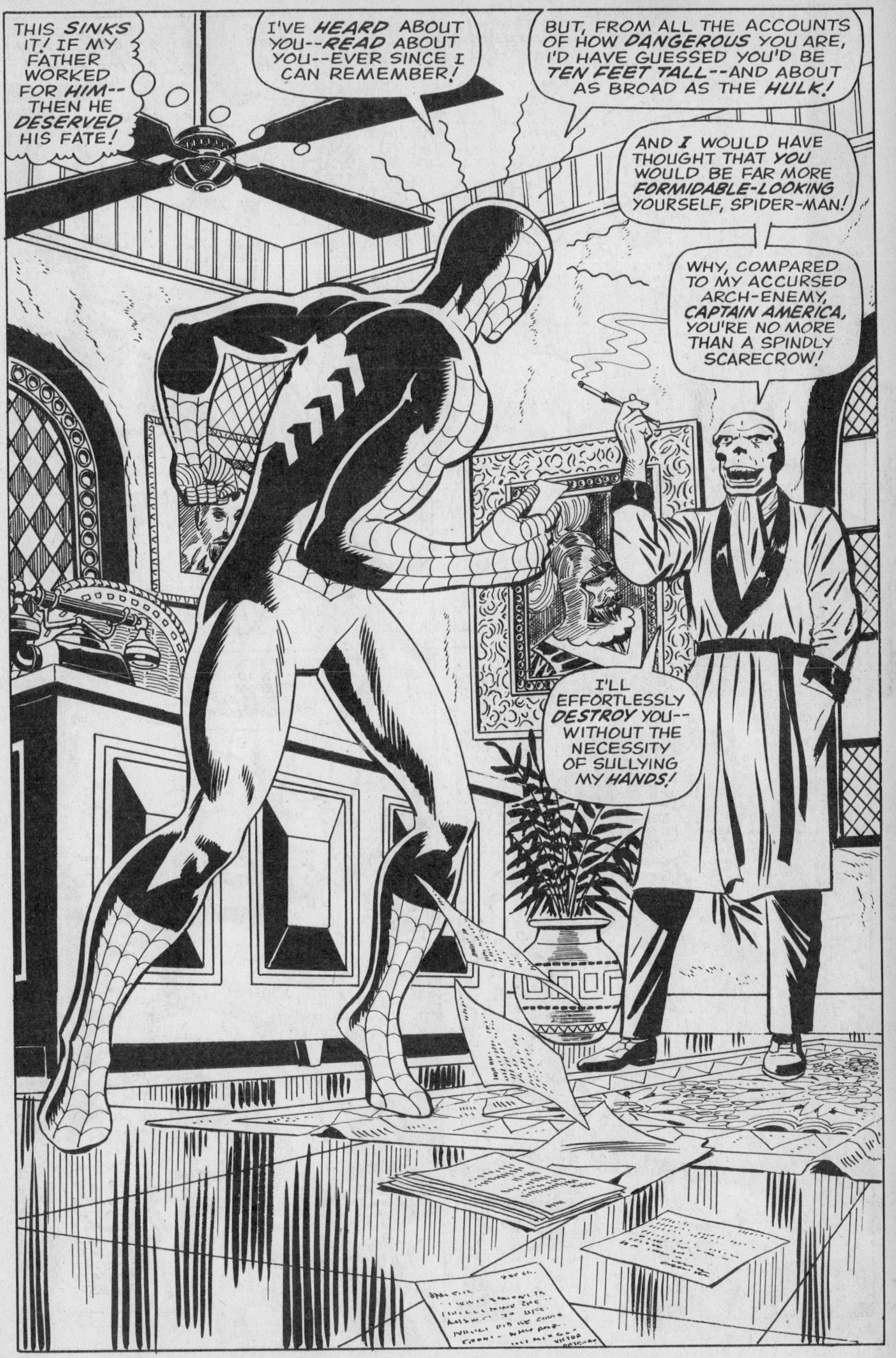
THIS SINKS IT! IF MY FATHER WORKED FOR HIM-- THEN HE DESERVED HIS FATE!
I'VE HEARD ABOUT YOU--READ ABOUT YOU--EVER SINCE I CAN REMEMBER!
BUT, FROM ALL THE ACCOUNTS OF HOW DANGEROUS YOU ARE, I'D HAVE GUESSED YOU'D BE TEN FEET TALL--AND ABOUT AS BROAD AS THE HULK!
AND I WOULD HAVE THOUGHT THAT YOU WOULD BE FAR MORE FORMIDABLE-LOOKING YOURSELF, SPIDER-MAN!
WHY, COMPARED TO MY ACCURSED ARCH-ENEMY, CAPTAIN AMERICA, YOU'RE NO MORE THAN A SPINDLY SCARECROW!
I'LL EFFORTLESSLY DESTROY YOU--WITHOUT THE NECESSITY OF SULLYING MY HANDS!

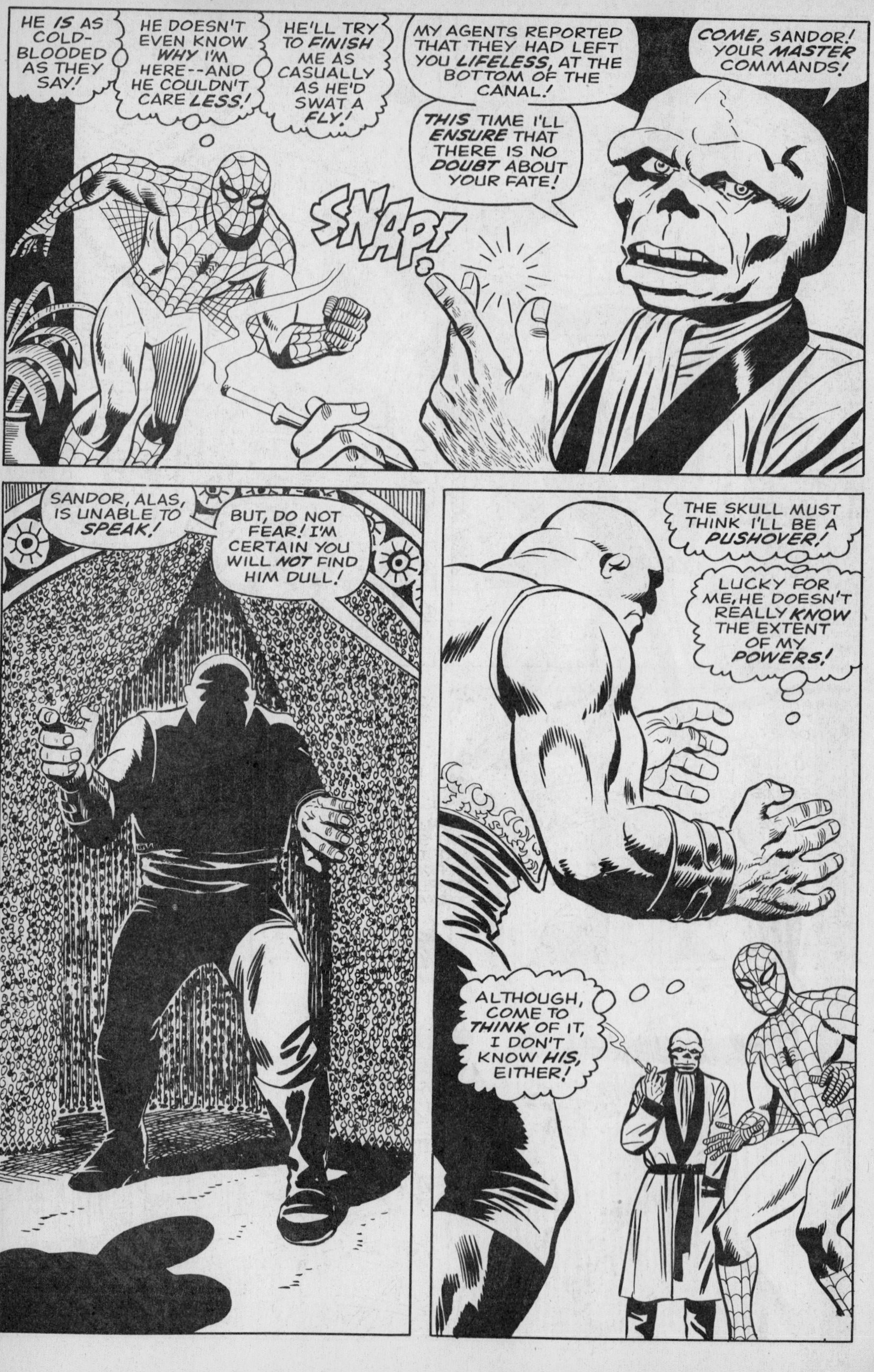
HE IS AS COLD-BLOODED AS THEY SAY!
HE DOESN'T EVEN KNOW WHY I'M HERE--AND HE COULDN'T CARE LESS!
HE'LL TRY TO FINISH ME AS CASUALLY AS HE'D SWAT A FLY!
MY AGENTS REPORTED THAT THEY HAD LEFT YOU LIFELESS, AT THE BOTTOM OF THE CANAL!
THIS TIME I'LL ENSURE THAT THERE IS NO DOUBT ABOUT YOUR FATE!
COME, SANDOR! YOUR MASTER COMMANDS!
SNAP!
SANDOR, ALAS, IS UNABLE TO SPEAK!
BUT, DO NOT FEAR! I'M CERTAIN YOU WILL NOT FIND HIM DULL!
THE SKULL MUST THINK I'LL BE A PUSHOVER!
LUCKY FOR ME, HE DOESN'T REALLY KNOW THE EXTENT OF MY POWERS!
ALTHOUGH, COME TO THINK OF IT, I DON'T KNOW HIS, EITHER!

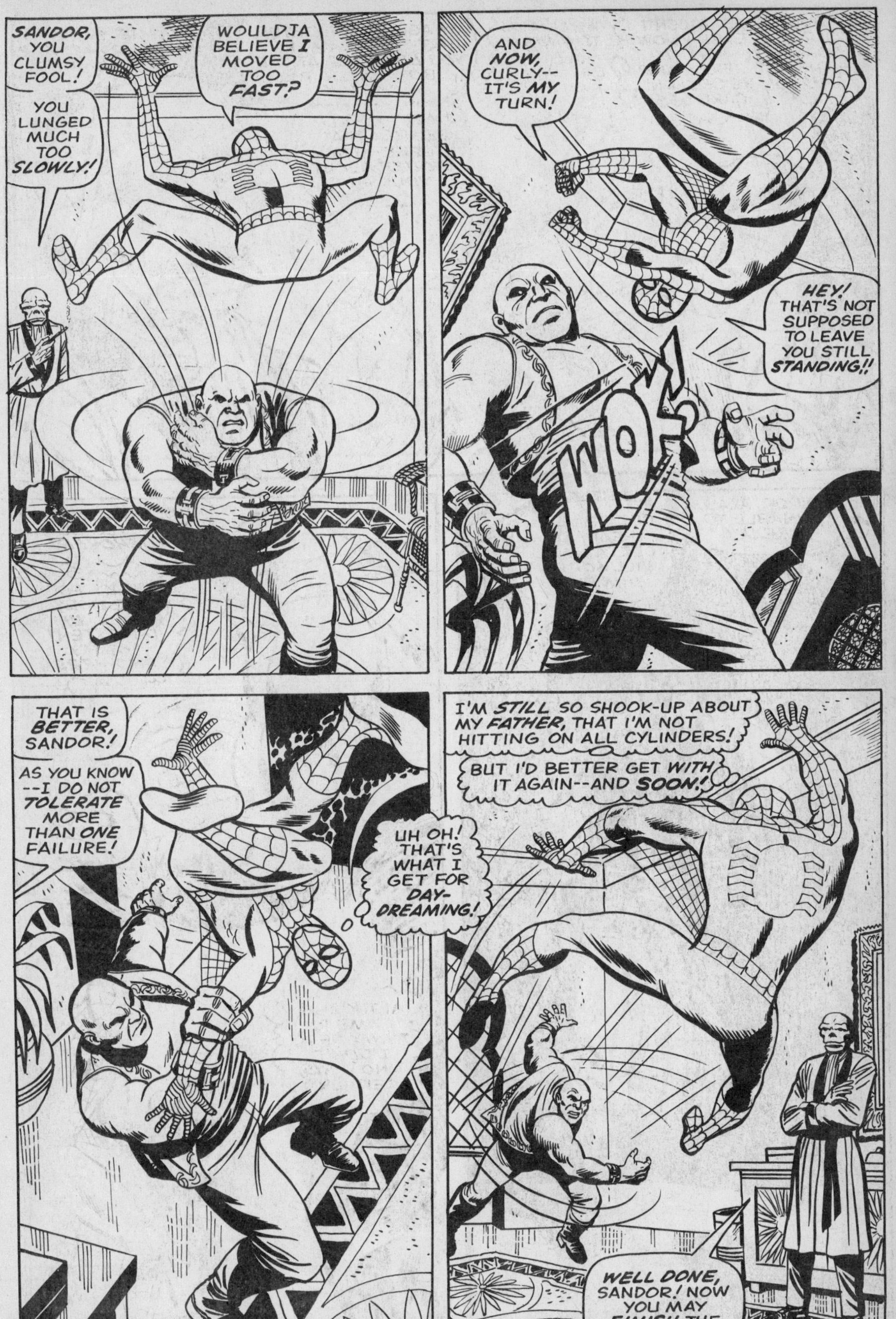
SANDOR, YOU CLUMSY FOOL!
YOU LUNGED MUCH TOO SLOWLY!
WOULDJA BELIEVE I MOVED TOO FAST?
AND NOW, CURLY-- IT'S MY TURN!
WOK!
HEY! THAT'S NOT SUPPOSED TO LEAVE YOU STILL STANDING!!
THAT IS BETTER, SANDOR!
AS YOU KNOW --I DO NOT TOLERATE MORE THAN ONE FAILURE!
UH OH! THAT'S WHAT I GET FOR DAY-DREAMING!
I'M STILL SO SHOOK-UP ABOUT MY FATHER, THAT I'M NOT HITTING ON ALL CYLINDERS!
BUT I'D BETTER GET WITH IT AGAIN--AND SOON!
WELL DONE, SANDOR! NOW YOU MAY FINISH THE JOB!

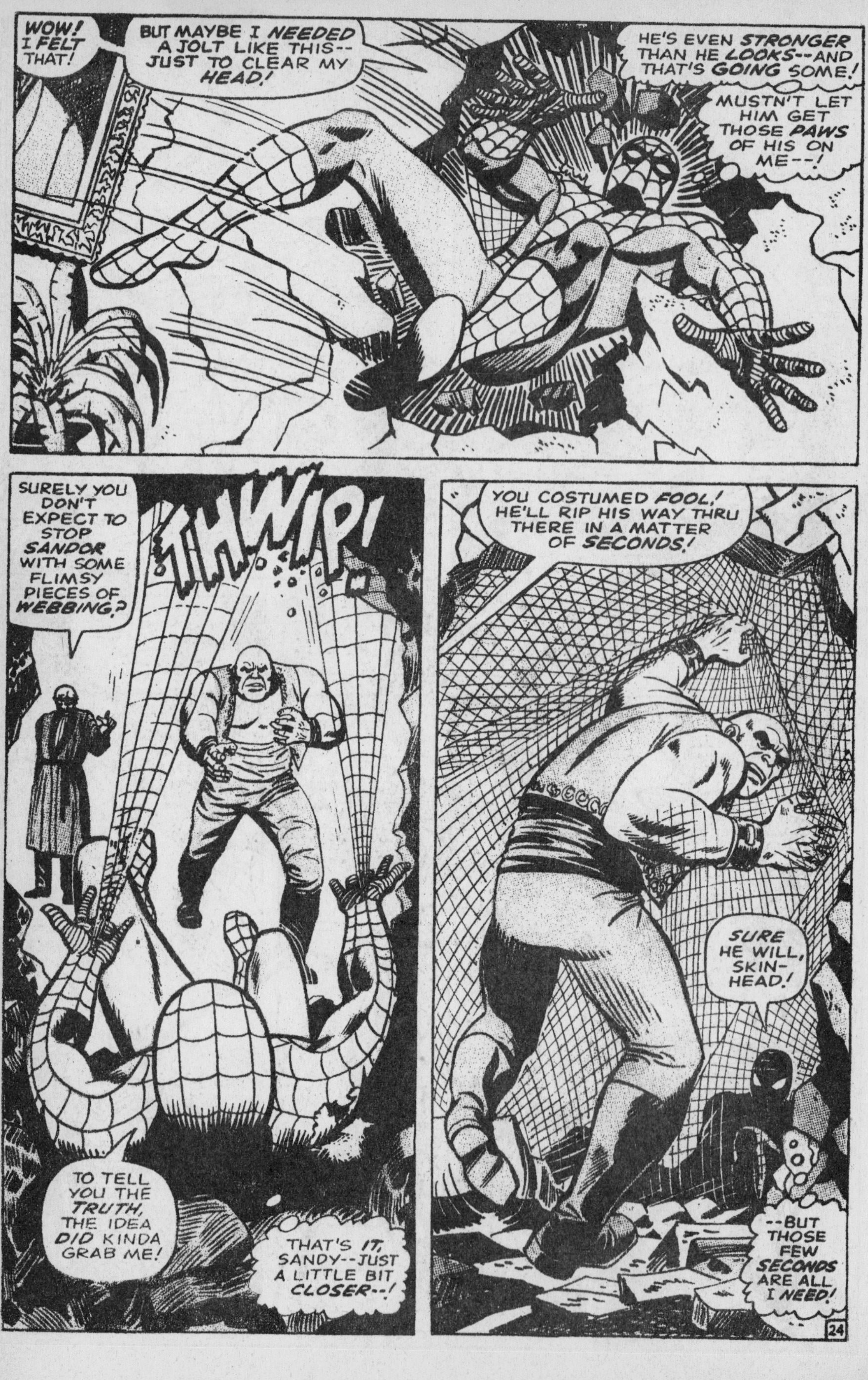
WOW! I FELT THAT!
BUT MAYBE I NEEDED A JOLT LIKE THIS-- JUST TO CLEAR MY HEAD!
HE'S EVEN STRONGER THAN HE LOOKS--AND THAT'S GOING SOME!
MUSTN'T LET HIM GET THOSE PAWS OF HIS ON ME--!
SURELY YOU DON'T EXPECT TO STOP SANDOR WITH SOME FLIMSY PIECES OF WEBBING?
THWIP!
TO TELL YOU THE TRUTH, THE IDEA DID KINDA GRAB ME!
THAT'S IT, SANDY--JUST A LITTLE BIT CLOSER--!
YOU COSTUMED FOOL! HE'LL RIP HIS WAY THRU THERE IN A MATTER OF SECONDS!
SURE HE WILL, SKIN-HEAD!
--BUT THOSE FEW SECONDS ARE ALL I NEED!
24

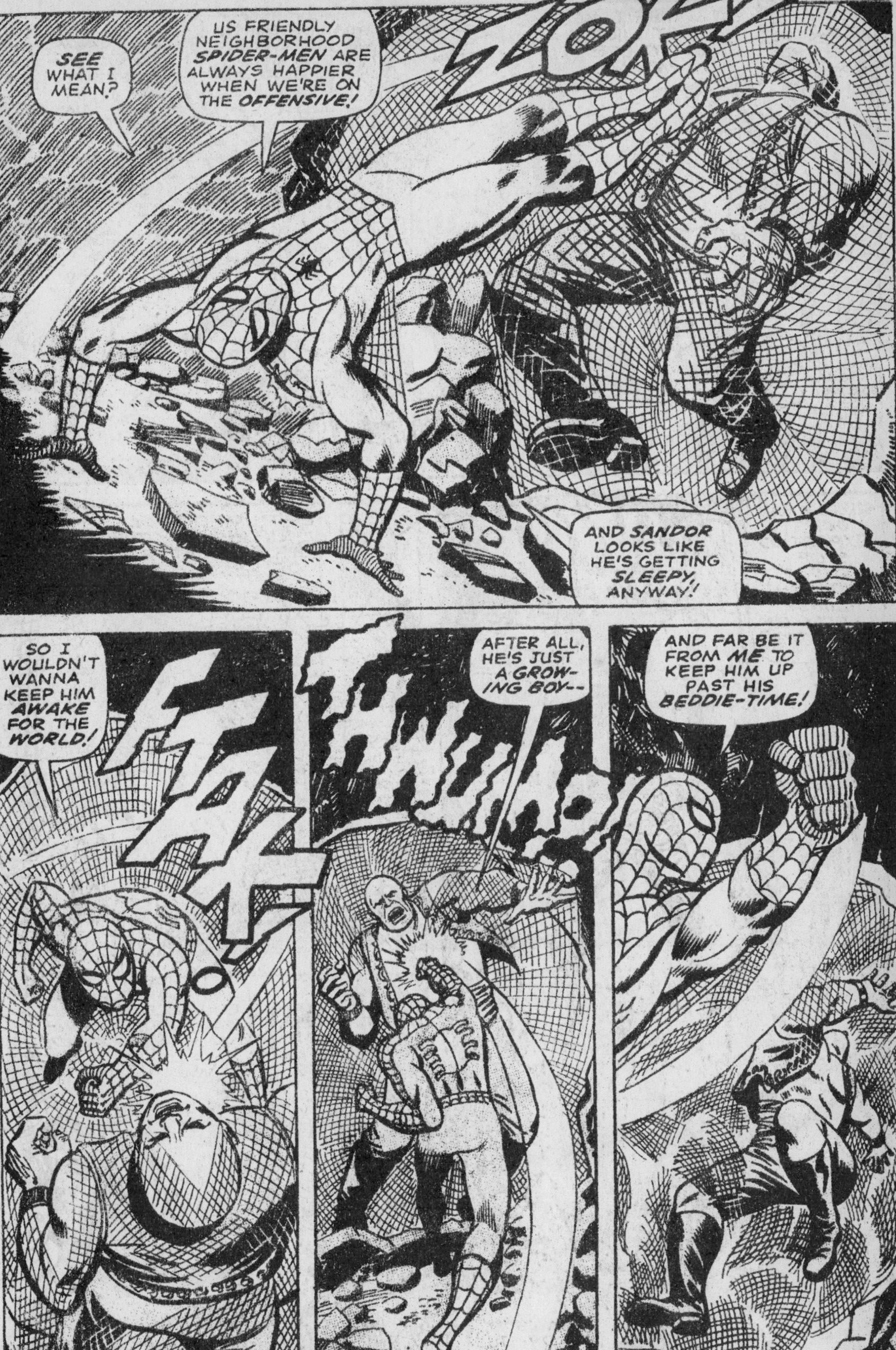

SEE WHAT I MEAN?
US FRIENDLY NEIGHBORHOOD SPIDER-MEN ARE ALWAYS HAPPIER WHEN WE'RE ON THE OFFENSIVE!
ZOK!
AND SANDOR LOOKS LIKE HE'S GETTING SLEEPY, ANYWAY!
SO I WOULDN'T WANNA KEEP HIM AWAKE FOR THE WORLD!
FTAK
THWUMP!
AFTER ALL, HE'S JUST A GROWING BOY--
AND FAR BE IT FROM ME TO KEEP HIM UP PAST HIS BEDDIE-TIME!
25

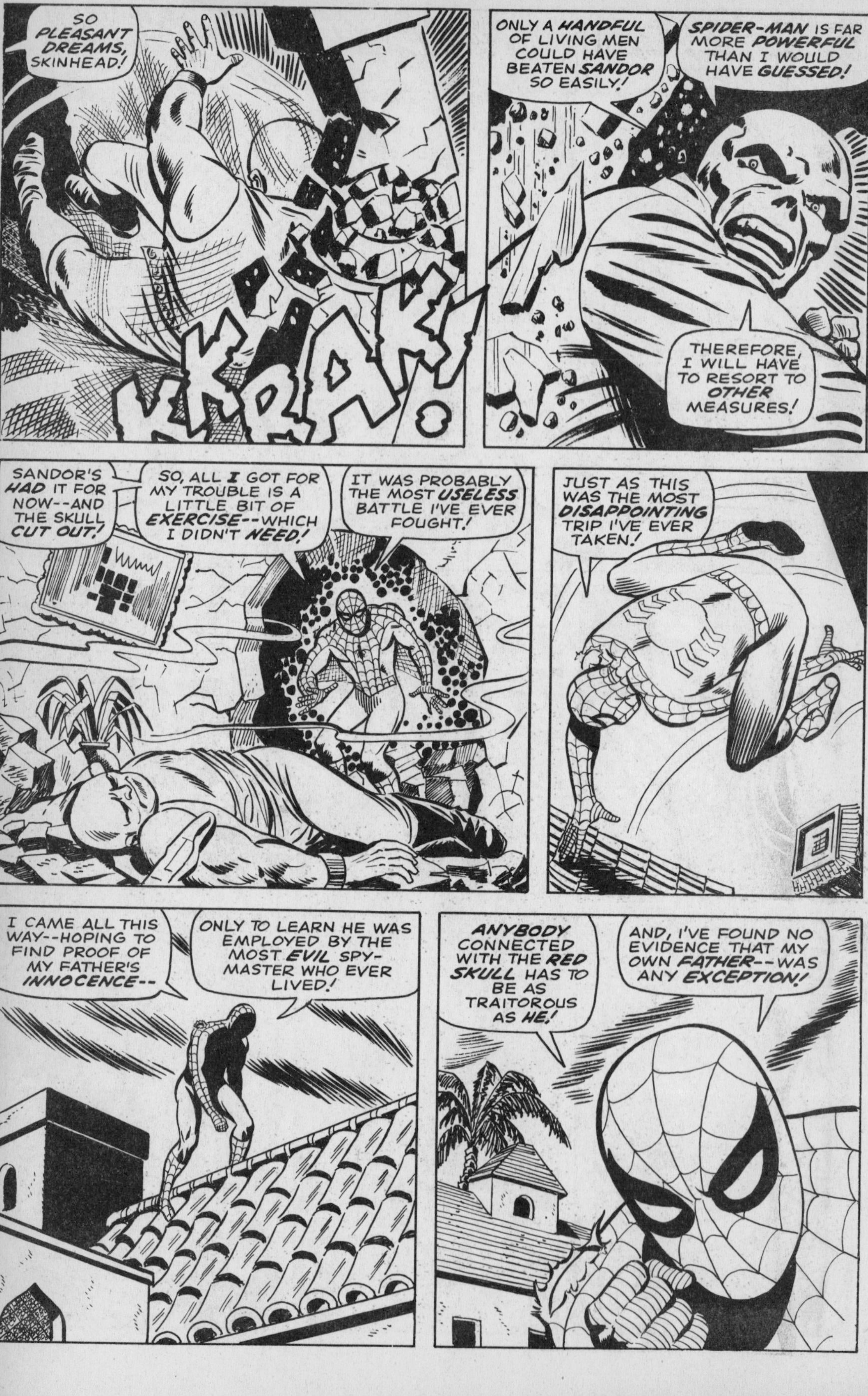
SO PLEASANT DREAMS, SKINHEAD!
KRAK!
ONLY A HANDFUL OF LIVING MEN COULD HAVE BEATEN SANDOR SO EASILY!
SPIDER-MAN IS FAR MORE POWERFUL THAN I WOULD HAVE GUESSED!
THEREFORE, I WILL HAVE TO RESORT TO OTHER MEASURES!
SANDOR'S HAD IT FOR NOW--AND THE SKULL CUT OUT!
SO, ALL I GOT FOR MY TROUBLE IS A LITTLE BIT OF EXERCISE--WHICH I DIDN'T NEED!
IT WAS PROBABLY THE MOST USELESS BATTLE I'VE EVER FOUGHT!
JUST AS THIS WAS THE MOST DISAPPOINTING TRIP I'VE EVER TAKEN!
I CAME ALL THIS WAY--HOPING TO FIND PROOF OF MY FATHER'S INNOCENCE--
ONLY TO LEARN HE WAS EMPLOYED BY THE MOST EVIL SPY-MASTER WHO EVER LIVED!
ANYBODY CONNECTED WITH THE RED SKULL HAS TO BE AS TRAITOROUS AS HE!
AND, I'VE FOUND NO EVIDENCE THAT MY OWN FATHER--WAS ANY EXCEPTION!

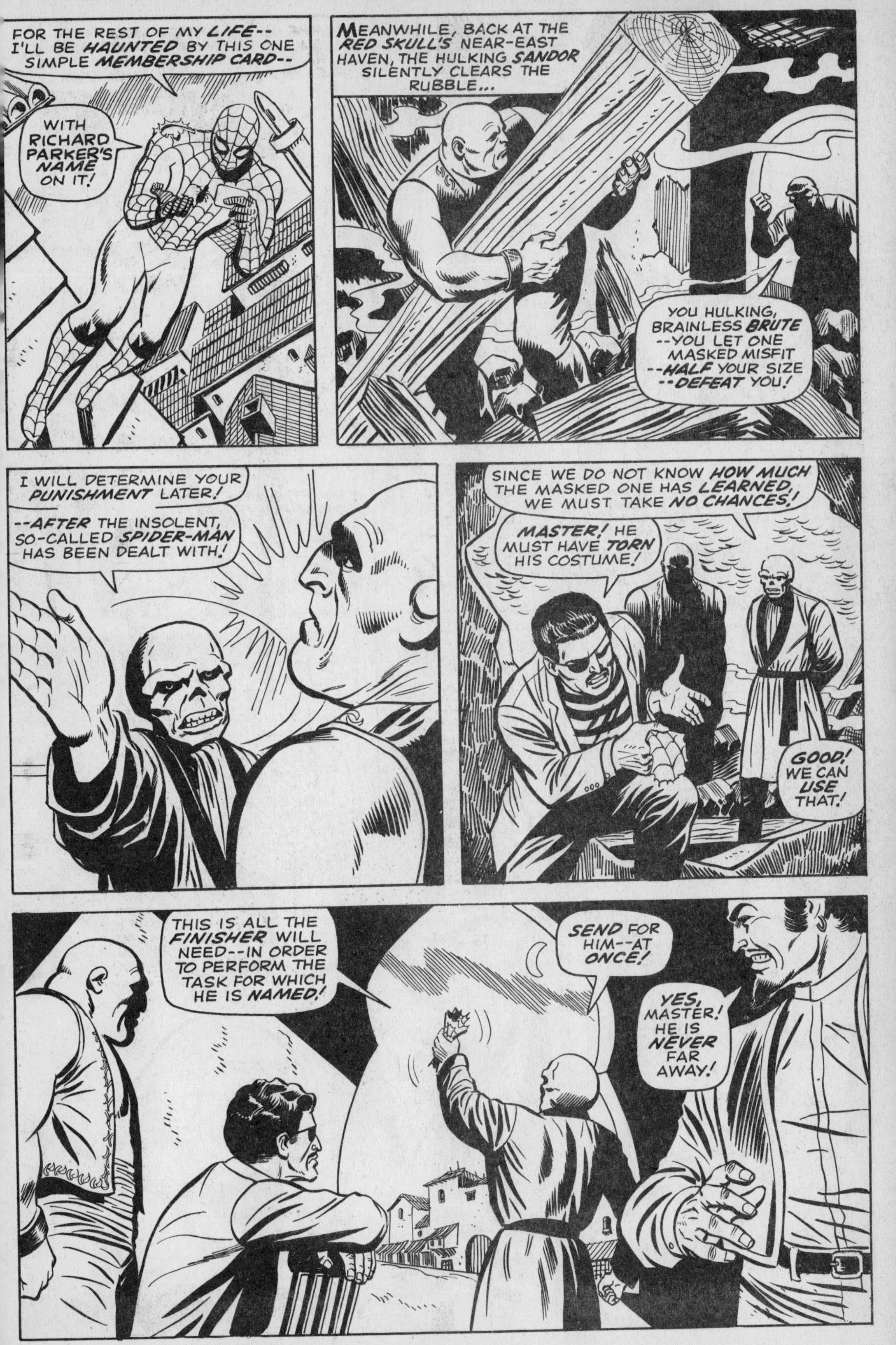
FOR THE REST OF MY LIFE-- I'LL BE HAUNTED BY THIS ONE SIMPLE MEMBERSHIP CARD--
WITH RICHARD PARKER'S NAME ON IT!
MEANWHILE, BACK AT THE RED SKULL'S NEAR-EAST HAVEN, THE HULKING SANDOR SILENTLY CLEARS THE RUBBLE...
YOU HULKING, BRAINLESS BRUTE --YOU LET ONE MASKED MISFIT --HALF YOUR SIZE --DEFEAT YOU!
I WILL DETERMINE YOUR PUNISHMENT LATER!
--AFTER THE INSOLENT, SO-CALLED SPIDER-MAN HAS BEEN DEALT WITH!
SINCE WE DO NOT KNOW HOW MUCH THE MASKED ONE HAS LEARNED, WE MUST TAKE NO CHANCES!
MASTER! HE MUST HAVE TORN HIS COSTUME!
GOOD! WE CAN USE THAT!
THIS IS ALL THE FINISHER WILL NEED--IN ORDER TO PERFORM THE TASK FOR WHICH HE IS NAMED!
SEND FOR HIM--AT ONCE!
YES, MASTER! HE IS NEVER FAR AWAY!

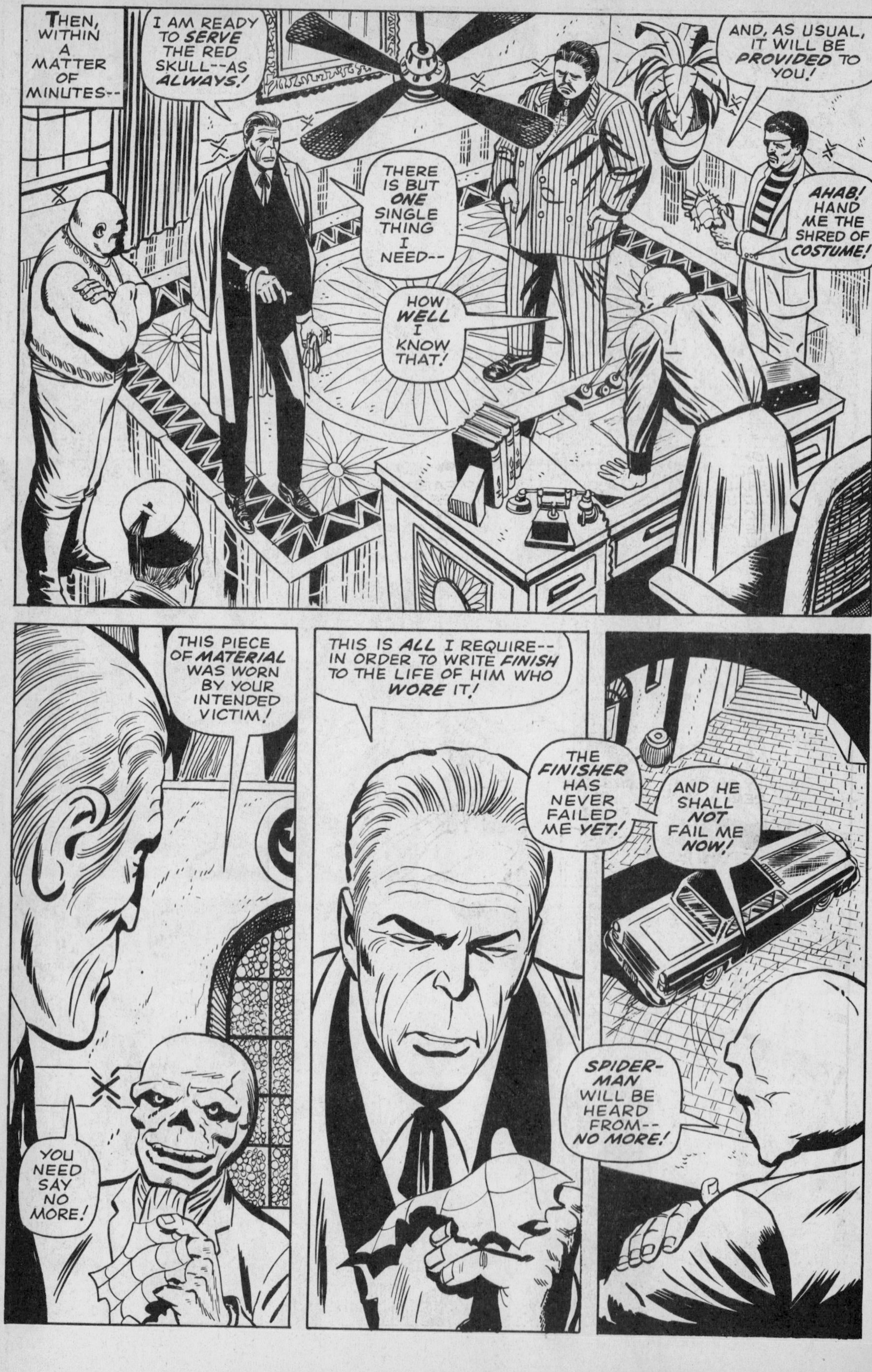
THEN, WITHIN A MATTER OF MINUTES--
I AM READY TO SERVE THE RED SKULL--AS ALWAYS!
AND, AS USUAL, IT WILL BE PROVIDED TO YOU!
THERE IS BUT ONE SINGLE THING I NEED--
HOW WELL I KNOW THAT!
AHAB! HAND ME THE SHRED OF COSTUME!
THIS PIECE OF MATERIAL WAS WORN BY YOUR INTENDED VICTIM!
YOU NEED SAY NO MORE!
THIS IS ALL I REQUIRE-- IN ORDER TO WRITE FINISH TO THE LIFE OF HIM WHO WORE IT!
THE FINISHER HAS NEVER FAILED ME YET!
AND HE SHALL NOT FAIL ME NOW!
SPIDER-MAN WILL BE HEARD FROM-- NO MORE!

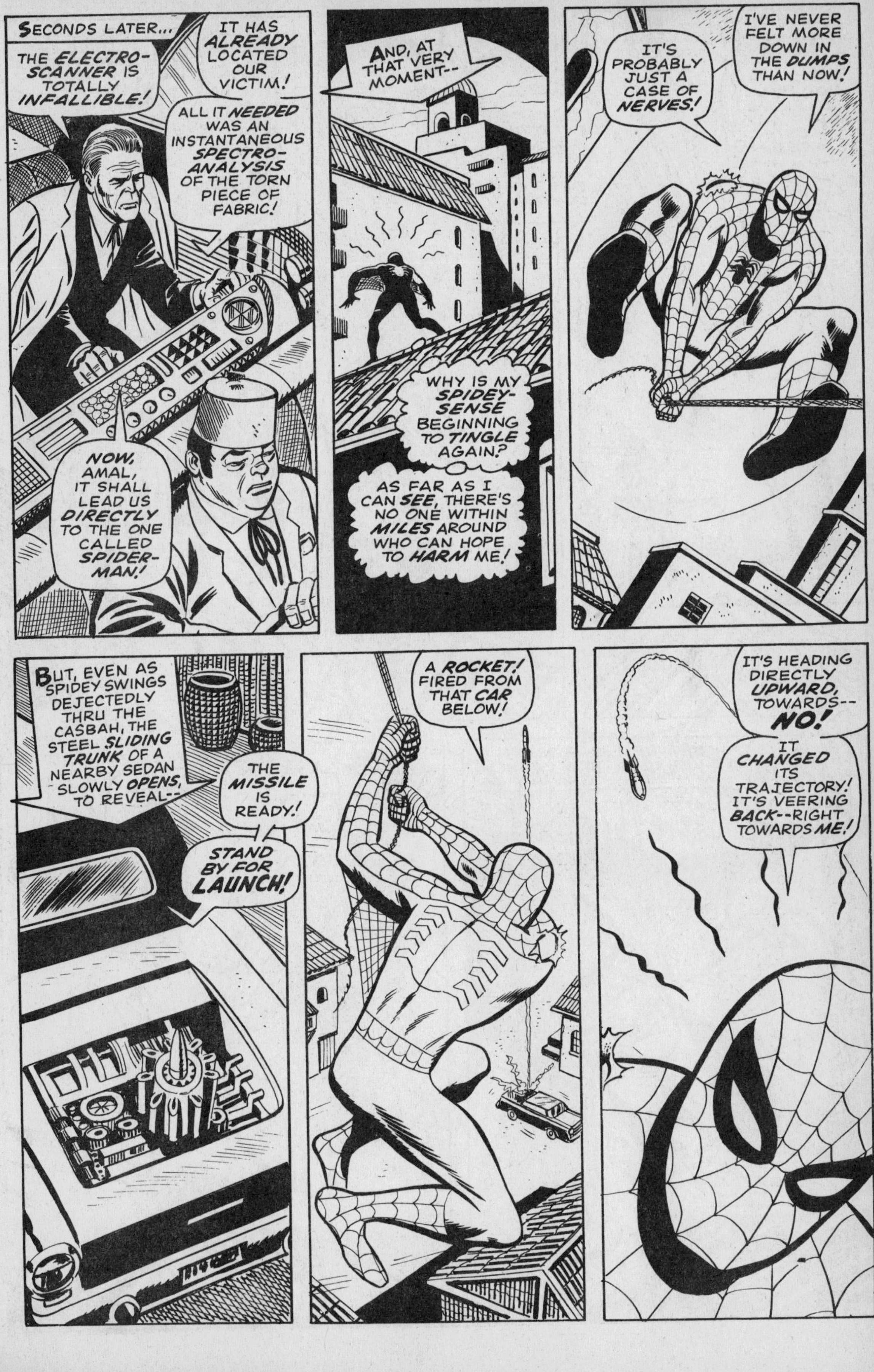
SECONDS LATER...
THE ELECTRO-SCANNER IS TOTALLY INFALLIBLE!
IT HAS ALREADY LOCATED OUR VICTIM!
ALL IT NEEDED WAS AN INSTANTANEOUS SPECTRO-ANALYSIS OF THE TORN PIECE OF FABRIC!
NOW, AMAL, IT SHALL LEAD US DIRECTLY TO THE ONE CALLED SPIDER-MAN!
AND, AT THAT VERY MOMENT--
WHY IS MY SPIDEY-SENSE BEGINNING TO TINGLE AGAIN?
AS FAR AS I CAN SEE, THERE'S NO ONE WITHIN MILES AROUND WHO CAN HOPE TO HARM ME!
IT'S PROBABLY JUST A CASE OF NERVES!
I'VE NEVER FELT MORE DOWN IN THE DUMPS THAN NOW!
BUT, EVEN AS SPIDEY SWINGS DEJECTEDLY THRU THE CASBAH, THE STEEL SLIDING TRUNK OF A NEARBY SEDAN SLOWLY OPENS, TO REVEAL--
THE MISSILE IS READY!
STAND BY FOR LAUNCH!
A ROCKET! FIRED FROM THAT CAR BELOW!
IT'S HEADING DIRECTLY UPWARD, TOWARDS-- NO!
IT CHANGED ITS TRAJECTORY! IT'S VEERING BACK--RIGHT TOWARDS ME!

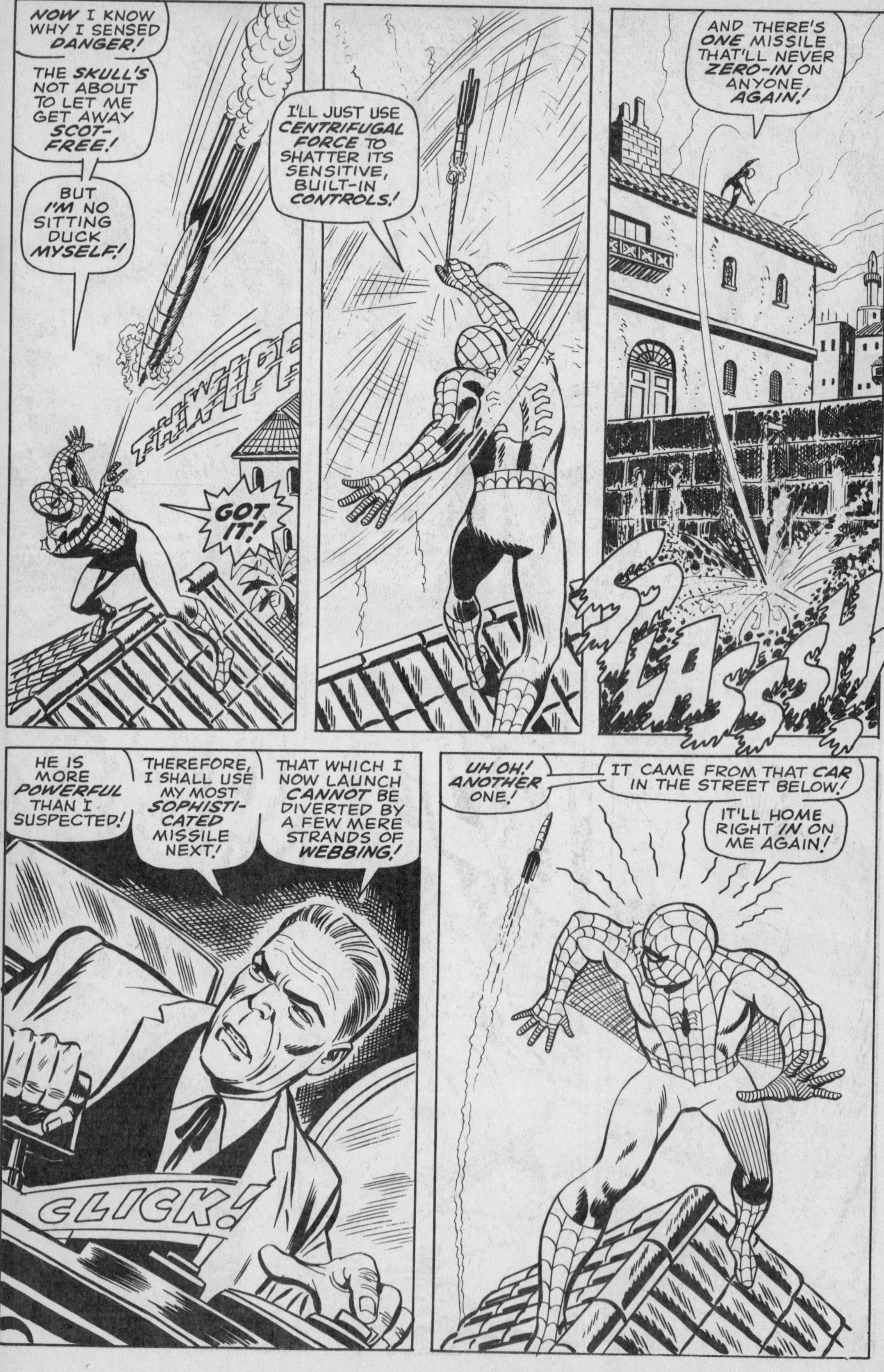
NOW I KNOW WHY I SENSED DANGER!
THE SKULL'S NOT ABOUT TO LET ME GET AWAY SCOT-FREE!
BUT I'M NO SITTING DUCK MYSELF!
THWIPP
GOT IT!
I'LL JUST USE CENTRIFUGAL FORCE TO SHATTER ITS SENSITIVE, BUILT-IN CONTROLS!
AND THERE'S ONE MISSILE THAT'LL NEVER ZERO-IN ON ANYONE AGAIN!
SPLASSH!
HE IS MORE POWERFUL THAN I SUSPECTED!
THEREFORE, I SHALL USE MY MOST SOPHISTI-CATED MISSILE NEXT!
THAT WHICH I NOW LAUNCH CANNOT BE DIVERTED BY A FEW MERE STRANDS OF WEBBING!
CLICK!
UH OH! ANOTHER ONE!
IT CAME FROM THAT CAR IN THE STREET BELOW!
IT'LL HOME RIGHT IN ON ME AGAIN!

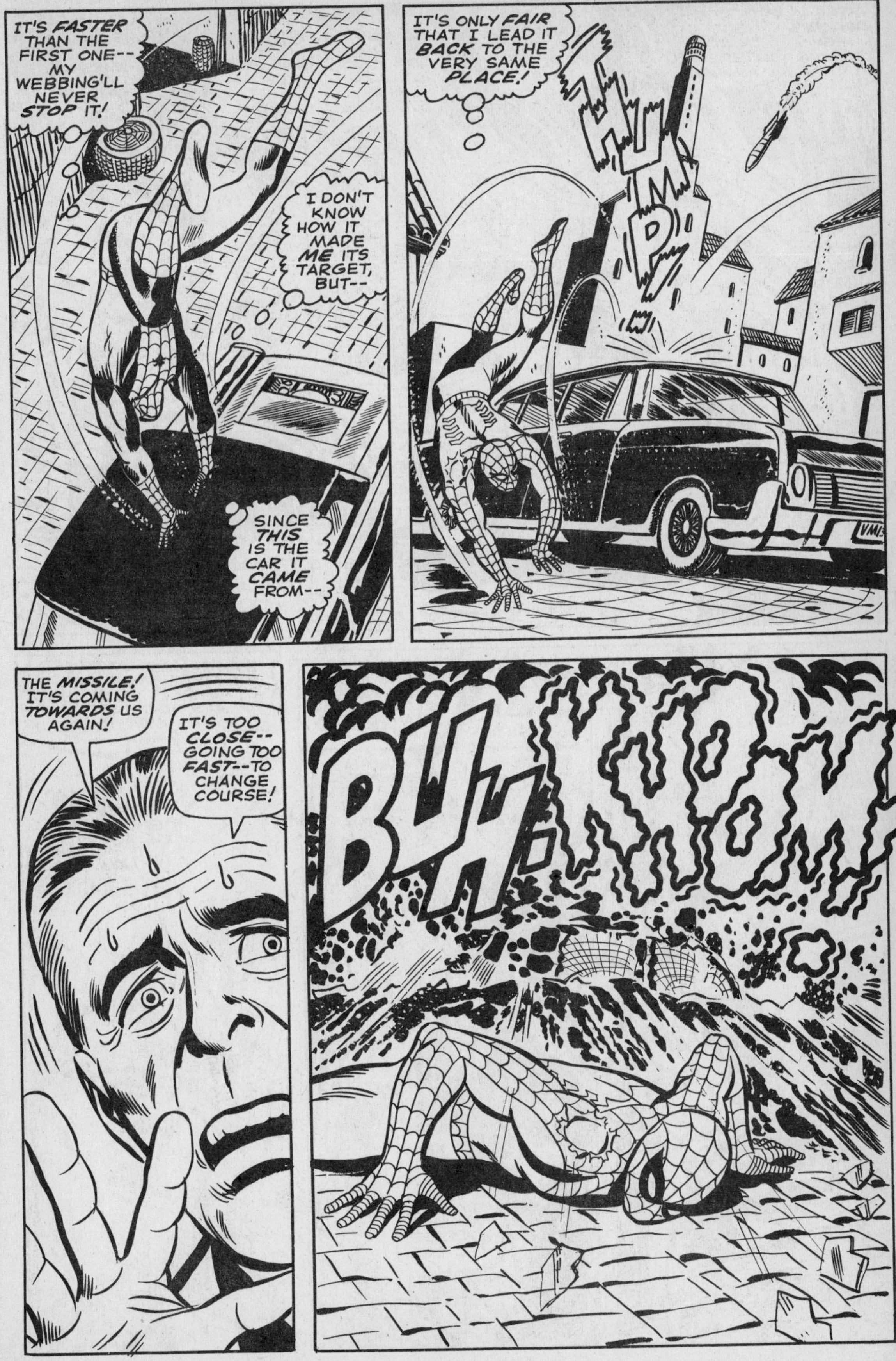
IT'S FASTER THAN THE FIRST ONE-- MY WEBBING'LL NEVER STOP IT!
I DON'T KNOW HOW IT MADE ME ITS TARGET, BUT--
SINCE THIS IS THE CAR IT CAME FROM--
IT'S ONLY FAIR THAT I LEAD IT BACK TO THE VERY SAME PLACE!
THUMP
THE MISSILE! IT'S COMING TOWARDS US AGAIN!
IT'S TOO CLOSE-- GOING TOO FAST--TO CHANGE COURSE!
BUH-WOW

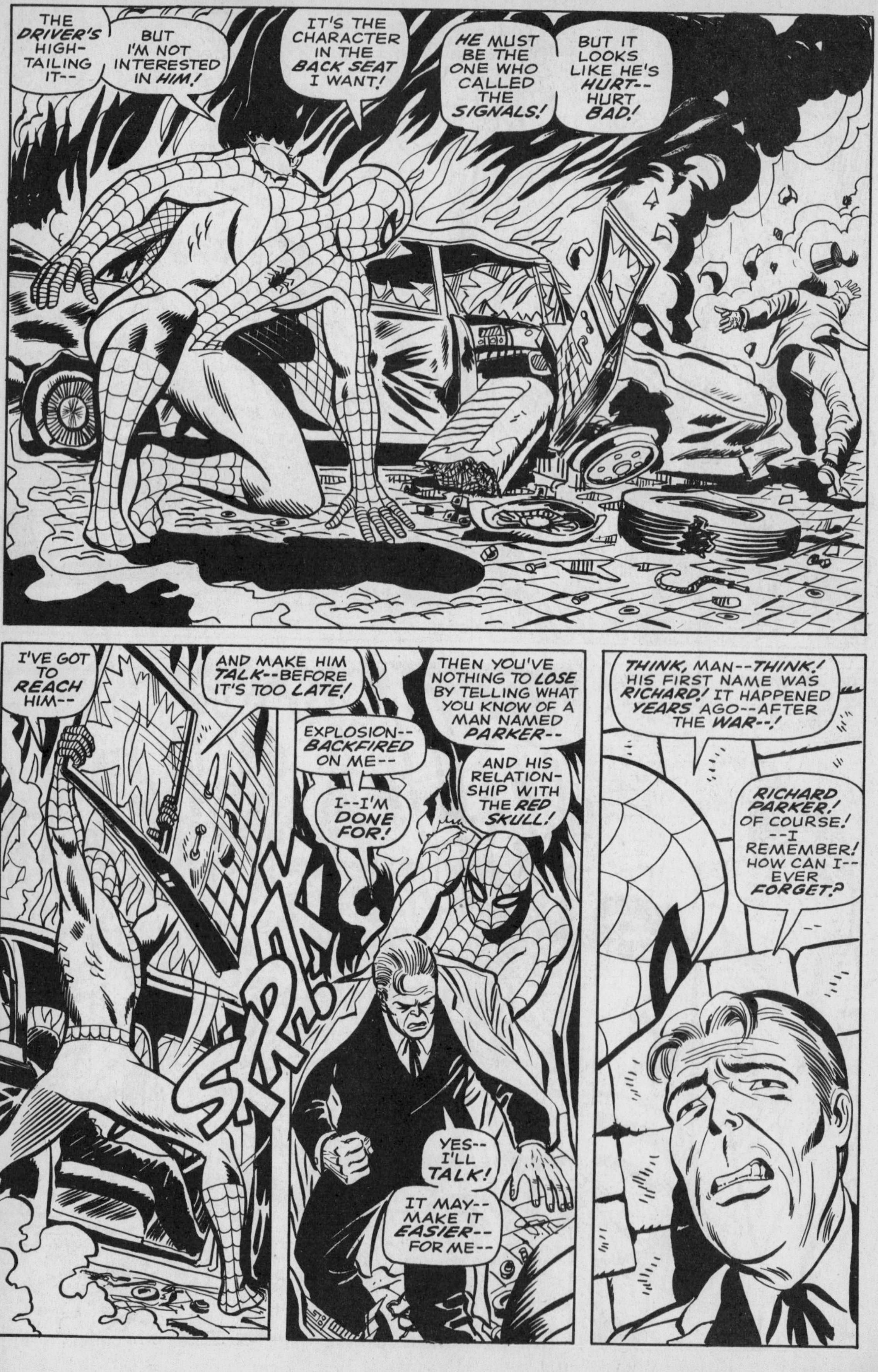
THE DRIVER'S HIGH-TAILING IT--
BUT I'M NOT INTERESTED IN HIM!
IT'S THE CHARACTER IN THE BACK SEAT I WANT!
HE MUST BE THE ONE WHO CALLED THE SIGNALS!
BUT IT LOOKS LIKE HE'S HURT--HURT BAD!
I'VE GOT TO REACH HIM--
AND MAKE HIM TALK--BEFORE IT'S TOO LATE!
SKRAK
THEN YOU'VE NOTHING TO LOSE BY TELLING WHAT YOU KNOW OF A MAN NAMED PARKER--
EXPLOSION--BACKFIRED ON ME--
AND HIS RELATIONSHIP WITH THE RED SKULL!
I--I'M DONE FOR!
YES--I'LL TALK!
IT MAY--MAKE IT EASIER--FOR ME--
THINK, MAN--THINK! HIS FIRST NAME WAS RICHARD! IT HAPPENED YEARS AGO--AFTER THE WAR--!
RICHARD PARKER! OF COURSE! --I REMEMBER! HOW CAN I--EVER FORGET?

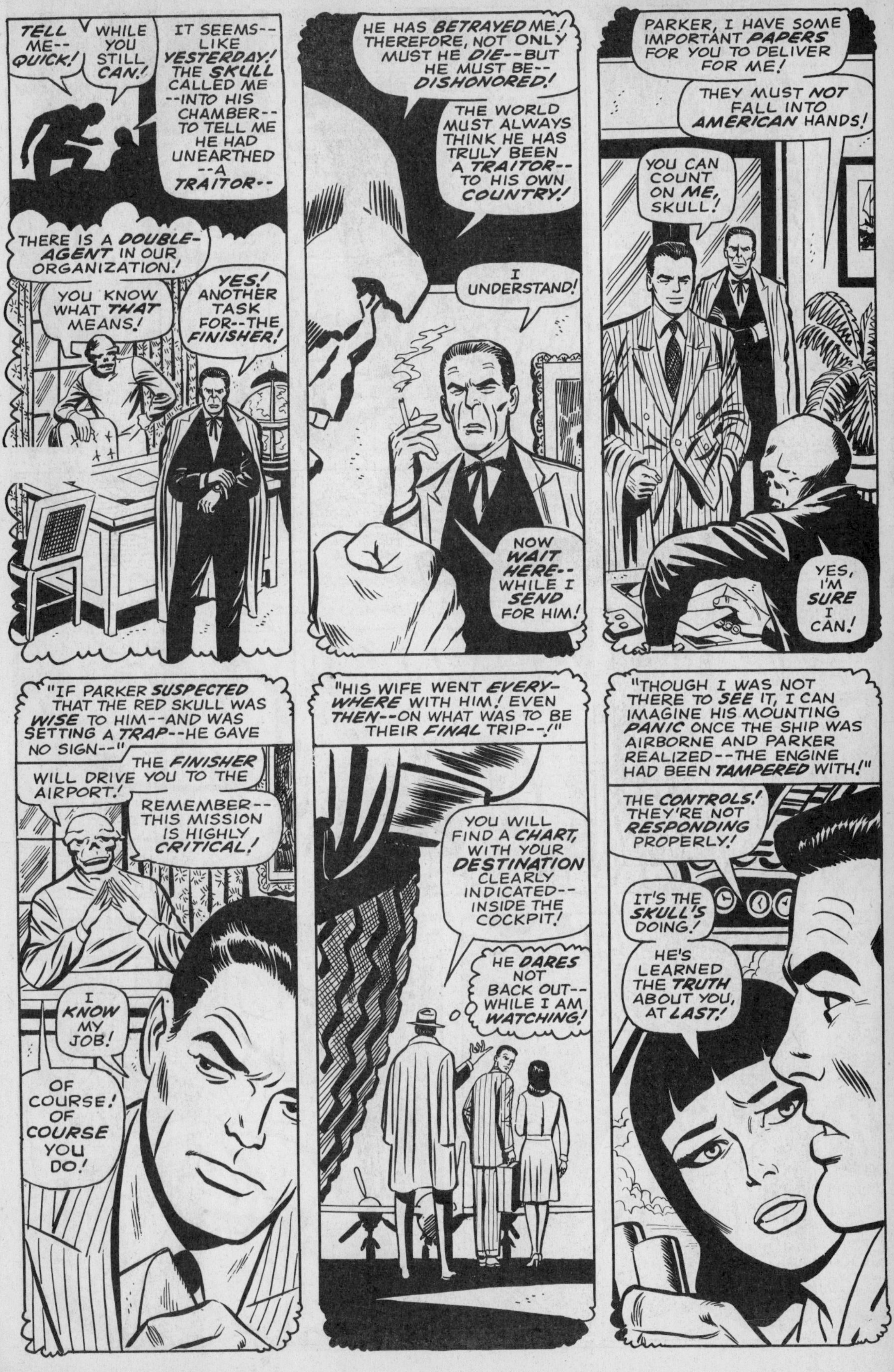
TELL ME--QUICK!
WHILE YOU STILL CAN!
IT SEEMS--LIKE YESTERDAY! THE SKULL CALLED ME --INTO HIS CHAMBER--TO TELL ME HE HAD UNEARTHED --A TRAITOR--
THERE IS A DOUBLE-AGENT IN OUR ORGANIZATION!
YOU KNOW WHAT THAT MEANS!
YES! ANOTHER TASK FOR--THE FINISHER!
HE HAS BETRAYED ME! THEREFORE, NOT ONLY MUST HE DIE--BUT HE MUST BE--DISHONORED!
THE WORLD MUST ALWAYS THINK HE HAS TRULY BEEN A TRAITOR--TO HIS OWN COUNTRY!
I UNDERSTAND!
NOW WAIT HERE--WHILE I SEND FOR HIM!
PARKER, I HAVE SOME IMPORTANT PAPERS FOR YOU TO DELIVER FOR ME!
THEY MUST NOT FALL INTO AMERICAN HANDS!
YOU CAN COUNT ON ME, SKULL!
YES, I'M SURE I CAN!
"IF PARKER SUSPECTED THAT THE RED SKULL WAS WISE TO HIM--AND WAS SETTING A TRAP--HE GAVE NO SIGN--"
THE FINISHER WILL DRIVE YOU TO THE AIRPORT!
REMEMBER--THIS MISSION IS HIGHLY CRITICAL!
I KNOW MY JOB!
OF COURSE! OF COURSE YOU DO!
"HIS WIFE WENT EVERY-WHERE WITH HIM! EVEN THEN--ON WHAT WAS TO BE THEIR FINAL TRIP--!"
YOU WILL FIND A CHART, WITH YOUR DESTINATION CLEARLY INDICATED--INSIDE THE COCKPIT!
HE DARES NOT BACK OUT--WHILE I AM WATCHING!
"THOUGH I WAS NOT THERE TO SEE IT, I CAN IMAGINE HIS MOUNTING PANIC ONCE THE SHIP WAS AIRBORNE AND PARKER REALIZED--THE ENGINE HAD BEEN TAMPERED WITH!"
THE CONTROLS! THEY'RE NOT RESPONDING PROPERLY!
IT'S THE SKULL'S DOING!
HE'S LEARNED THE TRUTH ABOUT YOU, AT LAST!

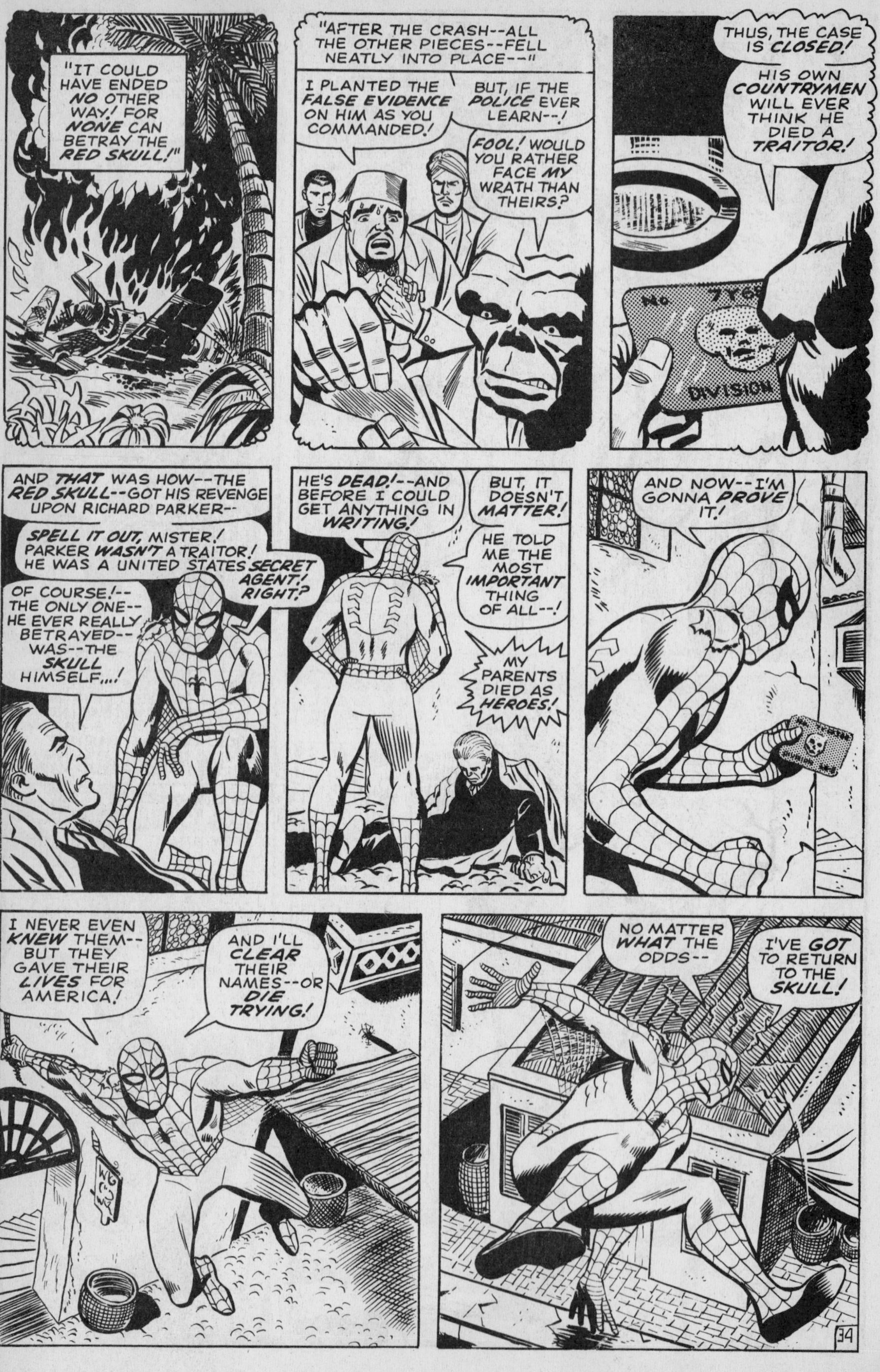
"IT COULD HAVE ENDED NO OTHER WAY! FOR NONE CAN BETRAY THE RED SKULL!"
"AFTER THE CRASH--ALL THE OTHER PIECES--FELL NEATLY INTO PLACE--"
I PLANTED THE FALSE EVIDENCE ON HIM AS YOU COMMANDED!
BUT, IF THE POLICE EVER LEARN--!
FOOL! WOULD YOU RATHER FACE MY WRATH THAN THEIRS?
THUS, THE CASE IS CLOSED!
HIS OWN COUNTRYMEN WILL EVER THINK HE DIED A TRAITOR!
DIVISION
AND THAT WAS HOW--THE RED SKULL--GOT HIS REVENGE UPON RICHARD PARKER--
SPELL IT OUT, MISTER! PARKER WASN'T A TRAITOR! HE WAS A UNITED STATES SECRET AGENT! RIGHT?
OF COURSE!--THE ONLY ONE--HE EVER REALLY BETRAYED--WAS--THE SKULL HIMSELF...!
HE'S DEAD!--AND BEFORE I COULD GET ANYTHING IN WRITING!
BUT, IT DOESN'T MATTER!
HE TOLD ME THE MOST IMPORTANT THING OF ALL--!
MY PARENTS DIED AS HEROES!
AND NOW--I'M GONNA PROVE IT!
I NEVER EVEN KNEW THEM--BUT THEY GAVE THEIR LIVES FOR AMERICA!
AND I'LL CLEAR THEIR NAMES--OR DIE TRYING!
NO MATTER WHAT THE ODDS--
I'VE GOT TO RETURN TO THE SKULL!

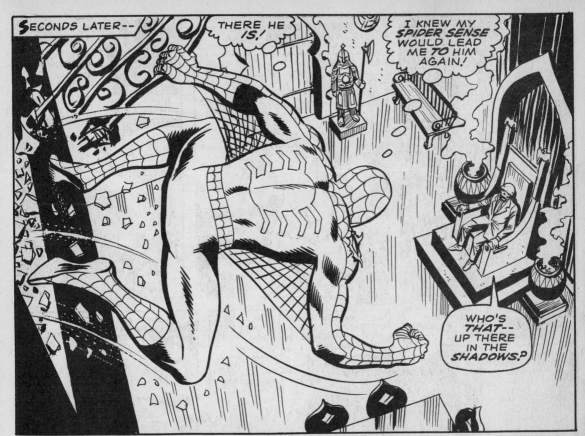

SECONDS LATER--

THERE HE IS!

I KNEW MY SPIDER SENSE WOULD LEAD ME TO HIM AGAIN!

WHO'S THAT-- UP THERE IN THE SHADOWS?

I WAS BEGINNING TO THINK YOU'D NEVER ASK!

YOU AGAIN!

WHAT DO YOU MEAN "AGAIN"? I'VE ALWAYS BEEN ME!

YOUR STUPID PERSISTENCE IS MATCHED ONLY BY YOUR ABYSMAL CARELESSNESS!

YOU SHOULD HAVE SURMISED THAT EVEN MY COMMAND CHAIR CONTAINS DEADLY, BUILT-IN WEAPONRY!

WHAT'S THE DIFF? YOU DON'T EXPECT THAT TO STOP ME!

SHZ ZZ

CLIK!

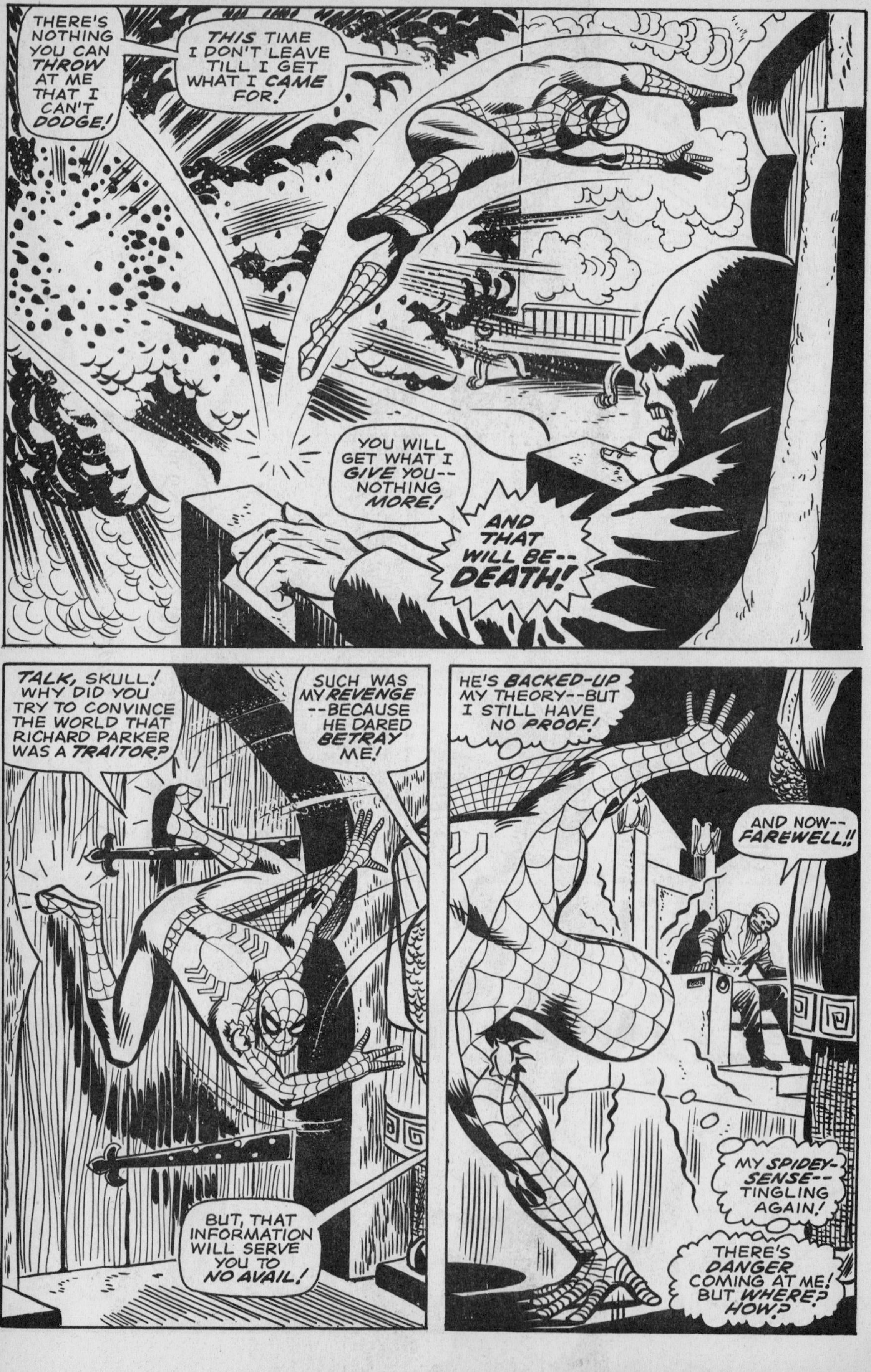
THERE'S NOTHING YOU CAN THROW AT ME THAT I CAN'T DODGE!
THIS TIME I DON'T LEAVE TILL I GET WHAT I CAME FOR!
YOU WILL GET WHAT I GIVE YOU-- NOTHING MORE!
AND THAT WILL BE-- DEATH!
TALK, SKULL! WHY DID YOU TRY TO CONVINCE THE WORLD THAT RICHARD PARKER WAS A TRAITOR?
SUCH WAS MY REVENGE --BECAUSE HE DARED BETRAY ME!
BUT, THAT INFORMATION WILL SERVE YOU TO NO AVAIL!
HE'S BACKED-UP MY THEORY--BUT I STILL HAVE NO PROOF!
AND NOW-- FAREWELL!!
MY SPIDEY-SENSE-- TINGLING AGAIN!
THERE'S DANGER COMING AT ME! BUT WHERE? HOW?

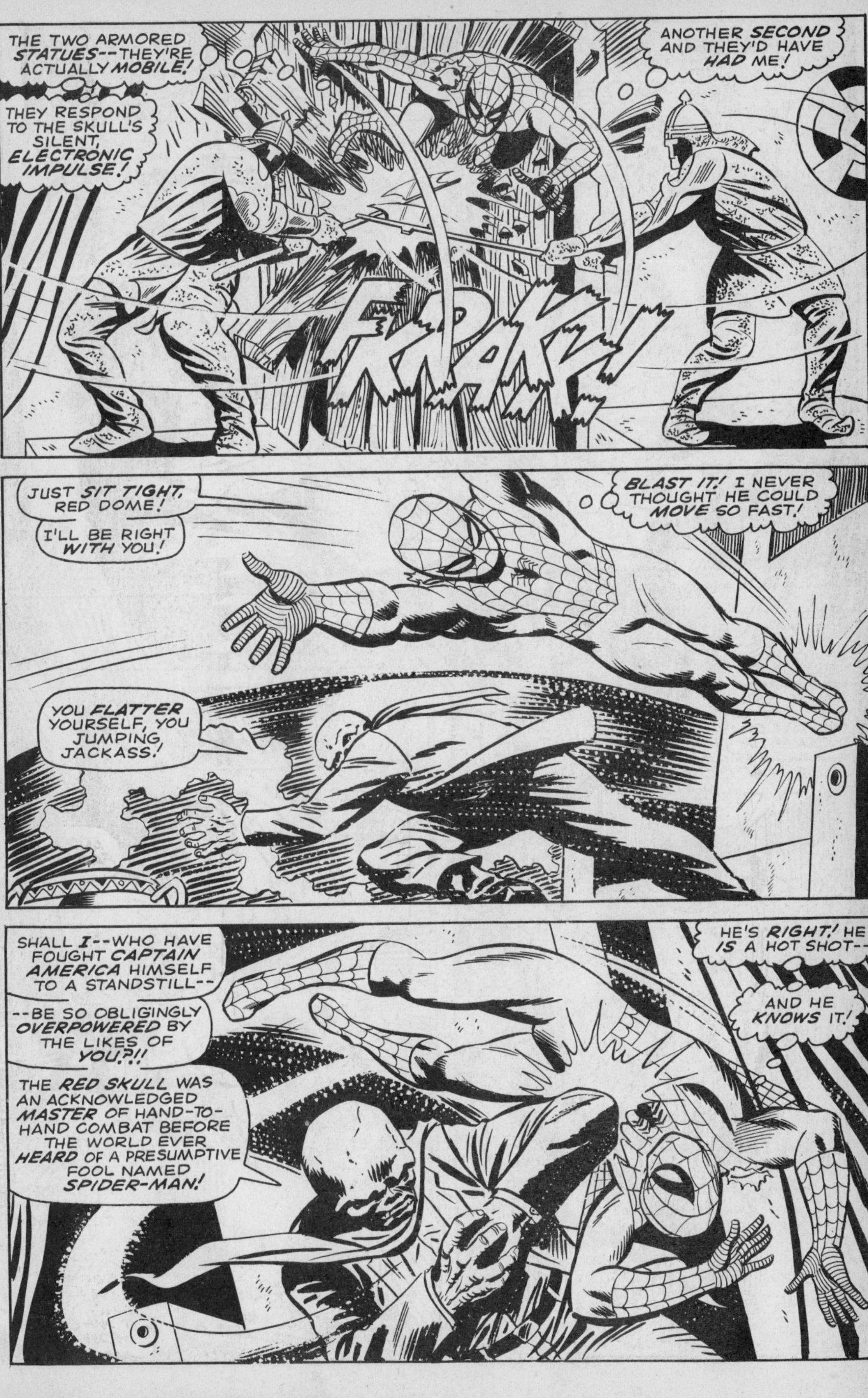
THE TWO ARMORED STATUES--THEY'RE ACTUALLY MOBILE!
THEY RESPOND TO THE SKULL'S SILENT, ELECTRONIC IMPULSE!
ANOTHER SECOND AND THEY'D HAVE HAD ME!
FRAAK!
JUST SIT TIGHT, RED DOME!
I'LL BE RIGHT WITH YOU!
BLAST IT! I NEVER THOUGHT HE COULD MOVE SO FAST!
YOU FLATTER YOURSELF, YOU JUMPING JACKASS!
SHALL I--WHO HAVE FOUGHT CAPTAIN AMERICA HIMSELF TO A STANDSTILL--
--BE SO OBLIGINGLY OVERPOWERED BY THE LIKES OF YOU?!!
THE RED SKULL WAS AN ACKNOWLEDGED MASTER OF HAND-TO-HAND COMBAT BEFORE THE WORLD EVER HEARD OF A PRESUMPTIVE FOOL NAMED SPIDER-MAN!
HE'S RIGHT! HE IS A HOT SHOT--
AND HE KNOWS IT!

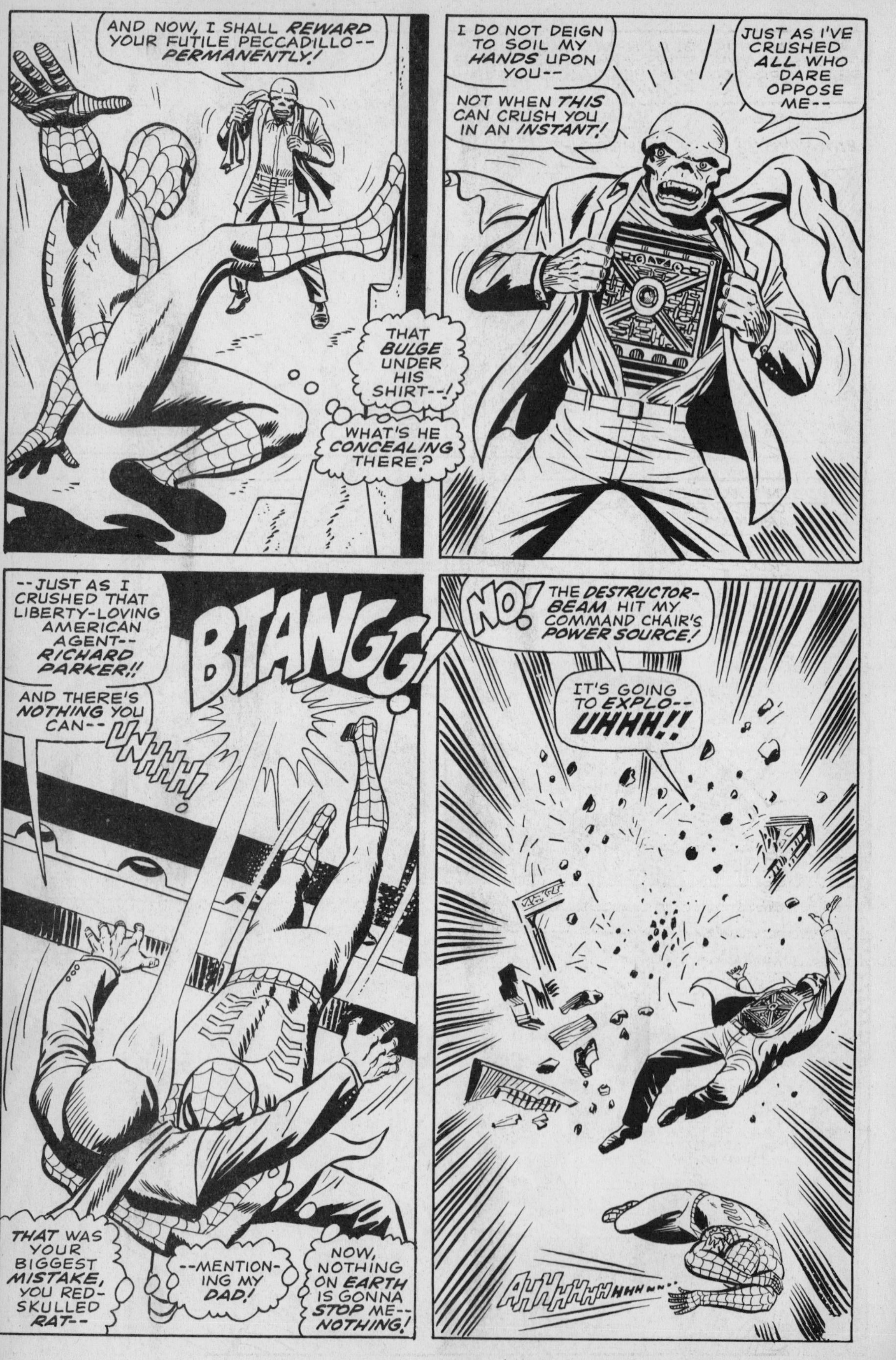
AND NOW, I SHALL REWARD YOUR FUTILE PECCADILLO-- PERMANENTLY!
THAT BULGE UNDER HIS SHIRT--!
WHAT'S HE CONCEALING THERE?
I DO NOT DEIGN TO SOIL MY HANDS UPON YOU--
NOT WHEN THIS CAN CRUSH YOU IN AN INSTANT!
JUST AS I'VE CRUSHED ALL WHO DARE OPPOSE ME--
--JUST AS I CRUSHED THAT LIBERTY-LOVING AMERICAN AGENT-- RICHARD PARKER!!
AND THERE'S NOTHING YOU CAN--
BTANGG!
UNHHH!
THAT WAS YOUR BIGGEST MISTAKE, YOU RED-SKULLED RAT--
--MENTIONING MY DAD!
NOW, NOTHING ON EARTH IS GONNA STOP ME-- NOTHING!
NO! THE DESTRUCTOR-BEAM HIT MY COMMAND CHAIR'S POWER SOURCE!
IT'S GOING TO EXPLO-- UHHH!!
AHHHHHHHHHHH...

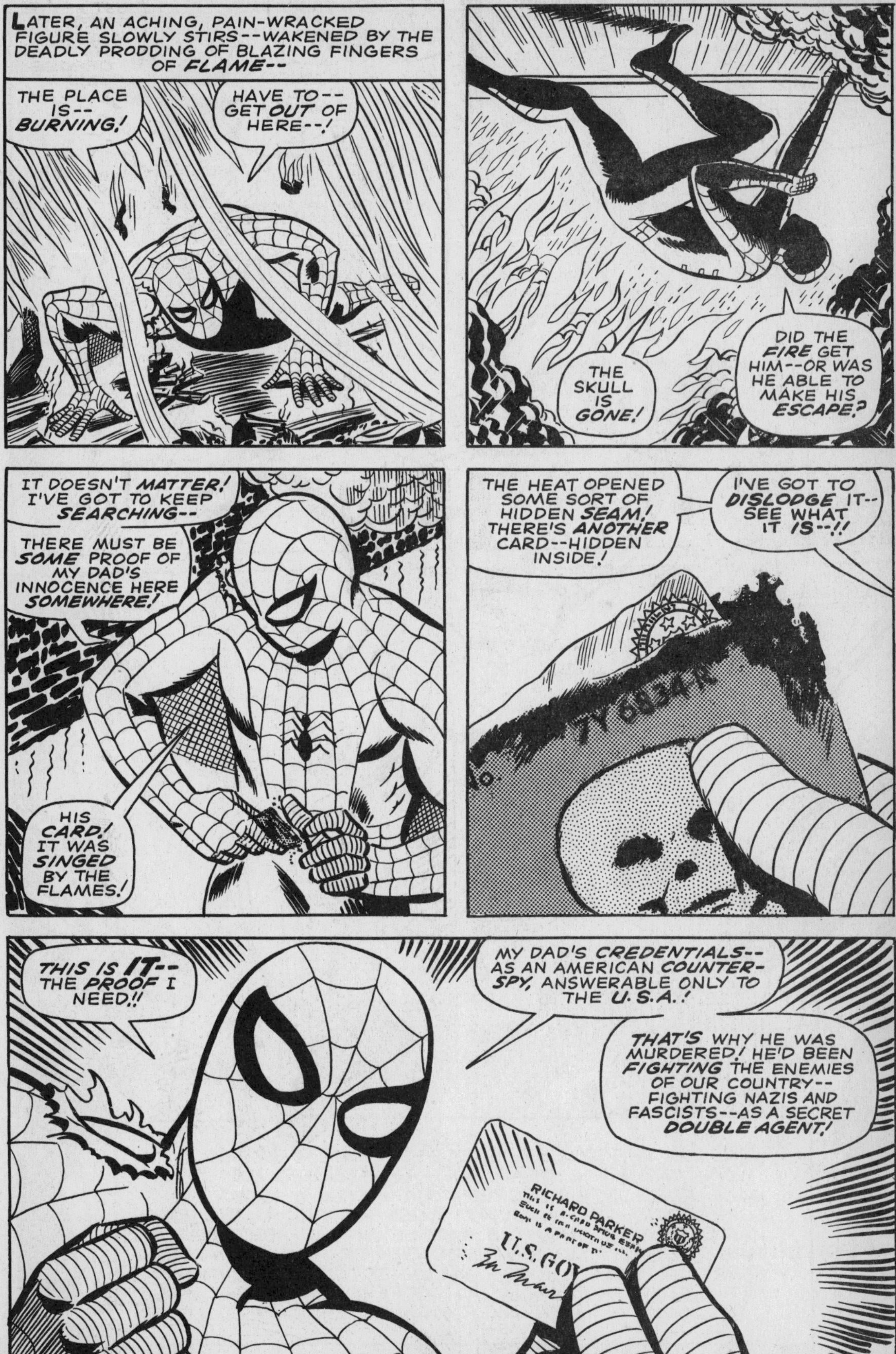
LATER, AN ACHING, PAIN-WRACKED FIGURE SLOWLY STIRS--WAKENED BY THE DEADLY PRODDING OF BLAZING FINGERS OF FLAME--
THE PLACE IS-- BURNING!
HAVE TO-- GET OUT OF HERE--!
THE SKULL IS GONE!
DID THE FIRE GET HIM--OR WAS HE ABLE TO MAKE HIS ESCAPE?
IT DOESN'T MATTER! I'VE GOT TO KEEP SEARCHING--
THERE MUST BE SOME PROOF OF MY DAD'S INNOCENCE HERE SOMEWHERE!
HIS CARD! IT WAS SINGED BY THE FLAMES!
THE HEAT OPENED SOME SORT OF HIDDEN SEAM! THERE'S ANOTHER CARD--HIDDEN INSIDE!
I'VE GOT TO DISLODGE IT-- SEE WHAT IT IS--!!
THIS IS IT-- THE PROOF I NEED!!
MY DAD'S CREDENTIALS-- AS AN AMERICAN COUNTER-SPY, ANSWERABLE ONLY TO THE U.S.A.!
THAT'S WHY HE WAS MURDERED! HE'D BEEN FIGHTING THE ENEMIES OF OUR COUNTRY-- FIGHTING NAZIS AND FASCISTS--AS A SECRET DOUBLE AGENT!
RICHARD PARKER
U.S. GOV

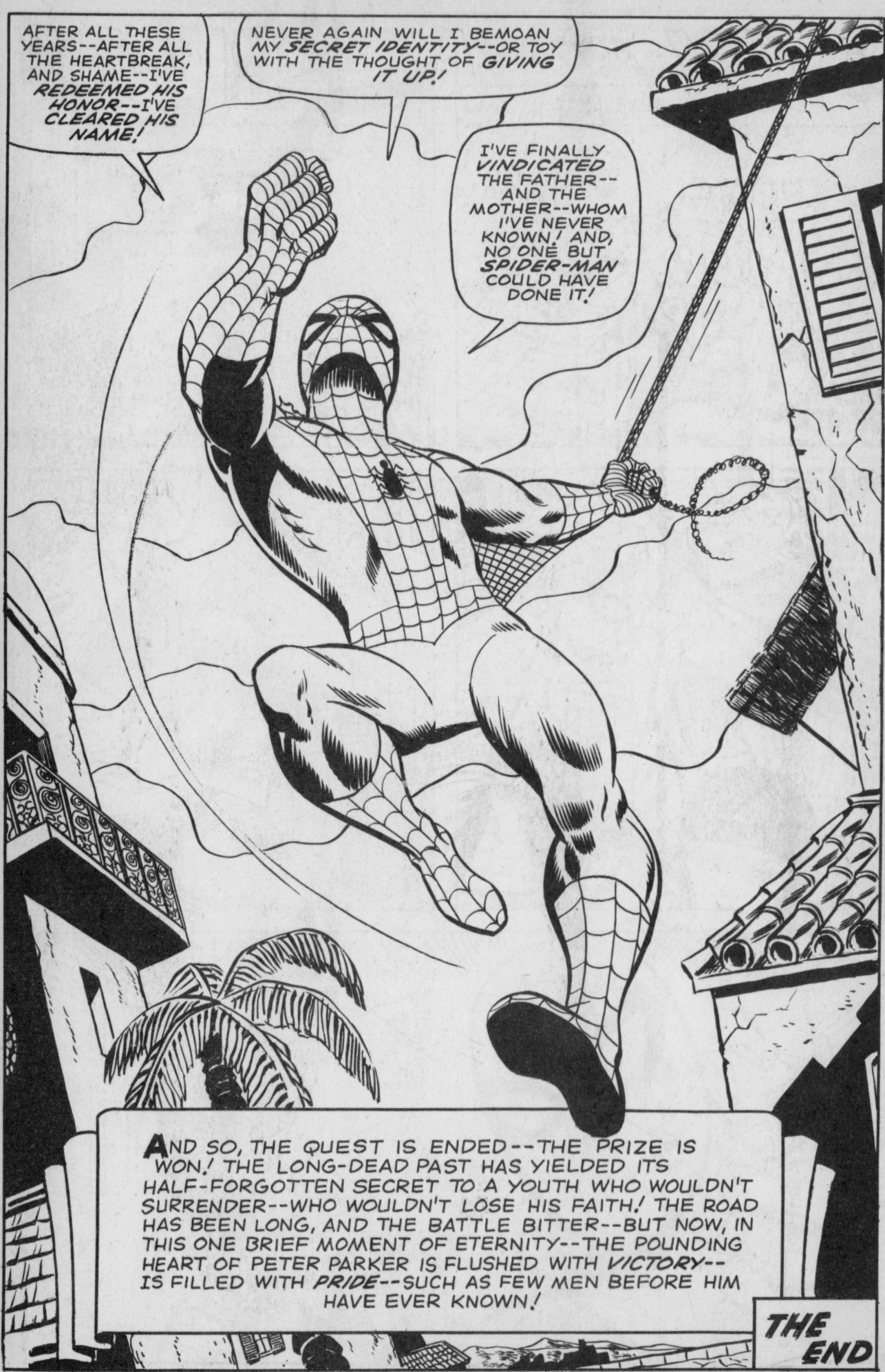
AFTER ALL THESE YEARS--AFTER ALL THE HEARTBREAK, AND SHAME--I'VE REDEEMED HIS HONOR--I'VE CLEARED HIS NAME!
NEVER AGAIN WILL I BEMOAN MY SECRET IDENTITY--OR TOY WITH THE THOUGHT OF GIVING IT UP!
I'VE FINALLY VINDICATED THE FATHER--AND THE MOTHER--WHOM I'VE NEVER KNOWN! AND, NO ONE BUT SPIDER-MAN COULD HAVE DONE IT!
AND SO, THE QUEST IS ENDED--THE PRIZE IS WON! THE LONG-DEAD PAST HAS YIELDED ITS HALF-FORGOTTEN SECRET TO A YOUTH WHO WOULDN'T SURRENDER--WHO WOULDN'T LOSE HIS FAITH! THE ROAD HAS BEEN LONG, AND THE BATTLE BITTER--BUT NOW, IN THIS ONE BRIEF MOMENT OF ETERNITY--THE POUNDING HEART OF PETER PARKER IS FLUSHED WITH VICTORY--IS FILLED WITH PRIDE--SUCH AS FEW MEN BEFORE HIM HAVE EVER KNOWN!
THE END

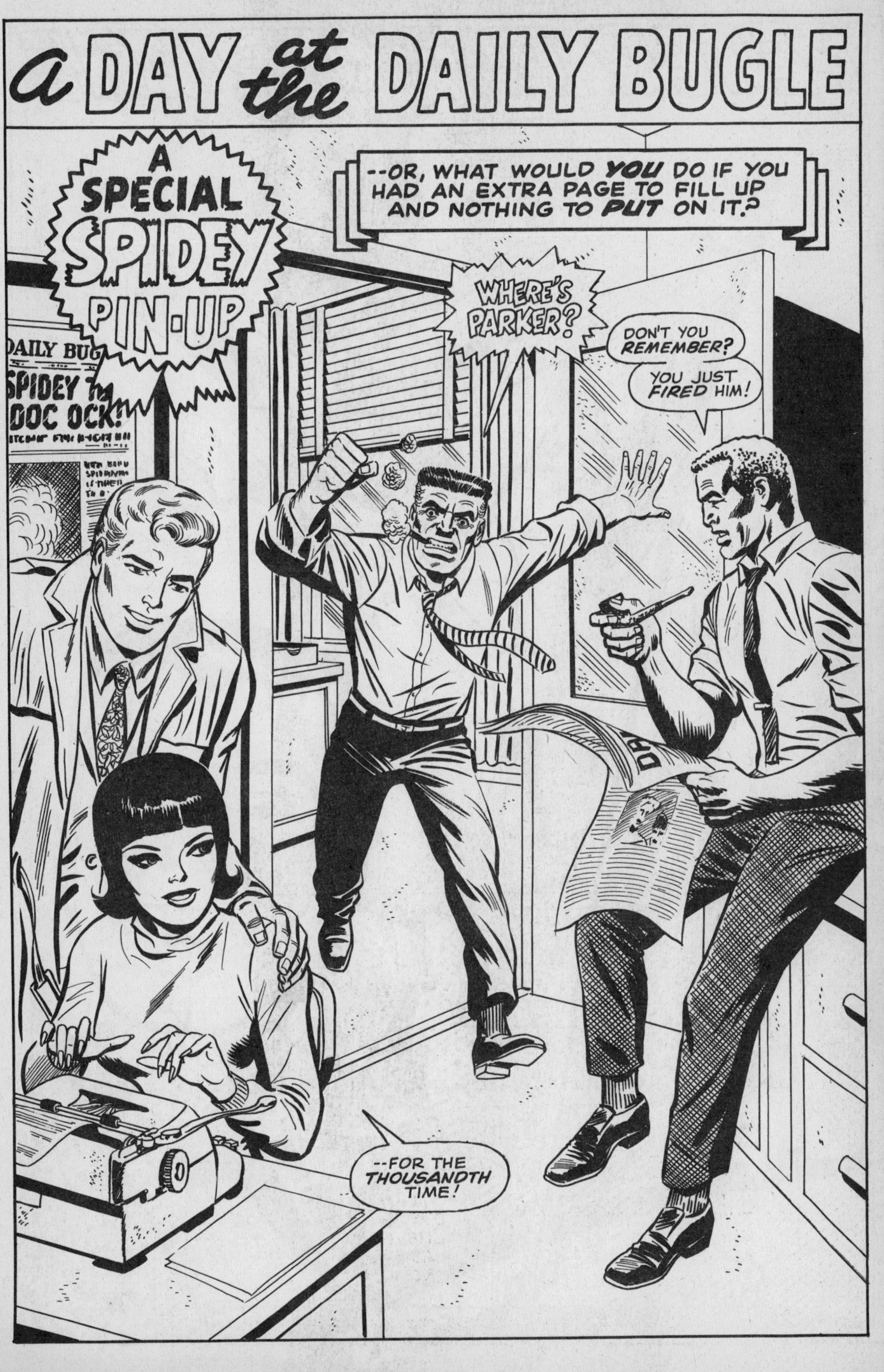
a DAY at the DAILY BUGLE
A SPECIAL SPIDEY PIN-UP
--OR, WHAT WOULD YOU DO IF YOU HAD AN EXTRA PAGE TO FILL UP AND NOTHING TO PUT ON IT.?
DAILY BUG
SPIDEY
DOC OCK!
WHERE'S PARKER?
DON'T YOU REMEMBER?
YOU JUST FIRED HIM!
--FOR THE THOUSANDTH TIME!

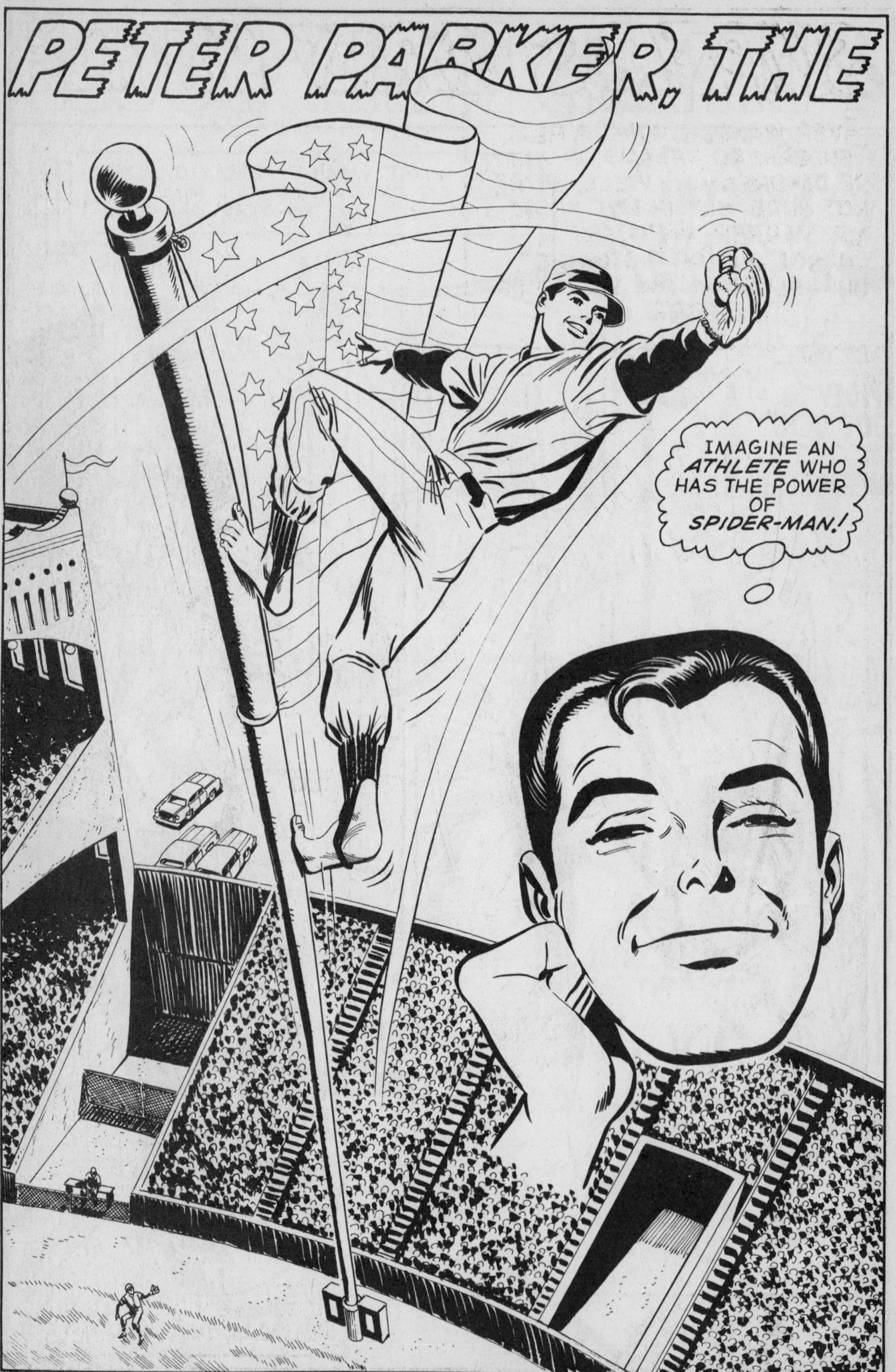
PETER PARKER, THE
IMAGINE AN ATHLETE WHO HAS THE POWER OF SPIDER-MAN!

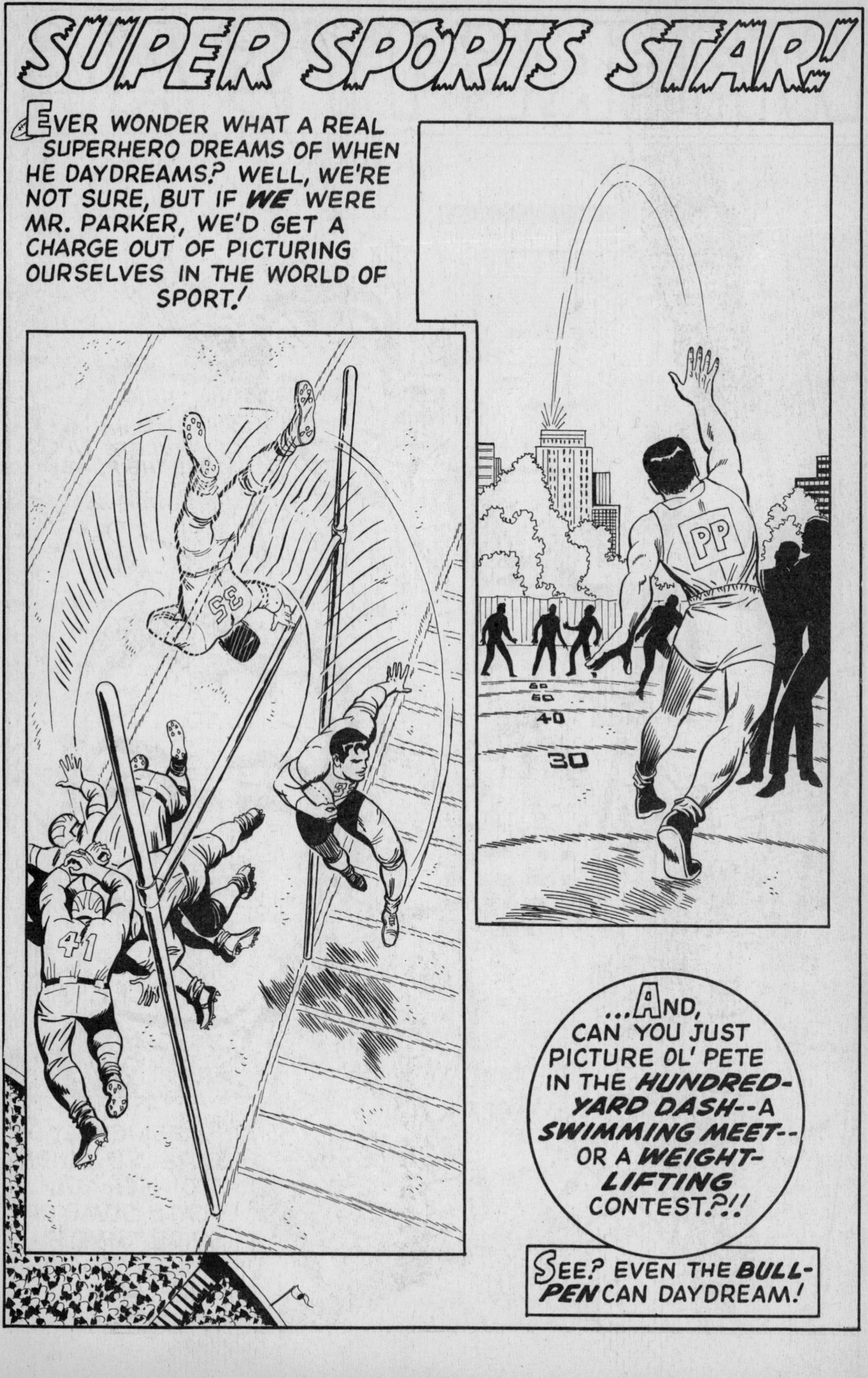
SUPER SPORTS STAR!
EVER WONDER WHAT A REAL SUPERHERO DREAMS OF WHEN HE DAYDREAMS? WELL, WE'RE NOT SURE, BUT IF *WE* WERE MR. PARKER, WE'D GET A CHARGE OUT OF PICTURING OURSELVES IN THE WORLD OF SPORT!
35
41
PP
40
30
...AND, CAN YOU JUST PICTURE OL' PETE IN THE *HUNDRED-YARD DASH*--A *SWIMMING MEET*--OR A *WEIGHT-LIFTING* CONTEST?!!
SEE? EVEN THE *BULL-PEN* CAN DAYDREAM!

WHERE IT'S AT!

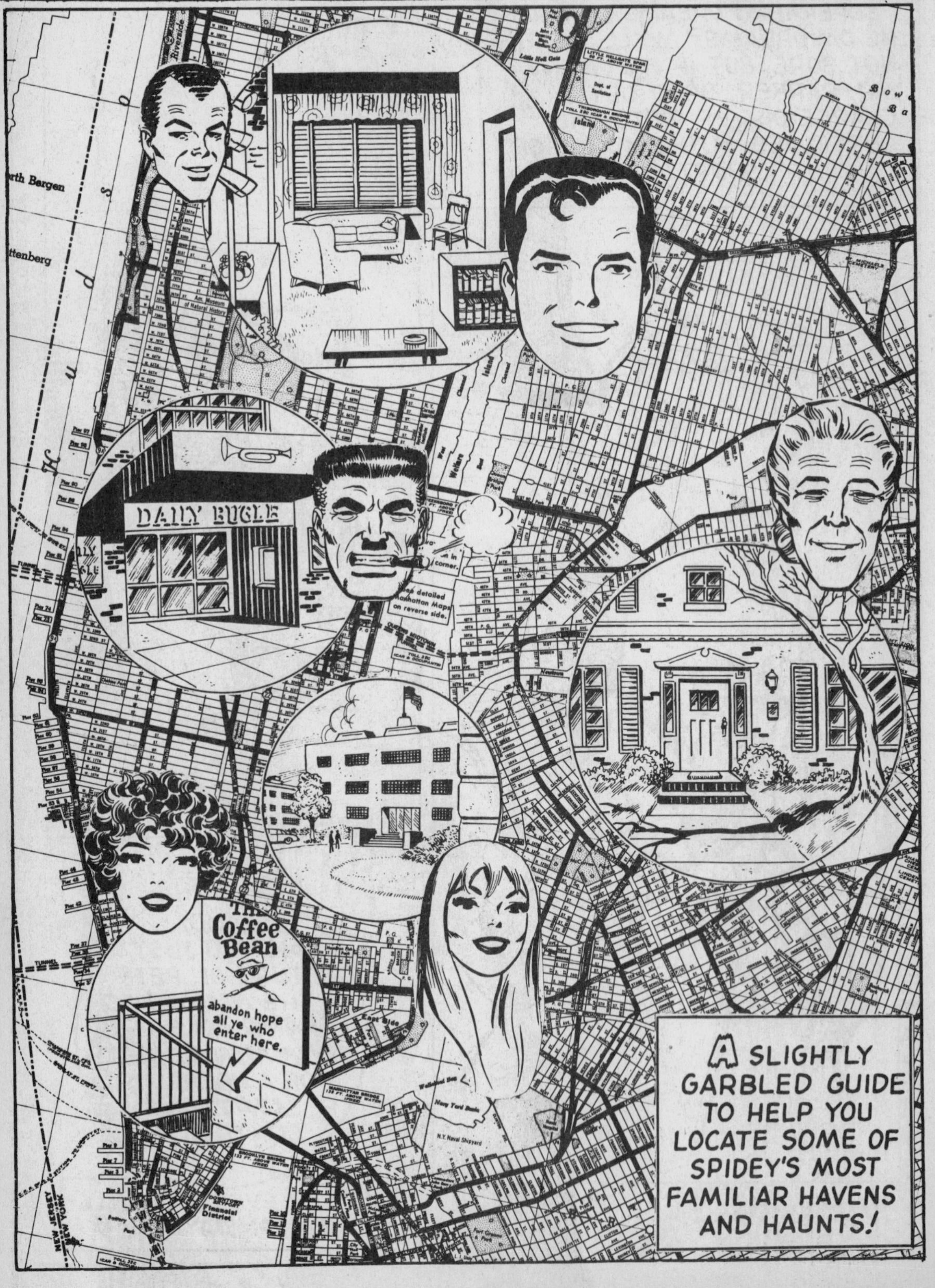
DAILY BUGLE
The Coffee Bean
abandon hope all ye who enter here.
A SLIGHTLY GARBLED GUIDE TO HELP YOU LOCATE SOME OF SPIDEY'S MOST FAMILIAR HAVENS AND HAUNTS!

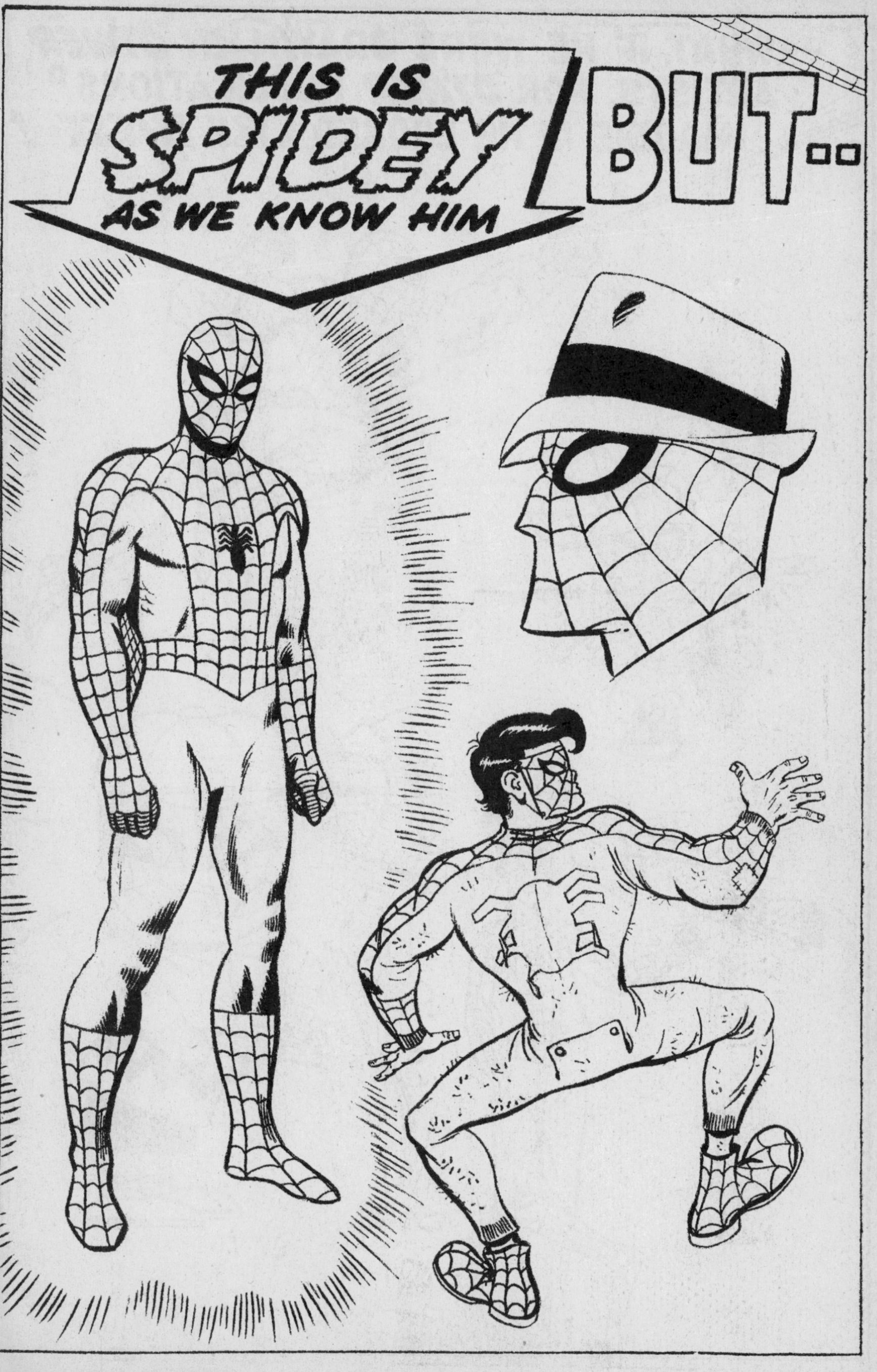
THIS IS SPIDEY AS WE KNOW HIM
BUT..

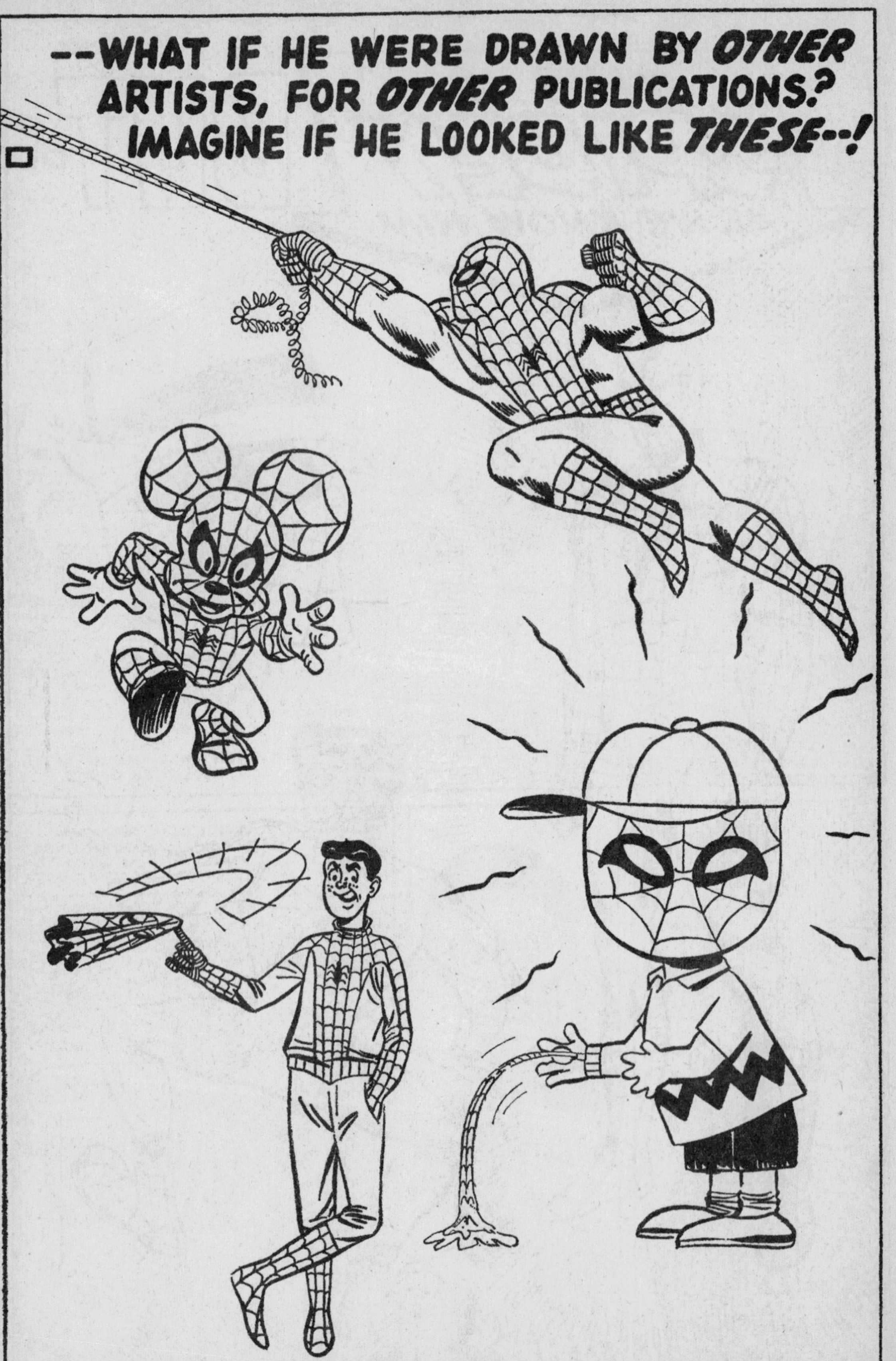
--WHAT IF HE WERE DRAWN BY *OTHER* ARTISTS, FOR *OTHER* PUBLICATIONS? IMAGINE IF HE LOOKED LIKE *THESE*--!

YOU MUST HAVE WONDERED...HOW WE CREATE ALL THE STORIES AND ART FOR *THE AMAZING SPIDER-MAN*...HERE IS A TYPICAL HONEST-AND-TRUE SITUATION FROM WHICH HIS ADVENTURES EVOLVE...

HERE WE GO- A-PLOTTING!

NOTHING HAS HAPPENED FOR 3½ MINUTES,/* WITH GROWING CONCERN, THE CREATORS WAIT FOR INSPIRATION...

GOOD OL' SMILEY

LARRUPIN' LARRY

JAZZY JOHNNY

SOUR BALLS

NO CREDITS FOR THIS ONE 'CAUSE NOBODY WILL TAKE THE BLAME!

BULLPEN PROGRESS RECORD

*THE RECORD FOR NOTHING HAPPENING WAS 4,003 MINUTES IN 1965--WHEN STAN THE MAN WAS TRANSFIXED (DURING A STORY CONFERENCE FOR THE MIGHTY THOR) BY THE APPARENT POWERS OF LEVITATION OF J. KIRBY (WHO HAD SAT UPON MR. LEE'S CIGAR.').

I GOT IT!

I KNEW I'D GET IT... I LOVE *GREEN* SOUR-BALLS, BUT THEY ALWAYS GIVE ME *HEARTBURN!*

THAT'S IT!! -- BRILLIANT! WHAT A GREAT EVERYDAY HUMAN EXPERIENCE! (FIRST PAGE) AUNT MAY HAS *HEARTBURN!* SPIDEY MUST GET HER *GREEN PILLS!*

OH--THIS IS TERRIBLE!

WHAT'S TERRIBLE?!!

NOW I GOT A SOUR BALL STUCK IN MY *THROAT!*

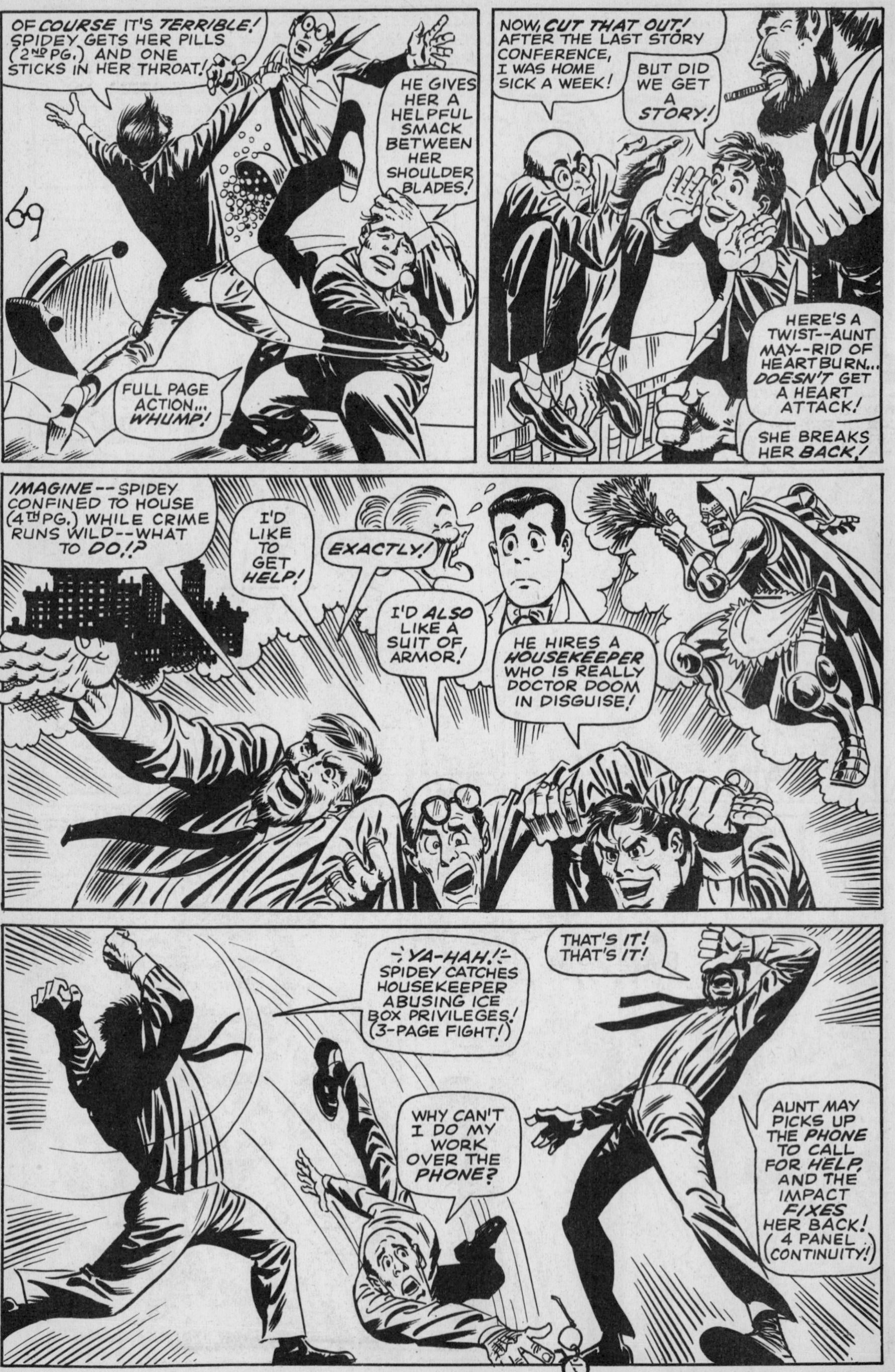
OF COURSE IT'S TERRIBLE! SPIDEY GETS HER PILLS (2ND PG.) AND ONE STICKS IN HER THROAT!
HE GIVES HER A HELPFUL SMACK BETWEEN HER SHOULDER BLADES!
69
FULL PAGE ACTION... WHUMP!
NOW, CUT THAT OUT! AFTER THE LAST STORY CONFERENCE, I WAS HOME SICK A WEEK!
BUT DID WE GET A STORY!
HERE'S A TWIST--AUNT MAY--RID OF HEARTBURN... DOESN'T GET A HEART ATTACK!
SHE BREAKS HER BACK!
IMAGINE--SPIDEY CONFINED TO HOUSE (4TH PG.) WHILE CRIME RUNS WILD--WHAT TO DO!?
I'D LIKE TO GET HELP!
EXACTLY!
I'D ALSO LIKE A SUIT OF ARMOR!
HE HIRES A HOUSEKEEPER WHO IS REALLY DOCTOR DOOM IN DISGUISE!
YA-HAH! SPIDEY CATCHES HOUSEKEEPER ABUSING ICE BOX PRIVILEGES! (3-PAGE FIGHT!)
THAT'S IT! THAT'S IT!
WHY CAN'T I DO MY WORK OVER THE PHONE?
AUNT MAY PICKS UP THE PHONE TO CALL FOR HELP, AND THE IMPACT FIXES HER BACK! (4 PANEL CONTINUITY!)

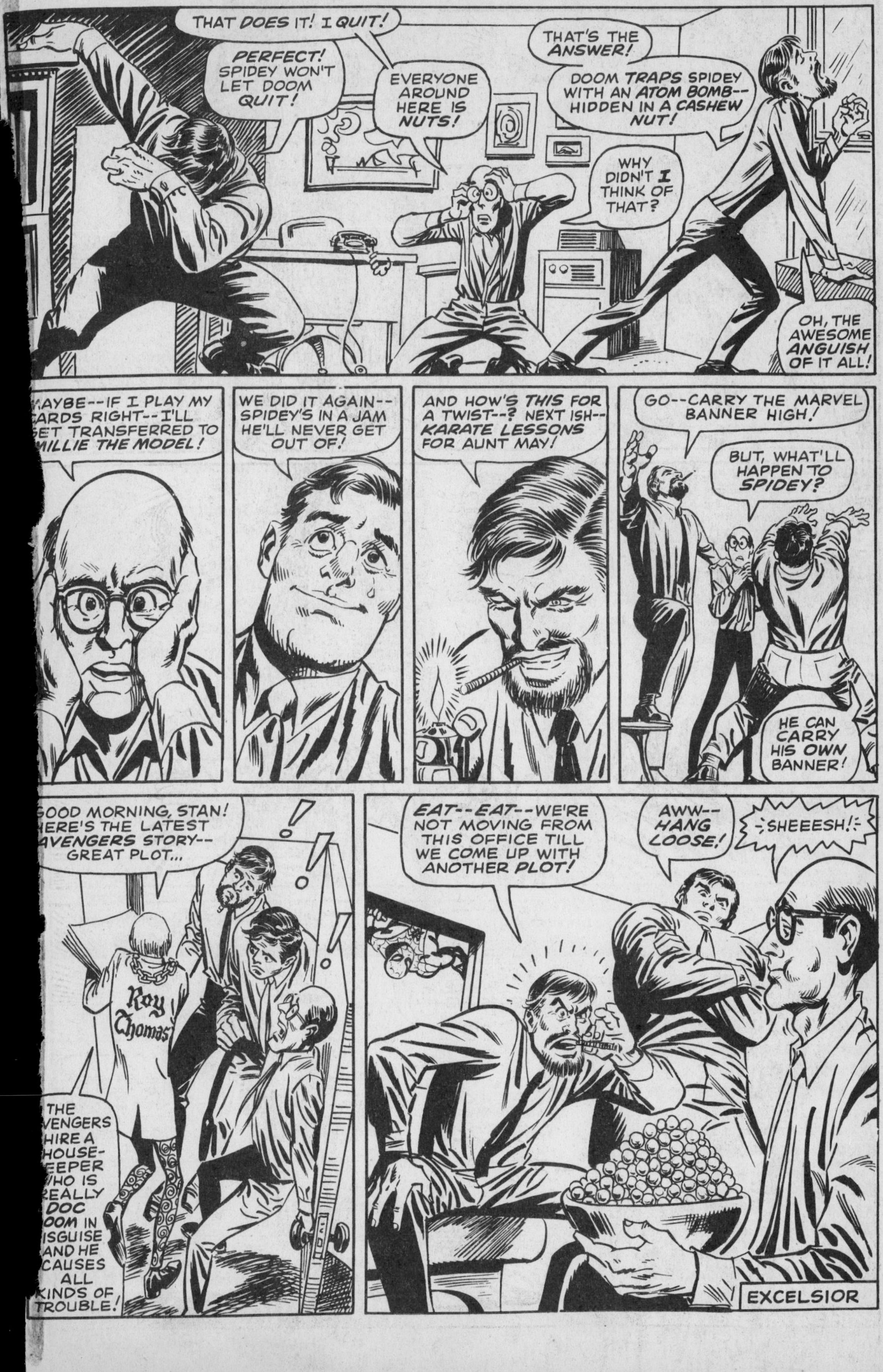
THAT DOES IT! I QUIT!
PERFECT! SPIDEY WON'T LET DOOM QUIT!
EVERYONE AROUND HERE IS NUTS!
THAT'S THE ANSWER!
DOOM TRAPS SPIDEY WITH AN ATOM BOMB-- HIDDEN IN A CASHEW NUT!
WHY DIDN'T I THINK OF THAT?
OH, THE AWESOME ANGUISH OF IT ALL!
MAYBE--IF I PLAY MY CARDS RIGHT--I'LL GET TRANSFERRED TO MILLIE THE MODEL!
WE DID IT AGAIN-- SPIDEY'S IN A JAM HE'LL NEVER GET OUT OF!
AND HOW'S THIS FOR A TWIST--? NEXT ISH-- KARATE LESSONS FOR AUNT MAY!
GO--CARRY THE MARVEL BANNER HIGH!
BUT, WHAT'LL HAPPEN TO SPIDEY?
HE CAN CARRY HIS OWN BANNER!
GOOD MORNING, STAN! HERE'S THE LATEST AVENGERS STORY-- GREAT PLOT...
!
!
Roy Thomas
THE AVENGERS HIRE A HOUSE-KEEPER WHO IS REALLY DOC DOOM IN DISGUISE AND HE CAUSES ALL KINDS OF TROUBLE!
EAT--EAT--WE'RE NOT MOVING FROM THIS OFFICE TILL WE COME UP WITH ANOTHER PLOT!
AWW-- HANG LOOSE!
SHEEESH!
EXCELSIOR